Scott Anguish
Erik M. Buck
Donald A. Yacktman

Cocoa Programming

SAMS

201 West 103rd Street, Indianapolis, Indiana 46290

Cocoa Programming

International Standard Book Number: 0-672-32230-7

Library of Congress Catalog Card Number: 2001089381

Printed in the United States of America

First Printing: September 2002

05 04 03 02 4 3 2 1

Trademarks

All terms mentioned in this book that are known to be trademarks or service marks have been appropriately capitalized. Sams Publishing cannot attest to the accuracy of this information. Use of a term in this book should not be regarded as affecting the validity of any trademark or service mark.

Warning and Disclaimer

Every effort has been made to make this book as complete and as accurate as possible, but no warranty or fitness is implied. The information provided is on an "as is" basis. The author(s) and the publisher shall have neither liability nor responsibility to any person or entity with respect to any loss or damages arising from the information contained in this book.

Executive Editor
Jeff Schultz

Acquisitions Editor
Betsy Brown

Development Editor
Susan Hobbs

Managing Editor
Charlotte Clapp

Project Editors
Elizabeth Finney
Katelyn Cozatt

Copy Editor
Chip Gardner

Indexer
Chris Barrick

Proofreaders
Andrea Dugan
Jody Larsen

Technical Editors
John Ray
Steve Munt

Team Coordinator
Amy Patton

Interior Designer
Gary Adair

Cover Designer
Alan Clements

Page Layout
D&G Limited, LLC

Contents at a Glance

Table of Contents

Part II The Cocoa Frameworks

Part III Cocoa Techniques

About the Authors

Scott Anguish (sanguish@digifix.com) started developing for the Macintosh in 1984. Upon seeing the NeXT development environment in 1992 he was hooked on the possibilities of a unified imaging model and a pure object-oriented system. In 1994, after several years of NeXT development, he created Stepwise, a portal for information related to NeXT technologies. Today, Stepwise serves as a hub for Apple's Mac OS X technology platform as well as Cocoa and WebObjects development. During the day he works to build better technology for the Center for Educational Technology at Middlebury College using Cocoa and WebObjects, of course.

Erik M. Buck (embassociates@qwest.net) is President of EMB & Associates, Inc., a technology leader in the aerospace and entertainment software industries. He is a contributor to Stepwise and has been developing software with Cocoa and its predecessor technologies, OPENSTEP and NeXTSTEP, professionally since 1989. Mr. Buck holds a BS in Computer Science from the University of Dayton.

Donald A. Yacktman (don@illumineX.com) has been using Cocoa and its predecessor technologies, OPENSTEP and NeXTSTEP, professionally since 1991. He is currently the Vice President of Development at illumineX, inc. illumineX is both an independent software vendor of Cocoa-based Mac OS X software and a WebObjects consulting firm. Mr. Yacktman is a member of the Stepwise editorial staff and the principal contributor to the MiscKit, a premier source of information and reusable software for the OPENSTEP and Cocoa communities. He holds BS and MS degrees in Electrical and Computer Engineering from Brigham Young University and has been programming professionally since 1981.

Acknowledgments

Scott Anguish

I would like to thank my wife Dorothy and my kids, Simon and Tori, for their love and support while I was working on this project. This book would have been much thinner if not for the heroic efforts of Don and Erik. I'd also like to thank the folks who contribute to the community and Stepwise in particular. I too have a long list of Cocoa programmers and developers who should be thanked both outside of Apple and within. I hope that we can continue this journey of Cocoa development for years to come.

Erik M. Buck

I would like to thank my wife Michelle and family for their support, which made writing the book both possible and enjoyable. I would also like to thank Don Yacktman, Scott Anguish, and the many supportive people who contribute to Stepwise and the community of Cocoa developers. Finally, I would like to thank the Cocoa programmers and enthusiasts for whom this book was written. It is my sincere hope that this book will both accelerate the process of learning Cocoa and help make using Cocoa fun.

Don Yacktman

I would like to thank my wife Marcie for her patience and support during the writing of this book. The support of my entire family is also greatly appreciated. I would also like to thank my co-workers at illumineX, especially CEO Gary Longsine, for their patience and understanding. Without the support of Marcie and Gary, this book would not have been possible. Many thanks are offered to the numerous friends at Apple who have taken time to verify facts in this book. Finally, I would like to thank all the people who helped me learn the skills used and described in this book. The people who have offered help and guidance over the years are too numerous to list, but this book exists in part because of their contributions.

We Want to Hear From You!

As the reader of this book, *you* are our most important critic and commentator. We value your opinion and want to know what we're doing right, what we could do better, what areas you'd like to see us publish in, and any other words of wisdom you're willing to pass our way.

You can email or write me directly to let me know what you did or didn't like about this book—as well as what we can do to make our books stronger.

Please note that I cannot help you with technical problems related to the topic of this book, and that due to the high volume of mail I receive, I might not be able to reply to every message.

When you write, please be sure to include this book's title and authors as well as your name and phone or email address. I will carefully review your comments and share them with the authors and editors who worked on the book.

Email: `opensource@samspublishing.com`

Mail: Mark Taber
Associate Publisher
Sams Publishing
201 West 103rd Street
Indianapolis, IN 46290 USA

Reader Services

For more information about this book or others from Sams Publishing, visit our Web site at `www.samspublishing.com`. Type the ISBN (excluding hyphens) or the title of the book in the Search box to find the book you're looking for.

Introduction

Software development for Mac OS X can be a great joy. The advanced programming tools and frameworks now provided by Apple astound many programmers. When programmers delve into the object-oriented technology called Cocoa, which is part of every Mac OS X system, they often describe the experience as life-changing. Claims of massive productivity increases are common. Developers describe Cocoa as eye-opening. Cocoa demonstrates the true power of object-oriented programming in a way that few programmers have experienced when using other technologies. Cocoa enables programmers to focus on the unique value of their applications by eliminating almost all the drudgery traditionally necessary when making complex graphical applications. The Cocoa technology exemplifies some of the best software design ever seen. Beyond providing tremendous functionality out of the box, the Cocoa technology inspires programmers to follow Apple's example and design excellent software.

Apple acquired much of the Cocoa technology in the last days of 1996 when Apple merged with a company called NeXT. When first seen publicly in 1988, the technology was called NeXTSTEP. Over the years NeXTSTEP became OPENSTEP, then Rhapsody, then Yellow Box, and finally Cocoa. Each name change brought additional features and maturity. Apple has significantly expanded and enhanced Cocoa for Mac OS X.

Although there are many ways to program an Apple computer, this book focuses on the Cocoa environment. Using Cocoa is the most advanced and arguably the most productive way to program a Macintosh—it's also the most fun. In presentations to developers, Apple representatives describe Cocoa as the future. Apple recommends that all new software development for the Mac use Cocoa.

This book contains all of the information necessary to build complex Cocoa applications. The major Cocoa concepts are explained and demonstrated with example code. With this book, an experienced developer can become immediately productive with Cocoa and Mac OS X.

Intended Audience

This book is intended for intermediate and advanced programmers who are familiar with C programming and many of the concepts of object-oriented programming. No prior experience with Mac OS X or other Apple products is required, but the reader must have access to a computer running Mac OS X and the Apple-provided development tools to use the example programs. Object orientation and a small set of object-oriented extensions to the C language are explained in this book, but this book is not a substitute for a comprehensive language reference or books solely dedicated to object technology. The two computer languages that Apple suggests for use with Cocoa are Java and Objective-C. Java is discussed, but the examples in this book are primarily implemented with Objective-C. Objective-C is the language in which Cocoa was written, and the reasons for choosing Objective-C are presented in the book.

Programmers familiar with other development technology including PowerPlant, Mac App, MFC/Win32, and Java Swing might experience culture shock when first learning Cocoa. Even though the core of Cocoa has been in use for more than a decade, it is still revolutionary. Revolutions do not always occur without discomfort, but few programmers ever look back after experiencing Cocoa. A common question posed after learning Cocoa is "why haven't we been doing it this way all along."

Conventions

The following typographical conventions are used throughout this book.

Italic type is used for introducing new terms and usage notes.

`Monospace` type is used for code examples, command-line output, filenames and file system paths, data types, URLs, and symbolic constants.

`Bold Monospace` type is used for required user input in examples.

`Italic Monospace` type is used to designate a placeholder for user input.

Learn By Example

Each major topic in this book is accompanied by a self-contained example. Examining and modifying the examples is often the best way to learn a new development environment and technology. Readers are encouraged to play with example code, experiment, and test their understanding. In many cases, the code in the examples can be copied into a new project to provide a jump-start. The authors have more than 30 years of collective experience with this technology. The examples embody the best practices, common programming idioms, and wisdom acquired by the authors.

There is a web site associated with this book at `http://www.cocoaprogramming.net/`. All the example code found in this book and more can be obtained from the Web site. The code is organized on the Web site by chapter and example name. Any updates to the material in this book, including errata, can be found there.

PART I
Overview

IN THIS PART

1

Cocoa and Mac OS X

IN THIS CHAPTER

- Understanding When to Use Cocoa
- Understanding Cocoa's Role in Mac OS X
- What You Need to Use Cocoa
- What's Included in Cocoa

Cocoa is a collection of software objects that implements almost all features common to Mac OS X applications. Programmers extend the Cocoa objects to implement application-specific features. The Cocoa objects are reused in every Cocoa application so that programmers can concentrate on adding unique value with each line of code rather than constantly reimplementing common features or struggling to access operating system services. Significant applications can be built with very little code.

Cocoa is the result of continuous evolution from the software development environment of NeXTSTEP, which was first released to the public in 1988. Cocoa takes advantage of common object-oriented design patterns and best practices. In fact, many of the common design patterns were first recognized in NeXTSTEP. Cocoa design patterns are described in Chapter 6, "Cocoa Design Patterns."

Cocoa is distinguished from other object-oriented development environments in several ways: Cocoa is mature, consistent, and broad. Cocoa is based on a cross-platform specification and has evolved from a cross-platform implementation. Cocoa is extraordinarily extensible, flexible, and dynamic in part because of Objective-C, the language used to implement it. Objective-C is described in Chapter 4, "Objective-C." Cocoa emphasizes the reuse of objects, dynamic loading of objects, and messaging between objects.

Many developers enjoy huge programmer productivity improvements by using Cocoa instead of other technologies. Several ground-breaking applications were originally developed with NeXTSTEP, including Apple's own Interface Builder, Lotus Improv, and the first World Wide Web browser. The initial implementations of the famous games Doom and Quake, and the custom development tools for the games were written using the predecessors to Cocoa. Developers such as Tim Berners-Lee, who invented the World Wide Web, claim that they could not have created cutting edge applications as easily if they had to use other technologies. The obstacles to overcome in other environments would have hampered the innovations.

NOTE

Screen shots of the first Web browser and commentary from Berners-Lee are available at `http://www.w3.org/People/Berners-Lee/WorldWideWeb.html`.

Understanding When to Use Cocoa

To understand why you would choose to use Cocoa, it is necessary to briefly explain the alternatives. Apple supports three principal software development environments for producing Mac OS X applications. The supported environments are Cocoa, Carbon, and 100% Pure Java. Each environment has strengths and weaknesses, and a developer's choice of environment is influenced by many factors.

Carbon

Carbon consists primarily of a subset of the traditional procedural Application Programming Interfaces (API)s used to program Mac computers. Apple updated, and in some cases, enhanced the C libraries used to program Macs before OS X. Carbon provides access to the modern and powerful features of OS X in a way that preserves compatibility with most of the software written for earlier Mac operating systems. Applications written using Carbon work on Mac OS 8 or Mac OS 9 with compatibility libraries installed, and on Mac OS X. Apple provides a free application called CarbonDater that analyzes software for compatibility with Carbon. In many cases, programmers can easily convert old applications written for the Mac to work with Carbon on OS X.

Cocoa applications do not work with Mac operating systems prior to OS X. If compatibility with Mac OS 8 or 9 is required, Carbon might be the best choice. On OS X, one advantage of Cocoa is that Cocoa programs written with the Objective-C language can freely call the C-based Carbon APIs. It is much more difficult for Carbon applications to benefit from Cocoa features. In some cases, Apple has already implemented Cocoa objects that shield programmers from underlying Carbon implementations.

The difficulty accessing Cocoa features from Carbon is expected to decline over time. Carbon is slowly gaining access to traditional Cocoa features. Cocoa solutions to common programming problems are preferred, and Apple has already exposed some parts of Cocoa to Carbon programs. For example, the Core Foundation API is used extensively in Carbon applications. Core Foundation is a procedural interface to the features of Cocoa objects. In some cases, Core Foundation functions are derived from previously private internal implementations of Cocoa objects.

Java

Java is both programming language and a set of cross-platform libraries. Mac OS X comes with a complete implementation of Sun's Java 2 Standard Edition version 1.3.1. Apple's Java Virtual Machine was developed in cooperation with Sun and uses many Sun technologies including Sun's Hot Spot JIT (Just In Time) compiler. 100% Pure Java applications can be developed on OS X using Apple's developer tools or third-party tools.

100% Pure Java applications are portable to many different operating systems. If portability is the primary requirement for a software project, 100% Pure Java might be the best development technology.

Java can be used to develop Cocoa applications, but the resulting applications only work on Mac OS X. The objects that comprise Cocoa are written in Objective-C, but Apple provides a technology called the Java Bridge that enables relatively seamless use of Cocoa objects from Java code and vise versa. Objective-C was one of the major influences that shaped the design of the Java language. Java and Objective-C have many similarities under the surface. Using Java to write Cocoa applications is explained in more detail in Chapter 2, "Cocoa Language Options."

Cocoa

Cocoa is the most mature development environment for OS X, as well as the most productive technology for implementing many types of applications. The cheapest, fastest, and most bug-free lines of code in any application are the lines a programmer didn't have to write. Cocoa's pervasive use and reuse of objects dramatically reduces the number of lines of code in applications. By following the example set by Cocoa, many developers achieve high levels of reuse with their own custom objects.

A simple comparison is the TextEdit application shipped with OS X versus the SimpleText Carbon example that Apple provides with their developer tools. TextEdit is a Cocoa application implemented in 1354 lines of code, whereas SimpleText is implemented in 5231 lines of code. TextEdit has many more features and fewer limitations than SimpleText, yet TextEdit requires approximately 1/4 the number of lines of code. Cocoa programmers often claim a 5–1 productivity advantage over alternative technologies, however, the TextEdit verses SimpleText comparison indicates a much greater advantage than 5–1.

Cocoa is the most flexible software development technology for Mac OS X. Cocoa is written in Objective-C, and that provides several advantages. Objective-C is a small superset of ANSI C. Objective-C programs can seamlessly use all the C libraries available in OS X, including Carbon and traditional Unix libraries. A variant of Objective-C called Objective-C++ includes support for direct use of C++ libraries along with Cocoa. Apple's Java bridge technology enables Java programs to use Cocoa, and allows Objective-C Cocoa applications to use existing Java libraries. Apple has even provided access to Cocoa from AppleScript, therefore, it is possible to write full-featured applications using AppleScript and Cocoa. Cocoa is the only development environment for Mac OS X that directly enables use of all other system components.

Cocoa is the most extensible software-development technology for Mac OS X. It is possible to add features to the objects provided by Cocoa without access to the source code for Cocoa. All Cocoa applications can take advantage of the addition without even being recompiled. It is possible to selectively replace Cocoa objects with custom versions. Cocoa provides powerful features for dynamically loading objects such as plug-ins. The dynamic loading capabilities of Cocoa are only partly available to Carbon programs. It is even possible to completely change the user interface of a Cocoa application without access to the application's source code.

Understanding Cocoa's Role in Mac OS X

Mac OS X traces its heritage to earlier Mac operating systems and to versions of Unix. Mac OS X melds the two operating systems into one.

Mac OS X uses the layered architecture shown in Figure 1.1. Cocoa is implemented to enable access to all the features of OS X. Cocoa applications can use the Quartz, OpenGL, and QuickTime graphics systems supported by Mac OS X. Cocoa provides high-level, object-oriented components that use Quartz and advanced font rendering capabilities built on top of Quartz. Cocoa objects exist to access OpenGL and QuickTime. Traditional Mac features are accessed through objects that internally use the Carbon API. Cocoa directly uses features provided by Darwin.

Cocoa contains objects that use the networking and file system features of Darwin. Many Cocoa objects are implemented to use the Core Foundation components of Darwin. The Objective-C language runtime used by Cocoa is implemented in Darwin.

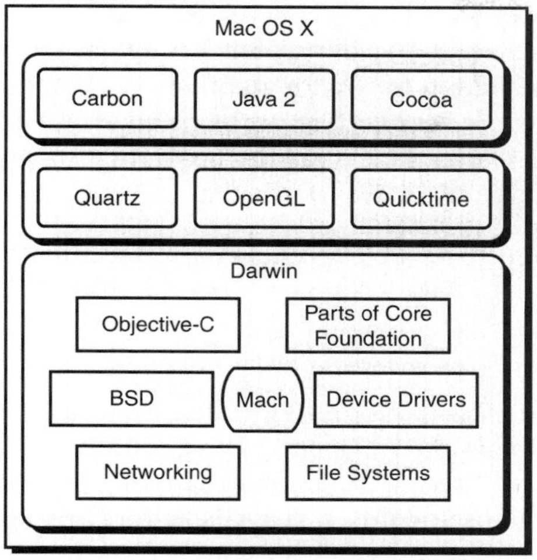

FIGURE 1.1 Mac OS X uses a layered architecture.

Quartz

Quartz is the term used to collectively identify the advanced 2D graphics capabilities of OS X, which are built on top of Darwin. Quartz consists of a window server process and a powerful library of 2D drawing functions based on Adobe's PDF imaging model.

The window server is a process that runs in the background and controls display access by applications. The window server provides device-independent color capabilities and color correction for displays. The window server manages the layering of windows owned by different applications and implements features such as translucency and live-window dragging. The window server can reposition windows, apply translucent drop shadows, and layer translucent windows without interrupting other applications. The window server also provides limited direct access to the video frame buffer for games, OpenGL, and QuickTime.

In addition to the window server, Quartz provides a graphics-programming API called Core Graphics. Core Graphics provides functions and data types that can be used from any of the programming environments supported by Mac OS X. In essence, Core Graphics is an API for producing graphics compatible with the powerful cross-platform Portable Document Format (PDF) standard from Adobe.

Core Graphics provides device-independent vector and bitmap graphics operations with support for antialiasing and transparency. Core graphics has set a new high standard for the presentation quality of graphics on a computer screen. Almost any graphics drawn with Core Foundation can be saved as PDF files for viewing on any computer with a PDF viewer. PDF is rapidly becoming the preferred format for What You See Is What You Get (WYSIWYG) printing and publishing.

Cocoa's use of Quartz and 2D graphics is described in Chapter 12, "Custom Views and Graphics: Part I," through Chapter 15, "Events and Cursors."

OpenGL

OpenGL is a standard cross-platform API for hardware accelerated 2D and 3D graphics. Mac OS X features optimized OpenGL drivers, and every recent Mac computer ships with hardware accelerated 3D graphics support. OpenGL is one of the most widely adopted graphics standards. It is available for Unix and Microsoft Windows in addition to OS X. Code that uses OpenGL can be very portable and produces consistent results across many platforms. OpenGL is frequently used to implement games, medical imaging software, and engineering applications. Cocoa includes an object for interfacing with OpenGL.

QuickTime

QuickTime is an Apple proprietary cross-platform technology for creating and presenting video, animation, sound, music, and virtual reality environments. QuickTime is extensible and supported for versions Mac OS 8 and higher, as well as all recent versions of Microsoft Windows. Mac OS X provides up-to-date QuickTime support including programming APIs, real-time streaming, and viewers.

QuickTime supports common graphics file formats for still images and video. QuickTime can be used with popular Internet protocols for streaming media, and plug-ins exist for most Web browsers including Internet Explorer, Netscape Navigator, and America Online. Cocoa provides an object that enables the use of QuickTime from Cocoa applications. Apple provides sample reusable objects that extend Cocoa's built-in support for QuickTime and enable the creation of simple movie editors without writing any code at all.

Darwin

Darwin is Apple's name for the lowest-level components in Mac OS X. Cocoa is implemented using the features of Darwin. Darwin consists of components that provide core essential services. The Mach kernel is the heart of Darwin. Device drivers, file systems, networking, Unix APIs, support for kernel extension, the Objective-C language runtime, and key programming APIs are all part of Darwin.

Darwin source code is available from Apple under the terms of Apple's flexible open-source license. By registering with Apple, any developer can download the Darwin source code. Ports of Darwin already exist for the Intel x86 family of processors. By making Darwin open source, Apple has empowered the broad community of Unix developers to inspect and enhance the lowest-level core of Mac OS X. Third-party developers have already contributed security enhancements and other features back to Apple.

Mach

Mach is the core of Mac OS X, and every software development technology in Mac OS X uses the features of Mach. The version of Mach used in OS X is based on Mach 3.0. Mach schedules CPU usage, supports symmetric multiprocessing with multiple CPUs, provides memory protection and dynamic virtual memory, provides real-time features, and implements an interprocess messaging system used by higher-level components to interface with the kernel.

Cocoa objects that manage processes, threads, and interprocess communication use features of Mach directly in their implementations. All Cocoa objects benefit from the memory protection, dynamic virtual memory, and real-time features provided by Mach.

Device Drivers

In some cases, Cocoa objects use the features of operating system device drivers directly. For example, Cocoa provides support for digital graphic tablets, mouse scroll wheels, and multiple mouse buttons by interoperating with the relevant device drivers. Device drivers for OS X are built as Mach kernel extensions. New device drivers can be dynamically loaded into a running Mach kernel. There is no need to recompile the kernel or even shut down the machine to install new device drivers.

BSD

Many Cocoa objects use traditional Unix features in their implementation on Mac OS X. The Darwin component called Berkley Standard Distribution (BSD) refers the University of California-Berkley standard distribution of Unix. The Berkley variant is one of the major branches on the Unix family tree. Several free implementations of BSD Unix are available. Apple uses code from some of the free versions in OS X and has contributed back to them as well. Mac OS X's Unix features are principally based on standard BSD 4.4 with networking components from FreeBSD 3.2.

Networking

Cocoa provides objects that enable seamless access to networking features of the operating system. Darwin includes networking support implemented as extensions to the Mach kernel. Most of the networking components are based on the network support architecture implemented in FreeBSD 3.2. Most of the POSIX standard API to access networking features via sockets is supported. Sockets-based communication originated with early versions of BSD Unix and has since become the most common technique. Sockets are supported by every recent version of Unix and Microsoft Windows.

File Systems

Cocoa relies on Darwin for file system support. Cocoa provides objects that abstract file system–specific issues. Cocoa programs work regardless of the underlying file system. The abstraction is particularly important because modern operating systems such as Mac OS X support so many different file systems. Avoiding the need to write code to handle different file system issues is an advantage of Cocoa.

Darwin includes advanced file system support implemented in a layer outside the Mach kernel. Mac OS X already supports Unix File System (UFS), Hierarchical File System plus (HFS+), ISO 9660, File Allocated Table (FAT), Network File System (NFS), Web-based Distributed Authoring and Versioning (WebDAV), and Universal Disk Format (UDF). UFS is a common Unix file system. HFS+ is the native file system used by prior Mac operating systems. HFS+ is the file system recommended by Apple because it best preserves compatibility with software written for prior Mac operating systems. The ISO 9660 file system is standard and commonly used on CD-ROMS. The FAT file system is used by Microsoft DOS and some Microsoft Windows installations. NFS implements a standard protocol for accessing file systems on one machine from another over a network. WebDAV is the file system implemented as extensions to the HTTP protocol. Apple uses WebDAV to provide remote access to each user's iDisk. An iDisk is simply storage allocated on a hard disk on a server at Apple. Mac users can use the storage to share files with other people over the Internet. UDF is a file system intended to replace the ISO 9660 file system. UDF is primarily used on DVDs.

Objective-C Runtime

One of the most critical features of Darwin that is used by Cocoa is Apple's Objective-C runtime. Cocoa is written in Objective-C. Apple uses the open source GNU Compiler Collection (gcc) compiler and provides the basic compiler and development tools for use with Darwin as a free download in source code or binary form. gcc is part of the Free Software Foundation's GNU project. The gcc compiler collection comes with Objective-C support, and a GNU Objective-C runtime that is slightly different from the one shipped with Apple's Darwin. Apple has stated plans to keep their own version of gcc synchronized with the standard GNU version and possibly unify the two Objective-C runtimes in the future.

Parts of Core Foundation

Darwin includes part of the implementation of the Core Foundation procedural APIs. Core Foundation is used by many of the higher-level APIs of Mac OS X including

Cocoa. Chapter 7, "Foundation Framework Overview," includes a brief introduction to the Core Foundation. The fact that some source code for Core Foundation is available with Darwin opens opportunities for third parties to inspect and enhance key elements of OS X's software development infrastructure.

What You Need to Use Cocoa

Apple provides everything needed to develop Cocoa applications for Mac OS X. Apple's developer tools are shipped on a CD-ROM in the same box with the Mac OS X operating system CD-ROM. Cocoa can be used with Java, AppleScript, C++, and other languages, but knowledge of C is required in most cases. The Cocoa objects are written in Objective-C.

This book provides an introduction to Objective-C for programmers who are already familiar with C. Objective-C consists of a small set of extensions to ANSI standard C. C programmers with experience using one or more object-oriented languages can learn Objective-C very quickly. When Objective-C is familiar, the more daunting task of learning the large and sometimes complex Cocoa frameworks begins.

The Cocoa frameworks are an excellent example of the power of object-oriented programming and Objective-C. Even though Cocoa is large and provides many features, it is consistent. The consistency helps programmers learn new parts of Cocoa by extending knowledge already gained. After a while, programmers often find themselves reusing Cocoa designs and programming idioms in their own code. Many programmers reaction to Cocoa is "why was software ever written another way?"

What's Included in Cocoa

Cocoa is composed of frameworks that contain libraries of objects and related resources, data types, functions, header files, and documentation. The two major Cocoa frameworks are the Foundation framework and the Application Kit framework. Figure 1.2 shows the Cocoa frameworks and the Mac OS X system components used by the frameworks.

The Foundation framework, shown in Figure 1.2, contains nongraphical objects that are useful in every Cocoa application. The Foundation framework uses the services provided by Darwin, and provides a foundation for other frameworks and applications to extend.

The Application Kit framework is built using the Foundation framework and OS X's graphics services that are, in turn, built on top of Darwin. The Application Kit provides graphical objects and graphical user interface elements. The Application Kit framework provides the look and feel of Mac OS X Cocoa applications. The Yellow Box version of the Application Kit provided Microsoft Windows, OpenStep, or traditional Mac OS looks on each platform, but the Application Kit on OS X only supports Apple's Aqua look and feel.

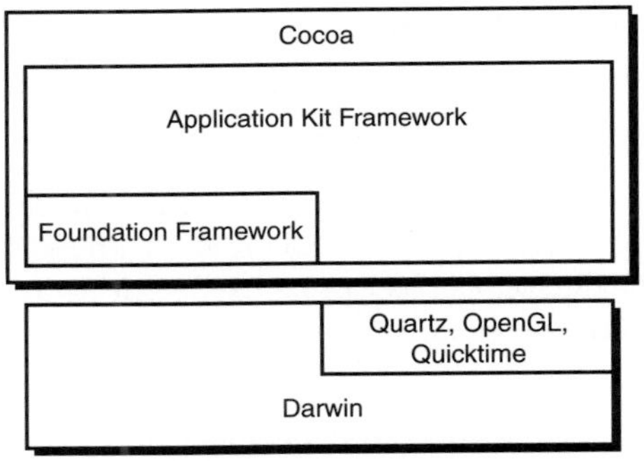

FIGURE 1.2 Cocoa contains layered frameworks of objects.

Cocoa is implemented in Objective-C. Objective-C is a dynamic language that supports a style of flexible programming well-suited to creating reusable objects and accommodating evolutionary change. Cocoa applications consist of interconnected objects. Apple provides some of the objects, and others are provided by other vendors. Finally, applications contain custom application-specific objects. The objects communicate with each other by sending messages, and all objects are equal. The objects that Apple provides are not special in any way. Custom objects, third-party objects, and Apple's objects all work together even though they are developed independently.

Apple provides several applications that contribute to the productivity of Cocoa programmers. Not surprisingly, most of Apple's own developer tools are Cocoa applications. Mac OS X is built using Cocoa applications. Even the Apple tools used to write Carbon and Java programs are Cocoa applications.

Summary

Cocoa is an advanced, mature, flexible, and extensible software development technology that uses frameworks of objects and related resources. Cocoa has a legacy of cross-platform support. Cocoa applications have access to all features of Mac OS X. Cocoa provides large programmer productivity advantages compared to other technologies available for software development on Mac OS X, but Cocoa applications only run on Mac OS X. Carbon and 100% Pure Java are alternative technologies that support multiple platforms.

The rest of this book explores Cocoa software development in detail. You'll start with Chapter 2, "Cocoa Language Options," which covers the range of languages used to develop Cocoa applications.

2 Cocoa Language Options

IN THIS CHAPTER

- Object Orientation
- Java
- Objective-C
- Other Languages
- Choosing a Language for Use with Cocoa
- The Use of Objective-C in This Book

Cocoa is a collection of object-oriented components written in the Objective-C language. Objective-C is a flexible and dynamic language that adds object-oriented extensions to ANSI standard C. Because of the flexibility of Objective-C, the Cocoa components can be used by a wide variety of languages besides Objective-C. The key language elements needed to use Cocoa are support for dynamic object orientation and compatibility with the C programming language.

This chapter describes the general features of all languages that can be used with Cocoa, and a brief overview of object-oriented terminology. Details about the most common languages used with Cocoa are provided. The available language options are explained along with some of the advantages and disadvantages of different languages. This book primarily uses the Objective-C language, and this chapter explains why.

Java and many scripting languages provide the required language features to use Cocoa directly. Other languages such as C and C++ are not sufficiently dynamic to use Cocoa objects directly. C and C++ programs can access Cocoa in two ways: They can use Cocoa indirectly via the C-based Objective-C runtime, or they can be recompiled using the Objective-C and Objective-C++ language compilers.

Details about using the Objective-C runtime from C or C++ without using the Objective-C language syntax are provided in Appendix A, "Unleashing the Objective-C Runtime." Because Objective-C is an extension of standard C and can compile all C programs, the best way to use Cocoa from C code is to actually use Objective-C. Parts of a program can be standard C (perhaps for portability reasons), whereas other parts can use Objective-C's object-oriented extensions to access Cocoa. A variant of Objective-C called Objective-C++ provides the same object-oriented extensions to C++ that Objective-C provides to standard C. The best way to mix C++ code and Cocoa is to use Objective-C++.

Object Orientation

Cocoa is a collection of objects. To understand how various languages use Cocoa, a brief explanation of objects and object orientation is needed. Object-oriented languages must use objects in a way that is compatible with Cocoa to be integrated with Cocoa. For example, Java is an object-oriented language that interfaces well with Cocoa. C++ is an object-oriented language that provides a model of objects incompatible with Cocoa.

The goals of object orientation are to make writing software easier, cheaper, and faster. The principal way that object orientation achieves its goals is through software reuse. The idea is that software can be organized into objects that are individually reusable. Each time a new software project begins, substantial parts of the project can be implemented using existing software objects. In theory, the only new code that is written for a project is the code that is truly unique to that project and cannot be shared by other projects.

By reusing objects, programmers hope to reduce the amount of new code written for each project and, therefore, finish the project faster. Reused objects are already well-tested in other projects. By reusing objects, programmers avoid bugs that might be created in new code. Existing objects that implement complex logic are used to make creating software for a new project easier. The idea is that the most complex and difficult to write code is provided by existing objects. Reusing objects is simpler than rewriting the logic implemented by the objects.

Encapsulation

Encapsulation is one of the principal ideas of object orientation. Encapsulation means that data and the logic that operates on the data are grouped together. Data is only modified via the operations encapsulated with the data. Encapsulation aids reuse and simplifies software maintenance. Encapsulation also ensures that related data and logic can be easily identified in one project and reused in another. Because data and logic are encapsulated together, it is not necessary to grab a line of code here and a data structure definition there, or search all the source code in a project for necessary lines of code to reuse just one feature of a project. Encapsulation aids software maintenance by localizing problem solutions. If a bug is detected, or a new feature must be added, encapsulation ensures that there is only one place in the code where changes are made. Without encapsulation, fixing a bug, or adding a feature might require changes to many different parts of a software project.

Modularity

Modularity is related to encapsulation. Modularity is the practice of implementing a software project in multiple modules. A module is a self-contained input to a compiler. The idea is that modules of code and data can be developed and compiled independently. The separately compiled modules are brought together to complete a project. In many cases, each module encapsulates some data and logic. Apple's Objective-C compiler enables the use of multiple modules to encapsulate one set of data and operations. It is also possible to implement multiple units of encapsulation in one module, but it is usually a bad practice.

Classes

In most object-oriented languages, something called a class is the basis of encapsulation. Each class encapsulates some data and all operations upon that data. Operations on data are sometimes called behaviors. Classes are implemented in one or more modules. Classes formalize the ideas of encapsulation, and in some languages the compiler enforces that encapsulation. The compiler prevents code that is not part of a class from modifying the data managed by the class. Classes are related to instances and inheritance.

Instances

A class is in some respects an abstract idea. A class describes data and operations on that data, but a class by itself is usually just an idea. For example, imagine a class called `Control` that describes certain characteristics of all graphical user interface elements. Those characteristics might include color and position. The class `Control` is not any particular user interface element, it describes all user interface elements. A particular button is an "instance" of the class `Control`. An instance of the class `Control` has a color and a position as described by the `Control` class.

A class describes data and behavior. An instance actually stores the data described by a class. There can be any number of instances of a class. The behaviors defined in a class are applied to instance's data.

NOTE

You will learn more about abstract classes and abstract Cocoa classes in Chapters 4 and 7. Chapter 4 also introduces the details of Objective-C as well as class methods versus instance methods. If these concepts are confusing to you now, you'll get more details in these two chapters.

Objects

Both classes and instances can be called objects. Classes are objects that describe instances. Instances are objects that store data described by a class. Object is a general term that applies to encapsulated data and logic and has different implications in different languages. Almost every object-oriented language endows objects with capabilities beyond just encapsulation, such as support for specialization.

Specialization

Object orientation promotes software reuse. Software objects from one project can be used in another project. But what happens when a new project needs an object similar to one that already exists, but needs just a few changes? The existing object can be specialized rather than starting from scratch to create a new object that meets the exact needs of the new project. Specialization is a technique for altering parts of the data and behavior of an existing object while reusing other parts. There are two types of specialization: instance-based and class-based. Cocoa uses both class-based specialization and instance-based specialization extensively.

Instance-based specialization is a technique for changing the behavior of just one instance object without necessarily modifying the behavior of other instances of the same class.

Class-based specialization applies changes to classes. The most common technique is to create a new class that includes all the data and operations of another class while adding additional data and new behaviors. Instances of the new class store the additional data and have the additional behaviors along with the data and behaviors of instances of the original class.

Inheritance

Inheritance is the most common form of class-based specialization. If a class called `Button` includes the data and behaviors of class `Control`, class `Button` is said to inherit from class `Control`. The terms subclass and superclass describe the inheritance relationship. `Button` is a subclass of `Control`. A subclass inherits all of the data and behavior of its superclass. In this example, `Control` is `Button`'s superclass. If class `Button` inherits from class `Control`, an instance of `Button` can be used in any context that an instance of `Control` is required.

Some languages such as C++ support multiple inheritance. Multiple inheritance means that a class has all the data and behavior described by two or more super classes. Java and Objective-C do not support multiple inheritance, and Cocoa does not use multiple inheritance.

Messages

Messages are one way that objects can communicate with each other. Messages enable objects to request that other objects invoke behaviors. A user interface object might send the `isEnabled` message to a `Control` instance as a way to request that the `Control` instance returns a `YES` or `NO` value. A message is an abstract idea and few assumptions are made about messages. For example, a message can be sent to an anonymous object. The sender of the message might not know the class of the receiver. The receiver might not even be in the same program as the sender. Messages promote object reuse by minimizing the dependencies between objects. The less one object knows about another, the better chance the objects can be reused separately. Messaging enables communication between objects without dependencies.

Many object-oriented languages do not directly support messaging. Messaging is one of the dynamic features of Objective-C that are essential to the implementation of Cocoa. Messaging is described in Chapter 4, and the technical implementation of messaging is described in Appendix A.

Polymorphism

Polymorphism is another technique that enables the reuse of software objects. Polymorphism allows the software that uses an object to work regardless of the specific class of the object. In other words, polymorphism enables an object to send the same message to different receivers without knowing precisely what behavior will be invoked by the message when it is received.

All messages in Objective-C use polymorphism. In many cases it is not possible for the sender of an Objective-C message to know the class of the object that receives the message. Each receiver will invoke different behaviors upon receipt of the message. Java and C++ also support polymorphism to various degrees. Along the spectrum of flexibility, C++ compilers require detailed knowledge about all objects whose behaviors are used. Objective-C does not require any knowledge about the objects that are used at compile time. Java falls between the two extremes.

Java

Java is one of the most popular programming languages used today. The designers of Java credit Objective-C as one of the influences that led to the creation of Java. In addition to the Java language syntax, Java provides standard libraries of objects and a standard runtime environment called the Java Virtual Machine (JVM). Apple supports the use of Java when creating Cocoa applications. Java implements classes, inheritance, and polymorphism in ways that are compatible with Cocoa. Java has several compelling features not shared by other languages used with Cocoa.

Automatic Garbage Collection

Dynamic memory management is one of the most difficult aspects of programming. The Java language and the JVM include technology called automatic garbage collection. Automatic garbage collection is a technique for automatically reusing dynamically allocated memory that is no longer being used by the objects that reserved it. Java programmers can usually ignore the issues of dynamic memory management because the language and JVM take care of that for them. However, to get the best possible performance with Java applications, programmers must still be sensitive to dynamic memory allocation issues. Objective-C does not have the same degree of support for automatic garbage collection.

Interfaces

Java includes a language feature called an interface. An interface specifies a set of behaviors that an object can invoke. Objects can have multiple interfaces. To promote reuse of objects, it is important that each object depend as little as possible on other objects. Java interfaces can be used to minimize the dependencies between objects. A Java object can be constructed so that it works with any other object that implements a particular interface without needing to know the class or other information about the other object. The less an object knows about other objects, the less likely it is to depend on the other objects.

Java interfaces are similar to Objective-C protocols. Cocoa uses protocols extensively. When Java is used with Cocoa, many of Cocoa's protocols are accessed with equivalent Java interfaces.

Security and Safety

Security was one of the design goals of Java. The JVM ensures that Java objects downloaded over the Internet cannot directly harm the computer on which they are run. Most computer languages do not have any security features and, therefore, it is not as safe to download and use objects written with other languages.

The Java Bridge

Apple provides a technology called the Java Bridge. The Java Bridge enables seamless interaction between Java objects and the Objective-C–based Cocoa objects. Java objects can specialize Objective-C objects. The Java Bridge handles issues such as the different dynamic memory management conventions between Java and Objective-C. Java programs that use Cocoa objects only run on Mac OS X.

100% Pure Java

Java is a cross-platform language because of the Java Virtual Machine. Any computer with a recent version of the JVM can run Java programs even if the programs were written on a different type of computer. Mac OS X includes an up to date JVM implementation and standard libraries.

Java programs that only use Java's standard libraries are called 100% Pure Java programs. Such programs run on any computer with an up to date Java implementation. Mac OS X is an excellent platform for writing 100% Pure Java applications. However, if a Java program uses Cocoa, it will not work on operating systems other than Mac OS X.

JavaBeans

The Java language includes JavaBeans, which are a standard for loading objects into running programs. The standard Java libraries include features for loading JavaBeans as well as identifying the interfaces and behaviors that the loaded JavaBeans support. JavaBeans have many features in common with a Cocoa technology called bundles.

Objective-C

Cocoa is implemented with Objective-C. Chapter 4, "Objective-C," describes Objective-C's object-oriented additions to the standard C language. This chapter provides information intended to help developers select a language to use with Cocoa. Some of the features of Objective-C not shared by the other languages used with Cocoa are presented here to aid the comparison of languages. The details are not presented until Chapter 4.

Categories

Categories are an Objective-C feature that enables the specialization of classes without using inheritance. Categories can be used to add behaviors to existing classes without recompiling them. The instances of specialized classes gain the new behaviors. Even pre-existing instances and instances created and used entirely within the implementations of Cocoa classes gain the new behaviors. Categories and their many advantages are used and described throughout this book. Chapter 26, "Application Requirements, Design, and Documentation," includes detailed analysis of the use of categories when designing an application.

Protocols

Objective-C protocols are similar to Java interfaces. Protocols specify the behaviors provided by objects independent of the class of the objects. Cocoa contains many protocols.

Perform

Objective-C objects can be asked to invoke behaviors in a dynamic way. For example, a program can accept input from a user that specifies a behavior to invoke in a running application. The capability to ask an object to invoke a behavior without the aid of a compiler contributes to the integration of Cocoa with scripting languages.

Posing

Posing is the capability to universally substitute one class for another. Every time an attempt is made to create an instance of a class, an instance of the posing class is created instead. Posing classes even work with compiled libraries such as Cocoa. If a Cocoa application includes an object that poses as a Cocoa object, the posing class is used instead of the original class in every case. Posing is a feature of Objective-C that conflicts with Java's security features and should not be used in Java Cocoa applications.

Runtime

Objective-C includes a runtime system similar in many ways to the Java Virtual Machine. Objective-C's runtime provides many of the dynamic features of Objective-C and enables the dynamic loading of Objective-C objects. Unlike the JVM, Objective-C's runtime is small and does not provide cross-platform support or security features. Objective-C's runtime is written in standard C and can be used from C or C++ programs even if those programs are not compiled with an Objective-C or Objective-C++ compiler.

Other Languages

Objective-C and Java are the two languages most commonly used with Cocoa, but many other languages operate with Cocoa to varying degrees. The languages used with Cocoa fall into two major categories: languages based on C and scripting languages.

ANSI C and C++

As mentioned previously, Cocoa is written in Objective-C, which is based on ANSI C. As a result, other languages that are based on C can be used with Cocoa. There are two strategies for using languages based on C with Cocoa. One strategy is to use only the C interface to the Objective-C runtime and a standard C or C++ compiler. The other is to use an Objective-C or Objective-C++ compiler to compile C or C++ code.

It is possible to write an ANSI C program that uses most features of Cocoa, and compile that program with a standard C compiler. The Objective-C runtime's C interface includes functions for creating and sending messages to Cocoa objects. As a superset of C, the C++ language can use the same techniques to access Cocoa objects.

The easiest way to use Cocoa from C programs is to use the Objective-C compiler to compile the standard C code along with modules containing Objective-C code. Apple provides an Objective-C++ compiler that enables the mixture of C++ code and Objective-C code in the same module.

Scripting Languages

Scripting languages usually have a runtime that can be interfaced with Cocoa. The most popular scripting languages used with Cocoa are AppleScript, TCL, and Python. Apple provides AppleScript Studio along with their other developer tools. AppleScript Studio enables the creation of full-featured Cocoa applications using AppleScript.

A product called Joy from AAA+ Software (`http://www.aaa-plus.com`) is used to integrate TCL, JavaScript, and other languages with Cocoa. An open source interface between Objective-C and TCL is available at `http://www-sfb288.math.tu-berlin.de/oorange/interpretedOC/interpretedOC.html`. The Usenix organization provides a technical paper discussing the integration between TCL and Objective-C at `http://www.usenix.org/publications/library/proceedings/tcl95/bogdanovich.html`.

Choosing a Language for Use with Cocoa

Cocoa can be used with many different languages, so how does a programmer choose the language to use? As always, the answer depends on many factors, including the programmer's familiarity with the languages and the special features of different languages that are applicable to the problem's solution. The pros and cons of the most common language choices for using Cocoa are described in this section. The bottom line is that any of the languages presented here can be used, and different programmers will make different choices.

Java Pros and Cons

Java is a powerful and modern language that emphasizes portability and security before performance and flexibility. Java is ideal for writing long-running server processes that heavily use network resources and databases. Java is well-suited for use in Web browsers where security is a concern. Java's use of automatic garbage collection simplifies application development and avoids whole classes of potential dynamic memory management errors. Java's standard libraries contain a broad range of features that provide a head start when developing many types of applications.

Java supports object orientation in a way that is compatible with Cocoa. Java applications can use Cocoa if portability is not important. Cocoa and the standard Java libraries have many features in common, but each contains objects that the other does not. Cocoa and standard Java libraries can be used well together.

Unlike Objective-C, Java is widely taught at universities and elsewhere. Many programmers who are learning Cocoa are already experienced with Java. For an experienced Java programmer, using Java with Cocoa might seem like less work than using Objective-C with Cocoa, but learning Objective-C takes little time for most programmers experienced with C and at least one object-oriented language. Because Cocoa is written in Objective-C, Cocoa programmers inevitably encounter Objective-C code even if that encounter is limited to example programs and documentation. Learning Objective-C makes learning Cocoa easier in the long run.

Java has several disadvantages for desktop applications. The cross-platform support and security features that make Java ideal for some applications can get in the way of others. The Java Virtual Machine that provides cross-platform support and security is large and takes a long time to load. When a Java desktop application is first started, the Java Virtual Machine must also be started and initialized. The JVM slows application start-up and consumes resources. For long-running server applications, the startup cost is negligible when averaged over the months or years that the program runs. Desktop applications are started and quit much more often.

Java Cocoa applications pay the price for the JVM, but they don't reap the benefits. When Cocoa is used, the Java application no longer has cross-platform support. Cocoa provides access to features that circumvent Java's security restrictions, which are probably inappropriate for a desktop application anyway.

Java is a popular language. Many libraries of Java objects are available, but it is inconvenient to use Java with most existing libraries that were written in different languages. To maximize the benefits of Java's portability and security, it is necessary to avoid existing non-Java libraries. The fact that it is inconvenient to reuse the millions of lines of existing C code and libraries from Java is a disadvantage.

Objective-C Pros and Cons

An advantage of Objective-C is its easy integration with existing C code. As a superset of ANSI C, Objective-C can be used with existing C libraries including traditional Mac and Unix libraries. The Objective-C++ compiler provided by Apple makes integration with existing C++ code convenient.

Objective-C is the implementation language of Cocoa, and some features unique to Objective-C are used by Cocoa. When Cocoa is used with different languages, small incompatibilities and features that do not translate well are exposed. Objective-C provides the most natural interface to Cocoa.

Objective-C is one of the most dynamic and flexible object-oriented languages, and Cocoa programming often benefits from these advantages. When Cocoa is used by less flexible languages, features and benefits of Cocoa are compromised to some degree. Java is also a flexible and dynamic language but not quite as flexible and dynamic as Objective-C.

Most existing Cocoa sample code and training resources use Objective-C. Familiarity with Objective-C maximizes the resources available to programmers who are learning to use Cocoa. Some of the features of Cocoa are based on unique features of Objective-C. Understanding how and why to use such Cocoa features is easier with an understanding of Objective-C.

Objective-C is a small extension of ANSI standard C. Unlike C++, which attempted to create a better C while adding a certain type of static strongly typed object support to C, Objective-C adds the minimum features necessary to support dynamic weak typed object support. Objective-C makes no attempt to improve the underlying C language. Objective-C is usually easy for C and C++ programmers to learn. The essential additions that Objective-C makes to C can be described in minutes.

Compared to existing implementations of the Java Virtual Machine, Objective-C's runtime makes more efficient use of system resources. For desktop applications and applications that occasionally need to resort to low-level system features and even assembly language, Objective-C is a better choice than Java. When performance is critical, the C subset of Objective-C can always be used to maximize performance.

There are two general types of applications: closed world and open world. Objective-C's flexibility and power are generally inappropriate for closed-world applications, but much more suited for open-world applications, as described in the following sections.

Closed-World Applications

The engine compartment of an automobile is analogous to closed-world applications. It is desirable to know in advance every component that will be inside the engine compartment and how they will fit together. Engines are carefully designed and their design is seldom modified after they leave the factory. Any variation in the connections between engine components is probably a manufacturing error. Languages such as C++ and to a lesser extent Java provide language-level features that are well-suited to solving closed-world problems. The static strong typing used by C++ and Java enables the compiler to verify that all components fit together as planned at the cost of making variation, redesign, and modification of existing applications more difficult. Some applications require the verifiability of static strong typing and can overcome the reduction in flexibility. Some programmers are just more comfortable solving closed-world style problems and might never be satisfied with Cocoa because it is designed to solve open-world problems.

Open-World Applications

The passenger compartment of an automobile is analogous to open-world applications. Any constraints on the type or number of people and things that can be placed in the passenger compartment detract from the utility of the automobile. Some constraints are inevitable, but the designer of a passenger compartment must strive for maximum flexibility. The price of that flexibility is that the designer cannot anticipate everything that might be put in the passenger compartment. The designer must work with incomplete information. Objective-C provides language-level support for solving open-world problems. Objective-C objects can operate with anonymous objects in different applications. It is possible to send messages to objects even though the receiver might not understand the message. It is possible to add behaviors to existing compiled objects without recompiling them. The flexibility provided by Objective-C aids the development and life-cycle modification of most desktop applications, but the cost is that the compiler cannot always verify that the components fit together. In some cases, errors that might have been caught by a compiler with a different language cannot be caught until an Objective-C application is running.

Most graphical user interfaces are examples of open-world applications. Restrictions on the type and number of graphical components available reduce the utility of user interfaces. Sometimes it is necessary to create new user interface components that were not anticipated by the original designers and still be able to integrate the new components with the old components. Plug-ins and context menus are other examples of open-world applications.

It is certainly possible to create open-world applications with static strongly typed languages, but it is more difficult. It is also possible to use strong static typing with Objective-C and gain many of the benefits at the cost of flexibility. Cocoa and Objective-C emphasize flexibility at the expense of compile time verifiability. Much of the increased programmer productivity attributed to using Cocoa results from Objective-C's flexibility.

Scripting Language Pros and Cons

Scripting languages are usually interpreted rather than compiled. Even scripting languages that can be compiled often also operate in an interpreted mode. In most cases, scripting languages promote rapid application development and programmer productivity before runtime performance and compile time verifiability. Scripting languages are often easy to learn and accessible to programming novices.

To access system resources that are only available from compiled languages, scripting languages almost always provide a mechanism to extend the language for use with compiled software written in other languages.

The extensibility of scripting languages combined with the power of Objective-C's runtime makes using Objective-C objects from within scripting languages possible. Details about allocating Objective-C objects and sending messages to them are provided in Appendix A. As long as a scripting language can call a small number of Objective-C runtime functions, Cocoa can be used in its entirety from the scripting language.

Scripting languages usually exhibit inferior performance and make producing large applications difficult in comparison to compiled languages. When the performance and scalability of scripting languages are acceptable, scripting languages can be an ideal way to use Cocoa.

The Use of Objective-C in This Book

Objective-C is used to present Cocoa in this book because Objective-C is the implementation language of Cocoa. Learning it is not a large obstacle to learning Cocoa. Understanding how and why to use Cocoa features is easier with an understanding of Objective-C. Cocoa is so large that the benefits derived from using Objective-C when explaining Cocoa outweigh the need for many readers to learn Objective-C. Programmers learn new languages all the time.

Summary

Cocoa can be used with many programming languages. For a language to use Cocoa, that language must support a degree of flexibility and a model of object orientation that is compatible with Cocoa. Objective-C, Java, and many scripting languages integrate well with Cocoa. Other languages such as standard C and C++ can use Cocoa either by using only the C functions provided by the Objective-C runtime or by using Objective-C and Objective-C++ compilers to mix Objective-C code with the standard C and C++ code.

Now that the languages used to write Cocoa applications have been explained, the next step is to learn the tools used to create Cocoa applications. Chapter 3, "Using Apple's Developer Tools," introduces the tools that Apple provides for creating Cocoa applications. Apple's developer tools can be used with C, C++, Java, Objective-C, Objective-C++, and AppleScript.

3

Using Apple's Developer Tools

IN THIS CHAPTER

- Obtaining Apple's Developer Tools
- Project Builder
- Interface Builder
- Frameworks
- Samples
- Terminal
- Other Tools

It is not possible to describe every feature of Apple's tools in one chapter, and the bulk of this book is dedicated to unleashing the power of Cocoa. Apple's tools have many features in common with other developer tools. This chapter describes the major tools that Apple provides and some introductory step-by-step ways to use them. Most developers become familiar with the tools quickly and discover features not mentioned here. Some of Apple's tools use unusual paradigms for development tasks. This chapter mentions some of those unusual aspects and assumes that the common aspects will be self-explanatory and second nature by the time several examples have been completed. Apple's own introductory documentation about the developer tools is available at `http://developer.apple.com/techpubs/macosx/DeveloperTools/devtools.html`.

Obtaining Apple's Developer Tools

Apple ships Mac OS X on one CD-ROM, and provides a second CD-ROM that contains developer tools. The Mac OS X Developer CD-ROM provides everything needed to write Cocoa applications using Apple's tools.

NOTE

The developer tools can also be downloaded from Apple's site for free at `http://developer.apple.com/tools/macosxtools.html`.

Apple's developer tools are high quality. They are competitive with similar tools from other vendors. The fact that

Apple distributes the tools with Mac OS X at no extra cost is not an indication that the tools are not valuable. Quite the contrary, the tools are powerful and in some cases indispensable for Cocoa development. Prior to the release of Mac OS X, Apple's tools had to be purchased separately at a cost of several thousand dollars. According to Apple, Mac OS X itself is built using Apple's tools.

Project Builder

The primary Cocoa development tool is called Project Builder. It provides an Integrated Development Environment (IDE) for writing, compiling, and debugging Cocoa applications using Objective-C, Objective-C++, AppleScript, or Java. Apple uses a modified version of `gcc`, the Gnu Compiler Collection, to compile Objective-C and Objective-C++. A modified version of `gdb`, the Gnu debugger, is used to debug applications. Project Builder wraps the Gnu tools and hides their command line nature from developers. Project Builder users do not need to use the Gnu tools directly. Project Builder integrates most development activities including editing code into one application.

NOTE

The Gnu project is a prominent open-source project. Details are available at `http://www.gnu.org/`.

Creating a New Project

To get familiar with Project Builder, create a new project to build a version of the classic "Hello World" program which is commonly the first program written in a new language. This example is so small that it barely uses features of Cocoa. It just shows how to create a new project and later how to edit, compile, and test code with Project Builder. The same techniques are used to create large Cocoa projects.

To get started, double-click the Project Builder icon in the `/Developer/Applications` folder. When Project Builder starts, select File, New Project from the menu bar to open the Assistant window. The Assistant window is used to select the type of new project to create. For this example, select the Foundation Tool project type, as shown in Figure 3.1. A Foundation Tool is a program that uses only nongraphical Cocoa objects. Tool programs do not have graphical user interfaces.

Click the Next button in the Assistant window. Project Builder requests the name and location of the new Foundation Tool project as shown in Figure 3.2. Type **`Hello World`** into the Project Name text field.

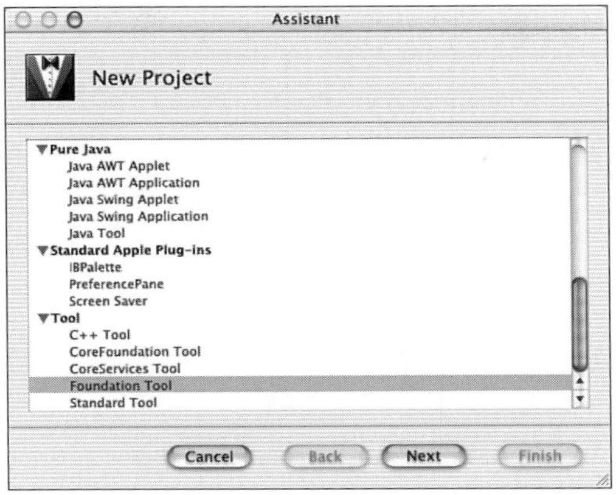

FIGURE 3.1 The Assistant window used to create new projects shows the Foundation Tool project type selected.

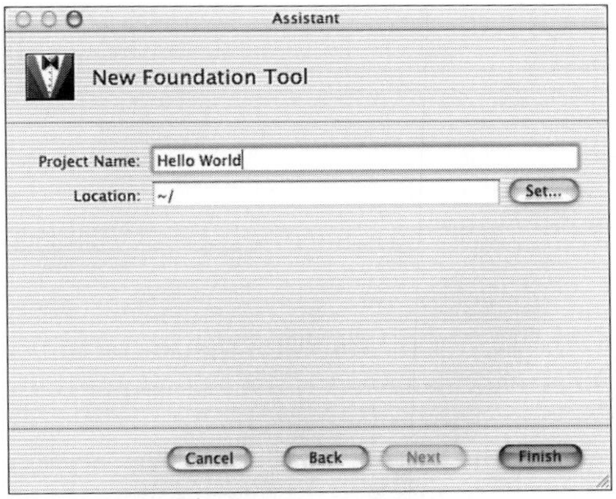

FIGURE 3.2 Specify the name and location of the new project.

Click the Finish button. Project Builder opens a new window for the Hello World project. Select the `main.m` file inside Project Builder's Source folder as shown in Figure 3.3. Each project document is divided into four main parts: Toolbar, Project pane, Editor pane, and Tool pane.

The Toolbar is user-configurable and accelerates access to frequently used Project Builder features. Every feature accessible with the Toolbar is also accessible through menus. The Project pane has several uses. Figure 3.3 shows the files that are used to build the Hello World program. The file `main.m` in the Source folder is selected. The contents of the `main.m` file are shown in the Editor pane. Figure 3.3 also shows the Tool pane closed, so that only tabs to access its features are visible.

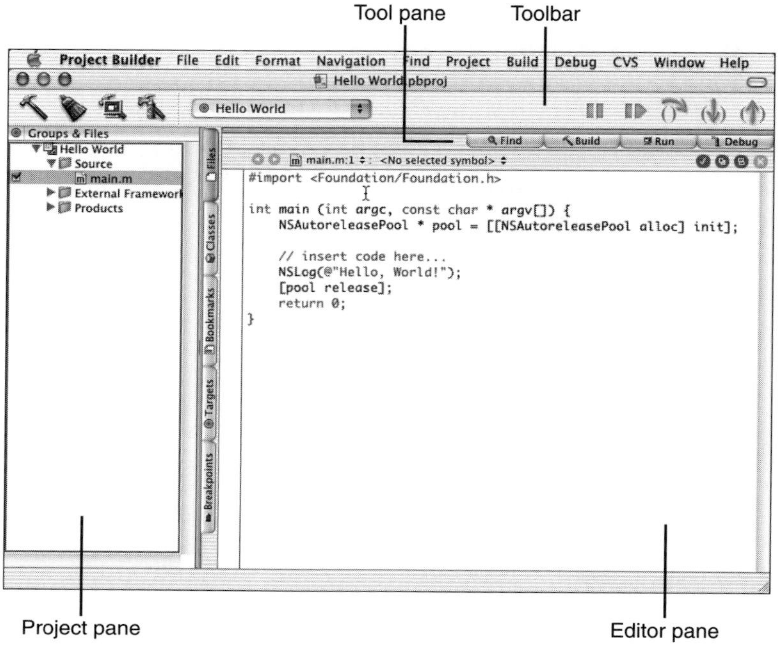

FIGURE 3.3 Each Project Builder document represents a project and has four main parts.

The `.m` extension on the `main.m` file indicates that it contains Objective-C code. In this example, the Objective-C language is used to output the string Hello, World!. Don't worry if you are not yet familiar with the Objective-C language. Chapter 4, "Objective-C," introduces the language. It is not necessary to write any code for this trivial example because by default, when Project Builder creates a new Foundation Tool project, it includes the file `main.m` exactly as shown in Figure 3.3. It even contains the following line that outputs the Hello, World! string.

```
NSLog(@"Hello, World!");
```

Building the Hello World Project

To build the Hello World example, use the Build, Build menu item or Cmd-b. Figure 3.4 shows Project Builder in the middle of compiling the Hello World program. The Tool pane shows the output from a variety of command-line tools used to build the project, including the gcc Objective-C compiler. If there are any errors or warnings generated during the build, they are displayed above the divider in the Tools pane.

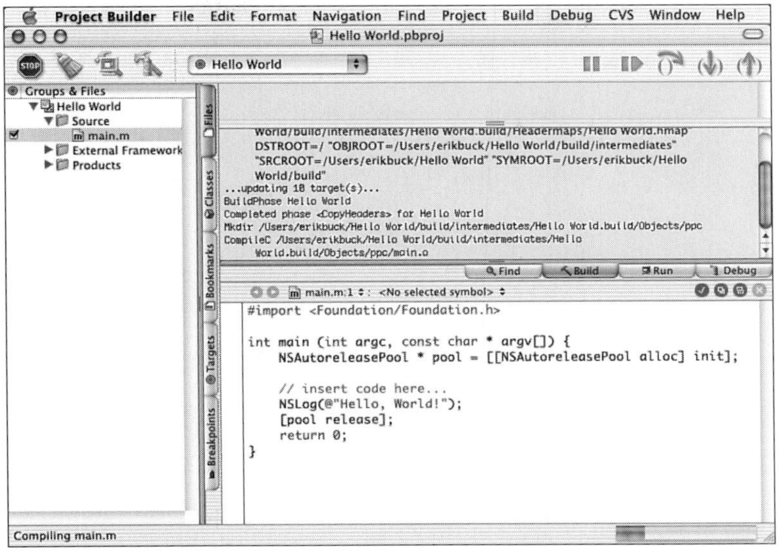

FIGURE 3.4 Project Builder shows the output from command-line build tools in the Tools pane.

Running Hello World

After the project has been built, it can be run. To run the Hello World program inside Project Builder, use the Build, Build and Run menu item, or Cmd-r. Figure 3.5 shows the output from Hello World in the Run tab of the Tools pane. The Cocoa `NSLog()` function used to output the string Hello, World!, prints information such as the date and program that produced the output followed by the output itself. The Hello World program outputs `2002-02-22 19:34:05.813 Hello World[567] Hello, World!`. The rest of the text in the Run tab of the Tools pane indicates that the process named Hello World exited with status 0, meaning that there were no errors.

Exploring the Project Pane

Two components are used to create the Hello World program; the `main.m` file has already been shown. The other component is `Foundation.framework` shown in the Project pane. The `Foundation.framework` is a collection of objects, functions, and resources used in Cocoa applications. For example, the `NSLog()` function used to output Hello, World! is implemented in `Foundation.framework`. Figure 3.6 shows all the folders in the Project pane expanded to reveal their contents.

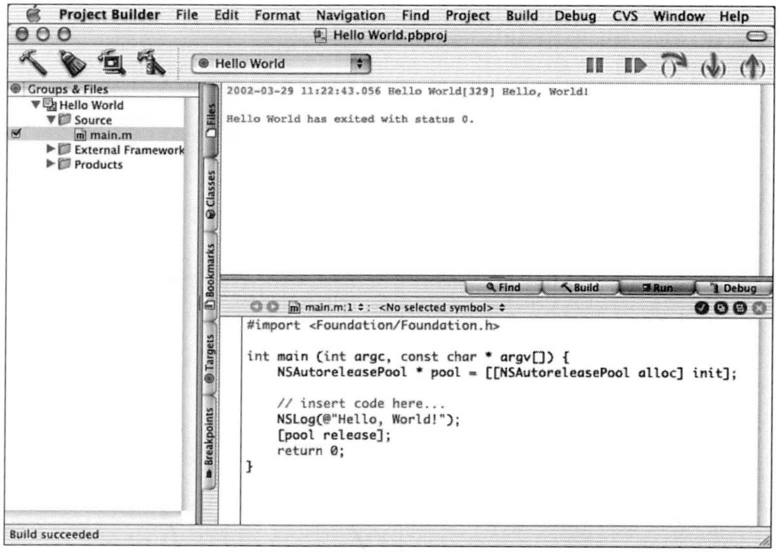

FIGURE 3.5 The output from running the Hello World program is shown in the Run tab of the Tools pane.

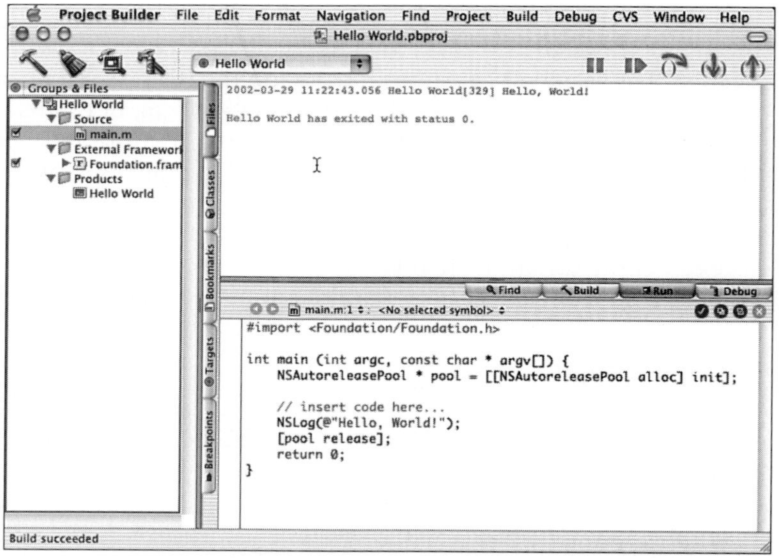

FIGURE 3.6 The components used to build the example are shown in the Project pane.

The folder labeled Products in the Project pane shown in Figure 3.6 lists the files that are created by building the project. In this example, the Hello World program is the only product that results from building the project.

There are five tabs that reveal different information in the Project pane. Figure 3.7 shows the tabs with the Targets tab selected.

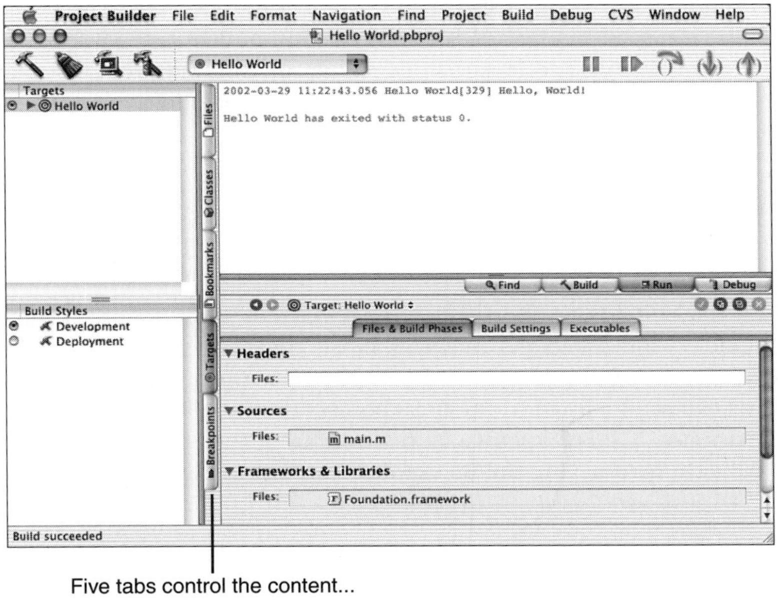

FIGURE 3.7 The Targets tab lists the products that are built by a project, and the build style used to produce the targets.

The tabs provide the following information:

- The Files tab organizes the components used to build the project and the output products from the project.
- The Classes tab lists the hierarchy of Cocoa classes available for use in applications. The Classes are introduced throughout the rest of this book.
- The Bookmarks tab shows and organizes the list of bookmarks set by the user. Bookmarks help users quickly jump to positions of interest within files.
- The Targets tab, shown in Figure 3.7, lists the applications, libraries, frameworks, and other products built by a project. A single project can have any number of targets, but there is usually only one. The Targets tab also lists available build styles that are described later in this chapter.

- The Breakpoints tab lists the places where the debugger should stop execution when debugging code. The previously set breakpoints can be disabled or deleted from within the Breakpoints tab.

A build style specifies the options that are passed to various command-line tools used by Project Builder to build projects. The two build styles shown in Figure 3.7 are Development and Deployment. The Development build style specifies build options that result in programs containing maximum debugging information. The Deployment build style specifies less debugging support, but produces smaller, faster programs. It is possible to create custom build styles and add them to the list as described in Project Builders online help.

Debugging with Project Builder

To start debugging an application, select the Build, Build and Debug menu item, or Cmd-y.

Figure 3.8 shows the Hello World program stopped on a breakpoint while running in Project Builder's integrated `gdb` debugger. Breakpoints can be added to a program by clicking in the margin to the left of a line of code in the Editor pane. Breakpoints that have been set are listed in the Breakpoints tab of the Project pane shown selected in Figure 3.8. Breakpoints are removed from the Breakpoints tab of the Project pane, or by dragging the Breakpoint icon out of the margin in the editor window.

NOTE

An online manual for the `gdb` debugger titled *Getting Started with GDB* is available at `http://developer.apple.com/technotes/tn/tn2032.html`

The Project Builder toolbar contains icons on the right side to control the basic functions of the debugger. The icons that look like VCR controls pause and resume execution of a program. The remaining icons enable various techniques for single stepping through code.

Using Project Builder's Find Tool

Another Project Builder feature that can be demonstrated with the Hello World example is the integrated Find tool. Figure 3.9 shows the Find tool in the Tools pane. Project Builder searches for strings within the files of a project and within online documentation and frameworks. One handy technique is to select an unfamiliar term in the Editor pane and use the Find, Find Selected Text menu, or Cmd-7, to search for the term in the online documentation. Figure 3.9 shows the results of searching for information about the selected word `NSAutoreleasePool`. Be sure to select the Find tab of the Tools pane to see the results of the find operation.

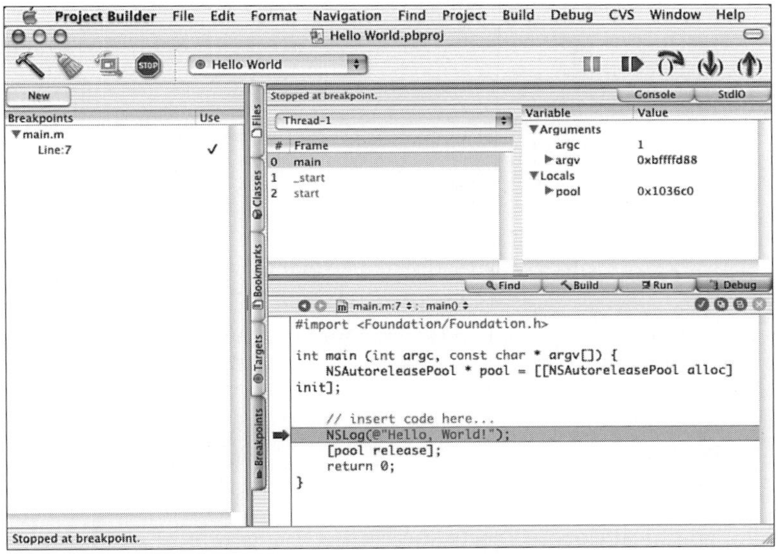

FIGURE 3.8 The Hello World program is stopped on a breakpoint while running in Project Builder's integrated `gdb` debugger. The Breakpoints tab of the Project pane is selected.

Project Builder has a related automatic symbol completion feature that reduces the amount of typing necessary. After the first few letters of a programming term have been typed, press the F5 function key, and Project Builder looks up the term with the Find tool and completes it, if possible. Typing `NSAutore` followed by pressing F5 completes the half-typed work to produce `NSAutoreleasePool`.

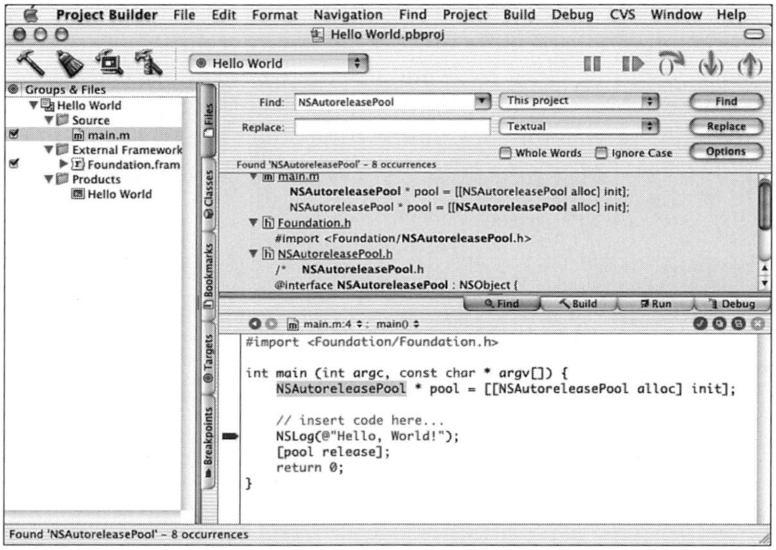

FIGURE 3.9 Project Builder's integrated Find tool searches for terms within a project or in the online documentation.

Interface Builder

Interface Builder is invaluable for Cocoa development. Interface Builder is a tool for positioning graphical Cocoa objects and connecting graphical and nongraphical objects together. Interface Builder is arguably the best and most flexible user-interface design tool available today for any platform. That is particularly impressive considering the fact that Interface Builder is more than 12 years old, and its basic features have not evolved much in that time. Interface Builder itself is a great example of a Cocoa application. It demonstrates the power and flexibility of Cocoa while helping developers create new Cocoa applications. Interface Builder can be extended and used with new reusable objects.

Interface Builder provides access to the full power and flexibility of the objects in the Cocoa frameworks. Without detailed descriptions of the objects and their interactions, there are limits to the amount of information that can be presented regarding the use of Interface Builder. In this section, the general features of Interface Builder and its idioms are presented without much explanation. Instead the role Interface Builder plays in Cocoa development is introduced.

The following example describes how to build a simple image-viewer application without writing or compiling any code at all. The example is similar in spirit to the nongraphical Hello World program. In the Image Viewer example, standard Cocoa objects are configured to allow drag and drop of image files from the file system and display the images in a window.

One of the features of Interface Builder that the following example demonstrates is the absence of required code. Interface Builder simply configures and connects existing objects such as windows, menus, and image-viewer widgets. The objects are stored in a file on the hard disk. When the file is read the objects and all their connections are restored and can be run immediately.

Creating a New Interface with Interface Builder

The first step in this example is to launch Project Builder from the `/Developer/Applications` folder. Next, select File, New Project to open the Assistant window, as shown in Figure 3.10. Select the Cocoa Application option and click Next.

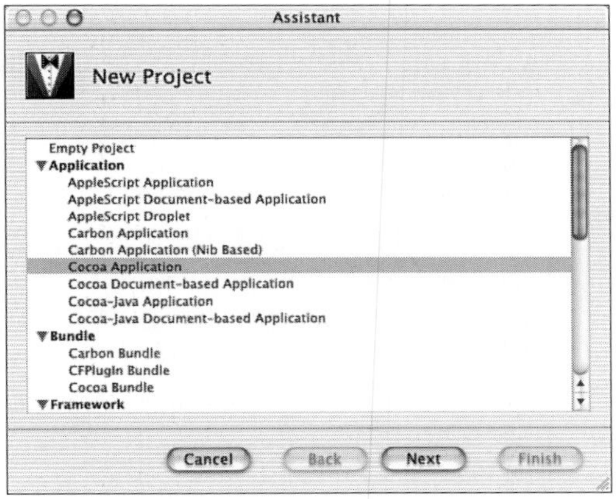

FIGURE 3.10 Select Cocoa Application in the Assistant window used to create new projects.

As shown in Figure 3.11, type the name `Image Viewer` into the Project Name text field, leave the default location in the Location text field unmodified, and click the Finish button.

Project Builder creates a new project with the name `Image Viewer.pbproj` in a folder called Image Viewer at the location specified. The new project is represented by the `Image Viewer.pbproj` document shown in Figure 3.12. Make sure that the Files tab of the Project pane is selected. Select the `MainMenu.nib` file in the Resources folder of the Project pane, as shown in Figure 3.12.

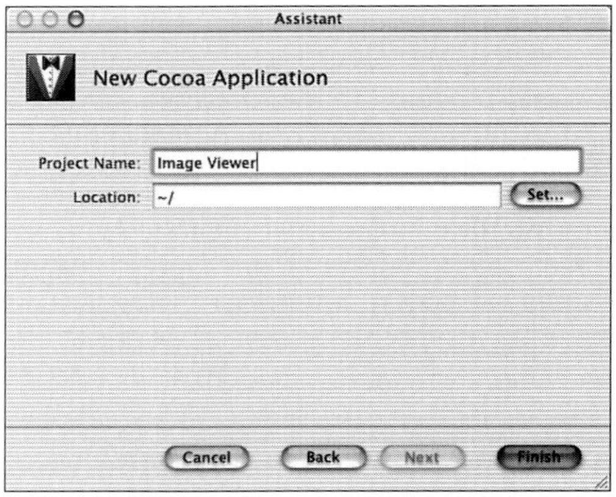

FIGURE 3.11 Name the new project Image Viewer.

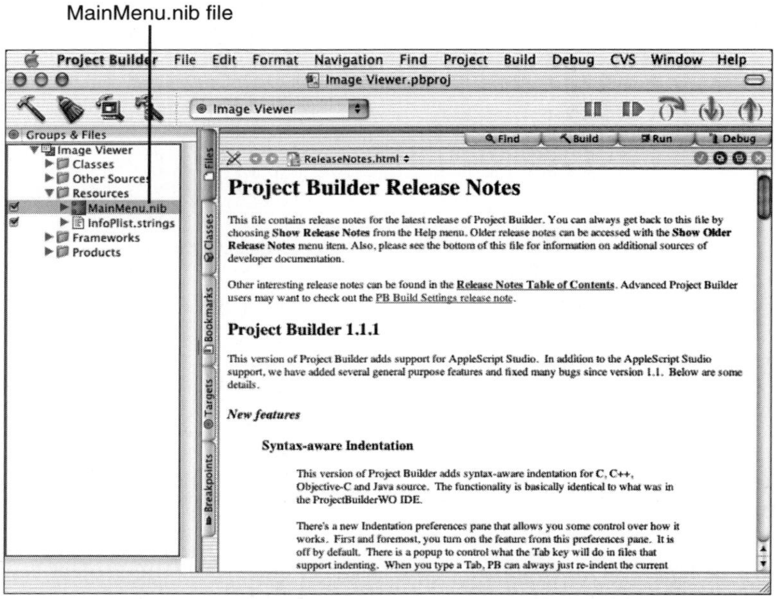

FIGURE 3.12 Select the `MainMenu.nib` file in the expanded Resources folder.

Double-click the `MainMenu.nib` file to start Interface Builder. When Interface Builder starts, select the Interface Builder, Hide Others menu to hide all applications except Interface Builder. Interface Builder is shown with the `MainMenu.nib` document open in Figure 3.13. By default, the `MainMenu.nib` document already contains several objects including a menu and an empty application window. Figure 3.13 shows Interface Builder configured with four open windows: one titled `MainMenu.nib`, another window titled `MainMenu.nib-MainMenu`, a window titled Window, and a window titled Cocoa-Other that contains a palette of reusable objects. The window titled Cocoa-Other in Figure 3.13 might have a different title and show different contents when Interface Builder starts. This window provides access to Cocoa objects that are used to build applications. Several different groups of objects exist. Each group is called a palette and can be shown by selecting one of the icons in a row just below the window's title bar. The last palette accessed in a previous session using Interface Builder is shown when Interface Builder is started. The title of the window changes based on the palette shown.

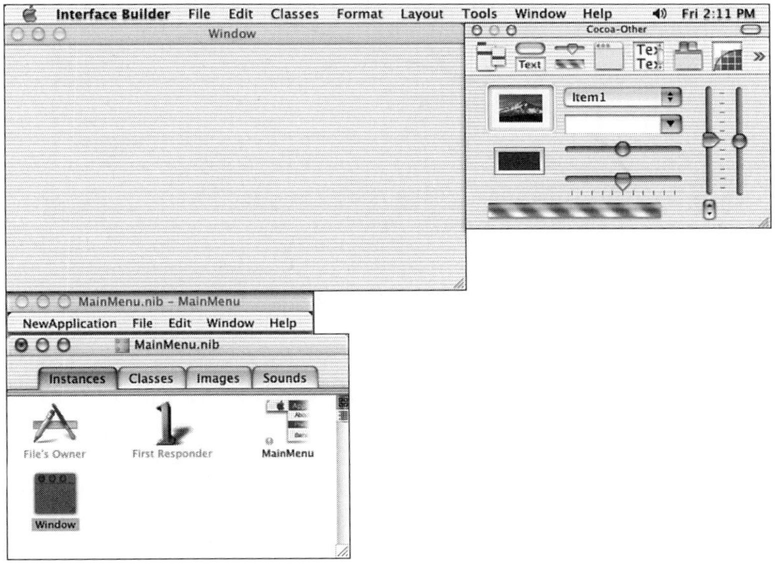

FIGURE 3.13 Four windows are open when Interface Builder starts and loads the `MainMenu.nib` file.

If the Interface Builder palette does not already show the collection of objects labeled Cocoa-Other, as shown in Figure 3.13, select the Cocoa-Other palette by clicking on the icon that depicts a slider and a progress indicator. It is third from the left in the window titled Cocoa-Other in Figure 3.13.

Drag an `NSImageView` object from the Cocoa-Other palette into the empty application window. Figure 3.14 shows the `NSImageView` being dragged from the palette.

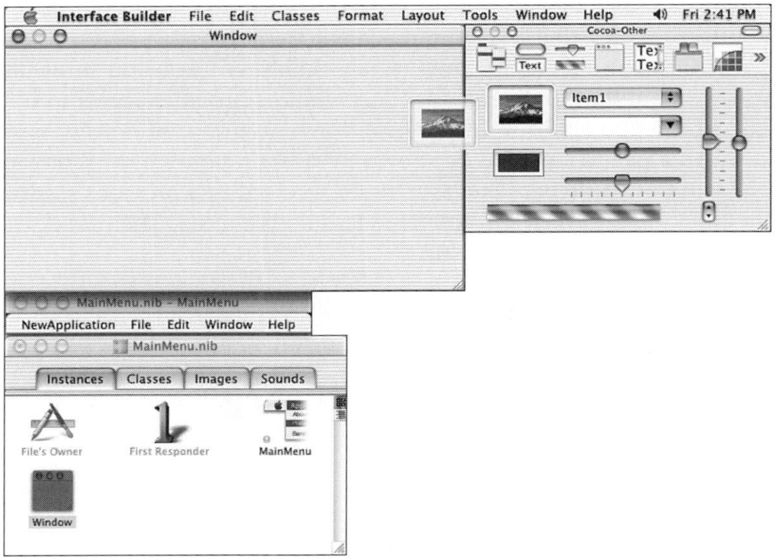

FIGURE 3.14 An `NSImageView` object is being dragged from the palette to the empty application window.

Figure 3.15 shows the `NSImageView` object that was dragged into the empty application window and selected. When the `NSImageView` object was dropped into the window, a copy of the object dragged from the palette was made, and then was added to the content of the window. The little boxes around the object in Figure 3.15 are control points that indicate the selected object. Selected objects can be moved and resized with the control points.

Resize the `NSImageView` object so that it almost fills the window. As the `NSImageView` is resized, Interface Builder shows dashed guidelines that indicate suggested placement of objects to conform to Apple's user-interface conventions. Figure 3.16 shows the `NSImageView` resized to extend to the guidelines.

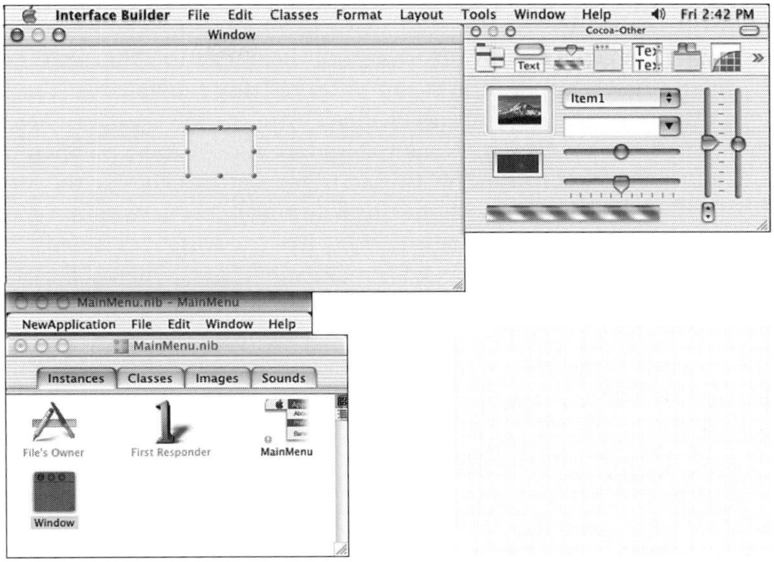

FIGURE 3.15 An `NSImageView` object is added to the content of the application window and selected.

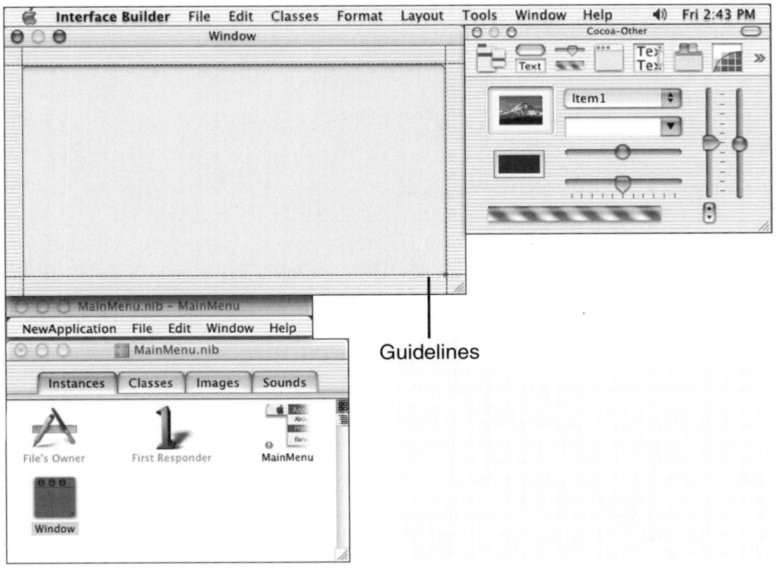

FIGURE 3.16 Interface Builder automatically shows guidelines for the placement and size of objects.

Configuring Objects

In this example, images are viewed by dragging them into the `NSImageView` object when the Image Viewer application is run. After resizing the `NSImageView`, the next step is to configure it to accept images dropped onto the `NSImageView`. Select Interface Builder's Tools, Show Info menu item or choose Cmd-1 to open the Show Info window. The Show Info window is used to inspect and change the attributes of selected objects. When first opened, the Show Info window's Attributes mode is visible. If the Show Info window does not look like the window labeled NSImageView Info, as seen in Figure 3.17, make sure that the newly positioned `NSImageView` is selected. The pop-up button labeled Attributes in Figure 3.17 is used to select the type of information shown in the window.

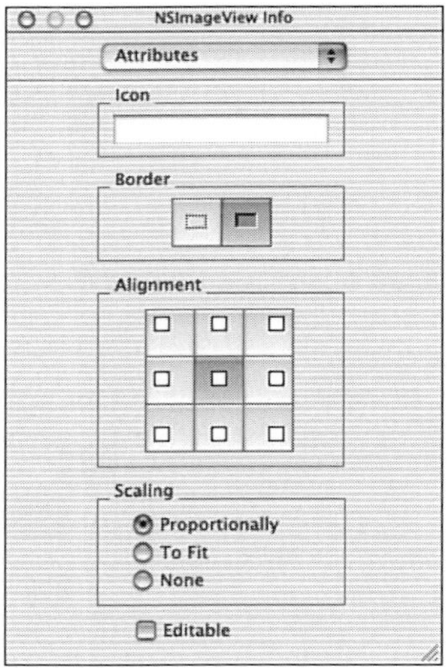

FIGURE 3.17 The Show Info window is used to inspect and change attributes of selected objects. It has the title NSImageView Info to indicate that it is showing information about a selected NSImageView object.

The `NSImageView` that was placed in the application window is an instance of a Cocoa class named `NSImageView`. Instances of the `NSImageView` class have many attributes that can be set, but for now the only attribute of interest is the Editable check box at the bottom of the Show Info window titled NSImageView Info in Figure 3.17. Select the Editable check box so the selected `NSImageView` is editable at runtime, as shown in Figure 3.18. Editable `NSImageView`'s accept dropped files, but noneditable ones do not.

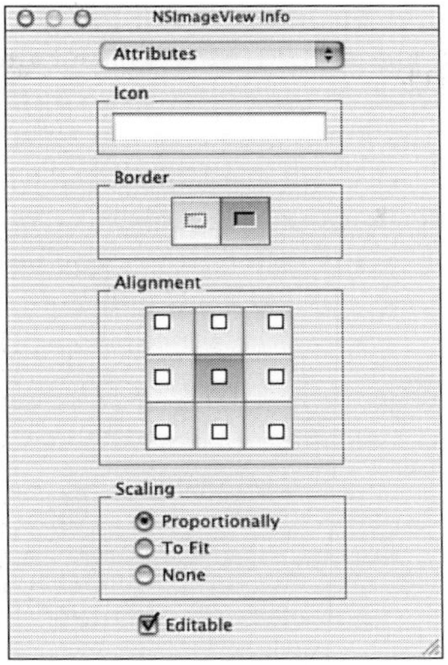

FIGURE 3.18 Make sure that the selected `NSImageView` is editable by selecting the Editable check box.

Next, configure the `NSImageView` to automatically resize when its window is resized. Select the Size mode of the Show Info window titled NSImageView Info using the pop-up button as shown in Figure 3.19, or use Cmd-3 to select the Size mode without using the pop-up button.

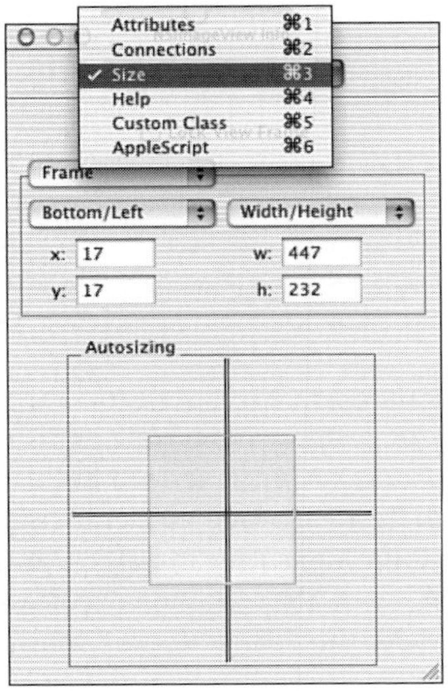

FIGURE 3.19 Change the Show Info window titled NSImageView Info to Size mode.

Click both of the lines within the inner box of the Autosizing area of the Show Info window until its similar to Figure 3.20. Most graphical Cocoa objects can be configured to automatically resize when the object that contains them changes size. By clicking the inner lines in the Autosizing area, the selected `NSImageView` is configured to always expand and contract to fill available space while leaving constant margins around the object. The outer lines in the Autosizing area control whether the margins can grow or shrink. Many different resizing behaviors can be set with the various springs and struts that look like coils and lines in the Autosizing area.

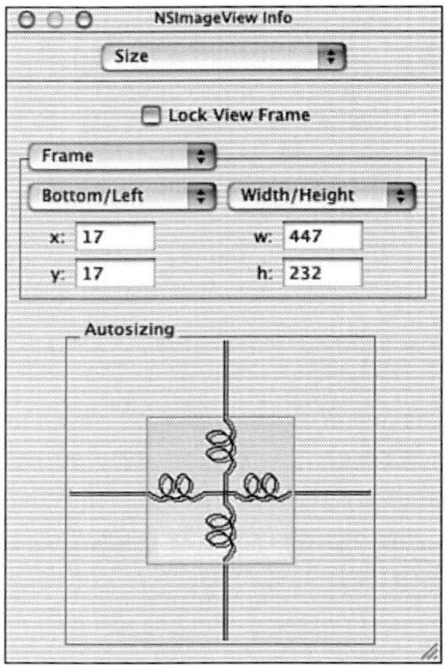

FIGURE 3.20 Set the Autosizing springs and struts for the selected `NSImageView` as shown.

NOTE

The size values shown in Figure 3.20 may be different if the window containing the `NSImageView` has been resized. The exact size specified does not matter.

The new interface can now be tested to determine if it is configured correctly. Select File, Test Interface, or use Cmd-r to put Interface Builder into Test Interface mode. When Interface Builder is in Test Interface mode, it copies the objects in the `.nib` file being edited, hides Interface Builder's user interface, and enables the copied objects to start running as if they were in a standalone application. When Interface Builder is put into Test Interface mode, the `Image Viewer` interface created looks like the one shown as in Figure 3.21.

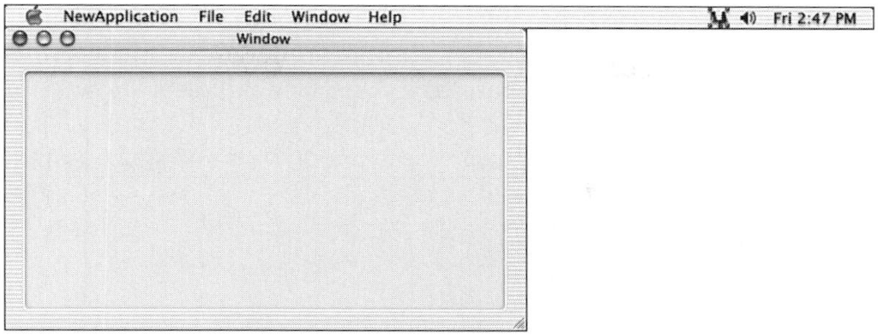

FIGURE 3.21 The interface being tested has its own menu and a single window titled Window that contains an editable `NSImageView`.

The interface being tested behaves just like it will in a standalone application. The window can be resized, and the `NSImageView` will resize with it. The interface has all the standard menus. To test the `NSImageView`, drag an image file from the Finder into the `NSImageView`. Image files can be found in the `/Library/Desktop Pictures` folder on most Mac OS X installations. Many types of images can be viewed including JPEG, TIFF, GIF, and BMP. Figure 3.22 shows an image file being dragged from the Finder to the `NSImageView`.

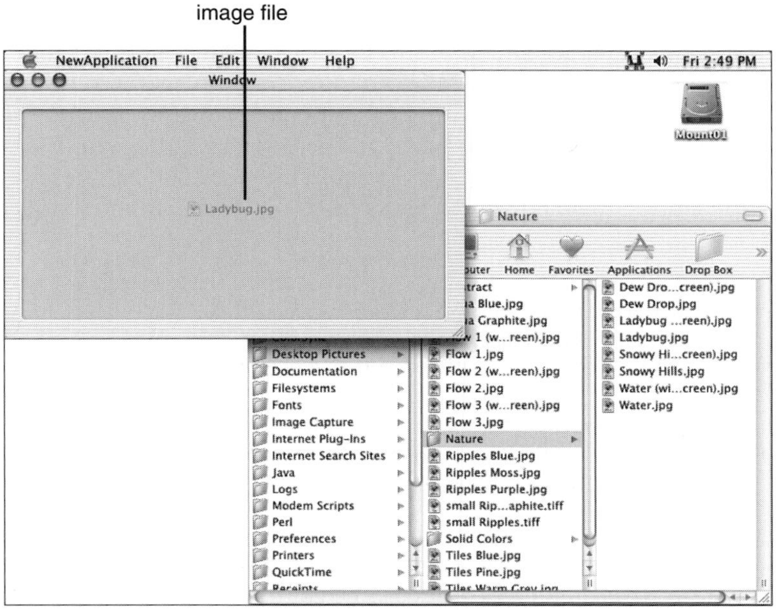

FIGURE 3.22 An image file is being dragged from the finder to the `NSImageView` being tested.

Figure 3.23 shows the image centered and scaled proportionally in the `NSImageView`. The default behavior of `NSImageView` is to proportionally scale images to fit within the view, and the default was not changed in Interface Builder's Show Info window.

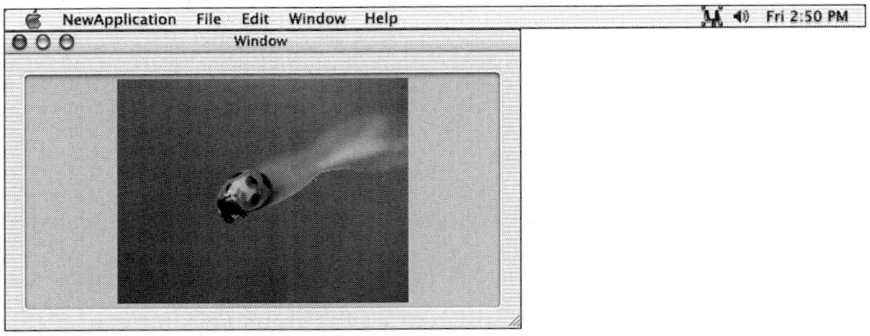

FIGURE 3.23 The interface being tested shows a ladybug image centered and scaled within the `NSImageView`.

As the window containing the `NSImageView` is resized, the image grows and shrinks to fit within the `NSImageView`. Try dropping other images on the `NSImageView`. The `NSImageView` can even be printed within the Interface Builder's test interface mode. Just select Cmd-p or the File, Print menu of the interface being tested.

To stop testing the interface and return to Interface Builder's normal mode, select the NewApplication, Quit NewApplication menu item, or use Cmd-Q. When Interface Builder is in its normal mode, make some additional changes to the `MainMenu.nib` interface. Change the title of the application's one window from Window to Dropped Image by selecting the Window icon in Interface Builder's `MainMenu.nib` window, and editing the name in the Show Info window's Attributes mode.

NOTE

When the Window icon is selected, the Show Info window is titled NSWindow Info. The Show Info window's title changes to reflect the selected object.

Select the Attributes mode of the Show Info window titled NSWindow Info. Enter the new title in the Window Title text field. Figure 3.24 shows the Window icon selected, and the title of the window being changed.

Change the name of the application's main menu by editing the menu as shown in Figure 3.25. Double-click the NewApplication menu in the window titled `MainMenu.nib—Mainmenu`. Menu names can be edited by double-clicking them. Change the NewApplication menu to the Image Viewer menu.

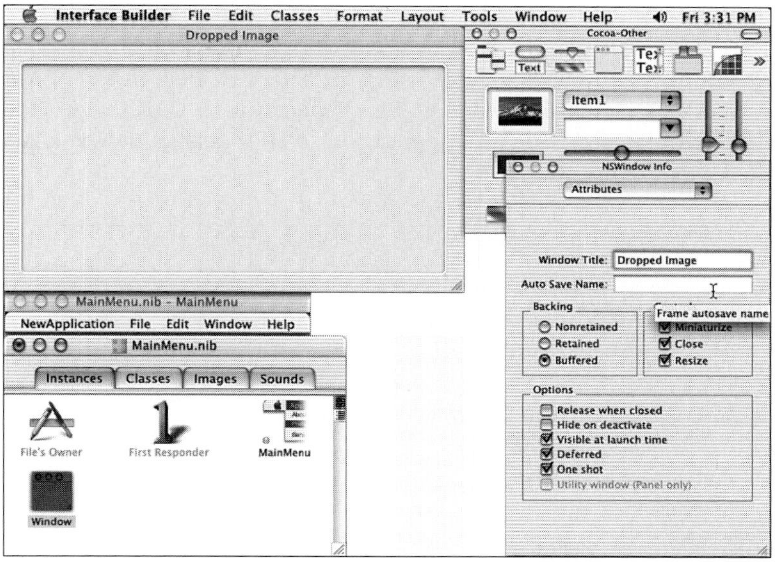

FIGURE 3.24 Change the application window's title to Dropped Image.

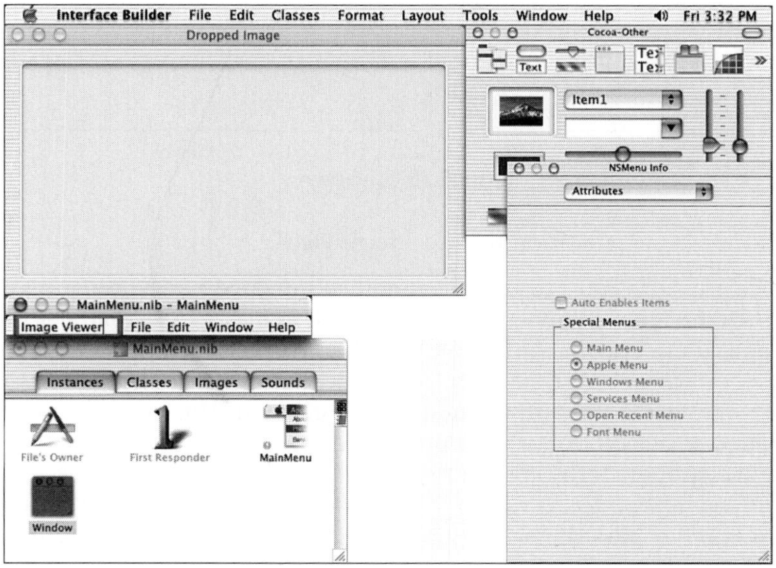

FIGURE 3.25 Change the application name in the main menu to Image Viewer.

Next, single-click the Image Viewer menu to show the menu's items. Change the item labeled About NewApplication to About Image Viewer by double-clicking the About NewApplication menu item or using the Title text field in the NSMenu Info window. Change the item labeled Quit NewApplication to Quit Image Viewer. Change the item labeled Hide NewApplication to Hide Image Viewer. Figure 3.26 shows the edited menu items.

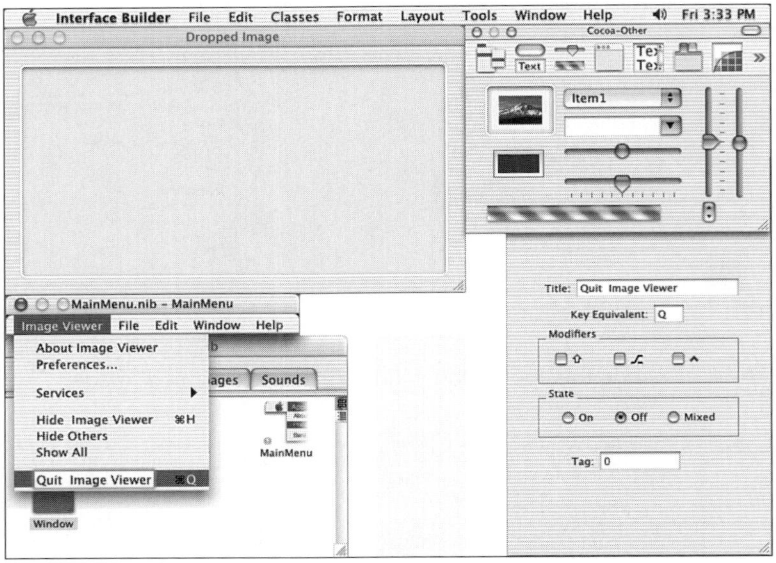

FIGURE 3.26 Edit the menu item labels as shown.

Change Hide NewApplication to Hide Image Viewer.

Select File, Save or Cmd-s to save the modified interface. Quit Interface Builder and single-click the Project Builder icon in the Dock to make Project Builder the front-most application. Use the Build, Build and Run menu item, or Cmd-r to build the project as shown in Figure 3.27. Project Builder builds the project and copies the edited `MainMenu.nib` file into the resulting application. The `.nib` file does not need to be compiled as part of the build process because it is just a resource. The `main.m` file that was automatically created for the new project must be compiled before the first time the new project is run, however. When Project Builder has finished compiling `main.m` and copied all necessary resources, the Image Viewer application is run.

Figure 3.28 shows the running standalone Image Viewer application with a displayed image and a standard Print panel accessed from the File, Print menu item.

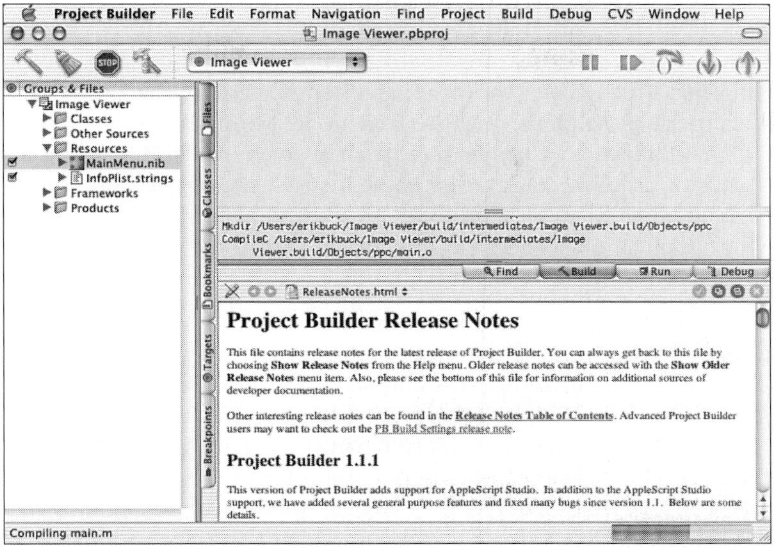

FIGURE 3.27 Project Builder compiles `main.m` and copies the `MainManu.nib` file as part of the build process.

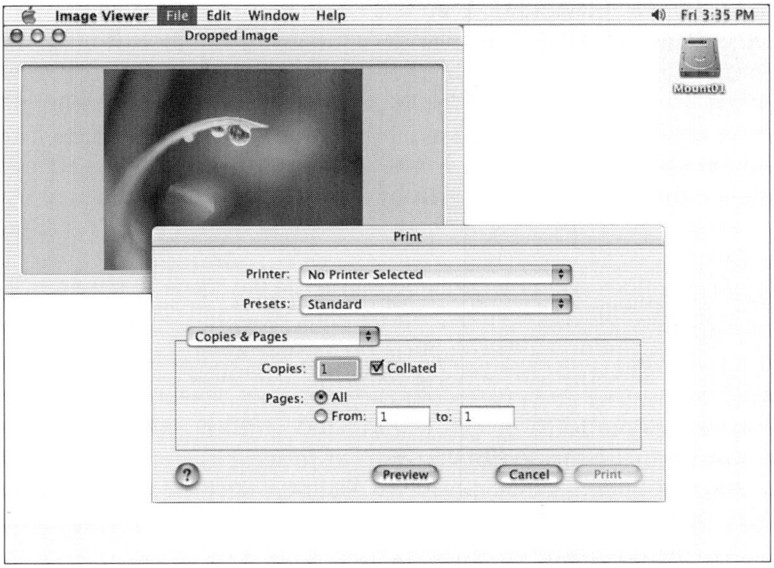

FIGURE 3.28 The Image Viewer application already supports printing and print preview.

Interface Builder Paradigms

Interface Builder has many features that have not yet been touched, but one of the key features has already been shown. The edited objects are live objects that can be run within Interface Builder's Test Interface mode. Minimal Cocoa applications support all standard menus and features such as live resize and printing. Interface Builder does not usually generate any code. Instead, the live objects being edited in Interface Builder are saved to a `.nib` file. Project Builder copies the `.nib` file into an already built application. When the application is run, the objects in the `.nib` file are loaded to create the application's user interface.

Interface Builder comes with several standard palettes and can be extended with more palettes. Palettes can contain nongraphical objects as well as graphical objects. Apple's developer tools include three sample custom Interface Builder palettes that demonstrate how to create new palettes. The samples are stored in the `/Developer/Examples/Interface Builder` directory. The bMoviePalette sample builds a palette that contains components useful for making a simple QuickTime movie editor within Interface Builder. The BusyPalette sample includes a variety of novel user-interface objects. The ProgressViewPalette sample is an introduction to creating new palettes. It demonstrates how to create a simple palette with minimal effort.

Most advanced features of Interface Builder are introduced in other parts of this book, but there are a few Interface Builder paradigms that must be understood now to effectively use the tool in examples. First, dragging an object from a palette creates a copy of the object. The copied object is configured with the Show Info window. So far, only the Attributes mode and the Size mode of the Show Info window have been used. There are usually six modes available, but under certain circumstances there can be more. Continuing the `Image Viewer` example, a few more changes are made to expose another paradigm employed by Interface Builder: nested views.

Nested Views

Start Interface Builder again by double-clicking the `MainMenu.nib` item in Project Builder's Resources folder. When Interface Builder has started, select the `NSImageView` that was previously added to the application's window. Choose Tools, Show Info, or Cmd-1 to open the Show Info window with the Attributes pane visible.

In the box labeled Border in the Show Info window titled NSImageView Info, select the button with the dashed outline icon. That specifies that the selected `NSImageView` does not have a border. In the box labeled Scaling, select the option labeled None. Figure 3.29 shows the `NSImageView` properly configured.

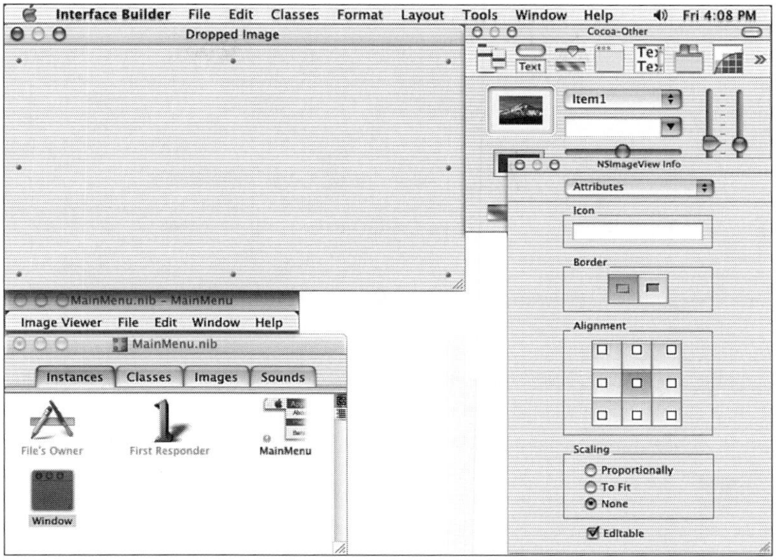

FIGURE 3.29 The `NSImageView` is selected and its attributes are shown in the window titled NSImageView Info.

This example is being modified to place the `NSImageView` inside a scroll view. In the modified example, the images that are dropped onto the `NSImageView` are shown at full size. If it is not possible to see the whole image at once, the scroll view is used to see other parts of the image.

To place the `NSImageView` in a scroll view, make sure it is selected and choose Layout, Make Subviews Of, Scroll View, as shown in Figure 3.30.

Using Layout, Make Subviews Of, Scroll View creates a new `NSScrollView` object, and nests the selected objects within the `NSScrollView`. The selected objects become the content that is scrolled. This capability to nest objects and make some views into subviews of other views is an important Interface Builder paradigm. Many powerful features are enabled by this paradigm. In addition to scroll views, objects can be nested inside box objects, split views, tab views, and even custom view objects. Scroll views, boxes, split views, tab views, and custom views are introduced in Chapter 8, "Application Kit Framework Overview," and further explained in Chapter 10, "Views and Controls."

After the `NSImageView` is nested within a `NSScrollView`, resize the `NSScrollView` so that it fills the window, as shown in Figure 3.31.

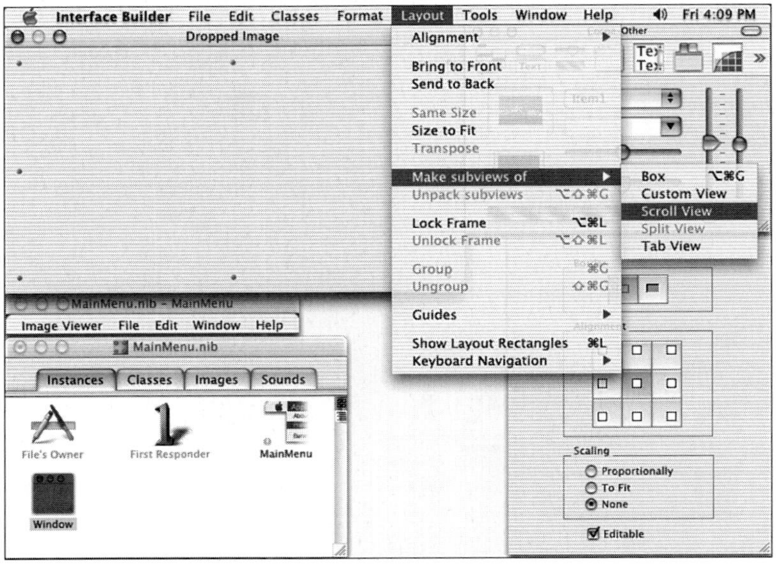

FIGURE 3.30 The Layout, Make subviews Of, Scroll View menu item is used to nest the selected objects inside a scroll view.

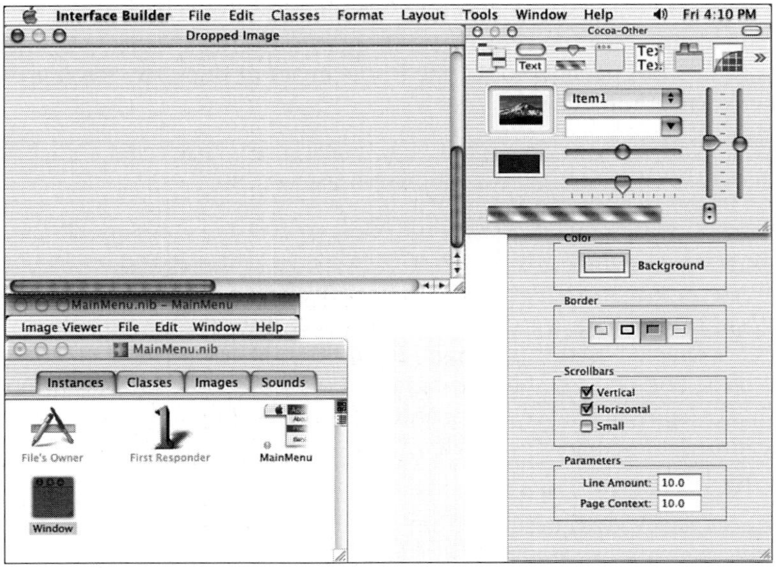

FIGURE 3.31 Resize the `NSScrollView` containing an `NSImageView` as shown.

Next, configure the automatic resizing behavior of the `NSScrollView`, so that is grows and shrinks with the window. Make sure the `NSScrollView` is selected and use Cmd-3 to reveal the Show Info window Size mode, or select the Size option in the Info Window's pop-up button. Figure 3.32 shows the `NSScrollView` configured to automatically fill available space and preserve constant margins.

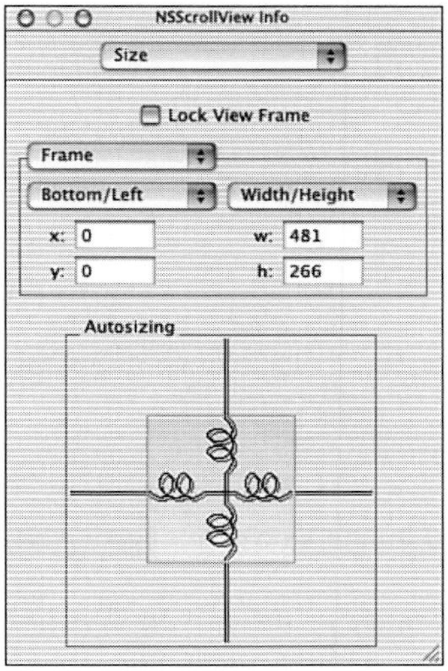

FIGURE 3.32 Set the `NSScrollView`'s automatic resize behavior to fill available space and preserve constant margins.

The modified interface can now be tested in Interface Builder's Test Interface mode. Save the modified `.nib` file using Cmd-s, or File, Save and quit Interface Builder. In Project Builder, use Build, Build and Run or Cmd-r to build and run the application. Project Builder does not have to compile anything to complete the build. It just copies the modified `.nib` file into the existing Image Viewer application and runs the application. Figure 3.33 shows the modified Image Viewer application displaying the Dew Drop (Wide Screen) `.jpg` image. The image is shown full size, but it is possible to scroll to reveal hidden parts of the image. As the Dropped Image window is resized, the scroll view resizes and the scrollbar elements automatically change size to reflect the proportion of the image that is visible. Experiment with dropping different images in the Image Viewer window to see the scroll behavior.

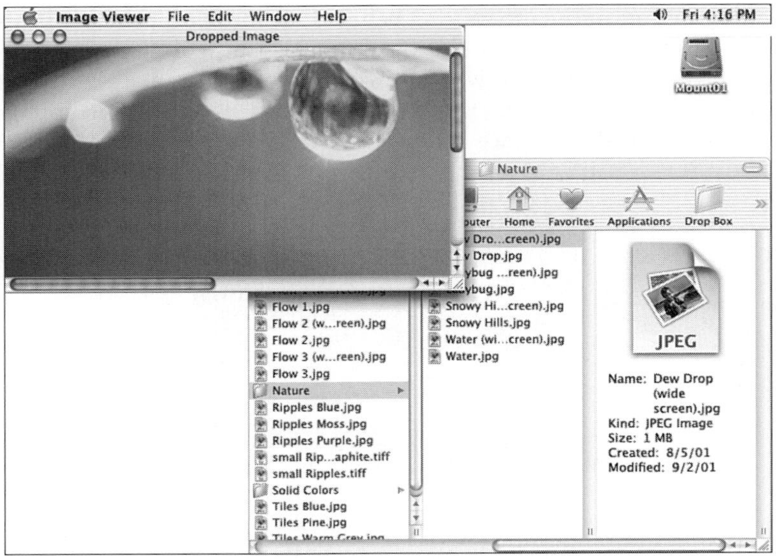

FIGURE 3.33 The modified Image Viewer application now enables scrolling to view full-sized images.

Two more important Interface Builder paradigms are presented next: Objects can be grouped to form a collection of cooperating objects arranged in a grid pattern called a matrix, and objects can be interconnected within Interface Builder.

Creating a Matrix

To create a matrix of objects, press the Alt key on the keyboard while dragging a selected object's control points.

NOTE

The Alt key is pressed by holding the Shift key and the Option key, simultaneously.

Figure 3.34 shows a matrix of buttons being created. The objects in a matrix are automatically configured to work together and resize as a group. Radio buttons, forms created from multiple text fields, and other groups of objects are implemented using a matrix in Interface Builder. Chapter 10 introduces the `NSMatrix` object. There is no need to experiment with creating a matrix in Interface Builder at this time, but it is important to know that the feature exists.

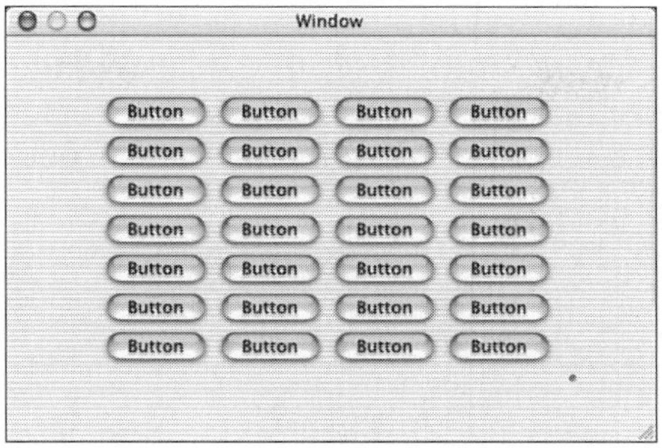

FIGURE 3.34 Drag the control points of a selected object while pressing the Alt key to create a matrix of objects.

In Project Builder, save the Image Viewer project, and then quit.

Interconnecting Objects

To briefly explore connections between objects, start Interface Builder and create a new empty interface. The Interface Builder application is located in the `/Developer/Applications` folder. Interface Builder shows a window titled Starting Point. If the Starting Point window is not visible, select File, New. Choose the option labeled Empty inside the Cocoa folder displayed in the Starting Point window. Then click the New button at the bottom of the Starting Point window to create a new empty user interface.

No windows are in the empty user interface yet. Select Interface Builder's Cocoa-Windows palette and drag a window object out of the palette and onto the desktop. A new empty-window object is created. Next, select the Cocoa-Other palette and drag a vertical slider object into the new window. Figure 3.35 shows a slider placed in the new window. Select the Cocoa-Views palette and drag a text-field object into the new window.

The slider's default configuration is to represent values from 0.0 to 100.0, and initially shows the value 50.0. If you are comfortable configuring objects with the Show Info window, configure the slider so its Continuous option is on, and its Marker Values Only option is off. These configuration options are not essential to the connections that will be made between the slider and the text field objects.

To make a connection from the slider to the text field, make sure the slider is selected. Press the Control key, and use the mouse to drag from the slider to the text field. A gray line will follow the mouse pointer to show the connection line being made. Release the mouse button over the text field. The Show Info window opens if it is not already and shows its Connections pane. A browser labeled Outlets is visible in the Connections pane, as shown in Figure 3.46. Select the target item in the browser, and then select the takeFloatValueFrom: item that appears in the browser's second column. Click the Connect button to make the connection.

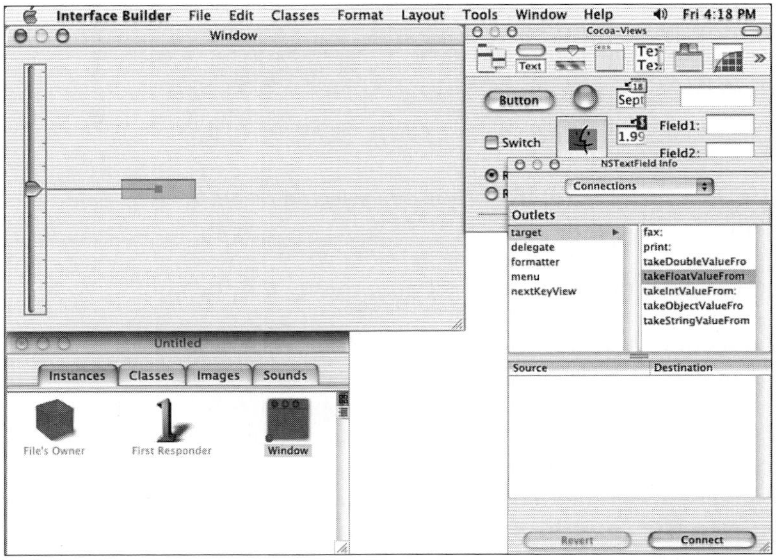

FIGURE 3.35 A slider and a text field are connected in Interface Builder so they show the same value.

The slider has just been configured to send a message to the text field whenever the slider's value changes. The message that is sent tells the text field to take its floating-point value from the slider's current value. If the slider has not been configured to be Continuous, the message is not sent until the slider is released after it is moved.

Next, connect the text field to the slider. Select the text field and Control-drag a connection line from the text field to the slider. Release the mouse over the slider. Select the target item in the Show Info window's Outlets browser, and then select the takeFloatValueFrom: item that appears. Click the Connect button to make the connection.

Put Interface Builder into Test Interface mode using Cmd-R, or File, Test Interface. Type a value between 0.0 and 100.0 into the text field being tested and press Return. The slider will move to show the entered value. Move the slider and the text field is updated with the slider's value. If the slider is configured to show Marker Values Only, as it was when originally dragged from the palette, the slider will hop from marker to marker as it moves. If the slider is not in Continuous mode, the value of the text field will not change until the slider is released after it is moved.

Objects are alive and can send messages to each other even in Interface Builder's Test Interface mode. The example barely touches on the power and flexibility of connections made in Interface Builder. It is possible to create significant applications entirely visually within Interface Builder. Menu items are connected to objects, and objects in different windows can be connected. Nongraphical objects that implement application logic can be connected to user interface objects.

Frameworks

In addition to tools, the developer CD contains frameworks and samples. Frameworks are directories full of compiled software libraries, header files, documentation, and resources. Frameworks keep related development information together. The libraries are present on all OS X installations so that Cocoa applications can run, but the developer CD-ROM provides alternate versions of the libraries to aid debugging and performance analysis. The header files are required to compile Cocoa applications.

A framework is a collection of libraries, header files, documentation, and resources organized so that Apple's developer tools can access the information. Apple's OS X developer CD-ROM contains frameworks for Carbon, 100% Pure Java, Cocoa, AppleScript, Perl, and more. Developer components of Apple technologies such as QuickTime and Text to Speech are also provided as frameworks on the CD-ROM.

When Apple's developer tools are installed, the frameworks that are stored in `/System/Library/Frameworks` on all OS X machines are extended. Additional versions of the libraries are added to support code profiling. Code profiling enables application developers to determine how many times functions are called and what percentage of an application's time is spent in each function.

Frameworks can contain multiple versions of libraries and resources at the same time. Apple might release beta libraries or new test frameworks to registered developers as they have in the past. In certain cases, such new components are added to existing frameworks rather than replacing the frameworks. By adding components rather than replacing them, backwards compatibility can be preserved, and applications that depend on the behavior of obsolete framework versions can continue to run.

Samples

When Apple's developer tools are installed, a wide range of sample applications with source code are copied into the `/Developer/Examples` directory. Samples that use

Carbon, 100% Pure Java, and Mac OS services such as Text to Speech are installed along with Cocoa specific examples.

Most Cocoa related examples are located in the /Developer/Examples/AppKit, /Developer/Examples/Foundation, and /Developer/Examples/InterfaceBuilder folders. Additional samples that use Cocoa are found in the /Developer/Examples/AppleScript Studio and /Developer/Examples/Java/AppKit folders.

Most topics demonstrated by the samples will not make any sense without a prior introduction to Cocoa programming. This book contains the information needed to gain maximum value from the samples that Apple provides. After Cocoa concepts are explained in this book, refer to Apple's examples along with this book's examples to see implementations of the concepts. The examples are an invaluable resource when learning Cocoa. Many developers prefer to learn new technology from complex examples. The Cocoa examples are presented here so that developers who are eager to jump into advanced topics can find suitable examples immediately and refer back to topics in this book for explanations.

Application Kit Framework Samples

The /Developer/Examples/AppKit directory contains the following samples:

CompositeLab	This example uses the NSView, NSBezierPath, NSAffineTransform, NSImage, and NSColorWell classes to demonstrate different compositing modes and transparency supported by the Quartz-graphics model and accessed with Cocoa's Application Kit framework. This example also uses drag and drop.
CircleView	This example creates a simple subclass of NSView to demonstrate drawing, event handling, coordinate systems, and text layout.
DotView	This example subclasses NSView to implement custom event handling and drawing. This is a good introductory example.
DragNDropOutlineView	This example implements drag-and-drop support in a NSOutlineView.
DrawerMadness	This example demonstrates the NSDrawer class.
HexInputServer	This example uses the NSInputManager class to create a custom input manager.
MenuMadness	This example demonstrates a wide range of features involving Mac OS X menus and the NSMenu class.

`OutlineView`	This example produces a simple file viewer using the `NSOutlineView` and `NSFileManager` classes. This is a good introduction that explains how to provide a data source for a `NSOutlineView` and how to access the file system using Cocoa.
`Rulers`	This example demonstrates custom units, rulers, and ruler drawing using the `NSRulerView` class.
`Sketch`	This is a complex example that builds a modest vector drawing application using the `NSDocument`, `NSWindowController`, `NSUndoManager`, and `NSBezierPath` classes. `Sketch` is a realistic application that provides most features that users expect from every application including AppleScript support.
`SimpleBrowser`	This example shows how to provide a data source for a `NSBrowser`. The `NSBrowserCell` and `NSFileManager` classes are also demonstrated.
`SimpleComboBox`	This example explains how to use the `NSComboBox` and `NSUndoManager` classes.
`SimpleImageFilter`	This example demonstrates the Cocoa Filter Service concept using the `NSBitmapImageRep` class.
`SimpleService`	This example explains the Cocoa Services menu.
`SimpleToolbar`	This example demonstrates a simple user-configurable toolbar using the `NSToolbar` and `NSDocument` classes.
`TextEdit`	This is the complete source code to the `TextEdit` application shipped with Mac OS X. `TextEdit` is a large application that provides mid-level word processing features. `TextEdit` uses many features of Cocoa and highlights Cocoa's text handling classes. This is an excellent example of a realistic full-featured application built with Cocoa.
`TextSizingExample`	This example demonstrates the interaction of the `NSTextView`, `NSTextContainer`, and `NSTextStorage` classes.
`UserDefaults`	This example shows how to store users preferences and default values using the `NSUserDefaults` class.

Foundation Framework Samples

The `/Developer/Examples/Foundation` folder contains the Authenticator, `ForwardInvocation`, and `MultiThreadedDO` samples. All these samples are built with a tool called `ProjectBuilderWO` that has not previously been mentioned.

ProjectBuilderWO is a version of Project Builder that predates the Project Builder application normally used with Mac OS X. WO refers to Apple's WebObjects product. ProjectBuilderWO is primarily used with older WebObjects applications, but is included with the other developer tools from Apple.

The Foundation samples have not been updated in many years. The concepts demonstrated are still relevant on OS X, but they are too esoteric to describe in detail here. Each of the examples deals with an aspect of inter-process communication. The Authenticator example shows how one process can authenticate requests from another process to make sure the requesting process has authority to make requests. The ForwardInvocation sample explores the low-level details of sending Objective-C messages between processes. The MultiThreadedDO sample shows how to use Distributed Objects to safely send messages between different threads in one process.

Interface Builder Samples

The /Developer/Examples/InterfaceBuilder folder contains sample custom Interface Builder palettes. The Interface Builder application can be extended in a variety of ways. These examples show how to create custom palettes of objects for reuse within Interface Builder.

One particularly interesting Interface Builder palette is created by the bMoviePalette sample. This palette contains components useful for making a simple QuickTime movie editor. The palette includes a custom NSFormatter object for time display and a novel user-interface element called a SoundFileWell that is used to add sounds to a movie via drag and drop.

Additional Samples

The /Developer/Examples/AppleScript Studio folder contains samples that demonstrate AppleScript Studio. AppleScript Studio is built with Cocoa and used the Cocoa objects. These samples explain many aspects of Cocoa programming from the perspective of a script writer. AppleScript Studio exposes Cocoa objects to AppleScripts and makes it possible to create Cocoa applications with logic implemented in scripts.

The /Developer/Examples/Java/AppKit folder contains several examples that show how to use Cocoa with Java. The Mac OS X developer tools can be used to create 100% Pure Java applications or use Java with the Cocoa frameworks. These samples examine Cocoa objects from the perspective of Java programmers.

Additional samples are provided at http://developer.apple.com/samplecode/Sample_Code/Cocoa.htm and http://developer.apple.com/samplecode/Sample_Code/Graphics_3D.htm. Apple updates the site regularly, so check it for new samples. A few important samples that are available from Apple's site include the following:

`RoundTransparentWindow`	This sample shows how to create windows that have transparent backgrounds and simulate windows that are not rectangular.
`Cocoa InitGL`	This sample shows how to initialize OpenGL for use with Cocoa applications.
`NSGL Teapot`	This sample demonstrates advanced OpenGL features accessed from a Cocoa application.
`Simple AppKit`	This sample shows how to interact with OpenGL using Cocoa from within Interface Builder.

Terminal

Mac OS X includes an application called Terminal in the /Applications/Utilities folder. Terminal provides access to a traditional Unix command line. Several developer tools that don't have graphical user interfaces use the command line. The command line is sometimes the most efficient way to use tools that do have a graphical user interface.

Project Builder is used from the command line to build the install version of an application. Normally, Project Builder preserves at least minimal debugging information in the applications that it builds. The command-line version of Project Builder is called `pbxbuild`. The command `pbxbuild -install` builds the project in the current directory using options appropriate for a final install version of the application. All debugging information is stripped out of the resulting application. The application built is optimized, and its resources are stored in the most compact form available. Using `pbxbuild install` produces the smallest and fastest applications. The pbxbuild tool is located in the `/usr/bin` folder.

NOTE

Finder hides the `/usr/bin` folder and other traditional Unix folders by default. The /usr/bin folder can be accessed from the Terminal application or by using Finder's Go, Go to Folder... menu and typing `/usr/bin` in text field presented.

The `pbxbuild` command is often used from automated scripts that build libraries and applications at night while nobody is present to push the buttons in a graphical user interface. `pbxbuild` can use any of the build styles defined in Project Builder. For example, the command `pbxbuild clean` cleans the project in the current directory and removes all intermediate files.

Other Tools

Several additional tools are provided on Apple's developer CD-ROM.

Concurrent Versions System (CVS)	This is a common open-source tool for text file version control. More information about CVS is available at `http://www.gnu.org/software/cvs/cvs.html`. CVS is installed with Apple's developer tools. Source code for many large projects, including Mac OS X itself, is controlled with CVS. The Concurrent in the name is a reference to the fact that unlike many other version control tools, CVS allows multiple developers to edit the same file at the same time. If conflicts arise between the different versions, a tool like the FileMerge application described in this section is used to reconcile the differences. CVS is installed in `/usr/bin`. Project Builder has limited built-in support for using CVS. Many of the less common, but important CVS tasks, must be performed using the command line unless additional software that is not provided by Apple is used. One free application that provides a graphical user interface for CVS is CVL available at `http://www.sente.ch/software/cvl/#Download`.
`nibtool`	This is a command-line program to convert Interface Builder `.nib` files to and from text files. It also verifies the correctness of `.nib` files. It is particularly useful when localizing an application for different languages and cultures. The list of strings used in a `.nib` file can be extracted with the `nibtool` simplifying translation. `nibtool` can also be used to produce textual descriptions of `.nib` files so that different versions can be compared with a tool like FileMerge. `nibtool` is installed in /usr/bin.

`otool`	This command-line tool shows information about compiled binary files. Lots of information is available, but `otool` is particularly handy for showing the install locations of all dynamic libraries needed by an application executable. The `otool` program can be used to list all Objective-C classes in a library or application. Otool is installed in `/usr/bin`.
Quartz Debug	This application highlights any drawing inefficiencies in OS X applications. Quartz Debug briefly flashes a yellow rectangle indicating each area of pixels that is being redrawn, each time it is redrawn. By watching the yellow flashes while an application is running, it is possible to detect unnecessary or redundant drawing. Quartz Debug is installed in `/Developer/Applications`.
Sampler	This is a noninvasive tool for profiling applications to determine where they are spending processor cycles. Sampler works with any Cocoa application. It can even attach itself to an already running application to find out what the application is doing. Sampler interrupts the execution of an application at regular intervals, records the current stack back-trace at an instant, and then resumes the execution of the application. Sampler then uses statistical analysis to provide a rough approximation of the percentage of program time spent in each function or method. Sampler is an alternative to using specialized profile libraries, when statistical sampling is a sufficient measure. Sampler is installed in `/Developer/Applications`.
FileMerge	This Cocoa application is used to compare and merge different versions of text files. FileMerge uses a nice graphical interface to show differences between files. The differences are then resolved in any of a variety of ways and a file optionally containing elements from both versions is saved. This is an outstanding Cocoa application that quickly becomes invaluable to developers. FileMerge is installed in `/Developer/Applications`.

Summary

Apple provides world-class developer tools for Mac OS X at no extra cost to Mac developers. Many of Apple's tools use open-source components that are common on other platforms, such as Linux. The Gnu gcc, gdb, and CVS tools are used from Apple's project Builder IDE. Interface Builder is an invaluable tool for Cocoa application development. Interface Builder configures and connects reusable objects. In some cases, entire applications can be created in Interface Builder without writing any code. Apple's developer tools include a rich collection of utilities that simplify application development and help with tasks such as performance profiling, version control, and file merging.

So far, the architecture of Mac OS X and the languages that are used for Cocoa development have been described. This chapter provided an overview of the tools used to create Cocoa applications. Chapter 4, "Objective-C," introduces the Objective-C language that was used to write Cocoa. Most of Apple's examples and documentation about Cocoa programming use Objective-C. Objective-C is a simple, small, and powerful extension to ANSI C that directly enables many of the features of Cocoa.

4
Objective-C

IN THIS CHAPTER

- Why Learn Objective-C?
- Additions to C
- Apple's Extensions
- The `NSObject` Base Class
- Runtime Functions
- Objective-C++

This chapter introduces the Objective-C language, and explains how Objective-C represents the concepts of object-oriented programming that were described in Chapter 2, "Cocoa Language Options." This book focuses on intermediate and advanced techniques that unleash the power of Cocoa; as a result, there is only room for a brief introduction to Objective-C. The information presented in this chapter and the next is sufficient for an experienced C++ or Java programmer to become immediately productive with Objective-C. Familiarity with C and at least one object-oriented language is a prerequisite for this chapter. The conventions described in Chapter 5, "Cocoa Conventions," are also essential to understanding how Objective-C is actually used in conjunction with Cocoa.

Why Learn Objective-C?

The Objective-C language is the implementation language for Cocoa itself. Because of this, an understanding of Objective-C is an important part of understanding Cocoa. It will help you better comprehend the design philosophies underlying Cocoa. Many of the available Cocoa code examples are implemented in Objective-C.

Objective-C is a superset of the ANSI C programming language. As a result, Objective-C code can be integrated with exiting C code. The ability to conveniently reuse C code makes Objective-C an ideal language for implementing modern object-oriented applications that use operating system features made available only as C code. Objective-C applications are capable of using every feature provided by the Mac OS X operating system.

Apple's rationale for selecting Objective-C is presented in the introduction to Apple's book, *Object-Oriented Programming and the Objective-C Language*. Cocoa includes an extremely flexible, extensible, and dynamic set of classes that can only be created with a flexible and dynamic language like Objective-C. Apple's engineers note that Cocoa could not have been written with a less dynamic language. The dynamism and flexibility of Objective-C contribute to the high degree of code reuse and productivity that Cocoa programmers enjoy.

Additions to C

Because Objective-C is an extension of the C language, you can use everything you know about C when programming in Objective-C. Parts of the C language are used less often in Objective-C, but they are all still available to anyone who wants to use them. On top of the C language, Objective-C adds a few new types, several keywords, and some new idioms. It is designed to be simple yet powerful. Because of this, it is easy to learn the key points in just a few minutes, if you already know the C language and have a basic understanding of object-oriented concepts.

The principal new idiom that Objective-C adds to C is the concept of messaging between objects. Objective-C includes the language elements needed to declare objects, specify the messages that the objects understand, and send messages to objects.

Messaging

Messaging is the reason that Objective-C is so dynamic. A message is a request for an object to do something. In Objective-C, the syntax for sending a message looks like this:

```
[someObject doSomething]
```

The square brackets (`[` and `]`) indicate the start and end of a message block. The variable `someObject` is the receiver of the message. The variable `doSomething` is called a selector and specifies the message to send. Messaging always takes the following form:

```
[receiver selector]
```

Messages can include arbitrary arguments and can return values. Any message can be sent to any receiver. If the receiver does not understand a message that is sent to it, a runtime error occurs. However, errors are easily avoided because at runtime it is possible to determine whether a particular receiver can understand a particular message before the message is sent.

The message sending syntax might look foreign at first. One of the reasons messaging syntax is so distinct from function calling syntax in Objective-C is that messaging is a very different operation from a function call. The two concepts are so different that representing them with the same syntax would be misleading.

Messaging is flexible and dynamic because both the receiver and the selector are variables. The determination of exactly which message is sent to which receiver is deferred until the program is running. At the time a program is compiled, it might not be possible to know what object or type of object will be the receiver. At compile time, the selector might be unknown. The selector might not even exist in the program at the time it is compiled. The selector could be added by dynamically loaded objects or typed in by a user. Because of messaging, it is relatively simple to integrate Objective-C with other dynamic languages as well as scripting languages.

The messaging system is so dynamic that the receiver might not even be in the same application as the code that sends the message. Messages sent between processes on the same or different computers are called distributed messages. The syntax for sending a distributed message is exactly the same as the stntax for local messages. In fact, the compiler cannot determine if a message is distributed or not at compile time.

Messaging is implemented by a simple, small, and efficient runtime. Most languages have a runtime to initialize the program stack and heap and call a program entry point like the `main()` function used in C. In Objective-C the runtime has a much more pervasive role. The Objective-C runtime is active throughout the running life of a program and is much more than just an initializer.

File Naming and Importing

Objective-C files are stored in the file system with the `.m` extension rather than the traditional `.c` extension used for C code. The `.m` extension tells the compiler to expect Objective-C code rather than standard C code. The source code of an Objective-C application is usually composed of header files with the `.h` extension, and implementation files with the `.m` extension, just as C uses `.h` and `.c`.

Objective-C files can include header files by using the standard C `#include` preprocessor directive or by using the `#import` preprocessor directive. The `#import` directive is similar to the `#include` directive. `#import` assures that no file is imported more than once. Objective-C header files that are imported don't need to be surrounded by "guards" (usually implemented with `#define`, `#ifndef`, and `#endif`) to keep them from being included multiple times. You must use the `#import` directive to import Cocoa headers because the Cocoa headers don't contain guards.

NOTE

In addition to the `#import` preprocessor directive, the Objective-C preprocessor understands `//` style comments. As with C++ and some dialects of C, the `//` symbol is used to start a comment that continues to the end of the line.

The `id` Type

As already mentioned, Objective-C is an object-oriented language. In the most general sense, Objective-C defines an object as anything that can receive messages. The receiver of an Objective-C message does not need to be known at compile time. The specific type of the receiver does not even need to be known. When sending a message, the only requirement is that receiver is an object.

Objective-C introduces a new type, `id`, that is a pointer to an object. A variable with the `id` type can be used as the receiver of any message. The `id` type is similar to the standard C `void *` type in the sense that the compiler knows very little about the memory being referenced.

The `id` type is used the same way as any other C type. The following code declares a variable of type `id`.

```
id     anObject;
```

As declared, the variable `anObject` is a pointer to any object. In C, any pointer can be set to the constant value, `NULL`. In Objective-C, any pointer to an object can be set to the constant `nil`. Messages sent to `nil` are not errors. The only caution is that the value returned from a message to `nil` is undefined in some cases.

Static Typing

The `id` type should only be used when very little information is known about an object and the maximum flexibility allowed by the language is needed. The compiler should be given as much information about objects as possible. When details about an object are known, static typing is used to convey the details to the compiler.

To use static typing, simply declare a pointer to an instance of a particular class of object. For example, given an existing class called `NSString`, a variable that stores a pointer to an instance of `NSString` is declared as follows:

```
NSString     *theString;
```

When the compiler subsequently encounters `theString` as the receiver of a message, the compiler can use the specified type information to verify that `theString` is an object that can understand the message being sent. If the compiler cannot find any appropriate declaration of the message being sent, a warning is generated. The compiler generates a warning rather than an error because the compiler cannot be certain that the message will not be understood. It is possible that the receiver does understand the message, but the message has not been declared in a way that the compiler can verify.

The following types are defined by the Objective-C runtime, and can be used in programs.

`SEL`: used to store selectors

`IMP`: used to store pointers to the C functions that implement messages

`Class`: used to store pointers to Objective-C class objects

`id`: used to store pointers to arbitrary Objective-C objects

`BOOL`: used to store the Boolean constants `YES` and `NO`

Static typing of objects may be used even when the class of the object is not fully declared. The `@class` keyword is used to inform the compiler that a type is a class as follows:

```
@class NSArray, NSString, NSNumber;
@class NSDictionary;
```

The declarations specify that `NSArray`, `NSString`, `NSNumber`, and `NSDictionary` are all valid class names that can be used for static typing. This form of class declaration is called forward declaration and is used in the same situations in which standard C structures are forward declared.

Declaring a Class

Declaring a class specifies the values that instances of the class will store, as well as the messages that the class itself and instances of the class will understand. It is not necessary to specify all the messages that can be understood by a class in the class declaration. Support for messages can be deliberately hidden or even added at runtime. The class declaration is only a hint to the compiler regarding messages, but the declaration is the only place that instance variables can be defined.

A class consists of two parts, an interface and an implementation. As described in Chapter 2, "Cocoa Language Options," classes are used to encapsulate data and behavior. The complexity of an implementation is hidden behind an interface through which the class is used.

Several new keywords exist to declare a class interface. Class interfaces begin with the @interface keyword and end with the @end keyword as follows:

```
@interface MYObject : NSObject
{
}

@end
```

In the example, a new class called MYObject is declared to be a subclass of the NSObject class. The NSObject class is part of Cocoa. Almost every class in Cocoa is directly or indirectly a subclass of NSObject. More information about NSObject is provided later in this chapter. At this time, it is only important to note that because MYObject is a subclass of NSObject, MYObject inherits all the NSObject class's instance variables and understands all the messages that NSObject understands. Objective-C does not allow multiple inheritance. It is only possible to declare at most one super class. A new class can be declared with no super class by omitting the colon (:) character and the superclass name.

Instance Variables

In the MYObject class interface, no instance variables beyond those inherited from NSObject are defined. If MYObject had additional instance variables, they would be defined between the curly braces ({ and }) in the interface declaration. The general form of a class interface declaration follows:

```
@interface CLASS-NAME : SUPER-CLASS-NAME
{
INSTANCE VARIABLE DECLARATIONS
}

METHOD DECLARATIONS

@end
```

The instance variables can have any previously defined type. For example, the following class interface declaration defines a class that encapsulates circles in a hypothetical drawing program:

```
@interface MYCircle : NSObject
{
  NSPoint         _myCenter;    // NSPoint is a Cocoa C structure
  float           _myRadius;    // float is a standard C type
  BOOL            _myIsFilled;  // BOOL is a Boolean type
```

```
  NSColor       *_myColor;     // NSColor is a Cocoa class
  id            _myExtraData;  // this can be any kind of object
}

@end
```

The `@public`, `@private`, and `@protected` keywords can be used to restrict the use (scope) of instance variables. Public instance variables can be accessed directly by any code. Protected instance variables can be accessed directly by instances of the class that declares the protected variables, and also subclasses of that class. Private instance variables can only be directly referenced by instances of the class that declares the private variables. When not otherwise specified, instance variables are protected. The `MYCircle` class could be modified as follows to use the instance variable scope keywords:

```
@interface MYCircle : NSObject
{
  NSPoint       _myCenter;     // NSPoint is a Cocoa C structure
@public
  float         _myRadius;
@private
  BOOL          _myIsFilled;   // BOOL is a Boolean type
@public
  NSColor       *_myColor;     // NSColor is a Cocoa class
  id            _myExtraData;  // this can be any kind of object
}

@end
```

All instance variables declared after one of the scope modifying keywords have that specified scope until another scope modifying keyword is specified. In the `MYCircle` example, `_myCenter` is protected because no scope is specified prior to its declaration. The `_myRadius`, `_myColor`, and `_myExternalData` instance variables have public scope, whereas the `_myIsFilled` instance variable has private scope.

It is seldom a good idea to puncture the encapsulation of instance variables by declaring them public. Public instance variables can be accessed just like the members of a C structure. For example, given a pointer to an existing instance of `MYCircle`, the `_myRadius` instance variable could be accessed from any code as follows:

```
MYCircle        *anInstance = someObject;
anInstance->_myRadius = 13.5f;
```

You should rarely use the private scope. When an instance variable is declared private, subclasses cannot directly use the instance variable they inherited. Not all uses of a class can be foreseen. Using the private scope might restrict valid uses of the variable in unanticipated future subclasses.

The protected scope is usually the best compromise between encapsulation and flexibility.

Methods

In Objective-C, an object is loosely defined as anything that can receive messages. Different objects can react in different ways upon receipt of the same message. In other words, different objects can have different methods of responding to a message. When declaring a class, it is possible to declare the methods that will be used to react to messages. Methods have the same name as the message they handle, and the terms message and method are sometimes used interchangeably when describing the behavior of an object. There is usually a correspondence between the set of methods that an object implements and the messages an object can understand. The phrase, "calling a method" is interchangeable with the phrase "sending a message."

When declaring a class interface, methods implemented by the class can be specified. Some, all, or none of the class's methods can be declared in the interface. The methods declared in the class interface aid the compiler when static typing is used, but they are just a hint. Methods that were never declared in a class interface can nevertheless be implemented and might even be added to a class dynamically at runtime.

Methods a class implements might be deliberately excluded from the class interface to discourage their use. In Objective-C, there is no way to declare a method private or protected. All methods are public. However, methods that should not be called in certain situations should not be declared in the class interface. If static typing is used, the compiler will generate a warning whenever a method that was not declared is used. The warning is a hint to programmers that they should not be calling that method. A technique for declaring methods so that the compiler generates the correct warnings for the use of methods in some situations and not others is presented when Objective-C categories are described later in this chapter.

Two types of methods can be declared in a class interface: instance methods and class methods. Instance methods are invoked when an instance of the class receives a message. Class methods are invoked when the class itself receives a message. Class methods are sometimes called factory methods alluding to the fact that most class methods are used to build new instances.

NOTE

In Objective-C, each class is represented at runtime by an object. Class objects can receive messages. Class objects are sometimes called Meta-Objects because they contain information about other objects. A class object encapsulates the definition of instance objects and is used to construct instances.

Method declarations occur after the closing curly brace of the instance variable declarations and before the `@end` that ends the interface declaration as follows:

```
@interface CLASS-NAME : SUPER-CLASS-NAME
{
INSTANCE VARIABLE DECLARATIONS
}

METHOD DECLARATIONS

@end
```

Instance methods are declared with a leading minus (-) as follows:

```
- (int)count;
```

The `-count` method handles any `count` messages that are received by an instance of the class that declares the `-count` method.

Class methods are declared with a leading plus (+) as follows:

```
+ (void)setVersion:(int)number;
```

The `+setVersion:` method handles any `setVersion:` messages that are received by the class itself.

The method's return type is after the plus or minus symbol in a method declaration. This looks like a C-language cast because it is written as a C type in parentheses. The return type is optional, however. If you don't provide it, the default return type assumed by the compiler is `id`. A method that doesn't have a return value should return `void`.

The method's name follows the return type and extends to the semicolon (;) that ends the method declaration. In the preceding examples, the `-count` method does not take input parameters. The `+setVersion:` method accepts a single integer parameter. Input parameters are always denoted by the presence of colons (:) in the method name.

The colon itself is part of the method name, so the methods `-init` and `-init:` are considered to be two different methods, each with a unique implementation. After each colon in a method name is a type, in parentheses, that specifies the type of the input parameter, and the variable name used inside the method's implementation code to refer to the input parameter. If no type is specified for an input parameter, the compiler assumes that the parameter has the type `id`.

The colons in method names enable the naming of parameters. Consider the following method declarations:

```
- (void)setArgument:(void *)argumentLocation atIndex:(int)index;
- (BOOL)lockWhenCondition:(int)condition beforeDate:(NSDate *)limit;
- (NSString *)descriptionWithCalendarFormat:(NSString *)format
      timeZone:(NSTimeZone *)aTimeZone locale:(NSDictionary *)locale;
```

Although these method declarations look complex, they all follow a simple pattern. After each parameter there is some space followed by another name, colon, type declaration, and input variable name. Any number of parameters of any type can be added to the method declaration this way.

Just as the colons are considered part of the method name, Objective-C method names include all the text before each input parameter. Therefore, the actual method names for the three previous methods are `setArgument:atIndex:`, `lockWhenCondition:beforeDate:`, and `descriptionWithCalendarFormat:timeZone:locale:`.

By interspersing parameter names with parts of a method name, it is possible for code to read almost as if it were natural language. This provides an advantage for code readability, maintainability, and clarity. Of course, badly chosen names can still lead to incomprehensible code. You cannot reorder the segments of a method name. The following are two different methods:

```
descriptionWithCalendarFormat:timeZone:locale:
descriptionWithCalendarFormat:locale:timeZone:
```

It is possible to leave out the text between the colons. Objective-C doesn't require anything other than a colon to specify a new parameter to a method, but it is usually poor style to not use some kind of brief explanatory text. The method declaration, `- (void)moveTo:(int)x :(int)y;`, is valid and declares the method named `moveTo::`, which takes two integer parameters, x and y, and returns nothing.

A method's name is the same as the message it handles. Methods are invoked upon the receipt of a message. The name of the message is used to select which method to execute. Message names are called selectors. Message names can be stored in variables with the type `SEL` defined by the Objective-C runtime. A method name can be converted into a `SEL` value by the compiler with the `@selector` keyword as follows:

```
SEL         aSelector;
aSelector = @selector(setObject:forKey:);
```

The value of the `aSelector` variable is set to the selector that represents the method named `setObject:forkey:`.

Selectors can be passed as arguments to methods and functions. For example, the `-(void)performSelector:(SEL)aSelector withObject:(id)anObject` method can be called to ask the receiver to execute the method identified by `aSelector` using `anObject` as an input parameter.

It is also possible to ask an object to provide a pointer to the function that implements a method identified by a selector. Such function pointers are stored in variables with the type `IMP`, which is defined by the Objective-C runtime. `IMP`s are only used as an optimization in rare cases. The use of IMPs is described in the optimization section of this chapter.

Implementing a Class

Class implementations begin with the `@implementation` keyword and end with the `@end` keyword. Class implementations contain the implementations of methods. Defining method implementations is done much the same as implementing C functions. The code that implements a method is defined after the method name and enclosed in curly braces. Consider the following class interface for the `MYAverager` class:

```
#import <Foundation/Foundation.h>

@interface MYAverager : NSObject
{
    float         _myValueArray[10];
}

- (float)avarageValue;
- (void)setValue:(float)aValue atIndex:(int)anIndex;

@end
```

The `MYAverager` class is simple. It stores ten floating-point values, each of which can be set by calling the `-setValue:atIndex:` method. The average of the ten stored values is returned from the -average method. The MYAverager class can be implemented as follows:

```
#import " MYAverager.h"

@implementation MYAverager

- (float)avarageValue
{
  int       i;
  float     sum = 0.0f;

  // sum the values
  for(i = 0; i < 10; i++) {
    sum = sum + _myValueArray[i];
  }

  // return the average
  return sum / 10.0f;
}


-(void)setValue:(float)aValue atIndex:(int)anIndex
{
  // set the value with the specified index
  if(anIndex >= 0 && anIndex < 10) {
    _myValueArray[i] = aValue;
  }
}

@end
```

self and super

When writing implementation code, sometimes it is helpful for an object to be able to send messages to itself, or to use itself as a parameter in a message to another object. To make this possible, Objective-C methods have a hidden parameter called self. In an instance method, self is a pointer to the instance object that received the message being handled by the method. In a class method, self is a pointer to the class object that received the message being handled.

The self variable can occur in any context that allows variables. It can be the receiver of a message such as [self setValue:10.0f atIndex:4]. The value of self can be assigned and it can be returned from methods. `self` is often passed as a parameter to other methods.

NOTE

All Objective-C methods also have another less-used hidden parameter, `_cmd`, which stores the selector that was used to invoke the method.

Objects often implement methods that are also implemented by a superclass. The `super` keyword can be used to invoke a superclass's implementation of a method. `super` is not a variable, and can only be used as the receiver of a message. The `super` keyword can only be used within a method implementation.

An `-init` method can be added to the `MYAverager` class previously declared. The following method demonstrates the use of `self` and `super`:

```
-(id)init
{
  int             i;

  // set the self variable to the value returned from the
  //   inherited implementation of -init
  self = [super init];

  // initialize the stored values by sending messages to self
  for(i = 0; i < 10; i++) {
    [self setValue:0.0f atIndex:i];
  }

  // return self
  return self;
}
```

Creating Instances

After a class has been implemented, instances of the class are created by calling the `+alloc` class method declared in the `NSObject` class. The need to inherit the `+alloc` method is one of the main reasons that almost all classes are subclasses of `NSObject`. After an instance is created it must be initialized by calling an instance method. The section about the `NSObject` base class in this chapter describes the role of the `NSObject` class in instance creation. The process of allocating and initializing instances is handled by conventions explained in the next chapter.

Apple's Extensions

No standard exists for the Objective-C language and runtime. The Apple and Gnu implementations of Objective-C include some powerful extensions to the language. The principal extensions are categories, protocols, type encoding, and constant string objects. The extensions are used throughout Cocoa and enable much of the power and flexibility that Cocoa programmers enjoy. The Apple and GNU compilers support the same extensions.

Categories

Categories enable the addition of methods to any class and can be used as an organizational tool or as an alternative to subclassing. Categories are declared to extend existing classes. The name of the category is specified in parentheses after a class name. The following category declaration extends the previously introduced `MYAverager` class to be able to add a `-max` method:

```
#import "MYAverager.h"

@interface MYAverager (SampleCategory)

- (float)max;

@end
```

The `-max` method can be implemented to return the maximum value stored in a `MYAverager` instance:

```
@implementation MYAverager (SampleCategory)

- (float)max
{
  int         i;
  int         result = myValueArray[0];

  for(i = 1; i < 10; i++) {
    if(myValueArray[i] > result) {
      result = myValueArray[i];
    }
  }
  return result;
}

@end
```

When categories were first introduced, NeXT recommended that they be used to break large implementation files into several smaller files so they could be used to organize the methods. For example, all the private methods that should not be called except by the class's author can be organized into a category that is concealed from other programmers. There is no way to restrict which methods of a class can be called in which contexts, but methods can be hidden from the users of a class. The extra effort to find out which hidden methods exist is usually enough to discourage their use.

Categories containing private methods are often added within implementation files so that there is no header file that declares the methods, and they can still be used within the object's own implementation without warnings. In fact, category declarations do not need an interface at all. Only the implementation is necessary.

Categories are useful for organizational purposes, but that barely touches the power and flexibility enabled by them. Methods can be added to any class without needing the source code for the class that is extended, or recompiling. Categories are an alternative to subclassing with some limitations. One limitation is that categories cannot be used to add instance variables to a class the way a subclass can. Nevertheless, using categories is preferable to subclassing in many situations. For example, suppose your application calls a method implemented by a Cocoa framework class to obtain an object. The class of the object returned by the framework was determined when the framework was written. Subclassing the returned object won't help because there might not be a way to get the framework to return your subclass instead of the class that was compiled into the framework. The class returned by the framework can be extended by a category implemented in your code to add the methods you need.

Methods added by a category can override existing implementations, and it is possible to patch bugs in classes to which you have no source code. To do so, replace the offending method with a correct implementation in a category. A restriction when replacing methods is that there is no convenient way to call the original implementation from the overriding implementation. The overriding method must duplicate the entire functionality of the replaced method. Also, if more than one category implements the same method, then it is unpredicitable which method will be chosen for use by the runtime.

Methods that are implemented in a category can access all the extended class' instance variables directly. At runtime, methods that are declared in a category are no different from methods declared in the class interface. All subclasses of the extended class also gain the category's methods. Even preexisting instances gain the category's methods when code containing a category is dynamically loaded during a program's execution. It is possible to have an object that does not understand certain messages when the application starts, but does understand them after a plug-in containing a category has been loaded.

Categories are a powerful feature that can be easily abused. A good practice is to add a unique prefix to the start of any method names defined in categories that modify framework classes. The prefix reduces the chance of an accidental clash with a hidden framework method or a method in another category, which can happen easily. After a while, programmers get in the habit of naming methods according to the conventions used in Cocoa. If you think of a method to add to a Cocoa class, there is a good chance someone else has thought of the same method and given it the same name. Another danger is that Apple will add the same method in a future release, but the method will be masked by a preexisting category. Even if a method added via a category does not create a conflict now, it may in a future version of Cocoa.

Protocols

Protocols enhance static-type checking and help optimize distributed messaging. An Objective-C class inherits all the methods and instance variables implemented by its superclass. This type of inheritance is sometimes called implementation inheritance. Protocols embody the related concept called interface inheritance. Interface inheritance means that method declarations are inherited, but not method implementations. A protocol declares a set of methods but does not provide any implementations. Protocols can be used in combination with static typing to assure the compiler that an object can understand the messages that are sent to it.

NOTE

An Objective-C protocol is analogous to a Java interface. An Objective-C interface is a different concept, and this terminology difference can be a point of confusion between Java and Objective-C programmers.

Declaring and Adopting Protocols

Working with protocols consists of two aspects. First, a protocol must be declared, and is then adopted by one or more objects. A protocol declaration defines methods, somewhat similar to an object interface, but it does not define instance variables or implementations for the methods. There are no implementation files for protocols.

A protocol is defined using the `@protocol` keyword. For example, a simple protocol defining two methods looks like this:

```
@protocol UpDown
- (void)increment;
- (void)decrement;
@end
```

The protocol's name follows the `@protocol` keyword. Between the `@protocol` and `@end` keywords are the protocol's method declarations. If our sample class, `MYAverager`, were to adopt the protocol, we would change the `MYAverager` class interface declaration to the following:

```
#import <Foundation/Foundation.h>
#import "UpDown.h"

@interface MYAverager : NSObject <UpDown>
{
    float          _myValueArray[10];
}

- (float)avarageValue;
- (void)setValue:(float)aValue atIndex:(int)anIndex;

@end
```

First, the header file that declares the `UpDown` protocol is imported so the compiler knows the protocol's details. Next, the protocol name is enclosed in angle brackets (< and >) and placed after the object's name and superclass declarations. To specify the adoption of more than one protocol, list the protocol names inside the angle brackets, separated by commas. The general form of a class interface that adopts protocols follows:

```
@interface CLASSNAME : SUPERCLASSNAME <PROTOCOL-LIST>
```

Category declarations can adopt protocols using the following syntax:

```
@interface CLASSNAME (CATEGORYNAME) <PROTOCOL-LIST>
```

One way of describing that a class is guaranteed to implement all the methods of a protocol is to say that the class conforms to the protocol. If a class adopts a protocol then that class conforms to the protocol. If a loaded category of a class adopts a protocol then that class conforms to the protocol. Finally, all the classes that inherit from a class that conforms to a protocol also conform to the protocol. Conforming to a protocol just means that all the methods declared in the protocol have been implemented either directly or through inheritance or a category.

After a class or category declares that it adopts a protocol, the compiler will require that all the methods found in the protocol are actually implemented. There is no requirement to place a protocol's method declarations in the class or category interface file because the protocol already declares them. Because categories can be loaded dynamically to add methods to existing classes at runtime, and protocols can be adopted by categories, it is possible to dynamically add protocol conformance to classes at runtime also.

NOTE

Protocol names have their own name space and do not conflict with class or function names. For example, the Cocoa frameworks declare the `NSObject` class and there is also an `NSObject` protocol.

Static-Type Checking with Protocols

Type declarations for variables, method parameters, method return types, function parameters, and function return types can include protocol conformance requirements to refine static-type checking. The following examples show several ways in which protocol conformance can be included in a type:

```
id <SomeProtocol> aVariable;
NSObject <SomeProtocol, AnotherProtocol> *anotherVariable;
id <NSObject> SomeFunction();
- (id <SomeProtocol>)methodThatReturnsAnObject;
- (void)methodThatAcceptsAnObjectParameter:(MYAverager <SomeProtocol> *)anObject;
```

Static type checking enables the compiler to verify correct type usage based on protocol conformance, class, and inheritance in any combination.

Types based on protocols uncouple the concept of class from the set of messages that can safely be sent to an object. Often, the only important information about an object is the set of messages it understands. Specifying that an object conforms to a protocol asserts that it doesn't matter what class is used as long as it responds to a set of messages. Information about the specific class and inheritance of an object constitutes implementation details. Protocols used in types enable the compiler to check type safety, and verify support for particular messages without unnecessary dependence on a particular class hierarchy.

Multiple-Interface Inheritance

Objective-C does not allow multiple-implementation inheritance, but multiple-interface inheritance is supported through protocols. A class can adopt any number of protocols, and protocols themselves can adopt other protocols. To declare that one protocol adopts another, just include the adopted protocol names in angle brackets (< and >) after the protocol declaration using the following syntax:

```
@protocol PROTOCOLNAME <PROTOCOL-LIST>
```

Any object that conforms to PROTOCOLNAME also conforms to all the protocols in PROTOCOL-LIST.

Protocol Objects

Protocols are similar to classes because they both declare methods. The Objective-C runtime encapsulates class definitions with class objects. Protocols are encapsulated by protocol objects. Apple's Objective-C runtime encapsulates protocols with a class called `Protocol`. The compiler creates class objects automatically from class declarations, and creates protocol objects automatically from protocol declarations.

References to class objects can be stored in variables and passed as arguments to methods. References to instances of the `Protocol` class can be used in the same ways. The `@protocol()` compiler directive accesses the instances of the `Protocol` class that are stored in the runtime as follows:

```
Protocol *aProtocol = @protocol(UpDown);
```

The variable, `aProtocol`, is a pointer to an instance of the `Protocol` class, and is initialized to reference the protocol called `UpDown`.

Protocols in Distributed Messaging

Another important use of protocols is to optimize distributed messaging. Messages can be sent to objects in a different process on a different computer. The Objective-C runtime routinely sends messages between anonymous objects, and has little knowledge about either the sender of the message or the receiver. Nothing special is done with the parameters and return values of messages sent to objects in the same process, but the runtime must package the messages' arguments and return value for network transport.

If the runtime does not know enough information about the receiver of a distributed message to correctly package the parameters and return value, the runtime must interrogate the remote object to get that information. The interrogation consumes some of the network bandwidth and performance.

Protocols can be used to optimize distributed messaging. The runtime can ask the remote object if it conforms to a particular protocol. Subsequent distributed messages that are defined by the protocol can be efficiently packaged and sent over the network. The protocol conformance only needs to be checked once, and that one check verifies the existence and types of all the methods declared in the protocol.

Type Encoding

Type encoding is used by the runtime to aid the dispatching of messages to objects. The encoding is essential when distributed messages are sent so that parameters and return types can be packaged and sent over a network. Type encoding is also a convenience that helps programmers avoid mistakes.

The Objective-C runtime encodes parameter types and return types as C strings. Each character in the string specifies a property of the type. The specific format of the encoded type strings is not important in this introduction. Details about type encoding are provided in Apple's online document at `http://developer.apple.com/techpubs/macosx/Cocoa/ObjectiveC/4MoreObjC/index.html`.

Encoded type information can be useful outside the Objective-C runtime, and is obtained by the `@encode()` compiler directive. The `@encode()` directive works in much the same way as the ANSI C `sizeof()` operator works, and can accept the same arguments as `sizeof()`. The value returned from `@encode()` can be assigned to a `char *` as follows:

```
char *aTypeString = @encode(int **)
```

Type encoding is particularly useful for encoding and decoding the instance variables of objects, as described in Chapter 5. The methods used to encode variables require a C string parameter that specifies the types to encode. The C string can be created as a constant string or via the `@encode()` directive. It is relatively easy to make mistakes when constructing type strings by hand. Therefore, the use of `@encode()` to automate the task is preferred.

Constant-String Objects

The Cocoa frameworks include the `NSString` class to encapsulate strings. The details of the `NSString` class are not important in this chapter, but using `NSString` instances instead of C strings has many advantages. However, C-string constants can be allocated by the compiler and stored as bytes within an executable program. Objective-C instances are typically dynamically allocated at runtime. It is possible to programmatically create an `NSString` instance that is initialized with a particular constant string at runtime. However, it is cumbersome to litter an application with hundreds of lines of code just to convert constant C strings into constant `NSString` instances.

Apple's Objective-C compiler includes an extension to enable the compiler to generate constant `NSString` instances. Constant string objects are both an optimization and a convenience for programmers. Programmers do not have to write code to explicitly create constant `NSStrings` at runtime. The CPU cycles and memory allocations needed to create the constant string objects at runtime are avoided.

To use constant strings in code, declare the strings as follows:

```
@"This is a constant string"
```

The leading @, before the quotes, informs the compiler that an NSString instance should be stored in the executable instead of storing a C string. Strings created with the @"" syntax can occur in any context that an NSString instance is allowed. It is safe to send messages to constant strings or return them from methods or functions.

The NSObject Base Class

The Objective-C language allows the creation of any number of base classes, sometimes called root classes. A base class is a class that does not have a superclass. However, Cocoa depends on the fact that almost all classes have a common base class. In Cocoa, the common-base class is NSObject.

The NSObject class is an abstract class meaning that programs use instances of classes that inherit from NSObject, but rarely use instances of NSObject itself. NSObject is a powerful class and a complete description of all its features is beyond the scope of this chapter. The NSObject class documentation that comes with the Apple developer tools is excellent and complete. Some key features of NSObject that enable much of the power and flexibility of Cocoa are described here.

There are many advantages to using a common-base class. Almost all the objects used in Cocoa inherit directly or indirectly from NSObject. As a result, messages that are understood by NSObject are understood by almost every Cocoa object. The NSObject class includes many powerful features that are ubiquitous because the common-base class provides them. Furthermore, methods can be added to the NSObject class via categories. Adding methods to NSObject effectively adds those methods to every Cocoa object.

NOTE

Methods that are added to the NSObject class by a category are sometimes called an informal protocol. Such methods are similar to the methods declared in a protocol because the programmer can safely assume that the methods are available in an anonymous object.

The NSObject class encapsulates much of the Objective-C runtime's functionality, and gives all objects basic, introspective abilities. NSObject conforms to the NSObject protocol, and declares only one instance variable called isa. This variable points to the class object that encapsulates the instance's class. The isa variable enables the runtime to determine the class of an instance. The isa variable is almost never accessed directly by code. The class of an object can be determined by sending it the -class message.

The NSObject class provides methods for dynamically allocating memory for new instances and initializing the newly created instances. The specific allocation and initialization techniques used by Cocoa are not part of the Objective-C language definition. Instead Cocoa introduces conventions, and `NSObject` implements the methods needed to support Cocoa's conventions. In Cocoa, an instance is allocated by sending the `+alloc` message to a class object. The instance that is returned from `+alloc` still needs to be initialized using a variant of the `-init` message. The `+alloc`, and `-init` methods are described in Chapter 5. Few classes override the `+alloc` method inherited from the `NSObject` class. As a result, `NSObject`'s `+alloc` method focuses almost all dynamic memory allocation into just one place in code, and that can be a useful attribute of Cocoa programming.

In addition to methods that allocate and initialize instances, the `NSObject` class provides methods for deallocating, copying, comparing, archiving, and sending objects to other computers over networks. `NSObject` has methods that interact with the Objective-C runtime to forward messages to other objects. `NSObject` also provides methods that implement one of the most powerful features of Cocoa, the capability to ask objects for information about themselves.

Object Introspection

The `NSObject` class includes methods that provide information about objects and expose runtime details about objects. For example, to find out if an anonymous object understands a particular message, send the `-respondsToSelector:` message with the selector for the message in question as a parameter. If `-respondsToSelector:` returns the `BOOL` value `YES`, then it is safe to send the message in question. The capability to obtain information about objects is called introspection because the objects look into themselves to provide the information.

To find out if an object responds to a message, use the following methods:

```
+ (BOOL)instancesRespondToSelector:(SEL)aSelector
- (BOOL)respondsToSelector:(SEL)aSelector
```

`NSObject` provides the `-class` method to determine the class of an object at runtime. A `-superclass` method returns the receiver's superclass as well. Two more introspective methods are `-isKindOfClass:` and `-isMemberOfClass:`.

```
- (BOOL)isKindOfClass:(Class)aClass
- (BOOL)isMemberOfClass:(Class)aClass
```

Both `-isKindOfClass:` and `-isMemberOfClass:` return `YES` if the receiver's class matches `aClass` exactly. The `-isKindOfClass:` method will also return `YES` if the receiver is a subclass of `aClass`. As a result, `-isKindOfClass:` is usually preferred. The need to use the more restrictive `-isMemberOfClass:` is relatively rare.

Beyond methods to determine the class of an object, whether an object can respond to a message, and whether an object inherits from a certain class, `NSObject` provides the `-conformsToProtocol:` method to determine if the receiver conforms to a particular protocol. The `-conformsToProtocol:` method is commonly used as follows:

```
If([someObject conformsToProtocol:@protocol(SomeProtocol)]) {
  // Safely send methods declared in SomeProtocol to someObject
}
```

The Introspective Format

C programmers are familiar with the idea of formats in functions such as `printf()`. Many Cocoa classes, such as `NSString`, and functions, such as `NSLog()`, use formats as well. Cocoa formats support most `printf()` formats and add an extra code, `%@`, to mean an object. The following example demonstrates the use of a Cocoa format used with the `NSLog()` function:

```
NSLog(@"Log the description of an object: %@", someObject);
```

`NSLog()` prints text messages to an error log. In this example, the constant string `"Log the description of an object: "` is output followed by a description of `someObject`. How should an object be rendered as text? Only the object itself knows. Whenever the `%@` format is used, one of the following methods will be used to determine how to print the corresponding object by asking it to describe itself:

```
+ (NSString *)description
- (NSString *)description
```

Optimization

Although the Objective-C message dispatcher is extremely fast, when a message must be sent multiple times to the same object in a tight loop, the messaging overhead might become significant. It is possible, in very specific circumstances, to bypass the message dispatcher to gain a slight boost in speed. This is dangerous and is discouraged, but if you feel you must do it, start by obtaining a pointer to the function, which implements the method for a given object by using one of these methods:

```
+ (IMP)instanceMethodForSelector:(SEL)aSelector
- (IMP)methodForSelector:(SEL)aSelector
```

The `IMP` is a pointer to a C function, which takes as its arguments `self` (a pointer to the instance), `_cmd` (the selector you used to obtain the `IMP`), and then whatever parameters the method itself requires. As an example of how you would use this, suppose we have an object which implements the method -incrementBy: and you want to call the method 100,000 times as quickly as possible with the loop variable as the parameter. It could be done this way:

```
SEL theSelector = @selector(incrementBy:);
IMP theIMP = [someObject methodForSelector:theSelector];
int i;

for (i=0; i<100000; i++) {
  theIMP(someObject, theSelector, i);
}
```

This use of IMPs is dangerous. Suppose you were cycling over an array of receivers. In that case, unless the receivers are instances of the same class, the IMP you should be using would vary from one instance to another. Furthermore, some classes might respond to a particular message, but not have a valid IMP. An example is presented later in this chapter where this can happen because of the use of forwarding. The Objective-C runtime takes care of all these details automatically for messages, but you must take care of them when using an IMP. Misuse of IMPs leads to strange, difficult-to-diagnose bugs.

Object Comparison

NSObject provides some basic facilities for comparing objects in the form of these two methods:

```
- (BOOL)isEqual:(id)object
- (unsigned)hash
```

Your subclasses probably need to reimplement these methods so that the suitable comparisons are performed. The default implementations simply use the pointer to the object as a comparison value; if the pointers are the same, the objects must be equal because they are the same object. However, your subclass's instances might be equal, even when the objects are different instances. Your implementation of -isEqual should reflect that.

The -hash method simply returns a value based on the value of a pointer to the receiving object. If you create a string class, or some other type of class for which a hashing function exists, you should probably reimplement the -hash method. The main idea of hashing is to provide some number that can be used to identify an object.

Cocoa imposes some rules that must be observed if the -isEqual method is overridden. First, if -isEqual: returns YES when comparing two objects then the –hash methods of the two compared objects must also provide equal values. Second, if `-isEqual:` returns `NO` then the return value of `-hash` may or may not be equal (the better the hashing, the less likely that they will be equal). Hashing in general is a complex subject and is beyond the scope of this book.

NOTE

If you want to learn more about hashing, check out *Sams Teach Yourself Data Structure and Algorithms in 24 Hours*. Part V of this book covers hash tables.

Runtime Integration

Many of the features of the Objective-C runtime can be accessed via `NSObject` methods. The `NSObject` class encapsulates most of the interaction between programs and the runtime.

Class Initialization

Two class methods are declared by `NSObject`, which the runtime calls automatically to initialize classes:

```
+ (void)load
+ (void)initialize
```

The first method, `+load`, is called when a class is linked into a running program. It is possible for programs to load new program code as they run (see the `NSBundle` class described in Chapter 7, "Foundation," for more information). If a class is loaded in this way, the `+load` method is called, offering the class an opportunity to take special actions. More commonly, `+initialize` is used for setting up a class object. This method is treated in a slightly special way: it will be called once and only once for each class object in the program. It will be called just before the program uses that object for the first time. Subclasses that implement this method should never call the super implementation of the method.

Posing

It is possible to have a particular class stand in for another class. This technique, known as posing, can be used to patch system classes or alter their behavior across the whole program. If you want one class to pose as another, use this method implemented by `NSObject`:

```
+ (void)poseAsClass:(Class)aClass
```

There are a few rules you absolutely must follow for posing to succeed. First, posing must be initiated before `aClass` is instantiated for the first time. If there are any instances of aClass already, then it is too late to pose. Second, the receiving class object must be a subclass of aClass, which adds no instance variables. Because of these restrictions, it is often much easier to use a category to add or patch some of a class's methods, instead of attempting to create a new object and have it pose as the class in question.

Performing

The Objective-C runtime also enables you to send a message that was not predetermined at compile time. There are three methods declared in NSObject that can be used to do this:

```
- (id)performSelector:(SEL)aSelector
- (id)performSelector:(SEL)aSelector withObject:(id)object
- (id)performSelector:(SEL)aSelector withObject:(id)object1
      withObject:(id)object2
```

A few other methods also do this, allowing for an optional delay in sending the message. These methods differ only in the arguments they accept. Which one you should use depends on aSelector. If aSelector takes no arguments, use the first. If it takes a single argument, use the second. If it takes two arguments, use the third. The arguments must all be of type id, or convertible to id, and the return value is id.

As an example of using these methods, suppose you have an instance variable that is a selector (SEL type) called action, and another that points to an object called target. Further assume that the selector is always known to have a single parameter, an id called sender. You might send the action message to target like this:

```
[target performSelector:action withObject:self];
```

See Chapter 8, "The Application Kit Architecture," for examples of targets and actions in use.

Forwarding Messages

The Objective-C compiler does not guarantee a given object will be able to respond to a given message. More importantly, the compiler cannot guarantee that a receiver can't respond to a message. As previously shown, methods can be added dynamically by categories, but an even more powerful facility exists. The Objective-C runtime and the NSObject class provide a way of trapping messages. Some objects can respond to a message and not yet have an implementation in machine code for that message. Messages can be transparently forwarded to another object.

Messages need to have a transport to get them from one place to another. In Objective-C the default transport is to use the underlying function call semantic, of the C language. However, it is possible to insert your own transport via forwarding. Here's how it works:

The Objective-C message dispatcher looks at the receiver of a message and checks to see if it can respond to the message using the default function call semantic. If it can, that will be used. If not, it asks the instance to attempt to deal with the message by calling this method:

```
- (void)forwardInvocation:(NSInvocation *)anInvocation
```

If the object cannot forward the message, or refuses to deal with it, this method is called to alert the runtime that the object simply refuses to receive the message:

```
- (void)doesNotRecognizeSelector:(SEL)aSelector
```

Given this process, you can override `-forwardInvocation:` so that it will handle methods for which the class has no implementation. Thus, even though a class might not handle a method, it can forward the message to another object. Perhaps the class has a pointer to an object in an instance variable, and that object can indeed handle the message. The `-forwardInvocation:` can be implemented to pass the message on to the object that can handle it.

Handling `-forwardInvocation:` can be as simple as reinvoking the message using a different receiver, or as complex as packaging up the `message` and sending it over a network connection. The possibilities are endless. Because any object can tap into the messaging resolution and sending process, Objective-C programmers should never make too many assumptions about what message will be delivered, to whom, or when. All the default behaviors can be changed simply by implementing `-forwardInvocation:`.

The `-forwardInvocation:` method can be used to simulate multiple implementation inheritance. Forwarding is also used by Cocoa's built-in undo mechanism, and implemented by the `NSUndoManager` class to capture messages and use them later during undo. The `NSUndoManager` class is described in Chapter 8. Messages to one object can be re-sent to multiple receivers, as implemented by the `MiscTee` class, available at `www.misckit.org`.

The `-doesNotRecognizeSelector:` method declared by `NSObject` is used whenever an object needs to tell the runtime "I don't want to respond to that message." For example, because `NSObject` defines the `-copy` method, almost all objects inherit an implementation of `-copy`. Suppose you have a subclass of `NSObject` for which `-copy` makes no sense. Perhaps the object encapsulates a system resource that cannot be copied. It might be best if attempts to copy that object triggered an exception or runtime error. In a case such as this, you would override the `-copy` method like this:

```
- (id)copy
{
  [self doesNotRecognizeSelector:_cmd];
}
```

This is exactly what the default implementation of `-forwardInvocation:` does, unless you override it.

Runtime Functions

The Apple Objective-C runtime provides many C functions for interacting with the runtime. Most of the runtime functions are described in Appendix A. However, four runtime functions are used commonly and deserve explanation here.

```
Class NSClassFromString(NSString *aClassName)
NSString *NSStringFromClass(Class aClass)
NSString *NSStringFromSelector(SEL aSelector)
SEL NSSelectorFromString(NSString *aSelectorName)
```

The first two methods convert from a string to a reference to the class named by the string and back. Uses of `NSClassFromString()` include allowing a user to input the name of a class to use. For example, an application could parse a text configuration file that specifies which classes to use in the application.

The `NSStringFromSelector()` and `NSSelectorFromString()` functions convert to and from strings containing message names and selectors. `NSSelectorFromString()` can be used to convert user input into messages to objects. Many scripting languages can be integrated with Cocoa just by converting the commands in the scripting language into similarly named messages in Objective-C. `NSStringFromSelector()` is useful when generating debugging or error output.

Objective-C++

Objective-C is a small set of extensions to ANSI C. Objective-C++ is the same set of extensions applied to C++. Apple's Objective-C compiler is also an Objective-C++ compiler.

One of the advantages of Objective-C is that, as a super-set of ANSI C, it can be easily mixed with the millions of lines of existing C code in the world. Objective-C++ can be mixed with the millions of lines of C++ code that already exist. C++ features, such as name mangling, are fully supported by Objective-C++ so that direct linkage between Objective-C++ code and existing C++ code is possible.

Objective-C source code files are identified by the `.m` extension. Apple's compiler treats files with the `.M` or `.mm` extensions as Objective-C++ source code. Additionally, the `-x` compiler option can be used to instruct Apple's compiler to treat any input file as Objective-C++ source code.

Apple's online documentation describes the features and limitations of Objective-C++ at `http://developer.apple.com/techpubs/`, and in the release notes that come with Apple's developer tools. In general, Objective-C classes and C++ classes can be intermixed so that an Objective-C method can call a C++ member function and visa versa or a C++ class can include a pointer to an Objective-C object as a member variable. Objective-C classes cannot inherit from C++ classes or the other way around. The two class hierarchies must remain distinct. The semantics regarding instance creation and deletion are dramatically different between C++ and Objective-C. As a result, mixing them can be tricky, but the benefit of reusing existing C++ code in new Objective-C projects outweighs the complications that it introduces.

Summary

Being able to cover the most important elements of the Objective-C language in a single chapter is a tribute to the language's simplicity. More details about the Objective-C runtime are presented in Appendix A. The appendix will help you harness the full power of Objective-C's runtime, and advanced techniques. In the meantime, with the information presented in this chapter and the next, you have all the language tools you need to start Cocoa programming.

Libraries of reusable code are needed to really take advantage of any language. Objective-C is a very rich language and the Cocoa frameworks comprise one of the most powerful libraries of reusable objects ever created. Just as libraries are needed to take full advantage of a language, conventions are often needed to take maximum advantage of the libraries. The need for conventions is nothing new. The Microsoft Foundation Classes library used with Microsoft Windows has its own conventions and rules for correct use. Many of the traditional Mac libraries require conventions such as Pascal style strings and specialized memory management. Chapter 5 introduces the conventions of the Cocoa frameworks that are required to use Cocoa effectively.

5 Cocoa Conventions

IN THIS CHAPTER

- Naming
- Initializers
- Managing Memory
- Accessors
- Using Memory Zones
- Encoding and Decoding

Several conventions are used throughout the Cocoa frameworks. Awareness of the conventions greatly enhances the readability of code and documentation that references the frameworks. Conventions exist within most software environments. The conventions soon become second nature to programmers. Because of consistency with which the conventions are applied within the Cocoa frameworks, programmers can often guess the name of a class or method without needing the documentation.

These conventions are not part of the Objective-C language. Some of the conventions, such as variable naming, were originally arbitrary, but have become standard and expected after many years of use. Many conventions, such as memory management of objects distributed over a network, are pragmatic solutions to problems. The conventions exist to reinforce the best programming practices. Adherence to the conventions can enhance the power and reusability of your code. In some cases, use of the conventions is not optional. For example, the memory-management conventions used by Cocoa unavoidably influence the code that you write. No Cocoa application will work correctly unless it follows the memory-management conventions.

This chapter describes the common Cocoa conventions and notes whether each convention is optional or not.

Naming

Naming conventions are used within the Cocoa frameworks. These conventions are optional, but they are a good standard to follow. The conventions indicate the intended scope and usage of the item being named. Scope refers to the region of a program in which a name is known, and is usually enforced by the compiler. Usage refers to the intended use of the named item. Even in cases where the compiler does not enforce the usage limitations, the usage clues should be respected.

If you do not follow Cocoa's naming conventions, your code will look odd when intermixed with code that uses Cocoa objects. Other programmers might be misled or confused about the meaning of your code.

Prefixes

Many symbol names in the Cocoa frameworks begin with the prefix NS. As long as other programmers do not create names that start with NS, Apple is free to create new names that begin with NS without fear of inadvertently using a name used by a third party and creating a conflict with existing code. Each company or programmer should adopt a unique two- or three-letter prefix for names. For example, the classes in the popular OmniFoundation Framework from Omni Development Corp. all begin with the prefix OF.

Use the prefix for all names that have global scope, and for all private instance variables.

At the time of this writing there is no way to register a prefix or find out if someone else is already using a prefix. Try to pick a prefix that is unlikely to be used by someone with whom you will need to share code, including the vendors of libraries and frameworks that you want to use. The need for unique prefixes is common in the C language, and languages derived from C, such as Objective-C. Java and C++ avoid the need for prefixes by providing a language construct called a Name Space. Future implementations of Objective-C may also support name spaces.

Capitalization and Scope

Items that have global scope should start with a capital letter or an underscore followed by a capital letter. Global scope means that the item named will be accessible anywhere in the program. In Objective-C all class names have global scope; therefore all class names should begin with a capital letter. For example, `NSObject` is a class name. In Objective-C, the following language constructs have global scope; names of classes, names of protocols, names of categories, names of types, names of enumeration constants, names of global variables, the names of C functions that are not declared static, and structure and union tag names.

Items that do not have global scope should begin with a lowercase letter, or an underscore followed by a lowercase letter. In Objective-C, method names do not have global scope. Methods only have meaning within the context of a particular class. All method names should begin with a lowercase letter. For example,

+initialize and -replaceObject:atIndex: are two method names. In Objective-C, the following language constructs do not have global scope: names of class/factory methods, names of instance methods, names of instance variables, names of C functions that are declared static, names of method and function arguments, names of local variables, and the names of individual structure and union elements.

Underscores and Usage

A leading underscore character in a name conveys usage information. Any name that begins with an underscore character refers to an item that should only be used by the programmers who maintain the module in which the item is referenced. Names that begin with an underscore are part of private application programming interfaces (APIs) and are subject to change without notice. In most cases, the Objective-C compiler will not enforce usage rules. For example, _MYPrivateClass is the name of a class that should not be used by programmers other than the maintainers. MY is the prefix, and like all class names, the first letter of the first word in _MYPrivateClass is capitalized because class names have global scope. The objective-C compiler will not prevent a programmer from creating an instance of _MYPrivateClass, but it is still a bad idea to do so.

In Objective-C classes, private instance variables should begin with an underscore and a unique prefix. The prefix is essential for private instance variables because Apple reserves the right to add or change instance variables that begin with a single underscore character and no prefix. Using a prefix ensures that your instance variable names will not conflict with the names of any private instance variables that Apple uses. For example:

```
int _myPrivateVariable;   // private instance variable with prefix "my"
```

Names that do not begin with an underscore refer to items that are intended for use by all programmers. For example, all programmers should use the NSString class.

Additional Capitalization

The second and subsequent words in each name should be capitalized. For example NSCaseInsensitiveSearch is the name of an enumeration constant. Some method names contain multiple name fragments separated by colon (:) characters. The first word in each fragment starts with a lowercase letter. For example, in the method -makeObjectsPerformSelector:withObject:, Objects, Perform, Selector, and Object are all capitalized. The word make is not capitalized because it is the first word in the name of a method, and methods do not have global scope. The word with is not capitalized because it is the first word in the second name fragment.

Nouns and Verbs

Class and object names should usually consist of nouns. For example: In class names, `NSNumber`, `NSArray`, and `NSWindow`, as well as the words number, array, and window are all nouns.

Method and function names should usually start with a verb. For example, in the method names, `-makeObjectPerformSelector:`, `-compare:`, `+initialize`, and `-isSelected`, the words make, compare, initialize, and is are all verbs.

Class Names

Most class names should include the name of the immediate super class. For example, `NSScrollView` is a subclass of `NSView`. There are a few exceptions to this convention. Most objects used with Cocoa are assumed to inherit from `NSObject`, and therefore it is never necessary to include Object in a class name. For example, the class `NSDocument` is not called `NSDocumentObject` even though it inherits directly from `NSObject`. Most of the classes in Cocoa follow this convention, but because the convention was adopted in the middle of the evolution of Cocoa, many of the oldest classes are not named this way. According to this convention, `NSControl` should have been called `NSControlView` and `NSTextField` should have been called `NSTextFieldControl`. Nevertheless, this is a wise convention and programmers should adhere to it when creating new classes.

Initializers

Instance methods that initialize a newly allocated instance are called initializers and, by convention, begin with the word `init`. The Objective-C compiler does not ensure correct initialization of object instances, therefore initialization must be handled by convention. The initialization convention is not optional for existing Cocoa classes or for most subclasses of Cocoa classes. By convention, object instances are created in two steps. First, memory for the new instance is reserved by calling the `+alloc` or `+allocFromZone:` class methods provided by the `NSObject` class. Almost all classes in the Cocoa frameworks inherit directly or indirectly from `NSObject`. After memory is reserved, the memory is initialized by calling an initializer. A class can provide any number of initializers.

In practice, this reliance on a mere convention for such an important aspect of using the language and the frameworks is not a problem. Programmers quickly become accustomed to the two-part creation of instances and the use of initializers. In fact, the most common way to create an instance of a class is to combine the allocation and initialization in one line as follows:

```
[[SomeClass alloc] init];
```

A class can provide any number of initializers. If there are multiple initializers, one should be the designated initializer. The designated initializer for the `NSObject` class is `-init`. The designated initializer for the `NSView` class is `-initWithFrame:`. Any initializer method can be the designated initializer for a class, but it must be clearly identified in documentation. When a class provides multiple initializers, the designated initializer is usually the one with the most arguments and options. Any other initializers are implemented to call the designated initializer with calculated or default arguments.

Documenting the designated initializer simplifies the creation of subclasses. Users of a class can call any of the initializers provided by the class, including all the initializers declared in that class's superclass. Without a documented designated initializer, the programmer creating a subclass cannot know which initializer a user will call. If the programmer creating a subclass does not know which initializer will be called then the new subclass must be implemented to override all the inherited initializers. That is the only way to be sure the instances of the new class will be correctly initialized. However, if there is a designated initializer, the programmer can override just the designated initializer in the subclass. The programmer can be confident that all other initializers are implemented to call the designated initializer.

When writing an initializer, it is important to call the superclass's designated initializer. Assuming that the superclass's designated initializer is `-init`, it should be called as follows:

```
self = [super init];
```

The assignment of `self` to the result of the superclass's designated initializer is important. In some rare cases, the inherited initializer can return a different instance from the one that received the message. In that case, an error will result if the assignment to `self` is not made.

When reading the Cocoa documentation provided by Apple, be sure to identify which initializer is the designated initializer for each class. When subclassing a class in the Cocoa frameworks, be sure to override the designated initializer if your subclass requires any special initialization. If a new class provides multiple initializers, be sure to document which initializer is the designated initializer, and make sure that the other initializers all call the designated initializer.

Managing Memory

Large portions of the errors in computer programs are byproducts of dynamic memory allocation. Dynamic-memory allocation enables a program to allocate as much memory as it needs on a case-by-case basis. When an application dynamically allocates memory, the operating system provides the requested memory as long as it is possible. The total memory allocated can be as large as the computer's physical memory, virtual memory, and addressing conventions will allow. The theoretical limit to the amount of memory that can be allocated by one application on Mac OS X is approximately four Gigabytes.

The difficulty with dynamic-memory allocation is that the application and/or the operating system have to keep track of memory that has been allocated, and remember to deallocate it (free it). When dynamically allocated memory is no longer being used, and has not been deallocated, the memory is called a memory leak. Memory leaks are wasteful and can cause serious performance problems as the program runs. If a program continues leaking memory, eventually it will drain the system of all its memory.

There are other ways of mishandling memory in addition to leaks. For example, in C, it is possible to have a pointer overrun or underrun. When memory is dynamically allocated, the program is given a pointer that tells it where the new memory is located. C allows a program to access data at some offset from a pointer. If the offset is larger than the amount of memory allocated, a pointer overrun occurs. The results are unpredictable and range from strange, unexpected program behaviors to crashes. As expected, attempting to access data that is in memory before the pointer (a negative offset) is a pointer underrun, and can have results similar to an overrun.

Automatic Garbage Collection

Because problems with memory handling are common, and mistakes are easily made, many programmers prefer to have the computer handle the memory automatically and flawlessly. As might be suspected, this is not easily done. One solution that has become popular is automatic garbage collection. Smalltalk, Java, and many other modern computer languages use automatic garbage collection. The basic idea is that there is an invisible garbage collector that periodically scans memory to see if it is still in use. If the garbage collector determines that the memory is no longer being used it frees up the memory. The programmer doesn't need to do anything special; automatic garbage collecting handles everything behind the scenes automatically.

The Objective-C Cocoa libraries don't use automatic garbage collection. By convention, Cocoa uses a form of garbage collection known as reference counting. The disadvantage to this is the programmer has to do a little bit of work to properly use reference counting; it isn't automatic. An advantage is reference-counting techniques can be more efficient than automatic garbage collection, and give the programmer more control. Additionally, Cocoa's Distributed Objects would not work well with automatic garbage collection, yet reference-counting works very well with remote distributed objects. Several other considerations are involved in deciding which type of garbage collecting to use, but they aren't germane to understanding how to use Cocoa's reference-counting technique. Correct use of the Cocoa memory-management conventions is essential.

Reference Counting

Reference counting is a simple idea. Every object has a reference count that indicates how many other objects are currently keeping a reference to it. When object `A` wants to reference object `B`, `A` increases `B`'s reference count by one. When object `A` is done referencing object `B`, `A` decreases `B`'s reference count by one. When no objects reference object `B`, its reference count will reach zero and `B` will be deallocated, thus freeing up memory for some other use. The process of deallocating `B` might decrease reference counts on objects used by `B`, perhaps causing them to be deallocated, too.

With Cocoa, newly allocated objects have a reference count of one. When a class is sent a `+alloc` or `+allocWithZone:` message, memory for a new instance is reserved and the new instance implicitly has a reference count of one. If this new instance is referenced by another object, then the reference count should be incremented. This is done by sending the `-retain` message:

```
[object retain];
```

Every `-retain` message causes the receiver's reference count to be increased by one. When code obtains a reference to an object through some means other than allocation and the code needs to keep a reference to the object, then the object should be sent a `-retain` message. If the code neglects to retain the object, it is likely that the object will be deallocated sometime in the future and it will be invalid when the code references it causing an error.

Now, when code is done using an object, the code should tell it by sending a `-release` message:

```
[object release];
```

The `-release` message decreases the object's reference count by one. If decreasing the reference count causes the count to reach zero, the object is immediately deallocated. It is a good idea at this point to reassign the reference to the object. A good strategy is to assign `nil` to the reference:

```
object = nil;
```

It is not a good idea to keep references to objects that might have been deallocated after being released. By assigning nil you are making sure that code doesn't erroneously attempt to send a message to an invalid object.

Your program can determine the reference count of an object at any time by sending the -retainCount message. -retainCount returns an integer count of the number of times the receiver has been retained including the initial value of one set when the object was allocated. There is seldom a need to call -retainCount in a working program. When using an object, the programmer should not care how many other ways the object is used. However, knowing the retain count of an object can be an invaluable debugging aid in some circumstances.

At this point, it should make sense that the number of release messages sent to an object over its lifetime should be equal to the number of -retain messages sent to the same object plus one. The extra one is for the initial +alloc or +allocWithZone: message that created the object in the first place. Also keep in mind that the -copy, -mutableCopy, -copyWithZone: and -mutableCopyWithZone: messages are like a +alloc message, so they need a matching -release.

This might seem complex, but it really isn't. You simply send one -release to match up with each +alloc, +allocWithZone, -copy, -mutableCopy, -copyWithZone:, -mutableCopyWithZone:, or -retain that you have sent.

Unfortunately, reference counting doesn't remain that simple. For example, suppose that we are writing a method that is expected to return a reference to an object. The following example shows one incorrect implementation:

```
-(NSObject *)incorrectMethod1
{
  NSObject        *result = [[NSObject alloc] init];

  return result;
}
```

The method, -incorrectMethod1, allocates a new instance of the NSObject class. The new instance has a retain count of one. The new instance is then returned. There is a serious problem with this method. First, the convention that we must send a -release message to balance the +alloc message has not been followed. The code that calls -incorrectMethod1 can ignore the object returned, at which point memory has been leaked. After return, the -incorrectMethod1 method no longer references the object. If the calling code ignores the value returned, there will not be any remaining reference to the object and no way to ever release it. The caller will not release the returned object because the caller did not explicitly call one of the alloc or copy methods that must be balanced with a release.

Another incorrect implementation calls `-release` inappropriately, as shown in the following code:

```
-(NSObject *)incorrectMethod2
{
  NSObject        *result = [[NSObject alloc] init];

  [result release];

  return result;
}
```

The method, `-incorrectMethod2`, adheres to the convention of sending a `-release` to balance the `+alloc`. Unfortunately, after sending the `-release` message, `result` can be deallocated. If the calling code relies on the reference returned, it might crash. The calling code is being given a reference to an invalid (deallocated) object.

How can an object reference be returned from a method without resulting in a memory leak, and without returning a potentially invalid reference?

The answer is very clever. Cocoa applications contain an auxiliary object called a release pool, which is a temporary holding place for objects during the short time in limbo between the end of one method and the point in the caller's code where the object is retained (if it is retained). When an object is added to a release pool, it is registered to receive a `-release` message at a later time. After an object has been added to a release pool, the object can be returned from the method without creating a leak or returning an invalid object. If the caller wants to keep a reference to the object, the caller will send a `-retain` message. At some later point, the release pool will be deallocated, and at that time it will release all the objects it contains. If the reference counts any of the objects in the release pool reach zero, those objects are then deallocated.

Figure 5.1 shows how an object can be allocated in a method and safely returned by adding the object to a release pool. Two timelines are shown. In Timeline 1, the caller retains the object returned from a method and the object is not deallocated when the release pool is deallocated. Because the caller retained the object, the caller must eventually release the object or else it will be a memory leak. In Timeline 2, the caller does not retain the returned object. As a result, when the release pool is deallocated, the object will also be deallocated. Because the caller did not retain the object, the caller does not ever need to release it.

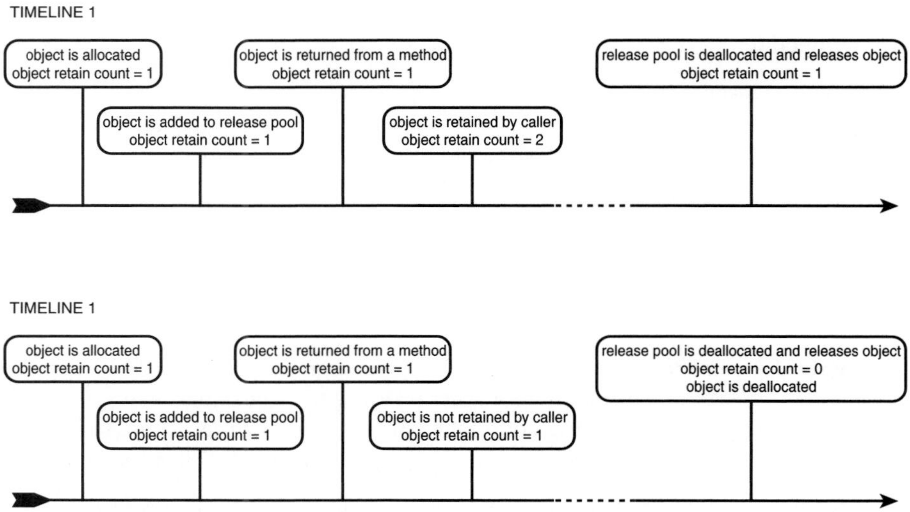

FIGURE 5.1 This Timeline illustrates the sequence in which an object is allocated, autoreleased, returned from a method, optionally retained by a caller, and released by a release pool.

The property of delaying a release message to a returned object until after the calling code has had a chance to retain the object allows for objects returned from a method to correctly handle reference counting.

In Cocoa, the `NSAutoreleasePool` class implements release pools. All the details of adding objects to a release pool are handled by a single method, `-autorelease`, declared in the `NSObject` class. To place an object in a release pool and thereby schedule the object's release at a later time, simply call `-autorelease` as follows:

```
[object autorelease];
```

The following code illustrates one correct way of returning an object from a method:

```
-(NSObject *)correctMethod
{
  NSObject        *result = [[NSObject alloc] init];

  [result autorelease];

  return result;
}
```

In the correct implementation, an object is allocated, initialized, and a reference to it is assigned to `result`. The object referenced by result has a reference count of one. When `result` is autoreleased, it is added to a release pool. After `result` is autoreleased, it still has a reference count of one and has not yet been deallocated.

If the code that calls `-correctMethod` does not retain the returned object, then the object's reference count will reach zero and the object will be deallocated when the release pool is eventually deallocated. If the calling code does retain the returned object, then object's reference count will temporarily be two. When the release pool is finally deallocated, the object's reference count will drop to one and the object will not be deallocated. The reference kept by the calling code remains valid.

The complete rules for using `-release` and `–autorelease` follow: Send one `-release` or `–autorelease` message to match up with each `+alloc`, `+allocWithZone`, `-copy`, `-mutableCopy`, `-copyWithZone:`, `–mutableCopyWithZone:`, or `-retain` message that you have sent.

A question might arise at this point. Who creates the release pool and how often does it get deallocated? It turns out that in Cocoa applications that use the Application Kit framework, a release pool is created automatically at the start of the internal event loop, and is cleared out at the end. Of course, you can always create your own pool and dispose of it as described in the `NSAutoreleasePool` class documentation. This can be done in special circumstances to enhance performance and reduce a program's memory requirements. If you are writing a command-line program that doesn't use the Application Kit framework, then you will have to create your own pool. It is really easy to do. The following line creates a pool:

```
NSAutoreleasePool *pool = [[NSAutoreleasePool alloc] init];
```

That's all you need to do; the `-autorelease` method will find it automatically. At the end of your run loop or when you want to clean out the pool simply release the pool:

```
[pool release];
```

One thing to be careful of is expecting an autoreleased object to be valid for too long. Normally, an autoreleased object will remain valid within the current scope (that is, current method) and can safely be returned from a method. It is wise, however, to send a `-retain` message as soon as you know you want to keep a reference to an object that was not obtained by calling one of the `+alloc`, `+allocWithZone`, `-copy`, `-mutableCopy`, `-copyWithZone:`, `–mutableCopyWithZone:` messages. Of course, if you don't need to keep a reference to an object don't send `-retain`, and it will go away automatically when the release pool is deallocated.

The `-release` method is much more efficient than `-autorelease`. Therefore, unless you need the special functionality of `-autorelease`, use `-release`. Applications that overuse `-autorelease` tend to run very slowly.

NOTE

Follow these guidelines religiously to avoid memory leaks and attempts to access deallocated objects:

- If you allocated, copied, or retained an object you are responsible for releasing the object with either `-release` or `-autorelease` when you no longer need it. If you did not allocate, copy, or retain an object you should not release it.
- When you receive an object by some means other than an alloc or copy method, the object will normally remain valid until the end of your method and it can be safely returned as a result of your method. You must either retain or copy the object if you need it to live longer than this (for example, if you plan to store it in an instance variable).
- Use `-autorelease` rather than `-release` when you want to return an object that you will no longer reference. Use `-release` rather than `-autorelease` wherever you can for performance reasons.

The online documentation that comes with the Cocoa development tools includes an excellent and detailed explanation of the `NSAutoreleasePool` class, as well as an analysis of the implications of nested release pools.

Retain Cycles

There is one final problem the preceding rules do not address: retain cycles. A retain cycle is a special kind of memory leak that can occur with a reference counting scheme. The problem occurs when two or more objects reference each other. For example, if object A is retaining object B and object B is retaining object A, the two objects never reach a zero-reference count because each references the other. If neither A nor B is referenced anywhere else in the program, then the memory used by A and B constitutes a memory leak. It is possible to have very complex retain cycles where the minimum reference count is higher than one (multiple objects depending upon each other), and also cases where a long chain of objects retain each other in what looks like a circular linked list.

The best solution to the retain-cycle problem is to avoid it. Be careful with your designs.

Tracking Memory Problems

By now it is obvious that reference counting, although a simple solution, also has its quirks and difficulties. Careful thought while designing objects can solve the difficulties, but even so, we all make mistakes. The Mac OS X development environment provides several tools to help you track down memory problems. Here is a brief synopsis to get you started:

- **gdb**—The debugger for the Cocoa environment that enables you to look at stack frames and variable values and trace execution of your program
- **ObjectAlloc.app**—An application that enables you to watch a graph showing the number of objects in a running application dynamically
- **MallocDebug.app**—Measures an application's use of dynamic memory
- **Sampler.app**—Displays the amount of time your application spends in each function and method

Understanding reference counting is fundamental to Objective-C Cocoa development. No Cocoa program is running correctly until it is following the reference counting rules.

Accessors

Accessors are methods used to query or change the internal state of an object. The internal state of objects is usually stored in instance variables. There is commonly a one-to-one correspondence between instance variables and accessor methods. The convention of using accessors is an extremely good practice that is ubiquitous in the Cocoa frameworks, but is optional.

The following simple class declaration shows how accessors are used.

```
@interface MYClass : NSObject
{
  NSRect _myRect;
}

- (void)setRect:(NSRect)aRect;
- (NSRect)rect;
- (void)getRect:(NSRect *)aRectPtr;

@end
```

`NSRect` is a C structure defined in `NSGeometry.h`. The `-setRect:` method passed the `aRect` argument by value even though `NSRect` is a structure. Similarly, the `-rect` method returns an `NSRect` value. By convention, accessor methods accept nonobject arguments by value, and return nonobject values even when the values have complex types like the `NSRect` structure.

An accessor method that sets a value begins with the word set, as in `-setRect:`. An accessor that returns a value is named after the value like `-rect`.

In some cases, an accessor method that returns a value by reference is provided. Accessors that return values by reference begin with the word get, as in `-getRect:` in this example. This type of accessor is very rare, and they are easy to spot because they begin with get. One example is the method `-(void)getBytes:(void *)buffer` in the `NSData` class, which returns bytes by reference in the buffer argument.

In this example of accessors for nonobject values, the accessors can be implemented as follows:

```
@implementation MYClass
/* Simple class to encapsulate _myRect */

- (void)setRect:(NSRect)aRect
/* Set _myRect */
{
  _myRect = aRect;
}

- (NSRect)rect
/* Return _myRect by value */
{
  return _myRect;
}

- (void)getRect:(NSRect *)aRectPtr
/* Return the value of _myRect by reference in the memory at aRectPtr */
{
  if(NULL != aRectPtr) {
    *aRectPtr = _myRect;
  }
}

@end
```

Consistent use of accessors in your own classes might seem like a chore, but it will simplify and promote reuse of your classes. Accessors are even more important when the values being accessed are objects.

Accessing Objects

The following code demonstrates a standard way to implement accessors for object-instance variables. The code provided here can be used as a template every time you write object accessors. Using this example and following the memory management conventions will prevent memory errors. Consistent use of object accessor methods can help localize the reference counting within your code.

```
@interface MYClassWithObjectAccessors : NSObject
{
  NSObject    *_myObject;
}
- (void)setObject:(NSObject *)anObject;
- (NSObject *)object;

@end

@implementation MYClassWithObjectAccessors
/* Simple class to encapsulate _myObject */

- (void)setObject:(NSObject *)anObject
/* Set _myObject the safe way */
{
  [anObject retain];
  [_myObject release];
  _myObject = anObject;
}

- (NSObject *)object
/* Return _myObject */
{
  return _myObject;
}

- (void)dealloc
/* Clean-up */
{
  [self setObject:nil];
  [super dealloc];
}

@end
```

Almost all memory management can be handled within the accessors. The `-setObject:` method sets the `_myObject` instance variable. Because the `_myObject` reference must remain valid indefinitely, the object to be referenced must be retained or copied. The objects referenced by instance variables should be retained or copied to make sure they are not deallocated while the instance is still using them. The object previously referenced by the `_myObject` instance variable will no longer be referenced after the assignment, so the obsolete object must be released. Finally, the assignment is made.

The order in which the new value is retained and the old value is released is very important. The new value must be retained before the old value is released. This order of operations assures correct behavior in all the circumstances in which the accessor might be used.

An accessor that sets an object value can be called in three general circumstances:

It can be called with a nil argument;

It can be called with an argument that is different from the receiver's existing value, or

It can be called with an argument that is identical to the receiver's existing value.

In any of the circumstances, the existing value could be `nil`.

When it's called with a `nil` argument, the `nil` argument is harmlessly retained. It is safe to send any message to `nil` as long as you do not count on any return value. The object that will no longer be referenced by the `_myObject` instance variable is released, and `_myObject` is set to `nil`. The instance variable ends up being set to `nil` as requested.

When it's called with an argument that's different from the receiver's existing value the new value is retained, the old value is released, and the instance variable references the new value as requested.

When its called with an argument that is identical to the receiver's existing value, the order of operations that is used is required. First, the argument, `anObject`, is retained causing its reference count to rise to at least two. Remember that `anObject` is the same as `_myObject` and has a retain count of at least one because `_myObject` was retained when it was initially set. Then `_myObject` is released causing its retain count to drop to no less than one. Finally, the argument is assigned to `_myObject`, which is a harmless operation because `_myObject` and `anObject` are the same. `_myObject` is left with the same retain count and value that it had before `-setMyObject:` was called. If retain and release are reversed, `_myObject` will be released and possibly deallocated. Therefore, the attempt to retain `anObject` will fail because `anObject` is the same as `_myObject` and has already been deallocated.

Finally, accessors can be used to confine the reference counting memory management of instance variables to just one method, the set accessor. A good strategy is to make sure that the only method that sends `-retain` and `-release` messages to instance variables is the set accessor. Instance variables are commonly released in a class's `-dealloc` method, but even that can be accomplished indirectly using set accessors. The following is an example of a dealloc method implementation that releases an object instance variable by calling an accessor with a `nil` argument:

```
- (void)dealloc
{
  [self setName:nil];          // accessor will release instance
                                    // variable and set it to nil
  [super dealloc];
}
```

Using Memory Zones

Memory zones are a technique that can be used to improve application performance. Memory zones optimize the location of memory for objects that are used together. The use of memory zones is the final wrinkle to Cocoa memory management.

Each application for Mac OS X has a very large amount of addressable memory. Each time an application requests more memory, the operating system provides memory even if all available RAM in the computer is already in use. To accommodate the application's request for memory, the operating system copies the contents of some RAM to the computer's hard disk. The operating system then makes the copied RAM available to the requesting application to reuse. When the memory that was copied to disk is needed again, the operating system chooses a different block of memory to copy to the disk, and brings the old memory back into RAM. The capability for applications to use more memory than the available RAM is called virtual memory. The process of copying the contents of memory to and from the hard disk is called paging or swapping. Accessing the hard disk and copying memory is time consuming. Too much swapping degrades system performance and is called thrashing.

In an application that allocates memory for many objects over time, the various objects might be far apart in memory. If two or more objects are used together, but stored far apart in memory, an inefficient situation can arise. When the memory for one object is needed, that memory is swapped into RAM from the hard disk. The object then needs to access another object that is still not in RAM, and even more memory must be swapped into RAM. In the worst case, the memory swapped in for the second object might force the memory for the first out of RAM. All the swapping dramatically slows the application.

One solution to this problem is to request locality of storage. In other words, store objects that are used together close in memory. When one of the objects is needed, the chances are good that all the needed objects will be swapped into memory at the same time. When the objects are not needed, they are swapped out together as well.

Cocoa provides a mechanism for requesting that objects are stored close together in memory. Cocoa provides functions for creating memory zones and allocating memory from specific zones. All the objects allocated from a specific zone will be close to the other objects in the same zone. Memory zones are represented by the `NSZone` type. `NSZone` and the functions for managing them are described briefly here. More details are available in the online Cocoa reference documentation. Zones are a very low level and somewhat esoteric topic. It is worthwhile to know that zones exist and can be used, but the Cocoa classes hide most of the details and make them work seamlessly without programmer intervention. The use of memory zones should be one of the last concerns of a Cocoa application developer. Get your code working and only then consider the use of zones as an optimization if and only if they are needed.

The function to create a memory zone is `NSCreateZone()`. To recycle a zone and make its memory available to other applications, use the `NSRecycleZone()` function. Arbitrary memory can be allocated from a zone with the `NSZoneMalloc()`, `NSZoneCalloc()`, or `NSZoneRealloc()` functions. These functions work like the traditional Unix memory-management functions, `malloc()`, `calloc()`, and `realloc()` to allocate uninitialized memory, allocate memory initialized to all zeros, and change the amount of the memory allocated respectively. Memory allocated with the `NSZoneMalloc()`, `NSZoneCalloc()`, or `NSZoneRealloc()` functions can be freed with `NSZoneFree()`, which is similar to the standard Unix `free()` function.

Cocoa objects are always allocated in a zone. The `+alloc` class method defined in `NSObject` actually calls the `+allocWithZone:` class method specifying a default zone. The default zone can be obtained by calling the `NSDefaultMallocZone()` function. Programmers can specify that an object instance should be allocated from a particular zone by using `+allocWithZone:` and providing the zone as an argument. A zone can also be specified when an object is copied. The `-copy` method declared in the `NSCopying` protocol is usually implemented to call `-copyWithZone:`.

You can determine the zone in which an object was allocated by sending the object a `-zone` message. If you decide to use zones explicitly in you application, it is a good idea to make sure objects that allocate other objects do so using the same zone. For example, the `-init` method of a custom class might allocate an instance of another class for use as the value of an instance variable, as shown here:

```
- (id)init
{
  self = [super init];
  _myInstanceVariable = [[MYHelperClass allocWithZone:[self zone]] init];

  return self;
}
```

`_myInstanceVariable` will be an instance of `MYHelperClass` that is allocated from the same memory zone as the object being initialized.

Encoding and Decoding

The Cocoa frameworks provide a convention for initializing an object instance by decoding data that has previously been encoded. Encoding and decoding object-instance data is the basis for storing objects on disk, and copying objects to different address spaces. Each class is responsible for encoding and decoding its own state by implementing two methods, `-encodeWithCoder:` and `-initWithCoder:`, which are declared in the `NSCoding` protocol. These methods are automatically called, under certain circumstances, by Cocoa framework classes such as `NSCoder`, `NSArchiver`, and `NSUnarchiver`. Almost all classes in the Cocoa frameworks conform to the `NSCoding` protocol and implement the two coding methods.

A file or block of memory that contains encoded objects is sometimes called an archive. The `NSArchiver` and `NSUnarchiver` classes are used to write and read archives, and they manage most of the details of the encoding and decoding process. For example, an object that is encoded more than once will only be stored once in an archive. When the objects in the archive are decoded, all the objects that referenced a shared object will be restored to reference a shared object that was decoded. Complex graphs of interconnected objects can be encoded and decoded, preserving all the interconnections. Encoded data is stored in a compact platform independent format.

Making your own classes conform to the `NSCoding` protocol is optional. In most cases, if your class inherits from a class in the Cocoa frameworks, your class will inherit the coding methods. You can override the inherited methods to call the inherited implementations, and then encode or decode the unique state of instances of your class.

The `NSObject` class does not conform to the `NSCoding` protocol. To add encoding and decoding support to a class that does not inherit `NSCoding` conformance, the class must adopt the `NSCoding` protocol and implement the `-encodeWithCoder:` and `-initWithCoder:` methods.

NOTE

Encoding and decoding are both used by Interface Builder. Interface Builder `.nib` files contain encoded objects. Instances loaded from nib files are sent the `-initWithCoder:` method so that they can reconstruct themselves from the encoded data. To use custom classes with Interface Builder, they must implement the `NSCoding` protocol.

Encoding Types

The methods `-encodeWithCoder:` and `-initWithCoder:` are called with an `NSCoder` argument. When an object receives an `-encodeWithCoder:` message, the object should encode its state using the methods of the `NSCoder` instance provided. Almost all types that can be represented by the `@encode` Objective-C compiler directive can be encoded. Objects, scalars, C arrays, C structures, C strings, and pointers to these types can all be encoded and decoded. C unions, void pointers, and function pointers cannot be encoded or decoded.

For example, consider the following class that stores a mixture of objects and other data types using instance variables:

```
@interface MYGrapnic : NSObject <NSCoding>
{
  NSString       *_myLabel;
  NSFont         *_myLabelFont;
  NSPoint        _myLabelPosition;
  id                 _myExtraData;
  float              _myLineWidth;
  NSMutableArray    *_myStyles;
  NSColor        *_myColor;
}

/* NSCoding methods */
- (void)encodeWithCoder:(NSCoder *)coder;
- (id)initWithCoder:(NSCoder *)coder;

@end
```

The `MYGraphic` class is a subclass of `NSObject`, which does not conform to the `NSCoding` protocol. Therefore, the `MYGraphic` class must adopt the `NSCoding` protocol explicitly to enable encoding and decoding. The `-encodeWithCoder:` method for the `MYGraphic` class might implement its `-encodeWithCoder:` method like this:

```
- (void)encodeWithCoder:(NSCoder *)coder
{
  [coder encodeObject:_myLabel];
  [coder encodeObject:_myLabelFont];
  [coder encodeValueOfObjCType:@encode(NSPoint) at:&_myLabelPosition];
  [coder encodeObject:_myExtraData];
  [coder encodeValueOfObjCType:@encode(float) at:&_myLineWidth];
  [coder encodeObject:_myStyles];
  [coder encodeObject:_myColor];
}
```

The `MYGraphic` class encodes all its instance variables, but classes that do not encode all their instance variables are possible also. There is no reason to encode the values of instance variables that can be computed from other data. There is no reason to encode the values of instance variables that are not important when the object is decoded.

Data that is encoded must be decoded in the same order using the same types with which it was encoded. Given the preceding implementation of `-encodeWithCoder:`, the corresponding `-initWithCoder:` method must be implemented as follows:

```
- (id)initWithCoder:(NSCoder *)coder
{
  self = [super init];
  _myLabel = [[coder decodeObject] reatin];
  _myLabelFont = [[coder decodeObject] reatin];
  [coder decodeValueOfObjCType:@encode(NSPoint) at:&_myLabelPosition];
  _myExtraData = [[coder decodeObject] reatin];
  [coder decodeValueOfObjCType:@encode(float) at:&_myLineWidth];
  _myStyles = [[coder decodeObject] reatin];
  _myColor = [[coder decodeObject] reatin];

  return self;
}
```

There are two key requirements for the implementation of `-initWithCoder:`. It must return `self`, and it must decode the same types in the same order that they were encoded. If `- initWithCoder:` is implemented in a class that does not inherit `NSCoding` conformance from its superclass, `- initWithCoder:` should then be implemented to call the superclass's designated initializer and assign the result to the `self` variable.

A class that overrides inherited -encodeWithCoder: and -initWithCoder: methods must call the inherited versions. The following class shows one correct technique for overriding the coding methods. The MYCircleGraphic class is a subclass of the MYGraphic class and is declared as follows:

```
@interface MYCircleGraphic : MYGraphic
{
    NSPoint             _myCenter;
    int             _myRadius;
}

/* NSCoding methods */
- (void)encodeWithCoder:(NSCoder *)coder;
- (id)initWithCoder:(NSCoder *)coder;

@end
```

There is no need for the MYCircleGraphic class declaration to explicitly adopt the NSCoding protocol because MYCircleGraphic inherits conformance from the MYGraphic class. The MYCircleGraphic class might implement its -encodeWithCoder: and -initWithCoder: methods like this:

```
@implementation MYCircleGraphic

/* NSCoding methods */
- (void)encodeWithCoder:(NSCoder *)coder
{
  [super encodeWithCoder:coder];
  [coder encodeValueOfObjCType:@encode(NSPoint) at:&_myCenter];
  [coder encodeValueOfObjCType:@encode(int) at:&_myRadius];
}


- (id)initWithCoder:(NSCoder *)coder
{
  self = [super initWithCoder:coder];
  [coder decodeValueOfObjCType:@encode(NSPoint) at:&_myCenter];
  [coder decodeValueOfObjCType:@encode(int) at:&_myRadius];

  return self;
}

@end
```

The key to these implementations is that they call their superclass, so that it has a chance to encode or decode its state. After the superclass's state is handled, the variables added by the subclass are encoded or decoded. Another detail is the assignment of `self` to the result of the superclass's `-initWithCoder:` method. In some rare cases, the inherited `-initWithCoder:` might substitute a different instance from the one that received the message. In that case an error will result if the assignment to `self` is not made.

Retaining Decoded Objects

Decoding objects follows the Cocoa reference counting conventions. If you obtain an object via decoding and you want to keep a reference to the decoded object, then you must retain it. Decoded objects that are not retained will be deallocated when the coder that provided them is deallocated. Objects can be decoded and retained in one line as follows:

```
_myName = [[coder decodeObject] retain];
```

If a class provides set accessors for its object instance variables, the set accessors can be used in conjunction with decoding as follows:

```
[self setName:[coder decodeObject]];
```

Using the accessors when they exist has advantages. Any logic applied to values when they are set can be implemented in one place, the accessor, rather than in two places, the accessor and also the `-initWithCoder:` method. Logic implemented by a set accessor can be arbitrarily complex, but at a minimum the set accessor will manage the reference count of the decoded instance variable, thus confining all reference counting of instance variables to just the accessors.

Conditional Encoding

The `NSCoder` class includes a method, `-encodeConditionalObject:`, to enable conditional encoding of objects. Conditional encoding means that a placeholder for the object being encoded is encoded instead of the object itself. When both classes are decoded they will be restored with a reference to the same object if the object conditionally encoded in one class is unconditionally encoded by another. If no class unconditionally encodes the object, then when the classes that conditionally encoded the object are decoded, they will decode a reference to `nil`.

Use conditional encoding to avoid encoding too many objects under certain circumstances. For example, if your application includes many interconnected objects in a complex data structure, conditional encoding can be used to enable the encoding and decoding of individual objects without inadvertently encoding all the interconnected objects. Figure 5.2 illustrates a possible configuration of interconnected objects using solid arrows to indicate which objects unconditionally encode references to other objects.

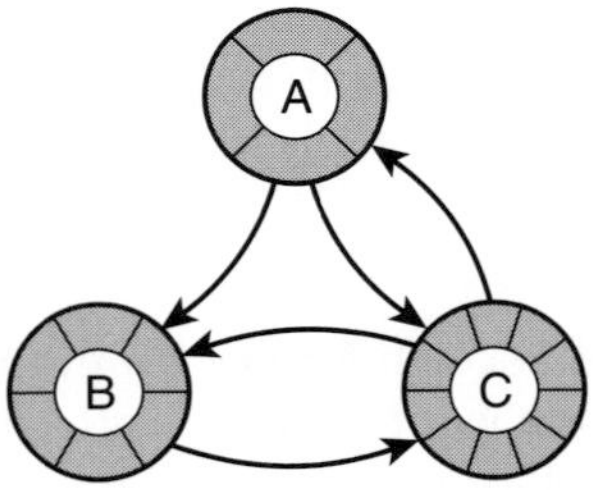

FIGURE 5.2 Interconnected objects can unconditionally encode referenced objects.

It is not possible to encode just one of the interconnected objects depicted in Figure 5.2 because each will encode all the others. Figure 5.3 shows an alternate configuration that uses conditional encoding and makes it possible to encode the entire graph of interconnected objects or encode individual objects. In Figure 5.3, solid arrows are used to indicate unconditionally encoded references and dashed arrows are used to indicate conditionally encoded references.

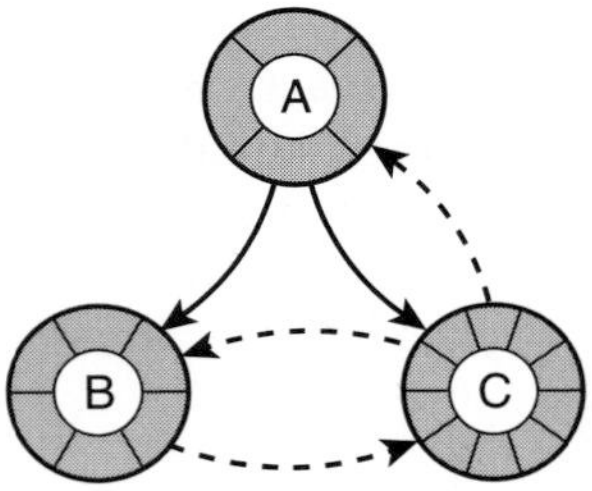

FIGURE 5.3 Interconnected objects can use both conditional and unconditional encoding.

If object A in Figure 5.3 is encoded, objects B and C, and all their interconnections, will also be encoded. When A is decoded, the entire graph of objects is restored. If either object B or object C is encoded by itself, just one object will be encoded. Due to the use of conditional encoding, when that object is restored, its references to other objects will be `nil`.

Using Version Numbers

The values that are encoded in -encodeWithCoder: must be decoded within -initWithCoder using the same order and the same types. What happens if a class is modified to store additional values or use different types? How can the modified class decode values that were encoded by prior versions of the class?

The Cocoa frameworks include a class versioning system that can be used to enable backward compatibility when decoding values. The version number of a class can be set with the +setVersion: method declared in the NSObject class. A good time to set the version of a class is in its +initialize method as follows:

```
@implementation MYClass
+ (void)initialize
{
  [MYClass setVersion:3];
}
@end
```

The +setVersion: message should be sent to the class itself using the class name rather than self because an inherited +initialize might be called by a subclass in which case self will be the subclass. You should not set the version of the subclass inadvertently.

The version number of a class can be obtained by sending the +version message to the class.

When decoding objects, you can obtain the version number of the object when it was encoded by calling the -versionForClassName: method of the coder. Based on the version of the class that was encoded, different decoding sequences can be used. For example, if the MYCircleGraphic class, which was previously introduced, is modified to store its radius as a float rather than an integer, backward compatibility can be maintained, as shown here:

```
@interface MYCircleGraphic : MYGraphic
{
    NSPoint           _myCenter;
    float            _myRadius;    // Changed to float
}

+ (void)initialize;
```

```
/* NSCoding methods */
- (void)encodeWithCoder:(NSCoder *)coder;
- (id)initWithCoder:(NSCoder *)coder;

@end


@implementation MYCircleGraphic

+ (void)initialize
{
  [MYCircleGraphic setVersion:1];    // Default is version 0
}

/* NSCoding methods */
- (void)encodeWithCoder:(NSCoder *)coder
{
  [super encodeWithCoder:coder];
  [coder encodeValueOfObjCType:@encode(NSPoint) at:&_myCenter];
  [coder encodeValueOfObjCType:@encode(float) at:&_myRadius];
}


- (id)initWithCoder:(NSCoder *)coder
{
  self = [super initWithCoder:coder];
  [coder decodeValueOfObjCType:@encode(NSPoint) at:&_myCenter];
  if([coder versionForClassName:@"MYCircleGraphic"] < 1) {
    // Versions prior to 1 saved an integer radius
    int        temp;

    [coder decodeValueOfObjCType:@encode(int) at:&temp];
    _myRadius = (float)temp;
  } else {
    [coder decodeValueOfObjCType:@encode(float) at:&_myRadius];
  }

  return self;
}

@end
```

Using Memory Zones When Decoding

By default, objects that are decoded are created in the default memory zone. In most cases, the default behavior is fine. If you need to decode objects using a different memory zone, set the zone to use via the coder's `-setObjectZone:` method before any objects are decoded. You can obtain the memory zone that a coder is using by sending the `-objectZone` message.

Substituting Objects

During encoding, the object being encoded can substitute a replacement class or instance for itself. Similarly, after an object is decoded, it can substitute another object for itself. The `NSCoder` class and its subclasses, `NSArchiver` and `NSUnarchiver`, call certain methods that are declared in the `NSObject` class to enable substitutions.

The `-classForCoder` method is called as an object is encoded. Override `-classForCoder` to return a different class that should be stored in the encoded data.

Next, the `-replacementObjectForCoder:` method of the object being encoded is called. Override `-replacementObjectForCoder:` to substitute a different instance for the instance being encoded.

After an object has been decoded, the `-awakeAfterUsingCoder:` method is called. Override `-awakeAfterUsingCoder:` to return a different instance than the one just decoded.

Using Alternative Techniques

The encoding support provided by the `NSCoder` class and its subclasses is powerful and flexible, but it has some shortcomings.

The binary data format of encoded values is compact and cross platform, but not documented by Apple. The encoded data cannot be decoded easily without using the Cocoa frameworks. As a result, using encoded values to store the document data of your custom applications is not a good choice. Users on other platforms will not be able to read your documents, even to import them into applications. Other Cocoa applications will not be able to read the document data unless the other applications include all the classes that can be encoded.

Although class versioning can be used to maintain backward compatibility when reading objects that were encoded by prior versions of the class, there is no way to reliably support forward compatibility. In other words, version 2 of a class can decode version 1, but version 1 cannot decode version 2.

Finally, because encoded values are stored in a cryptic binary format, there is no easy way to troubleshoot problems with encoded data. If an error was made encoding values, it might be impossible to ever decode the values.

Fortunately, freely available alternative coding techniques exist. One alternative is property-list encoding, which is available at `www.misckit.com`. Each object is encoded in a human-readable format. Both backward and forward compatibility is possible. Conditional encoding, substitutions, versioning, and memory zones are all supported. Objects that are encoded multiple times are only stored once in the encoded data. Property lists can be stored as XML data.

The disadvantage of property list encoding is that the encoded data can be large and slower to encode and decode than Apples binary implementation. Also, if your class supports both `NSCoder` encoding and property list encoding, you will have to implement the `NSCoding` methods as well as the property coding methods. Interface Builder and Cocoa's distributed objects technology only use the binary format.

Summary

Although this chapter describes the major conventions used throughout the Cocoa frameworks, there are many other conventions and examples of good practices to be found in the frameworks. An awareness of the conventions clarifies the frameworks. When the conventions are observed in use consistently, they become familiar and even comforting. In some cases, awareness of the conventions is essential for correct use of the frameworks.

A trend toward accentuation and documentation of conventions, best practices, and programming wisdom has swept the software industry. Best practices are sometimes called design patterns. Many of the design patterns used by the Cocoa frameworks are described in the next chapter.

6 Cocoa Design Patterns

IN THIS CHAPTER

- Understanding Design Patterns
- A Catalog of Cocoa Design Patterns

Design patterns are a popular way to describe an object-oriented design. A pattern usually doesn't include actual code. Instead, it describes general program elements (objects), and how they can interact to solve a particular type of problem. The key elements of a design pattern are the pattern's name, the problem it solves, the solution it presents, and the consequences of using the pattern.

Many class names and concepts are introduced in this chapter that might not yet be familiar. This chapter does not explain the use of any classes in detail, or even fully explain the design patterns; instead it provides an overview and terminology. The classes that are mentioned briefly in this chapter are described in detail throughout this book. One goal of this chapter is to enable effective use of additional references by correlating standard industry terminology with Cocoa's terminology. At a minimum, this chapter provides the definition of terms and patterns that recur throughout the Cocoa frameworks, and this book.

Understanding Design Patterns

In general, patterns offer a vocabulary of design solutions to software developers. Systems that use well-known patterns in their design are easier to comprehend. Having a collection of named patterns handy serves as a toolbox for developers. You can use these tools instead of being forced to create a new set of tools for every design you create.

A pattern's name offers a common vocabulary that can be used between developers. The details of the pattern, and all that it implies, can be communicated rapidly using the name. Cocoa has its own special set of terms to represent the key concepts around which it is built. Being familiar with these terms will make it easier to understand and use Cocoa, as well as make it easier to describe designs to other developers.

Each pattern might apply to a range of situations, which can represent several different design problems. Part of understanding a particular pattern is to know when to use it and when not to. Because that is largely a matter of experience, documenting the problems a pattern is meant to solve enables that experience to be shared with other developers.

The core of a pattern is the solution it offers. This includes the various program elements (usually objects) that participate in the pattern. How elements collaborate, and the responsibilities of each element, are also a part of the solution. Patterns don't include actual code, except perhaps as an example of how a pattern might be applied. Instead, they offer a generic template that can be modified to best match a particular problem. When a developer thoroughly understands a pattern she can usually implement it quickly and efficiently, even though she might not have specific code to cut and paste.

Most pattern definitions list the consequences of using the pattern. Every design decision includes trade-offs, and choosing whether to use a pattern is like every other design decision in this respect. Obviously, knowing the consequences of a decision enables you to make better decisions.

The Cocoa frameworks are remarkably self-consistent. The designers used and reused several common patterns, and even created a few of their own. Because these patterns recur throughout the frameworks, it is useful to describe the patterns before diving into the frameworks themselves. References to named patterns simplify the descriptions of the frameworks. When a pattern is identified, the problem being solved and the consequences of the solution are efficiently conveyed.

Design Pattern Terminology

Cocoa tends to use specific terms, which differ from the names that you might find in object-oriented design texts, for many of its underlying design patterns. It is useful to learn Cocoa's vocabulary and how it relates to these other terms. Sometimes the term is different because there really are subtle differences between the concepts. In other cases, they mean the same thing but the ideas were developed independently, and thus have different names.

The patterns listed here are presented using terminology that is common among Cocoa developers. Sometimes the patterns are unique to Cocoa, but in many cases, they are found by other names in other literature.

NOTE

If you want to know more about patterns in general, an excellent starting point is the seminal "Gang of Four" (GOF) book, *Design Patterns: Elements of Reusable Object-Oriented Software* by Erich Gamma, Richard Helm, Ralph Johnson, and John Vlissides (Addison-Wesley, ISBN 0-201-63361-2). Patterns from that book are commonly referred to as "GOF patterns" Many of the patterns found in Cocoa are also found in the GOF book and are presented in greater detail there. The name of the GOF pattern is provided along with the name used by Cocoa when this is the case. You don't need to know the GOF patterns to read this chapter or use Cocoa, but understanding them might help you to learn Cocoa more quickly.

A Catalog of Cocoa Design Patterns

The meat of this chapter is a catalog of common design patterns found in Cocoa. This catalog includes industry standard patterns and patterns unique to Cocoa. While this catalog is not comprehensive, it does present the most commonly encountered Cocoa patterns.

Model-View-Controller

Model-View-Controller, or MVC for short, is considered an architecture more than a pattern. This is because it is a general way of organizing an application, and is an architectural feature at a higher, more abstract level than most patterns. Because this approach to application design permeates Cocoa, it makes sense to discuss it as a part of the patterns and design philosophies encountered when working with Cocoa.

The MVC architecture was first used with the Smalltalk language in the 1970s, and has proven to be one of the most successful and commonly used top-level application designs. Every application has different architectural needs. MVC will not apply in every case, but it is well-suited to most graphical applications.

MVC divides an application into three major parts or layers. Each part is composed of many objects, and within the MVC paradigm their responsibilities and functions are well defined. The pattern is named for its layers.

Model: This is the heart of an application. It contains all the application-specific data structures and core logic.

View: Views are responsible for providing output to the user and collecting input. Views are generally graphical, but they can be textual, Web-based, and even script-based.

Controller: This handles synchronization between the model and views, as well as some input from the user. The purpose of the controller layer is to isolate the model and view, so that each can be changed independently of the other.

If you consider an application to be an "editor" for some well-organized chunk of data, then MVC becomes a natural means of internal-program organization. The data is all contained within the model, and the view is the window, or interface, to the data that the application presents to the user. The controller layer ties the two together.

Cocoa's emphasis on this type of application structure makes it valuable to offer more details about each layer.

Model

The model should contain the central algorithms and data structures of the application. The model is the core of the application, contains the application's internal state, and contains most of the code that is unique to a particular application. It should be possible to reuse a model with any number of different controller and view subsystems. To enable that reuse, it is best if the code in the model has no dependencies on the controller or view.

View

The view contains the user interface for an application. In most graphical applications, the purpose of the user interface is to enable users to view and modify the model's data via its algorithms. Remember this when a user interface seems to be the most critical and complex part of an application: A particular user interface has no value without a model to view and modify, but a model can be used with any number of different user interfaces. Furthermore, the historic necessity of designing applications around their user interfaces was the result of inflexibility and inherent complexity in the user interface development tools that were available. The user interface of a Cocoa application should not be more complex than the model being viewed. In many Cocoa applications, the view might not contain any code at all. For example, an application to view the file system might represent the file system as a columnar browser, an outline, a table, or as scrolling text like a terminal. None of those views of the file system necessarily require any custom code in the view subsystem of the application because of the rich classes in the Cocoa frameworks and Interface Builder.

The view should not contain any application state other than state that is intrinsic to a particular user interface. For example, the percentage of a document that is visible depends on the nature of the view of the document. The appearance of a button depends on the purpose of the button in the user interface. Those attributes are naturally part of the view. However, the information displayed by a document and the value set by a button should be stored in the model.

Ideally, the view subsystem and the model subsystem should have no interdependence. However, if avoiding dependence is impractical, the dependence should be entirely from the view to the model, and not the other way. Dependencies between subsystems result in the situation where a change to one subsystem necessitates a change in the other. The code in the model usually becomes stable and mature over time, but the user interface continually evolves. If a change in the model requires a change in the view, the cost of the change is mitigated by the fact that the view would likely change anyway. Furthermore, many changes in the view can be accomplished with Interface Builder, and do not require any code at all. A change in the model that is required by a change in the view can incur costs that would otherwise be avoided.

Controller

Ideally, the view subsystem and the model subsystem should have no interdependence. The controller subsystem exists to reduce the dependencies between the model and the view. The controller is a layer of insulation between the other subsystems. The controller's purpose is to prevent changes in the view subsystem from necessitating changes in the model, and visa versa.

Any change to either the model or the view usually necessitates changes in the controller. Therefore, the controller should be kept as small and simple as possible to reduce the cost of those changes. The controller should not contain any application state. For example, if a user presses a button to delete some information stored in the model, the action of the button is in the controller subsystem. The controller's action should be implemented to call the API of the model to delete the information. Then, the controller should use the API of the view to reflect the deletion, perhaps by requesting that the view redraw. If the controller is used in this way, the user interface to delete information can be changed to use a menu or a script command, or both, without impact on the model. Similarly, the model can be changed to disable the deletion of certain information without any change to the user interface.

MVC in Cocoa

By making this separation into three layers, an application's interface and internal data structures are decoupled. As a result, the potential for object reuse between applications is enhanced. A generic view object, such as a text field, could be created and then reused in many different, unrelated applications. A model could be used in different applications that provide different ways to access or modify the model's data. For example, perhaps you have a desktop application for manipulating some data and a secondary command line or Web interface that allows access to the same data. Just like generic-view classes and specialized-model classes can be reused, generic-controller classes can also be reused across unrelated applications.

The Foundation Kit offers many data structures that provide a basis upon which a model can be built. This allows you to concentrate on what makes your model special as opposed to reimplementing yet another standard data structure. In theory, this layer is where most of your code-writing time should be spent because the model is the part of your application, which makes it truly unique.

Cocoa supplies a wide variety of views in the Application Kit, therefore, many applications will not need to create their own custom views. This is a huge time saver, and one of the ways that Cocoa can improve your productivity.

If you are creating a document-centric application, then the various classes surrounding the `NSDocument` class will provide much of the controller logic you need. The `NSDocument` class is described in Chapter 9, "Applications, Windows, and Screens." Sadly, in other parts of the controller layer, Cocoa does not yet provide much help. The Application Kit focuses on the view layer, whereas the Foundation Kit focuses on the model. There is no generic "controller framework."

The lack of a controller framework is one area that could stand improvement. Note that Apple does have some generic controller objects that would help. They are in the `EOInterface` framework, which is a part of the Enterprise Objects Framework. Unfortunately, this is not a part of Cocoa, so it isn't something every Cocoa developer can use. Perhaps sometime in the future these classes, or something similar to them, will become a part of Cocoa.

Until that time, however, there is no controller framework that is a part of Cocoa itself. As a result you will often spend time writing code for your application's controller layer. Most developers don't design and create reusable, generic-controller classes because it is difficult to do well and takes much more time to create the objects. Few developers have the time and resources to "do it right," so most Cocoa application developers create their own controller classes each time. This is reasonable, especially given the time constraints of most projects. Unfortunately, very few of these custom classes are reusable from one application to the next.

Cocoa applications often have two features that do not fit well into the MVC architecture: undo and user preferences/defaults. Each can reasonably be implemented in the controller or the model, but each should be exclusively in one or the other. For example, setting and getting user preferences/defaults can be implemented in the controller on the grounds that the user defaults system is just another view, and the controller should communicate between the user defaults view and the model. On the other hand, user defaults often contain data (Application State) that is part of the model. Similarly, undo can be regarded as recorded commands to modify the model, and therefore just another view that is like a scripting system that communicates with the model via the controller. On the other hand, undo can be considered preserved application state, and therefore best implemented in the model.

A lot more could be said about how to design using the MVC approach, but it would require a complete book. Any good book on object-oriented design will give more information about it, so we recommend that you read a few books on design if you aren't comfortable with the concepts behind MVC. While working in the other sections of this book, keep MVC in mind to help you remember the proper uses of the various classes you encounter.

Class Clusters

Class clusters are a means of hiding complexity in the inheritance hierarchy. The general idea is similar to the GOF Facade pattern, which attempts to hide a complex graph of objects behind a single object. Instead of hiding a group of interacting objects, a class cluster hides several different classes behind one abstract superclass. Instead of knowing anything about the subclasses, you only interact with the API defined by the abstract superclass. The actual instances you manipulate will always be subclasses of the abstract superclass, but you never know the actual class you are dealing with, and you don't need to know.

The biggest impact of class clusters is that you'll see some unfamiliar class names in the debugger, usually with the word "Concrete" in the name. For example, you might see something like `NSConcreteArray` when you are working with an `NSArray`. A large portion of the classes in the Foundation Kit are actually class clusters. The collection classes and `NSString` are the ones you are most likely to encounter.

In the most general terms, you can write Cocoa programs without ever worrying about the details of a class cluster. Just don't be thrown if you see unexpected class names when running the debugger. The other important detail is that creating a subclass of a class cluster is a tricky proposition and should be undertaken with utmost care. For the gory details of class clusters, including how to subclass them, you should refer to Appendix A, "Unleashing the Objective-C Runtime."

Shared Objects

One of the simplest patterns seen in Cocoa is called the "shared object" in Cocoa's documentation. In GOF terms, this is known as a "Singleton." A shared object is used in cases where a particular class should be instantiated once and only once. One of the most obvious examples of a shared object is the central application object. Every Cocoa application has a single `NSApplication` instance. This makes sense; an object that represents a running application should only appear once per application.

Several other Cocoa classes you will learn about are also shared objects. `NSWorkspace` represents the Mac OS X Finder and is a shared object. Some of the standard panels Cocoa offers, such as the font and color panels, are also shared. Some of the scripting objects use the shared object pattern.

To implement this pattern, the class object provides a method that is globally accessible and can be used to obtain the shared-object instance. At the same time, the

+alloc method is disabled to prevent you from creating extra instances. The single, shared instance is created the first time you ask for it, and then the same instance is returned every time thereafter. Usually, the method used to obtain a shared instance includes the word "shared" and the name of the class minus the "NS" prefix as in these examples:

From NSWorkspace.h:

```
+ (NSWorkspace *)sharedWorkspace;
```

From NSApplication.h:

```
+ (NSApplication *)sharedApplication;
```

You might also see this more generic method used sometimes:

```
+ (id)sharedInstance;
```

Finally, shared instances can sometimes be obtained by calling the +new class method. This use of the +new method is left over from prior versions of the frameworks and is deprecated. The +new method plays a crucial role in the earliest frameworks that were developed for Objective-C, but should not be used with Cocoa.

For some classes it is also possible to find out whether or not the shared instance has already been created. For example:

From NSSpellChecker.h:

```
+ (NSSpellChecker *)sharedSpellChecker;
+ (BOOL)sharedSpellCheckerExists;
```

Because Cocoa is object oriented, it is important that developers be able to subclass a shared object and, instead of the original, use an instance of the subclass as the shared instance. It turns out that, thanks to Objective-C, this is easy. Simply create your subclass, and then call the appropriate accessor method, but with your subclass's class object as the receiver instead of the superclass. For instance, suppose you have a special subclass of NSSpellChecker. Before any other part of your application asks for a spell checker, you would ask for it yourself, like this:

```
[MySpellchecker sharedSpellChecker];
```

This should return an instance of your subclass even if you haven't overridden the +sharedSpellChecker method itself.

Enumeration

Cocoa's Foundation Kit offers enumerators for all its collection classes. This pattern is similar to the GOF Iterator pattern. Enumerators provide a way to loop through any collection of objects and do something with each object. Rather than requiring you to write a specialized loop for each kind of collection, you can enumerate all objects from any type of collection the same way. You simply ask the collection for an enumerator object, and then ask the enumerator for the next object in the sequence until it stops returning objects. Code to do this for an arbitrary collection class, `myCollection`, looks like this:

```
id instance;
id enumerator = [myCollection objectEnumerator];
while (instance = [enumerator nextObject]) {
    // do something with instance
}
```

The code first obtains an enumerator from the collection class. Next, the enumerator is asked for the next object in the sequence. When the enumerator runs out of objects, it will return `nil` and then the loop will exit.

Every collection class in the Foundation Kit offers some kind of enumerator. Some other objects offer enumerators, too, when it makes sense. The only thing that changes is the method you call to obtain the enumerator itself. This changes because sometimes more than one kind of enumerator is available. For example, `NSArray` enables you to pass over all its objects in forward or reverse order. The two methods available for this have obvious names:

From NSArray.h:

```
- (NSEnumerator *)objectEnumerator;
- (NSEnumerator *)reverseObjectEnumerator;
```

In the case of an unordered collection, only one enumerator may be available because there's no concept of forward or reverse. Other collections, such as an `NSDictionary`, might have more than one group of objects to enumerate over. A dictionary associates pairs of objects with one object being the key, and the other being the value. You can enumerate over just the keys or just the values:

From NSDictionary.h:

```
- (NSEnumerator *)keyEnumerator;
- (NSEnumerator *)objectEnumerator;
```

However, no matter how you get the enumerator, you always use it the same way. Sometimes it is also useful to work in the other direction and create a collection containing all the objects that would be returned by an enumerator. To do this, simply ask the enumerator for an `NSArray` containing all the objects it would have returned:

```
myArray = [myEnumerator allObjects];
```

Target/Action

When a user manipulates one of Cocoa's user interface objects, it will send a specific message to a specific object. This differs from many other application frameworks on other platforms that insert an event into the application's event loop for later interception and decoding. In Cocoa, this process of sending a direct message in response to a user action is known as target/action. Using this terminology, the target is the object that receives the message, whereas the action is the message that is sent.

Actions are invoked when buttons are clicked, when editing finishes on a text field, when a slider is moved, and so on. Each interface object can have its own unique target and action. Usually, only one interface object will send a particular action. This means there is rarely a need to test to see what happened or which interface item was activated. Sometimes an action might be sent by more than one object. For example, perhaps a particular button triggers the same action as an item in the application's main menu. In a case like this, you might want to know which control sent the action message. This is easy because all actions have a single parameter: the message's sender.

To make use of target/action, you must do two things. First, create objects that implement action messages. An action message will have a prototype that looks like this:

```
- (IBAction)someAction:(id)sender;
```

The name `-someAction:` will change depending on what your action method is supposed to accomplish. When you have implemented your action method, you can use InterfaceBuilder.app to connect an interface object with an instance of the class that implements the action method. When that interface is used in your application, the action message is sent to the target you selected in Interface Builder every time that the control is activated.

It is also possible to create a target/action connection between objects programmatically. Here's the code you would use to do it:

```
[myControl setAction:@selector(someAction:)];
[myControl setTarget:myTargetObject];
```

To determine what a control's target or action is, simply ask it using the `-target` or `-action` methods. If you are implementing a control of your own, you don't even have to know how to send an action because the `NSControl` class implements a method you can use to send action messages:

```
- (BOOL)sendAction:(SEL)theAction to:(id)theTarget;
```

You can invoke this on any control subclass to get it to send an arbitrary action message to an arbitrary target.

Commands

Those who are familiar with the GOF patterns might note that target/action seems to be an implementation of the Command pattern. Although the command pattern, or something like it, could be used to implement something like target/action, it is not needed in Objective-C. The command pattern is used in more static object-oriented languages to simulate the dynamic facilities that are missing. For an object to send a message that it has never seen before in a static language would be generally impossible. To get around this, you would create an abstract superclass called Command, which would implement a virtual method such as invoke. Then, you would create a subclass for *every* method that you might need to send. Finally, the sender would be handed an instance of some arbitrary Command subclass and call invoke on that object when it needs to send the message. By doing this, one object can send a message to another object even though the message was unknown when the sender class was compiled.

Because Objective-C is more dynamic, however, there is no need to jump through all these hoops to send an arbitrary message. Instead, selectors are passed to the sending object to specify which message should be sent. The sender then uses the `-performSelector:` method or, if appropriate, a variant such as `-performSelector:withObject:` to invoke the method.

Selectors only specify the message to be sent and not the receiver. In some cases this is desirable, but not always. If you need to specify both the message and the receiver with a single object, the `NSInvocation` class can be used. An `NSInvocation` encapsulates a message, a receiver, and all the parameters of the message. The `NSInvocation` class is the closest Cocoa equivalent to the GOF Command pattern.

Delegates

One of the most common mistakes made by a new Cocoa developer is to subclass a Cocoa object without really needing to. Normally, they want to change the object's behavior, and that's why they make a subclass. In most other object-oriented–application frameworks, subclassing is the only way to alter the behavior of a class. Instead, Cocoa introduces the concept of delegation as an alternative to subclassing. No specific GOF pattern describes delegation exactly; delegation is something of a hybrid of the Observer and the Chain of Responsibility GOF patterns.

Delegation is a way for a framework designer to defer design choices. Instead of doing everything one way and that way only, many Cocoa classes are equipped to ask some other object what they should do in a given situation.

For example, if the user clicks the close button in a window's title bar, the default action would be to close the window. But what if the window contains an altered document and the application needs to enable the user to save their changes before the window is closed? In Cocoa, the window will ask another object, "I want to close now, is that OK?" The object can then respond yes or no, perhaps after presenting a sheet to ask the user whether to save the document or cancel the window close. No subclassing is required to change the window's behavior. Instead, another object is provided that can answer the question in an application and context specific way.

This other object that gets to participate in the decision is known as the delegate. The messages sent by an object to its delegate are known as delegate messages. No standard terminology exists for the object that sends delegate messages to a delegate. For lack of a better term, this book will use the word delegator to identify such an object. Typically, the documentation and header for every delegator class describes all the messages that might be sent to its delegate.

Many of the more complex Application Kit classes, such as `NSApplication`, `NSWindow`, `NSTableView`, and `NSToolBar`, are delegators.

Some messages to delegates don't require a response from the delegate and are just sent to let the delegate do something before or immediately after a particular event has happened. For example, a delegate can receive a message just before and just after a window is placed onto the screen. This offers the delegate the opportunity to perform any special initialization or other operations at the appropriate time.

A delegate is not required to implement any particular delegate messages. It only needs to implement the messages that are interesting to it. The delegator will always check to see if its delegate responds to a particular message before trying to send the message. If the delegate doesn't respond to a given message, it simply won't be sent.

NOTE

Checking to see if a delegate responds to a message before sending the message might seem inefficient. The Cocoa implementation is actually a bit smarter. When a delegate is set, Cocoa will determine the messages it can handle and cache that information for use when a delegate message needs to be sent.

One limitation of delegates is the fact that there is only a specific set of delegate messages known to a delegator. If the designer of a delegator didn't send out a delegate message for some event that you want to catch or influence, a delegate won't work. In that case a subclass of the object might be the only solution. Luckily, there are not many places in Cocoa where a subclass is required. The existing sets of delegate messages provide a rich collection that covers nearly everything you'll need.

Another limitation of delegates is that objects usually have only one delegate. There is no way, for example, for an `NSApplication` instance to have multiple delegates. If there is a need to have more than one object receive delegate messages from a single delegator then have your delegate pass messages on to other delegates.

In the case of messages that require a response, such as "do I close the window?" forwarding the message to other objects is the only solution. On the other hand, if the other delegates only require notification of events, such as "the window closed," and they don't need to participate in any decisions, then the next pattern can be used to solve the multiple delegates problem.

Notifications

Cocoa often uses notifications to tell objects in an application that something important has happened. For any given notification, there can be multiple receivers of the message. Multiple objects can send or post a given notification, as well. Some notifications come with extra information detailing the event that they represent, and others do not.

The central figure of the notification pattern is the `NSNotificationCenter`, which is described in Chapter 7. In GOF terms, the objects that register for a notification would be known as observers. The `NSNotificationCenter` and `NSNotification` classes provide a generic, flexible, and reusable implementation of the GOF Observer pattern. Therefore, it should never be necessary for you to implement the pattern yourself.

To receive a notification, an object must register with a notification center. Usually, an application has only one notification center, known as the default center, although you can create more if necessary. When registering for a notification, an object can specify the details of how it wants to receive the notification. It is also possible to specify the objects from which a receiver accepts notifications.

When it is time to send out a notification, the sender "posts" the notification to the notification center. The notification is automatically passed on to all the objects that registered to receive it. Some notifications carry extra information about the event they represent in a user info parameter. It is up to the object posting a notification whether to add that information prior to posting.

Unlike delegates, notifications enable multiple objects to receive notification of a given event. There can be any number of observers. Another benefit of notifications is that an object can register for a notification without knowing who the sender is and the sender doesn't have to know anything about objects that observe the notifications it posts. As objects register and post notifications, the interactions between objects can emerge dynamically. This reduces the need for global variables to help an object find other objects it needs to communicate with.

One limitation of notifications is that the implementation is slower than that of delegate methods because the notification center adds a layer of indirection. Furthermore, objects that observe a notification cannot send a response directly back to the object that sent the notification in the same way a delegate can.

Proxies

Cocoa's Distributed Objects technology includes the concept of a proxy, which is more specific than the GOF Proxy pattern. This can be a point of confusion for those new to Cocoa. Because the same term can mean two different things depending on context, this section will take care to explicitly say "GOF Proxy," if that is what is meant.

In Cocoa, a proxy is a stand-in for another object that is in a different process or different thread. Sending messages to the proxy is the same as sending them to the actual object. The proxy transparently bundles the message, and sends it to the object in the other process. The programmer doesn't have to worry about whether or not a proxy is involved, or whether the ultimate receiver of a message is in the same process as the sender. Just send it a message and the right thing will happen. Some designers call this an Ambassador.

The GOF Proxy pattern includes this function. It can also serve other functions. Therefore, a Cocoa proxy is a GOF Proxy, but a GOF Proxy is not necessarily what Cocoa calls a proxy. The other types of GOF Proxy do appear in Cocoa. Some have different names while others have no specific name.

Another job of a GOF Proxy might be to allow for the lazy allocation and loading of an expensive resource. The `NSImage` class is an example of this kind of proxy. In this case, the object has two parts: The external part of the image, which is the interface you normally access, and the actual image data, which is an `NSImageRep` or image representation in Cocoa terms. The image can tell you information about itself without needing to load and decode all the data. In fact, the data can be kept on disk until it is actually used. This approach helps reduce memory usage in the case where some images might never be displayed.

`NSImage` takes this a bit further, however, and actually can act as a proxy for *multiple* image representations, choosing the best for a particular context. In this respect, the object acts as a GOF Facade. A Facade is an object that presents a single, simple interface to a more complex graph of underlying, cooperating objects.

Another Cocoa example that combines the Proxy and Facade patterns is the `NSWindowController`, which usually acts as a cover for the graph of objects inside one of Interface Builder's `.nib` files. It won't load the `.nib` itself until it absolutely has to. At the same time, a window controller subclass usually acts as the application's connection to the objects inside the `.nib`. In the process, it can also perform another potential proxy duty: managing access to the object(s) it is covering.

A final example of Proxy behavior is not yet found in Cocoa proper, but is found in Apple's Enterprise Objects Framework (EOF). Some proxies stand in for an object that hasn't yet been created and might never actually be needed. In the Enterprise Objects Framework, an `EOFault` performs this duty. It stands in for objects that are still in a database so that there is no need to fetch a large chunk of a database's contents as a result of fetching an object with references pointing all over the database. Because those references might never be touched by the application, a fault object is put in place to stand in for the real object and data. If the application ever tries to access the object, then the fault will automatically transform itself into the real object and fetch the requested data.

Although Cocoa has nothing like this at present, it might have a class with similar behavior in the future. Such fault objects can be useful for dealing with any type of object persistence, and not just for databases.

In general, the GOF Proxy and Facade patterns are used extensively throughout Cocoa, and often you will find both patterns in use together.

Facades

As explained in the previous sections on class clusters and proxies, a Facade is an object that presents a single, simple interface to a complex graph of cooperating objects. It is common throughout Cocoa to find the Facade pattern used in conjunction with other patterns.

Many of the Application Kit objects you use, especially the more complex ones, are Facades. Two of the Facades are the `NSText` and `NSImage` classes.

The way `NSText` is used is a great example of this; most Cocoa developers can just use `NSText` itself and not worry about what happens inside. This is easy for the developer and good enough for many situations. The trade-off is that you lose some flexibility, configurability, and extensibility in exchange for that ease of use. A few developers will want, or need, to make specific customizations and will pull back the Facade. In doing so, they expose themselves to a large collection of new classes that they have to learn in conjunction with a complex graph of objects that takes time to fully understand. The power and customizability comes with a huge price in complexity.

Prototypes

Some of Cocoa's objects make direct use of the GOF Prototype pattern. A prototype is an instance that is not used directly. Instead, it is used as a sort of template for creating new instances. When a new instance is needed, the prototype is cloned. This is very useful for generic containers such as the `NSMatrix`. When a matrix grows in size and needs more elements, it copies a prototype to obtain the new elements.

The Prototype pattern enables you to create any appropriate instance and configure it however you like. Because of this flexibility, the `NSMatrix` class doesn't need to know anything about the instances it contains, and can simply create and install them automatically, as needed, without requiring your intervention.

This is also useful for incorporating dynamically loaded code from bundles into your application. A developer could use this pattern with multiple prototypes to create a palette of preconfigured objects in their programs, too. The objects on an Interface Builder palette are all prototypes.

In the case of `NSMatrix`, it is even possible to edit the prototype itself in Interface Builder. Being able to control this from Interface Builder saves a lot of code when setting up new dynamic interfaces.

Some of the other views provided in the Application Kit use a slightly different kind of prototype. These prototypes are actually both shared and used between objects. Reuse of instances in this way is common throughout Cocoa, especially for input, input validation, and output formatting.

As an example, consider the `NSTextField` class. It presents a simple, editable field of text to the user. However, it uses an `NSText` object to handle the editing itself. Since `NSText` objects are heavyweight classes because of all the internal objects they use behind the Facade, it is inefficient to create an `NSText` object for every single field in the interface. Instead, all the text fields share a single `NSText` object, known as the field editor.

In another example, the `NSTableView` object has an internal object that formats the rows of a table for display. It is shared between the rows. The way this object is configured will determine the look of all the rows that it formats.

Archiving and Coding

Cocoa's Foundation Kit offers a way to "freeze dry" an object, so that it can be brought back to life at a later time. The object, when frozen, could be stored in memory, on a disk, in a database, or by some other means. The process of freezing an object is known as archiving or object serialization, and is performed by the `NSCoder` class. A coder can freeze any object that conforms to the very simple `NSCoding` protocol. It can also unfreeze any objects it or any other coder has frozen.

Encoding and decoding are described in Chapter 5, "Cocoa Conventions."

The frozen data produced by a coder contains the complete state of an object, and therefore is similar to the GOF Memento pattern. Archiving is a little different from Memento, though, because it is not usually used to restore an existing instance to a previous state. Instead, it is used to store an object so that the live object can be destroyed and later re-created exactly as it was. Another use for archiving is to create duplicate instances, or move an instance from one process to another.

NOTE

Another example of the Memento pattern in Cocoa is the undo system. Cocoa's undo system usually doesn't do archiving to save and restore the state of object, but archiving could be used as part of a brute-force undo implementation.

Nearly all Cocoa objects conform to the `NSCoding` protocol. This enables live objects to be manipulated and edited by Interface Builder. When the objects are saved into a `.nib` file by Interface Builder, they are first frozen by an `NSCoder` instance so that they can be written out as a part of the file. Coders are smart enough to freeze an entire graph of objects, even if it has cycles in it. They keep track of both the objects in the graph and the connections between the objects.

When an object is unfrozen, the coder will also send it a "wake up" message so that the object can take care of any special tasks it might need to perform to become fully "alive" again.

Subviews

In Cocoa, every area of screen real estate inside of a window is controlled by a subclass of the `NSView` object. Although views should not be laid out so they overlap each other, one view can completely enclose another. In this case, the enclosing view is known as a superview, and the view that is enclosed is called a subview. Often the superview will add some drawing around the subview or tile several subviews together to create a complex user interface element. This is a hybrid implementation of the GOF Composite and Decorator patterns, and not a specific pattern by itself.

The Composite pattern is a way for one view to build itself out of several others. An example of a composite view would be an `NSTableView` object. This object uses different objects to represent the table column headers, the cells, and the scrollbars. All these views are assembled and controlled by the enclosing table view.

The Decorator pattern is a way for one view to add extra "decorations" around another view. For example, the `NSScrollView` object can take any view and add vertical and horizontal scrollbars to it. The most common view to put inside a scroll view is an `NSText` instance, to create a scrollable text area. Any view could be put inside, though. Another decorator is the `NSBox` class, which can optionally add a border and/or title around a group of views.

All Cocoa views can have subviews and superviews, so they all can potentially be a composite, decorator, or both.

Responder Chain

The responder chain is not a pattern, but rather another implementation of a pattern. It is fully explained in Chapter 8, "Application Kit Framework Overview." It is mentioned here because it is a concrete implementation of the GOF Chain of Responsibility pattern. In short, the responder chain handles input from the user. Its job is to route input events to the right place.

For example, if the user chooses the Copy command from the Edit menu, what should the target for the menu item's `-copy:` action be? Whatever view currently has the focus and active selection is given the first opportunity to handle the message. If the focused view doesn't handle the message, it will be passed along to the control's window, and then, if it's still not handled, the application object. A message like `-quit:` will usually make it all the way to the application object. If an event isn't handled and drops off the end of the chain, the application will beep at the user to alert him that his action wasn't understood.

The Application Kit has created a chain of objects that might be able to respond to the event, and it includes the currently focused interface control at the start and the application at the end. The Application Kit updates and manages this chain as the user moves from control to control and window to window. In effect, the dispatching and routing of an application's input events becomes automatic. By design it happens as a consequence of the object graph's structure.

When a control's target is set to `nil`, it knows to send its action to whichever object is at the head of the chain. This allows targets to be dynamically updated in a contextual manner. Thus, you don't need to write any code to retarget your menu items. In fact, it is even possible to determine if any object in the responder chain will handle a given message or not. By making use of this information, Cocoa can automatically enable and disable menu items as the user changes focus.

Summary

With the responder chain, the target/action and the Chain of Responsibility patterns have been tied together in Cocoa's design. Several other examples of patterns being combined by Cocoa have been shown throughout this chapter. This type of interaction between the patterns is common. Because Cocoa consistently applies the patterns, you will probably find it easy to learn despite the huge size of the APIs. You will find that things tend to work the way you would expect when you are comfortable with the underlying patterns.

As you become more proficient, you'll even be able to guess at method names without ever having read an object's documentation. You will also find that if you try to use these same patterns as you write code, your objects will be better able to leverage the Cocoa's power.

This discussion of patterns in Cocoa is just an overview. This chapter offers only brief descriptions of the most common, most reused patterns found in the Cocoa frameworks, while focusing more on their application within the frameworks than on theory.

Keep in mind that entire books have been written to describe patterns. This chapter is just a starting point.

This chapter concludes the section of the book dedicated to background information, languages, conventions, and patterns. The background information presented so far will be essential for understanding the frameworks. Beginning in the next chapter, details about the Cocoa frameworks, and techniques to unleash their power, are presented.

PART II

The Cocoa Frameworks

IN THIS PART

7

Foundation Framework Overview

IN THIS CHAPTER

- Mutability
- Class Clusters
- Typed Storage
- Collections
- Property Lists
- Run Loops and Timers
- Support Types
- String Processing
- Bundles
- File System Access
- Defaults System
- Notifications
- Related Core Foundation

The Foundation framework contains the classes, functions, and data types that are used by all Cocoa applications. The Foundation framework is the foundation on which other Cocoa frameworks are built. Much of the power of the Cocoa frameworks results from the consistent use of foundation classes. Functions and methods throughout Cocoa use features provided by the Foundation framework. For example, methods that use strings use instances of the foundation `NSString` class.

The Foundation framework can be used for both nongraphical and graphical applications. It contains a wide range of classes including classes that implement strings, values, collections, dates, and timers. Operating system features such as file system access, networking, process information, threads, command-line arguments, and even user preferences are encapsulated by foundation classes. The Foundation framework is present in every copy of Mac OS X. A more or less complete reimplementation of the Foundation framework exists as part of the open source GNUstep project for Linux available at `www.gnustep.org`.

Mutability

Many of the classes in the Foundation framework are immutable meaning that instances are created with a particular value or content, and the value does not change for the life of the instance. If another value is needed or different information must be stored, a new instance is created with the new value rather than changing the value of an existing instance. The value stored by an immutable object never changes after the object is initialized.

In contrast to immutable objects, the value or content of mutable objects can be changed any number of times. In most cases, when the Foundation framework includes an immutable class, a mutable variant is also available. Mutable classes are commonly implemented as subclasses of immutable ones. The mutable classes extend their respective superclasses by adding methods to change the value or contents of instances. Many immutable classes also provide a `-mutableCopy:` method that returns a mutable copy of the immutable object.

NOTE

A common mistake made by programmers is the over use of mutable classes. Use mutable classes only when necessary to simplify an algorithm. Mutable classes do not share many of the optimizations of memory and performance that benefit immutable classes.

Immutable classes are implemented to enable efficient memory use. For example, when an instance of the immutable `NSString` class is initialized with a value, the exact storage needed for the string is allocated. When a mutable string is used, undesirable inefficiencies results from the need to handle changes in the length of the stored string. The same storage issues and optimizations apply to other classes that store arbitrary amounts of data including collection classes.

Common operations such as copying are optimized when immutable classes are used. Because the value of an instance of an immutable class cannot change, there is no need to allocate any new storage for a copy. Copying is implemented to return another pointer to the original instance. One instance can be safely shared.

Mutable Instance Variables

If a pointer to a mutable instance variable is returned from a method, the encapsulation of the class that owns the instance variable might be violated. In such cases, other code might change the value stored by the mutable object without using methods of the class that owns it. However, when a class uses an immutable instance variable, the class can safely return a pointer to the instance variable from accessor methods. There is no danger that the returned object will be modified without its owner's knowledge. Returning immutable objects from accessor methods simplifies implementation, promotes efficiency, and preserves the encapsulation of the object that implements the accessor methods.

In the following example, a simple class stores an immutable string using the `NSString` class described later in this chapter. The immutable string is safely returned from an accessor method:

```
@interface MYSimpleClass
{
```

```
  NSString        *_myStringValue;
}

- (NSString *)safeStringValue;

@end


@implementation MYSimpleClass

- (NSString *)safeStringValue
{
  // The instance variable can be safely returned
  return myStringValue;
}

@end
```

However, if `MYSimpleClass` is implemented with a mutable string and provides access to that mutable string, the encapsulation of the class might be violated:

```
@interface MYSimpleClass
{
  NSMutableString        *_myStringValue;
}

- (NSMutableString *)unsafeStringValue;

@end


@implementation MYSimpleClass

- (NSMutableString *)unsafeStringValue
{
  // The instance variable can not be safely returned
  // because it may be modified externally and violate the
  // encapsilation of MYSimpleClass
  return myStringValue;
}

@end
```

The mutable instance variable cannot be directly returned from an accessor method without inviting violations of `MYSimpleClass`'s encapsulation. The value stored by the mutable variable could be modified outside `MYSimpleClass`.

Two techniques are used to return a mutable object from a class without violating that class's encapsulation. A mutable instance variable is safely returned by a method typed to return an immutable object. Programmers might take advantage of the fact that the returned object is actually mutable, but a determined programmer can circumvent any protection. Programmers should respect the return type specified by a method and not assume that the returned value is actually a subclass of the specified type. Also, if it is necessary to return a mutable object with the intention that programmers will modify the returned object, return a mutable copy of the instance variable.

```
@interface MYSimpleClass
{
  NSMutableString        *_myStringValue;
}

- (NSString *)safeStringValue1;
- (NSMutableString *)safeStringValue2;

}


@implementation MYSimpleClass

- (NSString *)safeStringValue1
{
  // The instance variable can be safely returned.
  // The caller will have to cast the return value
  // to violate MYSimpleClass's encapsulation
  return myStringValue;
}


- (NSMutableString *)safeStringValue2
{
  // A mutable copy of the instance variable is returned
  return [[myStringValue mutableCopy] autorelease];
}

@end
```

Class Clusters

The Foundation framework and other Cocoa frameworks contain several class clusters. Class clusters consist of multiple hidden classes that are accessed through an abstract public superclass. In Objective-C, when an object is described as abstract it means that programs use instances of classes that inherit from the abstract class, but rarely use instances of the abstract class itself. Concrete subclasses of the abstract class are used. Chapter 6 introduced the class cluster design pattern. Apple provides excellent documentation about class clusters and the reasons for using them at `http://developer.apple.com/techpubs/macosx/Cocoa/TasksAndConcepts/ProgrammingTopics/Foundation/Concepts/ClassClusters.html`, and in the online documentation that comes with Apple's developer tools.

The primary motivation for using class clusters in a framework is to simplify the use of multiple complex classes. Simple concepts might sometimes require complex implementations for reasons of flexibility or optimization. Class clusters attempt to present simple class interfaces that match simple concepts and hide the true complexity of implementations from users of a framework. Having a few classes that conceal a multitude of hidden classes reduces the number of classes that must be learned to use a framework.

Prominent Foundation class clusters are accessed via the `NSArray`, `NSCharacterSet`, `NSData`, `NSDictionary`, `NSNotification`, `NSScanner`, `NSSet`, and `NSString` abstract classes. These classes are commonly used but seldom subclassed.

The class clusters in the Foundation framework simplify complex multiclass implementations, but the price of that simplification is increased difficulty when subclassing a member of a class cluster. An example of a custom subclass of a class cluster's abstract superclass is provided in Appendix B.

Typed Storage

Many programming languages provide built-in data types for the storage of common values. The C language contains only the bare minimum of built-in types that map well to the hardware limitations of almost every CPU family. The philosophy of the C language is to implement as little as possible in the language itself and execute complex ideas in libraries. As a small extension of C, Objective-C adheres to the same philosophy. Objective-C adds only a small number of standard data types, and they are all defined in terms of C built-in types such as `char *` and pointers to structures. Apple's Foundation framework contains classes that enhance the basic capabilities of Objective-C and manage data types that are more complex and powerful than the built-in types.

In some cases, the classes in the Foundation framework act as simple object wrappers around standard data types. The object wrappers encapsulate data along with the available operations on the data. The wrappers also aid memory management and storage of data in XML documents or other contexts. Storing simple data types as objects enables the use of those types in conjunction with collection classes.

Foundation classes that provide powerful features far beyond the limits of the built-in types are available. Strings with numerous encodings including 7-bit ASCII and Unicode are supported. Date and time management classes prevent the types of problems encountered with the year 2000 roll over. Classes that encapsulate large blocks of binary data in efficient ways are available. For example, arbitrary data from files on disk is mapped into virtual memory so that it can be accessed in random order without the need to load it all into memory at once.

Strings

Strings are one of the most common types used in any program. The C language does not have a built-in string data type. Strings are usually simulated via pointers and arrays. The Foundation framework provides classes that manage almost every detail of string manipulation including memory management, encoding systems including Unicode, searching, truncating, concatenating, and more.

`NSString`

The `NSString` class is the public face of a class cluster. Private subclasses exist to efficiently handle 7-bit ASCII strings, constant strings compiled into a program, Unicode strings, and gigantic strings that are mapped into virtual memory.

When an instance of `NSString` is initialized, an instance of one of the private subclasses is created based on the encoding and size of the requested string instance. `NSString` instances are immutable. They are initialized with a particular value that never changes. The immutability enables several optimizations in the implementation and usage of strings.

One of the most common ways to create `NSString` instances is the use of the `@""` construct provided as an extension to the Objective-C language in Apple's compiler and runtime. The open source Gnu implementation of Objective-C and the Gnu runtime include the same support. Any string declared between the quotes of a `@""` expression is created at compile time as a constant instance of `NSString` using 7-bit ASCII encoding. Such strings might be stored along with executable code in the resulting application's binary.

Constant strings created with `@""` are full objects and are used in any context that `NSString` instances created other ways are used. For example, messages can be sent to constant string objects as follows:

```
[@"This is a 7 bit ASCII string" length];
[@"The quick brown fox" stringByAppendingString:@" jumped over the log"];
```

Convenience allocators provide another common way to create NSString instances. Following the Cocoa conventions, class methods that include a variation of the class name return new autoreleased instances. The simplest convenience allocator for NSString is -stringWithString:. It accepts a string argument and returns a new immutable string instance with the same contents as the argument. The -stringWithString: method is used to copy strings and serves as an example of the power that class clusters provide. The subclass of NSString that is returned from -stringWithString: depends on the argument. If the argument is a multimegabyte string that is partially stored on the hard disk, an NSString implementation optimized for that case is used. If the argument is a short constant string compiled into the application, the string returned from -stringWithString: might just be another pointer to the same string contents.

Many convenience allocators and corresponding initializer methods are provided. The guidelines for using the convenience allocators versus the combination of +alloc and an initializer are the same as for other classes. If the instance that is being created is intended to be returned from a method and is not stored by the object that is creating the string, the convenience allocators should be used. Otherwise use +alloc and an initializer.

The online class documentation describes each of the available initializers and the convenience allocators, but three groups of methods deserve special recognition here. First, the NSPathUtilities category of NSString provides methods that manage file system paths. Methods such as -stringByDeletingLastPathComponent: are very handy, but they are frequently overlooked. Second, string objects are created from C pointers to characters via -initWithCString:, and the -lossyCString method returns a pointer to any 7-bit ASCII characters stored by the receiving string object, performing conversions as necessary. Third, NSString provides the following methods that accept formats and arguments similar to the printf() function in the standard C libraries: -initWithFormat:... and -stringWithFormat:... . For example, the following code produces a new instance of NSString containing a formatted string, a number, and a new line character:

```
[[NSString alloc] initWithFormat:@"Name: %s Number: %d\n",
   "John Smith", 42];
```

Most of the standard format string arguments are supported, but Mac OS X v. 10.1.2 and earlier versions contain some errors and omissions from the ANSI standard. Bug reports have been submitted and Apple is aware of the problems. They are not severe and will probably be resolved in future releases of the operating system and libraries.

An additional format beyond those supported by standard `printf()` is also available. The `%@` format uses the object argument's description. For example, the following code is similar to the previous format example, but it uses a constant string object instead of a C string constant:

```
[[NSString alloc] initWithFormat:@"Name: %@ Number: %d\n",
   @"John Smith", 42];
```

The distinction is subtle. Whenever a `%@` is encountered in a format string, the corresponding object argument is sent a `-description` message. The `-description` message returns an `NSString` instance, and that string is used to produce the formatted string. Because the `NSString` class implements `-description` to return itself, the format that uses a C string constant and the format that uses a string object both produce the same result. However, object descriptions enable many powerful uses. For example, the following code creates an instance of `NSString` containing the name of a private subclass of `NSString`:

```
[[NSString alloc] initWithFormat:@"Class name: %@", [@"Constant string" class]];
```

In the example, when the `-class` message is sent to the constant string instance, its class object is returned and used as the argument in the formatted string. The `-description` method is implemented by class objects to return the name of the receiving class. In this case, the name of the private subclass of `NSString` that was created by the compiler is returned.

NOTE

Objective-C class objects are true objects and can respond to any messages defined for the `NSObject` class. Because the `NSObject` class declares the `+description` message, all class objects can respond to it. The `-description` and `+description` methods are also used by Apple's version of the gdb debugger when the debugger's print-object (po) command is invoked.

Objects return arbitrary strings from their `-description` methods. In some cases, the strings are long and complex. For example, the foundation collection classes implement `-description` to return a string containing the descriptions of all the contained objects. When collections contain other collections, tremendous amounts of information might be revealed by one `-description` message.

The `NSString` class inherits the `-compare:` method from the `NSObject` class. The `-compare:` method is used to compare strings with arbitrary objects, but `NSString` also provides the `-isEqualToString:` method to perform optimized comparisons when the object being compared is known to be another string. Use `-isEqualToString:` instead of `-compare:` whenever possible.

Methods for searching strings and obtaining substrings are available. The online documentation that comes with Apple's developer tools lists available `NSString` operations. String objects are used extensively throughout the Cocoa frameworks, and the most common `NSString` methods quickly become second nature to Cocoa programmers. `NSString's -length` method returns the number of stored Unicode characters in the string. The `-characterAtIndex:` method returns the Unicode character at a particular index in the range `0` to `(length - 1)`.

NSMutableString

`NSMutableString` is a subclass of `NSString` and therefore inherits all `NSString`'s capabilities. `NSMutableString` adds methods to change the contents of existing instances. Use mutable strings when they simplify an algorithm, or when it is necessary to make several small changes to a single string without varying its length very much. Mutable strings do not share many of the optimizations of memory and performance that benefit immutable instances.

Raw Data

Strings are one of the most common types used in programs. Because the ANSI C language does not provide any high-level abstractions for strings, they are usually implemented as pointers to bytes or as arrays of bytes in ANSI C. The Foundation framework provides the `NSString` class to encapsulate true strings whether they store bytes or complex multibyte character encodings, but many programs still need to store and manipulate arbitrary bytes. Examples of arbitrary data stored as bytes include images, archived objects, and data received over a network connection. Traditional C programs commonly store such data the same way they store strings. Arrays of characters are used, and values are accessed via pointers to characters. The Foundation framework provides the `NSData` class to store and access arbitrary data that might not be correctly interpreted as strings.

NSData

The `NSData` class cluster encapsulates arbitrary bytes. No special meaning or significance is applied to the stored bytes. The data might represent a compressed `TIFF` format image, a sound loaded from the hard disk, or a complex graph of archived objects. The `NSData` class manages the memory used to store the bytes and controls access to the bytes. The `NSData` object is immutable.

Instances of the `NSData` class are used throughout the Cocoa frameworks. Some of the hidden classes in the `NSData` class cluster use virtual memory features of Mac OS X to optimize storage of large amounts of data. When `NSData` objects are initialized with the contents of large files on disk via methods such as `-initWithContentsOfFile:`, the files are mapped into the process's virtual memory address range and portions of the files are brought in and out of memory on demand. This behavior enables random access to the bytes stored by `NSData` objects without requiring that every byte be loaded into memory at once. Mapping existing files into virtual memory also avoids the need to ever load bytes that are not accessed. If an `NSData` object is initialized with the contents of a 100MB file, but only a few bytes of the file are ever read, only a small part of the file is ever loaded into memory.

`NSData`'s `-bytes` method returns a pointer to the data stored. The `-length` method returns the number of bytes stored. All other `NSData` methods are implemented using these two methods.

NSMutableData

The `NSMutableData` class extends the `NSData` class to enable modification of the stored data. The storage allocated by `NSMutableData` objects grows and shrinks automatically as bytes are added or removed. The `NSMutableData` class is used to avoid manual memory allocation using functions such as `malloc()` and `realloc()`. `NSMutableData` encapsulates memory management of arbitrary data using the standard Cocoa memory conventions and helps avoid dynamic memory allocation errors.

The decision to use mutable or immutable data is similar to the decision to use mutable or immutable strings. Immutable data objects benefit from many optimizations that are not possible with mutable objects, but some algorithms might require mutable data. Use the immutable `NSData` class to maximize operating system optimizations when very large amounts of memory are stored, or when the bytes stored are read only. Use `NSMutableData` in situations where dynamic memory allocation is required and when there is a need to modify the bytes that are stored.

`NSMutableData`'s `-mutableBytes` method returns a pointer to the bytes stored. The stored bytes are modified via the pointer. The `-setLength:` method expands or reduces the number of bytes stored. If the storage is increased, the new bytes are initialized to zero.

Values

The Foundation framework provides object wrappers for nonobject data types. The `NSValue` class, and its subclasses `NSNumber` and `NSDecimalNumber`, encapsulate nonobject types within objects so that they can be managed using Cocoa's memory management conventions and stored within collections such as `NSArray` and `NSDictionary` that only store objects.

NSValue

The `NSValue` class is immutable and provides an object wrapper around fixed-size, nonobject data types. `NSValue` only wraps values of fixed-size types such as `int`, float, pointers, and structures. NSValue does not store variable length arrays of values or arbitrary numbers of bytes. NSString and NSData are better suited to storing large or variable amounts of data.

NSValue instances are created and initialized with the value of a nonobject data type. The initializers and convenience allocators used to create an NSValue instance require a pointer to the value to be stored and a string that defines the type of the value being stored. The type of the data being stored can be obtained by using the @encode() compiler directive described in Chapter 4. For example, the following code creates an instance of NSValue that stores a double value and another one that stores a structure.

```
typedef struct _MYSampleStruct
{
  int             anInt;
  _MYSampleStruct    *nextStruct;
} MYSampleStruct;

{
  double              doubleValue = 5.5;
  MYSampleStruct      sampleStruct = {10, NULL};

  NSValue     *aDoubleValue = [NSValue valueWithBytes:&doubleValue
      objCType:@encode(doubleValue)];
  NSValue     *aStructValue = [NSValue valueWithBytes:&sampleStruct
      objCType:@encode(sampleStruct)];
}
```

The +valueWithBytes:objCType: convenience allocator is used in the example and returns autoreleased instances. The NSValue class provides additional dedicated convenience allocators for many of the data types commonly wrapped including pointers. If NSValue is used to store pointers, remember that only the pointer is stored. Do not deallocate the values referenced by the pointer before the NSValue instance is deallocated or the NSValue instance will be left storing an invalid pointer.

NSNumber

NSNumber extends the NSValue class with a set of methods for storing and accessing numeric values. The following standard C data types are directly supported by NSNumber in both signed and unsigned variants: BOOL, char, short int, int, long int, long long int, float, and double. NSNumber overrides the -compare: method inherited from NSObject to enable standard numeric ordering of NSNumber instances. The number stored by an NSNumber instance can be a obtained in any of the supported types, and standard numeric conversions are applied. For example, when the int value of an NSNumber that is storing a double value is requested, a conversion from double to int is performed using the same conversion rules as standard C. The NSNumber instance continues to store a double, the conversion only applies to the returned value.

NSDecimalNumber

NSDecimalNumber is a subclass of NSNumber that stores numbers in a format that reduces cumulative errors that occur when performing decimal arithmetic on binary values. Binary numbers stored in a computer do not have infinite precision and therefore must approximate some values that are stored. Decimal numbers stored in a computer do not have infinite precision either, but the two different number systems have different limitations. Each number system is forced to approximate different values. It is usually best to store decimal numbers, such as the balance of a bank account, in an encoding that preserves the expected precision of decimal numbers rather than converting back and forth to standard binary encoding.

NSDecimalNumber uses a decimal encoding and stores values with 38 digits of precision in the range from 10^{-128} to 10^{127}. Like NSNumber, NSDecimalNumber is an immutable class. Different rounding schemes and error handling behaviors are used with NSDecimalNumber. The NSDecimalNumberBehaviors protocol defines the available behaviors and is described in the online documentation that comes with Apple's developer tools.

Dates

The Foundation framework provides rich capabilities for storing dates and times, and comparing them. Dates are represented as seconds and fractions of seconds since a reference date, and can be output in a variety of forms including as a month within a year or a day within a week. Dates and times are represented by several different objects with different capabilities, but all dates are immutable and represent a single instant in time.

Dates and times are stored as time intervals from a reference time. Cocoa uses the first instant of January 1, 2001 GMT as its system-wide, absolute reference date. Double precision, floating-point values storing seconds provide greater than millisecond accuracy for dates 10,000 years apart.

NSTimeInterval

NSTimeInterval is the type used to store time intervals within Cocoa. NSTimeInterval is not a class. It is a type that refers to double precision, floating-point values. Time intervals are often obtained by calling the +timeIntervalSinceReferenceDate class method of the NSDate class. The returned time interval is the interval between the system's absolute reference date and the current date and time. After January 1, 2001, all time intervals returned from +timeIntervalSinceReferenceDate are positive.

One way to time the execution of code is to obtain NSTimeIntervals before and after the code executes and compare the intervals. For example, the following code calculates the number of seconds needed to execute a long-running calculation and provides better than millisecond accuracy:

```
NSTimeInterval       startInterval;
NSTimeInterval       stopInterval;
NSTimeInterval       elapsedInterval;

startInterval = [NSDate timeIntervalSinceReferenceDate];
// execute some long lasting calculation here
stopInterval = [NSDate timeIntervalSinceReferenceDate];

// calculate the time elapsed in seconds with
// sub-millisecond precision
elapsedInterval = stopInterval - startInterval;
```

NSDate

NSDate is the abstract public interface of a class cluster. When an instance of NSDate is initialized, an instance of one of the private subclasses of NSDate is returned. NSDate provides the foundation for all time storage within Cocoa.

NSDate provides an interface for creating and comparing dates. Time intervals between dates are computed. The private subclasses of NSDate are implemented to be efficient and immutable. Different subclasses of NSDate might use different reference dates and different calendar systems. The public NSCalendarDate subclass of NSDate provides dates using the Gregorian calendar and international time zones.

NSCalendarDate

NSCalendarDate extends NSDate to represent dates using the Gregorian calendar. NSCalendarDate uses an associated time zone to control the way times are displayed and interpreted. Like NSDate, NSCalendarDate stores a time interval from the system's absolute reference date. The time interval stored is independent of time zone, and NSCalendarDate can be compared with other NSDate objects without concern for time zone differences. The associated time zone only affects how dates are initialized and output.

NSCalendarDate instances are initialized with dates provided as strings or by values corresponding to year, month, day, hour, minute, and second. NSCalendarDate instances can also be initialized as offsets from other dates.

NSCalendarDate instances provide a string description of themselves using different location, language information, and formats. A wide range of output options are available for dates, and NSFormatter objects are used to fine-tune the way dates are presented to users.

NSTimeZone

NSTimeZone is an abstract class that helps date objects reflect time zone–related, location-specific information. The NSTimeZone class stores the name of a time zone, but it does not store a temporal offset from GMT for the zone. The Foundation framework includes subclasses of NSTimeZone that store offsets from GMT and Daylight Savings Time information.

Time zone objects are obtained by calling the +timeZoneWithName:, +timeZoneWithAbbreviation:, and +timeZoneForSecondsFromGMT: class methods of the NSTimeZone class. The default time zone in effect for the computer can be obtained via the +defaultTimeZone method.

Collections

Collections are an essential component of most applications, and the Foundation framework provides rich collection classes to meet most needs. All the collection classes take advantage of Cocoa's reference-counted memory management conventions and the power of Objective-C. The Foundation collection classes are able to store any type of object that conforms to the NSObject protocol. The collections even store heterogeneous objects. In other words, a single collection object stores many different classes of objects at the same time.

The Foundation framework includes classes for arrays, dictionaries, and sets. Arrays provide ordered storage that enables random access to stored elements via an index specifying a position within the collection. Dictionaries provide unordered associative storage. Each stored object has an associated key object. The stored objects are accessed via the keys. Sets provide unordered storage, which guarantees that no object is stored within the collection more than once.

The collection classes only store objects. It is possible to store nonobject values within a collection by wrapping the values within an object such as NSValue or NSNumber. It is not possible to store nil within the collections.

The Foundation collection classes are intended to solve common problems. They are highly optimized and handle a wide variety of uses. The collection classes are implemented as class clusters, and various private subclasses exist to optimize different uses. For example, a private subclass of NSMutableArray exists to optimize insertion at either the beginning or end of the collection. Nevertheless, some programs might have specific needs that are not well-suited to solutions using the standard collections. The Foundation collection classes are handy, but do not hesitate to write new classes if there is a specific need.

One consequence of the implementation of collection classes as class clusters is that they are difficult to subclass. An example of subclassing a class cluster is provided in Appendix B.

Arrays

Arrays provide ordered indexed storage. The objects stored in an array are accessed by index. The Foundation framework implements arrays using the `NSArray` class cluster. `NSArray` and `NSMutableArray` are abstract public interfaces. When an array is initialized, a private subclass of `NSArray` is created.

The Foundation framework provides array classes that are used extensively throughout Cocoa. Arrays are used to store the list of files in a directory, the list of documents open in an application, the list of file types that an application can open, and much more. Arrays can be loaded and saved from files and stored as property lists.

`NSArray`

`NSArray` is an immutable class. The array is initialized with certain contents and the contents do not change during the life of the collection. Each object stored in an array is automatically sent a `-retain` message and therefore is not deallocated until after the array is deallocated. `NSArray`'s `-count` method returns the number of objects stored in an array. The `-objectAtIndex:` method provides access to the object at a particular index in an array. Valid indexes are in the range 0 to count – 1. If an object at an invalid index is requested, `-objectAtIndex:` raises a `NSRangeException` exception.

A new autoreleased array with the sorted contents of an existing array is obtained by using the `-sortedArrayUsingFunction:context:` or `-sortedArrayUsingSelector:` methods. All the objects in an array can be asked to perform a particular method by calling `NSArray`'s `-makeObjectsPerformSelector:` or `-makeObjectsPerformSelector:withObject:` methods. Arrays can also be written to files via `-writeToFile:atomically:` or converted to strings via `-description` or `-componentsJoinedByString:`.

`NSMutableArray`

`NSMutableArray` extents the `NSArray` class to enable modifications to an existing array. As objects are added to a mutable array, additional storage is allocated as necessary, and the added objects are retained. As objects are removed from a mutable array, the objects are released. If an object removed from an array is not retained by any other object, the object is immediately deallocated when the array releases it.

Mutable arrays are sorted using either the `-sortUsingFunction:context:` method or the `-sortUsingSelector:` method.

Dictionaries

Dictionaries store associated key value pairs. Dictionaries provide an efficient way to retrieve data associated with a key. Each key is unique within a dictionary, but any number of different keys can be associated with the same value. The keys and values stored in a dictionary are not ordered.

`NSDictionary`

The `NSDictionary` class implements an immutable dictionary using a hash table. Because `NSDictionary` instances are immutable, they must be initialized with their key value pairs. The internal use of a hash table provides efficient access to values. Similar to all the Foundation collection classes, `NSDictionary` retains the objects that it stores.

The `NSDictionary` class is used extensively throughout Cocoa. For example, dictionaries are passed as arguments to notifications. User defaults and preferences are stored as dictionaries. Dictionaries can be stored in files and represented as strings in a variety of formats including XML.

`NSDictionary`'s `-count` method returns the number of key value pairs stored in the collection. The `-objectForKey:` method returns the object associated with a specified key or `nil` if the key is not stored in the dictionary. The `-keyEnumerator` method returns an enumerator object that can be used to iterate through all the keys stored in the dictionary.

`NSMutableDictionary`

The `NSMutableDictionary` class extends the `NSDictionary` class to enable modifications to the contents of an existing dictionary. When keys and values are added and removed from mutable dictionaries, the storage for the objects grows and shrinks automatically. If `-setObject:forKey:` is called with an existing key, the object associated with that key is replaced by the new object. Each key is only stored once in each dictionary.

The objects (values) that are added to a mutable dictionary are retained by the dictionary and released when they are removed. `NSMutableDictionary` stores copies of the keys specified when objects are added. Therefore, objects used as keys must conform to the `NSCopying` protocol. Any object that conforms to `NSCopying` may be used as a key as long as an additional constraint is met. The `NSObject` class declares the methods `-isEqual:` and `-hash`. If two keys are considered equal by the `-isEqual:` method, those two keys must also return the same value from their `-hash` methods.

NOTE

The NSCopying protocol, the -isEqual: method, and the -hash method are all defined in NSObject.h within the Foundation framework. NSObject provides many powerful methods that can be used with almost any object. NSObject's methods support Cocoa conventions described in Chapter 5, "Cocoa Conventions."

Although any object that has the capability to be copied might be used as a key in a mutable dictionary, dictionaries can only be used in property lists if all keys are NSString instances. Similarly, dictionaries can only be represented as property lists if all the values stored can be represented in a property list.

Sets

In the Foundation framework, a set is an unordered collection of objects with the property that each object is stored only once. That concept contrasts arrays and dictionaries, which store any number of references to the same object. Sets are used to efficiently determine if a particular object is contained within a collection. Sets are an alternative to arrays when the order of the contained objects is not important, but determining if an object is contained needs to be fast.

NSSet

NSSet is the public abstract interface to a class cluster. Its -count method returns the number of objects in the set. The -member: method returns non-nil if and only if the specified object is contained by the set. The -objectEnumerator method returns an enumerator that is used to access all the objects in the set.

The objects stored in a set must implement the inherited NSObject methods -isEqual: and -hash so that any two objects that are equal according to -isEqual: also return the same value from their –hash methods.

NSMutableSet

NSMutableSet extends the NSSet class to enable modifications to the contents of a set. Objects that are added to a set are retained, and objects that are removed are released. The storage for a mutable set grows and shrinks as needed. Objects are added with the -addObject: method and removed with the -removeObject: method.

NSNull

The Foundation collection classes cannot store nil values. When there is a need to store a placeholder value in a collection, the NSNull class is used. A single shared instance of the NSNull class is obtained by calling the +null class method.

Enumerators

An enumerator is an object that enables flexible access to the contents of a collection. Enumerators are called iterators in other frameworks. The Foundation framework provides the abstract `NSEnumerator` class. Foundation collection classes have methods that provide instances of concrete `NSEnumerator` subclasses to meet a variety of needs.

The following code shows one way to access all the objects stored in a preexisting collection referenced by `aCollection`:

```
NSEnumerator    *enumerator = [aCollection objectEnumerator];
id              object;

// loop to obtain each object in aCollection
while (nil != (object = [enumerator nextObject])) {
    // object is a pointer to one of the objects in aCollection
}
```

One of the key aspects of this example is the fact that the specific type of collection referenced by `aCollection` is not specified. The code works equally well if `aCollection` is an `NSArray`, `NSDictionary`, or `NSSet`. When an enumerator is initialized it is ready to return the first object in the associated collection. The first time `-nextObject` is called, the first object is returned. Each subsequent time `-nextObject` is called, another object in the collection is returned. When all the objects in the collection have been returned, the `-nextObject` method returns `nil`.

Do not modify mutable collections while an enumerator is in use. Addition, removal, and reordering of the contained objects corrupts the enumerator object. Enumerators retain their associated collection so that collections are not deallocated while an enumerator is in use.

All the Foundation collection classes implement the `-objectEnumerator` method to return an initialized and autoreleased instance of an `NSEnumerator` subclass. Some of the collection classes are also capable of providing specialized enumerators. For example, the `NSArray` class implements the `-reverseObjectEnumerator` method to enumerate the contents of the array in reverse order. The `NSDictionary` class provides the `-keyEnumerator` method for enumerating the keys used to store the objects enumerated by the `-objectEnumerator` method.

Enumerators provide a general mechanism for accessing all the elements in a collection regardless of the specific type of collection. In many cases, using an enumerator requires fewer lines of code than an alternative approach. Enumerators decouple the uses of a collection from the type of the collection and therefore enable the flexibility to change collection types later without breaking code all over an application. Enumerators also take advantage of optimizations that might not be obvious or practical when the contents of a collection are accessed in a different way.

Deep Versus Shallow Copying

Two different approaches to copying collections exist. A shallow copy is a copy of the collection itself, but not its contents. In other words, when a collection is shallow copied, the result is a second collection containing references to the same objects contained by the first. A deep copy copies the objects within the collection as well. When a deep copy is used, the result is two collections containing references to different objects.

By default, the Foundation collection classes all implement shallow copying. One technique for obtaining deep copies of collections is to use the `NSArchiver` and `NSUnarchiver` classes. Archiving is described in Chapter 5. If all the objects stored in a collection conform to the `NSCoding` protocol, the collection is copied using code like the following:

```
id MYDeepCopyObject(id <NSCoding> anObject)
// This function accepts an object conforming to
// the NSCoding protocol and returns a deep copy
{
  return [NSUnarchiver unarchiveObjectWithData:[NSArchiver
      archivedDataWithRootObject:anObject]];
}
```

The `MYDeepCopyObject` function accepts any object that conforms to the `NSCoding` protocol and returns a deep copy of that object. If `anObject` is a collection, the entire collection and all the contained objects are copied. In fact, `anObject` can be the root of an arbitrary graph of interconnected objects and the entire graph is copied.

Property Lists

Property lists enable convenient storage of application data without the need to write a lot of code or invent a new file format every time. Property lists are used extensively by Cocoa applications. User defaults and preferences are stored as property lists. Information such as the icon to use for a particular document type is stored in a property list. The Project Builder application uses property lists to store information about the project being built, such as which files to include in the build and which compiler options have been specified.

NOTE

Apple's developer tools come with a `PropertyListEditor` application that helps users graphically edit a property list. The `PropertyListEditor` application can be used to edit any property list including the user's preferences and defaults. When property lists are stored in files, the extension `.plist` is often used.

Property lists are a textual representation of `NSString`, `NSArray`, `NSDictionary`, and `NSData` objects. In fact, the `-description` method is implemented by each of these classes to return a string containing the property list representation of the receiver and any objects contained by the receiver. Almost any combination of `NSString`, `NSArray`, `NSDictionary`, and `NSData` objects can be read or written as a property list. For example, it is possible to store an array of dictionaries that each map string keys to data values in a property list.

There are two encoding styles for property lists. One is formatted to be very easy to read. The other uses industry standard `XML` formatting. Only `NSString`, `NSArray`, `NSDictionary`, and `NSData` objects are directly supported for use in both styles of property list. An additional constraint is that the keys used in a dictionary must be strings for the dictionary to be stored in a property list. XML property lists also store `NSNumber` and `NSDate` objects that cannot be directly stored in the other property list style.

Property lists obtained via the `-description` message use the more readable format. One reason for this is that the `-description` method is used within Apple's gdb debugger to show the contents of objects. XML data would be hard to read in that context. An existing string containing a property list can be used to recreate the objects described by the property list using `NSString`'s `-propertyList` method.

The `NSArray` and `NSDictionary` classes implement the `-initWithContentsOfFile:` method to read an XML property list stored in a file at a specified path. In each case, the property list read must define an array or dictionary as appropriate. If the file being read to initialize an array or dictionary contains errors, the `NSParseErrorException` exception is raised.

Convenience allocators are also available. `NSArray` implements `+arrayWithContentsOfFile:`, and `NSDictionary` implements `+dictionaryWithContentsOfFile:`. In each case, if the file being read to initialize an array or dictionary contains errors, nil is returned. An array or dictionary that contains only objects suitable for property lists is written to an XML property list file using the `-writeToFile:atomically:` method.

Using the non-XML property list style, numbers can be converted to and restored from strings easily by using `NSString` methods such as `-doubleValue` and `-intValue`. With both property list styles, many classes and structures are converted to and restored from strings. For example, the NSStringFromRect() and NSRectFromString() functions exist to convert rectangle structures to and from strings. Rectangle structures are briefly described in this chapter and in Chapter 12, "Custom Views and Graphics Part I." Objects that are not easily represented as strings are stored in property lists as data. Any object or graph of objects that all conform to the NSCoding protocol might be archived into an NSData instance. The following example demonstrates how an existing NSColor instance is encoded into data:

```
// Obtain an autoreleased NSData object initialized by encoding an
// existing instance of the NSColor class.
NSData    *tempData = [NSArchiver archivedDataWithRootObject:aColor];
```

When an object or graph of objects has been encoded as NSData, the data can be stored in a property list. This technique is used to store colors in each user's preferences property list.

Run Loops and Timers

Run loops are described with more detail in Chapter 8, "The Application Kit Framework Overview," because most features of run loops apply to applications with graphical user interfaces. However, run loops are implemented within the Foundation framework by the NSRunLoop class, and some features of the Foundation framework such as timers rely upon run loops. Each thread in a Cocoa application has one corresponding NSRunLoop instance that helps the thread communicate with the operating system. The run loop for the main thread in each application is created automatically. Other threads need to create an NSRunLoop instance in code.

NSRunLoop

An instance of the NSRunLoop class monitors a set of possible input sources from the operating system. The NSRunLoop class shields applications from requiring detailed knowledge of the underlying operating system to operate effectively. NSRunLoop simplifies the implementation of many common application features such as nonblocking file system access and timers.

NSTimer

The NSTimer class is used in conjunction with the NSRunLoop class to schedule delayed or periodic events. An NSTimer instance is created and initialized with the time interval of the delay, a selector that identifies a message to send when the interval has elapsed, and the object that should receive the message. Timers can be configured to send messages at repeating intervals.

NSTimer is used as an alternative to multithreading in some cases. Different processing jobs can be scheduled to execute at different times by using NSTimer to simulate concurrent execution. For example, a find panel in an application is used to start a repeating timer, which sends a message to search through the application's data structures a few at a time. The user can continue to use the application during the search while progressive results are displayed in the find panel.

Support Types

In addition to classes, the Foundation framework includes several functions and types based on C structures. The NSTimeInterval type has already been mentioned. NSTimeInterval is implemented using the C double type. Structures that store points, sizes, and rectangles are defined in the Foundation framework. Another type used extensively is NSRange.

NSRange

NSRange is a C structure used to identify a location and a length. For example, an NSRange can be used to specify a range of characters to delete from a mutable string using NSMutableString's -deleteCharactersInRange: method. The location is the index of the first character to delete. The length is the number of characters to delete. The NSRange structure is used by many Cocoa classes. NSRange is defined as follows:

```
typedef struct _NSRange {
    unsigned int location;
    unsigned int length;
} NSRange;
```

The Foundation framework contains a category that extends the NSValue to class to enable storage of NSRange values as follows:

```
@interface NSValue (NSValueRangeExtensions)

+ (NSValue *)valueWithRange:(NSRange)range;
- (NSRange)rangeValue;

@end
```

Ranges are converted to and from strings with the NSStringFromRange(NSRange range) and NSRangeFromString(NSString *aString) functions. NSMakeRange(unsigned int loc, unsigned int len) is used to obtain a new range. Ranges can be compared, intersected, and combined. The

NSLocationInRange(unsigned int loc, NSRange range) function is used to determine if a location is within a range.

NSGeometry

The NSGeometry.h header file that is part of the Foundation framework defines several data types that are useful for drawing and geometric operations. These types are part of the Foundation framework because they are used even in nongraphical applications. The NSPoint type is a C structure that stores the floating point X and Y coordinates of a point. The NSSize type is a structure that stores floating point width and height values. The NSRect structure consists of a point called the origin and a size:

```
typedef struct _NSPoint {
    float x;
    float y;
} NSPoint;

typedef struct _NSSize {
    float width;        /* should never be negative */
    float height;       /* should never be negative */
} NSSize;

typedef struct _NSRect {
    NSPoint origin;
    NSSize size;
} NSRect;
```

The Foundation framework contains the constant NSZeroPoint, NSZeroSize, and NSZeroRect global values that are useful for initializing geometric structures. NSMakePoint(float x, float y), NSMakeSize(float w, float h), and NSMakeRect(float x, float y, float w, float h) are also used to initialize structures. These types and functions are described and used in Chapter 12.

Just like the NSValue class is extended to store NSRange values, the Foundation framework contains a category that extends NSValue to store NSPoint, NSSize, and NSRect structures. A category also extends the NSCoder class to enable encoding and decoding of geometric types:

```
@interface NSCoder (NSGeometryCoding)

- (void)encodePoint:(NSPoint)point;
- (NSPoint)decodePoint;
```

```
- (void)encodeSize:(NSSize)size;
- (NSSize)decodeSize;

- (void)encodeRect:(NSRect)rect;
- (NSRect)decodeRect;

@end
```

Finally, the geometric types are converted to and from strings using `NSStringFromPoint(NSPoint aPoint)`, `NSStringFromSize(NSSize aSize)`, `NSStringFromRect(NSRect aRect)`, `NSPointFromString(NSString *aString)`, `NSSizeFromString(NSString *aString)`, and `NSRectFromString(NSString *aString)`. When converted to strings, the geometric types can be used in property lists.

String Processing

The Foundation framework contains powerful string processing capabilities. Some are implemented directly by `NSString` methods such as `-rangeOfString:` and `-componentsSeparatedByString:`. The Foundation framework provides the `NSCharacterSet` and `NSScanner` classes that are used together to enable additional types of string processing. A character set defines a set of Unicode characters, and a scanner is used to find patterns involving characters from a set.

NSCharacterSet

The `NSCharacterSet` class encapsulates a set of Unicode characters. `NSCharacterSet` is the public interface to a class cluster containing private classes optimized for different situations. For example, a character set composed solely of the ASCII subset of Unicode characters has different performance characteristics than a character set representing an Asian language using Unicode-composed character sequences. Character sets are primarily used when scanning for patterns in a string. `NSMutableCharacterSet` is a subclass of `NSCharacterSet` that adds methods to modify the contents of an existing set.

`NSCharacterSet` instances are usually obtained via convenience allocators such as `+alphanumericCharacterSet`, `+decimalDigitCharacterSet`, `+lowercaseLetterCharacterSet`, and `+characterSetWithCharactersInString:`. In many cases, the easiest way to generate a character set is to invert an existing set. `NSCharacterSet` implements the `-invertedSet` method to return an autoreleased `NSCharacterSet` instance containing all Unicode characters except the ones in the original set. The following example initializes the `nonWhiteSpaceSet` variable to a set containing all Unicode characters except spaces, tabs, and other white space characters:

```
NSCharacterSet        *nonWhiteSpaceSet = [[NSCharacterSet
    whitespaceCharacterSet] invertedSet];
```

`NSCharacterSet` is a CPU and memory resource intensive class. Profiling reveals that `NSCharacterSet` methods such as `-invertedSet` consume a large share of the processing time in applications that use `NSScanner` or perform a lot of complex operations with `NSString`. As with any powerful high-level technology, the best practice is to implement Cocoa applications using the most straightforward and simplest techniques available. Use `NSCharacterSet` and `NSScanner` when they save even a little work. When the application is working correctly, profile it, and determine where any performance problems exist. In most cases, slight changes to algorithms yield more performance improvements than avoiding `NSCharacterSet`, but `NSCharacterSet` is a common source of performance problems.

NSScanner

The `NSScanner` class is used to scan strings for patterns and return substrings or numeric values. `NSScanner` instances are usually initialized with a string to scan via `+scannerWithString:` or `-initWithString:`. The scanner can be configured to be case sensitive or not via `-setCaseSensitive:`. The `-isAtEnd` method can be used to determine that all characters from a string have been scanned.

The following example uses `NSScanner`'s `-scanUpToCharactersFromSet:intoString:` and `- scanCharactersFromSet:intoString:` methods to scan a string for substrings separated by punctuation and white space characters, and then stores the substrings in a mutable array.

```
#import <Foundation/Foundation.h>

int main (int argc, const char * argv[]) {
  NSAutoreleasePool *pool = [[NSAutoreleasePool alloc] init];
  NSMutableArray *resultArray = [NSMutableArray array];
  NSString      *testString = @"{Bush, George, W.},{Clinton, William, J.}";
  NSCharacterSet *nameCharacterSet = [NSCharacterSet alphanumericCharacterSet];
  NSScanner      *nameScanner;

  // Initialize a scanner with the string to scan
  nameScanner = [[NSScanner alloc] initWithString:testString];

  while(![nameScanner isAtEnd])
  {
```

```
    // Skip characters that can not be in a name and
    // discard the sub-string that does not include a name
    [nameScanner scanUpToCharactersFromSet:nameCharacterSet
                            intoString:nil];

    // if there are any characters left they must be part of a name
    if(![nameScanner isAtEnd])
    {
      NSString        *foundName; // this variable will hold pointer
                                  // to autoreleased string created
                                  // by the scanner
      [nameScanner scanCharactersFromSet:nameCharacterSet
                          intoString:&foundName];

      // Store the name in an array
      [resultArray addObject:foundName];
    }
  }

  [nameScanner release];

  // Output the description of resultArray
  NSLog(@"%@", [resultArray description]);

  [pool release];
  return 0;
}
```

The example code stores the strings `Bush`, `George`, `W`, `Clinton`, `William`, and `J` in `resultArray`.

`NSScanner` provides methods for extracting various numeric values from a string. The `-scanDecimal:`, `-scanDouble:`, `-scanFloat:`, `-scanInt:`, `-scanHexInt:`, and `-scanLongLong:` methods convert strings into numbers and store the numbers using the specified type. These methods return `YES` if a number was successfully scanned. The argument to each method is a pointer to storage of the correct type. Scanned values are stored at the specified address. In each case, excess digits are skipped so that the next character scanned is beyond the last digit in the number. If the scanner cannot find a string representation of a number, the methods for extracting numeric values return `NO`, and the value stored in the memory referenced by the argument is undefined.

Regular Expressions

The Foundation framework does not directly support string processing via regular expressions. Regular expressions describe complex patterns within strings and are used with many languages including Perl and shell scripts.

`NSString` supports multiple-string encoding systems including Unicode. Implementing regular expressions for complex encoding systems is very difficult. Unicode in particular is problematic. Even though `NSString` does not support regular expressions directly, the C `Regex` functions that are part of Mac OS X's `BSD` subsystem can be used with C strings obtained from the `NSString` class. In addition, several third-party libraries extend the `NSString` class via categories to directly support regular expressions with certain constraints.

Both the Omni Foundation framework available at `http://www.omnigroup.com/ftp/pub/software/Source/MacOSX/Frameworks` and the MOKit framework at `http://www.lorax.com/FreeStuff/MOKit.html` provide regular expression features for Foundation framework-based applications.

Formatters

Formatters format strings for presentation in a user interface. For example, formatters represent currency and dates using formats appropriate for different countries and languages. Formatters also validate user input to ensure that input values conform to specified formats. Formatters convert textual user input into objects such as `NSNumber` or `NSDate` instances.

The `NSFormatter` class is part of the Foundation framework, but it is used in combination with the Application Kit's `NSCell` class. `NSFormatter` is an abstract class. Subclasses such as `NSNumberFormatter` and `NSDateFormatter` exist to handle specific formatting needs. The `NSFormatter` class is described in more detail in Chapter 10, "Views and Controls." An example subclass of `NSFormatter` is provided in Chapter 11, "The Cocoa Text System."

Bundles

A bundle is a collection of executable code and resources such as images, sounds, strings, and user interface elements. The code and resources are stored together within a directory structure. Each resource is stored in its own file. In fact, bundles store multiple versions of resources to enable localization. Localization refers to the ability to use one set of executable code with different resources based on the language or culture preferences of the user. The different user interface elements, strings, images, and so on, appropriate for different languages and cultures are stored separately within a bundle.

Within the code that programmers write, bundles are commonly loaded into running applications to implement plug-ins. An application programmatically loads any number of bundles that contain Objective-C objects and resources. Bundles containing Objective-C categories are even used to extend existing classes within an application.

Bundles are implemented in several different forms within Mac OS X. Many bundles are loaded automatically without any programmer intervention. For example, each application is itself implemented as a bundle. The application bundle contains the application executable and the resources needed to launch the application. The application bundle is called the main bundle. Frameworks are bundles, which contain executable code that is automatically loaded into applications when they start. Frameworks can also contain resources such as user interface elements and strings. The Foundation framework itself is a bundle.

All types of bundles contain a file that stores a property list identifying important information about the bundle. The property list can be read and interpreted as an `NSDictionary` containing keys and values.

NSBundle

Every Cocoa application has at least one bundle for the application itself, and that bundle contains the application's `main()` function. Bundles are encapsulated by the `NSBundle` class. The application's bundle is called the main bundle. It is accessed from within any application by using the `NSBundle` class method, `+mainBundle`.

The bundle that contains the implementation of an Objective-C class is obtained using `NSBundle`'s `+bundleForClass:` method. The `+bundleForClass` method is usually used to access framework bundles. For example, `[NSBundle bundleForClass:[NSString class]]` returns the bundle for the Foundation framework itself because the `NSString` class is implemented in the Foundation framework.

Bundles in the file system are loaded using `NSBundle`'s `-initWithPath:` or `+bundleWithPath:` methods. There is never more than one instance of `NSBundle` for each bundle loaded. If an attempt is made to load the same bundle more than once, the `-initWithPath:` and `+bundleWithPath:` methods return the existing instance. Loaded bundles cannot be unloaded, but future support for unloading could be provided by Apple.

When a bundle is first loaded, code contained within the bundle is not yet linked into the loading application. The `NSBundle` class waits until a request to use code within the bundle is made. One way to force that code to be linked into a running application is to call `NSBundle`'s `-load` method. The `-principalClass` method also forces the linkage of loaded code. The `-principalClass` method returns a class object for the "principal class" within the bundle. The principal class can be specified when building a bundle with Apple's developer tools. If the principal class is not specified, the first class found within the executable code for the bundle is returned.

If the principal class for a bundle is specified when the bundle is built, the name of the principal class is stored in the bundle's info property list. All bundles contain an info property list containing information about the bundle. A `NSDictionary` initialized with the contents of the info property list can be obtained by calling `NSBundle`'s `-infoDictionary` method. The `NSPrincipalClass` key within the info dictionary is used to obtain the name of the bundle's principal class.

When a bundle has been loaded, any class defined within the bundle can be accessed using `NSBundle`'s `-classNamed:` method. For example, the class object for a hypothetical class named `MYApplicationPlugin` can be loaded by calling `[someBundle classNamed:@"MYApplicationPlugin"]`.

It is not necessary to explicitly load the application's main bundle or any framework bundles. Those are loaded automatically when the application starts. However, it is often necessary to use the main bundle and framework bundles to access their resources. The `-pathForResource:ofType:` method returns the path to a resource within the directory that stores a bundle. The following example initializes a string with the contents of a text file resource named `localizedText.txt` within the main bundle:

```
NSString    *resourcePath;
NSString       *result = nil;

resourcePath = [[NSBundle mainBundle] pathForResource:@"localizedText"
    ofType:@"txt"];

if(nil != resourcePath)
{
  result = [NSString stringWithContentsOfFile:resourcePath];
}
```

The `-pathForResource:ofType:` method automatically selects the resource with the specified name using the user's preferred localization. If the user's preferred language is German and a German language version of `localizedText.txt` exists within the bundle, the path to that version is returned. If no German language version is present, the user's preferences for other languages are used to determine which version's path is returned. The automatic support for localized resources applies to all resources regardless of their type. Different user interface components, images, sounds, and so on can be stored for each localization.

A bundle's resources can be loaded without loading any code from the bundle by using NSBundle's +pathForResource:ofType:inDirectory: class method and specifying a directory that contains an unloaded bundle. Localized resources are searched according to the user's language preferences until the specified resource is found. If the specified resource does not exist, -pathForResource:ofType: and +pathForResource:ofType:inDirectory: both return nil.

When a bundle is loaded, the NSBundleDidLoadNotification is automatically sent to the application's default notification center.

The NSBundle class is declared in the Foundation framework, but the Application Kit framework extends NSBundle in several ways using categories. The Application Kit adds methods for loading user interfaces, images, and other resources directly. The capability to extend classes that are declared in one framework with methods that depend on features of another framework is very powerful. Categories enable elegant designs. Methods are declared and implemented where they make the most sense. Unfortunately, spreading the commonly used methods of one class across multiple frameworks makes documenting the class very difficult. It does not make sense to describe how user interface objects are loaded from bundles before introducing user interface objects in a chapter about the Application Kit. Nevertheless, NSBundle is part of the Foundation framework. When reading Apple's documentation, always be sensitive to the fact that important methods might be documented separately from the main class documentation.

Localization

Resource files that are specific to a particular language or culture are grouped together. Each set of localized resources is stored within a different directory inside the bundle directory. The bundle's executable code works with any of the resources in the bundle. All versions of the same resource have the same name so that they can be found regardless of the directory that contains them.

NSBundle automatically selects the most appropriate resources when methods such as -pathForResource:ofType: are used. Each user's language preferences determine which resources are used in a running application. User preferences are stored in property lists and are edited using Mac OS X's System Preferences application. User language preferences are ordered. The user's most preferred language is stored first in an array, followed by the second most preferred, and so on. NSBundle's -localizations method returns an array of all available localizations within a bundle. The +preferredLocalizationsFromArray: class method returns an ordered array of localizations based on the user's preferences.

File System Access

File system access is one of the most common aspects of application development. Mac OS X includes file systems and APIs from Unix as well as the traditional Mac OS. The Foundation framework provides classes that encapsulate file system differences. An application written using the Foundation framework seamlessly accesses all of the available file systems on Mac OS X and can even access Windows file systems via Mac OS X's built in network file system support. All file system differences are hidden within the implementation of the Foundation framework.

In Mac OS X, the classes of the Foundation framework partially support features unique to Apple's HFS+ file system. The integration of the long-standing Unix file system support and the traditional Mac file system conventions is not yet complete in OS X version 10.1.3. As a result, many operations specific to the HFS+ file system must be accomplished using Apple's procedural Carbon APIs. However, most common file system operations, and all operations that are similar between traditional Unix file systems and HFS+, are supported by classes in the Foundation framework.

`NSFileHandle`

The `NSFileHandle` class encapsulates files and communications channels regardless of their underlying implementation. `NSFileHandle` is the public interface of a class cluster. Private subclasses of `NSFileHandle` are optimized for different operations.

Instances of `NSFileHandle` are initialized to use an existing file descriptor using the `-initWithFileDescriptor:` method. File descriptors are a Unix convention. Standard POSIX APIs exist to open files and communications channels for reading, writing, or both. When opened, the file descriptor for the file or communications channel is used with `NSFileHandle`. `NSFileHandle` takes care of closing the file descriptor when appropriate.

On Mac OS X, `NSFileHandle`'s convenience allocators `+fileHandleForReadingAtPath:`, `+fileHandleForWritingAtPath:`, `+fileHandleForUpdatingAtPath:`, `+fileHandleWithStandardError`, `+fileHandleWithStandardInput`, `+fileHandleWithStandardOutput:`, and `+fileHandleWithNullDevice:` avoid the need to use POSIX procedural APIs directly. These methods completely hide differences between file systems. The paths passed as arguments to these methods are usually obtained from a `NSBundle` instance's `-pathForResource:ofType:` method. Paths are also constructed using `NSString`'s path related methods such as `-stringByAppendingPathComponent:` and functions within the Foundation framework such as `NSHomeDirectory()` or `NSTemporaryDirectory()`.

After an `NSFileHandle` instance is created, data is read or written using the associated file or communications channel. In some cases, `NSFileHandle` enables random access to the contents of a file. Files can be truncated, and it is possible to read or write to specific locations within a file. `NSFileHandle` also works with communications channels such as pipes and sockets. Pipes are a Unix mechanism for using the output of one program as the input for another. Sockets provide cross-platform support for bidirectional network communications. The set of operations that work with a `NSFileHandle` instance depends on the type of file or communications channel being used.

The Foundation framework provides many different ways to access file systems. For example, some Foundation classes provide methods to directly write or read files. The `-writeToFile:atomically:` method is implemented by `NSArray`, `NSData`, `NSDictionary`, and `NSString` among others. `NSFileHandle` is a lower-level class that provides more flexible, but less convenient access to files and their contents.

Data is read from a file that is handled by a `NSFileHandle` instance using the `-readDataOfLength:` method. When `-readDataOfLength:` is called, data from the current position within the file is read up to the specified length or the end of the file (whichever comes first). To determine if all data has been read from a file, call `NSFileHandle`'s `-availableData` method. It returns `YES` if data is available and `NO` otherwise. However, if the `NSFileHandle` represents a communications channel, the `-availableData` method will block until data becomes available. That means an application cannot perform any more computations until data becomes available.

Blocking while waiting for data to become available is not usually acceptable in a Cocoa application. When users see the "spinning beach ball" cursor indicating that an application is not responding to user input, the usual cause is that the application is blocked waiting for data.

One solution for avoiding the "spinning beach ball" cursor is to perform file operations in a different thread from the one that controls the user interface. The separate thread for I/O blocks without harm to other threads. Multiple threads are sometimes the best solution, but they unavoidably make applications more complex.

`NSFileHandle` is optionally used to implement asynchronous background communication without the need to explicitly create multiple threads in an application. `NSFileHandle`'s `-readInBackgroundAndNotify` returns immediately. When data becomes available, `NSFileHandle` sends the `NSFileHandleReadCompletionNotification` to the default notification center. The notification includes the data read as an argument.

After receiving the `NSFileHandleReadCompletionNotification`, the object that received the notification must call `-readInBackgroundAndNotify` again to receive more data. Data is written to a file using NSFileHandle's -writeData: method. The current position in an open file is changed with the -seekToFileOffset: method. Files are truncated with the -truncateFileAtOffset: method. Finally, an open file is closed with the -closeFile method.

NSFileManager

The NSFileHandle class encapsulates operations on a specific open file or communications channel. The NSFileManager class is used to manipulate file systems. NSFileManager encapsulates file system management operations and abstracts many file system differences. By using NSFileManager, an application manipulates the file system regardless of whether the file system is based on Windows, Unix, or traditional Mac HFS+.

NSFileManager provides methods to create directories and change the current working directory. NSFileManager is used to copy, move, delete, or link files and directories. The attributes of files and directories are obtained and changed. The contents of files and directories can be read or compared. Finally, file system links and aliases can be evaluated.

One key to the implementation of NSFileManager is that it manages conversions between application string and file system string encodings. For example, if an attempt is made to create a file with a Unicode name in a file system that does not support Unicode, the name is automatically converted to an encoding suitable for the file system.

There is at least one instance of NSFileManager called the default manager in every Cocoa application. The default manager instance is obtained with NSFileManager's +defaultManager class method. The following example fills an existing mutable array with strings that each contain the name of a file or directory in the current working directory:

```
void getNamesInCurrentDirectory(NSMutableArray *resultArray)
{
  NSString              *fileName;
  NSFileManager         *fileManager = [NSFileManager defaultManager];
  NSDirectoryEnumerator *enumerator = [fileManager enumeratorAtPath:
      [fileManager currentDirectoryPath]];

  while (nil != (fileName = [enumerator nextObject]))
  {
    [resultArray addObject:fileName];
  }
}
```

NSFileWrapper

The `NSFileWrapper` class is part of the Application Kit framework and cannot be used by Foundation framework applications that do not also use the Application Kit framework. Nevertheless, it is worth mentioning here because it is closely related to the `NSFileManager` and `NSFileHandle` classes. `NSFileWrapper` provides a higher level and more abstract representation of files than `NSFileHandle`. `NSFileWrapper` is used with whole directories of files and provides high-level capabilities that would otherwise be implemented using lower-level `NSFileManager` methods.

`NSFileWrapper` is described in Chapter 8. `NSFileWrapper` helps an application treat files and whole directories of files as if they were all simultaneously present in the application's memory. `NSFileWrapper` encapsulates operations on the files and information such as the icon associated with a file. `NSFileWrapper` also synchronizes changes made to the portions of files stored in memory and changes files on disk.

Defaults System

Mac OS X provides rich support for storage of user preferences and application defaults. Traditional user preferences and defaults are both called defaults in Cocoa. Every user has a defaults database which is created automatically. Defaults are stored in several different domains. For example, a user can have defaults that apply to only one application or defaults that apply to all applications run by the user. Defaults domains are accessed by name. Mac OS X defines the following domains: argument, global, registration, application, and languages. The first three are referenced in code using the `NSArgumentDomain`, `NSGlobalDomain`, and `NSRegistrationDomain` constants respectively. The application domain uses the application's bundle identifier as its name. The languages domain uses the name of the user's preferred language as set in Preferences. It is seldom necessary to access defaults domains explicitly by name because the NSUserDefaults class uses domains automatically.

Values in each domain are stored in property lists that define dictionaries of key value pairs. Because defaults are stored in property lists, only object types supported for use in property lists can be stored. Types not directly supported are usually converted into `NSString` or `NSData` instances for storage.

Standard keys are used in each domain. The domain used to store a default value depends on the value's use. For example, the argument domain contains default values specified on the command line when an application is started. Applications can add new keys and values to any domain, but changes to the argument domain are not saved. When an application looks up a default value, the domains are searched in the following order: argument, application, global, languages, and registration. As a result, defaults stored in the application domain supercede defaults stored in the global domain. Default values specified on the command line supercede all other defaults. Default values are specified on the command line and added to the argument by preceding a default name with a hyphen and following it with a value. For example, adding the following argument to the command line when launching a Cocoa application will change the default units of measurement used by the application during that session:

```
-NSMeasurementUnit Inches
```

Even if the user's default value set with Apple's System Preferences application is "Centimeters," running an application from the command line and specifying "Inches" will supercede the default value for one execution session.

Apple's System Preferences application is used to graphically set many default values. In addition, each application can contain its own user interface for setting default values in any domain. Many default values such as default window positions are stored automatically by the relevant classes. Finally, a command-line tool called `defaults` is used to read or write default values. The following command typed into a terminal will set the user's default measurement unit for all applications:

```
defaults write -globalDomain NSMeasurementUnit Centimeters
```

The dictionary for the argument domain is constructed from command-line arguments. In contrast, the dictionary for the application domain is read from a property list of default values stored for each user. Application defaults apply to just one application. Each application can have different user specific default keys and values. Changes that an application makes to application defaults are automatically stored in a user's defaults property list when the application is quit.

The dictionary for the global domain is read from each user's defaults database. Default values in this domain apply to all applications that a user runs. Values such as the default units of measurement are usually set for all applications. The languages domain is also stored in a persistent property list. The languages domain stores preferences that depend on the user's preferred language. For example, the Foundation framework class, `NSCalendarDate`, uses values stored in the languages domain to determine how dates should be presented. Finally, the registration domain is used by applications to make sure that every expected default value exists. Defaults in the registration domain are not saved. When an application starts, it can initialize the values of all defaults that it requires to factory settings in the registration domain. If a user has set the same default in any other domain, the user's value is used. By setting all factory defaults in the registration domain when an application starts, the code that uses default values in the rest of the application is simplified. Using the registration domain eliminates the need to verify that a default value exists before each time it is used.

NSUserDefaults

The NSUserDefaults class encapsulates all operations involving Mac OS X's defaults domains. A single shared instance of the NSUserDefaults class is obtained by calling the +standardUserDefaults class method. The standard user defaults instance is created and initialized with all the user's default values from all the standard domains. The default values are cached to minimize the number of times the defaults database is accessed on disk.

To obtain the default value associated with a particular key, send the -objectForKey: message to the standard user defaults instance. The following function returns a string containing the user's preferred currency symbol:

```
NSString *GetPreferredCurrencySymbol()
{
  return [[NSUserDefaults standardUserDefaults]
      objectForKey:@"NSCurrencySymbol"];
}
```

A dictionary of all default values in effect is obtained by calling the standard user defaults object's -dictionaryRepresentation method. The returned dictionary contains key value pairs from all the domains. Values set in domains that are searched first supercede values set in lower priority domains.

Apple's online documentation for the NSUserDefaults class provides a partial list of default keys such as the NSCurrencySymbol key. Many others are used by Cocoa applications but aren't documented anywhere. For example, the NSWindowResizeTime key changes the number of seconds used to animate window resizing in Cocoa applications. Valid values are greater than 1.0. One reason that Apple has not documented many default keys might be that they are considered part of private APIs or deprecated APIs. There is no guarantee that undocumented keys will continue to work in new versions of Mac OS X.

Set default values by calling the -setObject:forKey: method of NSUserDefaults. When a default value is changed programmatically in a running application, the NSUserDefaultsDidChangeNotification is posted to the default notification center. Observers of this notification can check the defaults dictionaries to determine what changed. Apple's online documentation provides an example of an application domain default for setting whether backup files should be automatically deleted.

Use the -synchronize method of NSUserDefaults to copy any values set programmatically into to defaults database on disk. The -synchronize method is called automatically when an application quits. There is no reason to call -synchronize explicitly in application code unless changed values need to be saved prior to the automatic save that occurs when the application quits. The

`+resetStandardUserDefaults` class method invalidates previously cached default values. The next time `+standardUserDefaults` is called, the returned instance contains only the default values actually stored in the user's defaults database on disk. Code for an application-specific preferences panel can call `+resetStandardUserDefaults` to reset all default values to the ones stored on disk.

Notifications

Notifications are a flexible mechanism that enables multiple objects to communicate with each other without tightly coupling the objects together. An object called a notification center is used to register objects that need to be notified under certain circumstances. The objects registered to receive notifications are called observers. When objects post notifications with the notification center, the notification center distributes the posted notifications to interested observers by sending Objective-C messages to them. The notifications design pattern is described in Chapter 6.

The observers know about the notification center, but don't need to know anything about the objects that post notifications. The objects that post notifications don't need to know which objects, if any, observe the notification. The objects that post notifications and the observing objects are decoupled.

NOTE

As a general design goal, coupling between classes should be avoided. Another term for coupling is dependency. Coupling reduces the reusability of objects. Coupling makes designs inflexible and difficult to maintain.

Any number of objects can be observers for any notification. Any number of objects can post notifications. Notifications enable extremely flexible application designs. For example, when objects and resources are dynamically loaded into an application, the `NSBundleDidLoadNotification` is sent to registered observers. The observers might use the notification to gain access to the loaded resources or send messages to the loaded objects. The key is that the `NSBundle` class used to dynamically load objects and resources is not modified in each application that uses it. Instead, application specific logic is implemented in the objects that observe the notification. `NSBundle` is reusable and does not have dependencies on objects in particular applications, and applications can still perform specific processing when a bundle is loaded.

Many Foundation framework classes post notifications. Notifications posted by `NSBundle`, `NSFileHandle`, and `NSUserDefaults` classes have already been mentioned in this chapter. Notifications are also used extensively in the Application Kit framework. Notifications are posted in many situations including when a window is closed or an application has finished launching.

NSNotificationCenter

Instances of the `NSNotificationCenter` class enable communication between objects that don't know about each other. `NSNotificationCenter` instances receive posted `NSNotification` instances and distribute them to appropriate observer objects.

Every Cocoa application contains at least one instance of `NSNotificationCenter` called the default notification center. The default notification center is obtained using the `NSNotificationCenter`'s `+defaultCenter` class method. Most notifications posted by Foundation framework and Application Kit framework objects are posted to the default notification center.

An application can contain any number of `NSNotificationCenter` instances. Specialized communication between custom objects in an application might use notification centers created just for that purpose, but most application needs are met by the default notification center.

Notifications are posted by calling the `-postNotification:` method of an `NSNotificationCenter` instance such as the default notification center. The argument to `-postNotification:` is a `NSNotification` instance. The `NSNotification` class is described in this chapter. The `-postNotificationName:object:userInfo:` method is used to indirectly create and post an `NSNotification` instance. The first argument is the notification name. The second argument is the object posting the notification. The third argument is a dictionary that is passed as an argument when observers are notified.

Objects register as observers for particular notifications based on several criteria. The standard way to register for a notification is to call `NSNotificationCenter`'s `-addObserver:selector:name:object:` method. The first argument is the object that will observe notifications. The second argument is a selector that identifies the Objective-C message that is sent to the observer when an appropriate notification is posted. The selector must specify a method that takes one argument. The third argument is the name of the notification that is being observed. If the third argument is `nil`, the observer is registered to receive all notifications posted by the object specified in the fourth argument. The fourth argument is an object that posts notifications and can be used to restrict the notifications received by the observer to only those notifications posted by the specified object. If the fourth argument is `nil`, all notifications with the specified name are observed.

The method called to notify an observer must have exactly one argument. The argument is the `userInfo` dictionary that is provided when a notification is posted. The `userInfo` dictionary can contain any objects and must be interpreted based on the notification being received.

Notification centers do not retain the observer objects. When an object registered to observe notifications is deallocated, it must remove itself from all notification centers. `NSNotificationCenter`'s `-removeObserver:` method removes a specified observer completely, no matter how many notifications are being observed. The `-removeObserver:name:object:` method is used to selectively remove a registered observer for a particular notification or notification posting object.

NOTE

The Foundation framework provides the `NSDistributedNotificationCenter` class to enable notifications between objects in different applications. Notifications can be delayed or queued with the `NSNotificationQueue` class so that multiple redundant notifications are coalesced and sent to observers only once.

`NSNotification`

`NSNotification` instances store a name that identifies the notification, a reference to the object that posted the notification, and a dictionary that is passed as an argument to the methods registered by observers of the notification.

`NSNotification` instances are created with the `+notificationWithName:object:userInfo:` convenience allocator and posted with a notification center. Notifications are also indirectly created by `NSNotificationCenter`'s `-postNotificationName:object:userInfo:` method. The only reason to create instances with `+notificationWithName:object:userInfo:` is to keep an instance around so that it can be posted multiple times with exactly the same `name`, `object`, and `userInfo` dictionary.

Related Core Foundation

With the release of Mac OS X, Apple has extended and documented much of the low-level code used to implement the Foundation framework. The code is included in a standard C library that Apple calls Core Foundation. The Core Foundation library consists of a set of procedural APIs and data structures that can be used from Cocoa or Carbon applications. In some cases, Foundation framework classes are internally implemented using Core Foundation functions. In other cases, there is effectively no difference between Core Foundation data structures and corresponding Foundation framework objects. Such objects are said to be "toll free bridged," meaning that Core Foundation just provides a procedural API for accessing objects.

One toll free bridged object is NSString. Core Foundation defines a data structure called CFStringRef and a set of C functions for manipulating CFStringRefs. In fact, CFStringRef and a pointer to NSString are the same and can be safely cast from one to the other. In the following example, a CFStringRef is created and initialized. Then it is further manipulated using Objective-C messages. Finally, the NSString pointer is cast back to CFStringRef.

```
CFStringRef    authorNames = CFSTR("Scott Anguish, Erik Buck, Don Yacktman");
CFStringRef    credits;

credits = (CFStringRef)[@"Authors: " stringByAppendingString:
    (NSString *)authorNames];
```

Not all Core Foundation data types that seem to be toll free bridged to a Foundation object actually are. CFArray, CFCharacterSet, CFData, CFDate, CFDictionary, CFRunLoopTimer, CFSet, CFString, and CFURL are toll free bridged to NSArray, NSCharacterSet, NSData, NSDate, NSDictionary, NSTimer, NSSet, NSString and NSURL, respectively. Other Core Foundation types might be used in the implementation of Foundation objects or might be completely unrelated. In either case, they cannot be used interchangeably with the Foundation framework objects that have similar names.

Parts of the implementation of Core Foundation are available in source code as part of Apple's open source Darwin project. Several data structures that are supported by Core Foundation have no equivalent in the Foundation framework. The CFBinaryHeap type stores values sorted using a binary search algorithm and implements priority queues. The CFBitVector data type can be used to efficiently store large numbers of Boolean values. The CFTree data type implements a tree data structure. CFStorage uses a balanced tree to provide O(log n) or faster access to arrays of arbitrary but uniformly sized data structures.

The open source CFSocket functions can be used instead of standard Unix socket functions to abstract potential differences between operating systems. Unix sockets might not be available on all platforms that support Core Foundation in the future. CFSocket can be implemented using the native interprocess communication API on each target platform.

CFBundle and CFPlugIn provide similar features to the NSBundle class, but neither is toll free bridged to NSBundle. CFURL and CFURLAccess provide platform independent ways to read and write files and other resources from remote machines. CFPreferences provides a procedural API for accessing the keys and values stored in a user's defaults database. CFPreferences is not bridged to NSUserDefaults. CFUUID is used to produce universally unique 16-byte identifiers. The same identifier will not be produced twice regardless of the platform or machine. CFUUID provides features similar to the NSProcessInfo class's -globallyUniqueString method defined in the Foundation framework. CFUserNotification provides procedural access to notifications and enables the registration of call back functions that are called when a notification is posted. CFPropertyList provides procedural access to property lists. CFMessagePort and CFMachPort wrap low-level Mach messaging and interprocess communication.

Core Foundation contains data types and functions for reading and extracting data from XML documents. CFXMLParser and CFXMLNode are used together to procedurally manage nonverified XML structured documents. CFXMLParser is used to read XML property lists including the user defaults database.

Summary

This overview could hardly cover every topic of interest regarding the Foundation framework. The information provided in this chapter conveys the breadth of classes available and indicates where to look for more information. It identifies the practical implications of some Cocoa conventions including the ideas of mutability, immutability, and class clusters. Many of the public Foundation classes are abstract interfaces to class clusters, and that fact can have huge impacts on their use. Additional classes such as NSHost and NSProcessInfo, exist but are not described in this overview. Such classes are indispensable in certain circumstances, but are seldom used in practice. Before writing code, be sure that there is no existing Foundation class or function to solve the problem.

The next chapter provides an overview of the Application Kit framework that is built on top of the Foundation framework. Just as the Foundation framework provides a foundation for all Cocoa applications, the Application Kit contains the classes needed for graphical applications and graphical user interfaces. Neither this chapter nor the next contains the kind of in-depth information needed to really unleash the power of the frameworks. These chapters are truly overviews. The information introduced is expanded throughout the rest of this book in examples and explanations, but the conceptual grounding provided in this chapter and the next provide an essential foundation.

8

The Application Kit Framework Overview

IN THIS CHAPTER

- Events and the Run Loop
- Responders
- `NSApplication` Overview
- `NSWindow` Overview
- `NSView` Overview
- Delegates
- Target-Action Paradigm
- Archived Objects and Nibs
- `NSWindowController` Overview
- Multidocument Applications
- Undo and Redo
- Menu Validation
- Spell Checking

The Application Kit contains most of the classes that provide user interfaces and graphics for Cocoa applications. The Application Kit uses the Foundation framework extensively, and is very large. Much of the rest of this book is dedicated to unleashing its power. This chapter focuses on the key concepts and techniques employed to provide Cocoa user interfaces. These key concepts might be unfamiliar even to experienced developers accustomed to other user-interface toolkits. The Application Kit takes advantage of the dynamic nature of Objective-C and the Foundation framework to implement an extremely flexible and powerful framework of cooperating classes.

The information presented in this chapter is essential for understanding how to use the Application Kit and how the pieces fit together. It is often necessary to recognize the interaction of multiple classes to use the kit effectively. This chapter presents the big picture architecture of the Application Kit, the key classes, and details of a few key concepts used to implement the Application Kit. This chapter covers broad concepts and does not provide enough information to make effective use of most Application Kit features. It can be difficult to understand a complex framework when too many details are provided up front. There is always the danger of not seeing the forest because of all the trees. The Application Kit provides many classes to implement core concepts, and the classes interoperate in ways that are difficult to see without a big-picture overview. This chapter provides the big picture at the expense of details.

Events and the Run Loop

Most graphical user interface toolkits, including the Application Kit, use an event-driven model. That simply means applications react to events that are sent to the application by the operating system. The events can result from the user typing on a keyboard, or moving a mouse. Timer events can be sent at periodic intervals. The arrival or availability of any new data from a monitored input source is also conceptually an event.

Cocoa applications receive events from the operating system with the help of the `NSRunLoop` class. Every Cocoa application contains at least one instance of the `NSRunLoop` class. A run loop is created automatically for each thread in the application. In most cases, the programmer does not need to access the run loop directly. The run loop for each thread monitors input sources that are part of the operating system. If no monitored input sources have available data, the run loop does not consume CPU resources. In other words, the run loop blocks on pending I/O.

When data becomes available, the run loop recognizes the new data as an event and sends Objective-C messages to various objects notifying them of the event. The receivers of the messages and the messages that are sent depend on the type of data that becomes available.

The purpose of the run loop is to enable efficient communication between the operating system and an application. The implementation of the `NSRunLoop` class is platform specific. The implementation for Mac OS X uses Mach ports and the Unix `select()` function to detect and manage I/O. `NSRunLoop` abstracts the differences between various operating systems. If Apple ever renews cross-platform support for Cocoa technology, the `NSRunLoop` class will certainly be reimplemented for each platform.

Application code seldom interacts with the run loop directly. Many user interface toolkits make the run loop a key focus for developers, but in Cocoa, the run loop plays a minor role in an application. Graphical Cocoa applications wrap the functionality of the `NSRunLoop` class within the `NSApplication` class. One of the purposes of the `NSApplication` class is to manage the run loop on behalf of the entire application. The `NSApplication` class is a key component of the Application Kit's architecture, and is described in this chapter.

Responders

When keyboard events, mouse events, timer events, or other events are detected by the run loop and the `NSApplication` instance that manages the run loop, those events are converted into instances of the `NSEvent` class and dispatched to other objects using Objective-C messages. The use of messaging is an important difference from other user interface toolkits and results in much of the power and flexibility of Cocoa. The Application Kit does not use C-language switch statements or explicit tables of function pointers. The messaging capabilities built into the Objective-C runtime are ideally suited to event dispatching.

An object that can receive event messages is called a responder. Figure 8.1 illustrates the relationships and communications between the operating system, the run loop, an instance of the `NSApplication` class, and a responder.

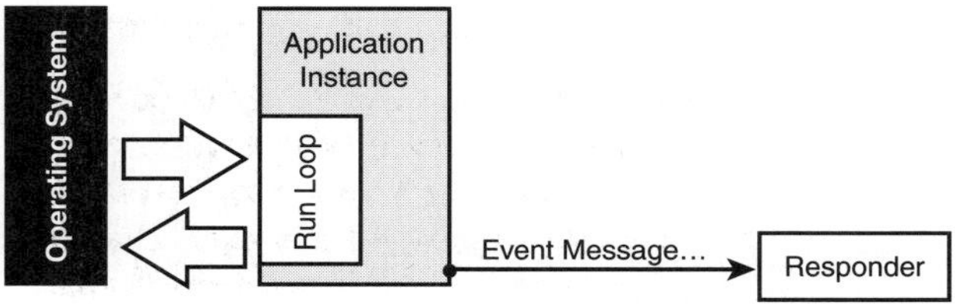

FIGURE 8.1 The operating system, the run loop, an instance of the `NSApplication` class, and a responder interact.

What Is a Responder?

Cocoa encapsulates the role of responders within the `NSResponder` class. `NSResponder` is an abstract class. Abstract classes are not intended for direct use by application programmers. Instead, abstract classes provide functionality that is used by subclasses. `NSResponder` provides the foundation on which some of the most prominent Cocoa classes are built. Subclasses of `NSResponder` include `NSView`, `NSWindow`, and `NSApplication`. These subclasses collaborate to manage the flow of events within an application.

The collaboration between the various subclasses of `NSResponder` within a Cocoa application is so powerful that many applications can be written without any custom event handling code at all. The event processing within the Application Kit framework takes care of almost all events automatically.

When application-specific, custom-event handling is needed, one or more of `NSResponder`'s event-processing methods can be overridden in a subclass. For example, to perform processing in response to a mouse button-press event, override `NSResponder`'s `-mouseDown:` method.

Each of `NSResponder`'s event-processing methods accepts a single argument, which is an instance of the `NSEvent` class. Within the event processing methods, the `NSEvent` instance can be interrogated to obtain more information about the event such as the location of the mouse or which modifier keys were pressed. The `NSEvent` class documentation describes all the information obtainable.

The following event-processing methods are declared in the NSResponder class:

```
- (BOOL)performKeyEquivalent:(NSEvent *)theEvent;
- (void)mouseDown:(NSEvent *)theEvent;
- (void)rightMouseDown:(NSEvent *)theEvent;
- (void)otherMouseDown:(NSEvent *)theEvent;
- (void)mouseUp:(NSEvent *)theEvent;
- (void)rightMouseUp:(NSEvent *)theEvent;
- (void)otherMouseUp:(NSEvent *)theEvent;
- (void)mouseMoved:(NSEvent *)theEvent;
- (void)mouseDragged:(NSEvent *)theEvent;
- (void)scrollWheel:(NSEvent *)theEvent;
- (void)rightMouseDragged:(NSEvent *)theEvent;
- (void)otherMouseDragged:(NSEvent *)theEvent;
- (void)mouseEntered:(NSEvent *)theEvent;
- (void)mouseExited:(NSEvent *)theEvent;
- (void)keyDown:(NSEvent *)theEvent;
- (void)keyUp:(NSEvent *)theEvent;
- (void)flagsChanged:(NSEvent *)theEvent;
```

These methods are presented here to provide a sense of the range of methods available. The uses for each of NSResponder's event processing messages are described in the class documentation for NSResponder. Many of the methods are used and described in examples within this chapter and the rest of this book.

The NSEvent passed to each event-processing method is only valid within that method's implementation. The Cocoa frameworks reserve the right to reuse existing NSEvent instances or otherwise tamper with their contents. To preserve the information in an NSEvent instance, copy it or store the information in a separate data structure. Simply retaining the NSEvent instance for later use is not sufficient.

The Responder Chain

Each instance of the NSResponder class stores a pointer to another instance of NSResponder called the next responder. NSResponder provides methods for setting and getting the next responder. Responders are chained together from next responder to next responder, and form a data structure called the responder chain. If an instance of NSResponder does not process a message that it receives, the message can be passed on to the next responder. The message travels along the chain until the message is processed or there is no next responder. Figure 8.2 shows event message processing including the responder chain.

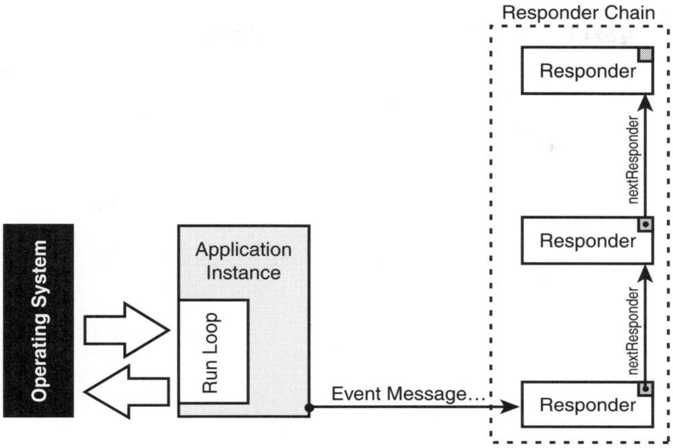

FIGURE 8.2 Event message processing includes the responder chain.

The responder chain plays a crucial role in applications that use the Application Kit. Many powerful features such as automatic menu validation, context sensitive menus, text entry, and automatic spell checking depend on the responder chain. The responder chain also provides opportunities for programmers to insert context-sensitive custom logic and event handling into applications. The responder chain is Cocoa's implementation of the "Chain of Responsibility" design pattern described in Chapter 6, "Cocoa Design Patterns."

The First Responder

The responder that gets the first chance to respond to an event message is called the first responder. The first responder is the first link in the responder chain. One of the keys to using the responder chain is the understanding of which responder will be the first responder in any circumstance. The first responder determines the chain that a message follows.

The responder chain and the first responder are managed by three `NSResponder` subclasses: `NSApplication`, `NSWindow`, and `NSView`. Applications contain exactly one instance of the `NSApplication` class, and that instance receives events from the operating system. The events are either sent on to a window represented by an `NSWindow` instance or consumed by the application object itself. Every window in an application stores a pointer to a first responder. The first responder for a window can change based on user actions or program code. The initial first responder in each window can be set in Interface Builder or through a `NSWindow` instance method. Sometimes the first responder for a window is the window itself. When a window receives an event from the application object, the event is either forwarded to a responder within the window or consumed by the window itself. The responders within a window are typically instances of `NSView` subclasses.

The first responder to receive an event message depends on the application object, the window that is most appropriate for the event, and a responder (view) within the window. Figure 8.3 expands the diagram of event-message processing to include windows and the responders within the windows.

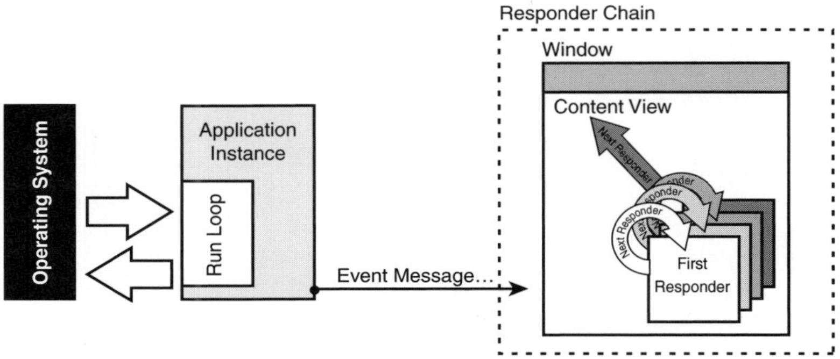

FIGURE 8.3 The first responder to receive an event message depends on the application object, a window, and the responders within the window.

The programmatic way to change a window's first responder is to call `NSWindow`'s `-makeFirstResponder:` method passing the responder that should become the new first responder as the argument. A sequence of messages are automatically sent when the first responder is changed via `-makeFirstResponder:`. First, the `-resignFirstResponder` message is sent to the current first responder asking it to accept the change in its status. If the current first responder returns `NO`, the first responder is not changed. If the current first responder returns `YES` from `-resignFirstResponder`, the argument to `-makeFirstResponder:` is sent a `-becomeFirstResponder` message. If the object that receives the `-becomeFirstResponder` message returns `NO`, the window that received the `-makeFirstResponder:` becomes the first responder.

Different types of events are dispatched to different first responders. For example, the first responder to receive an event message might be different for keyboard events and mouse-click events. The full implications of the first responder and the responder chain cannot be described without more information about the `NSApplication`, `NSWindow`, and `NSView` classes. In this chapter there is an overview of each of these classes which includes information about their roles in the responder chain.

NSApplication Overview

Each Application Kit-based application contains a single instance of the NSApplication class that extends the event handling capabilities of NSResponder to communicate with the operating system. NSApplication is a subclass of NSResponder and is implemented as a shared object or Singleton as described in Chapter 6, "Cocoa Design Patterns." The shared instance can be accessed with NSApplication's +sharedApplication method or through the NSApp global variable provided by the Application Kit framework.

NSApplication provides the interface between an application and the operating system. The NSApplication instance manages a run loop that receives events from the operating system. NSApplication converts events into instances of the NSEvent class and sends the events to responders. The NSApplication object also maintains the application's connection to the operating system for drawing, scripting, and notification of system-wide events such as the launch of other applications or the pending shutdown of the computer.

NSApplication stores the application's icon, manages all the application's windows, and provides access to the application's menus. NSApplication implements the standard behaviors of Mac OS X applications automatically. As a result, Cocoa applications behave consistently. Applications obtain many powerful features for free by using the NSApplication class.

The NSApplication class is seldom subclassed. Instead, the behavior of an application can be modified through the use of an application delegate and notifications. Delegation is a powerful technique that is described in the Delegation Versus Notifications section later in this chapter and also in Chapter 6.

NSWindow Overview

The NSWindow class is a subclass of NSResponder and extends the capabilities of responders to provide an area of the display for drawing as well as aid event dispatching. In Cocoa applications, every window onscreen is an instance of the NSWindow class or one of its subclasses such as NSPanel. A window is needed to display the output from an application on the display.

Windows are composed of three major parts: an optional title bar, the content view, and an optional resize control. Figure 8.4 indicates the parts of a window. The title bar might contain a title and controls to minimize, maximize, or close the window. The window automatically manages these controls. The application can be notified when one of the controls is activated, but the controls are not directly accessible from within a Cocoa application. The resize control is also managed automatically by the window itself. Every window has a content view. The content view is the portion of a window that is controlled by code unique to each application.

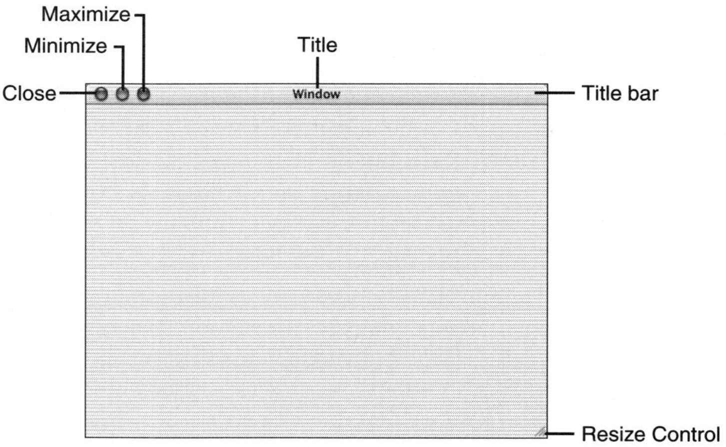

FIGURE 8.4 Windows are composed of an optional title bar, an optional resize control, and a content view.

Windows have a position and size onscreen. The position that is stored is the lower-left corner of the window, and it is stored as integer coordinates corresponding to pixels on the display. The size is stored as the integer width and height of the window in pixels.

Windows uses the `NSApplication` object's connection to the operating system to draw onscreen. The pixels drawn by a window are stored in memory that can be shared by the operating system and the window. Because the operating system has direct access to the memory, the operating system can move and uncover windows without intervention by the application that owns the window. For example, a window can be dragged while the application that owns it is busy performing other computations. The shared memory is also used by the operating system to implement transparency effects.

Backing Store

The shared memory is called the backing store for the window. The Application Kit supports three different configurations for backing store: buffered, retained, and nonretained.

Buffered backing store is the default. With buffered backing store, all pixels of the window are stored once in a buffer drawn by the window and again in a separate buffer used by the operating system. The pixels drawn by the window are copied or "flushed" into the buffer used by the operating system automatically. This style of buffering is often called double buffering because two separate buffers are used. Buffered windows provide the best presentation to users. Users do not see any partial drawing or delayed updates because the pixels of a window are not displayed until the window has been completely redrawn. The disadvantage of buffered windows is that they require memory to store two buffers.

Retained backing store uses one buffer to store the visible pixels of a window and a separate buffer to store pixels that are offscreen or obscured by other windows. Retained backing store uses less memory than buffered backing store because each pixel is only stored in one buffer. When a window is moved to reveal pixels that were formerly obscured, the operating system can transfer the pixel data from one buffer to the other without intervention by the application that owns the window. However, partial drawing of the portions of a window that are visible onscreen may be seen by users. Retained backing store is a compromise between memory usage and the quality of presentation to users.

Nonretained backing store uses only one buffer. Pixels that are not visible are just discarded. Nonretained backing store uses the least memory and provides the worst presentation to users. Each time the window is redrawn, users see partial drawing. If an area of the window that was obscured becomes visible, the application that owns the window must be alerted to redraw the newly visible pixels. If the application is busy with other computations and is not multithreaded, the user might see delays between when the window is uncovered and when it is redrawn. Use of nonretained backing store is discouraged.

NOTE

In many versions of Mac OS X, including version 10.1, only buffered backing store is supported. Apple might restore support for other backing store types in future releases.

The backing-store type for each window can be set in Interface Builder or programmatically. The backing store type is set when a window is initialized and via `NSWindow`'s `-setBackingType:` method.

Key Window and Main Window

The `NSApplication` class manages all the windows in an application. In addition to a list of all the application's windows, `NSApplication` also keeps track of which window, if any, is the key window and which is the main window. The key window and the main window are the windows in which the user is currently working. The key window receives keyboard events. The main window is the window that is effected by actions in the key window. The key window and the main window are usually the same, but in some cases they might be different. Figure 8.5 shows a typical situation in which the key window and the main window are different. In Figure 8.5, the Find panel is the key window because keyboard events are only sent to the key window and the user must be able to type the string to find into the Find panel's text field. The README.rtf window is the main window and contains the text that is searched. The user's actions in the Find panel are applied to the contents of the main window. The Untitled window is neither key nor main.

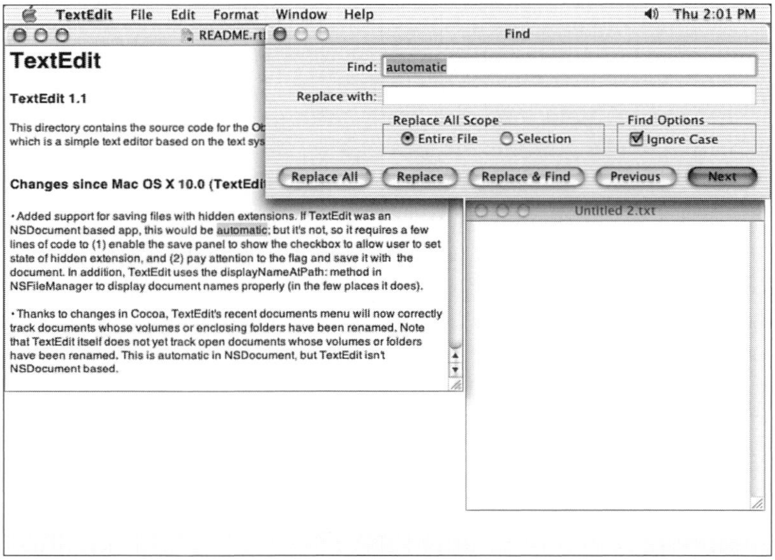

FIGURE 8.5 An application with separate key and main windows as well as a window that is neither key nor main.

The key window and main window have opaque window title bars. All other windows have translucent title bars. The key window is the only window to which keyboard events are sent.

Windows become the key window and main window automatically as the result of the user actions. If the main window and key window are different, the main window becomes key if the current key window is closed or minimized. In most cases, the user can make a window become the key by clicking the mouse within the window. Application developers can prevent a window from becoming the key window by subclassing `NSWindow` and overriding `NSWindow`'s `-canBecomeKeyWindow` method to always return `NO`. However, `NSWindow` is seldom subclassed for this purpose because the `NSPanel` class already provides the desired behavior when configured as a utility window in Interface Builder. A window can also be made the key or main window by calling `NSWindow`'s `-makeKeyWindow` or `-makeMainWindow` methods, respectively. The `-makeKeyAndOrderFront:` method is available to make a window the front-most or top-most window, and also the key window in one operation.

Windows in the Responder Chain

NSWindow is a subclass of NSResponder and can be part of a responder chain. The role that a window plays in the responder chain depends on the state of the application that owns the window. Windows are also integral to event distribution. Most events received by the application are sent on to a window. NSApplication selects the window to receive an event based on the type of the event.

Events outside the window's content view are handled automatically by the window. No programmer intervention is required to resize windows or manage the controls in the window's title bar. The NSWindow class handles all those details automatically and notifies the application of any changes so that the application can perform operations such as constraining the window's size or saving the contents of the window before it closes.

Mouse-down and mouse-move events are sent from the application object to the top-most window under the mouse pointer. The NSWindow class then distributes received mouse events to a responder within the window, or consumes the events itself. Mouse-up and mouse-drag events are sent to the window that received the corresponding mouse-down event. The window sends the mouse-up and mouse-drag events on to the same responder that received the mouse-down event. Keyboard events are sent to the first responder in the key window

NSView Overview

The NSView class extends the event-handling capabilities of NSResponder to enable drawing and printing. NSView is an abstract class meaning that instances of NSView are seldom used directly. Instead, many subclasses of NSView exist to implement particular combinations of event handling and drawing behavior. Almost everything drawn in a Cocoa application is drawn by a subclass of NSView. For example, buttons, text fields, sliders, and even the backgrounds of windows are directly or indirectly subclasses of NSView. The most prominent subclasses of NSView include NSControl, NSText, NSTabView, NSSplitView, NSScrollView, and NSBox.

The NSView class cannot draw without the help of a window. When a view is drawn, it writes the data for pixels into memory. A window is needed to provide the memory that stores the pixel data. NSWindow and NSView cooperate to implement user interfaces. Every NSWindow instance has at least one associated NSView instance called the content view. The content view is used to draw the content of the window.

View Hierarchy

Views exist in a hierarchy. A view can contain any number of subviews. Views are normally added to the content of a window by making them subviews of the window's content view. Each view has a reference to the view that contains it. The reference to the containing view is called the superview. Complex user interfaces are composed of many views arranged in a hierarchy of superviews and subviews. Figure 8.6 shows a representative user interface composed of a window, the window's content view, and subviews within the content view. The hierarchy of nested views in the window on the right is shown on the left.

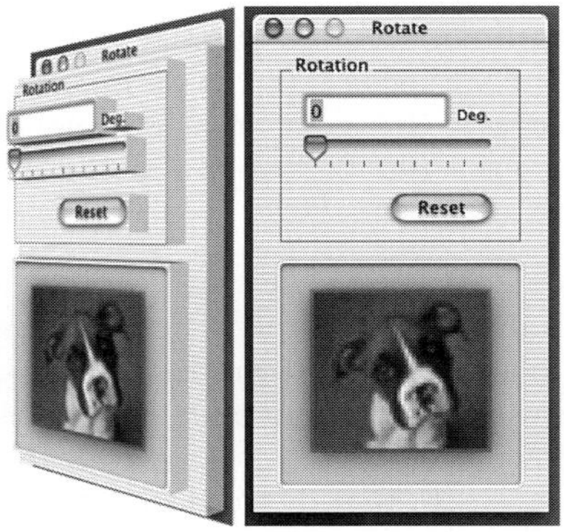

FIGURE 8.6 Views exist in a hierarchy in which views contain subviews.

Subviews are always drawn after their superview resulting in subviews always appearing on top of their superview graphically. Views clip their subviews so that no part of a subview can be drawn outside its superview. The order in which views with the same superview are drawn is not defined. As a result, sibling views should not be overlapped. If they are overlapped, changes in drawing order could result in incorrect display.

Each view can have its own coordinate system. By default, a window's content view has its origin in the lower-left corner, and has a width and height equal to the width and height of the window's content area in pixels. The positive-X axis is to the right, and the positive-Y axis is up. Views store two rectangles to define both the area of the view in its superview's coordinate system, and the area of the view in its own coordinate system. The area of a view in its superview coordinate system is called its frame. The same area stored in the view's coordinate system is called the bounds. Figure 8.7 depicts the relationship between a view's frame and its bounds.

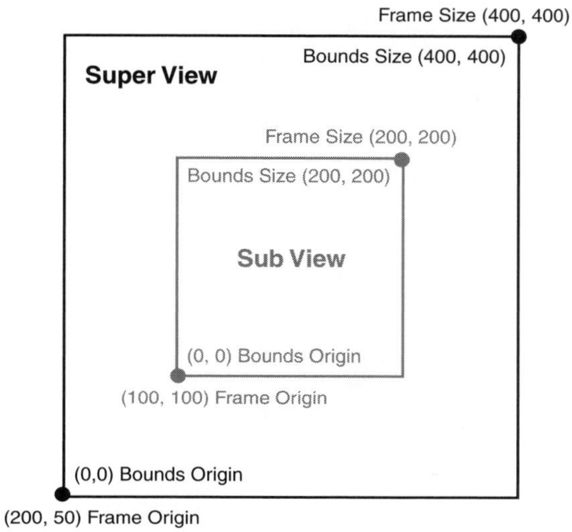

FIGURE 8.7 A view's frame is stored in its superview's coordinate system, and its bounds are stored in its coordinate system.

The view's frame, its bounds, and a transformation matrix define the coordinate system used by a view. The coordinate systems used by views are described in detail in Chapter 13, "Custom Views and Graphics Part II."

Views in the Responder Chain

As a subclass of `NSResponder`, `NSView` instances participate in the responder chain. Most responders in an application are actually subclasses of `NSView`. The next responder of a view is usually the view's superview. Arbitrary responders can be added to the responder chain by calling `NSResponder`'s `-setNextResponder:` method, and that technique can be used to insert responders in the responder chain between a view and its superview. If an event-processing message is sent to a view that does not handle the message, the message is sent to the view's next responder and its next and so on until the window's content view, the ultimate superview of all views in a window, receives the message. Figure 8.8 shows a view hierarchy in which a text field is the first responder. The responder chain, up to the window object, is depicted with arrows.

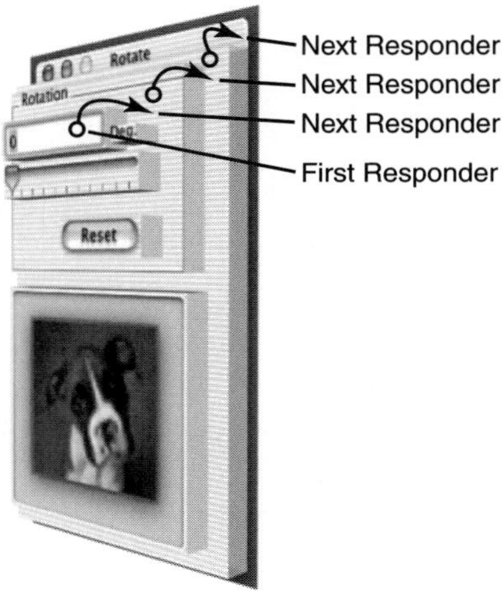

FIGURE 8.8 A responder chain consisting of views within a window is depicted.

The first view to receive an event-processing message depends on the type of the event. The first mouse-down event within a window that is not the key window is usually consumed by the window itself to make the window into the key window and bring it to the front. This behavior can be modified in several ways. For example, a subclass of `NSView` can override the `-acceptsFirstMouse:` method to return `YES`, meaning that it uses the first mouse click in an inactive window.

`NSWindow` sends mouse-down and mouse-move event messages to the top-most view under the mouse. Subviews are drawn after their superview. The top-most view under the mouse is, therefore, usually the most deeply nested view under the mouse. Mouse-move events occur frequently and are seldom used. `NSWindow` does not send mouse move event messages to views by default. If a subclass of `NSView` needs to receive mouse-move events, it must tell `NSWindow` to send them. `NSWindow`'s `-setAcceptsMouseMovedEvents:` method is used to tell the window to send mouse-move event messages to views. Mouse-drag and mouse-up event messages are sent to the view that received the corresponding mouse-down event. Keyboard event messages are sent to the first responder within the window.

The `NSView` class implements the `-acceptsFirstResponder` method to always return `NO`. As a result, most views never become the first responder within a window. Subclasses of `NSView` that implement text processing or allow the user to make selections usually override the `-acceptsFirstResponder` method to return `YES`. If a view accepts becoming the first responder, the first mouse-down event within the view automatically makes that view the first responder, unless the current first responder refuses to resign its status.

Details of handling events in subclasses of NSView are provided in Chapter 15, "Events and Cursors." The information presented here is just an overview to describe the roles of views in the Application Kit. Applications often include one or more custom subclasses of NSView. The NSApplication, NSWindow, and NSView classes cooperate and form the core of the Application Kit architecture. A detailed understanding of NSView and its relationships with other classes is needed to unleash the power of Cocoa.

Delegates

Delegates and delegate methods are used throughout the Application Kit. Delegates provide an alternative to subclassing when the behavior of classes must be refined to meet an application's needs. Application Kit classes such as NSApplication, NSWindow, NSBrowser, and NSMatrix are seldom subclassed. Delegation enables all the customization that most applications need.

A delegate is an object that is able to influence the behavior of another object by responding to delegate messages. A class that uses a delegate has a delegate instance variable and defines a number of delegate methods. An instance of that class sends delegate messages to its delegate for help deciding how to behave. For example, the NSWindow class has a delegate and declares the -windowShouldClose: delegate method. Before a window closes, the window sends the -windowShouldClose: message to its delegate. If the delegate returns NO, the window does not close.

The object that acts as a window's delegate might implement -windowShouldClose: to determine if a document represented by the closing window has been edited, and if so give the user a chance to save the changes or cancel the close. If the user cancels the close then -windowShouldClose: returns NO, and the window does not close.

Delegates are not compulsory, nor do they have to implement all delegate methods that might be called. If a delegate has not been set for an instance of NSWindow, the window simply closes when the user clicks the Close button. If a delegate has been set, the window checks to see if the delegate implements the -windowShouldClose: method. If the delegate does not implement -windowShouldClose:, the message is not sent and the window closes. The default behavior of the window is changed only if the window has a delegate and the delegate implements the -windowShouldClose: method to return NO.

Delegates can be part of an extended version of the responder chain. The NSWindow and NSApplication classes give their delegates a chance to handle messages that are sent up the responder chain. This important use of delegates is described in this chapter as part of the Target-Action paradigm.

Delegates can often be set within Interface Builder. Most classes that can have a delegate also provide a `-setDelegate:` method. Delegate messages are documented at the end of the online class documentation for each class that can have a delegate. Before attempting to subclass an Application Kit object, make sure that the desired behavior cannot be achieved with a delegate. Using a delegate is almost always preferred over subclassing.

Delegation Versus Notifications

Delegation is a powerful and dynamic feature of Cocoa. Delegation and notifications as described in Chapter 7, "The Foundation Framework Overview," are closely related. In fact, many delegate methods accept a notification as an argument. Delegate messages and notifications share many of the same benefits. Both decouple the sender of a message from the receiver. Objects know very little about their delegates. The determination of the messages that a delegate understands is made at runtime, just before the messages are sent.

The principal difference between a delegate and the receiver of notifications is that the delegate can affect behavior that the receiver of notifications can only observe. Delegate messages are sent directly to one object. Notifications are sent to a notification center that forwards the messages to any number of observers. The return value, if any, from a method that handles a notification is ignored. The returned values from methods that handle delegate messages can often modify the sender's behavior.

Methods that handle notifications accept exactly one argument, and that argument is a notification object. Delegate methods can have any number and type of arguments. Notifications are inherently slower than delegate messages. Delegate messages take direct advantage of the Objective-C runtime for fast dispatch. Notifications are processed through a hash table to determine which objects should be notified in any given situation.

Specialization of Behavior and Coupling

One of the lauded virtues of object-oriented software design is the potential for code reuse through specialization. The idea is that when a programmer tries to solve a new problem she can start from an existing solution to a similar problem and "specialize" that solution to solve the new one. Reusing all or part of someone else's work is better than starting from scratch each time, and the capability to "specialize" facilitates code reuse.

The most-common technique for specializing and achieving code reuse is subclassing of existing classes. Subclassing is arguably the most powerful and flexible way to specialize behavior. Subclassing enables a programmer to directly modify practically any detail of the behavior of the superclass. The code that is written in the subclass can be tightly integrated with the superclass implementation. Often that tight integration is necessary or desirable. Sometimes, however, loose integration and a loose coupling are better. Although subclassing is a powerful reuse tool, it is ironic that subclassing can also increase one of the most common obstacles to reuse, namely the unnecessarily tight coupling of code.

Delegation enables the specialization of a class without subclassing. The primary advantages of delegation over subclassing are loose coupling and code partitioning (modularization). The primary disadvantage of delegation is the sacrifice of some flexibility and power. The following illustrates loose coupling.

In a multidocument application that displays Web pages, each page is represented onscreen as a `NSWindow` instance that contains objects for displaying Web content. If the last open window is closed, the user should be asked if the current Internet connection should be closed. This can be handled by creating a class that implements the `-windowWillClose:` delegate method, and using an instance of that class as the delegate for each document window. `NSWindow` sends the `-windowWillClose:` message to its delegate just before closing. The delegate can determine if the last window is being closed, ask the user if the Internet connection should be closed, and close the connection if the user agrees.

The use of delegation in the example provides loose coupling in the following ways. Knowing if the window that is closing is the last window requires knowledge of (coupling with) all other open document windows. Knowing how to close an Internet connection requires coupling with that subsystem. If the behavior is implemented by subclassing `NSWindow` rather than using a delegate, the subclass is coupled to all other document windows and the Internet-connection subsystem. With delegation, a class that already knows about Internet connections can be used as the delegate of the windows. With delegation, the `NSWindow` class does not need to be extended to know about the Internet connection closing, and the class for managing Internet connections does not have to know anything about the `NSWindow` class. It just has to respond to the `-windowWillClose:` method.

The example also illustrates code partitioning. In the typical Model-View-Controller partitioning, the `NSWindow` that represents Web documents is clearly part of the View subsystem. The class that manages Internet connections is probably part of either the Model or the Controller partitions. Extending the `NSWindow` class via subclassing creates a class that is part of the View subsystem by virtue of being a window and simultaneously part of the Model subsystem because it manages Internet connections. In most cases, an object that acts as a delegate is part of the controller layer, acting as intermediary between the model and the view. The Model-View-Controller system is described in Chapter 6, and in Chapter 26, "Application Requirements, Design, and Documentation."

Delegation Versus Multiple Inheritance

Multiple implementation inheritance is not supported by Objective-C. Delegation can eliminate one of the common arguments in favor of multiple inheritance. Consider a subclass of `NSTextView` called `MYSquiggleTextView` for drawing squiggles under words, and a class called `MYSpeller` that can check the spelling of a word. Using multiple inheritance, a text view that draws squiggles under misspelled words can be created by inheriting from both `MYSquiggleTextView` and `MYSpeller`. Alternatively, an instance of `MYSpeller` can be attached to an instance of `MYSquiggleTextView` as a delegate.

Using a delegate is a more powerful and flexible technique than the proposed multiple inheritance. Subclassing requires a high degree of coupling. The delegate is loosely coupled enabling the optional use of a `MYEmphasiseTechnicalWords` instance as a delegate without any change to the `MYSquiggleTextView` class. There is no need to create one subclass of `MYSquiggleTextView` just for technical-word emphasis and another just for spelling emphasis. A user interface can even be provided so users can dynamically change the reason for drawing squiggles.

Delegation results in sufficiently loose coupling that many instances of `MYSquiggleTextView` can be specialized in different ways simply by having a different delegate. If `MYSquiggleTextView` is subclassed in the future, the changes need not affect either the `MYSpeller` or the `MYEmphasiseTechnicalWords` classes. The classes can all change independently.

Delegation avoids a tendency toward combinatorial classes. Consider `MYSquiggleTextView` mixed with `MYScientificSpeller` and `MYSquiggleTextView` mixed with `TheOtherGuysLegalSpeller`. Similarly, mix `MYSpeller` with an ordinary `NSTextView`, `MYStraightUnderlineTextView`, or some other class. If the only technique available is subclassing, there will be an awful lot of classes after a while.

Limitations of Delegation

The biggest limitation of delegation is that it is only possible if the need for specialization has been anticipated. The developers at NeXT and Apple were able to anticipate that programmers would want to do something special when a window is closed. They provided the `-windowWillClose:` delegate method and many others. Had they not anticipated the need, there would probably be no alternative but to subclass `NSWindow`. There are limits to the extent a delegate method can change the behavior of a class. A subclass is free to change anything.

Delegation and notification are two techniques pervasive in the Cocoa frameworks. Both offer alternatives to subclassing, but operate at the level of instances rather than of classes. Delegation typically allows one object to effect the behavior of another. Notification serves as a mechanism for informing an arbitrary number of observers of the actions of another. Delegation provides a means of specializing behavior without subclassing, and therefore allows loose coupling between objects. This facilitates object reuse, and sidesteps one of the common reasons for multiple inheritance.

Target-Action Paradigm

One of the most powerful features of the Application Kit is its use of the target-action paradigm. Objective-C messages that have one object argument are called actions. The one argument is usually the sender of the action message. A target is an object that can receive action messages. Targets and actions can be defined programmatically or in Interface Builder. The target-action paradigm is a key mechanism with which user interface elements respond to user actions. The target-action paradigm is implemented with four parts, the `NSControl` class, the `NSActionCell` class, the `NSApplication` class, and the responder chain. User interface elements such as menu items, buttons, and text fields are implemented as subclasses of either `NSControl` or `NSActionCell`.

For example, buttons in a user interface are represented by instances of the `NSButton` class, which is a subclass of `NSControl`. `NSControl` is a subclass of `NSView` so that it inherits the capability to handle events as well as draw. When a user presses a button, the button sends its action message to its target object. Because both the target and action are variables, button instances can be very flexibly configured. A button can be configured to send the `-selectAll:` action message to a target object that displays editable text. Another button might be configured to send the `-deleteSelectedText:` action message to the same text object target.

One of the strengths of the target-action implementation in the Application Kit is that actions are sent as Objective-C messages using the standard Objective-C messaging system. Other user interface toolkits use integer event IDs along with large switch statements or tables of function pointers. Another approach used by other toolkits is to use specialized command classes that must be subclassed for each different command and receiver combination. The Objective-C runtime eliminates the need for extra code and tables. Even more importantly, the target-action system used by the Application Kit takes advantage of the responder chain to enable a tremendous amount of flexibility.

When a user interacts with a user interface element that is derived from the `NSControl` class or the `NSActionCell` class, the user interface element asks the shared `NSApplication` object to send an action to a target by calling `NSApplication`'s `-sendAction:to:from:` method. When an action is sent using `-sendAction:to:from:`, the `to:` argument is the target of the action and the `from:` argument is the object that is sending the action. The `-sendAction:to:from:` method sends the action message to the target passing the sender as the argument. The target of an action message can use the sender argument to obtain additional information. For example, when the user moves a slider, the slider sends an action message to its target with the slider itself as the argument. The receiver of the action message can ask for more information such as the current value of the slider.

The role of the shared `NSApplication` object in the target-action implementation is important. If the target of a user interface element is specified, the shared application object just sends the action message to the target directly. However, if no target is specified (the `to:` argument is `nil`), `-sendAction:to:from:` uses an expanded version of the responder chain to select the object that receives the action message. Setting the target of a user interface element to `nil` makes the target context sensitive.

If the `to:` argument to `-sendAction:to:from:` is `nil`, the method searches the responder chain for an object that can respond to the action message. The search begins with the first responder in the key window. If the first responder cannot respond to the action message, the next responder is checked and so on until the key window itself is reached. After the key window gets a chance, the key window's delegate is checked. If the key window's delegate cannot respond to the action message, and the main window is different from the key window, the first responder in the main window is checked. The search for an object that responds to the action continues up the main window's responder chain to the main window itself, and then the main window's delegate. If no target has been found, the application object is tried. Finally, if the application object cannot respond to the action, the application object's delegate is given a chance. Figure 8.9 enumerates the order of the search for the target of an action message sent to `nil`.

NOTE

When the target of a user interface element is set to the First Responder in Interface Builder, the target is actually set to `nil`, so that the expanded responder chain is used to select the target at runtime.

The responder chain enables flexible, dynamic message processing that is context sensitive in conjunction with the target-action paradigm. For example, the target of a `-copy:` action sent from a menu item depends on the current first responder. If the first responder in the key window is an editable text object with selected text, pressing the Copy menu item places the selected text on the application's pasteboard. If the first responder has selected graphics, the graphics are placed on the pasteboard. The result of pressing the Copy menu item depends on the user's current selection identified by the first responder.

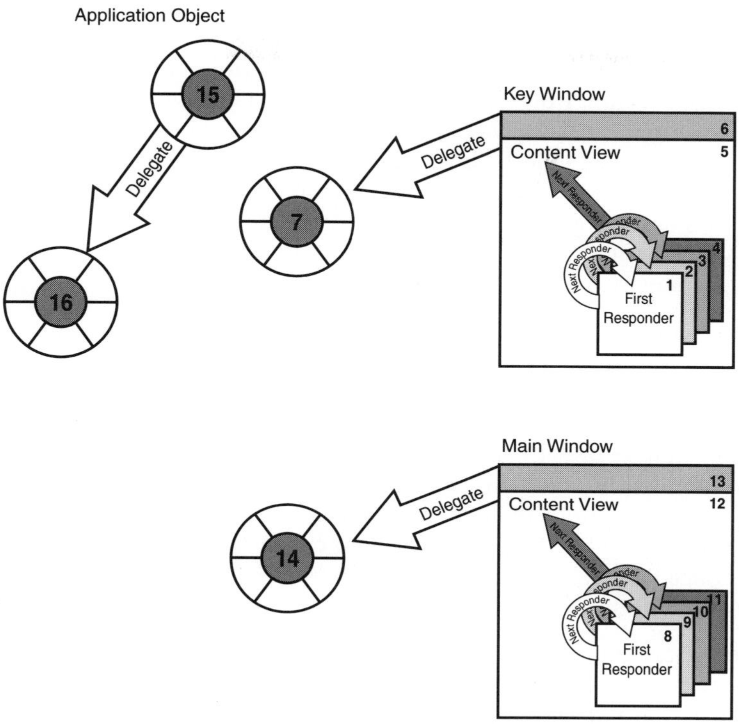

FIGURE 8.9 The extended responder chain is searched in the indicated order for the target of actions sent to `nil`.

The EventMonitor.app application described in Chapter 15, "Events and Cursors," and provided at `www.cocoaprogramming.net` demonstrates the responder chain.

Archived Objects and Nibs

The encoding and decoding of objects is briefly described in Chapter 5, as one of the conventions used by the Cocoa frameworks. Most objects defined in Apple's frameworks can be encoded and decoded whether they are nongraphical objects from the Foundation framework, or graphical objects like windows and buttons from the Application Kit. Encoding and decoding are frequently used to implement copy-and-paste operations, drag-and-drop operations, and distributed-object messaging. When interconnected objects are encoded as data into a block of memory or a file, the data is called an archive. One key to using the Application Kit effectively is the knowledge that user interface elements and their interconnections can be stored in just such an archive.

The objects stored in an archive are conceptually freeze dried. A freeze-dried object is an actual software object including data and code. It was running in memory at one time, but is now in cold storage. It can be decoded from an archive and revived, so that it begins running from right where it left off at the time it was frozen. In fact, when a user interface is designed in Interface Builder, the file that is saved is an archive of freeze-dried objects. Interface Builder names files that contain such archives with the extension `.nib`. Nib originally stood for Next Interface Builder, but the term has become generic and now just refers to an archive of user interface objects. When an application loads a `.nib` file, the objects are decoded to the same state they where in when encoded.

Most object-oriented environments include a visual tool for laying out user interfaces. Such tools usually generate code and resources, which much be edited and compiled. Cocoa's Interface Builder generates freeze-dried objects instead of code. This is an important distinction. Generating code is a static approach, whereas the freeze-dried objects present a dynamic solution. The static solution mimics the dynamic solution, but lacks much of its underlying power. Freeze dried objects retain all their interconnections including delegates, targets, actions, superviews, current displayed values, and so on. It is possible to create nontrivial applications entirely with Interface Builder, and run them in Interface Builder's Test Interface mode without ever compiling.

Interface Builder could have been called Object Connector because in addition to positioning and sizing graphical objects, Interface Builder enables the interconnection of objects. Interface Builder is not limited to editing the objects that Apple provides with Cocoa. New objects can be edited and connected within Interface Builder with varying degrees of sophistication. Any object can be instantiated and have outlets and actions that are set within Interface Builder. New Interface Builder palettes can be created to enable more complex editing and configuration as well.

It is possible to write Cocoa applications without using Interface Builder or any `.nib` files, but loading `.nib` files is so convenient and powerful that almost every application uses them. Unless the programmer intervenes, Cocoa applications automatically load a main nib file when launched. The main nib file contains the objects that define the application's menu bar. The main nib file for an application can be set in Project Builder's Application Settings tab.

Nib Awaking

A problem can arise when objects that have been encoded into a `.nib` file are decoded. As an object is decoded, it might need to access a reference to an object that has not yet been decoded. How does an object know when during decoding it is safe to access the objects to which it is connected? The answer is the `-awakeFromNib` method.

When objects are decoded from a `.nib` file, the Application Kit automatically sends the `-awakeFromNib` message to every decoded object that can respond to it. The `-awakeFromNib` message is only called after all the objects in the archive have been loaded and initialized. When an object receives an `-awakeFromNib` message, it's guaranteed to have all its outlet instance variables set. The `-awakeFromNib` message is also sent to objects when Interface Builder enters Test Interface mode because Interface Builder actually copies the interface before it is run. Interface Builder encodes objects into a nib archive in memory, and then immediately decodes them to create a fully functional copy, ready to test.

Implement `-awakeFromNib` to perform any initialization that needs to occur after all an object's outlets have been reconnected after decoding from a `.nib`.

`.nib` files can be loaded into an application multiple times to create multiple copies of the objects within the `.nib`. The multidocument architecture described in this chapter loads the `.nibs` that define document windows as many times as needed to create as many documents as needed.

The File's Owner

When direct communication between objects within a `.nib` and objects outside the `.nib` is required, the `.nib` file's owner provides that communication. The file's owner represents an object that is not in the `.nib` file. Figure 8.10 shows the Interface Builder icon that represents the file's owner of the nib being edited. Connections to the outlets and actions of the file's owner can be set in Interface Builder, but the actual object that is used as the file's owner is only specified when the `.nib` is loaded.

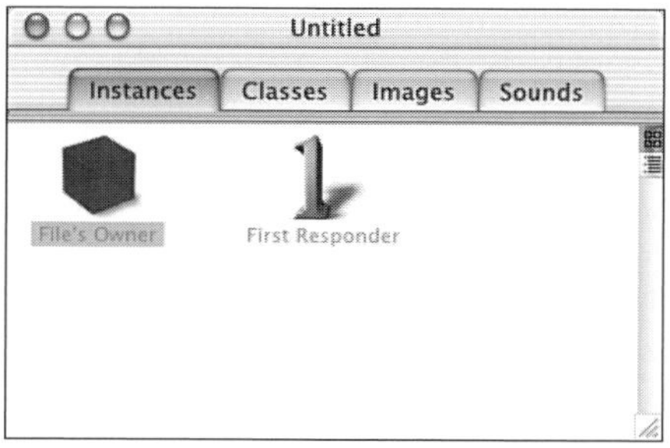

FIGURE 8.10 Interface Builder uses an icon labeled File's Owner as a placeholder for an object that is not in the `.nib`.

In many cases, direct connections between objects can be avoided by using notifications and the responder chain. For example, an object decoded from a `.nib` can register to receive notifications from within its `-awakeFromNib` implementation. Objects can also send notifications to anonymous receivers or to the current first responder. Objects within a .nib can use the shared NSApplication instance in every application by referring to the NSApp global variable or calling [NSApplication sharedApplication].

.nibs are explicitly loaded into an application by calling the -loadNibNamed:owner: method declared in a category of the NSBundle class. The category is part of the Application Kit. As a result, .nibs cannot be loaded by programs that do not link to the Application Kit, even if the .nib that is loaded does not contain any objects that depend on the Application Kit.

The owner argument to -loadNibNamed:owner: is the object that is used as the file's owner for the nib. Any connections made to the file's owner within the .nib are made to the owner, specified when the .nib is loaded. Connections that cannot be made because of inconsistencies between the owner used when the .nib is loaded and the outlets and actions specified for the file's owner when the .nib was created are discarded. The -awakeFromNib method is also sent to the file's owner specified with -loadNibNamed:owner:. The file's owner is not technically part of the .nib, but a .nib's owner can implement -awakeFromNib to perform any logic needed after a nib has been loaded. If several .nibs are loaded using the same owner, that owner's -awakeFromNib method is called multiple times.

The application's main .nib is loaded automatically by the NSApplication object when the application is launched. The NSApplication object itself is the file's owner of the main .nib.

NSWindowController Overview

The NSWindowController class is often used as the file's owner when loading a .nib containing the definition of a window. The NSWindowController class can be used to customize a window's title, preserve the window's position and size in the user's defaults database, cascade windows onscreen, and manage the window's memory when the window is closed. Unlike NSApplication, NSWindow, and NSView, the NSWindowController class is not a core part of the Application Kit architecture. NSWindowController is provided as a convenience to help implement a common feature of applications, the dynamic loading of windows from nibs and their subsequent management.

NSWindowController can be used to manage windows that are created programmatically as well as windows loaded from .nibs. The NSWindowController class can be used along with other classes to implement flexible multidocument support in applications. NSWindowController is not used in every Application Kit-based application, but it is available for use when appropriate and can eliminate lines of code that would otherwise be repeated in many applications.

NSWindowController can be subclassed to manage complex documents in an application. Custom subclasses of NSWindowController are a handy place to implement logic that ties the documents of an application to the application itself, particularly if other dedicated multidocument support classes are not used. The NSWindowController class is usually part of the Controller in the common Model-View-Controller application architecture as described in Chapter 6.

Multidocument Applications

Applications that enable users to open and manipulate multiple documents simultaneously are very common. Examples of multidocument applications include word processors, spreadsheets, and drawing programs. Because multidocument applications are so common, the Application Kit contains classes that automate most of the work needed to manage multiple documents simultaneously.

The following five classes interoperate to aid in the implementation of multidocument applications: NSApplication, NSDocumentController, NSDocument, NSWindowController, and NSFileWrapper. Every application contains an instance of NSApplication, but the other classes are strictly optional. NSDocumentController, NSDocument, NSWindowController, and NSFileWrapper are powerful classes that implement code that would otherwise be duplicated in many applications. Figure 8.11 shows the relationships between these classes used in a complex multidocument application.

Apple's documentation on the Application Kit's multidocument support is excellent and comprehensive. An overview of multidocument application design using the provided classes is provided in online documentation at http://developer.apple.com/techpubs/macosx/Cocoa/TasksAndConcepts/ProgrammingTopics/AppArchitecture/. The TextEdit.app sample application that is distributed with Apple's Cocoa developer tools is an example of a multidocument application that does not use the multidocument-support classes. The Sketch.app sample does use the built-in multidocument support. Examining TextEdit.app's source code and comparing it to Sketch.app is a good way to contrast the different approaches to multidocument support.

As a general rule, the built-in classes save a lot of work and ensure a high degree of compatibility and consistency with other applications. Using the NSDocument and NSDocumentController classes can also simplify the implementation of scripting and undo features in applications.

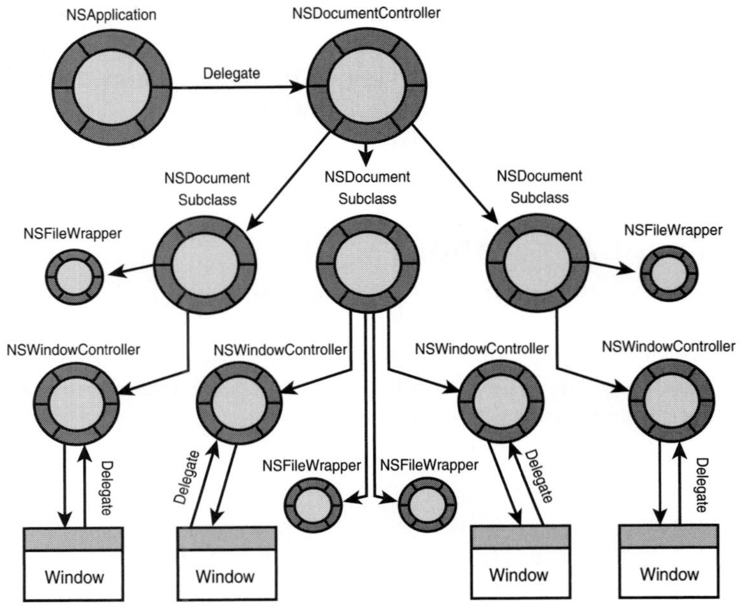

FIGURE 8.11 The `NSApplication`, `NSDocumentController`, `NSDocument`, `NSWindowController`, and `NSFileWrapper` classes interoperate to implement multidocument applications.

`NSApplication` Support

A certain amount of support for multidocument applications is built into the `NSApplication` class. `NSApplication` provides delegate methods that enable customization of standard application behaviors regarding multiple documents. For example, Mac OS X applications that support multiple documents are expected to open a new untitled document under some circumstances. The `-applicationShouldOpenUntitledFile:` delegate method can be implemented in an application object's delegate to control that behavior. The following delegate methods are provided to enable the application object's delegate to control multi-document behavior without using the built-in multidocument support classes:

```
-(BOOL)application:(NSApplication *)anApp
    openFile:(NSString *)filename

-(BOOL)application:(NSApplication *)anApp
    openFileWithoutUI:(NSString *)filename
```

```
-(BOOL)application:(NSApplication *)anApp
    openTempFile:(NSString *)filename

-(BOOL)application:(NSApplication *)anApp
    printFile:(NSString *)filename

-(BOOL)applicationOpenUntitledFile:(NSApplication *)anApp

-(BOOL)applicationShouldHandleReopen:(NSApplication *)anApp
    hasVisibleWindows:(BOOL)flag

-(BOOL)applicationShouldOpenUntitledFile:(NSApplication *)anApp

-(NSApplicationTerminateReply)applicationShouldTerminate:(NSApplication
*)anApp

-(BOOL)applicationShouldTerminateAfterLastWindowClosed:(NSApplication
*)anApp
```

The `NSApplication` class implements most of the standard behaviors expected of multidocument classes without intervention by its delegate. The delegate methods should only be used when there is a need to deviate from the standard behaviors. If the Application Kit's classes for supporting multidocument applications are used, the delegate methods are almost certainly unnecessary

`NSDocumentController` Overview

`NSDocumentController` class assists with the creation of new documents and opening existing documents. It also plays a role in saving, printing, and closing documents. There should be at most an instance of `NSDocumentController` in any application. The use of `NSDocumentController` is optional, but it provides many of the features of multidocument applications that must be tediously hand coded if it is not used.

When the multidocument application is created with Project Builder and Interface Builder, an instance of `NSDocumentController` is automatically created and added to the application's responder chain. Standard menu items such as New and Open in the File menu send actions to the first responder. The actions travel up the responder chain until handled. `NSDocumentController` handles many standard document-related actions including the actions sent by default from the New and Open menu items. If no object preceding the document controller in the responder chain handles such actions then the document controller will.

`NSDocumentController` handles the actions sent from the New menu item by creating a new instance of a `NSDocument` subclass and initializing it with the `-init` method. The subclass that is instantiated can be set within Project Builder by selecting the Edit Active Target menu item in the Project menu. Project Builder displays various properties of the current target including its Application Settings. Within the Application Settings tab, type the name of a `NSDocument` subclass into the Document Class field.

When `NSDocumentController` receives the action to open an existing document, it displays the Open panel, gets the user's selection, creates a new instance of a subclass of `NSDocument` as appropriate, and initializes the new document object by calling `-initWithContentsOfFile:ofType:`. The subclass of `NSDocument` that is instantiated might depend on the type of file being opened. The associations between file types and `NSDocument` subclasses are made in Project Builder's Application Settings tab.

Values entered via Project Builder's Application Settings interface are stored in a human-readable text file named project.pbxproj within the *.pbproj directory created by Project Builder for each project. When an application is built by Project Builder, a file named Info.plist is created based on the project's application settings and stored in the *.app directory which contains the resulting application executable. Both can be edited in any text editor if some care is taken to preserve the formatting.

NOTE

*.pbproj and *.app directories as well as many others are depicted as individual files in Apple's Finder. The contents of these folders can be revealed by selecting the Show Package Contents option of Finder's contextual menu. The contextual menu is shown if the Control key is held down when clicking on the folder.

`NSDocumentController` is rarely subclassed. It is included in the responder chain for action messages automatically if it is included in an application. `NSDocumentController` also registers for and receives notifications that are sent when documents might be affected by system events. For example, `NSDocumentController` responds when an application is notified that the system is shutting down so that unsaved documents can be saved. `NSDocumentController` does not do anything that cannot be done by other classes. In particular, the application's delegate can fill most of the roles of the document controller. If custom behavior not provided by `NSDocumentController` is needed, it is usually easier to create a custom class and use it as the application's delegate than it is to subclass `NSDocumentController`. A custom application delegate and `NSDocumentController` can both be used in the same application. `NSDocumentController` defers to the application delegate whenever both respond to the same delegate message or notification.

`NSDocument` Overview

`NSDocument` is an abstract class. Subclasses of `NSDocument` are used to encapsulate the data associated with documents. Subclasses of `NSDocument` can be used in multidocument applications and in other types of applications. A subclass of `NSDocument` is appropriate any time an application manipulates persistent data that is stored in the file system.

The `NSDocument` class provides methods that implement the standard actions sent by the Save, Save As, Print, Revert, and Close menu items and others. `NSDocument` handles most of the logic needed by all applications, such as showing the Save panel when the action message associated with the Save As menu item is received. The `NSDocument` class even provides partial support for undo, redo, and scripting features that can be expanded to meet the needs of particular applications. Subclasses inherit the standard behaviors and only have to override a handful of methods to enable application-specific data manipulation. Like with the `NSDocumentController` class and the `NSWindowController` class, using `NSDocument` is optional, but it provides standard behaviors that must be hand coded if it is not used.

A subclass of `NSDocument` is typically used in conjunction with one or more instances of `NSWindowController` to implement a user interface for documents. The `NSDocument` subclass stores the data that is represented by the document and has references to any window controllers associated with windows that display the data. The typical relationships between document controllers, documents, and window controllers are shown in Figure 8.11. Although the relationships might seem complex, each class has a narrowly defined role. They cooperate to provide a complete solution for document management and presentation.

Unlike `NSApplication`, `NSDocumentController`, and `NSWindowController`, `NSDocument` must be subclassed to be used in an application. The details of subclassing `NSDocument` and using the Application Kit's multidocument support classes are provide in Apple's documentation that comes with the developer tools. Several examples in this book use the multidocument classes, but the emphasis is unleashing the power of advanced features. The multidocument classes are presented as part of the infrastructure used to delve into more advanced topics. Detailed introductory tutorials for creating document-based applications with Apple's developer tools are available on the Internet. One good tutorial is at `www.stepwise.com/Articles/VermontRecipes/index.html`. The interoperation of the multidocument classes might seem complex or mysterious at first, but in reality they provide straightforward implementations that can be readily replicated as shown by the TextEdit.app sample application that comes with the developer tools. Working with the multidocument classes might be the first task when coding a new Cocoa application, but the task is highly automated by the tools and consumes a tiny fraction of the time invested in coding.

NSFileWrapper Overview

One additional class that aids the implementation of multidocument applications is NSFileWrapper. The NSDocument class is used to encapsulate the data stored by a document and the relationship between that data and its graphical presentation in one or more windows. The NSFileWrapper class is often used within the implementation of a NSDocument subclass. NSFileWrapper encapsulates the relationship between the data stored by a document and that data's representation in a file system. For example, many applications store the data for one document within many related files in a directory called a package. The package and all contained files appear to be a single file to users.

The use of packages provides a way for developers to store document data in the number of files and formats that is most convenient without inadvertently increasing the user's perception of complexity. Packages provide multiple-streams of data for one document and are conceptually similar to HFS resource forks. Packages can contain any number of different files and even other packages. One reason to use a package to store document data is so that document settings for page size and margins might be stored in one file, and document content in another. For example, in an application that displays standard image data formats, the standard format image data can be stored separately from application-specific data. To the user, the whole package appears to be a single file that can be copied and moved as a unit.

Undo and Redo

The Application Kit includes a powerful and flexible system to implement undo and redo operations by taking advantage of the Objective-C runtime to record the messages sent to objects and play them back later. Many Application Kit classes including the text management views already implement undo and redo.

Each instance of the NSDocument class optionally includes an instance of NSUndoManager. The NSUndoManager class stores recorded messages and works with the standard Undo and Redo menu items. NSUndoManager is actually part of the Foundation framework because nongraphical applications might include undoable operations. The NSUndoManager class can be used without the NSDocument class and visa versa, but using them together automatically provides several benefits. Each document can have its own list of undoable and redoable operations. The NSDocument class can use the undo manager to provide information about the state of the document, such as whether there have been any unsaved changes made before a document is closed.

NSUndoManager uses instances of the NSInvocation class to store Objective-C messages and their arguments. By default, all the messages that are stored in an undo manager, within one iteration of the run loop, are grouped into a single undoable operation. This is a sensible policy because all the messages that result from a single user action should be undoable by a single user action. Redo is automatically supported whenever an operation is undone. Just as messages for undo are recorded when an operation is originally performed, undoing the operation records messages that enable redo. Redo is essentially implemented as undoing undo.

Menu Validation

The Application Kit implements menus with the `NSMenu` class. After each user event, visible menu items are automatically validated. By default, a menu item is valid, and therefore enabled, if its target can respond to its action. If no object that responds to the menu item's action is found, the menu item is invalid and disabled.

When the target for a menu item is a specific object, default validation is simple. The target either responds to the action or it does not. When the target of a menu item is `nil` the expanded responder chain is searched to validate the menu item. If any object in the expanded responder chain responds to the action the menu item is valid. Otherwise, it is invalid.

The default validation can be enhanced by implementing the `-validateMenuItem:` method in object within the responder chain. When `NSMenu` has found an object that responds to a menu item's action, an additional check is made to determine if that object also implements `-validateMenuItem:`. If so, `NSMenu` calls `-validateMenuItem:` with the menu item being validated as the argument. If `-validateMenuItem:` returns `YES`, the menu item is the validated.

The `-validateMenuItem:` method enables fine control of a menu item's status. For example, a view in the responder chain might respond to the `-copy:` action message, but the Copy menu item should still be disabled if the view that contains no selection to be copied is the menu item's target. The view can implement `-validateMenuItem:` to return `YES` only if the user's selection within the view can be copied.

Automatic menu validation is disabled by calling `NSMenu`'s `-setAutoenamblesItems:` method. Menu items must be validated manually using the `-setEnabled:` method implemented by `NSMenuItem` if automatic validation is disabled. The `-setEnabled:` method should not be used in conjunction with automatic validation because the automatic validation might unpredictably reset any status set with `-setEnabled:`.

Spell Checking

The Application Kit contains support for spell checking of any selectable text. A single instance of the `NSSpellChecker` class provides access to system-wide, spell-checking services that can be used with the Application Kit's text objects. A standard panel for spell checking is also provided to let users select alternate spellings or add words to the system-wide dictionaries. Spelling in multiple languages is supported, but Mac OS X only ships with an American English dictionary. When additional dictionaries are added to a system, `NSSpellChecker` uses them automatically, based on user language preferences.

The text classes provided by the Application Kit already support spell checking, and a Spelling submenu is provided by default in every Application Kit based application. The menu items in the Spelling submenu send actions using the responder chain. The text classes already respond to the appropriate actions. The programmer must implement methods for the relevant action messages to enable spell checking in custom classes.

Enabling Spell Checking

The details of enabling spell checking in custom classes are provided here primarily to highlight another example of the way applications use dynamic features. Spell checking is implemented using the responder chain. Any class that responds to the necessary messages can benefit from built-in Application Kit features.

The Check Spelling menu item of the standard Spelling submenu is configured to send the `-checkSpelling:` action message using the responder chain. Enable spell checking in a custom class by implementing the `-checkSpelling:` method to implement the following code:

```
[[NSSpellChecker sharedSpellChecker] checkSpellingOfString:aString
                                                startingAt:0];
```

The `-sharedSpellChecker` method returns the shared instance of `NSSpellChecker`. The `aString` argument contains the string to be checked. An optional index into the string can be supplied to start checking at some position other than the start of the string. The `-checkSpellingOfString:startingAt:` method returns the range of the first word that is misspelled. The more complex `-checkSpellingOfString:startingAt:language:wrap:inSpellDocumentWithTag:wordCount:` method can be used to fine tune the spell checking by specifying a language and a set of words to ignore.

When the range of the first misspelled word is found, the spelling can be corrected via the `-changeSpelling:` action. Implement `-(void)changeSpelling:(id)sender` to replace the misspelled word with the string provided by the `sender` argument. If `-changeSpelling:` is not implemented, `NSSpellChecker` can identify spelling errors but cannot fix them.

If a custom object conforms to the `NSIgnoreMisspelledWords` protocol then `NSSpellChecker` enables the Ignore button in the standard-spelling panel.

Summary

This chapter provides an overview of the most prominent features built into the Application Kit, and the architecture used to provide those features. The Application Kit contains a core set of classes that all Application Kit-based applications must use. Those classes are the `NSResponder` and three of its subclasses, `NSApplication`, `NSWindow`, and `NSView`. Features that are common to most applications are implemented by classes that are optionally included to avoid work that would otherwise be repeated in many applications. Optional classes such as `NSDocumentManager`, `NSDocument`, and `NSWindowController` cooperate to enable many powerful features and save many lines of code. Each of the optional classes are integrated into the responder chain constructed by the core classes. Spell checking, undo, redo, and automatic menu validation all take advantage of the responder chain to simplify their implementation and enhance their value.

Concepts, overviews, language options, conventions, architecture, and design patterns have been covered so far. Starting with Chapter 9, "Applications, Windows, and Screens," the details of Cocoa programming with Objective-C are the primary focus. The conceptual information presented in the first eight chapters provides the information needed to understand where the upcoming details fit into the over all system. Pay attention to the recurring patterns and conventions. Programmers familiar with the idioms and conventions of other development environments should take note of the areas where Cocoa differs from other frameworks. In particular, the dynamic features of Objective-C are used extensively.

9
Applications, Windows, and Screens

IN THIS CHAPTER

This chapter builds on information about the principal Application Kit framework classes introduced in Chapter 8, "The Application Kit Framework Overview." To show how classes such as NSWindow and NSApplication are used in applications, this chapter extends the Image Viewer application started in Chapter 3, "Using Apple's Developer Tools." The Image Viewer application in Chapter 3 has many compelling features even though it does not contain a single line of custom code. In this chapter, custom classes are written to make Image Viewer into a multidocument application similar to Apple's Preview application. The complete implementation of Image Viewer is available at www.cocoaprogramming.net.

In addition to showing typical uses of the NSWindow and NSApplication classes, the new Image Viewer application uses Cocoa standard Open, Save, and Alert panels, and a technique for using panels as Aqua sheets is shown.

The New Image Viewer

Two custom classes are used to convert the Image Viewer application created in Chapter 3 into a multidocument application with the features that users expect: MYDocument and MYDocumentManager.

Cocoa includes the NSDocument and NSDocumentController classes that have many features in common with MYDocument and MYDocumentManager. Most multidocument Cocoa applications should use the existing NSDocument and NSDocumentController classes because they save work. In fact, they save so much work that they completely hide their interaction with other classes such as NSWindow and NSApplication. Because one of the purposes of this example is to show how NSWindow and NSApplication are used, this example does more work than is usually necessary.

The NSDocument and NSDocumentController classes are used in an example in Chapter 18, "Advanced Views and Controls." A side benefit of implementing MYDocument and MYDocumentManager in this chapter is that they dispel much of the mystery about how NSDocument and NSDocumentController work. Project Builder and Interface Builder simplify the creation of multidocument applications by hiding most of the configuration and communication that takes place between the document-related classes. This example makes the communication explicit.

In addition to requiring more work than necessary, the MYDocument and MYDocumentManager classes lack many features of NSDocument and NSDocumentController. For example, NSDocument handles undo, redo, and AppleScript support, whereas NSDocumentController maintains a persistent Recent Documents menu and supports the HFS file system's unique features. These features can be added to MYDocument and MYDocumentManager, but that is beyond the scope of this chapter.

NOTE

Apple's TextEdit sample shows another way to implement multidocument applications without using NSDocumentController. TextEdit supports undo, redo, AppleScript, the Recent Documents menu, and HFS file system features.

The Role of the MYDocument Class

The Image Viewer application built in Chapter 3 has one window for displaying images. It is necessary to modify Image Viewer so that it can have any number of open documents each represented visually by a window that contains an NSImageView.

The MYDocument class is created to encapsulate documents. Each MYDocument instance has an outlet connected to an NSImageView instance and stores information about the document such as its path in the file system. The MYDocument class is responsible for saving documents and giving users a chance to save unsaved documents when their associated windows are closed.

The Role of the MYDocumentManager Class

A single instance of the MYDocumentManager class creates new MYDocument instances and manages open documents. MYDocumentManager also cascades document windows and allows review and saving of unsaved documents when the application quits.

By convention, the use of the word "manager" in a class name implies that the class is responsible for allocating, storing, and releasing instances of some other class. For example, the NSFontManager class stores information about existing NSFont instances.

Working with NSWindow

The NSWindow class encapsulates windows in Cocoa. Each instance of MYDocument has an associated window that represents the document on the screen. Instances of MYDocument need to be informed when the user uses the standard File, Save and File, Save As menu items. MYDocument also needs to know when its associated window is closed so that it can prompt the user to save unsaved documents.

It is not necessary to subclass NSWindow to get it to interoperate with MYDocument. Classes such as NSWindow are seldom subclassed because they provide delegate methods that enable customization of behavior without the need to subclass.

The NSWindow class provides delegate methods to inform a delegate object when attributes of the window change. Delegate methods are able to influence the behavior of a window. For example, NSWindow calls its delegate's -windowShouldClose: method to ask permission to close. If the delegate's -windowShouldClose: returns NO, the window does not close.

Each instance of MYDocument is the delegate of its associated window.

NSWindow's Delegate

Each Cocoa class that sends delegate messages includes a section titled "Methods Implemented By the Delegate" in its class documentation. The NSWindow class documentation lists the following delegate methods:

```
- (void)windowDidResize:(NSNotification *)notification;
- (void)windowDidExpose:(NSNotification *)notification;
- (void)windowWillMove:(NSNotification *)notification;
- (void)windowDidMove:(NSNotification *)notification;
- (void)windowDidBecomeKey:(NSNotification *)notification;
- (void)windowDidResignKey:(NSNotification *)notification;
- (void)windowDidBecomeMain:(NSNotification *)notification;
- (void)windowDidResignMain:(NSNotification *)notification;
- (void)windowWillClose:(NSNotification *)notification;
- (void)windowWillMiniaturize:(NSNotification *)notification;
- (void)windowDidMiniaturize:(NSNotification *)notification;
- (void)windowDidDeminiaturize:(NSNotification *)notification;
- (void)windowDidUpdate:(NSNotification *)notification;
- (void)windowDidChangeScreen:(NSNotification *)notification;
```

```
- (void)windowWillBeginSheet:(NSNotification *)notification;
- (void)windowDidEndSheet:(NSNotification *)notification;
- (BOOL)windowShouldClose:(id)sender;
- (id)windowWillReturnFieldEditor:(NSWindow *)sender toObject:(id)client;
- (NSSize)windowWillResize:(NSWindow *)sender toSize:(NSSize)frameSize;
- (NSRect)windowWillUseStandardFrame:(NSWindow *)window defaultFrame:
    (NSRect)newFrame;
- (BOOL)windowShouldZoom:(NSWindow *)window toFrame:(NSRect)newFrame;
- (NSUndoManager *)windowWillReturnUndoManager:(NSWindow *)window;
```

The delegate methods that do not require any return value have a single argument that is an `NSNotification` instance. In each case, the `NSWindow` instance that sent the delegate message is obtained by sending the `-object` message to the notification argument. The delegate methods that return a value all include the `NSWindow` instance that sent the delegate message as an argument. Apple's class documentation describes how each delegate method is used and when it is called.

The `MYDocument` class implements only the following three `NSWindow` delegate methods:

```
/*" Window delegate methods "*/
- (BOOL)windowShouldClose:(id)sender;
- (void)windowWillClose:(NSNotification *)notification;
- (void)windowDidBecomeKey:(NSNotification *)notification;
```

Cocoa classes check to see if their delegate responds to each delegate message before sending it. As a result, it is common for delegates to implement only the methods they need. In the case of the `MYDocument` class, only three of the available delegate methods are needed.

Because each `MYDocument` instance is a window's delegate, each instance becomes part of the responder chain and can receive action messages. As explained in the "Target-Action Paradigm" section of Chapter 8, `NSWindow` instances include their delegates in the responder chain for actions. `MYDocument` handles the `-saveDocument:`, `-saveDocumentAs:`, and `-noteImageWasDropped:` action messages. Each `MYDocument` instance receives these action messages when user interface objects, such as menu items, send the actions up a responder chain that starts with the document's associated window.

The responder chain is also used to validate menu items. The `-validateMenuItem:` method is called automatically before menu items become visible. When a menu item is about to be displayed, the menu item searches the responder chain for an object that responds to its action. When a suitable object is found, the menu item sends the `-validateMenuItem:` message to that object passing the menu item to be validated as an argument. `MYDocument` implements `-validateMenuItem:` to enable or disable menu items that send the `-saveDocument:` or `-saveDocumentAs:` actions. For example, if a document has not been modified, the menu item that sends `-saveDocument:` can be disabled because there are no changes to save.

Configuring the Document's Window

Each `MYDocument` instance needs its own associated window and other objects used to represent the document. `MYDocument` gets its window by loading a `.nib` file that defines the interface for documents. Each time the `.nib` file that defines documents is loaded, new instances of the objects inside the `.nib` are unarchived. By loading the `.nib` file, each `MYDocument` instance gets its own instances of the user interface objects.

To make the Image Viewer interface ready to support multiple documents, the following changes must be made: Start Project Builder and open the project for the Image Viewer application developed in Chapter 3. Open Image Viewer's `MainMenu.nib` file by double-clicking it within the Resources folder in the Files tab of Project Builder's Project pane. Figure 9.1 shows the `MainMenu.nib` file selected in Project Builder.

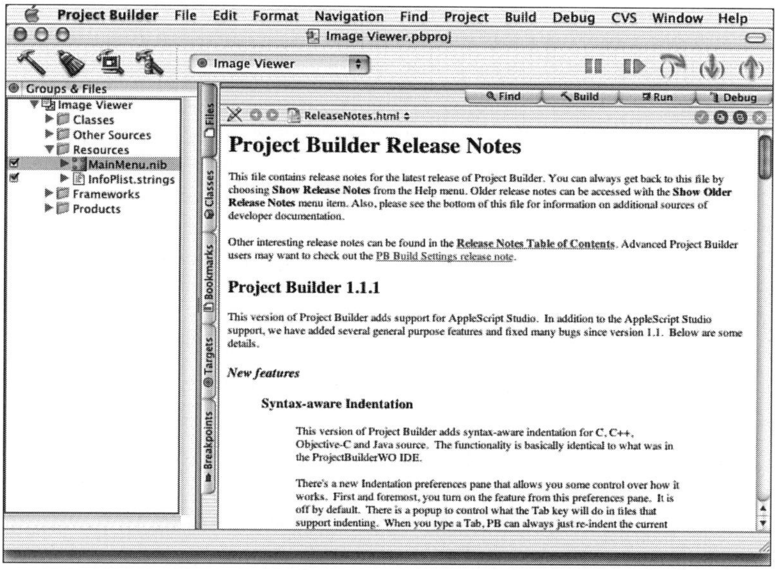

FIGURE 9.1 The `MainMenu.nib` file for Image Viewer is selected in the Files tab of Project Builder's Project pane.

The `MainMenu.nib` file contains only one window for displaying images. To provide the capability of having any number of open document windows, the interface for document windows needs to be stored separately from the other objects in

MainMenu.nib. By putting the definition of the document window in a separate .nib file, it becomes possible to load the document .nib file over and over to create as many windows as needed without also creating new copies of the main menu and other objects in MainMenu.nib.

In Interface Builder, create a new empty interface by using the File, New menu item. When Interface Builder displays the panel titled Starting Point, select an Empty Cocoa interface as shown in Figure 9.2 and click the New button. Interface Builder displays a window titled Untitled that represents the new empty .nib file. The new interface is used to define the interface for documents in the new Image Viewer application.

FIGURE 9.2 The Starting Point panel enables selection of the type of interface to create.

Two .nib files are now open at once: the MainMenu.nib file and the new empty .nib file represented by an Interface Builder window titled Untitled. In the Instances tab of the window titled MainMenu.nib, select the icon for the window that contains the NSImageView instance. Cut the window with Interface Builder's Edit, Cut menu item. Make the window titled Untitled key by clicking in its title bar, and then paste the cut window using Interface Builder's Edit, Paste menu item. Figure 9.3 shows the window containing the NSImageView cut from the MainMenu.nib and pasted into the Untitled .nib.

Save MainMenu.nib and close it for now. It will be edited more in the later example.

The next step is to create the MYDocument class. Select the Classes tab in the window titled Untitled and select the NSObject class as shown in Figure 9.4. Create a new subclass of NSObject using Interface Builder's Classes, Subclass NSObject menu item and name the new class MYDocument.

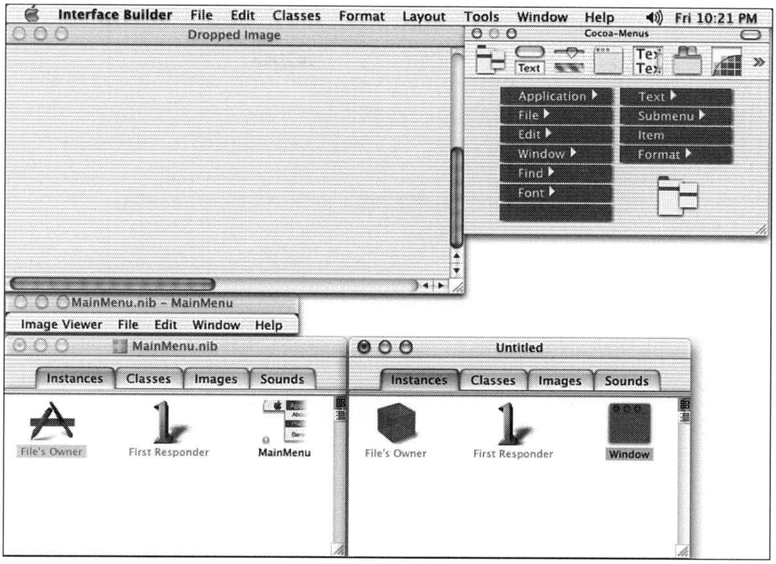

FIGURE 9.3 The window titled Dropped Image has been cut from the `MainMenu.nib` and pasted into Untitled.

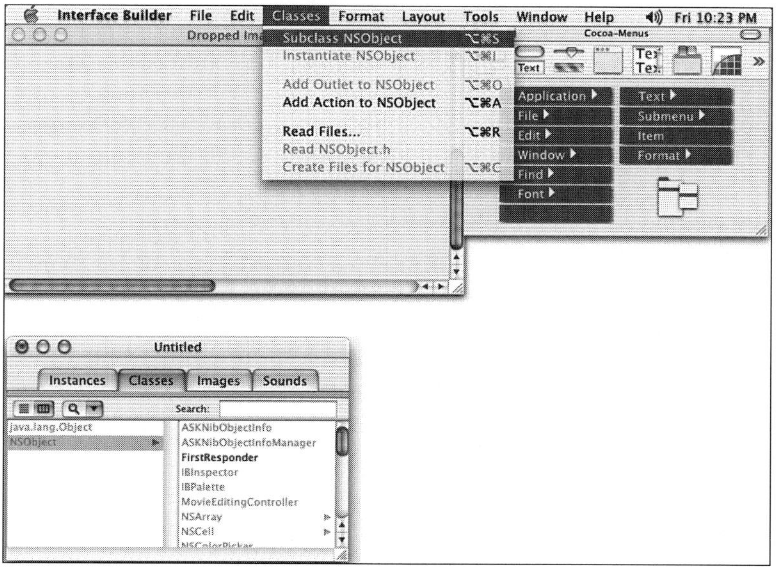

FIGURE 9.4 The `NSObject` class is selected in `MainMenu.nib`'s Classes tab.

With the MYDocument class selected in the Classes tab of the window titled Untitled, use Interface Builder's Classes, Add Outlet to the MYDocument menu item. If it is not already visible, Interface Builder displays the Show Info window titled MYDocument Class Info. In the window titled MYDocument Class Info, set the name of the new outlet to imageView and set its type to NSImageView as shown in Figure 9.5.

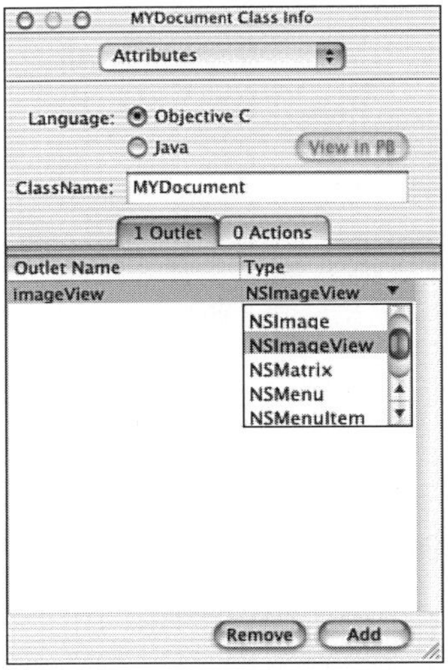

FIGURE 9.5 MYDocument's new outlet is named imageView and has the type NSImageView.

Select the tab labeled 0 Actions in the Show Info window titled MYDocument Class Info. Use the Add button in the lower-right corner to add an action method to the MYDocument class. Name the new action saveDocument:. Next, add two more actions. Name one saveDocumentAs: and the other noteImageWasDropped:.

Make sure the MYDocument class is still selected in the Classes tab of the window titled Untitled and use Interface Builder's Classes, Create Files for the MYDocument menu item to create the files that will contain the interface and implementation of the MYDocument class. Interface Builder displays a sheet asking where to store the new files. Select the folder that contains the Image Viewer project and click the Choose button at the bottom of the sheet.

Switch to the Instances tab in the window titled Untitled and select the Icon labeled File's Owner. The Show Info window's title changes to File's Owner Info. The File's Owner Info window shows a list of classes. Select the MYDocument class in the list. Interface Builder now knows that an instance of MYDocument will be the File's Owner of the .nib when the .nib is loaded.

Draw a connection line from the File's Owner icon to the area inside the scroll view in the Dropped Images window. Connection lines are drawn by pressing Ctrl and dragging the mouse. Connect the `imageView` outlet of the File's Owner to the `NSImageView` instance that is already inside the scroll view. Figure 9.6 shows the connection line from the File's Owner icon to the `NSImageView` instance inside the scroll view.

Draw a connection line from the icon for the window titled Dropped Image to the File's Owner icon. Make the File's Owner the window's delegate, as shown in Figure 9.7.

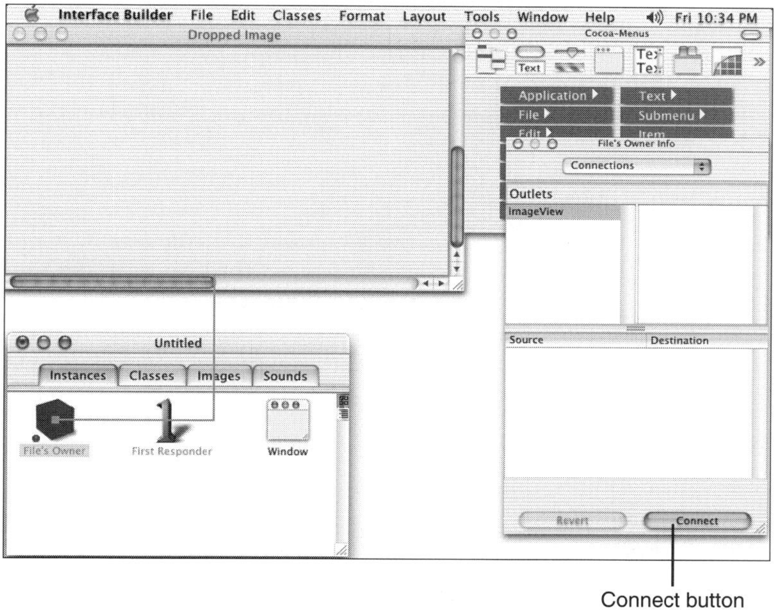

FIGURE 9.6 Click the Connect button to connect the `imageView` outlet of the File's Owner to the `NSImageView` instance inside the scroll view.

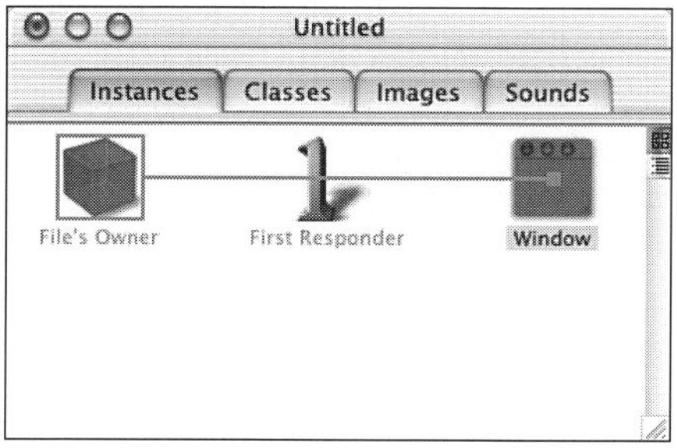

FIGURE 9.7 Make File's Owner the window's delegate.

Select the icon for the window titled Dropped Image. If the Show Info window titled NSWindow Info is not already visible, use Interface Builder's Tools, Show Info menu item to make it visible. In the Options section of the NSWindow Info window, make sure that the option Visible at launch time is off. For `.nib` files other than `MainMenu.nib`, the Visible at launch time options specifies whether the window should be visible when the `.nib` file that contains the window is loaded. In Image Viewer, it is better to have the windows that represent documents invisible at first so that the `MYDocument` class can make them visible at the right time.

Save the Untitled `.nib` as `ImageViewerDocument.nib` inside the `English.lproj` directory of the Image Viewer project. If Interface Builder displays a sheet asking if it should add the `.nib` file to the Image Viewer project, click the Add button on the sheet. Now close `ImageViewerDocument.nib`, hide Interface Builder, and return to working in Project Builder.

Implementing `MYDocument`

If the Image Viewer project does not already contain the `MYDocument.h` and `MYDocument.m` files created in Interface Builder, select the Classes folder in the Files tab of Project Builder's Project pane. Use Project Builder's Project, Add Files menu item to add `MYDocument.h` and `MYDocument.m` to the project. Project Builder displays a sheet asking how to reference the files added to the project. Click the Add button to accept the default reference style.

Edit the `MYDocument.h` file so that it defines the interface to `MYDocument` class as follows:

```
File MYDocument.h:

#import <Cocoa/Cocoa.h>

@interface MYDocument : NSObject
{
  IBOutlet NSImageView *imageView;

  NSString  *_myDocumentPath;     /*" Document's path "*/
  BOOL      _myHasEverBeenSaved;  /*" YES iff document has ever been saved "*/
}

/*" Supported document extensions "*/
+ (NSArray *)documentExtensions;

/*" Designated Initializer "*/
- (id)initWithPath:(NSString *)aPath;

/*" Alternate Initializer "*/
```

```
- (id)init;

/*" Document management methods "*/
- (NSString *)documentPath;
- (BOOL)safeClose;

/*" Access document's Window "*/
- (id)documentWindow;

/*" Document status "*/
- (BOOL)hasEverBeenSaved;
- (BOOL)isDocumentEdited;

/*" Actions "*/
- (IBAction)saveDocument:(id)sender;
- (IBAction)saveDocumentAs:(id)sender;
- (IBAction)noteImageWasDropped:(id)sender;

/*" Window delegate methods "*/
- (BOOL)windowShouldClose:(id)sender;
- (void)windowWillClose:(NSNotification *)notification;
- (void)windowDidBecomeKey:(NSNotification *)notification;

@end
```

The implementation of the `MYDocument` class begins here and is developed in the next few sections of this chapter as the Cocoa features used by the implementation are described. The first lines in `MYDocument.m` import the class interface and start the implementation of `MYDocument`.

```
#import "MYDocument.h"

@implementation MYDocument
/*" This class encapsulates documents in a multi-document application. "*/
```

The next part of the implementation defines some localizable strings that are presented to users and used to report errors that are detected when Image Viewer is run.

Localizable Strings

Localization is described in the Localization section of Chapter 7, "Foundation Framework Overview." When an application is localized for a particular language or culture, every string that is ever presented to users needs to be translated to the appropriate language. Even error messages need to be translated, so users can read them when they are displayed.

Many of the strings that users see are defined in .nib files. Cocoa applications are able to use different .nib files for every localization. When Cocoa applications load .nib files, they automatically load the available .nib files that best match the user's language preferences.

Any number of .nib files can be created to support localization without the need to edit or compile code for each one, but strings are also commonly defined in code. There needs to be a way to localize strings in code without having to edit and recompile the code for every localization. Cocoa provides the NSLocalizedString() macro that aids the localization of strings in code.

NSLocalizedString() accepts two arguments. The first is constant NSString containing words that need to be translated for each localization. The second argument is a short phrase that explains the meaning of the first argument. The second argument is intended to help translators make accurate translations. The NSLocalizedString() macro is explained in more detail at http://developer.apple.com/techpubs/macosx/Cocoa/Reference/Foundation/ObjC_classic/Functions/FoundationFunctions.html. Apple provides a program called genstrings in /usr/bin that is capable of reading source code and generating a file named Localizable.strings containing strings that need to be translated.

NOTE

Finder hides the /usr/bin folder and other traditional Unix folders by default. The /usr/bin folder can be accessed from the Terminal application or by using Finder's Go, Go to Folder menu and typing /usr/bin in text field presented.

Different versions of the Localizable.strings file are stored for each language along with the different .nib files. When a Cocoa application that uses NSLocalizedString() is run, it automatically uses the translated strings based on the user's language preferences. The same source code can be used with every localization without the need to edit or recompile the source code for each one. More information about genstrings is available at http://developer.apple.com/techpubs/macosx/Cocoa/TasksAndConcepts/ProgrammingTopics/Internationalization/Tasks/GeneratingStringsFiles.html.

The following localizable strings are used in MYDocument.m:

```
/*" Constant local strings "*/
#define MYDEFAULT_DOC_PATH NSLocalizedString(@"~/Untitled", @"")
#define MYCANCEL NSLocalizedString(@"Cancel", @"")
#define MYSAVE_CHANGES NSLocalizedString(\
    @"%@ has been edited. Do you want to save changes?", @"")
```

```
#define MYDEFAULT_CLOSE_ACTION NSLocalizedString(@"Close", @"")
#define MYSAVE NSLocalizedString(@"Save", @"")
#define MYDONT_SAVE NSLocalizedString(@"Don't Save", @"")
#define MYFILE_SAVE_ERROR NSLocalizedString(@"Document Save Error", @"")
#define MYFILE_SAVE_ERROR_MSG NSLocalizedString(@"Unable to save <%@>.", @"")
#define MYFILE_OPEN_ERROR NSLocalizedString(@"Document Open Error", @"")
#define MYFILE_OPEN_ERROR_MSG NSLocalizedString(@"Unable to open <%@>.", @"")
```

Document File Types

The MYDocument class adds the +documentExtensions class method to the class methods inherited from NSObject. The +documentExtensions method returns an array of file extensions for file types that can be used by an instance of MYDocument. The Image Viewer application can display any image file type supported by the NSImage class. The NSImage class is described in Chapter 14, "Custom Views and Graphics Part III." NSImage's +imageFileTypes method returns an array containing all the file types understood by NSImage.

```
+ (NSArray *)documentExtensions
/*" Returns the extensions supported by NSImage "*/
{
  return [NSImage imageFileTypes];
}
```

The Document's Path

Each instance of MYDocument stores the path to the file that it represents. A standardized version of the path is stored so that comparisons between paths provide accurate results. It is possible for any number of paths to refer to the same file due to file system links in the paths. Standardized paths expand all links. Two standardized paths can be compared with a simple string comparison to determine if they refer to the same file.

MYDocument's -_mySetDocumentPath: method is not declared in any class interface and is, therefore, considered private to the implementation of MYDocument.

```
- (void)_mySetDocumentPath:(NSString *)aPath
/*" Set the document's path by expanding tilde characters in aPath and
standardizing aPath. Also sets the title of the document window. "*/
{
  NSString     *standardPath = [aPath stringByExpandingTildeInPath];

  standardPath = [standardPath stringByStandardizingPath];
  [standardPath retain];
  [_myDocumentPath release];
```

```
  _myDocumentPath = aPath;
  [[self documentWindow] setTitleWithRepresentedFilename:_myDocumentPath];
}
```

In addition to storing the path to the file represented by the document, the `-_mySetDocumentPath:` method sets the title of the document's window. The expression `[self documentWindow]` is explained in Document Management Methods section of this chapter. It returns the window associated with the document. `NSWindow`'s `-setTitleWithRepresentedFilename:` sets the window's title to an easily readable variant of the document's path.

Loading Images and Using `NSRunAlertPanel()`

The private `_myLoadDocumentWithPath:` method loads the image data, if any, at a specified path and tells the document's image view to display the image.

This method uses the `NSAssert()` macro to perform error checking in the debug build of Image Viewer. The `NSAssert()` macro has two arguments. The first is a Boolean expression, and the other argument is an error message that is passed along with an exception that is raised if the first argument does not evaluate to `YES`. The `NSAssert()` macro is used to raise an `NSInternalInconsistencyException` exception and output an error message if some condition that should always be true turns out to be false.

In the `-_myLoadDocumentWithPath:` method, `NSAssert()` is used to assert that no attempt is made to load an image into a document that already has an image. The `NSAssert()` macro is automatically disabled in release builds. The `NSAssert()` macro helps programmers find errors when debugging and does not have any performance impact on released applications.

```
- (void)_myLoadDocumentWithPath:(NSString *)aPath
  /*" Sets documents image to the image stored aPath. "*/
{
  NSImage     *imageData;

  NSAssert(![self hasEverBeenSaved],
      @"Attempt to load document that is already loaded.");

  if([[NSFileManager defaultManager] fileExistsAtPath:aPath])
  {
    imageData = [[NSImage alloc] initWithContentsOfFile:aPath];

    if(nil == imageData)
    {
```

```
      // Unable to load image data
      NSRunAlertPanel(MYFILE_OPEN_ERROR, MYFILE_OPEN_ERROR_MSG,
                      nil, nil, nil, aPath);
    }
    else
    {
      [imageView setImage:imageData];
      [imageData release];   // imageData retained by imageView

      // Make the image view a reasonambe size for the image displayed
      [imageView setFrameSize:[[imageView image] size]];

      // Set the path and remeber that documnet has been saved
      _myHasEverBeenSaved = YES;
      [self _mySetDocumentPath:aPath];
    }
  }
  else
  {
    // The specified path does not exist.
    // Set the document window's title but don't set its path
    [[self documentWindow] setTitleWithRepresentedFilename:aPath];
  }
}
```

The expression `[self hasEverBeenSaved]` is explained in the "Document Status Methods" section of this chapter. It returns `YES` if the document has ever been saved and, therefore, has a valid path to the image data displayed. For now it is enough to know that `NSImage`'s `-initWithContentsOfFile:` method initializes a new `NSImage` instance with the image data in a specified file. The `-initWithContentsOfFile:` method releases the new image and returns `nil` if it is unable to load the image data.

If `-_myLoadDocumentWithPath:` is unable to initialize an `NSImage` with the image data at `aPath`, and alert panel is displayed with `NSRunAlertPanel()` to tell the user that the document could not be opened with the image at `aPath`.

`NSRunAlertPanel()`creates an alert panel, displays it onscreen, and runs it in a modal loop that requires the user to acknowledge the panel by clicking a button. The use of a modal loop means that all events received by the application are directed to Alert panel until the panel is closed. Modal loops are described in more detail in the "Modal Loops" section of this chapter. Each alert panel has a short title, some explanatory text, and up to three buttons. `NSRunAlertPanel()` is declared as follows:

```
int NSRunAlertPanel(NSString *title, NSString *msg, NSString *defaultButton,
    NSString *alternateButton, NSString *otherButton, ...);
```

`NSRunAlertPanel()` accepts a variable number of arguments. The `msg` argument that provides explanatory text can include `printf`-style formatting characters that are supported by NSString's `-stringWithFormat:...` method. The arguments used to replace the formatting characters are specified after the titles of the buttons at the end of `NSRunAlertPanel()` arguments list. `NSRunAlertPanel()` is documented at `http://developer.apple.com/techpubs/macosx/Cocoa/Reference/ApplicationKit/ObjC_classic/Functions/AppKitFunctions.html`.

`NSRunAlertPanel()` does not return until the user acknowledges the panel by clicking a button or closing the panel. It returns one of the following constants: `NSAlertDefaultReturn`, `NSAlertAlternateReturn`, or `NSAlertOtherReturn`. If the user clicked the button labeled with the `defaultButton` argument to `NSRunAlertPanel()`, `NSAlertDefaultReturn` is returned. If the user clicked the button titled by the `alternateButton` argument, `NSAlertAlternateReturn` is returned. Otherwise `NSAlertOtherReturn` is returned. If the `defaultButton` title is `nil`, the default button is titled `OK`. If any of the other button titles are `nil`, the corresponding button is not shown.

If `-_myLoadDocumentWithPath:` is able to load the image data at the specified path, the document's image view is told to display the image with `[imageView setImage:imageData]`. The allocated image is released because every method that allocates an object is responsible for releasing or autoreleasing the object. In this case, the document's image view already retains the image, so releasing it in `-_myLoadDocumentWithPath:` does not cause it to be deallocated immediately. The image view is responsible for releasing the image it retains. The fact that the document has a valid path is noted by setting the `_myHasEverBeenSaved` instance variable to `YES`. Finally, the document's path is set to the path of the image.

Initializing `MYDocument` Instances

The instances of the `MYDocument` class are initialized with the designated initializer, `-initWithPath:`. All other initializers must call the designated initializer. In the case of `MYDocument`, the only other initializer is `-init` inherited from `NSObject`. The `-initWithPath:` and `-init` methods are implemented as follows:

```
- (id)initWithPath:(NSString *)aPath
/*" Designated Initializer: Loads the objects that represent the document from
a nib file, configures the objects, and then loads the data at aPath.  Sets
the document's path to a standardized version of aPath. If aPath is nil, an
untitled document is created. "*/
{
  self = [super init];
```

```
  if(self)
  {
    // Load the user interface objects defined in a nib file using self as the
    // File's owner of the nib
    [NSBundle loadNibNamed:@"ImageViewerDocument.nib" owner:self];

    // Configure the loaded objects
    [imageView setTarget:self];
    [imageView setAction:@selector(noteImageWasDropped:)];
    [imageView setAutoresizingMask:NSViewNotSizable];
    [[imageView window] setReleasedWhenClosed:YES];

    if(nil != aPath)
    {
      [self _myLoadDocumentWithPath:aPath];
    }
    else
    {
      [self _mySetDocumentPath:MYDEFAULT_DOC_PATH];
    }
  }

  return self;
}


- (id)init
/*" Alternate Initilaizer: calls [self initWithPath:nil]. "*/
{
  return [self initWithPath:nil];
}
```

The key to the implementation of `-initWithPath:` is the `[NSBundle loadNibNamed:@"ImageViewerDocument.nib" owner:self]` expression. Each `MYDocument` instance gets its associated user interface objects by loading the `.nib` file that defines the objects and specifying the `MYDocument` instance as the File's Owner of the `.nib`. Connections that were made to the File's Owner in Interface Builder are automatically made to the `MYDocument` instance when the `.nib` file is loaded. As a result, the `MYDocument` instance becomes the delegate of its associated window, and `MYDocument`'s `imageView` instance variable is connected to the `NSImageView` instance inside the document's window.

The -initWithPath: method makes the document instance the target of the associated NSImageView and sets the action to -noteImageWasDropped:. As a result, the image view calls the document's -noteImageWasDropped: method whenever the user drags and drops an image onto the image view. This target/action connection could have been made in Interface Builder, but it is made here to show an alternative technique. The target of the image view could also have been set to nil. In that case, the image view would use the responder chain to find a target for its action. Unless another object earlier in the responder chain responds to the noteImageWasDropped: message, the document object would still receive the message when the user drags and drops an image onto the image view.

Another crucial part of the configuration of the document's user interface objects is the [[imageView window] setReleasedWhenClosed:YES] expression. The NSView class provides the -window method that returns the window containing the view. As a subclass of NSView, NSImageView inherits the -window method. In this case, the window that contains the image view is the window that represents the document. By telling the document's window to release itself when it is closed, the MYDocument class takes care of memory management for the user interface objects loaded from the .nib. When the window is closed, it releases itself. When the window is deallocated, it releases all the objects inside the window. The - setReleasedWhenClosed: property of the window can also be set in Interface Builder.

The -init method calls the designated initializer specifying a nil path. When -initWithPath: is called with a nil path, it initializes the document as an untitled document that has never been saved.

Document Management Methods

The MYDocument class provides several methods that are used by MYDocumentManager to manage open documents. The first document management method is -documentPath.

```
/*" Document management methods "*/
- (NSString *)documentPath
/*" Returns the document's path or nil. "*/
{
  return _myDocumentPath;
}
```

MYDocumentManager can use this method to identify documents. For example, if a user double-clicks an image file that is already represented by an open document, NSDocumentManager can make the existing document key instead of creating a second document instance that represents the same file. It is critical that the document's path is stored as a standardized path so that MYDocumentManager can simply determine if an open document represents a particular image file.

The document manager needs to be capable of closing open documents, and MYDocument provides the -safeClose method for that purpose. The -safeClose method calls [self _myShouldClose] to confirm that the user wants to close the document. If the document being closed has unsaved changes, an alert panel is displayed giving the user a chance to save the document, close the document anyway, or cancel the close. If the user cancels the close, -_myShouldClose returns NO and the document is not closed.

```
- (bool)_myShouldClose
/*" Gives users a chance to save edited documents before closing the document.
Returns NO if the user cancels the close.  Returns YES otherwise. "*/
{
  BOOL     result = YES;

  if([self isDocumentEdited])
  {
    int          userChoice;
    NSString     *documentName = [self documentPath];

    if(nil == documentName)
    {
      // document has no path so use its window's title instead
      documentName = [[self documentWindow] title];
    }

    // the document has been edited
    userChoice = NSRunAlertPanel(MYDEFAULT_CLOSE_ACTION,
        MYSAVE_CHANGES, MYSAVE, MYDONT_SAVE, MYCANCEL, documentName);

    switch(userChoice)
    {
      case NSAlertDefaultReturn:
      {
        // User chooses to save changes
        [self saveDocument:nil];
        result = YES;
        break;
      }
      case NSAlertAlternateReturn:
      {
        // User chooses NOT to save changes
        result = YES;
        break;
```

```
      }
      case NSAlertOtherReturn:
      {
        // User chooses to CANCEL close
        result = NO;
        break;
      }
    }
  }

  return result;
}


- (BOOL)safeClose
/*" Gives users a chance to save edited documents before closing the document.
Returns NO if the user cancels the close.  Returns YES otherwise. "*/
{
  BOOL      result = [self _myShouldClose];

  if(result)
  {
    // the user agrees to close the window
    // close the document window immediately without
    // letting the window call its -windowShouldClose: delegate
    // method.
    [[self documentWindow] close];
  }

  return result;
}
```

The window that represents each document is returned by the `-documentWindow` method. The `MYDocument` class could be implemented with an outlet that is directly connected to the associated window, but that is unnecessary. `MYDocument` already has an outlet for an image view, and the image view's window is the window that represents the document.

```
- (id)documentWindow
/*" Returns document's window "*/
{
  return [imageView window];
}
```

Document Status Methods

The MYDocument class uses the _myHasEverBeenSaved instance variable to store YES if the document has ever been saved. Knowing if the document has ever been saved is important because the results of opening and saving documents differ for documents that have been previously saved and documents that have never been saved. For example, documents that have been previously saved or opened from a file in the file system have a valid path, but unsaved untitled documents don't. MYDocument's -hasEverBeenSaved method returns the value of the _myHasEverBeenSaved instance variable.

```
- (BOOL)hasEverBeenSaved
/*" Returns YES iff document has ever been saved and has a valid path. "*/
{
  return _myHasEverBeenSaved;
}
```

MYDocument does not define a _myHasBeenEdited instance variable because each document already has access to an associated window, and NSWindow provides the -setDocumentEdited: and -isDocumentEdited methods to store information about whether the document has been edited since it was last saved. The value returned from NSWindow's -isDocumentEdited method is used to determine if the user should be given a chance to save changes before a document window is closed.

```
- (BOOL)isDocumentEdited
/*" Returns YES iff document has been edited since it was last saved. "*/
{
  return [[self documentWindow] isDocumentEdited];
}
```

Document Actions and the Save Panel

Because each MYDocument instance is the delegate of its associated window, document instances receive action messages that are sent up the responder chain. Two of the action messages handled by MYDocument are saveDocument: and saveDocumentAs:, which are sent up the responder chain by the File, Save and File, Save As menu items, respectively.

The private -_mySaveDocumentData method is called by both -saveDocument: and -saveDocumentAs: to actually save the document's image in a file specified by the document's path. If writing the file to the document's path fails for any reason, an alert panel is displayed with NSRunAlertPanel(). If the document's image is successfully saved, `[[self documentWindow] setDocumentEdited:NO]` is called to tell the window that the document has not been edited since it was saved. The `_myHasEverBeenSaved` instance variable is set to `YES`.

```
- (void)_mySaveDocumentData
/*" Save the document's image to the document's path. Displays an alert panel
if the image is not saved correctly. "*/
{
  NSData     *imageData = [[imageView image] TIFFRepresentation];

  if(![imageData writeToFile:[self documentPath] atomically:YES])
  {
    // The image was not saved correctly
    NSRunAlertPanel(MYFILE_SAVE_ERROR, MYFILE_SAVE_ERROR_MSG,
                    nil, nil, nil, [self documentPath]);
  }
  else
  {
    // The image was saved correctly
    [[self documentWindow] setDocumentEdited:NO];
    _myHasEverBeenSaved = YES;
  }
}
```

The primary difference between `-saveDocument:` and `-saveDocumentAs:` is that `-saveDocumentAs:` displays a standard Cocoa Save panel that gives the user a chance to specify the path at which the document is saved or the save is cancelled.

The `-saveDocument:` method checks to make sure the document's path specifies an existing file and not a directory. If the document's path does not exist or is a directory or the document has never been saved, `-saveDocument:` calls `-saveDocumentAs:` so that the user has a chance to specify a path. If there is no problem with the document's path, `-saveDocument:` calls `-_mySaveDocumentData` to save the document's image.

```
- (IBAction)saveDocument:(id)sender
/*" Save the image data displayed by the document "*/
{
  BOOL       pathExists;
  BOOL       pathIsDirectory;

  // check to see if a directory exists at document path
  pathExists = [[NSFileManager defaultManager] fileExistsAtPath:
      [self documentPath] isDirectory:&pathIsDirectory];
```

```
  if(![self hasEverBeenSaved] || pathIsDirectory || nil == [self documentPath])
  {
    // The image has never been saved or it has no path or there is a directory
    // at its path. Use -saveDocumentAs: because is shows a Save panel to find
    // out where the user wants to save the image.
    [self saveDocumentAs:sender];
  }
  else
  {
    // Save the image data
    [self _mySaveDocumentData];
  }
}
```

The `-saveDocumentAs:` method displays the standard Cocoa Save panel encapsulated by the `NSSavePanel` class. The Save panel enables users to specify a file system path by browsing in the file system. The Save panel can be configured with a custom accessory view. The accessory view is used to extend the Save panel without the need to subclass `NSSavePanel` or edit the `.nib` file that defines the Save panel. There is normally only one instance of `NSSavePanel` in each application, and that instance is accessed by calling `[NSSavePanel savePanel]`.

`NSSavePanel` supports many configuration options documented at `http://developer.apple.com/techpubs/macosx/Cocoa/Reference/ApplicationKit/ObjC_classic/Classes/NSSavePanel.html#//apple_ref/occ/instm/NSSavePanel/setAccessoryView`. `NSSavePanel`'s `-filename` and `-URL` methods return the full path to the file that the user selected. The `-directory` method returns the path to the directory that contains the file that the user selected.

`MYDocument`'s `-saveDocumentAs:` method uses `NSSavePanel`'s `- setRequiredFileType:` method to set the file type to `tiff`. It also uses `NSSavePanel`'s `-setTreatsFilePackagesAsDirectories:` to configure the panel so that users are not able to select paths inside file packages that do not look like directories in Finder.

The Save panel is displayed and run in a modal loop using `NSSavePanel`'s `-runModalForDirectory:file:` method. Modal loops are described in more detail in the "Modal Loops" section of this chapter.

If the user selects a path and clicks the Save panel's default button, the document's path is set to the selected path, and the document is saved using `-_mySaveDocumentData`.

```
- (IBAction)saveDocumentAs:(id)sender
/*" Displays a Save panel to find out where the user wants to save the
document's image data. If the user does not cancel the save, this method saves
```

```
the image data at the specified location. "*/
{
  NSSavePanel     *savePanel;
  NSString        *documentDirectory = [[self documentPath]
      stringByDeletingLastPathComponent];
  NSString        *documentName = [[self documentPath] lastPathComponent];

  savePanel = [NSSavePanel savePanel];
  [savePanel setRequiredFileType:@"tiff"];
  [savePanel setTreatsFilePackagesAsDirectories:NO];

  if (NSOKButton == [savePanel runModalForDirectory:documentDirectory
      file:documentName])
  {
    [self _mySetDocumentPath:[savePanel filename]];
    [self _mySaveDocumentData];
  }
}
```

The last action method implemented by `MYDocument` is `- noteImageWasDropped:`. `MYDocument`'s `-initWithPath:` method makes each document instance the target of the corresponding image view. The image view calls the document's `-noteImageWasDropped:` method when an image is dragged and dropped on the image view. The `- noteImageWasDropped:` is implemented to tell the document's window that the document has been edited.

```
- (IBAction)noteImageWasDropped:(id)sender
/*" Called by document's image view when the image changes. "*/
{
  // The image has changed so note that the document has been edited.
  [[self documentWindow] setDocumentEdited:YES];

  // Make the image view a reasonable size for the image displayed
  [imageView setFrameSize:[[imageView image] size]];
}
```

Menu Validation

`MYDocument` implements the `-validateMenuItem:` method to validate the menu items that send the `saveDocument:` and `saveDocumentAs:` actions. Menu validation is explained in Chapter 8.

```
- (BOOL)validateMenuItem:(NSMenuItem *)aMenuItem
/*" Validate menu items that send the saveDocument: and
saveDocumentAs: actions. "*/
{
  SEL         action = [aMenuItem action];
  BOOL        enableMenuItem = NO;

  if (action == @selector(saveDocument:))
  {
    // If the document has never been saved or has been edited since it was
    // saved then enable the menu item that sends saveDocument:
    enableMenuItem = [self isDocumentEdited] || ![self hasEverBeenSaved];
  }
  else if (action == @selector(saveDocumentAs:))
  {
    // Always enable the menu item that sends saveDocumentAs:.
    enableMenuItem = YES;
  }

  return enableMenuItem;
}
```

Using NSWindow Delegate Methods

MYDocument implements three window delegate methods: - windowShouldClose:, -windowWillClose:, and -windowDidBecomeKey:.

The -windowShouldClose: method is called by NSWindow when the window is about to close because the user clicked the Close button on the window's title bar. It is implemented to give users a chance to save unsaved documents before closing and returns the result of calling -_myShouldClose.

The -windowWillClose: method is called by NSWindow just before a window is closed. By the time -windowWillClose: is called, it is too late to cancel the close. MYDocument implements -windowWillClose: to set the document's imageView instance variable to nil and send the documentWillClose: action message using the responder chain. The argument to the documentWillClose: method is the document that is closing. Objects in the responder chain can implement -documentWillClose: to update references they might have to the document being closed. For example, when a MYDocumentManager instance receives the documentWillClose: message, it removes the document from an array of open documents.

The `-windowDidBecomeKey:` method sends the `makeDocumentActive:` action message up the responder chain with the document as the argument. When a `MYDocumentManager` instance receives the `makeDocumentActive:` message, it makes the document the active document.

```
- (BOOL)windowShouldClose:(id)sender
/*" Give users a chance to save edited documents before they close and/or
cancel the close. "*/
{
  return [self _myShouldClose];
}


- (void)windowWillClose:(NSNotification *)notification
/*" Tell document manager that document is closing. "*/
{
  imageView = nil;  // don't keep reference to closed window
  [NSApp sendAction:@selector(documentWillClose:) to:nil from:self];
}


- (void)windowDidBecomeKey:(NSNotification *)notification
/*" Tell document manager to make the receiver the active document "*/
{
  [NSApp sendAction:@selector(makeDocumentActive:) to:nil from:self];
}
```

The `-windowWillClose:` and `-windowDidBecomeKey:` methods use the responder chain to keep the document manager informed of changes in managed documents. These methods could have been implemented to send notifications that are observed by the document manager instead of using the responder chain. Messages could also have been sent directly to the application's delegate by calling `[[NSApp delegate] documentWillClose:self]` and `[[NSApp delegate] makeDocumentActive:self]` after first checking to make sure that the application's delegate responds to the messages. The choice to use the responder chain was arbitrary in this case. The responder chain, notifications, and delegates are all techniques for loosely coupling the sender of a message to the receiver. The "Delegation Versus Notifications" section of Chapter 8 describes some of the tradeoffs of using different techniques. The responder chain offers yet another option.

Concluding MYDocument's Implementation

Most classes that store object instance variables need to implement the -dealloc method to release the instance variables. MYDocument has the imageView and _myDocumentPath object instance variables.

There is no need to release imageView because it is set when the document's .nib file is loaded and MYDocument never explicitly retains it. When the window that contains the image view closes, it releases all the objects it contains. If no other object retains the image view, it is deallocated. MYDocument implements -windowWillClose to set imageView to nil when the window closes so that MYDocument does not have a reference to a possibly deallocated object.

MYDocument does retain its _myDocumentPath instance variable and, therefore, must release it in -dealloc.

```
- (void)dealloc
/*" Clean-up "*/
{
  [_myDocumentPath release];
  [super dealloc];
}
```

The MYDocument implementation is concluded with the @end compiler directive.

```
@end
```

Saving Window Frames in User Defaults

The Image Viewer application does not explicitly save the frames of any windows in the user's defaults database, but it is described here because NSWindow supports that feature. When a window's frame is saved in the defaults database, the window's position and size become persistent. The user can quit the application and when it is launched again, the windows are restored with the same position and size they had when the application was last quit. Because each user has a different defaults database, each user can store different window frames for the same windows.

NSWindow's -(void)saveFrameUsingName:(NSString *)name method saves the window's frame rectangle in the user's defaults database. The defaults database is described in Chapter 7. The name argument to -saveFrameUsingName: is the key used to retrieve the saved default value.

NSWindow's -(BOOL)setFrameUsingName:(NSString *)name method retrieves the window frame previously stored in the default database with the key name and sets the window's frame to the stored value. The - setFrameUsingName: method returns YES if the stored frame was successfully read and NO otherwise.

Windows can be configured to automatically save its frame in the user's defaults database by calling NSWindow's -(BOOL)setFrameAutosaveName:(NSString *)name method. After a window is given an autosave name, it automatically updates its frame stored in the defaults database when the window is moved or resized. The - setFrameAutosaveName: returns YES if the frame is successfully saved by using name as the key and NO otherwise.

Document windows shouldn't save their frames in the user's defaults database. If every window saves its frame, the defaults database will become very large, and users have no easy way to remove window frames from their defaults database. Reserve the use of saved frames for windows that benefit most from the feature. For example, Interface Builder stores the frames of its Palette window and Show Info window. Utility windows such as palettes and tool windows are good candidates for the frame saving feature because there are usually not very many of them and each user probably has a preferred arrangement and size for them.

Transparent Windows

Cocoa windows can be transparent, and Cocoa can simulate nonrectangular windows. Apple provides the RoundTransparentWindow sample at http://developer.apple.com/samplecode/Sample_Code/Cocoa/RoundTransparentWindow.htm. The key features of the sample show how to change the shape of a window and how to recalculate the window's drop shadow.

NSWindow's -setOpaque: method is used to make the background behind a window show through the window's transparent portions. The -setAlphaValue: method sets the overall transparency of the window. Calling -setAlphaValue: with 1.0 as the argument makes the parts of the window that are not drawn in a transparent color fully opaque. Setting the window's alpha value to zero makes the entire window invisible. The -setBackgroundColor: method is used to set the background to a transparent color. Finally, -setHasShadow: enables or disables the drawing of the window's drop shadow.

Working with NSApplication

The NSApplication class is the primary interface between Cocoa applications and the operating system. Each Cocoa application has exactly one instance of the NSApplication class. NSApplication is seldom subclassed. It provides delegate methods and notifications that enable customization of application behavior without the need to subclass.

To show how NSApplication's delegate methods are used, the MYDocumentManager class is created. An instance of MYDocumentManager is the application's delegate in the new Image Viewer application and manages open documents. MYDocumentManager also allows review and saving of unsaved documents when the application quits.

NSApplication's Delegate

The MYDocumentManager class needs to know when an application is terminating so that it can prompt the user to save unsaved documents. It also needs to know when users have double-clicked a document in Finder or dragged a document onto its application's icon.

An instance of the NSApplication class sends messages to its delegate informing the delegate when the application is terminating. Delegate methods are called when the application has finished launching, when files need to be opened or printed, and when AppleScript events are received.

The "Methods Implemented By the Delegate" section of NSApplication's class documentation lists the following delegate methods:

```
- (void)applicationWillFinishLaunching:(NSNotification *)notification;
- (void)applicationDidFinishLaunching:(NSNotification *)notification;
- (void)applicationWillHide:(NSNotification *)notification;
- (void)applicationDidHide:(NSNotification *)notification;
- (void)applicationWillUnhide:(NSNotification *)notification;
- (void)applicationDidUnhide:(NSNotification *)notification;
- (void)applicationWillBecomeActive:(NSNotification *)notification;
- (void)applicationDidBecomeActive:(NSNotification *)notification;
- (void)applicationWillResignActive:(NSNotification *)notification;
- (void)applicationDidResignActive:(NSNotification *)notification;
- (void)applicationWillUpdate:(NSNotification *)notification;
- (void)applicationDidUpdate:(NSNotification *)notification;
- (void)applicationWillTerminate:(NSNotification *)notification;
- (void)applicationDidChangeScreenParameters:(NSNotification *)notification;
- (NSApplicationTerminateReply)applicationShouldTerminate:
    (NSApplication *)sender;
- (BOOL)application:(NSApplication *)sender openFile:(NSString *)filename;
- (BOOL)application:(NSApplication *)sender openTempFile:(NSString *)filename;
- (BOOL)applicationShouldOpenUntitledFile:(NSApplication *)sender;
- (BOOL)applicationOpenUntitledFile:(NSApplication *)sender;
- (BOOL)application:(id)sender openFileWithoutUI:(NSString *)filename;
- (BOOL)application:(NSApplication *)sender printFile:(NSString *)filename;
- (BOOL)applicationShouldTerminateAfterLastWindowClosed:
    (NSApplication *)sender;
- (BOOL)applicationShouldHandleReopen:(NSApplication *)sender
    hasVisibleWindows:(BOOL)flag;
```

```
- (NSMenu *)applicationDockMenu:(NSApplication *)sender;
- (BOOL)application:(NSApplication *)sender delegateHandlesKey:(NSString *)key;
```

The delegate methods that do not require any return value have a single argument that is an `NSNotification` instance. In each case, the `NSApplication` instance that sent the delegate message is obtained by sending the `-object` message to the notification argument. The delegate methods that return a value all include the `NSApplication` instance that sent the delegate message as an argument. Apple's class documentation describes how each delegate method is used and when it is called.

The `MYDocumentManager` class implements the following application delegate methods:

```
- (NSApplicationTerminateReply)applicationShouldTerminate:
    (NSApplication *)sender;
- (BOOL)application:(NSApplication *)sender openFile:(NSString *)filename;
- (BOOL)applicationShouldOpenUntitledFile:(NSApplication *)sender;
- (BOOL)applicationOpenUntitledFile:(NSApplication *)sender;
```

The `-applicationShouldTerminate:` method is implemented to check for any unsaved documents and give users a chance to save them. The `-application:openFile:` method is implemented to open documents when they are double-clicked in Finder or dropped on an application icon. Finally, the `-applicationShouldOpenUntitledFile:` and `-applicationOpenUntitledFile:` methods control how the application handles untitled documents.

The `MYDocumentManager` class works closely with the `NSApplication` class to implement features that users expect from multidocument applications. Because an instance of the `MYDocumentManager` class is the delegate of the `NSApplication` instance, the document manager is automatically added to the responder chain and can receive action messages sent up the responder chain. `MYDocumentManager` implements three actions that are sent by user interface objects such as menu items: `-newDocument:`, `-openDocument:`, and `-saveAllDocuments:`. The `MYDocumentManager` instance receives these action messages when user interface objects send them up the responder chain and no other object handles them. `MYDocumentManager` also implements the `-documentWillClose:` and `-makeDocumentActive:` actions that are sent up the responder chain by `NSDocument` instances.

The `-validateMenuItem:` method implemented by `MYDocumentManager` is called automatically before menu items become visible. When a menu item is about to be displayed, it searches the responder chain for an object that responds to its action. When a suitable object is found, the menu item sends the `-validateMenuItem:` message to that object passing the menu item to be validated as an argument.

MYDocumentManager implements -validateMenuItem: to enable or disable menu items that send the -newDocument:, -openDocument:, or -saveAllDocuments: actions.

Creating and Configuring MYDocumentManager

To add the MYDocumentManager class to the Image Viewer project and make an instance of MYDocumentManager the application's delegate, Open Image Viewer's MainMenu.nib file in Interface Builder by double-clicking it within the Resources folder in the Files tab of Project Builder's Project pane. Figure 9.1 shows the MainMenu.nib file selected in Project Builder.

After Interface Builder has loaded Image Viewer's MainMenu.nib file, select the Classes tab in Interface Builder's window titled MainMenu.nib and select the NSObject class. Create a new subclass of NSObject using Interface Builder's Classes, Subclass NSObject menu item.

Name the new subclass MYDocumentManager. Make sure the MYDocumentManager class is selected and uses the Classes, Instantiate MYDocumentManager menu to create an instance of the MYDocumentManager class. When the new instance is created, Interface Builder automatically displays the Instances tab shown in Figure 9.8. Make sure the MYDocumentManager instance is selected as shown.

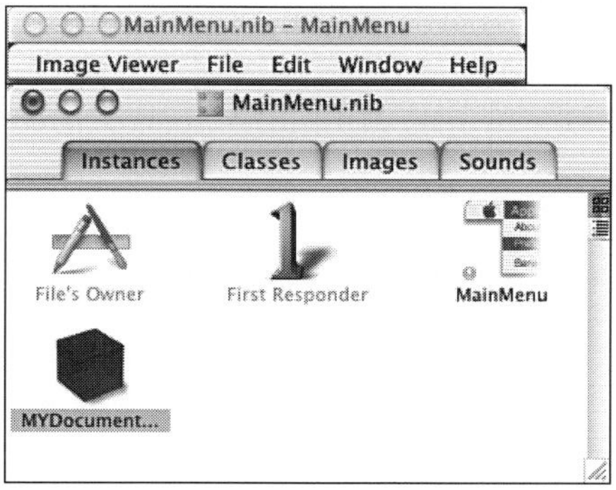

FIGURE 9.8 A new MYDocumentManager instance is selected in MainMenu.nib's Instances tab.

Drag a connection line from the icon labeled File's Owner to the new instance of MYDocumentManager as shown in Figure 9.9. Hold the Ctrl key while dragging with the mouse to draw connection lines. When the mouse button is released after drawing a connection line, Interface Builder automatically displays a Show Info window in Connections mode. Figure 9.9 shows the Show Info window titled File's Owner Info.

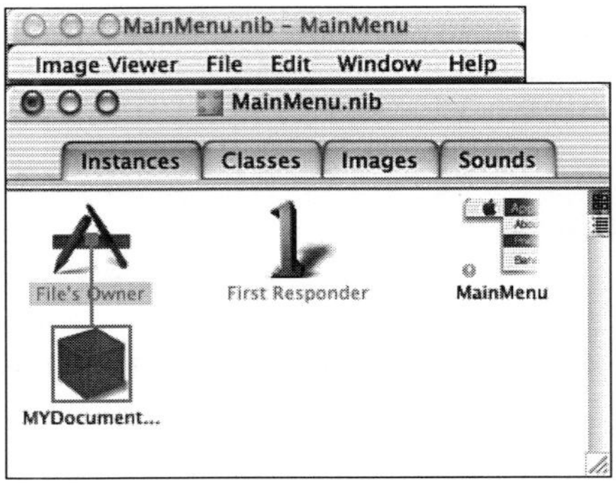

FIGURE 9.9 A connection line is drawn from File's Owner to the `MYDocumentManager` instance, and the File's Owner Info window is displayed ready to make a connection.

Select the `delegate` outlet displayed in the Outlets column of the window titled File's Owner Info and click the Connect button. The File's Owner of the `MainMenu.nib` file is the application object. The instance of `MYDocumentManager` is now the application's delegate.

Switch to the Classes tab of the `MainMenu.nib` window and select the `MYDocumentManager` class. Use Interface Builder's Classes, Create Files for `MYDocumentManager` menu item to create the files that will contain the interface and implementation of the `MYDocumentManager` class. Interface Builder displays a sheet asking where to store the new files within the Image Viewer project. Select the folder that contains the Image Viewer project and click the Choose button at the bottom of the sheet.

The next step is to make connections between the Image Viewer's menu items and the First Responder.

NOTE

The First Responder icon in Interface Builder is just a placeholder for whichever object is actually the first responder at any given moment while an application is running.

The user interface–related actions that `MYDocumentManager` implements are standard. Interface Builder already knows that `newDocument:`, `openDocument:`, and `saveAllDocuments:` are messages that can be sent to the First Responder. It is possible to add actions to First Responder so that custom actions can be used with the responder chain, but that is not necessary yet in this example.

Select Image Viewer's File, New menu item in the window titled `MainMenu.nib - Main menu`, which is shown in Figure 9.10. Draw a connection line from the File, New menu item to the First Responder Icon.

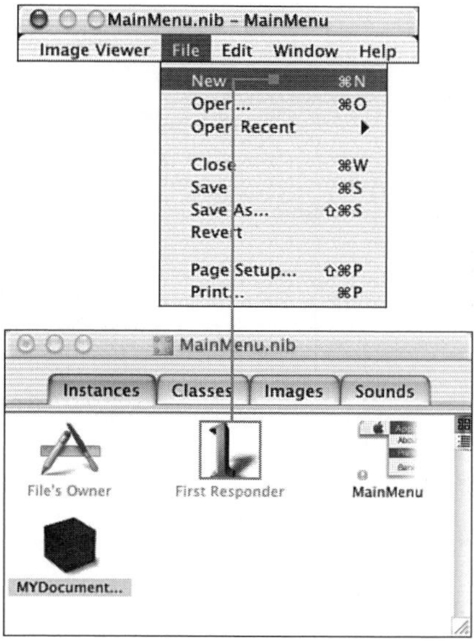

FIGURE 9.10 A connection line from the File, New menu item to the First Responder icon is shown with the `target` outlet and the `newDocument:` action selected.

Connect the `target` outlet to the `newDocument:` action, as shown in Figure 9.10. When Image Viewer is running and the File, New menu item is clicked, the `newDocument:` action will be sent up the responder chain. If no other object in the responder chain responds to `newDocument:`, `MYDocumentManager`'s `-newDocument:` method will be called.

NOTE

If Project Builder's Multi-Document Cocoa application project template is used when a project is created, Project Builder automatically makes the connections from standard File menu items to the First Responder. The connections are made manually in this example to show how the connections work.

Use the same technique to connect Image Viewer's File, Open menu item to the First Responder's `openDocument:` action. Connect the File, Save menu item to the First

Responder's `saveDocument:` action. Connect the File, Save As menu item to the First Responder's `saveDocumentAs:` action. Next, add a new menu item to Image Viewer's File menu by dragging a menu item from Interface Builder's Cocoa-Menus palette, as shown in Figure 9.11.

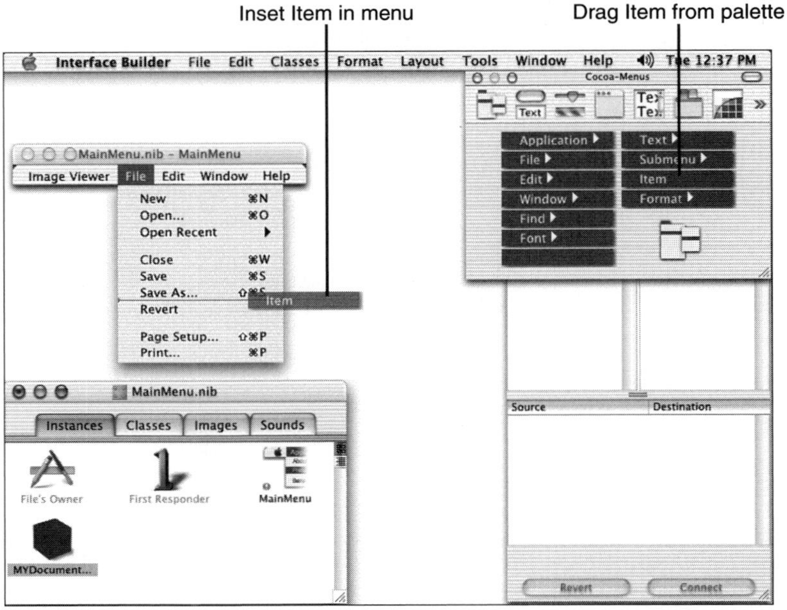

FIGURE 9.11 A new menu item is added to Image Viewer's File menu.

Name the new menu item Save All. Connect the File, Save All menu item to the First Responder's `saveAllDocuments:` action.

NOTE

The `-saveDocument:` and `-saveDocumentAs:` methods are implemented by `MYDocument` not `MYDocumentManager`. The connections made to the First Responder work for documents as well as the document manager because instances of both classes are in the responder chain when Image Viewer is run.

Save Image Viewer's `MainMenu.nib` and hide Interface Builder, and then return to Project Builder.

Implementing MYDocumentManager

The project for Viewer needs to contain the MYDocumentManager.h and MYDocumentManager.m files that were created with Interface Builder's Classes, Create Files for MYDocumentManager menu item. If they are not in the project, add them now using Project Builder's Project, Add Files menu item. Edit the MYDocumentManager.h file in Project Builder so that it contains the following code for the MYDocumentManager class interface.

```
File MYDocumentManager:

#import <Cocoa/Cocoa.h>


@interface MYDocumentManager : NSObject
{
  NSMutableArray    *_myOpenDocuments;     /*" Array of open documents "*/
  NSPoint           _myWindowCascadePoint; /*" Used to cascade windows "*/
}

/*" Designated initializer "*/
- (id)init;

/*" Document class "*/
- (Class)documentClass;

/*" Document loading "*/
- (NSArray *)documentExtensions;

/*" Accessing open documents "*/
- (NSArray *)existingOpenDocuments;
- (id)existingOpenDocumentWithPath:(NSString *)aPath;
- (id)activeDocument;

/*" Document actions "*/
- (IBAction)openDocument:(id)sender;
- (IBAction)newDocument:(id)sender;
- (IBAction)saveAllDocuments:(id)sender;

/*" Document communication actions "*/
- (void)documentWillClose:(id)sender;
- (void)makeDocumentActive:(id)sender;
```

```
/*" Application delegate methods "*/
- (NSApplicationTerminateReply)applicationShouldTerminate:
  (NSApplication *)sender;
- (BOOL)application:(NSApplication *)sender openFile:(NSString *)filename;
- (BOOL)applicationShouldOpenUntitledFile:(NSApplication *)sender;
- (BOOL)applicationOpenUntitledFile:(NSApplication *)sender;

@end
```

The implementation of `MYDocumentManager` begins by importing the class interfaces in `MYDocumentManager` and `MYDocument`.

```
#import "MYDocumentManager.h"
#import "MYDocument.h"


@implementation MYDocumentManager
/*" A single instance of this class is used as the application's delegate and
manages documents in a multi-document application.

There is a single "active" document at any time.  The "active" document is
usually the document that controls that last key window, but the active
document can be set programmatically.
"*/
```

The following localizable strings are used in `MYDocumentManager.m`:

```
/*" Constant local strings "*/
#define MYQUIT NSLocalizedString(@"Quit", @"")
#define MYOPEN NSLocalizedString(@"Open Error", @"")
#define MYOPEN_DOCUMENT_ERROR_MSG NSLocalizedString(\
    @"Unable to open document.", @"")
#define MYNEW_DOCUMENT_ERROR_MSG NSLocalizedString(\
    @"Unable to create new document.", @"")
#define MYUNSAVED_DOCS_MSG NSLocalizedString(\
    @"There are unsaved documents.\nReview them?", @"")
#define MYCANCEL NSLocalizedString(@"Cancel", @"")
#define MYQUIT_ANYWAY NSLocalizedString(@"Quit Anyway", @"")
#define MYREVIEW_UNSAVED NSLocalizedString(@"Review", @"")
#define MYUNTITLED NSLocalizedString(@"Untitled", \
    @"The name of untitled documents")
```

Initializing the MYDocumentManager Instance

The one and only instance of MYDocumentManager in the Image Viewer application is instantiated inside the MainMenu.nib file. Because the MYDocumentManager instance is never initialized programmatically, its designated initializer is never called. Instead, its -awakeFromNib method is called after it is loaded from MainMenu.nib. Objects that are instantiated in Interface Builder often need similar initialization logic in both -awakeFromNib and the designated initializer.

Instead of duplicating initialization code in both -init and -awakeFromNib, MYDocumentManager implements the private -_myInitInstanceVariables method that is called from -init and -awakeFromNib.

The -_myInitInstanceVariables method allocates and initializes a mutable array to store the open documents. It also initializes the _myWindowCascadePoint instance variable to the upper-left corner of the visible area of the main screen obtained by using the NSScreen class. NSScreen is described in the "Working with Screens" section of this chapter.

```
- (void)_myInitInstanceVariables
/*" Initialize instance variables: called by -init and -awakeFromNib. "*/
{
  NSRect    screenVisibleFrame = [[NSScreen mainScreen] visibleFrame];

  // Create array of open documents
  _myOpenDocuments = [[NSMutableArray allocWithZone:[self zone]] init];

  // Set initial cascade point
  _myWindowCascadePoint = NSMakePoint(0, NSMaxY(screenVisibleFrame));
}


- (id)init
/*" Designated initializer "*/
{
  self = [super init];

  if(nil != self)
  {
    [self _myInitInstanceVariables];
  }

  return self;
}
```

```
- (void)awakeFromNib
/*" Called automatically after receiver is fully loaded from a nib file. "*/
{
  [self _myInitInstanceVariables];
}
```

Document Information Methods

The -documentClass and -documentExtensions methods provide information about the types of documents managed by MYDocumentManager. The -documentClass method returns the class that is used to create document instances. It is currently hard coded to return the MYDocument class, but it could be reimplemented to return different document classes in different applications.

```
- (Class)documentClass
/*" Returns the class used to encapsulate documents "*/
{
  return [MYDocument class];
}
```

The -documentExtensions method returns an array of file extensions that identify files that can be opened by Image Viewer. It is implemented to return the array of extensions supported by the document class or an empty array. When the array returned by this method is used to limit files that can be opened with an Open panel, an empty array means that any file type can be opened.

```
- (NSArray *)documentExtensions;
/*" Returns an array of NSString file extensions for documents that can be
opened. This implementation returns an array containing elements obtained
by calling [[self documentClass] documentExtensions].  Override this method
to provide more sophisticated behavior and support multiple document classes.
To allow any opening of documents with any extension or no extension,
override this method to return an empty array. "*/
{
  NSMutableArray     *supportedExtensions = [NSMutableArray array];
  Class              documentClass = [self documentClass];

  if([documentClass respondsToSelector:@selector(documentExtensions)])
  {
    [supportedExtensions addObjectsFromArray:
        [documentClass documentExtensions]];
  }
```

```
  return supportedExtensions;
}
```

Accessing Open Documents

The -existingOpenDocuments method returns an array of open document instances. The -existingOpenDocumentWithPath: method returns the open document with the specified path or nil if no open document has that path. The use of standardized paths means that different paths that reference the same file through file system links are considered to be the same path. The -activeDocument method returns the current active document or nil. The active document is the usually the document associated with the last document window that was the key window.

```
- (NSArray *)existingOpenDocuments
/*" Returns an array of open documets. "*/
{
  return _myOpenDocuments;
}


- (id)existingOpenDocumentWithPath:(NSString *)aPath
/*" Returns the open document with the specified path or nil. "*/
{
  NSString        *standardPath = [aPath stringByStandardizingPath];
  id              result = nil;
  id              currentDocument = nil;
  NSEnumerator    *enumerator = [_myOpenDocuments objectEnumerator];

  while(nil == result && nil != (currentDocument = [enumerator nextObject]))
  {
    if([currentDocument respondsToSelector:@selector(documentPath)])
    {
      // the current document has a path
      if([[currentDocument documentPath] isEqualToString:standardPath])
      {
        // currentDocument has aPath
        result = currentDocument;
      }
    }
  }

  return result;
}
```

```
- (id)activeDocument
/*" Returns the active document or nil.  The active document is usually the
last document who's window was key. "*/
{
  // The last object in _myOpenDocuments is assumed to be the active document
  return (0 < [_myOpenDocuments count]) ? [_myOpenDocuments lastObject] : nil;
}
```

Creating Document Instances

When new untitled documents are created, it is important that they do not inadvertently have the same name as an existing file in the file system. If a new document has the same name as an existing file, the user might be misled to think that the new document shows the contents of the existing file when in fact it is a document that has never been saved.

The private `-_myNextUntitledDocumentName` method returns a variant of the path, `~/Untitled`, that does not reference an existing file in the file system.

```
- (NSString *)_myNextUntitledDocumentName
/*" Returns an NSString with a unique untitled document name by appending an
integer to the string "Untitled" and the first document extension in the array
returned by -documentExtensions. "*/
{
  static int    lastUntitledIndex = 1;
  NSString      *result = nil;
  NSString      *extension = @"";
  NSArray       *documentExtensions = [self documentExtensions];

  if(0 < [documentExtensions count])
  {
    // documentExtensions has at least 1 element so use last element as
    // default untitled document extension
    extension = [documentExtensions lastObject];
  }

  do
  {
    [result release]; // release string from previous iteration
                      //    (nil on first iteration)

    result = [[NSString alloc] initWithFormat:@"~/%@%d.%@", MYUNTITLED,
      lastUntitledIndex++, extension];
```

```
  }
  while([[NSFileManager defaultManager] fileExistsAtPath:
      [result stringByStandardizingPath]]);

  [result autorelease];

  return result;
}
```

The private -_myRegisterDocument: method is called by the -_myOpenDocumentWithPath: and -newDocument: methods. This method adds a document to the array of open documents, positions the document's window so that it cascades nicely with other document windows, and makes the document's window the key window. A side effect of making the document's window key is that the associated document becomes the active document.

The _myWindowCascadePoint instance variable is initialized to the top-left corner of the visible area of the main screen in -_myInitInstanceVariables. The first open document window is positioned at _myWindowCascadePoint. Then, _myWindowCascadePoint is set to a new position down and to the right so that the next window's position is offset enough not to obscure the title of the previous window.

```
- (void)_myRegisterDocument:(id)aDocument
/*" Adds aDocument to the receiver's array of open documents, makes
aDocument's window visible on screen, and makes aDocument the active
document. "*/
{
  [_myOpenDocuments addObject:aDocument];

  if([aDocument respondsToSelector:@selector(documentWindow)])
  {
    id     documentWindow = [aDocument documentWindow];

    // Cascade the registered document's window
    _myWindowCascadePoint = [documentWindow cascadeTopLeftFromPoint:
        _myWindowCascadePoint];

    // make registered document's window visible and key
    [documentWindow makeKeyAndOrderFront:self];
  }
}
```

The private -_myOpenDocumentWithPath: method checks to see if an existing open document already represents the specified path. If so, the window associated with the open document is made key and ordered front, which indirectly causes the open document to become the active document. If no open document references the specified path, a new document instance is created with the [[[self documentClass] allocWithZone:[self zone]] initWithPath:aPath] expression. MYDocumentManager's -documentClass method returns the MYDocument class. MYDocument implements the -initWithPath: method to load the image data at the specified path.

```
- (void)_myOpenDocumentWithPath:(NSString *)aPath
{
  id            newDocument = [self existingOpenDocumentWithPath:aPath];

  if(nil != newDocument)
  { // an existing open document already has currentPath
    [[newDocument documentWindow] makeKeyAndOrderFront:self];
  }
  else
  { // no open document already has currentPath
    newDocument = [[[self documentClass] allocWithZone:[self zone]]
        initWithPath:aPath];
    if(nil == newDocument)
    {
      NSLog(@"%@", MYOPEN_DOCUMENT_ERROR_MSG);
    }
    else
    {
      [self _myRegisterDocument:newDocument];  // Retains newDocument
      [newDocument release];
    }
  }
}
```

The - openDocument: action method displays the standard Cocoa Open panel encapsulated by the NSOpenPanel class. The Open panel enables users to select one or more file system paths by browsing in the file system. The Open panel can be configured with a custom accessory view. The accessory view is used to extend the Open panel without the need to subclass NSOpenPanel or edit the .nib file that defines the Open panel. There is normally only one instance of NSOpenPanel in each application, and that instance is accessed by calling [NSOpenPanel openPanel].

NSOpenPanel supports many configuration options documented at http://developer.apple.com/techpubs/macosx/Cocoa/Reference/ApplicationKit/ObjC_classic/Classes/NSOpenPanel.html. NSOpenPanel's -filenames method returns an array of the full paths selected by the user. The -directory method returns the path to the directory that contains the files selected by the user.

```
- (IBAction)openDocument:(id)sender
/*" Displays an open panel that allows selections of multiple paths and opens
the selected files. In this implementation, individual files can be selected
and directories can not. The paths that are selected must have one of the
extensions in the array returned by -documentExtensions. If the array
returned from -documentExtensions is empty, any path is accepted. "*/
{
  NSArray       *typesArray;
  NSOpenPanel   *openPanel;
  NSString      *directory;
  id            activeDocument;

  typesArray = [self documentExtensions];
  if(0 == [typesArray count])
  {
    // Set fileTypesArray to nil so that any type is accepted
    typesArray = nil;
  }
  activeDocument = [self activeDocument];

  if(nil != activeDocument && [activeDocument respondsToSelector:
      @selector(documentPath)])
  {
    // Use active document's directory as initial directory
    directory = [[activeDocument documentPath]
        stringByDeletingLastPathComponent];
  } else {
    directory = @"";
  }

  // Configure the open panel
  openPanel = [NSOpenPanel openPanel];
  [openPanel setAllowsMultipleSelection:YES];
  [openPanel setTreatsFilePackagesAsDirectories:NO];
  [openPanel setDirectory:directory];
  [openPanel setCanChooseDirectories:NO];
```

```
  [openPanel setCanChooseFiles:YES];
  [openPanel setResolvesAliases:YES];

  if (NSOKButton == [openPanel runModalForTypes:typesArray])
  {
    NSArray       *selectedPaths = [openPanel filenames];
    NSEnumerator  *enumerator = [selectedPaths objectEnumerator];
    NSString      *currentPath;

    while(nil != (currentPath = [enumerator nextObject]))
    {
      [self _myOpenDocumentWithPath:currentPath];
    }
  }
}
```

The -newDocument: action method creates a new document with an ~/Untitled path.

```
- (IBAction)newDocument:(id)sender
  /*" Creates a new instance of the class returned from the -documentClass.
The new document is given a unique title and made the active document. "*/
{
  id             newDocument;
  NSString       *newDocumentPath = [self _myNextUntitledDocumentName];

  newDocument = [[[self documentClass] allocWithZone:[self zone]]
      initWithPath:newDocumentPath];
  if(nil == newDocument)
  {
    NSLog(@"%@", MYNEW_DOCUMENT_ERROR_MSG);
  }
  else
  {
    [self _myRegisterDocument:newDocument];  // Retains newDocument
    [newDocument release];
  }
}
```

Saving All Open Documents

The -saveAllDocuments: action method could not be simpler. It just sends the saveDocument: message to every open document.

```
- (IBAction)saveAllDocuments:(id)sender
/*" This method sends the saveDocument: message to all open documents. "*/
{
  [[self existingOpenDocuments] makeObjectsPerformSelector:
      @selector(saveDocument:) withObject:sender];
}
```

Messages Sent by Documents

`MYDocument` instances send the `documentWillClose:` action message up the responder chain when the document's window is about to be closed. The `-documentWillClose:` method is received by the `MYDocumentManager` instance because it is the application's delegate. `MYDocumentManager` implements `-documentWillClose:` to remove the document that is closing from the array of open documents. The array of open documents releases the document instance that is removed from the array. If the array of open documents is the only object that retained the removed document, the document is immediately deallocated.

```
/*" Document communication actions "*/
- (void)documentWillClose:(id)sender
/*" Removes sender from receiver's open documents array "*/
{
  [_myOpenDocuments removeObject:sender];
}
```

`MYDocument` instances send the `makeDocumentActive:` action message up the responder chain when the document's window becomes the key window. `MYDocumentManager` implements `-makeDocumentActive:` to make the sender of `makeDocumentActive:` the active document.

```
- (void)makeDocumentActive:(id)sender
/*" Sets the receiver's active document to sender if possible.  If sender is
not an open document, this method does nothing. This method does not make
sender's window key. "*/
{

  if(0 < [_myOpenDocuments count])
  {
    // There is at least 1 open document
    int       index = [_myOpenDocuments indexOfObject:sender];

    if(index != NSNotFound)
    {
```

```
      // anObject is an open document
      // Swap positions in _myOpenDocuments: the last object in
      // _myOpenDocuments is assumed to be the active document
      [sender retain];
      [_myOpenDocuments replaceObjectAtIndex:index withObject:
          [_myOpenDocuments lastObject]];
      [_myOpenDocuments removeLastObject];
      [_myOpenDocuments addObject:sender];
      [sender release];
    }
  }
}
```

Menu Validation

MYDocumentManager implements -validateMenuItem: to validate menu items that send the openDocument:, newDocument:, and saveAllDocuments: actions.

```
/*" Menu validation "*/
- (BOOL)validateMenuItem:(NSMenuItem *)aMenuItem
/*" Validate menu items that send the openDocument:, newDocument:, or
saveAllDocuments: actions. "*/
{
  SEL         action;
  BOOL        enableMenuItem = NO;

  action = [aMenuItem action];

  // The -open:, -new: and -saveAll: actions are provided by this calss and
  // therefore validated by this class.
  if (action == @selector(openDocument:) || action == @selector(newDocument:))
  {
    enableMenuItem = YES;
  }
  else if (action == @selector(saveAllDocuments:))
  {
    enableMenuItem = (0 < [_myOpenDocuments count]);
  }

  return enableMenuItem;
}
```

Using NSApplication Delegate Methods

When user quits a graphical Cocoa application, NSApplication sends the applicationShouldTerminate: message to its delegate. The values that can be returned from - applicationShouldTerminate: are the constants NSTerminateNow, NSTerminateCancel, and NSTerminateLater. Returning NSTerminateNow gives the application permission to terminate immediately. Returning NSTerminateCancel cancels the termination. Returning NSTerminateLater postpones the decision to terminate or not until NSApplication's -replyToApplicationShouldTerminate: method is called with a YES or NO argument.

MYDocumentManager implements -applicationShouldTerminate: to give users a chance to save unsaved documents before the application terminates.

```
/*" Application delegate methods "*/
- (NSApplicationTerminateReply)applicationShouldTerminate:
    (NSApplication *)sender
/*" Implemented to Give user a chance to review and save any unsaved documents
before terminating "*/
{
  NSEnumerator                *enumerator;
  id                          currentDocument;
  int                         choice;
  NSApplicationTerminateReply result = NSTerminateNow;
  BOOL                        foundUnsaved = NO;

  // Catch exception during review and save

  // Determine if theer are any unsaved documents
  enumerator = [_myOpenDocuments objectEnumerator];
  while(!foundUnsaved && nil != (currentDocument = [enumerator nextObject]))
  {
    if([currentDocument respondsToSelector:@selector(isDocumentEdited)])
    {
      // Found at least one unsaved document
      foundUnsaved = [currentDocument isDocumentEdited];
    }
  }

  if(foundUnsaved)
  {
    // Find out of the user wants to review and possibly save the unsaved
    // documents, cancel the termination, or terminate anyway
```

```
    choice = NSRunAlertPanel(MYQUIT, MYUNSAVED_DOCS_MSG, MYREVIEW_UNSAVED,
                             MYQUIT_ANYWAY, MYCANCEL);
    if (choice == NSAlertOtherReturn)
    { // User selected Cancel
      result = NSTerminateCancel;
    }
    else if (choice != NSAlertAlternateReturn)
    {    // User selected Review Unsaved
      // Give the user the chance to review the edited document(s). */
      enumerator = [_myOpenDocuments objectEnumerator];
      while(result == NSTerminateNow &&
          nil != (currentDocument = [enumerator nextObject]))
      {
        if([currentDocument respondsToSelector:@selector(safeClose)])
        {
          // Cause unsaved documents to show a save panel
          if(![currentDocument safeClose])
          { // User selected Cancel
            result = NSTerminateCancel;
          }
        }
      }
    }
    else
    { // User chooses to quit without saving
    }
  }

    return result;
}
```

When a user double-clicks a file in Finder, the user's default application for the file is launched, if it is not already running, and notified that it should open the file that was double clicked. When that happens, `NSApplication` sends the `application:openFile:` message to its delegate. The `application:openFile:` message is also sent to the application's delegate when files are dragged and dropped onto the application's icon.

`MYDocumentManager` implements `-application:openFile:` to verify that the file to open is a supported type, and then calls `-_myOpenDocumentWithPath:` to open the file. If the file is opened, `-application:openFile:` returns `YES`; otherwise it returns `NO`. The value returned is sent back to Finder, which displays a short animation if files are not opened after a drag and drop.

```
- (BOOL)application:(NSApplication *)sender openFile:(NSString *)filename
/*" Called automatically when application is requested to open a document
either by drag and drop or double clicking in finder. Returns YES if the
file is successfully opened, and NO otherwise "*/
{
  int               result = NO;

  if([[self documentExtensions] containsObject:[filename pathExtension]])
  {
    // Filename has an accepted extension
    [self _myOpenDocumentWithPath:filename];
    result = YES;
  }

  return result;
}
```

According to Apple's user interface guidelines, when a document-based application is activated by the user, the application must display a document window. If there are no open document windows, a new untitled document must be created. `NSApplication` already implements most of that behavior. When Apple's guidelines require the creation of an untitled document, `NSApplication` calls its delegate's `- applicationShouldOpenUntitledFile:` method. If `- applicationShouldOpenUntitledFile:` returns YES, `NSApplication` calls the delegate's `-applicationOpenUntitledFile:` method to open the untitled file.

```
- (BOOL)applicationShouldOpenUntitledFile:(NSApplication *)sender
/*" Called automatically: returns YES meaning that it is OK to open an
untitled document. "*/
{
  return YES;
}


- (BOOL)applicationOpenUntitledFile:(NSApplication *)sender
/*" Called automatically when application is requested to open an untitled
document. This method is implemented to call [self newDocument:nil] "*/
{
  [self newDocument:nil];

  return YES;
}
```

Concluding MYDocumentManager's Implementation

MYDocumentManager implements the -dealloc method to release the _myOpenDocuments instance variable. When _myOpenDocuments is deallocated, it releases all the objects it contains.

```
- (void)dealloc
/*" Claen-up "*/
{
  [_myOpenDocuments release];
  _myOpenDocuments = nil;

  [super dealloc];
}

@end
```

Build and test the Image Viewer application. Drag image files from Finder and drop them in open Image Viewer document windows. Test the automatic creation of untitled documents by closing all open Image Viewer documents, making another application active, and then switching back to Image Viewer. Image Viewer now has almost all the features of Apple's Preview application. Image Viewer could have been implemented with more features and fewer lines of code by using Cocoa's NSDocument and NSDocumentController classes, but this implementation shows how the NSApplication, NSWindow, NSSavePanel, and NSOpenPanel classes are used. The NSDocument and NSDocumentController classes completely hide their interaction with NSApplication, NSWindow, NSSavePanel, and NSOpenPanel.

Modal Loops

A modal loop is a loop that consumes all events so that it is not possible for the user to interact normally with an application until the modal loop terminates. Modal loops are used when the user's attention is required before the application can continue processing. For example, modal loops are used when the user must acknowledge an error message before continuing or when input is required.

Modal loops consume all events in an application, but users can use other applications, move application windows, and hide applications even when modal loops are running.

Modal loops are started in two general ways: either an entire window is run in a modal loop controlled by the NSApplication class, or an individual view implements its own modal loop in code.

Using Modal Windows

To run an entire window in a modal loop, call NSApplication's -runModalForWindow: method sending a window as the argument. The -runModalForWindow: method does not return until the modal loop terminates. When -runModalForWindow: is called, NSApplication sends all events to the modal window until one of the NSApplication's -stopModal, -abortModal, or -stopModalWithCode: methods is called to terminate the loop. The -stopModal method is called to end a modal loop normally. For example, use -stopModal to end a modal loop with the user clicking an OK button to acknowledge an error message. The -abortModal method is called when abnormal termination is required. For example, -abortModal should be called if the user closes a modal window by clicking the window's close button in the title bar. Both -stopModal and -abortModal call -stopModalWithCode:. The argument passed to -stopModalWithCode: is the value that is ultimately returned from the call to -runModalForWindow: that started the loop. The -stopModal method calls -stopModalWithCode: with the NSRunStoppedResponse constant, and -abortModal calls -stopModalWithCode: with the NSRunAbortedResponse constant.

NOTE

Modal windows normally consume all events received by the application. However, NSWindow subclasses that override NSWindow's -worksWhenModal method to return YES are able to receive events even when a modal window is active. This capability should be used sparingly.

The NSRunAlertPanel() function used in Image Viewer is a convenience function that calls NSApplication's -runModalForWindow: method. Many standard Cocoa panels such as NSSavePanel, NSOpenPanel, and NSPrintPanel provide methods that start modal loops using NSApplication's -runModalForWindow:. For example, Image Viewer uses NSSavePanel's -runModalForDirectory:file: method that starts a modal loop and does not return until the user selects a path or closes the panel.

Apple provides a detailed explanation of modal loops controlled by the NSApplication class at http://developer.apple.com/techpubs/macosx/Cocoa/TasksAndConcepts/ProgrammingTopics/WinPanel/Concepts/UsingModalWindows.html. Apple's class documentation for the NSApplication class includes sample code for starting and ending modal loops. Apple's guidelines for when to use modal loops are provided at
http://developer.apple.com/techpubs/macosx/Essentials/AquaHIGuidelines/AHIGDialogs/Types_of_Di_to_Use_Them.html.

Using Modal Views

Individual views can create their own modal loops that consume all events until the loop terminates. This technique is described in Chapter 15, "Events and Cursors," with an example. Apple also provides an example at `http://developer.apple.com/techpubs/macosx/Cocoa/TasksAndConcepts/ProgrammingTopics/BasicEventHandling/Tasks/HandlingMouseEvents.html`.

Working with Sheets

Modal windows normally consume all events received by the application and prevent users for working in other windows within the same application. Modal windows require the user's undivided attention before the user can continue working with the application. However, users can switch to other applications even when another application is displaying a modal window. Modal windows are, therefore, called application modal windows because each window can only affect one application.

A sheet is a document modal window. Each sheet is attached to another window. When a sheet is visible, it consumes all events received by its associated window, but users can continue to use other windows in the same application. Using sheets instead of application modal windows gives users more flexibility. In addition, when a sheet displays an error or requires input for a particular document window, the association between the sheet and the effected window is clear. Application modal windows that display errors or required input related to a particular document can confuse users who lose track of which document is effected.

Only one sheet can be attached to a window at a time. Sheets emerge from another window's title bar with an animation to catch the user's eye. Sheets should not be used with windows that do not have a title bar.

Sheets work best when there is a clear association between the information presented by the sheet and the associated window. For example, a sheet for saving a document makes sense. The association between the sheet and the document window makes it clear to the user which document is being saved.

Apple provides guidelines for when to use sheets at `http://developer.apple.com/techpubs/macosx/Essentials/AquaHIGuidelines/AHIGDialogs/Document_Mo_ogs_Sheets_.html`.

To show how sheets are used with Cocoa, the Image Viewer application is modified to use sheets instead of application modal windows when appropriate.

Changes to `MYDocument` to Support Sheets

The first change is made to the `MYDocument` class interface. An addition instance variable is needed to keep track of whether the document's window should close when the user is finished with a Save sheet. Edit the `MYDocument.h` file so that it has the following instance variable section:

```
@interface MYDocument : NSObject
{
  IBOutlet NSImageView *imageView;

  NSString  *_myDocumentPath;     /*" Document's path "*/
  BOOL      _myHasEverBeenSaved;  /*" YES iff document has ever been saved "*/
  BOOL      _myShouldCloseAfterSave; /*" YES iff document is being closed "*/
}
```

Several changes must be made to MYDocument's implementation. The -_myShouldClose method currently displays a modal alert panel that asks users if they want to save changes made to a document before closing the document. The following implementation of -_myShouldClose uses the NSBeginAlertSheet() function instead of NSRunAlertPanel() to ask users if they want to save changes.

```
- (bool)_myShouldClose
/*" Gives users a chance to save edited documents before closing the document.
Returns NO if the document has unsaved changes.  Returns YES otherwise. "*/
{
  BOOL   result = YES;

  _myShouldCloseAfterSave = NO;  // set to deafult value

  if([self isDocumentEdited])
  {
    NSString    *documentName = [self documentPath];

    if(nil == documentName)
    {
      // document has no path so use its window's title instead
      documentName = [[self documentWindow] title];
    }

    // the document has been edited
    NSBeginAlertSheet(MYDEFAULT_CLOSE_ACTION, MYSAVE,MYDONT_SAVE, MYCANCEL,
        [self documentWindow], self,
        nil, @selector(_mySaveChangesSheetDidEnd:returnCode:contextInfo:),
        NULL, MYSAVE_CHANGES, documentName);

    result = NO;
  }
```

```
  return result;
}
```

NSBeginAlertSheet() is similar to NSRunAlertPanel(). NSBeginAlertSheet() is declared in Apple's header files as follows:

```
void NSBeginAlertSheet(NSString *title, NSString *defaultButton,
    NSString *alternateButton, NSString *otherButton, NSWindow *docWindow,
    id modalDelegate, SEL didEndSelector, SEL didDismissSelector,
    void *contextInfo, NSString *msg, ...)
```

The title, msg, defaultButton, alternateButton, and otherButton arguments all have the same meaning as the corresponding arguments to NSRunAlertPanel(). The docWindow argument specifies the window that the sheet references. The additional arguments, modalDelegate, didEndSelector, didDismissSelector, and contextInfo, exist because of the most important difference between NSRunAlertPanel() and NSBeginAlertSheet(): NSRunAlertPanel() does not return until the user acknowledges the panel, but NSBeginAlertSheet() returns immediately.

Because NSBeginAlertSheet() returns before getting input from the user, the alert sheet needs a way to tell the application what user input is received at some later time. The didEndSelector and didDismissSelector arguments to NSBeginAlertSheet() specify the messages that are sent when the user clicks a button on the alert sheet and when the alert sheet is closed, respectively. The modalDelegate argument specifies the object that will receive the messages identified by the didEndSelector and didDismissSelector selectors. The contextInfo argument is used to specify arbitrary data that is passed along as an argument to the didEndSelector and didDismissSelector messages.

When NSBeginAlertSheet() is called in the implementation of -_myShouldClose, the modalDelegate argument is self. The didEndSelector argument is nil, which means don't send any message to modalDelegate when the user clicks a button. The contextInfo argument is NULL, and the didDismissSelector is -_mySaveChangesSheetDidEnd:returnCode:contextInfo:.

Both didEndSelector and didDismissSelector must specify selectors that take three arguments. The first and last arguments are pointers. The second argument is an integer return code, which will be one of the NSAlertDefaultReturn, NSAlertAlternateReturn, or NSAlertOtherReturn constants when the message is sent to modalDelegate.

MYDocument implements -_mySaveChangesSheetDidEnd:returnCode:contextInfo: as follows:

```
- (void)_mySaveChangesSheetDidEnd:(id)sheet returnCode:(int)returnCode
    contextInfo:(id)contextInfo
{
  switch(returnCode)
  {
    case NSAlertDefaultReturn:
    {
        // User chooses to save changes
      [self saveDocument:nil];
      _myShouldCloseAfterSave = YES;  // note fact that close is pending
      break;
    }
    case NSAlertAlternateReturn:
    {
      // User chooses NOT to save changes
      [[self documentWindow] close];
      break;
    }
    case NSAlertOtherReturn:
    {
      // User chooses to CANCEL close
      break;
    }
  }
}
```

The private `-_mySaveChangesSheetDidEnd:returnCode:contextInfo:` method is added to the `MYDocument` class implementation right above the implementation of `-_myShouldClose` in `MYDocument.m` so that the compiler does not warn that `-_mySaveChangesSheetDidEnd:returnCode:contextInfo:` has not been declared when it is used in `-_myShouldClose`. If the `returnCode` argument that the alert sheet sends when it calls `-_mySaveChangesSheetDidEnd:returnCode:contextInfo:` is `NSAlertDefaultReturn`, the `_myShouldCloseAfterSave` instance variable is set to `YES`, which means that the document should be closed after the user has finished saving it. The instance variable is needed because the document cannot be closed until some time in the future. If `returnCode` is `NSAlertAlternateReturn`, the document can be closed immediately because the user does not want to save changes. Finally, if `returnCode` is `NSAlertOtherReturn`, the method does not do anything because the user has canceled the close.

The `-_myShouldCloseAfterSave` method is added to `MYDocument` to return the value of the `_myShouldCloseAfterSave` instance variable. If `_myShouldCloseAfterSave` is `YES`, the document is going to be closed after it is saved.

```
- (BOOL)_myShouldCloseAfterSave
/*" Returns YES if the document should be closed after it is saved.
NO otherwise. "*/
{
  return _myShouldCloseAfterSave;
}
```

MYDocument now uses an alert sheet instead of an alert panel when asking users to save changes to documents. The next step is to make the Save panel, which is used to select paths to save unsaved documents, is run as a sheet. NSSavePanel already provides the -beginSheetForDirectory:file:modalForWindow:modalDelegate: didEndSelector:contextInfo: method to run it as a sheet.

The first two arguments are the same directory and file paths used with -runModalForDirectory:file:. The modalForWindow argument is the associated document window. The didEndSelector argument specifies the message to send to the modalDelegate, and the contextInfo argument is passed to the modal delegate as an argument to the didEndSelector message.

The -_mySavePanelDidEnd:returnCode:contextInfo: method is called when the user clicks a button on the Save sheet. The returnCode argument is NSOKButton if the user saved the document and NSCancelButton if the user clicked the Cancel button on the Save sheet.

If the user canceled the save, the _myShouldCloseAfterSave variable is set to NO. The document should not be closed if it was not saved. An action message is sent up the responder chain to inform the document manager that the close was canceled. The need for the action message is explained in the "Changes to MYDocumentManager to Support Sheets" section of this chapter.

If returnCode is NSOKButton, the document is saved at the path selected by the user. After the save, if -_myShouldCloseAfterSave returns YES, the document is closed. The document cannot be closed before -_mySavePanelDidEnd:returnCode:contextInfo: is called because the save sheet is still active until then.

```
- (void)_mySavePanelDidEnd:(id)sheet returnCode:(int)returnCode
    contextInfo:(id)contextInfo
/*" Called when Save sheet is being closed. "*/
{
  if (NSOKButton == returnCode &&
      [sheet respondsToSelector:@selector(filename)])
  {
```

```
    // Cast is safe because we just verified that sheet responds to filename.
    [self _mySetDocumentPath:[sheet filename]];
    [self _mySaveDocumentData];

    if([self _myShouldCloseAfterSave])
    {
      [[self documentWindow] close];
    }
  }
  else
  {
    // User canceled save
    [NSApp sendAction:@selector(cancelPendingTerminate:) to:nil from:self];
    _myShouldCloseAfterSave = NO;
  }
}
```

The `-saveDocumentAs:` method is modified to use `NSSavePanel` panel as a sheet instead of a modal panel.

```
- (IBAction)saveDocumentAs:(id)sender
/*" Displays a Save panel to find out where the user wants to save the
document's image data. If the user does not cancel the save, this method
saves the image data at the specified location. "*/
{
  NSSavePanel     *savePanel;
  NSString        *documentDirectory = [[self documentPath]
      stringByDeletingLastPathComponent];
  NSString        *documentName = [[self documentPath] lastPathComponent];

  savePanel = [NSSavePanel savePanel];
  [savePanel setRequiredFileType:@"tiff"];
  [savePanel setTreatsFilePackagesAsDirectories:NO];

  [savePanel beginSheetForDirectory:documentDirectory file:documentName
      modalForWindow:[self documentWindow] modalDelegate:self
      didEndSelector:@selector(_mySavePanelDidEnd:returnCode:contextInfo:)
      contextInfo:NULL];
}
```

Changes to MYDocumentManager to Support Sheets

An additional instance variable must be added to the MYDocumentManager class interface to keep track of whether the application is in the process of terminating. Edit the MYDocument.h file so that it has the following instance variable section:

```
@interface MYDocumentManager : NSObject
{
  NSMutableArray *_myOpenDocuments;      /*" Array of open documents "*/
  NSPoint         _myWindowCascadePoint; /*" Used to cascade doc windows "*/
  BOOL            _myApplicationIsTerminating; /*" YES iff application is
                                                   terminating "*/
}
```

The logic for terminating the Image Viewer application needs to be changed to accommodate MYDocument's use of Save sheets. The problem is that when -applicationShouldTerminate: is called, the user is given a chance to save unsaved documents. The documents are saved with a sheet, which means that the application must wait an indeterminate amount of time before terminating so that the user can interact with the sheets.

The following implementation of -applicationShouldTerminate: returns NSTerminateLater if there are any unsaved documents and sets the _myApplicationIsTerminating instance variable to YES. NSApplication interprets NSTerminateLater to mean that it should wait until its -replyToApplicationShouldTerminate: is called to tell it whether the termination is canceled or should proceed. The behavior of -applicationShouldTerminate: is provided by NSApplication specifically to enable the use of sheets during application termination.

```
- (NSApplicationTerminateReply)applicationShouldTerminate:
    (NSApplication *)sender
/*" Implemented to Give user a chance to review and save any unsaved documents
before terminating "*/
{
  NSEnumerator                *enumerator;
  id                          currentDocument;
  int                         choice;
  NSApplicationTerminateReply result = NSTerminateNow;
  BOOL                        foundUnsaved = NO;

  // Determine if theer are any unsaved documents
  enumerator = [_myOpenDocuments objectEnumerator];
  while(!foundUnsaved && nil != (currentDocument = [enumerator nextObject]))
```

```
{
  if([currentDocument respondsToSelector:@selector(isDocumentEdited)])
  {
    // Found at least one unsaved document
    foundUnsaved = [currentDocument isDocumentEdited];
  }
}

if(foundUnsaved)
{
  // Find out of the user wants to review and possibly save the unsaved
  // documents, cancel the termination, or terminate anyway
  choice = NSRunAlertPanel(MYQUIT, MYUNSAVED_DOCS_MSG, MYREVIEW_UNSAVED,
                           MYQUIT_ANYWAY, MYCANCEL);
  if (choice == NSAlertOtherReturn)
  { // User selected Cancel
    result = NSTerminateCancel;
  }
  else if (choice != NSAlertAlternateReturn)
  {    // User selected Review Unsaved

    // Give the user the chance to review the edited document(s). */
    enumerator = [_myOpenDocuments objectEnumerator];
    while(result != NSTerminateCancel &&
        nil != (currentDocument = [enumerator nextObject]))
    {
      if([currentDocument respondsToSelector:@selector(safeClose)])
      {
        // Cause unsaved documents to show a save panel
        if(![currentDocument safeClose])
        { // User selected Cancel
          result = NSTerminateLater;

          // Note the fact that termination is still in progress
          _myApplicationIsTerminating = YES;
        }
      }
    }
  }
  else
```

```
    { // User chooses to quit without saving
    }
  }

    return result;
}
```

The -documentWillClose action method is called by MYDocument instances when their associated window is closed. The following implementation of -documentWillClose checks to see if the last open document has closed and the application is waiting to terminate. If so, the [NSApp replyToApplicationShouldTerminate:YES] expression tells NSApplication to go ahead and terminate now.

```
- (void)documentWillClose:(id)sender
  /*" Removes sender from receiver's open documents array "*/
{
  [_myOpenDocuments removeObject:sender];

  if(_myApplicationIsTerminating && 0 == [_myOpenDocuments count])
  {
    [NSApp replyToApplicationShouldTerminate:YES];
  }
}
```

The -cancelPendingTerminate: method is needed so that documents can cancel application termination if the user clicks the Cancel button on a sheet. If MYDocumentManager receives the -cancelPendingTerminate: action, the [NSApp replyToApplicationShouldTerminate:NO] expression tells NSApplication to cancel termination. The _myApplicationIsTerminating instance variable is set to NO so that the application does not terminate when the last document is closed.

```
- (void)cancelPendingTerminate:(id)sender
/*" Cancels the pending termination of the application. If no termination is
pending, this method does nothing. "*/
{
  if(_myApplicationIsTerminating)
  {
    [NSApp replyToApplicationShouldTerminate:NO];
    _myApplicationIsTerminating = NO;
  }
}
```

Working with Drawers

A drawer is similar to a sheet in some ways. A drawer is a window that is attached to, and associated with, another window. Unlike sheets, drawers are not modal. Drawers slide out of the sides of other windows instead of sliding down from a window's title bar.

Drawers are documented at `http://developer.apple.com/techpubs/macosx/Cocoa/TasksAndConcepts/ProgrammingTopics/Drawers/index.html` and `http://developer.apple.com/techpubs/macosx/Cocoa/Reference/ApplicationKit/ObjC_classic/Classes/NSDrawer.html`.

Drawers are usually created in Interface Builder and stored in a `.nib` file along with their associated window called the parent window. Interface Builder includes an `NSDrawer` object already on a palette. No code is needed to manage drawers. In Interface Builder, drag a drawer from the palette into the Instances tab of a `.nib`. Connect the drawer's `parentWindow` outlet to the parent window. Place a button somewhere in the parent window. Use Interface Builder to make the drawer the button's target and set the button's action to `toggle:`. Each time the button is clicked, the drawer opens or closes.

The contents displayed in a drawer can also be set in Interface Builder. `NSDrawer` provides a `contentView` outlet that can be connected to any view. Create a view in Interface Builder including views with subviews, scroll views, tables, and so on. Connect the drawer's `contentView` outlet to the view created in Interface Builder. Each time the drawer opens, it shows its `contentView`. Views are described in detail in Chapter 10, "Views and Controls."

Drawers should not be larger than their parent window. While opening and closing, the drawer slides behind the parent window. If the drawer is too big, it will emerge from the opposite side of its parent as it slides in or out.

Apple provides guidelines on when to use drawers at `http://developer.apple.com/techpubs/macosx/Essentials/AquaHIGuidelines/AHIGWindows/index.html`.

Working with Screens

The `NSScreen` class encapsulates the attributes of a computer display such as its size in pixels and the number of supported colors. Each computer can have more than one attached display, and each display can have different attributes. The `NSScreen` class provides the `+screens` class method that returns an array of `NSScreen` instances that each encapsulate a display connected to the computer. The `+deepestScreen` method returns an `NSScreen` instance that encapsulates the display that supports the highest color fidelity. The `+mainScreen` method returns an `NSScreen` instance for the display that is currently showing the key window.

NSScreen's -visibleFrame method was already used in the implementation of Image Viewer. NSScreen only has a few methods, and they are documented at http://developer.apple.com/techpubs/macosx/Cocoa/Reference/ApplicationKit/ObjC_classic/Classes/NSScreen.html.

Working with Panels

Panels are special windows that have auxiliary purposes in applications. Example of panels include the Save panel, Open panel, and Alert panels used in Image Viewer.

Panels have slightly different behavior than standard windows. Most panels are hidden when their application is not the user's current active application. The panels automatically reappear when the user switches to their application. Panels can float above other windows. For example, alert panels are always visually on top of other application windows. Panels can become the key window, but not the main window. The key and main windows are described in the "Key Window and Main Window" section of Chapter 8. Panels can be prevented from becoming the key window, and panels can be configured to receive events even when another window is being run in a modal loop.

The NSPanel Class and Subclasses

The NSPanel class encapsulates Cocoa panels. NSPanel is a subclass of NSWindow and, therefore, panels inherit all the attributes of windows.

NSPanel only adds the following public methods to the ones inherited from NSWindow:

```
- (BOOL)becomesKeyOnlyIfNeeded
- (BOOL)isFloatingPanel
- (void)setBecomesKeyOnlyIfNeeded:(BOOL)flag
- (void)setFloatingPanel:(BOOL)flag
- (void)setWorksWhenModal:(BOOL)flag
- (BOOL)worksWhenModal
```

NSPanel is documented at
http://developer.apple.com/techpubs/macosx/Cocoa/Reference/ApplicationKit/ObjC_classic/Classes/NSPanel.html.

Cocoa includes several subclasses of NSPanel that implement features common to most graphical applications. Cocoa's NSPanel subclasses include the NSOpenPanel and NSSavePanel classes used in Image Viewer and other examples in this book. The other standard subclasses of NSPanel are NSPrintPanel, NSFontPanel, NSColorPanel, and NSPageLayout.

The NSApplication class provides the -orderFrontColorPanel: and -runPageLayout: methods for displaying the standard NSColorPanel, and NSPageLayout instances, respectively.

The NSFontPanel class is described in Chapter 11, "Text Views." The NSPrintPanel and NSPageLayout classes are described in Chapter 25, "Printing," and the NSColorPanel class is introduced in Chapter 17, "Color."

Summary

This chapter covered two of the three most prominent classes in Cocoa's Application Kit framework: NSApplication and NSWindow. The NSApplication, NSWindow, and NSView classes collaborate to form the basis of every graphical Cocoa application. The Image Viewer example used most of the features provide by NSApplication and NSWindow, but it hardly touched the surface of the capabilities of NSView subclasses such as NSImageView.

The Application Kit framework includes subclasses of NSWindow such as NSPanel, but neither NSWindow nor NSApplication are commonly subclassed by Cocoa programmers. In contrast, NSView is subclassed in almost every Cocoa application. NSView is designed to be subclassed to implement application-specific features, custom drawing, and custom-event management. The next chapter describes many of the NSView subclasses provided by the Application Kit framework, but views are such a large subject that Chapters 10 through 15 all deal with aspects of views. Views are used in almost every chapter from here on because they play such a central role in Cocoa application development.

10

Views and Controls

IN THIS CHAPTER

- Controls
- Simple Views and Controls
- Container Views and Controls
- Compound Controls

This chapter focuses on using the wide array of user interface objects, or widgets, found in the Application Kit. Interactive widgets, such as sliders, buttons, and text fields, are known as controls in Cocoa because they all descend from the `NSControl` class, which is a subclass of `NSView`. Passive widgets, such as progress bars, are usually just known as views because they descend from `NSView`. This chapter covers nearly all the simpler Cocoa controls and views. A discussion of the remaining control and view classes, which are all considerably more complex than those in this chapter, can be found in Chapter 18, "Advanced Views and Controls."

Most of the Application Kit widgets are relatively simple and tend to work in a similar fashion. Most respond to a nearly identical set of methods, with only a few unique methods for each different kind of widget. Before diving into the details of these objects, it is imperative to understand all the concepts explained in Chapter 8, "Application Kit Framework Overview." This chapter assumes a basic understanding of the responder chain, target/action, overall Cocoa application structure, and the `NSResponder` and `NSView` classes as described in Chapter 8.

Controls

All Cocoa controls are subclasses of the `NSControl` class, which is in turn a subclass of `NSView`. The `NSControl` class is an abstract class and should not be instantiated. Understanding it is necessary to effectively use its subclasses, however.

The `NSControl` class performs three key functions. It must be able to draw the user interface element that it represents. The machinery to support this task is inherited from

`NSView`. It also needs to be able to respond to user input, in particular from the mouse and keyboard. This capability is inherited from the `NSResponder` class. Finally, a control needs to be able to send arbitrary action messages to arbitrary targets. This capability is added in the `NSControl` class itself.

`NSControl` Class

The `NSControl` class adds several methods to the `NSView` class. Because all interactive Cocoa user interface elements inherit from `NSControl`, all these methods are valid for such user interface objects. Some of these methods might not make sense for certain user interface elements. In those cases, these methods usually do nothing.

Methods to Define a Control's Appearance

Many controls display some text. Text fields are an obvious example of this. There are several `NSControl` methods to adjust how the control displays text. These methods are rarely used in program code. In most cases, the values altered by these methods are set in Interface Builder's inspector and stored in a `.nib` file.

The `-setFont:` method, which takes an `NSFont` object as its argument, sets the font used by the control to display text. The `-font` method returns the font currently in use by the control. Chapter 11, "Text Views," discusses the `NSFont` class. In Interface Builder, the standard font panel is used to change the font of a control.

The text alignment can be altered with the `-setAlignment:` method. This method takes one of the five constants `NSLeftTextAlignment`, `NSRightTextAlignment`, `NSCenterTextAlignment`, `NSJustifiedTextAlignment`, and `NSNaturalTextAlignment`. Many of the Interface Builder inspectors have a control for setting the alignment. Figure 10.1 shows how the control corresponds to these constants.

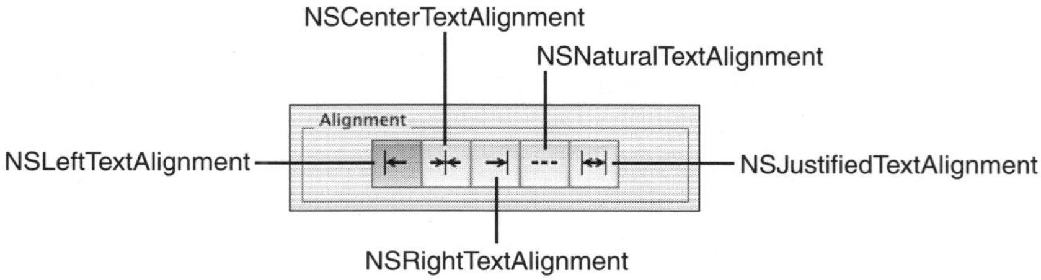

FIGURE 10.1 The alignment control in Interface Builder.

The default alignment for all controls is `NSNaturalTextAlignment`. This generally behaves like `NSLeftTextAlignment`, which renders the text at the left edge of the control. Multiline text has a jagged right edge. The difference is that natural text alignment takes localization into account. In a right to left language, natural alignment might imply a right text alignment. When `NSRightTextAlignment` is used, the text is rendered at the right edge of the control. Multiline text has a jagged left edge. Text drawn with `NSCenterTextAlignment` is horizontally centered in the control. Both the left and right edges are jagged if the text is multiline. The `NSJustifiedTextAlignment` constant refers to text that is adjusted so that it is flush with both the left and right edges. Extra space is inserted between words as necessary to justify the text. This is normally only observable with multiline text because the last line of text will not be stretched to fit. Figure 10.2 shows how the various text alignment modes are rendered for single line and multiline text.

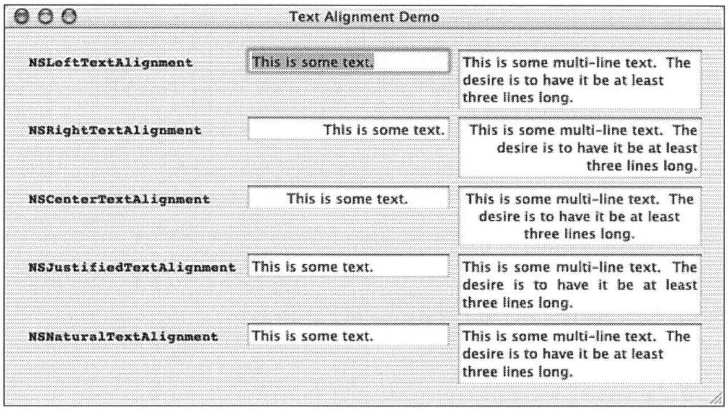

FIGURE 10.2 Demonstration of the five alignment modes supported by Cocoa.

There are several other methods for modifying a control's appearance, but they are implemented by the `NSCell` class. Refer to the section "`NSCell` Class" later in this chapter for a listing and description of these other methods.

Methods to Implement Target-Action

Several `NSControl` methods can be used to set up and modify a control's target-action behavior.

Setting up target-action requires that a control's target and action be defined. The action should be the selector of an action method (the `SEL` type). The target should be the `id` of an object or `nil`. If `nil`, the action is sent to the first responder and down the responder chain if necessary. The `-setAction:` and `-setTarget:` methods are used, respectively, to set action and target. The `-action` and `-target` methods can be used to determine a control's current action and target.

Usually, the action and target of a control are set up in Interface Builder by control dragging a connection between two objects. This could be done programmatically with these methods, but Interface Builder is generally the easier way to set up a target-action connection. For example, suppose that in Interface Builder a connection is control dragged from `myButton` to `myControllerObject` and the action is set to `-buttonClicked:`. This could be done in code as follows:

```
[myButton setTarget: myControllerObject];
[myButton setAction:@selector(buttonClicked:)];
```

Using either this code or Interface Builder gives the same result. If the button is clicked, the `-buttonClicked:` method of `myControllerObject` is invoked. Alternatively, setting the target to `nil` is the same as connecting to the `.nib` file's first responder icon.

To programmatically simulate a user clicking a control—such as a button—send the `-performClick:` message to the control. This causes the control's action message to be sent, just as if a user had clicked the control.

Some controls need to send an action message repeatedly. To do this, the `-setContinuous:` method is used. Use `YES` to make the control send multiple action messages, or `NO` for a single action message. The `-isContinuous` method can be used to obtain this setting. In Interface Builder, a control's inspector has a check box labeled Continuous that can be turned on and off to change this setting. Because this setting isn't useful for every type of control, not all controls have this check box.

The meaning of continuous can change from one type of control to another. For example, a continuous button sends its action message over and over at a fixed rate as long as the button is being pressed. A continuous slider sends action messages as the slider is moved, whereas a noncontinuous slider sends a single action message when the slider is released.

NOTE

Control subclasses that send actions periodically, such as buttons, have methods for changing how often the action is sent. The repeat speed can also be controlled by a user's preferences.

There is also an advanced method, `-sendActionOn:`, which can be used to specifically define which types of events should trigger sending the action. Common events for this would be mouse-dragged, mouse-down, or mouse-up. The argument to this method is a bitwise `OR` of event mask constants. See Chapter 15, "Events and Cursors," for a list of the event constants and what they mean. This method can radically alter a control's behavior, so it is normally best to avoid using it. Each control subclass sets up its action-sending behavior automatically, based on the Aqua guidelines. That is good enough for most situations.

Methods to Modify Event Response

Some of the NSControl methods determine how the control responds to mouse and keyboard events.

The most often used methods are -setEnabled: and -isEnabled. Using the constants YES or NO, the -setEnabled: method can be used to enable or disable the control. A disabled control is usually grayed out and will not respond to any user input. It will also refuse to become the first responder.

When a user double-clicks or triple-clicks a control, that action is usually interpreted as two or three distinct clicks on the control. To ask a control to ignore all but the first click, send it a -setIgnoresMultiClick: message with a value of YES. All clicks after the first will be forwarded to the control's superclass. Normally, the superclass ignores the extra clicks. The -ignoresMultiClick method can be used to determine whether the control is ignoring multiple clicks.

Finally, a control can choose to accept or reject first responder status. Use the -setRefusesFirstResponder: method to change this behavior, and -refusesFirstResponder to see how it is currently set. Changing this method also alters how the control responds to the inherited NSView method -acceptsFirstResponder. Sending a YES to -setRefusesFirstResponder: will cause -acceptsFirstResponder to return a NO and vice-versa.

Setting and Getting a Control's Value

Most controls have an internal value. For example, the value could be an integer or floating-point number representing a slider's position, or a text string representing the contents of a text field. The NSControl class implements many methods to set and get this value. Most of the methods described in this section are also defined by other Cocoa objects, such as NSString. This consistency through the frameworks makes it easier to remember what methods are available.

Several methods can be used to change the value of an NSControl. They are

```
- (void)setStringValue:(NSString *)aString;
- (void)setIntValue:(int)anInt;
- (void)setFloatValue:(float)aFloat;
- (void)setDoubleValue:(double)aDouble;
- (void)setAttributedStringValue:(NSAttributedString *)obj;
- (void)setObjectValue:(id)obj;
```

Note that all these methods can be sent to any control. Each control attempts to do the right thing if a value is sent in a form that isn't native to the control. For example, text fields display strings. Asking it to set its value to a number causes it to do a number-to-string conversion so that is has a new string to display.

The `-setAttributedStringValue:` method is somewhat special because it allows a string with multiple fonts and styles to be set. Most controls treat this as a regular string, but text fields use the extra text attributes to modify how the text is displayed.

The `-setObjectValue:` method is a little different from the others because usually no type conversion will take place, and the value displayed by the control will not be changed. Instead, the object is stored by the control and otherwise ignored. This allows a particular object, which can be retrieved later, to be associated with a given control.

Whenever any of the previous methods are used to change a control's value, the control immediately ends any in-progress editing and is marked as needing to be redisplayed.

To get the current value of a control, use one of these methods:

```
- (NSString *)stringValue;
- (int)intValue;
- (float)floatValue;
- (double)doubleValue;
- (NSAttributedString *)attributedStringValue;
- (id)objectValue;
```

Finally, there is a group of methods that can be used to get one control to take the value from another object and set itself to that value. The methods are

```
- (void)takeStringValueFrom:(id)sender;
- (void)takeIntValueFrom:(id)sender;
- (void)takeFloatValueFrom:(id)sender;
- (void)takeDoubleValueFrom:(id)sender;
- (void)takeObjectValueFrom:(id)sender;
```

There are a couple of things to note. The `sender` parameter should be an object that can respond to the previous get methods, such as `-intValue`, and so on. This is important because the `-take` methods will call the correlating accessor method. Usually, the sender will be an instance of another `NSControl` subclass, which implicitly guarantees this condition. Also, notice that there is no method for taking an attributed string value. A method for attributed strings would be expected for the sake of consistency, but as of Mac OS X 10.1 there is no such method.

To see how these methods work, try creating an Interface Builder file with a single window containing a slider and a text field. Drag a connection from the slider to the text field, setting the action to `-takeIntValueFrom:`. Enter Interface Builder's Test Interface mode and drag the slider. The text field will continuously update to show the value of the slider as the slider is dragged.

Tags

All controls can be assigned a tag. A tag is an arbitrary integer that can be used to identify the control to program code. The tag for a control can be set programmatically or in the control's inspector in Interface Builder. The tag is most often used by action methods to determine which control sent the action message. Often, it is unnecessary to know which control sent a message, in which case the tag can remain unset. The Interface Builder default is to set the tag to zero.

To determine a control's tag, use the `-tag` method, which returns an integer. To change a control's tag, use the `-setTag:` method, providing it with a new integer or change the tag in the Interface Builder inspector. Many advanced Cocoa programmers use a `#define` statement or an enumerated type to assign symbolic names to integers used as tags. This can enhance code readability and maintainability.

NOTE

For controls with titles, the title should not be used to identify the control in program logic. Titles change with localizations and are, therefore, unreliable. Tags, which are invisible to the user, are a much better way to identify control objects.

Relationship Between Controls and Cells

Nearly every Cocoa control is associated with a cell object. A cell is a lightweight object that behaves much like a view object. Cells don't manage a coordinate system or graphics context, however. Instead, they rely on a view, typically a control, to perform those tasks. Most controls use cells to implement the drawing behavior as well as some of the event-handling behavior. Although most controls are paired with a single cell object, some of the more complex controls use more than one cell. The extra cells are typically used as labels or as extra active areas of the control.

One of the most common questions for developers new to Cocoa is "why bother with cells at all when you can just use views everywhere?" The answer is that this is a performance enhancement that has the additional benefit of adding some extra flexibility to the design of control objects.

Using cells is a performance enhancement for a couple of reasons. First, view objects use much more memory for their instance variables than do cell objects. For controls that use more than one cell, the memory savings is significant. Second, each view has its own Quartz drawing context. (Drawing contexts are defined in Chapter 12, "Custom Views and Graphics Part I," and are described more fully in Chapter 13, "Custom Views and Graphics Part II.") To render a view, its drawing context needs to become active. For a control with multiple elements, all these context switches can eat up a lot of CPU cycles. Because a cell requires its parent view object to handle the context, a control with many cells doesn't need to switch contexts as each cell is drawn. All the cells use the same context. This makes drawing significantly faster.

Cells also increase the flexibility of Cocoa controls and reuse throughout the framework. By laying out several cells of different types, complex controls such as steppers can be created. A matrix control, which is used to implement radio buttons and other repeated types of controls, is also a collection of cells. Most controls can be turned into a matrix of cells in Interface Builder by dragging the resize handles while holding down the option (alternate) key. The only requirement for this to work is that the control have an associated `NSCell` subclass. Thus, the `NSButton` class has the associated `NSButtonCell` class, and so on.

Because cells are so prevalent, before diving into the individual types of controls, it is important to understand what the `NSCell` class has to offer.

`NSControl` Methods for Working with Cells

The `NSControl` class has a few methods for manipulating its associated cell classes. The `-cell` method returns the control's cell. The `-setCell:` method can be used to change a control's cell. Both methods are most useful with controls that have only a single associated cell. Controls that use multiple cells often have their own specific methods that are better choices to use than these two methods.

Much of a control's appearance is controlled by its cell object. Therefore, when configuring a control programmatically, most of the work is done by changing settings in the associated cell. The `-cell` method is used to obtain a pointer to the cell instance.

When a new control is initialized, it creates a default cell instance for itself. The class of the cell that is generated can be changed with the class method `+setCellClass:`. This method should normally be used with a specific subclass of `NSControl`. For example, to set `NSSlider` to use the custom class `MySliderCellSubclass` for all sliders, this code is used:

```
[NSSlider setCellClass:[MySliderCellSubclass class]];
```

The `+setCellClass:` method only changes the cell class for objects initialized after it has been invoked. Existing controls remain unaffected. It is common to change the class temporarily while programmatically building a user interface. To restore the previous cell class, the previous class needs to be obtained and stored. Use the `+cellClass` method to see what class a particular control is using at the moment.

`NSCell` Class

A large majority of the methods implemented by the `NSCell` class are duplicates of the methods implemented by the `NSControl` class. The methods described in the previous sections "Methods to Define a Control's Appearance," "Methods to

Implement Target-Action," "Setting and Getting a Control's Value," and "Tags," are all implemented by `NSCell`.

NOTE

Although the `NSCell` class defines methods for target-action, it is a passive object. It doesn't really store targets or actions, nor does it send actions. Subclasses that use target-action need to define instance variables for storing the target and action as well as implement the target-action–related methods. The `NSActionCell` class does this for most Application Kit cells.

The `NSCell` class offers many methods for defining its appearance. Some of these methods don't make sense for cells of a particular type. In such cases, the cell attempts to do the right thing, whatever that may be. Usually, a parameter that doesn't make much sense is ignored. Because many of these methods are specific to a particular type of control, such as a button or text field, they are discussed throughout this chapter in the appropriate section.

A few parameters apply to all cells, however. The way a cell is initialized determines how it will be used, favoring images or text. The control size (large or small) and control tint (aqua blue or graphite) can be changed. The border, highlight, and bezel can be turned on and off.

When a cell is initialized, it is generally set up to be primarily used for text or for images. As a result `NSCell` defines two designated initializers, `-initTextCell:` and `-initImageCell:`. Subclasses of `NSCell` tend to favor one method over the other. Because `NSCell` is abstract and shouldn't be instantiated, having two initializers doesn't cause any confusion. The initializer favored by a given subclass should be used for that subclass.

Cells can be converted between the two types of cell with the `-setType:` method and the current type is returned with the `-type` method. Both methods use the constants `NSTextCellType`, `NSImageCellType`, and `NSNullCellType`. (The null type is a cell that displays nothing.)

To change the control size of a cell object, use the `-setControlSize:` method. It takes either the `NSRegularControlSize` or `NSSmallControlSize` constant as its argument. The `-controlSize` method returns the current control size.

To change the tint of a cell object, use the `-setControlTint:` method. It takes either the `NSDefaultControlTint` or `NSClearControlTint` constant as its argument. The `NSDefaultControlTint` constant causes the control to be rendered in aqua blue or graphite, depending on the user's setting in preferences. The `-controlTint` method returns the current control tint.

The `-setBordered:`, `-setBezeled:`, and `-setHighlighted:` methods turn a cell's border, bezel, or highlight on or off, respectively. Each takes `YES` or `NO` as a parameter. These methods only turn these features on or off. Specific methods to change a cell's border or bezel type are found in the various `NSCell` subclasses. To see whether a feature is on or off, use one of the `-isBordered`, `-isBezeled`, or `-isHighlighted` methods.

Some cells have titles. This is usually the case with a cell that displays both an image and text, such as some buttons. The accessors for the title are `-setTitle:` and `-title`.

`NSActionCell` Class

Most controls use cells that are designed to manage user events and send an action at the appropriate time. `NSCell` objects, although they define target-action methods, are actually passive. A cell subclassed from `NSActionCell` actually makes use of the target-action information. It stores the target-action information and implements all the related methods. The `NSActionCell` class doesn't define any significant new methods not already defined in its superclass, `NSCell`.

Simple Views and Controls

Most of this chapter is concerned with cataloging the many user interface elements offered by Cocoa. This section covers the simplest views and controls. Buttons, sliders, and text fields are controls common to almost any graphical user interface. Passive views for displaying images and progress of a long task are also common. In Cocoa, each of these objects has a single cell instance associated with it.

These controls are normally laid out and configured in Interface Builder. Many methods can also be used to modify all Cocoa controls without the need for Interface Builder. It is important to realize that Interface builder is actually instantiating these objects and editing them. That means that internally Interface Builder is actually calling the methods described in this chapter. Anything that can be done in Interface Builder can be done in code. No special magic is involved.

Buttons

A button is a user-interface object that sends an action when it is clicked. Apple's Aqua user interface supports many different styles of buttons. In Cocoa, all these buttons are implemented by the `NSButton` and `NSButtonCell` classes. Because there are so many options available for buttons, these classes can at first seem somewhat complex. Normally, a user interface's buttons are configured in Interface Builder, which simplifies the process a little. It is also possible to change the details programmatically.

NOTE

The terminology between the Cocoa method names and the Interface Builder options is sometimes different. The programmatic interface is also much more detailed. In most cases, a single option in Interface Builder actually changes several of the programmatic options simultaneously. Because of these discrepancies, it is difficult to describe the underlying methods at the same time the Interface Builder options are being explained. Because of this, Interface Builder options are described first, and then all the programmatic options are discussed separately.

The following button-related sections explain the available button options and the methods offered by `NSButton` and `NSButtonCell` to change them. The described methods are technically `NSButtonCell` methods, but the `NSButton` class also implements them as a convenience. The `NSButton` implementations simply forward the messages on to the underlying `NSButtonCell` object.

Button Options in Interface Builder

The first option, which affects a button's appearance the most, is the button's type. Interface Builder supports six different button types as defined by Aqua: Rounded Bevel Button, Square Button, Push Button, Check Box, Radio Button, and Round Button. All six buttons are available on the Cocoa-Views palette in Interface Builder. Click the palette button with a small button and text field on it to open the Cocoa-Views palette. This palette and the six button types are shown in Figure 10.3.

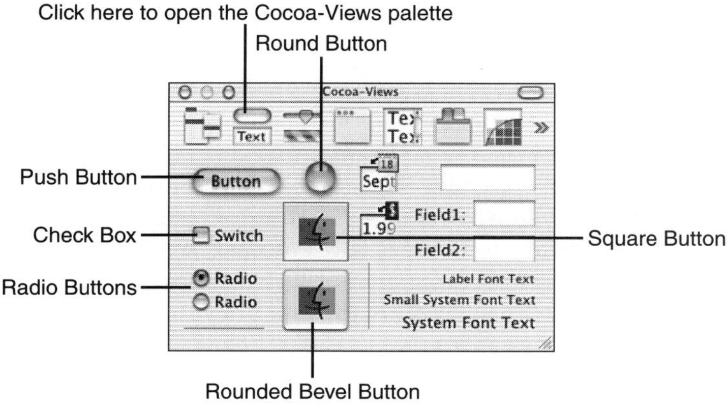

FIGURE 10.3 Buttons on the Cocoa-Views palette.

It is also possible to change the button type using the button inspector. Open the inspector by hitting Cmd-1 with a button selected. Figure 10.4 shows this inspector.

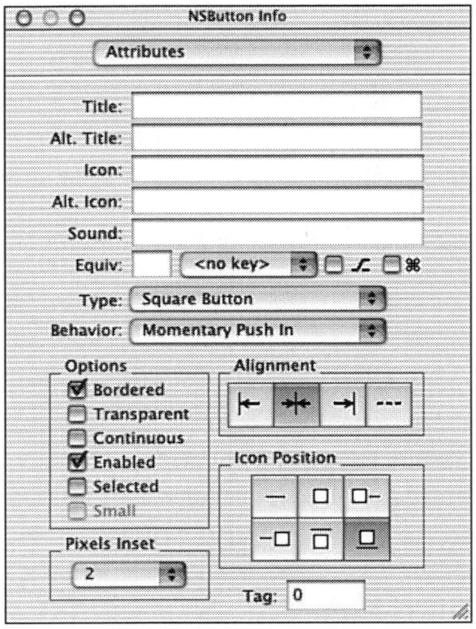

FIGURE 10.4 Interface Builder's button/button cell inspector.

To change the button type, use the pop-up list labeled Type. The rest of this section refers back to Figure 10.4 as the other options are described.

NOTE

In this case, the label Type in Interface Builder is not the same as the word type when seen in the Cocoa method names. The type pop-up in Interface Builder's inspector actually changes a button's bezel style, gradient, images, and more. There is a method `-setButtonType:`, but it refers to what Interface Builder labels Behavior.

At the top of the inspector are text fields for setting a button's title, image, and sound. The sound is played whenever the button is clicked. The title and/or image are displayed on the button to identify it to the user. When the button is in the off state, the normal title and image are displayed. When in the on state, the alternate title and icon are displayed. Normally, titles should be kept as short as possible while remaining clear. ToolTips, as described in Chapter 20, "Adding Online Help," can be used if more information than the title needs to be offered to the user. Images are typically small icons. In the case of radio buttons and switches (also known as check boxes), a special icon is used for the image and alternate image to show the button's state.

Buttons can have a key equivalent. When the key equivalent is typed, the button is triggered as if the mouse had clicked it. If the window doesn't have an active first responder, it acts as the first responder and looks for buttons that have key equivalents for anything typed at the keyboard. If the key equivalent uses the Cmd key, the window looks for a button to click even if it has a first responder. Buttons with Cmd-key equivalents take precedence over menu items with the same key equivalents when the window containing the button is the key window.

A button's key equivalent can be configured by the row of controls labeled Equiv in Interface Builder. The key is typed into the text field. Alternatively, special keys, such as Return or Tab, can be selected with the pop-up list. The two switches determine whether the Option or Cmd keys need to be pressed to trigger the key equivalent. Refer to Figure 10.4 to see these controls.

The Behavior pop-up controls how a button behaves. This setting varies between the button objects on the palette and is generally set to be the way a user would expect a button of a particular type to behave. It is very rarely changed because most changes would violate the Aqua guidelines. To prevent the worst offenses, this pop-up is disabled for some button types. It offers six options, as described in Table 10.1.

TABLE 10.1 Button Behaviors

Behavior Name	Behavior
Momentary Light	Redraws itself between mouse-down and mouse-up to be highlighted.
Momentary Change	Redraws itself between mouse-down and mouse-up to show the alternate image and title.
Momentary Push In	Redraws itself between mouse-down and mouse-up to be highlighted and, if bordered, pushed in.
Toggle	The first click turns the button on, the second turns it off. On buttons display their alternate text and image. Highlighting happens between mouse-down and mouse-up.
On/Off	The first click turns the button on, the second turns it off. On buttons are highlighted, but don't show alternate text or image.
Push On/Push Off	The first click turns the button on, the second turns it off. On buttons are highlighted and, if bordered, appear pushed in.

The key difference between these modes is whether the button is momentary or toggles state. The other difference is in whether the alternate title and image are used. The difference between appearing pushed in or not is actually moot in Mac OS X 10.1.

NOTE

A button that is highlighted and a button that is highlighted and pushed in are actually drawn the same in Aqua. The difference between the two was more apparent on versions of Cocoa prior to Mac OS X that implemented the classic Macintosh interface and the NeXT interface.

The options area of the button inspector controls miscellaneous button options. They can alter a button's appearance, event handling, and state.

Three check boxes control the appearance of a button. Some buttons have borders. The Border check box allows this to be changed for buttons that allow it to be changed. Some types of buttons, such as push buttons, don't allow the border to be turned off. Transparent buttons don't draw anything, but are still sensitive to being clicked. These buttons can be used to make certain areas of a user interface become live, even though there's not necessarily anything obvious to click. One use of this is as a secret button that triggers an Easter egg. The Small check box causes the small version of the button to be drawn, if such a thing applies. All the button types except for rounded bevel and square have small versions.

Continuous buttons are buttons that repeatedly send their action message while they are in the on state. The Continuous check box turns this behavior on or off. The Enabled check box can be used to disable a button. An enabled button can be clicked and sends its action, but a disabled button is grayed out and all clicks on the button are ignored. The Selected check box changes a button's state. A selected button is a button that is in the on state. This makes sense only for toggle, on/off, check box, and radio buttons.

The Icon Position buttons determine how buttons display their titles and images. Refer to Figure 10.5 to see the icons on each of these buttons and how they correspond to Cocoa constants. They behave similar to radio buttons because only one can be selected at a time. On the buttons, a line represents the text title and a square represents the image. Select just a line to display only the text title. Selecting the square displays only the image. The four remaining buttons cause the text and icon to be used, with the text to the top, bottom, left, or right of the icon. The Pixels Inset pop-up controls the spacing between the image and the text and is, therefore, only available when image and text are both to be rendered.

The final two controls on the inspector, alignment and tag, have already been explained in the previous sections "Methods to Define a Control's Appearance" and "Tags." The justified option is not available for buttons, but because buttons only display a single line of text, this is not a problem. Single line justified text looks just like left justified text.

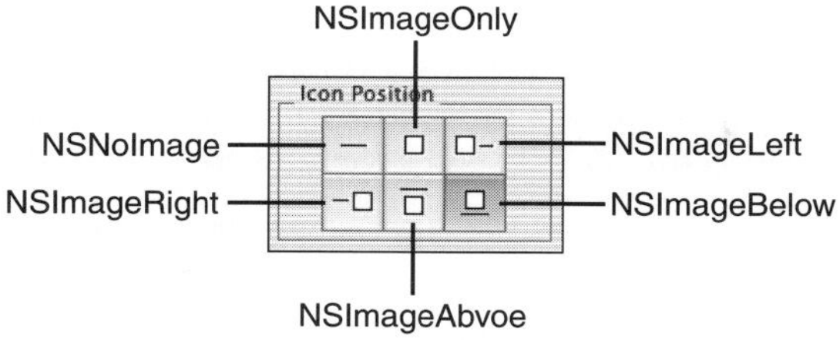

FIGURE 10.5 Icon Position control from Interface Builder's button/button cell inspector.

Configuring a Button's Titles, Images, and Sound

There are methods for setting a button's titles. The two types of titles are the normal and alternate, and each can be set with a string or attributed string. Thus, there are four methods, the function of each is obvious from the name:

```
- (void)setTitle:(NSString *)aString;
- (void)setAlternateTitle:(NSString *)aString;
- (void)setAttributedTitle:(NSAttributedString *)aString;
- (void)setAttributedAlternateTitle:(NSAttributedString *)aString;
```

Likewise, there are four methods for retrieving a button's title. They are `-title`, `-alternateTitle`, `-attributedTitle`, and `-attributedAlternateTitle`.

Use `-setImage:` and `-setAlternateImage:` to set a button's image and alternate image. The image and alternate image can be retrieved with the `-image` and `-alternateImage` methods. Both methods use the `NSImage` class. This class is explained in Chapter 14, "Custom Views and Graphics Part III."

The image position can be altered with the `-setImagePosition:` method. The possible constants that can be passed to this method are `NSNoImage`, `NSImageOnly`, `NSImageLeft`, `NSImageRight`, `NSImageBelow`, `NSImageAbove`, and `NSImageOverlaps`. The first six in that list correspond to the Icon Position control in Interface Builder's button inspector. The constant `NSImageOverlaps` cannot be set from Interface Builder. It can be used to make the image and title overlap.

Finally, `-setSound:` sets the sound the button plays when it is triggered. The `-sound` method returns the sound. Both methods use the `NSSound` object, which is described in Chapter 21, "Multimedia."

All the methods for altering a button's titles, images, and sound can be sent to instances of both the `NSButton` and the `NSButtonCell` class.

Configuring a Button's Rendering

Quite a few methods alter the way a button is rendered. Some of these methods correspond directly to counterparts in Interface Builder's inspector. However, most of the controls in the inspector actually call several of these methods at once.

To make a button transparent, use the `-setTransparent:` method. The `-isTransparent` method is used to determine if a button is transparent or not. These methods correspond to the Transparent switch in Interface Builder.

The border around a button is controlled by the `-setBordered:` and `-setBezelStyle:` methods. These values are accessed with the `-isBordered` and `-bezelStyle` methods. The border methods take and return the constants `YES` and `NO`. The bezel style constants are `NSRoundedBezelStyle`, `NSRegularSquareBezelStyle`, `NSThickSquareBezelStyle`, `NSThickerSquareBezelStyle`, `NSShadowlessSquareBezelStyle`, and `NSCircularBezelStyle`.

NOTE

For all cells that support borders and bezels, the border and bezel are mutually exclusive. Setting one turns off the other.

The bezel types loosely correspond to the Type pop-up list in Interface Builder. The `NSRoundedBezelStyle` constant corresponds to the Rounded Bevel button. A button using `NSCircularBezelStyle` is a Round button. The four square bezel style constants are variants of the Square button type. Other methods can be used to select the other types. A button using `NSShadowlessSquareBezelStyle` can be tiled with other buttons of the same bezel style, which is useful for tool palettes.

The Type button in Interface Builder sets a button's gradient as well as its bezel. Square buttons display a gradient that simulates a shadow. This makes them look as though they have a slightly curved surface. The gradient can be concave or convex and weak or strong. A concave gradient makes the button look like it curves slightly into the screen, whereas a convex gradient makes the button appear to be curved out of the screen. Weak versus strong refers to the contrast between the light and dark colors of the gradient. Strong gradients appear to have more curvature.

To set a gradient, use `-setGradientType:` with one of the constants `NSGradientConcaveWeak`, `NSGradientConcaveStrong`, `NSGradientConvexWeak`, or `NSGradientConvexStrong`. To use no gradient, use the constant `NSGradientNone` instead.

It is possible to alter how a button renders itself when it is highlighted with the `-setHighlightsBy:` method. The `-highlightsBy` method returns the current highlight mode. Both methods use a series of mask constants. The value can be either `NSNoCellMask` or the bitwise `OR` of the constants `NSContentsCellMask`, `NSPushInCellMask`, `NSChangeGrayCellMask`, and `NSChangeBackgroundCellMask`.

The `NSNoCellMask` constant specifies no change between highlighted and nonhighlighted buttons. The `NSContentsCellMask` constant causes the alternate title and image to be used. The `NSPushInCellMask` constant is supposed to make the button appear to be pushed in, but has no effect in Mac OS X. The `NSChangeGrayCellMask` and `NSChangeBackgroundCellMask` constants make the button appear to be darker when it is highlighted. The key difference is that `NSChangeBackgroundCellMask` is meant for buttons using images that have alpha channel data.

Similar to highlighting, it is possible to change the way a button renders itself when in the on state. The `-setShowsStateBy:` method changes this, and the `-showsStateBy` method returns the current setting. Both methods use the same set of masks as the `-setHighlightsBy:` and `-highlightsBy` methods.

NOTE

Depending on how a button is configured, it might make a distinction between being highlighted and being in the on state. Interface Builder sets up both parameters based on a combination of how the Type and Behavior pop-up lists are set.

A final rendering parameter controls the look of a disabled button. When a button with an image is disabled, normally the image should be dimmed along with the text. This is generally always the case in Mac OS X, even for switches and radio buttons. It is possible, however, to have the image remain undimmed when a button is disabled. In such a case, only the text is dimmed to indicate that the control is disabled. Sending `YES` or `NO` to the `-setImageDimsWhenDisabled:` method controls whether the image is dimmed and `-imageDimsWhenDisabled` returns the current setting.

Configuring a Button's Behavior

It is possible to modify the way a button behaves with the `-setType:` method. The Interface Builder pop-up lists Type and Behavior both send this message along with several other messages to modify the button's rendering. Remember that in the programming API, the word `type` is not used entirely the same as it is used in the Interface Builder interface. The various button types and their meanings are shown in Table 10.2. It might also be useful to refer back to the button behaviors in Table 10.1.

TABLE 10.2 Button Type Constants

Constant	Meaning
`NSSwitchButton`	Same as Switch Button in Interface Builder Type pop up
`NSRadioButton`	Same as Radio Button in Interface Builder Type pop up
`NSMomentaryLightButton`	Same as Momentary Light in Interface Builder Behavior pop up
`NSMomentaryChangeButton`	Same as Momentary Change in Interface Builder Behavior pop up
`NSMomentaryPushInButton`	Same as Momentary Push In in Interface Builder Behavior pop up
`NSToggleButton`	Same as Toggle in Interface Builder Behavior pop up
`NSOnOffButton`	Same as On/Off in Interface Builder Behavior pop up
`NSPushOnPushOffButton`	Same as Push On/Push Off in Interface Builder Behavior pop up

The `NSCell` methods `-setContinuous:` and `-isContinuous` affect `NSButtonCell` objects. Continuous buttons send their actions repeatedly until released. The following two methods control the timing of the repeats:

```
- (void)setPeriodicDelay:(float)delay interval:(float)interval;
- (void)getPeriodicDelay:(float *)delay interval:(float *)interval;
```

The delay is the time in seconds before the button starts sending repeated action messages. The interval is the time between each of the repeated action messages.

When a button is being held down, it normally remains highlighted until the mouse is dragged outside of the button's bounds. It is possible to make a border-based highlight remain on when the mouse strays outside of the button with the `-setShowsBorderOnlyWhileMouseInside:` method. The `-showsBorderOnlyWhileMouseInside` method returns the current setting. This only affects the button's border. It will not cause a button's other highlights to stay on when the mouse leaves the button's bounds.

Configuring a Button's Key Equivalents

Two methods exist for setting a button's key equivalent. The `-setKeyEquivalent:` method sets the actual key equivalent. An `NSString` containing a single character should be provided. To tell a button whether modifier keys, such as Cmd and Option, need to be pressed down, use the `-setKeyEquivalentModifierMask:` method. It requires the bitwise `OR` of the modifier key masks described in Chapter 15. The `NSCommandKeyMask` and `NSAlternateKeyMask` refer to the Cmd and Option keys, respectively, and are the only ones that can be set with Interface Builder. The current key equivalent setting can be obtained with the `-keyEquivalent` and `-keyEquivalentModifierMask` methods.

When a button is set to display text and an image, but the image has been set to `nil`, the key equivalent is shown in place of an image. Although Interface Builder doesn't allow the font used for the key equivalent to be altered, it can be changed programmatically. The following three methods can be used to get and set the key equivalent's font:

```
- (NSFont *)keyEquivalentFont;
- (void)setKeyEquivalentFont:(NSFont *)fontObj;
- (void)setKeyEquivalentFont:(NSString *)fontName size:(float)fontSize;
```

NOTE

The three methods for working with a key equivalent's font are only available in the `NSButtonCell` class. This differs from the other methods for modifying buttons. The others can be sent to either `NSButton` or `NSButtonCell`.

Configuring a Button's State

Normal buttons, created in Interface Builder, can have one of two states, on or off. The `-setState:` method can take the constants `NSOnState` or `NSOffState` to change the state. The `-state` method returns the current state of a button.

NOTE

The constants `YES` and `NO` can be used as synonyms for `NSOnState` and `NSOffState`, respectively, but this is implementation dependent and should be avoided. It is common to see `YES` and `NO` used in older example code, so it is useful to know that this works. It is stylistically discouraged, however, in part because it doesn't work well with mixed state buttons.

It is also possible to programmatically create buttons that are capable of displaying a third state, known as mixed. This is very common for check boxes that are displaying the attributes of a selection. If a selection contains objects with a particular attribute on, the check box is set to on. It is set off if none of the objects has the characteristic. But if the selection contains some objects with the setting on and some with it off, a mixed state is usually used. For example, suppose a check box is showing whether a text selection is in boldface. The text selection could be all in boldface, all in a nonbold style, or mixed, with some text in bold and some not.

To enable a button to have a mixed state, use the `-setAllowsMixedState:` method. The `-allowsMixedState` method can be used to see if this is already on or not. The `-setState:` and `-state` methods use the constant `NSMixedState` to denote the mixed state.

When a mixed state toggle button is clicked, instead of toggling between on and off it cycles through the three states. The order of the cycle is on, off, mixed, and so on. The `-nextState` method returns the next state the button takes on, but doesn't actually change the state. The `-setNextState` method moves the button into the next state in the cycle. Of course, `-setState:` can be used to set a particular state.

Sliders

A slider is a user interface element that can deal with a range of numeric values. On Mac OS X, sliders can be horizontal or vertical. Some sliders can be configured to have tick marks on one side or the other, whereas others can be configured to have no tick marks at all. A slider can be disabled, which causes it to be grayed out. Sliders also come in large and small forms. Figure 10.6 shows a wide variety of sliders displaying these various characteristics.

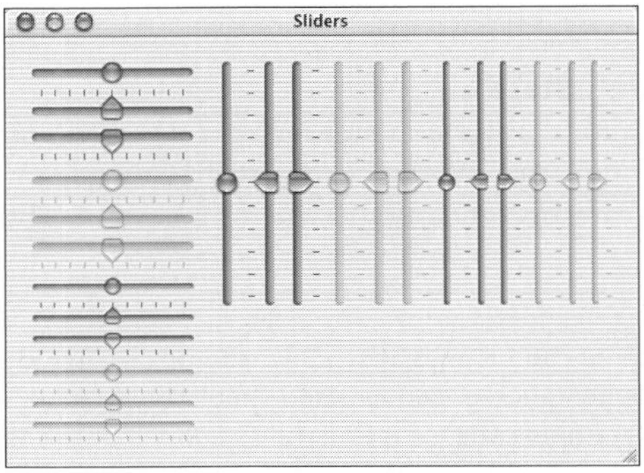

FIGURE 10.6 A variety of slider configurations.

A slider's knob is moved by clicking and dragging inside the slider. If the user clicks outside of the slider's knob, the knob jumps to the mouse location and can then be dragged from there. If a slider has tick marks, the knob movement can optionally be constrained to move in jumps aligned with the tick marks. Sliders can be configured to send their actions either continuously as the slider is moved or once when the mouse is released. Several preconfigured sliders are available on the Cocoa-Other palette in Interface Builder. This palette is shown in Figure 10.7.

The `NSSlider` object implements a single slider. It uses the `NSSliderCell` object in the same way `NSButton` uses `NSButtonCell` objects. Also like buttons, the methods supported by the `NSSliderCell` class can also be sent to the `NSSlider` class. Most messages to `NSSlider` are forwarded to its cell.

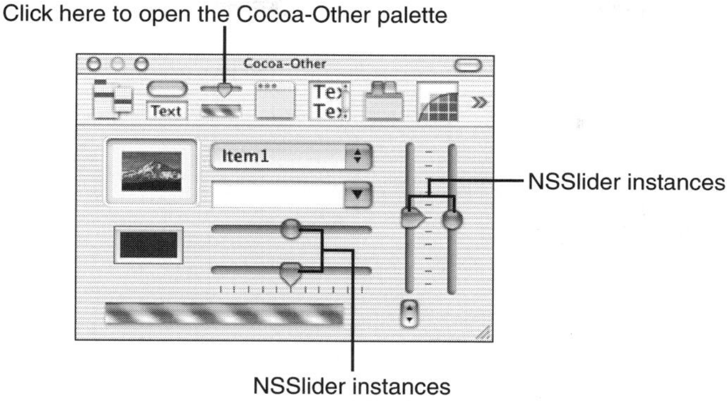

FIGURE 10.7 Sliders on the Cocoa-Other palette.

Cocoa offers a second object that acts much like a slider, the `NSScroller`. Scrollers and sliders both navigate a one-dimensional range, but cannot be used interchangeably. Sliders select a single point from within their range, whereas a scroller is designed to allow the user to select a fixed-size range within a range. Because scrollers are usually used indirectly as part of an `NSScrollView` object, they are discussed later in this chapter in conjunction with scroll views.

Slider Options in Interface Builder

All the options for configuring a slider can be found in Interface Builder's `NSSlider` inspector. This inspector, shown in Figure 10.8, is displayed by using the Cmd-1 key equivalent when a slider or slider cell is selected.

In the inspector, the minimum and maximum values control the range of the slider. The current value represents the slider's current position. When the slider's `.nib` is loaded, the slider will already be set to this value.

In the inspector, the Options box, with the Continuous, Enabled, and Small switches, and the Tag text field are all control options defined by `NSControl` and `NSCell`. All four of these options are described previously in this chapter.

The Markers box is used to set tick marks. Set the number of markers to zero for a slider with no tick marks. If the number is set to 1, there will be a single mark at the slider's center. If there are two or more marks, there will be a mark at each end of the slider with the remaining marks distributed evenly between the ends.

The Position radio buttons change their titles depending on whether the slider is vertical or horizontal and control which side of the slider has the tick marks. Depending on where the slider is located in a user interface, one layout might look better than another. Although this setting can be changed if there are no tick marks, doing so won't change the rendering of the slider until tick marks are added.

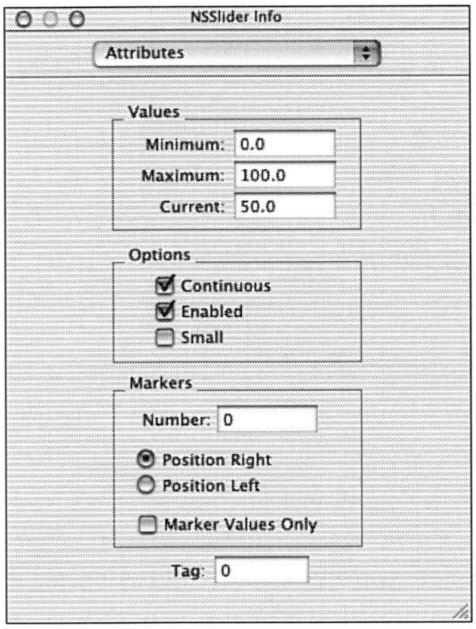

FIGURE 10.8 Interface Builder's slider/slider cell inspector.

The Marker Values Only switch forces the slider knob to always be over a tick mark. As the knob is dragged, it jumps from one tick mark to the next. Although Interface Builder allows this to be turned on for a slider with a single tick mark, doing so is somewhat useless because it renders the slider immobile. It can also be turned on for sliders with no tick marks, but there will be no change in the slider's behavior.

Slider Sizes

Some constraints are set by Aqua for `NSSlider` objects. Sliders dragged from Interface Builder's palette automatically follow these constraints. Sliders created programmatically should be created so that the correct sizes are used.

First, determine whether the slider should be horizontal or vertical. The `NSSlider` class automatically decides whether it is horizontal or vertical based on its size. A slider that is horizontal should be created so that it is wider than it is high. A vertical slider should be higher than it is wide. To see how a slider will be rendered, the `-isVertical` message can be used.

When the orientation is decided, there are certain limits to the shorter dimension. A horizontal slider's height should be 25 pixels for a large slider with tick marks or 21 pixels for a large slider without ticks. Small sliders should be 17 pixels high with tick marks and 15 pixels without.

NOTE

Curious readers will eventually discover that the horizontal slider with tick marks on Interface Builder's palette is actually 26 pixels in height. This is probably a bug because turning the ticks off and back on will change the height to 25 pixels. This is true for the April 2002 Mac OS X Developer tools release, future releases might fix this discrepancy.

For vertical sliders, the width is the constrained dimension. A large vertical slider with ticks should be 25 pixels in width. Without ticks, a large slider should be 21 pixels wide. A small slider with ticks should be 19 pixels wide. A small slider without ticks should be 15 pixels wide.

Configuring a Slider's Range

The range of a slider is set using the `-setMinValue:` and `-setMaxValue:` methods, both of which take a `double`. The `-minValue` and `-maxValue` methods return the current settings. These correspond to the Interface Builder inspector's minimum and maximum values. The current value setting in Interface Builder is set using the standard methods for setting a control's value, such as `-setFloatValue:`.

If the user holds down the Option key when dragging a slider knob, it is possible to have the knob move in precise increments instead of smoothly. This is somewhat like constraining a slider to only land on tick marks, except that it is optional. To set the increment size, use the `-setAltIncrementValue:` method. The `-altIncrementValue` method retrieves the current setting.

Configuring a Slider's Tick Marks

The options for setting tick marks in Interface Builder's inspector have obvious accessor method counterparts. To set the number of ticks, use the `-setNumberOfTickMarks:` method. The `-numberOfTickMarks` method returns the current setting. To control where tick marks are rendered, use the `-setTickMarkPosition:` method with the constants `NSTickMarkBelow`, `NSTickMarkAbove`, `NSTickMarkLeft`, and `NSTickMarkRight`. The `-tickMarkPosition` method returns the current setting. Finally, the `-setAllowsTickMarkValuesOnly:` method controls whether the slider knob is always forced to be over a tick mark or able to move smoothly. The `-allowsTickMarkValuesOnly` method returns the current setting.

A few other methods for dealing with tick marks might be useful. For a slider with n tick marks, each mark is given an index from 0 to n-1. Given an `NSPoint`, the nearest tick mark can be determined with the `-indexOfTickMarkAtPoint:` method. It returns the index of the nearest tick mark or `NSNotFound` if the point is too far away to be considered near any tick mark.

Given the index of a tick mark, the `double` value of the slider at that tick mark can be found using the `-tickMarkValueAtIndex:` method. The area of the view where the tick mark is drawn is obtained with the `-rectOfTickMarkAtIndex:` method. This is useful when overriding a slider's `-drawRect:` to do custom rendering.

Given a particular slider value, it is possible to determine the value represented by the nearest tick mark. The `-closestTickMarkValueToValue:` method takes a hypothetical `double` value and determines which tick mark is closest to that slider value. It then returns the `double` value that the slider would have if its knob were at that mark.

Configuring a Slider's Rendering

Prior to the Aqua user interface in Mac OS X, Cocoa supported two rendering options for sliders. The first option would alter the size of the slider's knobs, using the `-setKnobThickness:` and `-knobThickness` methods. The other option, using `-setImage:` and `-image`, would allow an image to be laid in the slider's track, much like the sliders in the standard color panel.

As of Mac OS X 10.1.4, neither of these rendering options works, even though the methods for controlling both can be found in the Cocoa headers. They are mentioned here to avoid frustration. Although Apple has taken the time to fully document these methods, they do nothing no matter how hard you try to make them work.

> **NOTE**
>
> It is obvious that images *could* be put in a slider's track because this is done in the color panel. The Application Kit actually uses an undocumented `NSSlider` subclass to implement this functionality.

Titles for Sliders

The `NSSlider` and `NSSliderCell` classes define several methods for drawing a title on the slider. If they are used, a separate cell is used to draw the slider's title. Unfortunately, the title is drawn in the middle of the slider, and can be obscured by the knob. Because of this, the title methods should be avoided for sliders. Instead, it is best to use a separate text field object placed near the slider to act as a label. This is also how labels should be placed to show the user a slider's range.

Text Fields

Text fields are controls that can display or edit text. A noneditable text field can be used as a text label in a user interface. It is possible to configure a text field so that the data it displays is given a specific format. Editable text fields can be used for data entry of string or numeric values. Such fields can be set up to validate input, rejecting unacceptable values.

Similar to other controls, text fields are implemented by two classes. The `NSTextField` class is a subclass of `NSControl`, and the `NSTextFieldCell` class is a subclass of `NSActionCell`. The `NSDateFormatter` and `NSNumberFormatter` classes, both subclasses of `NSFormatter`, work with text fields to implement formatting and validation.

The Cocoa-Views palette in Interface Builder contains four instances of `NSTextField`; three are configured as labels and one is editable. The palette also has instances of `NSDateFormatter` and `NSNumberFormatter`. Figure 10.9 shows where these objects are located on the Cocoa-Views palette. There is also an `NSForm` object on the palette. The `NSForm` class is more complex than a text field. It is described in the "Compound Controls" section later in this chapter. The separator objects are discussed in the "Boxes" section later in this chapter.

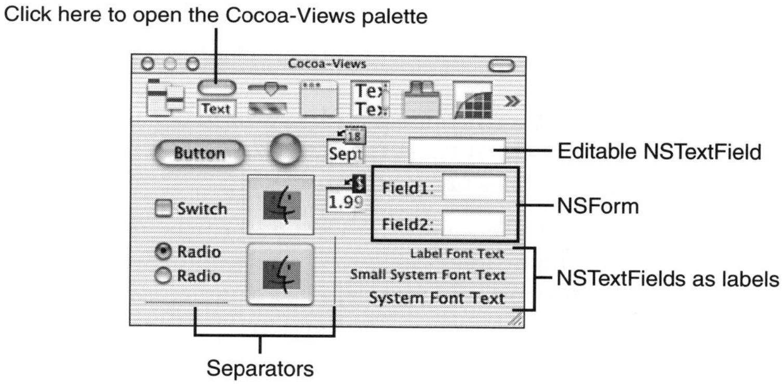

FIGURE 10.9 Text fields on the Cocoa-Views palette.

Text Field Options in Interface Builder

All the options for configuring a text field can be found in Interface Builder's `NSTextField` inspector. This inspector, shown in Figure 10.10, is displayed by using the Cmd-1 key equivalent when an `NSTextField` or an `NSTextFieldCell` is selected.

The title field in the inspector can be used to change the text displayed by the view. This can also be edited by double-clicking the text field in Interface Builder.

The color of the text and the background color of the field can be set with the two color wells. Dragging a color swatch and dropping it on the text field also changes the text color. The Draws Background switch can be used to suppress drawing the background for some border types.

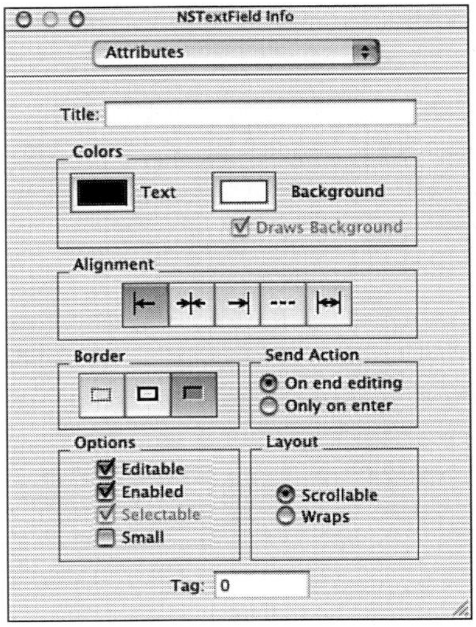

FIGURE 10.10 Interface Builder's text field/text field cell inspector.

The alignment control changes where the text is drawn in the field. The tag field at the bottom of the inspector is used to set the text field's tag. Both controls are described earlier in this chapter as part of the discussion of the `NSControl` class.

The border control selects between three border types. The left button, with the dashed line, is used to configure a text field to have no border. The middle button, with a solid black line, is for bordered text fields. The border is drawn as a 1-pixel thick black line. The border's color cannot be changed. The right button sets the text field to have a bezeled border. Figure 10.11 shows the border control. The setting of this control enables or disables the Draws Background switch. Bezeled fields always draw their backgrounds. The background can be turned off for bordered or unbordered text fields.

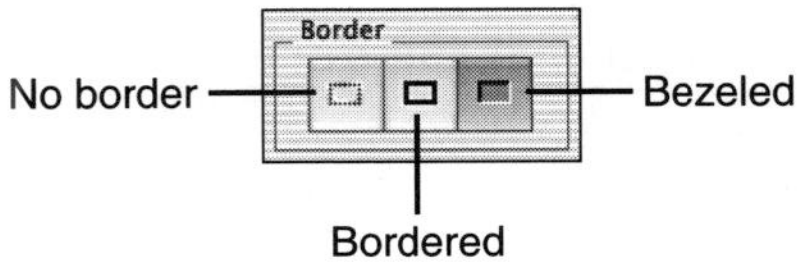

FIGURE 10.11 Border control in Interface Builder's text field/text field inspector.

The send action radio buttons control when the text field sends its action. The On end editing setting causes the action to be sent whenever the text field's editing ends. This happens when the user presses the Return key, tabs to a new field, or clicks in another field to change focus. This is the default behavior. The Only on enter setting causes the action to only be sent if the user hits the Return (or Enter) key.

The options box offers four options for text fields. The Editable switch determines whether the text field's value can be changed by the user. If the field is bezeled, making it noneditable lightens (dims) the color of the bezel. The Enabled switch can be used to disable a text field, even if it is editable. This setting is often changed as a program runs. A disabled text field dims its text.

The Selectable switch is always turned on for an editable text field. For noneditable fields, this switch controls whether the user can select the text and use the Copy command. Usually, text fields used as labels are not selectable. Making a field noneditable, but selectable is useful primarily to allow the user to copy data from the field while disallowing modification. For example, some programs use a unique host ID for generating licenses. The host ID is immutable, so a field displaying it should not be editable. Usually, such IDs are prone to being mistyped, however, so it is wise to allow the user to copy the value from the host ID field. It can then be pasted elsewhere, avoiding the possibility of typing mistakes.

The Small switch chooses a smaller version of the text field. It changes both the font and bounds of the text field object. This can be convenient, but is somewhat redundant because the font of the text field can be changed with the standard font panel, and the text field itself can be resized to any arbitrary size by dragging the object's resize handles.

The Layout radio buttons control how the text field renders text that is too wide to fit within its bounds. If it is set to Scrollable, the text always is a single line in height. As the user types, the text scrolls leftward to make room for new characters. This is generally the preferred behavior for simple data-entry text fields. The Wraps setting is used to make the text wrap to multiple lines. In Figure 10.2, shown earlier in this chapter, the text fields on the right side of the window are all set to wrap instead of scroll.

Configuring an `NSTextField`

As with all Cocoa controls, the `NSTextField` and `NSTextFieldCell` classes define methods that implement all the functionality accessible from the Interface Builder inspector. These methods can be used to programmatically configure text views or change their appearance as a program runs. Both classes implement the same set of methods.

The text field's value can be set using the standard `NSControl` methods, such as `-setStringValue:`. This is labeled as the Title in the Interface Builder inspector.

NOTE

Some of the more complex user interface controls have titles that are distinct from the values they contain and/or edit. Such controls use the `-setTitle:` and `-title` methods for the titles and the normal value accessors such as `-setStringValue:` and `-stringValue` for the data. Because the Interface Builder inspector's label says Title for a text field's value, it is common to mistakenly use the `-setTitle:` and `-title` methods instead of the appropriate value accessor methods when working with text fields.

A text field's colors are controlled by three pairs of accessor methods that correspond to the controls in the Color box of the Interface Builder `NSTextField` inspector. Set the colors by passing an `NSColor` object to the `-setTextColor:` and `-setBackgroundColor:` methods. The `-textColor` and `-backgroundColor` methods both return an `NSColor`. The `NSColor` class is described in Chapter 17, "Color." For text fields used as labels, it is common to not draw a background color, so that the window's background shows through. To turn the background color on or off, pass `YES` or `NO` to the `-setDrawsBackground:` method. The `-drawsBackground` method returns the current setting.

The text field's border is controlled by the `-setBordered:` and `-setBezeled:` methods. The current setting can be determined with `-isBordered` and `-isBezeled`. Only one feature, bezeled or bordered, can be active at a time. If both are set, the bezel will win out.

To change the way a text field lays out its text, use the `-setScrollable:` and `-setWraps:` methods. Use `-isScrollable` and `-wraps` to determine the current settings. The scrollable and wraps options are mutually exclusive. Setting one causes the other to be unset. These four methods correlate to the Layout radio buttons in Interface Builder.

Editability of a text field is controlled by the `-setEditable:` method. Selectability is controlled by the `-setSelectable:` method. These methods correlate with the Editable and Selectable switches in Interface Builder. The current settings are returned by the `-isEditable` and `-isSelectable` methods.

The `NSTextField` class also responds to the action message `-selectText:`. Sending this message attempts to make the text field become the first responder, and then all the text in the field will be selected. This method is the one to use to programmatically change the keyboard focus to a particular text field.

Tabbing Between Text Fields

Cocoa supports use of the Tab key to move focus from one text field to another. This process works as a loop within each window. Continually pressing Tab moves keyboard focus from one field to the next until it returns to the field where it started. When a window is first brought onscreen, focus will be on the first field in the loop.

Cocoa sets all this up automatically. The first text field in the loop is the field that is topmost and leftmost on the window. Focus then moves from left to right, and then from top to bottom across the window. Tabbing out of the bottommost, rightmost field returns the focus to the first field.

If Cocoa's automatic tab loop in unsuitable, it is possible to manually set up a different tab loop. To do this, each of the fields must be connected together. Drag a connection from a field to the next field in the Tab loop and set the connection to the `nextKeyView` outlet. This should be done for every field in the loop. To identify the first field in the loop, drag a connection from the window to the first field and set the connection to the `initialFirstResponder` outlet.

`NSTextField` Delegates

Text field objects can have delegates to help modify their behavior. As usual, the delegate accessor methods `-setDelegate:` and `-delegate` are available. `NSTextField` objects send the following messages to their delegate:

```
- (BOOL)textShouldBeginEditing:(NSText *)textObject;
- (BOOL)textShouldEndEditing:(NSText *)textObject;
- (void)textDidBeginEditing:(NSNotification *)notification;
- (void)textDidEndEditing:(NSNotification *)notification;
- (void)textDidChange:(NSNotification *)notification;
```

The methods returning a `BOOL` can be used to prevent the start or end of editing. The remaining methods notify of various changes in the text field's state.

Many text fields don't actually need to have a delegate. Many of the functions that would be performed by a delegate can be performed by formatter objects instead. To learn about formatter objects, see the "Validation and Formatters" section later in this chapter.

The Field Editor

Text rendering and editing is an extremely complex task. The `NSTextField` and `NSTextFieldCell` classes are too lightweight to handle all the complexities involved. Rather than lose functionality or duplicate code, all text fields share a single `NSText` object called the field editor.

The `NSText` class is extremely heavyweight and supports all the most advanced features of text handling Cocoa offers. Sharing a single instance helps to simplify the implementation of the text-field classes while amortizing the overhead of the `NSText` class across several `NSTextFieldCell` instances.

Normally, developers don't need to worry about the field editor. It remains behind the scenes, doing its thing. When subclassing `NSTextFieldCell`, however, it is often necessary to intervene and configure the field editor for the new subclass. This is usually done by overriding the `NSTextFieldCell` method `-setUpFieldEditorAttributes:`. This method is handed an `NSText` instance, the field editor, and should return the same instance after finishing. It is common to call the `super` implementation of the method when overriding.

Other methods are related to the field editor, but they are beyond the scope of this book. Refer to the documentation for the `NSControl` class for information about these methods. Furthermore, many of the `NSControl` delegate methods allow customization of field editor behavior without a need for subclassing.

Input Managers

All Cocoa text objects make use of input managers to handle complex input tasks. They allow the user to type characters not available on their keyboards. This is used heavily for oriental languages, but even European languages take advantage of this facility for adding accents and other diacritical marks to characters. The `NSText` class is the primary customer of input managers' services. Because text fields use an `NSText` as their field editor, all `NSTextField` and `NSTextFieldCell` instances can implicitly take advantage of this rich functionality.

Input managers are typically separate processes that communicate using RPC. The `NSInputManager` and `NSInputServer` classes implement the actual functionality. Under normal circumstances, developers never need to work with either class directly. All interation is handled automatically and transparently by `NSText`. Menus to allow users to change between input managers are also fully automatic. Cocoa adds the appropriate menus as necessary without any developer intervention.

Developers wanting to create custom input managers should consult the Cocoa documentation for the `NSInputManager` and `NSInputServer` classes. The developer example at `/Developer/Examples/AppKit/HexInputServer` is also very helpful.

Secure Text Fields

The `NSSecureTextField` and `NSSecureTextFieldCell` classes implement a special variation on the standard text field. Secure text fields override the normal field editor behavior so that the field's value is not displayed when the user types. For added security, it also prevents the standard cut, copy, and paste operations. This type of text field should always be used for extremely sensitive data such as passwords.

Unfortunately, all `NSSecureTextField` objects must be created programmatically because Interface Builder does not yet have an instance of this class on any of its palettes. A partial workaround for this is to create an `NSTextField` object where the secure field is wanted, and then change it to an `NSSecureTextField` in the Custom Class inspector (Cmd-5). The cell class is not changed, however, and there's no way to change it in Interface Builder as of Mac OS X 10.1.4. Therefore, when the `.nib` is unarchived, it is necessary to create a new `NSSecureTextFieldCell` object and pass it to the `NSSecureTextField` by using the `-setCell:` method.

The NSSecureTextFieldCell class can have one of two behaviors. It can echo a user's typing as either a series of bullets (small, black-filled circles), one per character typed, or by moving the cursor, but drawing nothing. The -setEchosBullets: method controls which behavior is used and the -echosBullets method returns the current setting. Unlike most methods used to configure control and cell pairs, these methods are only implemented by the cell subclass.

Validation and Formatters

Cocoa supports automatic validation and formatting of text field entries. When validation is being used, a user is not allowed to stop editing a field until it contains a legal value. The computer beeps if they try to click in another field or Tab to the next field. Formatting concerns how a field displays its values. Formatting includes instructions such as how many decimal places to display for numeric values or which separators to use for date strings. The abstract class NSFormatter is designed to perform both validation and formatting tasks. Cocoa supplies two concrete subclasses, NSNumberFormatter and NSDateFormatter.

For other types of validation, such as Zip codes, phone numbers, or application-specific validation a custom subclass of NSFormatter is required. Subclassing NSFormatter is shown in Chapter 11. The reader should also refer to the third-party frameworks listed in Appendix C, "Finding Third-Party Resources." Many of these frameworks have very good examples.

The easiest way to configure formatters is to use Interface Builder. There are two ways to attach a formatter to a text field in Interface Builder. The first is to drag a formatter off the Cocoa-Views palette and drop it onto a text field. The formatter will automatically be attached to the text field. The second is to drop the formatter into the main .nib window. Drag a connection from the text field to the formatter and connect it to the formatter outlet.

The interface between these two approaches is slightly inconsistent in Interface Builder as of the April 2002 developer tools release. When a formatter is dropped onto a text field, it can be adjusted with a formatter inspector brought up by Cmd-7. The formatter object remains invisible, so although a formatter is connected to the field, the connection won't be shown in the connections inspector. On the other hand, dragging an explicit connection between a text field and a formatter gives a connection that shows up in the text field's connection inspector. But the text field won't have a Cmd-7 format inspector available, even though there is a formatter attached. To get the formatter inspector, the formatter itself needs to be selected and its attributes inspector (Cmd-1) should be brought up.

The second approach, dragging an explicit connection to a formatter instance in the main .nib file, is the only approach that allows a single formatter to be shared between multiple text fields. Because formatters can be shared, it is a good idea to do so whenever possible.

Program code can use the `NSControl/NSCell` methods `-formatter` and `-setFormatter:` to retrieve and change the formatter for a given field, respectively.

Both of the formatters provided by Cocoa, for dates and numbers, are easiest to configure with Interface Builder. When set up, there is rarely a need to change them programmatically. In fact, `NSDateFormatter` instances are immutable. The date formatter's inspector in Interface Builder offers two options. The first is the date format to be used, and the second is whether to allow natural language. The date formatter inspector is shown in Figure 10.12.

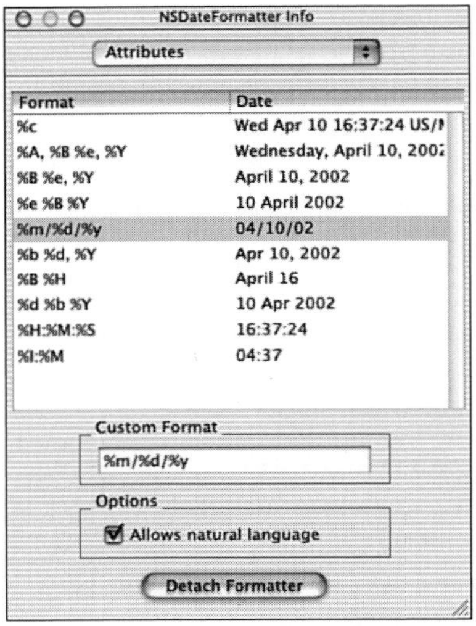

FIGURE 10.12 Interface Builder's `NSDateFormatter` inspector.

Clicking one of the preset formats in the table automatically fills the Custom Format field with the right value. Alternatively, any format can be typed into this field. The format should follow the format specifiers accepted by the `strftime()` C function. Type `man strftime` at the command line to see the function's manual page, which lists all the options.

Turning on the switch to allow natural language makes it possible for the user to type things like `yesterday`, `next week`, `today`, and so on. The phrase is parsed, the date is calculated, and the correct date is put into the text field being formatted. This is very useful, and works remarkably well, but it isn't perfect. For example, relative terms can be problematic. The phrase "two days ago" doesn't work at all and "day before yesterday" incorrectly fills yesterday's date into the field. So, although this is a really neat feature, it might not be acceptable for all uses.

To programmatically create a date formatter, use the designated initializer `-initWithDateFormat:allowNaturalLanguage:`. The `-dateFormat` and `-allowsNaturalLanguage` methods return the object's characteristics. `NSDateFormatters` are immutable, so there are no `-set` accessor methods.

The number formatter's inspector in Interface Builder offers several complex options. It is shown in Figure 10.13.

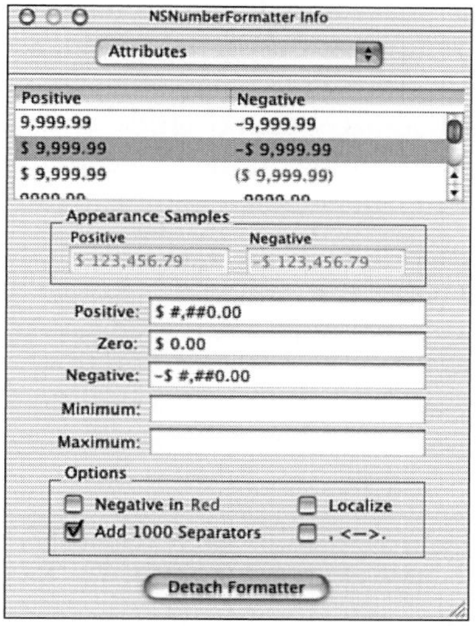

FIGURE 10.13 Interface Builder's `NSNumberFormatter` inspector.

The easiest way to set a number format is to use one of the preset formats available in the table at the top of the inspector. There are formats for floating-point numbers, integers, money, and percentages. Any format can be selected from the table by clicking on its row. The relevant settings will be made in the rest of the inspector panel.

The other way to set a number format is to provide a format for positive, zero, and negative numbers. In the formats, characters such as spaces, dollar signs ($), and percent signs (%) will be used verbatim in the output. Zeros are used as placeholders for digits that should always exist. These digits are zero-filled if necessary, allowing for leading or trailing zeros to be defined. Pound signs (#) are used for optional digits and repeat as necessary. They are used primarily in formats that have thousands separators. The Add 1000 Separators switch must be on for this to work. To get a better feel for how the formats are defined, it is best to play with the Interface Builder inspector a bit and watch how the appearance samples change.

The minimum and maximum settings allow the range of numbers to be constrained. This is especially useful for text fields associated with sliders. The Negative in Red switch can be used to make negative numbers be displayed in red instead of the field's normal text color. The normal text color is still used when editing the field, even if it contains a negative value, and the negative color can only be red.

The Add 1000 Separators switch enables and disables the separators, and takes precedence over what the formats in the fields above it say to do. In some locales, the character used for decimal points and thousands separators are swapped. In the United States, a period (.) is used as the decimal point, and a comma (,) is used as the thousands separator. This is reversed in many other countries. The , <-> . switch swaps the separators. The Localize switch overrides that setting and swaps the separators only when necessary, depending on the locale. In most cases, using the localize feature is preferred because it should always do the right thing for the current locale.

The Detach Formatter button in both the date and number formatters' respective inspectors can be used to delete the formatter instance. Clicking the button causes the formatter object to be deallocated with the side effect of severing any connections made to the formatter. This button works for both shared and private formatters, so it should be used with care. To detach a shared formatter from only one text field instead of all fields, select the field in question and disconnect the `formatter` outlet.

Dozens of methods can be used to adjust an `NSNumberFormatter`. Rather than discuss them all here, refer to the class reference sheet. It can be found as part of the developer documentation at `/Developer/Documentation/Cocoa/Reference/Foundation/ObjC_classic/Classes/NSNumberFormatter.html`. Many of the methods do not directly correspond to the controls in the Interface Builder inspector, though all the same functionality is available.

Image Display

Image views are used to display images. For instance, an image view can be used to *skin* a window's content area. Image views can also be used as a way for users to select images. When editable, a user can drag an image to an image view and drop it there. Image views are implemented in Cocoa with the `NSImageView` and `NSImageCell` classes.

NOTE

The class names `NSImageView` and `NSImageCell` don't follow the naming convention established between the other Cocoa control/cell pairings. There is already an `NSImage` class for representing images (described in Chapter 14) so that name is not available for this control. The name `NSImageViewCell` is cumbersome and misleading because the cell is not a view, so `NSImageCell` is used.

Image views are found on the Cocoa-Other Interface Builder palette. (Refer to Figure 10.7 shown earlier in this chapter to see this palette.) The `NSImageView` instance is the rectangular object with rounded corners that is displaying a picture of a mountain.

Image View Options in Interface Builder

All the options for configuring an image view can be found in Interface Builder's `NSImageView` inspector. This inspector, shown in Figure 10.14, is displayed by using the Cmd-1 key equivalent when an `NSImageView` or an `NSImageCell` is selected.

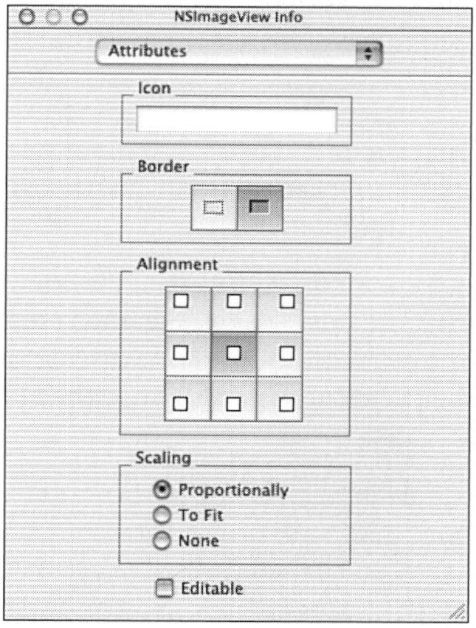

FIGURE 10.14 Interface Builder's image view inspector.

There are five configurable features in the `NSImageView` class—icon, border, alignment, scaling, and editability. The icon is the name of the image being displayed. This can be the name of an image in the project, one of the system bitmap names, or even the full path of an image anywhere in the file system. The border can be turned on or off. Cocoa actually supports other options for the border, but they are not Aqua-compliant. To avoid the temptation to use these extra options, they aren't available from within Interface Builder.

The alignment and scaling determine how the image is displayed. Alignment controls where the image is placed within the view, and scaling allows the image to be stretched. Each of the scaling options is worth examining. Proportional scaling means that the image will be shrunk in size if it doesn't completely fit within the view's bounds. The scaling will be done proportionally, which preserves the image's aspect ratio. Scaling to fit will expand or shrink the image as necessary to make it cover the entire bounds of the view. This can seriously distort the image if the view's aspect ratio differs significantly from the image's aspect ratio. No scaling will always render the image without any size adjustment or distortion. If the view is too small, the excess parts of the image will be clipped (cropped) so that the image stays within the bounds of the view.

The editable parameter determines whether the user is allowed to drag and drop new images into the image view. It is usually best to disable this for borderless image views because the user wouldn't know that there was an active control without the border to send the necessary visual cues.

Modifying Image View Instances

A few methods are available in `NSImageView` and `NSImageCell` to expose the functionality used in Interface Builder.

The image view's image, labeled Icon in Interface Builder, can be manipulated with the `-setImage:` and `-image` accessors. They take and return an `NSImage` instance, respectively. Refer to Chapter 14 for an in-depth discussion of `NSImage`. To make the view editable or not, or see the current setting, use the standard `NSCell` methods `-setEditable:` and `-isEditable`.

To work with the border of an image view, use the `-setImageFrameStyle:` and `-imageFrameStyle` methods. They take and return the constants `NSImageFrameNone`, `NSImageFramePhoto`, `NSImageFrameGrayBezel`, `NSImageFrameGroove`, and `NSImageFrameButton`. Only the `NSImageFrameNone` and `NSImageFramePhoto` constants should be used to keep within the Aqua guidelines.

Scaling options are accessed with the `-setImageScaling:` and `-imageScaling` methods. The constants used by these methods are `NSScaleProportionally`, `NSScaleToFit`, and `NSScaleNone`. Alignment is accessed with the `-setImageAlignment:` and `-imageAlignment` methods. The following constants can be used with the alignment methods:

```
NSImageAlignCenter

NSImageAlignTop

NSImageAlignTopLeft

NSImageAlignTopRight

NSImageAlignLeft
```

`NSImageAlignBottom`

`NSImageAlignBottomLeft`

`NSImageAlignBottomRight`

`NSImageAlignRight`

The default image scaling is `NSScaleProportionally`. The default image alignment is `NSImageAlignCenter`.

Progress Indicators

Progress indicators can be used to provide feedback about long-running processes. There are two types of indicator: indeterminate and determinate. An indeterminate progress indicator looks like a sideways barber pole. While a long-running task is being performed, it appears to spin. This animation tells the user that the program hasn't hung up. Determinate progress indicators start out empty and fill in their bounds from left to right as a process is completed. The filled-in part of the progress indicator has a subtle animation that makes it look somewhat like flowing water.

Progress indicators are implemented by the `NSProgressIndicator` class. This class is a subclass of `NSView`, not `NSControl`, and has no partner `NSCell` subclass. Because of this, progress indicators cannot be used in matrices or other objects requiring cells. A progress indicator instance can be found on Interface Builder's Cocoa-Other palette. (Refer to Figure 10.7 earlier in this chapter to see the palette.) It is set to be indeterminate, so it looks like a sideways barber pole.

Progress Indicator Options in Interface Builder

All the options for configuring a progress indicator can be found in Interface Builder's `NSProgressIndicator` inspector. This inspector, shown in Figure 10.15, is displayed by using the Cmd-1 key equivalent when an `NSProgressIndicator` is selected.

This inspector is very simple. The progress indicator's type, indeterminate or not, is set with the Indeterminate switch. The Small switch is used to choose a smaller version of the progress indicator.

If the progress indicator is determinate, the range parameters become meaningful. When a long task is running, it periodically updates the progress indicator's value to show how far the task has proceeded. The range is set beforehand to tell the indicator the range of values it should expect to see between starting and completing the task. Then, as the value changes, the progress indicator knows how much of its bar should be colored in. The default range of zero to 100 nicely matches the idea of percent complete. Of course, any range will work, so it is best to choose a range that best suits the task reflected by the progress indicator.

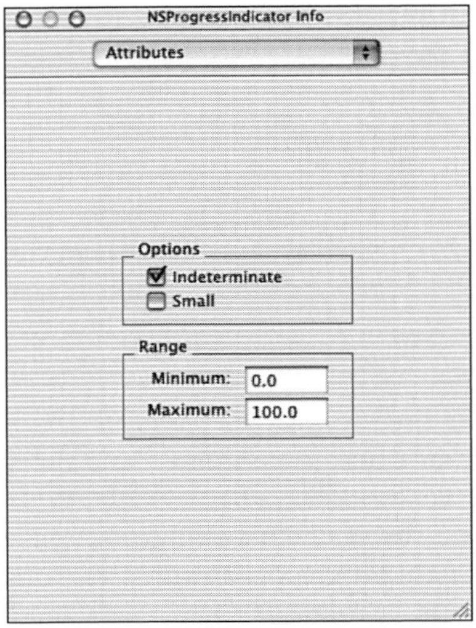

FIGURE 10.15 Interface Builder's progress indicator inspector.

There is no way to set the progress indicator's value in Interface Builder. This must be done through program code. In general, the `NSProgressIndicator` class requires some amount of code to be used properly.

`NSProgressIndicator` Methods

The basic options offered from Interface Builder are available from a set of self-explanatory accessor methods. They are

```
- (BOOL)isIndeterminate;
- (void)setIndeterminate:(BOOL)flag;
- (NSControlSize)controlSize;
- (void)setControlSize:(NSControlSize)size;
- (double)minValue;
- (double)maxValue;
- (void)setMinValue:(double)newMinimum;
- (void)setMaxValue:(double)newMaximum;
```

The `NSControlSize` type is enumerated and can be either `NSRegularControlSize` or `NSSmallControlSize`.

If a progress indicator is determinate, its value can be manipulated by using the `-setDoubleValue:` and `-doubleValue` methods. These are the only two value accessors available. Because this class isn't a control, it doesn't implement other value accessors such as `-setIntValue:`, and so on. The method `-incrementBy:` can be used to move the progress indicator forward by a set amount. It takes a double as its parameter. The `-incrementBy:` method is for convenience only, so the following two lines of code are equivalent:

```
[myIndicator incrementBy:someDelta];
[myIndicator setDoubleValue:[myIndicator doubleValue] + someDelta];
```

There are also several methods that can be used to start, stop, and control the animation of an `NSProgressIndicator`. To start the animation, use the `-startAnimation:` action method. The `-stopAnimation:` action method stops the animation. To manually advance the animation by one frame, call the `-animate:` action method. This method's `sender` argument is ignored.

The speed of the animation can be adjusted with the `-setAnimationDelay:` method. The `-animationDelay` method returns the current delay. These methods work with the `NSTimeInterval` type, which is a floating-point number representing seconds. So, an interval of 0.5 would mean two frames per second.

It is possible to have the animation of the progress indicator be run from an `NSTimer` in the main thread or from a separate thread. If the task being monitored runs in the main thread and blocks the main event loop until it is finished, it is usually best to run the animation from a separate thread. If a background worker thread is being monitored, running a separate thread might not be necessary. Chapter 24, "Subprocesses and Threads," describes threads in detail and includes an example that uses an `NSProgressIndicator`. To change the threading behavior of an `NSProgressIndicator` instance, use the `-setUsesThreadedAnimation:` method. Use the `-usesThreadedAnimation` method to see the current setting.

Container Views and Controls

Several of Cocoa's view subclasses can be wrapped around other Cocoa views. Because of these behaviors, they are often referred to as containers. Boxes, scroll views, tab views, split views, and matrices can all be considered containers. Boxes simply draw a pretty border around the views they contain. A scroll view allows a user to scroll around a view that is much larger than the scroll view itself. Tab views allow users to switch between several related views. Split views provide a separator that can be dragged to reallocate screen real estate between two views.

NOTE

Most Cocoa containers use both the GOF Decorator and GOF Facade patterns. Chapter 6, "Cocoa Design Patterns," briefly discusses these and other patterns found in Cocoa.

In Interface Builder, the Cocoa-Containers palette, shown in Figure 10.16, has tab view and box instances on it. These instances can be dragged into any window. Matrices, scroll views, and split views are not available on any palettes, however. Interface Builder offers an alternative means of creating these views. First, select one or more views that are to become subviews of the container. Next, select one of the items in the `Layout>Make subviews of>` menu. This enables arbitrary views to be wrapped in a box, scroll view, split view, tab view, or a custom view subclass.

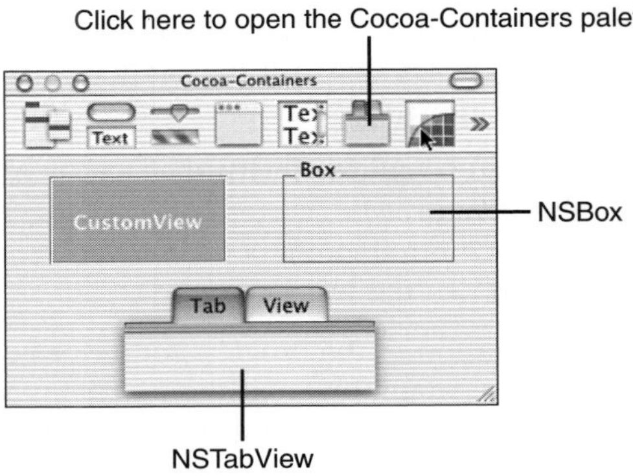

FIGURE 10.16 Interface Builder's Cocoa-Containers palette.

After a container instance has been created, double-clicking the container or clicking one of the container's visible subviews enables the contents of the container to be edited. Items can also be dragged from the palette into the container.

Boxes

Boxes are used to visually group user interface items. Normally, boxes draw a border around their bounds and a title at the top. Boxes do not accept user input. Boxes are implemented by the `NSBox` class. Figure 10.17 shows three variations of the basic box available in Interface Builder. There is an `NSBox` instance on the Cocoa-Containers palette, as shown in Figure 10.16. Refer to the previous section "Container Views and Controls" for instructions on how to create an `NSBox` instance in Interface Builder.

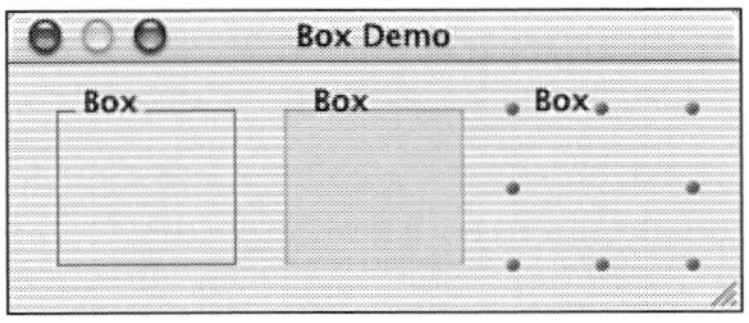

FIGURE 10.17 `NSBox` instances created with Interface Builder.

Some boxes are drawn to be very narrow. Look for the vertical and horizontal separator lines in the Cocoa-Views Interface Builder palette. (The palette is shown in Figure 10.9 earlier in this chapter.) These separators are actually instances of `NSBox`. It is not possible to change an `NSBox` instance from a rectangular box into a separator or vice-versa, even though they are the same class. Separators can't be changed between being vertical or horizontal, either. Interface Builder prevents such changes. Instead of changing existing instances, a new instance of the right kind would need to be dragged from the palette.

Box Options in Interface Builder

All the options for configuring a box can be found in Interface Builder's `NSBox` inspector. This inspector, shown in Figure 10.18, is displayed by using the Cmd-1 key equivalent when an `NSBox` is selected.

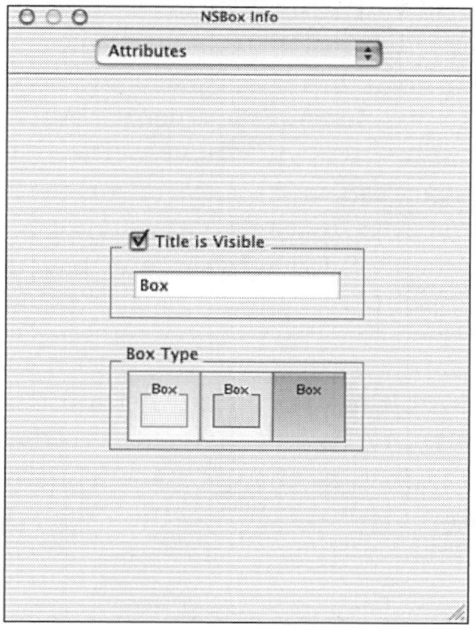

FIGURE 10.18 Interface Builder's `NSBox` inspector.

Interface Builder offers two options for boxes, changing the title and type of the box. The Title is Visible switch turns the title on or off. The title itself can be changed by modifying the text field under the switch. It can also be changed by double-clicking the title on the box itself and modifying the title in place.

NOTE

Setting the title to an empty string is not the same thing as making it invisible. A box actually obscures part of its border before drawing the title. An empty title still leaves a small gap in the border. Making the title invisible makes the box border seamless.

The Box Type control allows the choice between three styles of box, as shown in Figure 10.17. The rightmost box is actually borderless. Most boxes seen in Aqua are of the leftmost style.

`NSBox` Methods

It is easiest to configure an `NSBox` in Interface Builder and be done with it. Several accessor methods can be used to make changes programmatically, though. Several options that are available through code are not offered in Interface Builder. These extra options sometimes create boxes that are not Aqua compliant, so extra care should be taken with these methods to ensure a user interface that looks like it really belongs on Mac OS X.

To turn the border on or off, use the `-setBorderType:` method. Use `-borderType` to see the current setting. Four constants are available for use with these methods, `NSNoBorder`, `NSLineBorder`, `NSBezelBorder`, and `NSGrooveBorder`. The `NSNoBorder` constant gives a borderless box. `NSGrooveBorder` is the default setting for all boxes. To change the style of the box, use `-setBoxType:`. Use `-boxType` to see the current setting. Four constants can be used with these methods, `NSBoxPrimary`, `NSBoxSecondary`, `NSBoxSeparator`, and `NSBoxOldStyle`. The leftmost box shown in Figure 10.17 is a primary style box, whereas the center box exhibits the secondary style. Separators are thin lines placed between user interface elements and do not enclose any views. The old style box should be avoided because it is not Aqua compliant.

The title is manipulated with the `-setTitle:` method. The current title is returned by the `-title` method. The title font is changed with the `-setTitleFont:` method. The current title font is returned by the `-titleFont` method. The title's position can be changed with the `-setTitlePosition:` method. The current position is returned by the `-titlePosition` method.

The title position methods work with several different constants. Interface Builder uses the `NSNoTitle` and `NSAtTop` constants, controlled by the Title is Visible switch. These are the only two that are Aqua compliant. The other constants that are available, but should be avoided, are `NSAboveTop`, `NSBelowTop`, `NSAboveBottom`, `NSAtBottom`, and `NSBelowBottom`. The title position can be at the top or bottom border of the box. A title can also be above, below, or at the border. Titles at the border interrupt the border, whereas titles above or below the border do not.

Every box has a content view object. All the views enclosed by a box are subviews of the content view. To manipulate the content view of a box, use the `-setContentView:` method. The current content view is returned by the `-contentView` method. Using the normal `NSView` methods `-addSubview:` and `-replaceSubview:with:` will also do the right thing, adding the views to the content view of the box.

Borderless Boxes

A common use of borderless boxes is to implement inspectors such as the one in Interface Builder. The inspector changes its user interface based on the current selection. To support this, it is convenient to define an inspector view for each object that might be selected. An inspector view will typically be an `NSBox` instance containing the full user interface for the object's inspector.

When it comes time to swap one inspector interface with another, a tabless `NSTabView` or other appropriate container is used as a container, and the inspector views are swapped in and out. The container and inspector view are invisible to the user. All the user sees is that one set of controls has vanished and a new set has appeared. (Tab views are explained in the upcoming "Tab Views" section.)

Scroll Views

Scroll views allow a large view, such as a document, to be displayed in a much smaller window. The large view being scrolled is known as the scroll view's document view. By adding scrollbars around the edges of the document view, it becomes possible to navigate through extremely large views. Scroll views can also optionally manage rulers and ruler markers.

A scroll view is implemented in Cocoa with the `NSScrollView` class. A scroll view contains multiple subviews in addition to its document view. Instances of `NSScroller` implement the scrollbars. The content area of the scroll view, called the content view, is actually an `NSClipView` instance. The document view being managed by the scroll view is really a subview of the clip view. The clip view can be thought of as a window that displays only a portion of the document view at any given time. Scroll views that have rulers use instances of `NSRulerView` and `NSRulerMarker`. Figure 10.19 shows how these views are normally laid out by a scroll view.

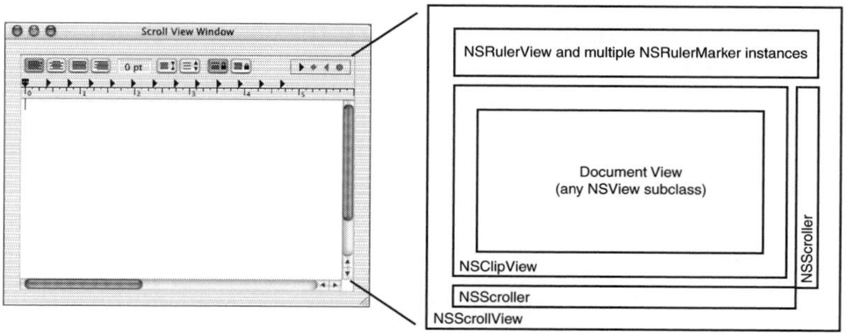

FIGURE 10.19 The layout of subviews inside an `NSScrollView` instance.

Refer to the previous section "Container Views and Controls" for instructions on how to create an `NSScrollView` instance in Interface Builder.

Scroll View Options in Interface Builder

All the options for configuring a scroll view can be found in Interface Builder's `NSScrollView` inspector. This inspector, shown in Figure 10.20, is displayed by using the Cmd-1 key equivalent when an `NSScrollView` is selected.

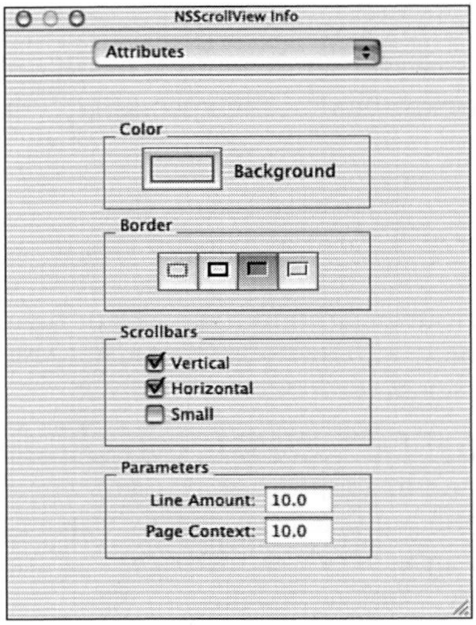

FIGURE 10.20 Interface Builder's `NSScrollView` inspector.

The background color is displayed as the scroll view's background if the views it encloses are transparent or do not cover the entire content area of the scroll view. It is common to set this color to a shade of gray if the default window background color is unacceptable.

The border setting allows there to be no border, a solid black line, a bezel, or a groove. Most user interfaces use the bezeled border if the scroll view is not the only user interface element in its window. If the scroll view is the only element, it is preferable to use no border and size the scroll view so that it covers the entire window content area. An example of this would be a document window in TextEdit.

The scrollbars are actually optional. Normally, it is best to have at least one scrollbar visible. It is entirely possible, though, to use a scroll view as if it were a sliding window over a view. In such a situation there would be no scrollbars and the application would programmatically move the scroll view, as necessary. The scrollers can also be set to use small versions. This is handy for cramped interfaces, but should not be done for full-window scroll views.

The Parameters box controls scrolling behavior. The first parameter, Line Amount, controls how many pixels the scroll view will move when an arrow is clicked on one of the scrollbars. The Page Context parameter is trickier. When a scroll arrow is Option-clicked, it asks the scroll view to scroll by a page instead of a line. The default behavior is to move the scroll view so that whatever was shown at the bottom of the scroll view before the page scroll is moved to the top of the scroll view after the scroll. The page context tells the scroll view how many pixels of data from the bottom (before the page scroll) should remain visible at the top (after the page scroll). A setting of zero means that the last row of pixels before the scroll will be just off the top of the screen after the scroll. A positive setting means that slightly less than a screenful will be considered to be a "page" for scrolling purposes.

Scroll views implement methods to expose all the functionality that is supported by Interface Builder. There is also a large amount of functionality that is not currently available from Interface Builder, so it is common to write some set up code to make final tweaks to a scroll view after it is loaded from a `.nib`.

Configuring `NSScrollView` Rendering

The background color of a scroll view is controlled with the `-setBackgroundColor:` and `-setDrawsBackground:`, methods. The current settings are returned by the `-backgroundColor` and `-drawsBackground` methods. In Interface Builder, background drawing is always turned on. Turning it off makes it possible for views underneath the scroll view to show through.

The border is manipulated with the `-setBorderType:` method. The current border type is returned by the `-borderType` method. These methods use the same four border type constants as boxes, `NSNoBorder`, `NSLineBorder`, `NSBezelBorder`, and `NSGrooveBorder`.

Scrolling Parameters

The scrollers are turned on and off with the `-setHasVerticalScroller:` and `-setHasHorizontalScroller:` methods. The scroller status is returned by the `-hasVerticalScroller` and `-hasHorizontalScroller` methods. To change the scroller size, it is necessary to manipulate the scroller objects themselves. The accessors for the scroller objects are `-setVerticalScroller:`, `-verticalScroller`, `-setHorizontalScroller:`, and `-horizontalScroller`. All four scroller accessors either accept or return `NSScroller` instances.

The `NSScroller` class implements scrollbars. Normally, there is little need to manipulate this class directly. The `NSScrollView` class takes care of all interaction with the class automatically. Scrollers are controls, so it is possible to use the standard

NSControl methods to configure them. Scrollers do not have an associated cell subclass.

The scrolling parameters for line amount and page context from Interface Builder are controlled by several methods. All these methods work with float values. The line amount is accessed with -setLineScroll: and -lineScroll. The page context is accessed with -setPageScroll: and -pageScroll. These methods treat the horizontal and vertical scrolling amounts identically. It is possible to treat the horizontal and vertical directions differently. The following methods control the scrolling parameters precisely in just the horizontal or vertical direction:

```
- (void)setHorizontalLineScroll:(float)value
- (void)setVerticalLineScroll:(float)value
- (float)horizontalLineScroll
- (float)verticalLineScroll
- (void)setHorizontalPageScroll:(float)value
- (void)setVerticalPageScroll:(float)value
- (float)horizontalPageScroll
- (float)verticalPageScroll
```

Rulers in Scroll Views

A scroll view wrapped around an NSText object is already set up to use rulers. To have rulers available for any other type of scroll view content requires some extra code. By convention, rulers are turned on and off by sending the -toggleRuler: method down the responder chain. The NSScrollView class doesn't support the -toggleRuler: action method. Instead, this method must be implemented by the class that is the scroll view's document view. This may seem odd because the ruler is actually laid out by the scroll view as one of its subviews. The NSText object in Interface Builder has the capability to show rulers because it implements the -toggleRuler: method. A -toggleRuler: method implementation should be written to cooperate with the enclosing scroll view to manage the rulers.

Prior to making the rulers visible, the ruler objects need to be set up. The -setHorizontalRulerView:, -horizontalRulerView, -setVerticalRulerView:, and -verticalRulerView accessors work with NSRulerView objects to set up and retrieve the rulers. The -setHasHorizontalRuler: and -setVerticalRulerView: methods can be used to turn the rulers on or off, individually. Finally, the -setRulersVisible: method causes the enabled rulers to be either displayed or not. The -rulersVisible method returns the current setting. The scroll view tries to automatically set up its rulers if possible. How this is done can be altered by telling the scroll view class which ruler class to use. Use the +setRulerViewClass: and +rulerViewClass class methods to do this.

Ruler views require a client view. The client view is the view being measured by the rulers. The scroll view will not automatically connect the document view to the ruler as a client. It is up to the document view to complete this part of the setup. The document view should use the `NSScrollView` `-horizontalRulerView` and `-verticalRulerView` accessors to obtain the rulers from the scroll view. After it has the rulers, the document view can call the `NSRulerView` `-setClientView:` method to set up the client relationship.

Rulers inside of scroll views are implemented by the `NSRulerView` class. Markers along the length of the ruler, such as tab stops, are implemented with the `NSRulerMarker` class. A single ruler view can have many markers. Both classes are highly configurable and relatively easy to use. The Sketch example at `/Developer/Examples/AppKit/Sketch` shows how to use rulers in the most basic form. The TextEdit example at `/Developer/Examples/AppKit/TextEdit` shows a much more complex ruler.

Using an `NSScrollView`

When working with the contents of a scroll view, it is important to remember that the content view is actually a clip view instance. The view that is scrolled is the document view, which is in turn a subview of the clip view. The clip view, an `NSClipView` instance, is accessed with `-setContentView:` and `-contentView`. The document view is accessed with `-setDocumentView:` and `-documentView`. The size of the content area is returned by `-contentSize`. The part of the document view currently being displayed is returned by `-documentVisibleRect`.

> **NOTE**
>
> It is rare to work directly with the `NSClipView` class because `NSScrollView` handles it automatically. It is, therefore, best to stick with the document view methods instead of using the content view methods.

Usually, the only reason to subclass `NSScrollView` is to add new controls to the interface. A common control is a zoom pop-up inside the horizontal scrollbar. The main method to override is the `-tile` method. This method is called by Cocoa to lay out the scroll view. Calling the `super` implementation, and then adjusting the subviews to make room for the new controls usually accomplishes the desired result. The TextEdit source code at `/Developer/Examples/AppKit/TextEdit` shows one way to do this in its `ScalingScrollView` class.

Another useful method is defined by the `NSView` class. The `-scrollRectToVisible:` method takes an `NSRect` and attempts to scroll so that the rectangle becomes visible; it returns `YES` if successful. This method should be sent to the document view of a scroll view. This is the primary means of scrolling programmatically. Search the

NSView class reference or header file for the word "scroll" to find a handful of other methods that are occasionally useful when working with scroll views.

Sometimes a scroll view's document view implements mouse-dragging and wants to scroll automatically in response to mouse-dragged events. To do this, it should invoke the enclosing clipview's -autoscroll: method, passing in the mouse-dragged event. Chapter 15 discusses events, such as mouse-drags, in detail. For now, it is enough to know that simply adding this line to a custom view's -mouseDragged: method usually suffices:

```
[[self superview] autoscroll:event];
```

It is always safe to call the -autoscroll: method because NSView defines it. The NSClipView class simply overrides -autoscroll: to work effectively with an enclosing scroll view. If a view isn't in a scroll view, the method call is ignored.

Adding this call in -mouseDragged: causes the scrolling to only happen when the mouse is moved. To have the scrolling happen continuously, even when the mouse isn't being moved, use an NSTimer to send the auto scroll message repeatedly. Doing auto scrolling with a timer often feels smoother to the user.

Tab Views

Tab views are containers that have multiple content views, but only one is available at any given time. Across the top is a row of labeled tabs that the user can click to move from one pane to another. Some tab views are tabless. Such views can still switch from pane to pane under program control, but the user is unaware that this is the case until they see it change. The Animal example from Chapter 24, "Subprocesses and Threads," puts a tabless tab view to good use. The tabless form is usually used to implement a wizard interface, where the user steps through a series of pages to accomplish a complex task.

Tab views are an economical means of putting many, many user interface controls into a reasonably sized window. The controls in a tab view should be grouped in a logical manner. Each grouping should be placed on a single tab. An example of putting tab views to good use is the System Preferences application. Many of the preferences panes it supports contain tab views.

Tab views are implemented by the NSTabView class. Each individual tab is represented by an NSTabViewItem instance. A typical NSTabView instance owns many NSTabViewItem instances. There is an NSTabView instance on the Cocoa-Containers palette, as shown in Figure 10.16 earlier in this chapter. Usually, Interface Builder is used to create tab views. Refer to the previous section "Container Views and Controls" for instructions on how to create an NSTabView instance in Interface Builder.

Tab View Options in Interface Builder

Options for configuring a tab view can be found in Interface Builder's `NSTabView` inspector. This inspector, shown in Figure 10.21, is displayed by using the Cmd-1 key equivalent when an `NSTabView` is selected.

FIGURE 10.21 Interface Builder's `NSTabView` inspector.

The most significant attribute is the number of items (tabs). Any number can be used, but there are some caveats. Tab views don't deal well with having too many tabs. They tend to clip out any tabs that don't fit within the tab view's bounds. To help this situation, the Allows truncated labels switch can be turned on to reduce the size of the individual tabs a little bit. The Small Tabs switch might help a little as well. If after all this the tabs are still too large, they will be clipped regardless. It is a good idea to make sure everything looks good in Interface Builder. Making the window larger and setting a relatively large minimum window size might be necessary to keep the user interface looking good.

The other key option is to choose whether the tab view should have tabs. If yes, the tabs will be at the top of the view. Even in a tabless view, there can still be an arbitrary number of items. Because tabless views don't have to worry about drawing tabs, any number of items is usable.

NOTE

There is a disabled pop-up button for tab view that is set to Has Tabs. The pop up looks like it allows the tabs to be put on a different side of the view, but it cannot be enabled. Tabs are always at the top. The fact that Apple added this pop up in the December 2001 developer tools release clearly implies that there are plans to allow tabs to be in other locations in the future.

Tabless tab views can display with or without a border. The Animal example in Chapter 24 uses a borderless, tabless tab view to implement its primary user interface. A bordered view looks like a raised box with drop shadow, floating just a tiny bit above the window containing it.

The Draws Background switch only affects tab views that are tabless and borderless. If it is on, the tab view's background will be drawn in solid black. There is no way to change this, so drawing the background isn't a terribly useful option at present.

Tab View Item Options in Interface Builder

Options for configuring a tab view item can be found in Interface Builder's `NSTabViewItem` inspector. This inspector, shown in Figure 10.22, is displayed by using the Cmd-1 key equivalent when an `NSTabViewItem` is selected.

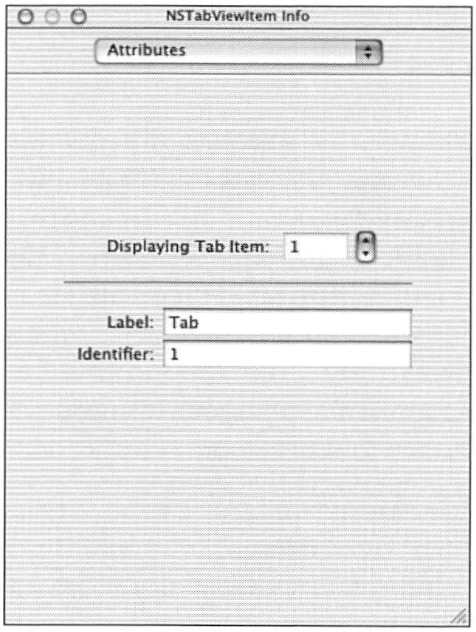

FIGURE 10.22 Interface Builder's `NSTabViewItem` inspector.

There are two settings in this inspector—the label and the identifier. The label is the text that appears on the tab itself, and can also be edited by double-clicking one of the tabs. The identifier is like a tag on a typical control except that it can be any string value. It doesn't have to be an integer. This identifier can be used in program code to find tab view items.

The control Displaying Tab Item: with the field and stepper is a convenient means of switching between tabs while working on a tab view in Interface Builder. This is especially handy for tab views that are tabless because, in that case, it is the only way to switch from tab to tab in Interface Builder. The tabs can be selected like normal to switch around, but only if they are visible.

Configuring an `NSTabView`

When configuring a tab view in code, the InterfaceBuilder controls for tabs/tabless and border type are combined into a single pair of accessor methods, `-setTabViewType:` and `-tabViewType`. The constants that can be used with these methods are `NSTopTabsBezelBorder`, `NSNoTabsBezelBorder`, `NSNoTabsLineBorder`, and `NSNoTabsNoBorder`. The `NSNoTabsLineBorder` constant is not available from Interface Builder.

> **NOTE**
>
> Three other constants are defined in the `NSTabView.h` header file: `NSLeftTabsBezelBorder`, `NSBottomTabsBezelBorder`, and `NSRightTabsBezelBorder`. A note in Mac OS X 10.1 says that these create a tab view with the tabs at the top, but implies that they will be supported in the future.

The `-setAllowsTruncatedLabels:` method controls whether the tab view will truncate the labels, if necessary, to make the tabs fit. The `-setDrawsBackground:` method turns the background on and off, but only for the `NSNoTabsNoBorder` (borderless) tab view type. The current settings of these attributes are returned by the `-allowsTruncatedLabels` and `-drawsBackground` methods.

Selecting Tabs

Selecting a tab is done by selecting one of the `NSTabViewItem` instances managed by the tab view. Tabs can be selected based on identifier with `-selectTabViewItemWithIdentifier:`. Tabs can also be selected by index with the `-selectTabViewItemAtIndex:` method. The indices run from zero to the number of tabs minus one. Both methods raise a range exception if a nonexistent tab is requested. When selecting by index number, examining the number of tabs first with the `-numberOfTabViewItems` method can prevent the exception.

A new tab can also be selected in a relative manner. Tabs are considered to run from left to right, so the first tab is the leftmost tab. The last tab is rightmost. In relation to the currently selected tab, the previous tab is to the left and the next tab is to the right. Four obvious action methods can be used to select tabs. They are `-selectFirstTabViewItem:`, `-selectPreviousTabViewItem:`, `-selectNextTabViewItem:`, and `-selectLastTabViewItem:`. These methods are useful when creating a wizard-like interface that steps the user through a series of tasks. The next and previous actions correspond directly to the buttons that would be at the bottom of the wizard to move from page to page.

There are also a few methods for looking up tab view items within the tab view. The `-tabViewItems` method returns an `NSArray` with all the items. This array is immutable, so tabs are not added and removed by manipulating this array. Refer to the "Adding, Removing, and Modifying Tabs" section later in this chapter to do that. The `-selectedTabViewItem` method returns the currently active tab view item or `nil` if no tab has been selected.

A particular tab view item can be obtained with the `-tabViewItemAtIndex:`, which returns an `NSTabViewItem` instance. As with the selection methods, exceptions are raised for numbers that are out of range. The `-indexOfTabViewItem:`, or `-indexOfTabViewItemWithIdentifier:` methods both return indices of the items or `NSNotFound`. There is no method to get an item based on its identifier. Instead, two messages must be sent—one to obtain the index, and another to obtain the item.

Adding, Removing, and Modifying Tabs

There are several methods for adding and removing tab view items. These methods function similarly to the `NSMutableArray` methods, but the names are more specific. To add an item to a tab view, it must first be created. The `NSTabViewItem` class uses the `-initWithIdentifier:` method as its designated initializer.

Add a newly created `NSTabViewItem` instance to a tab view with either `-addTabViewItem:` or `-insertTabViewItem:atIndex:`. The `-addTabViewItem:` method adds the tab at the end of the list. Remove an item with the `-removeTabViewItem:` method.

A tab view item can be modified in several ways. The identifier and label can be accessed through the standard accessor methods `-setIdentifier:`, `-identifier`, `-setLabel:`, and `-label`. The label is displayed on the tab itself, whereas the identifier is private to the application's internals. When set in Interface Builder, both are `NSString` instances, but identifiers don't have to be strings. An instance of any class is acceptable, so if something makes more sense than a string, feel free to use it.

A tab view item has a content view. The `-setView:` and `-view` methods allow the content view to be manipulated. As with windows, a tab item can have an initial first responder. This is the view that will become first responder when the tab is activated. The initial first responder is accessed with the `-setInitialFirstResponder:` and `-initialFirstResponder` methods.

`NSTabView` Delegates

Tab views can havedelegates. The usual accessor methods for delegates, `-setDelegate:` and `-delegate` are available. The tab view sends any of the following four methods to a delegate if it implements them:

```
- (BOOL)tabView:(NSTabView *)tabView
        shouldSelectTabViewItem:(NSTabViewItem *)tabViewItem;
- (void)tabView:(NSTabView *)tabView
        willSelectTabViewItem:(NSTabViewItem *)tabViewItem;
- (void)tabView:(NSTabView *)tabView
        didSelectTabViewItem:(NSTabViewItem *)tabViewItem;
- (void)tabViewDidChangeNumberOfTabViewItems:(NSTabView *)TabView;
```

The `-tabView: shouldSelectTabViewItem:` method allows the delegate to prevent the user from switching tabs. Because there's no way to disable a tab visually, it is not a good idea to simply return `NO` without offering the user some feedback as to why the tab can't be changed. An alert sheet to help the user along is recommended.

Delegates are usually used most often as part of the implementation of a wizard interface. Delegates can do tricky things such as inserting extra tabs based on user input in other tabs. Delegates often perform or coordinate input validation tasks as well.

Split Views

Split views lay out two or more views and draw divider bars between them. The user can drag the divider bars to change the relative sizes of the subviews. Split views lay out the subviews either horizontally or vertically, but never both ways at once. In other words, the layout is always in one dimension. Any number of subviews is supported, even though the most common layout is to have only two views, one atop the other.

The `NSSplitView` class implements split views in Cocoa. There are no instances on the palettes in Interface Builder, but it is possible to create an instance by wrapping multiple selected views in a split view. The menu item Layout, Make subviews of, Split View does this.

Split View Options in Interface Builder

Options for configuring a split view can be found in Interface Builder's `NSSplitView` inspector. This inspector, shown in Figure 10.23, is displayed by using the Cmd-1 key equivalent when an `NSSplitView` is selected.

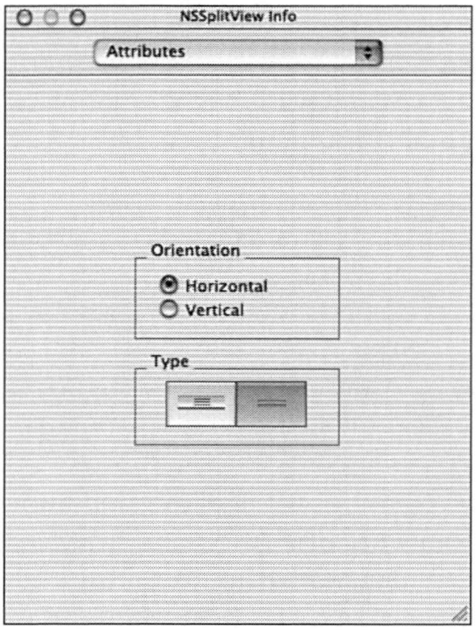

FIGURE 10.23 Interface Builder's `NSSplitView` inspector.

There are two parameters that can be modified. The first is the orientation of the divider drawn between the subviews of the split view, and the second is the way that the divider itself is rendered.

If horizontal orientation is selected, the divider runs horizontally and the subviews are stacked one atop the other (vertically). A vertical orientation has a vertical divider with the subviews stacked side by side (horizontally). This can be confusing; it is easiest to remember that this setting controls how the divider between subviews is drawn.

The type switches change the divider's rendering. The button on the left gives an opaque divider with a bubbly Aqua look. Split views configured this way are known as pane splitters. If the divider orientation is vertical, there is no difference between the two types, and there is also no marking drawn on the divider.

`NSSplitView` Methods

The two parameters that can be altered in Interface Builder have their own accessor methods. The `-setVertical:` and `-isVertical` methods work with the orientation. The `-setIsPaneSplitter:` and `-isPaneSplitter` methods change the divider's rendering. Pane splitters draw an opaque divider with a bubbly Aqua look. Split views that aren't pane splitters draw a wider marking on the divider, and have a background that matches the window's background pattern.

NOTE

As of Mac OS X 10.1.4, the `NSSplitView` class reference says that the default orientation of the split view is vertical in the description of the `-isVertical` method. In the description of the `-setIsVertical:` method, it says that the default orientation is horizontal. Clearly, both can't be right. The real default orientation is actually horizontal, so the documentation for `-isVertical` is incorrect. The documentation for the `-setIsPaneSplitter:` method is also in error, claiming both settings are achieved by sending `YES`. To get a separator without the bubbly Aqua look, a `NO` is what should actually be sent. These errors are likely to be fixed eventually, of course.

There are no methods to move the dividers. Instead, the frames of the subviews should be modified directly, and then the split view should be redisplayed. Care must be taken to be ensure that the views are laid out properly and that enough room has been left for the divider(s). To make this a little easier, the `-dividerThickness` method returns the size of the dividers. The `-isSubviewCollapsed:` method returns `YES` if the divider is placed such that no part of a subview is actually visible. In this case, the split view retains the subview, but doesn't display it until the divider is moved to expose it.

`NSSplitView` Delegates

Split views support delegates and implement the standard delegate accessor methods `-setDelegate:` and `-delegate`. There is a very rich collection of delegate methods available, as well as a pair of notifications. Delegates are allowed to lay out all the subviews at once when a split view is about to be rendered for the first time. They can also place maximum and minimum size constraints on the subviews. Delegates can also say whether a subview can be collapsed.

The `NSSplitViewWillResizeSubviewsNotification` notification is sent before resizing a subview. After resizing subviews, the `NSSplitViewDidResizeSubviewsNotification` notification is sent.

A full description of each delegate method is beyond the scope of this book. Refer to the `NSSplitView` class documentation at `/Developer/Documentation/Cocoa/Reference/ApplicationKit/ObjC_classic/Classes/NSSplitView.html` for full descriptions of each of the available methods.

Compound Controls

Compound controls use multiple cells to produce a more complex interface object. They often contain glue code that makes the cells work together in a specific way. Most of these controls still have their own specialized cell subclass. Much of the complexity of managing multiple elements falls to the associated cell class instead of the control object.

Steppers look like a pair of very small buttons with up and down arrows on them. The most complex and most flexible of the compound controls is the NSMatrix, a class for laying out an arbitrary number of cells of arbitrary classes in a uniform way. Forms look like a pair of text fields, one an uneditable label, and the other an editable text field. Forms are usually used in matrices. Pop-up buttons are special buttons that can open a menu when clicked. They can also be configured as pull-down menus.

Steppers

A stepper is a small control that draws an up and a down arrow. Clicking one of the arrows will increment or decrement its value. Clicking and holding down an arrow will make some steppers autorepeat. Steppers are normally used in conjunction with another control, usually a text field. They send their actions whenever the user changes their value.

Steppers are implemented by the NSStepper control subclass and the NSStepperCell cell subclass. An NSStepper instance can be found on the Cocoa-Other palette shown earlier in this chapter in Figure 10.7. The stepper is under the vertical sliders.

Stepper Options in Interface Builder

Options for configuring a stepper can be found in Interface Builder's NSStepper inspector. This inspector, shown in Figure 10.24, is displayed by using the Cmd-1 key equivalent when an NSStepper or NSStepperCell is selected.

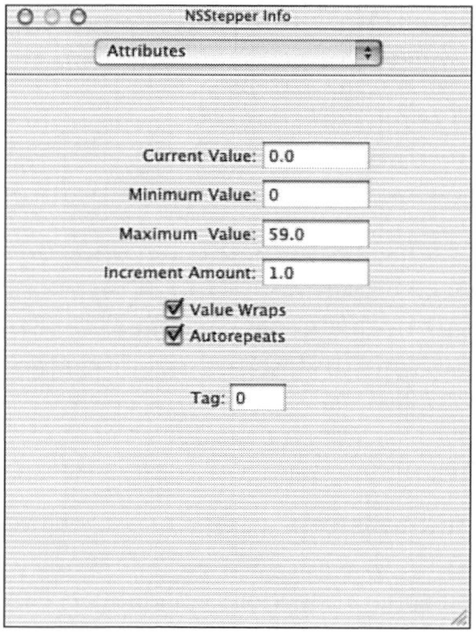

FIGURE 10.24 Interface Builder's NSStepper inspector.

The settings for steppers are straightforward. The value is the current value of the stepper. Similar to sliders, a minimum and maximum value is provided. The increment amount determines how much the stepper's value changes when an arrow is clicked. If the down arrow is clicked, the increment value is used as a decrement value.

The Value Wraps check box determines if the stepper should start over from the beginning of its range if the user attempts to increment or decrement beyond its minimum or maximum values. If this check box is off, the stepper stops changing its value when it hits the boundary of its range.

The Autorepeats check box turns autorepeat behavior on or off. If on, the stepper continues to increment or decrement periodically while the mouse is held down on one of the arrows. The stepper's action is resent for each autorepeat.

Similar to other controls, steppers support an integer tag that can be used to identify them uniquely in program code.

Configuring a Stepper

Like every control, both `NSStepper` and `NSStepperCell` respond to the standard accessor methods such as `-intValue` for their value. The standard `-setTag:` and `-tag` also work as expected.

Both classes also respond to a series of new accessor methods. The minimum value's accessors are `-setMinValue:` and `-minValue`. The maximum value's accessors are `-setMaxValue:` and `-maxValue`. The accessors for the increment amount are `-setIncrement:` and `-increment`. All six of these methods use `double` values.

The accessors for the boolean settings all take `BOOL` arguments. The `-setValueWraps:` and `-valueWraps` methods control whether the value wraps around. Autorepeat is manipulated and inspected with `-setAutorepeat:` and `-autorepeat`, respectively.

`NSMatrix` Class

The `NSMatrix` class can take a collection of cells and lay them out uniformly in one or two dimensions. It is commonly used with text fields and forms. When filled with button cells, a matrix can make them work in concert to behave like radio buttons. (Only one button can be on at a time, like the station selector buttons on an old-time car radio.) Selection lists, such as those used to select multiple files, are also possible. Matrices can contain cells of many different types, but place the restriction that all cells must be the same size.

To create a matrix, simply Option-drag one of the resize handles of a standard control. This works with any control that has an associated cell subclass. For example, color wells, described in Chapter 17, don't have an associated cell class, so they can't be turned into matrices. The Cocoa-Views palette, shown earlier in this chapter in Figures 10.3 and 10.9, contains two preconfigured NSMatrix instances, one populated with basic NSFormCell objects, and the other with NSButtonCell objects set up as radio buttons.

NSMatrix is a huge, complex class, so a full discussion of all its features is beyond the scope of this book. Be sure to refer to the Cocoa documentation when attempting to do complex manipulation of matrices. This discussion of NSMatrix leaves out several of the more advanced methods that are available.

Event Handling with NSMatrix Objects

Because a matrix has many cells, it tends to respond differently to user events when compared to a standard control. Matrices can handle drags between cells in special ways. Matrices support standard target/action, and they extend it by adding the idea of a double-click action.

When a user clicks inside a matrix, and then drags the mouse, the matrix has four ways to interpret the action. A matrix's mode determines which interpretation is used. The four matrix modes are described Table 10.3.

TABLE 10.3 Matrix Modes

Mode	Constant	Description
Track	NSTrackModeMatrix	Acts as if the cells were working individually. The cell where the mouse-down event occurred tracks the mouse until mouse-up.
Highlight	NSHighlightModeMatrix	Which cell tracks the mouse changes as the mouse moves over other cells. No cells remain selected after mouse-up.
Radio	NSRadioModeMatrix	Only one cell can ever be on at a time. Selecting a cell deselects all others.
List	NSListModeMatrix	Drag to select multiple cells. Shift and other selection modifiers work as expected. This works like selecting multiple files in the open and save panel's browsers.

Matrices extend target/action so that each cell can have its own target and action or a single target and action can be used for the whole matrix. NSMatrix offers a default target and action for any cells that don't have them set. It is important to be careful when making connections in Interface Builder. When connecting from a matrix, be sure the connection is coming from the right place, a single cell or the whole matrix. Any connections made for individual cells will override the connections made for the whole matrix. When connecting to a matrix, be careful to connect to the whole matrix or individual cells. It is easy to accidentally connect to a cell when a connection to the whole matrix is desired.

The NSMatrix class also adds the idea of a double-click action. This is an action sent when a double-click occurs inside the matrix. This is always sent to the matrix's target, never the target of an individual cell. This action cannot be set in the Interface Builder connection inspector. It can only be set programmatically, using the -setDoubleAction: method. The double action is returned by the -doubleAction method. The -sendDoubleAction method sends the action as if the user had double-clicked. One important consideration when using double-click actions is that the single-click action is always sent before the double-click action.

NOTE

Sometimes developers want to have a double-click action for a standard control. Controls don't support this, but turning a control into an NSMatrix with a single cell produces a control that looks just like a single control, but also implements a double-click action. This can save the trouble of subclassing.

Matrix Options in Interface Builder

Options for configuring a matrix can be found in Interface Builder's NSMatrix inspector. This inspector, shown in Figure 10.25, is displayed by using the Cmd-1 key equivalent when an NSMatrix is selected.

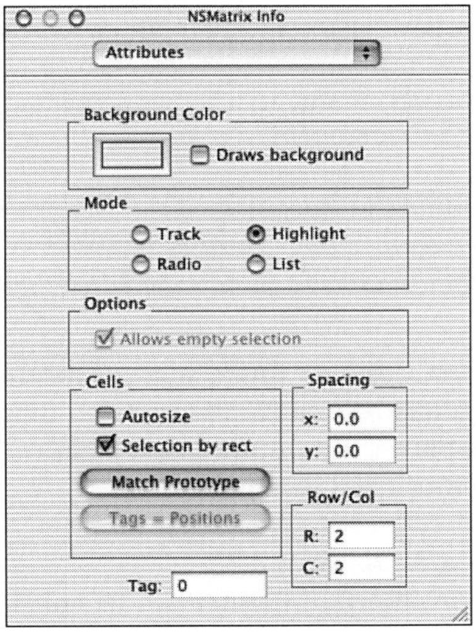

FIGURE 10.25 Interface Builder's NSMatrix inspector.

The color well and switch control the background of a matrix. The background color only applies to the area between cells (intercell spacing) and any cells that don't draw their backgrounds.

The Mode radio buttons set the matrix's selection mode. Refer to Table 10.3 for a description of the various modes. If the mode is set to Radio, the Allows empty selection check box is available. Radio mode only allows one cell to be selected. The check box tells the matrix whether one cell must be selected at all times.

When a matrix is created in Interface Builder, the first cell created is considered to be the prototype cell. Newly created matrix cells are created as copies (clones) of the prototype. This makes it easier to add new cells because they don't have to be reconfigured one at a time. It is important to configure a control completely before Option-dragging its handles to create a matrix. After the matrix is created, there is no way to edit the prototype.

NOTE

Older versions of Interface Builder, such as the version for NeXTSTEP, had a button to copy a selected cell in the matrix so that it would be used as the prototype cell. This functionality has sadly been lost, so now care must be taken to remember to preconfigure a control to its final settings before turning it into a matrix.

The Cells options refer to basic `NSMatrix` behaviors. Autosizing refers to how the matrix handles being resized. If autosizing is off, the cells will not change their frames as the matrix is resized. If autosizing is on, the cells will resize proportionally across the whole matrix.

The Selection by rect switch enables the user to drag out a rectangle to select multiple cells. This is especially useful for two-dimensional matrices in list mode. If this option is off, the user must move the mouse over every single cell they want to select.

The Spacing control determines how much space is inserted between the cells of the matrix. This can also be adjusted graphically by Cmd-dragging one of the resize handles. The Row/Col fields set the number of cells in the matrix. This can also be adjusted by Option-dragging a resize handle.

Methods for Configuring an `NSMatrix`

All the options available in Interface Builder can be adjusted programmatically through accessor methods.

To manipulate the background color, use the `-setBackgroundColor:`, `-backgroundColor`, `-setDrawsBackground:`, and `-drawsBackground` methods. The matrix's mode is accessed with the `-setMode:` and `-mode` methods. The four constants shown in Table 10.3 should be used to set the mode. If radio mode is selected, the -setAllowsEmptySelection: and -allowsEmptySelection accessors can be used.

Cell size is accessed for all cells with the -setCellSize: and -cellSize methods. The intercell spacing is adjusted with -setIntercellSpacing: and -intercellSpacing. The parameters and return values for these methods are NSSize structures.

The prototype cell is set using the -setPrototype: and -prototype methods. Individual cells can be looked up with the -cellWithTag: or -cellAtRow:column: methods. To get all the cells in the matrix, use the -cells method. It returns an NSArray. To add and remove cells, don't try to modify the immutable array. Instead, use the methods described in the "Methods for Manipulating Cells" section later in this chapter.

Autosize behavior is accessed by the -setAutosizesCells: and -autosizesCells methods. Selection by rectangle is controlled by -setSelectionByRect: and -isSelectionByRect.

Methods for Managing Cell Selection

To select a specific cell in the matrix, use either the -selectCellWithTag: or -selectCell: method. It is also possible to select a cell based on location in the matrix using the -selectCellAtRow:column: method. To select all cells, use the standard -selectAll: action method (the same as used by text fields for selecting all their text).

Cells can be deselected with -deselectSelectedCell or -deselectAllCells. Despite the name, the -deselectSelectedCell method will actually deselect all selected cells if a multiple selection is active. The only real difference between these two methods is that -deselectSelectedCell does not redisplay the matrix. Neither method will deselect a cell if the matrix is in radio mode and disallows empty selections.

There are two ways to determine which cells are selected. If the mode is radio mode, where only one cell can be selected at a time, it is safe to use the -selectedTag and -selectedCell methods inherited from NSControl. If multiple selections are possible, the -selectedCells method is best because it returns an array of all the selected cells.

Methods for Manipulating Cells

The -numberOfRows and -numberOfColumns methods return the current number of rows and columns in a matrix. There are several methods that can be used to add or remove columns or rows.

Add a column with -addColumn or -insertColumn:. The -addColumn method adds the column at the right side of the matrix. The -insertColumn: method inserts a new column before the specified column. A column can be removed with `-removeColumn:`.

Add a row with `-addRow` or `-insertRow:`. The `-addRow` method adds the row at the bottom of the matrix. A row can be removed with `-removeRow:`.

NOTE

Notice that the `-insertColumn:`, `-removeColumn:`, `-insertRow:`, and `-removeRow:` method names are one of the very few inconsistencies in the Cocoa framework. Based on how methods with a similar function are named elsewhere in Cocoa, the methods really should have been given names such as `-insertColumnAtIndex:`, and so on. Be careful to use the right names when writing your code! There is no compiler error if the `id` type is used instead of static typing with `(NSMatrix *)`. Programs using the wrong names will malfunction and report a runtime error.

Forms

Forms are controls that look like multiple text fields, each with a label. They provide a convenient means of treating multiple data entry fields as a single unit.

Forms are implemented by the `NSForm` and `NSFormCell` classes. Unlike other controls, the `NSForm` class does not have a one-to-one mapping of control to cell. `NSForm` is a subclass of `NSMatrix`, so it can handle many `NSFormCell` instances at once.

Interface Builder has an `NSForm` on the Cocoa-Views palette, as shown earlier in Figure 10.9. After dragging a form to a window, it can be Option-dragged so that it has the needed number of form cells. Although they descend from matrices, forms are constrained so that they can have only one column.

Form Options in Interface Builder

Options for configuring a form can be found in Interface Builder's `NSForm` inspector. This inspector, as shown in Figure 10.26, is displayed by using the Cmd-1 key equivalent when an `NSForm` is selected.

The options for forms and form cells are a limited combination of the options for text fields and matrices. The background color control works like the one for `NSMatrix` objects. The alignment controls work as expected. Alignment can be set independently for the title, or label, and the editable part of the form cell.

The various options in the Options box work like their counterparts in the text field and matrix inspectors. The only switch that is a little different is the Scrollable switch. If it is turned on, the editable part of the form behaves similar to a text field that has been set to Scrollable. If it is turned off, however, the text will not wrap; it will simply be cut off. Usually, the scrollable behavior is preferred.

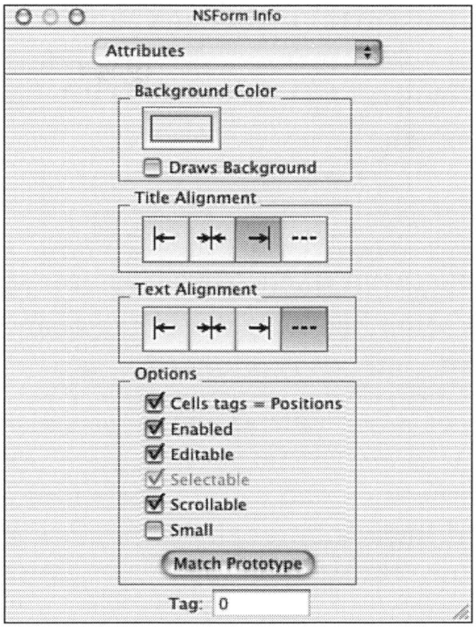

FIGURE 10.26 Interface Builder's `NSForm` inspector.

`NSForm` Methods

The `NSForm` class augments the `NSControl` and `NSMatrix` classes with a few new methods. Most manipulation of forms is done using methods from the superclasses. A few exceptions, however, are worth considering.

The alignment and font for all the cells can be set for both the title and the editable text. The methods to make these changes across the whole form are `-setTitleAlignment:`, `-setTextAlignment:`, `-setTitleFont:`, and `-setTextFont:`. The alignment methods take the same constants as text fields and other controls. They are `NSLeftTextAlignment`, `NSRightTextAlignment`, `NSCenterTextAlignment`, and `NSNaturalTextAlignment`. The `NSJustifiedTextAlignment` constant is meaningless for forms. The font methods work with `NSFont` instances.

The sizes and spacing of the cells in a form can be set using the `-setEntryWidth:` and `-setInterlineSpacing:` methods. The `-setEntryWidth:` method affects the entire width of all the cells. The `-setInterlineSpacing:` method is preferred over the `NSMatrix` `-setIntercellSpacing:` method for setting the spacing between cells.

Cells can be added with the `-addEntry:` and `-insertEntry:atIndex:` methods. Both require that a title, in the form of an `NSString`, be provided. The `-addEntry:` method adds the new cell at the bottom of the form. A cell can be removed with the `-removeEntryAtIndex:` method.

To find a particular cell, the `-cellAtIndex:` and `-indexOfCellWithTag:` methods are used. The selected cell's index is obtained with `-indexOfSelectedItem`. A particular cell can be activated and have all its text selected at the same time by calling the `-selectTextAtIndex:` method.

`NSFormCell` Methods

Working with an `NSFormCell` class is much like working with an `NSTextField`. The main difference is the addition of the title (label). All the normal `NSCell` methods for setting fonts, values, and so on, work on the editable portion of the field. To manipulate the title, a new set of methods is provided.

Change the title with `-setTitle:` if an `NSString` is available. The `-title` method returns the current title. The `-setTitleFont:`, `-titleFont`, `-setTitleAlignment:`, and `-titleAlignment` methods can access the title's font and alignment attributes. To work with the title and the attributes all at once, use an `NSAttributedString` with `-setAttributedTitle:` and `-attributedTitle`.

The title's width can be accessed with the `-setTitleWidth:` and `-titleWidth` methods. This width is what the cell uses to decide how to split itself between the title and editable portion.

Pop-Up Buttons and Pull-Down Lists

Pop-up buttons are a special kind of button that, when clicked, open a menu of options. There are two types of pop-up button in Cocoa. The first, a basic pop up, performs a function much like a set of radio buttons. It offers a list of choices, only one of which can be selected at a time. When the menu is not open, the button's title displays the title of the selected menu item. Radio buttons are preferred for this function when they fit in the interface. If space is cramped or there are more than ten options, a pop up is a good alternative.

A pull-down menu is different. The title on the button never changes. Selecting an item in a pull-down menu doesn't cause the item to be selected as it would in a pop up. Instead, it simply triggers an action to be sent. Pull downs are good for implementing verbs in the user interface. Opening a pull down offers users a series of actions that they can perform.

Pop-up buttons and pull-down lists are both implemented by the `NSPopUpButton` and `NSPopUpButtonCell` classes. Changing configuration parameters alters the pop up or pull down behavior of an instance.

Interface Builder offers an `NSPopUpButton` instance preconfigured as a basic pop up button on the Cocoa-Other palette. Figure 10.7 shows this palette. (There are no instances preconfigured as pull down menus.) The `NSPopUpButton` instance is found at the upper center of the palette. The text Item1 appears on the button. The preconfigured pop up has three items in it, named iItem1, Item2, and Item3. Double-clicking the button opens the button's menu for editing. It can be edited like any other menu. Refer to Chapter 16, "Menus," for information about manipulating menus.

Pop-Up Button Options in Interface Builder

Options for configuring a pop up button can be found in Interface Builder's `NSPopUpButton` inspector. This inspector, shown in Figure 10.27, is displayed by using the Cmd-1 key equivalent when an `NSPopUpButton` is selected. The individual items inside the pop-up button's menu are `NSMenu` items. They are discussed in Chapter 16.

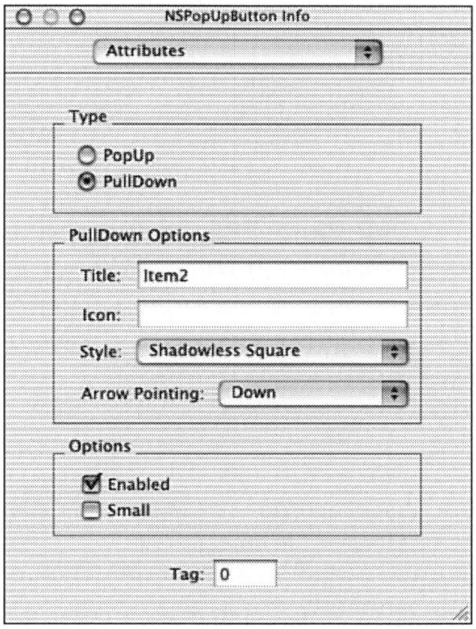

FIGURE 10.27 Interface Builder's `NSPopUpButton` inspector.

The Type control at the top of the inspector is used to change the pop-up button between basic pop-up and pull-down behaviors. The PullDown Options area only applies if the PullDown option has been chosen. The other options, Enabled, Small, and Tag all work the same as they do for other controls.

The pull-down options primarily affect the visual aspects of the pull down. The title and icon are shown on the pull down itself. The style and arrow direction determine rendering details of the pull down. The available styles are Rounded, Square, and Shadowless Square. The rounded type can only have a downward pointing arrow. The two square styles can have their arrow point either right or down. When the menu appears onscreen it appears below or to the right of the `NSPopUpButton` as indicated by the arrow. Figure 10.28 shows how the various different pop-up and pull-down list styles are rendered.

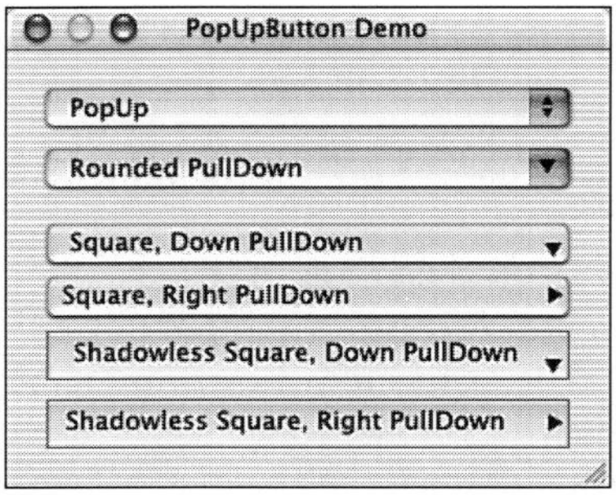

FIGURE 10.28 Different styles of `NSPopUpButton`.

`NSPopUpButton` Methods

The main behavior of a pop-up button is controlled with the `-setPullsDown:` and `-pullsDown` accessors. Set it to `YES` for a pull down menu and `NO` for a pop up.

The various items inside the pop-up button are menu items, and part of a menu object. The menu object is accessed with the `-setMenu:` and `-menu` methods. Chapter 16 explains these objects and shows how to manipulate them from within program code. The DynamicMenu example in Chapter 16 shows programmatic manipulation of the menu inside of a pop-up button.

NOTE

The `-setMenu:` and `-menu` accessors exist for all control classes and normally control contextual menus, as explained in Chapter 16. In the case of pop-up buttons, no contextual menu is possible or available because the control itself opens its own menu. Dynamically adding and removing items from the pop up's menu would make a contextual menu pointless anyway because the menu that pops up is effectively a contextual menu as it is.

Pop-up buttons also implement several convenience methods for manipulating the pop-up menu. Refer to the class reference at `/Developer/Documentation/Cocoa/Reference/ApplicationKit/ObjC_classic/Classes/NSPopUpButton.html` for more information about these methods.

Three methods exist for dealing with a pop-up button's current selection. These methods really only make sense when the button is in pop-up mode. The methods are `-selectItem:`, `-selectItemAtIndex:`, and `-selectItemWithTitle:`. Which method to use depends on whether it is more convenient to set a selection based on `NSMenuItem` object, `int` index, or `NSString` title, respectively.

The current selection is determined by `-selectedItem` or `-titleOfSelectedItem`. Surprisingly, there is no `-indexOfSelectedItem` method. That's easy enough to fix with the following `NSPopUpButton` category, though:

```
@interface NSPopUpButton(MyIndexOfSelectedItemCategory)
- (int)indexOfSelectedItem;
@end
@implementation NSPopUpButton(MyIndexOfSelectedItemCategory)
- (int)indexOfSelectedItem
{
    return [self indexOfItem:[self selectedItem]];
}
@end
```

`NSPopUpButtonCell` Methods

The `NSPopUpButtonCell` class is actually a subclass of the `NSMenuItemCell` class. It is the object that actually owns the menu associated with a pop-up button, so most of the `NSPopUpButton` methods work with this cell class as well.

There is one pair of accessors implemented by `NSPopUpButtonCell` that isn't available elsewhere. To change the direction an arrow points on a square pull-down menu, use the `-setArrowPosition:` and `-arrowPosition` methods. Use one of the `NSPopUpNoArrow`, `NSPopUpArrowAtCenter`, or `NSPopUpArrowAtBottom` constants. It isn't very clear how these constants correspond to the settings in Interface Builder. The `NSPopUpArrowAtCenter` constant gives a right-pointing arrow, whereas `NSPopUpArrowAtBottom` is a down pointing arrow. The `NSPopUpNoArrow` constant is not an option in Interface Builder.

Summary

Cocoa offers a wide variety of user interface controls. All the standard controls that you would expect to use, such as buttons, sliders, and text fields are present. Also, several view classes can be used to help organize the controls in a window. Boxes, scrolling views, tab views, and split views all add different ways to lay out a user interface.

As alluded to in the discussions of text fields in this chapter, handling text is a very complex function. Cocoa offers a rich set of objects for manipulating text. The next chapter discusses Cocoa's text-handling features in depth.

This chapter hasn't covered every view and control class Cocoa has to offer. Several more controls are available that are very complex. Chapter 18, "Advanced Views and Controls" discusses these additional `NSView` subclasses.

11

The Cocoa Text System

IN THIS CHAPTER

- Using the High-Level Text Classes
- The Text System Architecture
- Managing Fonts
- Text Input

Cocoa provides powerful text presentation and input capabilities that are not matched on any other platform. The classes that are used to store and present text are complex and include many hooks that provide flexibility and enable customization. This chapter begins with several examples that show how to use the basic high-level features of the text system. The examples demonstrate common tasks and use features that are sufficient for many applications. This chapter then delves into the architecture of the text systems and identifies the many classes that interact to implement high-level features and provide low-level flexibility.

Cocoa's font support is an essential and powerful feature of the text system. This chapter explains the classes used to represent and manage fonts. Interaction with the user and font selection with Cocoa's built-in Font panel are explained. An overview of the sometimes complex relationship between fonts and Unicode character sets is provided.

Finally, this chapter explains Cocoa's text-input system. Cocoa provides classes that assist with user input validation. Hooks are provided to enable programmatic restriction of user input. The interaction with the operating system and features to support bidirectional text input and Eastern language input are explained. Apple's overview documentation for the text system is available at `http://developer.apple.com/techpubs/macosx/Cocoa/TasksAndConcepts/ProgrammingTopics/TextArchitecture/index.html`.

Using the High-Level Text Classes

Cocoa's text system is extremely complex. The complexity is needed to support state-of-the-art features and a high degree of customizability. However, it is possible to use the text system without exposing the underlying complexity. High-level features common to most applications are easily accessed. The details and complexity are only encountered when using advanced or specialized features.

The easiest way to include formatted text display and input in a Cocoa application is to drag a text object from the Interface Builder Cocoa-Data palette. The `NSTextView` object on the Interface Builder palette is actually an instance of the `NSTextView` class embedded as the document view of a scroll view. Scroll views, the `NSScrollView` class, and document views are all explained in the "Scroll Views" section of Chapter 10, "Views and Controls."

The combination of the `NSTextView` instance and the scroll view provide sophisticated text features including display of arbitrary amounts of formatted text, rulers, undo and redo, multiple text justification options, multiple text alignment options, kerning, ligatures, underlining, spell checking, embedded graphics, copy and paste, drag and drop, and more. No programming is needed to use these features.

The Cocoa text classes are able to read, display, and write Rich Text Format (RTF) data. Apple provides an additional format called RTFD that extends RTF to store text and embedded graphics in a directory with multiple files instead of packing all the data in a single file. The text classes provide limited support for HyperText Markup Language (HTML) formatted text display.

If a text object dragged from the Interface Builder palette is configured via Interface Builder's attributes inspector to enable editing, users can edit the `NSTextView` directly. Even if the text object is not editable, it can be configured to be selectable. If so, users can select the noneditable text for use with copy and paste, searching, or services. Services are described in the "Services" section of Chapter 19, "Using Pasteboards." Text in Cocoa applications should usually be selectable even if it is not editable. Even the text of labels in the user interface can benefit from being selectable. If such text is selectable, users can select the words in the labels to search for them in online documentation or use a Service to define words that might be unfamiliar.

NOTE

Services provide a mechanism for all Cocoa applications to benefit from features such as dictionary lookup, email integration, automatic file format conversion, and text formatting. Each Cocoa application is able to use Services provided by other Cocoa applications. Services are described in the "Services" section of Chapter 19, "Using Pasteboards."

Setting the Text to Display

Text objects can be programmatically modified. One of the most common tasks is to programmatically set the text to be displayed by an instance of `NSTextView`. The easiest way to do that is to use the `-setString:` method. `NSTextView` is a subclass of `NSText`, which is in turn a subclass of `NSView`. The `-setString:` method is implemented by `NSText` and is, therefore, available for use with instances of `NSTextView`. As its name implies, the `-setString:` method accepts an `NSString` argument and replaces the entire content of the receiving text view with the string. `NSText`'s `-string` method is used to obtain the entire content of the text object.

`NSString` objects do not normally contain any formatting information. When text is set via `-setText:`, the new text is displayed with the formatting that was previously applied to the first character of the text that was replaced.

To change the formatting of the text, use `NSText`'s `-setBackgroundColor:`, `-setFont:`, `-setAlignment:`, and `-setTextColor:` methods. Formatting attributes can be applied to all or part of the text. `NSText` also provides `-backgroundColor`, `-font`, `-alignment`, and `-textColor` methods for retrieving the attributes.

Many of `NSText`'s methods such as `-changeFont:`, `-alignCenter:`, `-alignLeft:`, `-alignRight:`, `-superscript:`, `-subscript:`, `-unscript:`, and `-underline:` apply formatting to the currently selected range of text. The selected range of text can be set with the `-setSelectedRange:` method and obtained with the `-selectedRange` method. Ranges are stored in `NSRange` structures. `NSRange` is explained in the "`NSRange`" section of Chapter 7, "Foundation Framework Overview."

Appending, Inserting, and Replacing Text

There are several ways to append text to the existing content of a text object. The simplest, but least efficient, way is to use code such as the following:

```
// Append "Text to append" to a text object called aTextView
[aTextView setString:[[aTextView string]
    stringByAppendingString:@"Text to append"]];
```

`NSText` provides the `-replaceCharactersInRange:withString:`, `-replaceCharactersInRange:withRTF:`, and `-replaceCharactersInRange:withRTFD:` methods for replacing arbitrary ranges of text. The first argument to each of the methods is an `NSRange` structure. The second argument to `-replaceCharactersInRange:withString:` is an `NSString` instance containing the new text. The `-replaceCharactersInRange:withRTF:`, and `-replaceCharactersInRange:withRTFD:` methods accept a second argument that is an `NSData` instance containing RTF data or RTFD data, respectively.

To append text to an `NSTextView` instance, use code similar to the following:

```
// Append "Text to append" to a text object called aTextView
[aTextView replaceCharactersInRange:NSMakeRange(
    [[aTextView string] length], 0) withString:@"Text to append"]];
```

This code replaces zero characters just past the end of the existing text with the specified string.

NOTE

To automatically scroll the newly appended text so that it is visible to the user, use `NSText`'s `-scrollRangeToVisible:` method and pass an `NSRange` containing the appended text as the argument.

To insert text at a specific location, use code such as the following:

```
// Insert "Text to insert" at insertLocation in a text object called aTextView
[aTextView replaceCharactersInRange:NSMakeRange(
    insertLocation, 0) withString:@"Text to append"]];
```

Finally, to replace text, use one of the `-replaceCharactersInRange:` methods and specify a range with a length greater than zero to replace.

Programmatically Ending Editing

When an editable Cocoa text object becomes the first responder, a standard insertion cursor is displayed, and the user can begin entering text into the text object. When another object becomes the first responder, any current editing in the text object that is no longer the first responder is ended. Editing needs to be ended to trigger delegate messages that inform the application that editing is complete and application logic can be applied to the new input. Controlling user input and delegate messages are explained in the "Using Delegate Methods" section of this chapter.

Many applications need to programmatically end editing to trigger the delegate messages and other logic. For example, if a text object is inside a tab view and the user selects a different tab, the editing might not be ended until the user selects another text object and makes it the first responder. However, after changing the visible tab, the user can no longer see the text object that is being edited. Therefore, he might quit the application thinking that the edits made have been accepted and saved by the application when in fact the application is unaware of the changes because the editing was not ended.

The following code is recommended to programmatically end all editing within a window:

```
// gracefully end all editing in a window named aWindow
if([aWindow makeFirstResponder:aWindow])
{
  // All editing is now ended and delegate messages sent etc.
}
else
{
  // For some reason the text object being edited will not resign
  // first responder status so force an end to editing anyway
  [aWindow endEditingFor:nil];
}
```

This code gives the Cocoa frameworks maximum opportunity to end the editing gracefully. It works for ordinary text views as well as the window's field editor. The field editor is a shared text object used to handle input in text fields and other controls and is explained in "The Field Editor" section of Chapter 10.

The Text System Architecture

Many classes are used to implement the complete text system. The classes are organized using the Model-View-Controller (MVC) design introduced in the "Model-View-Controller" section of Chapter 6, "Cocoa Design Patterns." The text to be displayed and the attributes that affect that display are stored in the model. The visual representation of text and handing user input are the responsibility of the view layer. The logic that links the model and view is implemented in the controller layer. Figure 11.1 shows the classes used by the text system, and their role in the Model-View-Controller design:

This Model-View-Controller design reduces dependencies between objects in different layers and makes it easier to modify individual components without having to change the entire system. The MVC design also reduces the amount of information needed to accomplish common tasks. It is possible to manipulate text in many ways using only the `NSTextView` class.

The principal classes in the text system are `NSTextStorage`, `NSLayoutManager`, `NSTextContainer`, `NSTextView`. Only `NSTextContainer` is intended to be subclassed. The behavior of the other classes should be specialized by using delegates and notifications and only subclassed as a last resort. The advantages of using delegates and notifications are explained in the "Delegates" section of Chapter 8, "The Application Kit Framework Overview."

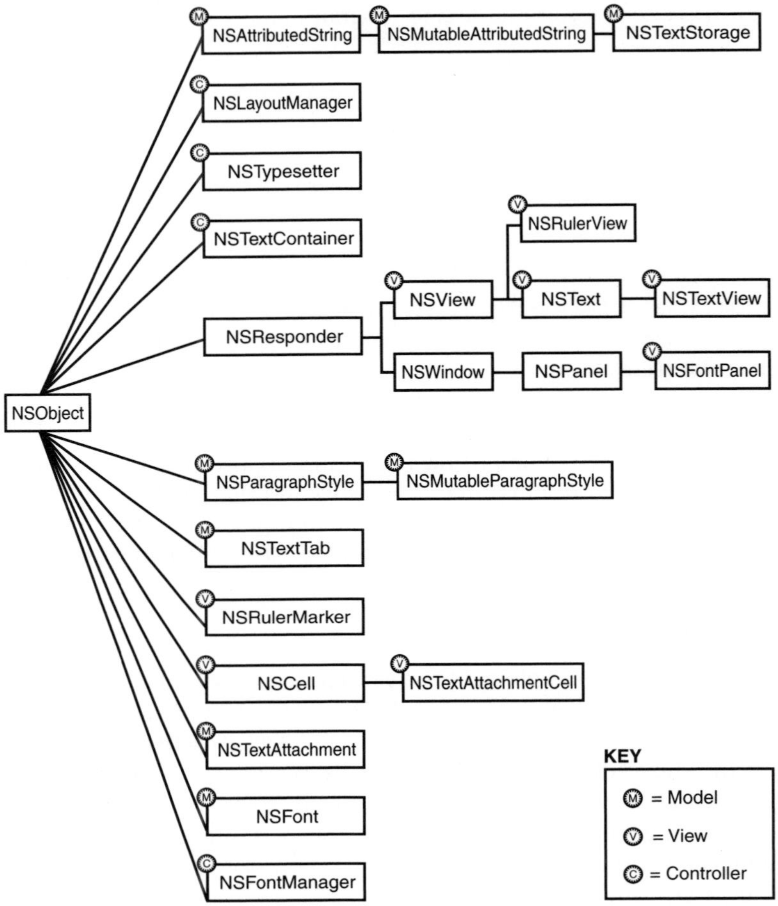

FIGURE 11.1 Many classes interact to implement Cocoa's text system.

Most applications that customize the text system work with either the Model layer or the View layer. Complex text can be created and processed entirely within the Model layer and displayed automatically by the View layer. In some cases, changes to the way text is displayed or edited by users must be made by an application. Those changes take place entirely in the View layer. There is seldom any need to interact directly with the Controller layer in Cocoa's text system, and there are not many modifications that can be made to the Controller layer without disrupting the View and Model layers.

Apple provides the following document to explain how to assemble the Model, View, and Controller parts of the text system without using the preconfigured object in Interface Builder at `http://developer.apple.com/techpubs/macosx/Cocoa/TasksAndConcepts/ProgrammingTopics/TextArchitecture/Tasks/AssembleSysByHand.html`.

The Model Layer: Text Storage and Attributed Strings

The Model layer of the text system can be used independently. For example, using only the Model layer, it is possible to search for text, specify formatting, load and save text, and apply application logic to the text. The Model layer can be used in nongraphical applications to perform text processing without the overhead of laying out and drawing text.

The primary class used to store text in the Model layer is `NSTextStorage`. `NSTextStorage` is a subclass of `NSMutableAttributedString`, which is in turn a subclass of `NSAttributedString`. Attributed strings store Unicode character strings as well as formatting commands that are applied to the strings when they are drawn. Mutable attributed strings can be modified after they are created. The `NSTextStorage` class extends the `NSMutableAttributedString` class to provide notifications when the attributes or strings are changed.

The `NSAttributedString` and `NSMutableAttributedString` classes are implemented in the Foundation framework so that even nongraphical applications can work with them. Applications can define custom attributes as needed. The Application Kit Framework extends the attributed string classes with categories to draw the strings and provide a standard set of attribute definitions such as font face, point size, color, paragraph style, tab stops, and more.

NOTE

Font dimensions are measured in Postscript Points (pts.), which equal 1/72 of an inch. Points are the standard unit of measurement in the printing industry. Points are also the standard unit of measurement for all graphical operations in Quartz.

Table 11.1 lists the attributes that are defined by the Application Kit framework. Attribute values are normally stored in `NSDictionary` instances using the attribute names as the keys for retrieving the values.

TABLE 11.1 Application Kit–Defined Text Attributes

Attribute Names	Attribute Type	Default Value
NSAttachmentAttributeName	NSTextAttachment	none
NSBackgroundColorAttributeName	NSColor	none
NSBaselineOffsetAttributeName	NSNumber	float 0.0
NSFontAttributeName	NSFont	Helvetica 12 pts.
NSForegroundColorAttributeName	NSColor	black
NSKernAttributeName	NSNumber	float 0.0
NSLigatureAttributeName	NSNumber	int 1
NSLinkAttributeName	id	none
NSParagraphStyleAttributeName	NSParagraphStyle	value returned by NSParagraphStyle's +defaultParagraphStyle method
NSSuperscriptAttributeName	NSNumber	int 0
NSUnderlineStyleAttributeName	NSNumber	int 0 (no underline)

Attachments such as images and files are stored in attributed strings by using a special character, `NSAttachmentCharacter`, within the string to identify the location of the attachment. The attributes applied to the `NSAttachmentCharacter` must include `NSAttachmentAttributeName` with an `NSTextAttachment` instance as the value. The `NSTextAttachment` instance stores the data of the attachment itself or information sufficient to load the data. The `NSTextAttachment` class is described at `http://developer.apple.com/techpubs/macosx/Cocoa/Reference/ApplicationKit/ObjC_classic/Classes/NSTextAttachment.html`, and in the documentation that comes with Apple's developer tools.

The `NSParagraphStyleAttributeName` attribute uses values that are `NSParagraphStyle` instances that define how strings are aligned when displayed. `NSParagraphStyle` instances also define tab stops and word wrapping. The `NSParagraphStyle` class is documented at `http://developer.apple.com/techpubs/macosx/Cocoa/Reference/ApplicationKit/ObjC_classic/Classes/NSParagraphStyle.html`, and in the documentation that comes with Apple's developer tools.

Initializing Attributed Strings

The Foundation framework implementation of `NSAttributedString` provides three methods to initialize instances. The `-initWithString:` method accepts an `NSString` argument and returns an `NSAttributedString` instance containing the string and default attributes. The `-initWithString:attributes:` method accepts a string for the first argument and a dictionary containing attribute names and values for the second argument. The returned NSAttributedString contains the string and attributes specified. Finally, the -initWithAttributedString: returns an attributed string containing a string and attributes identical to the ones specified in the NSAttributedString provided as an argument.

The Application Kit framework provides additional NSAttributedString methods to support initialization with HTML, RTF, or RTFD format data, and data that is convertible to one of those formats using Services. The
- initWithHTML:documentAttributes:, - initWithRTF:documentAttributes:,
- initWithRTFD:documentAttributes:, and
- initWithRTFDFileWrapper:documentAttributes: methods each accept an NSData instance containing appropriately formatted data as the first argument. The second argument is a pointer to a pointer to an NSDictionary instance. If the second argument is not NULL, it is used to return by reference an NSDictionary instance containing the attributes defined for the newly initialized attributed string. The dictionary returned must be retained if it is used outside the scope of the call to one of the initializers. The complete set of attributes that can be stored in the dictionary returned by reference in the documentAttributes: argument of one of these initializers is defined in Table 11.2.

TABLE 11.2 Keys and Values for documentAttributes: Arguments

Key	Attribute Type	Description
@"PaperSize"	NSValue	Contains an NSSize.
@"LeftMargin"	NSNumber	Contains a float value in pts.
@"RightMargin"	NSNumber	Contains a float value in pts.
@"BottomMargin"	NSNumber	Contains a float value in pts.
@"HyphenationFactor"	NSNumber	Contains a float value.
@"DocumentType"	NSString	Contains the value of one of the following constants: NSPlainTextDocumentType, NSRTFTextDocumentType, NSRTFDTextDocumentType, NSMacSimpleTextDocumentType, NSHTMLTextDocumentType.
@"CharacterEncoding"	NSNumber	Contains an int specifying the NSStringEncoding used. Present only in plain-text files.
@"ViewSize" to display in.	NSValue	Contains an NSSize representing the view size
@"ViewZoom"	NSNumber	Contains a float describing current zoom as a percentage.

TABLE 11.2 Continued

Key	Attribute Type	Description
`@"ViewMode"`	`NSNumber`	Contains an `int`. 1 indicates show page layout format such as page boundaries and margins. 0 indicates not to show page layout.
`@"CocoaRTFVersion"`	`NSNumber`	Contains an `int` if created by Cocoa. Value of 100 indicates Mac OS X, whereas lower values are earlier versions.
`@"Converted"`	`NSNumber`	Contains an `int`. If the file was converted by a filter service, the value will be 1 or greater. Absent or lower values indicate it was not converted by a filter service.

An additional initializer, `-initWithHTML:baseURL:documentAttributes:`, is similar to `-initWithHTML:documentAttributes`. It accepts an `NSData` instance containing the HTML data as the first argument. The attributes dictionary is returned by reference in the last argument. The additional `baseURL:` argument specifies a URL used to resolve relative URLs within the HTML data. The `baseURL:` argument must be an instance of the `NSURL` class. The `NSURL` class is described in the "`NSURL` and `NSURLHandle`" section of Chapter 23, "Networking."

NOTE

If the data passed to any of the Application Kit defined `NSAttributedString` initializers cannot be interpreted, the initializers return `nil`.

Finally, the `-initWithPath:documentAttributes:` and `-initWithURL:documentAttributes:` methods are used to initialize an attributed string with the contents of a file. These methods are not format specific. If the file contains one of the supported types of data returned by `NSAttributedString`'s `+textUnfilteredFileTypes` class method, the contents are loaded directly. Otherwise, an attempt is made to use Services to convert the data to a recognized format. The complete list of supported data types including the ones that require Services is returned by the `+textFileTypes` method.

The `-initWithPath:documentAttributes:` method expects the first argument to be an `NSString` containing a path. The first argument to `-initWithURL:documentAttributes:` must be a file location specified by an `NSURL` instance. Both methods return the attributes dictionary for the loaded data by reference in the second argument.

NOTE

The URL passed to -initWithURL:documentAttributes: must use the file:// URL scheme. It is not possible to use the http:// scheme or other remote formats with this method. To initialize an attributed string with remote data, use an NSURL instance to fetch the data from the remote location via NSURL's -resourceDataUsingCache: method, and then use the data to initialize an attributed string with -initWithHTML:baseURL:documentAttributes:.

NSAttributedString provides a convenience method to create an instance that contains an attributed string representing an attachment. The +attributedStringWithAttachment: method returns an autoreleased instance of NSAttributedString consisting of the NSAttachmentCharacter with attributes set to contain the NSTextAttachment passed as the argument.

Using Attributed Strings

The length of an attributed string instance is returned as an integer by calling the method -length. An NSString instance that contains the text portion of the NSAttributedString is returned by calling -string.

The -isEqualToAttributedString: method compares the receiver to the NSAttributedString passed as the argument. To be considered equal, the string and the attributes of both attributed strings must correspond. This method returns a Boolean value of YES if the strings are equal.

The -attributedSubstringFromRange: method returns an NSAttributedString instance that contains the text and attachments within the range specified using an NSRange structure. If the NSRange argument lies outside of the contents of the string—for example, beyond the end—this method raises an NSRangeException exception.

The attributes that are attached to an attributed string are accessed by calling -attributesAtIndex:effectiveRange:. This method expects an unsigned integer index for the first argument and returns an NSDictionary containing all attributes that apply to the character at the specified index. The second argument is an NSRange returned by reference that identifies the full range of characters to which the attributes in effect at the index apply. If the effectiveRange: argument is NULL, the range is not returned. If the index is past the end of the string, an NSRangeException is raised.

The -attribute:atIndex:effectiveRange: method is similar to -attributesAtIndex:effectiveRange:, but it allows specification of a particular attribute. The attribute: argument is an NSString instance containing an attribute name. If an attribute with the specified name is in effect at the specified index, the value of the attribute is returned. If the effectiveRange: argument is not NULL, and the specified attribute is in effect at the specified index, the range of characters to which the attribute applies is returned by reference. If the specified attribute is not in effect at the specified index, and the `effectiveRange:` argument is not `NULL`, the range that the attribute does not apply to is returned by reference.

The following example takes an `NSAttributedString`, finds any underlined text, and returns an `NSString` containing a version of the string in HTML format with underline formatting preserved.

```
- (NSString *)convertUnderlineTextToHTML:(NSAttributedString *)attributedString
// Returns a string containing HTML format text that preserves any underline
// formatting in attributedString but discards all other formatting
{
  unsigned int    length;
  NSRange         effectiveRange;
  NSMutableString *resultString = [NSMutableString string];

  length = [attributedString length];
  effectiveRange = NSMakeRange(0, 0);

  while (NSMaxRange(effectiveRange) < length)
  {
    id        attrVal;
    NSString *plainStr;

    // get the effective range that has the same value for the underline
    // attribute
    attrVal = [attributedString attribute:NSUnderlineStyleAttributeName
       atIndex:NSMaxRange(effectiveRange) effectiveRange:&effectiveRange];

    if (nil != attrVal)
    {
      // this range is underlined so insert the HTML code for underline
      [resultString appendString:@"<u>"];
    }

    // append the plain string to the result
    plainStr = [[attributedString string] substringWithRange:effectiveRange];
    [resultString appendString:plainStr];

    if (nil != attrVal)
    {
      // this range was underlined so insert the HTML code to end underline
      [resultString appendString:@"</u>"];
```

```
    }
  }

  return resultString;
}
```

Initially, the length of the attributed string is determined using the `-length` method, and the location of `effectiveRange` is set to the start of the string. The `while` loop continues as long as `effectiveRange` is within the attributed string.

The `-attribute:atIndex:effectiveRange:` method is called specifying the maximum position within `effectiveRange` as the index argument. This causes the search to begin at index 0 the first time through the loop and at the end of the previous search during each subsequent iteration. During each pass through the loop, `effectiveRange` is updated to store the next contiguous range of characters with the same value for the `NSUnderlineStyleAttributeName`. If the attributed string does have an `NSUnderlineStyleAttribute` for the requested index, the value returned by `-attribute:atIndex:effectiveRange` is `nil`, but effective range is still returned with the range of the string that does not have the attribute.

A similar example using `-attributesAtIndex:effectiveRange:` can be constructed. Each contiguous range of characters that have the same attributes is processed by the loop. The attributes can be analyzed inside the loop to implement almost any format conversion.

Additional variants of the `-attribute:atIndex:effectiveRange:` method are available. Each provides a slightly different way of searching for contiguous ranges of characters with similar formatting. Not all the methods are described here, but enough information is provided to enable the straightforward usage of all the variations.

The `-fontAttributesInRange:` method returns attributes related to the appearance of an attributed string. The returned `NSDictionary` contains any of the following attributes if they are in effect for the first character in the specified range: `NSBackgroundColorAttributeName`, `NSBaselineOffsetAttributeName`, `NSFontAttributeName`, `NSForegroundColorAttributeName`, `NSKernAttributeName`, `NSLigatureAttributeName`, `NSLinkAttributeName`, `NSSuperscriptAttributeName`, and `NSUnderlineStyleAttributeName`.

Similarly, the `-rulerAttributesInRange:` returns an `NSDictionary` containing the `NSParagraphStyleAttributeName` for the first character in the specified range. Apple has indicated that in the future there might be additional ruler-related attributes returned.

The method `-containsAttachments` returns a Boolean value of `YES` if the receiving attributed string instance contains any attachments and `NO` otherwise.

Several methods are available to convert a requested range of an attributed string to RTF and RTFD formats. The method `-RTFFromRange:documentAttributes:` returns an `NSData` instance with the appropriately generated RTF for the `NSRange` passed as the first argument. The *`documentAttributes`* argument is optional. If provided, it should be an `NSDictionary` with keys from Table 11.2, and their associated values. If the requested range is outside of the receiving attributed string, an `NSRangeException` is raised. This method strips out any attachments within the attributed string, but does not remove the `NSAttachmentCharacter` from the generated RTF.

The method `-RTFDFromRange:documentAttributes:` is identical except that the returned `NSData` instance contains a flattened RTFD representation of the attributed string, including any attachments.

`-RTFDFileWrapperFromRange:documentAttributes:` expects the same arguments, but returns the RTFD contents as an `NSFileWrapper` instance, which represents the contents of an RTFD-bundled document.

Also included in the Application Kit extensions to `NSAttributedString` is support for finding linguistic elements within an attributed string. The methods are `-doubleClickAtIndex:`, `-lineBreakBeforeIndex:withinRange:`, `-nextWordFromIndex:forward:`. They are primarily used for determining ranges of text affected by mouse clicks or user interaction with the keyboard.

The Application Kit framework adds `NSAttributedString` methods for drawing and calculating the graphical size of the attributed strings when they are drawn. These methods are described in the "`NSString` Drawing Methods" section of Chapter 14, "Custom Views and Graphics Part III."

Using Mutable Attributed Strings

The `NSMutableAttributedString` class extends the `NSAttributedString` class to enable modification of the strings and attributes. As with the `NSAttributedString` class, the implementation of `NSMutableAttributedString` is split across Cocoa's Foundation and the Application Kit frameworks.

There are methods to append, replace, and delete characters within the attributed string. `-appendAttributedString:` appends the attributed string passed as the argument to the end of the receiver. Similarly, an attributed string can be inserted at a specified location in an `NSMutableString` using the method `-insertAttributedString:atIndex:`. If the index is not a valid position within the receiver, an `NSRangeException` is raised.

The method `-replaceCharactersInRange:withAttributedString:` deletes the characters in the specified `NSRange` and replaces them with the attributed string passed as the second argument. Similarly, `-replaceCharactersInRange:withString:` replaces the characters within the specified `NSRange` with the characters in the `NSString` that is passed as the second argument. If `-replaceCharactersInRange:withString:` is used, the newly inserted characters have the attributes that were set for the location of the first deleted character in the range. In both methods, if the `NSRange` is outside the bounds of the `NSMutableAttributedString`, an `NSRangeException` is raised.

It is also possible to completely replace the contents of an `NSMutableAttributedString` using the method `-setAttributedString:` passing an attributed string to use as the replaced contents.

The characters within a given range of an `NSMutableAttributedString` can be deleted by using the method `-deleteCharactersInRange:`. If the `NSRange` passed as the argument is outside the bounds of the receiving `NSMutableAttributedString`, an `NSRangeException` is raised.

Attributes can be modified for a range of text in an `NSMutableAttributedString` using the methods `-setAttributes:range:`, `-addAttribute:value:range:`, `-addAttributes:range:`, and `-removeAttribute:range:`. The method `-setAttributes:range:` replaces any attributes set on the characters in the specified `NSRange` with those contained in the `NSDictionary` passed as the first argument. The method `-addAttributes:range:` adds the attributes in the `NSDictionary` passed as the first argument to the characters in the range. If an attribute already exists on the text, the value of that attribute is changed to the value in the dictionary. A simpler method, `-addAttribute:value:range:`, does the same thing, but expects only a single attribute identifier and value instead of an `NSDictionary`. Finally, attributes are removed from a range of characters by the `-removeAttribute:range:` method. In all cases, if the range is outside of the receiving string, an `NSRangeException` is raised.

`NSMutableAttributedString`'s `-mutableString` method returns the receiver's string as an `NSMutableString` instance.

The Application Kit adds methods to `NSMutableAttributedString` for dealing with font changes, attachment handling, and fixing attributes that have changed because of editing. The method `-applyFontTraits:range:` applies the font traits that are passed as a C bitwise mask in the first argument to the specified range. The mask consists of one or more of the `NSFontTraitMask` values combined using the C logical `OR` operator. `NSFontTraitMask` is described in the "Font Traits and Weights" section of this chapter.

A portion of a mutable attributed string can be given superscript or subscript traits by calling `-superscriptRange:` or `-subscriptRange:`, respectively; passing the character range as an `NSRange` argument. Any existing superscript or subscript traits can be removed from a range of characters by calling `-unscriptRange:`.

The alignment of paragraphs within a range can be modified by calling -setAlignment:range:. The alignment argument must have one of the following constant values: NSLeftTextAlignment, NSRightTextAlignment, NSCenterTextAlignment, NSJustifiedTextAlignment, or NSNaturalTextAlignment. NSNaturalTextAlignment uses the language-appropriate alignment for the characters in the selected range. For example, Japanese or Arabic characters have different natural alignment than common Western characters. Changes to the alignment only apply to paragraphs that begin within the specified range of characters. If the range is outside of the receiving string, an NSRangeException is raised.

The method -readFromURL:options:documentAttributes: replaces the contents of the receiving NSMutableAttributedString with the contents of the file at the NSURL passed as the first argument. The second argument is an NSDictionary that specifies how the contents of the file are handled. For plain-text files, the dictionary is consulted for the @"CharacterEncoding" key, which must have a corresponding NSNumber value containing the NSStringEncoding constant that should be applied to the characters in the file. NSStringEncoding is an enumerated type declared in NSString.h. NSStringEncoding values range from 1, which specifies NSASCIIStringEncoding, to 65536, which specifies NSProprietaryStringEncoding. The available encoding constants are documented at http://developer.apple.com/techpubs/macosx/Cocoa/Reference/Foundation/ObjC_classic/TypesAndConstants/FoundationTypesConstants.html. The @"DefaultAttributes" key has an NSDictionary value that defines the attributes to be applied to the characters loaded from the file. Table 11.1 lists the valid attribute keys and values. If the file being read from the URL is an HTML file, a dictionary passed as the options: argument might contain the @"BaseURL" key, which is consulted to resolve relative URLs within the file being read. The third argument to -readFromURL:options:documentAttributes: is a pointer to a pointer to an NSDictionary. If the third argument is not NULL, a dictionary that describes the document attributes of the file being read is returned by reference. Document attribute keys and values are listed in Table 11.2. If the file identified by the URL is successfully read, -readFromURL:options:documentAttributes: returns the Boolean value of YES. NO is returned otherwise.

There are several methods to ensure that the attributes for a requested range are appropriate: -fixAttributesInRange:, -fixAttachmentAttributeInRange:, -fixFontAttributeInRange:, and -fixParagraphStyleAttributeInRange:. The -fixAttachmentAttributeInRange: method removes any NSAttachmentAttributeName identifiers that don't apply to NSAttachmentCharacter characters within the specified range of characters. The -fixFontAttributeInRange: method ensures that the font settings on text within the range are correct. For example, characters that lie within the Chinese Unicode character set but have a Western font attribute are corrected to have an appropriate Chinese font attribute.

The method `-fixParagraphStyleAttributeInRange:` ensures that `NSParagraphAttributes` affect only complete paragraphs. The method `-fixAttributesInRange:` invokes each of the other methods, providing a single call to fix all the text within a range. Once again, ranges outside the bounds of the string cause an `NSRangeException` to be raised.

The View and Controller classes in Cocoa's text system make changes to `NSTextStorage` instances automatically as the result of user input. `NSTextStorage` is a subclass of `NSMutableAttribtedString`. A complex system of notifications keeps the View and Control layers synchronized with changes in the text storage. When an `NSTextStorage` instance is modified directly by program code, it's important to bracket the changes with calls to `NSMutableAttribtedString`'s `-beginEditing` and `-endEditing` methods. Doing so causes `NSTextStorage` to coalesce notifications for changes that occur between `-beginEditing` and `-endEditing` calls.

The classes in the View and Control layers of the text system need to perform time consuming layout and display calculations each time they are notified of changes to the underlying `NSTextStorage`. The most efficient way to modify an attributed string such as an `NSTextStorage` is to call `-beginEditing`, make as many changes as needed, and then call `-endEditing`. The `-beginEditing` and `-endEditing` block prevents the other objects in the text system from being notified until `-endEditing` is called.

The Control Layer: Text Layout and Containers

The visual representation of each character in an attributed string requires one or more glyphs. A glyph is a pictorial representation of a character. Glyphs are managed by font and are described in more detail in the "Managing Fonts" section of this chapter. The glyphs that are used to represent a character might depend on the context. Factors such as the preceding and following glyphs, the position of a glyph on a line, and the orientation of a glyph all contribute to the glyph that is ultimately displayed.

The `NSLayoutManager` class is responsible for selecting glyphs to represent the characters in attributed string based on the attributes and context. The `NSLayoutManager` class must also position glyphs relative to each other and the graphical area that contains the glyphs.

`NSLayoutManager` does not normally draw anything without the help of a view or accept user input. The View layer handles those tasks in the text system. `NSLayoutManager` has its hands full mapping the attributed strings, fonts, attachments, and paragraph styles in the Model layer to positioned glyphs ready for display in the View layer. `NSLayoutManager` requires an incredibly complex implementation to support diverse languages, writing styles, and fonts from around the world. It is one of the most complex and sophisticated classes in the Cocoa frameworks, but it exposes very little of its complexity to Cocoa programmers.

`NSLayoutManager` uses instances of the `NSTextContainer` and `NSTypesetter` classes to assist it with its task. The `NSTextContainer` class defines graphical areas within which the layout manager can place glyphs. By default, text containers are rectangular, but `NSTextContainer` can be subclassed to simulate almost any shape. Text containers can be used to force a layout manager to place glyphs around an irregular shape or leave gaps in the glyph placement. `NSLayoutManager` uses private subclasses of `NSTypesetter` to control word wrapping, hyphenation, line breaks, and even layout direction. Typesetters exist for right-to-left languages and vertical languages. The `NSSimpleHorizontalTypesetter` class is used for most Western languages.

Diagrams of different ways layout managers and text containers can be configured are available at `http://developer.apple.com/techpubs/macosx/Cocoa/TasksAndConcepts/ProgrammingTopics/TextArchitecture/index.html`.

One `NSTextStorage` instance can be used with multiple `NSLayoutManager` instances. One `NSLayoutManager` instance can have any number of ordered `NSTextContainer` instances. When the layout manager has filled one container with glyphs, it moves on to the next container until it either runs out of glyphs to place or runs out of containers. Each `NSTextContainer` instance is associated with at most one `NSView` instance. `NSLayoutManager` can be used with `NSTextContainer` instances even if the containers are not associated with views. In that configuration, the layout manager is used to calculate glyph placement and obtain information such as the amount of space needed to display all the glyphs. The layout manager can even perform precalculations and layout text in the background while other application threads continue to execute.

Apple provides the `CircleView` example in `/Developer/Examples/AppKit/CircleView`. The `CircleView` example uses a custom `NSView` subclass and `NSLayoutManager` to position and draw glyphs around the circumference of a circle. This example shows rudimentary use of `NSLayoutManager` in combination with `NSTextContainer` and `NSTextStorage`.

Apple's `TextEdit` example (`/Developer/Examples/AppKit/TextEdit`) and the `TextSizingExample` (`/Developer/Examples/AppKit/TextSizingExample`) both show complex use of `NSLayoutManager` in combination with `NSTextContainer` to implement multiple column text, text with margins, and text with complex sizing, wrapping and line break behaviors.

A new `TextViewConfig` example that is not distributed with Apple's Developer Tools prior to the release of Mac OS X 10.1.5 is available at `http://developer.apple.com/samplecode/Sample_Code/Cocoa/TextViewConfig.htm`.

This example shows how to use multiple instances of NSLayoutManager with a single NSTextStorage instance and multiple text containers.

The View Layer: NSTextView

The NSTextView class implements the View layer in Cocoa's text system. NSTextView handles display and input of text at the user interface level. NSTextView is a subclass of NSText. NSText provides a general interface to Cocoa's text system, but NSText is not normally used directly. Instead, NSTextView instances are used. NSTextView provides the highest-level interface to the text system and includes features not available in NSText.

Some simple uses of the NSTextView class have already been shown in the first sections of this chapter. The simplest configuration for an NSTextView instance is the one provided by the text view on Interface Builder's Cocoa-Data palette. That NSTextView is the document view of a scroll view and is preconfigured with one text container as wide as the text view and very tall. Only one layout manager is used, and only one text storage is used.

The NSTextView methods for setting the text to be displayed and configuring text attributes such as color and underline are all implemented to change the contents of the NSTextStorage instance associated with the view. The NSTextContainer associated with the view is configured to resize horizontally when the view is resized horizontally. The NSTextView instance is configured to automatically resize vertically to contain all the text in the associated text container. If either the text storage or the text container change, the layout manager associated with the NSTextView instance automatically lays out the text storage–attributed string within the text container to account for the changes.

If the NSTextView changes size to accommodate a change in the size of the text container after text layout has completed, the scroll view automatically adjusts the scrollbars to reflect the change.

NSTextView provides the -textStorage method that returns its associates NSTextStorage instance. The -textContainer method returns the associated NSTextContainer instance. The -layoutManager method returns the associated NSLayoutManager instance.

NSTextView provides a comprehensive set of methods for setting text attributes, controlling the display of text, configuring text-input behavior, interacting with rulers, managing the user's current selection, undo, spell checking, drag and drop, and even text-to-speech features. The NSTextView class is document at http://developer.apple.com/techpubs/macosx/Cocoa/Reference/ApplicationKit/ObjC_classic/Classes/NSTextView.html and in the documentation that comes with Apple's developer tools.

NSTextView is very seldom subclassed. Powerful techniques for controlling, validating, and formatting text input by users without subclassing are described in the "Text Input" section of this chapter. NSTextView's methods are largely self-explanatory after its interaction with NSLayoutManager, NSTextContainer, and NSTextStorage has been described. The complete documentation for NSTextView is available at http://developer.apple.com/techpubs/macosx/Cocoa/Reference/ApplicationKit/ObjC_classic/Classes/NSTextView.html and comes with Apple's developer tools. The remainder of this section is dedicated to providing a couple of examples that use NSTextView and the other text system classes.

Appending or Inserting an Image Attachment

One method for inserting or appending content to an NSTextView is by directly interacting with the NSTextView's text storage. For example, a common task is to insert an image attachment into a text view. This can be done at the NSTextStorage level using the following code:

```
NSTextAttachment    *att;
NSString            *path;
NSFileWrapper       *wrapper;
NSAttributedString  *attStr;

// determine the path to our image
path = [[NSBundle mainBundle] pathForResource:@"image" ofType:@"tiff"];

// construct an NSFileWrapper for the path
wrapper = [[[NSFileWrapper alloc] initWithPath:path] autorelease];

// construct an NSTextAttachment for the NSFileWrapper instance
att = [[[NSTextAttachment alloc] initWithFileWrapper:wrapper] autorelease];
attStr = [NSAttributedString attributedStringWithAttachment:att];

//Insertion Code Begins
[[theTextView textStorage] beginEditing];
[[theTextView textStorage] appendAttributedString:attStr];
[[theTextView textStorage] endEditing];
//Insertion Code Ends
```

The theTextView variable is a previously created NSTextView instance. The path to an image is used to initialize a new NSFileWrapper instance. The NSFileWrapper instance is then used to create a new NSTextAttachment. The NSAttributedString method, +attributedStringWithAttachment:, creates an instance of an attributed string configured to hold the image attachment. NSFileWrapper is described in

Chapter 7's "NSFileWrapper" section. NSBundle is described in the "NSBundle" section of Chapter 7.

After the attributed string is constructed, theTextView's associated NSTextStorage is notified that editing is going to begin by calling the -beginEditing method. The attributed string is appended directly to the text storage, and the NSTextStorage is notified that editing is complete using -endEditing. The -beginEditing and -endEditing methods cause NSTextStorage to coalesce change notifications for changes that occur between -beginEditing and -endEditing. This is not very important in this example, but if many changes are made at once, the -beginEditing and -endEditing block prevents the associated NSLayoutManager from expensively recalculating the layout after each change. Instead, the layout can be recalculated once including all the changes.

It is possible to insert the image at a specific location, using code such as the following:

```
//Insertion Code Begins
[[theTextView textStorage] beginEditing];
[[theTextView textStorage] replaceCharactersInRange:NSMakeRange(
       insertionLocation,0) withAttributedString:attStr];
[[theTextView textStorage] endEditing];
//Insertion Code Ends
```

To replace text with an image or attachment, use one the -replaceCharactersInRange: method and specify a range with a length greater than zero.

Inserting a Web Link

Inserting a Web link is similar to inserting an image. Begin by constructing an instance of NSDictionary that contains an NSString instance (the link) as the value for the NSLinkAttribute identifier; then create a new NSAttributedString with the text that should be displayed and the link requested.

The following NSAttributedString category provides an +attributedStringWithLink:labelString: method that returns a properly formatted NSAttributedString for a link:

```
@implementation NSAttributedString (_MYLinkSupport)

+ (NSAttributedString *)attributedStringWithLink:(NSString *)link
                                     labelString:(NSString *)text;
{
  NSDictionary *attrsDict;
```

```
  attrsDict = [NSDictionary dictionaryWithObject:link
      forKey:NSLinkAttributeName];
  return [[[NSAttributedString alloc] initWithString:text
      attributes:attrsDict] autorelease];
}

@end
```

The `+attributedStringWithLink:labelString:` method is used to append a link to the text in an `NSTextView` as follows:

```
NSAttributedString   *linkStr;

linkStr = [NSAttributedString
    attributedStringWithLink:@"http://www.cocoaprogramming.net"
    labelString:@"Go to Cocoa Developer's Handbook site"];
[[textView textStorage] beginEditing];
[[textView textStorage] appendAttributedString:linkStr];
[[textView textStorage] endEditing];
```

Managing Fonts

In the "The Control Layer: Text Layout and Containers" section of this chapter, it was stated that glyphs are managed by font objects. Each font can be thought of as a collection of glyphs. Each glyph depicts a character in a particular character set. Character sets are described in the "`NSCharacterSet`" section of Chapter 7. Character sets describe groups of Unicode characters. Because no font can contain glyphs for every possible Unicode character, a complex relationship between character sets, Unicode characters, and fonts is needed. The complexity is encapsulated within the `NSLayoutManager` class that is responsible for laying out glyphs corresponding to the characters and attributes in attributed strings.

Cocoa's text system can use Fonts specified in PostScript, Macintosh TrueType, Windows TrueType, or OpenType formats. Fonts are automatically available for use if they are located in the standard font locations (`/Network/Fonts`, `/Local/Library/Fonts`, `/Library/Fonts`, `~/Library/Fonts`, and `/System/Library/Fonts`). The standard locations and the logic used to search for fonts and other resources are described in the "Standard Locations" section of Chapter 22, "Integrating with the Operating System."

Cocoa provides three principal classes for managing fonts: `NSFont`, `NSFontPanel`, and `NSFontManager`. Fonts are grouped into font families. For example, Helvetica and Times are two common font families. Each family consists of one or more individual fonts, also called typefaces. Fonts exhibit one or more style traits. For example, bold and italic are traits of a font. The terminology used to describe fonts is almost as old as the printing press. A complete discussion of typography and fonts requires a book longer than this one. By necessity, only an overview of Cocoa's font support and font usage is provided here.

When working with fonts, an individual typeface is often referenced by its fully specified font name, which consists of the family name combined with the typeface's traits. Helvetica-BoldOblique, LucidaGrande-Bold, and Futura-CondensedExtraBold are examples of fully specified font names. Each typeface also has a weight, which refers to how visually heavy the font appears. Examples of font weights include ultralight, light, book, regular (also called plain or book), bold, extrabold, and black.

The Cocoa font managing classes use the Model-View-Controller architecture. The `NSFont` class is the model. It encapsulates the glyphs and traits of a font. The standard Font panel represented by an instance of the `NSFontPanel` class is the view component. It provides a way for users to view and select fonts. The `NSFontManager` class is the controller. It provides a list of available fonts, keeps track of which fonts are being used, converts fonts between typefaces and traits, and controls communication between the Font panel and an application.

The `NSFont` Class

Each `NSFont` instance represents a specific typeface and is created only once for each application. Each `NSFont` instance is stored and reused. When an `NSFont` instance is requested with a typeface that has been previously used, the existing instance is returned. If the no appropriate `NSFont` instance has been created for the requested typeface, a new instance is automatically created, stored for later reuse, and returned.

Getting an `NSFont` Instance

An instance of `NSFont` that corresponds to a specific font is returned by calling the method `+fontWithName:size:` passing an `NSString` as the name argument and a `float` as the size. The font name must be the fully specified font family name. The size is measured in Postscript Points (pts.). Passing 0.0 as the `size:` parameter causes `+fontWithName:size:` to return a font with a default size. The default size is determined by the user's preference the defaults database that is described in the "Defaults System" section of Chapter 7.

NOTE

Fonts created via `+fontWithName:size:` automatically flip themselves when drawing in an `NSView` that has a flipped coordinate system. Flipped views are described in the "Rectangle Tests" section of Chapter 12, "Custom Views and Graphics Part I."

There are a number of convenience methods available to access standard fonts. Using the standard fonts ensures a consistent appearance across applications. The +systemFontOfSize: method provides the font that is used for standard interface items such as buttons and menu items. Passing zero or a negative value as the size returns the system font with the default size. The default size for the system font is returned by +systemFontSize. The bold variation of this font is available using the method +boldSystemFontSize:, again passing the size as a float. The +smallSystemFontSize method returns the size to use when specifying a small system font. The +labelFontOfSize: method returns an instance of NSFont consistent with Apple's Aqua guidelines for labels in the user interface. The default size for such fonts is returned by +labelFontSize.

The user font (also called the Application font) is returned by calling the method +userFontOfSize:. This is the font used by default for text that the user is able to edit. The user's default fixed pitch font is returned by the method +userFixedPitchFontOfSize:. In both cases passing zero or a negative size results in the return of a font with the default size. A fixed pitch font is one in which all the glyphs require the same space when printed. Most fonts are proportionally spaced, meaning that different glyphs require different amounts of space. The user font for an application can be set by calling the method +setUserFont: passing an NSFont instance as the argument. The fixed pitch user font is set by calling +setUserFixedPitchFont:.

Obtaining Font Information

NSFont provides a myriad of methods for getting detailed information about a font and specific glyphs within a font. Only the most commonly used methods are described in this section. The complete documentation for NSFont is available at http://developer.apple.com/techpubs/macosx/Cocoa/Reference/ApplicationKit/ObjC_classic/Classes/NSFont.html, and in the documentation that comes with Apple's developer tools.

The fully specified name of a font is returned by NSFont's -fontName method. The family name is returned by -familyName. The method -displayName returns the name that should be used to identify the font in a user interface. The -displayName method returns a name in the user's preferred language.

To determine if a font is a fixed pitch font, call the method -isFixedPitch. This method returns a Boolean value of YES if the font has fixed pitch and NO if it is a proportionally spaced font.

NSFont's -pointSize method returns a float that represents the size of the font in Postscript Points. This is the overall height of the font from its lowest descender to its highest ascender, and because of this, two fonts with the same point size might appear to be radically different sizes. Figure 11.2 shows the critical dimensions of a font that are used to layout glyphs and calculate the area needed to display glyphs. The method `-ascender` returns the distance in Postscript Points from the baseline of the font to the highest ascender. Likewise, `-descender` returns the distance of the lowest descender from the font baseline.

FIGURE 11.2 Fonts are measured by their total point size as well as ascender, descender, xHeight, and capHeight dimentions.

Calling `-capHeight` returns a `float` that is the height in Postscript Points of a capital letter in the font. Individual letters might have ascenders that are larger or smaller than the `-capHeight` value. The `-xHeight` method returns the height of a lowercase letter in the font. `NSFont` approximates both the `-capHeight` and `-xHeight` values in some cases because not all font formats provide the information.

The `-defaultLineHeightForFont` method returns a `float` that is the sum of the ascender and descender of the font plus the default line gap (vertical distance between two lines of text).

The method `-maximumAdvancement` returns an `NSSize` structure that represents the maximum advancement of a glyph in the font. Depending on the type of font, the advancement can be horizontal or vertical. The `-boundingRectForFont` method returns an `NSRect` that is the union of the bounding rectangles for all the glyphs in the font. The bounding rectangle is the minimum rectangle that completely encloses a glyph. The union of those rectangles is the minimum rectangle that encloses all of the bounding rectangles.

Using the Font Manager

The `NSFontManager` class is the hub of font used in Cocoa. It tracks the available fonts and traits, displays the `NSFontPanel`, and notifies responders when a font is changed. There is a single shared `NSFontManager` instance in each graphical Cocoa application. The shared instance is retrieved with `NSFontManager`'s `+sharedFontManager` class method.

When a user changes font attributes with the Font panel, the shared `NSFontManager` object records the requested attribute, changes, and then sends a `-changeFont:` message up the responder chain. Objects in the responder chain implement

-changeFont: to call NSFontManager's -convertFont: method. The argument to -convertFont: is an NSFont instance that will be converted to be consistent with the user's choices in the Font panel. For example, if the user has changed only the point size selected in the Font panel, the font passed to -convertFont: is modified to have the specified size without affecting other attributes such as the font face or whether the font is italic.

The -convertFont: method can be called multiple times as the result of one -changeFont: message. For example, if the current selection in a text editor includes text with several different fonts, the -convertFont: method is called once for each font in the selection. Because -convertFont: only modifies the attributes that were explicitly set by the user, several convenient features are automatically provided to users. When the selection includes multiple fonts, the user is able to change only the size of each font without changing the font face. Similarly, the user is able to change all the selected text to one font face without changing the different font sizes in the selection.

NSFontManager methods such as -addFontTrait: and -removeFontTrait: simulate the corresponding changes made through the Font panel and cause NSFontManager to send the -changeFont: message up the responder chain.

The weight of an NSFont instance is returned by calling the method -weightOfFont: passing an NSFont instance as the argument. An NSFontTraitMask describing the traits of a font is returned by calling the -traitsOfFont: passing an NSFont instance as the argument. Font traits and weights are described in the next section.

Font Traits and Weights

Each typeface exhibits one or more style traits. A group of traits can be specified with an NSFontTraitMask value. NSFontTraitMask values are used to create new typefaces or modify existing typefaces. Table 11.3 lists common traits and their restrictions. This is not a complete list of the possible traits for a font. Only the traits used by NSFontManager to convert font into another are listed.

TABLE 11.3 Common Font Traits and Restrictions

Trait	Restrictions
NSBoldFontMask	Mutually exclusive with NSUnboldFontMask
NSUnboldFontMask	Mutually exclusive with NSBoldFontMask
NSItalicFontMask	Mutually exclusive with NSUnitalicFontMask
NSUnitalicFontMask	Mutually exclusive with NSItalicFontMask
NSNonStandardCharacterSetFontMask	None
NSNarrowFontMask	None
NSCondensedFontMask	Mutually exclusive with NSExpandedFontMask
NSExpandedFontMask	Mutually exclusive with NSCondensedFontMask

TABLE 11.3 Continued

Trait	Restrictions
`NSSmallCapsFontMask`	None
`NSPosterFontMask`	None
`NSCompressedFontMask`	None
`NSFixedPitchFontMask`	None

`NSFont` provides several methods for requesting a specific font using the fully specified typeface name. `NSFontManager` provides alternative methods that use the family name, the font traits, the font weight, and the size to specify a font. `NSFontManager`'s `-fontWithFamily:traits:weight:size:` accepts a family name passed as an `NSString` for the first argument. The `traits:` argument is the value of an `NSFontTraitMask`, or a C bitwise logical `OR` of multiple `NSFontTraitMask` values from Table 11.3. The weight is an integer value between 0 and 15 that represents the visual heaviness of a face. Table 11.4 lists the available integer weight values and the corresponding typographic term for the weight. Finally, the size argument is passed as a `float` value measured in Postscript Points.

TABLE 11.4 Font Weight Constants and Corresponding Typographic Terms

Weight Constant	Standard Term
1	ultralight
2	thin
3	light, extralight
4	book
5	regular, plain, display, roman
6	medium
7	demi, demibold
8	semi, semibold
9	bold
10	extra, extrabold
11	heavy, heavyface
12	black, super
13	ultra, ultrablack, fat
14	extrablack, obese, nord

NOTE

If the `NSBoldFontMask` trait is included in the `traits:` argument to `-fontWithFamily:traits:weight:size:`, the `weight:` argument is ignored.

The weight of an NSFont instance is returned by calling the method -weightOfFont: passing the NSFont instance as the argument. An NSFontTraitMask consisting of the logical OR of all the traits of an NSFont is returned by calling -traitsOfFont: passing the NSFont instance as the argument.

It is possible to determine if a font typeface has specific traits using the method -fontNamed:hasTraits:. This method requires a fully specified font typeface name such as an NSString for the first argument and a NSFontTraitMask value, or a logical OR of multiple NSFontTraitMask values, as the second argument. It returns the Boolean YES only if all the traits specified in the hasTraits: argument are true for the named font.

Determining Available Fonts

An application can get an array of all available font typefaces by calling NSFontManager's -availableFonts method. This method returns an NSArray containing fully specified typeface names. Similarly, an application can get a subset of the available fonts that correspond to a specific set of font traits by using the method -availableFontNamesWithTraits: passing a logical OR of NSFontTraitMask values as the argument. A value of 0 for the NSFontTraitMask returns fonts that are neither bold nor italic faces. In both methods, fonts that are not normally displayed to the user are prefaced with a . character.

A localized version of the family and face name is returned by the method -localizedNameForFamily:face:. Passing nil as the face string returns a localized version of the face name.

Converting Fonts

NSFontManager is able to provide NSFont instances by converting any of the family, face, size, weight, or traits of an existing NSFont instance. The conversion methods accept an NSFont instance argument used as the basis for changes.

The principal conversion method is -convertFont:. It returns an NSFont instance derived from the font passed as an argument. Attributes specified by the user via the standard Font panel or the standard Font menu are applied to the font being converted. For example, if the Font panel currently has no selected font family, but the size is set to 72.0 pts., and -convertFont: is called passing an NSFont instance that represents Helvetica-Bold 12.0 pts., the returned NSFont represents Helvetica-Bold 72.0 pts. If, however, the font panel specifies the Times family with 48.0 pts., the returned NSFont represents Times-Bold 48.0 pts. Only the font attributes explicitly specified by the user are changed when converting a font.

The method -convertFont:toFace: returns an NSFont instance with the font face name specified by a string passed as the second argument. All other attributes of the returned font are identical to the attributes of the font passed as the first argument.

The face should be a fully specified family-face font name such as Helvetica-BoldOblique. If `NSFontManager` is unable return the requested font, `nil` is returned.

The `-convertFont:toFamily:` method returns an `NSFont` belonging to the font family passed as an `NSString` name. The returned font has the same size and traits as the base font passed as the first argument. For example, if the passed `NSFont` instance represents Helvetica-BoldOblique, and the requested family is Optima, this method returns an `NSFont` representing Optima-BoldItatlic. If no face in the requested family has the same attributes as the font argument, the `NSFont` argument is returned unmodified.

The method `-convertFont:toHaveTrait:` returns an `NSFont` instance based on `NSFont` and the trait passed as the second argument. Only a single trait can be passed as the `toHaveTrait:` argument. If `NSFontManager` is unable to make the conversion, the `NSFont` passed as the first argument is returned unchanged. The `-convertFont:toNotHaveTrait:` returns an `NSFont` instance based on the passed `NSFont` and returns a variant that does not have the specified trait. Again, if the conversion does not take place, the passed `NSFont` argument is returned unchanged.

The `-convertFont:toSize:` method returns an `NSFont` instance with the same family, face, traits, and weight as the first argument and the `float` size in Postscript Points specified by the second argument.

The final method in `NSFontManager`'s conversion suite is `-convertWeight:ofFont:`. The weight argument, a Boolean, specifies if the returned font should be visually heavier (by passing a `YES` value) or lighter (by passing a `NO` value) than the supplied `NSFont` instance. If there is no heavier or lighter face available, the `NSFont` instance passed as the second argument is returned unmodified.

Current Font Selection

Applications notify the `NSFontManager` of changes in the current font using the method `-setSelectedFont:isMultiple:`. Graphical applications should call this method when the user's selection has changed and pass the font used by the current selection as the first argument. Cocoa's `NSText` and `NSTextView` classes already do this. It is only necessary to call `-setSelectedFont:isMultiple:` in applications that handle fonts directly. If the selection uses only a single `NSFont` instance, the Boolean value `NO` is passed as the `isMultiple:` argument. If there are multiple fonts used by the current selection, the application should call `-setSelectedFont:isMultiple:` once for each font used, passing the `NSFont` instances as the first argument. For the first font used, call `-setSelectedFont:isMultiple:` with `NO` as the `isMultiple:` argument. For each subsequent font, pass `YES` as the `isMultiple:` argument.

`NSFontManager`'s `-selectedFont` method returns the last `NSFont` instance passed to `-setSelectedFont:isMultiple:`. It is possible to determine if there are multiple fonts selected by calling the method `-isMultiple`, which returns a Boolean value.

NOTE

Using NSFontManager's -selectedFont method from within an implementation of -changeFont: is not a reliable way to obtain the user's font selection. Font attributes that the user has not explicitly set will have indeterminate values. Instead use the NSFontManager's -convertFont: method to convert an existing NSFont instance into one that corresponds to the user's chosen font attributes.

Triggering -changeFont: Programmatically

NSFontManager sends the -changeFont: up the responder chain when the user changes a selection in the Font panel or Font menu. The -changeFont: message is the key to informing the rest of Cocoa's text system that a change has been made. Custom objects that display editable text need to implement the -changeFont: method to call NSFontManager's -convertFont: and convert fonts in the user's current selection. It is possible to cause NSFontManager to send the -changeFont: message as the result of programmatic changes as well.

NSFontManager's -addFontTrait: specifies a font trait that will be applied the next time the NSFontManager receives a -convertFont: message. Calling -addFontTrait: causes the NSFontManager to send a -changeFont: message. The object that is passed as the argument to -addFontTrait: must respond to the -tag message by returning NSFontTrait. The -removeFontTrait: operates in a similar manner. It removes the trait returned by the -tag method of the argument and sends the -changeFont: message.

The method -modifyFontViaPanel: causes the -changeFont: message to be sent up the responder chain, and when the NSFontManager receives a subsequent -convertFont: request, the NSFontManager uses the NSFontPanel's -panelConvertFont method to return the new NSFont. The NSFontPanel class is described in the "Using the Font Panel" section of this chapter.

Finally, the method -modifyFont: is used to control how fonts are converted by calls to -convertFont:. The -modifyFont: method can be used to increase or decrease a font's size or weight. It triggers a -changeFont: message. The object passed as the argument to -modifyFont: must implement the -tag method to return one of the constants in Table 11.5. The constant returned determines which method will be used to convert fonts and consequently which attributes will change as the result of subsequent -convertFont: calls.

TABLE 11.5 Font Modification Actions and Corresponding Conversion Methods

Modification Action	Conversion Method
NSNoFontChangeAction	The font passed to -convertFont: is not changed.
NSViaPanelFontAction	The font passed to -convertFont: is changed by NSFontPanel's -panelConvertFont method.
NSAddTraitFontAction	The font passed to -convertFont: is changed by the -convertFont:toHaveTrait: method.
NSRemoveTraitFontAction	The font passed to -convertFont: is changed by the -convertFont:toNotHaveTrait: method.
NSSizeUpFontAction	The font passed to -convertFont: is changed by increasing its size using the -convertFont:toSize: method.
NSSizeDownFontAction	The font passed to -convertFont: is changed by reducing its size using the -convertFont:toSize: method.
NSHeavierFontAction	The font passed to -convertFont: is changed by increasing its weight using the -convertWeight:ofFont: method.
NSLighterFontAction	The font passed to -convertFont: is changed by decreasing its weight using the -convertWeight:ofFont: method.

NSFontManager normally sends the -changeFont: up the responder chain to indicate that a change to a font is needed, but a different message can be specified via NSFontManager's -setAction: method. Cocoa's text classes expect to receive -changeFont: messages and will most likely malfunction if it is not sent, but it might make sense to customize this behavior in some applications. The selector of the message sent by NSFontManager is returned from the -action method.

Interacting with the User

As a Controller in the Model-View-Controller architecture, NSFontManager is responsible for communications between the Model and the View layers. NSFont objects compose the model. NSFontManager methods for interacting with the model have already been described. NSFontManager doesn't provide any direct visual interaction with the user, but it does provide access to the two most common View layer objects that enable font manipulation: the Font panel and the Font menu. In addition, NSFontManager is used to enable and disable the user's ability to change fonts via an application's user interface.

A shared instance of the NSFontPanel class is from NSFontManager's -fontPanel: method. The argument to -fontPanel: is a Boolean that indicates whether the NSFontPanel instance should be created if it does not already exist. The NSFontManager method -orderFrontFontPanel: makes the standard Cocoa Font panel (creating it if necessary) the frontmost window.

The standard Font menu is returned from NSFontManager's -fontMenu: method as an NSMenu instance. The argument to -fontMenu: is a Boolean value specifying whether the menu should be created if it does not already exist. It is also possible to set the current font menu for an application by calling NSFontManager's -setFontMenu: passing the NSMenu instance to use as the Font menu as the argument.

The user interface objects that control interactive font changes can be disabled or enabled using the -setEnabled: method and passing a Boolean as the argument. The current status of the user interface is queried with -isEnabled, which returns a Boolean value.

Finally, the fonts that are shown to the user in the Font Panel are restricted by implementing the -fontManager:willIncludeFont: method in the NSFontManager's delegate. This method is called automatically if the delegate responds to it. The first argument is the shared NSFontManager instance. The second argument is the fully specified name of a font to be displayed in the Font panel. If -fontManager:willIncludeFont: returns YES, the font is present in the Font panel. Otherwise, the font is not shown and is not available for the user to select. The determination of the value to return can be based on many different criteria. For example, an application might restrict font selection to only fixed pitch fonts if a particular view that only displays fixed pitch fonts is the first responder in the main or key windows.

Using the Font Panel and Font Menu

The NSFontPanel class encapsulates the standard Cocoa Font panel. The Font panel provides a consistent and flexible user interface for selecting and modifying fonts. Figure 11.3 shows the standard Font panel and the standard Font menu.

NSFontPanel is a subclass of the NSPanel class. NSPanel is briefly described in the "NSWindow Overview" section of Chapter 8, "The Application Kit Framework Overview," and more extensively in the "Working with Panels" section of Chapter 9, "Applications, Windows, and Screens."

Each graphical Cocoa application has a single shared instance of the NSFontPanel class that is created the first time it is needed. The shared instance is returned by calling NSFontPanel's +sharedFontPanel method or by calling NSFontManager's -fontPanel: method. It is made visible to the user by calling the -makeKeyAndOrderFront: method inherited from the NSWindow class or by using NSFontManager's -orderFrontFontPanel: method.

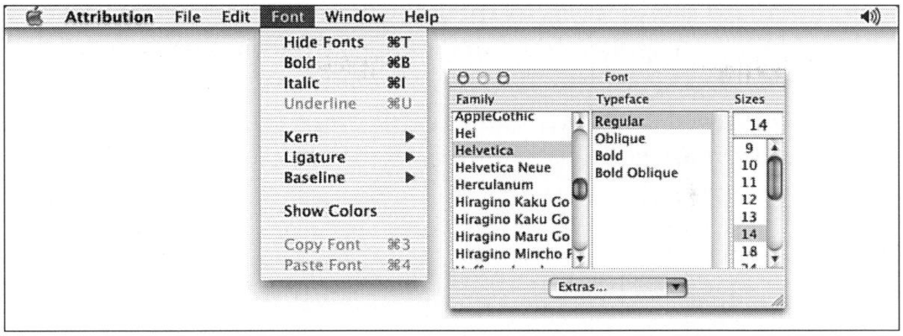

FIGURE 11.3 The standard Font panel and Font menu are shown.

As with most standard Cocoa panels, it is possible to add an accessory view through the use of `-setAccessoryView:` passing the `NSView` that should be added to the panel. The `-accessoryView` method returns the current accessory view or `nil` if none has been set. Accessory views are described in the "Document Actions and the Save Panel" section of Chapter 9.

`NSFontPanel`'s `-worksWhenModal` method ignores the `-setWorksWhenModal:` flag and always returns `YES`, enabling users to change fonts even in modal panels. The `-worksWhenModal` and `-setWorksWhenModal:` methods are explained in the "Using Modal Windows" section of Chapter 9.

The `NSFontPanel` class uses the `-panelConvertFont:` method to change an existing a font according to the Font Panel's current settings. The argument is the `NSFont` instance to change. This works similarly to `NSFontManager`'s `-convertFont:` method, returning only the changes that are selected in the Font panel. If changes cannot be made to the specified font, the original font instance is returned.

The method `-reloadDefaultFontFamilies` reloads the set of fonts displayed in the Font panel. This in turn calls the `NSFontManager`'s delegate's implementation of `-fontManager:willIncludeFont:` for each font allowing the application to filter the fonts shown to the user. The `-reloadDefaultFontFamilies` method can be called to update the Font panel after the filter criteria for `-fontManager:willIncludeFont:` has changed, or to detect new fonts added to the system while the application has been running.

The standard Font menu is available on Interface Builder's Cocoa-Menus palette. Most of the menu items in the Font menu send action messages up the responder chain. The menu items are automatically enabled if an object in the responder chain responds to their actions and disabled otherwise. The action messages are eventually received by a Cocoa text object, such as an `NSTextView` instance or a custom object that responds to the action.

Three of the standard menu items in the Font menu are preconfigured to send messages directly to the application's shared NSFontManager instance. The Font, Show Fonts menu item sends the -orderFrontFontPanel: message to the font manager. The Font, Bold and Font, Italic menu items send the -addFontTrait: message to the font manager.

Text Input

NSTextView uses helper objects called input managers to interpret user input and turn it into text or commands. NSTextView passes raw character input to an input manager. The input manager determines what the raw input means and sends messages to the NSTextView. If the input consists of characters to be inserted, the input manager sends an -insertText: message with the text to insert. If the input consists of commands such as cursor movement keys, the Enter key, or the Backspace key, the input manager sends a -doCommandBySelector: message with an appropriate selector as the argument. The selector specifies the action that the text view should take such as -moveDown:, -deleteBackward:, or -insertNewline:. The set of actions that input managers can send is documented at http://developer.apple.com/techpubs/macosx/Cocoa/Reference/ApplicationKit/ObjC_classic/Classes/NSResponder.html, and in the NSResponder documentation that comes with Apple's developer tools.

NSTextView gives its delegate an opportunity to intercept actions sent with -doCommandBySelector:. The -textView:doCommandBySelector: delegate method is described in the "NSTextView Delegate Methods and Notifications" section of this chapter. If the delegate implements -textView:doCommandBySelector:, and it returns YES, the text view does nothing further; otherwise, the text view performs the action specified by the command.

Input managers are encapsulated by the NSInputManager class and communicate with NSTextView instances via the NSTextInput protocol. Input managers are typically implemented as separate processes, and communication between the input manager and applications is handled by NSInputManager instances. Input managers are briefly described in the "Input Managers" section of Chapter 10, "Views and Controls." Apple provides an NSInputManager example in /Developer/Examples/AppKit/HexInputServer. Another example is available at http://developer.apple.com/samplecode/Sample_Code/Text/Inline_Input_for_TextEdit.htm.

Input managers play a small but crucial role in the Cocoa text system. Input managers offer a great degree of flexibility. For example, many Eastern languages require multiple keystrokes to compose a single Unicode character. An input manager is able to accept as many keystrokes as necessary, and then call

`-insertText:` only once with the fully composed Unicode. Apple provides handwriting recognition capabilities that are implemented as an input manager so that the characters, words, and commands that originate from a stylus and graphics tablet are sent to an `NSTextView`. Similarly, speech input can be gathered from a microphone and injected into Cocoa's text system. Because appropriate input managers exist, every Cocoa text object automatically works seamlessly with a wide variety of input sources.

Using Delegate Methods

The `NSText` class sends notifications and communicates with its delegate when changes are made. The delegate is given substantial control over text-editing behavior. As a subclass of `NSText`, `NSTextView` also uses the delegate. In fact, `NSTextView` extends the set of messages sent to the delegate to include all `NSText`'s delegate messages as well as its own.

NOTE

Use the notifications sent by `NSTextView` objects or implement a delegate to customize text-handing behavior. Many complex Cocoa classes including `NSTextView` are extremely difficult to subclass effectively. Subclassing `NSTextView` should always be a last resort.

`NSText` Delegate Methods and Notifications

The delegate method `-textShouldBeginEditing:` is called when an action that will change the contents or format of an `NSText` instance is about to take place. The argument to `-textShouldBeginEditing:` is the text object that sent the message. If the delegate implements `-textShouldBeginEditing:` and returns the Boolean value `NO`, the changes to the `NSText` object are not allowed. If `-textShouldBeginEditing:` returns `YES`, the text system operates as usual.

When an `NSText` object is about to stop editing, for example, when another `NSText` object is about to become active, the delegate's `-textShouldEndEditing:` method is called. The argument is the text object that sent the message. The delegate implementation allows editing to end by returning the Boolean value `YES`. If `NO` is returned, the text object that sent the message refuses to give up its First Responder status. Because the text object remains the First Responder, no other text object can become active and begin editing. A text object must be the First Responder to be edited. A text object can be forced to end editing even if `-textShouldEndEditing:` returns `NO` by calling `[aWindow endEditingFor:nil]` where `aWindow` is the window that contains the text object.

There are three notifications that can be posted by an `NSText` object: `NSTextDidBeginEditingNotification`, `NSTextDidChangeNotification`, and `NSTextDidEndEditingNotification`. There are corresponding delegate methods for each of these notifications. The delegate methods are called even if the delegate does not observe the notifications.

An `NSTextDidBeginEditingNotification` is sent when an action is about to change the contents or format of an `NSText` object that was not already being edited. Use `NSNotification`'s `-object` method to access to the text object that sent the notification. The delegate method `-textDidBeginEditing:` is automatically called when the `NSTextDidBeginEditingNotification` notification is sent. The argument to `-textDidBeginEditing:` is the notification object.

An `NSTextDidChangeNotification` is sent when the contents or format of an `NSText` object have just been changed. The `NSNotification` that is passed to any registered observers contains the affected `NSText` object as its `-object` value. The delegate method `-textDidChange:` is automatically called with an `NSNotification` argument when the notification is sent.

An `NSTextDidEndEditingNotification` is sent when a text object has ended editing. The `NSNotification`'s `-object` value is the text object that sent the notification. The delegate's `-textDidEndEditing:` method is called with the notification as the argument. The `NSNotification` instance sent for `NSTextDidEndEditingNotification` contains a dictionary with a single key, `NSTextMovement`. Calling the notification's `-userInfo` method accesses the dictionary. The value for the `NSTextMovement` key is one of the following constants that indicate why the editing ended: `NSReturnTextMovement`, `NSTabTextMovement`, or `NSBackTabTextMovement`.

`NSTextView` Delegate Methods and Notifications

The `NSTextView` extends the delegate methods provided by `NSText` to handle fine-grained control of attachments, links, selection changes, keyboard navigation, undo, and formatting.

The `-textView:clickedOnCell:inRect:atIndex:` delegate method is called after the user clicks an attachment embedded in an `NSTextView` instance. The first argument is the `NSTextView` instance that sent the message. The second argument is the cell that represents the attachment. The third argument is the rectangle that encloses the attachment cell in the text view's coordinate system. The fourth argument is the position within the text view's text storage of the `NSAttachmentCharacter` for the clicked attachment. The delegate can use this method to select the attachment or send an action message.

NOTE

The NSTextView object sent as the first argument to NSTextView's delegate messages is usually the first text view in the ordered collection of text views used by an NSLayoutManager. A single NSLayoutManager can layout text for multiple views. Because the change that caused a delegate message to be sent might have occurred in one of the other text views managed by the layout manager, there is no guarantee that the change happened in the text view passed as the first argument to the delegate method.

The most reliable way to process text within an NSTextView delegate method is to use the sending NSTextView's text storage directly, rather than using the NSTextView's methods.

The -textView:clickedOnLink:atIndex: delegate method is called after the user clicks a link embedded in an NSTextView instance. The first argument is the NSTextView instance that sent the message. The second argument is the link that was clicked. The third argument is the position within the text view's text storage of the link. If the delegate does not respond to this message or returns NO, the text view's next responder is given an opportunity to process the click. If the delegate handles the click, return YES from -textView:clickedOnLink:atIndex:.

The -textView:doCommandBySelector: delegate message gives delegates an opportunity to intervene in an NSTextView's command processing. The first argument is the text view that sent the message. The second argument is a selector that identifies an action to perform. If the delegate does not respond to -textView:doCommandBySelector: or returns NO, the text view processes the command by performing the action. If the delegate does handle the command on behalf of the text view, -textView:doCommandBySelector: should return YES informing the text view that no additional processing is required. Implement this delegate method to influence selection changes, insertion cursor movement, text insertion, text deletion, and scrolling. Apple provides an excellent example that uses this method at http://developer.apple.com/samplecode/Sample_Code/Cocoa/TextViewDelegate.htm.

The -textView:doubleClickedOnCell:inRect:atIndex: method is called after the -textView:clickedOnCell:inRect:atIndex: method if the user clicks a second time within the default double-click threshold. The arguments to -textView:doubleClickedOnCell:inRect:atIndex: are the same as the arguments to -textView:clickedOnCell:inRect:atIndex:. Implement this delegate method to perform special processing when an attachment is double-clicked.

The -textView:draggedCell:inRect:event:atIndex: message is sent to the delegate when the user attempts to drag an attachment within an NSTextView. The first argument is the NSTextView that sent the message. The second argument is the cell that represents the attachment. The third argument is the rectangle that encloses the attachment cell in the text view's coordinate system. The fourth argument is the

NSEvent that started the drag. The NSEvent class is described in the "Responders" section of Chapter 8. The fifth argument is the position within the text view's text storage of the NSAttachmentCharacter for the dragged attachment. The delegate can implement this method to initiate a dragging operation. Drag operations are explained in the "Drag and Drop in Custom View and Window Objects" section of Chapter 19, "Using Pasteboards."

The -textView:shouldChangeTextInRange:replacementString: method is used to control whether a particular range of characters can be modified. The first argument is the NSTextView that sent the message. The second argument is an NSRange structure that identifies the range of characters to be replaced. The third argument is a string containing the proposed replacement characters. The third argument is nil if only attributes are being changed. If the delegate implements this method to return YES or the delegate does not implement this method at all, the text view makes the change. If the delegate implements -textView:shouldChangeTextInRange:replacementString: to return NO, the change is not made.

The -textView:willChangeSelectionFromCharacterRange:toCharacterRange: delegate method is called before the selection is changed. The first argument is the NSTextView that sent the message. The second argument is an NSRange structure identify the range of characters currently selected. The third argument is the proposed range of characters that will be selected. Implement this method to return the range that should be selected. The delegate can return the proposed range unmodified or substitute any other range as appropriate.

The -textView:writablePasteboardTypesForCell:atIndex: delegate method is used to return an array of pasteboard types suitable for writing an attachment to the pasteboard. The first argument is the NSTextView that sent the message. The second argument is the cell that represents the attachment. The third argument is the position of the character that represents the attachment in the text view's text storage. Do not implement this method if the delegate implements -textView:draggedCell:inRect:event:atIndex:.

The -textView:writeCell:atIndex:toPasteboard:type: delegate method is used to write an attachment to a pasteboard. The first argument is the NSTextView that sent the message. The second argument is the position of the character that represents the attachment in the text view's text storage. The third argument is the pasteboard. The fourth argument is a pasteboard type. -textView:writeCell:atIndex:toPasteboard:type: should return YES if the attachment is successfully written to the pasteboard and NO otherwise.

The -undoManagerForTextView: method enables the delegate to control which NSUndoManager instance is used with a text view. The argument is the NSTextView that sent the message. Return an `NSUndoManager` instance. `NSUndoManager` is described in the "Undo and Redo" section of Chapter 8.

`NSTextView` posts the following notifications in addition to the ones posted by the `NSText` class: `NSTextViewDidChangeSelectionNotification` and `NSTextViewWillChangeNotifyingTextViewNotification`.

The `NSTextViewDidChangeSelectionNotification` is posted whenever the selection changes in a text view. This notification is posted once at the end of each selection operation. If the `NSTextView`'s delegate implements the `-textViewDidChangeSelection:` method, it is automatically called even if the delegate does not observe the notification. The argument to `-textViewDidChangeSelection:` is the `NSNotification` instance that was posted. Use `NSNotification`'s `-object` method to obtain the `NSTextView` that posted the notification. The notification's `-userInfo` dictionary contains a single key, `NSOldSelectedCharacterRange`. The value of the key is an `NSValue` instance containing an `NSRange` structure that identifies the previously selected range. The `NSTextView` that posted the notification can provide the current selection range.

The `NSTextViewWillChangeNotifyingTextViewNotification` is posted whenever one `NSTextView` is about to stop sending notifications and another is about to start. Observing this notification gives objects a chance to reregister for notifications from a new `NSTextView` instance. Calling `NSTextView`'s `-removeTextContainerAtIndex:`, `-textContainerChangedTextView:`, and `-insertTextContainer:atIndex:` methods results in this notification being posted. There's no delegate method that is called automatically when this notification is posted.

The `-object` of the `NSTextViewWillChangeNotifyingTextViewNotification` is the old notifying `NSTextView` or `nil`. The notification's `-userInfo` dictionary might contain zero, one, or two keys. The two possible keys are `NSOldNotifyingTextView` and `NSNewNotifyingTextView`. The value for the `NSOldNotifyingTextView` key is the old `NSTextView`, if it exists. The value for the `NSNewNotifyingTextView` is the new `NSTextView` if it exists.

Using Formatters

Cocoa's text system is very powerful, but also very complex. Many classes cooperate to make a single instance of `NSTextView` operate. Almost all text drawn by Cocoa applications is drawn by `NSTextView` instances, but it does not make sense to have separate text views for every label, button, or text field that draws text. Instead, each window has an instance of `NSTextView` that is shared by most of the other objects that need to draw text. The shared `NSTextView` instance is called the window's field editor. The field editor is described in "The Field Editor" section of Chapter 10.

The objects that use the field editor are usually subclasses of `NSControl` and `NSCell`. For example, `NSTextField` is a subclass of `NSControl`, and `NSTextField` uses an instance of `NSTextFieldCell` in its implementation. `NSTextFieldCell` is a subclass of `NSActionCell`, which is in turn a subclass of `NSCell`.

Controls such as `NSTextField`, and the corresponding `NSCell` instance, not only draw text with the aid of the field editor, they need to accept textual user input as well. Controls and cells optionally use `NSFormatter` instances to assist with the display of textual information and to control or validate user input. `NSFormatters` are described in the "Validation and Formatters" section of Chapter 10. The remainder of this section is used to explain the interaction between `NSFormatter` subclasses and the field editor or another `NSTextView`.

Formatters convert objects such as `NSCalendarDate` or `NSNumber` into instances of `NSString` or `NSAttributedString`, which are then displayed by the field editor. Formatters also accept characters input to the field editor and convert the characters into other objects.

To convert objects into strings for display, `NSFormatter` subclasses must implement the `-stringForObjectValue:` method. The optional `-attributedStringForObjectValue:` method can also be implemented. Both methods accept an arbitrary object argument. They return an `NSString` and an `NSAttribtedString`, respectively. If `-attributedStringForObjectValue:` is implemented by a formatter, `-stringForObjectValue:` will never be called unless `-attributedStringForObjectValue:` calls it. Controls and cells prefer attributed strings.

To convert strings into objects, `NSFormatter` subclasses must implement `-getObjectValue:forString:errorDescription:`. The first argument is a pointer to a pointer to an object. This method returns an object by reference in the first argument. The second argument is the string to convert. The third argument is a pointer to a pointer to an `NSString` object. If an error is detected during conversion, a message describing the error can be returned by reference in the third argument.

The following simple `NSFormatter` subclass formats 10-digit phone numbers with the standard USA notation. For example, `(800) 555-1234` is a correctly formatted phone number. The first three digits are an area code. The next three digits are a prefix. The last four digits complete the phone number. Including the parentheses, a space character, and the dash character between the prefix and the rest of the number, the formatted phone number requires 14 characters.

Create a new Cocoa Application Project Builder project. A good name for the new project is `MYPhoneNumberFormatterExample`. Add the following code for `MYPhoneNumberFormatter.h` and `MYPhoneNumberFormatter.m` to the project.

File MYPhoneNumberFormatter.h:

```
/* MYPhoneNumberFormatter */

#import <Cocoa/Cocoa.h>

@interface MYPhoneNumberFormatter : NSFormatter
{
}

@end
```

File MYPhoneNumberFormatter.m:

```
#import "MYPhoneNumberFormatter.h"

@implementation MYPhoneNumberFormatter
/*" Instances of this class format 10 digit numbers using standard USA phone
    number notation: (XXX) XXX-XXXX. "*/

/*" The number of characters needed to display a formatted 10 digit phone
    number "*/
static const int      MYNumberOfCharactersInFormattedPhoneNumber = 14;


- (NSString *)stringForObjectValue:(id)obj
  /*" Returns a string by converting obj into a string formatted with standard
      USA phone number notation.
  "*/
{
  NSString   *result = @"(   )    -    ";  // default result if obj is invalid

  if([obj respondsToSelector:@selector(longLongValue)])
  {
    // obj is able to provide a ten digit number to format
    long long      phoneNumber = [obj longLongValue];
    long long      areaCode = (phoneNumber / 10000000);    // first 3 digits
    long long      prefix = (phoneNumber / 10000) % 1000;  // (digits 5-7)
    long long      fourDigitNumber = phoneNumber % 10000;  // last 4 digits
```

```
    result = [NSString stringWithFormat:@"(%03d) %03d-%04d", (int)areaCode,
        (int)prefix, (int)fourDigitNumber];
  }

  return result;
}


- (BOOL)getObjectValue:(id *)obj forString:(NSString *)string
    errorDescription:(NSString **)error
  /*" Returns by reference in obj an NSNumber derived from string. The
      NSNumber stores a ten digit number using the long long type. If
      any errors are detected, this method returns NO and also returns
      an error message by reference in error. If an error is detected,
      the value returned by reference in obj is undefined. If no errors
      are detected, this method returns YES. "*/
{
  long long     phoneNumber = 0;      // the 10 digit phone number
  long long     areaCode = 0;         // the 3 digit area code
  long long     prefix = 0;           // the 3 digit prefix
  long long     fourDigitNumber = 0;  // the 4 digit number
  BOOL          result = NO;          // default result

  if(MYNumberOfCharactersInFormattedPhoneNumber == [string length])
  {
    // string has the proper length for a formatted phone number

    // 01234567890123   character position in formatted phone number string
    // (XXX) XXX-XXXX
    areaCode = [[string substringWithRange:NSMakeRange(1, 3)] intValue];
    prefix = [[string substringWithRange:NSMakeRange(6, 3)] intValue];
    fourDigitNumber = [[string substringWithRange:NSMakeRange(10, 4)]
        intValue];
  }

  // combine area code, prefix, and 4 digit number to create a 10 digit number
  phoneNumber = (areaCode * 10000000) + (prefix * 10000) + fourDigitNumber;
  if(phoneNumber >= 1000000000)
  {
    // the 10 digit phone number must be greater than or equal to 1000000000
    // because the first digit in the area code can not be 0
    if(NULL != obj)
```

```
    {
      *obj = [NSNumber numberWithLongLong:phoneNumber]; // return NSNumber
    }
    result = YES;
  }
  else if(NULL != error)
  {
    // There were too few digits in the phone number
    *error = @"Too few digits in phone number";  // return error by reference
  }

  return result;
}

@end
```

The code so far implements a minimal `NSFormatter` subclass. Both the `-stringForObjectValue:` and `-getObjectValue:forString:errorDescription:` methods are implemented. Compile the project to make sure there are no errors.

Double-click the `MainMenu.nib` file in the Resources folder of the new project. Interface Builder will start and display the user interface for this example. Drag the `MYPhoneNumberFormatter.h` file into Interface Builder's window titled `MainMenu.nib`. The `MainMenu.nib` window displays its Classes tab containing a class browser that shows the `MYPhoneNumberFormatter` class selected. Ctrl-click the selected `MYPhoneNumberFormatter` class in the class browser to display Interface Builder's contextual menu. Click Instantiate `MYPhoneNumberFormatter` in the context menu. After an instance of `MYPhoneNumberFormatter` is created in Interface Builder, the `MainMenu.nib` window switches to its Instances tab, which now contains the new `MYPhoneNumberFormatter` instance.

Next, drag two editable `NSTextField` objects from Interface Builder's Cocoa-Views palette into the window titled Window. The editable `NSTextField` object on the Cocoa-Views palette is shown in Figure 10.9 within the "Text Fields" section of Chapter 10. Resize the text fields so that they are wide enough to display 10 digits plus the formatting characters. Ctrl-drag a connection line from one of the text fields in the window titled Window to the instance of `MYPhoneNumberFormatter` in the `MainMenu.nib` window. Interface Builder's Connections inspector is automatically shown, if it is not already visible. In the Connections inspector, select the text field's `formatter` outlet and click the Connect button.

Save the user interface using Interface Builder's File, Save menu item, and then quit Interface Builder.

Build and run the new application in Project Builder. When the user interface for the new application appears, both text fields are shown. The text field that does not have a formatter accepts any characters typed into it, but only a very precise set of characters are accepted by the text field that has the connection to the `MYPhoneNumberFormatter` instance. The formatted text field does not allow editing to end until a number with the correct formatting such as `(555) 555-5555` is provided. The single-space character after the `)` character is required and there cannot be any spaces or other characters after the last digit. Experiment by entering different values into the two text fields to see the range of input allowed.

The new formatter is doing its job, but it does not provide a very nice experience for users. Currently, users must enter the digits using the specific notation; no variations are tolerated. In addition, the formatter is sloppy. If any three-digit number greater than 100 is typed into the area-code portion of the phone number, the rest of the input can be random characters as long as the total length of the input is exactly 14 characters.

The next step is to improve the user experience by modifying the formatter. Quit the running example application and return to Project Builder.

If a text field has a formatter, each time the text in the text field changes because of user input, the formatter's `-isPartialStringValid:newEditingString:errorDescription:` method is called. The first argument is a string containing the characters in the text field. The second argument is a pointer to a pointer to an `NSString` instance. The second argument is used to return a replacement for the contents of the text field. The last argument is a pointer to a pointer to a string used to return an error message by reference. If `-isPartialStringValid:newEditingString:errorDescription:` returns `NO`, the contents of the text field being formatted are replaced with the string return by reference in the second argument. If the method returns `YES`, the text field's content is left alone and continues to show the string passed as the first argument just the way the user entered it.

Add the following implementation of `-isPartialStringValid:newEditingString:errorDescription:` to the implementation of `MYPhoneNumberFormatter`. Each time a character is entered into the text field, the contents of the field are replaced with the new string returned by this method. The basic algorithm is to find each decimal digit typed by the user and insert the characters into a string that already has the correct formatting. Any characters typed by the user that are not decimal digits are ignored.

```
#define _MYNUM_VALID_DIGIT_POSITIONS (10)

/*" Array lists valid position for digits in a formatted phone number "*/
static int _MYValidPositionsInPhoneNumber[_MYNUM_VALID_DIGIT_POSITIONS] =
    { 1, 2, 3, 6, 7, 8, 10, 11, 12, 13 };

- (BOOL)isPartialStringValid:(NSString *)partial
    newEditingString:(NSString **)newString
    errorDescription:(NSString **)errorString
/*" This method is implemented to place digits within a formatted phone number
    string as the digits are typed.  This method always returns NO and always
    returns a formatted phone number string by reference in newString. This
    method does no set the value of errorString.
"*/
{
  BOOL                  result = NO;
  int                   lengthOfPartial = [partial length];
  NSMutableString       *formattedPartialString = [NSMutableString
      stringWithString:@"(   )    -    "];
  NSCharacterSet        *digits = [NSCharacterSet decimalDigitCharacterSet];
  int                   positionInPartial = 0;
  int                   currentDigit = 0;

  // while we have not run out of digits in partial string, place the digits
  // in order in the valid positions within formattedPartialString
  while(positionInPartial < lengthOfPartial &&
      currentDigit < _MYNUM_VALID_DIGIT_POSITIONS)
  {
    NSRange      remainingRangeInPartial = NSMakeRange(positionInPartial,
        lengthOfPartial - positionInPartial);
    NSRange      rangeOfNextDigit = [partial rangeOfCharacterFromSet:digits
        options:NSLiteralSearch range:remainingRangeInPartial];

    if(rangeOfNextDigit.location != NSNotFound)
    {
      [formattedPartialString replaceCharactersInRange:
          NSMakeRange(_MYValidPositionsInPhoneNumber[currentDigit], 1)
          withString:[partial substringWithRange:rangeOfNextDigit]];
      positionInPartial = rangeOfNextDigit.location + rangeOfNextDigit.length;
      currentDigit++;
    }
    else
    {
```

```
      // terminate the loop because there are no more digits
      positionInPartial = lengthOfPartial;
    }
  }

  *newString = formattedPartialString;

  return result;
}
```

Build and run the example application. Experiment entering values into the formatted text field. One shortcoming of this approach is that the text insertion cursor moves to the end of the text field after each character is entered. The insertion cursor can be moved to any location in the field with the mouse or arrow keys, but it cannot be moved more than one position with the Backspace or Delete keys. This is an unfortunate side effect of always returning a full-length formatted string from `-isPartialStringValid:newEditingString:errorDescription:`. A better behavior would be to have the formatter move the insertion cursor to the position just after the last digit entered. Unfortunately, there is no reliable way to do that from within a formatter's `-isPartialStringValid:newEditingString:errorDescription:` implementation.

The `NSControl` class has a delegate method that can be implemented to provide the desired text-insertion cursor behavior. If the `-control:didFailToValidatePartialString:errorDescription:` method is implemented by the control's delegate, the method is called whenever the formatter returns `NO` from `-isPartialStringValid:newEditingString:errorDescription:`. Because `MYPhoneNumberFormatter` always returns `NO` from `-isPartialStringValid:newEditingString:errorDescription:`, the control's delegate can implement `-control:didFailToValidatePartialString:errorDescription:` to position the insertion cursor just after the last digit.

Code similar to the following implementation of `-control:didFailToValidatePartialString:errorDescription:` can be implemented in a text field's delegate to set the insertion cursor's position. `NSControl`'s `-controlTextDidChange:` delegate method is another place where the insertion cursor can be positioned.

```
- (void)control:(NSControl *)control
    didFailToValidatePartialString:(NSString *)string
    errorDescription:(NSString *)error
/*" Move the insertion cursor of the field editor used to edit control to the
    location just past the last digit in string "*/
{
```

```
  if(0 < [string length])
  {
    id              fieldEditor = [[control window] fieldEditor:NO
        forObject:control];
    NSCharacterSet  *digits = [NSCharacterSet decimalDigitCharacterSet];
    NSRange         rangeOfLastDigit = [string rangeOfCharacterFromSet:digits
        options:NSLiteralSearch|NSBackwardsSearch];

    if(NSNotFound != rangeOfLastDigit.location)
    {
      [fieldEditor setSelectedRange:NSMakeRange(
          rangeOfLastDigit.location+1, 0)];
    }
  }
}
```

One last modification to the `MYPhoneNumberFormatter` class enables the display of attributes in the formatted strings. Add the following method to the implementation of `MYPhoneNumberFormatter` in `MYPhoneNumberFormatter.h`.

```
- (NSAttributedString *)attributedStringForObjectValue:(id)obj
    withDefaultAttributes:(NSDictionary *)attrs
  /*" Calls [self stringForObjectValue:obj] and returns an attributed string
      containing a formatted string and color attributes. "*/
{
  NSMutableAttributedString    *result = [[[NSMutableAttributedString alloc]
      initWithString:[self stringForObjectValue:obj] attributes:attrs]
      autorelease];

  if(MYNumberOfCharactersInFormattedPhoneNumber == [result length])
  {
    // The string to format has the correct length
    // Add color attributes to the various components of the formatted phone
    // number
    NSColor   *gray = [NSColor grayColor];
    NSColor   *black = [NSColor blackColor];

    [result addAttribute:NSForegroundColorAttributeName value:gray range:
        NSMakeRange(0, 1)];
    [result addAttribute:NSForegroundColorAttributeName value:black range:
        NSMakeRange(1, 3)];
    [result addAttribute:NSForegroundColorAttributeName value:gray range:
        NSMakeRange(4, 2)];
```

```
    [result addAttribute:NSForegroundColorAttributeName value:black range:
        NSMakeRange(6, 3)];
    [result addAttribute:NSForegroundColorAttributeName value:gray range:
        NSMakeRange(9, 1)];
    [result addAttribute:NSForegroundColorAttributeName value:black range:
        NSMakeRange(10, 4)];
  }

  return result;
}
```

Build and run the example to see the effects of the new method. Controls such as `NSTextField` call the `-attributedStringForObjectValue:` method in preference to `-stringForObjectValue:` if the attributed string variant is available.

For more examples, an excellent tutorial that explains how to create `NSFormatter` subclasses is available at
`http://www.stepwise.com/Articles/VermontRecipes/recipe05/recipe05.html`.

Summary

Few Cocoa applications need the full range of features and customization options that Cocoa's text system provides. The objects on Interface Builder palettes are extremely powerful, even in their default configuration; however, enough information was presented in this chapter to enable very sophisticated use of Cocoa's text system. The MVC architecture used to implement the text system makes it possible to customize parts of the system without affecting other parts. The examples provided show the most common ways the text classes are used, and the hooks needed to customize the text system.

The next chapter, "Custom Views and Graphics Part I," describes how to create custom subclasses of `NSView` and implement custom drawing features. All Cocoa's visible user interface objects are direct or indirect subclasses of `NSView` including the `NSText` and `NSTextView` classes explained in this chapter. `NSView` provides the common features needed to implement user interface elements as simple as `NSBox` or as complex as `NSTextView`.

12

Custom Views and Graphics Part I

IN THIS CHAPTER

- The Quartz Graphics Model
- Quartz Graphics Via the Application Kit
- Using the `NSBezierPath` Class
- Modifying Drawing

The Application Kit contains classes that provide the user interface elements common to most applications. However, some applications require the use of custom interface elements and graphics that none of the Application Kit classes provide. For example, the Application Kit doesn't contain any classes for plotting graphs. Therefore, it is necessary to subclass `NSView`, an Application Kit class, to create such graphics.

There are several ways to draw when implementing a subclass of `NSView`. The first and most common way is to use Quartz 2D graphics. Another is to use Cocoa's support for OpenGL 3D graphics. Finally, the Application Kit provides limited support for QuickDraw graphics from prior Macintosh operating systems.

Quartz 2D graphics are accessed via Application Kit classes or Core Graphics functions. In this chapter, only the Application Kit classes are discussed in depth. There are, however, a few things that can be done in Core Graphics that can't be done with Cocoa's Application Kit, such as capturing the screen and full-screen drawing. Using the Application Kit is as efficient as using Core Graphics. There is little gained by using Core Graphics directly, whereas much is lost when leaving behind the object-oriented features that Cocoa provides. For example, the `NSView` class provides all the basic logic needed to manage the Quartz drawing context so all the developer needs to add in a subclass is the minimal drawing code.

OpenGL 3D graphics are accessed by subclassing the `NSOpenGLView` class. `NSOpenGLView` provides OpenGL context management. This chapter only covers 2D graphics. 3D graphics and OpenGL are described briefly in Chapter 21.

The Quartz Graphics Model

To write effective code for 2D drawing in Cocoa, it is necessary to understand the graphics model that underlies the Quartz 2D graphics layer in Mac OS X. It is beyond the scope of this book to give every tiny detail of the graphics model, but this section provides, in the most general terms, a bird's eye view of what is available and the capabilities of those offerings. Most of the rest of this chapter and the two that follow flesh out the facilities described in this section.

The Quartz graphics model is fundamentally based on Adobe's PDF standard, which in turn takes most of its ideas from the PostScript graphics language. The graphics model is complex, and this book can only touch on the most basic concepts. For more detailed information, any good book on PostScript or PDF will prove invaluable.

Quartz graphics are designed to be both device and resolution independent. Quartz also allows for basic color management. It maintains a current drawing state that consists of a collection of parameters that affect future drawing. Similar to PostScript and PDF, Quartz uses transformation matrices to alter the base coordinate system for effects such as translation, rotation, scaling, and more. To actually draw something, a path or outline must be defined, and then either stroked or filled. All these features and terms are defined in more depth throughout this chapter.

Resolution Independence

To be resolution independent, the basic units of measurement used when specifying coordinates are points, as understood by the printing industry. On a high-resolution device a point still specifies the same distance as on a low-resolution device. As a result, the graphics drawn will look the same size to the user when they move from one device to another. The higher the resolution, the more pixels are painted when drawing a given geometrical object.

The point unit is defined as 1/72 of an inch. Thus, on a 1440 dpi printer, one point would be 20 dots long. A square one-point high and one-point wide covers an area of 400 dots total. Apple assumes that all monitors have a resolution of 72 pixels per inch. In other words, Apple assumes that one pixel on a monitor is one point in size (1/72 of an inch by 1/72 of an inch). Thus, when drawing to the screen, a point could actually be larger or smaller than a true point that is supposed to be 1/72 inch. The result is that if you specify a 10×10-point square, a 10×10-pixel rectangle, painting 100 pixels total, will be drawn on the screen. This one-to-one mapping is a direct result of Quartz's assumption that one screen pixel equals one printer's point. It is dangerous to assume that this will always be the case, however. Apple could, at some future date, choose to calibrate monitors' dpi ratings. This might make sense to do as monitors increase in resolution.

Device Independence

To be device independent, it is important that when you specify a color it looks the same on all devices. Quartz uses ColorSync to achieve this. You can bypass this and specify device-dependent colors, but usually that is not a good idea. Any serious graphics should use calibrated colors. Because Quartz itself uses ColorSync, you, as a developer, don't have to do anything special to support it.

Transparency

One other aspect of color permeates Quartz: transparency. Usually the term alpha or alpha channel is used to refer to transparency. Both bitmap images and the colors used to render paths can have varying levels of transparency. Generally, alpha of zero means completely transparent. Depending on context, alpha might be an integer in the range of 0–255 or, more commonly, a floating-point value from 0.0–1.0. The highest number in the range (1.0 or 255) denotes fully opaque. In the present implementation of Quartz, transparency is supported much better on the screen than it is on the printer or when printing to PDF. The PDF standard, however, is evolving to support transparency better. According to Apple, improved support for transparency when printing will eventually make its way into Quartz.

Paths

Paths support basic drawing. A path is an outline of a graphical shape. There are several commands to add line segments, arcs, and more to a given path. While under construction, a path is completely invisible. When the path is fully defined, the stroke or fill commands can be used. Stroking a path paints the outline that the path defines. Filling the same path creates a solid, filled shape instead.

The easiest way to think of a path being created is to envision an inkless pen tracing out the path, following given commands. For lines and curves, the commands use the pen's current position as an implied starting point. Note that the pen can be lifted by moving to a new point instead of tracing out a line to the point. When the pen has traced out the path, a pen with ink in it can actually follow the predefined path to put something visible onto the page. Remember, if stroke or fill isn't used after defining a path, nothing will be shown on your drawing canvas.

In Cocoa, there are a few convenience functions for laying out and drawing or filling rectangular paths. There is also the `NSBezierPath` class that is used for most path creation and manipulation.

Transforms

It is often convenient to define a basic path, and then repeat it multiple times, perhaps at different locations, sizes, or rotations. This can be accomplished with the current transformation matrix (CTM). A point can be thought of as a two dimensional vector, allowing it to be multiplied by a matrix. In doing so, it undergoes a transformation into a new vector. Depending on the contents of the matrix, the new vector could be at a different location (such as translated or moved), a different size (scaled), or rotated. Some matrices can cause shearing and other unusual effects as well.

With Quartz, you can specify an explicit matrix, or you can add a translation, rotation, or scaling to the current matrix. For most developers, the latter is the easiest way to work with the CTM. However, developers experienced with the CTM might choose to create and set their own matrices explicitly.

One of the special properties of transformation matrices is that multiple matrices can be multiplied together to create a new matrix that performs all the transformations that were specified by the original matrices. For example, if there are three matrices with the first one doing a translation, another one doing rotation, and the last one for scaling, by multiplying the three together a single matrix can be created that performs all three operations. This process of multiplying matrices together is known as concatenation.

Cocoa's `NSAffineTransform` class, described in Chapter 13, "Custom Views and Graphics Part II," helps manage the CTM and provides a simple way to manipulate these matrices. It can be given raw matrices or asked to concatenate scaling, rotation, or translation elements to the matrix it represents.

Bitmapped Images

When drawing, sometimes it is necessary to draw bitmapped graphics, as opposed to paths. Quartz offers several facilities for compositing bitmaps. Compositing combines an image with the graphics that are already on the drawing canvas. There are 13 different compositing operators available. In compositing terminology, the source is the image that is being composited, and the destination is the area of the canvas being drawn.

The simplest compositing operation is clear, which zeroes out the drawing area. Another simple operation, copy, copies the bitmap into the drawing area, completely replacing whatever was underneath. One of the most common operations is source over, which places the opaque parts of the source image on top of the destination, but enables the destination to show through the transparent parts of the source image. Many other modes are also available, and will be described more fully later.

The NSImage class described in Chapter 14, "Custom Views and Graphics Part III," can be used for managing and compositing images. NSImage instances are usually composed of one or more other objects called image representations. Various different NSImageRep subclasses are used in conjunction with NSImage to support different image formats.

Graphics Contexts

Quartz uses a graphics context to control what is drawn. The graphics context stores attributes such as the current line width, the current line end cap style, the current drawing color, the current transformation matrix, and the current path. All graphics commands are given to the context, and the context can modify them according to its settings.

There can also be multiple graphics contexts. Typically, each window has its own context. It is possible for a view object within a window to have its own context. Some contexts never draw to the screen. A context could be writing graphics commands to a file, a printer, or even drawing into an offscreen image buffer. Usually, a developer doesn't need to worry about what the current graphics context is doing. Cocoa's NSGraphicsContext class described in Chapter 13, is used to query and modify contexts.

Text Rendering

The final big function performed by Quartz is to draw text. Quartz doesn't work entirely alone because text is such a complex function. It uses Apple's ATSUI (an advanced text rendering technology) to do most of the hard work. Working with text at this level is very complex, so Cocoa offers a whole suite of classes for manipulating and displaying text. At the lowest level there are NSString and NSAttributedString. The Application Kit adds some categories to these objects for very simple text rendering. Drawing text with strings is covered in Chapter 14. The NSText object and its associated helper objects manage more complex rendering. This is complex enough that the text object is covered in its own chapter. For more information, see Chapter 11, "Text Views."

Quartz Graphics Via the Application Kit

The Application Kit provides several classes to assist in using Quartz to draw 2D graphics. It also provides functions that can be used to do some basic, common drawing tasks, such as rapidly drawing rectangles.

NOTE

Many Application Kit classes support Quartz drawing. For managing and drawing bitmaps, there is NSImage and several NSImageRep subclasses. To draw lines, rectangles, arcs, curves, polygons, and more, there is NSBezierPath. To adjust the parameters of the current graphics context, use the NSGraphicsContext and NSAffineTransform classes. To draw simple text, use the methods added to NSString and NSAttributedString by the Application Kit in the NSStringDrawing categories. If more complex or more efficient text drawing is required, an NSText object should be used.

New Types and Functions

Before continuing, a few types and structures that the Foundation Kit defines for graphics must be understood. There are several C functions and macros available for manipulating these types and structures.

Points, Sizes, and Rectangles

The NSPoint type stores the x and y coordinates of two-dimensional points as floating-point values. The NSPoint type is a C structure. Its x and y members can be accessed directly. For example:

```
NSPoint myPoint;
NSPoint *pointPointer;
myPoint.x = 10.0;
myPoint.y = 25.0;
pointPointer = &myPoint;
pointPointer->x = 6.0;
```

A similar structure, NSSize, also has two floating-point members. NSSize stores the size of a two dimensional area. Its two members are called height and width. One important thing to remember about the NSSize type is that its members should never be negative. The compiler won't automatically check this, so a developer must be careful with any code that manipulates NSSize structures. Again, the members are accessed directly. For example:

```
NSPoint mySize;
NSPoint *sizePointer;
mySize.width = 50.0;
mySize.height = 70.5;
sizePointer = &mySize;
sizePointer->width = 100.0;
```

A third frequently used type is NSRect. Cocoa defines rectangles as having an origin and a size. The origin member is an NSPoint structure and specifies the rectangle's lower-left corner. The size member is an `NSSize` structure, giving the rectangle's width and height. An `NSRect` is therefore a structure made up of two structures. The members are still accessed directly:

```
NSRect myRect;
NSRect *rectPointer;
myRect.origin.x = 10.0;
myRect.origin.y = 5.5;
myRect.size.width = 40.0;
myRect.size.height = 20.55;
rectPointer = &myRect;
rectPointer->origin.x = 21.43;
```

Each of these three types also has two companion types, one for a pointer to the structure, and the other for a pointer to an array of structures. These types are `NSPointPointer`, `NSPointArray`, `NSSizePointer`, `NSSizeArray`, `NSRectPointer`, and `NSRectArray`. The following two variable declarations are equivalent:

```
NSRect *rectPointer;
NSRectPointer rectPointer;
```

And so on for the other five companion types.

There is one final type, `NSRectEdge`, which is often used to specify a particular edge of a rectangle. `NSRectEdge` is an enumerated type and can have one of the following four values: `NSMinXEdge`, `NSMinYEdge`, `NSMaxXEdge`, and `NSMaxYEdge`.

Point, Size and Rectangle Constants, Creation, and Accessors

To help manipulate the point, size, and rectangle structures, Cocoa defines some constants and inline utility functions. Because these functions are inlined, don't be afraid to use them liberally. They are well tested and will continue to work even if the Cocoa definitions of these structures change in the future.

There is a constant zero version of each structure that has each member set to zero. They are named `NSZeroPoint`, `NSZeroSize`, and `NSZeroRect`. These can be handy for clearing or resetting the values of a point, size, or rectangle.

In many cases, a point, line, or rectangle structure needs to be provided to Cocoa and yet the structure in question is not readily available. Perhaps the individual values are available as separate variables, or need to be calculated. To make it easy to create a structure for Cocoa to use, a creation function can be used that corresponds to the structure needed: `NSMakePoint()`, `NSMakeSize()`, or `NSMakeRect()`.

The two arguments to `NSMakePoint()` are the x and y values, in that order. `NSMakeSize()` requires the two arguments width and height. To call `NSMakeRect()`, x, y, width, and height must be specified. For example, this code creates an NSRect structure and passes it as an argument to a hypothetical RectFunction() that accepts a single rectangle as its argument:

```
float x = 5.5;
float y = 10.0;
float w = x * 2.0;
RectFunction(NSMakeRect(x, y, w, y + 5.5));
```

Several other inline functions can be used to access special values or to obtain commonly calculated values from NSRect structures. Table 12.1 describes these functions.

TABLE 12.1 Inline Rectangle Functions

Function	Description
NSMinX(NSRect aRect)	Returns the leftmost x coordinate in the rectangle (aRect.origin.x)
NSMinY(NSRect aRect)	Returns the lowest y coordinate in the rectangle (aRect.origin.y)
NSMidX(NSRect aRect)	Returns the center x coordinate in aRect
NSMidY(NSRect aRect)	Returns the center y coordinate aRect
NSMaxX(NSRect aRect)	Returns the right most x coordinate in the rectangle (aRect.origin.x + aRect.size.width)
NSMaxY(NSRect aRect)	Returns the largest y coordinate in the rectangle (aRect.origin.y + aRect.size.height)
NSWidth(NSRect aRect)	Returns the width of the rectangle (aRect.size.width)
NSHeight(NSRect aRect)	Returns the height of the rectangle (aRect.size.height)

As an example, calculating the center point of a rectangle is accomplished like this:

```
NSPoint rectCenter = NSMakePoint(NSMidX(theRect), NSMidY(theRect));
```

Rectangle Tests

Several other functions can also be used to test the values of these structures in various ways. For example, NSEqualPoints(), NSEqualSizes(), and NSEqualRects() each take two arguments and return a Boolean (BOOL type) YES or NO. The arguments should both be of the same type, NSPoint, NSSize, or NSRect. Besides simply testing for equality, a single NSRect can be tested to see if it covers any actual area with NSIsEmptyRect(). A rectangle with zero width and/or zero height is considered to be empty.

There are also a few slightly more complex tests. To see if a point is inside a given rectangle, use `NSPointInRect()`, providing an `NSPoint` and an `NSRect` as arguments. To see if a rectangle is completely contained within another rectangle, use `NSContainsRect()` with two `NSRect` arguments. This function returns true if the first rectangle completely encloses the second rectangle. If the second rectangle is empty or touches an edge of the first rectangle, it returns `NO`. To see if two rectangles share any area between them, use `NSIntersectsRect()`, again with two `NSRect` arguments. If either rectangle is empty, this function returns `NO`. All these functions assume that the coordinate system has not been scaled, rotated, or translated. In such cases, some of the functions might not work exactly as expected.

A final test function, related to `NSPointInRect()`, is `NSMouseInRect()`. This function requires three arguments: an `NSPoint`, an `NSRect`, and a `BOOL`. The first two arguments work exactly like `NSPointInRect()`. The third argument, the `BOOL`, specifies whether or not the coordinate system has been flipped so that the origin is at the upper left. Use `NSMouseInRect()` to test the location of the cursor's hot spot.

NOTE

In a flipped coordinate system, the positive Y axis runs from top to bottom instead of the normal Quartz orientation that places the origin at the lower left with increasing Y values moving up the screen. Flipped coordinate systems are seen most commonly in text based views.

Rectangle Manipulation

There are six functions that produce new rectangles based on manipulation of existing rectangles in various ways. The first is `NSIntegralRect()`, which returns a new rectangle that has had its origin and size massaged so that each value is an integer. If the rectangle doesn't already have integral bounds, it expands slightly. If it has a zero or negative size, `NSZeroRect` is returned.

The next function is `NSUnionRect()`. This function takes two `NSRect` arguments and returns a new `NSRect` that completely encloses both of them. Note that if the two rectangles don't intersect, this would return a rectangle that is much larger than either of the original two rectangles. If one of the input rectangles has zero or negative values in their size member, the other rectangle is returned verbatim. If both input rectangles have invalid sizes, then `NSZeroRect` is returned.

To find the rectangular area of overlap between two rectangles, use `NSIntersectionRect()`, which takes two `NSRect` values. If the overlap is a point, a line, or there is no overlap at all, `NSZeroRect` is returned. Otherwise, a rectangle defining the area of overlap is returned.

To take a rectangle and create a smaller rectangle centered inside the original rectangle, use `NSInsetRect()`. This function takes the original rectangle and two floating-point values as arguments. The first floating-point number is the amount to move the left and right edges of the rectangle inward. The second number is the distance to move the top and bottom edges. Because both pairs of edges move inward by the same amount, the new rectangle that is returned is centered inside the original rectangle.

The `NSOffsetRect()` function moves a rectangle by a specified amount. For arguments, pass the original rectangle, a floating-point X offset and a floating-point Y offset. The rectangle's origin is moved by the specified amount and the size remains unchanged.

The final rectangle manipulation function is the most complex. `NSDivideRect()` is used to take a rectangle and split it into two new rectangles. It works by taking a slice off of an edge of the rectangle, leaving two new rectangles. The first is the slice itself, the second is what remains of the original rectangle after slicing. (Note that the original `NSRect` is left unaffected.) The parameters are input `NSRect`; a pointer to an `NSRect` where the slice is put; a pointer to the `NSRect` in which the remainder rectangle is placed; a floating-point number to specify how much of a slice to take; and an `NSRectEdge` to specify which side of the rectangle should be sliced.

For example, suppose we want to take a slice off the left edge of a rectangle that has a width of 10.0 points. The code would look like this:

```
NSRect startRect = NSMakeRect(8.0, 8.0, 200.0, 100.0);
NSRect slice, remainder;
NSDivideRect(startRect, &slice, &remainder, 10.0, NSMinXEdge);
```

After the previous code, `startRect`'s values have not changed, but slice contains a rectangle made up of the slice we took off the left edge. The remainder variable contains the original rectangle minus the area sliced off.

Storing Points, Sizes, and Rectangles in the Defaults Database

It is useful to be able to store points, sizes, and rectangles in the user defaults (preferences) database. However, there is no explicit property list type for these values. To make it easier to store any of these values in the database, there are six functions that can convert a point, size, or rectangle into an `NSString` or vice versa.

To convert an `NSPoint`, `NSSize`, or `NSRect` into a string, use `NSStringFromPoint()`, `NSStringFromSize()`, or `NSStringFromRect()`, respectively. Each takes a single argument of the expected type, and returns a pointer to an autoreleased `NSString` instance.

To go the other direction, use `NSPointFromString()`, `NSSizeFromString()`, or `NSRectFromString()`. They each take a pointer to a single `NSString` instance and return an `NSPoint`, `NSSize`, or `NSRect`, respectively.

In general, these functions are used together. The parsing functions are quite specific about how they expect the input string to be laid out, and the string-creation routines are designed to produce the exact output that the parsers want to see.

Subclassing `NSView`

To do any custom drawing in Cocoa, a subclass of `NSView` must be created. The easiest way to learn how to do this is by working through an example. The simplest possible path that can be drawn is a line segment so that is the example shown here.

The first step to drawing is to create a subclass of `NSView` and override the inherited `-drawRect:` method. This method is called whenever the Application Kit determines that the view needs to be redrawn. The developer should not call this method. Instead, to redraw the view, call the `-setNeedsDisplay:` method. This method can be used to tell the Application Kit that the view needs to be redisplayed. The Application Kit automatically takes care of redrawing the view at an appropriate time as well as setting everything up so that the graphics drawn are output to the correct place.

The most basic skeleton code possible for a view subclass that draws looks like this:

```
File MYLinesView.h:

#import <Cocoa/Cocoa.h>

@interface MYLinesView : NSView
{
}

- (void)drawRect:(NSRect)aRect;

@end

File MYLinesView.m :

#import "MYLinesView.h"

@implementation MYLinesView

- (void)drawRect:(NSRect)aRect
```

```
{
  [[NSColor blackColor] set];
  NSRectFill([self bounds]);
}

@end
```

Before going further, this example code should be integrated into a project to more easily work with it. Create a new Cocoa application project called Lines in Project Builder, and add `MYLinesView.h` and `MYLInesView.m` to the new project's Classes folder as shown in Figure 12.1.

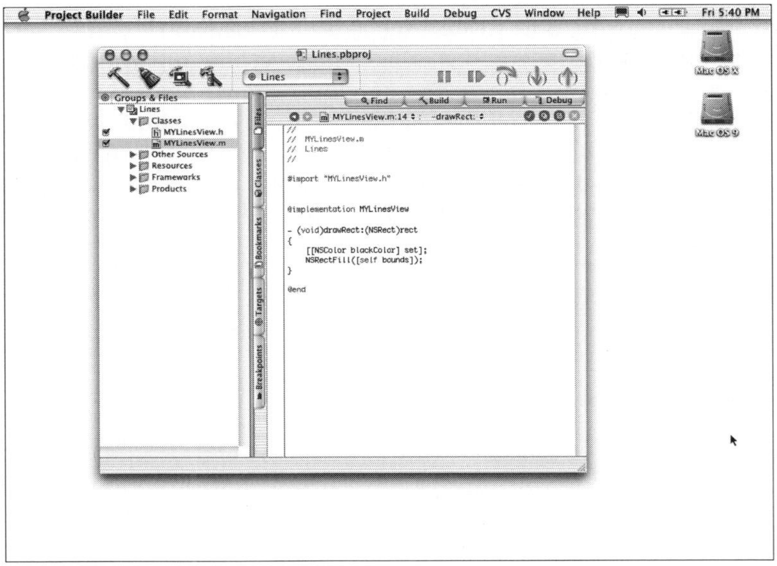

FIGURE 12.1 A new Project Builder project called Lines contains the files `MYLinesView.h` and `MYLinesView.m` in the Classes folder.

Next, open up `MainMenu.nib` in the new project's Resources folder. When Interface Builder has launched, select the Classes tab in Interface Builder's `MainMenu.nib` window and have Interface Builder read the `MYLinesView.h` file. Use Read Files from Interface Builder's Classes menu, or just drag the `MYLinesView.h` file into the `MainMenu.nib` window. Now, drag a Custom View object from Interface Builder's palette and drop it onto the window being edited. The Custom View object looks like a gray rectangle with the words CustomView on it. It can be found at the upper-left corner of the Cocoa-Containers palette. This is the palette that also contains the tab view and box. Figure 12.2 shows a CustomView object being dragged from Interface Builder's palette.

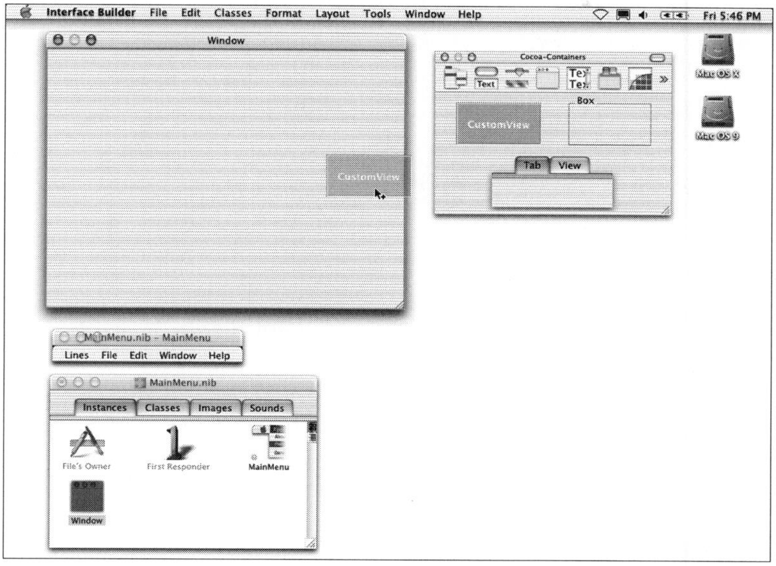

FIGURE 12.2 A CustomView object is dragged from Interface Builder's palette to a window.

When you have dragged a CustomView object onto your window, select the custom view and open the Show Info window (Cmd-1). With a custom view selected, the Show Info window contains a list of all the `NSView` subclasses known to Interface Builder. Interface Builder has already read the files defining `MYLinesView`, and the `MYLinesView` class appears at the top of the list as shown in Figure 12.3.

Select `MYLinesView` so that the custom view knows what class it should be. Figure 12.4 shows the custom view configured to be an instance of `MYLinesView` and filling the entire content area of a window.

Use the Size mode of Interface Builder's Show Info window to configure the `MYLinesView` instance to fill all available space when resized. Figure 12.5 shows the `MYLinesView` instance selected and the correctly configured resize springs in the Size mode of Interface Builder's Show Info window.

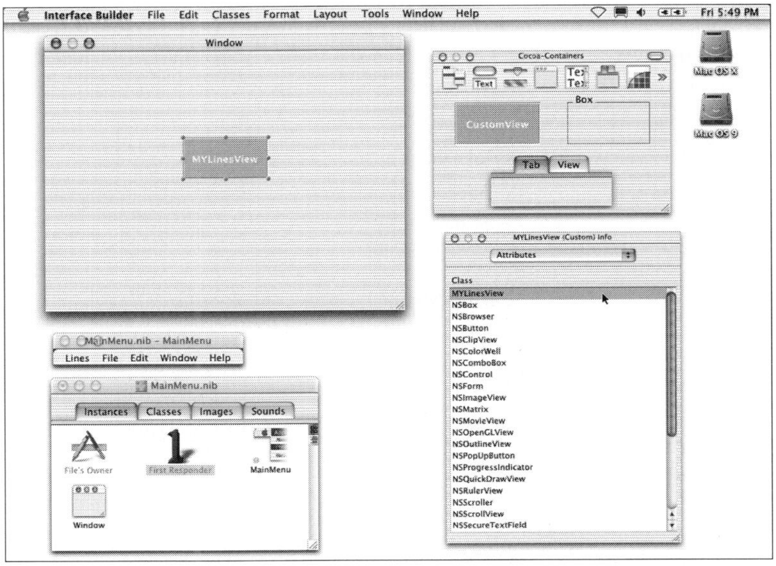

FIGURE 12.3 Because Interface Builder has already read the files defining `MYLinesView`, the `MYLinesView` class appears in the list.

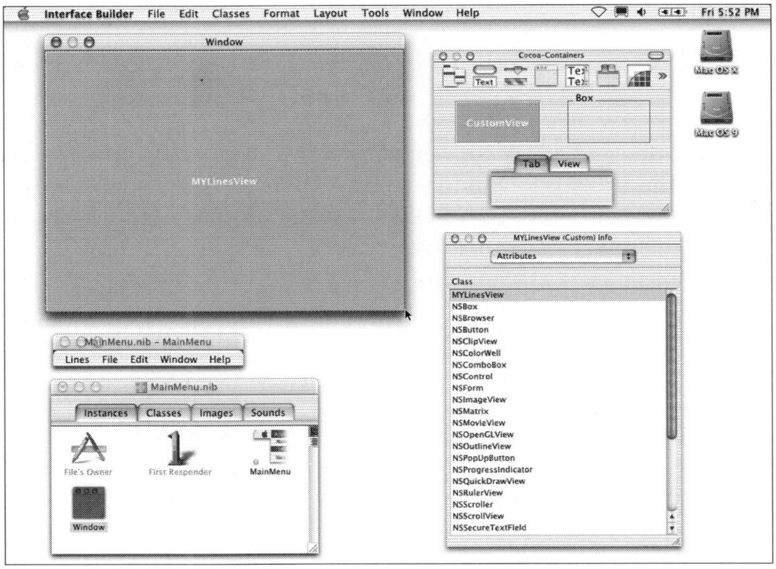

FIGURE 12.4 The custom view is configured to be an instance of `MYLinesView` and fills the entire content area of a window.

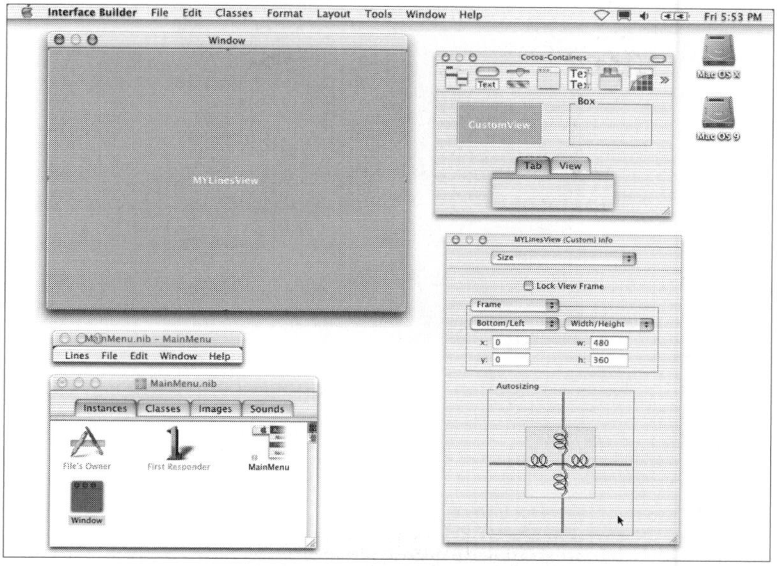

FIGURE 12.5 The `MYLinesView` instance is selected and the resize springs in the Size mode of Interface Builder's Show Info window are correctly configured.

Save the `MainMenu.nib` that you have edited in Interface Builder. At this point, the project can be built and run. Select Build and Run in Project Builder's Build menu. After a brief delay while the project is compiled, the new Lines application launches, and the window configured in Interface Builder to contain an instance of `MYLinesView` is displayed onscreen, as shown in Figure 12.6. The content of the window is black because the `MYLinesView` instance covers the entire area, and `MYLinesView` has been implemented to fill its bounds with the color black. If the window is resized, the `MYLinesView` instance grows and shrinks to fill all available space in the window's content area.

The code that implements `MYLinesView`'s `-drawRect:` method first sets the current color to black, and then fills the view's bounds rectangle with the current color. See Chapter 17, "Color," for more information about the `NSColor` class, and Chapter 8, "The Application Kit Framework Overview," for the description of a view's bounds. The view's bounds are obtained by calling the `-bounds` method inherited from the `NSView` class. The `NSRectFill()` function fills a rectangle with the current color.

This example, simple as it is, provides the basic framework for subclassing a view to perform custom drawing. It shows the bare minimum that must be done to draw custom graphics. The next examples expand on this foundation. The next section will add the promised ability to draw line segments.

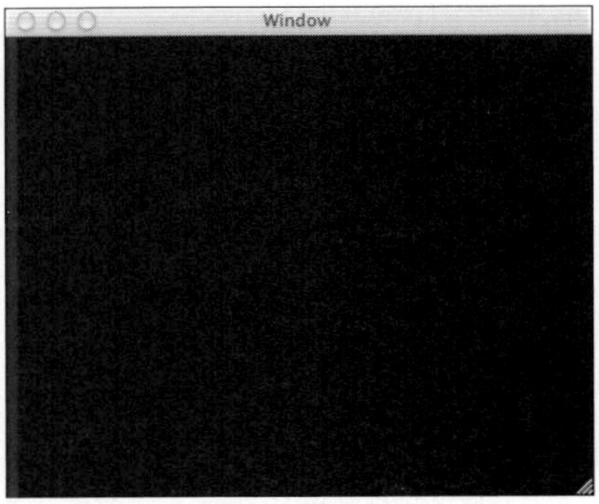

FIGURE 12.6 The Lines application displays a window containing a `MYLinesView` instance that draws a black-filled area.

Using the `NSBezierPath` Class

To draw something more than just colored rectangles, a bitmapped image must be rendered, or a Quartz path must be defined and subsequently stroked or filled. Because the sample application started in the previous section is supposed to draw random line segments, the latter option makes the most sense. Cocoa uses the `NSBezierPath` class to define and manipulate Quartz paths.

There are two ways to create an `NSBezierPath` instance. If an object is just temporary, using the `+bezierPath` method returns an autoreleased object with an empty path. Alternatively, for an object that will be kept around, use the standard Objective-C `+alloc`/`-init` pair to create a brand new, empty object.

After a path object is created, a path must be constructed. This tells the object where drawing takes place, but doesn't actually do any drawing. Next, the path is rendered. There are several options for how the path might be used in rendering. A single path object can be rendered multiple times in different ways. The next two sections of this chapter cover defining, and then rendering paths.

To get a jump start before going into these operations in depth, the example program that draws random line segments will be finished. When a developer has a feel for the basic work involved, the details of all the operations and options available can be discussed.

The first step is to obtain a path. For that, simply use the `+bezierPath` class method. The next step is to define the path. Because this path is a simple line segment, only two methods are needed. The starting point of the line is defined by using `-moveToPoint:`, and the end point is defined by using `-lineToPoint:`. Imagine someone with a pencil in hand. We tell them to lift the pencil off the paper and move to the start point, and then draw a line to the end point. However, there is still one step left, and that is to actually render the path. Use the `-stroke` method to do that. Stroking a path treats it as an outline and paints all the pixels that lay on the path as it is traced out, which is exactly what should be done to paint a series of line segments.

There is a little other code needed to set the drawing color to white, to create a loop to draw many line segments, and to randomly choose the coordinates of the start and end points. This code and the path code is displayed in this code listing:

```
File MYLinesView.m :

#import "MYLinesView.h"

#define NUM_LINES 50

@implementation MYLinesView

- (void)drawRect:(NSRect)aRect
{
    int i;
    NSRect bds = [self bounds];
    [[NSColor blackColor] set];
    NSRectFill(bds);
    [[NSColor whiteColor] set];
    for (i=0; i<NUM_LINES; i++) {
        NSPoint start = NSMakePoint(random() % (int)bds. size. width,
                random() % (int)bds. size. height);
        NSPoint end = NSMakePoint(random() % (int)bds. size. width,
                random() % (int)bds. size. height);
        NSBezierPath *line = [NSBezierPath bezierPath];
        [line moveToPoint:start];
        [line lineToPoint:end];
        [line stroke];
    }
}

@end
```

Try adding this code and running it. A window with a random collection of white line segments on a black background should be seen. If the window is resized, triggering a redraw, new line segments are chosen and drawn. (Try it!) This example provides a functional `NSView` subclass. The Paths example on `www.cocoaprogramming.net` contains the previous code as well as the code for many of the examples found throughout this chapter. Build it, run it, and then select the Simple Lines algorithm from the control panel, to see the code in action. It should look similar to Figure 12.7.

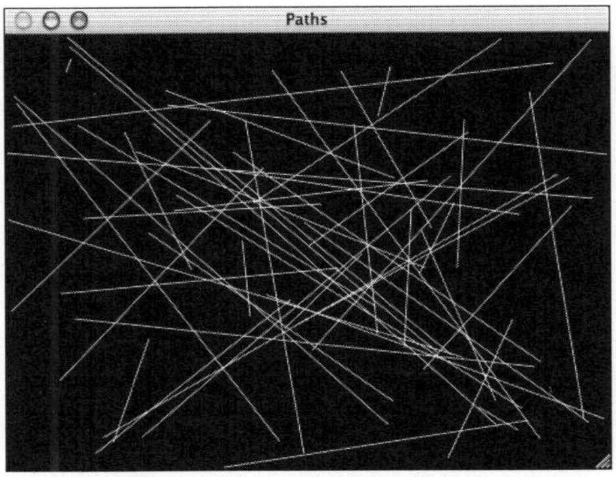

FIGURE 12.7 Select the Simple Lines algorithm from the control panel to see the described code in action.

The next section explores more of the details of constructing and rendering paths and `NSBezierPath` manipulation to gain familiarity with path objects.

Constructing a Path

After a developer has a path object, a graphics path can be constructed by appending a series of operations. The path object starts out empty, which means nothing would be drawn. Line, move, curve, and arc segments can be appended to the path to create an outline. Every operation begins at the current point. To understand the significance of the current point, imagine a pencil on a paper. Where the point rests at any given moment is the pencil. An operation, such as a line, only provides the destination of the pencil after the line has been drawn. The destination point becomes the new current point. Therefore, the line operation means "draw a line from the current point to this new point." Some operations require more than one point to be specified, but all implicity use the current point as the starting point for that operations segment. Each of the basic available operations that might be appended to a path is described in Table 12.2.

TABLE 12.2 Valid Path Operations

Operation	Purpose
Move	Moves the current point to a new location. ("Lift the pencil and move it to this new location.")
Line	Adds a line from the current point to a new location.

TABLE 12.2 Continued

Operation	Purpose
Curve	Adds a Bezier cubic spline from the current point to a new location. Two control points also need to be defined in addition to the destination.
Arc	Adds a circular arc and, if needed, a line segment.
Oval	Adds a complete oval or circle. Developer provides the desired bounding rectangle.
Glyph	Adds a glyph from a specified font at the current point.
Path	Adds another path.
Close	Adds a line segment from the current point to the starting point.

Inside the actual path object itself, all the different operations are stored as simple move, line, curve, and close operations. All the others can be built from these basic primitives.

Several of the operations in Table 12.2, namely move, line, and curve, also offer relative versions. The difference between absolute and relative operations is in how the points provided to the operation should be interpreted. In the absolute version, the points give a specific location on the drawing canvas. In the relative version, however, the points provided are interpreted to be relative to the current point. So, if the current point is (15, 35) and a line is drawn to (50, 40), the new current point is the endpoint of the line at (50, 40). If instead, the relative version is used with the same two points, the endpoint would be at (65, 75) instead of (50, 40) because the endpoint was specified relative to the starting point, which implies adding the new point's coordinates to those of the current point to calculate the endpoint.

Each of the path construction functions has corresponding methods that can be used with an instance of `NSBezierPath`. The following sections are a catalog of the methods and what they do.

Move to Point

There are two methods to change the current point to a new point.

```
- (void)moveToPoint:(NSPoint)point
- (void)relativeMoveToPoint:(NSPoint)point
```

Nothing is drawn between the original point and the new point. The result of this operation is analogous to lifting a pencil off the paper and moving it to a new location. With the relative version of the method, the new point is specified as if the current point were the origin. In mathematical terms, it is doing a vector addition instead of simply replacing the old value with the new. These methods correspond to the PostScript commands `moveto` and `rmoveto`, respectively.

The previous Lines example shows one way this method can be used. In the example, the first endpoint of each line segment is specified by moving to that point's location.

Line to Point

There are two methods to add a line segment to a path.

```
- (void)lineToPoint:(NSPoint)point
- (void)relativeLineToPoint:(NSPoint)point
```

The line segment starts at the current point and ends with the specified point. As with the move methods, the relative version specifies the new point relative to the current point, whereas the plain version, `-lineToPoint:`, does not. The current point is changed to the line segment's endpoint at the end of this operation. These methods correspond to the PostScript commands `lineto` and `rlineto`.

The Lines example shows one way this method can be used. In the example, several line segments are drawn by first moving to the start of the line segment with `-moveToPoint:`, and then using `-lineToPoint:` to specify the other end of the line segment.

Curve to Point

There are two methods for adding curved line segments to a path.

```
- (void)curveToPoint:(NSPoint)endPoint controlPoint1:(NSPoint)controlPoint1
        controlPoint2:(NSPoint)controlPoint2
- (void)relativeCurveToPoint:(NSPoint)endPoint controlPoint1:(NSPoint)controlPoint1
        controlPoint2:(NSPoint)controlPoint2
```

The curve starts at the current point and ends at the point specified by the `endPoint` parameter. The two `controlPoint` parameters specify Bezier control points that define exactly how the line segment curves. In simple terms, the curve starts out tangent to an invisible line from the start point to control point one and ends up tangent to an invisible line from control point two to the end point. Figure 12.8 shows this relationship. The exact quadratic equations that are used to calculate the curve can be found in any computer graphics text.

As with the line methods, the current point is moved to `endPoint` when this method is finished. These methods correspond to the PostScript commands `curveto` and `rcurveto`.

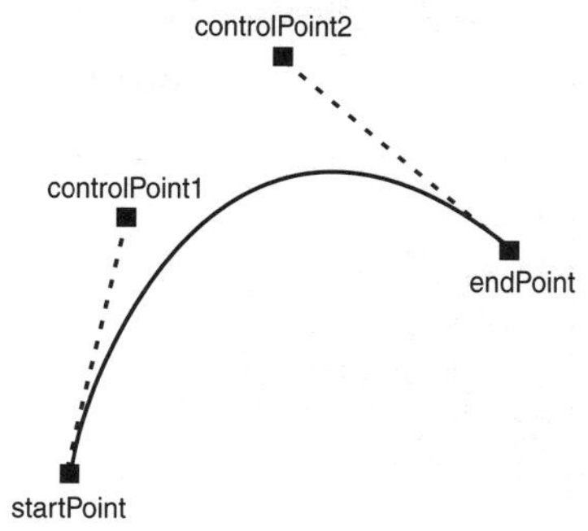

FIGURE 12.8 The curve starts out tangent to an invisible line from the start point to control point one and ends up tangent to an invisible line from control point two to the end point.

The Paths example contains code that draws random Bezier curves. Besides just drawing the curve itself, the code also draws a rectangle over each point: start, end, and both control points. Additionally, gray dashed lines are drawn between the endpoints of the curve and their associated control points. The output looks similar to the previous diagram. When running the example, choose the Bezier curves option from the control panel. Click Redraw several times to see a variety of examples. As more examples are viewed, the relationship between the points becomes much more clear. The code is as follows:

```
- (void)drawCurve
{
    NSBezierPath *curve = [NSBezierPath bezierPath];
    NSBezierPath *line1 = [NSBezierPath bezierPath];
    NSBezierPath *line2 = [NSBezierPath bezierPath];
    NSRect bds = [self bounds];
    NSPoint start = NSMakePoint(random() % (int)bds. size. width,
            random() % (int)bds. size. height);
    NSPoint end = NSMakePoint(random() % (int)bds. size. width,
            random() % (int)bds. size. height);
    NSPoint control1 = NSMakePoint(random() % (int)bds. size. width,
            random() % (int)bds. size. height);
    NSPoint control2 = NSMakePoint(random() % (int)bds. size. width,
            random() % (int)bds. size. height);
    float dash[1] = { 5. 0 };
    [[NSColor whiteColor] set];
    NSRectFill(bds);
    [[NSColor grayColor] set];
```

```
    // draw lines between the endpoints and their associated control points
    [line1 moveToPoint:start];
    [line1 lineToPoint:control1];
    [line1 setLineDash:dash count:1 phase: 0. 0];
    [line1 setLineWidth:2. 0];
    [line1 stroke];
    [line2 moveToPoint:end];
    [line2 lineToPoint:control2];
    [line2 setLineDash:dash count:1 phase: 0. 0];
    [line2 setLineWidth:2. 0];
    [line2 stroke];
    [[NSColor blackColor] set];
    // draw the curve itself
    [curve moveToPoint:start];
    [curve curveToPoint:end controlPoint1:control1 controlPoint2:control2];
    [curve setLineWidth:4. 0];
    [curve stroke];
    // draw rectangles around each point
    NSRectFill(NSMakeRect(start. x - 5. 0, start. y - 5. 0, 10. 0, 10. 0));
    NSRectFill(NSMakeRect(end. x - 5. 0, end. y - 5. 0, 10. 0, 10. 0));
    NSRectFill(NSMakeRect(control1. x - 5. 0, control1. y - 5. 0, 10. 0, 10. 0));
    NSRectFill(NSMakeRect(control2. x - 5. 0, control2. y - 5. 0, 10. 0, 10. 0));
}
```

Close Path

There is a special operation for drawing a line segment from the current point to the starting point of the most recent path segment. This is known as closing a path, so the method is named `-closePath`. It takes no arguments and returns nothing.

Every time a move operation is performed, a new path segment is started. Thus, the line segment that is added ends at the point specified by the most recent move operation and changes the current point to the same point. This operation is nearly always used when working with filled paths, but can also be used to complete the outline of a shape. The corresponding PostScript command is `closepath`.

NOTE

There is an important difference between adding a line segment with one of the previous line methods and using `-closePath`. For a continuous path, such as a circle, square, polygon, and so on, it is important to be sure that the start/end point of the loop is considered to be a corner as opposed to two separate line endings. This is accomplished by using `-closePath`. If `-closePath` is not used, an incorrect rendering of two line caps instead of a mitered corner will occur.

As an example of the difference between a path that uses -closePath and one that does not, consider the following code from the Paths example:

```
- (void)drawClosePathExample
{
    NSRect bds = [self bounds];
    NSBezierPath *leftTriangle = [NSBezierPath bezierPath];
    NSBezierPath *rightTriangle = [NSBezierPath bezierPath];
    double center = NSMidX(bds);
    double top = NSMaxY(bds) - 20.0;

    [[NSColor whiteColor] set];
    NSRectFill(bds);
    [[NSColor blackColor] set];
    // draw left triangle without a closepath
    [leftTriangle moveToPoint:NSMakePoint(20.0, 20.0)];
    [leftTriangle lineToPoint:NSMakePoint(center - 20.0, 20.0)];
    [leftTriangle lineToPoint:NSMakePoint(center * 0.5, top)];
    [leftTriangle lineToPoint:NSMakePoint(20.0, 20.0)];
    [leftTriangle setLineWidth:10.0];
    [leftTriangle setLineCapStyle:NSButtLineCapStyle];
    [leftTriangle setLineJoinStyle:NSRoundLineJoinStyle];
    [leftTriangle stroke];
    // draw right triangle with a closepath
    [rightTriangle moveToPoint:NSMakePoint(center + 20.0, 20.0)];
    [rightTriangle lineToPoint:NSMakePoint(NSMaxX(bds) - 20.0, 20.0)];
    [rightTriangle lineToPoint:NSMakePoint(center * 1.5, top)];
    [rightTriangle closePath];
    [rightTriangle setLineWidth:10.0];
    [rightTriangle setLineCapStyle:NSButtLineCapStyle];
    [rightTriangle setLineJoinStyle:NSRoundLineJoinStyle];
    [rightTriangle stroke];
}
```

When the previous code is run, the output looks like Figure 12.9. Note that the lower-left corner of the left triangle has a notch in it. Because the left triangle doesn't have a close path at the end, Quartz renders the end caps (square butts) instead of a line join (rounded corners in this case). This shows why -closePath should normally be used to finish defining the path of a closed polygon.

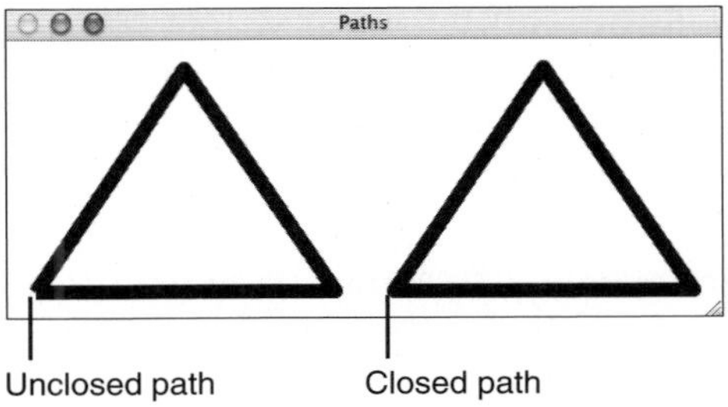

FIGURE 12.9 The difference between line cap without `-closePath` and line join with `-closePath` is shown.

Remove All Points

Use the `-removeAllPoints` method to completely erase the path stored inside of an `NSBezierPath` object and start over. After calling it, the path is empty. This method is handy when reusing an `NSBezierPath` to draw several different paths. It is similar, but not exactly the same as, the PostScript command `newpath`.

The most common reason to use `-removeAllPoints` is to avoid instantiating multiple `NSBezierPath` objects. Instead, the object can be reused by emptying out all the points, and then defining a new path. In the Paths example, the code for the `-drawClippedLines` method uses this technique. Each line is drawn, one at a time, by the same `NSBezierPath` object. The code for this method can be found in the rounded rectangle example at the end of the "Appending an Arc" section later in this chapter.

Appending a Rectangle

A convenience method is available to add a rectangular path to the current path.

```
- (void)appendBezierPathWithRect:(NSRect)rectangle
```

The effect of this method is the same as the following sequence of operations:

1. move to the origin of rectangle
2. line to the lower-right corner of rectangle
3. line to the upper-right corner of rectangle
4. line to the upper-left corner of rectangle
5. close path

Note that the rectangle is defined in a counterclockwise manner. If a clockwise rectangle is needed, the operations have to be explicitly performed by the developer instead of using this method. To quickly create a new path object that contains a rectangle, use the related class method `+bezierPathWithRect:` as a shortcut. It gives a new autoreleased path object that defines the rectangle as described previously.

Appending a Series of Lines

Another convenience method adds a continuous series of line segments to a path.

```
- (void)appendBezierPathWithPoints:(NSPointArray)points count:(int)count
```

This method adds a line operation to the current path for each point in the points array. If the path started out empty, the very first operation is a move instead of a line. If there is an array of points that define the corners of a polygon, this method can be used to add the polygon to the current path. The one caveat is that this method doesn't issue a close operation, so don't forget to close the path if necessary.

An example of drawing several lines with this method can be found in the Paths example. The Lines using points array option in the control panel activates this code:

```
- (void)drawLinesWithArray
{ // Single stroke method with points array
    int i;
    NSBezierPath *lines = [NSBezierPath bezierPath];
    NSRect bds = [self bounds];
    // clear the view to solid black background
    [[NSColor blackColor] set];
    NSRectFill(bds);
    // set up to draw with white
    [[NSColor whiteColor] set];
    // draw a bunch of random connected lines
    [lines moveToPoint:NSMakePoint(random() % (int)bds. size.
➥ width, random() % (int)bds. size. height)];
    for (i=0; i<numberOfLines; i++) {
        pointsArray[i] = NSMakePoint(random() % (int)bds. size.
➥ width, random() % (int)bds. size. height);
    }
    [lines appendBezierPathWithPoints:pointsArray count:numberOfLines];
    // render the lines all at once
    [lines stroke];
}
```

When this code is run, multiple random line segments are drawn. The end point of one line segment is the starting point for the next, so all the line segments are connected together. Figure 12.10 shows an example of the drawing produced by this code.

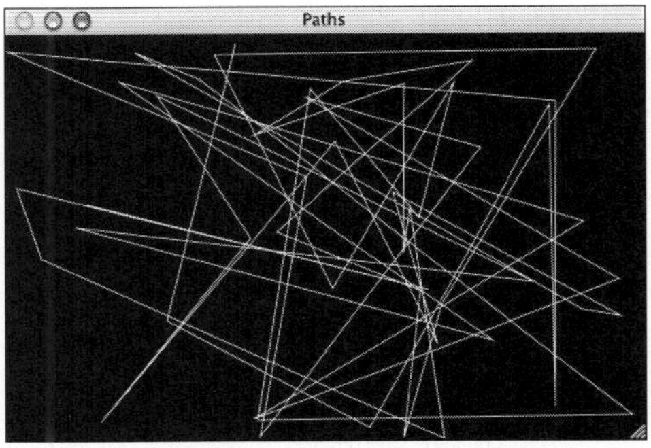

FIGURE 12.10 The end point of one line segment is the starting point for the next.

Appending an Oval

Curve to operations can be used to draw ovals and circles, given the right set of points. Rather than calculate all the points, it is easier to use a convenience function instead.

```
- (void)appendBezierPathWithOvalInRect:(NSRect)rect
```

This method adds a move and several curve segments to the path. The added shape is inscribed in the rectangle specified with `rect`. An oval is displayed for rectangular shapes and a circle is displayed if a square is specified. The circle or oval starts at the top center of the specified rectangle and continues counterclockwise around its circumference, finishing where it started.

To quickly create a brand new path object that contains an oval or a circle, use the related class method `+bezierPathWithOvalInRect:` as a shortcut. It returns a new autoreleased path object that defines an oval as described in the previous paragraph.

As an example of this method in action, take a look at the code for the `-drawDonuts` method in the Paths example. The code can be found in the "Strokes and Fills" section later in this chapter.

Appending an Arc

There are two convenience methods that add a circular arc to the path.

```
- (void)appendBezierPathWithArcWithCenter:(NSPoint)center radius:(float)radius
      startAngle:(float)startAngle endAngle:(float)endAngle
      clockwise:(BOOL)clockwise
- (void)appendBezierPathWithArcWithCenter:(NSPoint)center radius:(float)radius
      startAngle:(float)startAngle endAngle:(float)endAngle
```

The only difference between the two is in the clockwise parameter. If using the method that leaves it out, a counterclockwise direction for the arc is assumed. The arc itself is a portion of a circle with the specified radius and center point. The `startAngle` parameter determines, along with the `center` and `radius` parameters, the starting point of the arc. The arc will continue around the circle in the direction specified (clockwise or counterclockwise) until it reaches the point specified by the `endAngle` parameter. Both angles should be provided in degrees and not radians. These methods add a move and one or more curve operations to the path, leaving the current point at the end of the arc.

An example showing a few variations of this method call is found in the Paths example. The `-drawArcs` method, selected by choosing Arcs in the control panel, is coded like this:

```
- (void)drawArcs
{
    NSRect bds = [self bounds];
    NSPoint center = NSMakePoint(NSMidX(bds), NSMidY(bds));
    NSBezierPath *arc1 = [NSBezierPath bezierPath];
    NSBezierPath *arc2 = [NSBezierPath bezierPath];
    NSBezierPath *arc3 = [NSBezierPath bezierPath];
    NSBezierPath *arc4 = [NSBezierPath bezierPath];
    double radius = MIN(center.x, center.y) * 0.5 - 10.0;

    [[NSColor whiteColor] set];
    NSRectFill(bds);
    [[NSColor blackColor] set];
    // lower left
    [arc1 appendBezierPathWithArcWithCenter:
        NSMakePoint(center.x * 0.5, center.y * 0.5)
        radius:radius startAngle:0.0 endAngle:90.0];
    // upper left
    [arc2 appendBezierPathWithArcWithCenter:
        NSMakePoint(center.x * 0.5, center.y * 1.5)
        radius:radius startAngle:0.0 endAngle:90.0 clockwise:NO];
```

```
    // lower right
    [arc3 appendBezierPathWithArcWithCenter:
        NSMakePoint(center. x * 1. 5, center. y * 0. 5)
        radius:radius startAngle:0. 0 endAngle:90. 0 clockwise:YES];
    // upper right
    [arc4 appendBezierPathWithArcWithCenter:
        NSMakePoint(center. x * 1. 5, center. y * 1. 5)
        radius:radius startAngle:0. 0 endAngle:90. 0 clockwise:YES];
    [arc2 closePath];
    [arc4 closePath];
    [arc1 stroke];
    [arc2 stroke];
    [arc3 stroke];
    [arc4 stroke];
}
```

When this code is run, Figure 12.11 shows the drawing that is produced.

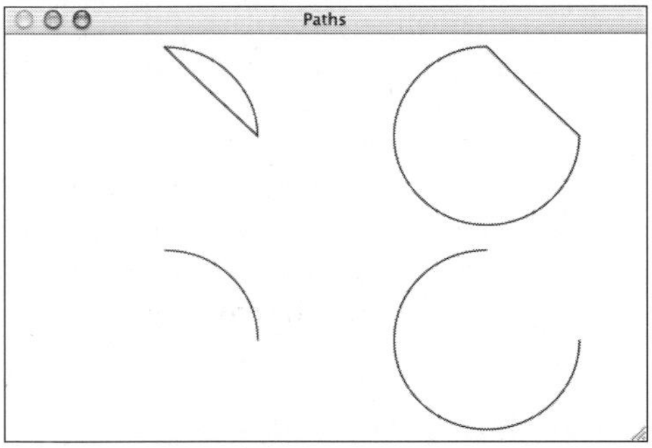

FIGURE 12.11 When the code described in the text is run, this is the drawing that is produced.

Another convenience method is available for drawing an arc with an attached line segment.

```
- (void)appendBezierPathWithArcFromPoint:(NSPoint)point1
        toPoint:(NSPoint)point2 radius:(float)radius
```

This method makes it easier to add rounded corners to a polygon. It adds a line segment and the arc of a circle to the path. Two tangent lines bound the circle from which the arc is taken—one from the current point to `point1` and the other from `point1` to `point2`. To uniquely specify the circle, it also uses the specified `radius`.

The line segment that is added to the path runs from the current point to where the tangent line from the current point to `point1` intersects the circle. The arc goes from that point to the point where the tangent from `point1` to `point2` intersects the circle. The current point is left at the arc's end point. Figure 12.11 should help visualize this; it sounds far more complex than it really is. The black line in Figure 12.12 shows what is actually added to the path object.

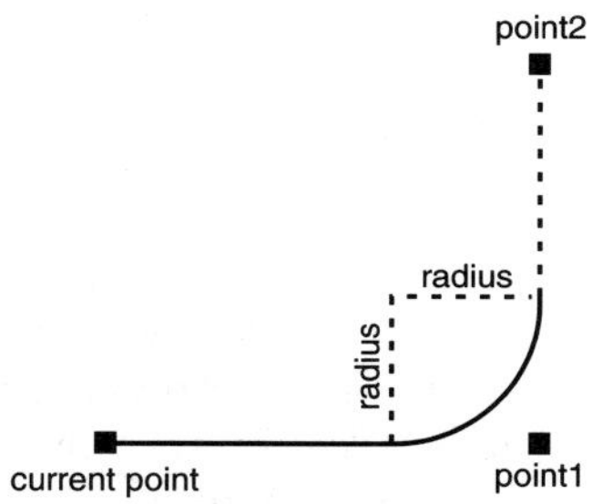

FIGURE 12.12 The black line shows what is actually added to the path object.

Because this operation relies on the existence of a current point, this method can't be used on an empty path or an exception is raised. A move operation must be used to set the current point first. This operation is similar to the PostScript `arcto` operator.

As an example of how you might use this method to build a polygon with rounded corners, draw a rectangle with rounded corners. Start at the midpoint of the top edge of the rectangle and work around the rectangle in a clockwise direction. Here is some code you can use for this example:

```
File RoundedRect. h :

#import <Cocoa/Cocoa. h>

@interface NSBezierPath(RoundedRect)

- (void)appendBezierPathWithRoundedRectangle:(NSRect)aRect
        withRadius:(float)radius;

@end
```

```
File RoundedRect. m :

#import "RoundedRect. h"

@implementation NSBezierPath(RoundedRect)

- (void)appendBezierPathWithRoundedRectangle:(NSRect)aRect
        withRadius:(float)radius
{
    NSPoint topMid = NSMakePoint(NSMidX(aRect), NSMaxY(aRect));
    NSPoint topLeft = NSMakePoint(NSMinX(aRect), NSMaxY(aRect));
    NSPoint topRight = NSMakePoint(NSMaxX(aRect), NSMaxY(aRect));
    NSPoint bottomRight = NSMakePoint(NSMaxX(aRect), NSMinY(aRect));
        [self moveToPoint:topMid];
    [self appendBezierPathWithArcFromPoint:topLeft toPoint:aRect.origin
            radius:radius];
    [self appendBezierPathWithArcFromPoint:aRect.origin toPoint:bottomRight
            radius:radius];
    [self appendBezierPathWithArcFromPoint:bottomRight toPoint:topRight
            radius:radius];
    [self appendBezierPathWithArcFromPoint:topRight toPoint:topLeft
            radius:radius];
    [self closePath];
}

@end
```

The previous method is defined as an Objective-C category of `NSBezierPath`. It could then be used like any other method of `NSBezierPath`. Simply call it with an `NSRect` defining the bounds of the rectangle and a radius for the curvature of the corners and it appends an appropriate rounded rectangle to the path. Note that if the rectangle's width or height is less than twice the radius, visual artifacts in the path are present as the arcs begin to overlap. Don't forget to stroke or fill the path to actually have drawing done; this sample code simply adds to the path definition.

To see this example code in action, look at the Paths example source code. The clipped lines option uses the rounded rectangle category to draw the outline of a rectangle with rounded corners and define a clipping area. No drawing takes place outside of the clipping area outlined by the rounded rectangle. The onscreen drawing is accomplished by calling this method from the `NSView's` `-drawRect:` method:

```
- (void)drawClippedLines
{ // Draw lots of random line segments, clipped to a rounded rect
    int i;
    NSBezierPath *line = [NSBezierPath bezierPath];
    NSBezierPath *rect = [NSBezierPath bezierPath];
    NSRect bds = [self bounds];
    // clear the view to solid black background
    [[NSColor blackColor] set];
    NSRectFill(bds);
    // set up to draw with white
    [[NSColor whiteColor] set];
    // save the current clipping path
    [[NSGraphicsContext currentContext] saveGraphicsState];
    // set up a new clipping path — a rect with rounded corners
    [rect appendBezierPathWithRoundedRectangle:NSInsetRect(bds, 20.0, 20.0)
            withRadius:30.0];
    [rect addClip];
    // draw a bunch of random lines inside the new clipped area
    for (i=0; i<numberOfLines; i++) {
        // get random start and end points
        NSPoint start = NSMakePoint(random() % (int)bds.size.width,
                random() % (int)bds.size.height);
        NSPoint end = NSMakePoint(random() % (int)bds.size.width,
                random() % (int)bds.size.height);
        [line removeAllPoints];
        // draw a line segment
        [line moveToPoint:start];
        [line lineToPoint:end];
        [line stroke];
    }
    // restore the original clipping path
    [[NSGraphicsContext currentContext] restoreGraphicsState];
    // now take the rect used as the path and draw it with a little
    // bit wider line width so that we have a nice looking frame
    [rect setLineWidth:2.0];
    [rect stroke];
}
```

When this code is run, output similar to Figure 12.13 is created.

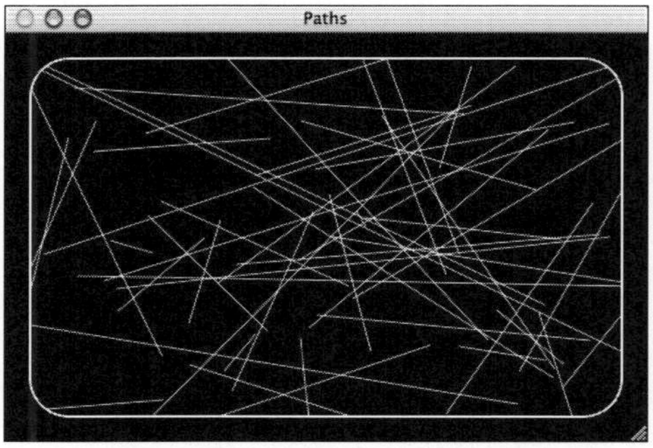

FIGURE 12.13 The -drawClippedLines method produces output similar to this.

```
- (void)appendBezierPath:(NSBezierPath *)path;
```

This method can be used to append the path defined by one NSBezierPath object to another. This can be used to build up complex paths by appending several path objects together.

The previous methods are the primary methods used to construct a path using the NSBezierPath class. There are also several other NSBezierPath methods that enable you to take individual character glyphs from the font of your choice and add them to a path. Because these methods are somewhat complex, a whole section of this chapter devoted to them. See "NSBezierPath and Glyphs" in Chapter 14 to learn how to use these methods.

Rendering a Path

When a path has been defined, it is ready to be rendered. Rendering is very easy because there are only a few ways to actually render the path: stroke, fill, or clip. Clip, the third operation, doesn't actually do drawing, but instead restricts further drawing.

Strokes and Fills

Stroking a path is similar to taking a paintbrush and using it to trace out the path that has been defined. In other words, this renders the outline of the shape the path defines. The star and donut shapes in Figure 12.14 are examples of stroked paths. To stroke a path, simply send it a -stroke message. No arguments are required.

Filling is like using the path as a wall, while pouring paint into the area enclosed by the path. A filled path gives a solid shape instead of an outline. To fill a path, send it a -fill message. There are no arguments.

There is a wrinkle with fills, however. Suppose there is a shape such as a five-pointed star, drawn with the outline at the left in Figure 12.14. Further suppose there are multiple paths defined in a shape that forms something of a donut shape, as in the shape to the right of the star.

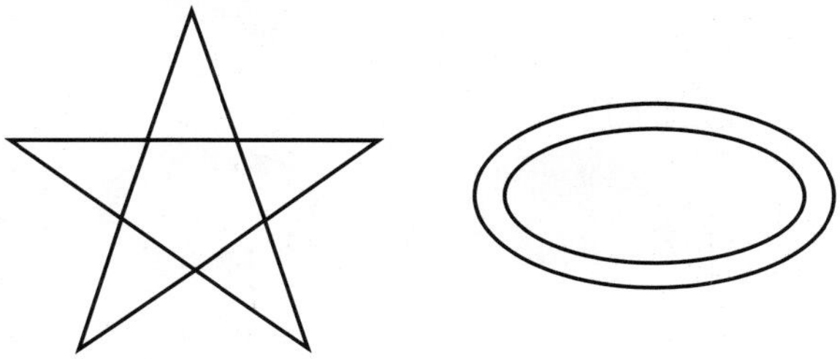

FIGURE 12.14 The star and donut shapes are examples of stroked paths.

When the star is filled, should the pentagon in the center be filled or not? What about the center of the donut, should it be filled? The answer depends on application. You would probably want to fill the whole star, but not the center of the donut. This is where the winding rule comes in. The winding rule determines how these situations should be handled. These situations do happen more often than you might think, especially when handling text.

Before issuing the fill command, a developer probably wants to specify a winding rule to get the fill behavior required. The enumerated type `NSWindingRule` defines two constants to represent the available winding-rule algorithms. The first, `NSNonZeroWindingRule`, is the default winding rule and represents the case where the center of the star and donut are filled in. The second is `NSEvenOddWindingRule`. With the even/odd rule, the filled star or donut would have a nonfilled hole in the middle. See Figure 12.15 for examples of each rule.

The winding rule for a particular path can be changed by using the `-setWindingRule:` method. The single parameter should be one of the constants (`NSNonZeroWindingRule` or `NSEvenOddWindingRule`). A developer can find out which rule is used by an `NSBezierPath` instance by querying with the `-windingRule` method, which returns one of these two values. Additionally, the default winding rule can be queried and changed by using the `NSBezierPath` class methods `+defaultWindingRule` and `+setDefaultWindingRule:`.

To demonstrate how the different rules can be used, the Paths example contains the code needed to draw the stars and donuts shown in Figures 12.14 and 12.15.

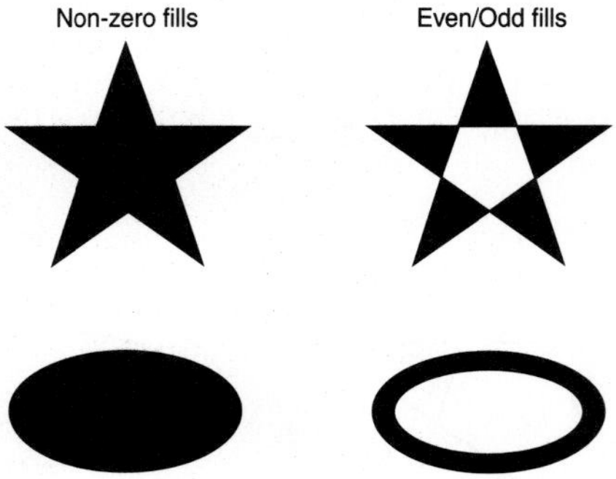

FIGURE 12.15 Using different winding rules produces the pictured fill behaviors.

To define the various ovals the code to draw the donuts uses `-appendBezierPathWithOvalInRect:`. Each oval is defined separately and the path object is emptied out after each donut is rendered. (The next chunk of example code, to draw the stars, does a better job of reusing the path data.) This example shows the results of a stroke, a fill without specifying a particular winding rule (the default winding rule) and each of the winding rules supported by Quartz (nonzero and even-odd). As in the rounded-rectangle example shown previously, this method is called from the `-drawRect:` method of the `NSView` subclass when it is time to do the drawing:

```
- (void)drawDonuts
{
// Draw four different ovals
//   2 non zero      3 even/odd
//   1 stroked       4 default winding
         NSBezierPath *path = [NSBezierPath bezierPath];
    NSRect bds = [self bounds];
    // divide the view into four rectangles
    NSRect r1 = NSMakeRect(bds. origin. x, bds. origin. y,
            bds. size. width / 2. 0, bds. size. height / 2. 0);
    NSRect r2 = NSMakeRect(bds. origin. x, NSMidY(bds),
            bds. size. width / 2. 0, bds. size. height / 2. 0);
    NSRect r3 = NSMakeRect(NSMidX(bds), NSMidY(bds),
            bds. size. width / 2. 0, bds. size. height / 2. 0);
    NSRect r4 = NSMakeRect(NSMidX(bds), bds. origin. y,
            bds. size. width / 2. 0, bds. size. height / 2. 0);
```

```
    // clear the view to solid white background
    [[NSColor whiteColor] set];
    NSRectFill(bds);
    // set up drawing parameters — draw black with linewidth of 2. 0
    [[NSColor blackColor] set];
    [path setLineWidth:2. 0];
    // Draw lower left donut (stroked)
    [path appendBezierPathWithOvalInRect:NSInsetRect(r1, 10. 0, 10. 0)];
    [path appendBezierPathWithOvalInRect:NSInsetRect(r1, 25. 0, 25. 0)];
    [path stroke];
    // draw lower right donut (default wind)
    [path removeAllPoints];
        [path setWindingRule:[NSBezierPath defaultWindingRule]];
    [path appendBezierPathWithOvalInRect:NSInsetRect(r4, 10. 0, 10. 0)];
    [path appendBezierPathWithOvalInRect:NSInsetRect(r4, 25. 0, 25. 0)];
    [path fill];
    // draw upper right donut (even/odd)
    [path removeAllPoints];
    [path setWindingRule:NSEvenOddWindingRule];
    [path appendBezierPathWithOvalInRect:NSInsetRect(r3, 10. 0, 10. 0)];
    [path appendBezierPathWithOvalInRect:NSInsetRect(r3, 25. 0, 25. 0)];
    [path fill];
    // draw upper left donut (non-zero)
    [path removeAllPoints];
    [path setWindingRule:NSNonZeroWindingRule];
    [path appendBezierPathWithOvalInRect:NSInsetRect(r2, 10. 0, 10. 0)];
    [path appendBezierPathWithOvalInRect:NSInsetRect(r2, 25. 0, 25. 0)];
    [path fill];
}
```

The donuts code produces the output shown in Figure 12.16 when the Paths application is run and Donuts is chosen on the control panel.

A similar approach to the one used with the donuts is used to draw the stars. However, rather than defining a new path for each star, a single `NSBezierPath` is defined and reused for each star. To accomplish this and cause each star to be drawn at a different location, the path is translated using an `NSAffineTransform` object. (This object is discussed in Chapter 13.) The translation operation causes the path to be drawn at a different location without affecting its size or shape. Except for this difference, the code is much like the donut drawing code shown previously:

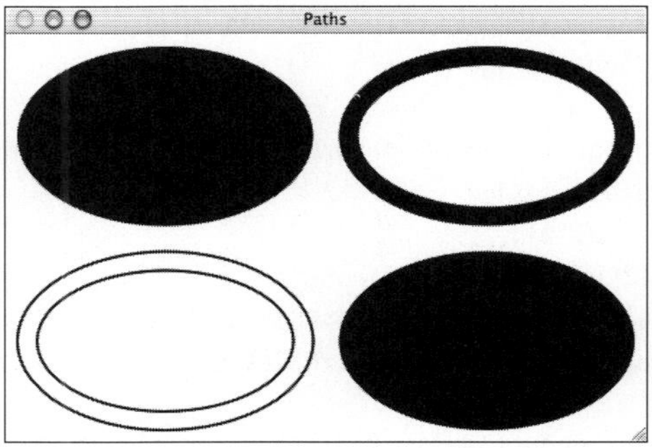

FIGURE 12.16 The pictured output is produced by the Paths example when Donuts is chosen on the control panel.

```
- (void)drawStars
{
// Draw four different stars
//   2 non zero      3 even/odd
//   1 stroked       4 default winding
    NSGraphicsContext *currentContext = [NSGraphicsContext currentContext];
    NSBezierPath *path = [NSBezierPath bezierPath];
    NSAffineTransform *transform = nil;
    NSRect bds = [self bounds];
    // divide the view into four rectangles
    NSRect r1 = NSMakeRect(bds. origin. x, bds. origin. y,
            bds. size. width / 2. 0, bds. size. height / 2. 0);
    NSRect r2 = NSMakeRect(bds. origin. x, NSMidY(bds),
            bds. size. width / 2. 0, bds. size. height / 2. 0);
    NSRect r3 = NSMakeRect(NSMidX(bds), NSMidY(bds),
            bds. size. width / 2. 0, bds. size. height / 2. 0);
    NSRect r4 = NSMakeRect(NSMidX(bds), bds. origin. y,
            bds. size. width / 2. 0, bds. size. height / 2. 0);

    // clear the view to a white background
    [[NSColor whiteColor] set];
    NSRectFill(bds);

    // set the drawing color to black and the line width to 2. 0
    [[NSColor blackColor] set];
    [path setLineWidth:2. 0];
```

```
    // define the star's path
    [path moveToPoint:NSMakePoint(NSMinX(r1) + 40. 0, NSMinY(r1) + 20. 0)];
    [path lineToPoint:NSMakePoint(NSMidX(r1), NSMaxY(r1) - 20. 0)];
    [path lineToPoint:NSMakePoint(NSMaxX(r1) - 40. 0, NSMinY(r1) + 20. 0)];
    [path lineToPoint:NSMakePoint(NSMinX(r1) + 20. 0, NSMaxY(r1) - 50. 0)];
    [path lineToPoint:NSMakePoint(NSMaxX(r1) - 20. 0, NSMaxY(r1) - 50. 0)];
    [path closePath];

    // stroke the star in r1.
    [path stroke];

    // do r4 — default winding rule
        [path setWindingRule:[NSBezierPath defaultWindingRule]];
    transform = [NSAffineTransform transform];
    [transform translateXBy:r4. origin. x yBy:r4. origin. y];
    [currentContext saveGraphicsState];
    [transform concat];
    [path fill];
    [currentContext restoreGraphicsState];

    // do r3 — even/odd winding rule
    [path setWindingRule:NSEvenOddWindingRule];
    transform = [NSAffineTransform transform];
    [transform translateXBy:r3. origin. x yBy:r3. origin. y];
    [currentContext saveGraphicsState];
    [transform concat];
    [path fill];
        [currentContext restoreGraphicsState];

    // do r2 — non-zero winding rule
    [path setWindingRule:NSNonZeroWindingRule];
    transform = [NSAffineTransform transform];
    [transform translateXBy:r2. origin. x yBy:r2. origin. y];
    [currentContext saveGraphicsState];
    [transform concat];
    [path fill];
        [currentContext restoreGraphicsState];
}
```

The output of the stars code is shown in Figure 12.17.

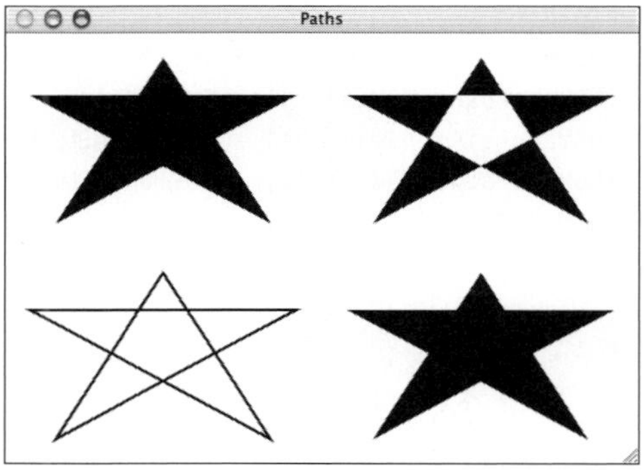

FIGURE 12.17 The output of the stars code looks like this.

Winding Rules

If a developer isn't familiar with PostScript or 2D graphics algorithms, she might wonder where the winding rule names come from or even why they are called winding rules. If you look at the paths used in the previous example (star and donut), you will note that the paths are closed. It could be said that the path winds around the area that it encloses. A winding rule is so named because it uses information about the path's winding to determine whether a pixel is in a fill area.

To simplify the result, move from outside of the figure toward its center and count how many winds have been passed through, starting with zero outside of the path. In the nonzero winding rule, whenever this count is nonzero, it is inside the object, therefore the fill paints the pixels. This is a very inclusive fill, and never has holes in it.

The complete rule for nonzero is slightly more complex than just counting path crossings. If the path section crossed is moving from left to right, add one to the crossing count. Conversely, subtract one from the count if the path segment moves from right to left. With the donut graphic, both ovals are drawn in the same direction. If the inner oval was drawn in the opposite direction from the outer oval, both the nonzero and even-odd rules would produce the same results.

In the even-odd case, note that one is in the filled area after crossing over the path once. Cross over again, to an area with count 2 in the center of the path, and one is in a nonfilled area. The generalization of this rule is that a section of the enclosed area is filled when the count is an odd number and not filled when the count is an even number.

NOTE

You might be interested to know that there are other types of winding rules as well, though Quartz and Cocoa only support the two rules described previously. To learn more about winding rules, consult a standard text on 2D graphics. OpenGL references might also be of interest because OpenGL supports some other winding rules, too.

Clipping

Now that strokes and fills are covered, there remains one other way to make use of a path—clipping. Clipping is a means of controlling where on the screen drawing is allowed to take place. For example, when `NSView's -drawRects:` method is called, Cocoa has already set up clipping so that all drawing is kept within the boundaries of the view. Any attempt to draw outside the view is simply thrown away by Quartz. No error is returned; the drawing simply doesn't appear on the screen.

This can be handy because a developer doesn't have to worry about whether he is drawing in a legal area. Just draw and only the parts that aren't clipped appear on the screen. This makes it easier for the developer when there are paths that are partly inside the clipping area and partly outside because he don't have to worry about what to draw and what not to draw. Quartz figures it out.

NOTE

If a path is completely outside the clipping area, then there's little point in sending it to Quartz. Some rendering time can be saved by not attempting to draw it at all. For more techniques to reduce drawing time see the section "Optimizing Drawing" in Chapter 13.

Quartz is not limited to just clipping by rectangles, however. Any arbitrary path can be used to define a clipping area. By sending the `-addClip` message to an `NSBezierPath` instance, it becomes a new clipping path. This can be used for some interesting special effects. As an example, small text can be used as a fill pattern for a headline or other large text. Using the large text's outline as the clipping path, and then rendering the smaller text accomplishes this. Only the smaller text that is actually inside the larger text is drawn. The parts of the smaller text that fall outside the outline are not drawn. The rounded-rectangle example uses the `-addClip` method to restrict drawing to be within the bounds of a rectangle with rounded corners.

The `-addClip` method actually intersects the path with the current clipping path, as opposed to replacing the clipping path. This means that using this method either leaves the current clipping unchanged or it makes the clipping more restrictive than it was already. It will not expand the clipping area.

Because the clipping area can't be expanded, you might wonder what to do to undo clipping changes before doing later drawing that shouldn't be clipped in the same way. The clipping area itself is a part of the current graphics context. As described in the section "Using `NSGraphicsContext`," in Chapter 13, the current context can be saved before changing the clipping area. By later restoring the context, any clipping changes that happened after the save can be undone. This is the primary approach that should be used to increase the clipping area back to what it was before clipping was altered.

Using a path for clipping respects the same winding rules as filling the path. After the `-addClip` operation, all future drawing only appears in the areas that would have been filled in had the path been sent a `-fill` message instead. Thus, if the star path were added to the current context's clipping, the winding rule would determine whether future drawing would be restricted to the whole outline of the star or just the star's points, excluding the center of the star.

Using a path for clipping does not change the path data in the `NSBezierPath` object. Therefore, the path can still be used later for fills or other operations as needed. To have the outline of the larger text drawn boldly, using the text within the earlier text example, the best approach is to follow these steps:

1. save the graphics context
2. add the large letters to the clipping path
3. draw the small letters
4. restore the graphics context
5. stroke the large letters

This assures that the smaller letters don't overwrite the outlines of the larger letters, and at the same time prevents the larger letter's outline from being restricted by the clipping path. Saving and restoring the graphics context is done with the `NSGraphicsContext` object, which is described in detail in Chapter 13.

A simpler example of this general technique is found in the rounded-rectangle example discussed previously in the "Appending an arc" section of this chapter. In the example, a rounded rectangle is used as a clip area for many random line segments. When it comes time to actually stroke the rounded rectangle itself, however, the clipping area needs to be undone. This is because the rounded rectangle is to be stroked with a line width of 2.0, half of that lies outside of the clipping area. To avoid clipping part of the outline, the graphics context is restored to its preclip state.

There is one other way to use an NSBezierPath to alter the Quartz graphic context's clipping path, but it is rather dangerous. By sending the -setClip method to a path instance it replaces the current clipping path with the path defined by the NSBezierPath. This is dangerous because it throws away the current clipping path entirely. That means the clipping area could be increased to include area outside the view's bounds. You still can't draw outside the window, but instead could risk scribbling all over inside the window. Drawing outside the view's bounds has all kinds of nasty side effects and can leave some ugly artifacts, so don't do it! If using this method, be sure to save the graphics context beforehand and restore the graphics context as soon as possible afterwards.

Drawing Shortcuts: Rectangle Functions and More

The NSBezierPath class object provides a few shortcut methods that can be used to define and render common paths without the tedium of instantiating a new object and sending all the individual method calls. The following self-explanatory methods can all be sent to the NSBezierPath class object as shortcuts:

```
+ (void)fillRect:(NSRect)rect;
+ (void)strokeRect:(NSRect)rect;
+ (void)clipRect:(NSRect)rect;
+ (void)strokeLineFromPoint:(NSPoint)point1 toPoint:(NSPoint)point2;
```

For example, to draw a filled rectangle:

```
[NSBezierPath fillRect:NSMakeRect(10.0, 10.0, 100.0, 100.0)];
```

This would draw a rectangle of dimensions 100×100 with the lower-left corner at (10.0, 10.0). It would be rendered as a filled rectangle in the current drawing color. The +strokeRect: method renders a rectangular outline with the line width and other parameters taken from the current settings in the active graphics context.

There are also several functions that can be used to deal with rectangles. The next three topics discuss these functions. The Rectangles example on the www.cocoaprogramming.net Web site shows most of the rectangle functions in action.

Basic Rectangle Functions

Because it can be rather tedious to create and use NSBezierPath for all drawing, Cocoa provides several functions that create a path and render it, all with a single function call. These specialized function calls are generally for drawing and manipulating rectangles and are highly optimized. In other words, for the best drawing performance, try to use these functions whenever they make sense. It should be noted that if using Core Graphics calls directly, many of these functions could cause settings within the graphics context (such as line width) to be changed. If a developer doesn't expect and account for this, seemingly mysterious bugs in rendering can occur.

The first set of functions is for drawing filled rectangles on the screen. Because rectangular paths can be highly optimized, these functions typically provide a significant speed boost over using `NSBezierPath`. With these functions a single rectangle can be filled in the simplest case, to filling a list of rectangles, each with a different color, using a particular compositing operator in the most complex case. The name of each function describes what it does well enough that little documentation is required, so the following descriptions are brief. The first function has already been used quite a bit in this chapter:

```
void NSRectFill(NSRect aRect);
```

This function, `NSRectFill()`, is the simplest of the rectangle rendering functions. Simply pass it an `NSRect` and that rectangle will be rendered, filled with whatever color is the current color in the graphics context.

```
void NSRectFillList(const NSRect *rects, int count);
```

If there is more than one rectangle to fill, then considerable function call and graphics context setup overhead can be saved by passing all the rectangles in a single function call. This is done with the `NSRectFillList()` call. Instead of passing a single `NSRect`, pass a pointer to an array of `NSRect` structures. The second parameter, `count`, tells the functions how many rectangles are in the array. It is very important that the count parameter be correct to prevent memory overruns. An example showing how to use this function is found later in the "Drawing Points and Rectangles" section in Chapter 13.

```
void NSRectFillListWithGrays(const NSRect *rects, const float *grays, int num);
void NSRectFillListWithColors(const NSRect *rects, NSColor **colors, int num);
```

By using `NSRectFillListWithGrays()` or `NSRectFillListWithColors()` each rectangle is rendered with a different shade of gray or different color. In the case of grayscale, the grays parameter is a pointer to an array of floating-point numbers in the range of 0.0 to 1.0. A 0.0 indicates black and a 1.0 indicates white. Numbers in between are varying shades of gray. For color, the `colors` parameter is a pointer to an array of pointers to `NSColor` objects. The remaining parameters, `rects` and `num`, are the same as for `NSRectFillList()`.

```
void NSRectFillUsingOperation(NSRect aRect, NSCompositingOperation op);
void NSRectFillListUsingOperation(const NSRect *rects, int count,
        NSCompositingOperation op);
```

```
void NSRectFillListWithColorsUsingOperation(const NSRect *rects,
        NSColor **colors, int num, NSCompositingOperation op);
```

The filled rectangle functions described previously in this section all assume the use of a Source Over-compositing operation. If using a specific operation that is different, use one of the `*UsingOperation()` functions. Each one works as its previous counterpart, simply adding the `op` parameter that specifies a particular compositing operation.

Three functions are available to draw a rectangular outline instead of a filled rectangle. They are

```
void NSFrameRect(NSRect aRect);
void NSFrameRectWithWidth(NSRect aRect, float frameWidth);
void NSFrameRectWithWidthUsingOperation(NSRect aRect, float frameWidth,
       NSCompositingOperation op);
```

The first function, `NSFrameRect()`, simply draws the specified rectangular frame, using color, line width, and so on as found in the current graphics context. The second function adds the capability to choose a specific line width, specified in dots per inch. The last function further adds the capability to choose a specific compositing operation.

Finally, there are two functions for changing the current clipping region:

```
void NSRectClip(NSRect aRect);
void NSRectClipList(const NSRect *rects, int count);
```

Both of these functions are called exactly like their `NSRectFill()` and `NSRectFillList()` counterparts. The difference, of course, is that instead of rendering filled rectangles, these functions further tighten the graphic context's existing clipping region.

Other Rectangle Functions

There are two functions for erasing rectangular regions.

```
void NSEraseRect(NSRect aRect);
void NSDrawWindowBackground(NSRect aRect);
```

The `NSEraseRect()` function paints the area defined by the `aRect` parameter with white, taking into account the current clipping path. Because a printed page is white, painting with white is akin to erasing the region. This function is functionally equivalent to this code:

```
[[NSColor whiteColor] set];
NSRectFill(NSRect aRect);
```

The `NSDrawWindowBackground()` function works like `NSEraseRect()` except that the area is painted with the default window background color or pattern. In Mac OS X, this is the horizontal striped pattern seen on most Aqua windows. Equivalent code would be

```
[[NSColor windowBackgroundColor] set];
NSRectFill(NSRect aRect);
```

Both `NSDrawWindowBackground()` and `NSEraseRect()` are handy shortcuts for filling rectangular areas with commonly used colors.

```
NSRect NSDrawTiledRects(NSRect boundsRect, NSRect clipRect,
        const NSRectEdge *sides, const float *grays, int count);
NSRect NSDrawColorTiledRects(NSRect boundsRect, NSRect clipRect,
        const NSRectEdge *sides, NSColor **colors, int count);
```

Both of these functions are used to paint bordered rectangular areas. Depending on how they are called, the result can look like a raised button, a recessed bezel, a basic border, or something else entirely. For example, `NSDrawColorTiledRects()` is used by the Application Kit to draw everything in `NSTextField` controls except for the text itself. Both functions are basically the same; the only difference is that one uses a list of floating point grayscale values (0.0 for black to 1.0 for white) for its drawing and the other uses a list of `NSColor` instances.

The tiled rectangle functions work by painting successive 1.0 point slices from the edge of the rectangular area being painted (remember that 1.0 point equals 1.0 pixel when drawing to the screen). Each time a slice is taken, the next slice is taken from the remaining area left to be painted. Any number of slices can be taken and it is possible to specify which side of the rectangle should be used for each slice as well as what color it should be painted. When all the slices have been taken, the remaining unpainted rectangle is returned. That returned rectangle can be filled if the bezel or border is to have an opaque background. If it is discarded, that area remains untouched.

The first parameter, `aRect`, specifies the area to be painted. Because this function is primarily meant to be used to create the border of an `NSView` subclass, usually `aRect` is the bounds rectangle of the view. The second parameter, `clipRect`, can be used to limit the actual painting to a particular area of `aRect`. Most often, it is equal to `aRect` or covers a larger area so that painting isn't restricted in any way.

The third and fourth parameters specify how the slices should be taken and whether each should have the same number of elements. That number of elements should be passed as the fifth parameter, count. The sides parameter is an array of NSRectEdge values. An NSRectEdge can be one of four predefined values: NSMinXEdge, NSMaxXEdge, NSMinYEdge, and NSMaxYEdge. The fourth parameter is either an array of floating-point–grayscale values or an array of pointers to NSColor instances. Because most drawing in Aqua is not grayscale, typically the color version of the tiled-rectangle function is used.

The easiest way to visualize what happens when these functions are called is to actually see an example. It also makes it easier to see how to set up the parameters. The Rectangles example demonstrates this function with the following code:

```
NSGraphicsContext *currentContext = [NSGraphicsContext currentContext];
NSAffineTransform *transform = [NSAffineTransform transform];
NSRect newBds = NSMakeRect(0. 0, 0. 0, bds. size. width / 4,
        bds. size. height / 4);
NSRectEdge sides[] = { NSMaxYEdge, NSMaxXEdge, NSMaxYEdge,
        NSMinXEdge, NSMinYEdge, NSMaxXEdge };
NSRect inside;
NSColor *colors[6];
colors[0] = [NSColor blackColor];
colors[1] = [NSColor blueColor];
colors[2] = [NSColor purpleColor];
colors[3] = [NSColor redColor];
colors[4] = [NSColor orangeColor];
colors[5] = [NSColor yellowColor];
NSDrawWindowBackground(bds);
[transform scaleBy:4. 0];
[currentContext saveGraphicsState];
[transform concat];
inside = NSDrawColorTiledRects(NSInsetRect(newBds, 5. 0, 5. 0),
        newBds, sides, colors, 6);
[[NSColor greenColor] set];
NSRectFill(inside);
[currentContext restoreGraphicsState];
```

Notice that the code uses an NSAffineTransform object to scale the drawing up by a factor of four. This makes it easier to see what is happening. The NSAffineTransform class and its uses for modifying drawing are described in detail in Chapter 13. Because different colors are used for each slice, it is easy to determine which slice is which and in what order they were drawn. The output of this code looks like Figure 12.18.

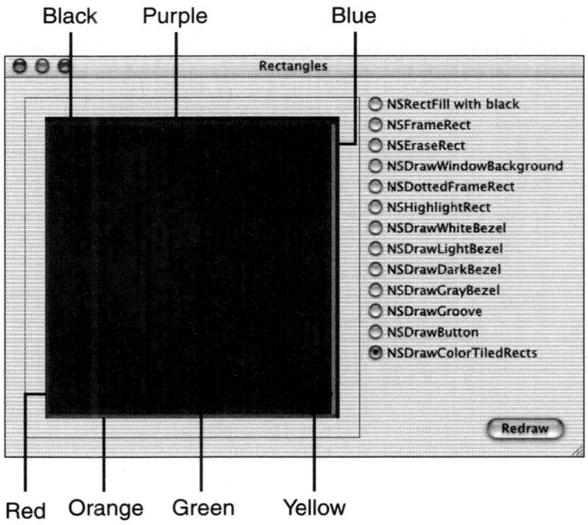

FIGURE 12.18 The scaled output of rectangle functions is shown.

The top edge is black, with a purple line below it. The right edge is blue, with yellow to the inside. The bottom edge is orange, the left edge is red, and the center is filled with green. This correlates with the color and edge values in the parameter arrays.

```
void NSCopyBitmapFromGState(int srcGState, NSRect srcRect, NSRect destRect);
void NSCopyBits(int srcGState, NSRect srcRect, NSPoint destPoint);
```

Both of these functions copy bitmap graphics (a rectangular region) from one view to another view or copy them within a single view. The difference between the functions lie in the final parameter. The destination can be given as a specific rectangular region or as a single point. In the case of a single point, the bitmap is copied at the same size as the original, with the origin (lower-left corner) placed at `destPoint`. A proper `srcGState` parameter can be obtained from an instance of `NSView` or one of its subclasses by using its `-gState` method. `NSNullObject` can be used for the `srcGState` parameter to signify that the source is the currently focused view. Note that these functions are designed to be used for copying graphics between views in the same application; copying bitmap images from arbitrary screen locations (as Grab.app does) requires dropping down to Quartz itself.

```
NSColor *NSReadPixel(NSPoint passedPoint);
```

This function enables the color of a particular pixel within the current context to be determined. The `passedPoint` parameter is the point in question; a pointer to an autoreleased `NSColor` instance is returned. This function could be used, for example, as part of the implementation of an eyedropper tool in a drawing program, the tool that allows the current color to be changed to the color of whatever pixel the user clicks. Note that this function is intended for use within the area owned by a particular NSView and not arbitrary screen locations. Quartz needs to be used for a more general way of reading pixels from the screen. Also, be aware that this function is not particularly fast and is therefore not well suited for capturing bitmaps a pixel at a time.

Obsolete Rectangle Functions

There are several rectangle functions that can be found in the Cocoa headers and documentation but are now obsolete. We describe them briefly here only so that a developer who encounters them in the Cocoa documentation won't be confused by their presence. All these functions should be ignored and avoided at present.

```
void NSDottedFrameRect(NSRect aRect);
void NSHighlightRect(NSRect aRect);
```

The NSDottedFrameRect() and NSHighlightRect() functions are carryovers from Cocoa's OpenStep roots and exist to allow older OpenStep source code to compile cleanly. The implementation of both functions has been removed from Cocoa. In other words, both functions do absolutely nothing. Although they are listed in the Cocoa headers and documentation, they should be ignored and not used.

```
void NSDrawWhiteBezel(NSRect aRect, NSRect clipRect);
void NSDrawButton(NSRect aRect, NSRect clipRect);
void NSDrawGrayBezel(NSRect aRect, NSRect clipRect);
void NSDrawGroove(NSRect aRect, NSRect clipRect);
void NSDrawDarkBezel(NSRect aRect, NSRect clipRect);
void NSDrawLightBezel(NSRect aRect, NSRect clipRect);
```

These six functions are also carryovers from Cocoa's OpenStep heritage. The implementations of these functions still exist, which means that each draw something. However, what they draw is a look and feel that is taken from OPENSTEP and does not look good on Aqua. Even NSDrawWhiteBezel(), which draws a rectangular area that looks similar to an empty NSTextField with a white background, isn't quite what Aqua would draw. The vertical sides are drawn too darkly for Aqua. Thus, all six of these functions should be avoided, even though they do work. Anyone who really wants to see what each does, however, can run the Rectangles example to see them in action.

The parameters to each function are as they would seem: aRect defines the area to be drawn, and clipRect allows the drawing to be restricted. Normally, clipRect covers the same area as, or more area than, the aRect argument.

Modifying Drawing

There are several ways to modify how things are drawn by Quartz. The `NSBezierPath` object itself allows a developer to modify several parameters that affect how a given path is rendered. Translating, rotating, scaling, and shearing a path with the `NSAffineTransform` class can affect the actual geometry. Finally, the `NSGraphicsContext` class allows a developer to modify a few global rendering options and control drawing. The `NSBezierPath` options are covered in this section. The other two classes are discussed in Chapter 13.

`NSBezierPath` Parameters

When a path is rendered, there are several parameters that can be set in the current graphics context that affect the rendering process. The first and most obvious is the current color. All paths are rendered with the current color. In Cocoa, the current color is set using the `NSColor` class. (You can read about this class in Chapter 17.) Besides setting the color, line width, line cap, line dash, line join, miter limit, and flatness can also be changed.

Examining the respective methods for controlling drawing demonstrates what the parameters do. Each group of methods follows a simple pattern. There are four methods for each parameter except the line dash. The first method, a class method, sets the default value for this parameter. This is the value that is used by all paths that aren't explicitly told to use something else. There is another class method that allows a developer to find out the current default value's setting. Third is an instance method to set the parameter for a particular `NSBezierPath` instance. Finally, the fourth method is an instance method to retrieve the value of the parameter. The line dash parameter only has the latter two methods, and nothing to control a default setting. Instead, the unchangeable default is to have no line dash at all.

Line Width

There are four methods for controlling the line width of a path.

```
+ (void)setDefaultLineWidth:(float)lineWidth;
+ (float)defaultLineWidth;
- (void)setLineWidth:(float)lineWidth;
- (float)lineWidth;
```

These methods control the width or thickness of all stroked paths. Larger values cause wider lines to be drawn. A value of zero has a special meaning here. It specifies the thinnest possible line that can be drawn on the current rendering device. On the screen, such lines are readily visible. On a very high-resolution printer, however, such a line could be so thin it would be nearly invisible. Many programmers use a value of 0.15 as something that is thin enough to always draw a 1-pixel wide line on the screen, and a line that is wide enough to be seen on all high-resolution devices.

Because of the rules Quartz uses to paint pixels, the actual width of the line could vary slightly (+/- 2 device pixels) from the actual value that is set. (Lines on pixel boundaries are one example where this could happen.) The current transformation matrix also affects line widths. If rendering into a scaled or otherwise altered graphics context, the line width could be distorted by the transformation. The end of the section "Using an `NSAffineTransform`," in Chapter 13 provides a code example showing how to avoid this distortion.

Line Cap

As with line width, there are four methods for choosing how line caps are drawn.

```
+ (void)setDefaultLineCapStyle:(NSLineCapStyle)lineCapStyle;
+ (NSLineCapStyle)defaultLineCapStyle;
- (void)setLineCapStyle:(NSLineCapStyle)lineCapStyle;
- (NSLineCapStyle)lineCapStyle;
```

Line caps are used to determine how the end(s) of a stroked path are rendered. There are three options available: `NSButtLineCapStyle`, `NSRoundLineCapStyle`, and `NSSquareLineCapStyle`. Use these three constants with the set methods; the get methods return one of the three constants. These parameters have an obvious effect on paths stroked with wider line widths. For paths with narrow line widths, there is little to no visual effect.

The first style, a butt end cap, is one where the path is drawn exactly from one point to the next. There is no end cap whatsoever, and the endpoints have squared-off corners.

The round line cap style produces rounded corners at the path's endpoints. The same effect can be achieved by rendering with a butt-style cap, and then drawing a circle with a diameter equal to the line width centered on each endpoint.

The last style, a square cap, looks much like the butt-style cap, but the length of the path is slightly extended. The same effect can be achieved by rendering with a butt-style cap, and then drawing a square with height and width equal to the line width centered on each endpoint.

Figure 12.19 shows what each line-cap style looks like. The thick black line is actually rendered by Quartz. The thin white line shows the location of the path defined before stroking.

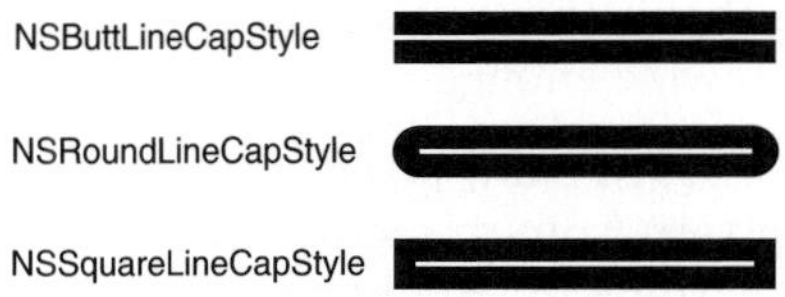

FIGURE 12.19 The results of applying line cap styles to paths are shown.

Line Dash

Two methods will allow control over stroking a path as a dashed line instead of a solid line.

```
- (void)getLineDash:(float *)pattern count:(int *)count phase:(float *)phase;
- (void)setLineDash:(const float *)pattern count:(int)count phase:(float)phase;
```

The line dash tells Quartz how to render stroked paths as dashed lines. There are two aspects to the line dash. First is the dash pattern, which specifies the sequence of dashes as determined by the rendered and nonrendered parts of the path. The second aspect is the phase. By altering the phase of the dash pattern, the dashes can be moved along the path.

The pattern is a list of floating-point values that are specified in typographical points. The dash pattern tells the renderer when to render the path and when not to. Each value in the pattern alternates between on and off. When the end of the dash pattern is reached, it starts over again from the beginning. For example, suppose the pattern {10.0, 20.0, 30.0, 40.0} is specified. This means that the path is rendered for the first 10.0 points of distance along the path, then 20.0 points will not be rendered, followed by 30.0 points rendered and 40.0 points not rendered. The cycle then repeats with 10.0 points rendered, and so on. Often, it is preferred to render a dash length proportional to the line width. This can be accomplished by scaling (multiplying) the values of a dash pattern by the line width.

Dash patterns can be as simple as a single value. A dash pattern of {10.0}, for example, draws a line with 10.0 on, 10.0 off, and so on. If a pattern has an odd number of values, then each time through the pattern a particular value changes whether it specifies off or on. For example, the pattern {10.0, 20.0, 30.0} indicates "10.0 on, 20.0 off, 30.0 on, 10.0 off, 20.0 on, 30.0 off, and repeat." As can be seen, each time through that pattern, the 10.0 alternates between on and off. In theory a pattern can be infinitely long and complex, but in general patterns with fewer values tend to look better because of their simplicity.

The `pattern` and `count` parameters to these methods are used to specify the dash pattern. The pattern parameter is a pointer to the first value in the floating-point array. The count parameter indicates how many values are in the pattern array. It makes little sense to have a value of 0.0 in the pattern array, and it is important that the array have at least one value.

The other parameter of these methods is the `phase`. This specifies where to start in the dash pattern when rendering begins. For example, again consider the simple pattern {10.0}. The 10.0 on, 10.0 off, and so on only truly applies to a phase of 0.0. If the phase were 5.0, the dash would be 5.0 on, 10.0 off, 10.0 on, 10.0 off, 10.0 on, and so on. The first dash starts 5.0 into the pattern (as specified by the phase), and then the pattern continues normally. Visually, for a line segment running left to right, it would appear as if the dashes had moved to the left, toward the starting point of the path. In this particular example, the value of the phase can range from 0.0 to 20.0. In fact, stroking the path with phase 20.0, 40.0, 60.0, and so on would appear exactly the same as if a phase of 0.0 had been used.

There is a simple general approach to determine the useful range of the phase value. The phase range always starts at 0.0. To find the maximum value, add up all the values in the line dash array. If there is an odd number of values in the array, this sum should be multiplied by two. There is no change for an even number of values. The result is the maximum useful value for the phase.

To offer some visual examples of line-dash patterns, the following method is a part of the Paths example:

```
- (void)drawLineDashes
{
    int i;
    NSRect bds = [self bounds];
    double spacing = bds.size.height / 10.0;
    double width = NSMaxX(bds) - 10.0;
    NSBezierPath *line[9];
    float dash0[] = { 30.0 };
    float dash1[] = { 30.0 };
    float dash2[] = { 30.0 };
    float dash3[] = { 30.0 };
    float dash4[] = { 30.0, 15.0 };
    float dash5[] = { 30.0, 15.0 };
    float dash6[] = { 30.0, 15.0, 5.0 };
    float dash7[] = { 30.0, 15.0, 30.0 };
    float dash8[] = { 40.0, 20.0, 30.0, 10.0 };

    [[NSColor whiteColor] set];
    NSRectFill(bds);
    for (i=0; i<9; i++) {
        double height = bds.origin.y + spacing * (i + 1);
```

```
        line[i] = [NSBezierPath bezierPath];
        [line[i] setLineWidth:5.0];
        [line[i] moveToPoint:NSMakePoint(10.0, height)];
        [line[i] lineToPoint:NSMakePoint(width, height)];
    }
    [line[0] setLineDash:dash0 count:1 phase: 0.0];
    [line[1] setLineDash:dash1 count:1 phase:15.0];
    [line[2] setLineDash:dash2 count:1 phase:30.0];
    [line[3] setLineDash:dash3 count:1 phase:60.0];
    [line[4] setLineDash:dash4 count:2 phase: 0.0];
    [line[5] setLineDash:dash5 count:2 phase:15.0];
    [line[6] setLineDash:dash6 count:3 phase: 0.0];
    [line[7] setLineDash:dash7 count:3 phase: 0.0];
    [line[8] setLineDash:dash8 count:4 phase: 0.0];
    [[NSColor blackColor] set];
    for (i=0; i<9; i++) {
        [line[i] stroke];
    }
}
```

When the `-drawLineDashes` method is called from within the `-drawRect:` method, the output shown in Figure 12.20 is produced:

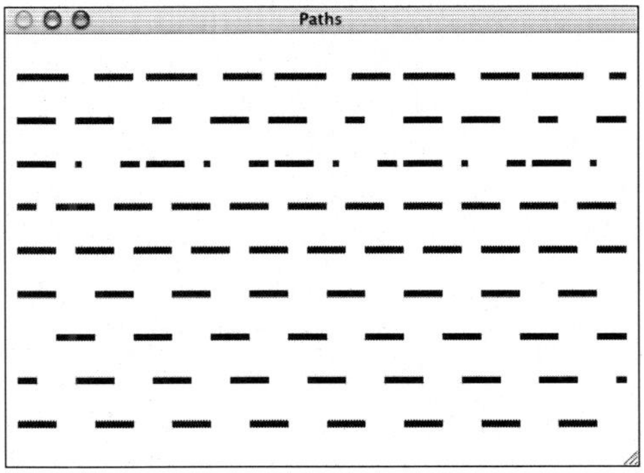

FIGURE 12.20 The `-drawLineDashes` method produces the pictured output.

Note that the lower four lines in the window show the exact same dash pattern at increasing phase values. The dash pattern is {30.0}, and the phases from bottom to top are 0.0, 15.0, 30.0, and 60.0. Because the range of phases for this pattern is 30.0×2=60.0, the line with a phase of 60.0 looks identical to the line with a phase of

0.0. The other lines in the example show a variety of different dash patterns, as can be seen in the source code.

Line Join

Four methods control how the joints between line segments of stroked paths are rendered:

```
+ (void)setDefaultLineJoinStyle:(NSLineJoinStyle)lineJoinStyle;
+ (NSLineJoinStyle)defaultLineJoinStyle;
- (void)setLineJoinStyle:(NSLineJoinStyle)lineJoinStyle;
- (NSLineJoinStyle)lineJoinStyle;
```

Three options are available: `NSMiterLineJoinStyle`, `NSRoundLineJoinStyle`, and `NSBevelLineJoinStyle`. Use these three constants with the set methods; the get methods return one of the three constants. These parameters have an obvious effect on paths stroked with wider line widths. For paths with narrow line widths, there is little to no visual effect.

The first style, a miter line join, is one in which the edges of the line segments are extended until they intersect. This gives a pointy or sharp corner. Note that the corner extends farther and farther from the end points of the path segments as the angle between them approaches zero. (See the miter limit discussion later in this section for more about this.)

The second style is a rounded corner. In this case, the corners are rounded, just as if the miter were masked by a circle of a diameter equal to the line width and centered on the path segments' intersection point.

The final style is a beveled line join. If you took the mitered line join, and then lopped off the sharp corner, you would have a beveled line join. To determine where the corner is cut off, draw a ray that bisects the angle between the two path line segments. The perpendicular line to that ray, running through the intersection point, is the cut line.

Figure 12.21 shows each line join style. The thick black line is rendered by Quartz. The thin white line shows the location of the actual path defined before stroking.

Miter Limit

Miter limit is used to keep mitered corners from becoming too long. Four methods control it:

```
+ (void)setDefaultMiterLimit:(float)limit;
+ (float)defaultMiterLimit;
- (void)setMiterLimit:(float)miterLimit;
- (float)miterLimit;
```

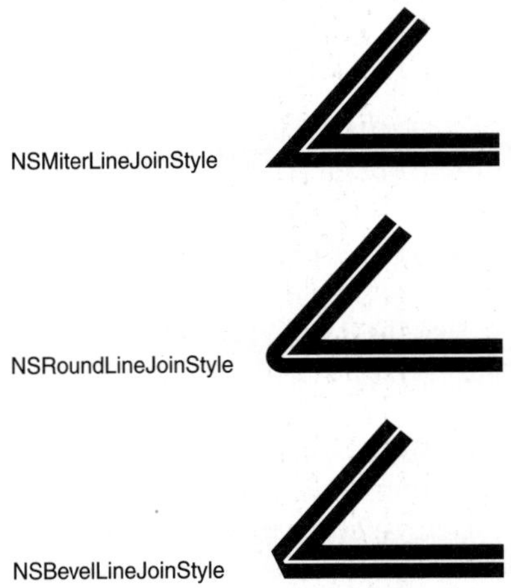

FIGURE 12.21 The `-line` join styles supported by Cocoa.

The miter limit is used as a way to keep mitered corners from becoming too long. As the angle between two path segments decreases, a mitered corner extends farther and farther from the intersection point. At an angle of zero, the corner would become an infinitely long spike. Thus, it is necessary to limit the miters so that they don't get out of hand. The miter limit limits this effect. If the angle between the two path segments becomes too small, the miter limit changes the corner from a mitered line join to a beveled line join. Note that the miter limit has no effect on rounded or beveled line joins.

The value of this parameter is somewhat arcane. It isn't just a simple cutoff angle. Instead, take a ratio of the diagonal length of the miter to the line width. If this ratio is greater than the miter limit, the beveled join is used. According to Apple's documentation, the default value of ten means angles of less than about 11 degrees become beveled.

Flatness

Flatness is one of the only graphics context parameters that affects both stroked and filled paths. It determines the accuracy of curved path sections. Whenever your path contains a Bezier curve or other arc, Quartz needs to flatten it into a series of line segments as part of the rendering process. By altering the flatness attribute you can trade rendering efficiency (execution time) with rendering accuracy. Four methods manipulate a curve's flatness. They are

```
+ (void)setDefaultFlatness:(float)flatness;
+ (float)defaultFlatness;
```

```
- (void)setFlatness:(float)flatness;
- (float)flatness;
```

The actual value passed to or returned from these methods is the maximum error tolerance in pixels for a given point along the curve; hence, it is device dependent.

Larger values of flatness mean less accurate curves, and smaller values give more accurate drawing at the expense of rendering time. Cocoa limits this parameter to be between 0.2 and 100. If the parameter is set to a value outside of this range, it is clamped to keep it within these limits. The standard value of 1.0 is fine for most applications.

Querying and Modifying a Path

Besides defining and rendering paths, an `NSBezierPath` object also enables a developer to query and modify the details of the path that it defines. There are several methods that can be used to query the points along the path and the operations acting on them, as well as determining more general information about the entire path such as its bounding box. There are also a few methods that can be used to alter the path. Some create a new path object and return that, without modifying the original `NSBezierPath`, and some modify the path object itself.

To determine if a given `NSBezierPath` object has any points defined yet, you can use the `-isEmpty` method. It returns a `BOOL` value, `YES` if there are no points defined yet and `NO` otherwise.

While a path is being defined, the `-currentPoint` method returns an `NSPoint` that indicates the current point in the path. Remember that all the path defining operations such as `lineto` and `curveto` always use the current point as the first endpoint of the path segment that they define.

Many times, a developer needs to know the bounding box of a given path. A path's bounding box is defined as the smallest rectangle that encloses the entire path. There are actually two bounding boxes that are significant. The first is the standard bounding box that encloses the visible path itself. The `-bounds` method returns an `NSRect` containing the standard bounding box. The second is the bounding box that encloses the path and any invisible control points from Bezier curve sections. Often, the control points of these curves can lie well outside of the bounds enclosing the visible parts of the path. If a path contains no `curveto` segments, both bounding boxes are the same. The `-controlPointBounds` method return an `NSRect` containing the bounding box that encloses both the visible path and the control points.

```
- (int)elementCount
- (NSBezierPathElement)elementAtIndex:(int)index
            associatedPoints:(NSPointArray)points;
- (NSBezierPathElement)elementAtIndex:(int)index;
```

Besides the queries that return information about the whole path, there are also several methods that provide specific information about each element of the path. The `-elementCount` method returns the number of path elements that are defined by a particular `NSBezierPath` instance.

To find out about a particular path element, use the `-elementAtIndex:associatedPoints:` method. The first parameter is an integer to specify which element to know about. The second parameter is an array of points. The actual points associated with the given element are placed into this array. Because a path element can have zero, one, or three points associated with it, the array you pass to the method should contain at least three points. (The `curveto` element has three points, and closing a path has zero points. The others have one point.) It is acceptable to pass in a pointer that references a portion inside of a larger point array as long as there are at least three points available to receive the information. In the case of a `curveto`, the points are returned in this order: control point one, control point two, and end point.

The return value of `-elementAtIndex:associatedPoints:` tells the actual type of element, and hence, how many of the points are filled in. The possible values, corresponding to the basic path elements described previously, are

```
NSMoveToBezierPathElement

NSLineToBezierPathElement

NSCurveToBezierPathElement

NSClosePathBezierPathElement
```

If the developer isn't interested in the values of the actual points associated with a given element, `-elementAtIndex:associatedPoints:` can still be used, but with `NULL` passed in as the points parameter. Alternatively, the `-elementAtIndex:` method can be used to do the same thing.

To modify an `NSBezierPath` object, there is currently only one method available:

```
- (void)setAssociatedPoints:(NSPointArray)points atIndex:(int)index;
```

The `-setAssociatedPoints:atIndex:` method can be used to change the positions of the points associated with a given path element. The index parameter specifies which element's point(s) should be modified. The points parameter contains the new data for the points in question. A `curveto` element would require an array with three points in it. One point is required for `moveto` and `lineto` elements. Because a `closepath` element has no points associated with it, this method leaves those elements unaffected.

Unfortunately, there are currently no methods available for removing path elements or for changing an element into an element of another type. If an `NSBezierPath` needs to be edited in this way, the only means of accomplishing this right now is to create a new path object. After instantiating the object, walk through all the elements in the original object, copying them to the new object while changing or deleting them as needed. When the new object has been built, it can replace the old path object.

There are two other methods of interest, both of which create new `NSBezierPath` objects. The first, `-bezierPathByFlatteningPath`, is for flattening a path. A flattened path is a path without any curve elements. Instead, it has only straight line segments. When paths are rendered to the screen or other output device, they must first be flattened; by obtaining a flattened path the previous element inspection methods can be used to find out how the curves will be approximated when rendered. Using the various flatness methods described earlier in this chapter under "Flatness" can control how curves are flattened.

The other method, also returning a new `NSBezierPath` object, is `-bezierPathByReversingPath`. Because the new path renders identically, it might not be immediately obvious why this would be useful. However, refer to the previous discussion of fills and recall that the direction a path is drawn is significant in determining how it is filled. By reversing a subpath, it is possible to change the fill behavior. It is possible to create a library of basic path shapes, each a different `NSBezierPath` instance, and then append them together to create a complete object. How each subpath is filled can be controlled by reversing it or not before appending it to the final path. This type of situation is where this method is most likely to be used.

Summary

This chapter introduced the techniques used to draw paths with a variety of attributes and styles. Custom drawing is implemented by subclassing the `NSView` class. A variety of Cocoa classes exist to aid the implementation of view subclasses. The `NSBezierPath` class is used to define paths that are stroked or filled. The built-in 2D graphics capabilities provided by Quartz and accessible using Cocoa rival those of expensive graphics applications. Complex and powerful graphics can be produced with the techniques described, but this chapter has only scratched the surface of Cocoa capabilities. Chapter 13 and Chapter 14 expand on the information already presented. The next chapter introduces more classes that enable drawing and delves into optimization issues.

13

Custom Views and Graphics Part II

IN THIS CHAPTER

- Using `NSGraphicsContext`
- Coordinate System Transformations
- Drawing Points and Rectangles
- Optimizing Drawing

This chapter extends the path drawing techniques described in Chapter 12, "Custom Views and Graphics Part I." Modifying the coordinate system used to draw paths enables the production of complex and powerful effects. Techniques for fast point and rectangle drawing are presented with examples, and the issues that impact drawing performance are described. This chapter presents methods of optimizing drawing and tools that help identify drawing inefficiencies. The combination of this chapter and Chapter 12 provide a firm grounding in the art of vector drawing with Cocoa.

Using `NSGraphicsContext`

The `NSGraphicsContext` class provides extra control over drawing. It is the main entity through which drawing commands flow, so it has a global control over all drawing sent to it. Seasoned Macintosh developers will find it useful to consider a graphics context to be analogous to a graphics port. Although there might be many graphics contexts in a given program, more often than not the current graphics context is the one of interest. The current context is the one that is being drawn right now, and generally represents the drawing surface of an `NSWindow`. All `NSView` instances in a given window will use that window's graphics context for their actual drawing unless previously instructed to create their own private context. To get a pointer to the instance of `NSGraphicsContext` object that is the current context, use the `+currentContext` method, like this:

```
NSGraphicsContext *currentContext = [NSGraphicsContext
currentContext];
```

There are several tasks that can be performed with an instance of NSGraphicsContext. It can be queried to find out information about the context, set some parameters that will affect drawing, and perform some basic actions.

Where Am I Drawing?

In Cocoa, it is generally not necessary to write different code for drawing to the screen versus printing. The Application Kit will use the NSView's -drawRect: method to perform both operations. To know whether the current drawing operations are going to the screen or being printed, send the -isDrawingToScreen method:

```
BOOL drawingToScreen = [currentContext isDrawingToScreen];
```

If a context is not drawing to the screen, then its output is being collected and stored as PDF, and could be saved to a file on disk or sent to a printer or fax. In other words, if this method returns YES the drawing is immediate, otherwise it will be deferred for later, stored as PDF data. This method is very handy if something in a drawing needs to be done differently when printing than when drawing to the screen. For example, a drawing program might display a grid in the onscreen document, and suppress drawing the grid when printing. This query would be used to control that decision.

To obtain the answer to this query without further use of the instance of NSGraphicsContext, do this:

```
BOOL drawingToScreen = [[NSGraphicsContext currentContext] isDrawingToScreen];
```

However, because this is done so frequently, Apple has provided the +currentContextDrawingToScreen method to simplify code slightly. This code does exactly the same thing as the previous code:

```
BOOL drawingToScreen = [NSGraphicsContext currentContextDrawingToScreen];
```

If it is necessary to use the current NSGraphicsContext instance further, don't use this shortcut. It is more efficient to obtain a copy of the current context and store it in a local variable than to send multiple +currentContext calls.

Flushing a Context

Although it was suggested in Chapter 12, "Custom Views and Graphics Part I," that drawing to the screen with Quartz is immediate, there are cases where drawing code is called, but nothing appears on the screen. This is particularly common when the drawing code is called as a result of an NSTimer firing, which would likely be the case for animation. This can be puzzling; it is clear that the drawing isn't quite as immediate as you might think. Cocoa tries to make drawing as efficient as possible. To this end, it stores up drawing commands until it is told to actually make them all appear onscreen at once, a process known as flushing. If the Application Kit invokes a `-drawRect:` method through the normal window and view display mechanism, it will take care of the flushing. In other cases, a developer must make sure that the flushing happens.

There are two ways to force drawing to be flushed to the screen, and which one to use will depend on how the code has been structured. Suppose that all drawing is done exclusively in the `-drawRect:` method. Instead of doing some drawing, and then flushing it to the screen, it might be easier to coerce the Application Kit into invoking its view redisplay mechanism. This forces the `-drawRect:` to be called, with all appropriate flushing done by the Application Kit. To do this, simply tell an `NSView` or `NSWindow` that it needs to be redrawn by sending a `-setNeedsDisplay:` message to it.

For example, suppose there is an `NSView` that displays an animation. Each frame is to be drawn at a certain time, and an `NSTimer` created to invoke the code that will set up the next frame. The code would look something like this, if the method were an instance method of the animated `NSView`:

```
- (void)timerPing:(NSTimer *)theTimer
{
    // the code or a call to the code to update the
    // internal model to the next frame goes here
    [self setNeedsDisplay:YES];
}
```

If this method were implemented in a controller object, the `-setNeedsDisplay:` method would go to any and all pertinent NSView objects and display the data that was updated for this frame of animation. The Application Kit, at the end of the event loop, will notice that the view needs to be redisplayed and will cause it to be redrawn at that time, flushing all drawing to the screen before starting another pass through the event loop. A display message could also be sent to the `NSView` to get it to redraw immediately, instead of waiting for the event loop to finish. This is not necessarily a good idea, however. If something else in the code also causes the same `NSView` instance to redraw, then it might get redrawn multiple times, possibly with the exact same frame contents being drawn each time. Obviously, coalescing all the redraw requests into one, and doing it just once, is the most efficient approach. This is what `-setNeedsDisplay:` attempts to do.

NOTE

The current version of Cocoa has a performance bug in it that affects the display methods. At present, -display is actually faster than -setNeedsDisplay:. Rather than using the methods incorrectly, it is best to use -setNeedsDisplay: anyway. To work around the problem, a category on NSView can be created to override -setNeedsDisplay: so that it calls -display. Anyone implementing such a workaround should check each release of Mac OS X and remove it as soon as Apple fixes the problem.

Sometimes finer granularity is needed to control when graphics are actually rendered on the screen. In that case, all pending drawing can be forced to be immediately rendered by using the NSGraphicsContext instance corresponding to the current context. Send it the -flushGraphics message, such as this:

```
[[NSGraphicsContext currentContext] flushGraphics];
```

If the drawing takes quite a while to render, put a few flushes into the code, so that the user sees the drawing take place in steps instead waiting for all the drawing commands to be issued. Sometimes a method might simply send -lockFocus to an NSView, scribble a bit, and then send -unlockFocus. It is legal to draw in an NSView outside of -drawRect: as long as the focus has been set to the view in question. For this drawing to actually be seen on the screen, however, flush the current graphics context before unlocking the focus. Although this does work, any drawing that isn't a part of the -drawRect: method can potentially be erased the next time the Application Kit decides to redraw the entire view, and most certainly won't appear when the view is printed. For temporary drawing, such as markers and guides, this might be preferred because it short circuits the more complex Application Kit redraw mechanism and the negative effects aren't undesirable. In most situations, though, it is best to stick with -drawRect: and -setNeedsDisplay:.

Controlling the Drawing

Drawing parameters can vary and a developer might want to restore them to their original state. Rather than querying, storing, and resetting the entire state of a graphics context, instruct the context to do this via the -saveGraphicsState and -restoreGraphicsState methods. Each save must be balanced by exactly one restore. The parameters are saved on a stack. If multiple saves are performed before issuing a restore, the settings will restore in the reverse order in which they were saved. For example:

```
NSGraphicsContext *currentContext = [NSGraphicsContext currentContext];
// initial settings, settings #1 in effect
[currentContext saveGraphicsState];
// change some settings
```

```
// settings #2 in effect
[currentContext saveGraphicsState];
// change some settings
// settings #3 in effect
[currentContext restoreGraphicsState];
// settings #2 in effect
[currentContext restoreGraphicsState];
// settings #1 in effect
```

This saving and restoring is very fast—much faster than trying to track all the parameters yourself. The stack size is limited only by available memory, but excessive saving and restoring could negatively impact performance. Only save when needed. Don't forget to match each save with a restore. Matching saves and restores ensures that the context is back to its original state at the end of drawing. Matching also makes sense because unmatched save operations waste memory and CPU cycles by saving something that is never intended to be restored.

There are two other ways to control drawing with the `NSGraphicsContext` class. The first is to turn antialiasing on or off. The second is to control image interpolation.

By default, all Quartz graphics are antialiased. This generally makes them look much nicer onscreen. However, in some situations, antialiasing might not be desirable. `NSGraphicsContext` implements two methods to deal with antialiasing. The first checks to see if antialiasing is on or off and the second sets the antialiasing to on or off:

```
- (void)setShouldAntialias:(BOOL)antialias;
- (BOOL)shouldAntialias;
```

The most common place to turn off antialiasing is with screensavers. Often, a screensaver will not redraw the entire view because it is such a large area of the screen. Instead, it will erase a line or other object by redrawing it in black. When drawing is antialiased, however, the black paint won't necessarily touch every pixel that was affected by the antialiasing. Other pixels along curves and lines will have been painted faintly in the antialiasing process. Because drawing in black won't erase these, there are two choices to not leave behind artifacts. The first is to paint a wider line, larger circle, and so on, so that the black paint covers some extra area. Although this works, it might make the screensaver look less appealing. Turning off antialiasing is the way to go. Any time drawing is leaving artifacts, check the antialiasing setting and make sure it is doing what is desired.

The other parameter that can be controlled via `NSGraphicsContext` is image interpolation. When Quartz scales an image up or down, it uses image interpolation to make the scaling look good. But interpolation is an expensive operation in terms of

CPU cycles. It is possible to squeeze out that last bit of performance by lowering the image interpolation quality or turning it off all together. Just like antialiasing, there are two associated `NSGraphicsContext` methods, one for querying and one to alter the setting:

```
- (NSImageInterpolation)imageInterpolation;
- (void)setImageInterpolation:(NSImageInterpolation)interpolation;
```

Note that these methods use a special type. `NSImageInterpolation` is an enumerated type and there are currently four self-explanatory options available: `NSImageInterpolationDefault`, `NSImageInterpolationNone`, `NSImageInterpolationLow`, and `NSImageInterpolationHigh`. Remember that changing this value from the default trades performance for quality. Because of this, use low quality or no image interpolation when drawing to the screen, but use full quality when printing. Additionally, if images are drawn without any scaling or rotation, and the image resolution matches exactly with the output-device resolution this setting will have no effect on actual output quality.

`NSGraphicsContext` Advanced Methods

So far, drawing into an `NSGraphicsContext`, which represents the drawing area of an `NSWindow` has been discussed. It is also possible to create an `NSGraphicsContext` that saves future drawing to an `NSData` instance or to a file on disk. It is important to understand that drawing code doesn't need to change when drawing to a different kind of `NSGraphicsContext`. In other words, the drawing that is done to the screen by an `NSView` can be sent to a different `NSGraphicsContext` without any need to change the drawing commands. What is captured on disk or sent to a printer will be identical to what is drawn on the screen.

The Application Kit `NSView` machinery, for example, already supports printing implicitly, without requiring a developer to write any code to support printing. The standard print panel will come up and, once the Preview or Print buttons are clicked, the `NSView` will create a special `NSGraphicsContext`, and then call its `-drawRect:` method to draw to the printer or to a file for the Previewer to open. A developer doesn't need to do any of this because the Application Kit takes care of it. If drawing code needs to know the drawing destination, it can find out by obtaining the current context and querying its attributes.

Some rare instances might occur where it makes sense to set up an `NSGraphicsContext` manually and use it, for example, writing to a PDF file. To create a
specialized `NSGraphicsContext` object, the `+graphicsContextWithAttributes:` method is used. The method is defined like this:

```
+ (NSGraphicsContext *)graphicsContextWithAttributes:(NSDictionary *)attributes;
```

This method will return a new context and requires an NSDictionary as its only parameter. To describe the type of graphics context desired, an NSDictionary instance with specific key and value pairs is required.

The first key/value pair uses the special Application Kit defined key NSGraphicsContextDestinationAttributeName. This key/value pair is required for this method to be called correctly. The value of this key in the NSDictionary should be an instance of NSWindow, NSData, or NSURL. The present implementation requires that the value be an instance of one of those three classes, or an instance of a subclass of one of those three classes. No other classes are accepted.

If an instance of NSMutableData or NSURL is chosen for the context destination, another key/value pair is possible. The key is NSGraphicsContextRepresentationFormatAttributeName, and it is used to define the file format for the graphics context's output. The two possible values for this key are NSGraphicsContextPSFormat and NSGraphicsContextPDFFormat. The first value will cause the output to be produced as PostScript data. The second value will cause PDF output.

As a shortcut to obtaining an NSGraphicsContext for a particular NSWindow, the +graphicsContextWithWindow: method can be used. This method takes an instance of NSWindow, or one of its subclasses, as an argument and returns an appropriate NSGraphicsContext. Therefore, the following two method calls are identical in functionality:

```
myContext = [NSGraphicsContext graphicsContextWithAttributes:
        [NSDictionary dictionaryWithObject:myWindow
                forKey:NSGraphicsContextDestinationAttributeName]];
myContext = [NSGraphicsContext graphicsContextWithWindow:myWindow];
```

Given an instance of NSGraphicsContext, it is possible to find out the specific attributes that were used to create it. The -attributes method will return an NSDictionary with the same key/value pairs as the dictionary used to create the instance.

To activate an instance of NSGraphicsContext, the NSGraphicsContext class needs to be sent the +setCurrentContext: method. Sending this method with an instance of NSGraphicsContext as the argument will cause that context to become active in the thread that sent the message. Until the current context is changed, all drawing in the thread will go through that context.

Although a discussion of low-level Quartz functions has been avoided, there are times when access to an NSGraphicsContext's underlying Quartz context is required for use in calling Quartz functions. The -graphicsPort method will return a

CGContextRef that can be used in this way. Because the method's return type is void *, it must be cast as a CGContextRef pointer to be able to use it.

```
CGContextRef *cgContext = (CGContextRef *)
        [[NSGraphicsContext currentContext] graphicsPort];
```

The -graphicsPort method's return value is platform dependent, so in the future it might have a different semantic. This will be true especially if Cocoa is ever ported by Apple, or another party, to run atop other operating systems. For the time being, Mac OS X is the only operating system that fully supports Cocoa, so this point is not yet critical, but could become so in the future.

Coordinate System Transformations

The NSAffineTransform class can warp the drawing canvas. The main purpose of this is to enable a single NSBezierPath object to define a path that can be used multiple times. In the star example in Chapter 12, four different stars are drawn at four different locations. They are all drawn using the same NSBezierPath object, without changing the object's path or the location of its points. Moving the canvas, or translation, is one of the ways that NSAffineTransform can alter drawing. It can also perform scaling (changing the size) and rotation. Other effects such as skew are also possible. Slanting is an example of skewing. After skewing, what was once a right angle is no longer a right angle.

Defining an NSAffineTransform

To get a new NSAffineTransform object, two approaches are possible—create an identity transform from scratch, or create one based on another instance. To obtain an identity transform, use the +transform method in this manner:

```
newTransform = [NSAffineTransform transform];
```

This method returns a brand new transform object that contains the identity transform. The identity transform is like a blank slate because it will cause no change in the drawing when it is applied. If a transform based on another existing transform is needed, then a different method, -initWithTransform:, should be used:

```
newTransform = [[NSAffineTransform alloc] initWithTransform:existingTransform];
```

This code will return a new transform object that is identical to the existingTransform object that was used as a parameter to the initialization method.

Translation

When you have a transform object, it can be instructed to translate, scale, or rotate. Translation causes drawing to be moved to a new location. Translation is added to a transform with the following method:

```
- (void)translateXBy:(float)deltaX yBy:(float)deltaY;
```

This method, `-translateXBy:yBy:`, causes drawing to take place at a new location. For example, suppose a circle is drawn with radius 10.0 with the origin (0.0, 0.0) as its center. After translation by (50.0, 40.0), the same path would actually be drawn with the point (50.0, 40.0) as its center, even though the path itself specifies the origin as its center point. In other words, translation moves the origin of the coordinate system to a new location. The star drawing example, shown in Chapter 12, uses translation to draw the same star, defined by a single `NSBezierPath` object in four different locations. This drawing is accomplished by using the `-translateXBy:yBy:` method. Many of the other algorithms in the Paths example code also demonstrate the use of this method, including the following scaling example.

Scaling

Two methods are used for scaling drawing. Scaling allows drawing to be expanded or shrunk.

```
- (void)scaleBy:(float)scale;
- (void)scaleXBy:(float)scaleX yBy:(float)scaleY;
```

The first, `-scaleBy:`, scales all drawing equally in both the X and Y directions. This is the most common case. However, the X and Y axes can be scaled by different amounts. This causes an effect where the drawing will appear to be stretched or squashed in one direction. For example, if the X axis was scaled by a larger number than the Y axis, a circle would become an oval that is wider than it is tall. Note that the following two lines of code are equivalent:

```
[transform scaleBy:scaleAmount];
[transform scaleXBy:scaleAmount yBy:scaleAmount];
```

A scaling value of 1.0 causes no change to the axis. A value greater than 1.0 will cause the axis to be stretched out. If a view's drawing area starts 100.0×100.0 it will be reduced to 50.0×50.0 after scaling both axes by 2.0. The view would still be the same size on the screen, but the drawing inside it would be twice as large. If the scaling value is between 0.0 and 1.0, then the affected axes will be shrunk. A view with a 100.0×100.0 drawing area scaled by 0.5 would display coordinates within a 200.0×200.0 area. Again, the view is still the same size on screen, but the drawing would be half as large as for an unscaled view.

As an example of scaling, the Paths example uses the `-drawScaling` method to draw four circles, each scaled differently. Here is the code:

```
- (void)drawScaling
{
    NSRect bds = [self bounds];
    NSPoint center = NSMakePoint(NSMidX(bds), NSMidY(bds));
    double radius = MIN(center.x, center.y) * 0.25 - 10.0;
    NSBezierPath *circle = [NSBezierPath bezierPath];
    NSAffineTransform *transform;
    NSGraphicsContext *currentContext = [NSGraphicsContext currentContext];
    [circle appendBezierPathWithArcWithCenter:NSZeroPoint
        radius:radius startAngle:0.0 endAngle:360.0];
    [circle closePath];
    [circle setLineWidth:4.0];
    [[NSColor whiteColor] set];
    NSRectFill(bds);
    [[NSColor blackColor] set];
    // lower left: normal size
    transform = [NSAffineTransform transform];
    [transform translateXBy:center.x * 0.5 yBy:center.y * 0.5];
    [currentContext saveGraphicsState];
    [transform concat];
    [circle stroke];
    [currentContext restoreGraphicsState];
    // upper left: x and y scaled by 2 (twice the size)
    transform = [NSAffineTransform transform];
    [transform translateXBy:center.x * 0.5 yBy:center.y * 1.5];
    [transform scaleBy:2.0];
    [currentContext saveGraphicsState];
    [transform concat];
    [circle stroke];
    [currentContext restoreGraphicsState];
    // lower right: x and y scaled by 0.5 (half the size)
    transform = [NSAffineTransform transform];
    [transform translateXBy:center.x * 1.5 yBy:center.y * 0.5];
    [transform scaleXBy:0.5 yBy:0.5];
    [currentContext saveGraphicsState];
    [transform concat];
    [circle stroke];
    [currentContext restoreGraphicsState];
    // upper right: x scaled by 2 and y scaled by 0.5
    // (distorted into a wide oval)
```

```
    transform = [NSAffineTransform transform];
    [transform translateXBy:center.x * 1.5 yBy:center.y * 1.5];
    [transform scaleXBy:2.0 yBy:0.5];
    [currentContext saveGraphicsState];
    [transform concat];
    [circle stroke];
    [currentContext restoreGraphicsState];
}
```

Figure 13.1 illustrates the output produced when the `-drawScaling` method is executed.

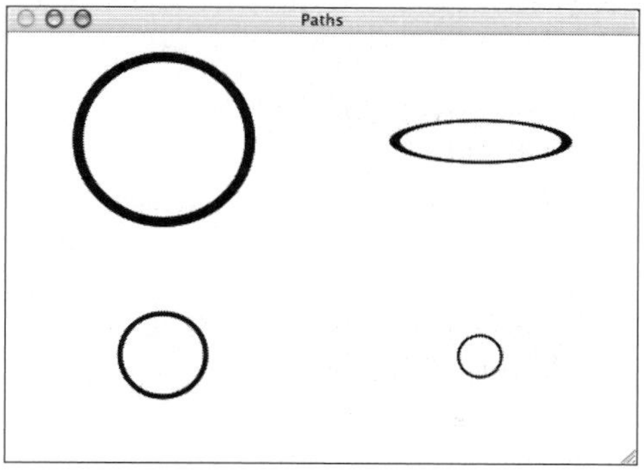

FIGURE 13.1 The output of the `-drawScaling` method is shown here.

Each circle is drawn with the same `NSBezierPath` object. The path object itself is not modified between strokes; the only difference between the circles is a change in the transformation matrix. Because the path is defined to be centered about the origin, there is a translation before each circle is rendered. In Figure 13.1, the circle at the lower left is the natural size. The circle at the lower right is scaled by 0.5, which results in it being half the normal size. The circle at the upper left is scaled by 2.0, a doubling in size. The circle at the upper right is scaled by 2.0 in the X axis and 0.5 in the Y axis. The resultant scaling reduces the height of the circle and widens it, causing it to be distorted into an oval shape.

Note also how the scaling affects the rendered line width as well as the path itself. It is possible to alternatively render the circles so the line width is not affected by the scaling. The `-drawDistortion` method, shown in the "Using an `NSAffineTransform`" section later in this chapter, demonstrates how to accomplish this.

Rotation

There are two ways to accomplish rotation, differing only in how the rotation angle is specified.

```
- (void)rotateByDegrees:(float)angle;
- (void)rotateByRadians:(float)angle;
```

Use the `-rotateByDegrees:` method if the angle is available in degrees. Use `-rotateByRadians:` if the angle is in radians.

Changing the rotation causes a rotation around the origin. This means that a path centered on the origin rotates in place. An object drawn some distance away from the origin is both rotated and translated similar to the square to the right in Figure 13.2.

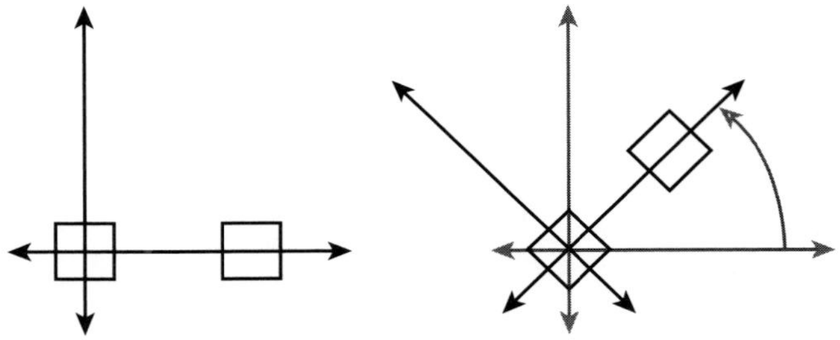

FIGURE 13.2 An object drawn some distance away from the origin is both rotated and translated, as with the square on the right.

The Paths example contains a sample of rotation in the `-drawRotation` method. The code draws two ovals (created as scaled circles) that have been rotated and two rotated squares:

```
- (void)drawRotation
{
    NSRect bds = [self bounds];
    NSPoint center = NSMakePoint(NSMidX(bds), NSMidY(bds));
    double radius = MIN(center.x, center.y) * 0.25 - 10.0;
    NSBezierPath *circle = [NSBezierPath bezierPath];
    NSBezierPath *rectangle = [NSBezierPath bezierPathWithRect:
    NSMakeRect(-radius, -radius, radius * 2.0, radius * 2.0)];
    NSAffineTransform *transform;
    NSGraphicsContext *currentContext = [NSGraphicsContext currentContext];
```

```
    [circle appendBezierPathWithArcWithCenter:NSZeroPoint
        radius:radius startAngle:0.0 endAngle:360.0];
    [circle closePath];
    [circle setLineWidth:4.0];
    [rectangle setLineWidth:4.0];
    [[NSColor whiteColor] set];
    NSRectFill(bds);
    [[NSColor blackColor] set];
    // lower left and upper right: squares normal size, rotated 45 degrees
    transform = [NSAffineTransform transform];
    [transform translateXBy:center.x * 0.5 yBy:center.y * 0.5];
    [transform rotateByDegrees:45]; // Counter Clockwise
    [currentContext saveGraphicsState];
    [transform concat];
    [rectangle stroke];
    transform = [NSAffineTransform transform];
    [transform translateXBy:center.x yBy:0.0];
    [transform concat];
    [rectangle stroke];
    [currentContext restoreGraphicsState];
    // upper left: scaled and rotated circle
    transform = [NSAffineTransform transform];
    [transform translateXBy:center.x * 0.5 yBy:center.y * 1.5];
    [transform rotateByDegrees:-30]; // Clockwise
    [transform scaleXBy:2.0 yBy:0.5];
    [currentContext saveGraphicsState];
    [transform concat];
    [circle stroke];
    [currentContext restoreGraphicsState];
    // lower right: x and y scaled by 0.5 (half the size)
    transform = [NSAffineTransform transform];
    [transform translateXBy:center.x * 1.5 yBy:center.y * 0.5];
    [transform rotateByRadians:M_PI / 6.0]; // Counter Clockwise
    [transform scaleXBy:2.0 yBy:0.5];
    [currentContext saveGraphicsState];
    [transform concat];
    [circle stroke];
    [currentContext restoreGraphicsState];
}
```

The previous code can be executed by choosing the Rotation Example option on the control panel of the Paths example. A sample of this method's output can be seen in Figure 13.3.

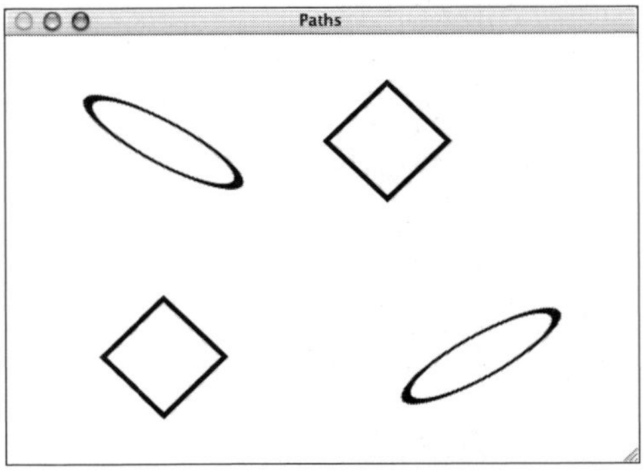

FIGURE 13.3 The output of the Rotation Example option is shown.

Reverse Transforms

At times it is useful to create a transform that does the opposite of an existing transform. The `-invert` method can be used to produce just that. An example of this follows:

```
reverseTransform = [[NSAffineTransform alloc] initWithTransform:existingTransform];
[reverseTransform invert];
```

After the invert message, reverseTransform would have the reverse effect on drawing that `existingTransform` has.

Combining Transforms

Multiple transforms can be combined into a single transform. The `NSAffineTransform` object can be thought of as a sequence of transformations that can be applied to drawing. The order of operations in the sequence is important (consider the previous combination of rotation and translation). Because order is important, there are two methods that can be used to build up a sequence of transformations:

```
- (void)appendTransform:(NSAffineTransform *)transform;
- (void)prependTransform:(NSAffineTransform *)transform;
```

The names of these methods are highly counterintuitive, so be very careful with them! The names match up with the math that is going on inside the `NSAffineTransform` object, as described in the "Expert Transforms" section later in this chapter. The effect the methods have is the opposite of what would be expected. To explain what will happen, consider the translation with rotation example shown in Figure 13.3. Suppose there are two objects, `translateTransform` and `rotateTransform`, and you want to create a third object that combines the two. Here are two of several possible ways to obtain the new objects:

```
NSAffineTransform *combinedTransform1;
NSAffineTransform *combinedTransform2;
combinedTransform1 = [[NSAffineTransform alloc]
        initWithTransform: translateTransform];
[combinedTransform1 prependTransform:rotateTransform];
combinedTransform2 = [[NSAffineTransform alloc]
        initWithTransform: translateTransform];
[combinedTransform2 appendTransform:rotateTransform];
```

The object `combinedTransform1` will perform a translation followed by a rotation. The other object, `combinedTransform2`, will be the reverse—a rotation followed by a translation. It might be expected that appending a transform would cause it to happen after what is already there, but that's not the case. If the transforms are listed from left to right, with prepend operation adding a transform to the left and an append operation adding a transform to the right, then the right-most transform is the one that takes effect first. The order of the transform operations will occur from right to left, with the left-most being the last transform applied. All the previous methods for scaling, rotation, and translation actually prepend their operation to the `NSAffineTransform` instance so they will take place after what is already there.

Although this is slightly confusing at first, the rule is simple and can easily be memorized: If a transform is to happen before what is there, use append. If it is to happen after, use prepend. Remember also that these terms are describing the underlying math rather than the expected effect. Although they might seem odd, they are actually following a common naming standard.

Prepending and appending transformations can offer a huge performance boost. This is because the cost of applying a transformation is constant no matter how many transform operations are aggregated together into a single `NSAffineTransform`. The reason for this becomes clearer in the "Expert Transforms" section later in this chapter. If a particular set of transformations occurs often, combining them into a single transformation with prepend and/or append operations will provide a performance boost. Rather than applying each transformation one by one, which can become time consuming, a single transform is applied that performs them all at once.

Using an NSAffineTransform

Defining a transform, as shown in the previous section, is not enough to actually alter drawing. For an NSAffineTransform to have any effect, it needs to be applied. It can be applied to an NSPoint or NSSize structure or to an NSBezierPath object. Doing so will return a new structure or object that represents the original entity after transformation. The transform can be applied to a graphic context, and after that it will affect all drawing.

To transform an NSPoint, use the -transformPoint: method. The method will return a new NSPoint, leaving the original NSPoint unaffected. For example:

```
NSPoint transformedPoint = [myTransform transformPoint:originalPoint];
```

To transform an NSSize, use the -transformSize: method. It works in a way similar to the -transformPoint: method. The -transformSize: method will return a new NSSize, leaving the original NSSize unaffected. For example:

```
NSSize transformedSize = [myTransform transformSize:originalSize];
```

There are two ways to transform an NSBezierPath object. If a new object, a transformed NSBezierPath, is required, the NSAffineTransform method -transformBezierPath: should be used, like this:

```
NSBezierPath *newPath = [myTransform transformBezierPath:originalPath];
```

Alternatively, if a new object is not desired, it is possible to transform an NSBezierPath object in place by sending it the -transformUsingAffineTransform: message like this:

```
[myPath transformUsingAffineTransform:myTransform];
```

In each of the previous methods, the effect of the transform is restricted to the structure or object upon which the message acts. More often, a transform is used to alter all subsequent drawing within a particular graphics context. To apply a transform to the current graphics context, send it a -concat message such as this:

```
[myTransform concat];
```

Note that this will always affect the current graphics context. Furthermore, the context's current transformation matrix (also called the CTM) is one of the things saved or restored when a graphics context is saved or restored as described in the "Using NSGraphicsContext" section later in this chapter. Just as with clipping areas, saving and restoring the graphics context can be used to undo changes to the CTM made with the -concat method.

The -set method can be used instead of -concat. Just as with clipping paths, the -set method is dangerous because it completely replaces the CTM rather than simply modifying it. This is important because when an NSView's drawRect: is called, the CTM is already set to account for the view's location, scaling, and rotation. By using -concat, the basic coordinate system of the view itself is being used as a starting point for any subsequent transformations. Using -set starts with the NSWindow's coordinate system instead. If all the specifics of the NSView's positioning are not taken into account within the window, -set will most likely not work as expected, and should therefore be avoided unless absolutely necessary. Similar to working with clipping areas, saving and restoring the graphic context is the preferred way to back out of a transformation.

When a transform has been applied to a graphics context, everything is affected. The path itself is altered by the transform. But line widths, dash patterns, fill patterns, and so on, are also all affected by the CTM. This can lead to unwanted distortion. The problem is that both the path and the rendering are being affected by the transformation. To affect only the path, and not the rendering, the NSAffineTransform's -transformBezierPath: method should be used instead of setting the transform as the graphics context's CTM. Here is some code to demonstrate this technique by drawing rectangles that have been stretched vertically and horizontally:

```
- (void)drawDistortion
{
// Draw four sheared rectangles
//   2 horiz stretch, correct       3 vert stretch, correct
//   1 horiz stretch, distorted     4 vert stretch, distorted
    NSGraphicsContext *currentContext = [NSGraphicsContext currentContext];
    NSBezierPath *path = [NSBezierPath bezierPath];
    NSAffineTransform *transform = nil;
    NSRect bds = [self bounds];
    // divide the view into four rectangles
    NSRect r1 = NSMakeRect(bds.origin.x, bds.origin.y,
            bds.size.width / 4.0 - 20.0, bds.size.height / 4.0 - 20.0);
    NSRect r2 = NSMakeRect(bds.origin.x, NSMidY(bds),
            bds.size.width / 2.0, bds.size.height / 2.0);
    NSRect r3 = NSMakeRect(NSMidX(bds), NSMidY(bds),
            bds.size.width / 2.0, bds.size.height / 2.0);
    NSRect r4 = NSMakeRect(NSMidX(bds), bds.origin.y,
            bds.size.width / 2.0, bds.size.height / 2.0);
```

```
// clear the view to a white background
[[NSColor whiteColor] set];
NSRectFill(bds);

// set the drawing color to black and the line width to 2.0
[[NSColor blackColor] set];
[path setLineWidth:10.0];

// define the star's path
[path appendBezierPathWithRect:r1];
//[path closePath];

// do r1 — horiz stretch, with distortion
transform = [NSAffineTransform transform];
[transform translateXBy:10.0 yBy:10.0];
[transform scaleXBy:2.0 yBy:1.0];
[currentContext saveGraphicsState];
[transform concat];
[path stroke];
[currentContext restoreGraphicsState];

// do r4 — vert stretch, with distortion
transform = [NSAffineTransform transform];
[transform translateXBy:r4.origin.x + 10.0 yBy:r4.origin.y + 10.0];
[transform scaleXBy:1.0 yBy:2.0];
[currentContext saveGraphicsState];
[transform concat];
[path stroke];
[currentContext restoreGraphicsState];

// do r3 — vert stretch, no distortion
transform = [NSAffineTransform transform];
[transform translateXBy:r3.origin.x + 10.0 yBy:r3.origin.y + 10.0];
[transform scaleXBy:1.0 yBy:2.0];
[currentContext saveGraphicsState];
[[transform transformBezierPath:path] stroke];
[currentContext restoreGraphicsState];

// do r2 — horiz stretch, no distortion
transform = [NSAffineTransform transform];
[transform translateXBy:r2.origin.x + 10.0 yBy:r2.origin.y + 10.0];
[transform scaleXBy:2.0 yBy:1.0];
```

```
    [currentContext saveGraphicsState];
    [[transform transformBezierPath:path] stroke];
    [currentContext restoreGraphicsState];
}
```

Figure 13.4 shows what this code's output looks like:

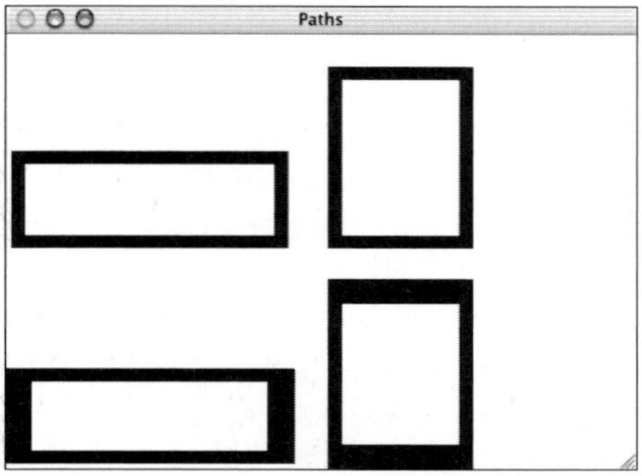

FIGURE 13.4 Output using `NSAffineTransform`'s `-transformBezierPath:` method is shown here.

Expert Transforms

There is another way to define an `NSAffineTransform`, but it is more complex than simple translation, scale, and rotation methods described in the "Defining an `NSAffineTransform`" section earlier in this chapter. Transforms are sometimes referred to as matrices because the underlying implementation uses a 3×3 matrix to define an affine transform. Matrix multiplication is used to get the new coordinates for a point from the original coordinates. By treating the input point as a vector, the matrix and vector can be multiplied to produce a new vector. The resultant vector is the new, transformed point.

By multiplying two 3×3 transformation matrices together, it is possible to create a new matrix. The new matrix, when used to transform a point, will perform both the transformations that the original matrices would have performed had they been applied individually. Several transforms can be multiplied together to create a single transform matrix that will perform all the operations of the original multiplicands. Matrix multiplication is not commutative like other more common types of multiplication. This means that order is important because the order the operations are applied changes the results, often dramatically. When a series of multiplications is written out, it might look like this (capital letters represent the matrices):

```
result = A × B × C × point
```

The order of the transforms actually affects the input point starting with the matrix closest to the point and ending with the matrix farthest from the point. Thus, transform C, then B, and finally A will be applied to the point to produce the result. If the matrix Z were defined to be the multiplication of the other matrices (A × B × C), then this equation would produce the same result:

```
result = Z × point
```

Note that if a matrix is prepended, or added to the beginning of the multiplications, then that matrix's transformation will be applied last. Conversely, if a matrix is appended (such as inserting a matrix D between C and point in the previous example), that transformation will occur before the others. This demonstrates why the prepend and append operations as described earlier do make sense according to the underlying mathematics.

The `-concat` method described previously works inside the current graphics context by performing a prepended multiplication with the CTM. The prepend and append methods do a matrix multiply inside the `NSAffineTransform` instance instead of inside the current graphics context.

There are several standard forms for defining matrices for translation, scaling, rotation, and shearing. The Cocoa documentation gives a good description of each kind of matrix, so they aren't repeated here. Refer to this page for the details:

`/Developer/Documentation/Cocoa/TasksAndConcepts/ProgrammingTopics/DrawBasic/Concepts/transforms.html`

One of the types of transformations mentioned at the start of the "Modifying Drawing" section of Chapter 12 was shearing. However, there is no `NSAffineTransform` method to explicitly do shearing.With that in mind, the next example will use direct manipulation of transform matrices to create a method for doing shearing.

First, code to actually modify an `NSAffineTransform`'s internal matrix is needed. For working with `NSAffineTransform` objects at this level, the Application Kit defines a special structure, `NSAffineTransformStruct`. This structure holds the six values required to specify a transformation matrix. It is defined as follows:

```
typedef struct _NSAffineTransformStruct {
    float m11, m12, m21, m22;
    float tX, tY;
} NSAffineTransformStruct;
```

Note that the structure members' names correspond exactly to the matrix and equations shown in the Apple documentation referenced previously. The

`NSAffineTransformStruct` for a given `NSAffineTransform` object can be obtained using the `-transformStruct` method as follows:

```
NSAffineTransformStruct myTransformStruct = [aTransform transformStruct];
```

This allows the actual matrix values of a given `NSAffineTransform` to be examined.

An `NSAffineTransformStruct` can alter the members in an arbitrary way. To change the entire matrix of an `NSAffineTransform` all at once, perhaps in a way that is not a typical translation, scaling, or rotation, the `-setTransformStruct:` method would be used:

```
[aTransform setTransformStruct: myTransformStruct];
```

Calling this method will remove any existing transforms the object has previously defined, and replace it with whatever transform is defined by `myTransformStruct`.

As an example of how to use these methods, a new transformation will be created. Because there is no `NSAffineTransform` method for shearing, one can be created as an `NSAffineTransform` category. To add a shear to the current transform, do the following:

1. Create a new transform object to hold just a shear transformation.
2. Set the new object's matrix coefficients to match a shear matrix.
3. Prepend the new shear transform to self.

The new matrix is prepended and not appended. Remember that order is important (consider rotation and translation, as in Figure 13.2). By prepending the shear, it is the operation that will affect the drawing last. The existing translation, scaling, and rotation methods are also all performing a prepend operation.

The code required to implement this algorithm looks like this:

```
File Shearing.h:

#import <Cocoa/Cocoa.h>

@interface NSAffineTransform(Shearing)
- (void)shearXBy:(float)shX yBy:(float)shY;
@end
```

File Shearing.m:

```
#import "Shearing.h"

@implementation NSAffineTransform(Shearing)

- (void)shearXBy:(float)shX yBy:(float)shY
{
    NSAffineTransform *shear = [NSAffineTransform transform];
    NSAffineTransformStruct shearStruct;
    shearStruct.m11 = 1.0;
    shearStruct.m12 = shY;
    shearStruct.m21 = shX;
    shearStruct.m22 = 1.0;
    shearStruct.tX = 0.0;
    shearStruct.tY = 0.0;
    [shear setTransformStruct:shearStruct];
    [self prependTransform:shear];
}

@end
```

The Paths example contains a method that will draw four sheared rectangles using the previous code. The complete implementation code is as follows:

```
- (void)drawShears
{
// Draw four sheared rectangles
//   2 y shear      3 x and y shear
//   1 no shear     4 x shear
    NSGraphicsContext *currentContext = [NSGraphicsContext currentContext];
    NSBezierPath *path = [NSBezierPath bezierPath];
    NSAffineTransform *transform = nil;
    NSRect bds = [self bounds];
    // divide the view into four rectangles
    NSRect r1 = NSMakeRect(bds.origin.x, bds.origin.y,
            bds.size.width / 4.0 - 20.0, bds.size.height / 4.0 - 20.0);
    NSRect r2 = NSMakeRect(bds.origin.x, NSMidY(bds),
            bds.size.width / 2.0, bds.size.height / 2.0);
    NSRect r3 = NSMakeRect(NSMidX(bds), NSMidY(bds),
            bds.size.width / 2.0, bds.size.height / 2.0);
    NSRect r4 = NSMakeRect(NSMidX(bds), bds.origin.y,
            bds.size.width / 2.0, bds.size.height / 2.0);
```

```
// clear the view to a white background
[[NSColor whiteColor] set];
NSRectFill(bds);

// set the drawing color to black and the line width to 2.0
[[NSColor blackColor] set];
[path setLineWidth:2.0];

// define the star's path
[path appendBezierPathWithRect:r1];
//[path closePath];

// stroke the rectangle in r1.
transform = [NSAffineTransform transform];
[transform translateXBy:10.0 yBy:10.0];
[currentContext saveGraphicsState];
[transform concat];
[path stroke];
[currentContext restoreGraphicsState];

// do r4 — x shear
transform = [NSAffineTransform transform];
[transform translateXBy:r4.origin.x + 10.0 yBy:r4.origin.y + 10.0];
[transform shearXBy:0.5 yBy:0.0];
[currentContext saveGraphicsState];
[transform concat];
[path stroke];
[currentContext restoreGraphicsState];

// do r3 — both shears
transform = [NSAffineTransform transform];
[transform translateXBy:r3.origin.x + 10.0 yBy:r3.origin.y + 10.0];
[transform shearXBy:0.5 yBy:0.5];
[currentContext saveGraphicsState];
[transform concat];
[path stroke];
[currentContext restoreGraphicsState];

// do r2 — y shear
transform = [NSAffineTransform transform];
[transform translateXBy:r2.origin.x + 10.0 yBy:r2.origin.y + 10.0];
[transform shearXBy:0.0 yBy:0.5];
```

```
    [currentContext saveGraphicsState];
    [transform concat];
    [path stroke];
    [currentContext restoreGraphicsState];
}
```

Figure 13.5 illustrates the output that results when the previous method is called from within the -drawRect: method in the Paths example.

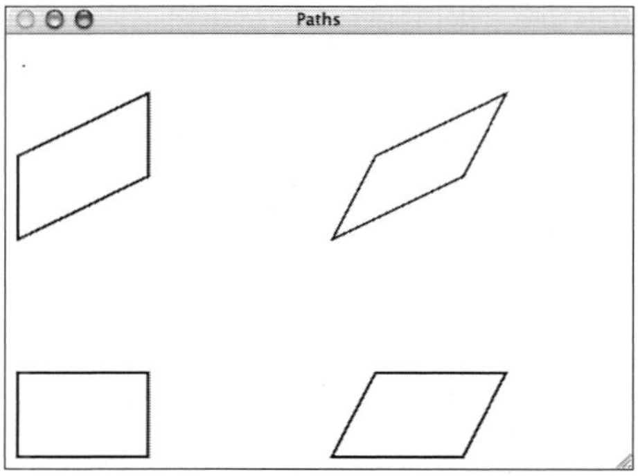

FIGURE 13.5 This is the output from the -drawRect: method in the Paths example.

A few things should be noted about this new -shearXBy:yBy: method. First, the values for shX and shY are not angles. In fact, values of 1.0 will produce 45° angles. Second, as the X-axis shear value increases the X axis rotates counter clockwise, but as the Y-axis shear value increases the Y axis rotates clockwise. This is opposite from what might at first be expected, but is amply illustrated in the output shown previously. A final important point is that when both the X- and Y-axis shear values are equal to 1.0, both axes are rotated towards each other 45°. This means they will have collapsed into a single axis running at a 45° angle. Because the axes are collapsed, attempts at drawing will not come out as expected. In fact, this line is mathematically infinitely narrow. That is why no drawing will appear whatsoever if a transform is used that shears both X and Y by 1.0.

NOTE

Direct manipulation of a transformation matrix's coefficients makes it possible to create a singular matrix. Such a matrix cannot be inverted; it is a mathematical impossibility. Therefore, be forewarned that code that strays from using the basic transform, scale, and rotation operations could produce an NSAffineTransform for which the -invert method cannot be called.

Drawing Points and Rectangles

Cocoa does not provide any methods, objects, or functions specifically intended for drawing points. Cocoa provides the `NSPoint` structure, yet there is no means of rendering an `NSPoint` onscreen. The reason has to do with the graphics model employed by Cocoa and Quartz. Apple describes the graphics model as being the same model as PDF and PostScript. This implies that all drawing should be considered to be both device and resolution independent. As a result, drawing a point is meaningless. In this graphics model, the term point is used to refer to a very precise, infinitely small point in the mathematical sense. If such a point was marked with ink, it still wouldn't be seen because it is infinitely small.

When drawing or plotting a point, the intent is to paint a single pixel. A single pixel on a display is much larger than a single dot on a high-resolution laser printer. To enable painting of pixels when it makes sense, the implementation of Quartz is not completely resolution independent when it comes to video devices. As a simplification, Quartz treats all video devices as if they are 72 dpi (dots per inch). When a coordinate is specified, the units used are typographical points, defined as 1/72 of an inch. If a square is drawn that is 1.0 in width and height, Quartz will paint a single pixel.

It seems inefficient to paint a filled rectangle every time a developer wants to draw a point on the screen. However, Quartz works very hard to notice things such as a 1.0×1.0 rectangle and optimize the `NSRectFill()` call. If there is more than one point of the same color to draw, using `NSRectFillList()` to draw multiple rectangles at once will offer reasonable performance for most applications. The advantage to using this approach is that when printed the drawing will still look right on the page. Extra pixels will be painted on the higher resolution devices so that the point plotted will truly be 1/72 of an inch on the page.

There is still a speed hit when rectangles are drawn. Another approach can be used to paint individual pixels. An `NSBitmapImageRep` can be used as a cover to raw pixel data. Because the pointer to the image data can be accessed directly, a function can be created to plot a point into the raw data and then copy the image onto the screen. Using raw image data is complex, and a complete description of the technique is not provided until Chapter 14, "Custom Views and Graphics Part III."

Drawing into a cache only provides a performance improvement when there are large batches of points to plot because it takes quite a bit of time to composite an image. Furthermore, in taking this approach any benefits of ColorSync and device resolution independence are lost unless extra effort is made to engage these features. One of the special tricks that can be used in conjunction with this caching method is to add it to an `NSImage`, and then ask Quartz to draw into the image, so drawing primitives don't necessarily have to be created by the developer.

Drawing Individual Rectangles

The following code segments implement each of these three techniques. The first segment draws individual rectangles. This is the easiest method.

```
File PointView.h :

#import <Cocoa/Cocoa.h>

#define NUM_POINTS 40000

@interface MYPointView : NSView
{
}

- (void)drawRect:(NSRect)aRect;

@end

File PointView.m :

#import "PointView.h"

@implementation MYPointView

- (void)drawRect:(NSRect)aRect
{
    int i;
    NSRect bds = [self bounds];
    [[NSColor blackColor] set];
    NSRectFill(bds);
    [[NSColor whiteColor] set];
    for (i=0; i<NUM_POINTS; i++) {
        NSRectFill(NSMakeRect(random() % bds.size.width,
                random() % bds.size.height, 1.0, 1.0));
    }
}

@end
```

This sample class needs no instance variables and no special initialization. The `-drawRect:` method simply has a loop to draw 1.0×1.0 rectangles at random locations inside the view's bounds. The `NSRectFill()` function is used to paint the rectangle defined by the `NSMakeRect()` function. The rectangles will be drawn with the color most recently `-set`, white in this example. Although simple to implement, the downside to this approach is that it is extremely slow. Unless all the points are different colors or there aren't many points to plot, this method is probably not the best choice.

Drawing Lists of Rectangles

The next method is to use lists of rectangles. Instead of using `NSRectFill()` to plot a single rectangle, use `NSRectFillList()` to fill several rectangles at once. It requires two parameters. The first is a pointer to a C array of `NSRect` structures. The second is an integer specifying how many rectangles are in the array. The array could be longer than the count specifies, but the extra rectangles won't be drawn in that case. The following code modifies the PointView object to use this technique.

```
File PointView.h :

#import <Cocoa/Cocoa.h>

#define NUM_PASSES 40
#define NUM_PER_PASS 1000
#define NUM_POINTS (NUM_PASSES * NUM_PER_PASS)

@interface MYPointView : NSView
{
    NSRect _myRectList[NUM_PER_PASS];
}

- (id)initWithFrame:(NSRect)frameRect;
- (void)drawRect:(NSRect)aRect;

@end

File PointView.m :

#import "PointView.h"

@implementation MYPointView

- (id)initWithFrame:(NSRect)frameRect
{
    int i;
    id ret = [super initWithFrame:frameRect];
```

```
    if (!ret) return nil;
    for (i=0; i<NUM_PER_PASS; i++) {
        myRectList[i].origin.x = 0.0;
        myRectList[i].origin.y = 0.0;
        myRectList[i].size.width = 1.0;
        myRectList[i].size.height = 1.0;
    }
    return ret;
}

- (void)drawRect:(NSRect)aRect
{
    int i, j;
    NSRect bds = [self bounds];
    [[NSColor blackColor] set];
    NSRectFill(bds);
    [[NSColor whiteColor] set];
    for (j=0; j<NUM_PASSES; j++) {
        for (i=0; i<NUM_PER_PASS; i++) {
            myRectList[i].origin.x = random() % bds.size.width;
            myRectList[i].origin.y = random() % bds.size.height;
        }
        NSRectFillList(myRectList, NUM_PER_PASS);
    }
}

@end
```

This approach is more complex because an array of rectangles and some special initialization is required. This rectangle array was filled with reasonable values as part of the view's initialization. The reason for this is that the width and height of each rectangle is known and constant. It makes sense to set it only once, and the initialization of the view is an excellent place for setting these values.

When it comes time to draw, use the loop with i as the loop variable to load the rectangle values into the list. When that is done, call `NSRectFillList()`. This is repeated for each batch of rectangles, using the j loop.

The previous code is rather simple. It assumes that the total number of points to plot is exactly the number of passes (batches) multiplied by the number of rectangles per pass. In a more realistic implementation, the last call to `NSRectFillList()` might send something less than `NUM_PER_PASS` as the number of rectangles to draw.

It turns out that this approach, lists of rectangles, is about ten times faster than the single-rectangle approach. If you have many rectangles of the same color, this is a very efficient way to get them drawn. The added complexity is not ten times worse to deal with, so in most cases this will probably be the preferred approach. If the rectangles vary in color, `NSRectFillList()` can't be used. Sort them by color into batches. If every rectangle's color is different, though, use `NSRectFillListWithColors()` instead. This function doesn't offer as much speed as `NSRectFillList()`, but it is faster than a sequence of `NSColor -set` and `NSRectFill()` calls.

Drawing with Bitmaps

The final technique is to use a bitmap cache and draw the points directly into it, as shown in the following code. This method is a bit more involved. First, set up the bitmap cache itself; then, the code must determine the location of the desired pixel(s), which requires a little math. When the bytes are altered, copy the bitmap to the view's onscreen area. The following code is one way to accomplish all of that.

```
File PointView.h :

#import <Cocoa/Cocoa.h>

#define NUM_POINTS 40000

@interface MYPointView : NSView
{
    NSBitmapImageRep *_myImageCache;
    unsigned char *_myDataPtr;
    int _myRowBytes;
}

- (id)initWithFrame:(NSRect)frameRect;
- (void)drawRect:(NSRect)aRect;

@end

File PointView.m :

#import "PointView.h"

@implementation MYPointView
```

```
- (id)initWithFrame:(NSRect)frameRect
{
    int i;
    id ret = [super initWithFrame:frameRect];
    if (!ret) return nil;
    myRowBytes = (((int)(frameRect.size.width / 4) + 1) * 4) * 4;
    myDataPtr = (unsigned char *)malloc(myRowBytes * frameRect.size.height);
    myImageCache = [[NSBitmapImageRep alloc]
            initWithBitmapDataPlanes:&myDataPtr
            pixelsWide:frameRect.size.width
            pixelsHigh:frameRect.size.height
            bitsPerSample:8 samplesPerPixel:4
            hasAlpha:YES isPlanar:NO
            colorSpaceName:NSDeviceRGBColorSpace
            bytesPerRow:myRowBytes bitsPerPixel:(8 * 4)];
    return ret;
}

- (void)drawRect:(NSRect)aRect
{
    int i, j;
    NSRect bds = [self bounds];
    for (i=0; i<myRowBytes*bds.size.height/4; i++) {
        ((unsigned int *)myDataPtr)[i] = 0;
    }
    for (i=0; i<NUM_POINTS; i++) {
        int x = random() % bds.size.width;
        int y = random() % bds.size.height;
        int baseIndex = ((bds.size.height - y - 1) * myRowBytes) + (x * 4);
        unsigned int *basePtr = (unsigned int *)&(myDataPtr[baseIndex]);
        *basePtr = 0xffffffff; // 0xrrggbbaa one whole pixel
    }
    [myImageCache draw];
}

- (void)dealloc
{
    free(myDataPtr);
    [myImageCache release];
    [super dealloc];
}

@end
```

The code for this third approach is more complex. It uses three new instance variables: `dataPtr`, `imageCache`, and `rowBytes`. The first of these, `dataPtr`, is a standard-C pointer that points to a chunk of bytes that will store the raw data for the image cache. The `imageCache` variable points to an `NSBitmapImageRep` object that will wrap around the data stored in `dataPtr`. This class will provide the ability to get the raw data onto the screen easily.

The third instance variable, `rowBytes`, is not strictly necessary. It is used to gain a little bit of efficiency. Normally, the number of bytes per image row is the number of bytes per pixel multiplied by the width of the image in pixels. However, it turns out that if this value is a multiple of 16, Quartz will kick in Altivec to draw the image. On a G4 Mac, this means a significant speedup. This example will be laying out our data as 32 bits per pixel (8 each for red, green, blue, and alpha). This means that the number of bytes per row will always be a multiple of four, but not necessarily a multiple of 16. Only images that have widths that are multiples of four would be able to take advantage of Altivec. Instead, adding a few wasted bytes to the end of each row will pad this number out to a multiple of 16. Because this calculation is more complex than just multiplying the number of pixels per row by four, cache the number of bytes per row in the rowBytes instance variable once the value is calculated.

Now initialize the variables in the `-initWithFrame:` method. Begin by calculating rowBytes. This calculation will always give a value that is divisible by 16. Next, use the standard `malloc()` function to allocate a pointer to a chunk of bytes large enough to store the raw image data. The number of bytes per row, multiplied by the number of rows provides the total number of bytes required by `malloc()`.

Finally, create an `NSBitmapImageRep` object to wrap around the data pointer. To create this object, tell it exactly how the image data is laid out, and provide it with a pointer to the raw image data. Instances can be created that wrap around TIFF or other image types, in this case a different initializer would be used to read and decode the image from an `NSData` object. Because an image cache is being used and there is no preexisting image data to decode, use the raw interface.

With the instance variables set up, implement the actual drawing code. The first thing to do is to clear the raw image data to all black. Rather than set each byte individually, treat the data pointer as a pointer to C's int type, which allows four bytes to be set simultaneously. For more speed, on G4 systems use Altivec and clear 16 bytes at once.

Next, draw all the points, one at a time, into the buffer by setting the raw bytes to the rgb color desired. Again, use the int shortcut to set four bytes at once. The for loop starts by randomly choosing a point's coordinates. Next, the location inside the raw data is calculated for the randomly chosen pixel. Note that the cached `rowBytes` value is being used, so that the padding at the end of each row is correctly taken into account.

Unlike the standard OS X coordinate system, which places the origin at the lower left, the image data is assumed to have its origin at the upper-left corner. Increasing y coordinates moves down the image, because it is flipped from the screen's coordinate system. This is why, in calculating the pixel's address, y is subtracted from the image's height. If this isn't done, the image cache will be drawn upside down.

After calculating the pixel's address, set the four bytes at that address to the new pixel values. The values are specified as hexadecimal numbers to make it easier to see what the r, g, b, and a values are. In this case white pixels will be drawn, so setting them all to 255, or hex 0xFF, is what is needed.

After the loop is complete and all the pixels have been drawn, send the image cache to the screen. Note that the `NSBitmapImageRep` object has only very rudimentary drawing facilities. The `-draw` method behaves like a copy operation, so the image will completely replace anything that was on the screen before it was drawn. To use more complex drawing, such as compositing operators, then use an `NSImage` object that contains the `NSBitmapImageRep` instance. A copy operation is what is desired in this example, so a `-draw` message is sufficient.

The final part of the code frees the image cache when deallocating. This is done with a straightforward override of the `-dealloc` method. Forgetting to do this would cause a memory leak.

The image cache technique is now implemented. Although the previous code works, one thing is missing. If the `NSView` subclass changes its size, the buffer doesn't change with it. This could create some problems. Because the calculations for buffer address use the view's current size, an incorrect address could be calculated. If the view becomes bigger, a buffer overrun could occur. The solution to this problem is to create a new image cache whenever the view is resized. One possible implementation of that would be to override the `NSView` method `-setFrame:` using this method:

```
- (void)setFrame:(NSRect)frameRect
{
    free(myDataPtr);
    [myImageCache release];
    [super setFrame:frameRect];
    myRowBytes = (((int)(frameRect.size.width / 4) + 1) * 4) * 4;
    myDataPtr = (unsigned char *)malloc(myRowBytes * frameRect.size.height);
    myImageCache = [[NSBitmapImageRep alloc]
            initWithBitmapDataPlanes:&myDataPtr
            pixelsWide:frameRect.size.width
            pixelsHigh:frameRect.size.height
            bitsPerSample:8 samplesPerPixel:4
```

```
            hasAlpha:YES isPlanar:NO
            colorSpaceName:NSDeviceRGBColorSpace
            bytesPerRow:myRowBytes bitsPerPixel:(8 * 4)];
}
```

First destroy the old buffer, and then allow super to set the new frame size. Finish up by creating a new buffer. It would be more efficient to first check and see if the new frame is a different size, and only destroy and recreate the buffer in cases where it really changes. Additionally, from a design perspective, the code is now poorly organized because there is duplicate code. Ideally, break the buffer creation and destruction out into their own private methods, and then use those throughout the code. The following code shows this change.

```
File PointView.h :

#import <Cocoa/Cocoa.h>

#define NUM_POINTS 40000

@interface MYPointView : NSView
{
    NSBitmapImageRep *_myImageCache;
    unsigned char *_myDataPtr;
    int _myRowBytes;
}

- (id)initWithFrame:(NSRect)frameRect;
- (void)drawRect:(NSRect)aRect;
- (void)setFrame:(NSRect)frameRect;

@end

File PointView.m :

#import "PointView.h"

@interface MYPointView(_private_methods)
- (void)_createCache;
- (void)_destroyCache;
@end

@implementation MYPointView
```

```
- (id)initWithFrame:(NSRect)frameRect
{
    int i;
    id ret = [super initWithFrame:frameRect];
    if (!ret) return nil;
    [self _createCache];
    return ret;
}

- (void)_createCache
{
    NSRect frameRect = [self bounds];
    if (myDataPtr || myImageCache) {
        [self _destroyCache];
    }
    myRowBytes = (((int)(frameRect.size.width / 4) + 1) * 4) * 4;
    myDataPtr = (unsigned char *)malloc(myRowBytes * frameRect.size.height);
    myImageCache = [[NSBitmapImageRep alloc]
            initWithBitmapDataPlanes:&myDataPtr
            pixelsWide:frameRect.size.width
            pixelsHigh:frameRect.size.height
            bitsPerSample:8 samplesPerPixel:4
            hasAlpha:YES isPlanar:NO
            colorSpaceName:NSDeviceRGBColorSpace
            bytesPerRow:myRowBytes bitsPerPixel:(8 * 4)];
}

- (void)_destroyCache
{
    free(myDataPtr);
    myDataPtr = NULL;
    [myImageCache release];
    myImageCache = nil;
}

- (void)setFrame:(NSRect)frameRect
{
    [self _destroyCache];
    [super setFrame:frameRect];
    [self _createCache];
}
```

```
- (void)drawRect:(NSRect)aRect
{
    int i, j;
    NSRect bds = [self bounds];
    for (i=0; i<myRowBytes*bds.size.height/4; i++) {
        ((unsigned int *)myDataPtr)[i] = 0;
    }
    for (i=0; i<NUM_POINTS; i++) {
        int x = random() % bds.size.width;
        int y = random() % bds.size.height;
        int baseIndex = ((bds.size.height - y - 1) * myRowBytes) + (x * 4);
        unsigned int *basePtr = (unsigned int *)&(myDataPtr[baseIndex]);
        *basePtr = 0xffffffff; // 0xrrggbbaa one whole pixel
    }
    [myImageCache draw];
}

- (void)dealloc
{
    [self _destroyCache];
    [super dealloc];
}

@end
```

Although this is better, there are still some issues remaining. For example, when setting the pixels to a particular color value, raw hex bytes are being used. This completely bypasses ColorSync. It would be better to find out what the RGB values should be, based on how the user has calibrated their computer's ColorSync profile for their monitor. Use an `NSColor` object to find out the proper RGB values; see Chapter 17, which concentrates on color, for how to do this.

Another problem is that this approach is not device independent. It makes assumptions about the size of a pixel. When doing the drawing, it would be better to find out whether it was destined for the screen, a file, printer, or some other medium. In Chapter 25, on printing, it is demonstrated how to determine where the view's drawing will end up. (The section "Using `NSGraphicsContext`" earlier in this chapter also discusses this.) Use the image cache method when the drawing is going to the screen, but use the list of rectangles method for all other types of drawing to retain device independence.

The Points example on the `www.cocoaprogramming.net` Web site provides sample code, which implements all three of these methods for drawing points in one single object. All the code shown previously has been combined into this one single example. It also can time the drawing to give a feel for each approach's performance. Try building it and experimenting with it. On a Pismo PowerBook, drawing 40,000 points takes approximately 2.2 seconds for individual rectangles, 0.22 seconds for rectangle lists, and 0.10 seconds with the bitmap cache.

Remember, however, that although the cache is faster, it is effectively bypassing most of Quartz, and in a real-world application, the speed up in drawing time might be insignificant compared to the rest of the application's calculations. Using the list of rectangles approach will make the most sense for the majority of applications. Very few will gain more than they lose when using image caches.

Optimizing Drawing

The documentation included with the Mac OS X Developer Tools includes an "Inside Mac OS X: Performance." This document talks about the tools for improving performance and how to use them. The file is found at `/Developer/Documentation/Essentials/Performance/Performance.pdf`.

Although all the techniques described in this document are useful for speeding up an application, there is not a lot of information about how to speed up drawing performance. It is worth reading this document because it will help with more general optimization and performance improvement.

There are many techniques that can be used to improve drawing performance. Most of this information is scattered throughout the Cocoa class references and other Mac OS X developer documentation.

When discussing drawing performance, there are some key rules throughout:

Rule #1: The fastest drawing is the drawing you don't do

The first rule suggests that unnecessary drawing should be avoided at all costs. Drawing is an inherently costly process because even a modestly sized drawing area can require huge amounts of data to be manipulated by the CPU and system bus. Consider, for example, a 128×128 pixel area. This is the size of an Aqua icon when at its largest. If this area is stored in a 32-bit RGBA buffer (8 bits each for red, green, blue, and alpha), the buffer would represent a total of $128 \times 128 \times 4 = 65536$ bytes. This can add up quickly. Therefore, don't ever draw more than what is needed, and be careful that the same things aren't drawn multiple times. More will be discussed about what this means and how to do it as specific optimization techniques are covered.

The rest of the optimization rules don't specifically apply to drawing, but they are critical to success.

Rule #2: Speed doesn't come for free

As with all optimizations, improved speed usually comes with an associated cost. Sometimes there is an up-front setup cost, so an optimization might only benefit an operation that is repeated many times. Other times the cost is in code complexity, and hence future maintainability and extensibility. Usually the cost is extra memory. For example, a chunk of complex drawing code might take quite a while to execute. It could be rendered once into an offscreen `NSImage`, and then composited whenever the drawing is needed onscreen. If the compositing operation is faster than the original drawing—which would be true for extremely complex drawing—then this results in a performance improvement. The downside is the extra memory required for the cache.

Because Mac OS X has a virtual-memory system, if there isn't enough RAM available, swapping will begin to occur. An application with too many offscreen buffers could cause swapping. Unless the drawing complexity is extreme, it is safe to assume that swapping in an image buffer from virtual memory will be a lot slower than just drawing everything to begin with. Therefore, it is critical to watch an application's memory usage both within the application and within the Quartz window server to make sure that won't cause a lower end, RAM-starved computer to swap too much. This leads right into the next rule:

Rule #3: Measure performance often

A given optimization might only be a true improvement in performance under certain circumstances. Because the parameters might be quite complex, it can often be easy to apply an optimization in a situation or in such a way that it actually reduces performance. A classic example is the one presented previously with Rule #2. If a set of optimizations uses so much memory that the computer begins to swap, performance will drop off very quickly. Therefore, every time an optimization, or set of optimizations, is applied, it is critical to measure the actual impact on real and perceived performance.

Experimentation is the key to getting things perfect. Try everything, measure it, and keep what works best. Don't forget to test on the lowest-end piece of hardware that the application will be targeting. Sometimes, optimizations need to be dynamically engaged and only turned on for machines that can use them to full advantage.

Measuring performance through profiling will expose the areas that will most impact an application's speed. It is more important to optimize code that is used thousands of times a minute than code that is used only once. Intuition commonly leads programmers astray here: Measure the execution so the true hot spots are known and receive attention, as opposed to the presumed hot spots.

As various optimizations are discussed later, they can only be presented in general terms, with the various tradeoffs highlighted. Because each situation differs slightly, there's no guarantee that a particular optimization approach will work or not. Performance measurement of actual code is often the best way to decide whether to use a given approach or not. Thus, it is up to the individual developer to take the optimization approaches, apply them both to a given situation, and determine if it is appropriate to do so.

Rule #4: Don't try to outsmart the Application Kit

More often than not, the Application Kit is already doing things as efficiently as possible. Even though this might not always be exactly what a given developer wants, trying to change the behavior in a dramatic way usually causes a lot of grief for little or no benefit. The Application Kit has certain ways it likes to do things, and going with the flow generally gives the most enjoyable development experience. The Application Kit provides plenty of hooks to enable a developer to do things their own way, of course. A more accurate way of stating this is to say that the Application Kit gives the developer plenty of rope to hang himself. The optimizations discussed generally center on how to do things so that they best fit what the Application Kit expects. When written with this in mind, code tends to run much faster in most cases.

Rule #5: Don't optimize too soon

The last rule is one of the most difficult, but it can also cause the most grief when not followed. Because increased code complexity and loss of flexibility is one of the hallmarks of optimizations, optimizing too soon can back a developer into a corner. Conversely, choosing a good algorithm over a poor one often makes a huge difference. A well-designed program, with good algorithms chosen up front, has a much better chance of success. So although good planning and efficient designs are very important, digging too deep into detailed optimizations early on can often negate the benefits of a good design.

These are good rules of thumb, and might seem like common sense. Yet over and over, not following these rules is the most common cause of slow code. It is possible to write Cocoa programs that use Quartz graphics and are absolutely blazing fast. It is also possible to create a real pig that will never fly. Being aware of what approaches tend to work best will make it much easier to create the former.

Finding Drawing Trouble Spots

Mac OS X comes with some special tools to help a developer diagnose performance problems, the most important of which for drawing is QuartzDebug. QuartzDebug is found in `/Developer/Applications`. When run, it opens the very simple control panel shown in Figure 13.6.

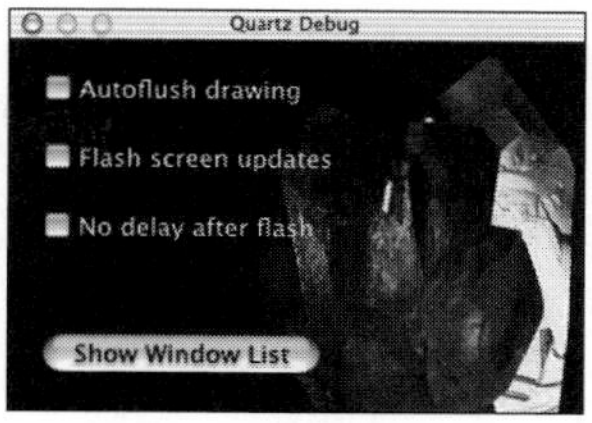

FIGURE 13.6 The QuartzDebug control panel looks like this.

The first check box, Autoflush drawing, will cause Quartz to flush drawing to the screen after each drawing operation. This slows things down a little bit, but it also helps make repeat drawing stand out. Because redraws are seen as they happen, it becomes clearer when something is being drawn more than once. Watching the Finder redraw on early versions of Mac OS X was a real eye-opener, for example.

The next check box is Flash screen updates. Turning this on causes a yellow rectangle to be drawn over an area that is about to be flushed to the screen. There is a slight delay before the flush, so that there is time to see the yellow rectangle. Turning this on is like putting the computer into slow motion. For some applications, this can become excruciating! Of course, wasted drawing effort will stand out like a sore thumb, making this one of the most valuable diagnostic techniques available to a Mac OS X developer.

If the delay after the flash is slowing things down too much, then the delay can be turned off with the third check box, No delay after flash. Quartz is really fast, though, so if this is turned off there's a good chance that some of the yellow flashes will escape perception.

One of the first things any developer should do before embarking on drawing-performance optimization is to start up QuartzDebug and turn on the check boxes. Many inefficiencies will simply jump out. When all the glaring problems have been fixed, the application's performance might even be good enough that no further optimization is required. If not, it is possible to dig much deeper.

Clicking the button labeled Show Window List will open a window that lists all the windows Quartz is maintaining. A sample of the Window List window is shown in Figure 13.7.

The Window List window contains a snapshot of Quartz's internal window list. Clicking the button again will append another snapshot to the end of the list already in the window. The window can be cleared by selecting Clear Window List (Cmd-Shift-C) from the Tools menu. The list contains quite a bit of data. A short description of each column's data is given in Table 13.1:

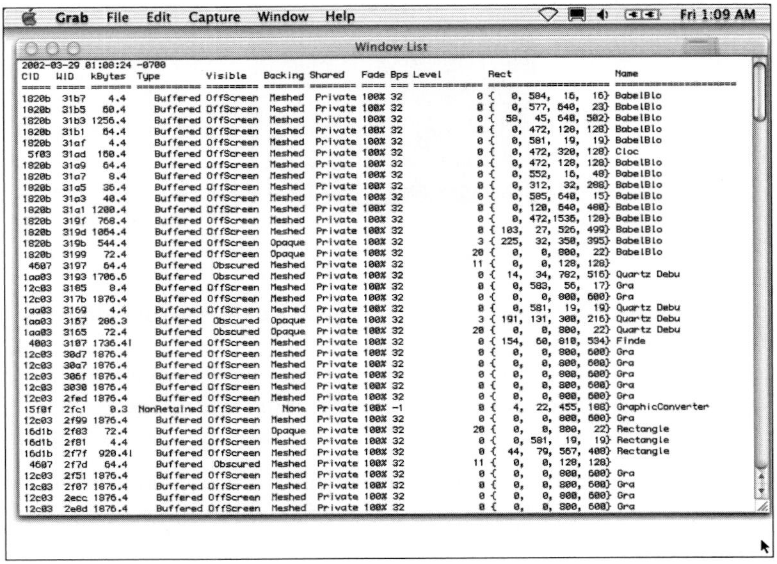

FIGURE 13.7 A window listing all the windows Quartz is maintaining.

TABLE 13.1 Properties of Quartz Windows

Property	Description
CID	The Connection ID. In general, each application, or thread, has a connection to Quartz. Windows with the same CID are being controlled through the same connection.
WID	This is Quartz's internal Window ID. Each window will have a unique ID.
kBytes	The amount of memory, in kilobytes, that the window is using. The larger the window, the more memory will be used. The letter I is appended to the size if the buffer is invalid, awaiting a redraw.
Type	The type will be Buffered, Retained, or NonRetained. The meanings of these are the same as with the `NSWindow` class.
Visible	Tells the status of the window. It will be OffScreen if it is not at all visible; Obscured if any portion of it is underneath another window; and OnScreen if it is on screen and no portion of the window is obscured.
Backing	This will be Meshed, Planar, Opaque, or None. These are slightly different from their Application Kit counterparts. Meshed means that each pixel in the buffer is stored as an

TABLE 13.1 Continued

Property	Description
	RGBA quad. The Planar configuration is a buffer with meshed color data (RGB triplets for each pixel) and alpha channel stored in a separate array. An opaque window has no associated alpha data. A window with no backing store, such as a nonretained window, will have None.
Shared	Most windows will be listed as Private, meaning they can only be modified by the application that owns them (see the Name column). Windows that are Shared allow other applications to draw in them.
Fade	The window's overall transparency percentage. All the pixels in the window's buffer, even the fully opaque ones, will pass through this fade percentage when being put onto the screen. A 0% window is completely transparent and 100% is fully opaque. However, even an opaque window can have transparent holes or translucent sections if its backing store has a fractional alpha value for a given pixel.
Bps	Stands for "bits per sample". This will usually match the screen's depth and is the sum of the bits per component values for all color components. Thus, this will be 32 for windows that have 8 bits each for their red, green, blue, and alpha components.
Level	The window's tier or level. Windows on a given level can obscure each other and windows on the levels below them, but they can never obscure a window on a higher level. The valid range of window levels is from LONG_MIN+1 to LONG_MAX-16.
Rect	This provides the onscreen location and size of each window. Offscreen windows that never appear onscreen will usually have an origin of (0.0, 0.0). These coordinates are given in screen pixels.
Name	The name of the application that owns the window. For private windows, it is the only application allowed to draw in the window.

The information about the Quartz window list can be used to see how an application impacts the window server. Each offscreen buffer and window will cause Quartz to use up more memory. This is one of the most important measurements available to a developer. It can be used to spot buffers that are no longer needed and can be released. It can also be used to determine how much memory is being used for buffering. In many cases this will encourage a developer to be more judicious about what is buffered and what is not.

QuartzDebug offers a lot of information that will quickly lead a developer to areas that need optimization. Sometimes, more information is required. The Application Kit supports several command-line options that can be used when an application is launched to turn on various debugging features. To engage these options, it is necessary to open a window in Terminal.app and use the Unix command line to launch the application.

To launch an application from the command line, follow these steps:

1. Launch Terminal.app. It can be found in the /Applications/Utilities folder.
2. Type **cd** in the terminal window, but do not press Return yet.
3. Switch to the finder and locate the application to run from the command line. Drag it to the terminal window and drop it there.
4. Switch to the Terminal window and press Return. The current working directory should now be the application's bundle wrapper.
5. Type **cd Contents/MacOS** to switch to the directory that contains the application's executable file.
6. Type **./*<application_name>* *<options>* &** and press Return to start the application. The *<application_name>* should be replaced with the application's name, without the .app extension. The *<options>* should be replaced with any options that are desired, or nothing if no options are wanted.

For example, to start up TextEdit this way, the commands would be as follows:

```
cd /Applications/TextEdit.app/Contents/MacOS
./TextEdit &
```

Note that this example uses no options. There are three debugging options that might be useful for investigating drawing performance. The first is -NSShowAllDrawing. This option, when turned on, will perform yellow flashes before NSViews are redrawn, similar to QuartzDebug. The key difference is that there will be a lot fewer flashes because not everything will be shown. In most cases, QuartzDebug provides better feedback. To use this option, the application is launched with a new command, including the option:

```
./TextEdit -NSShowAllDrawing YES &
```

Another option is `-NSShowAllViews`. This option will draw borders to highlight the bounds of every single `NSView`. This is useful for debugging the layout of views and to see if there are any unwanted overlaps. It is turned on like the previous option:

```
./TextEdit -NSShowAllViews YES &
```

The last option is `-NSShowAllWindows`. It permits all offscreen windows (buffers), including the caches for all `NSImages`, to be seen on the screen. All windows are also shown in retained mode instead of buffered mode, so there are no transparent or translucent windows. It is invoked like this:

```
./TextEdit -NSShowAllWindows YES &
```

It is possible to combine these options as well; they are not mutually exclusive. So, for example, to see all three options in action simultaneously, the application would be invoked like this:

```
./TextEdit -NSShowAllWindows YES -NSShowAllViews YES -NSShowAllDrawing YES &
```

The order of the options is not significant. Note that these options, when enabled, will tend to slow an application down quite a bit. They might also make it flaky, so they should only be used for testing and observation of the application's drawing behavior. The data collected with these options turned on can help the bug-hunting process, so it is worth experimenting with them.

A final means of collecting data about drawing performance is to actually instrument the drawing code, so that timing information can be extracted. Profiling tools can be used to see how long a particular subroutine takes to run, and they are often the simplest way to do this. Sometimes it is helpful to actually have even more detailed timing for only a particular algorithm or subsection of code. As an example of how to obtain this timing information, look at the Points example in the "Drawing Points and Rectangles" section. It uses three different algorithms for drawing points, and when run, determines how long it takes to use each algorithm for drawing. A similar technique can be used whenever optimized and nonoptimized code need to be run side by side for comparison. It can help determine which algorithm is the best choice.

Easy Optimizations

The first several optimizations are very simple. Many of the Application Kit classes have optimizations built into them that can be used by simply turning them on. Why aren't they turned on by default? Because they either have an undesirable side effect, or they can require significant memory resources when turned on. Therefore, it is beneficial to turn them on when it is known that their side effects won't be detrimental. The `NSBezierPath`, `NSView`, and `NSWindow` classes all have some of these simpler optimizations.

The `NSBezierPath` class can create a cache of its path inside Quartz. By caching the path data, a slightly faster rendering of the path is possible. The downside is that caching paths can have an impact on memory usage. Furthermore, there is an up-front cost to create the cache in the first place. This means that only paths that are used over and over should be cached. Paths that are used just once or twice, and then discarded, will see little or no benefit to caching. There are two methods that can be sent to an instance of `NSBezierPath` to control caching.

```
- (BOOL)cachesBezierPath
- (void)setCachesBezierPath:(BOOL)flag
```

The `-cachesBezierPath` method will report whether or not the path is cached. The `-setCachesBezierPath:` will actually turn caching on or off. The cache itself is created the first time the path is rendered, not when caching is turned on. The cache will be deleted from memory immediately upon turning it off, however. The impact of this optimization should be watched closely through careful measurement. It can be as harmful as it is helpful when misapplied or overused.

There are several ways that the basic `NSView` class can be speeded up. The first thing to understand is that locking and unlocking focus is a somewhat expensive operation. Therefore, it should be performed as infrequently as possible. There is no reason to unlock, do some calculations, and then relock. It is better to avoid locking and unlocking, and use them only when absolutely necessary.

That said, there is a way to slightly improve the performance of locking. To lock focus, an `NSView` will set up several parameters inside its graphics context. Every time focus is locked, these parameters need to be set up. A graphics context allows its current state to be stored as a graphics state, or gstate for short. The `NSView` class can allocate a private gstate object for itself and use that to set things up when focus is locked. Although this is certainly much faster than resending all the setup commands to Quartz, it does cost memory. In general, the faster the CPU, the less advantage this will offer. There are three `NSView` methods that can be used to manage a private gstate.

The `-allocateGState` method will allocate a private gstate for the view. This gstate will be used every time the view's focus is locked. If some of the view's basic parameters have changed, the gstate will need to be recreated with the new settings. The `-renewGState` method will invalidate the gstate and cause it to be recreated from scratch the next time it is needed. The `-releaseGState` method will invalidate the gstate and immediately free up the memory it has been using, turning off this optimization.

A few guidelines emerge once this behavior is understood. If a view doesn't get drawn very often, there won't be many `-lockFocus` operations and this optimization will be of minimal value. Most windows have many controls that don't change too often. For these views, there's little point to allocating a gstate. It would just take up space and provide little benefit. On the other hand, a view that is displaying animation and gets redrawn 30 or more times per second could probably benefit from a gstate because it is having focus locked on it quite often.

Also, if a view's settings are changing quite often, the gstate will need to be invalidated and recreated just as often. Because creating a gstate for the first time costs more than a simple focus lock, regular invalidation of gstates could make this optimization actually cause a slowdown. As usual, the key is to try it out, measure the performance change, and keep it helpful.

It should also go without saying that because it is expensive to lock focus, the following construct is an absolute no-no:

```
while (loop) {
    [self lockFocus];
    // do some drawing
    [self unlockFocus];
}
```

It is much better to move the focusing outside of the loop if at all possible, like this:

```
[self lockFocus];
while (loop) {
    // do some drawing
}
[self unlockFocus];
```

Another optimization offered by `NSView` is overlooked surprisingly often. When a view is asked to draw, there is a parameter that is usually ignored. Look at the method prototype:

```
- (void)drawRect:(NSRect)rect
```

The rect parameter is provided to tell the view which portion needs to be redrawn. It is true that there is nothing wrong with redrawing the entire view. This will work and it is certainly the easiest thing to do. However, drawing things that will never be seen is clearly inefficient. The rect parameter is a good place to look for an optimization. In most cases, simply using `NSIntersectionRect()` with the bounding box of a graphics object and the rect parameter as arguments will make it clear whether or not the object should be drawn. Of course, more complex schemes can also be employed. One popular technique is to sort graphical objects by their locations, so that only a handful of the view's objects even need to be considered at all for an intersection test. Remember that finding and eliminating work that can be avoided generally means a speedup.

There is a final optimization that an `NSView` subclass can use to gain more speed. Subclasses can override the `-isOpaque` method to return YES, instead of the default NO. Recall that views are generally nested within each other. When a view is redrawn, it will pass the redraw up the chain until it finds a 100% opaque view. That view will be drawn, then each of its nonopaque children, until finally the view in question is redrawn. Clearly, a view that is indeed opaque would be wasting time asking its ancestor views to redraw something that it only intends to cover up anyway. To eliminate that extra drawing, the view must declare itself to be opaque. It is a bad idea to declare a semitransparent view to be opaque because the views behind it will not be properly redrawn.

Finally, there is an optimization available in the `NSWindow` class. When a window redraws its views, it locks focus on them in a specific order. This order is especially important when views overlap. Unfortunately, algorithms for correctly drawing overlapping views can be somewhat more expensive than available alternates. The Application Kit can do it both ways, it just needs to know whether or not there are overlapping views. If there aren't, then it can safely kick in some optimizations that are essentially free. To engage these optimizations, send this message to an `NSWindow` instance:

```
- (void)useOptimizedDrawing:(BOOL)flag
```

If there are no overlapping views, the window will still render correctly and it will render more rapidly. The downside of turning it on is that overlapping views may or may not be drawn correctly. Precise behavior is unpredictable, so this should only be turned on when it is known that the views will not overlap each other.

Controlling Display and Flushing

When a window or a portion of a window is redisplayed, the Application Kit attempts to do so in the most efficient manner possible. Because it is aware of everything that needs to be redisplayed, it is usually most efficient to allow the Application Kit to decide when to update the graphics. Thus, although it is possible to ask a view to redisplay itself immediately, it is often better to only tell the view that it needs to be redisplayed. The Application Kit will take care of actually invoking the redisplay at the optimal time. To allow the Application Kit to make this choice, the view should be marked as needing redisplay by using one of these two methods:

```
- (void)setNeedsDisplay:(BOOL)flag
- (void)setNeedsDisplayInRect:(NSRect)invalidRect
```

With `-setNeedsDisplay:`, passing a YES will tell the view that its entire bounds need to be redisplayed. If the data model that the view is displaying has changed, then it would send this message to the view so that the onscreen information would be updated at an appropriate time. If only a part of the view has changed and it is known exactly what part of the view is out of date, then `-setNeedsDisplayInRect:` can be used to specify a particular rectangular region of the view to be redisplayed. When the actual redisplay eventually occurs, these rectangles will usually be merged so that only one redisplay occurs, covering all the dirty parts of the view.

In general, the Application Kit will do all requested redisplays at the end of the event loop after handling a user event. This makes the application feel more responsive to the user because the events will be handled as expeditiously as possible. Sometimes it is important to have redisplays happen at an exact moment in time and not wait for the Application Kit to decide that the time is right. A host of methods are available in the `NSView` class to force an immediate redraw:

```
- (void)display
- (void)displayRect:(NSRect)rect
- (void)displayRectIgnoringOpacity:(NSRect)rect
- (void)displayIfNeeded
- (void)displayIfNeededIgnoringOpacity
- (void)displayIfNeededInRect:(NSRect)rect
- (void)displayIfNeededInRectIgnoringOpacity:(NSRect)rect
```

Each of the `-displayIfNeeded` methods will only cause a redisplay if the view thinks it needs to do so. The others force an immediate display of the requested area. The methods that take a rectangular argument attempt only to redisplay those specified portions of the view (but how much is actually sent to Quartz to be rendered is determined by how well the implementation of `-drawRect:` handles its rect parameter). The methods that have IgnoringOpacity in their name allow for a rapid redraw that automatically assumes the view is opaque. Although such a display is certainly faster, it might not provide the desired result for semitransparent views. It might be good enough, though, when used for temporary drawing within a modal loop. Experimentation is the key here.

Because multiple objects might invalidate a view by telling it that it needs to be redrawn, it is generally advantageous to wait until the end of the event loop before invoking another display. If displays are done immediately, it is likely that a view will get redisplayed more than once in a given event loop. For animation, this might be acceptable and desirable, but in most cases it just wastes CPU cycles. Letting the Application Kit take over where possible usually yields the best results.

When views are redisplayed, that is not necessarily enough to actually get something on the screen. Even if the view is redrawn, the new graphics that were drawn into the window's backing store need to be flushed out to the screen. When the Application Kit is handling redisplay, the graphics context and the window are properly flushed. When a developer decides to force drawing early, all this needs to be done manually. Like redrawing a view, there are two ways to flush a window. The first is to flush the window whether it needs to be flushed or not. The second is to only flush the window if it needs to be flushed. The window itself is smart enough to keep track of what parts actually need to be flushed and only flushes those parts where something changed, so there is no way to request that only a particular portion of the window be flushed. Here are the `NSWindow` flushing methods:

```
- (void)flushWindow
- (void)flushWindowIfNeeded
```

Sometimes it is advantageous to flush more often than is actually needed. If a particular drawing operation takes a long time, the user will see no updates to the screen until the operation finishes. Waiting for this to happen might make the application feel slow to the user. By flushing occasionally throughout the drawing process, the user will see things happening on the screen. This makes the overall drawing take longer, but the user perceives it to be faster because their mind is being kept occupied by the changes being flushed to the screen. In other words, sometimes it actually pays to do something that is known to be inefficient. What the user perceives is far more important than what is actually happening because that perception will shape a user's opinion of the application far more than the facts.

It is also possible to disable and enable window flushing. Because a flush can be an expensive operation, it is usually counterproductive to flush a window over and over. If an operation is about to be performed that will likely cause a flush, this method can be used to temporarily disable flushing before all drawing is completed:

```
- (void)disableFlushWindow
```

When everything is ready, flushing should be enabled with this method:

```
- (void)enableFlushWindow
```

It is possible to detect whether a window has flushing disabled with this method:

```
- (BOOL)isFlushWindowDisabled
```

It is important that any code that disables window flushing not to forget to enable flushing after it is done. If flushing is not enabled, the window will be unable to update its contents on the screen.

The redraw of views and windows is automatic when the management is done by the Application Kit, thus no need to worry about any of it. However, it is possible to change the timing of when things get updated if so desired. The key here is that any developer who does this should be very careful to measure the effects of their changes. It is rare that a developer can use these methods in a way that significantly beats the Application Kit's built-in mechanisms. Remember, the Application Kit has been refined and optimized over more than a decade of use to be as fast as possible for the widest variety of situations. There will be specific cases where it is possible to do better, so it is sometimes worth the experimentation. Usually more benefit for the time spent will be achieved by concentrating on the best possible algorithms.

Caching Complex Drawing

A common technique for optimizing manipulation of complex graphics is to use an `NSImage` as an offscreen graphics cache. (See Chapter 14 for a complete description of the NSImage class.) To better understand what this is and why it is used, consider an example. In a drawing program, a common user operation is to select a group of graphics, and move them to a new location on the virtual canvas. In Aqua, solid user feedback is preferred. This means that the program should move the actual objects instead of moving an outline of the graphics. Because Aqua uses pervasive translucency, even better would be to redraw the canvas itself without the objects, and then redraw the objects as translucent ghosts. This would enable the user to see the area underneath the objects as they are moved. When released, the objects would become solid again, redrawn with the rest of the canvas.

The problem with implementing something like this is performance. If many graphics have been selected, the cost to redraw them all every time the mouse is moved can become prohibitive. The response to mouse movement could become choppy, making the application feel unresponsive. Furthermore, altering the drawing so it can or cannot conditionally draw translucently could make the code less maintainable because of the complexity added.

The solution is to cache the selected graphics in an `NSImage`. When a drag to move the objects commences, the affected areas of the canvas would be redrawn without the selected graphics. The selected graphics would be drawn into an `NSImage`. Then, the image would be composited repeatedly as the drag continues. By using a value less than one for the delta parameter after fraction: in the `-drawInRect:fromRect:operation:fraction:` method, the graphics appear translucent as they are dragged onscreen. At the same time, the graphics can be drawn using the normal, full-opacity rendering code when they are being drawn into the buffer. This removes the need for the rendering code to be able to draw both with and without translucency. When the drag completes, the graphics are redrawn as a part of the canvas. This method is effective when the selected graphics, or the graphics underneath them, are complex because in either, or both, cases it will be faster to do a single composite operation rather than redraw everything.

As usual, the downside is that this technique can use quite a bit of memory. If memory is tight, the extra memory usage could cause swapping. Therefore, it is important to do performance measurement to make sure that this optimization is actually helping more than hindering. For simpler applications, the memory requirements might make this method less useful. `NSBezierPath` and friends can potentially be very fast. For example, the old NeXTSTEP/OPENSTEP example application Draw used this caching technique extensively. On Mac OS X, the Draw.app example was renamed to Sketch. In the process, the code was rewritten from scratch to make better use of Cocoa's newest features. The new Sketch example no longer uses this technique, so at least in that case this optimization was not considered to be worth the implementation effort.

There is one more positive aspect of this approach. If the graphics program wants to allow the user to drag an object from one window to another, the Cocoa drag-and-drop system would normally be used. If the selected graphics have already been captured into their own image, that image can then be handed off to the drag-and-drop system. Instead of the graphics turning into a tiny icon the moment the mouse leaves the confines of the canvas's window, the solid graphics can be dragged right off the canvas and dropped onto another document. This will feel quite natural to the user and is definitely more Aqua-like. An example of this is the OmniWeb application. When images are dragged from it, even large images are dragged across the screen in their entirety, and not as icons. The Cocoa mechanisms for drag-and-drop text also redraw the text into an `NSImage` so that the text, in rendered form, is what is dragged as the mouse moves.

The `NSWindow` class supports some methods that are closely related to this approach. It can temporarily cache a portion of its raster image to be restored later.

Call the `-cacheImageInRect:` method to save a portion of the window in a cache. Remember that because this is an `NSWindow` method, the rectangle is in window coordinates, not view or screen coordinates. If this method is being called from an `NSView`, the `NSView` method `-convertRect:toView:` using nil for the argument after toView: will convert a rectangle from the view's coordinate system to the window's coordinate system.

When a portion of the window has been cached, temporary drawing can be done in that area. When it is time to remove the temporary drawing and restore the original window contents, the `-restoreCachedImage` method should be sent to the window. When the cached area is no longer needed, the `-discardCachedImage` method should be called to free up the resources consumed by the cache.

These methods would be ideal to use, for example, with rubber-banded lines, such as the user dragging out a selection rectangle in a graphics program. It is typically faster to quickly restore a window region from a cache than to redraw it through the `NSView` hierarchy. In general, the algorithm, in pseudocode, would look like this:

```
cache the applicable window region (perhaps the view's bounds)
while (mouse moves) {
    draw the rubber band
    flush graphics context
    restore the cached window region
}
discard cache
```

This works well as long as the view isn't moved or scrolled while the dragging continues. If the view scrolls, its contents change and need to be redrawn. In that case, it might be faster to just perform the necessary redrawing. Continually invalidating and recaching the window region might prove to be move expensive.

Custom Buffering

It is common, especially with animation, to carefully control cache-flushing behavior in an attempt to reduce the time required to flush the cache. Although this works well on most platforms, it should be avoided on Mac OS X. To understand why, it's best to understand what is commonly done as well as why it won't work on Mac OS X.

When a window is flushed on Mac OS X, the current algorithm will take a list of all the dirty regions and merge them into a single rectangular region. The resultant rectangle is the smallest rectangle that encloses all the areas that need to be flushed. That region is what will be flushed, in a single operation. The individual rectangles will not be flushed separately. To visualize this, consider Figure 13.8. The dashed rectangles are the areas that need to be redrawn. The flushing algorithm actually causes the area enclosed by the larger, solid rectangle to be redrawn. The areas in the upper-right and lower-left corners doesn't really need to be redrawn, but when rectangles overlap it is typically much faster to just redraw the whole area rather than to go through all the setup to do two separate redraws. Additionally, with two separate redraws, it is likely that the overlap area in the middle would be drawn twice.

NOTE

Dirty region is a term commonly used to refer to areas in a buffer that have changed since the last update. A region becomes dirty when drawing is performed in the buffer. The drawing is not visible because it is not on the screen yet. Flushing the dirty region to the screen makes the drawing visible and causes the region to become clean.

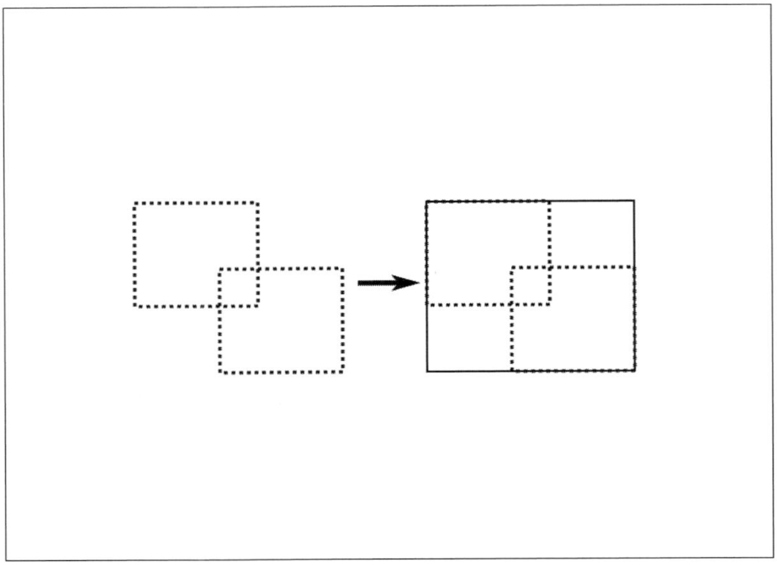

FIGURE 13.8 The dashed rectangles are the areas that need to be redrawn. The flushing algorithm causes the area enclosed by the larger, solid rectangle to be redrawn.

In many cases, this is a reasonable approach. Often, there are few regions that need updates, and they will usually be fairly close together. However, in a game, screensaver, or other animated view, it is common to have small dirty regions that are far apart. Imagine a classic arcade game where the object is to shoot and destroy rocks floating through space. The rocks move with each frame and are spread sparsely across the screen. The area that gets flushed will contain a lot of area that hasn't been modified at all. Another case where this might happen is when two scrollbars, or rulers, change at once. Consider the two cases illustrated in Figures 13.9 and 13.10.

In these cases, it is more efficient to do several flushes of just the smaller regions that have been affected. Theoretically, this could be done in Cocoa. The standard flushing algorithm should, in theory, be turned off when a nonretained or retained window is used instead of a buffered window. Furthermore, it is possible to use an `NSImage` which is the exact same size of the `NSView` subclass as a buffer for offscreen drawing. To do the flushes, first all the overlapping rectangles would be combined. Next, the remaining list of rectangles would be used to do several composites. The composites would copy only the changed areas of the offscreen `NSImage` onto the screen.

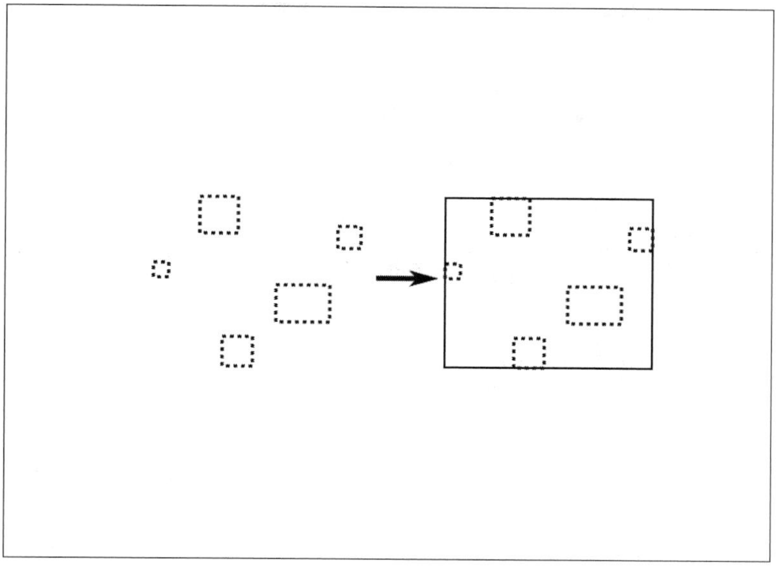

FIGURE 13.9 Many small areas that are far apart can result in large unmodified areas being flushed.

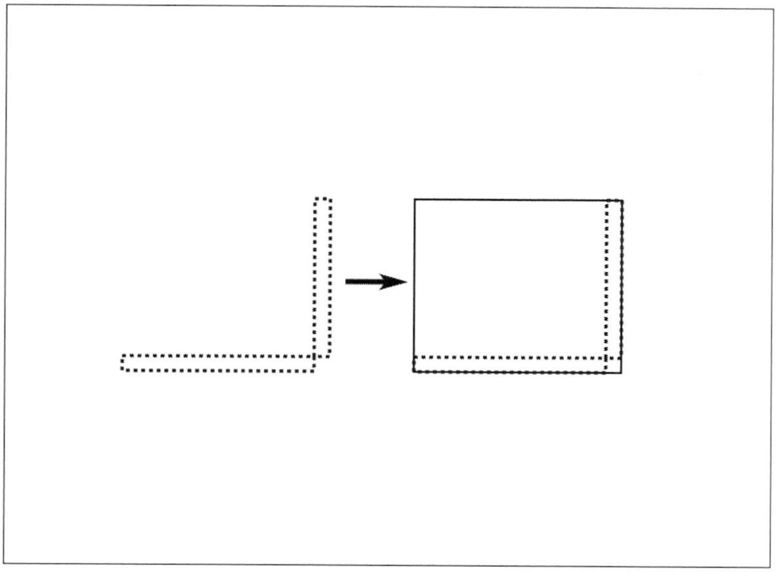

FIGURE 13.10 Long narrow areas like the areas used to display rulers or scrollbars can result in large unmodified areas being flushed.

This sounds great in theory and worked extremely well on NeXTSTEP, OPENSTEP, and the early Display PostScript (DPS) based versions of Mac OS X Server. It works well for many other platforms as well. On Mac OS X, and the newer Mac OS X Server platforms, DPS has been replaced by Quartz. It turns out that Quartz effectively buffers its drawing, even with nonbuffered windows. Flushes of the graphics context are still required to make drawing appear onscreen, even for nonbuffered windows. In the current implementation of Quartz, these flushes use the first, potentially less-efficient buffering algorithm. Therefore, any developer who attempts to bypass the flushing and manage it herself will discover that doing so actually slows down her drawing. The slowdown can be as much as two to five times slower!

Quartz tries to synchronize its flushing with the vertical blanking signal on devices that have one, such as a CRT. On a CRT, the flush will take place after the beam has passed the area to be flushed. Hopefully the flush will complete before the beam reaches the area being flushed. This prevents flicker and tearing effects, making screen updates feel very clean. Moving from one flush to multiple flushes could cause flushing to be paused while it waits for the beam to pass. Trying to take control over flushing risks creating a huge performance problem.

So why discuss this algorithm if is should be avoided? So that other developers don't have to go down that path just to discover that it is a dead end. Without understanding what the algorithm is, it is more difficult to avoid it. Because many texts on game development describe this technique and recommend using it, great importance needs to be placed on the fact that for the Mac OS X/Quartz platform this approach will do far more harm than good. Don't use it!

This might seem like bleak, depressing news. Quartz already has the information it needs to be able to do a better job. It just has a simple-minded flushing implementation at the moment. This should be considered an optimization that Apple just hasn't done yet, but might in the future. When Quartz Debug is turned on, it is quickly realized that many of Apple's own applications modify areas that are small and far apart, so there is a huge incentive to make flushing more intelligent. There are no specific promises, however, so it is important for developers to focus on what works well now. Unfortunately there is no API for modifying Quartz's flushing behavior.

NOTE

One minor caveat here is that Quartz is only storing a path's bounding box. The information it stores is not as specific as knowing which actual pixels were touched. This is significant because it implies that flushing diagonal lines might never be done at maximum efficiency.

So this optimization should be avoided on Mac OS X. Let Cocoa and Quartz choose what to flush. The environment is such that developers cannot actually implement it correctly. The OS itself needs to change to support it. There is the possibility that Apple will implement this optimization as part of Quartz. If that happens, it will be transparent to the developer, which equates to a performance enhancement from which all applications will benefit without any additional developer effort required. For the time being, this is reason enough to follow Apple's recommendations and avoid attempts to further optimize flushing.

Other Optimizations

Many methods and functions perform a single operation, and many have a counterpart that performs multiple operations at once. A great example of this would be the contrast between `NSRectFill()` and `NSRectFillList()`. It can be demonstrated by running the Points example from earlier in this chapter, that the list version is approximately ten times faster when enough rectangles are drawn. It has limitations, but it will provide huge performance boosts for situations where it can be used. Throughout the Cocoa classes, look for and use methods like this that allow for groups of operations to be performed at once.

Reusing `NSBezierPath` Objects

In the same vein, it is often worth retaining an `NSBezierPath` instance and reusing it, instead of recreating it from scratch every time the path needs to be drawn. If the path never changes, this is an especially good idea. Of course, this means some increased memory usage, especially if the path is being cached. Performance testing and evaluation is the key to determining when an instance should be saved as opposed to being recreated from scratch.

Because `NSBezierPath` objects can be specified in relative terms, a subpath can be stored that is defined as being completely relative to the current point. This usually makes it easier to create path objects that are indeed reusable and worth retaining. A path that can't be specified in relative terms can still be reused by doing a coordinate system transformation before rendering the path. Transformations can translate, scale, rotate, and otherwise warp a path, increasing the number of ways a given path can be reused. Looking for ways to reuse `NSBezierPath` objects is usually worth the effort. It is also important to make sure that the cost of using the transformations isn't greater than the cost of not reusing the paths. Again, performance measurement is valuable here.

Bit Depth Matching

The bit depth used for drawing is important. Drawing buffers should be created with bit depths that match the output device (usually the screen), unless there is a good reason for not doing so. If the screen is using 16-bit color, then 16-bit buffers are much more efficient than 32bit buffers. It might be easier to write code that always uses one particular bit depth. But doing so causes bit depth conversions and other time consuming operations to be performed. These operations would not need to be performed if the buffer and output device bit depths were an exact match. Not to mention that a 32-bit buffer requires twice the memory of a 16-bit buffer. Normally, Quartz will default to creating suitable buffers automatically. It is possible to override this behavior, especially when creating `NSImage` instances. Before doing such an override, make sure that the performance hit is worthwhile.

Using 16-bit buffers when the output device is 32 bit might be more efficient as far as memory usage goes, and therefore worth doing to conserve memory. There is still some depth conversion taking place as the image is rendered to the output device, and that might increase drawing time. Again, performance measurement is paramount in determining which approach is best.

Transparency

A topic related to bit depth is transparency. Many buffers are created without transparency by default. For a color buffer, one quarter of the buffer is usually dealing with transparency. If one quarter of the buffer can be omitted and doesn't need to be used for any rendering calculations, both memory and CPU time will be saved. It is best to use transparency only when it is needed and to avoid it otherwise. The trick is that transparency is infectious. When Cocoa tries to perform a rendering operation that will leave behind a nonopaque pixel in a buffer that has no transparency, the buffer will be promoted to contain transparency. With one single, seemingly innocuous rendering command, the buffer's size expands and future rendering will take longer.

In other words, a developer shouldn't just create an opaque buffer without alpha channel. It is also important that extreme care be taken ensure that the buffer won't be accidentally promoted to contain an alpha channel. Painting with an `NSColor` that isn't fully opaque is an obvious culprit that can easily be avoided. Most compositing operations will not promote the destination to contain alpha, either. But the Clear operation will always promote the destination to contain alpha information, and the copy operation will do so if there is transparency in the source image. To avoid this promotion `NSEraseRect()` or `NSRectFill()` with a solid color should be used in place of a composite Clear operation. The composite copy can be replaced with a Source Over operation or a Source Over preceded with an `NSRectFill()`, depending upon the desired result.

Another reason to be careful about using transparency in the current implementation of Quartz is that transparency is not yet supported for printing. PDF files created from captured drawing and printed output do not yet take advantage of transparency information. This means that when transparency is being used, WYSIWYG (What You See Is What You Get) is broken between screen and printer. Not using transparency is one way to avoid this problem. At WWDC 2001, Apple engineers suggested that this would be fixed in a future version of Mac OS X, but no promises were made as to when that would be. If Apple continues to track the PDF specification, however, it is safe to assume that this will indeed be the case because the latest emerging PDF specs support transparency.

Buffer Widths

Another optimization opportunity concerns a buffer's width. If a buffer is created with exactly the right width, Quartz can use Altivec to speed up compositing on G4 based Macintoshes. The magic width is any width that results in the number of bytes per image row being 16. For example, consider a 32-bit RGBA buffer. There are four bytes per pixel in such a buffer. Therefore, if this particular buffer's width is a multiple of four, then the Altivec optimization will be triggered. The Points example from earlier in this chapter makes use of this optimization in one of its algorithms when creating a buffer.

Drawing Text

Several text drawing functions in Cocoa are convenient to use, but will slow performance. All the `NSString` methods described in Chapter 14 for drawing text should generally be avoided when actual drawing performance is of any importance. The problem is that each time these methods are called they need to set up the current graphics context with fonts and other text attribute parameters. Because this is very expensive, these methods are by far the most inefficient way to render text. There are at least two alternative approaches to drawing text that might work well depending on the situation.

The first approach, and the easiest to implement, is to use the text-drawing methods to render the text into an `NSImage` buffer. When the text is needed, the image can be composited where it is required. This works well for any text that is unlikely to change, such as labels. The code to do this is still relatively simple to write. Chapter 14 discusses using images for offscreen drawing. Although the string rendering methods are slow, if they are used infrequently they won't have a significant impact on overall application performance.

Alternatively, an `NSText` object can be used as a helper to actually render the text. If the text is at all complex, this is by far the preferred approach. `NSText` is designed to be extremely efficient at rendering complex text and it transparently provides most of the benefits of Apple's advanced-type technologies. By inserting an `NSText` object as a subview, it is possible to use the `NSText` to render text inside of an arbitrary `NSView` subclass. The downside is that `NSText` is a complex object that can be difficult to use.

Despite the complexity, this technique is usually the best approach for achieving speed in text rendering. Even Cocoa itself uses it. All the `NSTextField` objects in any given application share a single `NSText` object, known as the field editor. The field editor is used to perform the fields' functionality. It is shared between the field objects because `NSText` is a very heavyweight object. Rather than waste resources instantiating an `NSText` object for every field, the same instance is shared between them. Refer to Chapter 11, "Text Views," for more information about `NSText` and how to use it.

Dashed Lines

Rendering dashed lines is also a relatively slow operation. Unfortunately, there is no good workaround for making this faster. Complex paths that are repeatedly rendered without being changed might benefit from some of the rendering techniques already described. One choice is to render the path into an `NSImage` cache, and then composite it when needed. If the path changes often or isn't very complex, however, using an image cache might be detrimental to performance. As usual, timing the application's performance is the only way to be sure which is the best approach. Either way, rendering dashed lines is an expensive process. If dashed lines are needed, however, there's simply no way to avoid this fact. If dashes can be avoided, doing so can lead to a performance improvement.

Context Saves

Another expensive operation is saving and restoring graphics contexts. It is important to limit context save/restore pairs to situations that truly require them. A common mistake is to save the context at the start of a `-drawRect:` implementation and restore it at the end. The `NSView` machinery already does this automatically, so doing it again would be superfluous. Furthermore, unless there is a demonstrable need to restore a graphics context to a previous state, there is little point in doing a save/restore.

Superfluous Drawing

Finally, when running with the `-NSShowAllWindows` command-line flag turned on, watch for panels that update themselves unnecessarily. There is no point in redrawing a control that is on an offscreen window. If it can't be seen, don't redraw it. Wait until it is brought on screen before asking it to be redrawn. Under normal circumstances, the Application Kit will update controls automatically before bringing them onscreen. When a developer tries to bypass or outsmart this machinery, the most common result is to cause this unnecessary updating. Therefore, it is worth watching for it when attempting to control display updates in a manner that is better than the Application Kit. The obvious danger is that such meddling can make things worse if the proper care isn't taken.

Path Intersections

When Quartz renders a path, it must perform special calculations to render antialiased path intersections correctly. This requires it to check every path segment against every other path segment to see if they intersect. Since this is a problem of n-squared complexity, paths with many elements will be drawn much more slowly than paths with just a few elements. If you don't care about correct rendering of intersections or you know that the segments in your path don't intersect, you can speed up rendering by splitting the path into several separate paths to be rendered one at a time. Be aware, however, that doing so could also cause rendering options such as end caps, corners, and line dash patterns to be rendered differently. When breaking up a path, care must be taken to preserve sections of the path where these rendering options matter.

Summary

This chapter described modifying the graphics context used for vector drawing to produce powerful and complex effects. The techniques for fast rectangle and point drawing enable applications such as scatter charts and control points. The optimization techniques presented can be used to speed up almost any Cocoa application. A lot of details of vector drawing have been covered, but techniques for drawing images and text have not yet been covered. Chapter 14, "Custom Views and Graphics Part III," dives into descriptions of Cocoa image and text support. Image manipulation and sophisticated text rendering are two of Cocoa's strongest attributes.

14

Custom Views and Graphics Part III

IN THIS CHAPTER

- Images and Bitmaps
- Drawing Text

This chapter continues the discussion of drawing with subclasses of `NSView` to detail the use of images and text. Cocoa provides powerful tools for drawing images with rotation, transparency, and other effects. Cocoa's text-drawing capabilities are state of the art, and in many cases, the built-in text-drawing capabilities of Cocoa exceed the features available in expensive desktop publishing applications. This chapter provides an overview of image and text drawing with examples.

Images and Bitmaps

Cocoa offers a suite of classes for managing bitmap images. This suite includes the `NSImage` and `NSImageRep` classes as well as several different `NSImageRep` subclasses. This group of classes can be used to decode many common bitmap image file formats (such as TIFF, GIF, JPG, and so on), and load them into memory for further manipulation. There are also facilities for manipulating vector-based images such as PDF. Support can be added for new image file formats, which makes them transparently available to all Cocoa programs via OS X's Services mechanism. An image can be created from raw byte data or even a drawing subroutine. Images can be further modified and drawn to the screen, or saved to a file or `NSData` object.

Compositing

When Cocoa renders images, the rendering is done by using a process called compositing. Compositing is a way to mix two images (a source and a destination) to produce a third image. There is more than one way to mix the two images. Each rendering approach is known as a compositing mode. Cocoa supports several compositing modes, described in Table 14.1. When compositing, the source image object is the one asked to render itself. The destination is the graphics context, the place where the result can be found after the operation is complete. The destination could be the screen, printed page, or another image object. Compositing behavior can be affected by what is already at the drawing destination. Table 14.1 provides the names of the available compositing modes, the constants used by Cocoa to identify them, and their rendering behavior.

TABLE 14.1 Cocoa Constants and Rendering Behaviors for Compositing Modes

Example	Compositing Mode	Constant	Rendered Behavior
	Clear	`NSCompositeClear`	Resultant image is made up of completely transparent (clear) pixels. Effectively, the source data is ignored and destination is erased.
	Copy	`NSCompositeCopy`	Destination image is replaced by the source image, pixel for pixel. The destination data is completely lost.
	Destination Atop	`NSCompositeDestinationAtop`	Where both images are opaque, the destination remains unchanged. Result uses source image in areas where destination is transparent, but source is not. Result is transparent everywhere source is transparent.
	Destination In	`NSCompositeDestinationIn`	Destination remains unchanged where both images are opaque. Result is transparent elsewhere.

TABLE 14.1 Continued

Example	Compositing Mode	Constant	Rendered Behavior
	Destination Out	`NSCompositeDestinationOut`	Destination remains unchanged where destination is opaque and source is transparent. Result is transparent elsewhere.
	Destination Over	`NSCompositeDestinationOver`	Destination is unchanged where destination is opaque. Where destination is transparent, result is the source image.
	Source Atop	`NSCompositeSourceAtop`	Destination is unchanged where source is transparent and destination is opaque. Source is used where source and destination are opaque. Result is transparent elsewhere.
	Source In	`NSCompositeSourceIn`	Source is used where destination and source are opaque. Result is transparent elsewhere.
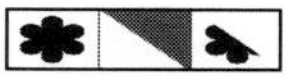	Source Out	`NSCompositeSourceOut`	Source is used where source is opaque and destination is transparent. Result is transparent elsewhere.
	Source Over	`NSCompositeSourceOver`	Source is used where source is opaque. Destination is unchanged where source is transparent.

TABLE 14.1 Continued

Example	Compositing Mode	Constant	Rendered Behavior
	Exclusive-Or	`NSCompositeXOR`	Result pixels are determined by the exclusive-or of the corresponding source and destination pixels. Where source and destination are both opaque or both transparent, the result is transparent. Where either source or destination is opaque and the other is transparent, the result is opaque.
	Plus Darker	`NSCompositePlusDarker`	Pixels are added together in such a way that the sum approaches a limit of zero (black).
	Plus Lighter	`NSCompositePlusLighter`	Pixels are added together in such a way that the sum approaches a limit of one (white).
	Highlight	`NSCompositeHighlight`	This mode is no longer supported, but still exists for backward compatibility. It now behaves like Source Over.

It might be difficult to imagine exactly what each of these modes does. The best way to visualize these operations is to actually manipulate some images to see what results are achieved when they are composited. Mac OS X Developer comes with an example application that allows just that. The example program, `CompositeLab`, can be found in /Developer/Examples/AppKit/CompositeLab. Try building and running it. For those who do not have this example program readily available, refer to Table 14.1. The leftmost column shows examples of each compositing mode. For each thumbnail, the source image is at the left, the destination in the center, and the result after compositing is on the right.

Two of the most common compositing modes are Copy and Source Over. Copy makes an exact copy of the source in the destination. The Source Over mode also copies the source to the destination, but it allows the alpha channel (transparency) of the source image to be taken into account as if it were a mask for the copy operation. When rendering an image, Source Over enables the source image to be added to the foreground of what is already in the destination.

The Source Over mode can be described mathematically. The following equation can be used per component to determine the resulting component values:

```
result = source * (source alpha) + destination * (1.0 - source alpha)
```

Each compositing mode can be described with a different, unique equation. Providing the mathematical details of each compositing mode is beyond the scope of this book. Any good computer graphics reference book should contain a complete discussion of all the mathematical details of compositing.

Returning to the operations themselves, usually the Atop, In, and Out modes are used for various masking operations. A mask image can be supplied as the source image. The various modes allow the mask to be used like a cookie cutter to punch holes in the destination image. Masks can also be used for cropping and framing. A semitransparent cropping mask can be used to feather the edges of an image, giving it a soft edge that fades out.

The Plus compositing modes are a bit more difficult to understand. Both can be used to aggregate images together and create a mask of the result. The resultant mask could then be used with the other modes for various effects. To better describe these two modes, look at the math behind calculating the result. In the case of Plus Lighter, imagine each color component being added together, and then clamped to the range [0.0, 1.0]. (That is, the result is kept within that range). For example, suppose the images being composited use the RGBA-color model. Focusing on one pixel, further suppose that the source pixel is the tuple (1.0, 0.5, 0.5, 1.0), and the destination pixel is the tuple (1.0, 0.5, 0.0, 1.0). Adding the two tuples and clamping the result gives the resultant tuple (1.0, 1.0, 0.5, 1.0) for the pixel in question.

Plus Darker is slightly more complex mathematically. First, each component is forced to be in the range from 0.0 to 1.0. Next, the result is determined per component by using this equation:

```
result = 1.0 - ((1.0 - source) + (1.0 - destination))
```

With a little algebra, this equation can be simplified to the following:

```
result = source  + destination - 1.0
```

As with Plus Lighter, the result is clamped to the range [0.0, 1.0] to produce the final result. As an example, the same pair of tuples used for the Plus Lighter example will produce this tuple for Plus Darker: (1.0, 0.0, 0.0, 1.0).

The `NSImage` Class

The `NSImage` class is the most commonly used interface for dealing with images. It can load images from disk or memory, and save images to disk or memory. It can render images to the screen, and even allow an image to be modified. The `NSImage` class can also supply some basic information about an image, such as its size.

The `NSImage` class does not, however, contain any of the image's actual data. Instead, it maintains a list of instances of `NSImageRep` (image representation) subclasses. This allows an `NSImage` to have more than one set of image data. For example, one image might contain a low-resolution representation that is 72 dpi, meant for use on the screen, and a high-resolution 1200 dpi representation for use with printing. Perhaps there are color and monochrome (black and white) versions as well. When an `NSImage` instance is rendered, it will go through its internal list of image representations and choose the one that best matches the current graphics context's output device. If an image has more than one representation, a different representation is often used for printing than is used for drawing to the screen.

Creating an `NSImage`

There are a few ways to obtain an `NSImage` instance. With most of the methods described in this section, there is the chance that an image will not actually be created. For example, image creation can fail because of corrupted files or data, missing files, stale URLs, undecipherable pasteboard data, and so on. If creation or initialization fails for some reason, `nil` will be returned. Therefore, it is wise to check the return values of these methods to make sure that the desired image was actually created.

If the image data of interest is stored on disk within an application's main bundle or one of the standard system images is desired, then the `NSImage +imageNamed:` method is the easiest way to obtain an `NSImage` object. The name passed to this method is provided without a file extension. For example, if an image file named `Grid.tiff` was added to the application's project in Project Builder, the file will be inside the application's bundle when the application is built. To obtain an `NSImage` capable of rendering this image file, the following code would be used:

```
NSImage *gridImage = [NSImage imageNamed:@"Grid"];
```

It is important to remember to retain this image if it will be used beyond the current execution scope. If this object will be archived at some point, it is important to know that an image created with this method will be archived without saving the image data. Instead, only the image's name will be archived. If the image isn't available within the bundle of the application that later unarchives the image, the original image will have been lost.

To avoid losing the image data when archiving an image object, the `NSImage` must be created differently. When loading an `NSImage` from a file, use the `-initWithContentsOfFile:` method. NSImage objects created this way will store image data when archived. In this case, the full path, including the filename extension, is required. Because `NSImage` can handle images of many different types and can be extended to handle new types, it is desirable to not provide the image's extension. The Application Kit adds the `-pathForImageResource:` method to `NSBundle` to make it easy to search for an image without knowing what type of image or what filename extension is being used. Put these two methods together to load the `Grid.tiff` image like this:

```
NSString *imagePath = [[NSBundle mainBundle] pathForImageResource:@"Grid"];
NSImage *gridImage = [[NSImage alloc] initWithContentsOfFile:imagePath];
```

This time the image was allocated, so it is the developer's responsibility to release the image when he is finished with it. Note that the archiving behavior of `+imageNamed:` can also be achieved by using `-initByReferencingFile:` instead of `-initWithContentsOfFile:`. If the full path to the image in question is known, that can be used instead of the `NSBundle -pathForImageResource:` method.

An instance of `NSImage` can also be obtained given a URL. Simply pass an `NSURL` instance to the `-initWithContentsOfURL:` method. The URL contents will be obtained and, if an image can be created from the data at that URL, a new `NSImage` instance will be returned.

An instance of `NSData` can also be used to initialize an `NSImage` object. The `-initWithData:` method can initialize an `NSImage` from an `NSDATA` object containing image data. The `NSData` should be a valid, recognizable image file format supported by the Application Kit. For example, TIFF, JPG, and GIF data are all legal. Using the `Grid.tiff` image example, it could be done this way instead:

```
NSString *imagePath = [[NSBundle mainBundle] pathForImageResource:@"Grid"];
NSData * imageData = [[NSData alloc] initWithContentsOfFile:imagePath];
NSImage *gridImage = [[NSImage alloc] initWithData:imageData];
```

Usually this wouldn't be done because it is less efficient than just initializing the image from the file directly. However, if there is already an `NSData` object available, the -initWithData: method could be helpful. Also, NSImages initialized with this method will save the image contents when archived.

When permitting a user to choose an image to open using the standard Open panel, Cocoa expects the allowable file types to be specified. Rather than specifying a particular file type, and including code for decoding that type in an application, use NSImage to load an image of any type that can be dealt with by the system. Because services can be installed to decode new types of image files, the types that can be accepted could change at any moment.

The NSImage class provides two methods that return an NSArray containing the allowable image types. The first method is +imageFileTypes, and the second is +imageUnfilteredFileTypes. Both methods return an NSArray populated with NSStrings. Each string is either a file extension as it would appear in a filename (tiff, gif, and so on) or a four character HFS file type enclosed in single quotes ('TIFF', 'GIFF', and so on). The array that is returned is usually used with open and save panels. It can, for example, be used directly as the argument to NSOpenPanel's -runModalForTypes: method. The array should never be cached. Because new filter services could be added to the system at any time, call NSImage every time this data is required.

These two methods differ in only one respect: The list returned by +imageUnfilteredFileTypes is a subset of the list returned by +imageFileTypes. The unfiltered types are the image types that are built into the system, and can be decoded without using filtering services. If an image filter service is installed, the +imageFileTypes method returns the types supported by the system as well as all types supported by the installed filter(s). In most circumstances, the +imageFileTypes method is the preferred choice because it lists all the image file types that can be supported one way or another.

The ImageTypes example provided on the book's Web site (www.cocoaprogramming.net) can be used to see what these methods return on a given system. Simply compile and run the application. The application is quite simple; it has a single controller object that acts as the NSApplication's delegate. When the application launches, this controller object runs the file-type methods and the pasteboard type methods discussed later. The result of each message is then put into its own NSTextView. The code for the controller object is as follows:

File Controller.h:

```
#import <Cocoa/Cocoa.h>
@interface MYController : NSObject
{
    IBOutlet NSTextView *imageFileTypesText;
    IBOutlet NSTextView *imagePasteboardTypesText;
```

```
    IBOutlet NSTextView *imageUnfilteredFileTypesText;
    IBOutlet NSTextView *imageUnfilteredPasteboardTypesText;
}
@end
```

File Controller.m:

```
#import "Controller.h"
@implementation MYController
- (void)applicationDidFinishLaunching:(NSNotification *)notification
{
    NSArray *imageFileTypes = [NSImage imageFileTypes];
    NSArray *imageUnfilteredFileTypes = [NSImage imageUnfilteredFileTypes];
    NSArray *imagePasteboardTypes = [NSImage imagePasteboardTypes];
    NSArray *imageUnfilteredPasteboardTypes =
            [NSImage imageUnfilteredPasteboardTypes];
    [imageFileTypesText setString:
            [NSString stringWithFormat:@"%@", imageFileTypes]];
    [imageUnfilteredFileTypesText setString:
            [NSString stringWithFormat:@"%@", imageUnfilteredFileTypes]];
    [imagePasteboardTypesText setString:
            [NSString stringWithFormat:@"%@", imagePasteboardTypes]];
    [imageUnfilteredPasteboardTypesText setString:
            [NSString stringWithFormat:@"%@", imageUnfilteredPasteboardTypes]];
    [[imageFileTypesText window] makeKeyAndOrderFront:nil];
}
@end
```

Given a pasteboard object, an `NSImage` can be created from the data on the pasteboard. Pasteboards are discussed in Chapter 19. The `NSImage` class method, `+canInitWithPasteboard:`, returns `YES` if it can initialize an `NSImage` instance from the data on the pasteboard, and `NO` otherwise. Because there are many image formats that might be placed on the pasteboard, this is the easiest way to tell if `NSImage` can interpret the data or not. When it is determined that the pasteboard data is useful, the `-initWithPasteboard:` method can be used. If given an `NSPasteboard` instance `myPasteboard`, the following code will create a new `NSImage` instance, if it is possible:

```
NSImage *newImage = nil;
if ([NSImage canInitWithPasteboard:myPasteboard]) {
    newImage = [[NSImage alloc] initWithPasteboard:myPasteboard];
}
```

The +canInitWithPasteboard: method only returns a YES or a NO. If there is a need to know the actual pasteboard types supported by NSImage, the +imagePasteboardTypes and +imageUnfilteredPasteboardTypes methods are available. These two methods work like their file type counterparts. The strings returned are different, however. Instead of file types, they are generally longer strings that identify a particular system pasteboard type.

Some of the strings that might be found as a pasteboard type are defined in the NSPasteboard.h header. For example, the constant NSTIFFPboardType is one of the types returned. On Mac OS X 10.1, this constant is actually NeXT TIFF v4.0 pasteboard type, as seen if you run the ImageTypes example. The system defined types defined as of Mac OS X 10.1 are NSPostScriptPboardType, NSTIFFPboardType, NSPICTPboardType, and NSPDFPboardType. The values of these should be ignored, however. It is recommended instead that the constant values always be used.

Of course, applications that publish image filter services might add other pasteboard types as well. Those types will appear in the +imagePasteboardTypes array but not in the +imageUnfilteredPasteboardTypes array. The Application Kit also adds several types to the +imagePasteboardTypes array. These extras aren't available as constants. The strings themselves are of the format NSTypedFilenamesPboardType:TYPE where TYPE is a file extension. These are added so a file reference placed on the pasteboard can be converted into an NSImage by loading the contents of the file. This is a good reason to use the more generic +imagePasteboardTypes method for most pasteboard operations. For example, if the unfiltered pasteboard types are used, drag and drop of image files from the Finder won't work.

Finally, if an NSImage needs to be created from scratch, as opposed to creating the object from preexisting data, use the -initWithSize: method. This is often used to create offscreen buffers (caches). Because all Quartz drawing is double buffered, it is usually not necessary for a developer to do caching. However, this can be a useful technique.

For example, suppose a drawing program is being developed. If the user chooses to drag a group of complex objects, it might be more efficient to render the objects into an NSImage. As the objects move, the NSImage can be redrawn to the view at a new location instead of rerendering the shapes themselves. The section "Drawing in an NSImage," later in this chapter describes how to direct drawing to an NSImage instance, and the section "Rendering an Image," (also later in this chapter) shows how to draw an image to the screen. The NSImage class is used when an offscreen drawing buffer is desired. It is common to want a buffer that matches an NSView instance in size. To create such an NSImage from within the NSView subclass, the following code could be used:

```
NSRect myBounds = [self bounds];
NSImage *backBuffer = [[NSImage alloc] initWithSize:myBounds.size];
```

Rendering an Image

When an NSImage is rendered, or drawn, it is composited as described in the "Compositing" section earlier in this chapter. The two basic methods for rendering an image are

```
- (void)drawAtPoint:(NSPoint)point fromRect:(NSRect)fromRect
        operation:(NSCompositingOperation)op fraction:(float)delta
- (void)drawInRect:(NSRect)rect fromRect:(NSRect)fromRect
        operation:(NSCompositingOperation)op fraction:(float)delta
```

The only difference between the two methods is in how the destination location is specified. In the first method, the destination is specified as a point. In this case, the destination point specifies where the image's origin is placed when the composite is performed. By changing the destination point, the image can be translated within the current graphics context. The destination is specified in terms of the active graphics context's current coordinate system, so that the existing scale, rotation, and translation are respected. The second form specifies a destination rectangle instead of a point. The image will be scaled as it is composited so that it is fitted exactly to the rectangle specified. The rectangle itself is specified in terms of the active graphics context's current coordinate system.

The rest of the parameters to these methods are identical in purpose. The second parameter is the `fromRect` parameter. It specifies the portion of the NSImage that is to be composited. This makes it possible to only composite a subimage from the NSImage. To composite the whole image, use a rectangle with origin (0.0, 0.0) and a size obtained from the NSImage `-size` method.

The next parameter specifies the compositing operation to be performed. The available operations are described in the "Compositing" section earlier in this chapter. The constants in Table 14.1 are the legal values for the `op` parameter.The last parameter, `delta`, specifies a fade value from 0.0 to 1.0. For a normal compositing operation, this is 1.0. If a fractional value is used, the final results of the compositing operation are a partial fade between the original destination image and the final, composited image.

The `SimpleAnimation` example shows how these methods can be used. It contains a custom NSView object with an animated object moving across a background. The animated object is a rotating, bouncing ball. There is an NSImage containing the background. Another NSImage contains the frames of the animated object, as shown in Figure 14.1. To erase the object before drawing it at a new location, a portion of the background image is composited to the NSView. The ball image contains all the animation frames, packed together into a single NSImage. To select the desired frame from the ball image, the `fromRect` parameter's origin, but not size, is changed with each frame of animation. While the ball itself moves, the `delta` parameter is changed to make it fade in and out.

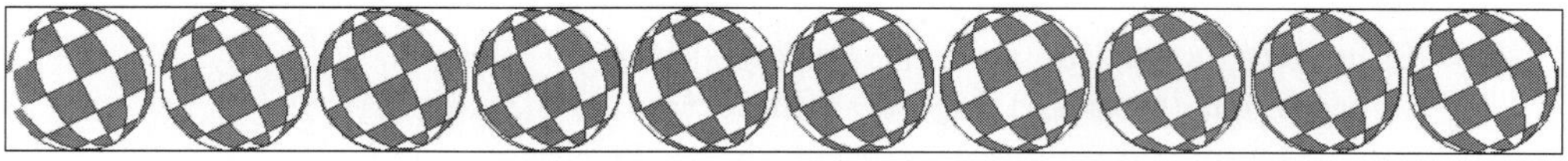

FIGURE 14.1 This NSImage contains the frames of the animated object in the SimpleAnimation application.

There is only one Interface Builder connection, setting the custom view as the application's delegate. All the code resides in the custom `NSView` object. For any real animation, this would not be an effective or scalable design. Instead, separate classes for the background and the ball would be created. The view would then call upon each class to contribute to rendering the final animation frame. Although this all has been lumped together into a single object to keep this example simple, an industrial-strength design would not do so. The code for the custom `NSView` is as follows:

```
File AnimationView.h:

#import <Cocoa/Cocoa.h>

#define BALL_FRAMES 10
#define FRAMES_PER_SECOND 30


@interface MYAnimationView : NSView
{
    NSTimer *_myFrameTimer;
    NSImage *_myBackgroundImage;
    NSImage *_myBallFramesImage;
    NSRect _myBallLocation;
    NSPoint _myBallVelocity;
    int _myBallFrame, _myFrameIncrement;
    float _myBallFade, _myFadeIncrement;
}

- (id)initWithFrame:(NSRect)frame;
- (void)applicationDidFinishLaunching:(NSNotification *)notification;
- (void)drawRect:(NSRect)rect;
- (void)eraseOldDrawing;
```

```
- (void)calculateNewFrame;
- (void)redrawFrame;
- (void)timerPing:(NSTimer *)theTimer;
- (void)startTimerWithInterval:(float)timeGap;
- (void)stopTimer;
- (void)dealloc;

@end

File AnimationView.m:

#import "AnimationView.h"

#define SECONDS_PER_FRAME (1.0 / (float)FRAMES_PER_SECOND)
#define BALL_WIDTH 104.0
#define BALL_HEIGHT 100.0
#define FADE_INCREMENT 0.02

@implementation MYAnimationView

- (id)initWithFrame:(NSRect)frame
{
    self = [super initWithFrame:frame];
    if (self) {
        myBallLocation = NSMakeRect(random() % 660 + 20,
                random() % 460 + 20, BALL_WIDTH, BALL_HEIGHT);
        myBallVelocity = NSMakePoint(random() % 5 + 5, random() % 5 + 5);
        myBallFrame = 0;
        myFrameIncrement = 1;
        myBallFade = 1.0;
        myFadeIncrement = -FADE_INCREMENT;
        myBallFramesImage = nil;
        myBackgroundImage = nil;
        myFrameTimer = nil;
    }
    return self;
}

- (void)applicationDidFinishLaunching:(NSNotification *)notification
{   // This will finish our initialization after the application has
    // been fully initialized. This object needs to be the
    // application's delegate in order to be sent this message.
```

```
    // load and cache animation frames for bouncing ball
    myBallFramesImage = [NSImage imageNamed:@"balls"];
    [myBallFramesImage retain];
    [myBallFramesImage lockFocus]; // forces image to be cached by Quartz
    [myBallFramesImage unlockFocus];
    // load and cache background image
    myBackgroundImage = [NSImage imageNamed:@"background"];
    [myBackgroundImage retain];
    [myBackgroundImage lockFocus]; // forces image to be cached by Quartz
    [myBackgroundImage unlockFocus];
    // start the animation timer
    [self startTimerWithInterval:SECONDS_PER_FRAME];
    // turn on a couple of minor speed-ups
    [self allocateGState];
    [[self window] useOptimizedDrawing:YES];
    // bring our window forward now that we're ready to draw
    [[self window] makeKeyAndOrderFront:nil];
}

- (void)drawRect:(NSRect)rect
{
    NSRect bds = [self bounds];
    NSRect ballFrameRect = NSMakeRect(myBallFrame * BALL_WIDTH,
            0.0, BALL_WIDTH, BALL_HEIGHT);

    // draw the whole background
    [backgroundImage drawInRect:bds fromRect:bds
            operation:NSCompositeSourceOver fraction:1.0];
    // draw the ball
    [ballFramesImage drawInRect:myBallLocation fromRect:ballFrameRect
            operation:NSCompositeSourceOver fraction:myBallFade];
}

- (void)eraseOldDrawing
{
    // erase the ball by splatting the background over it
    [backgroundImage drawInRect:myBallLocation fromRect:myBallLocation
            operation:NSCompositeSourceOver fraction:1.0];
}

- (void)calculateNewFrame
{
```

```
NSRect bds = [self bounds];
NSPoint ballLimit = NSMakePoint(bds.size.width - BALL_WIDTH,
        bds.size.height - BALL_HEIGHT);
BOOL bounced = NO;

// calculate new ball location
myBallLocation.origin.x += myBallVelocity.x;
if (myBallLocation.origin.x < 0.0) {
    myBallLocation.origin.x = 0.0;
    myBallVelocity.x = -myBallVelocity.x;
    bounced = YES;
}
if (myBallLocation.origin.x > ballLimit.x) {
    myBallLocation.origin.x = ballLimit.x;
    myBallVelocity.x = -myBallVelocity.x;
    bounced = YES;
}
myBallLocation.origin.y += myBallVelocity.y;
if (myBallLocation.origin.y < 0.0) {
    myBallLocation.origin.y = 0.0;
    myBallVelocity.y = -myBallVelocity.y;
    bounced = YES;
}
if (myBallLocation.origin.y > ballLimit.y) {
    myBallLocation.origin.y = ballLimit.y;
    myBallVelocity.y = -myBallVelocity.y;
    bounced = YES;
}

// calculate which frame to display next
myBallFrame += myFrameIncrement;
if (myBallFrame >= BALL_FRAMES) {
    myBallFrame = 0;
}
if (myBallFrame < 0) {
    myBallFrame = BALL_FRAMES - 1;
}
if (bounced) {
    myFrameIncrement = -myFrameIncrement;
}
```

```
    // calculate ball's fade
    myBallFade += myFadeIncrement;
    if (myBallFade < 0.0) {
        myBallFade = 0.0;
        myFadeIncrement = -myFadeIncrement;
    }
    if (myBallFade > 1.0) {
        myBallFade = 1.0;
        myFadeIncrement = -myFadeIncrement;
    }
}

- (void)redrawFrame
{
    NSRect ballFrameRect = NSMakeRect(myBallFrame * BALL_WIDTH,
            0.0, BALL_WIDTH, BALL_HEIGHT);
    // draw the ball
    [myBallFramesImage drawInRect:myBallLocation fromRect:ballFrameRect
            operation:NSCompositeSourceOver fraction:myBallFade];
}

- (void)timerPing:(NSTimer *)theTimer
{   // called by our NSTimer to render the next animation frame
    // This is the basic animation loop
    [self lockFocus];
    [self eraseOldDrawing];
    [self calculateNewFrame];
    [self redrawFrame];
    [[NSGraphicsContext currentContext] flushGraphics];
    [self unlockFocus];
}

- (void)startTimerWithInterval:(float)timeGap
{
    [self stopTimer];
    myFrameTimer = [NSTimer scheduledTimerWithTimeInterval:timeGap
            target:self selector:@selector(timerPing:)
            userInfo:nil repeats:YES];
    [myFrameTimer retain];
}
```

```
- (void)stopTimer
{
    if (myFrameTimer) {
        [myFrameTimer invalidate];
        [myFrameTimer release];
    }
}

- (void)dealloc
{

    [self stopTimer];
    [self releaseGState];
    [myBallFramesImage release];
    [backgroundImage release];
    [super dealloc];
}

@end
```

Several other rendering operations are less likely to be used. There are four `-composite:` methods and the two `-dissolveToPoint:` methods. The `-composite:` methods look like this:

```
- (void)compositeToPoint:(NSPoint)point operation:(NSCompositingOperation)op
- (void)compositeToPoint:(NSPoint)point fromRect:(NSRect)rect
      operation:(NSCompositingOperation)op
- (void)compositeToPoint:(NSPoint)point operation:(NSCompositingOperation)op
      fraction:(float)delta
- (void)compositeToPoint:(NSPoint)point fromRect:(NSRect)rect
      operation:(NSCompositingOperation)op fraction:(float)delta
```

These methods look suspiciously like the `-draw` methods described above, but there is a significant difference. The image will be composited in a way that ignores the current context's scaling and rotation. Only translation is respected. Because this is not usually what is desired, these methods are not often used.

These methods exist primarily for backward compatibility with older code. Versions of Cocoa prior to Mac OS X had the limitation that they couldn't composite images in a way that would respect the current coordinate system. The compositing destination point would respect the coordinate system, but the rest of the image would not. To keep old code from needing to be completely rewritten, these methods have been retained.

The parameters to these methods have the exact same meanings as the similarly named parameters of the `-draw` methods.

```
- (void)dissolveToPoint:(NSPoint)point fraction:(float)aFloat;
- (void)dissolveToPoint:(NSPoint)point fromRect:(NSRect)rect
        fraction:(float)aFloat;
```

Calling either of the dissolve operations is basically the same as calling the corresponding `-compositeToPoint:` method with the Source Over compositing mode. In other words, these two messages produce identical results:

```
[myImage compositeToPoint:point operation:NSCompositeSourceOver fraction:delta];
[myImage dissolveToPoint:point fraction:delta];
```

These two lines of code also have identical results:

```
[myImage compositeToPoint:point fromRect:rect
        operation:NSCompositeSourceOver fraction:delta];
[myImage dissolveToPoint:point fromRect:rect fraction:delta];
```

Just like the `-compositeToPoint:` methods, these methods have been retained for backward compatibility with older Cocoa code.

There is another way to get a bitmap onto the screen, but it is not recommended for general-purpose use. The `NSDrawBitMap()` function can take a pointer to raw image data and blast it onto the screen. It is a thin cover for a Quartz function that does the same thing. This function is briefly described in the "Bitmap Image Representations" section later in this chapter, but actually using it is often more trouble than it is worth. The `NSImage` class is efficient enough that there is no performance-based reason not to use it.

The `NSImage` method `-drawRepresentation:inRect:` might seem an obvious choice to use as an alternate rendering method. It is not, however, meant to be called directly. Instead, it is meant to be overridden in custom subclasses. It's primarily used as a way to alter how an `NSImage` will be rendered. Therefore, this method is discussed in the "Drawing in an `NSImage`" section later in this chapter.

Inspecting and Manipulating Image Properties

Several methods can be used to change the behavior of an `NSImage`, or inspect its settings and attributes.

When creating an `NSImage` there are many ways that the creation attempt might fail. In many cases, `nil` is returned to signal this. It is easy to check for that, however, sometimes an instance will be returned. Because an `NSImage` might load its image data lazily, depending on how it was initialized, a given instance might not really be usable. This normally wouldn't be known until the image attempted to render itself. To determine ahead of time whether an NSImage is valid and usable, send it the -isValid message. Either YES or NO will be returned. It is a good idea to use this method as part of the error checking when creating a new NSImage, or when unarchiving an image from the pasteboard or elsewhere.

One of the ways that a new NSImage is obtained is by using the class method +imageNamed: to look up the image. A new image can be created from scratch and assigned a name. When so registered, the image is available via that method. To assign a name or change an image's name, use the -setName: method. There is something unusual about this method's prototype:

```
- (BOOL)setName:(NSString *)string;
```

Unlike most -set methods, NSImage's -setName: returns a boolean value. If another image is already registered under the name used in the string parameter, this method will fail and return NO. If the receiving image is already registered under another name, it will first unregister itself, and then reregister with the new name. If this method succeeds, it will return YES. To see what name an image has been given, the -name method can be used. It will return either an NSString containing the image's name, or nil if no name has been assigned.

Because image data is expensive, sometimes it is desirable to have an NSImage only retain a reference to the file from which it was created instead of all the image data. When an image is archived, only the file reference would be stored instead of all the image data, thereby reducing the archive's size considerably. As previously discussed, the -initByReferencingFile: method enables creation of an image that only retains a file reference. To find out if an image will retain its data or not, use the -isDataRetained method. If YES is returned, all the image data will be stored with the image when it is archived. NO will be returned by objects that only store file references. This behavior can be altered by using the -setDataRetained: method. It takes a single boolean argument and returns nothing.

All NSImages can have a background color. This color is used when a nonscalable image representation is drawn in an image that is larger than the representation. The background color fills the pixels that are not covered by the representation. Cached image representations won't use this because all caches use a white background. Normally, the background color is transparent, the same color returned by the NSColor class's +clearColor method. To change an NSImage's background color, use the -setBackgroundColor: method, passing it an NSColor instance. To find out what the background color is set to be, the -backgroundColor method returns an NSColor object. Changing the background color doesn't cause the image to be recached. Recaching, if desired, must be forced by sending the -recache message to the image.

Maintaining a graphic context in Quartz can be a bit of a resource hog. To reduce the number of graphics contexts maintained in Quartz for `NSImage` caches, a single cache can contain the contents of multiple images. For images that don't change in size, this can be very efficient. In this scenario, each image owns a portion of the context and when it locks focus, it restricts all drawing to the portion of the cache that it owns, using a clipping rectangle. There is no need to worry about accidentally drawing into the area owned by a different `NSImage`. However, disable this behavior if an image changes its size often. In that case, it is more efficient to maintain a context just for that image.

To force an image to have its own private graphics context for its cache, as opposed to sharing caches, use the `-setCachedSeparately:` method with a `YES`. To allow an image to be part of a shared cache, send a `NO` to that method. To see what the current caching behavior of the image is, use the `-isCachedSeparately` method. Note that even when cache sharing is turned on, `NSImage` might decide to cache the image separately anyway. The choice is implementation dependent. In other words, this parameter is really just a hint to `NSImage`, and doesn't guarantee any specific behavior.

The cache for an `NSImage` can, in theory, take its bit depth from one of two sources. The most common, and the default case, is to make the cache match the depth of the screen, which is an application's default bit depth. Alternatively, the depth of the image cache could be determined from the image data itself. For example, a TIFF image has tags that specify how many bits of color there are per pixel. Not every image can use image data to determine a depth, of course. Basically, only bitmapped images loaded from a file, or from data in a particular image format, can do this.

To make an image take its bit depth from the image data itself, the `-setCacheDepthMatchesImageDepth:` method can be used. Send a `YES` to it and the cache's depth is taken from the image data. Send a `NO` to get the default behavior of matching the cache to the screen. Normally, matching the screen is the desired behavior, but this could cause a high-depth image to lose information. For some applications, such as a paint program, that would be unacceptable. Matching the cache depth to the image data makes sense in such a case. To find out how an `NSImage` instance is determining its cached depth, use the `-cacheDepthMatchesImageDepth` method, which will return `YES` or `NO`.

One of the few parameters concerning the image data that is actually maintained by an `NSImage` is the image's size. Because each image representation maintained by the `NSImage` might have a different size in and of itself, the parent `NSImage` stores a master size that is the canonical size of the image. Representations are scaled to that size if possible, or else uncovered pixels are painted with the image's background color to make sure that the image covers all the pixels specified by its size.

An image cannot be rendered until it has a size set. When initialized from image data, the NSImage takes its size from that. All bitmap image data formats specify dimensions for their image data in some way; NSImage uses that information, where available, to set its size. EPS and PDF files specify a bounding box for their vector graphics; NSImage uses bounding-box information where applicable to set its size. Where there is no image data provided, a size must be given. This is why a simple -init should be avoided for an NSImage; -initWithSize: must be used. It is legal, however, to call -initWithSize: with a zero size (0.0, 0.0). In this case, the size must be set at a later time before the image can be rendered. The image will be invalid until it has a nonzero size.

To set or change an image's size, use the -setSize: method. The method takes an NSSize as its single argument and returns nothing. When called, -setSize: will invalidate and release any image cache that might exist, forcing a recache to occur. The cache will be recreated at the new size the next time it is needed. To determine the size of an image, send it the -size method. An NSSize will be returned.

When an image is resized, any existing image representations might need to be scaled so they fit the new size exactly. However, because it might not always be desirable to scale the associated image representations, this can be turned on or off. NSImage's default behavior is to not scale image representations when the image's size changes. This behavior can be changed with the -setScalesWhenResized: method. This method takes a boolean argument and returns nothing. Changing this setting controls the NSImage's behavior in respect to all the image representations it is maintaining. Use the -scalesWhenResized method to determine the image's current behavior in this respect. It will return a boolean value.

When an image is rendered, it can be drawn with the Y axis flipped (that is, flipped over vertically). To make this happen, send a YES to the -setFlipped: method. The default behavior is NO, don't flip the image. To see whether an image is drawn flipped, use the -isFlipped method. It returns a boolean. When an image is flipped, it's still drawn in the exact same place it would have been if it weren't flipped. This is important to remember, especially with the -compositeToPoint: and -dissolveToPoint: methods. The image will not be drawn downward from the point specified. Usually, flipping an image doesn't seem like a very helpful function. However, if the image is being rendered into a flipped view, commonly seen with text, flipping the image causes it to be drawn correctly in that context.

NSImage's Relationship with NSImageRep

As has been previously described, the NSImage class maintains a list of image representations. The representations themselves contain the actual image data. NSImage doesn't know how to render anything by itself. It always asks one of its image representations to do the drawing. Each image representation is an instance of a subclass of the `NSImageRep` class. A discussion of the `NSImageRep` class, its subclasses, and how to use them directly can be found in the "Manipulating Image Representations" section later in this chapter. This section discusses exactly how the `NSImage` class makes use of its image representations.

One of the first questions to ask is how an `NSImage` chooses which representation to use for rendering itself on a given device. The selection algorithm uses three basic rules. Each rule can cause some image representations to be discarded from the list of candidates. If there is more than one candidate left after the rule has been applied, the `NSImage` will proceed to the next rule until just one image representation remains. Because the rules might need to be changed, depending upon the situation, `NSImage` also provides some ways to modify the rules and the order in which they are applied. The simplest set of rules, the default procedure, is as follows:

- **Rule 1**—Look for a representation that matches the device's color space. For example, if the device is monochrome, choose a monochrome representation, if available. Likewise, if the device is color, look for a color representation in the same color space, or failing that, any color representation.
- **Rule 2**—Choose a representation that matches the device's resolution. A representation that is an integral multiple of the device's resolution is considered to be a match. If there is more than one match, the representation closest to the device resolution will match. If there is no match, choose the representation with the highest resolution. This rule prefers a bitmap representation to a vector-based representation because vector graphics typically do not specify a resolution.
- **Rule 3**—Select a representation that most matches the device's bits per sample. If there is no exact match, choose the representation with the highest number of bits per sample.

These rules, as are, work great for drawing to a screen device. Because most drawing is to the screen, this is a reasonable default. However, there might be times where it makes sense to adjust this algorithm. The first change that can be made is to swap the order of Rules 1 and 2, thereby making a resolution match take precedence over a color space match. The two methods for controlling this are

```
- (void)setPrefersColorMatch:(BOOL)flag
- (BOOL)prefersColorMatch
```

Use `-setPrefersColorMatch:` to change the order of Rules 1 and 2. The default value is `YES`. Calling this method, and passing it the value `NO` causes a resolution match to take precedence over the color space match. To determine the current priority of these two rules, use the `-prefersColorMatch` method.

In Rule 2, which matches resolutions, an integral multiple of the device's resolution is considered to be a match. Although this can work well on the screen, sometimes an exact match is preferred. To require the rule to only look at exact resolution matches, use these methods:

```
- (void)setMatchesOnMultipleResolution:(BOOL)flag
- (BOOL)matchesOnMultipleResolution
```

The default setting is `YES`, which allows integral multiples of the device resolution to be considered a match. Setting this to `NO` causes only exact matches to be considered. The `-setMatchesOnMultipleResolution:` method changes the setting, and the `-matchesOnMultipleResolution` method returns the current value of the setting.

Rule 2 also favors bitmap-based representations to vector-based representations. For drawing to the screen, this makes a lot of sense. Often a vector-based image has an associated bitmap preview that is rendered to work well on a device with a given set of characteristics. When drawing to the screen, the preview is likely to be the better choice. This isn't always the case. Sometimes the vector representation is preferred. In cases where the vector-based representation takes precedence over bitmaps, the following methods can be used:

```
- (void)setUsesEPSOnResolutionMismatch:(BOOL)flag
- (BOOL)usesEPSOnResolutionMismatch
```

The value of this setting defaults to `NO`. Setting it to `YES` makes EPS-based representations take precedence over bitmap representations during the resolution match whenever a resolution match is not found. If a bitmap with an exact resolution match is available, it will still be used over the vector representation. Unfortunately there is no current API for making PDF or other vector-based representations take precedence.

To find out which representation would actually be chosen by the algorithm described previously, the following method can be used:

```
- (NSImageRep *)bestRepresentationForDevice:(NSDictionary *)deviceDescription;
```

This method returns the one image representation that the `NSImage` instance would choose to be used when rendering to a device matching the parameters found in the `deviceDescription` dictionary. The allowable keys for the device description dictionary are described in Table 14.2.

TABLE 14.2 Device Description Dictionary Keys

Key	Expected Value
NSDeviceResolution	This value is an NSValue instance containing an NSSize. (Use the +valueWithSize: method to create the NSValue). The size specifies the dots-per-inch (dpi) resolution of the device in each direction.
NSDeviceColorSpaceName	This is an NSString. The string is one of these color space identifier constants: NSCalibratedWhiteColorSpace, NSCalibratedBlackColorSpace, NSCalibratedRGBColorSpace, NSDeviceWhiteColorSpace, NSDeviceBlackColorSpace, NSDeviceRGBColorSpace, NSDeviceCMYKColorSpace, NSNamedColorSpace, NSPatternColorSpace, or NSCustomColorSpace. See Chapter 17 "Color," for more information about these constants.
NSDeviceBitsPerSample	This value is an NSValue containing an integer. Note that this is bits per sample, not bits per pixel. For example, a device with a 24-bit RGB color space would specify 8 bits per sample.
NSDeviceIsScreen	The value for this key is the NSString @"YES" only. Leave the key out of the dictionary if not specifying that the device is a screen.
NSDeviceIsPrinter	The value for this key is the NSString @"YES" only. Leave the key out of the dictionary if not specifying that the device is a printer.
NSDeviceSize	This value is an NSValue instance containing an NSSize. (Use the +valueWithSize: method to create the NSValue.) The size specifies the size of the drawing canvas that can be painted by the device.

Besides just asking for a single representation, the list of representations maintained by the NSImage can be manipulated. The following four methods can be used to retrieve the list and modify it:

```
- (NSArray *)representations;
- (void)addRepresentations:(NSArray *)imageReps;
- (void)addRepresentation:(NSImageRep *)imageRep;
- (void)removeRepresentation:(NSImageRep *)imageRep;
```

The first method, -representations, returns an NSArray containing all the representations available to the NSImage. This array is treated as a constant, as can be noted from the nonmutable return type. Don't try to modify the array directly.

To add representations to the NSImage's list one at a time, use the -addRepresentation: method. To add several representations at once, put them all into an NSArray, and then use the -addRepresentations: method. An NSImage retains any representations it is given. There is one important, nonobvious detail here. A given image representation can only be owned by one NSImage. There is no sharing between them. Don't try to add the same representation to multiple images.

To remove a representation from an NSImage, use the -removeRepresentation: method. This removes the representation from the list and releases it. If the image representation needs to be used elsewhere, perhaps handed to another image object, you should explicitly retain it before it is removed from the NSImage's list.

Finally, an NSImage object can be saved as a TIFF image. Two methods can be used for this:

```
- (NSData *)TIFFRepresentation
- (NSData *)TIFFRepresentationUsingCompression:(NSTIFFCompression)comp
        factor:(float)aFloat
```

Both methods return an NSData object and not an NSImageRep subclass. Note that a new NSImage could be initialized from the NSData object that is returned by these methods. To actually create a TIFF file, the NSData object needs to be saved to a disk. NSData's -writeToFile:atomically: can be used for that.

The -TIFFRepresentation method doesn't allow a compression type or factor to be specified. Instead, the default compression type is taken from the individual image representations. The default compression type depends on the image representation. If it was created from a file, that file's compression type is the default. Instances initialized from raw byte data default to uncompressed.

The -TIFFRepresentationUsingCompression:factor: method allows the compression type and factor to be specified. The comp parameter is specified from one of the constants offered by the NSBitmapImageRep class. Because the list is implementation dependent and could change from one release to the next, the NSBitmapImageRep class has facilities for discovering the list of valid compression types. The "Bitmap Image Representations" section later in this chapter discusses the available methods.

Some of the commonly used compression schemes in the current Cocoa implementation are NSTIFFCompressionNone, NSTIFFCompressionCCITTFAX3, NSTIFFCompressionCCITTFAX4, NSTIFFCompressionPackBits, and NSTIFFCompressionLZW. For no compression at all, the NSTIFFCompressionNone constant is used. For one bit per sample images, the two CCIITTFAX compression modes can be used. The PackBits and LZW compression modes both work for any bitmap. Both are lossless compression, which means the uncompressed image will be identical to the original image. The LZW compression tends to produce a more compact output than PackBits, so it is generally the preferred choice. None of these compression algorithms can use a compression factor, so the floating-point value passed to the NSImage for the factor is ignored. For a lossy compression scheme where image fidelity can be sacrificed to obtain more compression, the factor would be significant. The factor's values would be implementation dependent and specified by the compression type. An example of lossy compression is JPEG algorithm. Although this algorithm used to be supported by Cocoa, it is no longer available for generating TIFF images.

If the -TIFFRepresentationUsingCompression:factor: method fails for any reason, such as a discrepancy in the compression requested, it can raise an exception. Therefore, call this method from within the scope of an exception handler.

Drawing in an NSImage

A new NSImage can be created from scratch or can be modified an existing image. As discussed previously, the -initWithSize: method can be used to create an image to be used as a blank slate. When an image is available, the image can be drawn in the way drawing is done in a custom NSView subclass.

To begin drawing in an NSImage, send it the -lockFocus message. All drawing of any type is rendered in the NSImage (actually in an NSCachedImageRep, to be precise) until the focus is changed. To release focus, send the image the -unlockFocus message. Drawing is returned to the original drawing context.

The focus can be locked on a particular image representation. Obtain one of the image's image representations (recall that an array containing them all is returned by the -representations method), and pass it as the parameter to the -lockFocusOnRepresentation: method.

Whenever focus is locked on an NSImage, all drawing is done in the image itself. This allows an NSImage to be used as an offscreen buffer. (See the section "Caching Complex Drawing" in Chapter 13 for more information.) The full features of the Quartz graphics model are available when drawing into an NSImage, so everything discussed in Chapters 12 and 13 about NSBezierPath, NSAffineTransform, compositing, and so on, applies.

Locking focus is like working with a stack: every lock must absolutely be matched with an unlock to avoid problems. It is common to have nested locks. For example, when focus has been locked on an NSView, drawing might require temporary drawing in an NSImage. Without unlocking the view, focus is locked on the image, transferring drawing focus from the view to the image. Before unlocking the view, the image's focus needs to be unlocked. It is also important to remember to lock focus before doing drawing intended for an image. Attempting to do any drawing without any focus locked will cause a runtime exception because the Application Kit will not know where to send the drawing. If focus is locked, but not on the image, the drawing might go to an unintended destination. Such bugs are easy to spot because they usually have quite dramatic results onscreen.

A cache is automatically created for an image when focus is locked on it, so that there is someplace for the drawing to go. If the image won't be used very often, and redraws are cheap enough, it might be worth freeing the cache while the image is not in use. The `-recache` method invalidates and releases the image's cache. The cache will not actually be recreated until it is needed again, so memory resources can be freed up this way. To release and immediately recreate the cache, use the following sequence:

```
[myImage recache];
[myImage lockFocus];
[myImage unlockFocus];
```

There doesn't have to be any actual drawing between locking and unlocking the focus. Because locking the focus creates a cache immediately, this sequence causes the old cache to be thrown away and a new cache to be created.

By creating a custom subclass of `NSImage`, custom code can be inserted into the rendering path. Although not meant to be called directly, this method is available to be overridden:

```
- (BOOL)drawRepresentation:(NSImageRep *)imageRep inRect:(NSRect)rect
```

When an `NSImage` has chosen an image representation to be used for rendering itself in a particular context, it calls this method to actually create a cached image that can be used by Quartz for compositing.

The default implementation fills the cache with the image's background color, and then draws the image representation using standard Quartz commands. The drawing goes into the `NSImage`'s cache. The cache, which is matched to the resolution and color depth of the context's output device, is then used for the actual compositing. If the drawing was successful, this method returns `YES`. If the drawing failed, `NO` is returned and `NSImage` object will try again with another image representation or fall back to its delegate for help. In the standard implementation, if the `NSImageRep` passed in is unable to be scaled, only the origin of the rect parameter is respected.

When `-drawRepresentation:inRect:` is overridden, developers often choose to modify some graphics context parameters, such as scale and rotation, and then call the super implementation. Something completely different can also be done; imagination is the only limit.

Like many other Application Kit objects an `NSImage` can have a delegate. The normal `-setDelegate:` and `-delegate` methods exist to change and retrieve the delegate object, respectively. In the case of `NSImage`, the delegate has only one function.

When an NSImage is unable to render itself, due to a lack of image representations or for any other reason, the NSImage instance attempts to notify the delegate. The message that the delegate needs to implement to be notified is

```
- (NSImage *)imageDidNotDraw:(id)sender inRect:(NSRect)aRect
```

The NSImage returned by the delegate is used as a replacement to render the image. If the delegate returns nil, the NSImage object gives up on the compositing operation in progress. This means the delegate can take one of the three following courses of action:

- Return a replacement image to be used for rendering.
- Render the image itself, with custom drawing, a composite, or other operation. The sender parameter can be used to identify the original NSImage that couldn't draw itself, and the aRect parameter can be used to determine where to draw. In this case, nil is returned so that NSImage will give up trying to render.
- Give up and render nothing, returning nil so that the sending NSImage also gives up.

This delegation mechanism is really meant to be a way to deal with images which for some exceptional reason are unable to be rendered. Therefore, it is not the best place to insert custom code into the rendering process. Overriding the -drawRepresentation:inRect: method, described previously, is a better place for custom code.

Another delegation mechanism is employed via the NSCustomImageRep class. It allows a developer to hook into the rendering path and insert her own custom code, perhaps code that uses NSBezierPath or other means to render the image. This delegation mechanism is described later in this chapter in the "Cached and Custom Image Representations" section.

Manipulating Image Representations

The NSImage class does not actually manage an image's data. It uses a subclass of NSImageRep to do that. The previous discussion about NSImage talks about how the NSImage class uses image representations. Much of the time, this is all that is needed to get the desired results. When more complex circumstances require, an image representation can be manipulated directly. For most image manipulation, the NSImage interface is the best API to use. However, when direct manipulation of the underlying image data is required, it is often necessary to manipulate one or more individual image representations. The following sections discuss how to work with image representations. First, the base NSImageRep class is discussed. Then, specific subclasses for working with bitmaps, vector graphics, and more will be discussed.

NSImageRep Class

The NSImageRep class is a semiabstract class that is the basis for all image representation objects. It is abstract in that the NSImageRep class itself should never be instantiated. Its primary function is to define a basic interface common to all image representation objects. However, because it defines some instance variables and implements several methods, it is not completely an abstract class in the purest sense. The methods that are defined by this class include methods for drawing (rendering) the bitmap in the current graphics context, methods for accessing generic image properties, and several methods for managing the different image-representation subclasses. Several of the latter exist solely to help subclasses fit cleanly into the Application Kit, providing a clear way to extend the types of image data that the Application Kit can manipulate.

To obtain a new instance of NSImageRep, one of these messages can be used on a subclass. Note that the NSImageRep class itself does not implement these methods, but it is expected that all subclasses will.

```
+ (NSArray *)imageRepsWithData:(NSData *)data
+ (id)imageRepWithData:(NSData *)data
- (id)initWithData:(NSData *)data
```

The first two methods are essentially convenience methods. Many image file formats, such as TIFF, can contain multiple images. They can all be different, as in frames of an animation, or they can all be the same image at different resolutions, color depths, and so forth. Although either method can be used on any image file, the one that returns an array often is the better choice to avoid losing the other images in the data. Both methods ultimately call the designated initializer, -initWithData:. This method interprets the image data in the NSData passed to it to initialize the instance. If the data is corrupt or of the wrong type, the object is released and nil will be returned.

There exists a set of convenience methods implemented by the class object to create new image representations:

```
+ (NSArray *)imageRepsWithContentsOfFile:(NSString *)filename
+ (id)imageRepWithContentsOfFile:(NSString *)filename
+ (NSArray *)imageRepsWithContentsOfURL:(NSURL *)url
+ (id)imageRepWithContentsOfURL:(NSURL *)url
+ (NSArray *)imageRepsWithPasteboard:(NSPasteboard *)pasteboard
+ (id)imageRepWithPasteboard:(NSPasteboard *)pasteboard
```

These methods are relatively simple to understand. There are two methods each for obtaining an image representation from a file, a URL, and a pasteboard. For each pair, one of the methods returns a single NSImageRep subclass, whereas the other returns an array of one or more. Many image file formats, such as TIFF, can contain multiple images. They can all be different, as in frames of an animation, or they can all be the same image at different resolutions, color depths, and so forth. Although either method from each pair can be used on any image file, the ones that return arrays are often the better choice to avoid losing the other images in the file.

The `NSImageRep` class keeps a registry of available subclasses and the types each can handle. As a result, each of the previous methods can be sent to the `NSImageRep` class. From the registry, it selects the best class for handling the image data. If the message is sent to a specific subclass instead, only data of the type(s) handled by the subclass are interpreted. Whether the message was sent to the `NSImageRep` class or a subclass, if the data cannot be interpreted, these methods will return `nil`.

The next group of methods is used by `NSImage` to draw a bitmap in the current graphics context:

```
- (BOOL)draw
- (BOOL)drawAtPoint:(NSPoint)point
- (BOOL)drawInRect:(NSRect)rect
```

The `-draw` method draws the image representation at the coordinate system's origin and without any scaling or rotation. The second two methods are convenience methods. They adjust the current coordinate system to allow for translation in the case of `-drawAtPoint:`, or to allow for both translation and scaling in the case of `-drawInRect:`. If the image data was successfully rendered, these methods return `YES`. If the image representation couldn't render or has no size set, `NO` will be returned.

These three methods all use the copy compositing operation to render the image data. To use another compositing mode, the `NSImage` class draws the image representation into an offscreen buffer and composites from that buffer using the desired mode. If using an `NSImageRep` subclass directly, this same approach is needed to use a different compositing operator. The simplest approach is to just use `NSImage`.

Several methods allow various image representation attributes to be queried and modified:

```
- (void)setSize:(NSSize)aSize
- (NSSize)size
- (void)setPixelsWide:(int)anInt
- (int)pixelsWide
- (void)setPixelsHigh:(int)anInt
- (int)pixelsHigh
- (void)setAlpha:(BOOL)flag
- (BOOL)hasAlpha
- (void)setOpaque:(BOOL)flag
```

```
- (BOOL)isOpaque
- (void)setBitsPerSample:(int)anInt
- (int)bitsPerSample
- (void)setColorSpaceName:(NSString *)string
- (NSString *)colorSpaceName
```

Although `NSImageRep` defines all these methods, some of these parameters might not apply to a given subclass. Therefore, when using these methods, some care must be taken to assure that the method(s) in question make sense for the type of image representation being manipulated. The subclasses all respond to any of these methods, but the results might be meaningless.

The `size` parameter is different from the `pixelsWide` and `pixelsHigh` parameters. The image representation's size is provided in units of the base-coordinate system. The Quartz graphic model currently defines that as typographical points, or 72 dpi. The pixel parameters are based on the actual size in pixels, as defined by the image data. Supposing the image representation is a bitmap image at 72 dpi, which is 800×600 pixels in size. In that case, the size is (800, 600), matching the pixel dimensions exactly. Suppose instead that the bitmap was actually a 400-dpi image, but with the same (800, 600) size in pixels. In this case, the pixel dimensions would return the same values, but the size returned would be (144, 108). It is scaled by a factor of 72/400 to convert the dimensions from pixels to points. By setting these parameters correctly, the Application Kit can properly manage bitmaps of different resolutions.

At first glance, the `alpha` and `opaque` parameters might seem identical. There is a subtle difference, however. The `alpha` parameter specifies whether the image representation has an alpha channel or not. The `opaque` parameter specifies whether the image representation will paint every pixel when it is drawn. For example, a bitmap with an alpha channel that covers the entire area as defined by the image representation's size should say that it has `alpha` and is `opaque`, even though the alpha channel might make portions of the image translucent or transparent. The semantic is indeed unusual, so it is important to be careful how these methods are used.

The `bitspersample` parameter refers to the number of bits required to represent a single pixel. This parameter is most applicable to bitmapped image representations. It is relatively meaningless for vector-based images. The special value `NSImageRepMatchesDevice` can be used with these methods.

The following constants define the valid color-space names:

`NSCalibratedWhiteColorSpace`

`NSCalibratedBlackColorSpace`

`NSCalibratedRGBColorSpace`

`NSDeviceWhiteColorSpace`

```
NSDeviceBlackColorSpace
NSDeviceRGBColorSpace
NSDeviceCMYKColorSpace
NSNamedColorSpace
NSPatternColorSpace
NSCustomColorSpace
```

Any of these constants can be used as the color-space name for an image representation. Normally, use the device-independent, calibrated-color spaces. Doing so allows Apple's ColorSync technology to be used. These constants are discussed in more depth in Chapter 17, "Color."

To have a new `NSImageRep` subclass fit into the Application Kit architecture seamlessly, several methods need to be implemented. Some of these methods have already been discussed, but there are many more as well. The following methods must all be implemented to have a fully functional `NSImageRep` subclass:

```
+ (NSArray *)imageRepsWithData:(NSData *)data
+ (id)imageRepWithData:(NSData *)data
- (id)initWithData:(NSData *)data
+ (BOOL)canInitWithData:(NSData *)data
+ (BOOL)canInitWithPasteboard:(NSPasteboard *)pasteboard
+ (NSArray *)imageUnfilteredFileTypes
+ (NSArray *)imageUnfilteredPasteboardTypes
```

The first three methods have already been discussed; they are where the class will interpret the image data. Because the class object chooses the proper image representation based on the data, it is reasonable to expect that valid, already filtered data will be passed to these three methods. The very first method, which returns an `NSArray`, is actually optional. Implement it for any `NSImageRep` subclass that wraps around an image format that could contain multiple images (TIFF would be an example).

To choose the right subclass from the registry, `NSImageRep` requires that subclasses implement the `+canInitWithData:` method. The `+canInitWithPasteboard:` method is a convenience method that calls `+canInitWithData:`, so it doesn't normally need to be specially implemented by a subclass. Note that these methods, if sent to the `NSImageRep` class, will answer for all the subclasses in the registry. If any subclass responds `YES`, then these methods will respond `YES`. When sent to a specific subclass it will answer only for that subclass.

The last two methods return file and pasteboard types, respectively. The arrays that are returned contain NSString objects with contents that match the types the NSImageRep subclass supports. The ImageTypes example on the book's Web site at www.cocoaprogramming.net can be used to see what these strings look like. It shows all the entries for all subclasses and filtered types available to NSImage. The return values from a custom subclass should be identical to one or more of those values for types already listed there. Otherwise, they should be of a similar format. As with the +canInit... methods, these methods can be sent to either NSImageRep or one of its subclasses. NSImageRep merges the results from all the subclasses in the registry to provide an answer.

The NSImageRep class implements two methods to expand the unfiltered types to include types that can be filtered into one of the unfiltered types:

```
+ (NSArray *)imageFileTypes
+ (NSArray *)imagePasteboardTypes
```

These two methods work like their NSImage counterparts. They also don't need to be overridden by subclasses. When sent to NSImageRep, they respond for all the subclasses in the registry. When sent to a subclass, they only answer for that subclass. If a filtered type is used, the Application Kit filters the data prior to passing it to the -initWithData: method and related class methods.

The final set of methods implemented by the NSImageRep class itself is for manipulating the registry of NSImageRep subclasses. The registry is used by NSImage and NSImageRep to select an appropriate NSImageRep subclass given a chunk of image data. The following methods are for registry manipulation:

```
+ (void)registerImageRepClass:(Class)imageRepClass
+ (void)unregisterImageRepClass:(Class)imageRepClass
+ (NSArray *)registeredImageRepClasses
```

The first method adds a class to the registry. The second removes a class from the registry. When either method is called, an NSImageRepRegistryDidChangeNotification notification is sent to the default notification center. This allows objects to watch for changes in the registry.

Any subclass that adds new file or pasteboard types must be sure to register itself. Most NSImageRep subclasses will want to register once, as soon as possible. They probably won't ever want to unregister themselves, either. A good place to do such a registration is in the +load method. It is called only once, when a class is first incorporated into the runtime.

The third method returns an array containing the class objects for all the NSImageRep subclasses that have been registered.

To actually search the registry, `NSImageRep` implements three methods:

```
+ (Class)imageRepClassForFileType:(NSString *)type
+ (Class)imageRepClassForPasteboardType:(NSString *)type
+ (Class)imageRepClassForData:(NSData *)data
```

Given a file type, a pasteboard type, or an `NSData` object, the appropriate method searches the registry and finds a subclass that can handle the image type or data in question. When a match is found, that class object is returned. If none is found, `nil` is returned.

Bitmap Image Representations

One of the most common `NSImageRep` subclasses is the `NSBitmapImageRep`. As the name implies, it is meant to handle bitmap data. It is capable of handling data for a wide variety of common bitmapped image file formats. TIFF, GIF, JPEG, BMP, and PNG are all supported. This class can read and write images in these formats. It can also be created from raw pixel data or by taking a snapshot of the contents of an `NSView`.

As discussed previously in conjunction with the `NSImageRep` class, the following methods are implemented by this class to initialize it from existing data or an image file:

```
+ (NSArray *)imageRepsWithData:(NSData *)imagedata
+ (id)imageRepWithData:(NSData *)imagedata
- (id)initWithData:(NSData *)imagedata
```

These methods work exactly as previously described. There are two other ways to obtain a new `NSBitmapImageRep` object. The first, and most complex, is to create one from a raw-data buffer. This is complex because there are many ways to lay out an image data buffer. Quite a few parameters are required to specify a given buffer's layout. Here's the method that is used:

```
- (id)initWithBitmapDataPlanes:(unsigned char **)planes
        pixelsWide:(int)width pixelsHigh:(int)height
        bitsPerSample:(int)bps samplesPerPixel:(int)spp
        hasAlpha:(BOOL)alpha isPlanar:(BOOL)isPlanar
        colorSpaceName:(NSString *)colorSpaceName
        bytesPerRow:(int)rowBytes bitsPerPixel:(int)pixelBits
```

Because of the length of this method's name, it can be daunting at first. However, it isn't as bad as it looks. The `Points` example in Chapter 13, "Custom Views and Graphics Part II," uses this method to create a drawing buffer. It actually manipulates the raw data after creating the bitmap image representation directly, using the image representation only to simplify drawing the image on the screen. This method releases the object and returns `nil` if something fails during initialization.

Before looking at the parameters, it is important to understand the difference between meshed and planar buffer configurations. To explain the difference, consider a bitmapped RGBA image. Each pixel of the image has four components, one for red, green, blue, and alpha. Suppose that each component is a single byte. Then, each pixel requires four bytes. Given a stream of raw bytes, there are two common ways to determine where the RGBA components of the pixel are found in the stream.

One approach is to have the first four bytes be a single pixel. In this case, byte 0 would be the first pixel's red component, byte 1 would be green, byte 2 would be blue, and byte 3 would be the alpha. Bytes 4–7 would be the next pixel. Pixels would be laid out until the end of the row, and then the next row would begin. This would continue until the image is completed. This format is known as meshed because the component values are interleaved throughout the byte stream.

The other approach is to separate the components. In this case, byte zero would be the red component of the first pixel, byte 1 would be the red component of the second pixel, and so on. One quarter of the way through the data, the green components would begin in the same way. Blue would begin at the halfway mark, and the last quarter of the data would contain the alpha components.

Figure 14.2 graphically shows the differences between the meshed and planar layouts.

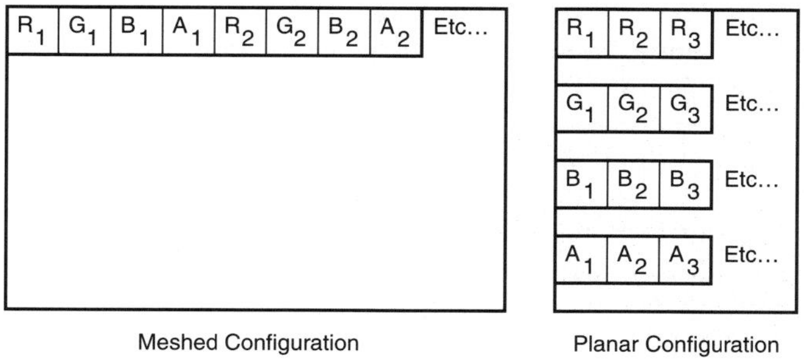

FIGURE 14.2 Notice the differences between the meshed and planar layouts.

The `planes` parameter of this method is an array of pointers to the buffers that contain the data planes. If the image data is in meshed format, then there will only be one plane of data. For a planar image, there could be between one and five planes of data. A grayscale image without alpha would be a single plane, whereas a CMYKA image would have five planes of data. The significance of each plane, and the order of the planes, is dictated by the color model. The planes must appear in the order they appear in the color-model name. For example, a planar RGB image would have three planes: red, green, and blue, in that order. The alpha channel, if it exists, always comes last. So CMYK with alpha (CMYKA) would have the five planes: cyan, magenta, yellow, black, and alpha.

The safest way to provide the planes' array is to provide an array with five elements, setting those that do not correspond to an actual data plane to `NULL`. This reduces the risk of memory overruns and invalid accesses.

If no buffer has been created, there is the option of having the `NSBitmapImageRep` class create one automatically. Simply pass `NULL` as the value for planes, and the necessary buffers will be allocated. Pointers to the buffer's plane(s) can still be obtained; even when the planes have been allocated by the class itself. Thus, no matter where the buffer comes from, there's no danger of losing the capability to have direct access to the raw image data.

When the `NSBitmapImageRep` object allocates a buffer, it takes responsibility for it. The buffer is freed when the object is deallocated. If the buffer was not allocated by the object, a reference is stored, but ownership is not transferred to the object. The data is copied and it won't be freed automatically. It is up to the original owner of the memory to free it when the time is right. This can be a problem because an object can be retained more than once. When the original owner releases it, he can only free the image data if the `-release` causes the object to be deallocated. There are several ways to avoid this problem, but the easiest is to just let the class create a buffer automatically.

The next two parameters to the method are `width` and `height`. They specify the image data's dimensions. These are the image's width and height in pixels, and both must be greater than zero. The `NSBitmapImageRep` assumes that the data is being provided at a 72-dpi resolution. To change the resolution, call the inherited `-setSize:` method to change the size in relation to the number of pixels. For example, to change the image representation's resolution from 72 dpi to 400 dpi, the current size needs to be multiplied by 72/400. This would also have the side effect of having the image render smaller onscreen, of course. Changing the size will not alter the number of pixels of width and height, nor will it modify the data buffer in any way. It only changes how the buffer is interpreted.

Next comes the bits per sample, `bps`, and the samples per pixel, `spp`. These two values are interrelated and depend on the image data's color model. A sample refers to a color component of a pixel. Thus, a 24-bit RGB image (no alpha channel) would have three samples per pixel and 8 bits per sample. (24 bits/pixel divided by 3 samples/pixel=8 bits/sample). Note that this assumes the bps is the same for each component. That places a minor constraint on what kinds of data layouts the `NSBitmapImageRep` class can support. Common values for `bps` for color images are 4 and 8. Black and white images might also be 1. It is a good idea to avoid other unusual values, because the current implementation of this class might not be support for them. The `spp` parameter can be anything from 1, for a grayscale image with no alpha, to 5 for a CMYKA image.

The `alpha` parameter is `YES` if there is alpha channel data and `NO` if not. The `isPlanar` parameter is a `YES` for image data in planar format and `NO` for data that is meshed.

The `NSImageRep` class discussion mentions color spaces. The same values that can be used there can also be used here for the `colorSpaceName` parameter. Remember, the following constants are all predefined by Cocoa:

```
NSCalibratedWhiteColorSpace
NSCalibratedBlackColorSpace
NSCalibratedRGBColorSpace
NSDeviceWhiteColorSpace
NSDeviceBlackColorSpace
NSDeviceRGBColorSpace
NSDeviceCMYKColorSpace
NSNamedColorSpace
NSCustomColorSpace
```

The next parameter, `rowBytes`, specifies how many bytes are in one horizontal line of pixels (scan line). This value is significant on a per-plane basis. One might expect that the `width`, `bps`, and `spp` parameters would be sufficient to determine how many bytes are in a row of image data. For a meshed image, the number of bytes in a row would normally be

```
rowBytes = width * bps * spp / 8
```

For a planar image, `spp` is left out of the equation. This is the default value, and passing a zero as `rowBytes` causes it to be calculated and used. If an image is laid out in memory so that the rows start on specific word or byte boundaries, however, there might be a few unused bytes at the end of the row. Doing this can actually be useful on Mac OS X. If, for example, image data is laid out so as to be on 16-byte boundaries, then Quartz can invoke Altivec to draw the image on a G4 processor. For an image so aligned, the `rowBytes` parameter would be greater than or equal to the value calculated in the previous equation.

The final parameter is `pixelBits`. Again, this is a parameter that normally can be calculated from the other parameters. For a meshed image, the following equation applies:

```
pixelBits = bps * spp
```

For a planar image, `pixelbits` would normally be the same as `bps`. However there might be some padding so that each pixel is aligned to a byte or word boundary. For an image without any per-pixel padding, passing a zero for `pixelBits` causes the default value to be calculated and used. The `NSBitmapImageRep` class only supports a few values for this parameter other than the default. In particular, a 12-bit RGB image can use a `pixelbits` of 16, and a 24-bit RGB image can use a value of 32.

Although there are a lot of parameters, this is the method most commonly used for obtaining an `NSBitmapImageRep` instance for direct manipulation. By creating an image representation this way, the byte buffer of the image can be directly manipulated. This is significant. Many game developers would like to get a pointer to the memory behind a Quartz buffer. However, there is no way to do this. Core Graphics can be used to access video memory directly after capturing a screen, but accessing Quartz's backing store cannot be done directly. For a game developer who doesn't capture the screen, this means she might not be able to write "to the metal" the way that she would like. The closest approximation to this in Cocoa is to use an `NSBitmapImageRep` object as a cover for a byte buffer, and to then composite that image to the screen to flush the buffer. As shown in the `Points` example in Chapter 13, this does work well and is very fast. It is, however, a lot more complex than simply using the normal drawing functions provided by the Application Kit.

There is one more way to obtain a new instance of `NSBitmapImageRep`. While focus is locked on an `NSView`, this method can be called:

```
- (id)initWithFocusedViewRect:(NSRect)rect
```

This takes a snapshot of the current state of the currently focused `NSView` object, taken from the specified rectangle. The image data is copied from Quartz into a new buffer maintained by the `NSBitmapImageRep` instance. Unfortunately, there isn't a method for taking a snapshot of an entire window or of the entire screen. This is one way to find out what is in a Quartz buffer, but it doesn't allow for direct manipulation. After the data is captured, the Quartz buffer might change further.

When an `NSBitmapImageRep` instance has been created and initialized, there are several properties that might be queried, but not changed. The following methods exist to query the layout of the `NSBitmapImageRep`'s internal data buffer.

```
- (BOOL)isPlanar
- (int)samplesPerPixel
```

```
- (int)bitsPerPixel
- (int)bytesPerRow
- (int)bytesPerPlane
- (int)numberOfPlanes
```

Each of these methods returns information about the buffer's layout. The meaning of each of these parameters was described previously in conjunction with the `-initWithBitmapDataPlanes:...` method. To obtain a pointer to the actual buffer itself, one of the following two methods can be used:

```
- (unsigned char *)bitmapData
- (void)getBitmapDataPlanes:(unsigned char **)data
```

For meshed image data, the `-bitmapData` method is sufficient. For data in planar format, this points to the first plane. Because planes are often contiguous in memory, making the assumption that this is true often works. However, planes are not required to be contiguous. In fact, they might actually be in some other order.

The safest approach is to get a pointer to the start of each data plane. To get these pointers, use the `-getBitmapDataPlanes:` method. The pointer array passed to this method needs to have room for at least five pointers because there could be as many as five planes. If there are fewer than five planes, the extra pointers are set to `NULL`. For meshed buffers, there is only one plane anyway.

It is legal to modify the data in the various planes directly, and then redraw the image. This is the approach taken with the `Points` example in Chapter 13 to achieve the fastest drawing rates.

The other primary function of the `NSBitmapImageRep` object is to enable the image data to be saved back out to a file. Because each file format has different supported features, this can be somewhat complex. This class originally only dealt with the TIFF file format, so many of its methods are specific to that image format. The TIFF format methods are covered first, and then the methods that are more general in nature are covered.

The TIFF image format supports many different kinds of compression, so there are several methods revolving around compression schemes.

```
+ (void)getTIFFCompressionTypes:(const NSTIFFCompression **)list count:(int *)
➥numTypes
```

The first method is used to obtain a list of all the available TIFF compression algorithms. Several constants are currently defined as values for the `NSTIFFCompression` type. Table 14.3 shows the constants and their meanings.

TABLE 14.3 `NSTIFFCompression` Constants and Meanings

Constant	Meaning
`NSTIFFCompressionNone`	No compression
`NSTIFFCompressionCCITTFAX3`	Standard fax compression algorithm for 1-bit images only
`NSTIFFCompressionCCITTFAX4`	See previous
`NSTIFFCompressionLZW`	Lempel-Ziv-Welch (LZW) lossless compression algorithm
`NSTIFFCompressionJPEG`	Lossy JPEG compression algorithm with variable compression factor; no longer supported
`NSTIFFCompressionNEXT`	Proprietary algorithm. Supported for input only, for backward compatibility
`NSTIFFCompressionPackBits`	Lossless PackBits compression algorithm
`NSTIFFCompressionOldJPEG`	Lossy JPEG compression algorithm with variable compression factor; no longer supported

To convert one of these constants into a localized string, for use in a user interface, the following method can be used:

```
+ (NSString *)localizedNameForTIFFCompressionType:(NSTIFFCompression)compression
```

To determine whether a particular compression method is applicable to a given instance, use this method:

```
- (BOOL)canBeCompressedUsing:(NSTIFFCompression)compression
```

When a compression type is chosen, the image representation can be told to use it with this method:

```
- (void)setCompression:(NSTIFFCompression)compression factor:(float)factor
```

Note that there is an additional parameter, `factor`. This is the compression factor and is used only by compression schemes that support variable compression rates. The values of factor are dependent on the algorithm. The only types in Table 14.3 that support different compression factors are the JPEG algorithms, where compression values from 0.0 to 255.0 are legal (0.0 means minimal compression). However, they are now listed in the documentation as no longer being supported. That means the `factor` value is currently ignored by the class.

When an `NSBitmapImageRep` instance is created from image data, the compression type is stored with the object. This method can be used to change the compression type. To see what compression type is currently set for the image, use this method:

```
- (void)getCompression:(NSTIFFCompression *)compression factor:(float *)factor
```

Note that both the compression type and factor are returned by reference instead of as return values. The object's data is stored in an uncompressed format. Any compression that is set is used only when writing the image representation to a file. Even this isn't set in stone, however. Some of the methods that save the data to a file allow the preset compression values to be overridden.

To save an NSBitmapImageRep as a TIFF file, two steps must be taken. First, the NSBitmapImageRep object has to be converted into an NSData object. Next, the NSData needs to be written to the output file. To obtain an NSData, one of four methods can be used:

```
- (NSData *)TIFFRepresentation
- (NSData *)TIFFRepresentationUsingCompression:(NSTIFFCompression)comp
        factor:(float)factor
+ (NSData *)TIFFRepresentationOfImageRepsInArray:(NSArray *)array
+ (NSData *)TIFFRepresentationOfImageRepsInArray:(NSArray *)array
        usingCompression:(NSTIFFCompression)comp factor:(float)factor
```

The first two methods are the basic means of producing a TIFF file from a single NSBitmapImageRep object. The first method uses the compression algorithm already set in the object. The second method overrides those settings.

Because a TIFF image can actually contain several different images within the file, there are also two class methods. Instead of being sent to an individual instance, an array of NSBitmapImageRep instances is sent to the class object. It combines them into a single, multiframe TIFF image. Like the first two methods, each instance can use its own compression algorithm, or with the latter method, an algorithm can be chosen to override for all the image representations.

With the addition of support for multiple bitmap image file formats, there are also two methods that are more generic in nature. These methods work much like the previous TIFF methods, but they require a properties dictionary to specify particular features of a given image file format. The two generic methods are

```
+ (NSData *)representationOfImageRepsInArray:(NSArray *)imageReps
        usingType:(NSBitmapImageFileType)storageType
        properties:(NSDictionary *)properties
- (NSData *)representationUsingType:(NSBitmapImageFileType)storageType
        properties:(NSDictionary *)properties
```

The first method is used for image formats like TIFF where multiple images are to be put into a single file. The second method is for creating a file from just a single image representation. Both methods require the file format and a properties dictionary to be specified.

The `storageType` parameter can currently be one of these predefined constants: `NSTIFFFileType`, `NSBMPFileType`, `NSGIFFileType`, `NSJPEGFileType`, or `NSPNGFileType`. They correspond to TIFF, BMP, GIF, JPEG/JPG, and PNG files, respectively.

The properties dictionary is a little more complex. It is an `NSDictionary` instance. The valid keys and expected values are shown in Table 14.4. Remember the keys that make sense depend on the value of the `storageType` parameter.

TABLE 14.4 Keys and Values for Image Property Dictionaries

Valid keys	Expected values
`NSImageCompressionMethod`	This is the compression method for TIFF files. An `NSTIFFCompression` value is placed into an `NSNumber`.
`NSImageCompressionFactor`	This is the compression factor for TIFF or JPEG/JPG files. For JPEG compression, the value is between 0.0 and 255.0, stored in an `NSNumber`. (255 is the maximum compression.)
`NSImageColorSyncProfileData`	This is ColorSync profile information stored in an `NSData` object. This is only applicable to the TIFF format. There is currently no specific way to obtain such an object from the Cocoa frameworks.
`NSImageDitherTransparency`	This is a boolean flag stored in an `NSNumber`. It is only applicable to GIF images that support transparent pixels, but not translucent (partially transparent) pixels. If `YES`, then translucency will be approximated by dithering with clear pixels.
`NSImageRGBColorTable`	This is a color map or palette that is used for a GIF image. It is an `NSData` object containing 256 tightly packed RGB triplets (a total of 768 bytes).
`NSImageInterlaced`	This is a boolean flag stored in an `NSNumber`. If `YES`, then the image will be interlaced. As documented, this is used for PNG images only, even though the GIF format can support interlacing.

The `NSBitmapImageRep` class can also perform one other interesting function. It can convert a grayscale image into a color image. The following method is used to do this:

```
- (void)colorizeByMappingGray:(float)midPoint toColor:(NSColor *)midPointColor
       blackMapping:(NSColor *)shadowColor whiteMapping:(NSColor *)lightColor
```

Note that three colors and a gray value need to be specified. A grayscale image's gray values run from 0.0 to 1.0. The value of `midPoint` should be chosen as a value between 0.0 and 1.0. This method will create a color continuum that goes from shadowColor to midPointColor to lightColor. The gray value will be linearly mapped onto that continuum to calculate the color for a given gray value.

If a pixel's gray value is equal to zero, then the resultant color is shadowColor. If the gray value equals midPoint then midPointColor is the resultant color. Gray values between zero and midPoint are converted into a color linearly interpolated between shadowColor and midPointColor. A gray value of 1.0 is mapped to lightColor.

The one limitation of this method is that it only works on images with 8 bits per pixel. This means it will only convert from an 8-bit grayscale to a 24-bit color image, with alpha optional. 12/16-bit color and 1 or 4 bit gray are not supported.

When working with raw bitmap data, if you want to bypass using an NSBitmapImageRep all together, a raw image data buffer can be rendered directly to the screen. This is a bad idea, but if you insist on doing it, then use this function:

```
void NSDrawBitmap(const NSRect rect, int pixelsWide, int pixelsHigh,
     int bitsPerSample, int samplesPerPixel, int bitsPerPixel,
     int bytesPerRow, BOOL isPlanar, BOOL hasAlpha,
     NSColorSpace colorSpace, const unsigned char *const data[5])
```

The parameters to this function directly correspond to the parameters previously described for the -initWithBitmapDataPlanes:... method. The correlation is obvious. The only new parameter is the first one, rect. If the size of rect differs from the pixelsWide and pixelsHigh parameters, the image is scaled as it is rendered.

The documentation warns that this method is "marginally obsolete." It is best to simply use an NSBitmapImageRep object to manage raw image data. Some developers might be tempted to use this function with the justification that it avoids the overhead of Objective-C. However, because of the complexities of setting up a Quartz context for drawing, it isn't surprising to find that the Application Kit is actually more efficient, and therefore faster than this function. Thus, there is little reason to use this function. For the fastest drawing, whether using this function or the NSBitmapImageRep class, it is important to match the layout of the image data to the layout of the screen to which it will be drawn. By matching them exactly, Quartz can use a very tight, optimized loop to render the image instead of a more general-purpose loop that can handle data format conversions.

Cached and Custom Image Representations

Two of the available NSImageRep subclasses are a little bit unusual. The NSCachedImageRep class is used to manage offscreen image caches. Although a developer is unlikely to create one of these, it is quite likely that one might be returned when dealing with an NSImage. Whenever Quartz drawing is performed inside an

NSImage, after locking focus on the image, the drawing is directed into a cached image representation created automatically by the NSImage. The other unusual class is NSCustomImageRep, which acts as a cover for a custom drawing method specified dynamically by the developer. It is used in the CompositeLab example provided by Apple with the Mac OS X developer tools to draw the various source images.

The cached image representation, as noted previously, is used by the NSImage class to manage any offscreen buffers it is using. When focus is locked on an image, an instance of NSCachedImageRep is created to act as a destination for the drawing. This class uses a region of an offscreen window for its drawing surface. It knows both the window and the area of the window that are assigned to it. This allows multiple NSCachedImageRep instances to share a single window. Because the original data to create the image isn't available, the cache itself is the image data managed by this representation. Because the drawing commands used to render the cache are not stored, a cached image representation is implicitly a kind of bitmapped image.

There are two ways to initialize an instance of NSCachedImageRep. The first is to tell it the window and area within the window that is to be used, using this method:

```
- (id)initWithWindow:(NSWindow *)win rect:(NSRect)rect
```

If an NSWindow to be used as the cache is not already available, then NSCachedImageRep can create one. To do this, several parameters to specify the nature of the window must be provided. This method creates or finds an appropriate NSWindow instance to use as a cache:

```
- (id)initWithSize:(NSSize)size depth:(NSWindowDepth)depth
        separate:(BOOL)flag alpha:(BOOL)alpha
```

The size parameter refers to the size of the cached image representation, not necessarily the size of the cache window. The flag parameter tells the NSCachedImageRep object whether it is allowed to share the window it is using with another NSCachedImageRep instance. If YES, it searches for an available NSWindow that it can use. If one isn't available, it creates a new window. Later on, another NSCachedImageRep object might then share the window. If flag is NO, then a brand new cache window is created and will never be shared. The alpha parameter specifies whether the window contains an alpha channel.

The window's depth is specified with the depth parameter. This is a little trickier, because there are no predefined constants that can be used for it. Instead, it must be obtained by using either the NSBestDepth() or the NSAvailableWindowDepths() function. These functions are defined as follows:

```
NSWindowDepth NSBestDepth(NSString *colorSpace, int bps, int bpp,
        BOOL planar, BOOL *exactMatch)
const NSWindowDepth *NSAvailableWindowDepths(void)
```

The `NSAvailableWindowDepths()` function returns a zero-terminated list of depths. Normally, the `NSBestDepth()` function is the best choice because it attempts to choose a depth that works well with the screen's depth.

All the parameters to the `NSBestDepth()` function are hints. It will try to find the closest match from the available window depths supported by Quartz and the underlying hardware. As such, all the parameters are optional. If a zero is passed in, default values are used. This makes it easy to get the window depth that matches the screen.

The `colorSpace` parameter takes a color-space name. See chapter 17, "Color," for a list and descriptions of the available color spaces. The `bps` parameter refers to bits per sample. This is the standard meaning, where each component of a pixel is considered to be a sample. Likewise, `bpp` refers to the number of bits per pixel. For example, in the case of 24-bit RGB, there are 8 bits per sample and 24 bits per pixel. To specify a meshed buffer layout, use `NO` for the planar parameter; obviously a `YES` produces a planar depth.

Finally, the `exactMatch` parameter returns by reference whether the depth returned matched the input specification exactly or not. If there is no available window depth to match exactly, the nearest match is chosen. The order of precedence to determine a match is `colorSpace`, `bps`, `planar`, and finally, `bpp`.

Given an `NSWindowDepth`, the various parameters can be determined using this set of functions:

```
BOOL NSPlanarFromDepth (NSWindowDepth depth)
NSString *NSColorSpaceFromDepth (NSWindowDepth depth)
int NSBitsPerSampleFromDepth (NSWindowDepth depth)
int NSBitsPerPixelFromDepth (NSWindowDepth depth)
```

These four functions are named to match up with the semantics of the first four parameters of the `NSBestDepth()` function. They can be used to determine the details of a given value for `NSWindowDepth`.

After an `NSCachedImageRep` instance has been initialized, the `-draw` method can be used. Generally, some drawing would be done in the cache first. `NSImage` usually manages this. To draw inside the cache directly, the window and drawing area are needed. Both can be obtained using these two methods, respectively:

```
- (NSWindow *)window
- (NSRect)rect
```

To draw in the cache, an NSView instance needs to be placed in the cache's window at the location and size specified by the cache's rect. Then, focus can be locked on the image, and drawing can take place. In this case, a plain NSView instance can be used; no custom subclass is needed. Because it is possible to lock focus on the view, draw in it, and then unlock focus, a subclass containing drawing code isn't strictly necessary. The lock/unlock machinery that is already there is all that is really needed. The view itself wouldn't even be needed if it were possible to directly lock focus on a window, but the Application Kit doesn't allow that to be done. Because of the complexity required to draw in the cache, it is best to use an NSImage to handle all the details automatically.

The other kind of image representation mentioned at the beginning of this section is the custom image representation. The NSCustomImageRep object is a cover for a custom drawing method. When it is asked to render itself, it sends a message to its delegate, requesting that the custom method be performed. For this to work, the object needs to know both the method's selector, and the object to which the selector is to be sent. The initialization method requires both to be specified:

```
- (id)initWithDrawSelector:(SEL)aMethod delegate:(id)anObject
```

For this to be meaningful, the delegate must respond to the specified method. The draw method itself can assume that focus is already locked, and that the image's origin is at (0,0). The method takes a single parameter, the NSCustomImageRep object that sent the drawing message. For example, a valid drawing method might have this prototype:

```
- (void)drawForImageRep:(NSCustomImageRep *)sender
```

The values used to initialize the object can be obtained with these two methods:

```
- (SEL)drawSelector
- (id)delegate
```

Note that neither the delegate nor the selector can be changed. Instead, a new NSCustomImageRep object must be created to replace the existing object.

To see an example of custom image representations in action, refer to the CompositeLab example that comes with Mac OS X Developer. It can be found in /Developer/Examples/AppKit/CompositeLab.

Other Image Representations

There are three other NSImageRep subclasses that have not yet discussed. They are NSPDFImageRep, NSPICTImageRep, and NSEPSImageRep. These classes are designed to allow NSImage to deal with PDF, PICT, and EPS images, respectively. Each of these classes has minor differences. The PDF object is the most useful in the Mac OS X environment. The other two classes, for PICT and EPS images, are primarily for baseline backward compatibility.

For all three types of image representation, it is preferable to use the following `NSImageRep` methods after initialization but before drawing to finish the setup:

```
-setColorSpaceName:
-setAlpha:
-setPixelsHigh:
-setPixelsWide:
-setBitsPerSample:
```

Of course, if any of the previous methods are omitted, Cocoa provides a default value. When the basic setup is complete, the `-draw` method can be used as normal to render the image representation. Each of the three classes offers a few methods specific to the class, which will be discussed class by class.

The first class is `NSPDFImageRep`, which is meant for dealing with PDF files. The subclass implements the `-initWithData:` method for reading PDF information from an `NSData` object. As a convenience, the `+imageRepWithData:` method could be used to allocate and initialize an instance. To get an `NSData` object containing the PDF data, use the `-PDFRepresentation` method.

Because a PDF file can have more than one page, this class has methods for manipulating pages. The three main methods are

```
- (int)pageCount
- (int)currentPage
- (void)setCurrentPage:(int)page
```

The `-pageCount` method returns the number of pages in the PDF image representation. The `-currentPage` method returns the page number of the page that is rendered when the image representation is drawn. The return value is zero based. This means that the first page is number zero, the second page is one, and so on, up to `pageCount-1` for the last page. To change pages, use the `-setCurrentPage:` method. Just like `-currentPage`, the page number passed to this method is zero-based.

Because each page could, in theory, have a different size, the `-bounds` method returns an `NSRect`, which contains the bounding box of the object's current page.

The `NSPDFImageRep` object does not handle many of the advanced features that the PDF format offers. However, it is an easy-to-use object that works well for most basic display purposes. As an example of how well it does or doesn't do, try looking at a PDF file in the Preview application that comes with Mac OS X.

The next class mentioned is the `NSPICTImageRep`. As the name implies, it is meant to handle Apple's PICT image format. Because of differences in graphics models, there is no guarantee that the image is rendered by Cocoa and Quartz exactly as it would be rendered by QuickDraw on Mac OS 9 or earlier. Apple's documentation specifically draws attention to transfer modes and region operations. Some of them render differently under Quartz than they do under QuickDraw.

Just like the `NSPDFImageRep` class, the `NSPICTImageRep` class implements both the `+imageRepWithData:` and `-initWithData:` methods to create and to initialize an instance, respectively, from an `NSData` object containing image data in the PICT format. The data object does not need the 512-byte header present on PICT files. If the header is present, it is ignored.

To obtain an `NSData` object with the PICT data in it, use the `-PICTRepresentation` method. The data object will not contain the 512-byte header required by the PICT spec. To write this data to a file, it is necessary to write the header first, and then the contents of the returned data object. It is valid, and simplest, to write out 512 bytes of zeroes as the header.

The last `NSPICTImageRep` method of interest is `-boundingBox`. This method returns an `NSRect` containing the bounding box of the PICT image. The bounding box is taken from the `picFrame` field in the PICT data's picture header. For more details about the data itself, consult Apple's documentation. The book, *Inside Macintosh: Imaging with QuickDraw* provides more information about the picture header and the PICT image format.

The final class is the `NSEPSImageRep` class. As the name suggests, it is meant to manage Encapsulated PostScript (EPS) images. When the Application Kit used Display PostScript as its graphics model, it was able to directly display any EPS image directly, without needing preview bitmaps. With the transition to Quartz, which lacks a PostScript interpreter, this capability has been lost, thereby reducing the utility of this class. As a result, while the Application Kit uses this class to manage EPS data, it is very likely that what is displayed is not what is printed.

Like the other classes, an `NSData` object containing the EPS data can be passed to either the `+imageRepWithData:` or `-initWithData:` methods to create and/or initialize an instance of this class. The actual EPS data can be obtained from the `-EPSRepresentation` method, which returns an `NSData` containing the EPS image data.

To obtain the bounding box of the EPS image, the `-boundingBox` method can be used. It returns an `NSRect`. This bounding box is obtained from the bounding box specified in the EPS header's comments. Specifically, the data comes from the "%%BoundingBox:" comment.

There is a final method used by the NSEPSImageRep object that is meant for subclasses to implement. Whenever the -draw method is called, the object first calls the -prepareGState method. Place any initializations to the graphics state that a subclass would like to make inside this method. The default implementation does nothing.

Drawing Text

Drawing text is an extremely complex process. Because of this, the Application Kit provides the NSText object just for this purpose. Because of the complexity of this object, a whole chapter of this book (Chapter 11, "Text Views") has been devoted to the NSText and related objects. Sometimes the NSText object is overkill for the type of text rendering that needs to be accomplished. At other times, it doesn't provide some of the special, in-depth manipulation options that would be useful in a heavy-duty graphically oriented application. In these cases, there are some other alternatives available that might make more sense.

The Application Kit adds drawing methods to the NSString and NSAttributedString classes. These methods are useful for adding simple text labels to graphics, but if a developer has multiple lines of text or anything much more complex than a simple label, using NSText should be considered. The NSBezierPath object has some methods that allows the path used to render a particular glyph from a given font to be captured. These methods would be useful, for example, in a font editor that might want to present the user with the details of the glyph's actual path. In this case, all the specialized text handling NSText provides would be moot.

Both of these types of drawing are discussed in the following two sections. As part of the discussion, the TextRendering example is described. This example shows code for implementing the text rendering techniques described here.

NSString Drawing Methods

The Application Kit adds a handful of methods to the NSString and NSAttributedString classes that render them as text in the current graphics context. The NSString methods require an NSDictionary listing the rendering attributes, such as font, to be used. Because only one dictionary can be provided, the entire string is rendered with that one set of attributes. Because an NSAttributedString instance stores attributes with the string itself, strings can be created with different attributes on different characters.

All the methods in this section also require some significant set up time when they are invoked, because they need to set several parameters in the graphics context, such as the active font. This can be relatively inefficient to do for each and every text string to be rendered. The result is that all the methods described in this section should be considered to be the slowest possible way to render text with the Application Kit. For text that isn't rendered very often or isn't very complex, these methods are quite convenient. Due to their performance penalty, however, avoid them.

The first NSString method of interest is

```
- (void)drawAtPoint:(NSPoint)point withAttributes:(NSDictionary *)attrs
```

This method renders the NSString at the specified point using the text attributes found in the attrs parameter. When the text is rendered, it will have a bounding box, defined as the smallest rectangle that completely encloses the touched pixels. The point that is passed to this method is used as the lower-left corner of the bounding box. This is significant because the lower-left corner of the bounding box is below the baseline. It is somewhat difficult to predict exactly where the baseline will be in the final rendered text, making this method rather imprecise.

Negative coordinates cause the rendering to be clipped aggressively. Passing points that are to the left or below the coordinate system's origin needs to be avoided. An NSAffineTransform can be used to translate the coordinate system to work around this limitation.

The attributes dictionary contains a series of predefined keys and values. If a parameter isn't provided, a default value is used. Table 14.5 describes each of the keys that might be used in this dictionary.

TABLE 14.5 Valid Keys and Values for Attributes Dictionary

Keys	Value
NSFontAttributeName	An NSFont object. Default is 12-point Helvetica.
NSForegroundColorAttributeName	An NSColor object. Default is NSColor's +blackColor.
NSBackgroundColorAttributeName	An NSColor object. For a transparent background, omit this key. The text is rendered with a composite-copy operation rather than a source-over operation, so using NSColor's +clearColor results in a black background. Default is nil (no background).
NSBaselineOffsetAttributeName	An NSNumber containing a floating-point number. The text baseline is moved up or down by this amount. (Down if it is negative.) Default is 0.0.
NSSuperscriptAttributeName	An NSNumber containing an integer greater than or equal to 0. Default is 0, no superscript. A positive integer indicates superscript level.
NSLigatureAttributeName	An NSNumber containing one of the integers 0 (no ligatures), 1 (default ligatures), or 2 (all ligatures). Default is 1.

TABLE 14.5 continued

Keys	Value
`NSUnderlineStyleAttributeName`	An NSNumber containing the integers 0 (no underline) or 1 (use underline). Default is 0, no underline.
`NSKernAttributeName`	An NSNumber containing a floating-point number representing the amount to modify the kerning. Positive spaces the glyphs farther apart (loosened); negative brings them closer together (tightened). Default is 0.0, no kerning.
`NSParagraphStyleAttributeName`	An NSParagraphStyle object. Default is +defaultParagraphStyle.
`NSAttachmentAttributeName`	An NSTextAttachment object. Default is nil.

The next `NSString` method is almost identical to the first:

```
- (void)drawInRect:(NSRect)rect withAttributes:(NSDictionary *)attrs
```

It still uses the same attributes dictionary as the previous method. The difference is that the rendering location is specified in terms of a rectangle instead of a point. The destination rectangle is used as a clipping path for the text rendering. Furthermore, the upper-right corner of the rendered text's bounding box is matched to the upper right of this rectangle. Therefore, if this rectangle is not tall enough, the bottom of the rendered text will be clipped. This is slightly counter-intuitive because most developers might have expected the origins to line up, causing the top of the text to be cut off instead.

Just like the other `NSString` method, there can be clipping problems with this method, especially if negative coordinates are used. An `NSAffineTransform` can be used to translate the coordinate system to get around this limitation.

The final new `NSString` method is not for rendering. Instead, it can be used to learn the size of the rendered text's bounding box, given a particular set of attributes:

```
- (NSSize)sizeWithAttributes:(NSDictionary *)attrs
```

It would be reasonable to assume that if the `-drawAtPoint:withAttributes:` method were used, the rectangle defined by the `point` parameter and the size returned by `-sizeWithAttributes:` would be the actual bounding box of the rendered text. This is not the case, however. The size is determined from the font's metrics and doesn't always match what is rendered. Consider it to be an approximation and not exact.

If the bounding box is defined as the smallest rectangle that encloses all the pixels touched by rendering, both the size and origin will not match up. The returned size will probably be taller than the actual touched area because it takes into account the space that might be used by ascenders and descenders. The true bounding box's origin might be horizontally offset slightly from the rendering origin, too. This can cause the drawing to extend outside the bounding box that you would assume to be correct. Note that an oblique font is far more likely to extend past the right edge of this box. Not all fonts extend outside this box; the accuracy of the box is very dependent on the font being used. Currently, no drawing will extend outside this box, so oblique fonts will often be clipped.

To better understand how this bounding box differs from the true bounding box, the `TextRendering` example provides a visual representation of the problem. In the example, the `TextStringView` object uses the `-drawAtPoint:withAttributes:` method to render text. It also paints a gray rectangle showing the box that is defined by using the point parameter to `-drawAtPoint:withAttributes:` and the return value from `-sizeWithAttributes:`. Comparing the location of this box to where the text was rendered makes it clear that getting an accurate bounding box is rather difficult. As an approximation, it might be good enough for most purposes, however. To help make it obvious where the point parameter of the `-drawAtPoint:withAttributes:` method lies inside the view, the code also draws a horizontal and a vertical line, both of which intersect that point.

The code for this example view looks like this:

```
File TextStringView.h:

#import <AppKit/AppKit.h>

@interface MYTextStringView : NSView
{
}

@end

File TextStringView.m:

#import "TextStringView.h"

@implementation MYTextStringView

- (void)drawRect:(NSRect)dirtyRect
{
    NSString *message = [NSString stringWithString:@"Hello World!"];
    NSFont *font = [NSFont fontWithName:@"Helvetica-BoldOblique" size:64.0];
    NSMutableDictionary *attributes = [NSMutableDictionary dictionary];
    NSBezierPath *path = [NSBezierPath bezierPath];
```

```
    NSRect textBounds = NSZeroRect;
    NSRect bds = [self bounds];

    // set up text attributes
    if (!font) {
        [[NSColor whiteColor] set];
        NSRectFill(bds);
        return;
    }
    [attributes setObject:font forKey:NSFontAttributeName];
    [attributes setObject:[NSColor blueColor]
            forKey:NSForegroundColorAttributeName];
    textBounds.size = [message sizeWithAttributes:attributes];
    textBounds.origin = NSMakePoint(
            (bds.size.width - textBounds.size.width) / 2.0,
            (bds.size.height - textBounds.size.height) / 2.0);
    [[NSColor whiteColor] set];
    NSRectFill(bds);
    [[NSColor greenColor] set];
    [path setLineWidth:2.0];
    [path moveToPoint:NSMakePoint(NSMinX(bds), textBounds.origin.y)];
    [path lineToPoint:NSMakePoint(NSMaxX(bds), textBounds.origin.y)];
    [path moveToPoint:NSMakePoint(textBounds.origin.x, NSMinY(bds))];
    [path lineToPoint:NSMakePoint(textBounds.origin.x, NSMaxY(bds))];
    [path stroke];
    [message drawAtPoint:textBounds.origin withAttributes:attributes];
    [[NSColor grayColor] set];
    NSFrameRect(textBounds);
}

@end
```

Figure 14.3 illustrates the output that is produced when this example is run on Mac OS X 10.1.

Notice that the top, left, and bottom edges of the bounding box all have a margin that makes the box larger than the true bounding box on those sides. Note also how the text extends outside of the box on the right side and is clipped. Furthermore, the horizontal line is not the same as the text's baseline. (Both the lines pass through the point that was used as a parameter to the `-drawAtPoint:withAttributes:` method.)

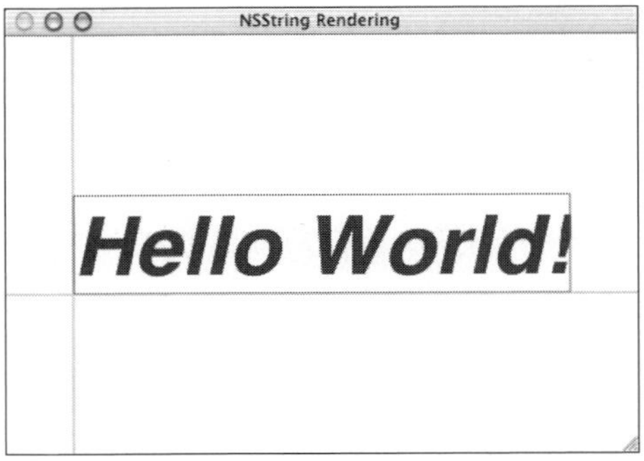

FIGURE 14.3 This is the output produced when `MYTextStringView` is run on Mac OS X 10.1.

NOTE

A workaround to avoid this clipping problem is to add a space character to the end of string being rendered. Instead of rendering "Hello World!" try modifying the previous example code to render "Hello World! " The bounding box will be clearly wider than necessary, but at least there will be no clipping.

Three methods are defined for the `NSAttributedString` class as well:

```
- (NSSize)size
- (void)drawAtPoint:(NSPoint)point
- (void)drawInRect:(NSRect)rect
```

These methods work exactly as the corresponding `NSString` methods. The most noticeable difference is that none of them take an attributes dictionary. Instead, the attributes are stored as part of the `NSAttributedString` itself. This allows for text with mixed attributes to be conveniently rendered. All the caveats to the `NSString` methods apply to these methods, however. It is strongly recommended that these methods be avoided for most text rendering. These methods might be acceptable for simple rendering that is not repeated very often and doesn't need to be particularly accurate. Beyond that application, though, a better technique is required.

`NSBezierPath` and Glyphs

The NSBezierPath object can be used to draw text. This rendering approach is more accurate than the `NSString` and `NSAttributedString` methods in many ways. Because the actual rendered path is known, bounding boxes are calculated from actual rendering as opposed to font metrics. Furthermore, when an `NSBezierPath` is asked to render at a particular point, that point is specified as being on the font's baseline, so it is much easier to accurately position the glyphs. Another aspect to this technique is particularly attractive. When a glyph has been added to an `NSBezierPath` object, the `NSBezierPath` methods can be used to inspect the path itself. Any developer who wants to extract glyph paths from fonts, perhaps for editing or other manipulation, can do so by using an `NSBezierPath` object. A final feature offered by this approach is that text can be rendered as outlines by using the `-stroke` method. The `NSString` rendering methods can only render filled text.

There is, at present, a serious difficulty with this approach. The `NSBezierPath` wants developers to tell it which glyphs to render. Because the methods work in terms of glyphs and not in terms of individual characters or strings of characters, it is a little bit more difficult to use these methods. The biggest problem is that Cocoa provides only one method for obtaining a glyph. The only public method in the Application Kit that returns a glyph is found in the `NSFont` class:

```
- (NSGlyph)glyphWithName:(NSString *)aName
```

The problem is that the Cocoa documentation offers absolutely no explanation of how glyphs are named, rendering this method almost useless. What would be preferred is a way to turn a `unichar` character into an `NSGlyph`. Unfortunately, using an `NSString` containing a single character in it for the glyph name does not work, so there's no clear way to get a glyph from a character. Even if it did work, it would probably be rather slow to convert a string into characters, convert those characters into some mystery string, and then have `NSFont` parse and convert that string into a glyph.

This is currently a very annoying flaw in Cocoa. Luckily, there is an easy, though slightly dangerous, way to work around this difficulty. By falling back to a private method in `NSFont` the problem is solved simply. The `NSFont` class implements this method:

```
- (NSGlyph)_defaultGlyphForChar:(unichar)theChar
```

Because this is a private method, it is not defined in the Application Kit headers, and it is subject to change at any future date. In other words, it can be used now and will work, but any code that uses it could break under any future release of Cocoa. It might never break, but there's always a lurking danger. Hopefully Apple will expose this method publicly in the future, but until then it is the easiest way to obtain an `NSGlyph` so the following example uses it, dangerous or not.

Because this method isn't in the headers, a category header needs to be added to any project that needs to use this method. Import this header for any code file that uses this method.

```
File NSFont+PrivateGlyph.h:

#import <AppKit/NSFont.h>

@interface NSFont(PrivateGlyph)
- (NSGlyph)_defaultGlyphForChar:(unichar)theChar;
@end
```

Now that there is a means of obtaining an `NSGlyph`, the `NSBezierPath` methods can be used. The first method of interest obtains the path for a single glyph:

```
- (void)appendBezierPathWithGlyph:(NSGlyph)glyph inFont:(NSFont *)font
```

This will append a glyph to the path object at the current point. An empty path object needs to first have a current point to add a glyph. Using `-moveToPoint:` first does the trick. Note that the glyph needs to be obtained from the font object that is passed to this method. Here is some code to render the outline of a character:

```
- (void)renderCharacterOutline:(unichar)theChar atPoint:(NSPoint)location
        withFont:(NSFont *)font andLineWidth:(float)width
{
    NSBezierPath *path = [NSBezierPath bezierPath];
    NSGlyph theGlyph = [font _defaultGlyphForChar:theChar];
    [myPath moveToPoint:location];
    [path appendBezierPathWithGlyph:theGlyph inFont:font];
    [path setLineWidth:width];
    [path stroke];
}
```

When rendering text one glyph at a time, the `NSFont` object can also be used to help determine where the next glyph is to be placed. The following `NSFont` method can be used to determine where the next glyph is to be drawn, given the glyph that was just drawn:

```
- (NSSize)advancementForGlyph:(NSGlyph)ag
```

By adding the size returned by this method to the point where the first glyph was drawn, the location where the second glyph should be drawn is produced. Using this approach takes into account the font's metrics, but it does not do any kerning and ignores any available ligatures. If there isn't an explicit `-moveToPoint:` operation before appending each glyph, then the resultant path will probably be something very different from what was expected. After appending a glyph, the current point is left at a random location that is dependent on the font being used. Try removing all but the first `-moveToPoint:` from the single glyph at a time code in the following

TextRendering example to see what happens. (The font used in the example causes the glyphs to be placed on an ascending diagonal from lower left to upper right, with the glyphs overlapping slightly.)

Rendering text one glyph at a time can be rather tedious. A series of glyphs can be added to an NSBezierPath object all at once with this method:

```
- (void)appendBezierPathWithGlyphs:(NSGlyph *)glyphs
        count:(int)count inFont:(NSFont *)font
```

This method uses NSFont's -advancementForGlyph: method to place the glyphs one after another, starting with the path's current point. The count parameter tells the method how many glyphs are in the glyphs array. Unfortunately, there is no method to take a string and return an array of glyphs based on it. Such a method would be nice because it could add ligatures, and so forth. Unfortunately, this is another gap in the Cocoa APIs. At present, the array of glyphs has to be produced manually, and there's no easy way to find out what ligatures are available in a given font. Again, using the full Cocoa text system makes these kinds of features available, but they aren't exposed publicly at this low a level.

Besides a simple array of glyphs, Cocoa also has an idea of a packed array of glyphs. Such an array can save as much as 50 percent of the memory used by the array, so it can be more efficient to deal with. There are two more NSBezierPath methods that can be used to manipulate arrays of glyphs, but they require a packed array. The Application Kit defines the following function to convert an array of glyphs into a packed array of glyphs:

```
int NSConvertGlyphsToPackedGlyphs(NSGlyph *glBuf, int count,
        NSMultibyteGlyphPacking packing, char *packedGlyphs);
```

There are four parameters to this function. The glBuf parameter is the unpacked array of glyphs that needs to be packed, and count tells how many glyphs are in the array.

The way the glyphs are actually packed is font dependent. Therefore, the packing parameter needs to be obtained from the font that was originally used to obtain the glyphs. The NSFont class defines this method:

```
- (NSMultibyteGlyphPacking)glyphPacking
```

The final parameter of this function is the output array, where the packed array of glyphs is stored. To avoid buffer overruns, this array needs to be at least count*4+1 bytes in length. Given the font myFont, input glyph array myGlyphArray, and array element count myNumGlyphs, an example call to this function looks like this:

```
char *outputArray = (char *)malloc(myNumGlyphs * 4 + 1);
NSConvertGlyphsToPackedGlyphs(myGlyphArray, myNumGlyphs,
        [myFont glyphPacking], outputArray);
```

After creating a packed array of glyphs, the following two `NSBezierPath` methods can be used:

```
- (void)appendBezierPathWithPackedGlyphs:(const char *)packedGlyphs
+ (void)drawPackedGlyphs:(const char *)packedGlyphs atPoint:(NSPoint)point;
```

The first method works like the methods already discussed. It appends the glyphs to the path, using the current font. The glyphs are spaced as dictated by the font's metrics. For this to work as expected, it is important to send a `-set` message to the font to be used for rendering. Note that focus must have previously been locked on a view or image to be able to set a font. Given a path object `myPath` and a location for the text `myTextOrigin`, this code could be appended to the glyph in the previous packing code:

```
[myFont set];
[myPath moveToPoint:myTextOrigin];
[myPath appendBezierPathWithPackedGlyphs:outputArray];
```

Following up with a stroke or fill would complete the rendering.

The other method is an `NSBezierPath` class method. It does exactly what it says, render the glyphs to the specified point. Like the related instance method, the font must be set first and focus must already be locked. The `+drawPackedGlyphs:atPoint:` methods use a fill for the text, not a stroke. If the capability to render outlined text or inspect the glyph paths is desired, use the instance methods instead.

The `TextDrawing` example uses each of these four methods to draw glyphs in its `TextGlyphView` object. Four text strings are rendered. At the top of the window is the string `@"Packed Glyphs"`, rendered with `+drawPackedGlyphs:atPoint:`. The next row is the same string rendered with the `-appendBezierPathWithPackedGlyphs:` method. It is rendered with a fill followed by a stroke, creating opaque letters that are outlined. The third row is the string `@"Glyph Array."` It is rendered without a packed array by using the `-appendBezierPathWithGlyphs:count:inFont:` method. It is also rendered with a fill followed by a stroke, but with a narrower line width on the stroke. Finally, the last line is rendered by adding the glyphs one at a time to the path object using the `-appendBezierPathWithGlyph:theGlyph inFont:` method. This line of text is stroked, but not filled, so only the character outlines are rendered. A horizontal line is also drawn at the same y coordinate as the one specified for the text to show that the text is accurately positioned on its baseline. The result of this rendering can be seen in Figure 14.4.

FIGURE 14.4 This is how the four text strings render in the TextDrawing application.

The code to create the drawing in the Figure 14.4 is listed here.

```
File TextGlyphView.h:
#import <Cocoa/Cocoa.h>
@interface MYTextGlyphView : NSView
{
    NSFont *_myFont;
    NSGlyph *_myGlyphArray;
    int _myGlyphArrayLength;
    NSGlyph *_myPackedGlyphArray;
    char *_myPackedGlyphs;
    int _myPackedGlyphArrayLength;
}

@end

File TextGlyphView.m:

#import "TextGlyphView.h"

#define ARRAY_STRING @"Glyph Array."
#define GLYPH_STRING @"Single Glyphs"
#define PACKED_GLYPH_STRING @"Packed Glyphs"


@interface NSFont(Exposing_Private_AppKit_Methods)
- (NSGlyph)_defaultGlyphForChar:(unichar)theChar;
@end
```

```
@implementation MYTextGlyphView

- (id)initWithFrame:(NSRect)frame
{
    int i;
    self = [super initWithFrame:frame];
    if (!self) return nil;
    myFont = [NSFont fontWithName:@"Helvetica-BoldOblique" size:64.0];

    // set up the unpacked glyph array
    myGlyphArrayLength = [ARRAY_STRING length];
    myGlyphArray = (NSGlyph *)malloc(sizeof(NSGlyph) * myGlyphArrayLength);
    for (i=0; i<myGlyphArrayLength; i++) {
        myGlyphArray[i] = [myFont _defaultGlyphForChar:
                [ARRAY_STRING characterAtIndex:i]];
    }

    // set up the packed glyph array
    myPackedGlyphArrayLength = [PACKED_GLYPH_STRING length];
    myPackedGlyphArray = (NSGlyph *)malloc(sizeof(NSGlyph) *
            myPackedGlyphArrayLength);
    myPackedGlyphs = (char *)malloc(4 * myPackedGlyphArrayLength + 1);
    for (i=0; i<myPackedGlyphArrayLength; i++) {
        myPackedGlyphArray[i] = [myFont _defaultGlyphForChar:
                [PACKED_GLYPH_STRING characterAtIndex:i]];
    }
    NSConvertGlyphsToPackedGlyphs(myPackedGlyphArray, myPackedGlyphArrayLength,
            [myFont glyphPacking], myPackedGlyphs);
    return self;
}

- (void)drawRect:(NSRect)rect
{
    NSBezierPath *path = [NSBezierPath bezierPath];
    NSRect bds = [self bounds];
    int i, length = [GLYPH_STRING length];
    NSPoint position = NSMakePoint(10.0, 20.0);

    [[NSColor whiteColor] set];
    NSRectFill(bds);
```

```
// draw baseline for the individual glyph text
[[NSColor blackColor] set];
[path moveToPoint:NSMakePoint(NSMinX(bds), 20.0)];
[path lineToPoint:NSMakePoint(NSMaxX(bds), 20.0)];
[path setLineWidth:1.0];
[path stroke];

// draw individual glyphs
[path removeAllPoints];
for (i=0; i<length; i++) {
    NSGlyph theGlyph = [myFont _defaultGlyphForChar:
            [GLYPH_STRING characterAtIndex:i]];
    NSSize advancement;
    [path moveToPoint:position];
    advancement = [myFont advancementForGlyph:theGlyph];
    position.x += advancement.width;
    position.y += advancement.height;
    [path appendBezierPathWithGlyph:theGlyph inFont:myFont];
}
[path setLineWidth:2.0];
[[NSColor purpleColor] set];
[path stroke];

// draw glyph array
[path removeAllPoints];
[path moveToPoint:NSMakePoint(10.0, 100.0)];
[path appendBezierPathWithGlyphs:myGlyphArray
        count:myGlyphArrayLength inFont:myFont];
[path setLineWidth:1.0];
[[NSColor yellowColor] set];
[path fill];
[[NSColor blueColor] set];
[path stroke];

// draw packed glyph array
[path removeAllPoints];
[myFont set];
[path moveToPoint:NSMakePoint(10.0, 180.0)];
[path appendBezierPathWithPackedGlyphs:myPackedGlyphs];
[path setLineWidth:4.0];
[[NSColor greenColor] set];
[path fill];
```

```
    [[NSColor blackColor] set];
    [path stroke];

    // draw packed glyph array with NSBezierPath class method
    [[NSColor orangeColor] set];
    [NSBezierPath drawPackedGlyphs:myPackedGlyphs
            atPoint:NSMakePoint(10.0, 260.0)];
}

@end
```

Summary

This chapter completes the description of drawing facilities offered by Cocoa. The facilities for rendering images are extremely powerful. Cocoa also offers several interfaces for drawing text. Basic text drawing is described in this chapter. This basic interface is extremely low level. Chapter 11, "Text Views," describes the NSText object suite that provides a high-level, text-rendering interface. Chapters 12, "Custom Views and Graphics Part I," and 13, "Custom Views and Graphics Part II," in combination with this chapter discuss custom NSView subclasses that draw. Custom drawing is one reason to subclass NSView. Customizing the handling of events such as mouse and keyboard input is another. Chapter 15, "Events and Cursurs," discusses NSView subclasses that customize event handling.

15

Events and Cursors

IN THIS CHAPTER

- Event Handling in Custom `NSView` Subclasses
- Managing Cursors

`NSView` is a subclass of `NSResponder`, and plays an important role in event processing. The role of views in the responder chain was briefly introduced in Chapter 8, "The Application Kit Framework Overview." This chapter expands that introduction and provides the details needed to effectively subclass `NSView` for event handling.

Events are handled the same way regardless of the graphics or drawing API used. In addition to handling events, views play a role in cursor management. As a cursor moves in and out of a view, the cursor can be changed to provide feedback to users. This chapter discusses event handling and cursor management in subclasses of `NSView` and provides examples.

Event Handling in Custom `NSView` Subclasses

The `NSView` class is a subclass of `NSResponder`. This means that any instance of `NSView`, or one of its subclasses, can be a part of the responder chain and potentially can become the first responder. As described in Chapter 8, the Application Kit automatically sends pertinent events to view instances. An event enters through the application object, which then distributes it to the appropriate window. The window passes the event to the appropriate view object. The type of the event and the state of the application determine the appropriate window and view. To receive events, an `NSView` subclass simply has to override the appropriate `NSResponder` method(s), such as `-mouseDown:` or `-keyDown:`.

This section doesn't go into much detail about how events pass from object to object. Instead, the focus is on what events can be received by a view class and what might be done with them. For information about how an event finds its way to a view object, refer to the "Responder Chain" section in Chapter 6, "Cocoa Design Patterns," and the "Responders" section in Chapter 8. Throughout this section on events, the EventMonitor example is discussed and used. The intended use of EventMonitor is to allow experimentation with various events and determine exactly what events are generated by various user actions. The application's main window is shown in Figure 15.1.

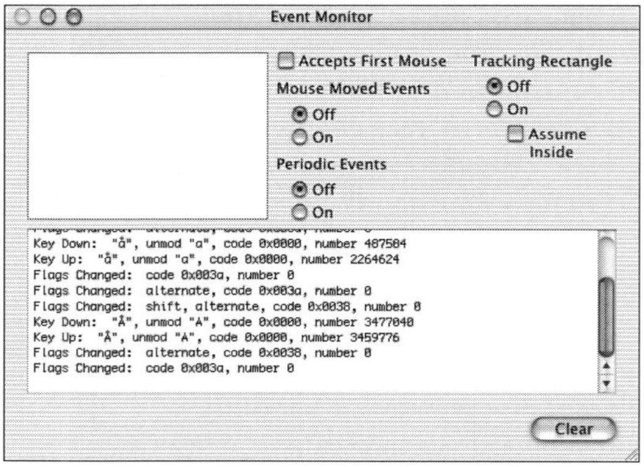

FIGURE 15.1 The main window of the EventMonitor application can be used to experiment with events and the responder chain.

Accepting First Responder Status

Subclasses of `NSView` can exert some control over which events they receive. The most important control is over whether the view can become the first responder. This can be controlled by overriding the `NSResponder` method `-acceptsFirstResponder` to return `YES` instead of the default `NO`. Because this defaults to `NO`, it must be overridden by any `NSView` subclass that wants to become the first responder. If it isn't overridden, the object will never become the first responder.

The capability to become the first responder is important to be able to receive several types of events. Mouse events generally are sent directly to the view where they occur. A mouse down and associated mouse up events are sent to the view that was clicked. Other events, such as keyboard events, won't be sent unless the view is the first responder. For example, a view that wants to receive key down events needs to be the first responder.

The `EventMonitor` example implements the `-acceptsFirstResponder` method in the `MYEventView` class. Because it is always willing to accept first responder status, the implementation always returns `YES`.

```
- (BOOL)acceptsFirstResponder
    return YES;
}
```

This is the most common implementation of the `-acceptsFirstResponder` method. Usually a view subclass either wants to be first responder or doesn't, and that won't be variable. Sometimes, a view only wants this status under certain circumstances. In that case, this method would need to determine the proper response based on its internal state and other context within the application.

A view is informed that it is about to gain or lose first responder status by being sent one of these `NSResponder` messages, as appropriate:

```
- (BOOL)becomeFirstResponder
- (BOOL)resignFirstResponder
```

Neither of these methods should ever be sent directly to a responder; instead, they are sent automatically by Cocoa. They are meant to be overridden by subclassers and can be used to further control the gain and loss of first responder status. Both methods are supposed to return a `YES` or `NO` answer to inform Cocoa whether they actually became or resigned first responder status, respectively. Usually, these methods are overridden in the following manner:

```
- (BOOL)becomeFirstResponder
{
    <determine if can become first responder>
    if (<can't be first responder>) {
        return NO;
    }
    return [super becomeFirstResponder];
}
```

`YES` is never returned in the previous pseudocode. Instead, the result of calling the super implementation is used. This is the preferred approach. These methods might be used in several ways. For example, consider an `NSTextField`. If the field is disabled for editing, it doesn't need to be the first responder. It would return a `NO` when `-becomeFirstResponder` is called. Suppose further that the field is using an `NSFormatter` to validate its input. It is important that the user enter correct data before moving to a new field. It could return a `NO` from `-resignFirstResponder` until there is valid input in the field. This would keep focus on the field until it contains a valid value.

NOTE

There are two places where first responder status can be refused. Typically, the `-acceptsFirstResponder` method returns `YES` if the object might ever accept the status, and `-becomeFirstResponder` is used to determine whether it will accept the status at a given moment.

Detecting Changes in First Responder Status

When the `-acceptsFirstResponder`, `-becomeFirstResponder` and `-resignFirstResponder` methods are overridden, they might make minor state changes in the object and not alter the super's return value. These methods, if used this way, inform you of status changes. In the `EventMonitor` application, the `MYEventView` draws a different color border to show whether it is the first responder. When it is not the first responder, it draws a blue border. When first responder status is gained, the border becomes red. Thus, the view needs to be redrawn whenever its first-responder status changes. This is done by overriding these two methods as follows:

```
- (BOOL)becomeFirstResponder
{
    [self setNeedsDisplay:YES];
    return [super becomeFirstResponder];
}

- (BOOL)resignFirstResponder
{
    [self setNeedsDisplay:YES];
    return [super resignFirstResponder];
}
```

Whenever the status of `MYEventView` changes, it flags itself for a redraw. When the view is redrawn, it can use its current status to determine which color or border to draw. Determining whether a view is actually the first responder is a two-step process. It must be the window's first responder, and the window itself must be the key window. Both conditions must be met for the view to truly be the application's first responder. Therefore, the `MYEventView` class implements this method to test both conditions:

```
- (BOOL)isFirstResponder
{
    if (![[self window] isKeyWindow]) return NO;
    if ([[self window] firstResponder] == self) return YES;
    return NO;
}
```

Because the window's status as key is a significant part of this, the view also needs to be redrawn whenever the window's key status is gained or lost. As shown so far, the view's border changes, as it should, except when the user switches to another application or another window within the application. This happens because although the key window's status changes, the view's status as first responder for its window has not. To fix this, the MYEventView instance is used as the window's delegate and implements two methods to detect changes in key window status:

```
- (void)windowDidBecomeKey:(NSNotification *)notification
{
    [self setNeedsDisplay:YES];
}
- (void)windowDidResignKey:(NSNotification *)notification
{
    [self setNeedsDisplay:YES];
}
```

With that change, the view correctly displays its status. Note that instead of becoming the window's delegate, the view could alternatively register with the default notification center to receive the NSWindowDidBecomeKeyNotification and NSWindowDidResignKeyNotification notifications. Either approach works. Notifications and delegation are described in Chapter 7, "Foundation Framework Overview," and Chapter 8, respectively.

First Mouse Clicks

Another way a view can control which events it receives is to override the NSView method -acceptsFirstMouse:.

```
- (BOOL)acceptsFirstMouse:(NSEvent *)theEvent
```

This method is expected to return a YES or NO answer. The answer determines how a mouse click is handled when the view's window is not the main window. The difference between the main window and the key window is explained in Chapter 8. A user click of a nonmain window normally makes that window the main and key window. The question is should the click that made the window main also be passed to the view that was clicked.

If the view is a button, should the first click on that button in a nonmain window be interpreted as a button click or not? The Aqua guidelines normally require that the first click not be used by the view. The first click just makes the window become the main window. Therefore, the implementation of -acceptsFirstMouse: inherited from NSView returns NO. If there is a good reason to override the default behavior, override -acceptsFirstMouse: to return YES. If a view returns YES from

-acceptsFirstMouse:, a first mouse click on the view is sent view as well as making the window become the main and key window.

The EventMonitor application allows the -acceptsFirstMouse: behavior to be turned on and off for a MYEventView instance. Try switching to another application, and then clicking the MYEventView; then click again. Try it all again after turning on the Accepts First Mouse switch. Notice that the first mouse-down event on the window will never even be sent to the EventView object unless Accepts First Mouse is on.

Controlling Key Status and Window Ordering

There is another related NSView method that subclassers might want to override:

```
- (BOOL)needsPanelToBecomeKey
```

The default implementation of this method returns NO. A view requires that its window become key in order for the view to receive keyboard events. An NSPanel might resist becoming key, however. By overriding this method to return YES, this problem can be overcome. Typically, a view that wants to receive keyboard events overrides this method to return YES. If this method is overridden, the -acceptsFirstResponder method also needs to be overridden to return YES. There's little point to asking a panel to become key if first responder status won't be accepted anyway.

There is a similar situation that might require an override to make drag and drop more reasonable for the end user. When dragging objects from one window to another, the normal Aqua behavior can get in the way. A mouse click is the first part of a drag operation. Normally, a mouse click brings the window to the front. This is a problem if the source window is large; it could come forward and obscure the drag target! Because this is extremely annoying, it is kinder to delay bringing the window forward until it is known whether that is the right thing to do. This delay can be introduced by overriding the following method:

```
- (BOOL)shouldDelayWindowOrderingForEvent:(NSEvent *)theEvent
```

The default implementation returns a NO. This causes the window to be brought forward immediately when a mouse-down event is received. If the event passed to this method is over a potential drag candidate, then YES should be returned. If YES is returned instead of a NO, the window won't be ordered forward until the mouse-up event is received. For anything other than a drag, the window still comes forward immediately. The delay only happens when the mouse is released instead of with the mouse down. If a drag is actually started, it is critical to send the -preventWindowOrdering message to the shared application object (NSApp) before the mouse up is received. This keeps the drag source window from ever being brought forward. Normally, the method that starts the drag would send the `-preventWindowOrdering` message. NSView's `-dragImage:at:offset:event:pasteboard:source:slideback:` and `-dragFile:fromRect:slideBack:event:` methods do this for you.

The `NSEvent` Class

When it is determined how first responder status is managed by a view subclass, it is time to start interpreting actual events. Before going into specific events and how to receive and use them, it is important to understand the `NSEvent` class. All events that are sent to a view are instances of `NSEvent`.

The `NSEvent` class encapsulates an event. Events can be related to the mouse. Mouse clicks, mouse movement, mouse drags, and scroll wheel movement are all mouse-related events. Other events, such as key up, key down, and flags changed are all related to the keyboard. There are several other internal events defined by the Application Kit, the OS, and the application.

When an event occurs, an `NSEvent` instance is created to hold all the data pertinent to the event. This instance is handed to the shared application object and placed into a queue. When there are events in the queue, the application removes them one at a time and attempts to send them to the correct object. Keyboard and mouse events go from the application object to the key window to be distributed. Keyboard events are sent from the window to the first responder, and then down the responder chain. Mouse events go to the view that is under the mouse when it is clicked, even if the view is not first responder. Events without an obvious destination remain in the application's event queue until they are explicitly removed by Application Kit or custom objects.

When events are sent to a view, the actual event object is sent to one of several methods defined by the `NSResponder` class. For example, Cocoa considers all mouse clicks to be mouse-down events. Such events are sent to the `-mouseDown:` method, with the event object as the argument. If the mouse is clicked on a view object, an `NSEvent` is created and follows the path described previously. It ends up as the argument to a `-mouseDown:` message being sent to the view where the mouse was clicked.

When an event is received by a specific method, such as `-mouseDown:` in the previous example, it is reasonable to assume what type of event the object represents. Despite this, the first thing that needs to be done when handling an event is to determine what the event's type is. The `-type` message can be sent to any `NSEvent` object to learn its type. One of several constants will be returned. Table 15.1 lists all the available event-type constants.

TABLE 15.1 Event-Type Constants

Event Constants	Event-Mask Constants
NSLeftMouseDown	NSLeftMouseDownMask
NSLeftMouseUp	NSLeftMouseUpMask
NSRightMouseDown	NSRightMouseDownMask
NSRightMouseUp	NSRightMouseUpMask
NSMouseMoved	NSMouseMovedMask
NSLeftMouseDragged	NSLeftMouseDraggedMask
NSRightMouseDragged	NSRightMouseDraggedMask
NSMouseEntered	NSMouseEnteredMask
NSMouseExited	NSMouseExitedMask
NSKeyDown	NSKeyDownMask
NSKeyUp	NSKeyUpMask
NSFlagsChanged	NSFlagsChangedMask
NSAppKitDefined	NSAppKitDefinedMask
NSSystemDefined	NSSystemDefinedMask
NSApplicationDefined	NSApplicationDefinedMask
NSPeriodic	NSPeriodicMask
NSCursorUpdate	NSCursorUpdateMask
NSScrollWheel	NSScrollWheelMask

Each of the event types also has a corresponding mask. The mask constants are the event-type constant names with "Mask" appended. For example, when fetching events from the application's event queue, it is possible to request that only events that match a certain mask be considered. The C language bitwise OR operator is used to build up a mask that selects multiple events. For example, the mask to select the mouse-down, mouse-dragged, or mouse-up events for the left mouse button would be

```
leftMouseMask = NSLeftMouseDownMask | NSLeftMouseUpMask | NSLeftMouseDragged;
```

It is also possible to create an event mask given an event type by using the `NSEventMaskFromType()` function. If all event types are to be considered, use the `NSAnyEventMask` constant.

Fetching Events

It is possible to fetch events that are waiting for processing in an application's event queue. The main method used to obtain an event from the shared application object is `NSApplication`'s `-nextEventMatchingMask:untilDate:inMode:dequeue:`. This method should only be sent to the shared application object. The shared application object can be obtained by calling `[NSApplication sharedApplication]` or by using the `NSApp` global variable. There are four arguments. The first, `mask`, is the bitwise OR of one or more of the eveny-mask constants in Table 15.1. The mask is used to choose which events are considered. Typically, only events of a certain type will be of any interest at a given time.

The `untilDate` argument is an expiration date used to limit the search. No events with a time stamp later than expiration are returned. Time wise, the earliest event is the one returned. If there are no events that happened before the time given, `nil` is returned. It is also allowable to use `nil` as the value for expiration. This enables the search to consider all events regardless of timestamp.

A final way to narrow the search is through the `inMode` argument. The mode is one of two predefined constants: `NSModalPanelRunLoopMode` and `NSEventTrackingRunLoopMode`. The latter constant is used for retrieval of normal events. The modal run loop mode is used only while retrieving events from within a modal loop. See Chapter 9 for an explanation of modal loops.

The `dequeue` argument tells the application what to do with the event. If it is `YES`, then the event is removed from the queue, and the application assumes that the event has been properly handled. When `NO` is used, the event remains in the application's event queue and is still dispatched by the application object. Passing `NO` as the `dequeue` argument is a way to see what events are coming without actually interfering with them.

This method is used in the `EventMonitor` application. The event monitor can set up a repeating event when the mouse is clicked and held down. The `-nextEventMatchingMask:` method is used to retrieve the periodic events and abort when a mouse up occurs. The code for this example is shown and described in the "Other Events" section later in this chapter.

There are a few other `NSApplication` methods that are useful for dealing with events. It is possible to remove events from the application's event queue in bulk. The following method can remove many events at once:

```
- (void)discardEventsMatchingMask:(unsigned int)mask
        beforeEvent:(NSEvent *)lastEvent
```

The `mask` argument is the same as before. Only events that match the mask are affected by a call to this method. The `lastEvent` parameter determines a time frame for event removal. Only events preceding `lastEvent` are deleted. This method can be used with mouse-dragged and mouse-moved events to discard extra events.

Posting Events

It is also possible to add an event to the application's event queue. To do that, it is necessary to obtain an event instance. A previously dequeued event could be added back into the queue. There are also several methods that can be used to create new events. Four class methods to do this are listed and described briefly in the "Creating

Events" section. Normally there is little need to add new events to the queue. The most common need for this functionality is for creating and queuing an application defined event. Add an event to the queue with this method:

```
- (void)postEvent:(NSEvent *)event atStart:(BOOL)flag
```

The event to be posted is passed in as the `event` parameter. The `flag` value is used to determine which end of the event queue will get the event. If the flag is `YES`, then the event will be added to the head of the queue and will be the next event to be dequeued by the application object. Using a flag value of `NO` will place the event at the end of the queue. It will not be dispatched until the events already in the queue have been handled. It is safe to post events from a subthread. All events are still handled in the main thread, however. Therefore, it is possible to create events in a thread and post them as a way to communicate with the main thread. Chapter 24, "Subprocesses and Threads," talks more about adding multiple threads to an application and communicating between them.

Finally, the `-currentEvent` method can be used to determine what event is currently being handled by the application.

Common Event Properties

Returning to the `NSEvent` class, it has already been mentioned that the `-type` method can be used to determine the event's type. There are many properties of the event that are dependent upon the event's type. For example, asking a key down event where the mouse was clicked is nonsensical. Likewise, asking a mouse-down event which key was pressed is unrealistic. As a result, there are many methods that can only be called on events of a specific type. For this reason, it is wise to check an event's type before sending it an event-type specific message.

On the other hand, there are several other properties that exist for all events. The following methods can all be sent to an event of any type:

```
- (NSEventType)type
- (unsigned int)modifierFlags
- (NSTimeInterval)timestamp
- (NSPoint)locationInWindow
- (NSWindow *)window
- (int)windowNumber
- (NSGraphicsContext*)context
```

The first method, `-type`, has already been discussed. The next method, `-modifierFlags`, is designed to tell which modifier keys were engaged when the event was created. The value returned is a bitwise `OR` of bit masks. The following predefined constants define the available modifier flags:

```
NSAlphaShiftKeyMask
NSShiftKeyMask
NSControlKeyMask
NSAlternateKeyMask
NSCommandKeyMask
NSNumericPadKeyMask
NSHelpKeyMask
NSFunctionKeyMask
```

More than one of these may be active at any given time. Use a bitwise `AND` operation between one of these masks and the return value of the `-modifierFlags` method to determine if a given modifier key is engaged. For example, to distinguish between a normal click and a command-click, use the following code:

```
BOOL commandKeyUsed = [mouseDownEvent modifierFlags] & NSCommandKeyMask;
```

If other flags are also relevant, then they can be tested too.

Each event has a timestamp that tells when it occurred. The `-timestamp` method will return an `NSTimeInterval` value. Note that this is not an object instance. Instead, it is the time in seconds since the system was last started up. Timestamps can therefore be sorted and compared against each other with standard C comparison operators. On the other hand, they require conversion to be used with `NSDate` and related objects.

The `-locationInWindow` method tells where the event occurred. This method doesn't make a whole lot of sense for key down and key up events, but it is still available to them. Normally, this is used to see where a mouse down or mouse up occurred or where the mouse ended up after a drag or move. The `NSPoint` that is returned is in the window's coordinate system. Because most relevant events are dispatched to a view subclass, the point needs to be converted to the view's coordinate system before it can be used meaningfully. This is easy to do by using code like this:

```
NSPoint windowLocation = [theEvent locationInWindow];
NSPoint location = [self convertPoint:windowLocation fromView:nil];
```

The previous code is used throughout the Event Monitor example to get a point within the view's coordinate system. This code is part of the view class itself, hence the latter message being sent to self.

The final three methods are used to determine the event's destination. The `-window` message tells which window is meant to receive the event. This is how the application knows where to send the event. The application can pass the event to the window and then the window object dispatches the event to a particular view based on the `-locationInWindow` return value. The `-windowNumber` message returns a unique integer ID that is used internally by Quartz. This is usually ignored unless one needs to deal directly with Quartz. Because `NSWindow` and other Application Kit classes cover most Quartz functionality, this is typically not necessary. The last method is `-context`. This returns the `NSGraphicsContext` instance that applies to the event. Generally, graphics contexts are associated with windows, so this is another value that isn't used very often.

As explained previously, there are also several methods that are more specific to the event type. These methods are discussed in later sections of this chapter that focus on mouse, keyboard, and other events.

Creating Events

The `NSEvent` class also has several class methods. These methods are primarily meant for creating new events that could then be posted to an application's event queue. Normally this is a bad idea. However, scripting and other operations might want to simulate user actions by creating events. The following methods can all create new events; each method specifies which type of event will be created and returned.

```
+ (NSEvent *)mouseEventWithType:(NSEventType)type location:(NSPoint)location
        modifierFlags:(unsigned int)flags timestamp:(NSTimeInterval)time
        windowNumber:(int)wNum context:(NSGraphicsContext*)context
        eventNumber:(int)eNum clickCount:(int)cNum pressure:(float)pressure

+ (NSEvent *)keyEventWithType:(NSEventType)type location:(NSPoint)location
        modifierFlags:(unsigned int)flags timestamp:(NSTimeInterval)time
        windowNumber:(int)wNum context:(NSGraphicsContext*)context
        characters:(NSString *)keys charactersIgnoringModifiers:(NSString *)ukeys
        isARepeat:(BOOL)flag keyCode:(unsigned short)code

+ (NSEvent *)enterExitEventWithType:(NSEventType)type location:(NSPoint)location
        modifierFlags:(unsigned int)flags timestamp:(NSTimeInterval)time
        windowNumber:(int)wNum context:(NSGraphicsContext*)context
        eventNumber:(int)eNum trackingNumber:(int)tNum userData:(void *)data

+ (NSEvent *)otherEventWithType:(NSEventType)type location:(NSPoint)location
        modifierFlags:(unsigned int)flags timestamp:(NSTimeInterval)time
        windowNumber:(int)wNum context:(NSGraphicsContext*)context
        subtype:(short)subtype data1:(int)d1 data2:(int)d2
```

Each event creation method is long and complex. It is beyond the scope of this book to give the complete details of each method and its parameters. However, careful inspection shows that it is required to provide all the general and specific data that would be part of a given event if it were real. The more specific data is described in the later sections dealing with each event type.

Handling Mouse Events

There are several mouse related events that can be sent to an NSView object. For a view to receive a mouse event, it needs to implement one of the methods that have been predefined by the NSResponder class for handling mouse events. These methods typically do nothing, simply absorbing the event. The methods in question are

```
- (void)mouseDown:(NSEvent *)theEvent
- (void)mouseUp:(NSEvent *)theEvent
- (void)mouseDragged:(NSEvent *)theEvent
- (void)rightMouseDown:(NSEvent *)theEvent
- (void)rightMouseUp:(NSEvent *)theEvent
- (void)rightMouseDragged:(NSEvent *)theEvent
- (void)scrollWheel:(NSEvent *)theEvent
- (void)mouseMoved:(NSEvent *)theEvent
```

The first three methods are the common mouse operations. A mouse-down event is the start of a click and a mouse-up is when the mouse button is released. Mouse dragged events are sent whenever the mouse moves while the button is being pressed.

Each of these three operations, mouse-down, mouse-up, and mouse-dragged, has a counterpart for the right mouse button as well. While Cocoa supports a second mouse button, write applications so that they can be used with only a single mouse button. Apple does not ship a multi-button mouse, so this is a very important point to remember when designing an application.

It is also possible to use a mouse with more than just two buttons. Getting events for other mouse buttons is a little bit thornier. The Application Kit does generate events related to other mouse buttons, but they are currently not documented. Because the interface is private and not normally used, it is beyond the scope of this book.

There are other mouse events. The scroll-wheel event can be sent by a mouse with a scroll wheel. Current mouse devices only support one scrolling axis. The Application Kit allows up to three scrolling axes to exist on the input device, however. Whether or not an input device that can actually use all these axes will ever appear is unknown, but they are there if ever needed.

Two final mouse events, not previously listed, are related to tracking rectangles. A tracking rectangle is a region of a view that is watched. An event is generated whenever the mouse enters or exits the region. The mouse entered and mouse exited events are discussed in the "Other Events" section later in this chapter.

The Event Monitor application implements all the previous mouse event methods. The implementations are bare bones. They simply obtain the most important attributes of their respective events and print out the information in a console.

Mouse-Related `NSEvent` Methods

The mouse-down, up, and mouse-dragged `NSEvent` objects each respond to a few additional methods. Each of the following three methods is implemented by the `NSEvent` class. The first two methods are only valid for mouse-up, mouse-down, and mouse-dragged events. The last method is also valid for the mouse-enter and mouse-exit events described later in this chapter.

```
- (int)clickCount
- (float)pressure
- (int)eventNumber
```

The first method is the most important. When the mouse button is pressed, a mouse-down event is generated. This is true for single, double, triple, or other clicks. The `-clickCount` method can be used to determine whether the mouse-down is a single, double, or other click. The count starts at one, so a single click will report 1 and a double click will report 2, and so on.

Each mouse-down event is reported. This means that a double click operation will generate an event for both a single and double click. A triple click will generate a single, double, and triple click mouse-down. When implementing a view's behavior it is easiest if higher click counts simply extend the action already taken by lower click counts. For example, double clicking in an `NSTextView` will select a word. A triple click selects the whole paragraph. Because the word selection is part of the paragraph, the triple click simply adds to the selection of the double click. This is easy to implement, because the action doesn't undo what has already been done and previous actions don't interfere.

There may be cases where the desired behavior is more complex. For example, suppose that a text area contains multimedia elements, such as an image. If the image is double clicked, a good behavior would be to launch it from the finder so that it can be manipulated in an image editor. If some text is already selected, this could pose a problem. The default behavior would cause the selection to be changed with the first click. However, if the user only wants to open the image for editing, changing the selection to the image is probably somewhat user-unfriendly. It would be better to leave the selection unchanged, but launch the double clicked image.

The TextEdit application that comes with Mac OS X follows this latter, more user-friendly course. To implement this in a mouse- down method, the first click would not necessarily change the selection or insertion point immediately. Instead, it would first check to see if the mouse click was on top of an attachment. If not, then the normal action can be taken. Otherwise, it sets up a delayed event to perform the standard single (or double) click operation using one of the -performSelector:...afterDelay: methods. If the double click never comes, the delayed perform will cause the normal action to happen. If the double click does come, the delayed action can be cancelled. The attachment can be opened with one of NSWorkspace's -openFile:... methods. Although somewhat complex, this approach does implement the desired behavior.

Aside from the click count, a mouse event can also report a pressure and an event number. The -pressure method returns the input device's pressure, if it has one. Most devices don't have pressure sensors. They simply report 1.0 on mouse-down and mouse drag and 0.0 on mouse-up. A pen-oriented device such as a tablet may offer pressure values that vary between 1.0 and 0.0. The -eventNumber method returns an integer that can be used as a unique ID to link a mouse-down event to its respective mouse-up event and any drag events generated between them. Each group of mouse events will use a new, different number. It is easy to see how this works from the following sample output from EventMonitor:

```
Left Mouse Down:  location (57.000000, 86.000000), 1 click, pressure 1.00, number
6185
Left Mouse Up:  location (57.000000, 86.000000), 1 click, pressure 0.00, number
6185
Left Mouse Down:  location (66.000000, 93.000000), 1 click, pressure 1.00, number
6186
Mouse Dragged:  location (68.000000, 93.000000), pressure 1.00, number 6186
Mouse Dragged:  location (68.000000, 92.000000), pressure 1.00, number 6186
Mouse Dragged:  location (69.000000, 90.000000), pressure 1.00, number 6186
Mouse Dragged:  location (70.000000, 88.000000), pressure 1.00, number 6186
Mouse Dragged:  location (70.000000, 87.000000), pressure 1.00, number 6186
Mouse Dragged:  location (71.000000, 87.000000), pressure 1.00, number 6186
Mouse Dragged:  location (71.000000, 86.000000), pressure 1.00, number 6186
Left Mouse Up:  location (71.000000, 86.000000), 0 click, pressure 0.00, number
6186
Left Mouse Down:  location (163.000000, 103.000000), 1 click, pressure 1.00, number
6187
Left Mouse Up:  location (163.000000, 103.000000), 1 click, pressure 0.00, number
6187
Left Mouse Down:  location (89.000000, 62.000000), 1 click, pressure 1.00, number
6191
```

```
Left Mouse Up:  location (89.000000, 62.000000), 1 click, pressure 0.00, number
6191
Left Mouse Down:  location (123.000000, 67.000000), 1 click, pressure 1.00, number
6192
Mouse Dragged:  location (123.000000, 66.000000), pressure 1.00, number 6192
Mouse Dragged:  location (123.000000, 65.000000), pressure 1.00, number 6192
Left Mouse Up:  location (123.000000, 65.000000), 0 click, pressure 0.00, number
6192
```

Note that the numbers are not always sequential; some numbers may be skipped. The numbers can reliably be used to match up the mouse-down, up, and drag events, however. Observe that the mouse-up event says 0 clicks whenever the mouse has been dragged. This is always the case. A mouse-up event will give the same number of clicks as the matching mouse-down event unless the mouse has been dragged.

Another event generated by a mouse is the scroll-wheel event. This event happens whenever the scroll wheel is moved, and the mouse is above a particular view. If the mouse is outside of a view's bounds, it will not receive these events even if it is first responder. The scroll-wheel event supports three axes of movement. Most mouse devices have only one scroll wheel, so there is only one axis of movement. To access the scroll amounts, the following methods are available for scroll-wheel events:

```
- (float)deltaX
- (float)deltaY
- (float)deltaZ
```

The events themselves can be received when a view overrides this `NSResponder` method:

```
- (void)scrollWheel:(NSEvent *)theEvent
```

Because most mouse devices implement only one wheel, the `-deltaY` method is used in a typical implementation of the `-scrollWheel:` method. As can be demonstrated with the Event Monitor example, scroll-wheel movement is expressed in the Y axis. When the wheel is rolled forward, `-deltaY` returns a value of 1.0. The `NSTextView` object implements this direction as scrolling back, toward the top of the document, that is, the scrollbar is moved upwards if possible. When the scroll wheel is rolled backward (toward the user), `-deltaY` returns -1.0. The `NSTextView` object interprets this as a scroll toward the end of the document. The scrollbar moves downward if it can. The other two axes, which aren't moving, both always return 0.0. On a mouse with multiple scroll wheels, if such a beast existed, the other axes would be assigned to the other scroll wheels.

Mouse-Moved Events

The last type of mouse event not yet discussed is the mouse-moved event. When the mouse moves, either a mouse-moved or a mouse-dragged event is generated. The difference is whether or not a mouse button is pressed while the mouse moves. If a button is pressed, it is a mouse-dragged event. Otherwise, it is just a mouse-move event. Because the mouse moves quite often, mouse-moved events are not usually dispatched. This is to avoid flooding the application's event queue. Normally, these events are turned on temporarily for a specific purpose, and then turned off again.

To begin receiving mouse-moved events a view class will tell its window that it wants them, using code such as this:

```
[[self window] setAcceptsMouseMovedEvents:YES];
```

Even when this is enabled, a view might not be sent mouse-moved events. Several conditions must be met. The application must be the active application. Also, the view's window must be the key window. Finally, the view itself must be the first responder. Even if a view doesn't want to receive keyboard events, it needs the capability to become key to receive mouse-moved events.

A much better way to track the position of the mouse is provided in many situations where mouse-moved events are wanted. For example, a somewhat famous "toy" application draws a pair of eyeballs that track the mouse as it moves around the screen. It seems obvious that mouse-moved events should be used to track the mouse as it moves. However, the previous conditions stipulate that the moment the user switches to another application, the stream of mouse-moved events will stop. The result is that the eyes stop moving. Obviously, this approach is unsatisfactory.

A better approach is to periodically poll the location of the mouse. If it has moved, the view can be redrawn as needed. A NSTimer or a repeating delayed perform can be used to trigger the polling method. The method itself needs to obtain the current location of the mouse, and then force the view to be redisplayed. The only thing that is new here is to determine the current location of the mouse. Two methods can be used:

```
NSEvent:   + (NSPoint)mouseLocation
NSWindow:  - (NSPoint)mouseLocationOutsideOfEventStream
```

Both of the previous methods return the current location of the mouse. The first method, an NSEvent class method, returns the mouse position in screen coordinates. The second method is sent to an instance of NSWindow and returns the mouse position in the window instance's base-coordinate system. There are readily accessible methods to convert mouse coordinates from the window's coordinate system to the view's coordinate system. This makes the NSWindow method the easiest to use. A view could use this code to get the current mouse location in the view's coordinate system:

```
NSPoint mouseBase = [[self window] mouseLocationOutsideOfEventStream];
NSPoint mouseLocation = [self convertPoint:mouseBase fromView:nil];
```

There are a few methods that are particularly good for working with mouse coordinates. The first is an NSView method for testing to see if a point is inside of a rectangle:

```
- (BOOL)mouse:(NSPoint)aPoint inRect:(NSRect)aRect
```

The point referenced by aPoint is usually the mouse's location in view coordinates, and aRect is the rectangle of interest. Either a YES or NO is returned. Remember that there is also a rectangle function NSPointInRect(). The -mouse:InRect: method is preferred to the NSPointInRect() function because it properly takes into account whether the view's coordinate system is flipped, whereas the function does not.

The Application Kit also provides a way to test if a given point is on a path. The following NSBezierPath method can be used for this:

```
- (BOOL)containsPoint:(NSPoint)point
```

This method does not take fills into account. It only returns a YES if the point is actually on the path itself. Furthermore, the point must be on the path, not just nearby. This is all that the Application Kit provides for hit detection. For more complex hit detection, it is necessary to create a custom method.

There is one more NSView method that is of interest when working with mouse events:

```
- (NSView *)hitTest:(NSPoint)aPoint
```

This method returns an NSView instance. It is another method that is meant to be subclassed, but not called directly. It is used by the NSWindow class to determine how to dispatch mouse events. The point passed to this method is assumed to be in the superview's coordinate system and not the receiver's coordinate system.

If aPoint lies outside of the receiver, nil is returned. If the point is inside the view, this method traverses as deep as possible into the view hierarchy and returns the farthest leaf found. The result could be the receiver itself, if it has no subviews. Another way to look at what is returned is to think of a view, and its subviews, as a group of concentric, nested rectangles. The innermost rectangle that encloses the point is the one that is returned by this method.

This behavior works as if a subview were on top of all its superviews. The main reason to override this method is to change the underlying semantic. Overriding provides the opportunity to give priority to a different subview, perhaps the receiver itself. A common reason to override this method is to hide mouse events from some or all subviews. By returning self, mouse events are sent to the receiver instead of its subviews.

Handling Key Events

There are three types of events related to the keyboard: key down, key up, and flags changed. As noted previously, for a view to receive keyboard events, it must be the first responder. This is true for all three types of keyboard events. Just like mouse events, there are several `NSResponder` methods that must be overridden in an `NSView` subclass for it to actually receive these events. The methods are

```
- (void)keyDown:(NSEvent *)theEvent
- (void)keyUp:(NSEvent *)theEvent
- (void)flagsChanged:(NSEvent *)theEvent
```

`NSEvent` doesn't implement any special methods for the last event type, flags changed. Typically, the `-modifierFlags` method, which is available for all events, is the main point of interest. Note that this event doesn't say which flags changed. It provides the current state of the modifier flags and the implication that something changed. To know what changed, you would have had to save the previous value of the flags, and then compare them. Normally, this is irrelevant because all that matters is the current state of the flags.

The two `-key` methods, especially `-keyDown:`, are the ones most commonly overridden.

Key-Related `NSEvent` Methods

Key-up and key-down event objects implement several methods specific to their event type, which are

```
- (BOOL)isARepeat
- (NSString *)characters
- (NSString *)charactersIgnoringModifiers
- (unsigned short)keyCode
```

When a key is held down, it repeats. Repeated key-down events return a `YES` when sent `-isARepeat`. The typical sequence of events in such a situation is a key-down (with repeats returning `NO`), several key-down events that return `YES` to `-isARepeat`, and then a key-up. The following output from the EventMonitor example shows how this works:

```
Key Down:  "a", unmod "a", code 0x0000, number 13554240
Key Down:  "a", unmod "a", repeat, code 0x0000, number 13518880
Key Down:  "a", unmod "a", repeat, code 0x0000, number 13554240
Key Down:  "a", unmod "a", repeat, code 0x0000, number 13518880
Key Down:  "a", unmod "a", repeat, code 0x0000, number 13554240
Key Down:  "a", unmod "a", repeat, code 0x0000, number 13518880
Key Up:  "a", unmod "a", code 0x0000, number 13510528
```

The two -characters methods return information about which keys went up or down. In both cases, an NSString instance is returned. Normally, the string contains only a single character. However, it is possible for multiple characters to be in the string. Because of this, it is always wise to check how many characters are in the string and not just blindly pick out the character at index 0, tossing away any others that potentially might be there. This usually happens whenever the application's event queue gets behind. Perhaps the processing of a previous event took a while to complete and multiple key-down events were received. Cocoa buffers the key events so they aren't lost. To allow the application a chance to catch up, all the key-down events are collected together and passed on as a single event. (This is sometimes called "coalescing" in the documentation.)

The difference between the -characters and -charactersIgnoringModifiers methods is straightforward. The first method takes into account all the modifier keys, such as the alternate key. The second method returns the event's characters ignoring all the modifier keys except for the Shift key. For example, an alternate-a and alternate-shift-a produce non-ASCII characters. In this situation, the -charactersIgnoringModifiers method would return "a" and "A," respectively. This is shown in the following output from the EventMonitor application:

```
Flags Changed:  alternate, code 0x003a, number 0
Key Down:  "å", unmod "a", code 0x0000, number 18168144
Key Up:  "å", unmod "a", code 0x0000, number 18167824
Flags Changed:  code 0x003a, number 0
Flags Changed:  alternate, code 0x003a, number 0
Flags Changed:  shift, alternate, code 0x0038, number 0
Key Down:  "Å", unmod "A", code 0x0000, number 13462032
Key Up:  "Å", unmod "A", code 0x0000, number 18120320
Flags Changed:  alternate, code 0x0038, number 0
Flags Changed:  code 0x003a, number 0
```

Because the characters generated by keyboard events are all provided in NSString instances, they are accessible as unicode characters (the unichar type). Besides the normal alphabet, there are many special keys, such as the arrows and function keys. There are many constants that can be used to refer to these special keys. All the constants in the following list are of the unichar type. The first part of this list has been abbreviated. There are 35 constants for function keys 1 through 35, only a few of which are shown.

```
NSF1FunctionKey                NSStopFunctionKey
NSF2FunctionKey                NSMenuFunctionKey
NSF3FunctionKey. . .           NSUserFunctionKey
NSF35FunctionKey               NSSystemFunctionKey
NSUpArrowFunctionKey           NSPrintFunctionKey
NSDownArrowFunctionKey         NSClearLineFunctionKey
NSLeftArrowFunctionKey         NSClearDisplayFunctionKey
NSRightArrowFunctionKey        NSInsertLineFunctionKey
NSInsertFunctionKey            NSDeleteLineFunctionKey
NSDeleteFunctionKey            NSInsertCharFunctionKey
NSHomeFunctionKey              NSDeleteCharFunctionKey
NSBeginFunctionKey             NSPrevFunctionKey
NSEndFunctionKey               NSNextFunctionKey
NSPageUpFunctionKey            NSSelectFunctionKey
NSPageDownFunctionKey          NSExecuteFunctionKey
NSPrintScreenFunctionKey       NSUndoFunctionKey
NSScrollLockFunctionKey        NSRedoFunctionKey
NSPauseFunctionKey             NSFindFunctionKey
NSSysReqFunctionKey            NSHelpFunctionKey
NSBreakFunctionKey             NSModeSwitchFunctionKey
NSResetFunctionKey
```

Clearly, not every keyboard has a key for every one of the previous constants. In fact, most keyboards only have 12 function keys, not 35. As an example of handling special keys, imagine an NSView subclass that responds to the arrow keys. A simple implementation of the -keyDown: method might look like this:

```
- (void)keyDown:(NSEvent *)event
{
    unichar theChar = [[event characters] characterAtIndex:0];
    if (theChar == NSLeftArrowFunctionKey) {
        [self leftAction:self];
```

```
    } else if (theChar == NSRightArrowFunctionKey) {
        [self rightAction:self];
    } else if (theChar == NSDownArrowFunctionKey) {
        [self downAction:self];
    } else if (theChar == NSUpArrowFunctionKey) {
        [self upAction:self];
    }
}
```

The previous code will work. Pressing an arrow key causes the appropriate action method to be called. The one simplification is that only the first character in the event is processed. If there are other characters, they will be effectively thrown out. For a game or an application that doesn't require complete precision, this might be acceptable. However, setting up a loop like this is the better approach, for most applications:

```
- (void)keyDown:(NSEvent *)event
{
    NSString *characters = [event characters];
    int i, length = [characters length];
    for (i=0; i<length; i++) {
        unichar theChar = [characters characterAtIndex:i];
        if (theChar == NSLeftArrowFunctionKey) {
            [self leftAction:self];
        } else if (theChar == NSRightArrowFunctionKey) {
            [self rightAction:self];
        } else if (theChar == NSDownArrowFunctionKey) {
            [self downAction:self];
        } else if (theChar == NSUpArrowFunctionKey) {
            [self upAction:self];
        }
    }
}
```

Another change to be considered is to call the super implementation of `-keyDown:` for unrecognized characters. This causes the standard beep, as would be expected when the user hits a key that is unrecognized. The previous implementations simply ignore invalid key presses.

There is one final method implemented by `NSEvent` for key events:

```
- (unsigned short)keyCode
```

This is a device-dependent code. While it is provided for key- down, key-up, and flags changed events, it is generally a very bad idea to use it. If an application never runs on more than one piece of hardware, the value returned is reliable. Apple is constantly changing their hardware in minor and major ways. Depending on the key code is a sure-fire way to ensure that an application breaks when new hardware is released. It is preferable to use the `-characters` method wherever possible because it always returns consistent results no matter what the underlying hardware does.

Key-Related NSView Methods

Besides the normal `NSResponder` methods such as `-keyDown:`, there are two `NSView` specific methods that can be overridden to handle certain kinds of keyboard events. The methods are

```
- (BOOL)performKeyEquivalent:(NSEvent *)theEvent
- (BOOL)performMnemonic:(NSString *)theString
```

Typically, if either of these methods is implemented, the `-keyDown:`, and other methods will not be. The first method is the one most commonly used. A key equivalent is a key that can be used to trigger the view, also known as a shortcut. An example of this is seen in the `NSButton` class. A common key equivalent is the Return key. Setting the Return key as the button's key equivalent makes it sensitive to the key being pressed. The button will be triggered and its action sent when the user hits Return. When a panel or window is key and the first responder view doesn't respond to the `-keyDown:` method, the window checks if any of its views respond to key equivalents. If not, the event is passed up the responder chain.

To see if the view responds to a particular key equivalent, the `-performKeyEquivalent:` method is sent to the view. If the view accepts the key equivalent, `YES` is returned and the search ends there. It is assumed that the key equivalent has been handled at that point. Otherwise, `NO` is returned and the search continues. The default implementation passes the message on to any subviews. Because of this, if a custom implementation doesn't return `YES`, it should return the result of calling the super implementation instead of returning `NO`. Custom implementations should use the `NSEvent` method `-charactersIgnoringModifiers` instead of `-characters` when checking to see if the key equivalent can be accepted.

The other method, `-performMnemonic:`, is meant for handling key mnemonics. This feature is a remnant from the Application Kit on OPENSTEP and Windows. In those environments, a button's title could be set so one of the characters would be underlined. That character is the mnemonic. When a mnemonic is triggered from the keyboard, the Application Kit follows a procedure similar to key equivalents, but using this method. Because Aqua doesn't actually use mnemonics, this method should normally be ignored. Of course, if Cocoa ever returns to being cross platform or mnemonics are added to Aqua, this method could once again become relevant. In that case, it would be overridden in a way similar to the `-performKeyEquivalent:` method previously described. The primary difference is that an `NSString` is used as the argument instead of an `NSEvent` object, removing the extra step of asking the `NSEvent` for its characters.

Other Events

There are other event types that don't fall into the standard mouse and keyboard event types. These other event types include tracking and cursor rectangles, system-defined events, Application Kit-defined events, application-defined events, and periodic events.

Tracking Rectangles

To simplify a common task in mouse-movement processing, the Application Kit adds the idea of a tracking rectangle. This is a rectangular area that covers all or a portion of a view. Whenever the mouse enters or exits the tracking rectangle, an event is sent to the view. This can be used to trigger redraws that highlight areas under the mouse, such as Web page mouse overs. Another use is to update a separate `NSTextField` that is acting as a status field, displaying data about whatever is under the mouse. It is common to change the cursor when it enters a tracking rectangle. Because this particular usage is so common, there is a special set of methods just for cursor manipulation. See the "Cursor Rectangles" section later in this chapter for more information on this special case.

To set up a tracking rectangle, call the following `NSView` method:

```
- (NSTrackingRectTag)addTrackingRect:(NSRect)aRect owner:(id)anObject
        userData:(void *)data assumeInside:(BOOL)flag
```

This method returns a special tag that is kept to remove the tracking rectangle later. It can also be matched with incoming enter and exit events to determine which rectangle was entered or exited.

The `aRect` argument specifies the rectangle of interest in the view's coordinates. This gives an invisible border, and an event is generated every time the mouse crosses this border.

The owner is the object that receives the mouse-entered and mouse-exited events. Often this method is being sent to `self`, and `anObject` is set to `self`. This is the case in the `EventMonitor` sample application.

The `data` is a pointer to untyped. It is wise to use an `NSDictionary` instance here because a dictionary can store arbitrary amounts of information for easy retrieval.

The data provided here is bundled up within the NSEvent objects that come back, so this is a way of passing data on to the tracking rectangle's owner object.

Finally, the flag argument tells the method which kind of event, entered or exited, is to be sent first. If it is set to YES, the assumption is that the mouse is already inside the tracking rectangle, regardless of its actual location. The first event sent in relation to this tracking rectangle is a mouse-exited event. If the mouse was already outside, no entered event is sent when the mouse enters the rectangle. The exited message is sent the moment the mouse leaves the rectangle. After the initial event, subsequent mouse-entered and mouse-exited events will all be sent as expected. If the value of flag is NO, the opposite happens. It is assumed that the mouse is outside of the rectangle. The first event related to this rectangle would then be sent the moment that the mouse moves from outside to inside, triggering an entered event.

This might seem a little confusing at first. The EventMonitor application can set up a tracking rectangle that can be the subject of various experiments. Try enabling the tracking rectangle, and then passing the mouse in and out of the rectangle. Notice that if the assumption made when the rectangle is turned on is incorrect, the first crossing in or out of the rectangle will not generate an event. This happens because the mouse is moving to where the Application Kit already thinks it is. Future crossings from there generate the appropriate event, of course.

To remove an existing tracking rectangle, use the following NSView method. Notice that it is necessary to provide the tag that was returned when the tracking rectangle was initially created.

```
- (void)removeTrackingRect:(NSTrackingRectTag)tag
```

Using these two methods for setting up and removing the tracking rectangle, the EventMonitor application implements the following code to toggle the state of the tracking rectangles:

```
- (IBAction)changeTrackingRect:(id)sender
{
    if ([[sender selectedCell] tag] > 0) {
        [self addTrackingRect];
    } else {
        [self removeTrackingRect];
    }
}

- (NSRect)rectToTrack
{
    return NSInsetRect([self bounds], 20.0, 20.0);
}
```

```
- (void)addTrackingRect
{
    NSString *message;
    if (haveTrackingRect) return;
    trackingRectTag = [self addTrackingRect:[self rectToTrack] owner:self
            userData:@"RectData" assumeInside:([insideSwitch state] ? YES : NO)];
    haveTrackingRect = YES;
    message = [NSString stringWithFormat:
            @"Tracking rect on:  tag %d\n", trackingRectTag];
    [[NSApp delegate] appendStringToConsole:message];
    [self setNeedsDisplay:YES];
}

- (void)removeTrackingRect
{
    NSString *message;
    if (!haveTrackingRect) return;
    [self removeTrackingRect:trackingRectTag];
    haveTrackingRect = NO;
    message = [NSString stringWithFormat:
            @"Tracking rect off:  tag %d\n", trackingRectTag];
    [[NSApp delegate] appendStringToConsole:message];
    [self setNeedsDisplay:YES];
}
```

To provide some visual feedback, the view object also uses the `NSFrameRect()` function to draw the outline of the tracking rectangle when it is enabled.

When a tracking rectangle has been set up, event methods need to be implemented to receive the mouse-entered and mouse-exited events. The owner of the tracking rectangle should implement both of these `NSResponder` methods:

```
- (void)mouseEntered:(NSEvent *)theEvent
- (void)mouseExited:(NSEvent *)theEvent
```

These methods are called when the mouse enters or exits the tracking rectangle. The supplied `NSEvent` instance implements these special, related methods:

```
- (int)trackingNumber
- (void *)userData
- (int)eventNumber
```

The first method, `-trackingNumber`, returns a tag that matches up with the tag returned when the tracking rectangle was created. The second method returns the untyped data that was used when creating the tracking rectangle. It needs to be cast to the appropriate data type before it can be used. As was noted previously, it is a good idea to use an NSDictionary here. However, other objects or 32-bit data types can certainly be used. The important thing is that because the programmer decides what to put here, she needs to be consistent with that when attempting to decode the data. This is an opportunity for pointer problems to surface if proper care isn't taken.

The last method returns the event number, similar to the mouse methods described in the previous section. In the case of mouse-enter and mouse-exit events, this event number does not necessarily match between them. If a mouse event such as mouse down or mouse up is received between an entered or exited event, the numbers differ. For this reason, the value returned by -eventNumber is only of marginal value when dealing with mouse-entered and mouse-exited events.

The EventMonitor application's implementation of the -mouseEntered: and -mouseExited: methods simply print lines in the console that contain the return values of these three methods.

Periodic Events

Another useful event type is the periodic event. These events are used within tracking loops to generate events at a constant rate.

An example of periodic event use within the Application Kit would be found within the arrow buttons associated with a scroller. When the button is clicked and held, there is a slight pause. The button then repeatedly sends its action at a constant rate until it is released. The loop to start, handle, and stop the periodic events happens within the -mouseDown: method. By doing this, the normal event dispatching system for mouse-up and mouse-drag events is bypassed.

Periodic events are not dispatched through the normal event process. To receive them it is necessary to explicitly grab them from the application's event queue. Normally, this is part of a tracking loop. To start a series of periodic events, the following method is sent to the NSEvent class object:

```
+ (void)startPeriodicEventsAfterDelay:(NSTimeInterval)delay
        withPeriod:(NSTimeInterval)period
```

The events won't actually start until the delay period, which is specified in seconds, has elapsed. The NSTimeInterval type is a floating-point type, so fractional values are acceptable. The period argument specifies how often the periodic event is to be sent. Sending the +stopPeriodicEvents message to the NSEvent object stops periodic events.

To dequeue periodic events, the NSPeriodic and NSPeriodicMask constants have been defined for the event type and mask, respectively.

The full implementation of the EventMonitor's -mouseDown: method shows a sample implementation of periodic events. When periodic events are enabled, it sets up a tracking loop. The loop watches for a mouse-up event, which is used to break out of the loop. Until the mouse up happens, periodic events are received at a regular rate. The code for this is as follows.

```
- (void)mouseDown:(NSEvent *)theEvent
{
    NSPoint windowLocation = [theEvent locationInWindow];
    NSPoint location = [self convertPoint:windowLocation fromView:nil];
    int clicks = [theEvent clickCount];
    NSString *message = [NSString stringWithFormat:
            @"Left Mouse Down:  location
➥(%f, %f), %d click%@, pressure %0.2f, number %d\n",
            location.x, location.y, clicks, ((clicks > 1) ? @"s" : @""),
            [theEvent pressure], [theEvent eventNumber]];
    [[NSApp delegate] appendStringToConsole:message];
    if (periodicFlag) {
        BOOL repeating = YES;
        [NSEvent startPeriodicEventsAfterDelay:2.0 withPeriod:0.5];
        while (repeating) {
            NSEvent *mouseUp = [NSApp nextEventMatchingMask:NSLeftMouseUpMask
                    untilDate:nil inMode:NSEventTrackingRunLoopMode dequeue:NO];
            if (mouseUp) {
                repeating = NO;
            } else {
                NSEvent *periodicEvent = [NSApp
                        nextEventMatchingMask:NSPeriodicMask
                        untilDate:nil
                        inMode:NSEventTrackingRunLoopMode
                        dequeue:YES];
                NSString *message = [NSString stringWithFormat:
                        @"Periodic Event:  number %d\n",
                        [periodicEvent eventNumber]];
                [[NSApp delegate] appendStringToConsole:message];
            }
        }
        [NSEvent stopPeriodicEvents];
    }
}
```

This technique is the preferred way to animate things in a tracking loop. The loop could have received mouse-drag events instead, which would cause some form of animation to occur, but only when the mouse is moved. The periodic events provide a constant rate and predictable behavior. Because a tracking loop temporarily bypasses the normal event dispatching system, it is necessary to use periodic events instead of an `NSTimer`. Messages sent by timers are temporarily put on hold while a tracking or modal loop is active. Periodic events get around this problem nicely.

Miscellaneous Event Types

There are a few other types of events that might be encountered when creating a custom view subclass. They are not commonly used, however. The other event types are system-defined, Application Kit-defined, and application-defined events. All these event types, like periodic events, must be explicitly retrieved from the application's event queue. There is no overrideable `NSResponder` method for them to be sent to. The constants `NSSystemDefined`, `NSAppKitDefined`, and `NSApplicationDefined` and the associated masks `NSSystemDefinedMask`, `NSAppKitDefinedMask`, and `NSApplicationDefinedMask` have been defined for use in identifying and dequeuing these events.

Each of these three types of custom events responds to these three `NSEvent` methods:

```
- (short)subtype
- (int)data1
- (int)data2
```

The `-subtype` method returns an event subtype to further define the event's semantics. There is currently only one subtype for system-defined events, `NSPowerOffEventType`. This is a predefined constant. There are several constants defined for Application Kit-defined events, as shown in the following list.

```
NSWindowExposedEventType

NSApplicationActivatedEventType

NSApplicationDeactivatedEventType

NSWindowMovedEventType

NSScreenChangedEventType

NSAWTEventType
```

The two data methods return information that is specific to the event's subtype. Specific data values' semantics are not documented at this time. In fact, the documentation recommends that programmers avoid working with these events. Because they are primarily internal to the Application Kit and made available through various Application Kit methods, there is little need to access them directly anyway.

Creating application-defined events is of the most value. Such events can be queued, and then retrieved as needed. The subtype and two data values can be used in whatever ways are useful to the application. Because events can be queued from subthreads, and then retrieved in the main event loop, they can be a valuable means of communicating with the main thread. For example, a subthread could be running a detailed calculation in the background. Although in a tracking loop, application-defined events could be retrieved to signal updates to the application's output or modify the tracking itself as the calculations progress.

Application-defined events, being by definition application specific in nature, are not shown in the EventMonitor application. However, the facilities already described are adequate for managing them.

Managing Cursors

Cocoa provides several ways to manage mouse cursors. The `NSCursor` class is central to this, but `NSView` and `NSWindow` classes both play an integral part in the more complex management options. For the simplest cases, such as a modal tool that temporarily changes the cursor on an application-wide basis, only knowledge of the `NSCursor` class is required. Because this class plays such a central role, it is discussed first, followed by more complex cursor management. Finally, cursor rectangles are covered. These special tracking rectangles provide a way to change the cursor automatically as it enters or exits a specific region.

The `Cursors` example at the `www.cocoaprogramming.net` Web site demonstrates all these techniques. It will be discussed throughout this section.

`NSCursor` Class

The `NSCursor` class encapsulates a mouse cursor. The cursor consists of two elements: an image and a hotspot. In Mac OS X, a cursor can be any full-color image, but it is limited to being 16×16 pixels in size. Although the image is 16-pixels wide and high, mouse itself is considered to be at a specific point on the screen.

To place the cursor image at the correct place on the screen in relation to where the mouse is located, a hotspot is defined. The hotspot of the image is always directly over the mouse. Because the image's meaning might change from cursor to cursor, the hotspot isn't always in the same place. For example, an arrow cursor would place the hotspot at the tip of the arrow. A crosshair would put the hotspot at the center. The wait cursor would put the hotspot at the center, too.

When cursors are set up to change as the mouse enters a particular region, the change occurs when the cursor's hotspot crosses the invisible line. The hotspot is also used to determine the location of a mouse click.

Creating an NSCursor

To create a new NSCursor object, both a cursor image and the hotspot need to be provided. The designated initializer is

```
- (id)initWithImage:(NSImage *)newImage hotSpot:(NSPoint)aPoint
```

The documentation discusses how the cursor has a flipped coordinate system. This can be confusing because it does not apply to the image itself. The image passed to the NSCursor instance is not flipped at all. It should be exactly as it would look onscreen. The coordinate system for the hotspot is flipped, however. The upper-left corner of the cursor is (0, 0), and the lower-right corner is (15, 15).

When an NSCursor has been initialized, it is immutable. The image and hotspot cannot be changed. Instead, a new instance needs to be created with the new values. There is one other -init... method that asks for foreground and background color hints. Because the two extra parameters are ignored by the current implementation of Cocoa, the method can safely be ignored.

Although a cursor cannot be changed once it has been created, it is possible to obtain an instance's image and hot spot. To see what a cursor's image is, use the -image method. It returns an NSImage. The -hotSpot method returns an NSPoint.

There are two NSCursor methods that can be used to obtain standard Mac OS X cursors. The NSCursor class method +arrowCursor returns the standard arrow cursor, a black arrow with a white outline. The +IBeamCursor method returns the I-beam cursor used with text fields. Figure 15.2 shows enlarged representations of the two cursors.

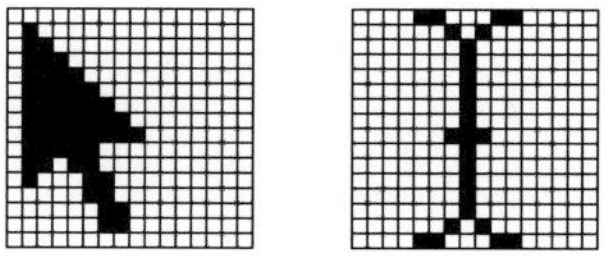

FIGURE 15.2 Enlarged representations of the +arrowCursor (left) and the +IbeamCursor (right) are shown.

Cursors Example

When an application defines its own cursors, it is convenient to have them accessible through a means similar to the +arrowCursor and +IBeamCursor methods. By using a category on the NSCursor class, this is possible.

The Cursors application uses two custom cursors. One is a crosshair, as seen in drawing applications such as sketch. Figure 15.3 shows an enlargement of the image.

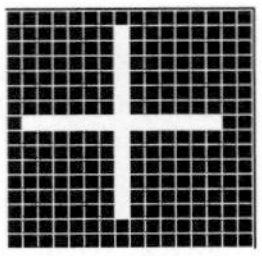

FIGURE 15.3 This is an enlarged representation of the crosshair cursor.

Because the hot spot is basically in the center of the image, the following code is a reasonable way to set up the cursor. This code is part of the `CustomCursors` category added to the `NSCursor` class in the `Cursors` application:

```
File NSCursor+CustomCursors.h:

#import <Cocoa/Cocoa.h>

@interface NSCursor(CustomCursors)

+ (NSCursor *)crossCursor;

@end

File NSCursor+CustomCursors.m:

#import "NSCursor+CustomCursors.h"

@implementation NSCursor(CustomCursors)

+ (NSCursor *)crossCursor
{
    static NSCursor *crossCursor = nil;
    if (!crossCursor) {
        NSImage *crosshair = [NSImage imageNamed:@"Cross"];
        NSSize crossSize = [crosshair size];
        NSPoint hotspot = NSMakePoint((crossSize.width / 2.0),
                (crossSize.height / 2.0));
        crossCursor = [[NSCursor alloc]
                initWithImage:crosshair hotSpot:hotspot];
    }
    return crossCursor;
}

@end
```

Because the cursor object is immutable, it only needs to be created once. Because the crossCursor variable is declared as static, it will start out nil and retain across method calls whatever value is assigned. Because the variable starts out as nil, it triggers the if statement and creates the cursor, and the cursor is then returned. Subsequent calls will return the original instance, saved in the crossCursor variable. This basic code pattern is commonly used as a way to make custom cursors readily available throughout an application. To obtain the custom cursor, the following code is all that is required:

```
[NSCursor crossCursor];
```

By using a category to add the method to the NSCursor class, it makes it much easier to remember where to go to get the custom cursor. The Cursors application adds a second custom cursor. This cursor looks like a pencil with the point at the lower left of the image. Figure 15.4 shows an enlargement of the cursor.

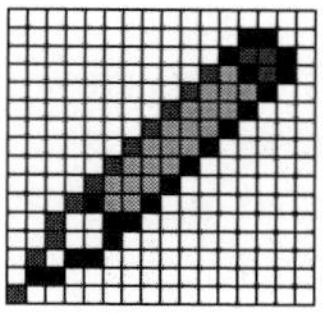

FIGURE 15.4 This is an enlargement of the pencil cursor.

For this cursor, the hotspot is at the lower left. Recall that the hotspot needs to be specified in a vertically flipped coordinate system. Furthermore, for a 16×16 image the coordinates run from 0.0 to 15.0. Therefore, the coordinates for the hot spot would be (0.0, 15.0). The code for setting up this cursor looks almost exactly like the code for setting up the crosshair cursor:

```
+ (NSCursor *)pencilCursor
{
    static NSCursor *pencilCursor = nil;
    if (!pencilCursor) {
        NSImage *pencil = [NSImage imageNamed:@"Pencil"];
        NSPoint hotspot = NSMakePoint(0.0, 15.0); // lower left
        pencilCursor = [[NSCursor alloc] initWithImage:pencil hotSpot:hotspot];
    }
    return pencilCursor;
}
```

Cursor Management

Most cursor management is done with the NSCursor class. Instance methods are available to make a given cursor active. The class object also maintains a stack of active cursors so that cursor changes can be done and undone easily. Additionally, the class object can be used to hide and unhide the mouse cursor.

The +currentCursor class method returns the NSCursor that is currently active. To make a cursor active, simply send it the -set method. In the case of an application-wide modal cursor, the cursor is often changed only temporarily. There are two ways to change the cursor back to what it was before it was engaged. The first is to save the current cursor before making the change and then using the -set method to change it back at a later time. Because this actually happens quite often, NSCursor provides an alternate means of changing the cursor.

Cursors can be placed onto a stack. Whatever cursor is at the top of the stack is the active cursor. When a cursor is sent the -push method, it is added to the top of the stack and made active. When the -pop method is received, the cursor is removed from the top of the stack and whatever cursor was active before it will once again be activated. Because the current cursor might not be known, simply sending a +pop to the NSCursor class pops the current cursor off the top of the stack.

By using this stack mechanism, it is not necessary to save the current cursor in a temporary variable. The NSCursor class tracks that all automatically.

When a user clicks on a text area and begins to type, the mouse cursor is hidden automatically. In a custom subclass of NSView, however, this needs to be done explicitly if it is appropriate. There are two ways to hide the cursor, and they are not to be mixed.

The first is to use the NSCursor class methods +hide and +unhide to hide and reveal the mouse cursor, respectively. This works, but if the application forgets to unhide the cursor it could be a major cause of irritation to the user. Therefore, it is not the preferred way to hide the cursor.

The other method of hiding the cursor is more user-friendly. The following method can hide or unhide the cursor:

```
+ (void)setHiddenUntilMouseMoves:(BOOL)flag
```

If the flag is YES, the cursor is hidden until the user moves the mouse. If the flag is set to NO, the cursor is revealed immediately without waiting for the user to move the mouse. Normally, when the cursor is hidden the user expects it to reappear when she moves the mouse. When this method is used, the computer feels very responsive because the application won't have to intervene to make the mouse cursor visible. The +hide and +unhide methods require the application to notice the movement and unhide the cursor.

These two methods are not to be mixed, however. If `+hide` was used to hide the cursor, then `+unhide` and not `+setHiddenUntilMouseMoves:` must be used to unhide it. Conversely, if the cursor was hidden with `+setHiddenUntilMouseMoves:`, the same method and not `+unhide` must be used to unhide it.

The `Cursors` application wraps all these methods inside action methods. For example, the `+hide` method is wrapped this way:

```
- (IBAction)hideCursor:(id)sender
{
    [NSCursor hide];
}
```

All these wrappers are found in the `MYCursorController` class. They are hooked up to a user interface that can be used to allow a developer to experiment with the methods by triggering them directly. The interface is shown in Figure 15.5.

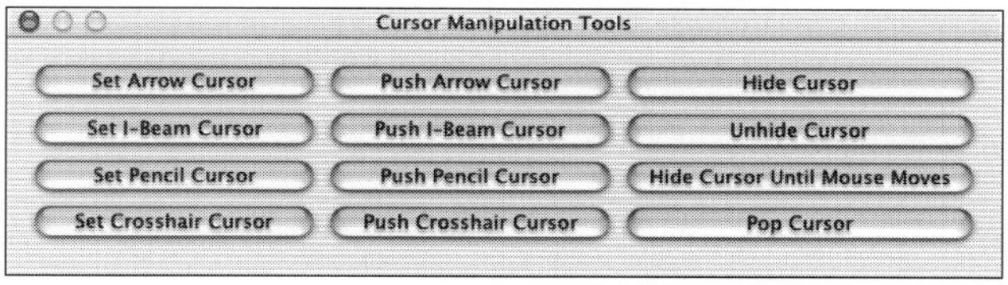

FIGURE 15.5 The Cursor Manipulation Tools window of the `Cursors` application can be used to set the cursor type.

Try experimenting with this panel to get a good feel of how these methods work together. Note that the Hide Cursor button hides the cursor for good until it is unhidden explicitly. Slowly moving the cursor to the unhide button and clicking works, but it's hard to do when the cursor is invisible. To get around this, the application also has a menu item for unhiding the cursor. This allows a Cmd-key combination to be used to bring back the cursor. To bring back the cursor without poking around blindly, use Cmd-Alt-U.

Changing the Cursor

Usually, cursor changes are wanted when the cursor moves over a particular area. For example, when the cursor is moved over the canvas of a drawing program, it might change from an arrow to a crosshair.

It is possible to track mouse-movement events, and then change the cursor when it enters a particular area. The code to do this would be somewhat involved, however.

Because this pattern for cursor manipulation is used so often, Cocoa provides several methods that make this functionality easy to implement. One is to set a cursor for an overall document and the other is to set up cursor rectangles within an `NSView` object.

Document Cursors

For a document that is displayed within an `NSScrollView`, give the scroll view an `NSCursor` instance that is to be used whenever the cursor is over the document itself. Send the following message to the document's scroll view:

```
- (void)setDocumentCursor:(NSCursor *)anObj
```

With this method, whenever the mouse moves over the scroll view's content view the cursor changes. The `-documentCursor` method can be used to retrieve the cursor that has been set.

This is demonstrated in the `Cursors` application. The Mandlebrot window contains an `NSScrollView` wrapped around an `NSImageView`. The `CursorController` class uses the `-awakeFromNib` method to set up the scroll view to display the crosshair cursor.

```
- (void)awakeFromNib
{
    [mandelScroll setDocumentCursor:[NSCursor crossCursor]];
}
```

When the cursor moves over the image, it changes to the crosshair as seen in Figure 15.6.

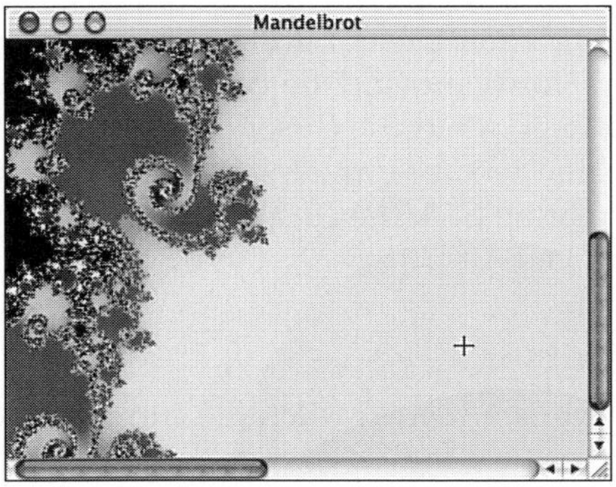

FIGURE 15.6 The cursor as it moves over the image.

There is one caveat. The cursor changes only if the window is key. This behavior is part of the look and feel of Aqua and it is something that the Application Kit offers for free. The programmer doesn't have to be aware of whether the window is key.

Simply tell the scroll view which cursor to use and the cursor appears whenever the time is right as specified by Apple's human-interface guidelines.

The `NSClipView` class also implements this method. This makes sense because an `NSScrollView` is actually using an `NSClipView` as a subcomponent. In a multidocument application, the `-awakeFromNib` method is not the best place for this code. Instead, it should be a part of the `NSDocument` subclass, typically in an implementation of the `-windowControllerDidLoadNib:` method.

This approach is very easy to use and for many situations it is enough. However, some views are even more complex and might need to change the cursor as it moves over different regions of the view. For example, an `NSMatrix` full of `NSTextFieldCell` objects would want to show the I-beam cursor when the mouse is over a text field and the arrow cursor when the mouse is between fields. Another example is the Web browser OmniWeb. When the cursor moves over a hyperlink, it changes from an arrow to a pointing finger. In these cases, setting a single cursor for the whole document or view is not sufficient.

Cursor Rectangles

A special tracking rectangle called a cursor rectangle can be used over a portion of a view to cause the cursor to change only when it is over that particular rectangle. The `NSView` class implements four methods for managing cursor rectangles, which are

```
- (void)addCursorRect:(NSRect)aRect cursor:(NSCursor *)anObj
- (void)removeCursorRect:(NSRect)aRect cursor:(NSCursor *)anObj
- (void)discardCursorRects
- (void)resetCursorRects
```

The only one of these methods that actually ever needs to be called is `-addCursorRect:cursor:`. Its function is obvious, pass it a rectangle in the view's coordinate system and a cursor. Whenever the mouse moves over that rectangle, the cursor changes. Effectively, the previous scroll-view method simply set up a single-cursor rectangle covering the entire content area.

The `-resetCursorRects` method is where all the calls to `-addCursorRect:cursor:` are to be placed. This method is never called directly. Instead, it will be called automatically by the Application Kit as needed. In this method, all the view's cursor rectangles are to be defined. It can be safely assumed that when this method is called, all previous cursor rectangles have already been removed. Therefore, it is important to set up all the cursor rectangles that apply to the view in this method.

The `-removeCursorRect:cursor:` method removes a cursor rectangle that was set up previously. The rectangle and cursor arguments must match exactly with a rectangle and cursor pair previously passed to the `-addCursorRect:cursor:` method for this to work, however. The -discardCursorRects method will remove all the cursor rectangles. However neither the -removeCursorRect:cursor: or -discardCursorRects methods are meant to be called directly. They exist primarily for use by subclassers wanting to trap these events. If overridden, the subclasser must remember to call the super implementation.

If neither removal method is to be called directly, a question arises. How are cursor rectangles supposed to be reset? It is done through the view's window and not directly through the view itself. The reason for this is in the implementation. Cursor rectangles are actually managed on a per-window basis by NSWindow instances and not by the views themselves. So, to remove cursor rectangles for a view, the -invalidateCursorRectsForView: method is sent to the view's window. For example:

```
[[someView window] invalidateCursorRectsForView:someView];
```

Because the window manages the cursor rectangles, they need to be reset whenever the window is resized or the view's bounds change. Whenever the view moves, for instance, through scrolling, the cursor rectangles also need to be reset. Moving a view to a new location in the view hierarchy is also reason to reset the rectangles. In all these cases, they are reset automatically by the Application Kit. The only time that cursor rectangles need to be reset manually is when a view's internal state changes in a way that causes the cursor rectangles to be changed.

Even though this isn't too terribly complex, in most normal implementations this is even simpler than it sounds. In the Cursors.app application, the CursorRects window shows the bare minimum implementation. The view draws two rectangles. The left rectangle has the pencil cursor assigned, whereas the right rectangle has the crosshair. The CursorRectsView class contains all the necessary code. The core is the implementation of the -resetCursorRects method, as follows:

```
- (void)resetCursorRects
{
    NSRect leftRect;
    NSRect rightRect;
    [self getLeftRect:&leftRect andRightRect:&rightRect];
    [self addCursorRect:leftRect cursor:[NSCursor pencilCursor]];
    [self addCursorRect:rightRect cursor:[NSCursor crossCursor]];
}
```

Nothing has to be done to invoke the -resetCursorRects method. It is invoked automatically by the Application Kit at the right time. Just by providing an implementation of the method, the rectangles become active automatically. In this implementation, the first method call is used to determine the actual two rectangles that are to be used; the latter two method calls do all the important work.

The example class adds a few other features besides just cursor management. It draws the cursor images in the center of the rectangles so the user knows at a glance which rectangle is which. Cursor rectangles are only active when the window is the key window, so the view tests to see if its window is key. If not, then the cursor images won't be drawn. By becoming the window's delegate, the view can be told of changes in the window's key status. This can be used to trigger the view to redraw itself. This way, it is clear when the cursor rectangles are active and when they are not. The sequence of screen shots in Figure 15.7 shows how the cursor changes as it moves from left to right across the view.

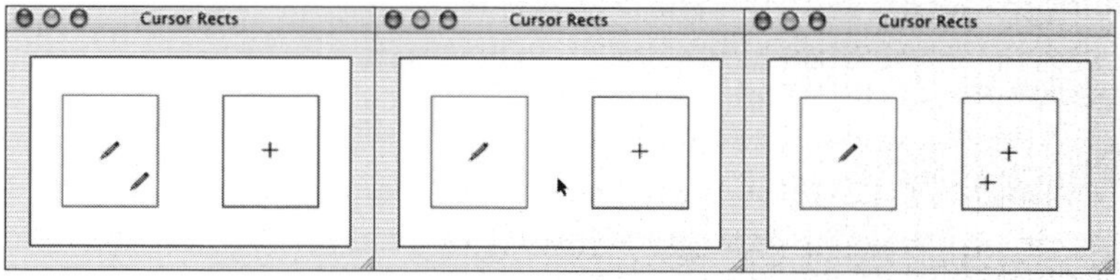

FIGURE 15.7 The cursor changes as it moves from left to right across the view.

The full code for this class, with all the features described previously, is shown as follows:

```
File CursorRectsView.h:

#import <Cocoa/Cocoa.h>

@interface MYCursorRectsView : NSView
{
}

- (void)getLeftRect:(NSRect *)leftRect andRightRect:(NSRect *)rightRect;

@end

File CursorRectsView.m:

#import "CursorRectsView.h"
#import "NSCursor+CustomCursors.h"


@implementation MYCursorRectsView

// Note that no special initialization is needed.
```

```
- (void)getLeftRect:(NSRect *)leftRect andRightRect:(NSRect *)rightRect
{
    // Split the view into two rectangles and then cause them to be inset by 20%.
    NSRect bds = [self bounds];
    float midX = bds.size.width / 2.0;
    float widthInset = midX * 0.20;
    float heightInset = bds.size.height * 0.20;

    *leftRect = NSMakeRect(0.0, 0.0, midX, bds.size.height);
    *rightRect = NSMakeRect(midX, 0.0, midX, bds.size.height);
    *leftRect = NSInsetRect(*leftRect, widthInset, heightInset);
    *rightRect = NSInsetRect(*rightRect, widthInset, heightInset);
}

- (void)drawRect:(NSRect)rect
{
    NSRect bds = [self bounds];
    NSRect leftRect;
    NSRect rightRect;
    BOOL windowIsKey = [[self window] isKeyWindow];

    [self getLeftRect:&leftRect andRightRect:&rightRect];

    // view is filled with white and has black border
    [[NSColor whiteColor] set];
    NSRectFill(bds);
    [[NSColor blackColor] set];
    NSFrameRect(bds);

    // left rectangle is red with pencil image in the middle
    [[NSColor redColor] set];
    NSFrameRect(leftRect);
    if (windowIsKey) {
        NSImage *leftImage = [[NSCursor pencilCursor] image];
        NSSize imageSize = [leftImage size];
        NSRect imageSrc = NSMakeRect(0.0, 0.0,
                imageSize.width, imageSize.height);
        NSPoint imageLoc = NSMakePoint(NSMidX(leftRect) -
                (NSWidth(imageSrc) / 2),
                NSMidY(leftRect) - (NSHeight(imageSrc) / 2));
```

```
        [leftImage drawAtPoint:imageLoc fromRect:imageSrc
                operation:NSCompositeSourceOver fraction:1.0];
    }

    // right rectangle is blue with crosshair image in the middle
    [[NSColor blueColor] set];
    NSFrameRect(rightRect);
    if (windowIsKey) {
        NSImage *rightImage = [[NSCursor crossCursor] image];
        NSSize imageSize = [rightImage size];
        NSRect imageSrc = NSMakeRect(0.0, 0.0,
                imageSize.width, imageSize.height);
        NSPoint imageLoc = NSMakePoint(NSMidX(rightRect) -
                (NSWidth(imageSrc) / 2),
                NSMidY(rightRect) - (NSHeight(imageSrc) / 2));
        [rightImage drawAtPoint:imageLoc fromRect:imageSrc
                operation:NSCompositeSourceOver fraction:1.0];
    }
}

- (void)resetCursorRects
{
    NSRect leftRect;
    NSRect rightRect;
    // set up the two rects' bounds as cursor rectangles
    [self getLeftRect:&leftRect andRightRect:&rightRect];
    [self addCursorRect:leftRect cursor:[NSCursor pencilCursor]];
    [self addCursorRect:rightRect cursor:[NSCursor crossCursor]];
}

// Use window delegate methods to detect gain or loss of key status.
// We want to draw or not draw the cursor images in the rects to reflect
// this status, so we need to know when it changes to force a redraw.

- (void)windowDidBecomeKey:(NSNotification *)notification
{
    [self setNeedsDisplay:YES];
}
```

```
- (void)windowDidResignKey:(NSNotification *)notification
{
    [self setNeedsDisplay:YES];
}

@end
```

Besides the -invalidateCursorRectsForView: method, the NSWindow class offers a few other methods for working with cursor rectangles:

```
- (void)disableCursorRects
- (void)enableCursorRects
- (BOOL)areCursorRectsEnabled
```

The first method turns off Cocoa's automatic management of the cursor rectangles in a particular window, whereas the second turns it back on. The last method allows the state of automatic cursor rectangle management to be determined. If some special cursor management is being done, and the Application Kit is interfering too much, disabling automatic management could help solve the problem.

There are two other methods, seen previously as NSView methods, which are also implemented by the NSWindow class:

```
- (void)discardCursorRects
- (void)resetCursorRects
```

Neither of these methods are meant to be called directly. Instead, they exist so that a subclasser can override them. Normally, the subclasser should call the super implementation at some point in their override.

It was mentioned in passing previously that an NSMatrix might need to set up cursor rectangles over some or all of the cells that it is displaying. There is a predefined protocol for this, too. A developer only needs to worry about it when they want to create an NSCell subclass that uses a cursor other than the arrow when the mouse is over it. The obvious example is the NSTextFieldCell class, which uses this protocol to set up an I-beam cursor. Because cells are more lightweight than views, they don't implement the -resetCursorRects method. Instead, the matrix sends this method to every cell it is displaying:

```
- (void)resetCursorRect:(NSRect)cellFrame inView:(NSView *)controlView
```

When a cell gets this message, it sets up any necessary cursor rectangles. A typical implementation would be something like this:

```
- (void)resetCursorRect:(NSRect)cellFrame inView:(NSView *)controlView
{
    [controlView addCursorRect:cellFrame cursor:myCustomCursor];
}
```

The cell's rectangle and the parent view are both sent as parameters to the method, so the only thing that needs to be determined is which cursor is to be used. This method should never be called directly and is meant for subclassers only. If an `NSCell` subclass doesn't need a special cursor, there is no need to include this method in the subclass.

There is one other programming interface of note in conjunction with cursor rectangles. An `NSCursor` class or subclass can receive both the `-mouseExited:` and `-mouseEntered:` events if it has explicitly been told to do so. The `NSCursor` methods relating to this are

```
- (void)setOnMouseExited:(BOOL)flag
- (BOOL)isSetOnMouseExited
- (void)mouseExited:(NSEvent *)theEvent
- (void)setOnMouseEntered:(BOOL)flag
- (BOOL)isSetOnMouseEntered
- (void)mouseEntered:(NSEvent *)theEvent
```

The methods that take `NSEvent` objects as arguments are not meant to be called directly; they are called automatically by the Application Kit as long as they have been turned on. They are listed here so that subclassers can take advantage of them. The other methods are for turning them on and off and determining whether or not they are on.

Summary

Subclassing `NSView` to handle events and manage the cursor enables the creation of complex views that accept user input. Application Kit classes such as `NSControl`, `NSScrollView`, and `NSSplitView` extend `NSView` using the techniques described in this chapter to provide the standard behaviors of Cocoa applications. After using Cocoa for a while, programmers can often guess exactly how the various Application Kit subclasses of `NSView` are implemented. The important realization is that there is no magic involved.

Views provide one of the most common ways to accept input from users. Another common way users interact with programs is via menus. Chapter 16, "Menus," delves into menu management, including the interaction of menu items and the responder chain.

16

Menus

IN THIS CHAPTER

- Standard Menu Layouts
- NSMenu Class
- NSMenuItem Class
- Menu Validation
- Contextual Menus
- Dock Menus
- Deprecated Functionality

Menus are an important feature of Mac OS X. Beyond the familiar menu bar across the top of a Macintosh's screen, there are also pop-up menus, pull-down menus, dock menus, and contextual menus. The Aqua user interface defines specific layouts and conventions for all menus in Mac OS X. Cocoa provides several facilities to make supporting the Aqua guidelines easy for developers.

In a Cocoa application, the menu displayed in the menu bar at the top of the screen is known as the main menu. It is composed of `NSMenu` and `NSMenuItem` objects. Both classes are also reused by Cocoa to implement all the other kinds of menus. Therefore, learning how to manipulate `NSMenu` and `NSMenuItem` objects enables a developer to work with the main menu and all pop-up, pull-down, dock, and contextual menus.

This chapter briefly highlights some of the Aqua interface's guidelines with respect to Cocoa, and then shows how to use the `NSMenu` and `NSMenuItem` classes. Menu validation, the automatic enabling and disabling of menus, is also discussed. Finally, contextual and dock menus are covered.

There are other Cocoa classes closely related to menus. One is `NSPopUpButton`, which controls both pop-up and pull-down menus. `NSPopUpButton` is discussed in Chapter 10, "Views and Controls." There are also the `NSStatusBar` and `NSStatusItem` classes, which control the little icons some programs add to the right side of the menu bar at the top of the screen. `NSStatusBar` and `NSStatusItem` are discussed in Chapter 18, "Advanced Views and Controls." Because pop-ups and status items are typically used in conjunction with `NSMenu` and `NSMenuItem` objects, the information in this chapter supplements the information in Chapters 10 and 18.

Standard Menu Layouts

The Aqua user interface guidelines specify a particular layout for an application's main menu. They also offer suggestions for how menus should be organized. The guidelines also offer suggestions for labeling menu items. Because this is a book about Cocoa and not Aqua, not every menu guideline is covered in detail. Every developer should read the Aqua guidelines at least once, however, to ensure that their menu layouts are consistent with other Mac OS X applications. The Aqua guidelines can be found at `/Developer/Documentation/Essentials/AquaHIGuidelines/AHIGMenus/index.html` on any Mac OS X machine with the developer tools installed.

Menu Support in Interface Builder

Interface Builder is designed to help developers follow the Aqua guidelines. A new `.nib` for a Cocoa application contains a default main menu holding many of the menus and menu items suggested by Aqua. The Cocoa-Menus palette also contains many of the standard Aqua submenus. The Cocoa-Menus palette is shown as part of Figure 16.1. Also shown is a `.nib` file that was created with Interface Builder's "Cocoa Application" document type. The preconfigured main menu is also visible. Additionally, a new `NSMenu` instance has been dragged into the `.nib` file.

Editing Menus with Interface Builder

For many programs, the main menu is built entirely in Interface Builder; no actual code is involved. To do this, drag menu items, dividers, and submenus from the palette and drop them onto an existing menu. The menu divider is the menu item on the palette without a title. It is a special `NSMenuItem` instance that is used to add white space between other menu items.

To rename an item, double-click it or change the title in the Attributes inspector (opened with Cmd-1). Key equivalents can also be set in the Attributes inspector. Dividers cannot have key equivalents, so these options are disabled when a divider is selected. Interface Builder allows a divider's title to be changed, but doing so does not change the appearance of the divider. (The Title text field ought to be disabled. A future revision of Interface Builder may fix this.)

NOTE

The menu item's Attributes inspector doesn't have a switch for enabling or disabling menu items. This is done dynamically by Cocoa. The "Menu Validation" section of this chapter explains how to control enabling of menu items.

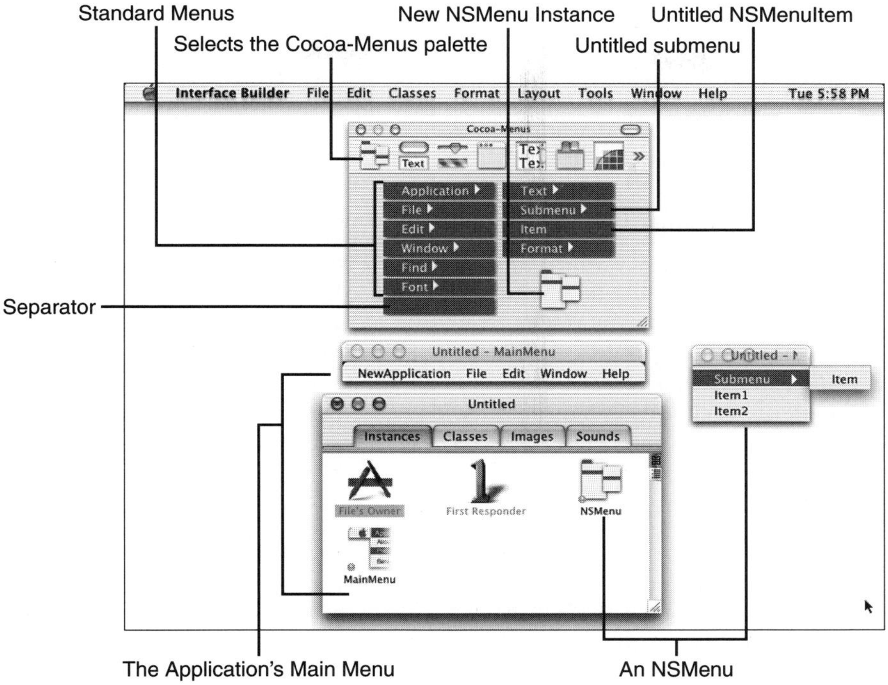

FIGURE 16.1 Interface Builder's Cocoa-Menus palette.

To change the order of the items, drag them to the new location. Items can be removed with the delete key or the Cut command. Menu items can also be copied and pasted. A pasted item is inserted in the menu just after the currently selected item.

Menu Connections

The final step of configuring the menu is to create connections from the menu items to objects in the application. Many menu commands are sent to the first responder object. This will allow them to be retargeted to whichever object is currently the active selection. For example, the Cut, Copy, and Paste commands, among others, are sent to the first responder because they should always apply to the current selection.

If a menu item should always call the same object, a connection to that object should be made. For example, the Quit item is usually configured to send a `-terminate:` message to the File's Owner. (In the main `.nib`, the File's Owner is the application object.)

NOTE

Submenus dragged off the palette are actually a pair of objects: an `NSMenuItem` with an associated `NSMenu`. The connection from the `NSMenuItem` to the `NSMenu` causes the submenu to be displayed. This connection is preconfigured on the palette and cannot be edited in Interface Builder.

Creating New Menus

The Cocoa-Menus palette also has an empty `NSMenu` instance. To create a new menu, drag this object from the palette into the `.nib`'s document window. The menu is created and opened on the screen, ready for editing. Double-click the instance to open the new menu for editing if it isn't visible. Menus created this way are typically used for contextual and dock menus, as described in the "Contextual Menus" and "Dock Menus" sections of this chapter. They are edited just like the main menu, in the same manner as previously described.

Menu Support in the Cocoa APIs

Everything that can be done with menus in Interface Builder can also be done using the `NSMenu` and `NSMenuItem` classes. There are also several other features of menus that can be performed only in code. All this functionality is covered in other sections of this chapter. At the time of this writing, none of the following API features are exposed by Interface Builder:

- Images in menu items (see "Configuring the Appearance" in the "`NSMenuItem` Class" section)
- "Radio" groups of menu items (see "Configuring State" in the "`NSMenuItem` Class" section)
- "Represented" objects (see "Configuring Identifiers" in the "`NSMenuItem` class" section)
- Explicit enabling and disabling of menu items (see "Menu Validation" section)

`NSMenu` Class

The `NSMenu` Class is the basis for all Cocoa menus. It manages a collection of `NSMenuItem` instances. It also handles the management of a borderless window used to display the menu. Because the `NSMenu` object acts as a collection containing several menu items, most of its methods are for manipulating a list of menu items. Aside from variations in the names, these methods are very similar to the methods defined by `NSMutableArray`.

NOTE

Because both the NSMenu and the NSMenuItem classes are nearly always used together, this section explains the NSMenu methods but does not provide specific code examples. Instead, the "NSMenuItem Class" section later in this chapter provides example code showing how both classes are used. You need to first learn how both objects work before trying to write code using them.

Creating an NSMenu

An NSMenu instance, like any other object, is created with +alloc. The designated initializer is -initWithTitle:. The title should be an NSString. Submenus are opened by NSMenuItem objects, so the title of an NSMenu destined to become a submenu should always match the title of the NSMenuItem that opens it. The -title method can be used to determine the title of an existing menu object.

Adding Items to an NSMenu

A newly created and initialized menu object contains no menu items. Items must be added to make the menu useful. There are two basic approaches to adding menu items. The simplest is to let the NSMenu create the items. Alternatively, a developer can create the NSMenuItem instances, and then add them to the menu. The latter approach is more flexible, but requires more code.

To have the menu object create the items, use one of these two methods:

```
- (id <NSMenuItem>)insertItemWithTitle:(NSString *)aString
        action:(SEL)aSelector keyEquivalent:(NSString *)charCode
        atIndex:(int)index;

- (id <NSMenuItem>)addItemWithTitle:(NSString *)aString
        action:(SEL)aSelector keyEquivalent:(NSString *)charCode;
```

The -insertItemWithTitle:action:keyEquivalent:atIndex: method will insert an item before the item currently at the index provided to the method. The -addItemWithTitle:action:keyEquivalent: method will append the item to the end of the menu. Both methods require a title, action, and key equivalent to be defined. The title can be any NSString.

The action is an Objective-C selector that will be invoked when the item is selected. Note that there is no parameter for the target. The target will be set to nil, which means the action message for a menu item created with one of these two methods will be sent to the first responder. To set an explicit target, it is necessary to create the menu item, and then add it to the menu.

The key equivalent should be an `NSString` containing the key equivalent. There is no way to set specific keyboard modifier flags using these methods. To set equivalents that use the option or control keys, it is necessary to create the menu item, and then add it to the menu. For an item without a key equivalent, do not pass `nil` as the `charCode`. Instead, use an empty string such as `@""`. Passing `nil` causes an exception to be raised.

If a menu item has already been created and configured, it can simply be added to the menu. The methods to do so are simpler because they don't take arguments required to create a new menu item:

```
- (void)insertItem:(id <NSMenuItem>)newItem atIndex:(int)index;
- (void)addItem:(id <NSMenuItem>)newItem;
```

Just as before, inserting an item places it in the middle of the menu as specified by the `index` argument, while adding an item puts it at the end of the menu.

Removing Items from an NSMenu

There are two ways to remove a menu item. The `-removeItemAtIndex:` method is most commonly used. It removes the item at the specified index. Be careful to use a valid index. The `-numberOfItems` method can be used to determine how many items are in the menu. Alternatively, if an actual `NSMenuItem` instance is available, the `-removeItem:` method can be used. For any change to the menu to occur the item passed as an argument should be a menu item that is actually in the menu receiving the message.

Finding Items in an NSMenu

One of the most common operations performed with an `NSMenu` is to retrieve one of its menu items. This makes sense because all the details of a menu's behavior are actually found in the individual items. Because there are so many ways to identify a menu item, there is a long list of methods for looking up either an item or its index in the menu:

```
- (int)indexOfItem:(id <NSMenuItem>)index;
- (int)indexOfItemWithTitle:(NSString *)aTitle;
- (int)indexOfItemWithTag:(int)aTag;
- (int)indexOfItemWithRepresentedObject:(id)object;
- (int)indexOfItemWithSubmenu:(NSMenu *)submenu;
- (int)indexOfItemWithTarget:(id)target andAction:(SEL)actionSelector;
- (id <NSMenuItem>)itemAtIndex:(int)index;
- (id <NSMenuItem>)itemWithTitle:(NSString *)aTitle;
- (id <NSMenuItem>)itemWithTag:(int)tag;
```

To find a menu item, use the method that matches the information available about the desired item. For example, if the menu item's tag is known, use `-itemWithTag:` or `-indexOfItemWithTag:`. Items can be searched based on title, tag, represented object, attached submenu, or target/action.

These methods return either the first item that matches the criteria or the index of the first item that matches. Because only one item or index is returned, but there might be multiple items that match the criteria, care should be taken to use a search criteria that can uniquely identify a particular menu item. For example, if many menu items use the same target/action pair, searching by tag is more likely to uniquely identify a menu item than would searching by target/action pair. This assumes that the menu's items were given unique tags when the menu was created, however.

Because there are fewer methods returning an actual `NSMenuItem`, it is common to combine one of the `-indexOf` methods with the `-itemAtIndex:` method. For example, because there is no `-itemWithSubmenu:` method, this code would do what is intended:

```
NSMenuItem * theItem = [myMenu itemAtIndex:
        [myMenu indexOfItemWithSubmenu:theSubmenu]];
```

Finally, there are two methods that are useful for developers wanting to inspect more than one menu item. The `-numberOfItems` method returns the number of items that the menu actually contains. The `-itemArray` method returns an immutable array containing all the menu's `NSMenuItem` objects. The items in the array will be in the same order that they are found in the menu itself, so object indexes from the array will match the indexes returned by the previous methods and can be used to determine insert locations for new menu items. Because the array is immutable, the `NSMenu` methods still need to be called to change the order of items or add or remove them.

`NSMenu` Notifications

Two groups of notifications are sent by `NSMenu` instances.

Whenever a menu item is selected, there is a notification both before and after the action has been sent. The notifications are named `NSMenuWillSendActionNotification` and `NSMenuDidSendActionNotification`, respectively. The most common use of these notifications is by loadable bundles. Objects in the bundle can register for these notifications as a way to be informed of events happening inside the parent application. This is especially useful if the application's bundle API doesn't offer all the desired notifications.

Both of these notifications include an NSDictionary as the notification's userInfo object. The dictionary contains a single key, @"NSMenuItem", which returns the NSMenuItem that has been selected. The actual action in question can be retrieved from this menu item.

The other type of notification from NSMenu objects is to announce changes to the menu. If an item is added to a menu, the NSMenuDidAddItemNotification notification is sent. The NSMenuDidRemoveItemNotification notification is sent when an object is removed and the NSMenuDidChangeItemNotification notification is sent when an item is changed. This includes changes in state, title, and enabling or disabling of the item.

All three of these change notifications include an NSDictionary as the notification's userInfo object. The dictionary contains a single key, @"NSMenuItemIndex", which returns an NSNumber containing the index of the item affected. This is necessary to determine which menu item was actually added, removed, or changed.

Other NSMenu Methods

The NSMenu class defines a few other methods. These methods can be used to manage submenus and supermenus or perform key equivalents and actions.

To attach a submenu to a menu item, use the -setSubmenu:forItem: method. Alternatively, the NSMenuItem method -setSubMenu: can be used before the item is added to an NSMenu.

Sometimes it is useful to know if an NSMenu has a supermenu. If an NSMenu is the submenu of another menu, that other menu is the supermenu. The -supermenu method returns the menu that is one level above the receiver. If the receiver isn't a submenu, -supermenu returns nil. When a menu becomes a submenu of another menu, the -setSupermenu: method is called. Developers should never call this method, but they can override it in a subclass. For example, this is a good way to find out if a menu has become a submenu.

To make an NSMenu perform a key equivalent or action, use either -performKeyEquivalent: or -performActionForItemAtIndex:, respectively. Key equivalents should be specified as NSEvent objects so that both the key and the modifier flags are available. Note that performing an action programmatically still causes the NSMenuWillSendActionNotification and NSMenuDidSendActionNotification notifications to be sent.

NSMenuItem Class

The NSMenuItem class contains all the information relating to a specific menu item. Several attributes, which are shown in Table 16.1, are common to all menu items.

TABLE 16.1 Menu Item Properties

Menu Item Property	Purpose
title	The text displayed on the item, such as Cut. An NSString object.
image	An optional NSImage that is displayed to the left of the menu item's title.
key equivalent	The key that can be used in conjunction with the Cmd key to activate the item from the keyboard. (Cmd-C for Cut) An NSString object.
target	The target object that will receive a message when the item is chosen. Often, this is nil, which sends the message to the first responder.
action	The Objective-C selector for the action message to be sent when the menu item is chosen.
state	The menu item's state, one of NSOffState, NSOnState, or NSMixedState.
tag	An integer that can be used to identify a menu item.
represented object	An object that can be used to identify a menu item. It can be any object.
menu	The submenu attached to this item, if any. An NSMenu instance.

Most of the work done to set up a menu programmatically is in creating and configuring NSMenuItem instances.

Creating an NSMenuItem

Like most objects, an NSMenuItem is created by using +alloc and -init. To set the title, action, and key equivalent at the same time the object is being initialized, another initialization method is provided:

```
- (id)initWithTitle:(NSString *)aString action:(SEL)aSelector
        keyEquivalent:(NSString *)charCode;
```

When using this method, be sure to always pass in valid string objects for aString and charCode, even if they are empty. Never use nil. It is acceptable for aSelector to be NULL, but be aware that doing so renders the menu item invalid and permanently disabled until a proper action is set.

This method doesn't allow the item's target to be set. Nor does it allow any key modifiers to be set in conjunction with the key equivalent. Because of this, it is likely that the new menu item will still require additional configuration.

To obtain a separator item, use the +separatorItem method. Don't use the methods above for separators.

Configuring an NSMenuItem

There are accessor and -set methods for each of the properties in Table 16.1. They allow a menu's appearance, key equivalents, target, action, state, and more to be inspected and configured.

Configuring the Appearance

The title and image properties affect the visual look of the menu item. The methods for changing the title and image a menu item are -setTitle: and -setImage:, respectively. An item's title and image can be retrieved with -title and -image. The title is an NSString, whereas the image is an NSImage. If a menu item lacks a title and an image, it might be a separator, but not necessarily. Use the -isSeparatorItem method to make sure.

Some menu items also display state, such as check marks and dashes. See the "Configuring State" section later in this chapter for information on setting state and controlling how it is displayed.

Configuring Key Equivalents

Key equivalents are set with a pair of methods, -setKeyEquivalent: and -setKeyEquivalentModifierMask:. The first sets the key and the other sets the modifier mask. Four constants can be used in a bitwise-or combination as the arguments for -setKeyEquivalentModifierMask:. The constants are NSCommandKeyMask, NSAlternateKeyMask, NSShiftKeyMask, and NSControlKeyMask. Note that Alternate and Option are the same key. Cmd and Apple are also the same key.

For example, to have the key equivalent be Cmd-Option-Y, the key is "Y" even though an Option-Y produces a yen symbol on most keyboards. Because all menu items should require the command key to be used, this example requires both option and command to be specified. The following code would be used to configure a menu item to accept Cmd-Option-Y as its key equivalent:

```
[myMenuItem setKeyEquivalent:@"y"];
[myMenuItem setKeyEquivalentModifierMask:
        (NSCommandKeyMask|NSAlternateKeyMask)];
```

To change this example to use Cmd-Shift-Option-Y, you would think that simply adding NSShiftKeyMask to the bitwise-or would be correct. It is not. Instead, the key equivalent is capitalized, as follows:

```
[myMenuItem setKeyEquivalent:@"Y"];
[myMenuItem setKeyEquivalentModifierMask:
        (NSCommandKeyMask|NSAlternateKeyMask)];
```

The NSShiftKeyMask constant is only used in conjunction with special keys, such as the F1 and F2 function keys, and navigation keys like Page Up, Home, and arrow keys. It is not used for letters or symbols painted on the key caps. As another example, use @"#" as the key equivalent instead of using @"3" with the NSShiftKeyMask set.

To see what the current key equivalent is, use the -keyEquivalent method. The -keyEquivalentModifierMask method returns the associated modifier flags.

Configuring Target and Action

Just like an NSControl subclass, the target and action are set with the -setTarget: and -setAction: methods. They can be retrieved with the -target and -action methods. As always, if the target is set to nil, the action is sent down the responder chain, starting with the first responder. If the action is set to NULL, the menu item remains disabled until a proper action has been set.

Configuring State

Some menu items show state. For example, a Bold menu item might show a check mark when the current selection is all bold text. That's an on state. If some of the selection is bold, but not all of it, a dash would be displayed to signify a mixed state. When none of the text is in boldface, that state display area on the menu item is blank, meaning off.

To set the state of a menu item, use the -setState: method. The argument should be NSOffState, NSOnState, or NSMixedState. The -state method returns the current state. Usually, a menu item's state is updated during menu validation. See the "Menu Validation" section later in this chapter for more information.

There are methods that can be used to change and retrieve the images used by an item to signal each of the three states. By default, a check mark is used for "on," a horizontal dash is used for "mixed," and a blank image is used for "off." The methods to manipulate these images are

```
- (void)setOnStateImage:(NSImage *)image;
- (NSImage *)onStateImage;
- (void)setMixedStateImage:(NSImage *)image;
- (NSImage *)mixedStateImage;
- (void)setOffStateImage:(NSImage *)image;
- (NSImage *)offStateImage;
```

Although these methods are available, they should be used sparingly. Using them is likely to lead to applications that violate Aqua's user interface guidelines.

Configuring Identifiers

All menu items offer two extra properties. Both are invisible to the user and are meant to have significance to developers only. Cocoa ignores them. The first is the tag. Like controls, menu items can have integer tags. If the tags assigned to the items are unique, each item can be distinguished by its tag. Tags are manipulated with the `-setTag:` and `-tag` methods.

For menu items, it is sometimes useful to be able to store more than a tag. For example, it might be useful to associate a color object with each menu item in a pop-up list of colors. To do this, `NSMenuItem` objects allow a represented object to be tracked. The represented object is an object that is represented by the menu item, usually a one-to-one mapping. In the color example, the represented objects would all be `NSColor` instances.

The methods to manipulate a represented object are `-setRepresentedObject:` and `-representedObject`. A represented object can be literally anything. For example, `NSString` keys, full-file paths, colors, and window objects could all be good choices for some situations.

Configuring a Submenu

Some menu items have submenus attached to them. Use `-hasSubmenu` to determine if this is the case. If there is a submenu, `-submenu` will return it.

To set a submenu for an `NSMenuItem`, use the `-setSubmenu:` method. Pass it an `NSMenu` instance. It is considered good form to make sure that the submenu and the menu item it is attached to both have the same title.

When a submenu is attached to an `NSMenuItem`, the menu item's target will become the submenu. The action sent to the submenu is always `-submenuAction:`. The supermenu of an `NSMenu` will be set automatically as well. Be aware that if a menu item previously had a different target and/or action, the original target and action will be lost when a submenu is assigned.

NOTE

The `NSMenu` action method `-submenuAction:` causes the menu to be validated, and then to be displayed in the correct place on the screen. When a user selects a menu item with a submenu, this action is what makes the submenu appear onscreen. This action should be invoked only by the menu item that opens the submenu. It should never be invoked directly, but it can be overridden.

The DynamicMenu Example

The DynamicMenu example on the www.cocoaprogramming.net Web site demonstrates four different things. The interface is shown in Figure 16.2.

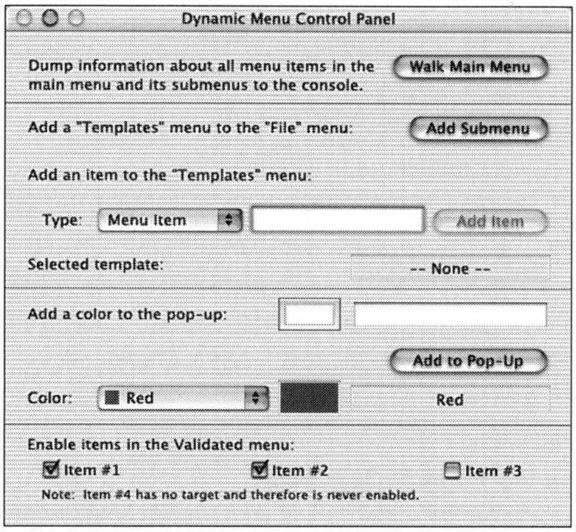

FIGURE 16.2 The user interface of the DynamicMenu example.

It can walk through its main menu and dump information about every menu item to the console. It can also add a new submenu to the File menu when the user clicks a button. It then allows the user to add arbitrary items to the new menu. The third demonstration is of adding items to a pop-up list. It is a list of colors, so images are used in the menu items to display swatches of color. The last demonstration is of menu validation. The first three parts of this example are described in this section, whereas the validation is discussed in the "Menu Validation" section later in this chapter.

Only code excerpts are shown in the description of this example. The whole example should be downloaded from the book's Web site at www.cocoaprogramming.net.

Walking Through the Main Menu

Walking through the main menu is remarkably simple. The example code defines the method `-walkMenu:withIndent:` to walk through one `NSMenu`. An enumerator is used to pass over each item in the menu. It calls itself recursively for every submenu found in the menu it is processing. This touches every menu item in the main menu. An `NSLog()` call is made to dump information about each item to the console. The code for this method and an action method to kick off the process are shown here:

```
- (IBAction)walkMainMenu:(id)sender
{
    [self walkMenu:[NSApp mainMenu] withIndent:@""];
}

- (void)walkMenu:(NSMenu *)menu withIndent:(NSString *)indentString
{
    NSArray *items = [menu itemArray];
    NSEnumerator *enumerator = [items objectEnumerator];
    id item = [enumerator nextObject];
    while (item) {
        BOOL hasSubmenu = [item hasSubmenu];
        NSLog(@"%@%@ 0x%08x: \"%@\" tag: %d action: %@ target: 0x%08x",
                indentString, (hasSubmenu ? @"Menu" : @"Item"), item,
                [item title], [item tag], NSStringFromSelector([item action]),
                [item target]);
        if (hasSubmenu) {
            [self walkMenu:[item submenu]
                    withIndent:[NSString stringWithFormat:@"%@    ",
                    indentString]];
        }
        item = [enumerator nextObject];
    }
}
```

Adding a Submenu

Adding a submenu to the File menu involves several steps and is more complex than simply walking the main menu. Both an `NSMenu` and an `NSMenuItem` need to be created in which the menu is set as the menu item's submenu. Next, the location where they are to be inserted needs to be determined. Finally, the new menu item needs to be inserted.

In the following code, this order is followed. The `while()` loop is used to find the File menu's Revert item. The action method is used to determine which menu item is the Revert item, just in case the title has been localized. The new submenu will be added after that item along with a separator. The new item and the separator are both inserted at the same index. This means that the separator will appear in the menu *above* the new submenu.

```
- (IBAction)addSubmenu:(id)sender
{
    NSMenuItem *newItem;
    NSMenu *newMenu;
```

```
    NSEnumerator *enumerator = nil;
    id item;
    NSMenu *fileMenu = [[[NSApp mainMenu] itemAtIndex:1] submenu];
    NSMenuItem *revertItem = nil;
    int insertIndex = 0;

    newItem = [[NSMenuItem alloc] init];
    newMenu = [[NSMenu alloc] initWithTitle:NewMenuName];
    [newItem setTitle:NewMenuName];
    [newItem setSubmenu:newMenu];
    enumerator = [[fileMenu itemArray] objectEnumerator];
    while ((!revertItem) && (item = [enumerator nextObject])) {
        if ([item action] == @selector(revertDocumentToSaved:)) {
            revertItem = item;
            insertIndex = [fileMenu indexOfItem:revertItem] + 1;
        }
    }
    [fileMenu insertItem:newItem atIndex:insertIndex];
    [fileMenu insertItem:[NSMenuItem separatorItem] atIndex:insertIndex];
    [newItem release];
}
```

Manipulating a Pop-Up List

The DynamicMenu application has a pop-up list with items representing colors. Users can choose a color, name it, and add it to the pop-up list. When a new item is chosen from the list, the associated color and name are copied into a noneditable color well and text field, respectively. Because `NSPopUpButton` objects use `NSMenu` instances internally, the implementation of this functionality exercises the `NSMenu` and `NSMenuItem` methods described in this chapter. To show a swatch of color on each item in the list, an `NSImage` is created and used as the image for the associated menu item.

The method that adds an item to the pop-up list is `-addPopUpColor:name:`. The first thing it does is to create a small `NSImage` to be used as the menu item's image. Large images will not be scaled to fit well into the pop-up's button when the menu is not being displayed. A size of 12.0 square seems to fit well and vertically centers nicely on the button. After creating the image, it is filled with the color.

Because of the way `NSPopUpButton` works, it is best to let it create any new items. The `-addItemWithTitle:` method creates a new `NSMenuItem`, sets its title accordingly, and adds it to the list. Because additional configuration is needed, it is necessary to retrieve the menu item from the list. Seemingly against all the other advice in this chapter, it is obtained using the `-itemWithTitle:` method. In this case, it is acceptable because the exact title is known. Having just created the menu item, the code can safely and uniquely identify the menu item with the title that was used when the item was created.

After the new menu item is obtained, final configuration is done. A new, unique tag is set. All further manipulation of the menu item will be done using the tag, not the title. Finally, the image is added to the menu item. After the image has been added, it must be released to avoid a memory leak. The menu item will retain it.

Here is the code to implement the `-addPopUpColor:name:` method:

```
- (void)addPopUpColor:(NSColor *)theColor name:(NSString *)theColorName
{
    NSMenuItem *theItem;
    NSImage *swatch = [[NSImage alloc] initWithSize:
            NSMakeSize(12.0, 12.0)];
    NSNumber *tagKey = [NSNumber numberWithInt:nextTag];

    [swatch lockFocus];
    [theColor set];
    NSRectFill(NSMakeRect(0.0, 0.0, 12.0, 12.0));
    [swatch unlockFocus];
    [colorPopUp addItemWithTitle:theColorName];
    theItem = [colorPopUp itemWithTitle:theColorName];
    [theItem setTag:nextTag];
    nextTag++;
    [theItem setImage:swatch];
    [swatch release];
}
```

Menu Validation

Enabling and disabling menu items is done automatically by Cocoa. A menu item will be disabled automatically if it has no action assigned or its target doesn't respond to its action. In the case of a `nil` target, the responder chain is queried to see if there is an object that can respond to the action. If not, the menu item will be disabled. In many cases, this is all that needs to be done, and there is nothing required of developers to make it happen. Menu items will be enabled and disabled automatically as selections change.

For menu items that do not send actions to the first responder, however, further validation might be required. Sending a particular message to an object might not make sense when the object is in a certain state. For example, a `-togglePause:` action sent to a controller object in a game doesn't make much sense if a game isn't in progress. In cases where a menu item's target does respond to an action, the target is offered an opportunity to validate whether it is willing to receive the action. If not, the menu item will be disabled.

Implementing the `-validateMenuItem:` Method

To perform this validation, the `NSMenuItem` sends a `-validateMenuItem:` message to its target before its enclosing `NSMenu` appears onscreen, or just before dispatching an action invoked by a key equivalent. According to the return value of that message, the item will be enabled or disabled accordingly. If a target doesn't implement the `-validateMenuItem:` message, then the menu item doesn't send the message. In this case the menu item defaults to an enabled state. This is very much like delegation. The difference is that `NSMenuItem` objects do not have delegates, so the message is instead being sent to the target object.

For the previous pause game example, the controller object would implement the method something like this:

```
- (BOOL)validateMenuItem:(id <NSMenuItem>)menuItem
{
    SEL theAction = [menuItem action];
    if (theAction == @selector(togglePause:)) {
        return (gameIsRunning ? YES : NO);
    }
    return YES; // we'll assume all else is OK, which should be the default
}
```

The DynamicMenu example on the `www.cocoaprogramming.net` Web site shows a similar example with three switches in a window being used to enable or disable three different menu items. The most important thing to do is to correctly determine which menu item is being validated. All menu items connected to this object are validated through this method. There are many ways to tell which menu item is being validated. Examining the item's action, tag, or represented object is the best approach.

Doing a string comparison against the menu item's title is the one approach that should be avoided at all costs. Because localizations of an application could cause titles to be different from what is expected, comparing titles is prone to failure. Unfortunately, the most obvious example of validation in Apple's documentation compares titles. Again, do *not* do this! It is the most common beginner mistake related to menu item validation. Most Cocoa experts usually compare actions, but tags and represented objects exist just for this purpose and will work fine.

If tags are compared, a C `switch` statement can be used. If actions are compared, a series of `if-then` statements are needed instead. The downside to using tags is that it is easy to forget to set a tag properly in Interface Builder. On the other hand, Interface Builder visually flags menu items that don't have an action set, so developers are much less likely to forget to connect it to something. Represented objects are sometimes a good choice, but configuring them always requires extra code, which can be cumbersome. That's why Cocoa experts tend to gravitate towards checking the action. It is the least error prone method, and also the easiest to set up in Interface Builder.

NOTE

The `-validateMenuItem:` method implementation is also an excellent place to update the state of any menu items that display state such as check marks and dashes.

Disabling Automatic Validation

If automatic menu validation doesn't behave as needed, it is possible to turn it off for a given menu. Use `-setAutoenablesItems:` with a `YES` or `NO` argument to turn it on or off. By default, it is set to `YES` of course. If validation is turned off, it becomes the programmer's responsibility to enable or disable all items in the menu manually using each item's `-setEnabled:` method. In nearly all cases, this should be avoided because it is cumbersome and does not offer much, if any, improvement over the automatic system.

The `NSMenu` method `-autoenablesItems` can be used to see if validation is enabled for a particular menu. The `NSMenuItem` method `-isEnabled` can be used to see if a given item is enabled or not.

Sometimes, rather than disabling automatic validation, it is better to force a menu to update its state dynamically. If a menu has become stale while it is open, sending `-update` to it will cause it to revalidate all its menu items. This might happen, for example, if a thread finishes while a menu is open. If the menu contained a `-stop:` action, clearly the action should be disabled as soon as the thread completes. The notification signaling completion of the thread could send an `-update` to the menu to make sure that the menu correctly reflects the status of the application. For more about threads, see Chapter 24, "Subprocesses and Threads."

Contextual Menus

In addition to an application's main menu, Cocoa supports contextual menus. A contextual menu is a menu that pops up when the user Control-clicks on a user interface object. The menu changes depending on the item clicked. The idea is to offer a menu of commands that are available for that particular user interface item. For example, clicking the document area of the TextEdit application opens a menu similar to the one shown in Figure 16.3.

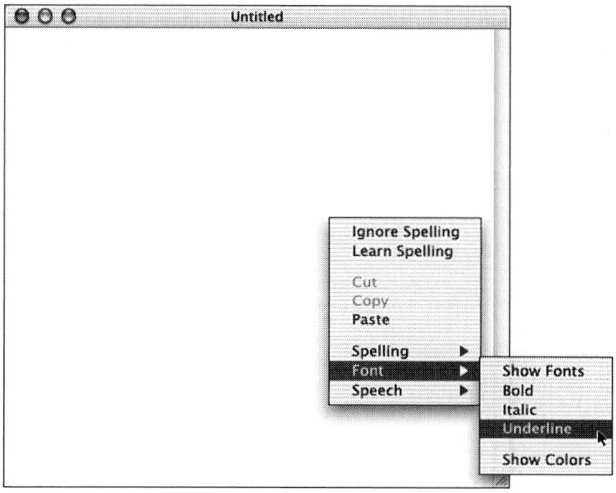

FIGURE 16.3 A contextual menu in TextEdit.

Contextual menus are defined on a per-view basis. There are three places that a contextual menu can be defined.

With the lowest priority, is the `NSView` class method `+defaultMenu`. This method should return an `NSMenu` to be used for any views not implementing one of the other techniques. It enables a particular menu to be used for every instance of a class. The default implementation in the `NSView` class returns `nil`. To change this behavior, override `+defaultMenu` in your custom `NSView` subclasses.

To change the menu on a per-instance basis and override the default menu for the class, an `NSMenu` can be set for a given view with the `-setMenu:` method. The `-menu` method returns the view's contextual menu. If no menu has been set for the view, `-menu` returns whatever is returned by `+defaultMenu`.

For more complex views, the contextual menu might need to change depending on where the user has clicked. For example, a vector drawing program might need to present a different menu depending on the type of object under the mouse. To do this, the `-menuForEvent:` method should be overridden. This method is passed an `NSEvent` object with the details of the event that is causing the contextual menu to open. The event object can be used to determine the location of interest. An appropriate `NSMenu` instance or `nil` should be returned. The default implementation returns whatever the `-menu` method returns. The implementation of `-menuForEvent:` is quite straightforward, so no example is shown here.

Dock Menus

All Cocoa applications have dock menus. When the application's icon in the dock is Control-clicked, the dock menu is shown. The default dock menu shows a list of all the application's open windows, a Show In Finder command, and a Quit command. If a window item is chosen, that window will be brought forward. In addition, the application will be activated if it isn't already the active application. Figure 16.4 shows an example of a dock menu taken from the TextEdit application.

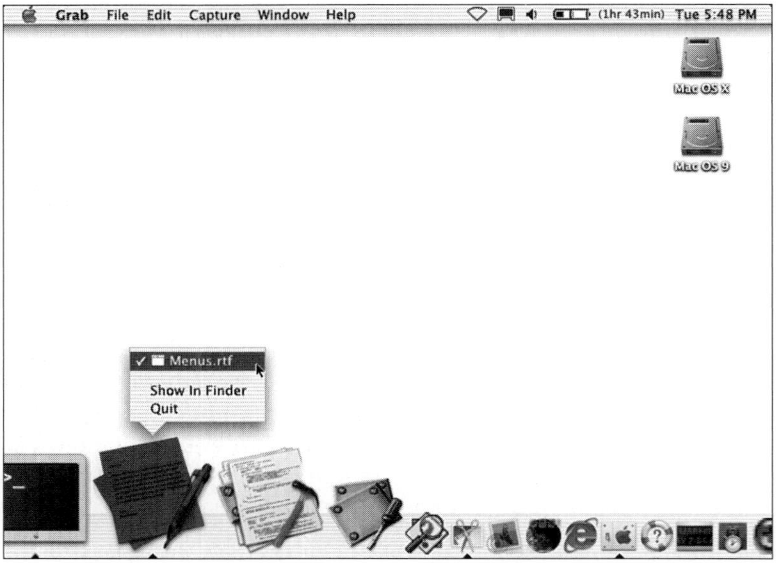

FIGURE 16.4 The dock menu for TextEdit.

It is easy to add additional items to the dock menu. Removing the default items, however, is not possible. There are two ways to extend an application's dock menu. The first is done with only Project Builder and Interface Builder. The second involves writing some code in the application's delegate object.

Extending the Dock Menu Without Code

This is the easiest way to extend an application's dock menu. Start in Interface Builder by creating a new `.nib` file, and choose Empty under Cocoa when creating it. Save it immediately with an appropriate name, such as DockMenu. Be sure it is added to the project. Next, change the class of the file's owner to `NSApplication` or whatever class is being used as the application object. If a class other than `NSApplication` is desired, the class headers will need to be added to the `.nib` first, of course.

Drag an `NSMenu` object off the Cocoa-Menus palette and drop it into the `.nib` file. Drag a connection from the application object (file's owner) to the menu and make the connection to the `dockMenu` outlet.

Add menu items and submenus from the palette as desired. The next step is to hook up each menu item to an appropriate action. The dock menu's items cannot be connected to the first responder. Dock menus are not allowed to have nil-targeted actions, which means no messages can be sent to the `.nib` file's first responder. Because the only object in the `.nib` file other than the menu is the file's owner (the application object), it might be necessary to create a "helper" object to forward messages from the dock menu to their desired targets.

NOTE

The dock menu cannot have nil targets. This is the case because the dock menu is actually running as part of the Dock application. It sends its messages, over a Distributed Objects connection, to its corresponding application. Because DO needs to have an explicit target, the menu items must be wired up to a real object instead of the first responder. See the Helper Objects sidebar for ways to work around this.

The final step in configuring the dock menu is to tell the application where to find the menu. This is done in Project Builder by adding a key to `Info.plist`. Go to the application target, select the Application Settings tab, and select the Expert button. Click New Sibling and name the new key `AppleDockMenu`. Set the value of the key to be the name of the `.nib` file minus the extension. For example, if the `.nib` is called `DockMenu.nib`, the key's value should be `DockMenu`.

The DockMenu example on the book's Web site (`www.cocoaprogramming.net`) shows an application configured with a dock menu `.nib`. It adds a menu item to the dock menu that opens the application's About panel.

HELPER OBJECTS

Creating a helper object to be the target of a dock menu's menu items can solve two problems at once. Dock menus in their own `.nib` files can't be connected directly to other objects in the application. Also, there is no way to send a message to the first responder because `nil` targets are not allowed. The helper object is an object that is instantiated inside the dock menu's `.nib` file. It is the target for all dock menu items and will then forward the actions on to other objects in the application. Although it won't have direct connections to application objects inside the `.nib`, it can query `NSApp` or its `delegate` to find the objects with which it communicates. This object can also dispatch appropriate messages to the first responder and down the responder chain. This starts by asking `NSApp` for the `-keyWindow`. Windows respond to `-firstResponder`.

Extending the Dock Menu with a Delegate

The other way to add items to an application's dock menu is through the application object's delegate. The application's delegate object simply implements the `-applicationDockMenu:` method so that it returns a preconfigured `NSMenu` instance. Every time the user requests a dock menu, this method is called. This is by far the most flexible option because the menu that is returned from the method can be reconfigured dynamically before it is displayed.

The DockMenu example implements this method so that the user can choose which of two menus should be shown when the dock menu is called up. The implementation is simple. It checks the setting of a radio button to determine which menu to show. If the radio button is set to show the menu from the `.nib` file, `nil` is returned. Returning `nil` signals the application to use the default dock menu, as described previously.

```
- (NSMenu *)applicationDockMenu:(NSApplication *)sender
{
    if ([[menuRadio selectedCell] tag] == 0) {
        return nil;
    }
    return dockMenu;
}
```

Returning an `NSMenu` as shown in this code causes that menu to override any menus set previously with `.nib` files and `Info.plist` keys. A more realistic implementation would dynamically create a menu that reflects the application's current state and return it.

Deprecated Functionality

When perusing the Cocoa reference and Application Kit headers, you are bound to discover some classes and methods not discussed in this chapter. Most of them have not been covered because they have become obsolete. With so many obsolete classes, protocols, and methods, it is useful to at least list them here so that they don't confuse new developers. It is important to know what can safely be ignored!

For example, prior to Aqua, each `NSMenu` had an associated `NSMenuView` object to lay out and draw the menu. Each `NSMenuItem` had an `NSMenuItemCell` object to render the menu item. The present version of Mac OS X uses Carbon functions to render menus, so Cocoa no longer uses the `NSMenuView` and `NSMenuItemCell` classes.

Although the documentation and headers for `NSMenuView` and `NSMenuItemCell` remain, neither class should be used. The "How Menus Work" documentation is also out of date. It still refers to the `NSMenuView` and `NSMenuItemCell` classes, even though they are no longer used.

For a while Cocoa didn't specify the `NSMenuItem` class and instead used an `NSMenuItem` protocol. The protocol still exists and is used throughout the Cocoa headers, but it is now deprecated in favor of the `NSMenuItem` class. References to the protocol should be avoided. Only the class should be used in new code.

Cocoa also supports the concept of tear-off menus. A submenu could be dragged off of the title bar and left on the screen indefinitely. A torn off menu has a close button and floats above all other windows on the screen. Users would typically use it like a palette of options or utility panel. With the move to the underlying Carbon menu functions, this functionality has been lost. There are several methods for dealing with tear off menus that are not discussed in this chapter. Apple has not explicitly marked them as deprecated, but they should be avoided as long as Mac OS X lacks support for this feature.

Apple documentation also makes a few suggestions that developers should use to make their applications "friendly" to tear-off menus. The most important is that additions to the main menu that can be made during the "will finish launching" notification should be made there instead of at a later time. It is wise to follow this as long as it will not alter the behavior of current code. It will ensure that the code continues to function correctly should Apple return this feature to Mac OS X in the future.

A final feature supported by Cocoa, but missing in Mac OS X, is the capability for users to define preferred key equivalents in Preferences. These preferred equivalents override the settings in the menu items, whether they were set in `.nib` files or programmatically. When set, these user-preferred key equivalents are consistent across all Cocoa applications. However, Carbon applications cannot have their key equivalents so easily overridden. As a result, this functionality is disabled in Cocoa. Having only some applications support this feature while others do not would lead to a large amount of user confusion. The `NSMenuItem` methods referring to user key equivalents should be ignored unless this functionality returns to Mac OS X. Like tear-off menus, these methods are not yet deprecated, so they may again be significant someday.

Summary

This chapter discussed the details of working with menus in Cocoa. The main menu, pop-up menus, pull-down menus, contextual menus, and the dock menu were described. The `NSMenu` and `NSMenuItem` classes were explained in depth, and the role of the responder chain in handling menu actions and validation was covered. Creating menus in Interface Builder and programmatically was also explained.

The next chapter explains how to use color with Cocoa. Cocoa provides a standard color selection panel and color well user interface widget. Cocoa also offers the `NSColor` class and a color list object, which together provide a rich set of functionality for manipulating colors.

17 Color

IN THIS CHAPTER

- `NSColor` Class
- Color Wells
- Color Panels
- Customizing the Color Panel
- `NSColorList` Class

Most applications have some use for color, whether as part of a document or to highlight certain information. Cocoa supplies a fairly rich set of color creation and management classes. This chapter explores the basic color storage object, `NSColor`, the associated color list management class, `NSColorList`, and user interface items associated with color, `NSColorPanel` and `NSColorWell`.

`NSColor` Class

The `NSColor` class is the public interface to a class cluster that encompasses the concept of a color in Cocoa. It is an immutable class, meaning a new instance can be created, but it is not possible to modify the contents of an existing `NSColor` instance.

An `NSColor` instance represents a unique location in a color space. The most common color space when dealing with computer displays is RGB (red, green, blue), whereas in printing CMYK (cyan, magenta, yellow, black) is the standard.

The location components of an `NSColor` are float values between 0.0 and 1.0. For example, in RGB color space, 0.0,1.0,0.0 would represent a pure green.

Each color can also have a transparency level associated with it, referred to as an alpha value. An alpha value of 1.0 is completely opaque, whereas an alpha value of 0.0 is completely clear. Alpha transparency is very useful when combined with the available drawing modes in Cocoa.

Colors can be device-dependent or device-independent. In Cocoa, device-independent colors are referred to as calibrated colors. Calibrated colors should display the same on any monitor or printer, provided that they have appropriate ColorSync entries. Device-dependent colors aren't guaranteed to look the same on another device as they do on the one on which they were created.

Another type of color space supported by Cocoa is a named color space, which is a simple list of color values indexed by name. These usually correspond to some real-world color; for example specific ink, thread, or paint colors. Color lists can be useful for keeping a set of application-specific colors in a configurable file rather than in code.

An `NSColor` can also be defined as a repeated image. This enables the implementation of complex patterns when used in conjunction with `NSImage` instances that use varied alpha transparency. Colors of this type reside in the pattern color space.

Table 17.1 contains a summary of the common color spaces and the constants used to refer to them.

TABLE 17.1 Color Space Constants

Device Color Spaces (Device Dependent)

Constant	Color Components
`NSDeviceCMYKColorSpace`	Cyan, magenta, yellow, black (and alpha) components
`NSDeviceWhiteColorSpace`	White (and alpha) components
`NSDeviceRGBColorSpace`	Red, green, blue (and alpha) or hue, saturation, brightness (and alpha)

Calibrated Color Spaces (Device Independent)

Constant	Color Components
`NSCalibratedWhiteColorSpace`	White (and alpha) components
`NSCalibratedRGBColorSpace`	Red, green, blue (and alpha) or hue, saturation, brightness (and alpha)

Miscellaneous Color Spaces

Constant	Color Components
`NSNamedColorSpace`	Catalog name and color name components
`NSPatternColorSpace`	`NSImages` used as a fill pattern

Creating Color Objects

A number of class methods are available to create both calibrated and device-dependent `NSColor` instances:

```
+ (NSColor *)colorWithCalibratedWhite:(float)white alpha:(float)alpha
+ (NSColor *)colorWithCalibratedHue:(float)hue saturation:(float)saturation
       brightness:(float)brightness alpha:(float)alpha
+ (NSColor *)colorWithCalibratedRed:(float)red green:(float)green
       blue:(float)blue alpha:(float)alpha
+ (NSColor *)colorWithDeviceWhite:(float)white alpha:(float)alpha
+ (NSColor *)colorWithDeviceHue:(float)hue saturation:(float)saturation
       brightness:(float)brightness alpha:(float)alpha
+ (NSColor *)colorWithDeviceRed:(float)red green:(float)green
       blue:(float)blue alpha:(float)alpha
+ (NSColor *)colorWithDeviceCyan:(float)cyan magenta:(float)magenta
       yellow:(float)yellow black:(float)black alpha:(float)alpha
```

Each of these class methods requires a float value for each component appropriate for the color space and returns an `NSColor`. All values should be between 0.0 and 1.0. Values outside that range are pinned to the closest legal value.

Working with a color list creation of a new `NSColor` requires the specification of a color catalog name as well as the color name.

```
+ (NSColor *)colorWithCatalogName:(NSString *)listName
       colorName:(NSString *)colorName;
```

If the list name and color name do not exist, the method returns `nil`.

Common colors are used by many applications, and Cocoa provides a number of convenience methods for creating appropriate `NSColor` objects:

```
+ (NSColor *)blackColor
+ (NSColor *)darkGrayColor
+ (NSColor *)lightGrayColor
+ (NSColor *)whiteColor
+ (NSColor *)grayColor
+ (NSColor *)redColor
+ (NSColor *)greenColor
+ (NSColor *)blueColor
+ (NSColor *)cyanColor
+ (NSColor *)yellowColor
+ (NSColor *)magentaColor
+ (NSColor *)orangeColor
+ (NSColor *)purpleColor
+ (NSColor *)brownColor
+ (NSColor *)clearColor
```

Each of these returns a color in a calibrated color space. The specific calibrated color space is dependent on the color requested and should not be assumed from the method name.

`NSColor` is also able to represent a pattern that should be used when drawing. An `NSImage` can be set for the current color using

```
+ (NSColor*)colorWithPatternImage:(NSImage*)image
```

The `NSColor` returned is in the `NSPatternColorSpace`. The `NSImage` is not scaled when the pattern is used to draw, rather it is offset and repeated as needed.

Setting the Current Color

Having created a color, the next most common task is to use it in a drawing operation. This is usually accomplished with the `-set` method.

```
- (void)set
```

This method sets the color to the receiver for the current graphics context.

```
// draw a black box
[[NSColor blackColor] set];
NSRectFill(theRect);

// draw a red circle
[[NSColor redColor] set];
theCirclePath=[NSBezierPath bezierPathWithOvalInRect:theRect];
[theCirclePath fill];
```

Querying `NSColor` Settings

An `NSColor` can be queried to access its color components by using the methods that are appropriate for the color space. For the `NSCalibratedRGBColorSpace` and `NSDeviceRGBColorSpace` color spaces, the components can be returned in either RGB or HSB values using

```
- (float)redComponent
- (float)greenComponent
- (float)blueComponent
- (float)hueComponent
- (float)saturationComponent
- (float)brightnessComponent
```

```
- (void)getRed:(float *)red green:(float *)green
        blue:(float *)blue alpha:(float *)alpha
- (void)getHue:(float *)hue saturation:(float *)saturation
    brightness:(float *)brightness alpha:(float *)alpha
```

To retrieve individual component values in `NSCalibratedCMYKColorSpace` or `NSDeviceCMYKColorSpace` color space, use

```
- (float)cyanComponent
- (float)magentaComponent
- (float)yellowComponent
- (float)blackComponent
- (void)getCyan:(float *)cyan magenta:(float *)magenta yellow:(float *)yellow
        black:(float *)black alpha:(float *)alpha
```

Likewise, individual components of colors in the `NSCalibratedWhiteColorSpace` or `NSDeviceWhiteColorSpace` can be extracted using

```
- (float)whiteComponent
- (void)getWhite:(float *)white alpha:(float *)alpha
```

When a color is in the `NSNamedColorSpace` color space the color catalog name and the color name itself can be returned. Methods also exist that allow the return of the name in the localized language (if available).

```
- (NSString *)catalogNameComponent
- (NSString *)colorNameComponent
- (NSString *)localizedCatalogNameComponent
- (NSString *)localizedColorNameComponent
```

The localized versions of the catalog name and the color name are typically used in the user interface portion of an application, whereas the other implementations are used internally because they will not change dependent on the user's language selection.

Regardless of the color space, the alpha transparency of an `NSColor` can be retrieved using

```
- (float)alphaComponent
```

If the receiving `NSColor` does not have an alpha component, the value for full opacity (1.0) is returned.

When using an NSColor in the NSPatternColorSpace the image rendered as the pattern is returned by a call to

```
- (NSImage*)patternImage
```

Visually Representing an NSColor

If an application needs to draw a representation of an NSColor solely for the purpose of displaying the selected color, it's desirable to use the method:

```
- (void)drawSwatchInRect:(NSRect)rect
```

Subclasses of NSColor can display a visual indicator for the color, as shown in Figure 17.1. CMYK colors draw an indicator in the upper-right corner, and all colors have a triangle in the background that shows through any semitransparent colors. This method displays the color as well any appropriate adornments.

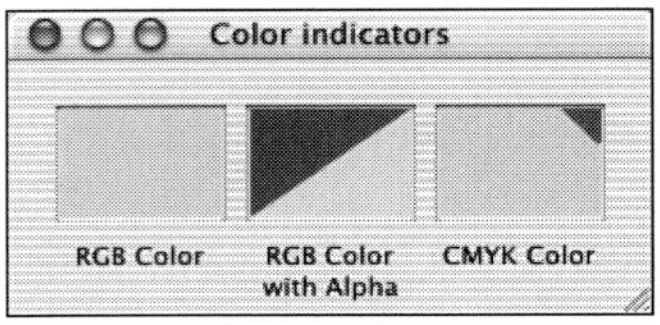

FIGURE 17.1 The visual representations for NSColor adornments.

Color Space Conversion

When a color is returned by a method other than those that specify the color space explicitly, it is often desirable to convert the color specifically to a known color space. This is accomplished using one of the following methods:

```
- (NSColor *)colorUsingColorSpaceName:(NSString *)colorSpace
- (NSColor *)colorUsingColorSpaceName:(NSString *)colorSpace
        device:(NSDictionary *)deviceDescription
```

The method -colorUsingColorSpaceName: assumes that the current device (printer, screen, or window) attributes should be used for the conversion. A target device can also be specified using -colorUsingColorSpaceName:device:. Device description dictionaries are available from the NSScreen, NSWindow and NSPrinter classes using -deviceDescription. In both cases, if the color can't be converted to the target color space, nil will be returned.

It is possible to leave the target color space name unspecified, passing in `nil` instead of an `NSString`. In this case the most appropriate color space is used based on the current device.

Caution is required, however, because these methods can be lossy. Not all colors in all color spaces can be fully represented in other color spaces. For example, there are RGB colors that cannot be reproduced in CMYK space. In such a case, a close value is substituted. It is best to be aware of this limitation and encourage the appropriate use of color space based on the application's target market.

The color space of an `NSColor` can be returned using the `-colorSpaceName` method.

```
- (NSString *)colorSpaceName
```

An example of using `-colorUsingColorSpaceName:` would be a method that can create a string version of an `NSColor` that can be used in HTML. The following example method can be used as a category on `NSColor` to create a string with the appropriate hex representation of the `NSColor`.

```
- (NSString *)hexRepresentation {
    NSColor *rgbColorRepresentation;
    int red, green, blue;

    // create an NSCalibratedRGBColorSpace version of the color
    rgbColorRepresentation=[self colorUsingColorSpaceName:
NSCalibratedRGBColorSpace];

    // collect the components and scale them to the
    // web representation color space of 0 to 255
    red=[rgbColorRepresentation redComponent]*255;
    green=[rgbColorRepresentation greenComponent]*255;
    blue=[rgbColorRepresentation blueComponent]*255;

    // return a formatted string with the hex value
    return [NSString stringWithFormat:@"%02x%02x%02x",red,green,blue];
}
```

Creating Derived Colors

`NSColor` offers a method for blending colors together to create a new color:

```
- (NSColor *)blendedColorWithFraction:(float)fraction ofColor:(NSColor *)color
```

The -blendedColorWithFraction:ofColor: method makes it simpler to create a gradual blend from one color to another in NSCalibratedRGBColorSpace. The fraction is a number between 0.0 and 1.0 that represents the weighting of the color passed as an argument and the receiving object. As the value approaches 1.0, the returned color becomes more like the passed NSColor. The following code can be used to draw a horizontal blend (or gradient) between two colors.

```
- (void)drawRect:(NSRect)rect {
// compute the size of each of the individual rectangles
    // that need to be drawn
    float stepRectWidth=[self bounds].size.width/([self numberOfSteps]+1);
    NSRect baseRect=NSMakeRect(0.0,0.0,stepRectWidth,[self bounds].size.height);
    int stepsIndex;

    // clear the contents of the view by
    // filling with a clear color, this is required
    // so that the underlying window contents are visible
    [[NSColor clearColor] set];
    NSRectFillUsingOperation([self bounds],NSCompositeSourceOver);

    // iterate over the number of steps required
    for (stepsIndex=0;stepsIndex<=[self numberOfSteps]+1;stepsIndex++) {
        NSRect localRect;
        NSColor *sourceColor=[self sourceColor];

        // calculate the fraction for the current step
        float fractionForStep=(float)(stepsIndex)/[self numberOfSteps];

        // use blendedColorWithFraction:ofColor: to create the new color
        NSColor *fillColor;
        fillColor=[sourceColor blendedColorWithFraction:fractionForStep
            ofColor:[self destinationColor]];

        // offset the rectangle that we're going to draw
        localRect=NSIntegralRect(NSOffsetRect(baseRect,
            stepsIndex*baseRect.size.width, 0.0));
        // calculate the next rectangle that we're going to draw
        nextRect=NSIntegralRect(NSOffsetRect(baseRect,
            (stepsIndex+1)*subRectWidth, 0.0));

        // adjust the current rectangle to not overlap the next
        // one, this prevents anti-alias problems
        localRect.size.width = nextRect.origin.x - localRect.origin.x;
```

```
        // set the current color
        [fillColor set];

        // draw, but use the NSCompositeSourceOver operator so that the
        // transparency is also used
        NSRectFillUsingOperation(localRect,NSCompositeSourceOver);
    }
}
```

This example implementation (a -drawRect: implementation in an NSView subclass) draws a color gradient starting at the source color and ending up at the destination color in the specified number of steps, shown in Figure 17.2.

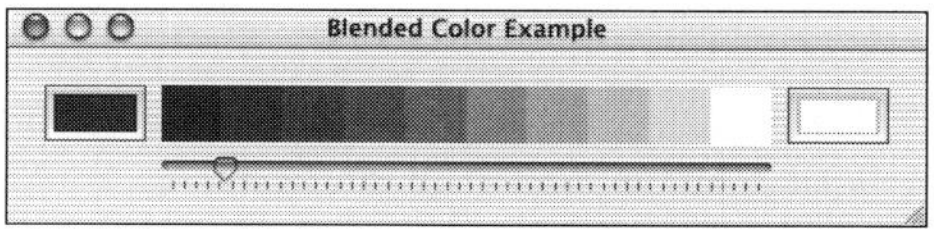

FIGURE 17.2 The Blended Color example user interface.

The -blendedColorWithFraction:ofColor: method includes the alpha component in the blended color just as it does the other color components. Blends from opaque to transparent are therefore possible. If the receiving color, or the specified color are unable to be converted to NSCalibratedRGBColorSpace, nil is returned.

There are two shorter forms of the -blendedColorWithFraction:ofColor: method.

```
- (NSColor *)highlightWithLevel:(float)highlightLevel
- (NSColor *)shadowWithLevel:(float)shadowLevel
```

Both of these methods return an NSColor that is the specified level (fraction) between the receiving color and the System colors defined to display as a highlight and shadow, and returned by the methods -highlightColor and -shadowColor, respectively. Both methods also return nil if the receiving color can't be converted to NSCalibratedRGBColorSpace.

To create an NSColor that has the same color components as an existing color object, but with a different transparency use

```
- (NSColor *)colorWithAlphaComponent:(float)alpha
```

This method attempts to create a new color in the same color space with the specified alpha for transparency. It will return nil if the color is not able to support alpha. An example of this would be an NSColor created in the NSPatternColorSpace.

System Color Values and Notification

In the user preferences of Mac OS X it is possible to personalize the environment. These colors can be retrieved using the NSColor class methods:

```
+ (NSColor *)selectedControlColor
+ (NSColor *)selectedTextColor
```

When a user changes their preferences, an NSSystemColorsDidChangeNotification is posted allowing currently running applications to refresh their displays to coordinate with the new settings.

Storing and Retrieving Colors

NSColor conforms to NSCoding, so it is simple to archive them as part of the standard object tree; however, there are additional situations that can arise when dealing with NSColor. An NSColor can be dragged into an application from another application. To facilitate that interaction these methods are used

```
+ (NSColor *)colorFromPasteboard:(NSPasteboard *)pasteBoard
- (void)writeToPasteboard:(NSPasteboard *)pasteBoard
```

The method +colorFromPasteboard: returns an NSColor from the pasteboard if one is present, otherwise it returns nil. Calling -writeToPasteboard: writes the receiving color to the pasteboard, provided that the pasteboard accepts color. If the pasteboard doesn't accept color, no action is taken.

When importing colors from the pasteboard, it is necessary to determine if an application can support alpha transparency or not. Your application can specify that it does accept alpha by passing NO to the NSColor class method +setIgnoresAlpha:.

The current value for an application can be accessed through the method +ignoresAlpha, which returns a Boolean. The default value for an application is YES.

Perhaps the most common storage task is storing an NSColor in the user defaults as part of an application's preferences. NSUserDefaults supports several object types, but not NSColor, so it's necessary to work around this limitation. This is accomplished by first encoding the NSColor data using NSArchiver, and then storing the returned NSData in the user defaults. When a color default is requested the NSData is read from the defaults, and the NSColor is unarchived and returned.

```
- (void)setColor:(NSColor *)color forKey:(NSString *)key
{
    NSData *data=[NSArchiver archivedDataWithRootObject:color];
    [self setObject:data forKey:key];
}
```

```
- (NSColor *)colorForKey:(NSString *)key
{
    NSData *data=[self dataForKey:key];
    return (NSColor *)[NSUnarchiver unarchiveObjectWithData:data];
}
```

The previous methods can be added to a category on `NSUserDefaults`, and then the application can directly request and set colors in the user defaults.

Color Wells

Color wells are the user interface that Cocoa provides for selecting and displaying a color. A color well displays a swatch representing the current color settings, and when clicked, the color panel is presented to the user. Most color wells are configured to show a border around them, which indicates if the color well is the active color well in the application, as shown in Figure 17.3. Color wells can be the target of a color dragging operation as well as an originator.

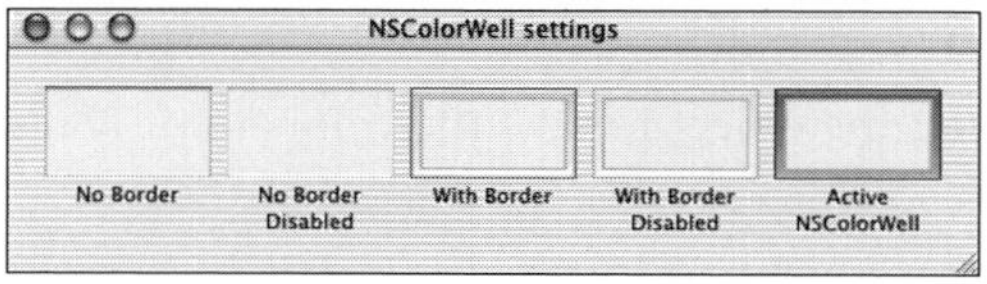

FIGURE 17.3 The possible NSColorWell visual states.

`NSColorWell` Class

`NSColorWell`, a subclass of `NSControl`, is the implementation class of the color well user interface. They can be created via code as any other `NSControl`, but the most common method of adding them to an application's user interface is by dragging from the controls palette in Interface Builder.

The `NSColorWell` inspector in Interface Builder allows setting of the initial color, as well as the state of the continuous, border, and disabled flags (see Figure 17.4).

```
- (NSColor *)color
- (void)setColor:(NSColor *)color
```

The current color reflected by an `NSColorWell` can be obtained by sending a `-color` message to the object. A new color can be set on a color well by calling `-setColor:` and passing the new color as the argument. A color well can also take another object's color by calling

```
- (void)takeColorFrom:(id)sender
```

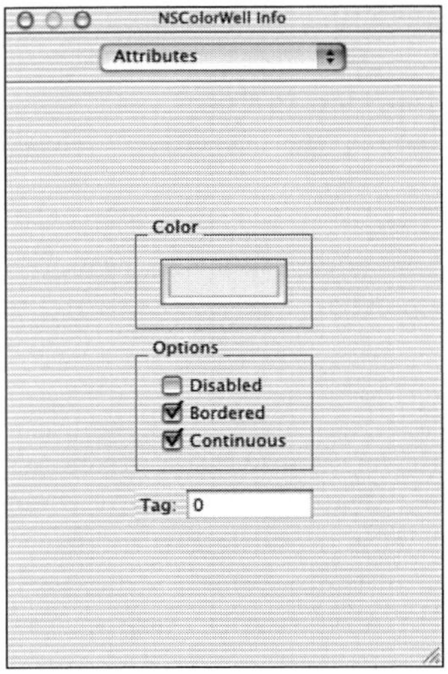

FIGURE 17.4 The Interface Builder Inspector for `NSColorWell` attributes.

with the sender being the object to take the color from. That object must implement the `-color` method.

```
- (void)activate:(BOOL)exclusive
- (void)deactivate
- (BOOL)isActive
```

Only a single `NSColorWell` can be active at a time in an application. The active state of a color well can be changed using either the `-activate:` or `-deactivate` methods. Determining if a specific color well is active is done using the `-isActive` method.

Because an `NSColorWell` is a subclass of `NSControl`, it can have a target object and an action method assigned using `-setTarget:` and `-setAction:`, respectively. When a color is dragged into the color well from the color panel (or another color well) the target object is sent the action method.

NOTE

Unlike other controls, the `NSColorWell` lacks an associated cell object. This means they can't be used directly inside of an `NSMatrix`, or any other place that requires a cell.

`NSColorWell` also implements the `NSControl` methods `-isContinuous` and `-setContinuous:`. If this is set to `YES`, the color well calls the target/action when the color in the well is changed (either via the Color Panel, or by dragging a color into the well from another source).

If `-isContinuous` is `NO`, however, the behavior is less predictable. If a noncontinuous color well is made active, and the color is changed in the color panel, the color well will update, but does not call the target/action method. Colors dragged into the well while active also do not cause the target action to trigger. If the color well is inactive, dragging colors into the well causes the target action to be called. This is likely a bug in the Mac OS X 10.1 implementation, but it is something that developers should be aware of.

```
- (BOOL)isBordered
- (void)setBordered:(BOOL)bordered
```

A color well that can bring the color panel to the front and can be activated has a border visible around it. This can be turned on and off using the method `-setBordered:` and passing `YES` or `NO` for the argument. The current state can be retrieved using `-isBordered`.

A subclass of `NSColorWell` might need to draw its contents differently than the standard display. This is accomplished by overriding `-drawWellInside:`, which is passed an `NSRect` representing the area that the `NSColorWell` subclass should draw within.

Color Panels

The Color Panel is the System-wide user interface for selecting and applying color. The panel itself is a floating utility window, which is divided into four distinct areas: color picker selection; color picker swap view area (which is different for each color picker); the user area (which consists of a color well displaying the current color and the user's customized colors area); and the optional accessory area, where an application can add functionality to the color panel, as seen in Figure 17.5.

`NSColorPanel` Class

The `NSColorPanel` is a subclass of `NSPanel`, and a shared object, there is only one instance of it for an entire application. The shared instance can be retrieved using the class method:

```
+ (NSColorPanel *)sharedColorPanel
```

This method returns the shared `NSColorPanel` object, creating it, if necessary.

The default instance of an `NSColorPanel` has all the color picker modes available. An application can control which of the pickers are available in the user interface by logically `OR`ing the following constants (defined in `AppKit/NSColorPanel.h`).

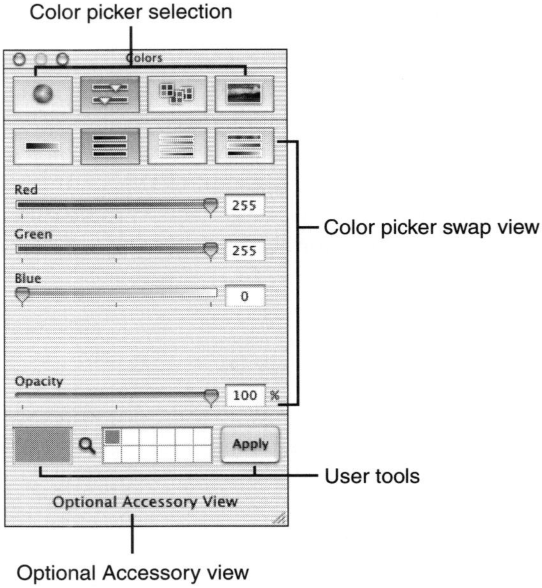

FIGURE 17.5 The anatomy of an `NSColorPanel`.

```
NSColorPanelGrayModeMask

NSColorPanelRGBModeMask

NSColorPanelCMYKModeMask

NSColorPanelHSBModeMask

NSColorPanelCustomPaletteModeMask

NSColorPanelColorListModeMask

NSColorPanelWheelModeMask

NSColorPanelAllModesMask
```

Pass the resultant mask to

```
+ (void)setPickerMask:(int)mask
```

For example, the following code would enable only the RGB slider picker and the color wheel picker.

```
[[NSColorPanel sharedColorPanel] setPickerMask:
        (NSColorPanelRGBModeMask || NSColorPanelWheelModeMask)];
```

The picker mask is usually set early in the execution of the program, often in the `-applicationDidFinishLaunching:` method of an `NSApplication` delegate. Another setting that is often initially set in the `-applicationDidFinishLaunching:` method is the support for setting the alpha transparency of colors. Alpha support is not necessary for many applications, and the default behavior is to have it turned off. If your application wants the color panel to support assignment of the alpha level, use the method

```
- (void)setShowsAlpha:(BOOL)flag
```

It is also possible to get the current value of this setting using `-showsAlpha`, which returns a `BOOL` value. It is possible to also set the initial color mode for the `NSColorPanel` using the method `-setMode:` and passing in one of the following constants (declared in `NSColorPanel.h`) as the mode:

```
NSGrayModeColorPanel
NSRGBModeColorPanel
NSCMYKModeColorPanel
NSHSBModeColorPanel
NSCustomPaletteModeColorPanel
NSColorListModeColorPanel
NSWheelModeColorPanel
```

The color panel is made visible by using the `NSApplication` method `-orderFrontColorPanel:` passing the requesting object as the sender. Applications that support color should have a Show Colors menu item under the Format menu. This menu item is connected to the first responder in Interface Builder to send the `-orderFrontColorPanel:` message. The standard Format menu on the Interface Builder Cocoa-Menus palette already includes a menu item connected appropriately. The other common way for a color panel to be presented is in response to the user clicking the border of an `NSColorWell`, which requires no action on the developer's part.

The color panel's currently selected color is accessed with the `-color` method. It returns the value as an `NSColor` instance. The current color of the `NSColorPanel` is changed with a `-setColor:` message, passing the `NSColor` it should be set to as the value.

An application can be notified when the `NSColorPanel` makes a change. There are three techniques for being notified when a color has been set using the `NSColorPanel`: a target/action can be triggered, the first responder is sent a `-changeColor:` message with the `NSColorPanel` as the argument, and an `NSColorPanelColorDidChangeNotification` is sent.

In the case of the target/action trigger, if the color panel has a target object set using `-setTarget:` and an action set using `-setAction:` then that method is called on the target object when the color changes.

If the target and action values are not set for an `NSColorPanel`, a check is run to determine if the current first responder implements a method called

```
- (void)changeColor:(id)sender
```

If it does, `-changeColor:` is called with the `NSColorPanel` as the sender argument. The implementation of `-changeColor:` can obtain the current color by calling `[sender color]`.

Finally, each time the color panel makes a change, the `NSColorPanel` posts an `NSNotification` with the identifier `NSColorPanelColorDidChangeNotification`. The notification object passed to any objects registered for this notification contains the `NSColorPanel`.

If the `NSColorPanel` is in continuous mode, which is the default, the appropriate methodology is triggered whenever the color changes, including in response to dragging the mouse in the color wheel, or as changing slider values. If the color panel has been set to noncontinuous mode by passing it a `-setContinuous:` message with `NO` as the argument, the changes are only updated when the mouse is released in the `NSColorPanel`.

Dragging Colors

Another feature of the `NSColorPanel` class is that it is responsible for providing the capability to drag colors from one user item to another. The class method

```
+ (BOOL)dragColor:(NSColor *)color withEvent:(NSEvent *)anEvent
        fromView:(NSView *)sourceView
```

makes it possible to drag a color to destination in response to a mouse down or mouse dragging. The following is a simple example.

```
- (void)mouseDragged:(NSEvent *)theEvent {
    [NSColorPanel dragColor:[self viewColor]
            withEvent:theEvent fromView:self];
}
```

This fragment from an `NSView` subclass will respond to any mouse dragging by attempting to drag the current color for this view (the `-viewColor`). The result from `+dragColor:withEvent:fromView:` is always `YES`.

Customizing the Color Panel

Like the other standard application panels, `NSColorPanel` functionality can be extended by attaching an accessory view. To do this, use the `-setAccessoryView:` method. Pass the `NSView` that contains the controls as the argument. This is discussed in more depth in Chapter 9, "Applications, Windows, and Screens," which discusses standard System panels.

Custom Color Pickers

Although Apple provides basic color picking methods, applications can also require custom color selection behavior. A custom color picker class needs to implement both the `NSColorPickingDefault` and `NSColorPickingCustom` protocols. Because the class `NSColorPicker` already implements the `NSColorPickingDefault` protocol, most custom pickers are implemented as a subclass of that class, overriding selected methods. All custom color pickers must fully implement the `NSColorPickingCustom` protocol completely. This means writing code for the following methods declared in the `NSColorPickingCustom` protocol:

```
- (void)setColor:(NSColor *)color
- (BOOL)supportsMode:(int)mode
- (int)currentMode
- (NSView *)provideNewView:(BOOL)initialRequest
```

It's also common to override the following methods in the `NSColorPicker` subclass.

```
- (id)initWithPickerMask:(int)mask
        colorPanel:(NSColorPanel *)owningColorPanel;
- (NSImage *)provideNewButtonImage;
- (void)alphaControlAddedOrRemoved:(id)sender;
```

The following sample code implements a color picker that uses Web-style color coding to create a six-digit hex color string, as shown in Figure 17.6. It is a basic reimplementation of the standard RGB slider picker, returning hex values in place of decimal values. Full code for the picker and the test harness are available at `www.cocoaprogramming.net`.

The custom color picker subclass should implement the method `-initWithPickerMask:colorPanel:`. This gives the subclass the opportunity to determine if it is appropriate with the selected color masks. The Web-style color picker requires one of the RGB color spaces to be available. If those are not available, the `super` implementation is not called.

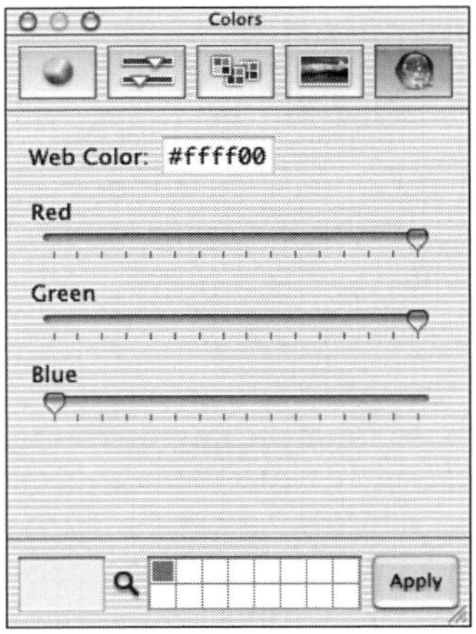

FIGURE 17.6 The example Web Color custom color picker.

```
- (id)initWithPickerMask:(int)mask colorPanel:(NSColorPanel *)owningColorPanel
{
    if (mask && NSColorPanelRGBModeMask) {
        // NSColorPanelRGBModeMask is enabled
        self=[super initWithPickerMask:mask colorPanel:owningColorPanel];
    }
    return self;
}
```

The custom color picker is asked for an `NSImage` to represent it in the color picker. To provide the image, implement the `-provideNewButtonImage` method returning the appropriate `NSImage`.

```
- (NSImage *)provideNewButtonImage {
    return [NSImage imageNamed:@"WebColorPicker"];
}
```

When a user clicks on the image button for the custom color picker it needs to return the `NSView` that should be swapped into the `NSColorPanel`. This is done using `-provideNewView:`. The argument is a Boolean that indicates if this is the first time that the view has been requested. If it is the first time, a class should load any custom nib file, or do any computational intensive preparation rather than in `-initWithPickerMask:colorPanel:`. This prevents doing any unnecessary tasks when loading the color panel initially, which could provide a significant delay if all the color pickers required loading nibs. The Web color picker implementation loads the nib with itself as the owner, causing the outlets and actions set in Interface Builder to interact with this specific instance of the class.

```
- (NSView *)provideNewView:(BOOL)initialRequest;
{
    if (initialRequest) {
        [NSBundle loadNibNamed:@"MyCustomColorPicker" owner:self];
    }
    return containerView;
}
```

Each color picker identifies itself by returning a unique value in it's implementation of `-currentMode:`. An individual color picker can also implement submodes. For example, standard color panel implementation that allows the setting of RGB/CMYK/Grayscale/HSB color modes is implemented in this manner. Each of these is implemented as a different mode, in spite of them appearing as submodes. If the custom picker supports multiple modes, it should return a unique value for the current mode when `-currentMode` is called. In addition, it should override `-supportsMode:` so that it can inform the color panel as to whether it supports a requested mode, which is passed as the argument. Finally, if it does support multiple modes, it should implement `-setMode:` to ensure that the appropriate mode is displayed. The Web color picker implements only a single mode.

```
- (int)currentMode;
{
    return CPWebColorPicker;
}

- (BOOL)supportsMode:(int)mode;
{
    return (mode == CPWebColorPicker);
}

- (void)setMode:(int)theMode
{
    return;
}
```

Only one more method must be implemented, `-setColor:`. This is called any time the color is changed in the color picker, and when the custom color picker is selected in the color panel. This provides an ideal opportunity to update the user interface to coincide with the currently selected color.

```
- (void)setColor:(NSColor *)color
{
    NSString *hexString;
    NSColor *forcedRBGColor;
    float red, green, blue;
    int scaledRed, scaledGreen, scaledBlue;

    // convert the color to calibrated RGB
    forcedRBGColor=[color colorUsingColorSpaceName:NSCalibratedRGBColorSpace];

    // break out the components, values will be between 0 and 1
    red=[forcedRBGColor redComponent];
    green=[forcedRBGColor greenComponent];
    blue=[forcedRBGColor blueComponent];

    // update the sliders to reflect the current values of the color
    // the minimum and maximum values for the sliders are set to 0 and 1
    // respectively, so they directly map to the NSColor components
    [redSlider setFloatValue:red];
    [greenSlider setFloatValue:green];
    [blueSlider setFloatValue:blue];

    //  scale the color components to the web rgb color range
    scaledRed = red * 255;
    scaledBlue = blue * 255;
    scaledGreen = green * 255;

    // update the text field that displays the web encoded value
    hexString=[NSString stringWithFormat:@"#%02x%02x%02x",scaledRed,
        scaledGreen,scaledBlue];
    [webColorTextField setStringValue:hexString];
}
```

All these methods are required for implementation by the protocols. Each custom color picker needs to interact with the various user interface elements on a custom basis. When the user interface has changed, and the color should be updated in the color picker, call the NSColorPanel method `-setColor:` passing the current color as the argument. In the Web color picker implementation the target action for all three sliders has been set to a single method that determines the color that should be set by getting the current values from the `NSSliders`. The color picker can determine the color panel that it belongs to by calling `-colorPanel`.

```
- (void)updateColorInResponseToUIChange:sender
{
    NSColor *theColor;
    theColor=[NSColor colorWithCalibratedRed:[redSlider floatValue]
                                      green:[greenSlider floatValue]
                                       blue:[blueSlider floatValue]
                                      alpha:1.0];
    [[self colorPanel] setColor:theColor];
}
```

Having created a custom color picker, it is necessary to now make it available to an `NSColorPanel`. This isn't done programmatically, but rather by creating a bundle within the application's wrapper that is stored in a directory called `ColorPickers`. The name of the bundle without the suffix should match the class name of your custom color picker. The bundle can be copied to the `ColorPicker` directory within the application wrapper by adding a Copy Files Build Phase to the project target.

NOTE

As of 10.1.3, the code that implements a custom color picker can't reside within the color picker bundle.

`NSColorList` Class

An `NSColorList` enables the storage of an ordered set of color presets, accessible by a key. `NSColorList` can replace hard-coded color values in source code, allowing for easier customization and changing of an application's user interface.

A new `NSColorList` instance can be created in memory by calling `-initWithName:` and passing an `NSString` with the name of the color list.

When an application is launched the standard library paths are searched for `Color` directories containing files ending with the suffix `.clr`. A list of the currently available color lists can be retrieved using the class method `+availableColorLists`. This list only includes color lists read from disk. Newly created `NSColorList` instances are not included in this list unless they have already been written to disk using `-writeToFile:` with the path to the file as the argument.

Color lists stored in one of the standard Library locations can be referenced by name using the class method `+colorListNamed:` passing the name of the color list. This name is the filename without the `.clr` suffix.

Another common requirement is to load an archived color list from within the application's wrapper. This can be done using `-initWithName:fromFile:` passing the name that the color list should be referred to in the `NSColorPanel` and the full path to the `.clr` file. An example of this would be

```
thePathString=[[NSBundle mainBundle]
        pathForResource:@"CustomColors" ofType:@"clr"];
theColorList=[[NSColorList alloc]
        initWithName:@"CustomColorList" fromFile:thePathString];
```

This example code loads a color list from the file `CustomColors.clr` within the application wrapper and will be referred to by the name `CustomColorList`. Localization of these files is done by putting the translated versions into the appropriate language, `.lproj`. One caveat is that the color list name that is passed to `initWithName:` needs to be localized independently by passing the localized version of the name string to the `initWithName:` method, and referring to that color list by the localized name throughout the code.

A color list is editable only if it is created within memory or is stored on the disk in a writable file. The editable state of a specific color list instance can be discovered using the `-isEditable` method, which returns `YES` or `NO`.

An application can remove an archived `NSColorList` file from disk by using the `-removeFile` method. This removes the file provided that it is within the standard Library search path and is writable by the user. Upon success, the color list is removed from the `+availableColorLists`.

An `NSColorList` that is created in memory, or read from within an application's wrapper, is not available to the `NSColorPanel` automatically. They must be explicitly attached by calling the shared `NSColorPanel` method `-attachColorList:` like so:

```
[[NSColorPanel sharedColorPanel] attachColorList:theColorList];
```

By calling the `NSColorPanel` method `-detachColorList:` and passing the color list as the argument, it can be removed from the `NSColorPanel`. Currently there is no method of preventing the user from modifying an `NSColorList` that is attached to an `NSColorPanel`, but does not reside on disk. They are always editable.

The approach for dealing with specific entries in an `NSColorList` is largely the same as working with `NSMutableDictionary`. The main difference is that keys in color lists are ordered. The method `-allKeys` returns an array of `NSString` objects with the available keys. A specific color key can be requested from the color list using `-colorWithKey:`, and can be removed using `-removeColorWithKey:` in both cases passing the key name as the argument. The `-setColor:forKey:` method behaves similar to the `NSMutableDictionary` method `-setObject:forKey:`. The one extension to the basic functionality is the capability to insert a new color at a specific index in the color list using `-insertColor:key:atIndex:`. This method attempts to insert the specified color with the key at the index provided. If a color already exists with that key, it is moved to this new index.

Summary

The Cocoa color objects offer a rich framework for working with color in all applications. Support for ColorSync technology is automatic with calibrated colors. Most applications will be able to use the Cocoa classes without modification. Some applications can benefit from the capability to customize and extend the supported color models and color picking user interfaces.

The next chapter begins to move the discussion into more advanced topic areas. It covers complex Cocoa views such as table views, outline views, and browsers.

18 Advanced Views and Controls

IN THIS CHAPTER

- NSTableView, NSOutlineView, and NSBrowser Concepts
- Table Views
- Outline Views
- Browsers
- Combo Boxes
- Custom Controls
- Toolbars
- Status Bars
- NSQuickDrawView Class

Chapter 10, "Views and Controls," discussed most of the Cocoa user interface widgets, but a handful were left out intentionally because of their complexity. This chapter covers the remaining widgets, which are NSTableView, NSOutlineView, NSBrowser, NSComboBox, NSStatusBar, and NSToolBar. This chapter also briefly touches on how to create custom controls to supplement what the Application Kit offers. Finally, a short discussion of the NSQuickDrawView class is provided. Before diving into these classes, this chapter introduces a few new concepts that permeate the design of most of these remaining user interface widgets.

Because the objects described in this chapter are some of the most complex classes Cocoa has to offer, most of the example code in this chapter is abbreviated to highlight the topic under discussion. The complete source code and project folders for all the examples in this chapter can be found on the book's Web site, www.cocoaprogramming.net. To help keep the examples simple and concentrate on the mechanics of using these complex views, most of the examples are based on the NSDocument architecture described in Chapter 8, "Application Kit Framework Overview." Additionally, all the internal data models are built using standard Foundation Kit classes instead of using custom model classes.

NSTableView, NSOutlineView, and NSBrowser Concepts

Cocoa's Application Kit framework contains the NSView subclasses NSTableView, NSOutlineView, and NSBrowser.

These views are designed to display large amounts of structured data and are usually laid out inside of an `NSScrollView` instance. For convenience, the instances on Interface Builder's Cocoa-Data palette are already wrapped in a scroll view. Figure 18.1 shows where to find instances of each class on the Cocoa-Data palette in Interface Builder.

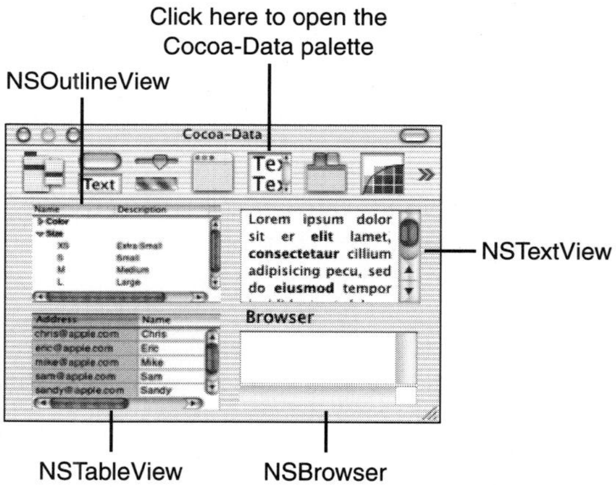

FIGURE 18.1 Interface Builder's Cocoa-Data palette.

Developers new to Cocoa often struggle with these three classes. Typically, there are two key points of confusion. First, developers should rarely subclass these three classes. Instead, a special helper object called a data source is created. This is different from the approach taken by most other application frameworks, where subclassing is the norm. The following "Data Sources" section explains the concepts behind data sources. The second point of confusion is when to use which class. The "Selecting an Appropriate User Interface" section later in this chapter gives some general guidelines.

Data Sources

When using user interface widgets, developers normally think in terms of putting data values into the user interface item. For example, if a `myTextField` is to display the text "Hello," a `[myTextField setStringValue:@"Hello"]` message would be sent to put the string "Hello" into the widget. For really large user interface objects such as an `NSTableView`, which could have thousands of items to display, this approach is extremely inefficient.

A better approach is to be aware of what items a view is displaying and only send the visible items to the view. Unfortunately, keeping track of when things need to be updated can be rather tedious. An even better approach is possible. To reduce the amount of code written by Cocoa developers, Apple has taken the idea of putting information into the view and turned it inside out. Instead of putting values into the view, the view asks for the values that it needs, when it needs them. This is sometimes known as lazy loading and is the most efficient way to handle these larger view objects.

One of the biggest advantages of lazy loading is achieved when data items are expensive to find, store, and/or initialize. For example, reading a file system's directories can be expensive. Rather than read an entire filesystem hierarchy into an object all at once, only the directories that are displayed need to be loaded. If a directory is never displayed, it never needs to be read. Also, old information can be thrown away to make room for new information. This allows for more efficient memory usage. Other examples where performance savings might be noticeable include interfaces for displaying values from databases or very large documents, such as spreadsheets.

To facilitate lazy loading, Cocoa uses a special object known as a data source. A data source is usually part of an application's controller layer, acting as a liaison between model and view. The view can ask it questions such as "How much data is there?" and "What's the data at this specific location?" The data source responds to these queries by looking up the answer inside the model and returning what it finds. The `NSTableView`, `NSOutlineView`, and `NSBrowser` classes all require a data source to provide them with information to display. Until an appropriate data source is provided, they display nothing.

NOTE

The `NSComboBox` class can also use a data source, but in this one case the data source is optional.

Data sources are conceptually similar to delegates. Just like delegates, data sources enable the behavior of a view to be modified, based on how they answer the view's questions. The Cocoa classes that use data sources also have outlets for delegate objects, however. The data source and the delegate could be the same object or they could be two separate objects. In addition, any delegate or data source can be the delegate and/or data source for more than one view.

Selecting an Appropriate User Interface

Each of the `NSTableView`, `NSOutlineView`, and `NSBrowser` classes works best for displaying or manipulating data with a particular kind of structure. For instance, data that is suitable for a table view is often not suitable for an outline view. Each view subclass also has different screen real estate requirements that will further affect user interface design.

A table view is an excellent way to display tabular data. Any data set that can be displayed as a two-dimensional sheet of cells, like a spreadsheet, is a candidate for display in a table view. Tables tend to be two-dimensional in nature and might contain a lot of data. As a result, they are generally the largest, and often the only, interface element in a given window.

Browsers are specifically meant to display hierarchical data. Anything organized in a tree-like structure, such as a file system, is a good candidate for an `NSBrowser`. The deeper the hierarchy, the better the browser is at providing easy navigation while still offering the user information about where they are at in the hierarchy. It is easy to see the path traversed to a particular point in the hierarchy. Not all browsers are multicolumn, however. A single-column browser or a single-column table view can both be used to display one-dimensional lists of items. An example would be the list of screen savers in System Preferences. Although single column browsers tend be vertically oriented like any list, multicolumn browsers are definitely horizontal in nature. If the layout of an interface can't accommodate a wide interface element, a browser element might be a less than ideal choice.

The outline view is good for data that exhibits both two-dimensional and hierarchical properties simultaneously. It can display multiple columns containing additional attributes for the item starting each row. For example, to display filesystem attributes beyond just a filename, an outline view might be a reasonable choice. Outlines are primarily vertical in nature, so they work well in layouts where this can be exploited. Consider Project Builder's Files tab on the left side of the project window as an example. One drawback with outlines is that they waste a lot of screen space when the hierarchy has many levels. Outline views can become cumbersome for the user when the data set is deep and/or very large. If the model has a deep hierarchy and the interface layout can accommodate a browser's width, the browser might be the better choice.

Terminology Used with Hierarchical Data

Both outline views and browsers can be used to display hierarchical data. It is worth reviewing some of the terminology commonly used when describing hierarchical data to avoid confusion later in this chapter. If these concepts or terms are new or unfamiliar, it is worth reading through an introductory computer science text on data structures. This chapter assumes that these concepts are already understood.

When data is hierarchical, it is commonly called a tree. Tree structures are commonly drawn from top to bottom. At the top is a single item, or node, called the root. The root connects to several nodes on the next row down, and those nodes in turn connect to nodes below them. When a node connects to nodes below it, it is called a branch node. If a node has no nodes below it, it is the last node in its branch and is called a leaf node.

A common tree structure is the family tree, as found in genealogy. It is common to use some genealogical terms for nodes in a tree. Consider any node as an example. Connected nodes below it are called its children. Connected nodes above it are called its parents. Parent and child are used to denote relationships between nodes. Therefore, a given node could be parent to some nodes and child to others. If two nodes are both children of the same parent, they are sibling nodes. Figure 18.2 illustrates this terminology as it would apply to some of the nodes in a sample tree.

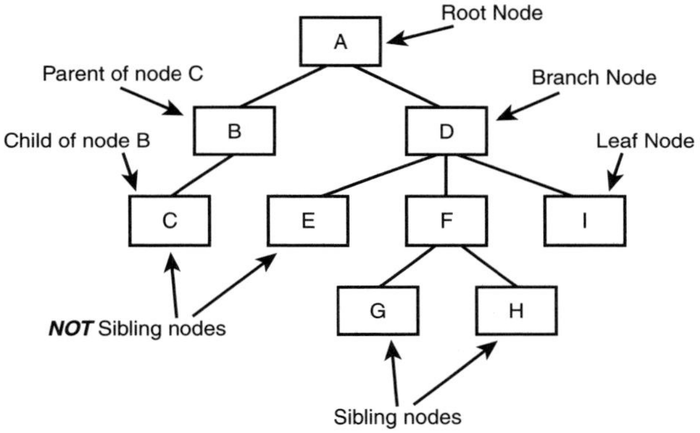

FIGURE 18.2 The terminology used in tree data structures.

The models used in this chapter place some restrictions on the tree hierarchy. Each node has only one parent, but can have unlimited children. Cycles are disallowed, which means that a node cannot be the parent of a node higher up the tree. Foundation Kit classes are used to implement all the models in this chapter. Each node is represented by an `NSMutableDictionary` instance containing its attributes. Each dictionary contains an `NSMutableArray` object that points to all its children.

Table Views

Table views are extremely complex objects. There isn't room enough in this book to list every method of the table view classes or to explain everything that can be done with table views. Instead, three examples are presented. The first example shows the basic setup of a table view and the simplest possible data source. The second example expands on the first by doing some custom formatting of the data displayed by the table view. The third and final example shows a complex data source that implements a master-detail interface.

NOTE

In a master-detail interface, a table view (the master) or other complex data-display objects display several data records. Selecting a particular record in the master causes a detail area, made of many controls such as text fields and switches, to be updated to show all the details of the record. The detail area can display extra details about the record that are not shown in the table.

One additional feature of table views is shown in a later example. In Chapter 19, "Using the Pasteboard," the master detail example in this chapter is extended to support drag and drop. These examples should be enough to demystify the table view, but they should only be viewed as a starting point.

Table views are implemented by a suite of classes that form a Facade. The `NSTableView` class is the main interface. Most developers can deal with it exclusively unless they need specialized behavior. Each table view is composed of several `NSTableColumn` instances, one for each column. This class is used when it is necessary to add, delete, or change columns. It is common to subclass `NSTableColumn` to change a table's formatting. The `NSTableHeaderView` and `NSTableHeaderCell` classes are used to render the column titles. They are rarely accessed.

The entries in the table are by default all `NSTextFieldCell` objects, often with one cell per column that is shared by all the rows. Creating a subclass to override methods in the `NSTableColumn` class can change the cell class and its formatting. The "Custom Formatting the Cells in an `NSTableView`" section later in this chapter shows how to do this.

Setting Up an `NSTableView`

The first example program shows the basics of getting a table view up and running. The finished example is named MultiplicationTable and can be found on `www.cocoaprogramming.net`. The program displays a multiplication table for the numbers one through ten. There are 10 rows and 11 columns. The extra column is for the multiplicands and its cells serve as row labels.

To set up the example, create a new Cocoa Application project called MultiplicationTable in Project Builder and open the main `.nib` file.

Creating and Configuring an `NSTableView` in Interface Builder

Create an `NSTableView` instance by dragging one from the Cocoa-Data palette into the default window. (Only a masochist would attempt to create a table view programmatically.) Figure 18.1 shows where to find the table view on the Cocoa-Data palette. Resize the table view to fill the window. Open the table view's attributes inspector by selecting the table view object and using Cmd-1. Add some columns by changing the 2 in the # Colms field to an 11. Figure 18.3 shows the table view from the example and the `NSTableView` attributes inspector. The `NSTableView` inspector controls are self explanatory, or mirror parameters seen on and described for other Cocoa objects in Chapter 10.

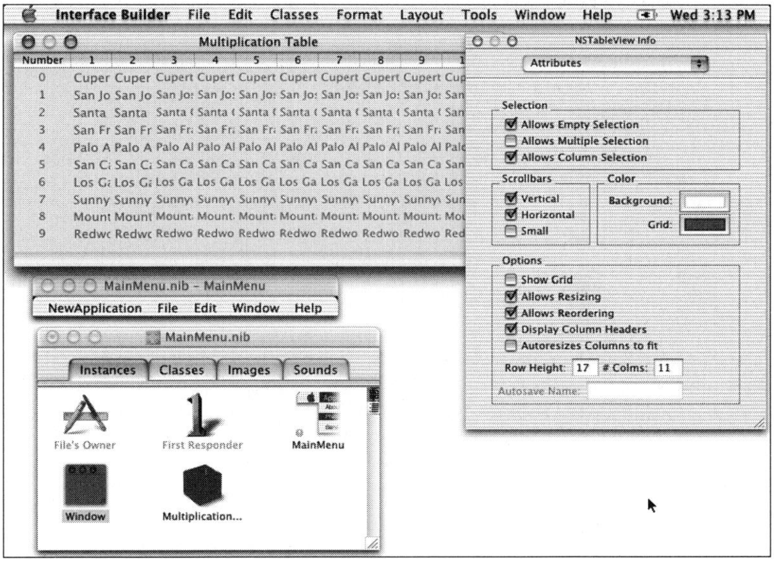

FIGURE 18.3 The MultiplicationTable example in Interface Builder with `NSTableView` inspector is shown here.

Finally, configure each of the individual columns. Double-click the table view so that the columns can be edited. Select each column, one by one. (Columns are selected by clicking their titles.) For each column, set the title alignment to be centered and the contents alignment to be right justified. Set the column titles to be Number for the first column and 1 through 10 for the remaining columns. A column's title can be modified by double-clicking a column title and modifying it directly or by changing the Column Title field in the inspector. Set each column's identifier. The identifier should be zero for the Number column and 1 through 10, matching the column title, for the rest of the columns. Figure 18.4 shows the `NSTableColumn` inspector with the column titled 5 selected.

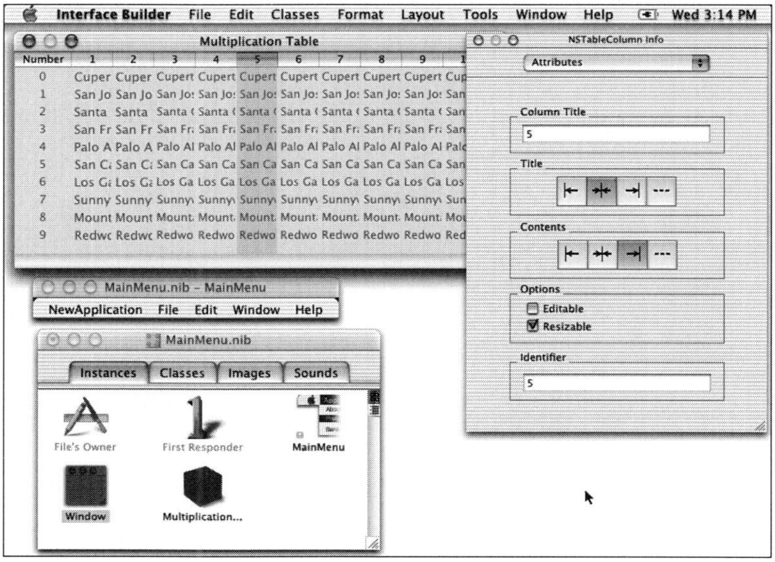

FIGURE 18.4 Configuring a table view column with Interface Builder's `NSTableColumn` inspector.

A Minimal `NSTableView` Data Source

To use a table view in an application, a suitable data source must be provided. The minimal data source must implement these two methods:

```
- (int)numberOfRowsInTableView:(NSTableView *)tableView;
- (id)tableView:(NSTableView *)tableView
        objectValueForTableColumn:(NSTableColumn *)tableColumn
        row:(int)row;
```

The `-numberOfRowsInTableView:` method should return the number of rows in the model. The table view uses this to determine its vertical size and decides which rows are visible, based on the size and position of its enclosing scroll view.

The `-tableView:objectValueForTableColumn:row:` method is called once for every visible cell in the table view. The table view uses this method to determine the contents of every cell. The data source should return the model object that should be displayed at the specified location. This method is called often, so implementations of it should be as fast as possible.

This example is so simple that no model is even required. There are always exactly ten rows, so a constant `10` can be returned from the `-numberOfRowsInTableView:`

method implementation. The cell contents can be calculated on-the-fly by multiplying the row and column together. Because row numbers from the table view will be from 0–9, the row number needs to be incremented by one before the multiplication. In Interface Builder, the column identifiers are already set to be the numbers 1 through 10, to match the column titles. The column number can, therefore, be obtained by taking the `-intValue` of the column identifier. The identifier for the "Number" column is zero, which is handled in code as a special case. The following code implements the `MultiplicationTableController` data source object.

File `MultiplicationTableController.h`:

```
#import <Cocoa/Cocoa.h>

@interface MultiplicationTableController : NSObject
@end
```

File `MultiplicationTableController.m`:

```
#import "MultiplicationTableController.h"

@implementation MultiplicationTableController

- (int)numberOfRowsInTableView:(NSTableView *)tableView
{
    return 10;
}

- (id)tableView:(NSTableView *)tableView
        objectValueForTableColumn:(NSTableColumn *)tableColumn
        row:(int)row
{
    int column = [[tableColumn identifier] intValue];
    int product = (row + 1) * (column == 0 ? 1 : column);
    return [NSString stringWithFormat:@"%d", product];
}

@end
```

Finishing the MultiplicationTable Example

After the data source code is created, parse the header in Interface Builder and create an instance of `MultiplicationTableController` in the main `.nib` file. Drag a connection from the table view to the controller and set the `MultiplicationTableController` instance to be the data source. The program can now be built and should provide output resembling that of Figure 18.5.

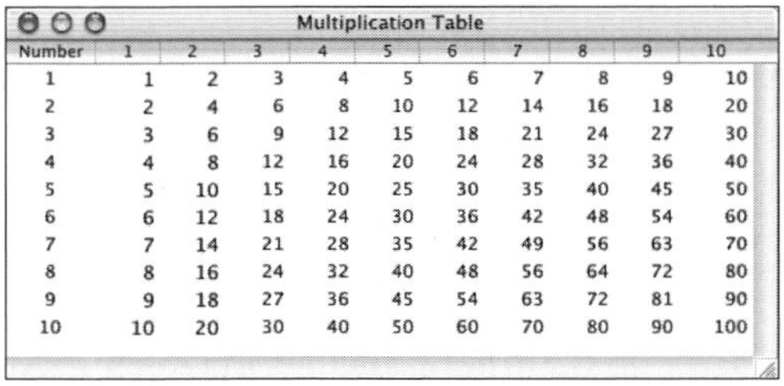

Multiplication Table

Number	1	2	3	4	5	6	7	8	9	10
1	1	2	3	4	5	6	7	8	9	10
2	2	4	6	8	10	12	14	16	18	20
3	3	6	9	12	15	18	21	24	27	30
4	4	8	12	16	20	24	28	32	36	40
5	5	10	15	20	25	30	35	40	45	50
6	6	12	18	24	30	36	42	48	54	60
7	7	14	21	28	35	42	49	56	63	70
8	8	16	24	32	40	48	56	64	72	80
9	9	18	27	36	45	54	63	72	81	90
10	10	20	30	40	50	60	70	80	90	100

FIGURE 18.5 The MultiplicationTable example.

Custom Formatting the Cells in an `NSTableView`

The next example shows how to change the way a table view's data cells are formatted. This example is a modification of the MultipliationTable example described in the "Setting Up an `NSTableView`" section of this chapter. The code for this example is found on `www.cocoaprogramming.net` under the name TableRowFormatting.

This example changes the way the table's cells are rendered. Every other row uses a light-green background for the cells instead of the default white. Every column uses a different text color, ranging from red (column 1) to blue (column 10), with the Number column in black. To make it even more interesting, the text color changes for each row, fading from black (row 1) to the full color (row 10). This is all implemented with a custom subclass of `NSTableColumn`.

Subclassing `NSTableColumn`

One way to customize the way a table column is formatted is to make a custom subclass of `NSTableColumn`. Create a new class called `MyTableColumn` and add it to the example's project. The header should look like this:

```
#import <Cocoa/Cocoa.h>

@interface MyTableColumn : NSTableColumn

+ (NSColor *)oddRowColor;
+ (NSColor *)evenRowColor;
- (NSColor *)textColorForRow:(int)row;

@end
```

Three methods can be used to calculate the background color and foreground (text) color for the cells. The `+oddRowColor` and `+evenRowColor` methods return a constant `NSColor`. The `-textColorForRow:` method uses the column's identifier and the `row` parameter to determine a text color. Some of the methods described in Chapter 17, "Color," are used to implement these three methods.

To actually change the formatting of a cell in the column, the -dataCellForRow: method is overridden. Before drawing a data cell, the table view asks the column for a cell to use in the rendering. It is possible to return a different cell for each row and column, but the default NSTextField cell is fine for this example. The overridden method takes the default cell from super, and then reconfigures the background and text colors as needed. The cell is then returned.

To make all this work, the implementation file for the MyTableColumn class should look like this:

```
#import "MyTableColumn.h"
#import "MultiplicationTableController.h"

@implementation MyTableColumn

+ (NSColor *)oddRowColor
{
    static NSColor *oddColor = nil;
    if (!oddColor) {
        oddColor = [NSColor colorWithCalibratedHue:0.3333333
                saturation:0.25 brightness:1.0 alpha:1.0];
        [oddColor retain];
    }
    return oddColor;
}

+ (NSColor *)evenRowColor
{
    return [NSColor whiteColor];
}

- (NSColor *)textColorForRow:(int)row
{
    NSColor *textColor = nil;
    int column = [[self identifier] intValue];
    if (column != 0) {
        float hue = 1 - ((float)column / ((float)TABLE_COLUMNS * 3.0));
        float brt = ((float)row / ((float)TABLE_ROWS - 1.0));
        textColor = [NSColor colorWithCalibratedHue:hue saturation:1.0
                brightness:brt alpha:1.0];
```

```
    } else {
        textColor = [NSColor blackColor];
    }
    return textColor;
}

- (id)dataCellForRow:(int)row
{
    id theCell = [super dataCellForRow:row];
    NSColor *textColor = [self textColorForRow:row];
    if (row % 2) {
        [theCell setBackgroundColor:[[self class] oddRowColor]];
    } else {
        [theCell setBackgroundColor:[[self class] evenRowColor]];
    }
    [theCell setTextColor:textColor];
    return theCell;
}

@end
```

Before compiling the code above, add the following lines of code to the top of the `MultiplicationTableController.h` file:

```
#define TABLE_COLUMNS 10
#define TABLE_ROWS 10
```

Using a Custom Subclass of `NSTableColumn`

There are two ways to use a custom `NSTableColumn` subclass. The hardest is to empty all columns out of the `NSTableView` created in Interface Builder when the `.nib` loads, and then programmatically replace each column with a new column of the correct class. The easy way is to just change the class in Interface Builder. We'll take the easy route.

First, get Interface Builder to parse the header for the `MyTableColumn` class. Next, select each column of the table view and change it to the `MyTableColumn` class in its Custom Class inspector (Cmd-5). When the application is rebuilt, it should make use of the new table column class, coloring the cells as specified for this example. (No screenshot is shown because the color changes won't be apparent in a black and white figure.)

It is time for a small confession: The TableRowFormatting example is contrived. Although it shows how to use a custom `NSTableColumn` class, subclassing is actually not necessary at all to achieve the desired result. The `NSTableView` class sends the following message to its delegate before it renders each cell in the table:

```
- (void)tableView:(NSTableView *)tableView willDisplayCell:(id)cell
      forTableColumn:(NSTableColumn *)tableColumn row:(int)row
```

The delegate has the opportunity to reconfigure the cell for each position in the table. If the data source is also connected as the table view's delegate, the data source can implement this method to color the cells instead, removing the need for a custom subclass of `NSTableColumn` and greatly simplifying the example. The TableRowFormatting2 example shows how to use the delegate method instead of a subclass.

NOTE

In both cell-formatting examples, a minor issue has been glossed over. `NSTableView` objects from the Interface Builder palette have the wrong kind of cells in them. The background color for these cells cannot be set. But columns added with the inspector do have cells where the background color can be set. The workaround used to construct the examples was to add 11 new columns and delete the original two columns so that all columns have the same kind of cell. This was easier than using code to work around the issue.

The two approaches to formatting table cells highlight the fact that there's often more than one way to get something done in Cocoa, and one of the approaches will invariably be more difficult. As a general rule, subclassing should always be avoided whenever possible. Implementing the proper delegate method works in this case.

If formatting is being done on a per-column basis, with no changes from row to row, an even simpler approach exists. By default, each table column has a single cell instance that is shared by all rows in the column for rendering and data entry. The shared cell can be changed to any arbitrary cell with the `NSTableColumn` `-setDataCell:` method. Also, more `NSTableColumn` methods are listed in Apple's documentation that can be used to make other advanced customizations.

NOTE

The TaskOutliner example later in this chapter creates a column of check box buttons in an outline view. An `NSButtonCell` is handed to one of the columns to use as the shared cell for all rows in that column. No subclassing is used to accomplish this. The technique works the same way for both outline and table views because `NSOutlineView` is a subclass of `NSTableView`.

Controlling Selectability in an NSTableView

The current example application allows any row or column to be selected. It doesn't make much sense to select the Number column, though. By implementing an NSTableView delegate method, it is possible to make the Number column unselectable.

First, drag a connection from the table view to the MultiplicationTableController instance in the main .nib file and set it to be the delegate. This object is already the data source. Now it will do double duty by performing as both data source and delegate. Complex applications might use different objects, but there's nothing wrong with using the same object for both functions in a simple design such as this example.

To control whether a table view will allow a column to be selected, the -tableView:shouldSelectTableColumn: method must be implemented. Other table view delegate methods can control selections of rows and notify the delegate of changes in the selection. To make the Number column unselectable, add this code to MultiplicationTableController.m:

```
- (BOOL)tableView:(NSTableView *)tableView
        shouldSelectTableColumn:(NSTableColumn *)tableColumn
{
    int column = [[tableColumn identifier] intValue];
    return (column > 0 ? YES : NO);
}
```

When you rebuild the application, it should no longer be possible to select the Number column.

Master-Detail Interfaces with NSTableView

The ScoreTable example on www.cocoaprogramming.net shows how to implement a master-detail interface with a table view. This example acts as an editor for high score tables. Each table row is a score entry with name, score, level, game time, and whether the player cheated. The basic interface is shown in Figure 18.6.

In a master-detail interface such as this, one user interface object acts as a master, controlling what the associated detail objects display. In this example, the table view at the top of the window is the master. The Details box in the lower half of the window is the detail. The detail changes to reflect the row selected in the table view.

This example is implemented using the NSDocument application architecture. This architecture uses the Model-View-Controller paradigm (MVC) introduced in Chapter 6, "Cocoa Design Patterns." For this example, the view portion is built entirely within Interface Builder using standard Cocoa classes. The MyDocumentModel class implements the model portion. It is an `NSObject` subclass. The `MyDocument` class implements the controller portion. `MyDocument` is a subclass of `NSDocument`.

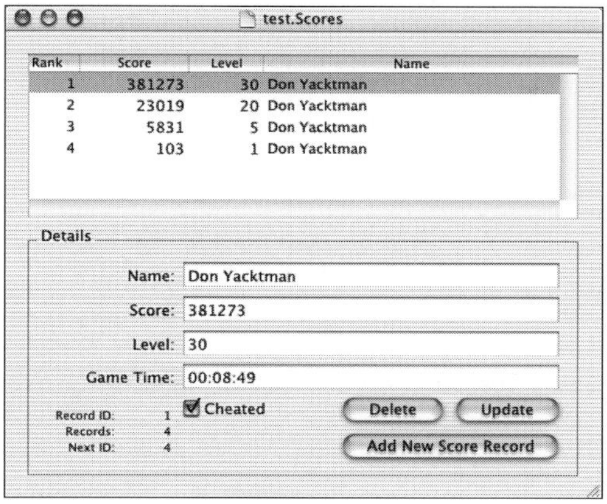

FIGURE 18.6 Master-detail interface in the ScoreTable example.

To remain relatively simple, the document model is implemented using Foundation Kit objects. Each row of the table is represented by an `NSMutableDictionary`. The whole table is represented by an `NSMutableArray` containing all the dictionary objects. As dictionaries are added, removed, and modified the array is always kept in sorted order. The model implements methods to pack and unpack itself into `NSData` objects. It also implements several accessor methods that can be used to discover various information about the model's contents. Because it only contains relatively straightforward manipulation of Foundation Kit objects, and to save space here, the source code for the model class will not be shown. Refer to the full source code for this example on `www.cocoaprogramming.net`.

`NSDocument` Methods in ScoreTable's `MyDocument` Class

The `MyDocument` class implements the controller for the ScoreTable example. It has two primary purposes. First, pass the results of user input on to the model. Second, reflect changes to the model in the user interface. As a subclass of `NSDocument`, it must implement a basic set of methods to complete the Cocoa document initialization, loading, and saving functionality. The implementations are

```
- (NSString *)windowNibName
{
    return @"MyDocument";
}
```

```
- (void)windowControllerDidLoadNib:(NSWindowController *) aController
{
    [super windowControllerDidLoadNib:aController];
    [self performSelector:@selector(updateDetail:) withObject:nil afterDelay:0.01];
}

- (NSData *)dataRepresentationOfType:(NSString *)aType
{
    return [[self model] dataRepresentationOfType:aType];
}

- (BOOL)loadDataRepresentation:(NSData *)data ofType:(NSString *)aType
{
    return [[self model] loadDataRepresentation:data ofType:aType];
}
```

The `-windowNibName` method returns the name of the `.nib` file that implements the document's user interface. A copy of the `.nib` will be loaded for each document opened. The `-windowControllerDidLoadNib:` method handles final initialization details by sending a delayed invocation of the `-updateDetail:` method to self. The `-updateDetail:` method synchronizes the detail user interface to match whatever is selected in the master table view.

The data methods implement save and load functionality, respectively, and simply forward the messages on to the model, returning the results from the model. The `-model` method returns the document's model class. It is an instance of `MyDocumentModel` and is created and configured the first time it is needed. The code for `-model` looks like this:

```
- (MyDocumentModel *)model
{
    if (!_model) {
        _model = [[MyDocumentModel alloc] init];
        [_model setDocument:self];
    }
    return _model;
}
```

`MyDocument` Communication with `MyDocumentModel`

A few methods are required to keep the user interface in synchronization with the model. An important part of that is to keep the master and detail interfaces in sync. That is the `-updateDetail:` method's primary purpose. The code for it looks like this:

```
- (void)updateDetail:(id)sender
{
    int row = [tableView selectedRow];
    MyDocumentModel *model = [self model];
    NSMutableDictionary *theRecord;

    [nextIDField setIntValue:[model nextID]];
    [totalRecordsField setIntValue:[model rowCount]];
    if (row < 0) {
        [currentIDField setStringValue:
            [[NSBundle mainBundle] localizedStringForKey:@"NoSelectionID"
                                               value:@"None" table:nil]];
    } else {
        [currentIDField setIntValue:[model recordIDForRow:[tableView
selectedRow]]];
    }
    [updateButton setEnabled:NO];
    [deleteButton setEnabled:NO];
    if (row < 0) {
        return;
    }
    theRecord = [[self model] recordForRow:row];
    [nameField setStringValue:[theRecord objectForKey:NAME_KEY]];
    [scoreField setStringValue:[theRecord objectForKey:SCORE_KEY]];
    [levelField setStringValue:[theRecord objectForKey:LEVEL_KEY]];
    [timeField setStringValue:[theRecord objectForKey:TIME_KEY]];
    [cheatedSwitch setState:[[theRecord objectForKey:CHEAT_KEY] intValue]];
    [currentIDField setIntValue:[[theRecord objectForKey:ID_KEY] intValue]];
    [deleteButton setEnabled:YES];
}
```

The implementation begins by copying attributes of the model into the detail user interface. It then disables the delete and update buttons. The update button will be enabled only after the user changes something in the detail. (There's nothing to update unless something is changed!) The delete button will be re-enabled near the end of the implementation if there is an actual selection.

If there's no selection, the table view will claim that the selected row is –1. If no row is selected, as would be the case in an empty document, this method returns without modifying the rest of the detail interface. It could have alternatively set all the detail's fields to some default values.

If there is a selection, the model's dictionary for the selected row is retrieved. The various detail fields are populated with values looked up from the dictionary that represents the selected row. Finally, because there's actually a row selected, the delete button is enabled.

The model can send two messages to the `MyDocument` class. The first, `-modelChanged`, is sent whenever the model's data changes. Both the master and detail views need to be updated to reflect the model's changes. The code for `-modelChanged` is as follows:

```
- (void)modelChanged
{
    [tableView reloadData];
    [self updateDetail:nil];
}
```

The model can also send the `-selectRecordWithID:` method to change the master's selection programmatically. This is done when a new record is added so that the new record is automatically selected by the master. The code determines which row should be selected, and then sends a message to the table view, asking it to change its selection.

```
- (void)selectRecordWithID:(int)recordID
{
    int row = [[self model] rowForRecordID:recordID];
    [tableView selectRow:row byExtendingSelection:NO];
}
```

`NSTableView` Methods in ScoreTable's `MyDocument` Class

The important part of this example is the methods that connect the table view to the model. The `MyDocument` class functions as both the data source and delegate for the table view. The required table view data source methods simply query the model's attributes, as follows:

```
- (int)numberOfRowsInTableView:(NSTableView *)tableView
{
    return [[self model] rowCount];
}

- (id)tableView:(NSTableView *)tableView
        objectValueForTableColumn:(NSTableColumn *)tableColumn row:(int)row
{
    return [[self model] stringForColumnNamed:[tableColumn identifier] row:row];
}
```

The model implements the `-rowCount` method to return the number of objects in its internal array. The model method `-stringForColumnNamed:row:` returns a string taken from one of the dictionaries stored in its array. It uses the row parameter to choose the dictionary from the array, and the column name to choose which key to return from the dictionary.

The column identifiers have been set in Interface Builder to match the dictionary keys used by the model. This makes the implementation very straightforward. The column identifier can be used without modification as a dictionary key. This also means that items stored in the dictionary that are shown only in the detail could easily be added to the table by simply adding a column with the correct identifier. This technique of using column identifiers as dictionary keys is common. That's why identifiers can be any string and aren't restricted to only integers the way that control tags are.

The `MyDocument` class also implements the `NSTableView` delegate method `-tableViewSelectionDidChange:`. When the table view's selection is changed, the controller needs to know about it so that the detail can be updated. Here's the method implementation:

```
- (void)tableViewSelectionDidChange:(NSNotification *)notification
{
    [self updateDetail:nil];
}
```

`MyDocument` Action Methods

The only other important methods remaining in the `MyDocument` class implementation are four action methods to respond to user input in the detail interface. Each of the three buttons (add, update, and delete) needs its own action message. Another action for all the other user interface elements is used to alert the document to the fact that the user has edited something in the detail.

To delete a record, the ID of the currently selected record is passed on to the model. The model will delete the record. The code for the delete action is

```
- (IBAction)deleteSelectedRecord:(id)sender
{
    MyDocumentModel *model = [self model];
    int selectedID = [model recordIDForRow:[tableView selectedRow]];
    [model deleteRecordWithID:selectedID];
}
```

To change the values in an existing record, the values in the detail and the selected row are sent to the model. It replaces the values in the dictionary for the selected row with the new values. The code looks like this:

```
- (IBAction)updateSelectedRecord:(id)sender
{
    MyDocumentModel *model = [self model];
    int selectedID = [model recordIDForRow:[tableView selectedRow]];
    [model changeRecordWithID:selectedID
                         name:[nameField stringValue]
                        score:[scoreField intValue]
                        level:[levelField intValue]
                         time:[timeField stringValue]
                      cheated:[cheatedSwitch state]];
}
```

To add a new record, the information in the detail interface is sent to the model with a request to generate a new record. By specifying an ID of –1, the model calculates and assigns a new, unique ID to the record. The only time an actual ID is specified is when the undo machinery wants to undelete a record that was deleted by the user. Undeleted records need to be reinstated with the same ID they originally had, not a new one. Here's the add action's code:

```
- (IBAction)addNewRecord:(id)sender
{
    [[self model] addRecordWithID:-1
                         name:[nameField stringValue]
                        score:[scoreField intValue]
                        level:[levelField intValue]
                         time:[timeField stringValue]
                      cheated:[cheatedSwitch state]];
}
```

The last action method is called whenever the user alters a text field or check box in the detail. If there's a row selected in the master, the change means that updates are now possible. Therefore, the update button is enabled. The code for the `-detailChanged:` action is

```
- (IBAction)detailChanged:(id)sender
{
    if ([tableView selectedRow] >= 0) {
        [updateButton setEnabled:YES];
    }
}
```

Adding Undo/Redo Support to ScoreTable

The source code for the MyDocument action methods on the www.cocoaprogramming.net Web site also includes basic support for undo. The add, delete, and update actions send the -setActionName: message to the document's default NSUndoManager so that the undo and redo menu items can be named something more intelligent than just Undo or Redo. For example, the add action sets the undo action name to a localized version of @"Add Record". After the user adds a record to the document, the undo menu item reads "Undo Add Record." The single line of code added to the -addNewRecord: action is this:

```
[[self undoManager] setActionName:
    [[NSBundle mainBundle] localizedStringForKey:@"AddRecordUndoAction"
            value:@"Add Record" table:nil]];
```

The -deleteSelectedRecord: and -updateSelectedRecord: actions have similar calls to set the undo action's name to Delete Record or Change Record, respectively.

Inside the model itself, the undo stack is given actions to undo changes to the model. The method to add a record records a delete action on the undo stack. To do this, the undo manager needs to know a message to send to reverse the operation. It also needs to know where to send the message.

The -prepareWithInvocationTarget: message tells the undo manager the message's destination. The prepare message returns the undo manager to allow for a nested message send. The next message sent to the undo manager is captured and stored for later use if the user wants to do an undo. So, inside the add record method of the model is the following line of code:

```
[[[document undoManager] prepareWithInvocationTarget:self]
        deleteRecordWithID:newID];
```

If the user later chooses to undo the add record operation, the undo manager sends the captured message. It would be as if this code had been invoked:

```
[modelObject deleteRecordWithID:newID];
```

The model's delete method performs a similar call to the undo manager to add the deleted record back to the model. The change record method sets up an undo call to itself to revert the values.

NOTE

No specific calls are needed to set up redo. The calls that set up undo also implicitly set up redo. The undo manager knows that any undo operation set up while it is in the process of doing an undo amounts to a redo operation. It handles these appropriately.

The complete implementation of undo in ScoreTable amounts to six lines of code. Three messages are sent from the action methods in `MyDocument` to set the names of undo operations. They are optional, but add a nice touch to the user interface. The other three messages are the ones sent from the `MyDocumentModel` to add undo operations to the undo stack. The undo manager handles everything else.

Outline Views

Outline views display hierarchical information as an outline. Each branch node has a disclosure triangle to indicate that it has children. Clicking the triangle toggles it between pointing right or down. If the triangle points right, none of its children are displayed. If the triangle points down, all the children are displayed.

In Cocoa, the `NSOutlineView` class implements outline views. `NSOutlineView` is actually a subclass of `NSTableView`. This chapter's discussion of table views is a prerequisite to understanding outline views. If that material is unfamiliar, it should be reviewed before proceeding.

Because an outline view displays a model that is hierarchical and not tabular, the `NSOutlineView` class has all new data source and delegate methods. These new methods are similar to what a table view would use, but are crafted to better match a hierarchical data model. There are also a few new methods implemented by `NSOutlineView`, but many of the inherited `NSTableView` methods are still used to manipulate outline views. In Interface Builder, the Attributes inspectors for an outline view and its columns are identical to those used for table views.

The TaskOutliner example from `www.cocoaprogramming.net` is referenced throughout the discussion of the outline view class. The example is based on `NSDocument` and uses foundation classes for its data model. The interface for a document is a single outline view with three columns. The columns contain a check box to indicate task completion, the task name and outline, and a description of the task. Figure 18.7 shows the user interface.

Internally, the TaskOutliner model uses an `NSMutableDictionary` for each node. The children of each node are stored in `NSMutableArray` objects. The root level of the model is an `NSMutableArray`, containing all the node objects (dictionaries) that are at the outline's top level. Besides the children array, each node also contains `NSString` objects for its name and description and an `NSNumber` for the state of the check box.

The discussion of this example doesn't show all the `NSDocument` code or the code for manipulating the model. Only code relating to the outline view's data source and delegate methods are shown in this book. Download the example from `www.cocoaprogramming.net` to see the rest of the code.

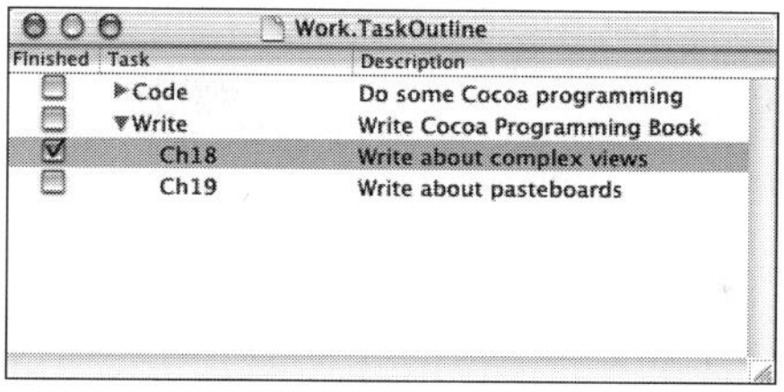

FIGURE 18.7 The user interface of the TaskOutliner example.

The Outline Table Column

Outline views treat exactly one of their columns as the hierarchical or outline column. The outline column usually displays the node's name and the disclosure triangles. All other columns are optional. Any additional columns would be used to display node attributes other than the node's name. All columns other than the outline column are standard `NSTableColumn` instances, so they can be manipulated just as they would be for a table view.

When setting up an outline view in Interface Builder, the leftmost column is always the outline column. If columns are dragged around so that a different column is moved into the leftmost slot, that column becomes the outline column. This is only a limitation of Interface Builder, however. In code, any column can be designated at the outline column. Just pass one of the outline view's `NSTableColumn` instances to the `-setOutlineTableColumn:` method to mark it as the outline column. The current outline column is returned by `-outlineTableColumn`. The `-tableColumnWithIdentifier:` method inherited from `NSTableView` can be used to find an `NSTableColumn` instance.

Another way to have a column besides the leftmost column being the outline column is to programmatically move another column into the leftmost slot. The TaskOutliner example takes that approach when setting up a new document. In the `-windowControllerDidLoadNib:` method of the `MyDocument` class, one of the columns is reconfigured to display its cell contents as a check box instead of a text string. That column is then moved into the leftmost slot. The code looks like this:

```
- (void)windowControllerDidLoadNib:(NSWindowController *)aController
{
    int checkboxColumnIndex;
    NSTableColumn *checkboxColumn =
            [outlineView tableColumnWithIdentifier:CHECK_KEY];
    NSButtonCell *checkbox = [NSButtonCell new];
    [checkbox setButtonType:NSSwitchButton];
    [checkbox setTitle:@""];
```

```
    [checkbox setImagePosition:NSImageOnly];
    [checkboxColumn setDataCell:checkbox];
    checkboxColumnIndex = [outlineView columnWithIdentifier:CHECK_KEY];
    [outlineView moveColumn:checkboxColumnIndex toColumn:0];
}
```

This code first obtains the `NSTableColumn` that should display the check boxes. It then creates an `NSButtonCell` object and sets it up to be a check box. That cell is set as the data cell for the column. All rows in that column will display check boxes instead of a text string. Finally, the `-moveColumn:toColumn:` method is used to move the check box column to the leftmost position. Because `-moveColumn:toColumn:` requires column indices and not column objects, the index has to be looked up with the `-columnWithIdentifier:` method.

NOTE

Avoid confusing the `-tableColumnWithIdentifier:` and `-columnWithIdentifier:` methods. The first returns an `NSTableColumn` instance, whereas the second returns an integer index.

`NSOutlineView` Data Sources

Data sources for outline views are similar to those for table views. The outline view keeps track of which disclosure triangles are expanded and handles assigning rows to each visible item in the hierarchy. As a result, the questions it asks of the data source are primarily about the model's hierarchy.

Instead of asking for things by row index, the outline view asks the data source about items. An item is an arbitrary object that is passed back and forth between an outline view and its data source to identify a particular node in the hierarchy. The item itself is a token; its purpose is like that of a tag or identifier in a control class. The outline view will never send a message to the item itself. The root level of the hierarchy is a special case. It is always specified as a `nil` item.

NOTE

It is common to use the model object that actually represents a particular model node as the item passed between outline view and data source for that node. Doing this reduces the need to search through the model to find nodes as the outline view requests them.

Required Methods

These four methods must all be implemented by an outline view's data source:

```
- (BOOL)outlineView:(NSOutlineView *)outlineView
        isItemExpandable:(id)item
- (int)outlineView:(NSOutlineView *)outlineView
        numberOfChildrenOfItem:(id)item
- (id)outlineView:(NSOutlineView *)outlineView
        child:(int)index ofItem:(id)item
- (id)outlineView:(NSOutlineView *)outlineView
        objectValueForTableColumn:(NSTableColumn *)tableColumn
        byItem:(id)item
```

NOTE

When implementing these four methods, it is important to take care to make them as efficient as possible. The `NSOutlineView` object calls these methods very often, so the performance of an outline view depends heavily upon these methods being fast.

The `-outlineView:isItemExpandable:` method is used to determine if a given item has children. If `NO` is returned, the node for the item in question is treated as a leaf node and no disclosure triangle appears. Returning `YES` tells the outline view that there are children and a disclosure triangle appears.

If a disclosure triangle is opened, the outline view needs to expand that part of the outline. It asks the data source how many rows need to be added for all the children of the expanding node. The `-outlineView:numberOfChildrenOfItem:` method is used to get this number.

After the outline view knows how many children belong to the node, it sends the `-outlineView:child:ofItem:` message multiple times to obtain each of the children. If model objects are being used as the items, this method simply needs to return the requested child node. The child indices run from zero to one less than the number returned previously by the `-outlineView:numberOfChildrenOfItem:` method. If the model stores its nodes' children in `NSArray` objects, the index can be used directly to find the child object in the array.

The final required method is the `-outlineView:objectValueForTableColumn:byItem:` method. This is the only method that actually puts a value into a cell in the outline view. This method is called for every row of every column, including the outline column. The return value should be an `NSString`, `NSNumber`, or other object that can be used as an argument to the `NSCell` method `-setObjectValue:`. As with the table view, the column's identifier makes a nice key for looking up information in an NSDictionary. If model objects are used as items and the model object for a node is an NSDictionary, the implementation of this method becomes trivial, as seen in the TaskOutliner example.

Required Methods as Implemented by TaskOutliner

The TaskOutliner example implements all four required outline view data source methods by using model objects as the item objects passed between data source and outline view. The model is composed of an NSArray at the root level. The array contains all the top-level nodes. A completely unexpanded outline view displays only these nodes. Each node in the model is an NSDictionary. The constant CHILD_KEY is used as a key in every node's dictionary to return an NSArray containing a list of all the children nodes.

To simplify the implementation of the data source methods, a macro is used to obtain the children array. The macro is given an item, or node, in the hierarchy with the name item. If item is nil, the root level NSArray object, named dataStore, is used as the child array. Otherwise, the child array is retrieved from the node/item itself. The code is as follows:

```
#define GET_CHILDREN  NSArray *children; \
if (!item) { \
    children = dataStore; \
} else { \
    children = [item objectForKey:CHILD_KEY]; \
}
```

With this macro, the data source methods become simple. The item is expandable if the children array exists and contains at least one object. The number of children is equal to the object count of the children array. And the child for a particular index is the object at that index in the child array. The object value for a given cell is found by using the table column's identifier as a dictionary key. Remember that the item passed to these methods is always a node object from the model, an NSDictionary. Here is the code for all four required data source methods in TaskOutliner:

```
- (BOOL)outlineView:(NSOutlineView *)ov isItemExpandable:(id)item
{
    GET_CHILDREN;
    if ((!children) || ([children count] < 1)) return NO;
    return YES;
}

- (int)outlineView:(NSOutlineView *)ov numberOfChildrenOfItem:(id)item
{
```

```
    GET_CHILDREN;
    return [children count];
}

- (id)outlineView:(NSOutlineView *)ov child:(int)index ofItem:(id)item
{
    // item is an NSDictionary...
    GET_CHILDREN;
    if ((!children) || ([children count] <= index)) return nil;
    return [children objectAtIndex:index];
}

- (id)outlineView:(NSOutlineView *)ov objectValueForTableColumn:
        (NSTableColumn *)tableColumn byItem:(id)item
{
    return [item objectForKey:[tableColumn identifier]];
}
```

Optional Methods

The main optional method for outline views enables cells to be edited in place. Most data sources will want to allow this. The prototype for the delegate method is long:

```
- (void)outlineView:(NSOutlineView *)outlineView setObjectValue:(id)object
        forTableColumn:(NSTableColumn *)tableColumn byItem:(id)item
```

Implementations of this method should use the column's identifier to determine what attribute of the item's node should be changed. In the case of the TaskOutliner example, the item passed to this method is an `NSMutableDictionary`, a node in the model, so the new object value can be inserted right into the dictionary. The method also sets up an undo action to call itself with the old value so that the user can revert the change. Here's the code.

```
- (void)outlineView:(NSOutlineView *)outlineView setObjectValue:(id)object
        forTableColumn:(NSTableColumn *)tableColumn byItem:(id)item
{
    NSString *theKey = [tableColumn identifier];
    NSString *oldValue = [item objectForKey:theKey];
    if (([theKey compare:CHECK_KEY] == NSOrderedSame) ||
            ([oldValue compare:object] != NSOrderedSame)) {
        [[[self undoManager] prepareWithInvocationTarget:self]
                outlineView:outlineView setObjectValue:oldValue
                forTableColumn:tableColumn byItem:item];
```

```
        [item setObject:object forKey:theKey];
        [outlineView reloadItem:item];
    }
}
```

Notice that this whole method is bracketed inside of an if/then statement. The change to the node's dictionary is not made if the value is a string that is the same value as what's already there. Without the if/then, the user action of entering a cell to edit it, and then exiting immediately without making a change, would cause a spurious undo operation to be added to the stack.

The actual method implementation of the `-outlineView:setObjectValue:forTableColumn:byItem:` method in the TaskOutliner example is actually a bit more complex than the code shown here because it uses more intelligent names for undo actions based on the column that was altered.

NOTE

In this implementation, the outline view is forced to reload the changed item. If the outline view is calling this method, the reload is actually unnecessary because the outline view already knows about the change and has already redisplayed the cell. The reload is needed only when the undo manager is making the call in response to an undo or redo because the outline view needs to be alerted to the change in the model.

Two additional data source methods are used to translate an item object into a persistent object and vice versa. They are required for outline views that want to automatically save persistent state data about which nodes are expanded and which are not. These features are beyond the scope of this book and, therefore, aren't discussed here. The two methods in question are

```
- (id)outlineView:(NSOutlineView *)outlineView
        itemForPersistentObject:(id)object;
- (id)outlineView:(NSOutlineView *)outlineView
        persistentObjectForItem:(id)item;
```

There are also several optional data source methods that enable drag-and-drop support. Chapter 19 presents these methods and discusses how they are implemented in TaskOutliner.

`NSOutlineView` Delegate Methods

Because outline views reference everything by item instead of by row number, the standard table view delegate methods are not called by outline views. However, many of the new outline view methods are nearly identical to the table view delegate methods, so understanding one set of methods makes the other easy to understand as well. For example, the following outline view delegate methods function just like their table view counterparts except for using an item instead of a row index and `outlineView` instead of `tableView` in the method name:

```
- (void)outlineView:(NSOutlineView *)outlineView willDisplayCell:(id)cell
      forTableColumn:(NSTableColumn *)tableColumn item:(id)item
- (BOOL)outlineView:(NSOutlineView *)outlineView
      shouldEditTableColumn:(NSTableColumn *)tableColumn item:(id)item
- (BOOL)selectionShouldChangeInOutlineView:(NSOutlineView *)outlineView
- (BOOL)outlineView:(NSOutlineView *)outlineView shouldSelectItem:(id)item
- (BOOL)outlineView:(NSOutlineView *)outlineView
      shouldSelectTableColumn:(NSTableColumn *)tableColumn
```

Two outline view-specific delegate methods can be used to restrict the expanding or collapsing of an item:

```
- (BOOL)outlineView:(NSOutlineView *)outlineView shouldExpandItem:(id)item
- (BOOL)outlineView:(NSOutlineView *)outlineView shouldCollapseItem:(id)item
```

Return `YES` or `NO` to signal whether to expand or collapse operation should be allowed to proceed.

Several notifications are sent by outline views to notify of changes in selection, changes in column position and size, and expanding or collapsing nodes. Each notification has an associated delegate message. Rather than listing them all here, refer to the Cocoa documentation for all the details.

Other `NSOutlineView` Methods

Outline views are dealt with primarily through implementing the data source and delegate methods. They do implement several useful methods, however. For example, an outline can be controlled with the following methods:

```
- (void)expandItem:(id)item expandChildren:(BOOL)expandChildren
- (void)collapseItem:(id)item collapseChildren:(BOOL)collapseChildren
- (void)reloadItem:(id)item reloadChildren:(BOOL)reloadChildren
- (void)expandItem:(id)item
- (void)collapseItem:(id)item
- (void)reloadItem:(id)item
```

Expanding an item is like clicking a disclosure triangle to open a branch of the outline. Collapsing an item hides its children. Reloading an item causes it to be redisplayed, and should be used to notify the outline view of any model changes.

The three methods that take a `Children` argument allow for recursive expanding, collapsing, or reloading of items. The other methods assume a value of `NO` and do no work recursively. To see whether an item is expanded, use the `-isItemExpanded` method.

Outline views do the hard work of tracking which nodes are expanded and mapping all the visible items to rows. To access that mapping facility, use the `-itemAtRow:` and `-rowForItem:` methods.

Indentation amounts for each row are also tracked by the outline view. To see what the indentation level is, use `-levelForItem:` or `-levelForRow:`. The indentation level is an integer from 0 on up. Pass a floating-point number to `-setIndentationPerLevel:` to set how many pixels the outline is indented per indentation level. The current amount is returned by `-indentationPerLevel`.

When the outline column is rendered, it is actually rendered with two cells. One displays the disclosure triangle, if any, and the other displays the column's contents. The contents cell is indented as necessary. The disclosure triangles can be indented or not. The default is to indent the triangles with the contents, so the marker can be said to "follow" the content cell. The other option is to have all the disclosure triangles aligned vertically. Sending `NO` to the `-setIndentationMarkerFollowsCell:` method aligns the disclosure triangles vertically. The current setting is returned by `-indentationMarkerFollowsCell`.

Browsers

Browsers present a multiple column interface and are designed to display hierarchically organized information. For example, the column mode of the Finder uses a browser to navigate the file system.

Cocoa uses the `NSBrowser` and `NSBrowserCell` classes to implement browsers. An `NSBrowser` instance is a composite of many other objects. The object itself is normally contained within a horizontally scrolling scroll view and offers the option of showing or hiding the horizontal scrollbar. Each column of the browser is a single column `NSMatrix` containing one cell for each row. The cells are usually `NSBrowserCell` instances. The column matrix is wrapped inside of a vertically scrolling scroll view. Because each column has its own scroll view, each column can be scrolled independently. By having a different matrix for each column, the number of rows can vary per column as well. Figure 18.8 shows how the various subview components of an `NSBrowser` are laid out.

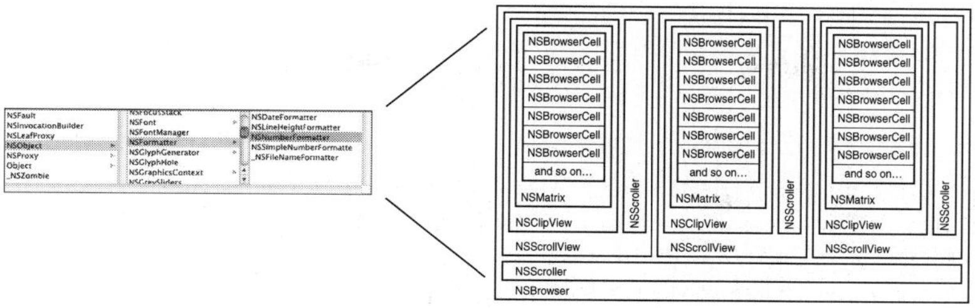

FIGURE 18.8 The subview layout used by the `NSBrowser` class.

Configuring an `NSBrowser` in Interface Builder

Because of the complexity of configuring browsers using code, they are usually set up in Interface Builder. The Cocoa-Data palette, shown in Figure 18.1, has an `NSBrowser` instance on it. Figure 18.9 shows the Interface Builder attributes inspector for `NSBrowser` instances.

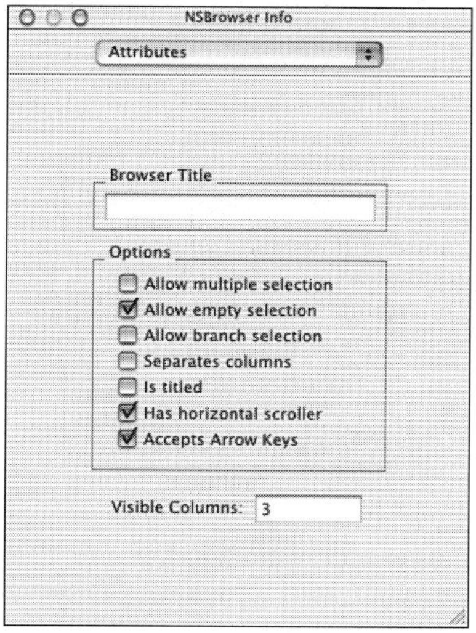

FIGURE 18.9 Interface Builder's `NSBrowser` attributes inspector.

The browser's title, if present, appears in the browser's upper-left corner. It is set in the Browser Title box, but the Is titled switch must also be turned on for the title to appear. The `NSBrowser` methods `-setTitle:`, `-title`, `-setTitled:`, and `-isTitled` each correspond to this field and switch pair.

There are three switches to control what the browser allows regarding selections. One allows empty selections, and another allows multiple selections. The third controls the selection of branches (cells with right pointing arrows) and leaves simultaneously.

If empty selections are allowed, the rightmost column doesn't have to have any items selected. Typically, a multiple column browser allows empty selections. Single column browsers sometimes require that something always be selected. The `-setAllowsEmptySelection:` method can be used to manipulate this setting programmatically. The current setting can be determined with the `-allowsEmptySelection` method.

If multiple selection is allowed, the rightmost column will allow more than one cell to be selected simultaneously. The `-setAllowsMultipleSelection:` method can be used to control this. The `-allowsMultipleSelection` method can be used to determine if multiple selections are allowed.

When multiple selection is allowed, the "Allow branch selection" switch has an effect. Although this switch is always enabled, it only affects multiple selections. If turned on, a multiple selection can include a branch node. If turned off, only leaf nodes can be selected. It is most common to allow branch selection. Consider the browser in the Finder, where multiple selections can include files and folders. Sometimes a model precludes selecting branches and leaves simultaneously, however. Use the `-setAllowsBranchSelection:` method to control this from code. Use `-allowsBranchSelection` to see what the setting is.

The Separates columns switch is sometimes disabled. If the Is titled switch is on, the browser always separates its columns. If there is no title, the Separates columns switch can be turned off to make the browser layout its columns flush up against each other horizontally. Separated columns have a small gap between them. The `-setSeparatesColumns:` method manipulates this setting. The `-separatesColumns` method can be used to inspect this setting.

There is a scrollview enclosing the `NSBrowser`. The Has horizontal scroller switch turns on the scroll view's horizontal scrollbar. There is no vertical scrollbar for the enclosing scroll view because all vertical scrollbars are handled by scroll views inside of the browser. There is a separate scroll view for each column, and each always has a vertical scrollbar that can't be turned off. Turning off the horizontal scrollbar is common for single column browsers and browsers displaying a hierarchy of a known depth that are guaranteed to have enough room to show all the columns they will ever display. Turning off the horizontal scrollbar should usually be avoided for multiple column browsers because the user would have difficulty returning to columns that have scrolled out of view. As a convenience, the `NSBrowser` class implements `-setHasHorizontalScroller:` to turn the horizontal scroller of its enclosing scroll view on or off. Use `-hasHorizontalScroller` to see if the horizontal scroller is available to the user.

Users can navigate a browser using the arrow keys if the Accepts Arrow Keys switch is on. The `-setAcceptsArrowKeys:` method also controls this and the `-acceptsArrowKeys` method returns the current setting.

All browsers created in Interface Builder send their actions when the user clicks a new cell or uses an arrow key to move to a new cell. The behavior of sending an action when arrow keys are used can be turned on or off programmatically using the `-setSendsActionOnArrowKeys:` method. There is no way to do this from Interface Builder directly. The `-sendsActionOnArrowKeys` method returns the current setting.

The final setting in the inspector is Visible Columns. This sets how many columns will be shown simultaneously and only affects what the user sees at a given moment. It does not set a cap on the total number of columns that the browser can have; the model being displayed by the browser controls that. The content area of the scroll view, whatever size it is, is distributed evenly between all the visible columns. As the browser changes in size, perhaps in response to resizing the window, the number of columns remains constant, but their widths change. The `-setMaxVisibleColumns:` method can be used to change this setting. The `-maxVisibleColumns` method returns the current setting.

The primary strength of browsers is that they offer contextual information about a hierarchy as it is navigated. Therefore, the more visible columns there are, the more useful the browser is for the end user. A single column browser should be set for only one visible column, of course, because it is really just displaying a list. Multiple column browsers should almost always display at least three columns so that there's enough navigation context to help the user keep his bearings. The exception to this rule of thumb is a hierarchy that is only two levels deep or a narrow interface such as the Open and Save panels.

Important `NSBrowser` Methods

Interface Builder lets the target and action of a browser be set. A browser can also have a double-click action, but that cannot be set in interface builder. It must be set programmatically using the `-setDoubleAction:` method. The `-doubleAction` method returns the selector of the current double click action. The double action is sent to the same target as the regular action. Double actions enable the user to use single-clicks to navigate and double-clicks to perform an operation on the selection. For example, a browser showing the filesystem would typically use the double-click action to open selected files and launch selected applications.

When a browser is first displayed, it loads up the leftmost column with the items for the root of the hierarchy automatically. There is also a method to trigger it to reload the root column. Because columns are numbered from left to right, starting at zero, the -loadColumnZero method should be used to reload the browser from scratch if a change in the model necessitates it. If a model change only affects one level of the hierarchy, there's no need to reload the entire browser. A single column can be reloaded with the -reloadColumn: method. Only that column is reloaded, so the method might need to be called more than once if a change requires children columns (those to the right) to be reloaded. The -isLoaded method can be used to determine if a browser has been loaded.

When a selection is made in a browser, it is tracked internally as a path through the model's hierarchy. Many of the methods dealing with NSBrowser selections work in terms of the browser's path. For example the -path method returns the current path selected in the browser. The return value is an NSString containing all the path elements separated by a separator string. The separator is manipulated with the -setPathSeparator: method. The current path separator string is returned by the -pathSeparator method. To programmatically set the browser to a new path, use the -setPath: method, but remember to use the correct path separator.

If the path to the selection is unimportant, any of the -selectedColumn, -selectedRowInColumn:, -selectedCellInColumn:, -selectedCell, or -selectedCells methods can be used to get the selection. Unless a browser disallows multiple selections, though, the -selectedCells method should be favored over the -selectedCell method. While -selectedCell still works for browsers that allow multiple selections, the method only returns one item from the current selection. Code that always assumes there is only one item in a selection is likely to not behave the way the user expects. The -selectedCellInColumn: method can be used to get a single path element, but shouldn't be called for the last column in the browser, as returned by the -selectedColumn method, if multiple selections are allowed. Again, in the last column, there may be more than one cell selected. When changing the selection programmatically, in lieu of the -setPath: method, a specific cell can be selected with the -selectRow:inColumn: method.

Horizontal scrolling of the browser can be manipulated programmatically as well. The -scrollColumnToVisible: method guarantees a particular column will be made visible. The -numberOfVisibleColumns, -firstVisibleColumn, and -lastVisibleColumn methods return information about what columns are visible.

A few other methods implemented by the NSBrowser class haven't been discussed here because they are used more rarely. Consult the documentation to learn about the advanced functionality NSBrowser can offer that goes beyond what is discussed here. The NSBrowser documentation is in the file /Developer/Documentation/Cocoa/Reference/ApplicationKit/ObjC_classic/Classes/NSBrowser.html.

NSBrowserCell Class

Browsers use the `NSBrowserCell` class. This cell class adds the little arrow icon on the right side of the cell. The arrow is used to differentiate between branch and leaf cells. A leaf cell is at the end of a hierarchy. It can be selected, but won't cause an extra column to be added. A branch cell, when selected, causes the next column to the right to be created and loaded.

When configuring a browser cell, the normal `-setTitle:`, `-title`, `-setImage:`, `-image`, and other cell accessor methods apply. The `-setLeaf:` and `-isLeaf` accessors are added to change or determine, respectively, whether the cell is a leaf or branch.

> **NOTE**
>
> A common mistake is to equate `YES` and `NO` with the presence of the arrow in a browser cell. The message `[browserCell setLeaf:YES]` removes the little arrow from the cell. Branches have arrows and leaves do not. If the cell should have an arrow, you should send the `[browserCell setLeaf:NO]` message.

NSBrowser Delegates

Unlike table and outline views, browsers don't make a distinction between their data sources and delegates. The browser's delegate is its data source. Furthermore, the browser doesn't ask for the string to be displayed in a cell. Instead, it passes the cell to the delegate and lets the delegate configure the cell itself. This typically amounts to setting the cell's title and flagging it as a leaf or branch in the hierarchy.

There are two types of browser delegates. A passive delegate allows the browser to manufacture cells as necessary. This is the easiest way to implement browser delegates. All the examples in this chapter use this approach. If custom cells are required, however, an active delegate would be used. Active delegates manufacture all the cells for the browser. The browser determines whether its delegate is passive based on what methods it implements. A passive delegate implements this method:

```
- (int)browser:(NSBrowser *)sender numberOfRowsInColumn:(int)column
```

The number of rows for the specified column should be returned. The browser uses the return value to manufacture the needed cells to populate the column's matrix. An active delegate should implement this method instead:

```
- (void)browser:(NSBrowser *)sender createRowsForColumn:(int)column
        inMatrix:(NSMatrix *)matrix
```

This method creates the cells for the requested column and puts them into the column's matrix. One these two methods must be implemented. However, it is illegal to implement both. A delegate must be passive or active; it cannot be both simultaneously.

This delegate method is used to configure the cell used for a given row in a particular column:

```
- (void)browser:(NSBrowser *)sender willDisplayCell:(id)cell
        atRow:(int)row column:(int)column
```

It is called for every cell that is visible. Cells that aren't visible are not configured until they have been scrolled into sight, so this method is often called as the user scrolls through a column for the first time. The implication is that showing a new column happens very fast because only the bare minimum of cells are configured when the new column is selected.

The `-browser:willDisplayCell:atRow:column:` method is required for passive delegates, but is optional for active delegates. If an active delegate chooses to configure all its cells in the `-browser:createRowsForColumn:inMatrix:` method, it doesn't need to implement the `-browser:willDisplayCell:atRow:column:` method.

Several other delegate methods described in the `NSBrowser` documentation allow the delegate to provide column titles and affect programmatic changes in the browser's selection. There are also methods to notify the delegate of any horizontal scrolling performed by the user. The details of these methods won't be covered in this book. Refer to the documentation for the specifics.

Single-Column Browser Delegates

It is easy to create a browser delegate for a single column browser. As an example, the ClassBrowser example on `www.cocoaprogramming.net` implements the `ArrayBrowserDelegate` class to display an array of `NSString` objects in a single-column browser. This is a generic, reusable class that works well as the delegate for any single-column browser.

There are two instance variables in the `ArrayBrowserDelegate` class. The first, `browserElements`, is the array of strings to be displayed in the browser. Get and set accessor methods are implemented for this instance variable. The other instance variable, `browser`, is a pointer to the browser that displays the array of values. The pointer to the browser is used in the `browserElements` set accessor so that the browser can be notified that the array changed and that it needs to have its data reloaded. The code for the set accessor is as follows:

```
- (void)setBrowserElements:(NSArray *)newArray
{
    [newArray retain];
    [browserElements release];
```

```
    browserElements = newArray;
    [browser loadColumnZero];
}
```

Two other important methods are the browser delegate methods. To keep this class simple, it is implemented as a passive delegate. That means it enables the browser object to create all the row cells. A passive delegate implements the `-browser:numberOfRowsInColumn:` method. Because it is displaying a one-dimensional array, column zero should have as many rows as there are elements in the array. Any other column has zero rows. Therefore, the method is implemented this way:

```
- (int)browser:(NSBrowser *)sender numberOfRowsInColumn:(int)column
{
    return ((column == 0) ? [browserElements count] : 0);
}
```

The other required delegate method is `-browser:willDisplayCell:atRow:column:`. This method is required to configure each browser cell before it is displayed. Because the `-browser:numberOfRowsInColumn:` method returns zero for every column other than zero, it is safe to assume that the column argument to this method will always be zero. With that in mind, the row argument is used to pick a string from the array. That string is used as the title for the browser cell. The implementation looks like this:

```
- (void)browser:(NSBrowser *)sender willDisplayCell:(id)cell
        atRow:(int)row column:(int)column;
{
    [cell setTitle:[browserElements objectAtIndex:row]];
    [cell setLeaf:YES];
}
```

The call to set the browser cell as a leaf ensures that the cell will not display the little arrow that would lead to the next column. There is only one column in this browser, so all cells are leaf cells.

Multiple-Column Browser Delegates

Writing a delegate for a full-blown, multiple-column browser is more difficult than the single column case. The browser asks for the number of rows in a given column by specifying column number. Column numbering starts at the left and moves to the right. The leftmost column is the root of the hierarchy and is column zero.

The difficulty with multiple-column delegates is in associating the column number with a particular node in the hierarchy. This process usually starts with a `-path` call to the browser. The browser's path is a string that lists every column that is traversed to arrive at the currently selected cell. A path separator string separates the elements of the path. The default is the Unix path separator /, but it can be set to anything. Code to take a path string and turn it into an array of path element strings is as follows:

```
NSString *path = [classBrowser path];
NSString *separator = [classBrowser pathSeparator];
NSArray *selectionArray = [path componentsSeparatedByString:separator];
```

The column number passed to the delegate methods can be used as an index into `selectionArray`. It is also possible to find a particular node in the hierarchy by traversing `selectionArray` as far as needed. Normally, the root column (column zero) will have to be treated as a special case. Element zero of `selectionArray` is always an empty string.

A complete example showing the implementation of a delegate for a multiple column browser is shown in the ClassBrowser example on `www.cocoaprogramming.net` and is explained in the following section.

ClassBrowser Example

The ClassBrowser example shows how to create both multiple and single column browsers in a master-detail relationship. The basic interface uses a multiple-column browser at the top of a window to browse the Objective-C class hierarchy. The class browser is the master. The lower half of the window is a detail area to show information about whatever class is selected in the master. The detail shows the class name and the superclass name in text fields. It also contains two single-column browsers. One lists the name of all the instance variables in the class, whereas the other browser lists all the methods implemented by the class. Figure 18.10 shows a screenshot of the example program.

ClassBrowser's Internal Model

This example uses two classes. The `ArrayBrowserDelegate` class has been described previously in this chapter in the "Single Column Browser Delegates" section. The `ClassBrowserController` class implements a multiple column browser delegate and manufactures the model used by the class browser.

The model displayed by the master class browser is built of standard Foundation Kit classes. For every class in the Objective-C runtime, there is a class dictionary. The class dictionary has two keys. The first is `NAME_KEY`, which points to an `NSString` instance containing the class name. The other is `SUBCLASSES_KEY`, which points to an `NSMutableArray`. The array contains pointers to the class dictionaries of all the subclasses. This structure creates a tree, with a dictionary at each node and the subclasses array defining the branches.

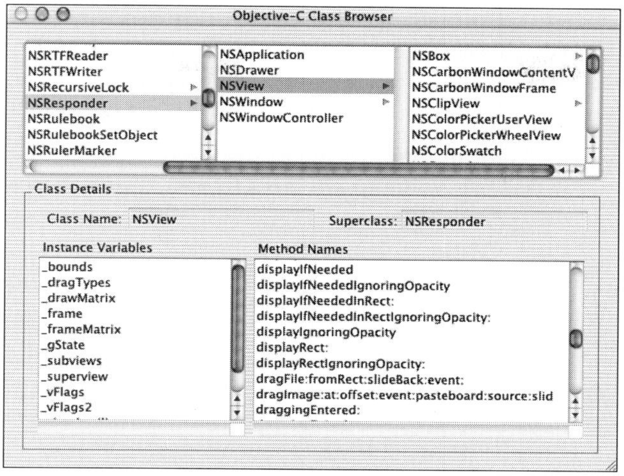

FIGURE 18.10 User interface of the ClassBrowser example.

To define the top of the hierarchy, there is a `rootClasses` array containing the class dictionaries of all root objects, or those that do not have superclasses. There is also a dictionary called `classes`, which contains all the class dictionaries referenced by using the class names as keys. This makes it easy to look up a given class without having to traverse the hierarchy. Because class names must be unique, this works well. (It wouldn't work for a filesystem where node names aren't unique.)

Walking through the Objective-C runtime structures creates the model. The code to do this isn't shown here. Appendix A, "Unleashing the Objective-C Runtime," shows example code to obtain a list of all the Class objects in the runtime. It also shows how to obtain lists of every instance variable and methods in a given class. The code used by `ClassBrowserController` to build its internal model mirrors those examples.

NOTE

One interesting aspect of building the data structure should be mentioned because the question arises fairly often. The Objective-C runtime doesn't maintain a list of subclasses for each class. It only knows the superclass of a given class. Because the model needs a list of each object's subclasses, how do we get it? To do this, the model-creation code creates subclass lists as it walks through the class objects creating class dictionaries. Each class is registered as a subclass of its superclass. One by one, objects are added to the appropriate subclass array or the root class array. After the code has passed through all the objects, the list of subclasses for every object is complete. Walking through all the objects in the runtime in this manner is the only way to get a list of all the subclasses of a particular class.

ClassBrowser Interface Builder Connections

The main .nib for the ClassBrowser example contains two instances of ArrayBrowserDelegate, one instance of ClassBrowserController, and a single window. The window contains the interface shown in Figure 18.10.

The instance variable and method browsers are each connected to their respective ArrayBrowserDelegate object. The ArrayBrowserDelegate is connected as a delegate of the browser, and the browser is connected to the browser outlet of the ArrayBrowserDelegate. The ivarController and methodController outlets of the ClassBrowserController instance are connected to the appropriate ArrayBrowserDelegate instance.

The ClassBrowserController object also has connections to the master class browser and the class and superclass text fields. The master class browser has the ClassBrowserController set as its delegate. The master class browser is also connected for target/action using the ClassBrowserController instance as a target with the action -classBrowserChanged:.

Download the ClassBrowser example from www.cocoaprogramming.net, if you haven't already, and explore the .nib file to see how these objects are connected together. Figure 18.11 shows a graph of all the connections in the main .nib file.

ClassBrowserController Model Accessors

A few methods to access the model are needed to be able to implement the browser delegate methods. The -subclassCountForClassNamed: method returns the number of subclasses that a particular class has. This is used to determine how many rows a particular column has. In the class browser, a given column shows all the subclasses of the class selected in the column to its left. Therefore, a handy way to get the count of subclasses is required. This method can also be used to determine if a class is a leaf or branch node. If no subclasses exist, it is a leaf. The code for -subclassCountForClassNamed: is

```
- (int)subclassCountForClassNamed:(NSString *)className
{
    NSDictionary *classDictionary = [classes objectForKey:className];
    NSArray *subclassArray = [classDictionary objectForKey:SUBCLASSES_KEY];
    return [subclassArray count];
}
```

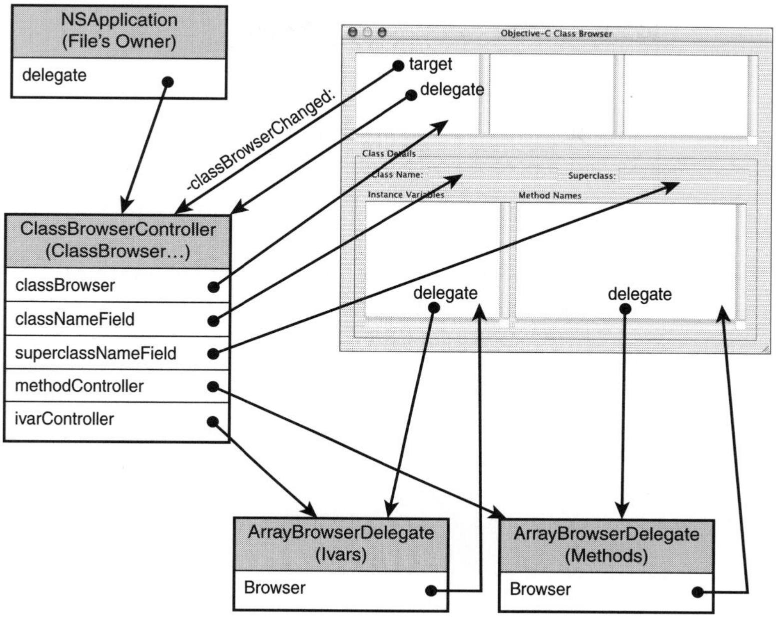

FIGURE 18.11 The Interface Builder connections use by the ClassBrowser example program.

A more complex method is used to determine the class name that should be displayed at a given row and column in the browser. To make this determination, it is necessary to parse the browser's path. The column name can be determined from the parsed path array. The column name is the superclass of all the classes in the column, so the row number can be used as an index into the subclass array of the superclass's class dictionary. A special case is made for column zero, where the row number is the index into the root class array. The code looks like this:

```
- (NSString *)classNameAtRow:(int)row column:(int)column
{
    NSArray *selectionArray = [[classBrowser path]
            componentsSeparatedByString:[classBrowser pathSeparator]];
    NSArray *classArray = nil;
    NSString *className = nil;
    if (column == 0) {
        classArray = rootClasses;
    } else if (column <= [selectionArray count]) {
```

```
        NSDictionary *classDictionary;
        className = [selectionArray objectAtIndex:column];
        classDictionary = [classes objectForKey:className];
        classArray = [classDictionary objectForKey:SUBCLASSES_KEY];
    }
    className = [[classArray objectAtIndex:row] objectForKey:NAME_KEY];
    return className;
}
```

`ClassBrowserController` Implementations of `NSBrower` Delegate Methods

Because passive delegates are simpler to implement, the `ClassBrowserController` object acts passively. Therefore, it must implement the `-browser:numberOfRowsInColumn:` method. The implementation is straightforward. Column zero is the root, so the number of objects in the root class array is returned for that column. For all other columns, the browser's path is parsed to get the name of the column. The number of rows is the number of subclasses for the class with the column name. Using the `-subclassCountForClassNamed:` model accessor, the number of subclasses is returned. The code is as follows:

```
- (int)browser:(NSBrowser *)sender numberOfRowsInColumn:(int)column
{
    NSArray *selectionArray = [[sender path]
            componentsSeparatedByString:[sender pathSeparator]];
    NSString *columnSuperClassName;
    if (column == 0) {
        int rootCount = [rootClasses count];
        return rootCount;
    }
    columnSuperClassName = [selectionArray objectAtIndex:column];
    return [self subclassCountForClassNamed:columnSuperClassName];
}
```

Passive browser delegates must also implement the `-browser:willDisplayCell:atRow:column:` method. The `-classNameAtRow:column:` accessor is used to get the class name that should be displayed in the cell. The subclass count for that class name is used to determine whether the cell is a branch. The method implementation configures the browser cell based on this information.

```
- (void)browser:(NSBrowser *)sender willDisplayCell:(id)cell
        atRow:(int)row column:(int)column;
{
    NSString *className = [self classNameAtRow:row column:column];
    int subclassCount = [self subclassCountForClassNamed:className];
```

```
    [cell setTitle:className];
    [cell setLeaf:((subclassCount == 0) ? YES : NO)];
    return;
}
```

`ClassBrowserController`'s Action Method

The final method is the action method. This action is sent whenever the user clicks a cell in the browser or uses the arrow keys to move to a new cell. The `ClassBrowserController` treats it as a notification that the class browser's selection has changed. When the selection changes, the detail needs to be updated. The very last element in the browser's selection path is the currently selected object, parsing the path and taking the last object gives the class name.

In the action method implementation, the class name and superclass name fields are updated with the relevant information. The two controllers for the method and instance variable lists are also updated. The `MethodNamesForClass()` and `InstanceVariableNamesForClass()` functions return arrays of method or instance variable names. Passing these to the `ArrayBrowserDelegate` instances cause the associated browsers to be reloaded. The code looks like this:

```
- (IBAction)classBrowserChanged:(id)sender
{
    NSArray *selectionArray = [[classBrowser path]
            componentsSeparatedByString:[classBrowser pathSeparator]];
    NSString *selectedClassName = [selectionArray lastObject];
    Class selectedClass = NSClassFromString(selectedClassName);
    Class superClass = selectedClass->super_class;
    NSString *superclassName = @"";

    if (superClass) {
        superclassName = [NSString stringWithCString:superClass->name];
    }
    [classNameField setStringValue:selectedClassName];
    [superclassNameField setStringValue:superclassName];
    [ivarController setBrowserElements:
            InstanceVariableNamesForClass(selectedClass)];
    [methodController setBrowserElements:MethodNamesForClass(selectedClass)];
}
```

With this method, the implementation of `ClassBrowserController` is complete. For the full source of the `ClassBrowserController` class, including the model creation code, refer to the ClassBrowser example on `www.cocoaprogramming.net`.

Combo Boxes

Combo boxes are a cross between a text field and a pop-up button. A combo box contains an editable text field cell and a button to the right of the text field cell. The button cell has a down pointing arrow, similar to a pull-down list. Clicking the button opens a list of items from which the user can choose a value. Combo boxes also support autocompletion as an option.

Cocoa uses the `NSComboBox` and `NSComboBoxCell` classes to implement combo boxes. These classes inherit from `NSTextField` and `NSTextFieldCell`, respectively. All the text field manipulations described in Chapter 10 apply to the text field portion of the combo box.

Because a combo box has a pull-down list from which a user can choose, it acts much like a pop-up button, a collection of radio buttons, or single-column browser. Of these user-interface elements, the combo box is the least preferred. The only time it should be used is when the user might want to be able to choose something that isn't on the preset list of items. The other selection controls offer the user a rigid set of options. Combo boxes offer that same list combined with a text field's capability to accept arbitrary data.

Although a combo box is a cell-based control, it has some additional complexity. The list portion of the combo box can be maintained by the combo box or by a data-source object. When setting up a combo box, it is important to decide early on whether it will use an external data source to manage the pop-up list. The methods that can be sent to an `NSComboBox` or `NSComboBoxCell` without raising exceptions depend on the type of data source.

Combo Boxes in Interface Builder

An `NSComboBox` instance can be found in Interface Builder on the Cocoa-Other palette between the pop-up button and the horizontal sliders. Figure 10.7 in Chapter 10 shows this palette. Most of the features in the `NSComboBox` inspector manage the text-field aspects of the combo box and work as described in Chapter 10 for text fields. Also, a few controls are specific to combo boxes. The inspector is shown in Figure 18.12.

The Options box in the inspector adds three controls that aren't in the `NSTextField` inspector. The Uses data source check box determines whether the combo box uses an external data source. If turned on, be sure to connect a suitable object to the combo box's `dataSource` outlet. The Completes check box turns on auto completion. The Number of visible items field determines how big the pop-up list is. The list has a scrollbar, so this number should normally be kept small; the default value of five is usually best. These methods can be used with `NSComboBox` or `NSComboBoxCell` to access these settings from code:

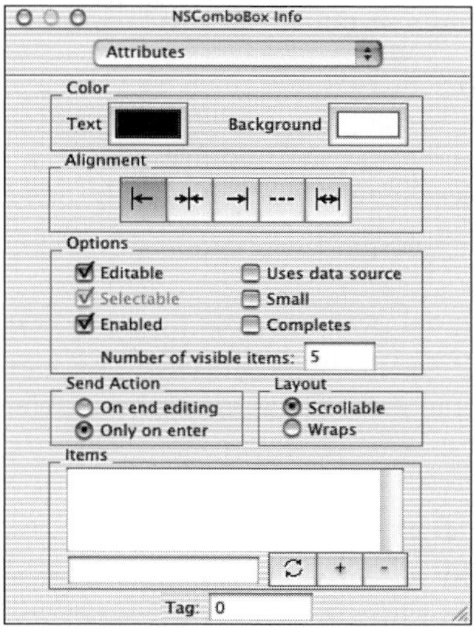

FIGURE 18.12 The `NSComboBox` inspector in Interface Builder.

```
- (BOOL)usesDataSource
- (void)setUsesDataSource:(BOOL)flag
- (BOOL)completes
- (void)setCompletes:(BOOL)completes
- (int)numberOfVisibleItems
- (void)setNumberOfVisibleItems:(int)visibleItems
```

The other addition to the inspector beyond the text-field inspector is the Items box. This box only applies if the Uses data source switch is off. This enables the list of items to be edited. Type an item into the text field and click the plus (+) button to add it to the list. Select an item in the list, change it in the text field, and click the button with the two circular arrows to change an item's value. Select an item in the list and click the minus (–) button to delete it. The section "Managing a Combo Box Item List" later in this chapter shows how to manage the list of items programmatically.

Other Combo Box Methods

A few combo box configuration options are not exposed by the Interface Builder inspector.

To get rid of the scrollbar in the pop-up list, use the `-setHasVerticalScroller:` method. Use the `-hasVerticalScroller` method to see if the scroller is present. If the user moves the mouse pointer near the top or bottom edge of the pop-up list, it autoscrolls. So a list without a scrollbar can still be useful, though they might seem unfriendly to most users.

The height of the items in the pop up list can be changed and accessed with the `-setItemHeight:` and `-itemHeight` methods, respectively. Both methods use `float` values. The spacing between items in the list is set by sending an `NSSize` structure to the `-setIntercellSpacing:` method. The `-intercellSpacing` method returns an `NSSize`.

The `-scrollItemAtIndexToVisible:` method makes sure that a particular item is found among the visible items in the pop-up list. This can be sent even if the list is not currently visible. (In that case, the item will be visible when the list pops up next.)

Managing a Combo Box Item List

The way the list of items in a combo box is managed depends on whether there is a data source. The methods for manipulating internal data sources will raise exceptions if the combo box has an external data source and vice versa. Regardless of how the item list is maintained, the `-numberOfItems` method always works. It returns the number of items in the pop-up list.

Internal Data Sources

Several methods can be sent only to combo boxes that do not use a data source. They all raise exceptions if the combo box is set to use an external data source. These methods work just like the `NSMutableArray` methods with the similar names:

```
- (void)addItemWithObjectValue:(id)object
- (void)addItemsWithObjectValues:(NSArray *)objects
- (void)insertItemWithObjectValue:(id)object atIndex:(int)index
- (void)removeItemWithObjectValue:(id)object
- (void)removeItemAtIndex:(int)index
- (void)removeAllItems
- (NSArray *)objectValues
```

External Data Sources

An external data-source object must be provided when a combo box is set to use a data source. The `-dataSource` and `-setDataSource:` methods are the accessors for the combo box's data-source outlet. Both methods will raise an exception if the combo box isn't set to use a data source. The external data source is expected to maintain the list of items by itself. When the list is changed, `-reloadData` should be sent to the combo box.

The data source is required to implement two methods. The first is `-numberOfItemsInComboBox:`. It must return the number of items in the combo box list as an integer. The second is `-comboBox:objectValueForItemAtIndex:`. The object value returned should be a standard object such as an `NSString` or `NSNumber`. Other object classes are usable only if the combo box has previously been provided with a custom formatter to deal with the class in question. Both methods are quite basic. For example, an object with a list of `NSString` instances inside the `NSMutableArray` `itemArray` could implement these two methods like this:

```
- (int)numberOfItemsInComboBox:(NSComboBox *)aComboBox
{
    return [itemArray count];
}

- (id)comboBox:(NSComboBox *)aComboBox objectValueForItemAtIndex:(int)index
{
    return [itemArray objectAtIndex:index];
}
```

NOTE

Two other optional data-source methods exist. They aren't discussed here because they are rarely needed. The primary function of these extra methods is to speed up searches through the list of items when doing autocompletion. Autocompletion works fine without them, however. For most lists, the simple linear search done by `NSComboBox` is fast enough.

Selecting an Item Programmatically

The `-selectItemAtIndex:`, `-deselectItemAtIndex:`, and `-indexOfSelectedItem` methods deal with the selection in a combo box. These only affect the pop-up list portion of the object. They do not change the value of the text field portion. Conversely, the `-setStringValue:` and other value setting methods don't change the selection in the combo-box list.

To make it easier to change both simultaneously, use the `SetAndSelect` category to `NSComboBox` and `NSComboBoxCell`. The code is as follows:

File `NSComboBox+SetAndSelect.h`:

```
@interface NSComboBoxCell(SetAndSelect)

- (void)setAndSelectStringValue:(id)stringValue;
- (void)setAndSelectItemAtIndex:(int)index;
```

```
@end

@interface NSComboBox(SetAndSelect)

- (void)setAndSelectStringValue:(id)stringValue;
- (void)setAndSelectItemAtIndex:(int)index;

@end
```

File NSComboBox+SetAndSelect.m:

```
@implementation NSComboBoxCell(SetAndSelect)

- (void)setAndSelectStringValue:(id)stringValue
{
    [self setStringValue:stringValue];
    [self selectItemWithObjectValue:stringValue];
}

- (void)setAndSelectItemAtIndex:(int)index
{
    id objectValue;
    if ([self usesDataSource]) {
        int selectedIndex;
        id ds = [self dataSource];
        [self selectItemAtIndex:index];
        selectedIndex = [self indexofSelectedItem];
        objectValue = [ds comboBox:self
                objectValueForItemAtIndex:selectedIndex];
        [self setObjectValue:objectValue];
    } else {
        [self selectItemAtIndex:index];
        objectValue = [self objectValueOfSelectedItem];
        [self setObjectValue:objectValue];
    }
}

@end

@implementation NSComboBox(SetAndSelect)
```

```
- (void)setAndSelectItemAtIndex:(int)index
{ // pass it through to the cell object
    [[self cell] setAndSelectItemAtIndex:index];
}

- (void)setAndSelectStringValue:(id)stringValue
{ // pass it through to the cell object
    [[self cell] setAndSelectStringValue:stringValue];
}

@end
```

This category adds the `-setAndSelectStringValue:` and `-setAndSelectItemAtIndex:` methods to `NSComboBoxCell`. Both methods are implemented so that they work correctly for both internal and external data sources. A parallel category adds the same methods to `NSComboBox`, but implements them to call the cell's counterpart methods. For most controls, the cell does all the work, so the methods on the `NSControl` subclass just forward the message to the cell.

Combo Box Delegate Methods

Combo boxes can have delegates. The delegates will be warned when the combo box list is about to appear or disappear. Delegates are also notified of any change in the selection. The following four methods are sent to delegates that implement them:

```
- (void)comboBoxWillPopUp:(NSNotification *)notification
- (void)comboBoxWillDismiss:(NSNotification *)notification
- (void)comboBoxSelectionDidChange:(NSNotification *)notification
- (void)comboBoxSelectionIsChanging:(NSNotification *)notification
```

Custom Controls

Cocoa offers a rich set of user interface controls. Even so, there are times when a custom control is desired. Usually, the controls provided in Cocoa are sufficient if enough creativity is employed. New kinds of controls can be confusing to users, so they should be avoided unless absolutely necessary.

Much of the time it is possible to subclass an existing control, making just a minor alteration in the standard behavior. Because each control is a little different, it is beyond the scope of this book to show the subtle details of how to subclass every kind of control. Instead, an example of subclassing the `NSControl` and `NSActionCell` classes directly is shown. The techniques used in the example show more about the internals of controls and provide a starting point for working with the other classes. Subclassers should also study the Cocoa documentation provided by Apple. Space limitations prevent this discussion from covering every option available.

The PieWidget example on www.cocoaprogramming.net shows how to create a simple pie widget. Visually, the object is a circle. The value, representing an angle, is displayed by drawing a pie-shaped wedge. Figure 18.13 shows the user interface of the completed example.

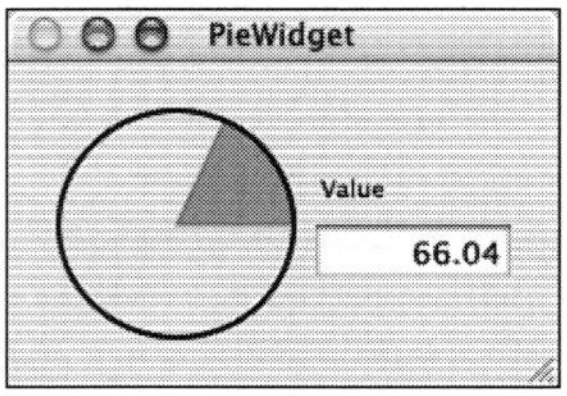

FIGURE 18.13 The user interface of the PieWidget example.

The user interface is built in Interface Builder. Use a CustomView object off the Interface Builder Cocoa-Containers palette as a stand-in for the PieWidget object. After the source code is part of the project, parse the `PieWidget.h` file and set the custom view to the `PieWidget` class. Only two custom connections are in the `.nib` file. The text field and the pie widget are each other's target, and each sends the `-takeDoubleValueFrom:` action message. This way a change in the value of either the text field or the pie causes the other object to change its value to match.

Subclassing `NSControl`

When subclassing `NSControl`, the one thing that absolutely must be done is to specify what cell subclass the control uses. This is done by overriding the `+cellClass` method to return the desired cell class object. In the case of the PieWidget, the cell subclass is `PieWidgetCell`. The code, therefore, looks like this:

```
+ (Class)cellClass
{
    return [PieWidgetCell class];
}
```

The `NSControl` subclass should also implement methods that mirror any methods the cell subclass adds to `NSCell` and/or `NSActionCell`. This allows other programmers to send messages to the control or the cell without having to know which kind of object they have. These are called cover methods because they simply pass the message on to the control's cell and return anything the cell returns. The

PieWidgetCell doesn't implement anything special, so no cover methods are needed.

The final thing to add to the control subclass is overrides of any NSView or NSResponder methods. The default implementations provided by NSControl are surprisingly rich, so normally very few methods actually need to be overridden. Because the PieWidget behaves like a slider, it does need to override the -acceptsFirstMouse: method, like this:

```
- (BOOL)acceptsFirstMouse:(NSEvent *)theEvent
{
    return YES;
}
```

That's all the code there is in the PieWidget class. There are no added instance variables, and only two one-line methods. The PieWidgetCell class does all the real work. In most control/cell pairings, this is the case.

Subclassing NSCell

A custom cell subclass typically has two primary functions. First, it needs to draw itself. Second, it needs to handle user events. If a custom cell is to participate in target/action, NSActionCell should be subclassed instead of NSCell.

Cells that hold a value need to add one or more instance variables to maintain the value. Accessor methods also need to be written. In the case of the PieWidgetCell, the value is an angle in degrees, so an instance variable name value of type double is declared in the class. The basic accessors for this are

```
- (double)doubleValue
{
    return value;
}

- (void)setDoubleValue:(double)aDouble
{
    value = aDouble;
    [[self controlView] setNeedsDisplay:YES];
}
```

Accessors that use the float type, int type, and NSString objects are also implemented in the example code, but they are not shown here. There is no need to implement methods such as -takeDoubleValueFrom: because the NSCell implementations do the right thing.

Initialization of Custom Cells

Cells have two designated initializers. Certain cells generally favor one over the other. The two methods are

```
- (id)initImageCell:(NSImage *)image
- (id)initTextCell:(NSString *)aString
```

It is wise to provide a sane implementation of both methods so that things work well, no matter which method is called. The `-init` method should also be overridden to call one of the designated initializers. The `-init` method is used by a control subclass to set up its cell, so an implementation that calls the designated initializer is necessary.

The `PieWidgetCell` class is set up from the `PieWidget` class using a call to `-init`. The `PieWidgetCell` class implements all three methods. They aren't shown here because they don't do very much beyond setting the control's `double` value to 0.0.

Custom Drawing in Cells

Most custom cells need to do custom drawing. Two methods can be overridden. The `-drawWithFrame:inView:` method is used to draw the entire cell. If the custom drawing needs to control everything, including borders around the cell, this is the method to override. If just the cell's contents are special, the `-drawInteriorWithFrame:inView:` method can be overridden instead. It is only meant to draw the inner contents of the cell.

The `PieWidgetCell` overrides the `-drawInteriorWithFrame:inView:` method. The code is as follows:

```
- (void)drawInteriorWithFrame:(NSRect)cellFrame inView:(NSView *)controlView
{
    NSBezierPath *path = [NSBezierPath bezierPath];
    NSRect drawFrame = cellFrame;
    double theAngle = [self doubleValue];

    theAngle = in360(theAngle);
    if (cellFrame.size.width > cellFrame.size.height) {
        drawFrame.size.width = cellFrame.size.height;
    }
    if (cellFrame.size.height > cellFrame.size.width) {
        drawFrame.size.height = cellFrame.size.width;
    }
    drawFrame = NSInsetRect(drawFrame, 1.0, 1.0);
    center = NSMakePoint(cellFrame.size.width / 2.0 + cellFrame.origin.x,
                         cellFrame.size.height / 2.0 + cellFrame.origin.y);
    radius = center.x - 1.0;
```

```
    [[[self class] _fillColor] set];
    [path setLineWidth:1.0];
    [path moveToPoint:center];
    [path appendBezierPathWithArcWithCenter:center radius:radius
            startAngle:0.0 endAngle:theAngle clockwise:NO];
    [path closePath];
    [path fill];

    [[[self class] _borderColor] set];
    [path setLineWidth:1.0];
    [path moveToPoint:center];
    [path appendBezierPathWithArcWithCenter:center radius:radius
            startAngle:0.0 endAngle:theAngle clockwise:NO];
    [path closePath];
    [path stroke];
    [path removeAllPoints];

    [[NSColor blackColor] set];
    [path setLineWidth:2.0];
    [path appendBezierPathWithOvalInRect:drawFrame];
    [path stroke];
}
```

The variables radius and center are instance variables of the double and `NSPoint` types, respectively. They are both used by the event methods to cache information about the cell's geometry. This method takes the cell's current value and geometry and uses that information to calculate its center, radius, and angle for drawing the pie wedge. An `NSBezierPath` object is used to do all the drawing.

Custom Event Handling in Cells

Event handling inside of a cell is handled by a tracking loop. The method that implements the tracking loop has this prototype:

```
- (BOOL)trackMouse:(NSEvent *)theEvent inRect:(NSRect)cellFrame
        ofView:(NSView *)controlView untilMouseUp:(BOOL)flag
```

The `-trackMouse:inRect:ofView:untilMouseUp:` method is called by the cell's view when a mouse-down event occurs within the cell's bounds. It sets up a loop to read mouse events until a mouse-up event occurs. Through the process, the following three methods are called:

```
- (BOOL)startTrackingAt:(NSPoint)startPoint inView:(NSView *)controlView
- (BOOL)continueTracking:(NSPoint)lastPoint at:(NSPoint)currentPoint
```

```
        inView:(NSView *)controlView
- (void)stopTracking:(NSPoint)lastPoint at:(NSPoint)stopPoint
        inView:(NSView *)controlView mouseIsUp:(BOOL)flag
```

These three methods are the ones that should be overridden to customize a cell's behavior. It is normal to call the super implementations of these methods when overriding them.

The `-startTrackingAt:inView:` method is sent when the initial mouse-down is received. The point where the mouse-down occurred and the cell's view object are sent as parameters. This method should handle anything that needs to be taken care of when the mouse-down occurs, such as becoming the first responder. The super implementation returns `NO` if the cell isn't configured to deal with mouse drags, or is not continuous. If `NO` is returned, this is the only event-handling message that is sent.

The `PieWidgetCell` implementation claims first-responder status for the control. It also sets a new value for the cell based on the location where the mouse-down occurred. By calling the `super` implementation from `NSActionCell`, the cell's action is sent. Here is the code:

```
- (BOOL)startTrackingAt:(NSPoint)startPoint inView:(NSView *)controlView
{
    BOOL ret = [super startTrackingAt:startPoint inView:controlView];
    float theAngle = angle(startPoint.x - center.x, startPoint.y - center.y);
    NSView *cv = [self controlView];
    [[cv window] makeFirstResponder:cv];
    [self setDoubleValue:theAngle];
    return ret;
}
```

Every time the mouse moves during the tracking loop, the `-continueTracking:at:inView:` method is sent. This method provides the point from the previous event as well as the current event's point. As with the start of tracking, `NSActionCell` subclasses can call the `super` implementation so that the cell's action is sent. Returning `NO` ends the tracking loop. The `PieWidgetCell` implementation changes the cell's value:

```
- (BOOL)continueTracking:(NSPoint)lastPoint at:(NSPoint)currentPoint
        inView:(NSView *)controlView
{
    BOOL ret = [super continueTracking:lastPoint
            at:currentPoint inView:controlView];
    float theAngle = angle(currentPoint.x - center.x,
            currentPoint.y - center.y);
```

```
    [self setDoubleValue:theAngle];
    return ret;
}
```

When the mouse exits the cell's boundaries or a mouse-up is received, the tracking ends. The `-stopTracking:at:inView:mouseIsUp:` message is sent at that time. As with the continue messages, the previous and current points are provided. Calling the `super` implementation in an `NSActionCell` subclass causes the cell's action to be sent.

The mouse-up flag can be used to determine why the tracking ended. If it is `YES`, the mouse-up event was received. If the mouse hasn't been released, and is dragged back within the bounds of the cell, the tracking starts all over again with the start message. Overriding the `+prefersTrackingUntilMouseUp` to return `YES` alters the tracking behavior so that the tracking never ends until the mouse is released.

The `PieWidgetCell` class overrides the stop method to set the cell's value. The code is

```
- (void)stopTracking:(NSPoint)lastPoint at:(NSPoint)stopPoint
        inView:(NSView *)controlView mouseIsUp:(BOOL)flag
{
    float theAngle = angle(stopPoint.x - center.x, stopPoint.y - center.y);
    [self setDoubleValue:theAngle];
    [super stopTracking:lastPoint at:stopPoint
            inView:controlView mouseIsUp:flag];
}
```

To get a cell to handle a complete tracking loop all the way until mouse-up, some of the cell's default settings need to be changed when the cell is initialized. In particular, the cell needs to know that it is interested in handling mouse drags, and it needs to know when to send actions. The `PieWidgetCell` class implements the following method, which is called from the `-init` methods:

```
- (void)_setup
{
    [self setDoubleValue:0.0];
    [self setShowsFirstResponder:YES];
    _cFlags.actOnMouseDragged = YES;
    _cFlags.actOnMouseDown = YES;
    _cFlags.dontActOnMouseUp = NO;
    _cFlags.refusesFirstResponder = NO;
    [self setContinuous:YES];
}
```

Control Tint

Mac OS X supports two user-selectable tinting schemes for Aqua controls, blue and graphite. Blue is the default. Graphite is a nearly, but not quite, grayscale color scheme. Custom controls should attempt to draw themselves according to the user selected color scheme. The `PieWidget` class is designed to do this. The class methods `+_borderColor` and `+_fillColor` return the two main colors used to render the cell. The current tint setting is determined by using the following code:

```
int tint = [[NSUserDefaults standardUserDefaults]
        integerForKey:@"AppleAquaColorVariant"];
```

The value of `tint` is 6 for graphite and 1 for blue. The code in `PieWidgetCell` uses the graphite color scheme if `tint` is 6 and defaults to blue for any other value. (There do not seem to be any constants in the Cocoa headers for these values as of Mac OS X 10.1.) The code for the `PieWidgetCell` color handling isn't shown here, but it can be found on `www.cocoaprogramming.net`. The full example caches the color values the first time they are requested so that they can be looked up quickly thereafter.

When the user changes the tint in Preferences, the `NSControlTintDidChangeNotification` notification is sent inside every Cocoa application on the system. The `PieWidgetCell` class object receives this notification and resets its drawing colors to match the new tint setting. If the drawing colors aren't cached, there is no need for the control itself to receive this notification. Cocoa ensures that all windows and controls are redisplayed automatically whether they listen to the notification or not.

Toolbars

Toolbars in Cocoa are strips of controls that can be used as shortcuts. A toolbar can display its items as a text menu or as a graphical item. Items that don't fit across the window are put into an overflow menu accessed by a right-pointing double arrow at the right edge of the toolbar. Toolbars are displayed in a strip across the top of the window, just under the title bar, and are managed by the window itself.

The `NSToolbar` class implements a toolbar, and the `NSToolbarItem` class implements the individual items in a toolbar. A toolbar item normally acts like a borderless button, sending an action message when it is clicked. This kind of item needs to be assigned an image, title, target, and action. Toolbar items can also be configured to contain any custom view or control instead. Subclassing `NSToolbar` and `NSToolbarItem` is very rare. Both classes are flexible so customization can be done by calling instance methods instead of through subclassing. Custom code is concentrated in the toolbar's delegate.

All toolbars require a delegate to function. The delegate actually acts as a delegate and a data source. Several methods must be implemented before an object can be used as an `NSToolbar` delegate. As of the April 2002 developer tools release, Interface Builder doesn't support creation or modification of toolbars. Toolbars are set up completely in code, primarily in the delegate implementation.

The ToolbarExample on `www.cocoaprogramming.net` shows the basics of setting up a toolbar in an `NSDocument`-based application. It demonstrates the creation of a toolbar delegate. It also shows how to create an `NSToolbarItem` that uses a custom view class. In this case, the `PieWidget` control developed in the "Custom Controls" section of this chapter is embedded in the toolbar. Figure 18.14 shows a document window with the toolbar and pie widget.

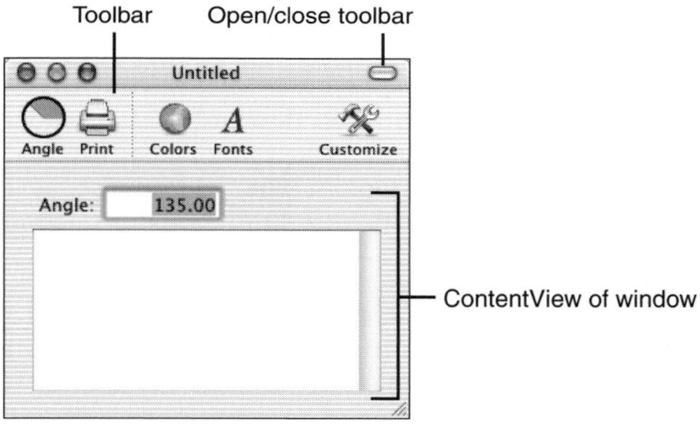

FIGURE 18.14 A document window with its toolbar visible.

`NSToolbar` Class

The `NSToolbar` class implements the toolbar itself. It must have a proper delegate to function correctly. Most of the interaction with `NSToolbar` instances takes place when it is initially set up. The "Toolbar Setup" later in this chapter section describes the methods commonly called when configuring a new toolbar instance. The "Other `NSToolbar` methods" section covers other available toolbar methods.

Toolbar Setup

The first step in setting up a toolbar is to determine which object will perform as the toolbar's delegate. Any object in the controller layer is appropriate. In an `NSDocument`-based application, it is most convenient for the `NSDocument` subclass to be the toolbar's delegate. Some object, usually the delegate, needs to implement some method that can be called to create the toolbar and attach it to the window. In the ToolbarExample code, the `MyDocument` class implements `-initializeToolbar` and calls it from the `-windowControllerDidLoadNib:` method.

The toolbar creation method needs to create a new toolbar instance, set basic toolbar attributes, set the toolbar's delegate, and attach the toolbar to the window.

A new toolbar is initialized with the `-initWithIdentifier:` method. Identifiers for toolbars are a little different from identifiers for other controls. Most controls use them as a unique way to identify the control. Toolbars use identifiers as a means of determining the toolbar's type. Often, many instances of `NSToolbar` within a single application have the same identifier. All toolbars that have the same identifier are automatically kept in sync across the entire application. The identifier is also used for autosaving a toolbar's configuration. As a result, all toolbars for a particular kind of document should use the same identifier. The `-identifier` method will return a toolbar's identifier. There is no way to change the identifier after initialization.

The delegate object is accessed with the standard `-setDelegate:` and `-delegate` accessor methods. The `-setAllowsUserCustomization:` method can be used to allow or disallow customization of the toolbar. The `-allowsUserCustomization` method returns the current setting. In most cases, this should be enabled to provide the greatest flexibility to the user.

The toolbar's configuration can be automatically saved in user preferences. The `-setAutosavesConfiguration:` method controls autosaving. The `-autosavesConfiguration` method returns the current setting. Autosaving is normally the easiest way to save and restore configuration information. It's not usually worth the trouble to turn off autosaving, but those who insist on doing things the hard way have the option to do so. The class documentation describes how to access the configuration dictionary for manual save and restore of this information.

The toolbar's display mode determines whether the toolbar items are displayed as icons, text, or icons with text. It can be controlled programmatically with the `-setDisplayMode:` method. The `-displayMode` method returns the current setting. Both of these methods can work with one of four constants: `NSToolbarDisplayModeDefault`, `NSToolbarDisplayModeIconAndLabel`, `NSToolbarDisplayModeIconOnly`, and `NSToolbarDisplayModeLabelOnly`.

After a toolbar has been created and is ready to be used, it must be attached to a window. The `NSWindow` method `-setToolbar:` is used to assign a toolbar to a window. The toolbar initialization code in ToolbarExample's `MyDocument` class creates a toolbar, configures it, and attaches it to the document's window. It looks like this:

```
- (void)initializeToolbar
{
```

```
    NSToolbar *toolbar = [[NSToolbar alloc]
            initWithIdentifier:MyDocumentToolbarIdentifier];
    [toolbar setAllowsUserCustomization:YES];
    [toolbar setAutosavesConfiguration:YES];
    [toolbar setDisplayMode:NSToolbarDisplayModeIconOnly];
    [toolbar setDelegate:self];
    [[self window] setToolbar:toolbar];
    [toolbar release];
}
```

Other `NSToolbar` Methods

A few other methods implemented by `NSToolbar` might come in handy.

The `-setVisible:` method shows or hides the toolbar as if the user had clicked the lozenge at the upper right of a window that has a toolbar. The current state can be determined with `-isVisible`. The customization palette is brought up by calling the `-runCustomizationPalette:` action method. The `-customizationPaletteIsRunning` method returns `YES` when the palette is in use.

The toolbar items can also be manipulated and reconfigured programmatically. Remember that changes to a toolbar are automatically propagated to all other toolbars with the same identifier. The `-items` and `-visibleItems` methods return immutable arrays listing the toolbar items. All items are returned with `-items`. If items have spilled off the toolbar because it isn't wide enough to display them all, the `-visibleItems` method returns a list omitting the items that have spilled off the right side of the toolbar.

Items can be removed with the `-removeItemAtIndex:` method. The index should match with the item's index in the `-items` array. New items are added with the `-insertItemWithItemIdentifier:atIndex:` method. It is important to realize that an identifier for the item is passed to this method, but not an actual `NSToolbarItem` instance. The toolbar always uses its delegate to create the actual toolbar item.

Configuring `NSToolbarItem` Instances

Before describing how to implement a delegate for the `NSToolbar` class, it is necessary to explain how to configure `NSToolbarItem` objects. This is because the toolbar delegate is required to create and configure toolbar items.

Toolbar items are initialized by specifying their identifier with the `-initWithItemIdentifier:` method. Several predefined identifiers exist, as shown in Table 18.1. Toolbar items other than those in the table require the developer to define their own identifiers. An item's identifier is returned by the `-itemIdentifier` method. After the item has been added to a toolbar, the toolbar containing the item is returned by the `-toolbar` method.

TABLE 18.1 Standard Toolbar Item Identifiers

Constant	Item Description
`NSToolbarSeparatorItemIdentifier`	Draws a thin vertical separator line.
`NSToolbarSpaceItemIdentifier`	Draws a fixed size gap between items.
`NSToolbarFlexibleSpaceItemIdentifier`	Draws a variable-sized gap that will use up any available space in the toolbar. Items to the right of this item are pushed to the right edge of the toolbar.
`NSToolbarShowColorsItemIdentifier`	Shows the standard color panel.
`NSToolbarShowFontsItemIdentifier`	Shows the standard font panel.
`NSToolbarCustomizeToolbarItemIdentifier`	Sends `-runCustomizationPalette:` to its toolbar.
`NSToolbarPrintItemIdentifier`	Sends `-printDocument:` to the first responder.

After an item has been initialized, it can be further configured. Most toolbar items are icon-based and behave like buttons. When clicked, they send their action. Some items are configured to use a custom view instead. Any arbitrary view subclass can be used. To set up an icon-based item, access the toolbar's icon image using `-setImage:` and `-image`. To match the other icons, the image should be 32×32 pixels in size or smaller.

To use an arbitrary view, don't use the image methods. Use `-setView:` and `-view` instead. If a custom view is being used, the `-setMinSize:`, `-minSize`, `-setMaxSize:`, and `-maxSize` methods can be used. These methods define the acceptable sizes for the toolbar item. If there's room in the toolbar, the item will be at the maximum size. As the toolbar gets crowded, the size will be shrunk to the minimum size. The custom view should be usable and look good at all sizes within the range set by these methods. Be aware that toolbars are only 40 pixels high, therefore, items taller than 32 pixels will look cramped in that space. The height of the sizes passed to these methods should take that into account.

Whether the toolbar item uses a custom view or an icon, it can have a label. There are actually two labels: One label is used in the toolbar itself, the other is used in the configuration palette. The label used in the toolbar is accessed with `-setLabel:` and `-label`. The label for the palette is accessed with `-setPaletteLabel:` and `-paletteLabel`. All four methods work with `NSString` objects. A ToolTip can be set and inspected for the item using the standard ToolTip accessors `-setToolTip:` and `-toolTip, respectively`. Refer to Chapter 20, "Adding Online Help," to learn more about ToolTips.

When a toolbar is in text-only mode, its items behave like menu items. This is also true for items that have been pushed off the right end of the toolbar into the overflow menu. For icon-based toolbar items, this is not a problem. For custom view–based items, the standard menu item form is always disabled. This can be changed by creating a menu item and, perhaps, a submenu for the toolbar item. Use the normal `NSMenu` and `NSMenuItem` methods to configure a menu item and submenu as appropriate. Use the `NSToolbarItem` `-setMenuFormRepresentation:` and `-menuFormRepresentation` methods to set and get the `NSMenuItem` used to represent the toolbar item when it is forced into a text-only mode.

The `NSToolbarItem` class also implements several of the typical `NSControl` and `NSCell` methods even though it isn't a subclass of either class. The `-setTarget:`, `-target`, `-setAction:`, and `-action` methods are supported for configuring the toolbar item's target and action. A tag can be manipulated with `-setTag:` and `-tag`. The item can be explicitly enabled or disabled with the `-setEnabled:` and `-isEnabled` methods.

NOTE

Enabling can also be handled through automatic validation. The "Toolbar Item Validation" section later in this chapter explains how to use automatic validation.

Creating an `NSToolbar` Delegate

The majority of code required to set up a toolbar is found in the toolbar's delegate. The delegate is required to implement three methods that are much like data source methods.

The first of these required delegate methods, `-toolbarAllowedItemIdentifiers:`, tells the toolbar what items it can legally contain. An `NSArray` containing item identifiers should be returned. This array must be all-inclusive; items such as spaces, dividers, and so on all need to be included. All custom identifiers that can be used should be returned in this array. The order of the items in the returned array determines the order that they appear in the customization sheet. This method is implemented as follows by ToolbarExample:

```
- (NSArray *)toolbarAllowedItemIdentifiers:(NSToolbar *)toolbar
{
    return [NSArray arrayWithObjects:
        AngleToolbarItemIdentifier, SaveToolbarItemIdentifier,
        NSToolbarPrintItemIdentifier, NSToolbarShowColorsItemIdentifier,
        NSToolbarShowFontsItemIdentifier,
        NSToolbarCustomizeToolbarItemIdentifier,
        NSToolbarFlexibleSpaceItemIdentifier, NSToolbarSpaceItemIdentifier,
        NSToolbarSeparatorItemIdentifier, nil];
}
```

The next required delegate method is `-toolbarDefaultItemIdentifiers:`. It also returns an `NSArray`. This time, the array contains the identifiers of the default toolbar configuration. It determines what appears in the toolbar the first time the application is run. It is also shown in the toolbar configuration sheet, allowing the user an easy way to reset the toolbar to the factory default settings. The implementation from ToolbarExample looks like this:

```
- (NSArray *)toolbarDefaultItemIdentifiers:(NSToolbar *)toolbar
{
    return [NSArray arrayWithObjects:
        NSToolbarPrintItemIdentifier, NSToolbarSeparatorItemIdentifier,
        NSToolbarShowColorsItemIdentifier, NSToolbarShowFontsItemIdentifier,
        NSToolbarFlexibleSpaceItemIdentifier,
        NSToolbarCustomizeToolbarItemIdentifier, nil];
}
```

The last required method is `-toolbar:itemForItemIdentifier:willBeInsertedIntoToolbar:`. This method is required to return new `NSToolbarItem` instances that have been configured to match the identifier specified. A flag is also provided to let the method know whether the item is destined for the toolbar or the configuration sheet. Implementations of this method tend to be long because they have to completely configure each kind of custom item supported by the toolbar. A typical implementation consists of a large if/then that has a clause for each type of supported item.

NOTE

This delegate method is only called to configure custom items. Cocoa's predefined items, such as `NSToolbarSeparatorItemIdentifier`, are configured by the toolbar itself. They are not the delegate's responsibility.

The code in ToolbarExample creates two custom toolbar items. The first, `SaveToolbarItemIdentifier`, is a simple icon-based toolbar item. The labels, ToolTip, image, target, and action are all configured appropriately.

The other toolbar item uses the `PieWidget` custom control, which was developed previously in this chapter. An instance of `PieWidget` is created and configured. Some developers prefer to configure a control in Interface Builder and connect it to an outlet of the delegate. This can save some code in the delegate's implementation if a control that is supported by Interface Builder is used. After the `PieWidget` is created, it is added to the toolbar item, and then the toolbar item's configuration is completed.

Finally, if the toolbar item identifier isn't recognized, nil should returned. Here is the code for the entire method:

```
- (NSToolbarItem *)toolbar:(NSToolbar *)toolbar
     itemForItemIdentifier:(NSString *)itemIdent
 willBeInsertedIntoToolbar:(BOOL)willBeInserted
{
    NSToolbarItem *toolbarItem = [[NSToolbarItem alloc]
            initWithItemIdentifier:itemIdent];

    [toolbarItem autorelease];
    if ([itemIdent isEqual:SaveToolbarItemIdentifier]) {
        [toolbarItem setLabel: @"Save"];
        [toolbarItem setPaletteLabel: @"Save"];
        [toolbarItem setToolTip:@"Save Document"];
        [toolbarItem setImage:[NSImage imageNamed: @"SaveDocumentItemImage"]];
        [toolbarItem setTarget: self];
        [toolbarItem setAction: @selector(saveDocument:)];
    } else if([itemIdent isEqual:AngleToolbarItemIdentifier]) {
        PieWidget *itemView = [[PieWidget alloc]
                initWithFrame:NSMakeRect(0.0, 0.0, 32.0, 32.0)];
        [itemView setDoubleValue:[angleField doubleValue]];
        [itemView setTarget:angleField];
        [itemView setAction:@selector(takeDoubleValueFrom:)];
        [angleField setTarget:itemView];
        [angleField setAction:@selector(takeDoubleValueFrom:)];
        [toolbarItem setLabel: @"Angle"];
        [toolbarItem setPaletteLabel: @"Angle Control"];
        [toolbarItem setToolTip: @"Set Angle"];
        [toolbarItem setView:itemView];
        [toolbarItem setMinSize:NSMakeSize(32.0, 32.0)];
        [toolbarItem setMaxSize:NSMakeSize(32.0, 32.0)];
        angleItem = toolbarItem;
    } else {
        return nil;
    }
    return toolbarItem;
}
```

There are two optional `NSToolbar` delegate methods, and both are also available as notifications. The first is the `-toolbarWillAddItem:` method. This method is parallel to the `NSToolbarWillAddItemNotification`. This method gives the delegate the opportunity to adjust the configuration of a toolbar item before it is added to the toolbar. The notification's `userInfo` dictionary contains the `item` key to provide access to the toolbar item about to be added.

All items, including the built-in ones, pass through this method. The ToolbarExample uses this fact to catch the `NSToolbarPrintItemIdentifier` item. The ToolTip and target are changed. Here is the implementation's code:

```
- (void)toolbarWillAddItem:(NSNotification *)notification
{
    NSToolbarItem *addedItem = [[notification userInfo] objectForKey: @"item"];
    if ([[addedItem itemIdentifier] isEqual:NSToolbarPrintItemIdentifier]) {
        [addedItem setToolTip: @"Print Document"];
        [addedItem setTarget:self];
    }
}
```

The `-toolbarDidRemoveItem:` method and `NSToolbarDidRemoveItemNotification` notification are sent when an item is removed from a toolbar. The ToolbarExample program connects a user interface element in the document to the item in the toolbar, so that connection needs to be reset as part of the cleanup. The code for this is as follows:

```
- (void)toolbarDidRemoveItem:(NSNotification *)notification
{
    NSToolbarItem *removedItem =
            [[notification userInfo] objectForKey: @"item"];
    if (removedItem == angleItem) {
        [angleField setTarget:nil];
    }
}
```

Toolbar Item Validation

Toolbar items are validated in a manner similar to the way menu items are validated. In fact, if the toolbar item is text only or in the overflow menu, normal menu item validation is used. Toolbar items that are based on a custom view might need to be validated explicitly by called `-setEnabled:`. Items that use icons are automatically validated by calling the `-validateToolbarItem:` method on their targets. This method should be implemented just like the `-validateMenuItem:` method. See Chapter 16 for more information about automatic control validation in Cocoa.

In the ToolbarExample program, the toolbar item for saving the document is validated by checking to see if the document has been edited. The print item is always validated, whereas other items are disabled by default. The code for this is as follows:

```
- (BOOL)validateToolbarItem:(NSToolbarItem *)toolbarItem
{
    BOOL ret = NO;
    if ([[toolbarItem itemIdentifier] isEqual:SaveToolbarItemIdentifier]) {
        ret = [self isDocumentEdited];
    } else if ([[toolbarItem itemIdentifier]
            isEqual:NSToolbarPrintItemIdentifier]) {
        ret = YES;
    }
    return ret;
}
```

Status Bars

Cocoa programs can create their own status bar items. These are views that are inserted at the right side of the main menu bar. When the status bar item's icon is clicked, a custom view appears in a fashion similar to opening one of the menus in the menu bar. Some status items, such as the monitor resolution and airport controls, open menus. Others, such as the sound volume control, open as a slider for system volume. Some example status items can be seen in Figure 18.15 in the "StatusItems Example" section later in this chapter.

Status bar items have limitations. They are only available when the application that provides them is running. If space is at a premium, they might not be available at all. If the active application's menu is so big that it would overlap a status bar item, the item is dropped from the menu bar to make room for the application's menu. Some or all the items might not be visible at any given time, especially on smaller resolution screens.

This means that status bar items should be created as handy shortcuts and should not contain any user interface controls that aren't available in some other way from their host application. For example, many of the status bar items offered by Apple, such as the monitors and sound controls, can be accessed through the Preferences application. Also, any application that can add an item to the status bar should offer a user preference to turn the item on and off.

Working with `NSStatusBar` and `NSStatusItem`

The status bar portion of the menu bar is represented by the `NSStatusBar` class, which is a Singleton. It is used to create new items. New items created by `NSStatusBar` are instances of the `NSStatusItem` class. These objects are not available directly from within Interface Builder. Custom code is always required to create and manage status bar items.

Creating an `NSStatusItem`

The `NSStatusBar` class is used to create a new status bar item. It is a Singleton, so it is never allocated directly. Instead, the shared instance is obtained with the `+systemStatusBar` class method. The main function of the status bar class is to act as a factory, manufacturing instances of `NSStatusItem`. Never allocate instances of `NSStatusItem` directly. Use the `NSStatusBar` `-statusItemWithLength:` method to obtain an autoreleased `NSStatusItem`.

> **NOTE**
>
> Because new `NSStatusItem` instances are autoreleased, they must be retained as long as they are to remain a part of the status bar. When an item is deallocated, it is removed from the status bar. If an item isn't appearing in the status bar, either there isn't room for it or the `-retain` was forgotten.

The length passed to `-statusItemWithLength:` really refers to the width of the status item. It can be one of three things. For status items that are text-based, such as the menu bar clock, the length should be the constant `NSVariableStatusItemLength`. This is the most flexible because it automatically adjusts the item's width to match its size as the title is changed. For icon-based status items, such as the sound, display, and airport items built into Mac OS X, use the constant `NSSquareStatusItemLength`. The icon should fit in the menu bar, which means it should be no larger than 22×22 pixels. The third way to specify the length argument is by passing a constant width for the status item. This is usually avoided because it is so inflexible.

The process of creating a status item causes it to automatically be added to the system-wide status bar. Nothing special needs to be done to add it to the status bar.

Configuring an `NSStatusItem`

Status items are not `NSControl` subclasses; they inherit only from `NSObject`. However, `NSStatusItem` instances respond to many of the `NSControl` methods and behave much like controls. For instance, status items can have a target and action as if they were controls. The standard `-setTarget:`, `-target`, `-setAction:`, and `-action` methods control the target and action.

Most status items actually have an associated menu instead of a target and action. In this case, the target and action are used to invoke the menu. The menu is attached to the status item with the `-setMenu:` method and returned by the `-menu` method. Both methods work with `NSMenu` instances. Refer to Chapter 16, "Menus," for information on creating and manipulating menus. To make the status item behave like the other main menu entries, the status item should be sent `[myItem setHighlightMode:YES]`.

Whether the status item uses target/action or has a menu, it can be enabled and disabled. Use the `-setEnabled:` and `-isEnabled` methods to control and inspect this setting, respectively. Because menu bar space is at such a premium, it is often preferable to remove an item instead of just disabling it.

If the status item has a text title, such as the menu bar clock, the `-setTitle:` and `-title` methods can be used to change the text. The item resizes as necessary to accommodate the text. Because menu bar space is limited, keep the text as short as possible—a single word is best. If the text requires special font or formatting attributes, use the `-setAttributedTitle:` and `-attributedTitle` methods.

Status items that use an icon instead of text should use an `NSImage` instance with the `-setImage:` and `-image` methods to change the image used for the icon.

The final type of status item uses an arbitrary `NSView` object to render itself. This is far more flexible than using text or an image, but also requires more work from the developer. View-based status items don't make use of their target/action abilities. The view itself has to appropriately handle all events it receives. The `-setView:` and `-view` methods can set up a view-based status item.

Removing an `NSStatusItem`

When a status item is no longer needed, it should be removed from the status bar. Use the `NSStatusBar` method `-removeStatusItem:` to do this. After removing an item, be sure to release the item itself. Simply releasing an item removes it from the status bar, but usually leaves an unsightly gap and/or artifacts in the bar. It is best to remove the item explicitly before releasing it.

StatusItems Example

In the StatusItems example on `www.cocoaprogramming.net`, two status items can be added to the system-wide status bar. One item creates a menu, named Menu, in the status bar. The other is a progress view that doesn't have an associated menu and does nothing if the user clicks it. There is a check box to turn each item on and off. The `StatusItemsController` class implements action methods for each of the check boxes to call. The interface for this example is shown in Figure 18.15.

A Menu-Based `NSStatusItem`

The `-toggleMenuStatusItem:` action method is used to turn the menu-based status item on and off. The item is turned on by asking the system-wide `NSStatusBar` to create a new `NSStatusItem` of variable length. The new item is retained and stored in the `menuItem` instance variable. The Title is set to be Menu, and the menu is taken from the `menuItemMenu` outlet. The outlet was set in Interface Builder to point to a custom configured `NSMenu` instance. To turn the item off, it is removed from the status bar and released. The code for the `-toggleMenuStatusItem:` method is

```
- (IBAction)toggleMenuStatusItem:(id)sender
{
    if ([sender state]) {
        if (!menuItem) { // turn it on
            NSStatusBar *bar = [NSStatusBar systemStatusBar];
            menuItem = [bar statusItemWithLength:NSVariableStatusItemLength];
            [menuItem retain];
            [menuItem setTitle:NSLocalizedString(@"Menu",@"")];
            [menuItem setHighlightMode:YES];
            [menuItem setMenu:menuItemMenu];
        }
    } else { // turn it off
        [[NSStatusBar systemStatusBar] removeStatusItem:menuItem];
        [menuItem release];
        menuItem = nil;
    }
}
```

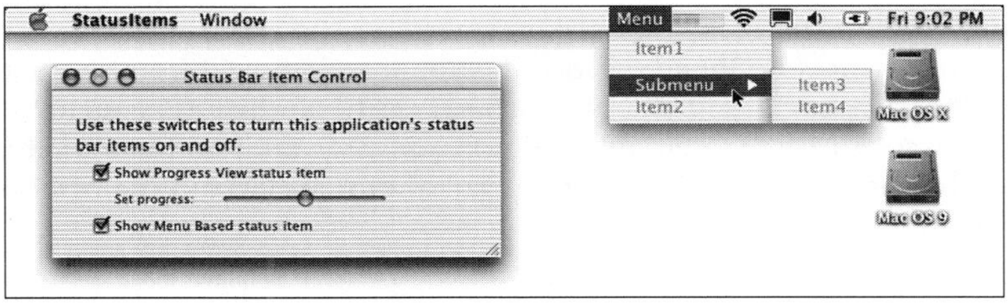

FIGURE 18.15 Interface for StatusItems example with both status items turned on.

A View-Based `NSStatusItem`

The `-toggleProgressStatusItem:` action method is used to turn the view-based status item on and off. The key difference is that no title or menu is set. Instead, the status item's view is set from the `progressItemView` outlet. This outlet is connected to a tiny `NSBox` that contains an `NSProgressView`. The box enables the progress view's position in the menu bar to be more carefully controlled. It is important to make the box exactly 22 pixels high, just like the menu bar. The code for the `-toggleProgressStatusItem:` method is

```
- (IBAction)toggleProgressStatusItem:(id)sender
{
    if ([sender state]) {
        if (!progressItem) { // turn it on
```

```
            NSStatusBar *bar = [NSStatusBar systemStatusBar];
            progressItem = [bar statusItemWithLength:NSVariableStatusItemLength];
            [progressItem retain];
            [progressItem setView:progressItemView]; // instead of title
            [progressView startAnimation:nil];
        }
    } else { // turn it off
        [progressView stopAnimation:nil];
        [[NSStatusBar systemStatusBar] removeStatusItem:progressItem];
        [progressItem release];
        progressItem = nil;
        [progressItemView removeFromSuperview];
    }
}
```

Removing the status item is a little different from before because the progress view's animation needs to be stopped. Also, the box needs to be explicitly removed from its superview to avoid leaving artifacts behind in the menu bar.

NOTE

Because the view used for this status item can be added to and removed from a visible location multiple times, the `StatusItemsController` class retains it in the `-awakeFromNib` method. This keeps the `progressItemView` outlet from ever being released accidentally.

`NSQuickDrawView` Class

The `NSQuickDrawView` class is an `NSView` subclass designed to make it easy to use QuickDraw from within Cocoa. Just like any other view subclass, custom drawing code should be put in the `-drawRect:` method implementation. The big difference is that QuickDraw drawing commands, such as `PaintRect()`, `FrameOval()`, and so on can all be used instead of Quartz calls.

NOTE

It is beyond this book's scope to discuss the QuickDraw API. Refer to Chapters 11 and 12 of *Carbon Programming* by K.J. Bricknell, Sams Publishing, ISBN 0-672-32267-6 for a discussion of QuickDraw.

During the time that a QuickDraw view is focused, the `-qdPort` method returns a QuickDraw `GrafPtr`. A view is always focused before the Application Kit calls `-drawRect:`, so custom drawing code in that method can safely assume that the return value of `-qdPort` is valid. Because the `GrafPtr` returned is only valid when focus is locked on the view, the return value shouldn't be kept past the view's next `-unlockFocus`.

Although the `NSQuickDrawView` class allows QuickDraw commands, it doesn't require them. It is possible to mix Quartz and QuickDraw drawing arbitrarily while doing custom drawing. The QuickDraw example on `www.cocoaprogramming.net` shows an example of this intermingling of drawing models. In the example, the two models are shown side by side in the same view. Some of the differences between models, such as antialiasing, become very apparent.

When mixing the two drawing models, it is important to remember that QuickDraw uses what Quartz and Cocoa would call a flipped coordinate system. The origin is at the upper-left corner of the view, and y-axis values increase as you move down the view. For example, a point with a y-coordinate of 100 is below a point with a y-coordinate of 50. To make sure that (0.0, 0.0) in Quartz refers to the same point in the view as (0, 0) in QuickDraw, all `NSQuickDrawView` instances have flipped coordinate systems. This means that coordinates passed to QuickDraw will work as expected, whereas the same coordinates passed to Quartz will work as would be expected for a flipped coordinate system instead of the default Quartz coordinate system.

Summary

This chapter describes several of the more complex Cocoa views and controls. The `NSTableView`, `NSOutlineView`, `NSBrowser`, and `NSComboBox` classes are explained in detail. Examples of data sources are provided for the table view, outline view, and browser classes. Toolbars and status items are also covered. Several examples are provided to show how to use some of the more complex options available.

The next chapter discusses the Mac OS X pasteboard and the Cocoa classes that work with it. The pasteboard underlies the implementation of cut, copy, and paste as well as drag and drop and services. Some of the examples from this chapter are extended to show how to add drag and drop to them. New examples are also provided.

19

Using Pasteboards

IN THIS CHAPTER

- Pasteboard Concepts
- Implementing Cut, Copy, and Paste
- Implementing Drag and Drop
- Implementing Services

Pasteboards are pervasive throughout Cocoa. They implement the Mac OS X clipboard, drag and drop, file-type filters, and services. This chapter begins by discussing the basic concepts underlying pasteboards on Mac OS X, and it explains the `NSPasteboard` object in detail. It also shows how to implement basic cut, copy, and paste as well as drag and drop. The chapter ends with information about implementing filters and services.

Pasteboard Concepts

Before diving into code, it is important to explain the basic concepts relating to pasteboards. Although the code to work with pasteboards is generally simple, it is hard to follow without understanding the concepts and designs employed in Cocoa and Mac OS X.

Mac OS X allows for multiple pasteboards. Every pasteboard is meant to be used for a different purpose. For example, one pasteboard is the general pasteboard, also known as the clipboard. Data involved in cut, copy, and paste operations pass through this pasteboard. Another pasteboard is the drag and drop pasteboard. Any item being dragged is placed on and retrieved from the drag and drop pasteboard. The "Obtaining a Pasteboard" section later in this chapter describes all the available pasteboards.

NOTE

Don Yacktman also describes the concepts discussed in this chapter in broad terms in the "Pastries" and "Service Call" developer articles on `www.stepwise.com`. "Pastries" is found at `http://www.stepwise.com/Articles/Technical/Pastries.html`, and "Service Call" is at `http://www.stepwise.com/Articles/Technical/Services.html`.

Pasteboard Server

So that pasteboard data can be passed between applications easily, Mac OS X has a pasteboard server. The pasteboard server is a hidden program running at all times. When data is placed on the pasteboard, it is sent to the pasteboard server. When data is retrieved from the pasteboard, the data comes from the pasteboard server.

The `NSPasteboard` class manages all communication with the pasteboard server automatically. There should never be any need to deal with the pasteboard server directly.

NOTE

Curious developers might be interested in some other details of the pasteboard server. The program's binary is found at `/System/Library/CoreServices/pbs` and it is launched by the `loginwindow` program. To see details about the running process, look for `pbs` in the list of processes in ProcessViewer.

Pasteboard Data Types

Data can be represented in many different formats. Not every application or object can be expected to deal with every data type. Pasteboards are aware of this and offer a solution.

Pasteboards call a particular data format a type. For example, data could be presented as a Unicode string. The same data could also be a rich text string in HTML, RTF, or RTFD format. The various types supported natively on Mac OS X are discussed in the "Pasteboard Types" section later in this chapter.

To facilitate greater interoperability and communications between applications, developers are encouraged to place data on a pasteboard in as many different types as possible. For example, a string copied from a word-processor document should be placed on the pasteboard as both RTF and Unicode data. The word processor might even choose to place the data on the pasteboard in a custom, internal format that preserves formatting features not representable in RTF. When the data is pasted, the recipient can look through the available data types and take the one it prefers. If the paste happens in the word processor, the custom format can be used. Pasting into other applications will still work well, though, because the RTF and Unicode formats that they are more likely to understand are also available.

When taking data off the pasteboard, developers are encouraged to take the richest data type that they can handle. For example, an application that can deal with RTF should always choose the RTF data type instead of Unicode, if both are available.

Lazy Evaluation

Putting the same data on the pasteboard in many different formats could be a very expensive operation. Because the data is probably only required to be in one of the possible types, it is also wasteful. Ideally, only the needed data format(s) would be placed on the pasteboard. The pasteboard doesn't know which data formats are needed until the paste operation occurs, however.

The solution to this is to allow lazy evaluation of pasteboards. When data is being placed on a pasteboard, the program tells the pasteboard all the types that are valid for the data. However, some or all the data types are not actually placed on the pasteboard at that time. Instead, the object placing data on the pasteboard declares itself as the owner of that pasteboard data type.

When it comes time to do a paste, the recipient requests the data type it wants. At that time, the pasteboard returns to the owner object to request the data. The required data type is provided to the pasteboard. The pasteboard then passes the data on to the object that is trying to do the paste.

Lazy evaluation is optional. If an owner provides the data in all the declared types up front, there is no need to call on it to provide other data types. The object doing the pasting doesn't need to know if the pasteboard's data is being evaluated lazily. The pasteboard handles all the details automatically.

If the application containing the pasteboard data's owner is about to quit and some of the data types haven't been provided to the pasteboard yet, the owner is required to provide the additional data types before the application is allowed to quit.

Applications that handle multiple documents should be careful to force pasteboard evaluation if a document containing the pasteboard owner is about to be closed. If the data owner is deallocated when the pasteboard is in an incomplete state, it could cause a crash when the pasteboard tries to perform evaluation later. If all the data has already been put on the pasteboard, it is safe to release the owner and the data. The pasteboard retains the information it requires.

Services

Services is a simple, but very powerful, concept. The premise is that users prefer their applications work well together. Also, a small application that does one thing really well is better than a monolithic application that does a lot of things only half as well. If the small applications can all communicate together, the user can choose the application they prefer for a particular function and put them together to form their own custom suite of tools. The hard part is getting that communication between applications.

Because pasteboards already exist and provide a common language for communication between applications, the communication problem can be solved. Services adds a little bit of structure to the whole process. Services can receive data from another application, send data to another application, or both.

For example, Grab is an application that offers services to take different kinds of screen shots. If one of the services is invoked while typing in a word processor, the screen shot is inserted in the document at the current cursor location. This is a service that provides data. An example of a service that sends data is Mail's Mail Text. The selected text is sent to Mail and placed in a compose window. A bidirectional service replaces the current selection with something new. For example, a list of items could be replaced by a sorted version of the list. An image could be run through a redeye filter. Services can even return types that differ from what they receive. One possibility is a service to convert an image into text by running it through optical character recognition.

In implementation, a service that receives data is really just a shortcut. The user could switch applications, copy the desired data onto the clipboard, switch back to the original application, and paste the data. The service does all this in one shot without having to switch applications. A bidirectional service uses this sequence: copy, switch applications, paste, perform some operation, copy, switch back, and paste—all in one click from the user.

Services can be published by any application. After a service is published, every application containing a services menu will offer that service. In effect, adding one application to the system extends the abilities of every other application.

When a user logs in for the first time, Mac OS X scans all the installed applications to see what services are offered and builds a database containing the information. Future logins update the database to reflect changes caused by new, upgraded, or deleted applications. Cocoa takes this database and automatically builds a services menu as part of an application's launch. A developer doesn't have to do anything to take advantage of services. Cocoa sets everything up.

Publishing and using services takes a little bit of effort. Existing Application Kit responder objects are already set up to make use of services automatically. If a custom responder subclass implements cut and paste, adding the capability to use services is almost trivial. Publishing services requires a bit more work, but is still easy to do. It is nearly always worth the minimal amount of effort needed to publish and use services. The concepts behind services might seem very simple to a developer, yet they are extremely powerful for the user.

Filters

Data can come in a wide variety of formats. For example, bitmapped images can be TIFF, PICT, GIF, JPG, PNG, or one of many other formats. It is unreasonable to expect every application to be able to natively handle every possible format of data. Mac OS X tends to favor certain data formats such as TIFF, PDF, AIFF, and so on. When data is available in another format, though, it would be nice for it to be available to all applications.

Through its services functionality, Mac OS X supports the capability to have one application perform data conversion for all other applications on the system. For example, a GIF to TIFF converter could be installed. From that point on, every application that could deal with TIFF data would instantly gain the capability to read GIF data. A service such as this is known as a filter service because it filters data from one type into another.

All services, including filter services, use pasteboards. Pasteboards and Application Kit classes work in concert to do filtering transparently. It is also possible to invoke filtering explicitly or to determine what filters are available.

Implementing Cut, Copy, and Paste

Custom subclasses of `NSView` and `NSControl` need to implement the `-cut:`, `-copy:`, and `-paste:` action methods if they want to support cut, copy, and paste operations. Because these actions are only sent to the first responder, it only makes sense to implement them for objects that accept first responder status. Sometimes, it might make sense to implement these actions in an `NSDocument` class instead of a view. (Any class in the responder chain could implement them.)

NOTE

The `NSTextView` class is different. The `-cut:`, `-copy:`, and `-paste:` actions should not be overridden in subclasses of `NSTextView`. Instead, there is a large group of methods that should be overridden to extend the existing `NSTextView` cut, copy, and paste support. There's not room to describe all the methods here, so refer to the class documentation and header file for all the details. Start with the "Managing the pasteboard" group of methods in `/Developer/Documentation/Cocoa/Reference/ApplicationKit/ObjC_classic/Classes/NSTextView.html`.

Throughout this chapter, cut, copy, paste, and drag and drop support are added to the `PieWidget` control from Chapter 18, "Advanced Views and Controls." The PieWidget2 example on `www.cocoaprogramming.net` contains the updated project.

The functionality of the cut, copy, and paste commands centers around the `NSPasteboard` class. When working with a pasteboard, the main tasks are to obtain a pasteboard, declare or check a pasteboard's types, and read data from or write data to the pasteboard.

Obtaining a Pasteboard

When implementing a `-cut:` or `-copy:` command, the data needs to be put on a pasteboard. The first task is to obtain a pasteboard. Any one of three `NSPasteboard` class methods can be used.

The `+generalPasteboard` method returns the pasteboard used for normal cut, copy, and paste operations. This is the pasteboard that is known to Mac users as the clipboard.

A more specific way to get a particular pasteboard is to ask for it by name. The `+pasteboardWithName:` method returns a specific pasteboard. It takes an `NSString` argument containing the pasteboard's name. Any name can be used. If a pasteboard with a particular name doesn't yet exist, it is created. There are five predefined pasteboard names. The constants for the predefined pasteboards and the intended uses for the pasteboards are shown in Table 19.1. It is always possible to send a `-name` message to an `NSPasteboard` instance to see what its name is.

TABLE 19.1 Pasteboard Constants and Uses

Constant	Purpose
`NSGeneralPboard`	Used by cut, copy, paste
`NSFontPboard`	Stores fonts
`NSRulerPboard`	Stores paragraph formatting
`NSFindPboard`	Stores the current find string
`NSDragPboard`	Used by drag and drop

The font and ruler pasteboards are used by the TextEdit application to store text and paragraph formatting information. Look in the Text and Font submenus of the Format menu to see the menu items that control copy and paste of font and ruler information. The `NSText` object implements actions that can make use of these pasteboards.

The find pasteboard is used by find panels to store the most recently used search string. When applications pay attention to this pasteboard, it is possible for the user to use the "find next" or "find previous" commands to search for the most recently used search string, even if the last search was performed in another application

NOTE

There's often more than one way to do something in Cocoa. The messages `[NSPasteboard generalPasteboard]` and `[NSPasteboard pasteboardWithName:NSGeneralPboard]` both return the same object.

Sometimes a private pasteboard is needed to perform a particular operation. Pasteboards excel at moving data around quickly, so private pasteboards are often used as a relatively inexpensive form of interprocess communication. To obtain a private, temporary use pasteboard, use the `+pasteboardWithUniqueName` method. The pasteboard is only accessible to applications that know the name. Of course, the `-name` method returns the name and the name can be passed on to any clients that need access to the pasteboard. There is no documented way to obtain a list of the pasteboards currently in existence.

When a unique pasteboard or custom named pasteboard is no longer needed, the `-releaseGlobally` message should be sent to it. This method releases the pasteboard server resources consumed by the pasteboard. It does not release any pasteboard objects. The normal reference counting mechanisms still apply for the `NSPasteboard` instances.

Pasteboard Types

All pasteboard data is typed. Many of the `NSPasteboard` methods require the names of pasteboard types. All type names are `NSString` objects. Several constants refer to predefined type strings. Table 19.2 shows the constants and the data type they represent. The Object column of the table shows the type of object normally passed to the pasteboard object to put the data on the pasteboard. Usually, a conversion to an `NSString` or `NSData` object is required to place data on the pasteboard.

TABLE 19.2 Pasteboard Types

Constant	Object	Data Type
`NSStringPboardType`	`NSString`	Unicode string
`NSFilenamesPboardType`	`NSString`	Tab Unicodedelimited list of filenames
`NSPostScriptPboardType`	`NSData`	Image Unicode data (EPS format)
`NSTIFFPboardType`	`NSData`	Image Unicodedata (TIFF format)
`NSRTFPboardType`	`NSData`	Rich Unicodetext (RTF format)
`NSTabularTextPboardType`	`NSString`	Generic Unicode tab-delimited data
`NSFontPboardType`	`NSData`	Font Unicode information
`NSRulerPboardType`	`NSData`	Paragraph Unicode information
`NSFileContentsPboardType`	`NSData`	File Unicode contents
`NSColorPboardType`	`NSColor`	UnicodeColor
`NSRTFDPboardType`	`NSData`	Rich Unicodetext (RTFD format)

TABLE 19.2 Continued

Constant	Object	Data Type
NSHTMLPboardType	NSData	Rich Unicodetext (HTML format)
NSPICTPboardType	NSData	Image Unicodedata (PICT format)
NSURLPboardType	NSURL	URL Unicode
NSPDFPboardType	NSData	Image Unicode data (PDF format)

Filtering an `NSPasteboard`

To learn what type of filtering is available on the system, the class method `+typesFilterableTo:` can be used. Pass it a target type and it returns an `NSArray` containing a list of all the types that can be turned into the target type. The three `NSPasteboard` methods can be used to invoke filter services are

```
+ (NSPasteboard *)pasteboardByFilteringFile:(NSString *)filename
+ (NSPasteboard *)pasteboardByFilteringData:(NSData *)data
       ofType:(NSString *)type
+ (NSPasteboard *)pasteboardByFilteringTypesInPasteboard:(NSPasteboard *)pboard
```

These methods create new pasteboard objects that contain all the possible data types available post-filtering. They are not terribly expensive to invoke, though, because the pasteboards that come back are all lazily evaluated. A filter is actually invoked only when it is needed.

NOTE

The `NSImageRep` and `NSSound` classes support several methods to make filtering easier and more transparent. Refer to their class documentation to learn more.

Writing Data to an `NSPasteboard`

Data is written to a pasteboard in two steps. First, the pasteboard is told what types of data can be provided. Sending the `-declareTypes:owner:` method to a pasteboard object does this. This method must be sent before writing anything to the pasteboard. The first argument is an array of `NSString` pasteboard types. The constants from the previous section “Pasteboard Types” are used most commonly.

The second argument is the pasteboard types’ owner. This should be the object that knows how to put data on the pasteboard in the types specified. Most often, `self` is used for this argument. If and only if all the data is to be provided immediately for all types declared, a `nil` owner is acceptable.

NOTE

Be careful about releasing any pasteboard-type owner objects provided to `NSPasteboard` instances. Problems might occur if an owner object is released before providing its data to the pasteboard. If the pasteboard later determines that it needs the data, a message is sent to the released owner. This usually crashes the application.

The `-declareTypes:owner:` method returns an integer representing the pasteboard's change count. The change count increments when new types are declared to indicate that the pasteboard's contents have been altered. It is common to ignore the return value since it is usually unnecessary to know the actual change count of a pasteboard. The `-changeCount` method returns the current change count if it is needed.

A pasteboard type owner object that wants to be released can monitor the change count of its associated pasteboard. When the count changes, it can be assumed that the data on the pasteboard has been altered and the owner is therefore no longer needed.

A complex program might not know all the types that can be added to the pasteboard without calling several other methods in the controller or model. These other methods can add new types to the pasteboard with the `-addTypes:owner:` method. This works just like declaring types. The owner that can produce the added types should be sent as the second argument. Each type can have its own owner. The pasteboard keeps track of which object can produce a particular data type.

After a data type has been declared or added to a pasteboard, the actual data of that type can be sent to the pasteboard. Many methods can be used to do this. The `NSPasteboard` class implements the following methods:

```
- (BOOL)setData:(NSData *)data forType:(NSString *)dataType
- (BOOL)setPropertyList:(id)plist forType:(NSString *)dataType
- (BOOL)setString:(NSString *)string forType:(NSString *)dataType
- (BOOL)writeFileContents:(NSString *)filename
- (BOOL)writeFileWrapper:(NSFileWrapper *)wrapper
```

The data and string methods are by far the most commonly used. The `NSURL`, `NSSound`, and `NSColor` classes all implement the `-writeToPasteboard:` method as a convenience. Because the Foundation Kit doesn't know about `NSPasteboard` objects, the `NSURL` support for `-writeToPasteboard:` is added by an Application Kit category. It converts the receiver into an `NSData` and places it on the pasteboard with the correct type. A view object can be asked to put EPS or PDF data onto a pasteboard with one of these two methods:

```
- (void)writeEPSInsideRect:(NSRect)rect toPasteboard:(NSPasteboard *)pasteboard
- (void)writePDFInsideRect:(NSRect)rect toPasteboard:(NSPasteboard *)pasteboard
```

The PieWidget2 example shows how to write data to the pasteboard. It implements `-cut:` and `-copy:` in the `PieWidget` control class. There is no way to delete a control's value; it always has a value. Therefore, the `-cut:` method calls the `-copy:` method to do the work. The `-copy:` method registers the control as being able to provide a string value or a TIFF bitmap. Only the string value is placed on the pasteboard immediately. The TIFF is provided lazily, upon request. The code is as follows:

```
- (IBAction)copy:(id)sender
{
    BOOL success;
    NSArray *types = [NSArray arrayWithObjects:
            NSStringPboardType, NSTIFFPboardType, nil];
    NSPasteboard *pb = [NSPasteboard pasteboardWithName:NSGeneralPboard];
    [pb declareTypes:types owner:self];
    success = [pb setString:[self stringValue] forType:NSStringPboardType];
    if (!success) { // very unlikely!
        NSBeep();
    }
}

- (IBAction)cut:(id)sender
{
    [self copy:sender];
}
```

Providing Data Lazily

When data of a particular type is not written to the pasteboard, an owner for the data must be provided. The owner needs to be able to provide the data in the requested format at any later time. If the data is required, this owner method is called

```
- (void)pasteboard:(NSPasteboard *)sender provideDataForType:(NSString *)type
```

The required type is passed in as an argument to the method. The pasteboard that needs the data is also passed into the method. Data of the requested type should be placed onto the `sender` pasteboard. If it is not, there is a good chance that the owner's application will crash or face other undesirable consequences.

The hardest part of implementing this method is that the data that needs to be put on the pasteboard might be long gone. For example, suppose the user copies a selection out of a bitmap image, and then changes the selection. When a copy or cut takes place, the application then needs to keep track of the data that was copied or cut so that the correct data can be placed on the pasteboard later.

This is even true for simple controls. With the `PieWidget` control, the user could have moved the control after copying the value. The PieWidget2 example doesn't save the value, however. It knows that the value it needs is saved on the pasteboard already. The solution is to set the pie to the value on the pasteboard, render the image, and then restore the pie's value. The user never sees the value change because no screen updates happen while the image is rendered.

To make this easier, `PieWidget` implements another method. The `-imageValue` method returns an `NSImage` snapshot of the control in its current state. The implementation of `-imageValue` and `-pasteboard:provideDataForType:` in PieWidget2 are

```
- (NSImage *)imageValue
{
    NSRect bds = [self bounds];
    NSImage *ret = [[NSImage alloc] initWithSize:bds.size];
    [ret lockFocus];
    [self drawRect:bds];
    [ret unlockFocus];
    [ret autorelease];
    return ret;
}

- (void)pasteboard:(NSPasteboard *)sender provideDataForType:(NSString *)type
{
    NSImage *imageValue;
    NSData *tiffData;
    double trueValue;
    NSString *pbString = [sender stringForType:NSStringPboardType];
    if ([type compare:NSTIFFPboardType] != NSOrderedSame) {
        NSLog(@"Pasteboard type \"%@\" requested, unable to comply.", type);
        [sender setString:pbString forType:type]; // put something on
return;
    }
    trueValue = [self doubleValue]; // save original value
    [self setStringValue:pbString]; // set ourselves to value on pasteboard
    imageValue = [self imageValue]; // draw an image of ourself at pb value
    [self setDoubleValue:trueValue]; // restore original value
    tiffData = [imageValue
            TIFFRepresentationUsingCompression:NSTIFFCompressionLZW factor:0];
    [sender setData:tiffData forType:type];
}
```

One other method can be sent to a pasteboard data type owner. If the pasteboard's owner is changed, the previous owner is warned by being sent a `-pasteboardChangedOwner:` method. This method is optional and most owners don't bother with it. It is only needed in the rare circumstance that a change in ownership is significant.

Reading Data from an `NSPasteboard`

Reading data from a pasteboard is similar to writing data. First, the available types must be queried. When the available types are known, then data for a particular type can be read. Even if the type of data that should be on the pasteboard is known, the pasteboard won't allow anything to be read until a type query is performed.

To determine what types are on the pasteboard, use either the `-types` or `-availableTypeFromArray:` method. The `-types` method returns an `NSArray` containing all the types the pasteboard can offer. The `-availableTypeFromArray:` method returns a single type. Pass it an `NSArray` containing the types that can be accepted in order of priority (preferred types first). The method returns the first type in the array that the pasteboard supports, or `nil` if nothing matches.

After a type query has been performed, data can be read from the pasteboard. The following `NSPasteboard` methods are available for reading data:

```
- (NSData *)dataForType:(NSString *)dataType
- (id)propertyListForType:(NSString *)dataType
- (NSString *)stringForType:(NSString *)dataType
- (NSString *)readFileContentsType:(NSString *)type toFile:(NSString *)filename
- (NSFileWrapper *)readFileWrapper
```

An `NSColor` object can be read from the pasteboard with `+colorFromPasteboard:`. An `NSURL` object can be read from the pasteboard with `+URLFromPasteboard:`. `NSSound` and `NSImage` objects can be initialized from a pasteboard with `-initWithPasteboard:`.

To implement a paste operation, data must be read from the pasteboard. The PieWidget2 example breaks the paste operation into two private methods. One method evaluates the pasteboard to see if it contains a type that the `PieWidget` class can handle. It returns a `YES` or `NO`:

```
- (BOOL)_canTakeValueFromPasteboard:(NSPasteboard *)pb
{
    NSArray *typeArray = [NSArray arrayWithObjects:NSStringPboardType, nil];
    NSString *type = [pb availableTypeFromArray:typeArray];
    if (!type) {
        return NO;
```

```
    }
    return YES;
}
```

The next private method reads a value off the pasteboard, if possible, and sets it as the control's value. If a value cannot be read, an alert panel is provided to the user to show that the operation failed. If there was success, the control's action is also sent so that the target knows the value changed. Here is the code:

```
- (BOOL)_takeValueFromPasteboard:(NSPasteboard *)pb operationName:(NSString *)op
{
    NSString *stringValue;
    if (![self _canTakeValueFromPasteboard:pb]) {
        NSRunAlertPanel(@"Paste",
                @"Unable to perform %@ operation for PieWidget.",
                @"OK", nil, nil, op);
        return NO;
    }
    stringValue = [pb stringForType:NSStringPboardType];
    [self setStringValue:stringValue];
    [self sendAction:[self action] to:[self target]];
    return YES;
}
```

With the previous two methods, the implementation of `-paste:` becomes almost trivial:

```
- (IBAction)paste:(id)sender
{
    NSPasteboard *pb = [NSPasteboard pasteboardWithName:NSGeneralPboard];
    [self _takeValueFromPasteboard:pb operationName:@"paste"];
}
```

The previous code is sufficient to implement pasting. However, if the user has copied something like an image onto the pasteboard, the pie widget won't be able to do a paste. An alert will be shown, but that's a bit of a pain for the user. Because the pasteboard can be examined prior to a paste operation, it makes sense to validate the `-paste:` menu item so that the user can only invoke a paste operation when the pasteboard contains valid information. The added advantage is that looking at the Edit menu's Paste item will provide immediate feedback about the pasteboard without having to do a paste. Here's the menu validation code from the `PieWidget` class:

```
- (BOOL)validateMenuItem:(id <NSMenuItem>)menuItem
{
    if ([menuItem action] == @selector(paste:)) {
        NSPasteboard *pb = [NSPasteboard pasteboardWithName:NSGeneralPboard];
        return [self _canTakeValueFromPasteboard:pb];
    }
    return YES;
}
```

Implementing Drag and Drop

Drag and drop on Mac OS X is implemented using a few standard protocols and pasteboards. All drag and drop operations have three major elements, a source, a destination, and the data being dragged. The source and destination are usually `NSView` objects, but any `NSWindow` can also be a source or destination. The data being dragged is placed on a pasteboard. A standard pasteboard, `NSDragPboard`, has been set aside for drag and drop, but it is possible to use a private pasteboard instead if desired.

The term *dragging session* (or just *drag session*) is used to describe the whole process from the initiation of a drag at mouse-down until the mouse-up event is received. The source, destination, data, and all mouse-dragged events between mouse-down and mouse-up are all properties of a drag session.

Drag and Drop in Custom View and Window Objects

Objects that are to be used as drag sources implement the `NSDraggingSource` informal protocol. Dragging destinations implement the `NSDraggingDestination` informal protocol. While a drag operation is in progress, the destination is given an object that implements the `NSDraggingInfo` formal protocol. A dragging info object encapsulates data about the drag, including the pasteboard containing the dragged data.

Initiating a Drag

A dragging source must call a method to initiate a drag when it determines it is time to start a drag. Both `NSWindow` and `NSView` implement this method to initiate a drag:

```
- (void)dragImage:(NSImage *)anImage at:(NSPoint)viewLocation
        offset:(NSSize)initialOffset event:(NSEvent *)event
        pasteboard:(NSPasteboard *)pboard source:(id)sourceObj
        slideBack:(BOOL)slideFlag
```

This method should be sent from within a `-mouseDown:` or `-mouseDragged:` event-handling implementation. It might be sent when a particular modifier key is held down or when the mouse has been dragged a certain distance and/or direction. The data to be dragged needs to be placed on a pasteboard before calling this method.

The method name is very long, but it's not as bad as it looks. Taking the arguments one at a time in order, let's start with `anImage`. This is the image that is displayed under the mouse as the user drags. The `viewLocation` is the location of the drag image's lower-left corner in the coordinate system of the object starting the drag. For example, if the drag image is a rendering of the entire view, the point would be (0,0).

The argument `initialOffset` is used to handle drags that start when a mouse-dragged event is received. It should be the difference between the current event location and the initial mouse-down event. If calling from within `-mouseDown:`, this is (0, 0). If a drag might be started later, the `-mouseDown:` method should save the mouse-down event so that an offset can be calculated when the drag actually starts.

The mouse-down event that initiated the drag needs to be provided as the `event` argument. In a `-mouseDown:` method, this is the event passed in to the method. If the call is made from a `-mouseDragged:` method, the `-mouseDown:` method should have retained the mouse-down event so that it can be used here.

The data to be dragged should already be on a pasteboard. The pasteboard is provided as the `pboard` argument. Any pasteboard, even a private one, can be used. The pasteboard is handed off to any drag destinations. The `sourceObj` argument is an object that implements some or all of the methods in the `NSDraggingSource` informal protocol, usually `self`.

Finally, `slideFlag` determines what should happen if the drag fails. If `YES`, the image slides back to where the drag started. If `NO`, it disappears. Most drags use `YES`. If the drag performs a delete or remove operation, such as dragging an icon out of the dock, `NO` would be used.

In the PieWidget2 example, this method is called from within the `-mouseDown:` method. To preserve the normal operation of the control when the mouse is dragged, a drag operation is only started when the option key is held down.

It is generally bad form to have a window come to the front when initiating a drag because it is likely to obscure the destination. To get around this, the `PieWidget` class implements the `-shouldDelayWindowOrderingForEvent:` method to signal to the application that perhaps the window should not be brought forward.

The `-shouldDelayWindowOrderingForEvent:` message is sent before the mouse-down is processed. After the `-mouseDown:` knows that a drag is starting, it sends the `-preventWindowOrdering` message to the application object to disable bringing the window forward. If no drag is started, no message is sent. When the application finishes the event loop, it assumes that it is okay to bring the window forward and does so.

Here is the code used by `PieWidget` to initiate the drag operation:

```
- (BOOL)shouldDelayWindowOrderingForEvent:(NSEvent *)theEvent
{
    return YES;
}

- (void)mouseDown:(NSEvent *)theEvent
{
    unsigned int flags = [theEvent modifierFlags];
    if (flags & NSAlternateKeyMask) { // option click starts a drag
        NSSize dragOffset = NSMakeSize(0.0, 0.0);
        NSPoint dragPoint = NSMakePoint(0.0, 0.0);
        NSPasteboard *pboard = [NSPasteboard pasteboardWithName:NSDragPboard];
        NSImage *image = [self imageValue];
        NSArray *pbTypes = [NSArray arrayWithObjects:NSTIFFPboardType, nil];
        [pboard declareTypes:pbTypes owner:self];
        [pboard setData:[image TIFFRepresentation] forType:NSTIFFPboardType];
        [NSApp preventWindowOrdering];
        [self dragImage:image at:dragPoint offset:dragOffset event:theEvent
                pasteboard:pboard source:self slideBack:YES];
    } else { // normal click gets normal operation
        [super mouseDown:theEvent];
    }

    return;
}
```

There is one other way to initiate a drag operation from an `NSView` object. This method allows a file icon to be dragged from a view:

```
- (BOOL)dragFile:(NSString *)filename fromRect:(NSRect)rect
      slideBack:(BOOL)slideFlag event:(NSEvent *)event
```

The `filename` argument should be the full path to the file being dragged. The `rect` argument is used to position the file icon under the mouse and should be expressed in the coordinates of the view being sent this message. The `slideFlag` and `event` arguments should be the same as with the other `-dragImage:` method. The return value indicates success in starting the drag, but says nothing about whether the drag succeeded.

`NSDraggingSource` Informal Protocol

Drag source objects must implement the `NSDraggingSource` informal protocol. It is an informal protocol because not every message in the protocol has to be implemented. Because some methods in the protocol are optional, it is not defined as a formal Objective-C protocol.

Implementing this informal protocol usually requires only a few lines of code. The one method that must be implemented by the dragging source is this:

```
- (NSDragOperation)draggingSourceOperationMaskForLocal:(BOOL)flag
```

This method is expected to return a bit-mask listing which drag operations are allowed. The flag passed in tells whether the drag destination is local, meaning that it is in the same application, or in another application. Because the local or nonlocal status might change, this method could be invoked more than once for a given drag session.

To create the return value, all the applicable masks from Table 19.3 should be combined using the C bitwise OR operator. For example, if copy and move operations are allowed, the expression `(NSDragOperationCopy | NSDragOperationMove)` should be returned.

TABLE 19.3 Drag Operation Mask Constants

Constant	Meaning
`NSDragOperationNone`	No drag operation allowed
`NSDragOperationCopy`	The destination gets a copy of the source
`NSDragOperationLink`	The source and destination share the same data
`NSDragOperationGeneric`	A generic operation, usually a copy
`NSDragOperationPrivate`	The operation is application-defined
`NSDragOperationMove`	The source is moved to the destination
`NSDragOperationDelete`	The source is deleted
`NSDragOperationEvery`	All drag operations allowed

The `NSDragOperationNone` mask is special. If no drag operation is allowed, it should be returned without being combined with any other mask. The mask that is returned is compared with what operations the destination can perform to see if a drag is possible between source and destination. The drag operation will also determine the mouse cursor that is shown as the drag proceeds. For example, a copy cursor has a little plus sign next to the cursor arrow. If more than one operation is allowed, the cursor changes automatically as needed when the user presses different modifier keys.

There are four other dragging source methods, all optional. Three are basically notifications. The `-draggedImage:beganAt:` method is called when a dragging session begins. Every time the mouse moves during the session, the `-draggedImage:movedTo:` method is called. When a session ends, the `-draggedImage:endedAt:operation:` method is called. The operation argument tells how the drag ended, offering one of the masks from Table 19.3. Unsuccessful drags end with `NSDragOperationNone`.

The other optional method allows the drag source to control whether the modifier key changes can be used mid-drag to change the drag operation. To change this, implement the `-ignoreModifierKeysWhileDragging` method to return `YES` or `NO`. The default if this method is not implemented is to respond to modifier key changes as if `NO` had been returned.

Making `PieWidget` a Dragging Source

The PieWidget2 example can only implement a drag copy operation. Because changing modifier keys won't change that, it also specifies that modifier keys should be ignored. Here is the implementation of the `NSDraggingSource` informal protocol used in the `PieWidget` class:

```
- (NSDragOperation)draggingSourceOperationMaskForLocal:(BOOL)flag
{
    return NSDragOperationCopy;
}

- (BOOL)ignoreModifierKeysWhileDragging
{
    return YES;
}
```

Try Option-dragging from a pie widget into a TextEdit document. A snapshot of the pie widget should be inserted into the document. Figure 19.1 shows a drag entering a TextEdit document.

`NSDraggingInfo` Protocol

On the destination side of a drag, an object that conforms to the `NSDraggingInfo` protocol is provided. This object is really just a container that holds information about the drag operation in progress. The destination queries this object to get any information it needs.

The dragging info object responds to `-draggingSourceOperationMask` to provide the drag operations allowed by the source. `-draggingLocation` and `-draggedImageLocation` return the location of the mouse and the image under the mouse, respectively. Both return points in the base coordinate system of the destination's window. The destination's window is returned by `-draggingDestinationWindow`.

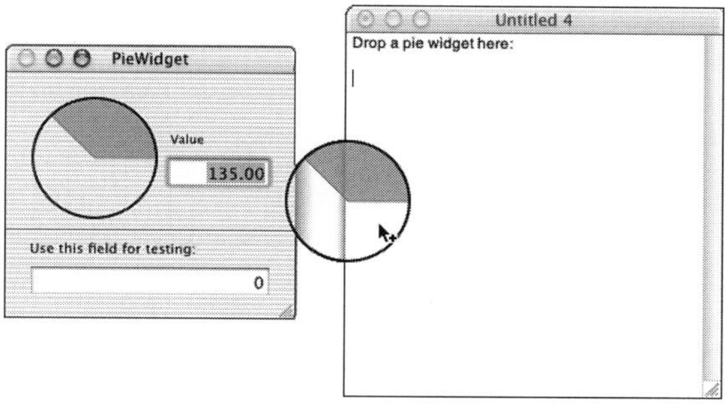

FIGURE 19.1 Option-dragging from a PieWidget to a TextEdit document.

The image being dragged, displayed under the mouse cursor, is returned by `-draggedImage`. The pasteboard containing the drag data is returned by `-draggingPasteboard`. Because the pasteboard is explicitly provided to the drag destination, any pasteboard can be used for a drag operation. The `NSDragPboard` pasteboard is usually used, but doesn't have to be. The source object is returned by `-draggingSource`, but only if the source is in the same application. If the source is in another application, `nil` is returned instead.

Setting Up a Drag Destination

To become a drag destination, a view or window must be registered. Registration requires a list of pasteboard types in an `NSArray`. The array should be used as the argument to the `-registerForDraggedTypes:` method sent to either a view or a window. If a drag containing data in any of the registered types moves over the view or window, it becomes a potential destination. Usually, the `-registerForDraggedTypes:` method is sent in a view's `-initWithFrame:` or `-awakeFromNib` methods. The `-unregisterDraggedTypes` method can be sent if the view or window is no longer accepting drags. It is rarely used.

NOTE

The most common mistake when implementing a drag destination is forgetting to register to receive drags. A view or window can be the destination only for drag types it has registered to receive. When debugging, the first thing to check is that the registration really happened.

`NSDraggingDestination` Informal Protocol

The `NSDraggingDestination` informal protocol is implemented by the dragging destination. If the destination is a window, the window's delegate can implement the methods instead of the window. This way windows that act as destinations don't have to be subclassed. None of the methods in this informal protocol are specifically required, but a drop won't do much without implementing some subset of these methods. All methods in this informal protocol take a single argument. The argument is always an object that implements the `NSDraggingInfo` protocol.

When a drag enters a target, be it view or window, the `-draggingEntered:` message is sent. An NSDragOperation should be returned (see Table 19.3 for the constants to use). Normally, this method examines the operations the source allows and returns one of them. The returned operation should specify what operation will happen if a drop actually happens over this destination in the current session. If none of the source's operations work with this destination, `NSDragOperationNone` is returned, signaling that a drop over the destination would fail.

As the mouse is moved within the target's area, the `-draggingUpdated:` message is sent. It should also return a drag operation. If this method isn't implemented, the drag operation from `-draggingEntered:` is used by the dragging machinery. If dragging leaves the destination's area without a drop occurring, `-draggingExited:` is sent. It doesn't have to return anything.

If the drag reenters the destination, the whole thing starts all over with `-draggingEntered:`. When an enter message is sent, it is possible to tell if it is the same drag session. Each session is given a unique number, known as the sequence number. If the sequence number is the same as before, it is still the same session. To obtain the sequence number, use the `-draggingSequenceNumber` method of the dragging info object.

If a drop actually happens on the destination, the `-prepareForDragOperation:` message is sent. This method is supposed to set things up so that the drop can proceed, but does not actually read the data off the pasteboard yet. It should return `YES` for the drop to proceed. If for some reason the drop needs to be aborted, a `NO` should be returned.

If the dragging image is going to land in a specific location within the drop target, the `-slideDraggedImageTo:` message should be sent to the dragging info object. An `NSPoint` should be used as the argument. This makes the drag image appear to snap into place. This method can only be sent to a dragging info object from within a `-prepareForDragOperation:` implementation.

The next method sent to the destination is `-performDragOperation:`, which is where the drop happens. The implementation should read the data from the pasteboard and do whatever else is needed to perform a drop operation. If the operation succeeded, a YES is returned. If something went wrong, NO is returned. Although an implementation of this method isn't strictly required, a drop won't do very much if this method isn't implemented.

One last method is sent to the destination. The -concludeDragOperation: method is expected to do any remaining clean up after a drop has finished.

Making PieWidget a Dragging Destination

In the PieWidget2 example, the PieWidget control displays a red border around itself when a valid drag enters the view. To provide this feedback, the BOOL instance variable dragSessionInProgress is added to the class. When true, the -drawRect: method adds the rectangle. The overridden -drawRect: is as follows:

```
- (void)drawRect:(NSRect)theRect
{
    [super drawRect:theRect];
    if (dragSessionInProgress) {
        [[NSColor redColor] set];
        NSFrameRect([self bounds]);
    }
}
```

The view's initialization is also overridden, so that the PieWidget can be registered to receive string-based pasteboards. Here's the code:

```
- (id)initWithFrame:(NSRect)myFrame
{
    NSArray *typeArray;
    self = [super initWithFrame:myFrame];
    if (!self) return nil;
    typeArray = [NSArray arrayWithObjects:NSStringPboardType, nil];
    [self registerForDraggedTypes:typeArray];
    dragSessionInProgress = NO;
    return self;
}
```

The next methods implement the NSDraggingDestination informal protocol. When a drag enters the view, the -draggingEntered: method tests the drag operation to see if the source allows a copy. If so, the copy operation is returned after setting dragSessionInProgress to YES. By redisplaying the view, the view provides the red rectangle as feedback for the drag operation. Here is the code for the -draggingEntered: method:

```
- (NSDragOperation)draggingEntered:(id <NSDraggingInfo>)sender
{
    NSPasteboard *pboard = [sender draggingPasteboard];
    unsigned int mask = [sender draggingSourceOperationMask];
    unsigned int ret = (NSDragOperationCopy & mask);

    if ([[pboard types] indexOfObject:NSStringPboardType] == NSNotFound) {
        ret = NSDragOperationNone;
    }
    if (ret != NSDragOperationNone) {
        dragSessionInProgress = YES;
        [self setNeedsDisplay:YES];
    }
    return ret;
}
```

If dragging exits the view without a drop occurring, the `PieWidget` needs to get rid of the red rectangle. The `-draggingExited:` implementation takes care of that:

```
- (void)draggingExited:(id <NSDraggingInfo>)sender
{
    dragSessionInProgress = NO;
    [self setNeedsDisplay:YES];
}
```

When a drop occurs on the `PieWidget`, the widget is sent the `-prepareForDragOperation:` method. The method doesn't need to do anything as far as `PieWidget` is concerned, but to finish the drag operation a `YES` must be returned, as follows:

```
- (BOOL)prepareForDragOperation:(id <NSDraggingInfo>)sender
{
    return YES;
}
```

The `-performDragOperation:` method is where the drop actually happens. It retrieves the pasteboard and calls the `-_takeValueFromPasteboard:operationName:` private method. The private method was created so that it could be used to implement both drop and paste support. Because both require data to be taken from a pasteboard, it is common to implement both functions with one method. The code for `-performDragOperation:` is

```
- (BOOL)performDragOperation:(id <NSDraggingInfo>)sender
{
```

```
    NSPasteboard *pb = [sender draggingPasteboard];
    return [self _takeValueFromPasteboard:pb operationName:@"drop"];
}
```

The last method to implement is the `-concludeDragOperation:` method. It performs any necessary cleanup. In this case, the cleanup is to turn off the red border now that the dragging session has concluded in a successful drop. The code in this method is the same as for the `-draggingExited:` method, though that is not always the case:

```
- (void)concludeDragOperation:(id <NSDraggingInfo>)sender
{
    dragSessionInProgress = NO;
    [self setNeedsDisplay:YES];
}
```

Drag and Drop for Table and Outline Views

The `NSTableView` and `NSOutlineView` objects already implement methods from both the `NSDraggingSource` and `NSDraggingDestination` informal protocols. To complete the implementation of drag and drop for these two classes, a special set of data source methods must be implemented. If the data source doesn't implement the necessary drag-and-drop support methods, drag-and-drop support is disabled for the table or outline view.

Although table and outline views are already set up to implement the `NSDraggingSource` and `NSDraggingDestination` informal protocols, they must still be registered as destinations. Implementing the data-source methods does not register these views to be drag destinations. It is very easy to implement the data-source methods and forget to call `-registerForDraggedTypes:`. Remember that it needs to be called from somewhere. The call is usually from an `-awakeFromNib` method in the data source so that the outlet to the table or outline view is already connected.

Drag and Drop for `NSTableView`

Implementing drag and drop for table view objects is much easier than for any generic view or window subclass. The table view object already implements the necessary drag-and-drop protocols. To implement drag and drop, three methods must be implemented by the data source. The first method is for enabling dragging. The method prototype is as follows:

```
- (BOOL)tableView:(NSTableView *)tv writeRows:(NSArray*)rows
        toPasteboard:(NSPasteboard*)pboard
```

The -tableView:writeRows:toPasteboard: method expects the data source to write the data for the specified rows to a pasteboard. The rows that should be written are provided in the rows array. The objects in the array all respond to -intValue. It is common to use a custom pasteboard type for the pasteboard. This allows all the attributes of the row's model object to be copied intact. For better interoperation with other applications, it is nice (but not required) to also write the data in a tabular data format and a plain-string format. This method is expected to return a YES if the data was successfully placed on the pasteboard and NO otherwise.

Implementing the -tableView:writeRows:toPasteboard: method enables dragging from the table view. The ScoreTable2 example on www.cocoaprogramming.net is an extension of the ScoreTable example in Chapter 18. ScoreTable2 adds drag-and-drop support to the table view. Here's the implementation of the -tableView:writeRows:toPasteboard: method from the MyDocument class:

```
- (BOOL)tableView:(NSTableView *)tv writeRows:(NSArray*)rows
        toPasteboard:(NSPasteboard*)pb
{
    NSMutableArray *rowArray = [[NSMutableArray alloc] init];
    NSEnumerator *enumerator = [rows objectEnumerator];
    id object;
    NSData *rowData;
    while (object = [enumerator nextObject]) {
        int theRow = [object intValue];
        NSMutableDictionary *rowRecord = [[self model] recordForRow:theRow];
        [rowArray addObject:rowRecord];
    }
    rowData = [self encodeDataRepresentationForObjects:rowArray];
    [pb declareTypes:[NSArray arrayWithObjects:MY_DRAG_TYPE, nil] owner:self];
    return [pb setData:rowData forType:MY_DRAG_TYPE];
}
```

To enable drop support, two methods must be implemented. The first validates the drop, and the second performs the drop operation. The method prototype for validation is as follows:

```
- (NSDragOperation)tableView:(NSTableView*)tv
        validateDrop:(id <NSDraggingInfo>)info proposedRow:(int)row
        proposedDropOperation:(NSTableViewDropOperation)op
```

The -tableView:validateDrop:proposedRow:proposedDropOperation: method is expected to return something to indicate whether the drop is legal. The dragging info should be examined to determine if it is possible to accept the data on the dragging pasteboard. The operations allowed by the source and the proposed operation should be examined along with the data to determine which drop operation is the correct one. That operation should then be returned. The `NSDragOperationNone` operation should be returned if no kind of drop can be performed.

The validation method can also retarget a drop. The drop defaults to being at or on a table view item depending on the mouse location. In a sorted table such as the ScoreTable example, however, a drop can actually be assimilated at only one location. Calling the table view method `-setDropRow:dropOperation:` causes the drop's location to be set to a specific location. The drop row should be the row where the dropped item will really end up.

The drop operation argument should be either the constant `NSTableViewDropOn` or `NSTableViewDropAbove`. Dropping on a row causes the row to be highlighted with a box around it. Dropping above a row causes a line to be drawn between rows. To indicate that the item will be added after the last row, use the `NSTableViewDropAbove` operation with a row value equal to the row count. Remember that the rows start at zero, so a row number equal to the count actually refers to a row beyond the end of the table.

The ScoreTable2 example implements the `-tableView:validateDrop:proposedRow:proposedDropOperation:` method in `MyDocument` like this:

```
- (NSDragOperation)tableView:(NSTableView*)tv
        validateDrop:(id <NSDraggingInfo>)info proposedRow:(int)row
        proposedDropOperation:(NSTableViewDropOperation)op
{
    NSPasteboard *pboard = [info draggingPasteboard];
    NSData *rowsData = [pboard dataForType:MY_DRAG_TYPE];
    NSArray *rows = [self decodeDataRepresentation:rowsData];
    NSDictionary *record = [rows objectAtIndex:0];
    int rownum = [[self model] dropRowForRecord:record];
    [tableView setDropRow:rownum dropOperation:NSTableViewDropAbove];
    return NSDragOperationCopy;
}
```

The document model class adds a method to find the drop's target row. It uses the sorting compare function to find where an insertion would take place. Here's the code:

```
- (int)dropRowForRecord:(NSDictionary *)record
{
    int i, count = [_records count];
    for (i=0; i<count; i++) {
        if (NSOrderedDescending == MYOrderScoreElements(
```

```
            [_records objectAtIndex:i], record, NULL)) return i;
    }
    return count;
}
```

The final method to implement drop support is the method that actually accepts the drop and adds the data to the data source's model. The method prototype is

```
- (BOOL)tableView:(NSTableView*)tv acceptDrop:(id <NSDraggingInfo>)info
        row:(int)row dropOperation:(NSTableViewDropOperation)op
```

This method should take the data from the dragging info's pasteboard and incorporate it into the data source's model. The type of operation that should be performed is also specified. Return a `YES` or `NO` to indicate success or failure. Here's how the method is implemented in `ScoreTable2`'s `MyDocument` class:

```
- (BOOL)tableView:(NSTableView*)tv acceptDrop:(id <NSDraggingInfo>)info
        row:(int)row dropOperation:(NSTableViewDropOperation)op
{
    NSPasteboard *pboard = [info draggingPasteboard];
    NSData *rowsData = [pboard dataForType:MY_DRAG_TYPE];
    NSArray *rows = [self decodeDataRepresentation:rowsData];
    NSEnumerator *enumerator = [rows objectEnumerator];
    id record;
    if (record = [enumerator nextObject]) {
        [[self model] addRecordWithID:-1
                              name:[record objectForKey:NAME_KEY]
                             score:[[record objectForKey:SCORE_KEY] intValue]
                             level:[[record objectForKey:LEVEL_KEY] intValue]
                              time:[record objectForKey:TIME_KEY]
                           cheated:[[record objectForKey:CHEAT_KEY] intValue]];
    }
    return YES;
}
```

For drop operations to even be tested, it is important to remember to register the table view to receive drops. To do this, the following code is added to the `MyDocument` class `-windowControllerDidLoadNib:` method:

```
[outlineView registerForDraggedTypes:
        [NSArray arrayWithObjects:MY_DRAG_TYPE, nil]];
```

Drag and Drop for `NSOutlineView`

Because outline views are subclasses of table views, it comes as no surprise that adding drag and drop to an outline view is much like adding it to a table view. As with the table view, enabling drag and drop is done by implementing three methods. The names are slightly different to accommodate the hierarchical layout of the data, but their purpose remains the same. The method prototypes are

```
- (BOOL)outlineView:(NSOutlineView *)olv writeItems:(NSArray*)items
        toPasteboard:(NSPasteboard*)pboard
- (NSDragOperation)outlineView:(NSOutlineView*)olv
        validateDrop:(id <NSDraggingInfo>)info proposedItem:(id)item
        proposedChildIndex:(int)index
- (BOOL)outlineView:(NSOutlineView*)olv acceptDrop:(id <NSDraggingInfo>)info
        item:(id)item childIndex:(int)index
```

As with the table view, a drop can be retargeted from within the validation method. To retarget a drop on an outline view, call the `-setDropItem:dropChildIndex:` method.

The implementations of these three methods work much like the table view methods. To see an example, look at the TaskOutliner example from Chapter 18, available on `www.cocoaprogramming.net`. It already supports drag and drop on the outline view, even though this support wasn't discussed in Chapter 18. Here is the code from the TaskOutliner `MyDocument` class that implements the drag-and-drop data source methods:

```
- (BOOL)outlineView:(NSOutlineView *)ov writeItems:(NSArray*)items
        toPasteboard:(NSPasteboard*)pboard
{
    NSData *data;
    data = [self encodeDataRepresentationForObjects:items];
    [ov registerForDraggedTypes:[NSArray arrayWithObjects:CAT_DRAG_TYPE, nil]];
    [pboard declareTypes:
            [NSArray arrayWithObjects:CAT_DRAG_TYPE, nil] owner:self];
    [pboard setData:data forType:CAT_DRAG_TYPE];
    return YES;
}

- (unsigned int)outlineView:(NSOutlineView*)ov
        validateDrop:(id <NSDraggingInfo>)info proposedItem:(id)item
        proposedChildIndex:(int)index
{
    return NSDragOperationCopy;
}
```

```
- (BOOL)outlineView:(NSOutlineView*)ov acceptDrop:(id <NSDraggingInfo>)info
        item:(id)item childIndex:(int)index
{
    NSPasteboard *pboard = [info draggingPasteboard];
    NSData *data = [pboard dataForType:CAT_DRAG_TYPE];
    NSMutableArray *items = [self decodeDataRepresentation:data];
    NSMutableArray *children = [item objectForKey:CHILD_KEY];
    int realIndex;
    if (!item) { // root level drop
        children = dataStore;
    }
    if (index == NSOutlineViewDropOnItemIndex) {
        realIndex = 0;
    } else {
        realIndex = index;
    }
    if (children == nil) {
        [item setObject:items forKey:CHILD_KEY];
    } else {
        int i;
        for (i=([items count]-1); i>=0; i—) {
            [children insertObject:[items objectAtIndex:i] atIndex:realIndex];
        }
    }
    [ov reloadData];
    return YES;
}
```

NOTE

In the example, only copy operations are supported. The model doesn't offer any way to delete an item. Implementing moves would require a little bit of extra model manipulation code to be added.

Implementing Services

Cocoa offers several facilities to help developers take advantage of services. The Services menu is automatically populated by the application object. Existing responder subclasses, such as the `NSApplication`, `NSWindow`, and many controls are already set up to make use of services. Custom controls need to implement a few special methods to take advantage of services. Also, a function call is available for invoking services programmatically. To publish a service, a service provider object is created and changes are made in the application's `Info.plist`.

Using Services

Several steps are required to take advantage of services in custom `NSResponder` subclasses. First, each object that can respond to a service must register the pasteboard types that it can accept. Next, the object implements a services validation method that works like menu item validation. Finally, methods to send data to a service and accept data back from a service are implemented.

Registering Pasteboard Types

The first step is to register for pasteboard send and return types. The services menu is automatically populated. If a service uses a data type that hasn't been registered, it won't even appear in the menu. Application Kit objects already register for many types, but not all types. If a services item isn't appearing in the menu, it could be because it uses an unregistered type.

To register pasteboard send and return types for the services menu, send the `-registerServicesMenuSendTypes:returnTypes:` method to `NSApp`. Both arguments are `NSArray` objects that contain pasteboard types (`NSString` objects). This method is usually sent from within an object's `+initialize` method. Any object that wants to use services should register the types it handles. All objects in the responder chain except for the main window get an opportunity to have services invoked on them. This includes custom control, application, window, and document objects as well as window and application delegate objects.

NOTE

An object can respond to types that it didn't register as long as some other object in the application registered the type. Registration is used by the application only to collect a list of types that might ever be used. It doesn't track which object registered for what type.

The `PieWidget` class in the PieWidget2 example implements methods to take advantage of services. Because it uses only one pasteboard type, `NSStringPboardType`, and that type is already registered by the Application Kit, it has no need to implement special code to register for the type. If it did register, the code would look like this:

```
+ (void)initialize
{
    NSArray *sendTypes, *returnTypes;
    static BOOL initialized = NO;
    if (initialized == YES) return;
    initialized = YES;
```

```
    sendTypes = [NSArray arrayWithObjects:NSStringPboardType, nil];
    returnTypes = [NSArray arrayWithObjects:NSStringPboardType, nil];
    [NSApp registerServicesMenuSendTypes:sendTypes
            returnTypes:returnTypes];
}
```

Validating Services Menu Items

When the services menu is displayed, all its items are validated. Validation for these items is not done in the normal way for menu items. Validation still traverses the responder chain, but a different validation method is sent:

```
- (id)validRequestorForSendType:(NSString *)sendType
        returnType:(NSString *)returnType
```

This method is expected to examine the send and return types and determine if that pairing can be supported. If so, the object that can support the services call must also be determined. The return value is not a boolean. It is the object, if any, that could make use of a services request that has the specified types. If no object is known, `nil` should be returned. This object is known as the requestor because the service is performed on its behalf. Normally, the object receiving the validation message is the requestor, so it is common to return `self` from this method. It is possible that a delegate or model object would be better suited to deal directly with services. In that case, the appropriate object should be returned.

In the PieWidget2 example, the `PieWidget` object implements this method as follows:

```
- (id)validRequestorForSendType:(NSString *)sendType
        returnType:(NSString *)returnType
{
    BOOL ret = NO, sendOK = NO, retOK = NO;
    if ([sendType compare:NSStringPboardType] == NSOrderedSame) sendOK = YES;
    if ([returnType compare:NSStringPboardType] == NSOrderedSame) retOK = YES;
    if (sendType && (!returnType) && sendOK) ret = YES;
    if (sendType && returnType && sendOK && retOK) ret = YES;
    if ((!sendType) && returnType && retOK) ret = YES;
    return (ret ? self : nil);
}
```

Sending Data to Services

When a service that takes input data is invoked, the validated object is sent the `-writeSelectionToPasteboard:types:` method. A pasteboard and array of types are passed as arguments to this method. The receiver's current selection, the selection that services is to operate on, must be placed on the pasteboard. The pasteboard has not had its types declared yet, so that has to be done before data can be placed on the pasteboard. Implementations of this method should return `YES` or `NO` to indicate success or failure.

The implementation of this method is often used as a core for implementing `-cut:`, `-copy:`, and the drag initiation so that a single method is written to place information on the pasteboard. In the PieWidget2 example, that is not done. Instead, each implementation does things a little differently. This is to show a variety of ways to interact with pasteboards. Unfortunately, it is at the expense of good object design. The `PieWidget` class implements `-writeSelectionToPasteboard:types:` to check the types and to make sure they match what it wants to do. If everything is in order, the types are declared on the pasteboard and the data is set immediately. The code looks like this:

```
- (BOOL)writeSelectionToPasteboard:(NSPasteboard *)pb types:(NSArray *)types
{
    NSArray *declareTypes = [NSArray arrayWithObjects:NSStringPboardType, nil];
    if ([types count] != 1) return NO;
    if ([NSStringPboardType compare:[types objectAtIndex:0]] != NSOrderedSame)
        return NO;
    [pb declareTypes:declareTypes owner:self];
    return [pb setString:[self stringValue] forType:NSStringPboardType];
}
```

This method could have used lazy evaluation instead of putting the data on the pasteboard immediately. Because there's only one type and it is guaranteed to be used, lazy evaluation doesn't make much sense for `PieWidget`. If lazy evaluation is used, it should be implemented exactly as described previously in the "Providing Data Lazily" section of this chapter.

Receiving Data from Services

When data comes back from a service, the `-readSelectionFromPasteboard:` method is called. Data should be read from the pasteboard argument and used to replace the current selection. If the selection is an insertion point as opposed to a range, an insertion might be performed. A `YES` or `NO` is returned to indicate success or failure.

The PieWidget class already has a method for reading a pasteboard, so its implementation of `-readSelectionFromPasteboard:` simply forwards the message:

```
- (BOOL)readSelectionFromPasteboard:(NSPasteboard *)pb
{
    return [self _takeValueFromPasteboard:pb operationName:@"services"];
}
```

Invoking Services Programmatically

It is easy to invoke services programmatically. The `NSPerformService()` function can be used to call any service. It requires two parameters. The first argument is the name of the service. The name is an `NSString` containing the nonlocalized name of the service as defined by the service providing application. (It can be found in the `Contents/Info.plist` file inside the `.app` wrapper.) For example, the name of Grab's screenshot service, Grab, Screen, is `@"Grab/Screen"`.

The second argument to `NSPerformService()` is an `NSPasteboard` instance. The pasteboard should be a custom, privately named pasteboard. If the service takes input, the input should be put on the pasteboard before the `NSPerformService()` call is made.

The `NSPerformService()` function returns `YES` if the service call succeeded. Any return data coming back from the service will be on the pasteboard that was passed to the function originally. If the call fails, `NO` is returned.

The ScreenShotTool example program on `www.cocoaprogramming.net` shows how a simple Foundation Kit–based tool can invoke a service. It will invoke Grab to take a screenshot, and then store the tiff in the specified file. Besides the `NSPerformService()` call, there are two other important things. First, to have access to the `NSPerformService()` function, the tool must be linked against `Cocoa.framework`, not `Foundation.framework`. Second, a connection to the pasteboard server is needed to make the services work. Simply asking `NSApplication` for the `+sharedApplication` object is enough to get the needed connections set up automatically. Here's the full source code for `ScreenShotTool`'s `main.m`:

```
#import <Cocoa/Cocoa.h>

NSData *getScreenshot()
{
    NSString *type;  BOOL success;
    NSArray *typeArray = [NSArray arrayWithObjects:NSTIFFPboardType, nil];
    NSPasteboard *pb = [NSPasteboard pasteboardWithName:@"Screenshot Board"];
    success =  NSPerformService(@"Grab/Screen", pb);
    if (!success) return nil;
    type = [pb availableTypeFromArray:typeArray];
    if (!type) return nil;
    return [pb dataForType:type];
}

int main (int argc, const char * argv[]) {
    NSString *filename;  NSData *screenshot;
    NSAutoreleasePool *pool = [[NSAutoreleasePool alloc] init];
```

```
    if (argc != 2) {
        fprintf(stderr, "Usage:  %s <filename>\n", argv[0]);
        fprintf(stderr, "    Stores a screenshot in <filename>\n");
        exit(1);
    }
    [NSApplication sharedApplication];
    screenshot = getScreenshot();
    if (!screenshot) {
        NSLog(@"Error:  unable to obtain screen shot.");
        exit(1);
    }
    filename = [NSString stringWithCString:argv[1]];
    [screenshot writeToFile:filename atomically:NO];
    [pool release];
    return 0;
}
```

NOTE

Grab requires a mouse click somewhere on the screen to actually have a screen shot taken. The service invocation waits for the mouse click. If the click doesn't happen within 30 seconds, the service will time out and fail. Keep this in mind when running the example.

Implementing Service Providers

Implementing a service provider is a simple process. The first step is to define an object to act as an application's service provider. An application can only have one service provider. All services invocations call one of the methods defined by the service provider. The next step is to install an instance of the service-providing object as the service provider. The last step is to add an `NSServices` entry to the application's `Info.plist`.

The MathService example on `www.cocoaprogramming.net` demonstrates how to implement a service provider. It is discussed throughout the sections on providing services. The example implements several services. The Insert Date service inserts the current date at the selection or insertion point of a text view. The Set Date Format service sends the current selection to the service provider for use as the date format for subsequent insert date invocations. The Halve and Double services take the current selection, interpret it as a floating-point number, and return a halved or doubled version of the number.

Defining a Service Provider Object

A service provider object can be an object of any class. The primary responsibility of the service provider object is to respond to messages that invoke the services its application offers. The messages have a very specific method signature, where only the <name> portion can be changed:

```
- (void)<name>:(NSPasteboard *)pb userData:(NSString *)userData
        error:(NSString **)error
```

For example, the MathService example defines these three services methods in the `MYServiceProvider` class:

```
- (void)dateService:(NSPasteboard *)pb userData:(NSString *)userData
        error:(NSString **)error
- (void)setDateFormatService:(NSPasteboard *)pb userData:(NSString *)userData
        error:(NSString **)error
- (void)multiplicationService:(NSPasteboard *)pb userData:(NSString *)userData
        error:(NSString **)error
```

The pasteboard argument is the pasteboard containing the service's input data. When the service finishes, any output data it provides should be on the pasteboard. Services that don't take input can skip taking data off the pasteboard. Likewise, those that do not return data don't need to put anything on the pasteboard.

The user data argument is an arbitrary string. The developer sets the value when writing the `Info.plist` `NSServices` entry. The main purpose is to allow a single method implement multiple services. The Halve and Double services from MathService both use the `-multiplicationService:` method. The `userData` parameter tells the object which service was invoked so that it can do the right thing.

The last argument, the error string, should be set if something goes wrong while attempting to perform the service. If everything goes fine, it should be left alone. The error string is returned by reference.

MathService's `MYServiceProvider` Class

The MathService example implements only one class, `MYServiceProvider`. The application has a small user interface, shown in Figure 19.2, that allows a date format to be set. The `MYServiceProvider` class has two outlets, `dateFormatField` and `dateExampleField`, that connect to the user interface. It also implements the `-dateFormatChanged:` action method. The `dateFormatField` field sends the `-dateFormatChanged:` action to the `MYServiceProvider` object. The `MYServiceProvider` also acts as the application's delegate.

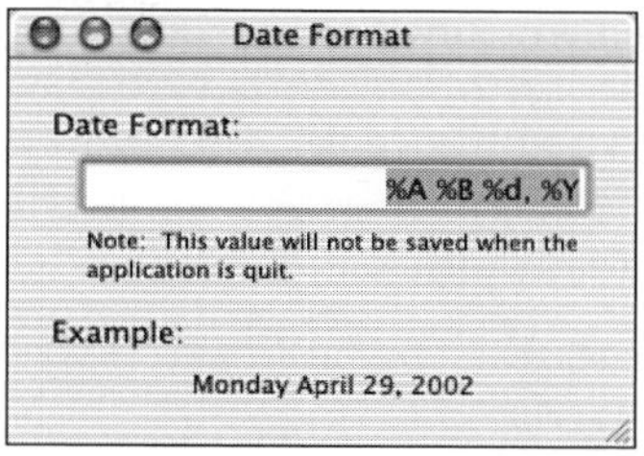

FIGURE 19.2 MathService user interface.

The user interface glue is implemented with this code:

```
- (NSString *)formattedDate
{
    return [[NSCalendarDate calendarDate] descriptionWithCalendarFormat:
            [dateFormatField stringValue]];
}

- (IBAction)dateFormatChanged:(id)sender
{
    [dateExampleField setStringValue:[self formattedDate]];
}
```

To make pasteboard manipulation simpler for the service methods, the following two convenience methods are implemented:

```
- (NSString *)getStringFromPasteboard:(NSPasteboard *)pb
{
    NSArray *types = [pb types];
    if (![types containsObject:NSStringPboardType]) {
        return nil;
    }
    return [pb stringForType:NSStringPboardType];
}

- (void)putString:(NSString *)outputString onPasteboard:(NSPasteboard *)pb
{
    NSArray *types = [NSArray arrayWithObject:NSStringPboardType];
    [pb declareTypes:types owner:nil];
    [pb setString:outputString forType:NSStringPboardType];
}
```

The three services methods mentioned in the "Defining a Service Provider Object" section earlier in this chapter are implemented in terms of the code already presented. They use the constants NO_READ_STRING and NO_WRITE_STRING, which are NSStrings defined with @"". In a professional application, these strings would be localized. Here is the code for all three methods:

```
- (void)dateService:(NSPasteboard *)pb userData:(NSString *)userData
        error:(NSString **)error
{
    NSString *outputString = [self formattedDate];
    if (!outputString) {
        *error = NO_WRITE_STRING;
        return;
    }
    [self putString:outputString onPasteboard:pb];
}

- (void)setDateFormatService:(NSPasteboard *)pb userData:(NSString *)userData
        error:(NSString **)error
{
    NSString *inputString = [self getStringFromPasteboard:pb];
    if (!inputString) {
        *error = NO_READ_STRING;
        return;
    }
    [dateFormatField setStringValue:inputString];
    [self dateFormatChanged:nil];
    [[dateFormatField window] makeKeyAndOrderFront:nil];
    [NSApp activateIgnoringOtherApps:YES];
}

- (void)multiplicationService:(NSPasteboard *)pb userData:(NSString *)userData
        error:(NSString **)error
{
    double output;
    NSString *outputString;
    NSString *inputString = [self getStringFromPasteboard:pb];
    if (!inputString) {
        *error = NO_READ_STRING;
        return;
    }
    output = [inputString doubleValue] * [userData doubleValue];
    outputString = [NSString stringWithFormat:@"%f", output];
```

```
    if (!outputString) {
        *error = NO_WRITE_STRING;
        return;
    }
    [self putString:outputString onPasteboard:pb];
}
```

The -setDateFormatService: method implements a service that receives data but returns nothing. This kind of service usually causes the service provider application to become active, because it generally implies that the user will follow through with further actions in the service provider application. Two good examples of this are the Mail Text and Mail To services implemented by the Mail application. That is why the -setDateFormatService: method brings a window forward and activates the application with the -activateIgnoringOtherApps: method. Those steps might be omitted for other applications where such behavior doesn't make sense.

The -multiplicationService: method makes use of the user data. It uses the user data as a multiplicand. This means that the Double user service needs to define the user data as 2.0 and the Halve service would define a user data of 0.5. User data could be anything, it is up to the developer to decide what its meaning is. Many simple services don't use it at all. The -dateService: and -setDateFormatService: methods completely ignore it.

Declaring a Service Provider Object

After a class that can act as a service provider has been written, it needs to be registered as the application's service provider. This is done in one of two ways. If the service providing application is a full Cocoa application, with an NSApplication object, the -setServicesProvider: method is sent to the application object. The -servicesProvider method returns the current services provider. In a Foundation Kit–based program, which has its own run loop, the NSRegisterServicesProvider() function call is used instead of -setServicesProvider:.

In the case of the MathService example, the application's delegate, a MYServiceProvider instance, does the registration by calling the NSApplication method -setServicesProvider: from the -applicationDidFinishLaunching: method. Here's the code for the entire method:

```
- (void)applicationDidFinishLaunching:(NSNotification *)notification
{
    [self dateFormatChanged:self];
    [NSApp setServicesProvider:self];
}
```

For an example of a Foundation-based program, refer to the SimpleService example in /Developer/Examples/AppKit. The main() for the program looks like this:

```
int main (int argc, const char *argv[]) {
    NSAutoreleasePool *pool = [[NSAutoreleasePool alloc] init];
    ServiceTest *serviceProvider = [[ServiceTest alloc] init];
    NSRegisterServicesProvider(serviceProvider, @"SimpleService");
    NS_DURING
        [[NSRunLoop currentRunLoop] configureAsServer];
        [[NSRunLoop currentRunLoop] run];
    NS_HANDLER
        NSLog(@"%@", localException);
    NS_ENDHANDLER
    [serviceProvider release];
    [pool release];
    return 0;
}
```

A service provider object is allocated and initialized, and then declared as the services provider. The first argument to NSRegisterServicesProvider() is the object that can provide services. The second argument is the program's services port. Normally, it should be the name of the program. Foundation-based programs, such as SimpleServices, don't have a user interface. Therefore, the application's icon should never appear in the dock. To keep the application out of the dock, set the key NSBGOnly to 1 in the Expert Applications Settings of the application's target in Project Builder.

NOTE

An object could start receiving services invocations the moment it is declared as a service provider. Don't declare an object as the services provider until it is completely ready to respond to services requests.

Configuring an Application's Info.plist for Providing Services

The final step in providing services is to properly configure the application's Info.plist. The key NSServices should refer to an NSArray that lists all the services an application can provide. Each item in the array is an NSDictionary that defines one service. Any number of services can be defined. Table 19.4 shows the keys that can be used in the dictionary that defines a service.

TABLE 19.4 Keys Found in Service Dictionaries

Service Dictionary Key	Contents
NSMessage	The service provider object method to invoke.
NSUserData	The string to use as the userData argument.
NSPortName	The services port name.
NSTimeout	The timeout in milliseconds, default is 30000 (30 seconds).
NSMenuItem	An NSDictionary containing the name of the services menu item.
NSKeyEquivalent	An NSDictionary containing the menu item's key equivalent.
NSSendTypes	An NSArray containing the service's input pasteboard types.
NSReturnTypes	An NSArray containing the service's output pasteboard types

The NSMessage key should point to an NSString that contains the partial name of the service provider message that should be invoked to perform the service. It should be the <name> portion of the method name, as shown in the "Defining a Service Provider Object" section. For example, the method -myService:userData:error: would use myService as the NSMessage name. The NSMessage key is required.

The NSUserData key is where the service's user data is set. It should be an NSString. The string can contain anything. It is passed verbatim as the userData argument when the service is invoked. The service method can then interpret it in any way it wants. This key is optional.

The NSPortName is the application's services port, a named Mach port. For an NSApplication-based program, it is the name of the application. For a Foundation Kit–based program, this should match the port name declared when calling the NSRegisterServicesProvider() function. This key is required.

NSTimeout controls the timeout length. This tells the operating system the maximum amount of time to wait for the service to finish before generating an error. The default is 30 seconds, which should be enough time for an application to launch and provide its service. If an application is likely to take longer, add this key to the services definition to extend the timeout period. The value is an NSString giving a time in milliseconds. This key is optional. The default value when the key is omitted is 30000.

The NSMenuItem and NSKeyEquivalent keys are used to define how the service appears in the services menu. Both are NSDictionary objects. Each has a single key/value pair. The key is default and the value is an appropriate NSString. The NSMenuItem key is required, but the NSKeyEquivalent key is optional.

The menu item specifies both the menu item's name as well as where it belongs in the services menu's hierarchy. The notation used separates menu levels with a / character, much like specifying a Unix file path. For example, the string Make Sticky creates a menu item in the top-level services menu. The string `TextEdit/Open File` specifies the item Open File in the TextEdit submenu. An application that offers only one service should not use a submenu. Applications vending multiple services should use a submenu. The services menus are always alphabetized. There is no way to specify a separator item or the order of the items in the menu.

The key equivalent's value should be a single character such as `d` or `D`. There is currently no way to specify key equivalents that take the option or control key.

The `NSSendTypes` and `NSReturnTypes` keys are both `NSArray` objects that contain a list of pasteboard types such as `NSStringPboardType`. Custom types can be specified, just use the string that is used when declaring the type on a pasteboard. The send types are the types that can be sent to the service as input. The return types are the types that come back from the service. One or both of these keys can be provided. It is necessary to at least declare one or the other.

MathService's `Info.plist`

The MathService example shows how to use `Info.plist` for services that send data, receive data, or both. To edit the `Info.plist` of an application, select the application's target in Project Builder, select the Application Settings tab, and click the Expert button. A property list editor will appear.

The Insert Date service uses the `-dateService:userData:error:` method. This means that the message name should be `dateService`. There is no send type, and only the `NSStringPboardType` return type. The menu item is Insert Date in the DateService submenu, so the menu item is specified as `DateService/Insert Date`. Figure 19.3 shows the `NSServices` entry for this service.

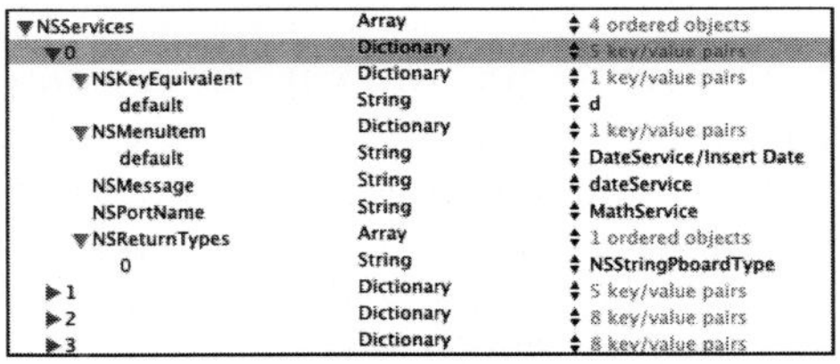

NSServices Array 4 ordered objects
0 Dictionary 5 key/value pairs
NSKeyEquivalent Dictionary 1 key/value pairs
default String d
NSMenuItem Dictionary 1 key/value pairs
default String DateService/Insert Date
NSMessage String dateService
NSPortName String MathService
NSReturnTypes Array 1 ordered objects
0 String NSStringPboardType
1 Dictionary 5 key/value pairs
2 Dictionary 8 key/value pairs
3 Dictionary 8 key/value pairs

FIGURE 19.3 The `NSServices` entry for the Insert Date service.

The Set Date Format service is much like Insert Date. The message name changes to `setDateFormatService` and there is a send type instead of a return type. The `NSServices` entry is shown in Figure 19.4.

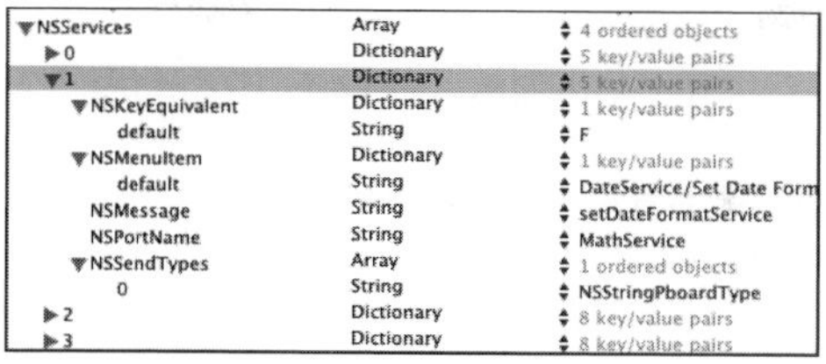

FIGURE 19.4 The `NSServices` entry for the Set Date Format service.

The Halve service uses the `multiplicationService` message. This method requires a proper `userData` setting. Because multiplying numbers by 0.5 halves them, the `NSUserData` key is set to `0.5`. A timeout entry of 20 seconds has also been set. It isn't necessary to change the timeout length, but this shows how it is done. Figure 19.5 shows the Halve service's `NSServices` entry.

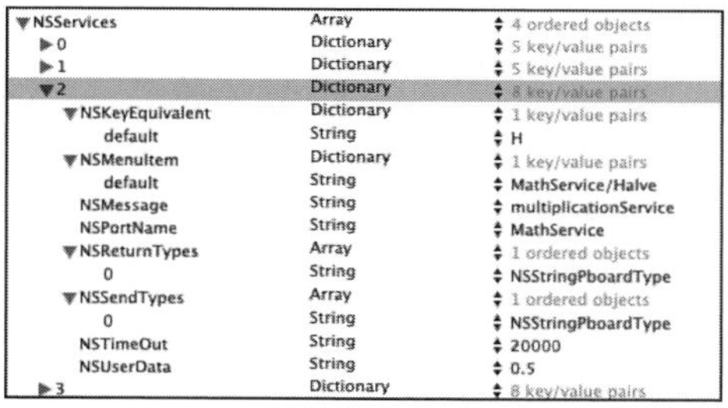

FIGURE 19.5 The `NSServices` entry for the Halve service.

The last service is the Double service. It is set up like the Halve service. It even calls the same method, so the `NSMessage` key is the same. The major difference is that the `NSUserData` key changes to 2.0. This `NSServices` entry is shown in Figure 19.6.

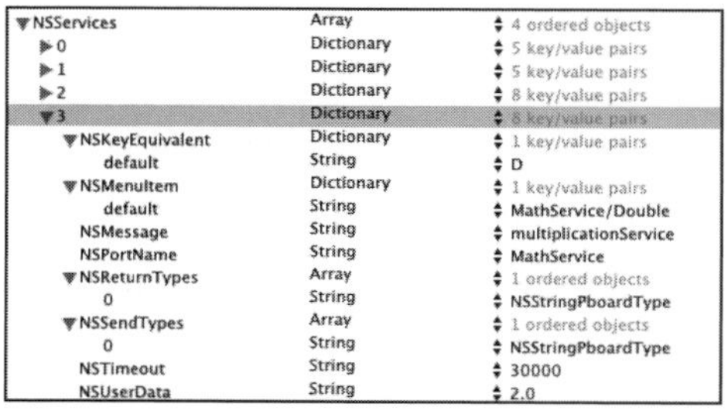

FIGURE 19.6 The `NSServices` entry for the Double service.

Both the Double and Halve services place their menu items in the MathService submenu, whereas the Insert Date and Set Date Format services insert their menu items in the DateService submenu. This is perfectly legal; items can be placed in any services menu that makes sense. By convention, the application's name is used as a submenu and all services items offered by that application are offered in that submenu. This helps to prevent conflicts between applications.

Key equivalents can also conflict between menu items. The items in an application's main menu override any key equivalents used by services items. Furthermore, services items take precedence over each other by where they fall in the menu. They are defined in alphabetical order, and the first item to request a key equivalent gets it. This means that even if a key equivalent is defined, there's a good chance it won't be available in every single application. For example, the key equivalent for Insert Date of d is lost within TextEdit. TextEdit already uses the D key for something else.

Installing Applications That Offer Services

For Mac OS X to make services available to other applications, it must first know about the service. It won't find a service unless the application that offers the service is installed in the standard application path. Installing the application in `~/Applications`, `/Applications`, or one of the other standard paths is necessary.

Applications can also be installed in the Services folder of one of the standard library paths. The `~/Library/Services` and `/Library/Services` folders are common locations. This works well for applications that offer services but don't have user interfaces. Because there's little point in launching them directly, they can be put in a services folder to keep the regular applications folders uncluttered. Putting the application in the right place isn't enough, though. After it has been installed, the services database needs to be rebuilt. This is done whenever the user logs in. So, logging out and logging back in can discover new services.

Unfortunately, there is no command-line tool to rebuild the database programmatically, even though there used to be one called `make_services`. Cocoa applications can call the `NSUpdateDynamicServices()` function, however. It takes no arguments and returns nothing. Although it does indeed update the services database, only applications launched after the `NSUpdateDynamicServices()` call display the new services. Running applications are not updated and must be quit and restarted to reflect any changes in the services menu. Programs that dynamically extend their `NSServices` entry on the fly should call this function after making modifications.

After the MathService example is correctly installed, all four of its services are available. Figure 19.7 shows the two date-related services in action.

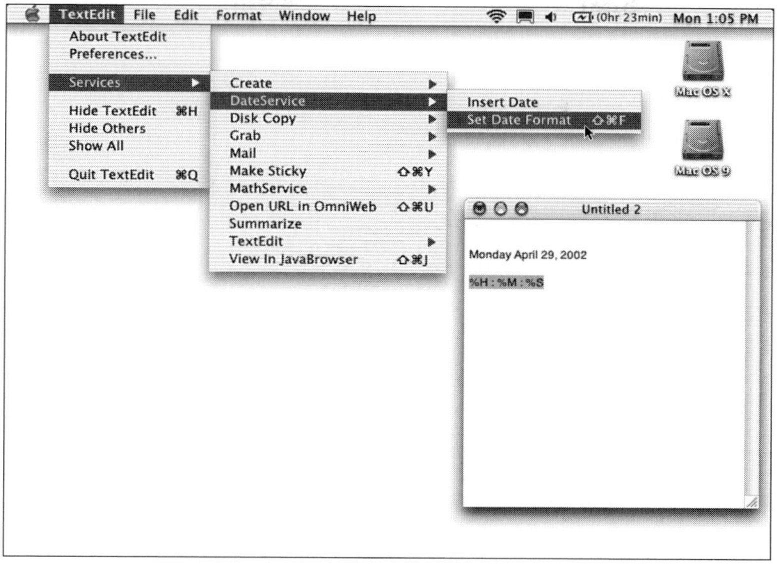

FIGURE 19.7 The date-related services offered by the MathService example.

The services for halving and doubling numbers are demonstrated in Figure 19.8. A TextEdit window shows some values that have already been run through the services. The MathService submenu of the Services menu is also shown.

Filter Services

It is also possible to create filter services to convert data from one type to another. Filter services are useful for adding a system-wide capability to open non-native image and sound formats. For example, the IFF image file type is not built into Mac OS X. By building and installing the SimpleImageFilter example in `/Developer/Examples/AppKit`, a rudimentary capability to import IFF images is available to all Cocoa applications.

To create a filter service, create a new Cocoa application project. Delete the main `.nib` file and set the `NSBGOnly` key to `1` in expert application settings. Finally, rewrite the application's main. Main should take the filename of the data to be converted from `argv[1]`. The converted data should be sent to `stdout`. The program should set its exit status to `0` for success or `1` for failure. In most cases, run loops are unnecessary. The filter program is run once for every filtering job. An autorelease pool will probably be required, though.

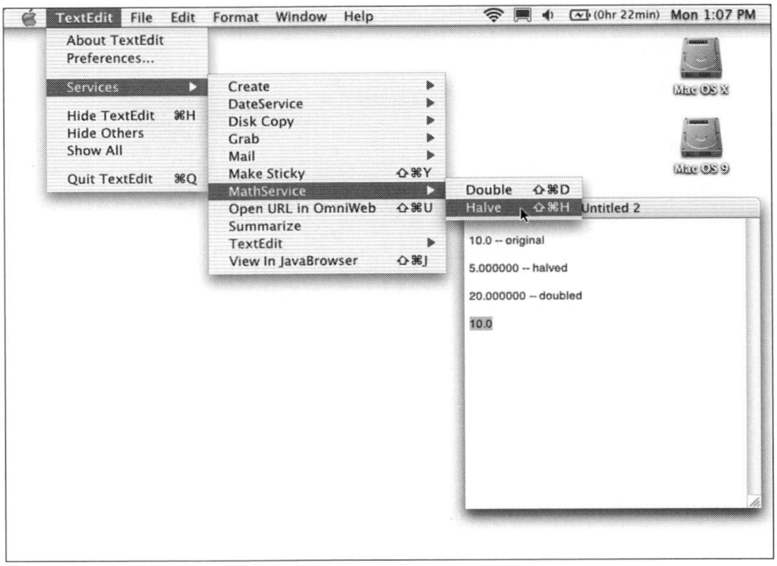

FIGURE 19.8 The math-related services offered by the MathService example.

The `NSServices` array's dictionaries have two new keys in them. The key `NSFilter` must appear in the service dictionary to flag the filter as a service. The value should be left empty. The key `NSInputMechanism` should also appear in the service dictionary, with the value `NSUnixStdio`. The return types should be a standard image or sound format. The send (input) types are usually set to a filename type with the extension added. For example, the IFF filter declares `NSTypedFilenamesPboardType:iff` and `NSTypedFilenamesPboardType:IFF` as send types.

Filter services should always be installed in a Services folder in one of the standard library paths. Refer to the SimpleImageFilter example in `/Developer/Examples/AppKit` for complete example of a filter service.

Summary

This chapter shows how to use the `NSPasteboard` class and all the major system features that revolve around pasteboard objects. A simple implementation of cut, copy, and paste is demonstrated. Drag and drop is also demonstrated in several formats. Working with services as both a client and provider is also described.

Because all these features are so closely related, it is easy to implement them all if one has been implemented. It is to an application's advantage to fully implement these features. Users appreciate applications that are willing to talk to each other, and pasteboards make it possible for developers to enhance the abilities of applications to communicate with each other.

The next chapter shows how to add online help to an application. Comprehensive help, in the form of Apple Help Books, and ToolTips are described. To improve the user's experience on Mac OS X, all Cocoa applications should implement help.

20 Adding Online Help

IN THIS CHAPTER

- Apple Help
- ToolTips
- Context-Sensitive Help (`NSHelpManager`)

Mac OS X and Cocoa offer two primary means of providing application help to users: comprehensive help and ToolTips.

Comprehensive help corresponds to the application's complete manual. It is stored in a folder inside the application as a collection of HTML pages. It is displayed by the Apple Help Viewer application that is a part of Mac OS X. The first section of this chapter describes how to use Apple Help from within a Cocoa application.

ToolTips are short messages that appear when the mouse pointer rests for a moment above a user interface element. They disappear when the mouse is moved again. ToolTips usually contain a short phrase that identifies the purpose of a control, but do not provide any in-depth information. The second part of this chapter discusses ToolTips.

Apple Help

Apple Help uses specially formatted HTML-based documents called help books to provide comprehensive help for an application. In its simplest form, a help book is a self-contained folder with HTML files and graphics. In more complex cases, some or all the help content is actually stored on an Internet server and retrieved on demand by the Help Viewer application. Figure 20.1 shows Help Viewer displaying the help book for the RoX application.

The HTML documents used by Help Viewer contain standard HTML 3.2 tags, but because of limitations in the Help Viewer application, the HTML files cannot contain any frames, forms, plug-ins, or Java. They can contain tables, images, anchors, and basic text formatting tags. Several additional meta tags are defined by Apple to customize the behavior of Apple's Help Viewer and are used by indexing applications.

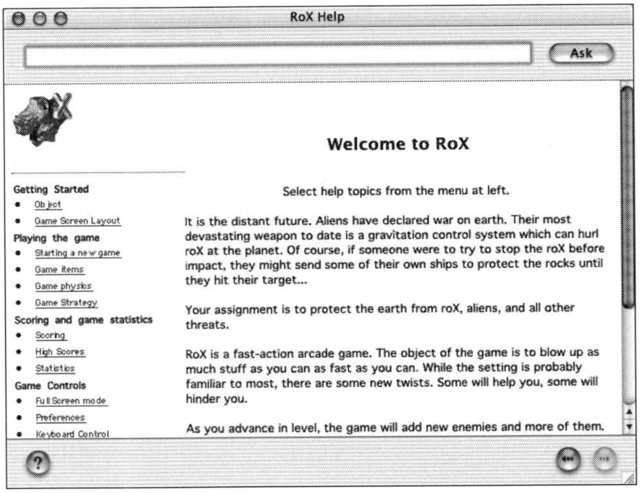

FIGURE 20.1 Apple's Help Viewer application displays comprehensive help.

NOTE

There are many features of help books that are beyond the scope of this book. Developers should read Apple's documentation about the help book format at `/Developer/Documentation/Carbon/HumanInterfaceToolbox/AppleHelp/ProvidingUserAssitAppleHelp/index.html`. The documentation is installed automatically when Apple's developer tools are installed. Details about specific Apple Help meta tags are provided in the Concepts section of the help documentation.

For those who want to dig in without reading all the documentation, just a few things are needed to create a minimal help book. The `BasicHelpExample` on the `www.cocoaprogramming.net` Web site is used as an example in this chapter.

The first task is to create a folder for the new help book. A good name would be something such as `<appname> Help`, where *<appname>* is the name of the associated application. The `BasicHelpExample` on `www.cocoaprogramming.net` uses `Basic Help` as the folder name. Help is typically a localized resource, so the help folder should be created in a localized folder such as the project's `English.lproj` folder. Put all the HTML and graphics files that are needed inside the new folder. The `BasicHelpExample` contains three HTML pages and a small GIF icon. The start page is named `index.html`, and it links to `license.html` and `release_notes.html`.

The contents of the `index.html` file used in `BasicHelpExample` are shown here. The file contains two interesting meta tags—`"AppleTitle"` and `"AppleIcon"`.

```
File index.html:

<HTML>
<HEAD>
<TITLE>Basic Help Book Example</TITLE>
<META NAME="AppleTitle" CONTENT="Basic Help Book Example">
<META NAME="AppleIcon" CONTENT="Basic%20Help/icon.gif">
</HEAD>
<BODY>
<CENTER><H1>
Basic Help Book
</H1></CENTER>
<P>
This is a very simple example of an Apple Help Book which can be
viewed in the Help Viewer application.
<P>
There's a
<A HREF="license.html">License</a>
page in this book as well as a
<A HREF="release_notes.html">Release Notes</a>
page.  Check them out!
<P>
</BODY>
</HTML>
```

The `"AppleTitle"` tag specifies the title of the help book. Clicking the ? button at the lower-left corner of the Help Viewer's window opens a listing of all the available help books, one per line. The title provided in the `"AppleTitle"` tag is shown in that listing.

To the left of each help book's title in the list of titles is a small icon. The `"AppleIcon"` meta tag specifies the filename of the icon. The icon should be a 16×16 GIF image according to Apple. Help Viewer displays a small translucent diamond if no icon is specified with the `"AppleIcon"` meta tag. Some experimentation by the authors has determined that animated GIF images and larger GIF images also work, but Help Viewer automatically scales them down to 16×16.

After the HTML files are added to the folder for the new help book, they need to be indexed. Indexing enables the Apple Help Viewer's search functionality. The Apple Help Indexing Tool application can be found in `/Developer/Applications`.

The Apple Help Indexing Tool depends on HFS file settings to tell it which files to index. This means that some command-line witchery is required before the indexer will work on OS X. Open a Terminal window and change to the help book's directory. When there, run the following command:

```
/Developer/Tools/SetFile -c 'hbwr' -t 'TEXT' *.html
```

The command sets the HFS creator code to `hbwr` and the HFS type code to `TEXT` for all files ending in the five characters, `.html`.

After the creator and type codes are set, the index can be created. The indexing application doesn't have an Open command in the File menu. The only way to get a help book indexed is to drag and drop the help book folder on the indexing tool's icon. If the indexing tool isn't already running, it will be invoked. If all goes well, a file called `<foldername> idx` will be created where `<foldername>` is the name of the folder dropped on the Apple Help Indexing Tool application icon. In the `BasicHelpExample` example, the help book's folder is `Basic Help`, so the index file is called `Basic Help idx`. The `BasicHelpExample` project already has an index in it, but feel free to delete the index and recreate it yourself.

A help book can be displayed by Help Viewer even if it does not have an index, but searches will not work without an index. Therefore, despite the inconvenience of creating an index, it is worth doing. A future version of Project Builder might have a feature to automatically create help indexes when building an application. Until then, the cumbersome manual process is required.

The process outlined so far produces valid indexed Apple Help books. The Basic Help book created in the `BasicHelpExample` example only takes advantage of the most basic features of Apple Help. To use more complex features, consult Apple's help documentation found at `/Developer/Documentation/Carbon/HumanInterfaceToolbox/AppleHelp/applehelp.html`.

Integrating a Help Book into Your Application

After a help book is available, Cocoa simplifies integration of it into an application. All the necessary steps can be performed in Project Builder.

The help book must first be added to the Project Builder project for the associated application. Copy the folder containing Help Viewer documents into the proper localized directory, such as `English.lproj` for English-language documentation. Next select Add Files from Project Builder's Project menu (Cmd-Option-A). In the sheet that appears, select the help folder and click Open. A new sheet appears. Select the Create Folder References for any added folders option, and then click the Add button.

After the folder containing Help Viewer documents has been added to Project Builder, the next step is to set up the proper bundle info keys so that Cocoa can find the help book when the application is run. Select the Targets tab in Project Builder, and then select the application's target. For most simple projects, that will be the only target shown. Choose the Application Settings tab from the target editor, and click the Expert button that appears at the upper right of the target editor area. Two new key/value pairs need to be added. Use the New Sibling button to add them. The keys and values to add follow in Table 20.1:

TABLE 20.1 Apple's Help Viewer Meta Tags

Key	Value
`CFBundleHelpBookFolder`	*<folder name>*
`CFBundleHelpBookName`	*<help book name>*

The first key, `CFBundleHelpBookFolder`, specifies the help book folder's name. Its value must exactly match the name of the folder containing the help book. In the case of the `BasicHelpExample`, the folder is named `Basic Help`, which is the value used in the example for the `CFBundleHelpBookFolder` key.

The second key, `CFBundleHelpBookName`, specifies the name of the help book. The value must be the same as the title specified with the `"AppleTitle"` meta tag in the index page of the help book. In our example, the value of this key is Basic Help Book Example. If the value of this key doesn't exactly match the `"AppleTitle"` meta tag, the Help Viewer application will still open, but it will not show the correct help book. Instead, it will show the list of all available help books on the system.

The main `.nib` file template used for Cocoa applications already contains a Help menu connected to the correct action, so at this point the application is ready to be tested. Build and run the application. Choosing the help item from the running application's Help menu (Cmd-?) opens the new help book as expected. If some aspect of help isn't working, be sure that each of the steps in this section were followed exactly. Also be sure that there are valid values for all the Basic Information target settings in the target editor in Project Builder (Application Settings tab with the Simple button selected).

To use another object such as a menu item, button, or control to open a help book, simply connect the object to the First Responder object and have it send the `-showHelp:` message. This action method is defined by the `NSApplication` class and will open an application's help book as long as it has been properly specified by the key/value pairs given in Table 20.1.

There has been no need to write code to implement Apple help, so far. It is possible to use Apple Help in a Cocoa application without writing a single line of code. As shown previously, all that is needed is to create a help book, and then set two bundle info keys in Project Builder. Everything else has already been set up automatically by Cocoa.

Extending Help Functionality Using Carbon

It is possible to implement more sophisticated behavior than just opening a help book to its title page when the Help menu item is selected. An application might need to open to a specific page in a help book or provide more than one help book. These features can be added, but some code is required. Unfortunately, Cocoa provides no direct API for this functionality. It is only available from Carbon. To make it easier for Cocoa developers to access this functionality, the `MiscHelpManager` class has been created. `MiscHelpManager` is adapted from Apple sample code provided with the Apple Help documentation.

NOTE

`MiscHelpManager` is part of the MiscKit. The MiscKit is a third-party resource and is available for free at `www.misckit.com`. The `MiscHelpManager` class is also available from the `www.cocoaprogramming.net` Web site.

The source code for the `MiscHelpManager` class is shown here primarily as a simple example of wrapping procedural Carbon APIs in objects.

File `MiscHelpManager.h`:

```
#import <Foundation/Foundation.h>


@interface MiscHelpManager : NSObject
{
}

- (void)goToUserHelpCenter;
- (void)goToDeveloperHelpCenter;
- (void)registerBook;
- (void)goToTableOfContents;
- (void)goToPage:(NSString *)pagePath;
- (void)goToAnchorNamed:(NSString *)anchorName;
- (void)goToAnchorNamed:(NSString *)anchorName onPage:(NSString *)pagePath;

@end

File MiscHelpManager.m:#import "MiscHelpManager.h"
#import <Carbon/Carbon.h>
```

```
@interface MiscHelpManager (_private)

- (OSStatus)_gotoHelpToc:(AHTOCType)theTOC;
- (OSStatus)_registerMyHelpBook;
- (OSStatus)_goToAnchorNamed:(CFStringRef)anchorName onPage:(CFStringRef)pagePath;
- (OSStatus)_goToAnchorNamed:(CFStringRef)anchorName;
- (void)_reportError:(OSStatus)err forMethodNamed:(NSString *)methodName
        withData:(NSString *)data;

@end

@implementation MiscHelpManager

- (void)goToUserHelpCenter
{
    OSStatus err = [self _gotoHelpToc:kAHTOCTypeUser];
    if (err != noErr) {
        [self _reportError:err forMethodNamed:@"goToUserHelpCenter" withData:@""];
    }
}

- (void)goToDeveloperHelpCenter
{
    OSStatus err = [self _gotoHelpToc:kAHTOCTypeDeveloper];
    if (err != noErr) {
        [self _reportError:err forMethodNamed:@"goToDeveloperHelpCenter"
                withData:@""];
    }
}

- (void)registerBook
{
    OSStatus err = [self _registerMyHelpBook];
    if (err != noErr) {
        [self _reportError:err forMethodNamed:@"registerBook" withData:@""];
    }
}

- (void)goToTableOfContents
{
    OSStatus err = [self _goToAnchorNamed:NULL onPage:NULL];
    if (err != noErr) {
```

```
        [self _reportError:err forMethodNamed:@"goToTableOfContents" withData:@""];
    }
}

- (void)goToPage:(NSString *)pagePath
{
    OSStatus err = [self _goToAnchorNamed:NULL onPage:(CFStringRef)pagePath];
    if (err != noErr) {
        [self _reportError:err forMethodNamed:@"goToPage:" withData:pagePath];
    }
}

- (void)goToAnchorNamed:(NSString *)anchorName
{
    OSStatus err = [self _goToAnchorNamed:(CFStringRef)anchorName];
    if (err != noErr) {
        [self _reportError:err forMethodNamed:@"goToAnchorNamed:"
                withData:anchorName];
    }
}

- (void)goToAnchorNamed:(NSString *)anchorName onPage:(NSString *)pagePath
{
    OSStatus err = [self _goToAnchorNamed:(CFStringRef)anchorName
            onPage:(CFStringRef)pagePath];
    if (err != noErr) {
        [self _reportError:err forMethodNamed:@"goToAnchorNamed:onPage:" withData:
                [NSString stringWithFormat:@"%@:%@", pagePath, anchorName]];
    }
}

- (void)_reportError:(OSStatus)err forMethodNamed:(NSString *)methodName
        withData:(NSString *)data
{
    if (err == noErr) return;
    if (err == fnfErr) {
        NSLog(@"IXHelpManager %@: File not found.  (\"%@\")", methodName, data);
    } else if (err == paramErr) {
        NSLog(@"IXHelpManager %@: Invalid parameter.  (\"%@\")",
                methodName, data);
    } else {
```

```
        NSLog(@"IXHelpManager %@: Unknown error %d.  (\"%@\")",
                methodName, err, data);
    }
}

- (OSStatus)_gotoHelpToc:(AHTOCType)theTOC
{
    return AHGotoMainTOC(theTOC);
}

- (OSStatus)_registerMyHelpBook
{
    // The code for this method comes from Apple's Carbon docs.
    // I touched it up so it would compile. - DAY
    CFBundleRef myAppsBundle;
    CFURLRef myBundleURL;
    FSRef myBundleRef;
    OSStatus err;

    // set up a known state
    myAppsBundle = NULL;
    myBundleURL = NULL;

    // Get our application's main bundle from Core Foundation
    myAppsBundle = CFBundleGetMainBundle();
    if (myAppsBundle == NULL) {
        err = fnfErr;
        goto bail;
    }

    // retrieve the URL to our bundle
    myBundleURL = CFBundleCopyBundleURL(myAppsBundle);
    if (myBundleURL == nil) {
        err = fnfErr;
        goto bail;
    }

    // convert the URL to a FSRef
    if (!CFURLGetFSRef(myBundleURL, &myBundleRef) ) {
        err = fnfErr;
        goto bail;
    }
```

```
    // register our application's help book
    err = AHRegisterHelpBook(&myBundleRef);
    if (err != noErr) goto bail;

    // done
    CFRelease(myBundleURL);
    return noErr;

bail:
    if (myBundleURL != NULL) {
        CFRelease(myBundleURL);
    }

    return err;
}

- (OSStatus)_goToAnchorNamed:(CFStringRef)anchorName onPage:(CFStringRef)pagePath
{
    // The code for this method comes from Apple's Carbon docs.
    // I touched it up so it would compile. — DAY
    // If pagePath is NULL, goes to main TOC
    // If anchorName is NULL, goes to top of page
    CFBundleRef myAppsBundle;
    CFTypeRef myBookName;
    OSStatus err;

    // set up a known state
    myAppsBundle = NULL;
    myBookName = NULL;

    // Get our application's main bundle from Core Foundation
    myAppsBundle = CFBundleGetMainBundle();
    if (myAppsBundle == NULL) {
        err = fnfErr;
        goto bail;
    }

    // get the help book's name
    myBookName = CFBundleGetValueForInfoDictionaryKey(myAppsBundle,
            CFSTR("CFBundleHelpBookName"));
```

```
    if (myBookName == NULL) {
        err = fnfErr;
        goto bail;
    }

    // verify the data type returned
    if (CFGetTypeID(myBookName) != CFStringGetTypeID()) {
        err = paramErr;
        goto bail;
    }

    // go to the page
    err = AHGotoPage(myBookName, pagePath, anchorName);
    if (err != noErr) goto bail;

    // done
    return noErr;

bail:
    return err;
}

- (OSStatus)_goToAnchorNamed:(CFStringRef)anchorName
{
    // The code for this method comes from Apple's Carbon docs.
    // I touched it up so it would compile. — DAY
    CFBundleRef myAppsBundle;
    CFTypeRef myBookName;
    OSStatus err;

    // set up a known state
    myAppsBundle = NULL;
    myBookName = NULL;

    // Get our application's main bundle from Core Foundation
    myAppsBundle = CFBundleGetMainBundle();
    if (myAppsBundle == NULL) {
        err = fnfErr;
        goto bail;
    }
```

```
    // get the help book's name
    myBookName = CFBundleGetValueForInfoDictionaryKey(myAppsBundle,
            CFSTR("CFBundleHelpBookName"));
    if (myAppsBundle == NULL) {
        err = fnfErr;
        goto bail;
    }

    // verify the data type returned
    if (CFGetTypeID(myBookName) != CFStringGetTypeID()) {
        err = paramErr;
        goto bail;
    }

    // go to the page
    err = AHLookupAnchor( myBookName, anchorName);
    if (err != noErr) goto bail;

    // done
    return noErr;

bail:
    return err;
}

@end
```

The `MiscHelpManager` class can't be used by itself; it is meant to be called by a controller within an application. It doesn't provide any action methods that could be used directly within Interface Builder. To see this object in action, refer to the `MiscHelpManagerExample` code on `www.cocoaprogramming.net`. The Basic Help book used in the `BasicHelpExample` example is also used in the `MiscHelpManagerExample`. The Basic Help book has three pages: an index page, a license, and release notes. The `MiscHelpManagerExample` application uses the `CFBundleHelpBookFolder` and `CFBundleHelpBookName` keys in Project Builder's target editor just like `BasicHelpExample`.

The `MiscHelpManagerExample` application contains a controller object called `AppDelegate` that provides five action methods for Interface Builder to call. Each method makes a corresponding call to an instance of `MiscHelpManager`, as shown in the following source code:

File AppDelegate.h:

```
#import <Cocoa/Cocoa.h>

@class MiscHelpManager;

@interface AppDelegate : NSObject
{
    MiscHelpManager *helpManager;
}

- (IBAction)openHelp:(id)sender;
- (IBAction)openHelpCenter:(id)sender;
- (IBAction)openDeveloperHelpCenter:(id)sender;
- (IBAction)openReleaseNotes:(id)sender;
- (IBAction)openLicense:(id)sender;

@end
```

File AppDelegate.m:

```
#import "AppDelegate.h"
#import "MiscHelpManager.h"

@implementation AppDelegate

- (id)init
{
    self = [super init];
    if (!self) return nil;
    helpManager = [[MiscHelpManager alloc] init];
    [helpManager registerBook];
    return self;
}

- (void)dealloc
{
    [helpManager release];
    [super dealloc];
}

- (IBAction)openHelp:(id)sender
```

```
{
    [helpManager goToTableOfContents];
}

- (IBAction)openHelpCenter:(id)sender
{
    [helpManager goToUserHelpCenter];
}
- (IBAction)openDeveloperHelpCenter:(id)sender
{
    [helpManager goToDeveloperHelpCenter];
}

- (IBAction)openReleaseNotes:(id)sender
{
    [helpManager goToPage:@"release_notes.html"];
}

- (IBAction)openLicense:(id)sender
{
    [helpManager goToPage:@"license.html"];
}

@end
```

A `MiscHelpManager` instance is created in `AppDelegate`'s `-init` method, and it is asked to register the bundle's help book(s). If there is only one help book, Cocoa will automatically register it. However, it is possible to have a bundle specify multiple help books. In such cases, it is necessary to explicitly register all the help books.

The first three action methods are straightforward. The `-openHelp:` method does the same thing as `NSApplication`'s `-showHelp:` method. It opens the associated help book to its index page. The only difference is that the `MiscHelpManager` object is being used to do the opening. Two other methods, `-openHelpCenter:` and `-openDeveloperHelpCenter:`, access the standard user and developer help centers shipped with OS X. Each help center provides a list of help books available on the system. The user help center lists books oriented toward typical users' concerns. The developer help center has more technical content.

The last two action methods, `-openReleaseNotes:` and `- openLicense:`, are more interesting and show how a developer most commonly would use a `MiscHelpManager` instance. They open the current help book to a specific page, in this case either the license or release notes page. These methods use the

MiscHelpManager -goToPage: method to open to a particular page in a help book. An NSString is used to specify a page. Pass in the filename of the page to be displayed. This filename should be a relative path, treating the help book folder as the current directory.

With MiscHelpManager, it is possible to ask the Help Viewer to jump to a specific anchor within the HTML files (as specified with an HTML <a name="*<anchor_name>*"> tag). To do this, use one of the MiscHelpManager methods -goToAnchorNamed: or -goToAnchorNamed:onPage:. Because information about all the anchors is stored in the help book's index, the first method, which doesn't require the page name, will search the index to find the right page for the requested anchor. This is usually the best way to look up an anchor because it prevents introducing dependencies on the help book's layout into the application's code. The second method can be used to specify a particular page just like the -goToPage: method.

ToolTips

ToolTips are short messages that appear when the mouse pointer rests for a moment above a user interface element, shown in Figure 20.2. They disappear when the mouse is moved again. A ToolTip is usually a short phrase that helps identify a control and does not provide any in-depth information. Interface Builder offers direct support for ToolTips, and that support is often sufficient. Cocoa also provides some APIs to handle more complex situations.

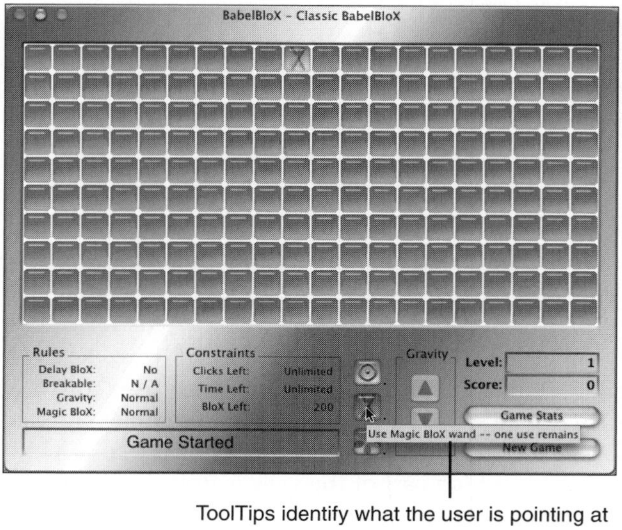

FIGURE 20.2 ToolTips display short identifying phrases.

Using Interface Builder to Set ToolTips

As with comprehensive help, Cocoa makes it possible to use ToolTips without writing any code at all. In Interface Builder there is a Help inspector for every view object that can have an associated ToolTip. Select an object in Interface Builder, and then use Apple-4 to open the help inspector. Type a short phrase into the text field labeled "Tool Tip" to set the ToolTip for that interface object. See Figure 20.3 to see a ToolTip set for the Open Help Book button in the `BasicHelpExample` application. The tip states, "Open example Apple Help Book." When the application is running and the user's mouse hovers over the button, the tip will automatically appear. ToolTips don't appear in Interface Builder unless it is in Test Interface mode.

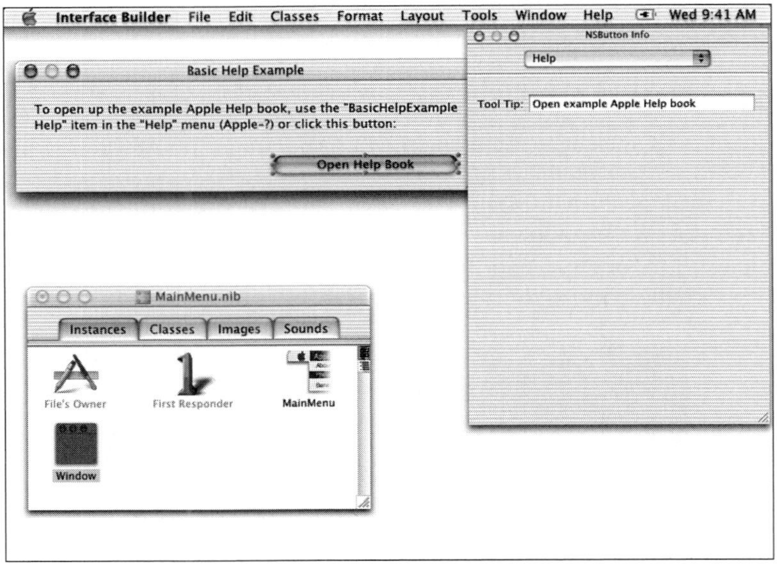

FIGURE 20.3 Set ToolTips using Interface Builder.

Cocoa APIs for ToolTips

Although Interface Builder presents an easy way to set ToolTips, it is rather limited. Only one ToolTip can be set per interface object. A complex interface object such as a `NSTableView`, a `NSMatrix`, or a custom view might need to display different ToolTips depending on which part of the view is underneath the mouse. Some code is required to do this.

The `NSView` class defines five methods for working with ToolTips. The functionality provided by the Help inspector in Interface Builder is accessed programmatically by passing an `NSString` to the `-setToolTip:` method. Passing `nil` to this method will remove the ToolTip. The `-toolTip` method returns any previously set ToolTip string.

For more advanced ToolTip functionality, there are three other methods. The first is for setting the ToolTip and looks like this:

```
- (NSToolTipTag)addToolTipRect:(NSRect)aRect owner:(id)anObject
        userData:(void *)data;
```

This method specifies a rectangular area of the view for the ToolTip. If the mouse comes to rest inside this rectangle, this ToolTip will be activated. Note, however, that the text of the ToolTip is not specified by this method call. Instead, when the ToolTip is needed, the owner object will be sent a message requesting a string to use for the ToolTip. The user data argument will be sent to the owner as part of that message. It should therefore either contain data useful to the owner or be set to `NULL`. When this method is used, an `NSToolTipTag` is returned. The tag can be used later by the owner to identify which ToolTip was activated. It can also be used to later remove the ToolTip.

The owner object itself can provide ToolTips for multiple different views. The owner could be one of the application's controller objects or could even be the view itself. For any of this to work, though, the owner object must implement this method from the `NSToolTipOwner` informal protocol:

```
- (NSString *)view:(NSView *)view stringForToolTip:(NSToolTipTag)tag
    point:(NSPoint)point userData:(void *)data;
```

When a ToolTip defined by `-addToolTipRect:owner:userData:` is activated, the `-view:stringForToolTip:point:userData:` message will be sent to the ToolTip's owner object. This message provides the owner with a wealth of information that can be used to determine which ToolTip text should be returned. It identifies which view object needs a ToolTip, what the ToolTip's tag is, the point within the view where the mouse is located, and the user data that was provided when the ToolTip was set up. Any or all these pieces of information can be used to determine the ToolTip text. When the text is known, it should be returned from this method as an `NSString`. This method is called before the ToolTip is displayed, so it is possible to dynamically return different strings based on the application's current state.

Finally, there are two methods defined by `NSView` objects that remove a ToolTip that has been attached to a rectangle. One, `-removeToolTip:`, removes a single ToolTip, as identified by the tag returned when the ToolTip was originally set. The other method, the aptly named `-removeAllToolTips`, removes all ToolTips for the view.

The `ToolTipExample` program on `www.cocoaprogramming.net` demonstrates how to use these methods. The example contains a custom `NSView` subclass that draws two colored rectangles. Each of the rectangles is a ToolTip area. For simplicity, the ToolTip owner object is the view itself. To add a little interest to the example, if the mouse is near the center of the red (right) rectangle a different ToolTip string will be returned.

The view also resets the ToolTip rectangles whenever it is resized. To do this, the view sets itself up to observe itself and watch for the `NSViewFrameDidChangeNotification` notification. Whenever this notification is received, the view declares the rectangles "dirty" and recalculates them the next time it is drawn. The dirty instance variable is used to keep track of this status. The tags for the ToolTips and the rectangles themselves are also stored in instance variables.

In the implementation, the end of the `-_resetRects` method in the ToolTipExampleView class is where the ToolTips are set up. Because there might already be some ToolTip rectangles set, all rectangles are removed with the `-removeAllToolTips` method. Then `-addToolTipRect:owner:userData:` is used to actually set the ToolTip rectangles. The ToolTip that is shown is determined in the view's implementation of the `-view:stringForToolTip:point:userData:` method. The implementation uses the ToolTip tag to determine which rectangle contains the mouse pointer. In the case of the right rectangle, the point parameter is used to decide if the mouse is near the center of the rectangle.

The rest of the view's code is typical initialization and drawing code. The complete code for the `ToolTipExampleView` object is shown here.

File `ToolTipExampleView.h`:

```
#import <AppKit/AppKit.h>

@interface ToolTipExampleView : NSView
{
    BOOL dirty;
    NSRect leftRect, rightRect;
    NSToolTipTag leftTag, rightTag;
}

- (NSString *)view:(NSView *)view stringForToolTip:(NSToolTipTag)tag
        point:(NSPoint)point userData:(void *)data;

@end
```

File `ToolTipExampleView.m`:

```
#import "ToolTipExampleView.h"

@interface ToolTipExampleView(PrivateMethods)
- (void)_frameChanged:(NSNotification *)theNotification;
- (void)_resetRects;
@end

@implementation ToolTipExampleView

- (id)initWithFrame:(NSRect)frame
{
    self = [super initWithFrame:frame];
    if (!self) return nil;
    dirty = YES;
    [self setPostsFrameChangedNotifications:YES];
    [[NSNotificationCenter defaultCenter] addObserver:self
            selector:@selector(_frameChanged:)
            name:NSViewFrameDidChangeNotification object:self];
    return self;
}

- (void)_frameChanged:(NSNotification *)theNotification
{
    dirty = YES;
}

- (void)_resetRects
{
    // determine the left and right rectangles
    NSRect bds = [self bounds];
    double midX = (bds.size.width / 2);
    NSRect leftSide = NSMakeRect(0.0, 0.0, midX, bds.size.height);
    NSRect rightSide = NSMakeRect(midX, 0.0, midX, bds.size.height);
    double xInset = (bds.size.width / 20.0);
    double yInset = (bds.size.height / 20.0);
    leftRect = NSInsetRect(leftSide, xInset, yInset);
    rightRect = NSInsetRect(rightSide, xInset, yInset);
    // add tooltips for the rectangles
```

```
    [self removeAllToolTips];
    leftTag = [self addToolTipRect:leftRect owner:self userData:NULL];
    rightTag = [self addToolTipRect:rightRect owner:self userData:NULL];
    dirty = NO;
}

- (NSString *)view:(NSView *)view stringForToolTip:(NSToolTipTag)tag
        point:(NSPoint)point userData:(void *)data
{
    // use the tags to determine which rectangle is under the mouse
        if (tag == leftTag) {
        return NSLocalizedString(@"The Blue rectangle", @"");
        }
    if (tag == rightTag) {
        // for the red rectangle, we'll look at the point and return a
        // different string if the mouse is near the center of that rectangle
        NSRect centerRect = NSInsetRect(rightRect, (rightRect.size.width * 0.4),
                (rightRect.size.height * 0.4));
        if (NSPointInRect(point, centerRect)) {
            return NSLocalizedString(@"Center of the Red rectangle", @"");
        }
        return NSLocalizedString(@"The Red rectangle", @"");
    }
    // we should never get to here!
    return NSLocalizedString(@"Unknown tooltip area", @"");
}

- (void)drawRect:(NSRect)rect
{
    NSRect bds = [self bounds];
    if (dirty) {
        [self _resetRects];
    }
    [[NSColor blackColor] set];
    NSRectFill(bds);
    [[NSColor blueColor] set];
    NSRectFill(leftRect);
    [[NSColor redColor] set];
    NSRectFill(rightRect);
}

@end
```

When the `ToolTipExample` project is built and run, you can see one minor flaw with the ToolTips. The example runs mostly as expected, but when a ToolTip has been shown for the right rectangle, it doesn't change until the mouse moves out of the rectangle and back in again. Thus, to see the different ToolTip message for the center of the rectangle, the mouse needs to keep moving until it is near the center of the rectangle. Whichever ToolTip is set first is the one that will be displayed until the mouse has exited and re-entered the rectangle.

ToolTip rectangles work just like tracking rectangles. Because of this limitation, it is best to set up another ToolTip rectangle for the center of the rectangle instead of using just the single ToolTip rectangle. This is a flaw left in the example to demonstrate that the ToolTips can be changed dynamically, but with the limitation that ToolTips only change when the mouse crosses a ToolTip rectangle's boundary.

Context-Sensitive Help (`NSHelpManager`)

A quick perusal of the Cocoa reference material, or the API header files, uncovers a final Help related API, the `NSHelpManager` class. From the class's interface, it might seem that the class manages contextual help.

Historically, under Openstep, the user could hold down the Help key (or the F1 key or the Ctrl-Alt keys) to change the cursor into a question mark. The user could then click a user interface object to open a small help window briefly describing the purpose of that control. The window would disappear when the user subsequently clicked anywhere in the application.

Although the API remains, this functionality has been removed in Mac OS X. In the current implementation of Cocoa, the `NSHelpManager` object does not work and should simply be ignored. We mention this object only because a casual observer might stumble across its interface, try to use it, and become quite frustrated. Hopefully, by explaining this situation, any confusion can be avoided until Apple decides to either remove this interface or restore the functionality.

Summary

This chapter explains the basic integration of help books into Cocoa applications. Help books are viewed with Apple's Help Viewer application. The `MiscHelpManager` class wraps Carbon procedural APIs to access sophisticated features of Help Viewer from Cocoa applications. Simple ToolTips set within Interface Builder and more complex, context position–dependent ToolTips are shown in the `ToolTipExample` example application.

The next chapter describes the integration of Apple's multimedia technologies with Cocoa applications. Just like with Apple's application help features, basic multimedia support can be added to Cocoa applications with little or no code. Sophisticated use of multimedia requires the use of procedural APIs. Chapter 21, "Multimedia," describes the Cocoa support for rich media.

21 Multimedia

IN THIS CHAPTER

- Sound
- QuickTime
- 3D Graphics

This chapter explores the options available from Cocoa for working with multimedia. Cocoa provides classes for sound playback, QuickTime movie playback, and OpenGL drawing. Additional technologies such as advanced QuickTime manipulation, speech recognition, and speech synthesis are also available as part of Mac OS X and can be accessed from Cocoa.

Sound

The Cocoa Application Kit includes the `NSSound` class that provides limited direct support for sound playback, but not recording. More powerful and flexible sound playback is supported through QuickTime. QuickTime can read a wide variety of sound file formats including the popular MP3 and CD audio formats. The Core Audio API underlies both QuickTime and `NSSound`. Even though there is no support for sound recording via Cocoa's `NSSound` class, the Core Audio APIs can be used by Cocoa applications to record sounds that are later played by `NSSound`.

`NSSound` Class

The Application Kit provides the `NSSound` class as a simple method of playing sound. It natively supports playback of `.aiff`, `.wav`, and `.snd` files, and can be extended through the use of filter services to play additional sound formats. The "Creating an `NSImage`" section of Chapter 14, "Custom Views and Graphics Part III," describes filter services for converting image types. Filter services for converting sound and other types are created in substantially the same way. Apple provides a filter service example called `SimpleImageFilter` in the `/Developer/Examples/AppKit` directory installed when Apple's developer tools are installed.

A number of methods exist for creating a new NSSound instance that can play the sound from a disk file. The simplest to use is the class method +soundNamed:. The argument, an NSString, identifies the sound that will be played. NSSound first searches for any sounds that have been previously loaded and assigned the provided name using -setName:. If no sound is located that fills that criteria, the search is expanded to include the named System sounds located in the /System/Library/Sounds folder. If there is still no matching sound found, the application's wrapper is checked next. Finally, the Sound directories in the standard library path locations are searched. If the named sound is still not located, nil is returned. If an NSSound object that is created with this method is archived using the NSCoding protocols, only the name is stored, not the sound data itself.

If the sound file resides outside of the directories searched by +soundNamed:, use the method -initWithContentsOfFile:byReference:. The first argument is the path to the file. The second argument allows explicit specification when archiving the object. A value of YES causes only the path to be saved, whereas NO causes the sound data to be archived as well.

As an alternative to using the +soundNamed: search method, NSBundle provides a method for finding a sound file with a specified filename by calling -pathForSoundResource:, passing the filename without the suffix as the argument. Only natively understood file types are supported.

Similar to the -initWithContentsOfFile:byReference: method, -initWithContentsOfURL:byReference: creates an NSSound based on the contents located at the provided NSURL. This can be a local file or a remotely stored Web resource. Again, the byReference parameter controls whether the sound data is archived, or just the URL.

If the raw sound data is available in an NSData format, a new instance of NSSound can be created using the method -initWithData: passing the data as the argument. The data must have the appropriate magic number and sound header intact. Only formats that Cocoa natively understands are supported for this method.

After an NSSound object has been created, the sound name can be set using setName: method. If the name is already registered to another existing NSSound instance, it re-registered with the new sound. The name of an NSSound can be retrieved using the method -name. If the sound was not initially created using +soundNamed: and has not been explicitly named since creation, the return value will be nil.

Sound objects can also be created from an application's pasteboard contents. An application can test a pasteboard to see if there are any suitable sound types available using the class method +canInitWithPasteboard: passing an NSPasteboard instance as the argument. This method tests the provided pasteboard for any contents that match one of the types returned by `+soundUnfilteredPasteboardTypes`. If a matching pasteboard type is found, `+canInitWithPasteboard:` returns `YES`. After an appropriate pasteboard type is found, an `NSSound` can be instantiated using the method `-initWithPasteboard:`.

An existing `NSSound` instance can be written to the pasteboard by calling `-writeToPasteboard:` with an `NSPasteboard` as the argument.

Similar to the method used to determine what types of sounds can be created from the contents of an `NSPasteboard`, `+soundUnfilteredFileTypes` can be used to get an array of all the file types that can be read from disk. The `NSArray` returned by this method is suitable to pass directly to an `NSOpenPanel` for restricting opening files to supported types.

Having created an `NSSound` instance, applications need the capability to control playback. Play a sound by calling an `NSSound` instance's `-play` method. If the sound can be played, a `YES` is returned, otherwise `NO`. To see if an instance of `NSSound` is currently playing, pass it an `-isPlaying` message. This will return `YES` if it is playing, `NO` if not. To pause a playing sound, call `-pause`. This method returns a `boolean` indicating success or not. Having paused a sound, playback can be resumed using the `-resume` method.

Detection of the completion of sound playback is accomplished by setting a delegate for the `NSSound` instance with `-setDelegate:` and having the delegate implement `-sound:didFinishPlaying:`. This method is called when playback has been completed.

Cocoa's sound playing support is documented at `http://developer.apple.com/techpubs/macosx/Cocoa/TasksAndConcepts/ProgrammingTopics/Sound/index.html`.

Core Audio and Core MIDI Frameworks

The Core Audio Framework provides sophisticated and flexible multichannel sound to Mac OS X. Core Audio is made up of a number of distinct APIs, which range from providing low-level driver access, an audio device to Musical Instrument Digital Interface (MIDI) sequencing, and playback. The Core Audio Frameworks are implemented in C and C++ and provide a procedural C-based API.

Core Audio attempts to provide a standard API onto hardware via the Audio Hardware Abstraction Layer. This enables multiple clients to simultaneously access the audio devices regardless of the interface to the device (PIC, USB, Firewire, and so on).

The Core MIDI Framework supports multiport MIDI playback, including MIDI stream and configuration management. The component Audio Toolbox provides sequencing capabilities, which can be built into a custom MIDI editing/playback application. Core Audio is documented at http://developer.apple.com/audio/coreaudio.html.

Two open source Objective-C frameworks provide object-oriented access to these APIs. The SndKit and MusicKit are based on sound and music frameworks originally shipped by NeXT. Together they can be used in music, sound, signal processing, and MIDI applications. Both are available from www.musickit.org.

Speech Synthesis and Recognition

The Speech Synthesis Manager provides a standardized API for applications to synthesis human speech. The speech APIs allow an application to choose a voice, set it's pitch, and specify a callback routine that will be run when the speech has completed playback.

Along with synthesis, Mac OS X provides for Speech Recognition. To make an application capable of recognizing speech requires the building of a speech model, and a method of being notified when a phrase has been spoken. This notification is provided through callbacks or AppleScript.

Raphael Sebbe has written SpeechUtilities.framework, which provides both synthesis and recognition capabilities for Cocoa applications. It provides a thin Objective-C wrapper for the Apple C-based APIs and is available here at http://softrak.stepwise.com/display?pkg=1631.

Apple's documentation for the Speech Synthesis Manager is available at http://developer.apple.com/techpubs/macosx/Carbon/multimedia/SpeechSynthesisManager/Speech_Synthesis_Manager/index.html. The Speech Recognition Manager is documented at http://developer.apple.com/techpubs/macosx/Carbon/multimedia/SpeechRecognitionManager/Speech_Recognition_Manager/index.html.

NOTE

Mac OS X 10.2 includes additional Cocoa support for speech synthesis and speech recognition.

QuickTime

QuickTime is Apple's solution for cross-platform multimedia APIs. It provides the capability to manipulate video data, still images, animations, vector graphics, multichannel sound, MIDI music, 360-degree panoramic objects, and more. It supports more than 70 different types of file formats encompassing the most common multimedia and compression standards including MP3, Flash 4, MPEG-1, JavaScript, JPEG, PhotoShop, and more.

The QuickTime `Movie` data structure is used to represent any time-based data. The Application Kit provides two classes for working with QuickTime: `NSMovie`, an Objective-C wrapper object for the `Movie` structure; and `NSMovieView`, a user-interface element to support playback and basic editing of an `NSMovie`.

Complete procedural QuickTime API references and samples are available at `http://developer.apple.com/quicktime/`.

`NSMovie` Class

`NSMovie` provides a simple Objective-C wrapper for a QuickTime `Movie` structure. It is very similar in implementation to `NSSound`, but it does not provide any playback capabilities directly. The `NSMovieView` class provides all onscreen playback control.

An `NSMovie` instance can be created from a movie source using the method `-initWithURL:byReference:`. The URL provided in the first argument can be a local file, or a remotely stored file on a Web server or QuickTime Streaming Server. The second argument is a `boolean`, which indicates whether the data should be stored directly when the `NSMovie` instance is archived, or if a simple reference to the URL is sufficient.

Both `http:` and `rtsp:` protocols are supported for remote movie resources. When dealing with remote streaming sources, download progress is monitored using the QuickTime function `GetMovieLoadState` on the QuickTime `Movie` structure returned by `-QTMovie`.

Passing an existing QuickTime Movie type pointer to the method `-initWithMovie:` can also create an `NSMovie`. The instantiated `NSMovie` will be the owner of the `Movie` data passed as the argument, releasing it when it is deallocated.

`NSMovie` instances can also be created from an application's pasteboard contents. An application can test a pasteboard to see if there are any QuickTime-supported data types available using the class method `+canInitWithPasteboard:` passing an `NSPasteboard` instance as the argument. This method tests the provided pasteboard for any contents that match one of the types returned by `+movieUnfilteredPasteboardTypes`. If a matching pasteboard type is found, `+canInitWithPasteboard:` returns `YES`. After an appropriate pasteboard type is found, an `NSMovie` object can be created using the method `-initWithPasteboard:`.

The class method `+movieUnfilteredFileTypes` returns an array of filename extensions that are supported for reading from disk. The results can be used directly in an `NSOpenPanel` to filter available file types.

The Objective-C Cocoa wrapper for `NSMovie` only scratches the surface of QuickTime's capabilities. Much more functionality is available by retrieving a pointer to the QuickTime `Movie` structure, and then directly using the procedural QuickTime APIs. A pointer to the `Movie` structure is returned by `-QTMovie`.

Apple has provided an excellent `NSMovie` exampled called bMovie, which is available from Apple's sample code site at `http://developer.apple.com/samplecode/Sample_Code/Cocoa/bMoviePalette.htm`. It implements a basic QuickTime movie editor in an Interface Builder palette. The `MyMovie` object is a subclass of `NSMovie` and allows for splitting a single movie into multiple movies, appending one movie on to another, inserting an `NSImage` into a movie, determining movie length, and more.

NSMovieView

The `NSMovieView` is an `NSView` subclass used to display an `NSMovie` in an application. It can optionally display a standard QuickTime movie controller as an inherent part of the view as shown in Figure 21.1.

FIGURE 21.1 Example `NSMovieView` with movie controller.

An `NSMovieView` is an `NSView` subclass, and can be created programmatically in the same manner. There is no specialized initialization method available for the class, `-initWithFrame:` is the designated initializer.

Often an `NSMovieView` is added to an application by dragging it from the Cocoa-GraphicViews Palette as seen in Figure 21.2.

An `NSMovieView` instance created in Interface Builder can set certain attributes through the `NSMovieView` Inspector (See Figure 21.3).

FIGURE 21.2 Cocoa-GraphicViews palette in Interface Builder.

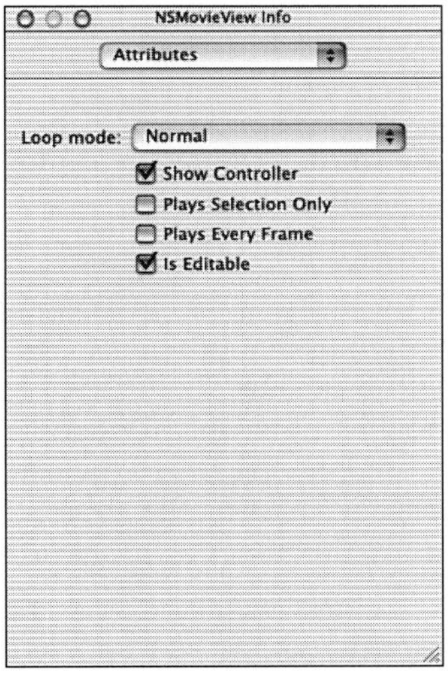

FIGURE 21.3 `NSMovieView` Inspector in Interface Builder.

If Show Controller is checked, the standard QuickTime control area is shown as part of the view. Programmatically this is controlled by the method called `-showController:adjustingSize:`, passing a `boolean` value for the first argument specifying whether it should be shown or not. The second argument, also a `boolean`, indicates whether the `NSMovieView` should change its onscreen size when the movie controller visibility is changed. If set to `YES`, and the controller is being removed, the `NSMovieView` itself will become smaller, but the area that the movie is displayed in would remain the same. If the controller was being removed and the adjusting size argument was `NO`, the area in which the movie is displayed would increase to include the area where the controller had been. The visible state of the movie controller can be ascertained through the use of `-isControllerVisible`, which returns a boolean value. It is also possible to obtain the QuickTime data structure, MovieController, for the controller using -movieController. This will return the MovieController if there is an NSMovie set for the NSMovieView, otherwise it will return NULL. After obtained, a MovieController can then be used in subsequent calls to QuickTime APIs.

The NSMovieView Interface Builder inspector also allows the setting of the playback-looping mode via a pop-up menu. Movies can be set to play once, play continuously, or play forward, and then backwards. In an application this can be done programmatically using the -setLoopMode: method, passing one of the following NSQTMovieLoopMode constants as the argument.

```
NSQTMovieNormalPlayback
NSQTMovieLoopingPlayback
NSQTMovieLoopingBackAndForthPlayback
```

The current looping mode can be determined by calling -loopMode, which will return one of the NSQTMovieLoopMode constants.

Whether the entire movie is played back each time or not is controlled by the checkbox Plays Selection Only in the NSMovieView inspector. If this is enabled, only the selected portion of the movie, indicated in the movie controller, is played. Manipulation of this selection is possible by the user during the program use, however, it is necessary to resort to the QuickTime APIs directly to accomplish this programmatically. Playback can be restricted to the current selection using the method -setPlaysSelectionOnly: passing the appropriate boolean value. The state of this can be determined using the method -playsSelectionOnly, which returns a boolean value.

The Play Every Frame setting ensures that each frame of the movie is played, even if that means playing the movie at a rate slower than what is specified by the movie's settings. Normally, this would be disabled. NSMovieView provides for setting this attribute via the method -setPlaysEveryFrame: with a boolean value for the argument. The current state of this setting can be retrieved using -playsEveryFrame, which returns YES or NO.

The final option in the NSMovieView inspector enables control of editing the movie in the NSMovieView. When enabled, a user can cut, copy, paste, and remove content for the NSMovie, as well as drag a new QuickTime movie onto the NSMovieView. This setting can be changed using the method called -setEditable: passing a boolean. The current status of editing can be accessed with the method -isEditable.

The editing functionality is accessible using the methods: -cut:, -copy:, -clear:, -paste:, -undo:, and -selectAll:. These methods all expect the sender as the argument, allowing them to be easily used as targets for Interface Builder actions.

A QuickTime movie is associated with an NSMovieView using the method -setMovie: passing an NSMovie as the argument. The current movie is available by calling -movie, which returns an NSMovie instance if there is a movie for the NSMovieView.

NSMovieView provides a number of target actions for playback functionality. All expect an argument consisting of the sender object. As with the editing functions, these allow for easy connections in Interface Builder.

Movie playback can be started using the method -start:, and stopped using the method -stop:. The location for playback can be changed by using -gotoBeginning:, -gotoEnd:, -stepBack:, and -stepForward:. It is also possible to go directly to the poster frame using -gotoPosterFrame:. This is a frame in the movie that can be shown statically, often before the movie is started.

An application can determine if an NSMovieView is currently playing a movie using the method -isPlaying, which returns YES or NO.

QuickTime movies have a playback rate associated with them. This rate is the optimum playback speed and is maintained by dropping frames if necessary; it is dependent on the -playsEveryFrame setting. The speed of playback relative to the movie's optimum rate is set using the method -setRate: passing a float value. The value of 1.0 causes the movie to play at normal speed, smaller values to play slower, larger values faster. Negative values cause reverse playback at the specified relative rate. This value is only taken into account when called by the -start: method, playback initiated by the movie controller is always at normal speed. The current relative rate can be determined by calling -rate, which will return a float.

The sound level the movie is played at is set between 0.0 and 1.0 and is relative to the volume set for the System. The volume is set by calling -setVolume: and passing a float as the volume. The current relative volume for playback is retrieved using -volume. Volume can also be muted using the method -setMuted: passing a boolean value. The current mute status is available from -muted.

The method -sizeForMagnification: will return an NSSize with the appropriate width and height for the specified magnification. This method assumes that the controller is always visible. An NSSize that is dependent on the visibility of the movie controller can be returned by the following method as a category on NSMovieView:

```
#import <Cocoa/Cocoa.h>

@implementation NSMovieView (MYMaginifcationSupport)

- (NSSize)exactSizeForMagnification:(float)magnification {
    NSSize tempSize;
```

```
    tempSize=[self sizeForMagnification:magnification];
    if (![self isControllerVisible]) {
        // the standard movie controller is 16 pixels high
        // it would be better to get the moviecontroller object
        // and determine the size at runtime.
        tempSize.height=tempSize.height-16.0;
    }
    return tempSize;
}

@end
```

Calling the method `-resizeWithMagnification:` resizes the `NSMovieView` to allow the display of the current `NSMovie` with the magnification specified by the argument. A value of 1.0 shows the movie at the full size.

The view is resized with the assumption that the movie controller is visible, regardless of the current state. If it is not visible, the view is stretched vertically to fill that additional space. It might be useful to set the movie view controller to show the controller without resizing, then call `-resizeWithMagnification:` and, finally, set the controller state explicitly as in the following code fragment:

```
wasControllerVisible=[self isControllerVisible];
[movieView showController:YES adjustingSize:NO];
[movieView resizeWithMagnification:1.0];
[movieView showController: wasControllerVisible
           adjustingSize:YES];
```

3D Graphics

Cocoa provides a direct interface for 3D drawing by supporting OpenGL. OpenGL is a multiplatform graphics standard that provides a portable set of 2D and 3D APIs for graphic applications. Apple provides several Cocoa-based sample applications at `http://developer.apple.com/samplecode/Sample_Code/Graphics_3D.htm`. Several examples that use OpenGL with Cocoa are provided including Cocoa_InitGL, NSGL_Teapot, OpenGLFastTexDemo, and Simple_AppKit.

OpenGL is a large and complex subject that is beyond the scope of this book, but support for OpenGL is an important aspect of Mac OS X and Cocoa. The definitive printed reference for OpenGL is *OpenGL Reference Manual Third Edition* by the OpenGL Architecture Review Board, edited by Dave Shreiner, published by Addison Wesley, ISBN 0-201-65765-1.

Application Kit Frameworks

The Application Kit provides three basic OpenGL building blocks. The `NSOpenGLView` is the onscreen view for an application to draw OpenGL. An `NSOpenGLView` consists of an `NSOpenGLContext` as well as an `NSOpenGLPixelFormat`. The context is used for all the OpenGL drawing, whereas the pixel format specifies the type of buffers used. Using the default `NSOpenGLContext` and `NSOpenGLPixelFormat` created by an `NSOpenGLView` will be sufficient for many applications. The additional classes come into effect in more complex cases, such as running in full-screen mode.

`NSOpenGLView` Class

An `NSOpenGLView` can be created programmatically, or by dragging an `NSOpenGLView` from the Cocoa-Graphics Views palette in Interface Builder (see Figure 21.2). When created in Interface Builder it is possible to set the type of renderer used, as well as the buffer's color/alpha format, depth, stencil depth, and accumulation buffer format, as seen in Figure 21.4.

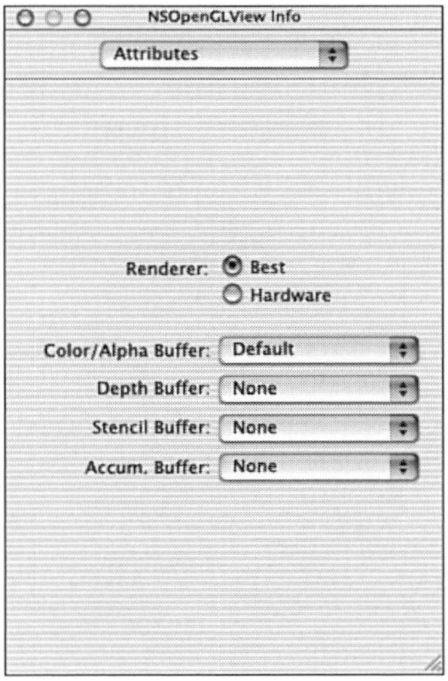

FIGURE 21.4 `NSOpenGLView` Inspector in Interface Builder.

Programmatic creation of an `NSOpenGLView` is accomplished by calling `-initWithFrame:pixelFormat:` passing the frame, and an `NSOpenGLPixelFormat` object as the arguments. It is necessary to subclass an `NSOpenGLView` to do any drawing, so this is often done as part of the `-initWithFrame:` in the subclass. The following implementation will create a 32-bit-deep pixel format, and then call the `-initWithFrame:pixelFormat:` with the `NSOpenGLPixelFormat` object.

```
- (id) initWithFrame: (NSRect) frameRect
{
    NSOpenGLPixelFormatAttribute attrs[] =
    {
        NSOpenGLPFADepthSize, 21,
        NSOpenGLPFAAccelerated,
        0
    };

    NSOpenGLPixelFormat* pixFmt = [[[NSOpenGLPixelFormat alloc]
        initWithAttributes:attrs] autorelease];
    self = [super initWithFrame:frameRect pixelFormat:pixFmt];
    return self;
}
```

As with other `NSView` subclasses, drawing in an `NSOpenGLView` is implemented by overriding the `-drawRect:` method. Neither Cocoa drawing classes nor methods should be used in an `NSOpenGLView` subclass; standard OpenGL primitives are used instead. It is often necessary to initially setup the textures and other OpenGL details during the first execution of the `-drawRect:` method.

The following example code will set up the instance, initialize the OpenGL environment, and draw a rectangle. It assumes that the `MyOpenGLView` class is set up in Interface Builder.

```
#import <AppKit/AppKit.h>
#import <OpenGL/OpenGL.h>
#import <OpenGL/gl.h>
#import <OpenGL/glu.h>

@interface MyOpenGLView : NSOpenGLView {
    bool _initializedOpenGL;
}

@end


#import "MyOpenGLView.h"

@implementation MyOpenGLView
```

```
- (void)awakeFromNib {
    _initializedOpenGL=NO;
}

- (void)drawRect:(NSRect)rect {
    if (!_initializedOpenGL) {
        glEnable(GL_DEPTH_TEST);
        glShadeModel(GL_SMOOTH);
        _initializedOpenGL=YES;
    }

    // erase the screen
    glClearColor (0.0, 0.0, 0.0, 0.0);
    glClear(GL_COLOR_BUFFER_BIT | GL_DEPTH_BUFFER_BIT);

    //set up transformation matrix and projection
    glLoadIdentity();

    //construct the rectangle
    glBegin(GL_QUADS);
    glColor3f(1.0f,0.0f,0.0f);
    glVertex3f( 0.5f, 0.5f, 0.5f);
    glVertex3f(-0.5f, 0.5f, 0.5f);
    glVertex3f(-0.5f,-0.5f, 0.5f);
    glVertex3f( 0.5f,-0.5f, 0.5f);
    glEnd();
    glFlush();
}
@end
```

A default NSOpenGLPixelFormat for the NSOpenGLView can be created using the class method +defaultPixelFormat. The current pixel format can be queried using -pixelFormat, whereas a new NSOpenGLPixelFormat can be set using -setPixelFormat: passing the new pixel format object as the argument.

Dealing with the NSOpenGLContext for the NSOpenGLView is accomplished using the methods -clearGLContext, -openGLContext, and -setOpenGLContext:. The -clearGLContext method disassociates the NSOpenGLContext from the view. A context can be set for the NSOpenGLView using the method -setOpenGLContext: passing the NSOpenGLContext as the argument. The NSOpenGLContext that is passed must also have its relationship established to the NSOpenGLView instance by calling the NSOpenGLContext method -setView: passing the view as the argument. Calling the method -openGLContext returns the view's OpenGL context. This method creates a new NSOpenGLContext instance if no instance is set for the view.

Subclasses of NSOpenGLView might want to override the -update and -reshape methods. The -reshape method is called when the window changes size or the visible bounds change, allowing an application to react. The default implementation does nothing. The -update method is called when the window moves, or if the view moves or resizes. The default of -update simply calls the -update method for the NSOpenGLContext.

NSOpenGLContext **Class**

All OpenGL rendering in a Cocoa application takes place in an NSOpenGLContext. A context can be offscreen, full-screen, or drawn into an NSView.

To initialize a newly allocated NSOpenGLContext call -initWithFormat:shareContext: passing an NSOpenGLPixelFormat as the first argument. The second argument specifies another NSOpenGLContext to share texture and display lists with. If sharing is not required, pass nil for the share context argument.

It is possible to get the current NSOpenGLContext that is being used for drawing by calling +currentContext. An instance of NSOpenGLContext can be made the current context by calling the method -makeCurrentContext, causing OpenGL calls to be rendered in this context. The current context can be detached from the NSOpenGLView by calling +clearCurrentContext. Contexts are accessed on a per-thread basis. Only drawing within the current thread will be affected by changing the context.

An NSOpenGLContext can also take over the entire screen to draw by using the call -setFullScreen. This requires that the NSOpenGLContext has been created using the attribute NSOpenGLPFAFullScreen. The attributes of an NSOpenGlContext and the pixel formats supported by a context are described in the "NSOpenGLPixelFormat Class" section of this chapter. An application should capture the screen using the Core Graphics Direct Display API before calling -setFullScreen. This prevents other applications from attempting to draw onto screen areas, which should be reserved for the application.

The view that an NSOpenGLContext is associated with can be set using the method -setView:. The context's view port is set to the size of the passed NSView argument. The current view, if any, that a context is associated to can be queried using -view. The context can be disassociated from all views by calling -clearDrawable. This also exists in full-screen or offscreen mode. The -update method should be called whenever the size or location of a context's drawable area changes.

Offscreen rendering can be specified by using the method `-setOffScreen:width:height:rowbytes:` passing a memory pointer as the first argument, and the width, height, and number of row bytes as the remaining arguments. The memory pointer must be sufficiently large to hold the data. The `NSOpenGLPFAOffScreen` must have been specified for the `NSOpenGLPixelFormat` for an offscreen context.

Attributes from an existing `NSOpenGLContext` can be copied to the receiving context using the method `-copyAttributesFromContext:withMask:`. The first argument is the source `NSOpenGLContext`, and the second is the result of a logical `OR` operation of the OpenGL attributes to copy. The attributes' values are specified using values suitable for the OpenGL call `glPushAttrib`, which is declared in Apple's `agl.framework`. Many good online reference documents for OpenGL that describe `glPushAttrib` are available including `http://www.3dlabs.com/support/developer/GLmanpages/glpushattrib.htm`.

`NSOpenGLPixelFormat` Class

Before rendering OpenGL calls into an `NSOpenGLContext` you must specify the pixel format, which details the buffer type, format, and depth amongst other settings.

A newly allocated `NSOpenGLPixelFormat` is initialized with a call to the method `-initWithAttributes:` passing a standard C array (not an `NSArray`) consisting of one or more of the `NSOpenGLPixelFormatAttribute` constants. There are two types of attributes, `boolean` attribute constants, which are presented here:

```
NSOpenGLPFAAllRenderers
NSOpenGLPFADoubleBuffer
NSOpenGLPFAStereo
NSOpenGLPFAMinimumPolicy
NSOpenGLPFAMaximumPolicy
NSOpenGLPFAOffScreen
NSOpenGLPFAFullScreen
NSOpenGLPFASingleRenderer
NSOpenGLPFANoRecovery
NSOpenGLPFAAccelerated
NSOpenGLPFAClosestPolicy
NSOpenGLPFARobust
NSOpenGLPFABackingStore
NSOpenGLPFAWindow
NSOpenGLPFAMultiScreen
NSOpenGLPFACompliant
```

and attributes that require an additional constant value:

```
NSOpenGLPFAAuxBuffers
NSOpenGLPFAColorSize
NSOpenGLPFAAlphaSize
NSOpenGLPFADepthSize
NSOpenGLPFAStencilSize
NSOpenGLPFAAccumSize
NSOpenGLPFARendererID
NSOpenGLPFAScreenMask
```

For example, to create a new `NSOpenGLPixelFormat` with a 32-bit pixel depth that can use accelerated hardware, but also runs on devices that don't support acceleration, the following code would suffice:

```
NSOpenGLPixelFormatAttribute attrs[] = {
    NSOpenGLPFADepthSize, 32,
    NSOpenGLPFAAccelerated,
    0};
NSOpenGLPixelFormat *pixFmt;
pixFmt = [[NSOpenGLPixelFormat alloc] initWithAttributes:attrs];
```

If a render that fulfills the attributes requirement is not available, `-initWithAttributes:` returns `nil`.

The number of available virtual screens can be retrieved with the call `-numberOfVirtualScreens`. This correlates to the number of video cards installed on the computer. Specific OpenGL attributes can be queried using the `-getValues:forAttribute:forVirtualScreen:` for a virtual screen. An array of values will be returned in the first argument, and the `NSOpenGLPixelFormatAttribute` passed as the second for the specified virtual screen.

In addition to the `NSOpenGLView`, `NSOpenGLPixelFormat`, and `NSOpenGLContext` classes, there are function calls available to query details about the overall `NSOpenGL` implementation. `NSOpenGLGetVersion()` returns the major and minor version numbers by reference. This should not be confused with the OpenGL version. The global `NSOpenGL` options can be queried and set using `NSOpenGLGetOption()` and `NSOpenGLSetOption()` functions, respectively, with one of the `NSOpenGLGlobalOption` constants as the first argument. In the case of the `NSOpenGLGetOption()` the second argument is a pointer to a variable with the C `long` type that will return the value by reference. The second argument to `NSOpenGLSetOption()` is the value to set the global to.

Procedural OpenGL

In addition to the Cocoa OpenGL classes, Apple provides an implementation of the GL Utility Toolkit (GLUT). GLUT is a platform-independent set of interfaces to window management, menus, and input devices. Apple's implementation gives an Aqua-style interface to a GLUT application. GLUT provides easy compatibility with existing OpenGL code and allows applications to maintain platform independence if required at the expense of flexibility. Apple includes a GLUT example projects in `/Developer/Examples/GLUTExamples`.

Apple also provides the AGL APIs that extends the OpenGL procedural APIs. These are detailed in Apple's Carbon OpenGL documentation.

Extensive OpenGL documentation is available at `www.opengl.org`.

Summary

Cocoa exposes basic functionality for video and sound playback. Complex applications can leverage the basic classes by using QuickTime directly. Cocoa's OpenGL support provides simple integration of a 3D drawing with the Aqua user interface.

The next chapter explores the integration of Cocoa applications with other applications and the operating system.

22

Integrating with the Operating System

IN THIS CHAPTER

- Getting System Information
- Authentication and Security
- Communicating with the Workspace

The Cocoa frameworks abstract most operating system details so that Cocoa applications are written at a very high level. It is usually unnecessary to have detailed knowledge of the underlying operating system and its features when using Cocoa. Cocoa's frameworks contain classes that enable an application to interact with the underlying operating system without dropping to low-level system-specific APIs. This chapter introduces Cocoa features that provide information about the host operating system, and the operating environment in which an application is running. This chapter also explains how to access standard directories, work with operating system security features, and manipulate the user's workspace.

Getting System Information

It is seldom necessary for Cocoa applications to use system information directly. Cocoa provides enough abstraction of system features that the need to know details about the system is rare. Nevertheless, Cocoa's Foundation framework provides classes that identify the operating system, provide information about the host computer, and provide access to the system environment in which an application is running. Information about the current user of an application and standard file systems locations is also available.

`NSProcessInfo` Class

Every application that runs on Max OS X is a separate operating system process. Cocoa applications access information about the operating system and processes using the `NSProcessInfo` class. With the `NSProcessInfo` class, a

Cocoa application can obtain information about its own process, the operating system that is running the process, and the computer that is running the operating system. A single shared instance of the NSProcessInfo class is obtained by calling [NSProcessInfo processInfo]. The first time the method is called, an instance is created. All subsequent calls return the same instance.

NSProcessInfo's -operatingSystem method returns an enumerated constant that identifies the operating system that is running the Cocoa application. On Mac OS X, -operatingSystem always returns NSMACHOperatingSystem. Information about the other operating system constants is provided in Apple's online documentation for the NSProcessInfo class. NSProcessInfo also has the -operatingSystemName method that returns the name of the host operating system. On Max OS X, the name returned is always NSMACHOperatingSystem.

The -arguments method returns an array of the strings that were specified as command-line arguments to the current process. The first string in the array is always the path to the executable for the process. Most applications that are launched from the Mac OS X desktop do not have any other command-line arguments. Project Builder provides a way to specify command-line arguments when an application is run from Project Builder. Command-line arguments can be specified when an application is run from a Unix shell or an NSTask. The NSTask class is described in Chapter 24, "Subprocesses and Threads."

The -environment method returns a dictionary of the system environment variables that are defined for the current process. Each key in the dictionary is the name of an environment variable, and the corresponding value is the value of the environment variable. Project Builder provides a way to specify environment variables to use when an application is run from Project Builder. Normally, the environment variables for a process are specified by the parent process that started it. For example, applications started from a Unix shell have the environment variables defined for that shell. Processes started from the Dock have the environment variables defined by the Dock process, and applications started from Finder have the environment variables defined by Finder. In practice, because the Dock and Finder are child processes started by a process called loginwindow, they have the environment variables defined for loginwindow. The loginwindow process reads its environment variables from a file at ~/.MacOSX/environment.plist in the current user's home directory. A partial list of environment variables that control the behavior of Cocoa applications is provided in Appendix B, "Optimizing and Finding Memory Leaks." Apple provides a technical note explaining the ~/.MacOSX/environment.plist file at http://developer.apple.com/qa/qa2001/qa1067.html.

The -processIdentifier method returns the operating system's internal identifier for the current process. This identifier can be used in low-level system calls that require it. The -processName method returns the name of the current process. The name of each running process is shown by Apple's ProcessViewer application located in the /Applications/Utilities folder. The process name is used to access the defaults database and is output by the NSLog() function to identify the process that generated log information. The defaults database is described in Chapter 7, "Foundation Framework Overview." The NSLog() function is introduced in Chapter 3, "Using Apple's Developer Tools." Mac OS X allows multiple processes to have the same name. The name returned by -processName is, therefore, not sufficient to uniquely identify a process.

The -hostName method returns the host name of the computer running the current process. Computers can have multiple host names and can exist simultaneously on multiple networks, or a host might not be networked at all. Because of the common variation in host names for a single computer, the string returned from NSProcessInfo's -hostName method is not very useful in practice. The NSHost class provides the -names method that returns an array of host names and is a better way to get host name information. The NSHost class is described in the next section.

One of the handiest NSProcessInfo methods is -globallyUniqueString. This method returns a string composed of the host name, the process identifier, a time stamp, and a counter. Each time the method is called, it returns a different string. No two processes running on computers on the same network will ever return the same string from - globallyUniqueString. This method should be used whenever a unique name or identifier is needed.

NSHost Class

Each instance of the NSHost class encapsulates information about a computer on an accessible network. Instances can be created with the +currentHost, +hostWithAddress:, and +hostWithName: methods. The +currentHost method returns a shared instance for the host that is executing the application. The +hostWithAddres: method returns an instance that encapsulates the host identified by a string argument containing an Internet address such as 192.42.172.1. The +hostWithName: method uses any available network naming services, such as Domain Name Service (DNS), to return an instance that encapsulates the named host.

NOTE

The NSHost class maintains a cache of previously created NSHost instances to avoid time-consuming network name searches when the same host is accessed multiple times via +currentHost, +hostWithAddress:, and +hostWithName:. The cache is enabled or disabled with the +setHostCacheEnabled: method. The cache is emptied with the +flushHostCache method.

After an instance of `NSHost` has been created, it can be used to obtain information about the host it represents. The `-addresses` method returns all the Internet addresses for the host as an array of strings. The `-names` method returns all the names for a host as an array of strings. Two `NSHost` instances can be compared with the `-isEqualToHost:` method that returns `YES` only if the receiver and the `NSHost` instance passed as an argument both identify the same host.

Users

Modern operating systems such as Mac OS X support multiple simultaneous users of one computer. A Cocoa application can get the logon username of the current user by calling the `NSUserName()` function in the Foundation framework. The `NSFullUserName()` function returns the full username that was entered when the account for the current user was created.

It is not safe to assume that the name returned by `NSUserName()` identifies the user logged into the Mac OS X console. The user that started an application could be remotely logged in or logged in via a Unix shell. Cocoa does not currently provide any way to identify the user logged into the console. Apple provides several technical notes on the subject. A Carbon function and example code to identify the current console user is available at `http://developer.apple.com/qa/qa2001/qa1133.html`. Like all Carbon functions, it can be called from Cocoa applications.

Standard Locations

Mac OS X uses several standard file system locations to store applications and files. The standard locations are based on the owners of the files, the purpose of the files, and whether the files are stored on a local hard disk or accessed via a network. The standard locations are called domains.

Mac OS X currently defines four domains: User, Local, Network, and System. The User domain specifies the location of files controlled by the current user. The User domain is the user's home directory, and it can be on a local hard disk or accessed via a network. The Local domain specifies the location of files shared by all users of a particular computer. Files stored in the Local domain are stored on a local hard disk, but are not needed for the computer to run. The Network domain specifies the location of files shared by all users of a network. The Network domain usually specifies a location on a file server that is accessed via a network. Finally, the System domain specifies the location on a local hard disk of system files provided by Apple. Many files in the System domain are needed for the computer to run. Files in the System domain cannot be modified by users.

Each domain normally contains both an Applications folder and a Library folder. For example, the Applications folder in the Network domain contains applications that are available to all users on the network. The Applications folder in the Local domain contains applications available only to users logged into a particular computer. The Applications folder in the User domain stores applications that are only available to the current user. The Library folder in each domain stores files that are not part of applications.

Cocoa provides the `NSSearchPathForDirectoriesInDomains()` function to search for files and applications within the domains. This function should be used instead of hard coding paths to files for two important reasons: The location specified for each domain can change, and searching provides flexibility for users.

The domains can be searched in any order, but a common order is User, Local, Network, and then System. That order provides maximum configuration options to users. For example, shared resources such as fonts are available in the System domain. In a particular work environment, an administrator might install a version of a font in the Network domain that differs from the system font with the same name. Because of the domain search order, each application will find the font in the Network domain before it finds the version in the System domain. Applications, therefore, prefer to use the Network domain version instead of the system version. Similarly, a user can install a replacement font in his own User domain, which supercedes any version in other domains.

The `NSPathUtilities.h` file in the Foundation framework defines the `NSSearchPathDomainMask` enumerated type for domains as follows:

```
// Domains
typedef enum {
   NSUserDomainMask = 1
   NSLocalDomainMask = 2,
   NSNetworkDomainMask = 4,
   NSSystemDomainMask = 8,
   NSAllDomainsMask = 0x0ffff
} NSSearchPathDomainMask;
```

The standard locations within domains are defined by the `NSSearchPathDirectory` enumerated type. Not all directories are available in all domains.

```
typedef enum {
    NSApplicationDirectory = 1,
    NSDemoApplicationDirectory,
    NSDeveloperApplicationDirectory,
    NSAdminApplicationDirectory,
    NSLibraryDirectory,
    NSDeveloperDirectory,
    NSUserDirectory,
```

```
    NSDocumentationDirectory,
    NSDocumentDirectory,
    NSCoreServiceDirectory,
    NSAllApplicationsDirectory = 100,
    NSAllLibrariesDirectory = 101
} NSSearchPathDirectory;
```

The `NSSearchPathForDirectoriesInDomains()` function accepts three arguments. The first is one of the directory values enumerated by `NSSearchPathDirectory`. The second argument specifies the domains to use in the search. Any of the domains enumerated by the `NSSearchPathDomainMask` type can be combined with C's logical `OR` operator. To search in only the User and Network domains, specify `(NSUserDomainMask | NSNetworkDomainMask)` as the second argument. The `NSAllDomainsMask` value specifies all domains. The third argument is a Boolean that specifies whether the "~"(tilde) character, which specifies paths relative to the user's home directory, should be expanded with the complete path to the user's home directory.

The following program outputs the path to the file that defines the Arial font in the Fonts directory within a Library directory using the standard domain search:

```
#import <Foundation/Foundation.h>

NSString  *MYFindPathToFileInLibraryWithStandardSearch(NSString *fileName)
/*" Retuns the path to the first occurrence of fileName in a Library
directory within the standard domains using the standard domain search
order. "*/
{
  NSString      *result = nil; // the returned path
  NSString      *candidate;        // candidate paths
  NSArray       *pathArray;        // array of standard locations
  NSEnumerator  *pathEnumerator;// used to enumerate pathArray

  // search in the library directories of all domains
  pathArray = NSSearchPathForDirectoriesInDomains(NSLibraryDirectory,
      NSAllDomainsMask, YES);
  pathEnumerator = [pathArray objectEnumerator];

  while(nil == result && (nil != (candidate = [pathEnumerator nextObject])))
  {
    result = [candidate stringByAppendingPathComponent:fileName];
    if(![[NSFileManager defaultManager] fileExistsAtPath:result])
    {
```

```
      result = nil;
    }
  }

  return result;
}


int main (int argc, const char * argv[])
{
  NSAutoreleasePool * pool = [[NSAutoreleasePool alloc] init];

  // Logs the path to the first occurrence of "Fonts/Arial" in a Library
  // directory within the standard domains using the standard domain search
  // order.
  NSLog(@"path = %@", MYFindPathToFileInLibraryWithStandardSearch(
      @"Fonts/Arial"));

  [pool release];
  return 0;
}
```

Experiment with the program by copying the Arial font from the `/Library/Fonts` directory into the `~/Library/Fonts` directory. The program will find the file in `~/Library/Fonts` instead of the one in `/Library/Fonts`.

NOTE

The Foundation framework provides the `NSHomeDirectory()` function that returns the path to the current user's home directory. Use domain searching even when the User domain is the only one searched. Appending a hard-coded path such `Library/Fonts` to the path returned from `NSHomeDirectory()` is not a reliable way to identify files because users might change the names of directories within their home directory. Domain searching has the potential to find files even if directories are renamed.

Authentication and Security

To provide security and prevent accidental or malicious damage to the operating system, Mac OS X restricts the use of certain system files and applications. Individual users can restrict the uses of their own files; however, some applications might need to modify restricted files or run restricted applications. Examples of such applications include software installation programs, network administration programs, and many standard Unix command-line programs. An installer that needs to write files in the /Applications folder must overcome the restriction that prevents the /Applications folder from being modified.

The capability to overcome a security restriction is called a privilege. Applications normally have the same privileges as the user who launched the application. Each user's privileges are set when the user's account is created by an administrator. On Mac OS X, even the administrator does not normally have sufficient privileges to do everything; however, a select few applications have privileges beyond the privileges of their user. Such applications are called set uid applications. The term uid is a reference to the capability of an application to run with a user identity other than the user who launched the application. The implications of set uid Cocoa applications are described in the Set uid Cocoa Applications section of this chapter.

NOTE

Administrators can explicitly log into the computer using a special account called root or use a special command-line utility called sudo to temporarily gain root privileges. The root users privileges are sufficient to overcome all operating system restrictions.

Apple does not provide a direct way to overcome security restrictions with Cocoa, but Cocoa applications can use the Carbon Authorization Services API. The Authorization Services API provides C functions that enable programs to call other programs and run them with administrator or root privileges. However, the users of applications that use the Authorization Services API must be able to authenticate that they are who they say they are. Authentication usually requires the user to type the Administrator's password or provide some other form of identification.

Apple provides a document that explains authentication and authorization at http://developer.apple.com/techpubs/macosx/CoreTechnologies/securityservices/authorizationconcepts.pdf. Authentication is handled by a special Mac OS X process called the Security Server. The Security Server is able to display a panel requiring the user to provide a password or other identification. Reference information about authentication and security is available at http://developer.apple.com/techpubs/macosx/CoreTechnologies/securityservices/authservref.pdf. Finally, Apple provides an example that uses the Carbon Authorization Services API at http://developer.apple.com/samplecode/Sample_Code/Security/AuthSample.htm.

Set uid Cocoa Applications

Cocoa applications should never be set uid applications. Cocoa applications provide too many ways in which they can be hijacked and used to circumvent the operating system's security features. The problems can be subtle. Apple has shipped Cocoa applications that inadvertently enabled any user to perform privileged operations without authenticating themselves.

By their very nature, set `uid` applications have privileges that their users do not have. Such applications need to be very carefully written to restrict the actions of users. For example, a set `uid` application for configuring the computer's network interface should not allow users to delete unrelated system files. To minimize opportunities for malicious use of set `uid` applications, the applications are typically very small and very straight forward.

Even the simplest and smallest set `uid` Cocoa applications contain vulnerabilities that might defeat the operating system's security features. For example, services run from the Services menu of a set `uid` Cocoa application are executed with the privileges of the set `uid` application. It is trivial to write a Service provider that deletes files. If such a service is ever run from a set `uid` Cocoa application, the application is able to delete system files that are not related to whatever other functions the application might have. Several of Apple's applications have this flaw.

Any Cocoa application that dynamically loads code can fall victim to Objective-C runtime hacks. The Objective-C runtime can be used to modify the behavior of a Cocoa application without the need to recompile the application. Using the Objective-C runtime, a method intended to copy files into a restricted folder could be replaced with a method that deletes all the files in the restricted folder.

Generally speaking, every Cocoa application dynamically loads code. Even if the application does not have explicit plug-in support, every Cocoa application that contains at least one text field can fall victim to a custom `InputManager` bundle. `InputManager` bundles are loaded automatically to handle text input. A user might install a custom `InputManager` bundle that deletes system files. The next time a set `uid` Cocoa application is run, the custom `InputManager` could destroy the file system.

The bottom line is that it is nearly impossible to make a set `uid` Cocoa application that does not create serious security vulnerabilities. The best solution is to write small set `uid` tools without Cocoa, and execute those tools from a larger Cocoa application that provides a graphical user interface. The Carbon Authorization Services API is used to authenticate the user and execute the small set `uid` tool.

Communicating with the Workspace

Cocoa applications benefit from bidirectional communication with the Mac OS X applications that provide the user's workspace. The term workspace refers to the combination of the Desktop, Dock, Finder, and operating system services that collectively implement the user's view of the computer. Cocoa applications are notified when changes to the workspace are made. For example, Cocoa applications are informed when the computer is about to be powered off, when applications are launched, and when network volumes are mounted. Cocoa applications can ask the workspace to perform operations such as copying files, launching applications, and selecting files in Finder.

`NSWorkspace` Class

A single shared instance of the `NSWorkspace` class encapsulates a Cocoa application's interface with the workspace. The `NSWorkspace` class is used by applications that need features provided by Apple's Finder. The shared instance is obtained by sending the `+sharedWorkspace` message to the `NSWorkspace` class as follows: `[NSWorkspace sharedWorkspace]`.

Many of `NSWorkspace`'s methods do not work at all in Mac OS X version 10.1.3. Apple's online documentation for `NSWorkspace` identifies the methods that do not currently work and describes how they used to work. This section focuses on the methods that are used to integrate Cocoa applications with the workspace. Only the key features of `NSWorkspace` are presented here. Apple's online documentation is comprehensive.

`NSWorkspace`'s methods fall into two general groups: methods for receiving information from the workspace, and methods for asking the workspace to do work on behalf of an application.

Getting Information from the Workspace

One way to receive information from the workspace is to observe notifications that are posted to `NSWorkspace`'s notification center. Most notifications are sent to an application's default notification center, but workspace related notifications are sent to a separate notification center controlled by the `NSWorkspace` class. After an application's shared `NSWorkspace` instance is obtained via `NSWorkspace`'s `+sharedWorkspace` method, the `-notificationCenter` message can be sent to obtain the notification center for workspace notifications.

The following notifications are sent to `NSWorkspace`'s notification center: `NSWorkspaceDidLaunchApplicationNotification`, `NSWorkspaceDidMountNotification`, `NSWorkspaceDidPerformFileOperationNotification`, `NSWorkspaceDidTerminateApplicationNotification`, `NSWorkspaceDidUnmountNotification`, `NSWorkspaceWillLaunchApplicationNotification`, `NSWorkspaceWillPowerOffNotification`, and `NSWorkspaceWillUnmountNotification`.

NOTE

Contrary to Apple's online documentation, in Mac OS X version 10.1.3 most of the workspace notifications are not sent unless the operations that prompted the notifications are initiated by the `NSWorkspace` class. For example, the `NSWorkspaceDidLaunchApplicationNotification` is not always sent when applications are started from Finder. Apple is aware of this bug and might restore the documented behavior in a future release.

Each notification that is sent provides a `userInfo` dictionary that contains additional information about the notification, such as the name of an application that is launching or the path of a mounted network volume. The following `MYWorkspaceNotificationObserver` class observes all the workspace notifications and logs messages when they are received:

```
File MYWorkspaceNotificationObserver.h:

#import <Cocoa/Cocoa.h>

@interface MYWorkspaceNotificationObserver : NSObject
{
}

/*" Designated initializer "*/
- (id)init;

@end

File MYWorkspaceNotificationObserver.m:

#import "MYWorkspaceNotificationObserver.h"

@implementation MYWorkspaceNotificationObserver
/*" An instance of this class observes all workspace notifications and outputs
information when  notifications are received. "*/

- (void)_myWorkspaceDidSendNotification:(NSNotification *)aNotification
/*" Called when any notifications are sent to shared workspace's notification
center. "*/
{
  NSLog(@"%@ userInfo:%@", [aNotification name], [aNotification userInfo]);
}
```

```
- (id)init
/*" Designated initializer "*/
{
  self = [super init];

  if(nil != self)
  {
    // Observe workspace notifications
    NSNotificationCenter  *workspaceNotificationCenter;

    workspaceNotificationCenter = [[NSWorkspace sharedWorkspace]
        notificationCenter];

    // add self as observer of all notifications
    [workspaceNotificationCenter addObserver:self
        selector:@selector(_myWorkspaceDidSendNotification:) name:nil
        object:nil];
  }

  return self;
}

- (void)dealloc
/*" Clean-up "*/
{
  // Stop observing workspace notifications
  [[[NSWorkspace sharedWorkspace] notificationCenter] removeObserver:self];

  [super dealloc];
}

@end
```

The `MYWorkspaceNotificationObserver` class is enhanced in the "Requesting Workspace Operations" section of this chapter to show information about selected files. `MYWorkspaceNotificationObserver` can be tested in its current form by adding it to a Cocoa application project and creating an instance of it in the application's main `nib` file.

In addition to workspace notifications, the `NSWorkspace` class provides several methods to obtain information from the workspace. The `-fileSystemChanged` method returns `YES` if the file system has changed since the last time the method was called. The `-userDefaultsChanged` method returns `YES` if current user's default settings have changed since the last time the method was called.

NOTE

The `-fileSystemChanged` and `-userDefaultsChanged` methods always return `NO` in Mac OS X version 10.1.3. Apple might correct this behavior in a future release.

`NSWorkspace` provides a group of methods for getting the icons that Finder displays for files and determining the applications used to open files. The `-iconForFile:` method returns an `NSImage` with the icon for a file specified by its path. The `-iconForFileType:` method returns an `NSImage` with the icon for a type specified as either a filename extension or an `HFS` file type. The `-iconForFiles:` method accepts an array of file paths and returns a single icon that represents all the files. The `-getInfoForFile:application:type:` method gets information about a file including the type of the file and the name of the application that would be used to open the file if it was double-clicked in Finder. The type provided by `-getInfoForFile:application:type:` can be used with `-iconForFileType:`.

The `-fullPathForApplication:` method returns the full path to a named application by searching the standard paths as described in the "Standard Locations" section of this chapter.

Methods for obtaining information about mounted file systems are provided. The `-mountedLocalVolumePaths` and `-mountedRemovableMedia` methods return arrays containing the paths to mounted file system volumes. The `- getFileSystemInfoForPath:isRemovable:isWritable:isUnmountable:description:type:` method is used to get information about a mounted file system volume at a specified path.

Requesting Workspace Operations

The `NSWorkspace` class includes methods used to ask the workspace to do work such as launching applications, opening files in applications, copying files, deleting files, and mounting file systems.

Applications can be launched using the `-launchApplication:` and `-launchApplication:showIcon:autolaunch:` methods. `NSWorkspace`'s `-hideOtherApplications` method hides all other running applications. Call `-openFile:` to open a file at a specified path using the Finder's default application for that file. The `-openFile:fromImage:at:inView:` is similar to `-openFile:`, but it displays an animation that provides feedback to users that a file is opening. The `-openFile:withApplication:` method is used to open a file with a specified application. Finally, the `-openURL:` method works like `-openFile:` and takes an `NSURL` argument instead of a path to the file to open.

The -findApplications method searches for applications in the standard locations described in the "Standard Locations" section of this chapter. Each Cocoa application's Services menu contains items for services provided by applications found with -findApplications. Call -findApplications to update the contents of the Services menu with items for applications added since the last time -findApplications was called. It is usually not necessary to call the -findApplications method directly because it is called automatically when Cocoa applications are launched.

One of the most powerful and handy methods provided by NSWorkspace is -performFileOperation:source:destination:files:tag:. This method is used to move, copy, link, or delete a group of files within a single directory. The operations that can be specified are NSWorkspaceMoveOperation, NSWorkspaceCopyOperation, NSWorkspaceLinkOperation, NSWorkspaceCompressOperation, NSWorkspaceDecompressOperation, NSWorkspaceEncryptOperation, NSWorkspaceDecryptOperation, NSWorkspaceDestroyOperation, NSWorkspaceRecycleOperation, and NSWorkspaceDuplicateOperation. The NSWorkspaceDestroyOperation deletes a group of files permanently. NSWorkspaceRecycleOperation just moves the files to the workspace's recycler. NSWorkspaceDuplicateOperation makes copies of the specified files and leaves them in the same directory with the originals. The copies all have slightly altered names.

NOTE

NSWorkspaceCompressOperation, NSWorkspaceDecompressOperation, NSWorkspaceEncryptOperation, and NSWorkspaceDecryptOperation do not work in Mac OS X version 10.1.3.

The -selectFile:inFileViewerRootedAtPath: method selects a specified file in Finder. If no root path is provided, the file is selected in an existing open Finder window. Otherwise, a new Finder window is opened to show the selected file.

Finally, NSWorkspace provides methods to mount and unmount file systems. The -checkForRemovableMedia method attempts to mount any available removable media such as Zip disks, floppy disks, and CD-ROMs. The -checkForRemovableMedia method returns immediately and tries to mount the file systems asynchronously in the background. The -mountNewRemovableMedia method is similar to -checkForRemovableMedia, but it does not return until the file systems have been mounted. The -mountNewRemovableMedia method returns an array of paths to all file systems mounted as a result of the call.

In the following code, the `MYWorkspaceNotificationObserver` class is enhanced to allow the selection of files, show information about the selected files, and open the files in appropriate applications using the `NSWorkspace` class:

```
File MYWorkspaceNotificationObserver:

#import <Cocoa/Cocoa.h>

@interface MYWorkspaceNotificationObserver : NSObject
{
  IBOutlet NSImageView  *_myIconView;       /*" displays icon for files "*/
  IBOutlet NSTextField  *_myNameField;      /*" displays selected name "*/
  IBOutlet NSTextField  *_myTypeField;      /*" displays selected type "*/
  IBOutlet NSTextField  *_myAppField;       /*" displays app for type "*/
  IBOutlet NSButton     *_myOpenButton;     /*" used to enable button "*/
  NSArray               *_mySelectedFiles;  /*" paths of selected files "*/
}

/*" Designated initializer "*/
- (id)init;

/*" Actions "*/
- (IBAction)selectFiles:(id)sender;
- (IBAction)openFiles:(id)sender;

@end
File MYWorkspaceNotificationObserver.m:

#import "MYWorkspaceNotificationObserver.h"

@implementation MYWorkspaceNotificationObserver
/*" An instance of this class observes all workspace notifications and outputs
information when  notifications are received. "*/

- (void)_myWorkspaceDidSendNotification:(NSNotification *)aNotification
/*" Called when any notifications are sent to shared workspace's
notification center. "*/
{
  NSLog(@"%@ userInfo:%@", [aNotification name], [aNotification userInfo]);
}
```

```
- (id)init
/*" Designated initializer "*/
{
  self = [super init];

  if(nil != self)
  {
    // Observe workspace notifications
    NSNotificationCenter  *workspaceNotificationCenter;

    workspaceNotificationCenter = [[NSWorkspace sharedWorkspace]
        notificationCenter];

    // add self as observer of all notifications
    [workspaceNotificationCenter addObserver:self
        selector:@selector(_myWorkspaceDidSendNotification:) name:nil
        object:nil];
  }

  return self;
}


- (void)_mySetSelectedFiles:(NSArray *)anArray
/*" Safely set _mySelectedFiles "*/
{
  [anArray retain];
  [_mySelectedFiles release];
  _mySelectedFiles = anArray;
}


- (IBAction)selectFiles:(id)sender
/*" Presents an Open Panel and gets one or more selected files from user.
Then updates various controls to show the path(s) to the selected file(s),
the icon for the selected file(s), the type(s) of the selected file(s), and
the application(s) used to open the selected file(s). "*/
{
  NSOpenPanel         *openPanel = [NSOpenPanel openPanel];
  int                 selection;
```

```
[openPanel setAllowsMultipleSelection:YES];
[openPanel setCanChooseDirectories:NO];
[openPanel setCanChooseFiles:YES];
[openPanel setResolvesAliases:YES];
selection = [openPanel runModalForTypes:nil];

if(NSOKButton == selection)
{
  // user selected one or more files
  [self _mySetSelectedFiles:[openPanel filenames]];
}

if(0 < [_mySelectedFiles count])
{
  // at least one file is selected
  [_myIconView setImage:[[NSWorkspace sharedWorkspace]
      iconForFiles:_mySelectedFiles]];

  if(1 < [_mySelectedFiles count])
  {
    // more than one file is selected
    [_myNameField setStringValue:@"Multiple Selected Files"];
    [_myTypeField setStringValue:@""];
    [_myAppField setStringValue:@""];
  }
  else
  {
    // exactly one file is selected
    NSString     *applicationName;
    NSString     *fileType;

    [_myNameField setStringValue:[_mySelectedFiles objectAtIndex:0]];
    [[NSWorkspace sharedWorkspace] getInfoForFile:
        [_mySelectedFiles objectAtIndex:0]
        application:&applicationName type:&fileType];
    [_myTypeField setStringValue:fileType];
    [_myAppField setStringValue:applicationName];
  }
  [_myOpenButton setEnabled:YES];
}
else
{
```

```
    // no file is selecetd
    [_myIconView setImage:nil];
    [_myNameField setStringValue:@""];
    [_myTypeField setStringValue:@""];
    [_myOpenButton setEnabled:NO];
  }
}


- (IBAction)openFiles:(id)sender;
/*" Opens the selected files in the default application for the respective
files "*/
{
  NSEnumerator   *enumerator = [_mySelectedFiles objectEnumerator];
  NSString       *currentPath;

  while(nil != (currentPath = [enumerator nextObject]))
  {
    [[NSWorkspace sharedWorkspace] openFile:currentPath];
  }
}


- (void)dealloc
/*" Clean-up "*/
{
  // Stop observing workspace notifications
  [[[NSWorkspace sharedWorkspace] notificationCenter] removeObserver:self];

  [super dealloc];
}

@end
```

A sample application that uses `MYWorkspaceNotificationObserver` is available at `www.cocoaprogramming.net`. The class can be tested by connecting its outlets to appropriate objects in Interface Builder. Connect buttons or menu items to `MYWorkspaceNotificationObserver`'s actions.

Summary

This chapter describes how to obtain information about files, processes, and the operating system. Cocoa applications can be integrated with the operating system's workspace and use applications such as Finder to manage files. This chapter also provides general information about operating-system security, and the security vulnerabilities of Cocoa applications.

The next chapter explains how to use operating system networking features from Cocoa including ways to communicate with other applications such as Finder. Networking and interapplication communication features enable tight integration of Cocoa applications with the operating system and other applications.

23
Networking

IN THIS CHAPTER

- NSURL and NSURLHandle
- Email Messages
- Directory Services
- Interapplication Programming

This chapter explores the networking facilities available to Cocoa applications from basic URL data types and downloading to complex interapplication communication using distributed objects. A general overview of network programming using Cocoa and several small examples are provided.

NSURL and NSURLHandle

URLs, Uniform Resource Locators, are the World Wide Web equivalent of a file system path. They specify where and what protocol to use to find a resource.

The canonical format that defines the pattern required for all URLs follows:

```
<scheme_Component>://<authority_Component>/<path>;
➥<params>?<query>#<fragment>
```

Each component of the URL format serves a specific purpose and helps identify the resource that is specified. For example, <scheme Component> is often http, https, file, or ftp and defines the protocol or communications scheme used to access a resource. The <authority_Component> defines the computer that can provide the resource. The <authority_Component> is often an Internet domain name or IP address. The <path>, <params>, <query>, and <fragment> components all help to identify a resource accessible by the <authority_Component>.

The Foundation Framework classes NSURL and NSURLHandle provide Cocoa applications with basic support for URL management and downloading data identified by URLs from the Internet.

NSURL and NSURLHandle work together to provide basic access to common Internet-based data types. NSURL specifies the location of a resource by providing an Objective-C wrapper around URLs. Various NSURLHandle subclasses provide the means for downloading the data. NSURL is toll-free bridged to the CoreFoundation data type CFURLRef. Toll-free bridging is described in the "Related Core Foundation" section of Chapter 7, "The Foundation Framework Overview."

NSURLHandle currently supports a limited subset of the various standard Internet protocols: http, https, and file. In Mac OS X 10.1, passing usernames and passwords via NSURL is not supported, nor are proxy servers. Apple has indicated that future versions of Mac OS X will add support for the ftp protocol, proxy servers, usernames, and passwords.

Creating a New NSURL

New autoreleased instances of NSURL are created using the convenience class method +URLWithString: passing an NSString as the argument. The -initWithString: initializer is also available. URLs that represent files in the local file system are created using the file:// URL scheme component. NSURL provides the +fileURLWithPath: and -initFileURLWithPath: methods that accept valid file system paths and return file:// URLs.

It is possible to initialize a new NSURL instance by specifying the scheme, host, and path components as individual NSString instances using the method -initWithScheme:host:path:, as shown in the following example:

```
theURL=[[NSURL alloc] initWithScheme:@"ftp"
                                host:@"www.cocoaprogramming.net"
                                path:@"/pub/somefile.txt"];
```

Not all characters that can be stored in an NSString can be used as part of a URL. A standard called RFC 2396 specifies the characters allowed in URLs. Apple provides the CFURLCreateStringByAddingPercentEscapes() function to make strings conform to RFC 2396. CFURLCreateStringByAddingPercentEscapes() is documented at http://developer.apple.com/techpubs/macosx/ReleaseNotes/CoreFoundation.html as part of a release note for Apple's Core Foundation framework and Carbon. The following category implementation shows one technique for extending the NSString class to support the creation of URLs. The two methods take advantage of the toll-free bridging between NSString and CFString.

```
@implementation NSString (MY_RFC2396Support)

- (NSString *)stringByAddingPercentEscapes
/*" Returns an autoreleased NSString composed of the characters in the
receiver modified (escaped) as necessary to conform with RFC 2396 for
use in URLs "*/
```

```
{
   return [(NSString *)CFURLCreateStringByAddingPercentEscapes(NULL,
       (CFStringRef)self, NULL, NULL,
       CFStringConvertNSStringEncodingToEncoding(NSASCIIStringEncoding))
       autorelease];
}

- (NSString *)stringByReplacingPercentEscapes
/*" Returns an autoreleased NSString composed of the characters in the receiver
represented directly as Unicode characters rather than RFC 2396 escaped
characters. "*/
{
   return [(NSString *)CFURLCreateStringByReplacingPercentEscapes(
      kCFAllocatorDefault,(CFStringRef)self, CFSTR("")) autorelease];
}

@end
```

To create an NSURL that is relative to an existing NSURL the class method +URLWithString:relativeToURL: is used. If a retained instance is preferred, the instance method -initWithString:relativeToURL: is used. The following example creates an NSURL instance the represents the README.html file in the /Developer/Documentation directory using +URLWithString:relativeToURL:.

```
baseURL=[NSURL fileURLWithPath:@"/Developer/Documentation"];
resultURL=[NSURL URLWithString:@"README.html" relativeToURL:baseURL];
```

The next example creates an NSURL instance that references the same network location (scheme, host, port, and so on) as an existing URL, but specifies a different file:

```
base = [[NSURL alloc] initWithString:@"http://localhost/somefile.html"];
result = [[NSURL alloc] initWithString:@"/newfile.html" relativeToURL:base];
```

The result URL in this example references http://localhost/newfile.html.

Decomposing an NSURL

NSURL's -absoluteString method returns an instance of NSString that represents the resolved location of a URL, either relative or absolute. The method -standardizedURL returns a new NSURL instance with any ".." or "." values within the URL path resolved. Combining these two methods as follows provides a URL suitable for feedback to the user:

```
theString = [[theURL standardizedURL] absoluteString];
```

NSURL instances created with -initWithString:relativeToURL: and +URLWithString:relativeToURL: methods contain both the base URL as well as the relative path. The base URL is retrieved using the method -baseURL. The path relative to the base is returned by -relativePath.

Sending the -absoluteURL message to an NSURL instance created with the relative methods returns a new absolute NSURL instance. If -absoluteURL is sent to an absolute URL it returns self.

NSURL also responds to the method -relativeString. In the case of an NSURL created relative to a base URL, -relativeString returns an NSString representing the relative portion of the URL. If the NSURL is an absolute URL, or the base URL value of a relative URL is nil, -relativeString returns the same results as a call to -absoluteString.

The -relativePath and -relativeString methods are similar to each other, but they handle the query and fragment portions of a URL differently. The following test program shows the difference between -relativePath and -relativeString.

```
#import <Foundation/Foundation.h>

int main (int argc, const char * argv[]) {
  NSAutoreleasePool * pool = [[NSAutoreleasePool alloc] init];

  {
    NSURL *url = [NSURL URLWithString:@"/tmp/foo" relativeToURL:
      [NSURL URLWithString:@"http://www.myserver.com/"]];

    NSLog(@"path: %@\nstring: %@", [url relativePath], [url relativeString]);
  }
  {
    NSURL *url = [NSURL URLWithString:@"/tmp/foo%20bar" relativeToURL:
      [NSURL URLWithString:@"http://www.myserver.com/"]];

    NSLog(@"path: %@\nstring: %@", [url relativePath], [url relativeString]);
  }
  {
    NSURL *url = [NSURL URLWithString:@"/tmp/foo#fragment" relativeToURL:
      [NSURL URLWithString:@"http://www.myserver.com/"]];

    NSLog(@"path: %@\nstring: %@", [url relativePath], [url relativeString]);
  }
  {
```

```
    NSURL *url = [NSURL URLWithString:
        @"http://www.myserver.com/tmp/foo#fragment"];

    NSLog(@"path: %@\nstring: %@", [url relativePath], [url relativeString]);
  }

  [pool release];
  return 0;
}
```

The following output shows that the string returned by `-relativeString` contains characters unmodified from the characters in the string used to create the relative portion of the URL. The `-relativePath` method returns a string representing the relative portion of the URL with query and fragment parts stripped, and URL escape sequences replaced with ordinary characters.

```
2002-03-21 19:53:53.518 TestURL[357] path: /tmp/foo
string: /tmp/foo
2002-03-21 19:53:53.520 TestURL[357] path: /tmp/foo bar
string: /tmp/foo%20bar
2002-03-21 19:53:53.520 TestURL[357] path: /tmp/foo
string: /tmp/foo#fragment
2002-03-21 19:53:53.521 TestURL[357] path: /tmp/foo
string: http://www.myserver.com/tmp/foo#fragment
```

The final distinction in the output is the way the URL created with `-URLWithString:` instead of `-URLWithString:relativeToURL:` is handled. The `-relativePath` method returns the relative portion of the URL obtained by actually parsing the URL to find its parts. The `-relativeString` method returns the entire string used to initialize the URL.

It is possible to retrieve specified components of the URL with the following instance methods. Table 23.1 shows the values returned by each method for the example URL `http://tori:pword@www.somehost:2704/path/to/resource;parameter?key=value&key=value#fragment`.

TABLE 23.1 `NSURL` Component Results

Method	Result
`-scheme`	http `-resourceSpecifier` `//tori:pword@www.somehost:2704/path/to/resource;parameter?key=value&key=value#fragment`
`-user`	tori
`-password`	pword

TABLE 23.1 Continued

Method	Result
`-host`	www.somehost
`-port`	2704
`-path`	/path/to/resource
`-parameterString`	parameter
`-query`	key=value&key=value
`-fragment`	fragment

The `NSURL` method `-isFileURL`, returns the Boolean value of `YES` if an `NSURL` was created using the file scheme and `NO` otherwise.

Downloading Data

There are several different ways of downloading data when working with the `NSURL` and `NSURLHandle` classes. The simplest is to download the data in the foreground, which blocks the application until the download is complete or has failed. Downloading data in the background (asynchronously) requires more code, but allows the application to respond interactively with the user while the download takes place.

`NSURLHandle` supports the concept of a cache. When beginning a download or creating a new `NSURLHandle` instance, an application can specify whether the cache is used or ignored. If the cache is used, an existing instance of `NSURLHandle` can service multiple `NSURL`s that reference different resources at the same base URL. Using the cache can reduce the number of network connections needed to download data, but some servers do not permit downloading of multiple resources from one network connection.

Foreground (Synchronous) Downloading

The simplest method of downloading text specified by an `NSURL` is actually provided by `NSString`. The `NSString` class method `+stringWithContentsOfURL:` returns a string initialized with the contents of the resource referenced by a URL. The string is encoded using the system's default string encoding, unless a resource referenced by a URL begins with a byte order marking `U+FEFF` or `U+FFFE` in which case the string has Unicode encoding.

Retrieving the data pointed to by an `NSURL` into an `NSData` is accomplished by calling the `NSURL` method `-resourceDataUsingCache:`. This returns an `NSData` that contains the contents of the referenced resource or `nil` if the data is not available. If the argument passed to this method is `YES`, and the contents of the referenced URL have already been retrieved, the cache is used instead of creating a new network connection. If the use cache flag is `NO`, or if it is `YES` but the data hasn't been cached, a new network connection is created and the data is downloaded and returned. The application will block until the data is retrieved, an error is encountered, or the attempt times out.

NSURLHandleClient **Protocol**

Downloading asynchronously requires direct use of the NSURLHandle class and use of the NSURLHandleClient protocol.

An object is assigned as the client of an NSURLHandle. This client then receives messages from the NSURLHandleClient protocol during the download. The NSURLHandleClient protocol defines the following messages:

```
- (void)URLHandleResourceDidBeginLoading:(NSURLHandle *)sender
- (void)URLHandleResourceDidCancelLoading:(NSURLHandle *)sender
- (void)URLHandleResourceDidFinishLoading:(NSURLHandle *)sender
- (void)URLHandle:(NSURLHandle *)sender resourceDataDidBecomeAvailable:
    (NSData *)newBytes
- (void)URLHandle:(NSURLHandle *)sender resourceDidFailLoadingWithReason:
    (NSString *)reason
```

An NSURLHandle client object receives the -URLHandleResourceDidBeginLoading: message when the download initially begins. The NSURLHandle beginning to load is the sender argument. The client receives -URLHandleResourceDidFinishLoading: when the download has completed successfully.

If the download encounters an error, the -URLHandle:resourceDidFailLoadingWithReason: message is sent to the client. The sender argument is the affected NSURLHandle, and the reason is an NSString that can be presented to the user as an error message.

As a download progresses, NSURLHandle sends newly acquired data to the client object with the -URLHandle:resourceDataDidBecomeAvailable: message. The data received since the last time this message was sent is provided in the second argument.

The client method -URLHandleResourceDidCancelLoading: is called if the download has been cancelled because the NSURLHandle instance received the -cancelLoadInBackground message.

Creating and Working with NSURLHandle Instances

NSURLHandle is an abstract class with various subclasses that provide concrete implementations. To create a new NSURLHandle, it is necessary to first determine the type of NSURLHandle class that needs to be created by calling +URLHandleClassForURL: and passing an NSURL as the argument. This returns the class that should be allocated and initialized for the scheme specified by the URL. The following example creates an NSURLHandle instance capable of handling the http scheme:

```
NSURL *theURL = [NSURL URLWithString:@"http://www.cocoaprogramming.net/"];
Class theClass = [NSURLHandle URLHandleClassForURL: theURL ];
theURLHandle = [[theClass alloc] initWithURL:theURL cached:NO];
```

NSURL provides the convenience method -URLHandleUsingCache: that also provides a suitable NSURLHandle instance. The following example creates an NSURLHandle instance capable of handling the http scheme:

```
theURLHandle = [[NSURL URLWithString:@"http://www.cocoaprogramming.net/"]
    URLHandleUsingCache:NO];
```

A newly initialized instance of NSURLHandle does not have a client object assigned to it. The client is specified by calling the NSURLHandle method -addClient: and passing the client object as the argument. The client must implement the NSURLHandleClient protocol. A client of an NSURLHandle instance is removed by sending the NSURLHandle -removeClient: message passing the client object.

Having initialized an NSURLHandle and assigned a client object, it is now possible to begin a download. A foreground download is initiated by sending -loadInForeground to the NSURLHandle instance. The -loadInForeground method returns an NSData instance containing all the data from the download.

Sending the -loadInBackground message to an NSURLHandle instance starts an asynchronous download. As the download takes place, the NSURLHandle client object receives the appropriate messages specified in the NSURLHandleClient protocol.

NSURL provides a convenience method to create a new NSURLHandle, assign a client object, and begin a background download through the use of -loadResourceDataNotifyingClient:usingCache:. The first argument specifies a client object that implements the NSURLHandleClient protocol. The second argument is a Boolean that specifies if the cache should be used or not.

A background download can be cancelled by sending the -cancelLoadInBackground message to the NSURLHandle instance performing the download. Canceling the download causes the client object to receive the -URLHandleResourceDidCancelLoading: message.

The status of a download is queried by sending the -status message to the NSURLHandle instance. This method returns an NSURLHandleStatus constant with one of the values in Table 23.2.

TABLE 23.2 NSURLHandleStatus Constants

Constant	Definition
NSURLHandleNotLoaded	The resource data has not been loaded.
NSURLHandleLoadSucceeded	The resource data was successfully loaded.
NSURLHandleLoadInProgress	The resource data is in the process of loading.
NSURLHandleLoadFailed	The resource data failed to load.

If the status of a download is `NSURLHandleLoadFailed`, a call to the `NSURLHandle` instance method `-failureReason` returns an `NSString` that contains a description of the error. If there is no error, `-failureReason` returns `nil`.

Calling `-availableResourceData` returns the data retrieved by an `NSURLHandle`. This method returns an `NSData` instance containing only the contents that have been received at the time the `-availableResourceData` message is sent. It returns `nil` if a previous attempted download failed.

Calling `-resourceData` returns the complete `NSURLHandle` resource contents blocking, if necessary, until all data has been received.

Adding Support for Additional Download Schemes

By subclassing `NSURLHandle` it is possible to add support for downloading from additional URL schemes, or to replace the existing handlers for the `http`, `https`, and `file` schemes.

The best example of an `NSURLHandle` subclass is Dan Wood's `CURLHandle` implementation. It is a wrapper around the CURL library (`http://curl.haxx.se/`). `CURLHandle` extends `NSURLHandle` capabilities with additional support for `http`, `https`, and `ftp` as well as support for Internet proxy servers. It is available as open source at `http://curlhandle.sourceforge.net`.

Email Messages

There are two principal techniques of sending email messages programmatically with Cocoa. The first is to open an email in the user's selected email application and allow them to edit or augment the message before sending. The second is to send the message directly from a Cocoa application.

Creating a Message in the User's Email Client

A compose window can be opened in the user's email client by creating an `NSURL` that uses the `mailto` scheme, and then calling the `NSWorkspace` method `-openURL:`.

The parameters that can be passed in a `mailto` URL are listed in Table 23.3.

TABLE 23.3 mailto URL Parameters

Query Key	Definition
CC	Carbon-copy address
BCC	Blind carbon-copy address
SUBJECT	Subject text
BODY	Body text

Each of the values for the query keys as well as the destination email address need to be escaped to protect the characters that are used in URLs for other purposes. This example uses the `-stringByAddingPercentEscapes` method defined in the `NSString` (`MY_RFC2396Support`) category shown in the "Creating a New `NSURL`" section of this chapter.

```
EncodedSubject = [NSString stringWithFormat:@"SUBJECT=%@",
    [subject stringByAddingPercentEscapes]];
encodedBody = [NSString stringWithFormat:@"BODY=%@",
    [body stringByAddingPercentEscapes]];
encodedDestinationUser = [destinationuser stringByAddingPercentEscapes];
encodedURLString = [NSString stringWithFormat:@"mailto:%@?%@&%@",
    encodedDestinationUser, encodedSubject, encodedBody];
mailtoURL = [NSURL URLWithString:encodedURLString];
[[NSWorkspace sharedWorkspace] openURL:mailtoURL];
```

This example opens the user's email client and creates a new compose window with the subject, body, and email address values already filled in.

Message Framework

It is also possible to send email without going through the user's email client. This is accomplished by using the `NSMailDelivery` class in Apple's Message framework located in `/System/Library/Frameworks`. The only documentation that Apple provides for this framework at the time of this writing is in the header files provided with the framework. This framework uses the settings that have been configured by the user in the System Preferences application to send the email.

`NSMailDelivery` provides two class methods used to send email:

```
+ (BOOL)deliverMessage:(NSString *)messageBody
              subject:(NSString *)messageSubject
                   to:(NSString *)destinationAddress;
```

```
+ (BOOL)deliverMessage: (NSAttributedString *)messageBody
              headers: (NSDictionary *)messageHeaders
               format: (NSString *)messageFormat
             protocol: (NSString *)deliveryProtocol;
```

The `+deliverMessage:subject:to:` method is the simplest to use. You provide `NSStrings` for the message body, subject, and email address, and the mail is sent via whatever `SMTP` host has been configured in System Preferences.

The `+deliverMessage:headers:format:protocol:` method allows control over the type of mail being sent as well as the specification of additional email headers. The `messageFormat` argument is one of two values: `NSMIMEMailFormat` or `NSASCIIMailFormat`. Specifying `NSASCIIMailFormat` causes any formatting and attachments in the `messageBody` argument to be removed before sending.

The `messageHeaders` dictionary contains at minimum an `NSString` value for the key To. If you want to send the message to multiple users at the same time, you can pass an NSArray for the To, Cc, or Bcc keys.

The `deliveryProtocol` is usually set to `nil` so that the default delivery configuration for the user's machine is used. The only other supported option is `NSSMTPDeliveryProtocol`.

The following example sends a document to three users by using a Cc header. It encodes the file `/tmp/ExampleDocument.rtfd` as a multipart MIME enclosure. The actual encoding that is done depends on the attributed string that specified the message body. If the string is created from an RTF or RTFD document, the email is encoded as MIME-rich text, which is not capable of reproducing all the details that an RTFD document contains. If the string is created from an HTML file, the email contains a text/html encoding of the document.

```
theMessage=[[[NSMutableAttributedString alloc]
    initWithPath:@"/tmp/ExampleDocument.rtfd"
    documentAttributes:NULL] autorelease];
[headersDict setObject:@"user@some.place" forKey:@"To"];
[headersDict setObject:[NSArray arrayWithObjects:@"secondUser@some.place",
    @"thirdUser@some.place",nil] forKey:@"Cc"];

[headersDict setObject:@"My Example Document" forKey:@"Subject"];
[headersDict setObject:@"Extra Header Contents 1.0" forKey:@"X-MyExtraHeader"];
result=[NSMailDelivery deliverMessage:theMessage
                              headers:headersDict
                               format:NSMIMEMailFormat
                             protocol:nil];
```

Directory Services

Directory services are repositories for information about various services, machines, and clients on a network. They provide mappings from TCP/IP port numbers to processes and machine names to IP addresses. Directory services also aid network file systems and provide user identification and password verification.

Apple's Directory Services APIs provide a layer of abstraction that helps Cocoa applications work regardless of the underlying network and directory services implementation. To do this, the Directory Services APIs support the development of plug-ins. Mac OS X version 10.1.3 provides a Directory Services plug-in for Apple's own NetInfo service, and in future versions will fully support OpenLDAP and Microsoft's Active Directory.

NOTE

NetInfo, OpenLDAP, and Active Directory all store information about available network services. The particular system used is controlled by the network administrator who set up the network. By supporting all three systems, Mac OS X will work seemlessly on almost any network.

Most applications do not need to directly access the information provided by directory services. Cocoa classes such as `NSHost`, `NSSocketPort`, `NSSocketPortNameServer` provide information using available services. Apple also provides the Security Framework briefly described in Chapter 22, "Integrating with the Operating System," and documented at `http://developer.apple.com/techpubs/macosx/CoreTechnologies/securityservices/authorizationconcepts.pdf`.

Apple's NetInfo directory service is part of the open source Darwin project and is available at `http://developer.apple.com/darwin/projects/opendirectory/`. NetInfo is documented at `http://www.apple.com/macosx/server/pdf/UnderstandingUsingNetInfo.pdf`.

Interapplication Programming

Cocoa applications can communicate with each other in several ways. The lowest levels of the Mac OS X kernel provide interapplication communication features. Deep within the implementation of the operating system, processes communicate using Mach messages and Mach ports. Just above the kernel level, Mac OS X provides standard BSD Unix sockets. Sockets are a cross-platform API for interprocess and network communications. Services such as the Message framework and Directory Services described in this chapter are implemented using Mach messages and/or sockets.

Mac OS X provides several high-level, interapplication communication APIs that are based on sockets and Mach messages, but shield programmers from low-level implementation details. The highest-level communication API is Apple Events. The remainder of this chapter describes the high-level communications APIs and places to look for information about the low-level APIs.

Apple Events

Apple's AppleScript system enables direct communication with applications including Finder by sending Apple Events. Apple Events are commands that are sent from one application to another locally or over a network. Applications that support AppleScript receive the Apple Events, perform the commanded operations, and return data to the application that sent the Apple Events. Most Cocoa applications automatically provide basic AppleScript support and can receive Apple Events.

Cocoa applications benefit from AppleScript support provided by the Foundation and Application Kit frameworks. The frameworks convert received Apple Events into script command objects that work with application objects to perform the commanded operations. Although most Cocoa applications can automatically receive Apple Events, Cocoa does not provide any way to send Apple events in Mac OS X version 10.1.3. Cocoa applications must use the Carbon Apple Event Manager API to send Apple Events.

The best way to get started using Apple Events is to read Apple's overview documentation at `http://developer.apple.com/techpubs/macosx/Carbon/interapplicationcomm/AppleEventManager/appleeventmanager.html`.

Cocoa's support for AppleScript and Apple Events is described at `http://developer.apple.com/techpubs/macosx/Cocoa/TasksAndConcepts/ProgrammingTopics/AppArchitecture/index.html` and `http://developer.apple.com/techpubs/macosx/Cocoa/TasksAndConcepts/ProgrammingTopics/Scriptability/index.html`.

Distributed Notifications

Notifications were introduced in Chapter 6, " Cocoa Design Patterns," and are used in most chapters of this book. Cocoa provides a mechanism for posting notifications that are transmitted to all applications running on the same computer. These distributed notifications have some limitations and are relatively inefficient compared to other interapplication communication techniques, but they are very simple to use.

Each Cocoa application has an instance of the `NSDistributedNotificationCenter` class that is accessed via `NSDistributedNotificationCenter`'s `+defaultCenter` method. The default-distributed notification center sends and receives notifications sent between applications on the same computer.

Posting Distributed Notifications

Notifications are posted to a distributed notification center with the following methods:

```
- (void)postNotificationName:(NSString *)notificationName
    object:(NSString *)anObject
- (void)postNotificationName:(NSString *)notificationName
    object:(NSString *)anObject userInfo:(NSDictionary *)userInfo
- (void)postNotificationName:(NSString *)notificationName
    object:(NSString *)anObject userInfo:(NSDictionary *)userInfo
    deliverImmediately:(BOOL)deliverImmediately
```

The `-postNotificationName:object:` method calls `-postNotificationName:object:userInfo:deliverImmediately:` with a `nil` `userInfo:` argument and `NO` for the `deliverImmediately:` argument. The `-postNotificationName:object:userInfo:` method calls `-postNotificationName:object:userInfo:deliverImmediately:` with `NO` for the `deliverImmediately:` argument. The `deliverImmediately:` argument controls the behavior of distributed notifications when the receiving applications are suspended and is described in the "Observing Distributed Notifications" section of this chapter.

Observers filter notifications so that only notifications with particular `object:` arguments are received. For local notifications, the addresses of the `object:` arguments can be used to determine if a notification should be dispatched to observers. Notifications posted using the `NSNotificationCenter` class do not have any restriction on the class of the `object:` argument. With distributed notifications, the `object:` arguments originate in different processes from the observers. Address comparisons between processes are meaningless. Therefore, distributed notifications are filtered based on the string value of the `object:` argument instead of its address. As a result, the `object:` argument to distributed notifications must be an instance of `NSString`.

The `userInfo:` argument to distributed notifications is encoded with `NSArchiver` and decoded with `NSUnarchiver`. As a result, only objects that conform to the `NSCoding` protocol should be used in the `userInfo:` dictionary. `NSArchiver`, `NSUnarchiver`, and `NSCoding` are described in the "Encoding and Decoding" section of Chapter 5, "Cocoa Conventions."

Observing Distributed Notifications

An object can be registered to observe distributed notifications with two `NSDistributedNotificationCenter` methods:

```
- (void)addObserver:(id)anObserver selector:(SEL)aSelector
    name:(NSString *)notificationName object:(NSString *)anObject
```

```
- (void)addObserver:(id)anObserver selector:(SEL)aSelector
    name:(NSString *)notificationName object:(NSString *)anObject
    suspensionBehavior:(NSNotificationSuspensionBehavior)suspensionBehavior
```

The `-addObserver:selector:name:object:` method calls `-addObserver:selector:name:object:suspensionBehavior:` with `NSNotificationSuspensionBehaviorCoalesce` as the `suspensionBehavior:` argument.

Notifications are not always received immediately when they are posted. `NSDistributedNotificationCenter`'s `-setSuspended:` method is used to suspend distribution of distributed notifications to observers. If `-setSuspended:` is called with `YES` as the argument, the distributed notification center for that application temporarily stops receiving notifications. The `NSApplication` object in Application Kit–based applications automatically calls `-setSuspended:YES` when the application is inactive and calls `-setSuspended:NO` when the application becomes active. Cocoa applications that do not use the Application Kit framework need to explicitly manage suspension of distributed notifications by calling `-setSuspended:` when appropriate.

The notifications that are posted, but not received by a suspended application, are handled in one of four ways depending on the `suspensionBehavior:` argument to `-addObserver:selector:name:object:suspensionBehavior:`. The available behaviors are enumerated by the `NSNotificationSuspensionBehavior` type that defines the following constants: `NSNotificationSuspensionBehaviorDrop`, `NSNotificationSuspensionBehaviorCoalesce`, `NSNotificationSuspensionBehaviorHold`, and `NSNotificationSuspensionBehaviorDeliverImmediately`.

If `NSNotificationSuspensionBehaviorDrop` is used, distributed notifications with the `name:` and `object:` arguments to `-addObserver:selector:name:object:suspensionBehavior:` are not received and are not queued. When `-setSuspended:NO` is called, notifications that were dropped while reception was suspended are not sent to observers.

If `NSNotificationSuspensionBehaviorCoalesce` is used, only one notification with each name and object is queued until `-setSuspended:NO` is called. When the application resumes receiving distributed notifications, only one notification is sent to each observer for each name and object pair no matter how many notifications were posted.

If `NSNotificationSuspensionBehaviorHold` is used, notifications are queued until `-setSuspended:NO` is called. The number of notifications that can be queued is undefined. When the application resumes receiving distributed notifications, all queued notifications are sent to observers. This suspension behavior should not be used for applications that may suspend notification reception for long periods of time because if the number of queued notifications exceeds Apple's undocumented limit, notifications might be lost.

Finally, if `NSNotificationSuspensionBehaviorDeliverImmediately` is used, notifications are sent to observers immediately regardless of whether the distributed notifications are suspended with `-setSuspended:YES`.

When distributed notifications are posted, the `deliverImmediately:` argument to `-postNotificationName:object:userInfo:deliverImmediately:` is used to force immediate reception of the notification by all applications even if they have suspended reception. If the `deliverImmediately:` argument is `YES`, the suspension status and suspension behavior of the applications that observe the notification are ignored. The `deliverImmediately:YES` option should only be used for critical notifications that cannot be delayed or ignored.

Observers can be removed for the distributed notification center with the `-removeObserver:name:object:` method that `NSDistributedNotificationCenter` inherits from its superclass, `NSNotificationCenter`. Notification centers do not retain the observer objects. When an object registered to observe notifications is deallocated, it must remove itself from all notification centers or there is a risk that notifications will be sent to deallocated objects and cause the application to crash.

Distributed Objects

Objective-C's features for sending messages between applications on the same or different computers were introduced in Chapter 4, "Objective-C." Distributed Objects are objects that take advantage of distributed messaging between applications. Distributed objects are very easy to use. In most cases, distributed objects work exactly the same way as local objects. Objects that reside in one application are represented by special objects called proxies in other applications. When a proxy receives an Objective-C message, it forwards the message to the actual object in another process. The forwarding of messages is handled automatically by the runtime.

Vending Objects

The first step when using distributed objects is to vend an object for use by other applications. The following code implements a very simple class called `MYMessageServer`:

```
#import <Foundation/Foundation.h>

@protocol MYMessageServerProtocol
```

```
- (void oneway)addMessageClient:(id)aClient;
- (BOOL)removeMessageClient:(id)aClient;
- (void oneway)broadcastMessageString:(NSString *)aString;

@end

@interface MYMessageServer : NSObject <MYMessageServerProtocol>
{
  NSMutableArray      *_myListOfClients;
}

@end


@implementation MYMessageServer

- (void oneway)addMessageClient:(id)aClient
{
  if(nil == _myListOfClients)
  {
    _myListOfClients = [[NSMutableArray alloc] init];
  }
  [_myListOfClients addObject:aClient];
  NSLog(@"Added client");
}


- (BOOL)removeMessageClient:(id)aClient
{
  [_myListOfClients removeObject:aClient];
  NSLog(@"Removed client");

  return YES;
}


- (void oneway)broadcastMessageString:(NSString *)aString
{
  [_myListOfClients makeObjectsPerformSelector:@selector(appendMessageString:)
      withObject:aString];
}
```

```
- (void)dealloc
{
  [_myListOfClients release];
  _myListOfClients = nil;

  [super dealloc];
}

@end
```

Instances of the `MYMessageServer` class maintain arrays of client objects registered with the `-addMessageClient:` method. Client objects are unregistered with `-removeMessageClient:`. Each time `MYMessageServer`'s `-broadcastMessageString:` method is called, the string argument to `-broadcastMessageString:` is sent to every registered client using the `-appendMessageString` method that clients must implement.

The following `main()` function creates an instance of `MYMessageServer` and vends that instance to other applications using a default connection. The `NSConnection` class is explained after this example.

```
int main (int argc, const char * argv[])
{
  NSAutoreleasePool *pool = [[NSAutoreleasePool alloc] init];
  MYMessageServer   *server = [[MYMessageServer alloc] init];
  NSConnection      *defaultConnection;

  defaultConnection = [NSConnection defaultConnection];
  [defaultConnection setRootObject:server];
  [defaultConnection registerName:@"server"];

  [[NSRunLoop currentRunLoop] configureAsServer];
  [[NSRunLoop currentRunLoop] run];

  [server release];
  [pool release];
  return 0;
}
```

The `MYMessageServer` class and the `main()` function are all that is needed to implement a server that sends and receives messages via distributed objects. To run the message server, create a Foundation Tool–style project in Project Builder. Enter the code for MYMessageServer into the main.m file that Project Builder automatically creates. Replace the existing implementation of the main() function in main.m with the main function that vends the MYMessageServer object. Build the project and run it.

The message server waits for other applications to connect to the vended object. The server runs until Project Builder or Process Viewer stops it. Before implementing a client application that communicates with the message server, it is worthwhile to analyze exactly what the server is doing.

Every thread in a Cocoa application has a default NSConnection instance. NSConnection instances manage network connections for distributed objects. NSConnection is only used directly when vending an object to other applications, when accessing objects vended by other applications, and when configuring attributes of distributed objects such as how long to wait for distributed messages before giving up. After a remote application has access to a vended object, the object is used just like local objects.

The message server's main() function obtains the default NSConnection instance for the application's main thread with the expression defaultConnection = [NSConnection defaultConnection]. The object to be vended is set with [defaultConnection setRootObject:server]. Then, a name is registered with the operating system so that client applications can find the server's connection by its name. The [defaultConnection registerName:@"server"] expression registers the connection with the name server.

A run loop needs to be running for an application to receive messages from clients. The expression [[NSRunLoop currentRunLoop] configureAsServer] tells the current run loop not to terminate just because no input is currently available. Then, [[NSRunLoop currentRunLoop] run] starts the run loop. Ordinarily, NSRunLoop's -run method returns immediately if no input is pending, but the -configureAsServer method prevents that. The NSRunLoop class is described in Chapter 7.

When configured as a server, [[NSRunLoop currentRunLoop] run] never returns. However, NSRunLoop's -runUntilDate: method can be used to specify a timeout after which the run loop stops waiting for input and returns.

Accessing Vended Objects

Figure 23.1 shows client applications running and broadcasting messages to each other via the message server that is running in the background. Two clients are shown, but any number of clients can connect to the server and broadcast messages.

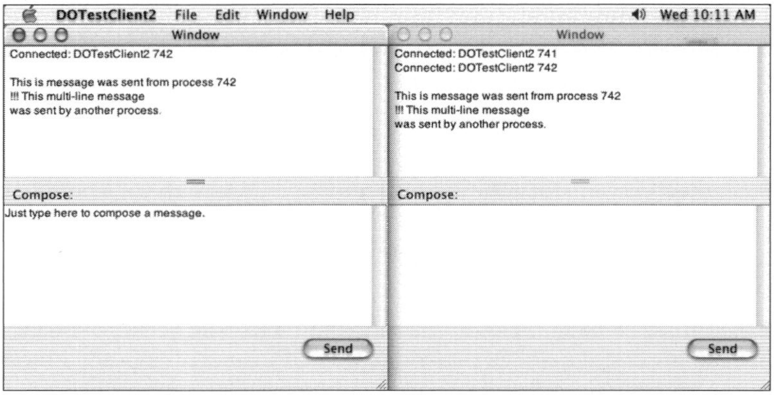

FIGURE 23.1 Two client applications communicate using distributed objects and a background server process.

The client application is implemented with a single instance of the `MYMasterController` class and `.nib` file. The interface of the `MYMasterController` declares outlets for two text fields. The text fields are used to compose messages to send and display messages that are received. The only other instance variable is a reference to the message server that is connected when the client application has finished launching:

```
File MYMasterController.h:

#import <Cocoa/Cocoa.h>

@interface MYMasterController : NSObject
{
  IBOutlet NSTextView          *composeView;
  IBOutlet NSTextView          *messageView;

  id                           server;
}

/*" Actions "*/
- (IBAction)sendMessage:(id)sender;

/*" Append Messages "*/
- (void oneway)appendMessageString:(NSString *)aString;

@end
```

The -sendMessage: action is sent by the Send button in the client's user interface. The -appendMessageString: is called by the message server to notify clients that a message string has been broadcast to all clients.

The implementation of MYMasterController is straightforward:

```
File MYMasterController.m:

#import "MYMasterController.h"

@protocol MYMessageServerProtocol

- (void oneway)addMessageClient:(id)aClient;
- (BOOL)removeMessageClient:(id)aClient;
- (void oneway)broadcastMessageString:(NSString *)aString;

@end


@implementation MYMasterController

/*" Actions "*/
- (IBAction)sendMessage:(id)sender
{
  // Braodcast the message and clear compose view
  [server broadcastMessageString:[composeView string]];
  [composeView setString:@""];
}


/*" Append Messages "*/
- (void oneway)appendMessageString:(NSString *)aString
{
  NSRange    appendRange = NSMakeRange([[messageView string] length], 0);

  // Append text and scroll if neccessary
  [messageView replaceCharactersInRange:appendRange withString:aString];
  [messageView scrollRangeToVisible:appendRange];
}


- (void)applicationDidFinishLaunching:(NSNotification *)aNotification
{
```

```
  server = [[NSConnection rootProxyForConnectionWithRegisteredName:@"server"
      host:nil] retain];

  if(nil == server)
  {
    NSLog(@"Error: Failed to connect to server.");
  }
  else
  {
     [server setProtocolForProxy:@protocol(MYMessageServerProtocol)];
     [server addMessageClient:self];
     [server broadcastMessageString:[NSString stringWithFormat:
          @"Connected: %@ %d\n",
          [[NSProcessInfo processInfo] processName],
          [[NSProcessInfo processInfo] processIdentifier]]];
  }
}


- (void)applicationWillTerminate:(NSNotification *)aNotification
{
  if(NO == [server removeMessageClient:self])
  {
    NSLog(@"Error: Failed to remove client.");
  }
  [server release];
  server = nil;
}

@end
```

After `MYMasterController.h` is imported, the protocol that server objects implement is defined. The protocol is not strictly necessary, but it is always a good idea to tell the distributed objects system what protocols distributed objects implement so that the distributed messages can be sent efficiently. The importance of protocols for distributed messaging is explained in the "Protocols" section of Chapter 4.

An instance of `MYMasterController` in the client application's `.nib` is used as the application's delegate. The application automatically sends the `-applicationDidFinishLaunching:` method to its delegate when the application has finished launching. The `-applicationWillTerminate:` message is sent to the delegate just before the application terminates. `MYMasterController` implements

-applicationDidFinishLaunching: to connect to the server application identified by the name "server," gets access to the object vended by the server, retains it, and registers the client to receive messages. The - applicationWillTerminate: method is implemented to remove references to the client from the server. The connection to the server is broken when the client application actually terminates.

In the implementation of MYMasterController's -applicationDidFinishLaunching: method, the server instance variable is set to the object returned from [NSConnection rootProxyForConnectionWithRegisteredName:@"server" host:nil]. The -rootProxyForConnectionWithRegisteredName: method establishes a connection to the service, identified by name if possible, and returns either a proxy to the root object vended by the server or nil. The significance of proxies is described in the next section. Specifying nil for the host: argument tells NSConnection to look for the named service on the local host. To make connections over a network, a host name such as lists.apple.com or an IP address string such as 172.92.42.1 must be provided as the host: argument.

If the connection to the server is established, the protocol supported by the server is set with [server setProtocolForProxy:@protocol(MYMessageServerProtocol)]. After that, messages can be sent to the server instance variable.

The implementation of -applicationWillTerminate: sends the -removeMessageClient: message to the server and then releases the server object. MYMessageServerProtocol declares that -removeMessageClient: returns a Boolean value. The return value is important in this case because it makes the message sent to the server synchronous. The client application cannot continue processing until the server returns a value or a timeout occurs. If the client does not wait for a reply from the server, the client application may terminate before the server has finished removing the client from its array of clients. Waiting for a return value assures that there is no chance that the server will be left with a reference to a terminated client.

The -sendMessage: action uses the server's -broadcastMessageString: method to broadcast any text that has been typed into the compose text view; then the compose text view is cleared.

The -appendMessageString: method is called by the server. It is implemented to append a string to the message text view and, if necessary, scroll the text view so that the new message text is visible.

With the server application running in Project Builder, experiment running the client application. Multiple copies of the client application can be run by using the Terminal application to launch the application. Assuming the client application is called DOTestClient.app and is installed in ~/Applications, the Terminal command to run the client follows:

```
>~/Applications/DOTestClient.app/Contents/MacOS/DOTestClient &
```

The & character at the end of the command tells the Terminal application to run the application in the background. The same command can be run any number of times to launch any number of clients.

The Role of Proxies

To establish distributed objects–based communication, the applications that need to communicate form connection represented by the `NSConnection` class for that purpose. After the connection is established, an object called the root object is shared by the connected applications. One application vends the root object. The other applications create proxies for the root object. The root object is the rendezvous point for communication.

A proxy is a stand-in for the actual object. Each application has a proxy that exists in its own address space. Any messages sent to the proxy are encoded and sent over the connection to the corresponding real object. Each application treats the proxies as if they were all the same object.

Proxies are not copies of remote objects. Proxies do not have any public methods of their own and require only a small fixed amount of storage no matter what objects they represent. Proxies forward messages that they receive to the actual object in another application.

Cocoa implements proxies with the `NSProxy` root class and its subclass, `NSDistantObject`. `NSProxy` conforms to the `NSObject` protocol. It is always safe to send `NSObject` protocol messages such as `-retain` to proxies. For example, when a proxy receives a `-retain` message, the message is forwarded to the proxy's represented object. The represented object is the one whose reference count is increased. The objects represented by proxies must conform to the `NSObject` protocol. In almost every case, the objects represented by proxies are subclasses of the `NSObject` class, and therefore inherit conformance with the `NSObject` protocol.

After a proxy for a vended root object is obtained, messages sent to the proxy and forwarded to the actual root object can accept object arguments and return objects. The root object's proxy is just a starting point. Apple's implementation of Objective-C provides keywords that define what should happen when pointers and objects are passed over a connection as arguments or return values.

Objective-C Keywords for Distributed Messaging

The default behavior when objects are sent from one application to another as the arguments or return values of distributed messages is to create new proxies to represent the objects in the remote application. The client example application in this chapter passes `self` to the server with the server's `-addMessageClient:` method. The server receives a proxy for the client object and stores the proxy in an array of clients. The array retains its elements. When the client proxy is added to the array, the `-retain` message sent by the array is forwarded back to the actual client object in the client application.

In some cases, the default behavior of creating proxies is not the best behavior. The `bycopy` keyword in the type specification of a message argument or return value forces the runtime to create a copy of the object in each process rather than using a proxy. The `bycopy` objects are encoded by the sender and then decoded by the receiver using a subclass of `NSCoder` called `NSPortCoder`. Objects sent `bycopy` must conform to the `NSCoding` protocol.

Some classes in the Cocoa frameworks are implemented to use `bycopy`. For example, when collection classes such as `NSArray` are passed over a connection, the collection itself is copied, but the objects contained in the remote copy of the collection are proxies to the original objects. The `byref` keyword is used to force the creation of a proxy instead of a copy if that is the desired behavior.

NOTE

The `bycopy` and `byref` keywords can only be used in protocol declarations, and they only apply to object arguments and return values.

The `oneway` keyword is used in the return type of messages. Specifying `(oneway void)` as the return type for a message indicates that sending application can continue processing immediately without waiting for the receiving application to acknowledge receipt or return a value. The `oneway` keyword only makes sense when used with `void` because with any other type the sender must wait for the return value. Without the `oneway` keyword, all messages are synchronous. The sender must wait for acknowledgement of the message before it can continue processing.

The `oneway` keyword should be used whenever possible because it reduces the communications traffic between applications. Without `oneway`, a minimum of two pieces of information are sent across the connection between applications: the message itself and the confirmation of receipt. Communications traffic can be reduced to one piece of information per message by using the `oneway` keyword.

The last three keywords that support distributed messaging are `in`, `out`, and `inout`. These keywords are used to specify what should happen when pointers are sent as arguments to distributed messages. Because pointers are only valid in one process, the pointers themselves cannot be sent to other applications. Instead, the memory referenced by the pointers is copied into the remote applications, and the remote applications are given pointers to their own local copies of the memory.

The `in` keyword specifies that the memory referenced by pointers is copied from the sender's application to the receiver's application, but changes made to the memory in the receiver are not copied back to the sender. The `out` keyword specifies that the memory referenced by the sender's pointer is not copied, but the values set by the receiver are copied back to the sender. The `inout` keyword specifies the default behavior. The memory referenced by pointer arguments that have the `inout` type modifier is copied from the sender to the receiver and copied again from the receiver to the sender when the method completes. The `in` and `out` keywords should be used whenever possible to minimize the number of times memory is copied between applications.

NOTE

Only pointers to fixed-size types can be passed as arguments or return values from distributed messages. The runtime needs to copy the memory referenced by pointers, and therefore must be able to determine how much memory to copy. The general rule is that pointer's to any type that can be used with C's `sizeof()` operator can be used with distributed objects.

Handling Errors

Most errors that occur as the result of distributed messaging are handled the same way other errors are handled. For example, unhandled exceptions raised as the result of a distributed message are raised in the application that sent the message, just like they would be for local messages. However, the termination of one of the applications using a distributed objects connection is a special case. If one application terminates, the other may need to perform cleanup operations such as removing proxies to objects in the terminated application.

When a communications connection is broken because one application has been terminated or become unresponsive, the `NSConnection` instance that encapsulates the broken connection sends the `NSConnectionDidDieNotification` to the default notification center in the surviving application.

Register for the `NSConnectionDidDieNotification` notification with code like the following:

```
[[NSNotificationCenter defaultCenter] addObserver:self
        selector:@selector(connectionDidDie:)
        name:NSConnectionDidDieNotification
        object:nil];
```

After registered with the default notification center, the `-connectionDidDie:` method is sent if any `NSConnection` instance posts the `NSConnectionDidDieNotification` notification. The `-connectionDidDie:` method must be implemented to perform any application specific cleanup needed.

The client application can implement -connectionDidDie: to simply report an error as follows:

```
- (void)connectionDidDie:(NSNotification *)aNotification
{
  NSLog(@"Error: Connection to server is broken");
}
```

Modify MYMasterController's -applicationDidFinishLaunching: method to observe the NSConnectionDidDieNotification notification:

```
- (void)applicationDidFinishLaunching:(NSNotification *)aNotification
{

  server = [[NSConnection rootProxyForConnectionWithRegisteredName:@"server"
      host:nil] retain];

  if(nil == server)
  {
    NSLog(@"Error: Failed to connect to server.");
  }
  else
  {
    [[NSNotificationCenter defaultCenter] addObserver:self
        selector:@selector(connectionDidDie:)
        name:NSConnectionDidDieNotification
        object:nil];
    [server setProtocolForProxy:@protocol(MYMessageServerProtocol)];
    [server addMessageClient:self];
    [server broadcastMessageString:[NSString stringWithFormat:
        @"Connected: %@ %d\n",
        [[NSProcessInfo processInfo] processName],
        [[NSProcessInfo processInfo] processIdentifier]]];
  }
}
```

Finally, call NSNotificationCenter's -removeObserver: method within MYMasterController's implementation of -applicationDidFinishLaunching:.

```
- (void)applicationWillTerminate:(NSNotification *)aNotification
{
  if(NO == [server removeMessageClient:self])
  {
    NSLog(@"Error: Failed to remove client.");
```

```
  }
  [[NSNotificationCenter defaultCenter] removeObserver:self];
  [server release];
  server = nil;
}
```

The server needs more sophisticated handling of client terminations. The server must find all invalid proxies in its client array whenever a connection dies. Add the following method to the `MYMessageServer` class:

```
- (void)connectionDidDie:(NSNotification *)aNotification
{
  NSConnection     *deadConnection = [aNotification object];
  int              i;

  NSLog(@"Connection to client is broken.");

  // remove proxies with dead connections from client list
  for(i = [_myListOfClients count] - 1; i >= 0; i—)
  {
    id    currentClient = [_myListOfClients objectAtIndex:i];

    NS_DURING
      if([currentClient respondsToSelector:@selector(connectionForProxy)])
      {
        if(deadConnection == [currentClient connectionForProxy])
        {
          // remove proxy with dead connection
          [_myListOfClients removeObjectAtIndex:i];
          NSLog(@"Removed client from client list.");
        }
      }
    NS_HANDLER
      [_myListOfClients removeObjectAtIndex:i];
      NSLog(@"Removed client from client list.");
    NS_ENDHANDLER
  }
}
```

The reverse order search through the list is necessary because items are removed from the list inside the loop. The `NS_DURING`, `NS_HANDLER`, `NS_ENDHANDLER` block handles exceptions that are raised when trying to remove a client proxy. Exception handling is described at http://developer.apple.com/techpubs/macosx/Cocoa/TasksAndConcepts/ProgrammingTopics/Exceptions/Tasks/HandlingExceptions.html. Proxies are in an indeterminate state when their associated connections have died. Any proxy that raises an exception within the loop needs to be removed.

Modify the server's main() function to register its MYMessageServer instance as an observer of the NSConnectionDidDieNotification notification:

```
int main (int argc, const char * argv[])
{
  NSAutoreleasePool *pool = [[NSAutoreleasePool alloc] init];
  MYMessageServer   *server = [[MYMessageServer alloc] init];
  NSConnection      *defaultConnection;

  defaultConnection = [NSConnection defaultConnection];
  [[NSNotificationCenter defaultCenter] addObserver:server
      selector:@selector(connectionDidDie:)
      name:NSConnectionDidDieNotification
      object:nil];
  [defaultConnection setRootObject:server];
  if ([defaultConnection registerName:@"server"] == NO)
  {
    NSLog(@"Error registering server");
  }

  [[NSRunLoop currentRunLoop] configureAsServer];
  [[NSRunLoop currentRunLoop] run];

  [[[NSNotificationCenter defaultCenter] removeObserver:server];
  [server release];
  [pool release];
  return 0;
}
```

With these changes, both the client and the server handle errors gracefully. Experiment running the server and the client in Project Builder. Use Project Builder to run and stop the applications in different orders and see what happens.

Low-Level Interprocess Communication

Apple provides an overview of interapplication communication techniques using Mac OS X at http://developer.apple.com/techpubs/macosx/Essentials/SystemOverview/InverEnvironissues/Interproces_mmunication.html. Low-level network programming using BSD Unix APIs and Mach kernel APIs is beyond the scope of this book, but more information is available at the following locations:

A document titled "BSD Sockets: A Quick And Dirty Primer" is available at `http:// world.std.com/~jimf/papers/sockets/sockets.html`. More comprehensive sockets documentation is available at `http://www.lowtek.com/sockets`.

Apple provides detailed instructions for using the `NSFileHandle` class with sockets at `http://developer.apple.com/techpubs/macosx/Cocoa/TasksAndConcepts/ProgrammingTopics/LowLevelFileMgmt/Concepts/FileHandle.html`.

Apple also provides the Cocoa `NSSocketPort` class and the Core Foundation `CFSocket` type to assist programmers with the integration of sockets with run loops implemented by `NSRunLoop`. `NSSocketPort` and `CFSocket` do not provide access to the complete set of features supported by sockets, however, and detailed knowledge of sockets programming is needed to effectively use them.

Information about Mach messages and Mach interprocess communication is available at `http://developer.apple.com/techpubs/macosx/Darwin/General/KernelProgramming/boundaries/Mach_Messag_cation_IPC_.html`.

Summary

Cocoa provides powerful interapplication programming and network communication features. In most cases, detailed knowledge of network protocols and operating system details are not required to create applications that download data or communicate with other applications. Cocoa provides extensible access to directory services, and the Message framework provides the `NSMailDelivery` class for communicating with the operating system's built in email-delivery features.

Chapter 24, "Subprocesses and Threads," covers the Cocoa classes that encapsulate operating system tasks and threads. Each application running on Mac OS X consists of one task and each task has at least one thread. Applications can start other tasks, send data to the tasks, and get data returned by the tasks. Chapter 24 also describes techniques for communicating between tasks and threads that complement and extend the information presented in this chapter.

24

Subprocesses and Threads

IN THIS CHAPTER

- Choosing Between Subprocesses and Threads
- Using the `NSTask` Class
- Using the `NSThread` Class
- Locking
- Threading Issues

Each program running on Mac OS X uses an underlying Unix process (sometimes also called a *task*). Mac OS X, like most operating systems, offers facilities for launching and controlling other programs. The `NSWorkspace` class offers facilities to launch another GUI application. Chapter 22, "Integrating with the Operating System," covers the `NSWorkspace` class.

For launching and controlling command-line tools or faceless programs, such as daemons (servers), Cocoa also offers the `NSTask` class. This class offers much more control over the launched process than the `NSWorkspace` facilities.

Each running process can have one or more threads. Threads are a lightweight execution context running within a single process. A thread shares memory and resources with other threads in the same process. Each thread has its own execution context, which allows it to run independently of the other threads in the process. On Mac OS X, threads are preemptively multitasked just like processes. On computers with multiple processors, threads can run simultaneously on different processors. The `NSThread` class is used to spawn and control threads.

Choosing Between Subprocesses and Threads

Both threads and subprocesses can be used to perform work in the background. This allows long running operations to proceed without locking up a user interface. Sometimes it is difficult to choose whether to solve a problem using a subprocess or a thread.

A common use for subprocesses is to wrap Unix commands. There are many useful programs available from the Unix community, but they generally lack a good graphical user interface. With some, the command-line interface borders on the incomprehensible. By launching such a command from an `NSTask`, it is possible to have the Unix command do all the heavy lifting while the program that launched it presents a logical user interface. The program that the user actually interacts with is known as a *wrapper* for the Unix command because it wraps itself around the command, isolating the command from the user. For some applications, it might make sense to create a Unix command, and then proceed to wrap it. This would make it possible to distribute a program that comes with both a graphical and command-line–based interface. For some markets, such an approach might be advantageous.

The "Using the `NSTask` Class" section of this chapter shows how to use the `NSTask` class. Two examples show how `NSTask` can be used to wrap a Unix command. The first is very simple, merely capturing the output of a Unix command. The second example is far more complex because it uses nearly all the `NSTask` facilities to wrap around an interactive Unix command.

The sections after the "Using the `NSTask` Class" section cover threads. Each process begins with one thread of control. The program's code is executed one statement at a time by this thread. However, it is possible to split the program's flow into multiple threads. Each thread will asynchronously execute its own series of instructions.

Threads are a good way to make use of computers that have multiple CPUs. For example, each CPU could potentially be running a different thread. A very CPU-intensive calculation could be split into as many threads as there are CPUs available. This would help the OS achieve maximum CPU utilization.

Threads can also be used to make a user interface more responsive. Normally, a long-running calculation would lock up a program until it is complete. No user input would be accepted until the calculation finishes and returns control to the event loop. The calculation can instead be performed in a thread separate from the main thread. Because the user interface runs in the main thread, it can continue to respond to user input while the other, background thread works towards a result. The result would then be communicated to the main thread when the calculation is complete.

It is more expensive to create a new process than to create a thread. Processes are generally very heavyweight. They have their own copy of the Unix environment variables, their own private memory context, and so on. Threads are different because they live in the same process space; they share memory contexts. This means that threads are subject to race conditions. Synchronization with locks is one of the techniques used to prevent race conditions. Unfortunately, synchronization can cause deadlock situations, so it must be used carefully.

The terms race condition, synchronization, and deadlock are each rather large topics of discussion. Later in the chapter they are briefly defined and discussed. Most of the discussion is found in the section "Threading Issues." For more details on the specifics of threads and processes and the theory behind them, the reader should consult a good operating systems textbook. This chapter shows how to use threads and subprocesses from Cocoa, but these topics are complex enough that there is no way all their theoretical aspects can be covered. You might find it helpful to consult such a text before proceeding with this chapter to become familiar with the principles being leveraged by `NSTask` and `NSThread`. One book that can serve as a reference is *Modern Operating Systems (Second Edition)* by Andrew S. Tanenbaum (Prentice Hall, ISBN 0130313580).

Because of all the complexities associated with threads, writing multithreaded applications can be a very challenging task. It should only be undertaken when a developer is really sure that threads truly are the best solution. This cannot be stressed enough. In fact, it is often wise to initially create a single-threaded application as a proof of concept, and then later partition it into threads. Designing up front so that such a partitioning will be natural is also wise, even if the future use of threads is not anticipated. Many of the tenets of good object-oriented design, if employed, will help to create such a partitionable design.

Using the `NSTask` Class

The `NSTask` class can be used to launch another process. In conjunction with other Cocoa classes, such as `NSPipe`, it can also set up communications between your program and the launched `NSTask`. To understand what facilities are available, it is instructive to first consider some of the ways you can communicate with another process.

Each process can take input from its environment variables, command-line arguments, files, and `stdin` (standard input). It can send output to a file, `stdout` (standard output), or `stderr` (standard error). Each process also has an integer return value, which is normally set to zero when a process exits successfully. Processes can also open up Unix pipes and sockets to communicate with each other. Any process linked with the Foundation Kit can also use distributed objects to communicate with other processes.

Of all these communication pathways, the command-line arguments, environment variables, `stdin`, `stdout`, and `stderr`, are all set up when the process is launched. `NSTask` has facilities to allow programmers to control the details of each of these communications channels. It is possible to later set up any of the other channels as desired, but this chapter won't discuss how to do that.

In using the `NSTask` object itself, it often helps to consider the object to have a life cycle consisting of three phases: setup, execution, and cleanup. The first, setup, is where most of the interaction with the object takes place. All the communications with the process and other relevant details are specified.

After everything is set up as desired, the task is launched. The two ways to launch a task are synchronously and asynchronously. In the synchronous case, the task will run to completion before control is returned to the program that launched the task. This is useful for tasks that run and exit quickly, but most of the time an asynchronous launch will be preferred. This will allow the task to run in the background without freezing the application that launched it. After the `NSTask` starts executing, none of the setup methods are valid anymore. In this phase, if the process was launched asynchronously, it can be suspended (paused), resumed, or aborted (terminated).

After the process exits, whether normally or by being terminated, the `NSTask` object moves to the cleanup phase. The setup methods are still invalid, and now the execution methods are also invalid. The object can be queried to see what the process' exit status was and that's about all that can be done with it. After the final data has been collected from the `NSTask` instance, it can be released. An `NSTask` cannot be relaunched after the subprocess has exited. Instead, a new object must be created and launched.

The next two sections show how to take `NSTask` through each of these phases of its lifecycle. The first example, Calendar, shows a very simple case where synchronous operation is acceptable. The second example, Animal, uses an asynchronous task to communicate with an interactive command.

`NSTask` Synchronously: Calendar Example

For this first example, a GUI wrapper around the Unix `cal` command is created. To learn about what this command can do, simply type `man cal` in a Terminal window. Basically, given a month and year, it will produce a small calendar, like this:

```
% cal 5 2002
      May 2002
 S  M Tu  W Th  F  S
          1  2  3  4
 5  6  7  8  9 10 11
12 13 14 15 16 17 18
19 20 21 22 23 24 25
26 27 28 29 30 31
```

The complete Calendar example can be downloaded from www.cocoaprogramming.net.

Calendar Example User Interface

As a simple GUI interface, create a window in Interface Builder like the one shown in Figure 24.1. Most of the window is taken up by an NSTextView at the top, which is used to display the output of the cal command. Because this output depends on a fixed-width font being used, set the object's font to some fixed-width font such as Courier New. The text view should also be selectable, but not editable.

FIGURE 24.1 The user interface for the Calendar example.

To allow the user to choose the month, a pop-up list of all twelve months is provided. The items should be in order from January to December. Each item should have an appropriate tag from 1 to 12 to correspond to the month of the year.

An NSForm with one field is used to specify the year. The cal command has one extra feature that should be exposed in the GUI. It can produce a calendar with Julian dates, where the day numbers are day of the year instead of day of the month. An NSButton set up as a switch is used to select this feature.

There is one feature of cal that will not be exposed with this example. The command has the capability to display a calendar for an entire year. This could be added easily by making a "whole year" entry at the end of the pop-up list and making a few code changes to detect its tag and change how the command is called.

After the interface has been laid out, a new object needs to be created. This can be done in either Project Builder or Interface Builder. Either way, create an object class called CalendarController, which is a subclass of NSObject. It should have four outlets: calendarText, julianSwitch, monthPopUp, and yearField. One action should be defined: -getCalendar:.

Make sure Interface Builder knows about the class and instantiate it in the `.nib` file. Next, hook up each of the outlets. All the elements will be hooked up to an outlet except for the Get Calendar button. It should be obvious which UI widget connects to which outlet. For all the GUI objects except the text view, connect them to send the `-getCalendar:` action to the `CalendarController` instance. This way, when the user changes the month, year, or julian setting the calendar will change automatically. In fact, this makes the Get Calendar button superfluous. It could even have be left out of the interface, but its presence is probably comforting to most users.

The `CalendarController` instance should also be connected up as the application's delegate (a connection from the File's Owner object). Finally, edit the main menu to suit—it probably makes sense to remove commands that don't apply to this program. It might be nice to add some ToolTips, as well.

`CalendarController` Class

After the interface is complete, it is time to start coding. Add two more method declarations to the header file so that it looks like this:

File `CalendarController.h`:

```
#import <Cocoa/Cocoa.h>

@interface CalendarController : NSObject
{
    IBOutlet id calendarText;
    IBOutlet id julianSwitch;
    IBOutlet id monthPopUp;
    IBOutlet id yearField;
}

- (void)applicationDidFinishLaunching:(NSNotification *)notification;
- (NSString *)runCommand:(NSString *)command withArguments:(NSArray *)args;
- (IBAction)getCalendar:(id)sender;

@end
```

When the program starts up, the interface will be set to show the current month of the year, based on today's date. This is the purpose of the `-applicationDidFinishLaunching:` method. It will obtain the current month and year, set the interface controls to these values, and then run the calendar for the first time, as if the Get Calendar button had been clicked. The code to do this is as follows:

```
- (void)applicationDidFinishLaunching:(NSNotification *)notification
{
```

```
    NSCalendarDate *today = [NSCalendarDate calendarDate];
    int month = [today monthOfYear];
    int year = [today yearOfCommonEra];
    [julianSwitch setState:0];
    [monthPopUp selectItemAtIndex:(month - 1)];
    [yearField setIntValue:year];
    [self getCalendar:self];
}
```

The -getCalendar: action method needs to be implemented next. It needs to obtain the parameters from the user interface, run the cal command, and then put the result in the text view. This is broken into two parts, running the command and everything else. The code to run the command will be placed in another, more general, method that can be reused in other programs as needed. Thus, the method to run the command will take the command's path as an argument along with an ordered NSArray containing NSStrings to be used as the command-line arguments. It will return the command's output as an NSString. There is a call to this function in the middle of the action method. The code for the action method looks like this:

```
- (IBAction)getCalendar:(id)sender
{
    NSString *calString;        NSMutableArray *args = [NSMutableArray array];
    BOOL julian = [julianSwitch state];
    int month = [[monthPopUp selectedCell] tag];
    int year = [yearField intValue];

    if (julian) {
        [args addObject:@"-j"];
    }
    [args addObject:[NSString stringWithFormat:@"%d", month]];
    [args addObject:[NSString stringWithFormat:@"%d", year]];
    calString = [self runCommand:@"/usr/bin/cal" withArguments:args];
    {
        int length = [[calendarText string] length];
        [calendarText setSelectedRange:NSMakeRange(0, length)];
        [calendarText setEditable:YES];
        [calendarText insertText:calString];
        [calendarText setEditable:NO];
    }
}
```

An array for the arguments (args) needs to be provided. A variable to hold the string that comes back (calString) is also needed. The variables for that are defined first.

Next, three variables, `julian`, `month`, and `year`, are defined. They are used to get the state of the user interface. The arguments array is configured next. To better understand this, consider what the command would look like if typed at the command line. To get a calendar for May, 2002, type

```
cal 5 2002
```

Type this to get it in Julian dates:

```
cal -j 5 2002
```

Therefore, the first argument is a `-j` if the Julian option is requested. The `if` statement adds this as the first object in the arguments array if appropriate. After that, the month and year are added to the array in order after they have been converted from integers to strings.

With the arguments array prepared, it is time to call the `-runCommand:withArguments:` method to run the command and get the result. For security, it is best to provide the command's full path name. In this case, the full path name is `/usr/bin/cal`. This can be determined for commands installed on a computer by typing `which` *<command>* in a Terminal window. For example:

```
% which cal
/usr/bin/cal
```

The `calString` variable contains everything that cal sent to both `stdout` and `stderr`. (This can be tested for output to `stderr` by forcing an error; when this example is complete, run it and choose a year greater than 9999.)

The final chunk of code selects the entire contents of the text view and inserts the command's result string. Because everything in the text view is selected when the insert happens, any text that was there before is replaced with the new text.

Running an `NSTask` Synchronously

Now, for the core work. It is necessary to create an `NSTask` object and have it run the command. The `-runCommand:withArguments:` method sets up an `NSTask`, run it synchronously, and then retrieve the task's output.

To capture the output, a pipe needs to be created. A pipe is a one-way communications channel. A process writes data into one end and another process retrieves the data from the other end. In this case, an `NSPipe` object is used to handle all the Unix details for controlling a pipe. The pipe object can be passed to the `NSTask` and assigned to `stdin`, `stdout`, or `stderr`. To capture both `stdout` and `stderr`, it is legal to connect a single pipe to both of them. Alternatively, to keep the streams separate, two pipes could be used.

NOTE

A single pipe can only send data in one direction between two processes. Don't ever attempt to connect a pipe to `stdin`, and then connect the same pipe to `stdout` and/or `stderr`. It won't work. Create multiple pipes instead, using at least one pipe per communication direction.

The `-runCommand:withArguments:` method begins by declaring all the needed variables:

```
- (NSString *)runCommand:(NSString *)command withArguments:(NSArray *)args
{
    NSTask *task = [[NSTask alloc] init];
    NSPipe *newPipe = [NSPipe pipe];
    NSFileHandle *readHandle = [newPipe fileHandleForReading];
    NSData *inData;
    NSString *tempString;
```

An `NSTask` and an `NSPipe` are allocated. Because the pipe will be used to read the output of the command, the pipe's read handle, which is an `NSFileHandle` object, is obtained. The `-fileHandleForReading` method is used to obtain the read handle. The `NSTask` connects the write handle of the pipe to the command's output. The output of the command is handed to us as an `NSData` object, so the `inData` variable is used for that. The `tempString` will be our return value and comes from the `NSData` object.

Next, the `NSTask` object is set up. Here is the code:

```
    [task setCurrentDirectoryPath:NSHomeDirectory()];
    [task setLaunchPath:command];
    [task setArguments:args];
    [task setStandardOutput:newPipe];
    [task setStandardError:newPipe];
```

The first message sets the current directory in the task's runtime environment with the `-setCurrentDirectoryPath:` method. The task might change the current directory as it runs; only the starting value is being set. The chosen starting value is the user's home directory, which is a reasonable default. For a command that is inside a bundle or app wrapper, it might make more sense to set this path to the app wrapper. The Unix `/tmp` directory or a temporary scratch directory might be better for some situations, depending on the command used.

The second message, `-setLaunchPath:`, sets the task's launch path. This is the full path to the command. The command argument to our method suits nicely.

(Remember, in this example `/usr/bin/cal` is the path that is used when this method is called.)

The `-setArguments:` method is used to set the command-line arguments of the task. The argument args is directly passed on to the `NSTask` object.

The last two messages, `-setStandardOutput:` and `-setStandardError:` give the `NSTask` the previously created `NSPipe` object to be connected to `stdout` and `stderr`, respectively. With that, the task is now ready to be run. A single line of code runs the task, invoking the `-launch` method:

```
    [task launch];
```

The task is launched and runs to completion. When it finishes, our program will continue. The next step is to obtain all the data written to `stdout` and `stderr`. The read handle provides it as an `NSData`, which is then converted into an `NSString`:

```
    inData = [readHandle readDataToEndOfFile];
    tempString = [[NSString alloc] initWithData:inData
            encoding:NSASCIIStringEncoding];
```

There are several ways to read data from a file handle. The `-readDataToEndOfFile` method obtains all the data in one shot. The example in the next section shows how data can be read from a file handle a chunk at a time.

The conversion to an `NSString` uses the `NSASCIIStringEncoding` encoding. Because Unix commands' output is typically ASCII, this is a sensible choice. If a custom command-line program is being used for the task, and it is known that it uses a different encoding, that would be specified here instead of ASCII.

The final step to finish off the method is to clean everything up. Because two objects are allocated in this method, the method must finish by releasing them. Because one of the objects (`tempString`) is to be the return value, it will be autoreleased. The other object, the `NSTask`, is no longer needed, so a simple `-release` is best. The method ends with this code:

```
    [task release];
    [tempString autorelease];
    return tempString;
}
```

That completes all the code needed to build this example. It should be possible to get output that looks similar to the screenshot in Figure 24.1.

Although this example works well, it is not perfect. For example, as mentioned previously, the cal command can provide a calendar for the whole year. The application could be updated to offer that feature.

Another improvement would be to do error checking and validation on the input to prevent error messages from the cal command. At the very least, presenting a localized alert sheet instead of exposing the raw error text from the Unix command would be clearly preferable. Separating the output and error streams and catching the command's errors to present a sheet would be preferred for any errors that can't be prevented with input validation. As a rule, when a Unix command is wrapped by a Cocoa application, the command should be hidden as far as possible from the user's view.

NSTask Asynchronously: Animal Example

The next NSTask-based takes the previous example much further. The full project and all files referenced in this section can be found on www.cocoaprogramming.net in the Animal example.

The example starts with a new implementation of the classic Animal program. This program is an interactive program. It asks the user to think of an animal, and then asks yes/no questions in an attempt to figure out the animal. If it can't guess the animal, it asks the user to provide another question that can be used to determine the new animal.

To wrap around this program, it is important to know what the program expects to see for input. Knowing what output to expect from the program is equally important. An example session from the command line might look something like this:

```
% ./animal_tool -f test.plist
Does your animal live in water?
y
Is this animal a mammal?
y
Is this animal usually very big?
y
Is your animal a whale?
y
Excellent!  I got it!
Would you like to play again?
y
Does your animal live in water?
n
```

```
Is it commonly found as a house pet?
y
Does the animal use a leash?
n
Can it be taught to talk?
n
Does this animal like to run inside a wire wheel?
n
*** Is your animal a cat?
n
Darn!  I don't know what animal it could be!
What is the name of your animal?
parakeet
What is a yes/no question I can use to distinguish between a parakeet
➥ and a cat?
Can it fly?
If someone answers "yes" to that question, is the animal a parakeet?
y
Would you like to play again?
n
```

The command-line program itself is written using the Foundation Kit and is an interesting example of how to use Foundation in a non-GUI program. However, because it doesn't use `NSTask` itself, the code isn't displayed here. It can be found in the `animal_main.m` file of the Animal example (it is 272 lines long, remarkably short considering the functionality and stability of the code).

Likewise, the controller object at the core of the example, `AnimalController`, will not be shown here in full. The header and implementation files for this class total nearly 600 lines of code! The important parts of the code, dealing with `NSTask`, will all be shown. For the support sections of the code, and the code for the command-line program, please refer to the example code at `www.cocoaprogramming.net` in the Animal example. The general design of the program is discussed here so that the code portions not explained in the text can be followed more easily.

Animal Example User Interface

The approach taken for a user interface in the Animal example is somewhat like a wizard. The interface is in a single window. As play progresses, the interface inside the window changes. A total of six different panels can appear. The `currentPage` variable is used to keep track of the interface's state. Figure 24.2 shows screenshots of each of the six panels.

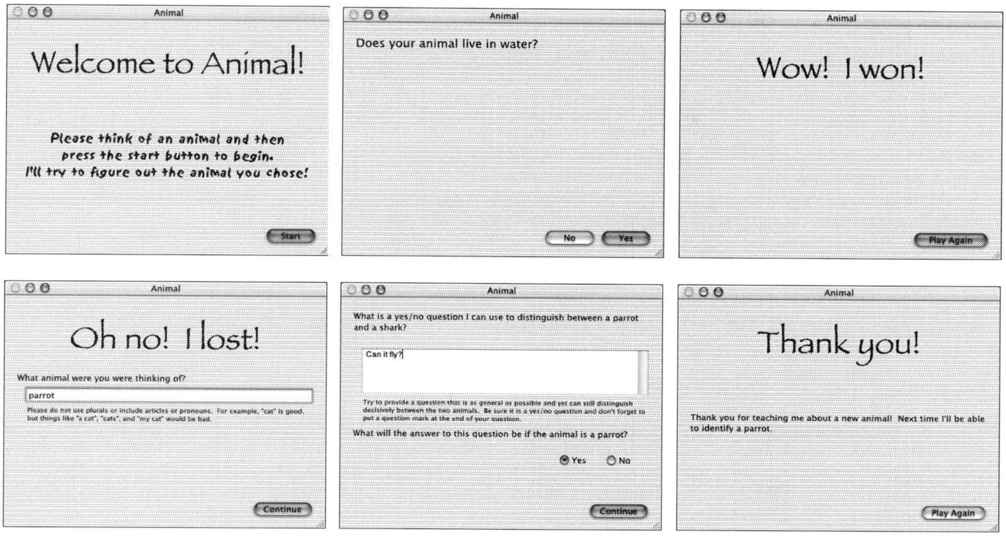

FIGURE 24.2 The user interface for the Animal example.

To implement this interface, start with an NSTabView. Configure it to have six tabs, and then set it to be tabless and borderless. Resize it to fill the window's entire content view area. Double-clicking the tab view allows UI elements to be dragged into the currently visible tab. The Interface Builder attributes inspector also switches to the NSTabViewItem inspector. By using the inspector it is possible to switch between the tabs so that the whole interface can be constructed. It is also important to give each NSTabViewItem a unique identifier. The pages have been given numbers from 1 to 6; these identifiers are used by the program code to switch from tab to tab. This inspector is visible in Figure 24.3.

To round out the interface, there is a preferences panel that allows the user to change the data file used by the underlying command-line program. Also, a debug console echoes the communications between our GUI and the command-line program. Figure 24.3 shows both the preferences window and the debug console in addition to the NSTabViewItem inspector.

When the application is running, the debug console is sort of like a noneditable Terminal.app window, in that it shows both the input to the Unix command as well as the output of the command. However, to help the user follow along, it uses different fonts for each type of information it displays. It puts the command's output in a normal font, whereas input to the command is in a bold font. Anything sent to stderr appears in italics. Also a few comments are in bold italics to give details about the Unix process being started and stopped. The text in bold italics is not part of the actual input to or output from the command-line program.

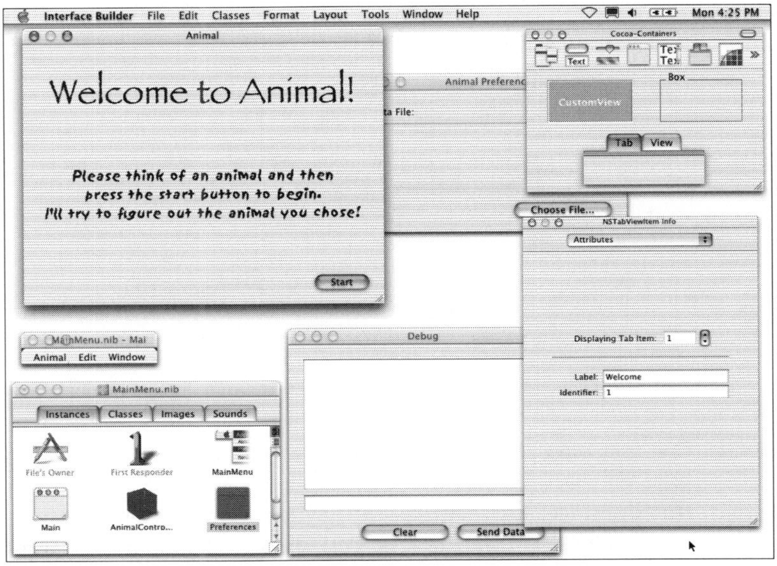

FIGURE 24.3 The preferences window and debug console for the Animal example.

Animal Example Application Delegate Methods

The first part of the code to consider is two `NSApplication` delegate methods. The `AnimalController` object is connected up as the application's delegate. It responds to both `-applicationDidFinishLaunching:` and `-applicationShouldTerminate:`. The first method does some basic initialization and launches the `animal_tool` command-line program by calling the `-_startAnimalProcess`. The code is as follows:

```
- (void)applicationDidFinishLaunching:(NSNotification *)aNotification
{
    NSWindow *mainWindow = [tabView window];
    [mainWindow center];
    [mainWindow makeKeyAndOrderFront:self];
    [self _setUpDataFile];
    [self _startAnimalProcess];
    currentPage = 1;
    [self _gotoPage:currentPage];
    gotLastQuestion = NO;
}
```

The other delegate method cleans things up when the application quits. The important part here is to call the -_killTask method to stop the animal_tool program. The tool should not be left running when the application quits.

```
- (NSApplicationTerminateReply)applicationShouldTerminate:
        (NSApplication *)sender
{
    [self _killTask];
    [animalTask release];
    animalTask = nil;
    [dataFilePath release];
    dataFilePath = nil;
    return NSTerminateNow;
}
```

Configuring NSTask for Asynchronous Operation

To understand how to control the animal_tool, it is easiest to consider how NSTask is used. The NSTask object encapsulates the running process. This time, the process is to run in the background. The process is handed three pipes, one each for stdin, stdout, and stderr. The AnimalController object sets itself up as an observer. Because the task will be run in the background, the GUI will continue processing its event loop. Instead of having to poll for data, a notification is sent when data comes in on the file handle for the stdout or stderr pipe. When the task ends, another notification will be sent. Therefore, all output from the command will arrive through notifications.

Here is the basic code used to launch the task and set up all the pipes and notifications. Note that it makes heavy use of several instance variables defined in AnimalController.h. For simplicity, the code used to send text about the task's launch to the debug console has been omitted from this listing. The full source can be found on the book's Web site, www.cocoaprogramming.net.

```
- (void)_startAnimalProcess
{
    NSNotificationCenter *defaultCenter = [NSNotificationCenter defaultCenter];
    NSString *toolPath = [[NSBundle mainBundle]
            pathForResource:@"animal_tool" ofType:@""];
    NSArray *arguments = [[NSArray alloc]
            initWithObjects:@"-f", dataFilePath, nil];
    NSDictionary *defaultEnvironment =
            [[NSProcessInfo processInfo] environment];
    NSMutableDictionary *environment = [[NSMutableDictionary alloc]
            initWithDictionary:defaultEnvironment];
```

```
    // set up the task
    animalTask = [[NSTask alloc] init];
    [defaultCenter addObserver:self selector:@selector(taskCompleted:)
            name:NSTaskDidTerminateNotification object:animalTask];
    [animalTask setLaunchPath:toolPath];
    [animalTask setArguments:arguments];

    // set up the environment
    [environment setObject:@"YES" forKey:@"NSUnbufferedIO"];
    [animalTask setEnvironment:environment];

    // set up pipe for stdout
    outputPipe = [NSPipe pipe];
    taskOutput = [outputPipe fileHandleForReading];
    [defaultCenter addObserver:self selector:@selector(taskDataAvailable:)
            name:NSFileHandleReadCompletionNotification object:taskOutput];
    [animalTask setStandardOutput:outputPipe];

    // set up pipe for stderr, just like stdout
    errorPipe = [NSPipe pipe];
    errorOutput = [errorPipe fileHandleForReading];
    [defaultCenter addObserver:self selector:@selector(errorDataAvailable:)
            name:NSFileHandleReadCompletionNotification object:errorOutput];
    [animalTask setStandardError:errorPipe];

    // set up pipe for stdin
    inputPipe = [NSPipe pipe];
    taskInput = [inputPipe fileHandleForWriting];
    [animalTask setStandardInput:inputPipe];

    // start the task and start looking for data
    [animalTask launch];
    [taskOutput readInBackgroundAndNotify];
    [errorOutput readInBackgroundAndNotify];

    // clean-up
    [arguments release];
    [environment release];
}
```

There is one other important point of note in the previous code. Rather than using the default environment, taken from the current process' environment, the environment variable `NSUnbufferedIO` is added, setting it to `YES`. This is a necessary addition to make sure that the output of the command-line program is received as soon as it is sent. If this variable is not set, the output from the program will wait in a buffer until the buffer is filled. Because this program is interactive, the data needs to be passed on immediately without any buffering. The `animal_tool` program expects to see responses back before it ever sends enough text to fill the buffer. (To learn more about buffering on Unix-based systems, such as Mac OS X, and why it is important, consult a textbook or try `man setbuf` in a Terminal window.)

Buffering can often cause puzzling problems when working with `NSTask`. If the environment change is taken out of the previous code, the GUI still works when the program is launched from within Project Builder. However, when launched from the finder, it won't work! Try it. Take out the code, build the example, run it, and open the debug console. Note the difference: When launched from the Finder, the first question from `animal_tool` won't appear. Why? If an `NSTask` is launched without first setting its environment, it will use the environment of the process launching it. When an application is launched from Project Builder, the `NSUnbufferedIO` environment variable is set to `YES`. The Finder doesn't set it, though, so the application's behavior changes. This is solved by explicitly setting it in the previous code.

For further illumination, take a look at the code for the `-applicationDidFinishLaunching:` method on the Web site. There is some code in it that is commented out. If the comments are removed, it will print the application's environment variables to the console. Using code such as this can help to diagnose problems caused by differences in a running program's environment. The lack of the `NSUnbufferedIO` environment variable becomes obvious when this code is run.

Stopping, Pausing, and Signaling an `NSTask`

The next method for controlling the task is for stopping it. The `-_killTask` method stops the subprocess by sending the `-terminate` message to the `NSTask` object. The `-terminate` message should only be sent after the task is launched and should not be sent if the task has completed. Therefore, the `-isRunning` method is used to determine if the task is actually running or not. The code looks like this:

```
- (void)_killTask
{
    if ([animalTask isRunning]) {
        [animalTask terminate];
    }
}
```

The `-terminate` method actually sends a Unix signal, `SIGTERM`, to the subprocess. Some processes will catch this signal, possibly ignoring it. This method is therefore not a fail-safe way to stop a subprocess. The `-interrupt` method sends `SIGINT`, which by default also stops a process.

The only way to send another signal, such as SIGKILL (which is uncatchable and will *always* terminate the process), is to use the NSTask method -processIdentifier to obtain the Unix process ID (pid) of the task, and then use the C library call kill() to send the signal. Note that although the function's name is kill, it won't necessarily kill the process. It all depends on what signal is sent with it. To definitively stop an NSTask, the code would be

```
kill([myTask -processIdentifier], SIGKILL);
```

It is best to use that only as a last resort, however, because it's a rather severe way to stop a process. In most cases, the -terminate method is sufficient. For more information on Unix signals, consult a textbook or peruse the signal, sigaction, kill, and related Unix manual pages.

To pause a process temporarily, as opposed to stopping or signaling it, send the -suspend method. Use -resume to make it continue. These method calls should be balanced just like retain/release pairs. If multiple -suspend messages are sent, the process remains paused until the same number of -resume messages have been received.

Restarting an NSTask

Returning to the Animal example, there is also a method for restarting the task. NSTask objects actually cannot be restarted after they have been run. Instead, a new NSTask must be created each time a Unix task needs to be started.

The restart method in the example is used to stop the task and restart it when the user uses the preferences panel to change the data file. This method kills the task, resets the GUI, and sets a flag that causes the task to be restarted. The flag is noticed when the task termination notification is sent and causes the notification handler to relaunch the task.

NOTE

A flag is used to delay the restarting of the task, instead of just calling -_startAnimalProcess outright because the termination notification handler closes up all the pipes that have been set up. If the task is restarted before the handler is called, the handler closes the pipes to the new task instead of the pipes to the old task, which would be disastrous. All communications with animal_tool would be lost! To solve this, the code must wait for the notification that the task has ended before the next task can be started.

The code looks like this:

```
- (void)_restartSubprocess
{
    [self _killTask];
    [animalTask release];
```

```
        animalTask = nil;
        doRestart = YES;
        currentPage = 1;
        [self _gotoPage:currentPage];
        gotLastQuestion = NO;
    }
```

NSTask Termination Status and Cleanup

Next, consider the methods that are used to handle the notifications from the NSTask and NSFileHandle. As can be seen from the previously shown code for -_startAnimalProcess, the -taskCompleted: method is set to receive the NSTaskDidTerminateNotification notification. The first thing it does is determine why the task exited by asking for the task's return code. The NSTask method -terminationStatus can be used to obtain this value. Most Unix tasks exit with a value of zero if everything finished successfully, so if the task exits with an error condition a message is printed with the NSLog() function.

The object then removes itself as an observer of the NSTask and NSFileHandle objects. Finally, the doRestart flag is consulted. If it is set to YES, the task is restarted and the flag is cleared, as shown in the following code:

```
- (void)taskCompleted:(NSNotification*)aNotification
{
    int exitCode = [[aNotification object] terminationStatus];

    if (exitCode != 0) {
        NSLog(@"Error: animal_tool exited with code %d", exitCode);
    }
    [[NSNotificationCenter defaultCenter] removeObserver:self];
    if (doRestart) {
        [self _startAnimalProcess];
        doRestart = NO;
    }
}
```

Receiving Output from an NSTask

To handle output from the task, the -taskDataAvailable: method handles data coming from the task's stdout pipe, and the -errorDataAvailable: method handles data coming from the task's stderr pipe. Both methods are very similar, so both are considered simultaneously.

Each method retrieves the data from the file handle, as in the previous example. However, this time the code doesn't read all the data at once using the file handle's

`-readDataToEndOfFile` method. Instead, a notification is sent each time data is received from `animal_tool`. The data itself can be found in the user info object with each notification. If the pipe has been closed, or the data has ended, the data object is `nil`. Therefore, the code checks for a non-nil, non-empty data object before proceeding.

The `NSData` object is then converted to an `NSString`. In the case of `stdout`, the string is passed to another method, `-_handleIncomingDataString:`, which updates the GUI appropriately. For `stderr`, the data is logged with `NSLog()` instead. A more industrial-strength program might try to parse the error and attempt some sort of recovery or abort based on the contents.

Finally, each method ends by asking the file handle to continue looking for data on the pipe. The code is as follows:

```
- (void)taskDataAvailable:(NSNotification*)aNotification
{
    NSData *incomingData = [[aNotification userInfo]
            objectForKey:NSFileHandleNotificationDataItem];
    if (incomingData && [incomingData length]) {
        NSString *incomingText = [[NSString alloc] initWithData:incomingData
                encoding:NSASCIIStringEncoding];
        [self _handleIncomingDataString:incomingText];
        [taskOutput readInBackgroundAndNotify];  // go back for more.
        [incomingText release];
        return;
    }
}

- (void)errorDataAvailable:(NSNotification*)aNotification
{
    NSData *incomingData = [[aNotification userInfo]
            objectForKey:NSFileHandleNotificationDataItem];
    if (incomingData && [incomingData length]) {
        NSString *incomingText = [[NSString alloc] initWithData:incomingData
                encoding:NSASCIIStringEncoding];
        NSLog(@"animal_tool error: %@", incomingText);
        [errorOutput readInBackgroundAndNotify]; // go back for more.
        [incomingText release];
        return;
    }
}
```

Sending Data to an NSTask

One aspect of communication with the NSTask remains: A method for sending data to the subprocess is needed. This is actually quite simple. The NSFileHandle method -writeData: on the file handle for the stdin pipe does the trick. The only other issue is that the string needs to be converted to an NSData before being sent to the file handle. The code looks like this:

```
- (void)_sendData:(NSString *)dataString
{
    [taskInput writeData:[dataString dataUsingEncoding:
            [NSString defaultCStringEncoding]]];
}
```

One important thing to remember when sending data is to include the newline character. For example, many of the responses sent to the animal_tool are yes/no answers. Here's a method that, given a BOOL, will send a yes/no answer to the subprocess:

```
- (void)_sendBoolean:(BOOL)flag
{
    if (flag) {
        [self _sendData:@"y\n"];
    } else {
        [self _sendData:@"n\n"];
    }
}
```

Parsing NSTask Output in the Animal Example

The -_handleIncomingDataString: method, as mentioned earlier, parses the data coming from the NSTask. It is a big switch() statement based on the currentPage variable. The data is passed to it as an NSString. The raw string could potentially contain multiple lines of data and will definitely contain newline characters. This line is used as the first step of parsing:

```
NSArray *lines = [aString componentsSeparatedByString:@"\n"];
```

The rest of the code for this method looks at the incoming lines for the text that is expected at each point of the game. It is not shown here because it is rather long and primarily contains NSString manipulations that aren't particularly special.

A group of messages also handles the various actions when a user clicks a button in the user interface. The method names are

```
- (IBAction)start:(id)sender; // sent by page #1
- (IBAction)answer:(id)sender; // sent by page #2
- (IBAction)playAgain:(id)sender; // sent by page #3 and page #6
- (IBAction)setAnimalName:(id)sender; // sent by page #4
- (IBAction)setAnimalQuestion:(id)sender; // sent by page #5
```

Each of these actions handles sending the appropriate data to the `NSTask` and advancing to the next "page" in the interface. Again, the code for each method is not shown here because it is simply typical GUI glue code. It handles the debug console, preferences panel, and programmatically changing the `NSTabView` from one tab to the next. Although this code isn't shown here, it is worth spending a little time examining it. Of course, it can be found on the book's Web site, `www.cocoaprogramming.net`.

As you consider this implementation of the Animal program, it is quickly realized that creating a command-line program, and then wrapping it, is a lot more work than just creating either the command line or a 100% GUI application. The one advantage is that there are two interfaces—command line and GUI—for accessing the same data. Some users might like this, especially for a program the user might want to run remotely over an `ssh` connection. (Type "`man ssh`" in a Terminal window to learn about `ssh`.) For a program such as Animal, however, that's not enough of an advantage to counteract the liability caused by the increased complexity of this approach.

In a case like this example, where the command-line tool's source code is under the developer's control, it might make more sense to put the core code into a framework. A GUI interface and a command-line interface can be created independently of each other, each taking advantage of the framework. This enables them to share their code while avoiding the complexity of wrapping a Unix command. Chapter 27, "Creating Your Own Frameworks," describes how to create a custom framework and use it in a project.

Using the `NSThread` Class

Several features of the Application Kit make use of threads. For example, in the previous `NSTask` examples, the task itself is actually run from a separate thread. Many of the animations in Aqua, such as throbbing buttons and progress meters, are also run from other threads. All these threads are entirely transparent to the programmer. For programmer-controlled threads, however, the `NSThread` class is the Cocoa interface to the operating system's thread functionality. On Mac OS X, the pthreads library is the underlying functionality being tapped. Although the full functionality of pthreads is not available through the `NSThread` interface, the careful programmer can get away with calling the pthread functions when and if the functionality is needed.

The ThreadExample Program

The ThreadExample program on the book's Web site (www.cocoaprogramming.net) shows a basic example of how you might take advantage of multithreading. It doesn't show everything that can be done with threads, but it should be enough to get you started with the class. Be sure to also read all the way through the last section of this chapter, on threading issues, before jumping headlong into multithreading. Threads introduce many ways to create huge, difficult-to-find bugs. It's best to know a little bit about what lies ahead before jumping into the thick of it.

ThreadExample User Interface

The user interface for the ThreadExample program is shown in Figure 24.4. It is divided into two sections. Each section is a simulation of a long-running calculation. In the top section, clicking Start Server Calculation starts the thread. The thread can be paused or resumed by clicking Pause/Unpause Server Calculation or stopped by clicking Stop Server Calculation. The `NSProgressIndicator` shows how far the server's calculation has progressed. The lower sections work a little differently. Clicking the Run Console Feeder button starts the thread. Every few seconds, the thread will append a new line to the scrolling text console. The user can also append strings to the console by entering text in the text field and clicking Append. As demonstrated in Figure 24.4, both threads can be run at the same time.

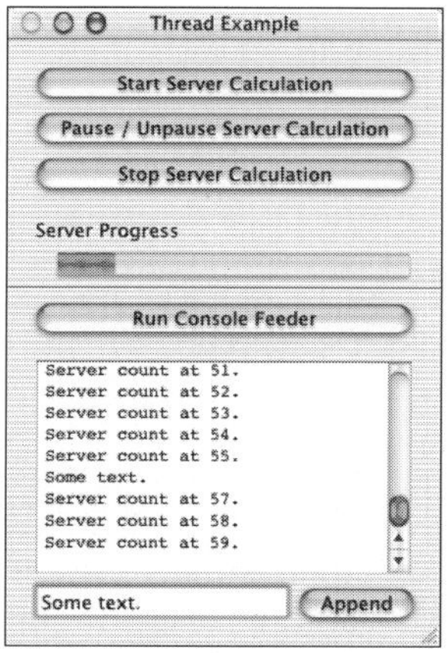

FIGURE 24.4 The user interface for the ThreadExample program.

Internally, there are four object classes. A controller class, `ApplicationDelegate`, which manages the GUI. The `ServerObject` class encapsulates all the details of launching a new thread. It is meant to be a reusable, abstract superclass, which is used by both example threads. The `ProgressServerObject` encapsulates the thread that sits behind the top section of the GUI. The `MessageServerObject` handles the lower half of the window. The last two objects provide a demonstration of how you might subclass `ServerObject`. The `ApplicationDelegate` class shows how to use these subclasses in a custom program.

Detaching Threads

Let's start by looking at the `ServerObject` class. This is the meat of the example because this is the class that actually deals with the `NSThread` class directly. A thread can be as simple as a single method that gets called, runs to completion, and then exits. If that is all that is needed, a single call to `NSThread` is all that is needed. The method to call is

```
+ (void)detachNewThreadSelector:(SEL)aSelector toTarget:(id)aTarget
        withObject:(id)anArgument
```

Unfortunately, instead of taking an `NSInvocation` as the single argument, which would be more flexible, `NSThread` can only perform a very specific invocation. Provide a target, action, and a single object and the thread is detached and run. The thread exits when the method call is completed. The selector for the action should have a method signature of the normal form for an Application Kit action, to wit:

```
- (void)selectorName:(id)anObject;
```

So, suppose a programmer wanted to send the following message:

```
[target someAction:anObject];
```

To have that message invocation run in a thread of its own, the call would change to this:

```
[NSThread detachNewThreadSelector:@selector(someAction:) toTarget:target
        withObject:anObject];
```

Kicking off a new thread is that simple. However, as threading issues begin to rear their ugly heads, it is generally important to do a little more than this for all but the most simple calls. Because all an application's threads have access to the same memory space, communication can take place by simply altering global or otherwise shared variables while taking extra care to not alter data that is in use by another thread. (The section "Locking," later in this chapter, discusses how to do this safely.)

Messages Between Threads

If one thread wants to send an Objective-C message to another thread, things become more complex. The common answer is to use Distributed Objects. That is where the ServerObject comes in. It will launch a thread, set up an event loop in that thread, and set up a Distributed Objects (DO) connection between the new thread and the thread that launched it. In the example program, all communication takes place over DO. This makes locking and other complexities unnecessary—for this example, at least.

The source code for the header begins by defining two protocols. One is for the server object, the other for the controller object. The server object, answering to the ServerMethods protocol, is in the new thread. The controller is in the original thread, answering to the ServerObjectController protocol. Here is the header file:

```
#import <Foundation/Foundation.h>

@protocol ServerMethods

- (void)start;
- (void)togglePause;
- (void)pause;
- (void)resume;
- (void)stop;

@end

@protocol ServerObjectController

- (void)setServer:(id)anObject tag:(int)serverTag;
- (void)setServerProgress:(double)newStatus finished:(BOOL)running
        tag:(int)tag;

@end


@interface ServerObject : NSObject <ServerMethods>
{
    int amountDone, tag;
    BOOL paused, running, suppressProgress;
    id <ServerObjectController> parent;
}

+ (NSConnection *)startServerThreadWithTag:(int)tag
        forController:(id <ServerObjectController>)controller;
```

```
- (id <ServerMethods>)initForParent:(id)theParent withTag:(int)theTag;
- (void)doCalculationStep;
- (float)delayBetweenSteps;

@end
```

The +startServerThreadWithTag:forController: class method is where the ServerObject is created and the thread is detached. The three other methods are all meant to be overridden by subclasses.

An important design point to notice is that many methods take a tag argument, and the server object itself keeps track of its own tag. This is to allow a single controller object to control multiple server objects. The objects are identified by their tag, which is really only of significance to the controller. The servers just hold the tag and pass it back as needed. Of course, the tag selected by the controller should be unique for each server it starts. If only one server is ever used, the tag could just be set to zero and ignored.

Let's look at how the server thread itself is actually created and set up. There are actually two methods involved. The public method starts the thread and the setup process finishes with a private method that runs within the new thread. Here is the code for the first half:

```
+ (NSConnection *)startServerThreadWithTag:(int)theTag
        forController:(id <ServerObjectController>)controller
{
    NSPort *port1 = [NSPort port];
    NSPort *port2 = [NSPort port];
    NSArray *portArray = [NSArray arrayWithObjects:port2, port1,
            [NSNumber numberWithInt:theTag], nil];
    NSConnection *serverConnection = [[NSConnection alloc]
            initWithReceivePort:port1 sendPort:port2];
    [serverConnection setRootObject:controller];
    [NSThread detachNewThreadSelector:@selector(_connectWithPorts:)
            toTarget:self withObject:portArray];
    return serverConnection;
}
```

As expected, a call to NSThread is needed to start a new thread at the end of the method. The rest of the code is to set up Distributed Objects. To set up DO, a connection to the remote process or thread is needed. Because in this case it does not exist yet, it isn't possible to just look up a connection. Instead, a pair of NSPort objects is created to be used for communications between the threads. The ports are used to create an NSConnection object. Two ports are needed because ports are unidirectional. One port is used to send data while the other receives data. Obviously, the port that is a receive port for the main thread needs to be the send port for the new thread and vice-versa. To swap the ports for the new thread, the ports are put into the portArray in reverse order, port2 before port1.

The DO connection also is handed the controller object as its root object. When the other side of the connection is established, a proxy for the root is obtained. Initially, that object receives all messages that come from the server thread. It could, however, return pointers to other objects to the server so that it can send direct messages to other objects in the main thread, if that is desired. Also of note is the fact that this DO connection is anonymous. This means that it is private between just these two threads. Other threads and processes will not be able to tap into the connection.

The portArray variable is interesting. Remember from the preceding discussion that only a single object can be an argument of the method that will be run in the new thread. However, it is necessary to pass two ports and a tag to the new method, a total of three objects. The way around this is to use a collection object such as an array or a dictionary to hold all the arguments. By turning the integer tag into an NSNumber and adding it to the array, it is passed through to the other side along with the ports.

The method ends by returning the NSConnection to the caller in case it wants to do any advanced manipulation. In most cases, the caller simply ignores this object. At this point, the method exits and the main thread continues executing.

Meanwhile, a new thread has been created and the ServerObject method +_connectWithPorts: starts executing in the new thread. This is a private method, so it is not exposed by the header. To complete the setup, it creates a ServerObject instance, finishes connecting DO, and then starts a run loop. Here is the code:

```
+ (void)_connectWithPorts:(NSArray *)portArray
{
    NSAutoreleasePool *pool = [[NSAutoreleasePool alloc] init];
    NSConnection *serverConnection = [NSConnection connectionWithReceivePort:
            [portArray objectAtIndex:0] sendPort:[portArray objectAtIndex:1]];
    int theTag = [[portArray objectAtIndex:2] intValue];
    id rootProxy = (id)[serverConnection rootProxy];
    ServerObject *serverObject = [[self alloc] initForParent:rootProxy
            withTag:theTag];
    [rootProxy setServer:serverObject tag:theTag];
    [serverObject release];
    [[NSRunLoop currentRunLoop] run];
    [pool release];
}
```

The first line of code creates a new autorelease pool. It is imperative to ensure that every thread that uses Cocoa objects has its own autorelease pool. Because this method is executing in a new thread, the first thing it must do is create the pool. To balance this creation, the pool is released as the very last statement in the method.

Next, the new thread's DO connection is created. The connection is set up using the same ports that were created in the first method before the thread was spawned. After that the tag is retrieved and a proxy to the root object of the connection is obtained. Remember that the root was previously set to be the server's controller.

The root proxy is *not* the controller object itself, but it does act as its representative inside the server thread. Any messages that are sent to the root proxy will be passed across the DO connection, and then be handled by the actual controller object in the main thread. In other words, this thread has no pointers to the actual root object. The controller does live in the same memory space, so a pointer to it would be valid. Messages could be sent to it directly. Such messages would be executed in the server thread, though, which is probably not what is wanted. DO is therefore being used as a partitioning device. Messages sent to a proxy actually cross thread boundaries and are executed in the other thread. This is also true of messages sent to the server from the controller.

The next line of code creates the actual server object instance. The object is given the proxy to the controller and its tag. Then, the controller is handed the serverObject and the tag. The tag will help the controller know which server object is being handed to it. Because this message is being sent to the root proxy, it crosses the thread boundary. Specifically, the message is bundled up and passed to the main thread. There, the main event loop unpacks the message and sends it to the controller object. In the unpacking, a proxy to the server object is created, and that is passed to the controller. In other words, the controller never gets a pointer to the actual server object. It gets a proxy that passes messages over DO to the server object. Thus, DO keeps a solid partition between the threads.

Because the controller object retains the server object, it is now safe to release it. Finally, an `NSRunLoop` is started. This is important because without a run loop, messages coming over DO will not be received. When the run loop is exited, then the autorelease pool will be cleaned up and the method will exit. When it exits, the thread will also exit. As long as the run loop is alive, the thread will be running as well.

When the controller gets the `-setServer:tag:` message, it knows that the server has been set up and is ready to go. At that point the run loop will be idling, waiting for messages to come in over DO. In general, the `-start` method would then be sent to the server at some point; in the example it is sent when the user clicks the start button. In the meantime, the server thread is in a "blocked" state, waiting for a message. While blocked, the thread uses up no CPU resources. It remains blocked until the controller sends a message. This is much more efficient than continually polling to see if it is time to do work yet.

Because the remainder of the code for the ServerObject class is straightforward, it won't be shown here. Look at the example code on the book's Web site (www.cocoaprogramming.net) to see it in its entirety. Instead of showing all the code, a summary of what it does and how it can be subclassed is explained.

The run loop is needed to receive messages from the main thread. As a result, it is important that the server object occasionally return to the top of the run loop to see if there are any new messages. To make this automatic, the subclass should define -doCalculationStep to perform just a part of the computations expected of the server. The server calls this method continually until the calculations are completed. Between each call, the run loop has a chance to respond to any messages coming from the parent thread.

Recall that NSThread has no means of pausing a thread. Although the pthreads functions can be used to do this, the fact that there is a run loop can be used to avoid having to drop down to those functions. Instead, the server object implements the -pause method to simply stop sending the -doCalculationStep messages until the -resume method is called. Likewise, the -start method starts the calculation steps, and the -stop method resets the server back to an idle state. The -delayBetweenSteps method tells the run loop how long to wait before sending the next -doCalculationStep message. The default implementation returns zero, which means there will be no waiting.

NOTE

There is no method to actually exit the run loop, thereby stopping the thread. A good enhancement to this class would be to implement an -exit method to terminate the run loop. This implementation, with a run loop and the associated overhead, might seem somewhat inefficient, but the flexibility that is gained far overshadows any inefficiencies that have been introduced.

Subclassing ServerObject

Now it is time to consider the concrete subclasses of ServerObject. The first subclass, ProgressServerObject, handles the top part of the UI, which has a progress bar that slowly advances in short jumps. To make the jumps happen at random times, and be somewhat spaced out, the -delayBetweenSteps method is overridden to return a random value between 0.5 and 1.0 seconds.

The ServerObject class actually manages tracking the progress of the calculations. To facilitate this, it expects that the -doCalculationStep method sets the amountDone instance variable to a new value after each calculation step. The value should be an integer between 0 and 100. If it is greater than or equal to 100, that signals the computation has completed. The server stops sending itself `-doCalculationStep` messages and starts waiting for a new `-start` message. Each time a calculation step is performed, if `amountDone` changed, the `ServerObject` code sends a message to the main thread updating it on the progress of the calculation. In our example, this causes the `NSProgressIndicator` to be updated.

If the `suppressProgress` instance variable is set to `YES`, the automatic progress message updates to the main thread are suppressed. For applications lacking progress indicators, this makes the server run slightly more efficiently.

Given all this information, all this subclass needs to do is to increment the `amountDone` variable by a random amount each time a calculation step is performed. (A random number from 1 to 6 is used.) The implementation of the entire subclass is rather trivial; here is the code:

```
#import "ProgressServerObject.h"

@implementation ProgressServerObject

- (void)doCalculationStep
{
    amountDone += (random() % 5) + 1;
}

- (float)delayBetweenSteps
{
    return ((random() %  500) + 500) / 1000.0;
}

@end
```

For the other `ServerObject` subclass, a different approach to subclassing is taken. This time, all the calculations take place inside a single invocation of the `-doCalculationStep` method. This means that the server won't return to the run loop until the long running computation has completed. The implication is that the overhead of multiple calls will be eliminated at the expense of rendering the `-pause`, `-resume`, and `-stop` methods impotent. This is certainly a valid tradeoff, and `ServerObject` was designed to still be functional if subclassed in this manner.

Because the progress happens in a single call, the automatic progress messages are suppressed by setting the `suppressProgress` instance variable to `YES` in an overridden `-initForParent:withTag:` method. It is important to remember to call the super implementation of this method in any overrides. There is no need to override the `-delayBetweenSteps` method, so the default implementation is left alone.

Finally, the `-doCalculationStep` method holds the meat of this class's functionality. Because the class of the controller is known, this method sends a message back to the controller that isn't part of the formal controller protocol. To suppress warnings, a cast is used to move from the `parent` instance variable's anonymous `id` type to the `ApplicationDelegate` type. This introduces a dependency between the controller and server, which, for our purposes here, is fine. Most real-world implementations would probably require some degree of this.

The implementation of the `-doCalculationStep` method simply posts a `Starting server.` message to the console, and then enters a loop to count from one to 100. Each time through, a message is sent to the console with the number, and then the thread sleeps for a second. The Unix `sleep()` function will put a thread to sleep for a specified period of time. During that time, the thread is blocked, using no CPU resources. When it wakes after the allotted time, execution proceeds as normal. When the loop exits, a `Server finished.` message is sent to the console and the method returns. In all, this method simulates a calculation that takes 100 seconds to complete.

Here is the implementation file for the `MessageServerObject` class:

```
#import "MessageServerObject.h"
#import "ApplicationDelegate.h"
#include <unistd.h>

@implementation MessageServerObject

- (id)initForParent:(id)theParent withTag:(int)theTag
{
    self = [super initForParent:theParent withTag:theTag];
    if (!self) return nil;
    suppressProgress = YES;
    return self;
}

- (void)doCalculationStep
{
    int i;
    ApplicationDelegate *castedParent = (ApplicationDelegate *)parent;
    [castedParent appendStringToConsole:
            NSLocalizedString(@"Starting server.\n", @"")];
```

```
    for (i=1; i<=100; i++) {
        NSString *theString = [NSString stringWithFormat:
                NSLocalizedString(@"Server count at %d.\n", @""), i];
        [castedParent appendStringToConsole:theString];
        sleep(1);
    }
    [castedParent appendStringToConsole:
            NSLocalizedString(@"Server finished.\n", @"")];
    amountDone = 100;
}

@end
```

Using `ServerObject` Subclasses

The final piece of code to complete this example is the controller class, `ApplicationDelegate`, which provides the glue between the GUI and the server objects. It uses instance variables server and `messageServer` for pointers to the two servers thread objects. There are also three outlets to connect to the progress indicator, the scrollable text view, and the text field near the bottom of the UI. The object adopts the `ServerObjectController` protocol and implements five action methods, one for each of the buttons on the window. There is also the `-appendStringToConsole:` method to add text to the end of the text view, and the `-launchServerThreads` method to start the two threads going. Here is the header file:

```
#import <Cocoa/Cocoa.h>
#import "ServerObject.h"

@interface ApplicationDelegate : NSObject <ServerObjectController>
{
    id <ServerMethods>server;
    id <ServerMethods>messageServer;
    IBOutlet NSProgressIndicator *progressView;
    IBOutlet NSTextView *console;
    IBOutlet NSTextField *appendText;
}

- (id)init;
- (void)applicationDidFinishLaunching:(NSNotification *)notification;
- (void)launchServerThreads;
```

```
- (IBAction)startServer:(id)sender;
- (IBAction)stopServer:(id)sender;
- (IBAction)pauseServer:(id)sender;

- (IBAction)runFeeder:(id)sender;
- (IBAction)appendText:(id)sender;
- (void)appendStringToConsole:(NSString *)aString;

@end
```

The implementation begins with initialization code that is called when the application's launch completes. It starts the two server threads and resets the user interface. The `+startServerThreadWithTag:forController:` method, sent to the class objects for the `ProgressServerObject` and `MessageServerObject` classes, is used to start each thread. The tags 0 and 1 are used to distinguish between the two objects.

```
- (void)applicationDidFinishLaunching:(NSNotification *)notification
{
    [self launchServerThreads];
    [progressView setDoubleValue:0.0];
}

- (void)launchServerThreads
{
    [ProgressServerObject startServerThreadWithTag:0 forController:self];
    [MessageServerObject startServerThreadWithTag:1 forController:self];
}
```

The `ServerObjectController` protocol requires that two different methods be implemented. The first is the `-setServer:tag:` method. It gives us a proxy to the server object after it has been created. The `-setProtocolForProxy:` method is used so that Distributed Objects can be more efficient with communications. This eliminates the need for the DO connection to determine if the target object responds to a method or not. It will be able to check for all the methods in the protocol at once instead of individually. The new proxy is retained and the previous proxy (if any) is released. Finally, the appropriate instance variable is assigned the pointer to the proxy. Note that the tag is used to determine which server object is being dealt with. This matches up with the tags assigned in the previous `-launchServerThreads` method.

```
- (void)setServer:(id)anObject tag:(int)serverTag
{
    [anObject setProtocolForProxy:@protocol(ServerMethods)];
    [anObject retain];
```

```
    if (serverTag == 0) { // progress view server
        [(id)server release];
        server = (id <ServerMethods>)anObject;
    } else if (serverTag == 1) { // console "feeder" server
        [(id)messageServer release];
        messageServer = (id <ServerMethods>)anObject;
    }
}
```

The next method required by the protocol is for dealing with progress reports from the server as it performs its calculations. The `-setServerProgress:finished:tag:` method can safely ignore the tag. It is already known that the `MessageServerObject` instance will never send this message because of its implementation. The `ProgressServerObject` instance is the only one that will send it. Therefore, the information can be passed on to the `NSProgressIndicator` without filtering, like this:

```
- (void)setServerProgress:(double)newStatus finished:(BOOL)running tag:(int)tag
{
    [progressView setDoubleValue:newStatus];
    if (!running) [progressView stopAnimation:self];
    else [progressView startAnimation:self];
}
```

The short method `-appendStringToConsole:` is used to append a text string to the end of the console represented by the scrollable text view. It simply places the selection point at the end of the text, and then calls a text insertion method. Because the view is not editable, it needs to be made editable before doing the insert. The code then reverts it to noneditable status. This method will be called by both the `MessageServerObject` instance's thread and one of the action methods. The text in the console can come from both the GUI and the background thread. Here's the code:

```
- (void)appendStringToConsole:(NSString *)aString
{
    int length = [[console string] length];
    [console setSelectedRange:NSMakeRange(length, 0)];
    [console setEditable:YES];
    [console insertText:aString];
    [console setEditable:NO];
}
```

Finally, there are the five action methods. The first four simply pass the message from the GUI on to the appropriate server object. The last one simply takes the text in the append text field and adds it to the end of the text in the console. The rest of the implementation of the `ApplicationDelegate` class is as follows:

```
- (IBAction)startServer:(id)sender
{
    [server start];
}

- (IBAction)stopServer:(id)sender
{
    [server stop];
}

- (IBAction)pauseServer:(id)sender
{
    [server togglePause];
}

- (IBAction)runFeeder:(id)sender
{
    [messageServer start];
}

- (IBAction)appendText:(id)sender
{
    NSString *fieldString = [appendText stringValue];
    NSString *withNewline = [NSString stringWithFormat:@"%@\n", fieldString];
    [self appendStringToConsole:withNewline];
}
```

And that completes the `ThreadExample` program. Build it and try running it. Click the buttons and monkey with the interface to see how it all works. Try running both threads simultaneously.

In a real application, it would be good practice to determine how many processors are available, and then create exactly that many server threads. Because threads can be scheduled so that each processor takes its own thread, this will allow for maximum processor utilization. Of course, this means that the code needs to be designed well enough to be able to be partitioned into a reasonable chunk of work for each processor. To determine the number of processors that are available, use this Carbon call:

```
ItemCount MPProcessors();
```

For example, try adding this line to the ThreadExample's -`applicationDidFinishLaunching:` method, and then run the program from within Project Builder so that the logging output can be readily examined:

```
NSLog(@"Number of processors available:  %d", MPProcessors());
```

Locking

When writing multithreaded programs, it is often necessary to find ways to ensure that certain resources or code sections can only be used by one thread at any given time. A special term, *critical section,* is used to refer to segments of code that require this special protection. For example, if two threads both attempt to do Application Kit drawing at the same time, the drawing commands sent to Quartz will be coming from both threads and could interleaved with each other. The resulting drawing will be an utter mess.

The use of Distributed Objects to isolate threads can provide a partial answer to this need, but it is not a complete solution. DO causes requests sent to a given thread to be *serialized* because the requests will be queued up and executed one at a time by the thread's event loop. If all Application Kit drawing is performed by the main thread with all subthreads sending drawing requests over DO to the main thread, the drawing will be done in an orderly manner. If two threads access the same variables or run the same section of code, however, the serialization provided by DO is effectively bypassed. Because running everything in the same thread defeats the purpose of multithreading, something else is needed.

One way to complete the picture is to use locks. Although other techniques might be described in textbooks, locking is the approach supported by Cocoa. A lock, also known as a mutex in some texts, is a special flag that can only be set (or owned) by one process or thread at a time. If another thread already owns the lock, no others can obtain it until it has been relinquished. If multiple threads attempt to obtain a lock simultaneously, only one will actually get it.

The operating system guarantees that only one thread can have a given lock at any point in time. This means that a lock can be used to protect a resource or critical section. Each resource and critical section of code needs its own lock. For a lock to work, all code accessing a protected resource must by convention obtain the lock before accessing the resource and release the lock as soon as the resource is no longer needed.

By following a locking convention, access to a resource can be serialized. Only one thread at a time will use the resource in question, and each will have to take its turn with the resource. Some important implications of this are discussed in the "Threading Issues" section later in this chapter. Before going into that detail, however, it is important to explain how to use the various lock classes provided by Cocoa.

Using the `NSLock` and `NSConditionLock` Classes

In Cocoa, the most common locking class is the `NSLock` class. It adopts the extremely simple `NSLocking` protocol. Only two methods exist, `-lock` and `-unlock`. Neither takes any arguments nor do they return anything. An `NSLock` would be shared between two threads, probably as a global variable. Code to protect a section of code would look something like this:

```
[theLock lock];
// critical section of code here
[theLock unlock];
```

If the lock is unavailable, the thread will block until it becomes available. The critical section and any resources used by the protected section of code will only be accessed by one thread at a time. For this code to work, the variable `theLock` should be a global variable that was initialized before the application spawns any threads. This guarantees that `theLock` will be assigned a value only once, which is very important. Somewhere early in the application's initialization code would be something like this:

```
NSLock *theLock = nil; // global variable

+ (void)initialize
{ // or in a did finish launching method, etc.
    theLock = [[NSLock alloc] init];
}
```

That's all there is to using a lock in its most basic way.

Locks Without Blocking

Sometimes, though, it is nice to be able to try to obtain a lock without blocking the thread. If the thread can't get the lock, it can go do something else in the meantime and try again later. To do this, just send `-tryLock` instead of `-lock`. The `-tryLock` method returns immediately with a `YES` or `NO` answer. If `YES` was returned, the lock was obtained. The critical code can be executed and the lock should be sent `-unlock` as soon as the code finishes. If NO was returned, the thread should not enter the critical section and no -unlock message should be sent because the lock was not obtained. It can try again later, or take some other appropriate action.

There is one other way to obtain a lock. It is somewhere between the two extremes of blocking and not blocking at all. By sending -lockBeforeDate: to the NSLock, the thread will block, but it will be blocked only until the NSDate passed with the message. If the lock is obtained before that time, the method returns YES. The thread can safely proceed with the critical section, and then send -unlock when it is finished. If NO is returned, the date passed and no lock was obtained. The thread will have to decide what to do from there. This method is nice because it means that the thread will not be blocked indefinitely. It also relieves the programmer of having to do continuous polling with -tryLock. Because there's no need for polling, there is none of the CPU overhead that would be caused by polling the lock.

Locks for Interthread Communication

A lock can be thought of as a cheap interthread communications system. The message conveyed by the lock is a simple yes/no answer to some question. The way suggested previously for using the lock asks the question "Can I proceed through this next chunk of code?" However, locks could be used to pass yes/no answers to *any* question a thread might want to ask of another. Usually a simple -tryLock would be used to get the answer to the question to avoid blocking the thread when using locks in this manner. Although locks are considered to be expensive performance-wise, they are definitely cheaper than sending a round-trip DO message to get a YES/NO answer to a given question.

To use this little trick, however, care must be taken. Unlike just inspecting a global Boolean value, using -tryLock actually changes the value of the lock if it is set to no. Here are two methods that could be used as get/set for a lock's value when using this scheme:

```
+ (void)setLockBoolean:(BOOL)flag
{
    [theLockProtector lock];
    [theLock tryLock]; // make sure the lock is set
    if (!flag) {
            [theLock unlock]; // unset it if we want it to be "NO"
    }
    [theLockProtector unlock];
}

+ (BOOL)lockBooleanValue
{
    BOOL current;
```

```
    BOOL ret = YES;
    [theLockProtector lock];
    current = [theLock tryLock];
    if (current) { // lock was at "NO"
        [theLock unlock]; // return it to its previous value
        ret = NO;
    }
    [theLockProtector unlock];
    return ret;
}
```

Both methods require the existence of two global variables called `theLock` and `theLockProtector`. The first is the actual signal between threads, the latter is used to keep the implementation threadsafe. Both methods are critical sections of code in and of themselves, so they need to be protected by a lock.

NOTE

It is very important to understand that these methods should *not* be used to protect critical code! They do not follow the proper locking conventions for doing so. They should only be used to pass a message between threads. Also, remember that these are globals. A new pair of methods would be needed for each flag that needs to be passed between threads.

Condition Locks

Although that code works, it isn't necessarily the best way to pass a message. The most obvious limitation is that the information that is shared can only be a yes/no answer. Another Cocoa locking class can be used to pass an integer value between threads and it is better designed to handle this type of communication. The class is `NSConditionLock`. It defines a whole new set of methods that parallel the names of the `NSLock` methods. The most important methods are

```
- (id)initWithCondition:(int)condition
- (int)condition
- (void)lockWhenCondition:(int)condition
- (BOOL)tryLockWhenCondition:(int)condition
- (BOOL)lockWhenCondition:(int)condition beforeDate:(NSDate *)limit
-   (void)unlockWithCondition:(int)condition
```

The designated initializer `-initWithCondition:` sets up the lock's initial *condition*. The condition is an arbitrary integer that has meaning only to the code that uses the lock. It is like a tag; the lock just passes the value around. For example, it is common for the condition's meaning to be the state number of a state machine's current state.

To determine what the lock's current condition is, simply use `-condition` to find out. It will not block and simply returns the value.

The three new methods for obtaining the lock all require that a condition be provided. They will block or will not block in the same way as the parallel methods in `NSLock`. Thus, `-lockWhenCondition:` will block and `-tryLockWhenCondition:` will not. Of course, `-lockWhenCondition:beforeDate:` will block, but only until the date passed in. The lock will only be obtained if and when the condition of the lock is equal to the condition passed into the method. Even if the lock is available, these locking methods will not actually obtain the lock until the condition is also met.

The last method, `-unlockWithCondition:`, will relinquish the lock and set it to a new condition at the same time. This is the only way to change the lock's condition to a new value. Clearly, the lock must be obtained before it can be changed.

NOTE

The `NSConditionLock` class also responds to all the standard `NSLock` methods, as well. If the `NSLock` methods are used, the lock's condition value will be ignored. This presents two ways that the `NSConditionLock` might be used.

The first application is to make a thread block until a certain condition is met or an event has occurred. When the condition is met or the event occurs in another thread, that thread will then obtain the lock and release it with a condition value that will flag that the change has happened. For example, suppose thread A wants to wait for something to happen in thread B. The condition lock is set to zero and when thread B does its thing, it will set the lock to 1. The code would look like this:

```
// in thread A, wait for a condition of 1
[myConditionLock lockWhenCondition:1]; // will block until condition is 1
[myConditionLock unlock];
// execution continues....

// in thread B, we do stuff
// critical event happens....
[myConditionLock lock];
[myConditionLock unlockWithCondition:1];
// we continue on our way; thread A will be woken up
```

Of course, multiple threads could set up a cascade of conditions or other complex cause/effect relationships with this technique. The other application of the condition lock is to simply pass an integer value between threads as a form of threadsafe global communications. Here's how you would do the get/set of the value:

```
value = [myGlobalValueLock condition];  // this is the "get"

// here's a "set" operation:
[myGlobalValueLock lock];
[myGlobalValueLock unlockWithCondition:newValue];
```

Usually, it is best to go to the trouble of using an `NSConditionLock` instead of just using a global integer variable. The reason is that using the lock is threadsafe, whereas the global variable is not. To make a global integer threadsafe, all accesses to it need to be protected by an `NSLock`. What the `NSConditionLock` does is combine the two into a single construct, which makes it easier to consistently follow the conventions needed to keep the code threadsafe.

It is common to ask what to do to communicate more information than just an integer value between threads. Of course, messages can always be sent over Distributed Objects. Another option is to associate a condition lock with a collection of data to be shared. For example, the sending thread would obtain the lock, prepare the data, and then unlock by setting it to a condition that signals "data is ready." The receiving thread would wait for the "ready" condition by blocking on the lock, requesting that condition. It would then do whatever is necessary with the data, such as copying it to a private area, and then release the lock with a "data is used up" condition. It could then process the data further. Releasing the lock with the "data used up" condition could signal the sender thread to start stuffing in more data, and so on. Obviously, many variations on this theme are possible.

Using the `NSDistributedLock` Class

Locks aren't used only with multithreaded programming. Different processes often need to coordinate their actions in the file system in the same way threads need to coordinate their accesses to memory. For example, imagine if one process was writing to a file. If another process comes along and tries to write to the same file before the first process is finished, the resultant file will probably end up an unholy mess.

The locking classes described in the previous section won't help solve this problem because they only exist within one process's memory space. They don't cross process boundaries. On the other hand, most operating systems do provide a means of locking files in the filesystem. Sometimes it is a special function that sets a file attribute flag on the file, locking other processes out of being able to modify that file. In other cases, locking is done by convention. For example, for a file `blahblah.log` the existence of another file `blahblah.log.lock` would be taken to mean that the file is locked and shouldn't be modified until the lock file has been deleted.

To isolate the programmer from the operating system–specific means of locking, Cocoa introduces the NSDistributedLock class. It uses the current OS convention for locking files, and is consistent. As long as all applications accessing a particular resource each use this class, accesses to the resource will be safe.

Creating an NSDistributedLock object is simple. Just use one of these two methods:

```
+ (NSDistributedLock *)lockWithPath:(NSString *)aPath
- (NSDistributedLock *)initWithPath:(NSString *)aPath
```

The only difference is that the class method returns an autoreleased instance. The alloc plus init approach returns an object with a retain count of one. Both methods require a path. This is the path of the resource to be protected. The resource must exist and be writable to the program attempting to create the lock. If either condition is not met, the lock cannot be created. The NSFileManager and other Foundation classes can be used to see if either condition is a problem as well as attempt to fix it.

After an object is returned, it does not mean that the application actually has the lock. To obtain the lock itself, the -tryLock method must be invoked. As with NSLock, this method does not block and will return a YES or NO immediately. If YES, the lock was obtained. If NO, the lock is already owned by another process. No methods will block, so the programmer will need to set up some kind of polling loop, perhaps with a timeout, if such behavior is desired. This method will raise an exception if a file system problem occurs.

To relinquish the lock, an -unlock message should be sent. This will raise an exception if the lock isn't already owned by the process trying to do the unlock. This is different from the previous locking classes because the thread-based locks can't really tell which thread owns a given lock. That is controlled by adherence to conventions only. In the case of a distributed lock, however, the owner *is* known, so exceptions can be raised.

It is possible for processes to die or to freeze up. If that happens to a process that owns a lock, there's really no way to tell. But it would be disastrous to have a lock in place with no way to release it. Thus, the distributed lock does provide a way to "break" the lock. This forces the lock to be relinquished, no matter what process owns the lock. Breaking a lock is a very bad thing to do unless it is certain that the process owning it has died or is frozen. (It is bad because effectively it defeats the very purpose of the lock itself.) To aid in determining whether a lock should be broken, it is possible to check how old the lock is. If it is very, very old (stale), breaking it might be the right thing to do. The methods to do this are

```
- (NSDate *)lockDate
- (void)breakLock
```

The `-lockDate` method can also be used by a program to see if somebody else has broken a lock it holds. If the date isn't the same as when the lock was obtained, the lock has been broken. It is a good idea to get the current date when obtaining a lock and storing it so that this check can be performed later. If the lock has been broken, further modification of the protected resource would be dangerous.

Threading Issues

This section discusses some of the issues that must be taken into account when writing multithreaded programs. It is beyond the scope of this book to describe every detail of multithreading. Furthermore, the discussions of each of the issues will be necessarily abbreviated. As such, if you are interested in further discussion it is strongly recommended that you obtain a good computer-science textbook that discusses the issues surrounding multithreaded and concurrent programming. Most operating systems textbooks provide in depth discussions of all the threading issues described in this chapter.

Performance Issues

The first issue is performance. Multithreading can affect a program's performance in several ways. It can affect a user's perception of performance as well. Surprisingly, the effects on perceived and actual performance aren't always the same.

On a single CPU system, multithreading can hurt performance. This is because each thread has an overhead associated with it. The first time a new thread is spawned, the Objective-C runtime moves into a thread-safe mode that adds a small overhead to all message calls. When the operating system switches from one thread to another, some CPU work is required to make the switch. That's all work that wouldn't have to be done in a single-threaded application.

On a multiple CPU system, this changes. Threads won't be switched as often, if at all because they don't have to all be scheduled on the same CPU. The optimal situation is to have one CPU for every thread so that no context switches will, in theory, be necessary. Obviously, with other processes also competing for CPUs, there will be an unavoidable number of context switches no matter how many threads are used. The idea, though, is to keep the number of switches to a minimum. Clearly, if a process spawns more threads than there are CPUs, there will be some degree of extra overhead to support the extra threads.

There is also an overhead associated with thread synchronization. Locking code sections, something that is necessary for thread safety, takes longer to do than no locking at all. The Distributed Objects communication commonly used between threads takes much longer to perform than a normal Objective-C message. The first time a thread is spawned, Cocoa and Objective-C will move into a threadsafe mode.

In that mode, the various locking code and other conventions required by multithreading will be turned on and there will be an application-wide performance hit that can be on the order of 15% or so.

Perceived performance is a very different beast, however. Suppose that a calculation takes two seconds to complete. If the user clicks a button to initiate the calculation, a single threaded application will freeze up for two seconds while the calculation completes. That's not very long, but during that time the application won't respond to user input such as keystrokes or mouse clicks and drags. That two seconds is long enough for the user to notice and probably long enough to momentarily trigger the dreaded spinning disk wait cursor. To the user, the application feels slow because the two-second wait is almost emphasized by the computer's behavior.

Now consider the same situation with that calculation being performed in a background thread. The user clicks the button and the main event loop continues immediately. The user can click other buttons, type somewhere else, and do other things while the calculation completes. And, most important of all, there is no spinning disk! The calculation still takes about two seconds before it shows its results in the interface, but the user won't have that wait emphasized as strongly by the user interface, so the delay tends to not be noticed as much. The possibly surprising result is that a multithreaded application can feel like it is faster than its single-threaded counterpart even if that is not actually the case.

An operation such as saving a file to disk is an excellent example of where the user thinks there's a real speed-up because there's no interface verification that the save completed. If the file is saved in the background, the user has no idea how long it actually took! To them, the file save was instantaneous. Now, if the user is allowed to continue modifying a document while the save proceeds, the data could be corrupted. That can be solved by making a copy of the document in memory first. After the copy is made, the save thread is spawned to save the copy. That's extra work, but a copy operation is much faster than writing to disk, so the user perceives a speed up even though reality is quite the opposite.

Critical Sections

Critical sections of code present all sorts of problems for multithreaded code. Access to critical sections must be serialized. That means that only one thread at a time can be using that code. If too much of the code is critical and serialized, then at the extreme a multithreaded program is behaving just like a single-threaded program. If things can't be done simultaneously, especially on a multiple CPU machine, the threads aren't helping at all. All the overhead is experienced with none of the gains.

To alleviate this, the best multithread code has as few critical sections as possible and keeps them as short as possible. If all the threads hit bottlenecks when trying to access critical sections, performance suffers. Throwing more CPUs at the problem won't help. The speed of the slowest CPU is the limiting factor as the code becomes over-serialized.

Some programs lend themselves to multithreading nicely because there are very few, if any, critical sections. Other programs should never be made multithreaded. This should be determined early on in the design phase by analyzing what code sections are critical. If there are too many—or any of them will have a long execution time—multithreading might not be a good idea. There's no clear heuristic other than experience to make this decision, but a little common sense up front certainly goes a long way.

By carefully analyzing your code, it might also be possible to shorten a critical section. Anything that doesn't need to be in the critical section should always be moved before or after the locking code whenever possible. Because this optimization happens later in the development stage, it almost never makes up for poor planning of critical sections early in the design phase.

Global Variables

Global variables, of course, are a great way to make data available between threads. All threads can see globals. The problem is that they also create critical sections. Any access touching a global, read or write, is a potential critical section. If it can be guaranteed that no other thread will *ever* touch the variable, the thread can use it safely. That's a big if, and it can be hard to prove for all cases. When in doubt, use a lock. It might hurt performance a little bit, but creating unsafe code would be far worse.

Sometimes it is nice to have a global variable that is really global only within the context of a thread. Such a variable would be accessible from anywhere, but yet would not be visible to other threads. Because all threads share the same memory space, this might not seem possible. A variable is either global or not; there are no compiler directives to say a variable is "global to a thread, make one copy of the variable for each thread."

Of course, Cocoa comes to the rescue here. One variable is global to a thread, with exactly one copy of it for each thread. And, even better, it is an `NSDictionary`, so it is possible to put any amount and any kind of data into it. All the "thread globals" can be stored in this dictionary. Here's how to obtain a thread's dictionary:

```
threadDictionary = [[NSThread currentThread] threadDictionary];
```

This dictionary is unique to the thread, so items stored in it won't be seen by other threads. It is still accessible throughout the entire thread, just like any real global variable. It is true that there is a minor performance penalty in obtaining the dictionary and extracting a data object from it, but this is certainly better than not having this functionality at all.

This dictionary is in use by Cocoa already. Each thread has its various default objects. Some of these thread-wide objects are kept in the thread's dictionary. The dictionary is usually empty for new threads, though. Because of this, it is best to use keys that do not begin with the prefix "NS" to avoid collisions.

Race Conditions

One of the most common bugs in multithreaded code is the race condition. This is basically what happens when a critical code section or resource isn't protected by a lock. It can happen if one thread forgets to use a lock, too, even if other threads are properly using the lock.

To explain what a race condition actually is, an example will help. Consider this C statement:

```
x += 1;
```

This statement, when compiled, actually could translate into several instructions. Retrieve `x`, add one, store `x`. Other statements or groups of statements might be broken up in different ways depending on the compiler. The important thing here is that thread context switches happen between CPU instructions, *not* necessarily between C or Objective-C statements. It all depends on the compiler and CPU. A context switch could happen between the retrieve and add instructions, for example.

Next, suppose there are two threads that both need to increment `x`. This is the desired sequence:

```
Variable x starts at 0.
Thread A increments x, so it is now 1.
Thread B increments x, so it is now 2.
```

If the increment is broken down into separate statements, and then has an unfortunate context switch right in the middle, this situation could happen:

```
Variable x starts at 0.
Thread A retrieves x.  It sees a 0.
<context switch to thread B>
Thread B retrieves x.  It sees a 0.
Thread B increments x to 1.
Thread B stores x.  Now x = 1.
<context switch back to thread A>
Thread A increments x to 1.  (Remember, it saw a zero.)
Thread A stores x.  Now x = 1.
```

So at the end of this, x should be 2, but instead it is 1. That is an incorrect result. That's a race condition: two or more threads all racing to do something first, interfering with each other. The outcome all depends on which thread gets there first. This means that each time the program is run, something different could happen. If the critical section is short, the bug only happens once in a blue moon. But it is there, lurking, waiting to bite at most inopportune moment.

The solution, of course, is to remember to use locks whenever data, resources, or code are shared between threads. The more locks there are, the more overhead and the more risk of over-serialization. On the other hand, having too few locks leads to unpredictable behavior that is difficult to find and fix. This is why experts warn to avoid multithreading unless there's a clear need for it.

Deadlocks

It is possible for a multithreaded program to get some or all its threads wedged or frozen. This state is called deadlock. It is generally avoidable through good design. To understand how things could get locked up, let's look at an example.

Suppose there are two resources, A and B. Two threads, 1 and 2, want to access both resources. Suppose that thread A obtains the lock for A, and then the lock for B before proceeding. Next, suppose that thread 2 obtains the lock for B, and then the lock for A, and then proceeds. Here's what could happen:

```
Thread 1 obtains the lock on A.
Thread 2 obtains the lock on B.
Thread 1 is now blocked waiting for lock B.
Thread 2 is now blocked waiting for lock A.
```

Note that neither thread can proceed. Thread 1 has the A lock and is waiting for the B lock. That lock is held by thread 2. Thread 2 can't release it until it gets the A lock because it needs it to proceed. But the A lock won't be given up by thread 1 until it gets the B lock, hence a deadlock. Neither lock can be released. Neither thread can continue. The whole situation is reminiscent of the Dr. Seuss story where two stubborn creatures are walking opposite directions on a pathway and meet up. Neither is willing to step aside for the other, so their progress is halted until one or the other makes a move. In computer programs, neither side will budge unless they've been programmed to do so.

Clearly, in the previous example, there's a simple solution. Just have both threads obtain the locks in the same order. If they both grab A before B, there is no deadlock. Also note that this example is really just a special case of a race condition, because if thread 1 obtained both locks before thread 2 tried for lock B, there would have been no problem. This serves to remind us that even if locks are used, if they aren't used correctly, there is still a danger of race conditions.

Most deadlock situations are more complex than the previous example. For example, there might be a chain of resources that create a large multistep circle of waiting. Any good operating systems text has a discussion on how to prevent, avoid, detect, and correct deadlock situations. A complete discussion of this topic is beyond the scope of this book.

Before leaving the topic of deadlocks, there are two other situations where deadlock can occur, which should be considered. First, deadlock can happen between processes. It isn't just an interthread problem. Applications using `NSDistributedLock` can end up deadlocked waiting for locked files. If a process dies before releasing a lock, there is no cycle as in the previous example, yet there is still a potential deadlock. That is why the `-breakLock` method exists. Of course, telling the difference between a resource hog and a true deadlock situation can be somewhat difficult, so you must be very careful about breaking locks.

Finally, deadlock doesn't even require two threads or two resources to occur. Consider a thread that obtains a lock, and then forgets it has the lock and tries to obtain it again. It will block, waiting for itself to give up the lock so that it can get it again. That sounds like a pretty stupid hole for a programmer to dig himself into, but it can and does happen. Sometimes, the design of some code practically mandates it. Obviously, if the lock is obtained and released from within the context of a single method and that method doesn't send any messages or make any function calls, this is easy to avoid. But if the lock and unlock statements are farther apart, or there are method calls in between them, this situation can be a lot harder to avoid and track down.

This last case is common enough that Cocoa offers another class to help out. The `NSRecursiveLock` class is a lock that can be obtained multiple times by a given thread. It cannot be obtained by more than one thread at a time, so it still behaves like a lock should behave. But once a thread has obtained the lock, the *same* thread is allowed to obtain it again as many times as it wants. The stipulation is that the thread must unlock it exactly as many times as it was locked. In other words, the `-lock` and `-unlock` messages must be paired up exactly, just like `-retain` and `-release`. This class responds to the same set of messages as the `NSLock` class, so `-lockBeforeDate:` and `-tryLock` also exist and work as expected. Just like the `-lock` message, each of these other messages must be paired with an `-unlock` message if the lock was obtained.

Starvation

Sometimes it might seem like a thread is deadlocked when that is not actually the problem. In the case of deadlock, the locks actually become dead. They are being held and are never given up. It sounds like a deadlock if a thread is blocked waiting for a lock and never gets it. But in some cases it is simply that there are so many threads contending for a lock that the blocked thread is never given a chance.

For example, suppose there are four threads A, B, C, and D. Threads B, C, and D are waiting for a lock that is being held by thread A. Suppose that A releases the lock and C gets it. Then, C unlocks and D gets it. Meanwhile, C decides it wants the lock again, as does A. When D drops the lock, suppose it goes to A, and then C gets it next. Thread B still hasn't seen the lock, and might never see it if the contention for the lock doesn't quiet down.

Many operating systems use a round-robin system or other scheduler to avoid this problem. With round-robin scheduling, as the locks are requested the requests are put into a queue (a line). The requestor that has been waiting longest is always the next in line to get the lock. Note that if the contention for the lock is really this bad, eventually all the threads but one will be waiting in line at any given time. That is the extreme limit of the problem. At that point the operation has been fully serialized, and a single-threaded design would be more efficient.

The round-robin approach does prevent starvation, but not all operating systems do this. Considering the issue, it is clear that the high contention for the lock is a problem. Having fewer threads or changing the design to reduce the need for locked resources decreases the risk of starvation. If the critical sections and resource usage are kept to a minimum, contention will be reduced. The less communication between threads, the less likelihood that this will be a problem.

If Distributed Objects are being used, the messages sent will be coming through the run loop and will be queued up. Once again, using DO offers an advantage. And, as before, the same techniques to reduce overhead and decrease the negative impact of critical sections will help to prevent starvation.

Debugging

Debugging multithreaded programs is extremely hard to do. Period. The previous discussions of threading issues should convince any reader of this fact. Good, solid design up front helps a lot here, but it won't fix everything.

Even with the most careful design work, race conditions will happen. Things slip through the cracks. It is possible to test, test, and test again and never see them. Worse, it sometimes seems like the first customer to pick up the application gets "lucky." Now there's a bug that has never been seen, can't be reliably reproduced, but is being randomly experienced by users. Sometimes the bug pops up months after a release. Either way, a bug such as this is a programmer's nightmare!

The `gdb` debugger can peek into all a program's threads, but it only gives snapshots for a single point in time. It can't tell a developer how threads are interacting with each other as time marches forward. All it can do is provide a series of snapshots from which the in-between parts must be inferred, which is a hit-or-miss proposition. With experience, developers can improve at this ability, but very few people are experts at it. For many, it seems as bad as trying to stumble through a minefield in a thick fog. Instrumenting the code to log progress often disturbs the code enough to lessen or remove the race condition, so careful code analysis is often the only way to find the problem.

Luckily, most of the other threading issues can be dealt with a bit more easily than race conditions. Deadlocks are pretty easy to spot; they tend to happen more reliably than race conditions, as well. Differentiating between starvation and deadlock can be difficult at first, but careful consideration of the bugs' symptoms usually makes it possible to sort out the difference. Complete starvation is rare, so even a starved thread usually gets a little bit of work done. Deadlocked threads are blocked and don't get anything done. Running the program in the debugger and stopping execution to look at a stack backtrace will usually help, too. If the backtrace shows a thread waiting to obtain a lock, the problem may be a deadlock.

There are many techniques for debugging multithreaded programs, and it is beyond the scope of this book to dive into all the possible techniques. Developers should obtain books on concurrent programming and operating systems to learn more about this topic. Many good texts exist that will make the task of multithreaded programming much less daunting.

Using `NSTimers` Instead of Threads

Because of the difficulty of using threads, it is valuable to consider the use of `NSTimer` objects as an alternative. To do this, the code in question is first broken up into smaller parts. When each part is finished, a timer is set up to call the next part. Between timer firings, the application's event loop is free to continue normally.

An example of applying this technique is the SimpleAnimation program from Chapter 14, "Custom Views and Graphics Part III." The animation loop for the program is what is broken up into parts. Each animation frame is calculated and rendered every time a repeating timer fires, so the loop itself executes only one pass per firing of the timer. In this way, the application seems to be multithreaded because the animation continues while the menus and other application features remain usable. No spinning cursor appears while the animation runs.

Using timers in this way is far simpler to write and debug than multithreading. The user is provided with many of the same benefits as with multithreading. There is only one downside. This technique is not true multithreading, and, therefore, applications that make use of it cannot take full advantage of multiple processors on machines that have them.

Summary

This chapter discusses running Unix tasks from Cocoa and how to use multithreading in a Cocoa application. It also discusses many of the issues surrounding threading. All this might scare a developer away from trying to use multiple threads. That is not the intent, though. Yes, it is hard, but it can also be very rewarding. Developers need to carefully think through the decision to jump into multithreading and only use it where it is necessary and makes sense. Knowing what to expect before making the jump will hopefully help with the decision and make the jump, if taken, much less painful. Advance knowledge enables the possibility of making preparations with the intent of avoiding potential pitfalls.

The next chapter talks about how Cocoa handles printing. There are several objects to help Cocoa programs integrate seamlessly into the Mac OS X printing architecture.

25

Printing

IN THIS CHAPTER

- Basic Printing
- Overview of the Printing Classes
- NSView's Printing Support
- Printing and Pagination Example
- Printing in NSDocument-Based Applications

This chapter explores the classes encountered when adding printing support to Cocoa applications. The Cocoa framework classes automatically provide basic printing features. There is a standard File, Print menu item included by default in Cocoa application user interfaces designed with Interface Builder. The menu item sends the `-print:` message up the responder chain. Cocoa views and windows in the responder chain respond to the `-print:` message to automate printing. This chapter explains how to modify and extend the default printing capabilities. The `NSPrintInfo`, `NSPageLayout`, `NSPrintPanel`, and `NSPrintOperation` classes are described, and techniques for printing views are presented. This chapter also focuses on printing support in `NSDocument`-based multidocument applications.

Basic Printing

Printing is usually handled by `NSView` and its subclasses. The code executed to print a view is most often the same code used to draw the view onscreen. When a view receives the `-print:` message it displays a standard Cocoa Print panel. If the user clicks the Print panel's Print or Preview buttons, the view's `-drawRect:` method is called, much like when the view is requested to draw to the screen. The main difference is that when printing, the current graphics context is a printing context instead of a display context.

When implementing the `-drawRect:` method of an `NSView` subclass, it is possible to determine if the view is drawing to the screen or to another device, such as a printer, by calling `[[NSGraphicsContext currentContext] isDrawingToScreen]`. When not printing to the screen, don't draw elements such as the user's highlighted selection and other view-specific features that should not show up in the printed output. Little or no extra code is needed to support basic printing. The details about printing views are provided in the "NSView's Printing Support" section later in this chapter as well as in Apple's NSView class documentation.

NOTE

If a window is the first responder when the -print: message is sent up the responder chain, the entire window is printed—including its title bar.

The default printing features provided by Cocoa are enough for many applications. Cocoa provides additional printing functionality including automatic pagination, customized pagination, and specialized drawing on each page, such as headers and footers. The rest of this chapter describes the classes used to control printing and advanced-printing features.

Overview of the Printing Classes

Cocoa supports printing with the NSPrintInfo, NSPageLayout, NSPrintPanel, and NSPrintOperation classes. Each class controls a different aspect of printing and of the resulting output.

NSPrintInfo

The NSPrintInfo class encapsulates information used to control printing. It provides methods to access the dimensions of the user's selected paper size, the type of pagination to use, whether the output should be centered horizontally or vertically on the page, and the orientation of the paper. It also provides information about the selected printer and the current print job status. NSPrintInfo instances store a dictionary containing detailed information about printing options.

Creating an NSPrintInfo Instance

A graphical Cocoa application automatically has a single shared instance of NSPrintInfo that is accessed by calling [NSPrintInfo sharedPrintInfo]. It is very common to need several different NSPrintInfo instances, especially in multidocument applications. For example, each open document might be configured to print with a different paper size or orientation. Additional instances of NSPrintInfo are best created by copying an existing instance, as shown in the following line of code:

```
documentPrintInfo = [[NSPrintInfo sharedPrintInfo] copy];
```

`NSPrintInfo` instances can also be created by allocating them, and then using the `-initWithDictionary:` designated initializer. `NSPrintInfo` instances store many attributes, however, and most should be set to the default values chosen by the user. By copying an existing instance, all the default values are preserved, and it is only necessary to change a handful of attributes instead of setting them all.

The shared `NSPrintInfo` instance is set by calling `+setSharedPrintInfo:`. An application can use this feature to set the default printing attributes. For example, if the application's views are usually printed with a landscape orientation, the shared `NSPrintInfo` instance can be set to default to a landscape orientation.

Using `NSPrintInfo`'s Paper Attributes

The type of paper that the user has selected (for example, Letter, Legal, A4) is obtained by calling `NSPrintInfo`'s `-paperName` method that returns an `NSString` containing a localized name. The size of the selected paper type is returned by the `-paperSize` method that returns an `NSSize` structure containing the width and height of the page in points (1/72 inch).

The margins (the empty space around the edge of the paper) are returned by `-topMargin`, `-bottomMargin`, `-leftMargin`, and `-rightMargin`. These methods return a `float` representing the width of the respective margin in points. Each of these margins is set by using the `-setTopMargin:`, `-setBottomMargin:`, `-setLeftMargin:`, and `-setRightMargin:` methods.

NOTE

It is possible to set margins outside of the printable area supported by a printer. An application should warn a user if he attempts to set the values out of the appropriate range for the selected printer.

The content area of a page is calculated with the following code, which subtracts the margins from the paper size:

```
printableWidth = [printInfo paperSize].width -
    ([printInfo leftMargin]+[printInfo rightMargin]);
printableHeight = [printInfo paperSize].height -
    ([printInfo topMargin]+[printInfo bottomMargin]);
```

The content width and height are used extensively during pagination and can also be used in representing the page visually onscreen.

Using NSPrintInfo's Pagination Attributes

Pagination is the action of breaking a single large view into smaller chunks that represent each printed page. Figure 25.1 shows one form of pagination in which a single large view is broken into four pages.

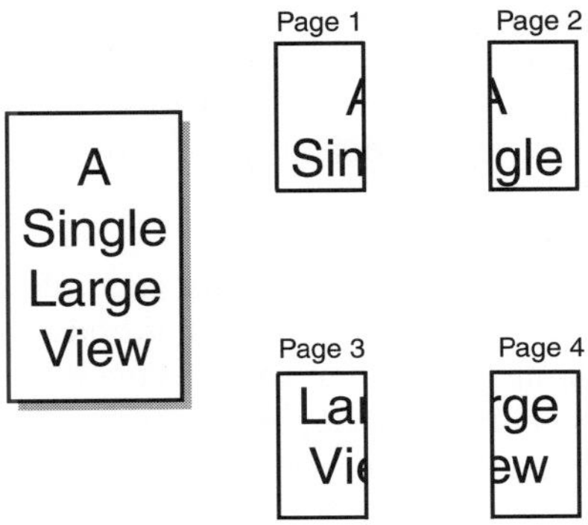

FIGURE 25.1 Pagination is used to break a single large view into multiple pages when printed.

NSPrintInfo's -setVerticalPagination: and -setHorizontalPagination: methods control the type of pagination that is used. The argument to these methods is one of the NSPrintingPaginationMode constants identified in Table 25.1.

TABLE 25.1 Pagination Type Constants

Pagination Constant	Description
NSAutoPagination	The drawing produced by the view being printed is split up into the number of pages required to print the view.
NSFitPagination	The drawing produced by the view being printed is scaled to produce one row or one column of pages. Note that setting this will cause the other pagination direction to scale as needed to preserve the view's aspect ratio.
NSClipPagination	The drawing produced by the view being printed is clipped to a single row or column of pages.

By default, the vertical pagination is set to NSAutoPagination, and horizontal pagination is set to NSClipPagination. This results in only the far-left column of pages represented by a view being printed. Horizontal NSAutoPagination should usually be explicitly set when creating an NSPrintInfo instance or a copy so that the entire view is printed.

NOTE

The shared `NSPrintInfo` instance is used to control printing when a `-print:` message is received by a view. A good practice is to set the shared instance's pagination mode before the first time `-print:` is called.

The current pagination mode is queried by calling `NSPrintInfo`'s `-horizontalPagination` and `-verticalPagination` methods. The methods return the `NSPrintingPaginationMode` constants in effect for horizontal and vertical pagination, respectively.

The position of the output on each page is controlled through the `-setHorizontallyCentered:` and `-setVerticallyCentered:` methods. Each accepts a `BOOL` argument. The output is only centered if it isn't larger than a single page. If multiple pages are needed, the output is always positioned on the pages to reflect the pagination. The current values for centering are obtained using `-isHorizontallyCentered` and `-isVerticallyCentered`, which return `BOOL` values.

A page can be printed either in portrait orientation (with the long edge of the page vertical) or landscape orientation (the long edge is horizontal). The orientation is set by calling `-setOrientation:` and passing one of the `NSPrintingOrientation` constants: `NSPortraitOrientation` or `NSLandscapeOrientation`.

Using `NSPrintInfo`'s Job Disposition

The disposition of a currently running print job is provided by `NSPrintInfo`'s `-jobDisposition` method, which returns an `NSString` instance. The possible values returned in the string are shown in Table 25.2.

TABLE 25.2 Pagination Type Constants

Disposition String	Meaning
`NSPrintSpoolJob`	Normal print job
`NSPrintPreviewJob`	The output is sent to the Preview application
`NSPrintSaveJob`	The output is being saved to a file
`NSPrintCancelJob`	The print job was cancelled
`NSPrintFaxJob`	The output is sent to a fax

Using `NSPrintInfo`'s Dictionary

All the data managed by an `NSPrintInfo` instance is stored in an `NSMutableDictionary` instance that can be accessed by calling `NSPrintInfo`'s `-dictionary` method. The returned dictionary can be archived along with a document's data or stored in an application's defaults database. A new `NSPrintInfo` instance with the same dictionary is initialized using `NSPrintInfo`'s `-initWithDictionary:` method.

Many NSPrintInfo dictionary keys are defined in the NSPrintInfo.h header file. Table 25.3 contains the dictionary keys supported in Mac OS X 10.1.3. Keys that have a type of float, int, BOOL, or a constant are stored as NSValue objects.

TABLE 25.3 NSPrintInfo Dictionary Keys

Dictionary Key	Type	Description
NSPrintPaperName	NSString	Paper name: Letter, Legal, A4, and so on.
NSPrintPaperSize	NSSize	Height and width of paper.
NSPrintMustCollate	BOOL	Output must be collated.
NSPrintOrientation	NSPrintingOrientation	Portrait or Landscape.
NSPrintLeftMargin	float	Left margin, in points.
NSPrintRightMargin	float	Right margin, in points.
NSPrintTopMargin	float	Top margin, in points.
NSPrintBottomMargin	float	Bottom margin, in points.
NSPrintHorizontallyCentered	BOOL	Pages are centered horizontally.
NSPrintVerticallyCentered	BOOL	Pages are centered horizontally.
NSPrintHorizontalPagination NSPrintingPaginationMode	int	One of the enumerated constants.
NSPrintVerticalPagination NSPrintingPaginationMode	int	One of the enumerated constants.
NSPrintScalingFactor	float	Scale before pagination.
NSPrintAllPages	BOOL	Include all pages in the job.
NSPrintReversePageOrder	BOOL	Print last page first.
NSPrintFirstPage	int	First page to print in job.
NSPrintLastPage	int	Last page to print in job.
NSPrintCopies	int	Number of copies to spool.
NSPrintPrinter	NSPrinter	Printer to use for print job.
NSPrintJobDisposition	NSString	The job's disposition; one of the constants in Table 25.2.
NSPrintSavePath	NSString	Path use to save a print job.

The string obtained with the NSPrintJobDisposition key contains one of the strings identified in Table 25.2

If the print job disposition string is NSPrintSaveJob, the NSPrintSavePath key in the NSPrintInfo dictionary is used to obtain the path to which the print job is saved.

Accessing the Selected Printer

The printer to use for a print job is obtained with NSPrintInfo's -printer method. The -printer method returns an instance of the NSPrinter class.

NOTE

Apple has licensed the Common Unix Printing System (CUPS) printing technology for use in the next major version of Mac OS X, 10.2. This may lead to changes in the way the selected printer is accessed.

NSPrinter

The NSPrinter class encapsulates the properties and capabilities of a printer. It is possible to obtain specific attributes of a printer, but they cannot be set via the NSPrinter class. Each printer's attributes and capabilities are defined by an appropriate PostScript Printer Description (PPD) file, or by the operating system driver for the printer.

NSPrinter instances are created to represent printers attached to the computer or accessible on the network.

The NSPrinter class method +printerWithName: returns an instance of NSPrinter for the named printer passed as an NSString argument. If no printer with the requested name is available, nil is returned.

The class method +printerWithType: returns an NSPrinter instance for a specified type of printer. An array of available printer types is obtained by calling NSPrinter's +printerTypes method. The type of printer represented by an existing NSPrinter instance accessed with NSPrinter's -type method.

It is also possible to get a list of the available printers using the +printerNames method. It returns an NSArray of NSStrings containing the names of available printers. The name associated with an existing NSPrinter instance is returned by the -name method. NSPrinter's -name method returns nil if the NSPrinter represents a type of printer rather than a specific printer.

NSPageLayout

The NSPageLayout class handles the user interface for presenting page layout information to the user. The standard File, Page Setup menu item in graphical Cocoa applications sends the -runPageLayout: message up the responder chain. If -runPageLayout: reaches the application object, NSApplication's -runPageLayout: method displays the Page Setup user interface as either a modal panel or as a sheet. Figure 25.2 shows the Page Setup panel used as a standalone panel.

Figure 25.3 shows the Page Setup user interface as a document modal sheet attached to a document window.

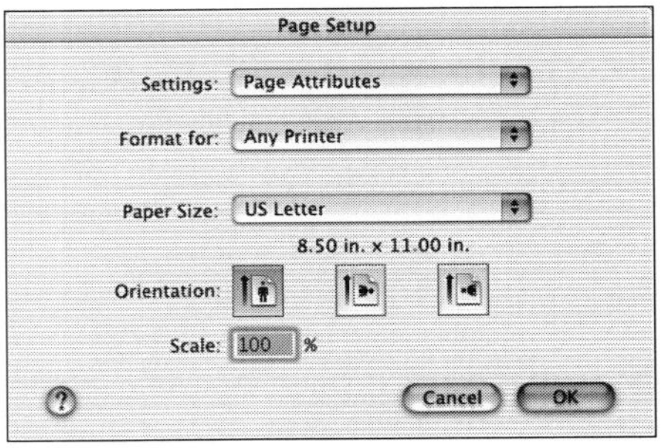

FIGURE 25.2 The Page Setup user interface controlled by an instance of the NSPageLayout class is displayed as a panel.

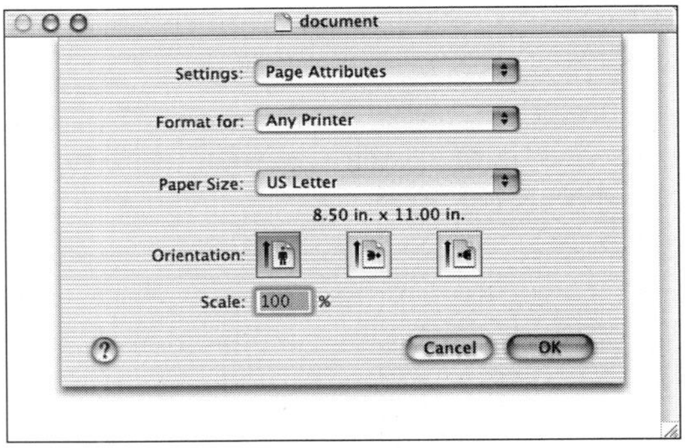

FIGURE 25.3 The Page Setup user interface controlled by an instance of the NSPageLayout class is displayed as a document modal sheet.

When a new Cocoa application is created in Project Builder using either the Cocoa Application or Cocoa Document–based Application templates, the File, Page Setup menu item is automatically included in the user interface. There are three common ways to change the standard page layout behavior of Cocoa applications: subclass `NSApplication` override its `-runPageLayout:` method, implement `-runPageLayout:` in an object earlier in the responder chain than `NSApplication`, or change the target and action of the standard Page Setup menu item.

Configuring an `NSPageLayout` Instance

An `NSPageLayout` instance is created by calling the `NSPageLayout` class method `+pageLayout`.

Similar to many of Cocoa's standard panels, the `NSPageLayout` panel can be augmented by adding an accessory view. This is done using `NSPageLayout`'s `-setAccessoryView:` method and passing an `NSView` instance as the argument.

Accessory views are described in the "Document Actions and the Save Panel" section of Chapter 9, "Applications, Windows, and Screens." Chapter 17, "Color," describes accessory views used with the standard Color panel. If an `NSPageLayout` instance has an accessory view, it is returned by the `-accessoryView` method.

Presenting the Page Setup Panel

The Page Setup panel is presented using either `NSPageLayout`'s `-runModal` or `-runModalWithPrintInfo:` methods. The `-runModal` method uses the shared `NSPrintInfo` instance as the source of information displayed by the panel. The `-runModalWithPrintInfo:` method uses the `NSPrintInfo` instance provided as an argument. Both methods return an integer value corresponding to the button on the Page Setup panel that is clicked by the user to close the panel. If the OK button is clicked, the integer constant `NSOKButton` is returned. If the Cancel button is clicked, the `NSCancelButton` constant is returned.

To present the panel as a document modal sheet, the following method is used:

```
- (void)beginSheetWithPrintInfo:(NSPrintInfo *)printInfo
           modalForWindow:(NSWindow *)docWindow
                   delegate:(id)delegate
             didEndSelector:(SEL)didEndSelector
                contextInfo:(void *)contextInfo
```

An `NSPrintInfo` instance is passed as the first argument. Document-based applications use an instance of `NSPrintInfo` that is associated with the active document, applications that don't support documents can use `[NSPrintInfo sharedPrintInfo]` instead. The window to which the sheet is attached is passed as the `docWindow` argument. The object passed as the `delegate` argument is automatically sent the message identified by the `didEndSelector` selector when the sheet's OK or Cancel buttons are clicked. The `contextInfo` argument specifies additional information to be passed to the `didEndSelector` method. The use of sheets, sheet delegates, `didEndSelector`, and `contextInfo` are described in the "Changes to `MYDocument` to Support Sheets" section of Chapter 9.

NOTE

If the `contextInfo` argument is not `null`, it should be retained before passing it to `-beginSheetWithPrintInfo:modalForWindow:delegate:didEndSelector:contextInfo:`. Otherwise, the object could be inadvertently deallocated before the sheet is closed. Release the `contextInfo` object in the associated `didEndSelector` method.

The method identified by the `didEndSelector` must take three arguments like the following `-pageLayoutDidEnd:returnCode:contextInfo:` method:

```
- (void)pageLayoutDidEnd:(NSPageLayout *)pageLayout
             returnCode:(int)returnCode
            contextInfo:(void *)contextInfo
```

When the method identified by the `didEndSelector` is called, the `NSPageLayout` instance that sent the `didEndSelector` message is passed as the first argument. The `returnCode` is an integer value corresponding to the button clicked to close the sheet; `NSOKButton` for the OK button and `NSCancelButton` for the Cancel button. The `contextInfo` associated with the sheet is passed as the third argument.

After the Page Setup panel or sheet has been presented to the user, the `NSPrintInfo` instance returned by `NSPageLayout`'s `-printInfo` stores the page layout information entered by the user.

NSPrintPanel

The `NSPrintPanel` class handles Cocoa's standard Print panel user interface, which can be presented as a normal panel or as a document modal sheet. Figure 25.4 shows the standard Print panel.

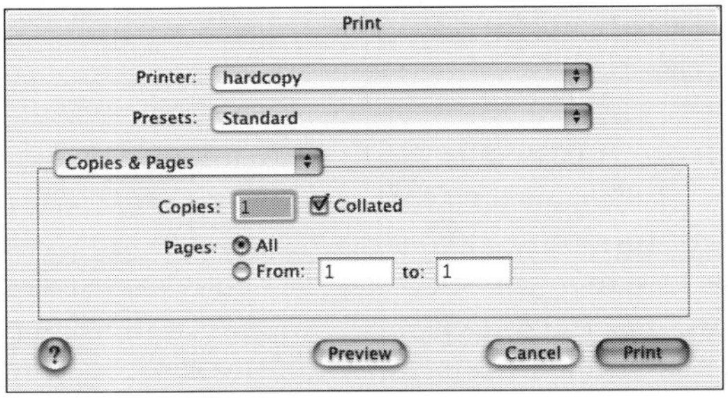

FIGURE 25.4 The Print user interface controlled by an instance of the `NSPrintPanel` class is displayed as a standalone panel.

Figure 25.5 shows the Print user interface as a document modal sheet attached to a document window.

The Print panel or sheet is presented in response to the user selecting the File, Print menu item.

When a new Cocoa application is created in Project Builder using either the Cocoa Application or Cocoa Document-based Application templates, the File, Print menu item is automatically included in the user interface. The File, Print menu item is normally configured to send the `-print:` message up the responder chain as described in the introduction to this chapter. Views and windows implement the `-print:` method to display a standard Print panel controlled by an instance of the `NSPrintPanel` class in cooperation with an instance of the `NSPrintOperation` class.

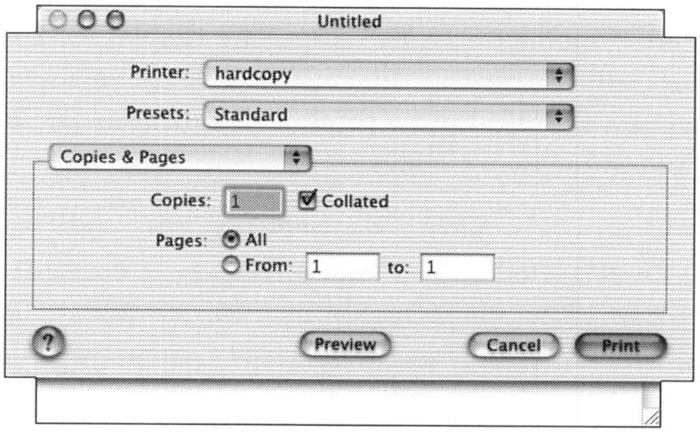

FIGURE 25.5 The Print user interface controlled by an instance of the `NSPrintPanel` class is displayed as a document modal sheet.

Direct programmer interaction with the `NSPrintPanel` class is rarely necessary. It's creation, configuration, and presentation are automatically handled by an instance of the `NSPrintOperation` class.

NSPrintOperation

The `NSPrintOperation` class coordinates the interaction between an `NSPrintInfo` instance and an `NSView` instance while printing takes place. The `NSPrintOperation` class is also used to create PDF and EPS representations of an `NSView`'s contents suitable for copy and paste between applications. Specified areas of a view are converted to cross-platform standard Encapsulated Postscript (EPS) or Portable Document Format (PDF) data. The use of EPS and PDF data is described in the "Pasteboard Types" section of Chapter 19, "Using Pasteboards."

Creating and Configuring an NSPrintOperation

A new `NSPrintOperation` instance is created by calling `NSPrintOperation`'s `+printOperationWithView:` class method. The NSView instance to be printed is passed as the argument. The `+printOperationWithView:` method returns an autoreleased `NSPrintOperation` instance configured to print with the attributes specified by the shared `NSPrintInfo` instance. `NSPrintOperation` also provides the `+printOperationWithView:printInfo:` method that is used to specify an `NSPrintInfo` instance other than the shared instance.

The `NSPrintInfo` instance used by an `NSPrintOperation` instance is returned by `NSPrintOperation`'s `-printInfo` method. A print operation's `NSPrintInfo` instance is set by calling `-setPrintInfo:`. The `NSView` instance that is being printed is returned by `NSPrintOperation`'s `-view` method.

An `NSPrintOperation` instance is able to display the standard Print panel controlled by an instance of `NSPrintPanel`. It is also able to display a progress indicator to indicate the status of a print operation to the user. The display of the Print panel and the progress indicator happens automatically unless `NSPrintOperation`'s `-setShowPanels:` method is called with the `BOOL` argument `NO`. The `-showPanels` method returns the value set by `-setShowPanels:`.

`NSPrintOperation` provides the `-setAccessoryView:` method that is used to specify an accessory view to be attached to the `NSPrintPanel` used by the printing operation. The current accessory view is returned by calling `NSPrintOperation`'s `-accessoryView`.

In the unlikely situation when a custom `NSPrintPanel` subclass is required by an application, the `NSPrintOperation` class provides the `-setPrintPanel:` method that accepts an instance of an `NSPrintPanel` subclass as the argument. The `NSPrintPanel` instance used by an `NSPrintOperation` instance is returned by `-printPanel`.

Print Operation Attributes

The order that pages are printed by an `NSPrintOperation` instance is set using the `-setPageOrder:` method and passing one of the following `NSPrintingPageOrder` constants as the argument, as shown in Table 25.4:

TABLE 25.4 `NSPrintingPageOrder` Constants

Constant	Description
`NSAscendingPageOrder`	Prints pages in ascending (back to front) page order.
`NSDescendingPageOrder`	Prints pages in descending (front to back) page order.
`NSSpecialPageOrder`	Pages are printed in the order the print spooler receives them.
`NSUnknownPageOrder`	No page order is specified.

The default page ordering for a print operation is `NSAscendingPageOrder`. The page order constant used by an `NSPrintOperation` instance is returned by the `-pageOrder` method.

An `NSPrintOperation` is configured to create a new thread to run the printing operation by calling `-setCanSpawnSeparateThread:` and passing a `BOOL` value of `YES` as the argument.

Running a Print Operation

An `NSPrintOperation` instance begins printing when its `-runOperation` method is called. The Print panel and progress indicator are displayed unless the

-setShowPanels: method was called to prevent that. The -runOperation method returns YES if the print operation was successful.

The Print panel can be presented to the user as a sheet instead of a standalone panel by using the following NSPrintOperation method that is similar to the -beginSheetWithPrintInfo:modalForWindow:delegate:didEndSelector:contextInfo: method already presented:

```
-(void)runOperationModalForWindow:(NSWindow *)docWindow
                        delegate:(id)delegate
                  didRunSelector:(SEL)didRunSelector
                     contextInfo:(void *)contextInfo
```

This method displays the Print interface as a sheet attached to docWindow. When the sheet's OK or Cancel buttons are clicked, the delegate object receives the didRunSelector message. The contextInfo argument is passed to the method identified by didEndSelector. The contextInfo argument can be NULL. The following method declaration is representative of the type of method that didEndSelector should identify:

```
- (void)printOperationDidRun:(NSPrintOperation *)printOperation
                     success:(BOOL)success
                 contextInfo:(void *)contextInfo
```

When the sheet is dismissed, the delegate method identified by didRunSelector is called with the sending NSPrintOperation instance as the first argument. The success argument has a BOOL value of YES if the printing operation completed successfully, and NO if there was an error or the sheet's Cancel button was clicked.

The NSPrintOperation instance that is currently printing, if any, is returned by NSPrintOperation's +currentOperation class method. The +currentOperation method returns nil if there isn't a print operation in progress. Although a print operation is still sending pages to a printer, the integer page number of the page currently being sent to the printer is returned by NSPrintOperation's -currentPage method.

Creating EPS and PDF Data with NSPrintOperation

NSPrintOperation is used to create either EPS or PDF representations of an NSView's contents. This feature is often used for exporting a view's representation to the pasteboard.

NSPrintOperation's +EPSOperationWithView:insideRect:toData: class method returns an autoreleased NSPrintOperation instance configured to generate EPS data that represents the portion of the specified view drawn within the specified rectangle. When the NSPrintOperation returned by this method is sent a -runOperation message, it generates the EPS data and appends it to the NSMutableData instance passed as the toData argument. The shared NSPrintInfo instance is used to control the generation of the EPS data. The +EPSOperationWithView:insideRect:toData:printInfo: method is used to obtain an NSPrintOperation instance that uses a specified NSPrintInfo instance when creating EPS data.

To generate a PDF representation of the drawing within a rectangle of a view, use NSPrintOperation's +PDFOperationWithView:insideRect:toData: or +PDFOperationWithView:insideRect:toData:printInfo: methods. Both methods operate in the same manner as the EPS variants, but produce PDF data instead.

An application can determine if the current print operation is printing to a printer or generated EPS/PDF data by calling NSPrintOperation's -isCopyingOperation. This method returns a BOOL value of YES if the NSPrintOperation is generating EPS or PDF data and NO otherwise.

NSView's Printing Support

NSView subclasses in Cocoa applications are responsible for drawing to the screen and to the printer. During a print operation, the -drawRect: method of a view being printed is called once for each page that is printed. The view is responsible for drawing the appropriate content within the rectangle passed to -drawRect: for each printed page. Basic printing is handled automatically by NSView's implementation of the -print: method, which creates a print operation, uses the shared NSPrintInfo instance, displays a print panel, and, unless the user cancels the print operation, prints the view including all subviews.

It is often desirable to draw slightly differently if the drawing is being sent to a printer instead of the screen. Within the implementation of an NSView subclass's -drawRect: method, it is possible to determine if the drawing is going to the screen or not by calling [[NSGraphicsContext currentContext] isDrawingToScreen]. In the following example implementation of -drawRect:, a background grid is drawn only when drawing to the screen:

```
- (void)drawRect:(NSRect)rect
{
  [[NSColor whiteColor] set];
  NSRectFill(rect);

  // draw the grid if we're drawing to the screen
  if ([[NSGraphicsContext currentContext] isDrawingToScreen]) {
    [self drawGrid];
```

```
    }

    // draw the regular contents of the view
    [self drawViewContents];
}
```

The custom -drawGrid and -drawViewContents methods are not shown here.

Additional Printing Features

When views are printed, NSView methods are called at various stages of the printing operations. NSView's implementations of the methods can be overridden to enable detailed control of printing.

NSView's -printJobTitle is called before the first page of a print operation is printed. NSView's implementation of -printJobTitle returns a string based on the title of the window that contains the view being printed. A subclass of NSView can override -printJobTitle to return a different job title string for the printing operation.

At the start of a printing operation, the -beginDocument method is called. NSView's implementation of -beginDocument configures the view's graphics context for printing. This method can be overridden in a subclass to perform operations such as modifying the shared NSPrintInfo instance. If -beginDocument is overridden, the superclass's implementation must be called.

Just before each page is printed, NSView's -beginPageInRect:atPlacement: method is called. NSView implements this method to set up the view's coordinate system and scaling for the page being printed. If this method is overridden, the superclass's implementation must be called.

Views are given two chances to add extra drawing to each printed page. Extra drawing can include items such as headers, footers, page numbers, crop marks, fold lines, and watermarks. The -drawPageBorderWithSize: method is called once for each page printed. The -drawSheetBorderWithSize: method is called once for each sheet of paper used in a print operation. To understand the difference between the two methods, consider the situation in which multiple pages are printed on a single sheet of paper when 2-up printing is used. The -drawPageBorderWithSize: method is called twice for each sheet of paper printed (once for each logical page on the sheet of paper). The -drawSheetBorderWithSize: method is called only once for each sheet of paper printed.

After each page is printed, NSView's -endPage method is called. This method calls -unlockFocus, and then ensures that the output of the page is properly terminated. Subclasses must call the superclass's implementation.

Finally, after the last page of a view is printed, the `-endDocument` method is called. Subclasses that override `-endDocument` must call the superclass's implementation.

Printing and Pagination Example

The example project, PaginationDemos, (available at `www.cocoaprogramming.net`) contains three application targets: AutomaticPagination, AdjustedPagination, and CustomPagination. These targets show different ways to use pagination.

The PaginationDemos application draws a representation of student's desks in a classroom with their names and seat numbers labeled on each desk, as shown in Figure 25.6.

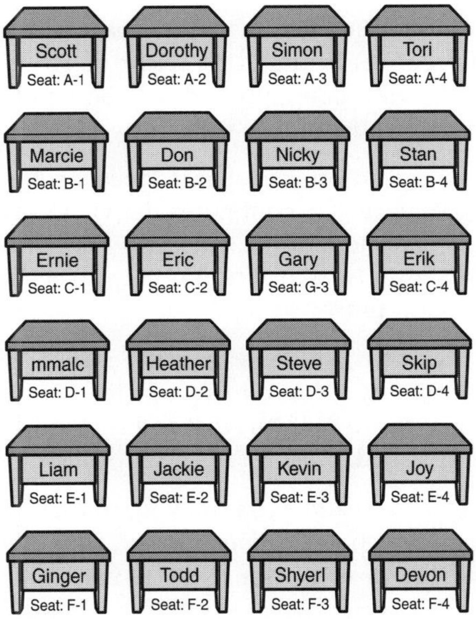

FIGURE 25.6 A single large view that displays images of student desks is shown unpaginated.

The desks are drawn by an `NSView` subclass called `ClassDeskView`. The `ClassDeskView` is instantiated inside the application's `MyDocument.nib` file and is 700 Postscript Points wide by 1050 Postscript Points tall. Because Postscript Points equal 1/72 inches, the view is approximately 9.7 inches wide and 14.6 inches tall. A view of this size requires pagination to print on multiple 8.5 by 11 inch sheets of paper.

The view initialization and drawing code for the `ClassDeskView` class are implemented within the `ClassDeskView.m` file that is part of the PaginationDemos project.

AutomaticPagination

AutomaticPagination is used when the NSPrintInfo instance for the current printing operation has had its horizontal and vertical pagination modes set to NSAutoPagination. The NSPrintInfo -setHorizontalPagination: and -setVerticalPagination: methods are described in the "Using NSPrintInfo's Pagination Attributes" section of this chapter. AutomaticPagination generates pages that are tiled together at the edges to recreate the entire view contents.

```
//
//  ClassDeskView.m
//  AutomaticPagination
//
//  Created by Scott Anguish on Mon Jun 03 2002.
//

#import "ClassDeskView.h"

#define CP_IMAGEDISTRIBUTION 175.0
#define CP_HORIZONTALITEMS 4
#define CP_VERTICALITEMS 6


@implementation ClassDeskView

- (float)imageDistribution
{
    return CP_IMAGEDISTRIBUTION;
}

- (int)numberOfHorizontalItems
{
    return CP_HORIZONTALITEMS;
}

- (int)numberOfVerticalItems
{
    return CP_VERTICALITEMS;
}


- (void)initializeImage
{
```

```
    theImage=[[NSImage imageNamed:@"Desk"] retain];
    [theImage setScalesWhenResized:YES];
    nameArray=[[NSArray arrayWithObjects:@"Ginger",@"Todd",@"Shyerl"
        ,@"Devon",@"Liam",@"Jackie",@"Kevin"
        ,@"Joy",@"mmalc",@"Heather",@"Steve"
        ,@"Skip",@"Ernie",@"Eric",@"Gary",@"Erik",
        @"Marcie",@"Don",@"Nicky",@"Stan",@"Scott",
        @"Dorothy",@"Simon",@"Tori",nil] retain];
}

- (id)initWithFrame:(NSRect)frame {
    self = [super initWithFrame:frame];
    if (self) {
        [self initializeImage];
    }
    return self;
}

- (void)awakeFromNib
{
    [self initializeImage];
}

- (void)dealloc
{
    [theImage release];
    [nameArray release];
    [super dealloc];
}

- (void)drawRect:(NSRect)rect {
    int x,y;
    NSString *letterConstants;
    NSMutableDictionary *seatTextAttributes;
    NSMutableDictionary *nameTextAttributes;

    [[NSColor whiteColor] set];
    NSRectFill(rect);

    // This string is used in the labelling of the
    // vertical repeating elements
    letterConstants=@"ABCDEFGHIJKLMNOPQRSTUVWYZ";
```

```
// setup the attributes dictionary that is
// used repeatedly to draw the labels on the
// repeating elements
seatTextAttributes=[NSMutableDictionary dictionary];
[seatTextAttributes setObject:[NSFont labelFontOfSize:14.0]
                       forKey:NSFontAttributeName];
[seatTextAttributes setObject:[NSColor blackColor]
                       forKey:NSForegroundColorAttributeName];
nameTextAttributes=[NSMutableDictionary dictionary];
[nameTextAttributes setObject:[NSFont labelFontOfSize:24.0]
                       forKey:NSFontAttributeName];
[nameTextAttributes setObject:[NSColor blackColor]
                       forKey:NSForegroundColorAttributeName];

// start looping over the pages
// note that drawing is done from the bottom to the top
for (y=0;y<[self numberOfVerticalItems]; y++)
{
    for (x=0;x<[self numberOfHorizontalItems]; x++)
    {
        float horizontalCenter, verticalBottom;
        float labelHLoc, labelVLoc;
        NSString *imageLabel;
        NSSize overallTextSize;
        NSRange theRange;
        NSString *imageLetter;
        float nameHLoc,nameVLoc;
        NSPoint compositeLocation;
        NSString *nameForDesk;

        // draw the repeating element at
        // the location for the current x and y
        // positioning
        compositeLocation=NSMakePoint(x*[self imageDistribution],
                                      y*[self imageDistribution]);
        [theImage compositeToPoint:compositeLocation
                         operation:NSCompositeSourceOver];

        // determine the letter to use for this
        // repeating element in labelling
        // and then construct the string
        theRange=NSMakeRange([self numberOfVerticalItems]-1-y,1);
```

```
            imageLetter=[letterConstants substringWithRange:theRange];
            imageLabel=[NSString stringWithFormat:
                    @"Seat: %@-%d",imageLetter,x+1];

            // we want to center the text, so first order of duty
            // is to determine the size of the text with the
            // given attributes, then determine the center of the
            // current element, and move left, down half the appropriate
            // sizes
            horizontalCenter=x*[self imageDistribution]+
                    [self imageDistribution]/2;
            verticalBottom=y*[self imageDistribution];
            overallTextSize=[imageLabel sizeWithAttributes:seatTextAttributes];
            labelHLoc=(horizontalCenter-overallTextSize.width/2);
            labelVLoc=verticalBottom+20;
            // draw the element's label
            [imageLabel drawAtPoint:NSMakePoint(labelHLoc,labelVLoc)
                    withAttributes:seatTextAttributes];

            // do the same to figure out the name
            // to print on each desk
            nameForDesk=[nameArray objectAtIndex:
                    (y*[self numberOfHorizontalItems]+x)];
            overallTextSize=[nameForDesk sizeWithAttributes:
                    nameTextAttributes];
            nameHLoc=(horizontalCenter-overallTextSize.width/2);
            nameVLoc=verticalBottom+56;
            [nameForDesk drawAtPoint:NSMakePoint(nameHLoc,nameVLoc)
                    withAttributes:nameTextAttributes];
        }
    }
}

@end
```

The `NSPrintInfo` is configured when the `MyDocument` class (an `NSDocument` subclass) responds to `-windowControllerDidLoadNib:`.

```
- (void)windowControllerDidLoadNib:(NSWindowController *) aController
{
    [super windowControllerDidLoadNib:aController];
    [self setPrintInfo:[[[NSPrintInfo sharedPrintInfo] copy] autorelease]];
```

```
    [[self printInfo] setHorizontalPagination:NSAutoPagination];
    [[self printInfo] setVerticalPagination:NSAutoPagination];

}
```

For this example, the horizontal and vertical pagination is set to `NSAutoPagination`. To enable the document to print, it is necessary to override the `-printShowingPrintPanel:` method in `MyDocument`. The example creates an `NSPrintOperation` for the `demoView`, and then runs the print operation as a document sheet.

```
- (void)printShowingPrintPanel:(BOOL)flag
{
    NSPrintOperation *printOp;

    printOp=[NSPrintOperation printOperationWithView:demoView
                                           printInfo:[self printInfo]];
    [printOp setShowPanels:flag];
    [printOp runOperationModalForWindow:[demoView window]
                               delegate:nil
                         didRunSelector:NULL
                            contextInfo:NULL];
}
```

The output from running the Automatic Pagination application is shown in Figure 25.7. Notice how the automatic pagination cuts the pages without regard to the location of the desks.

To prevent the desks from being cut off, the application can adjust the pagination.

Customizing Automatic Pagination

Implementing these methods can modify the automatically provided pagination:

```
- (void)adjustPageWidthNew:(float *)newRight
                      left:(float)left
                     right:(float)proposedRight
    ....             limit:(float)rightLimit

- (float)widthAdjustLimit
```

The `-adjustPageWidthNew:left:right:limit:` method can be overridden by an `NSView` subclass to allow for adjustments to the right hand edge of the page. This is useful to prevent an element on the page from overlapping two pages. The `left` argument contains the horizontal location (in pixels) of the left side of the page to be imaged. The argument `proposedRight` is the location where the right side of the page will break by default. The argument `rightLimit` indicates the smallest value that the `proposedRight` location could be adjusted to. The adjusted value that should be used for the right hand page break is returned by reference in the `newRight` new argument.

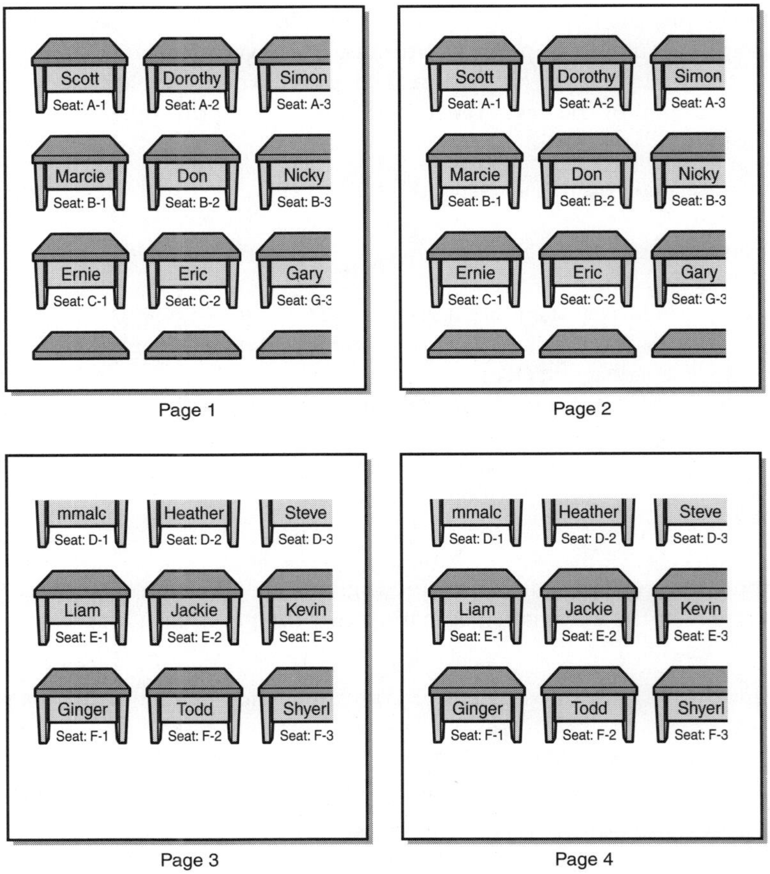

FIGURE 25.7 The printed output doesn't respect the location of the desks when cutting pages with automatic pagination.

The value of `rightLimit` is determined by the method `-widthAdjustLimit`. This method can be overridden to limit the amount of change that can be made to the `proposedRight` location by returning a float value between 0 and 1. The default value is 0.2.

The default implementation will iterate over any subviews, allowing each the opportunity to return the newRight value. A custom implementation should call super with the new value for newRight.

```
- (void)adjustPageHeightNew:(float *)newBottom
                        top:(float)top
                     bottom:(float)proposedBottom
                      limit:(float)bottomLimit

- (float)heightAdjustLimit
```

The method -adjustPageHeightNew:top:bottom:limit: is the vertical equivalent of the -adjustPageWidthNew:left:right:limit: method. This can be overridden to cause elements to be pushed onto the next page that would otherwise be disturbed by a page break.

The top argument contains the vertical location (in pixels) of the top edge of the page to be imaged. The argument proposedBottom is the location where the bottom edge of the page will break by default. The argument bottomLimit indicates the minimum value that the proposedBottom location could be adjusted to. The adjusted value that should be used for the bottom edge page break is returned by reference in the newBottom new argument.

The value of bottomLimit is determined by the method -heightAdjustLimit. This method can be overridden to limit the amount of change that can be made to the proposedBottom location by returning a float value between 0 and 1. The default value is 0.2.

In the example project PaginationDemos, the application AdjustedPagination implements these methods to ensure that none of the students' desks are split across pages. The code that implements this is contained within the ClassDeskView+AdjustPagination.m file. This category on the ClassDeskView class contains the following code.

```
//
//  ClassDeskView+AdjustPagination.m
//  AdjustedPagination
//
//  Created by Scott Anguish on Tue Jun 04 2002.
//

#import "ClassDeskView+AdjustPagination.h"


@implementation ClassDeskView(AdjustPagination)
```

```
- (void)adjustPageWidthNew:(float *)newRight
                      left:(float)left
                     right:(float)proposedRight
                     limit:(float)rightLimit
{
    // inherit the superclass behaviuor
    [super adjustPageWidthNew:newRight
                         left:left
                        right:proposedRight
                        limit:rightLimit];

    // adjust the page such that any partial images are
    // bumped to the next page
    *newRight=((int)(proposedRight / [self imageDistribution])
              * [self imageDistribution]);
}

- (float)widthAdjustLimit
{
    // allow up to half a page to be bumped to
    // the next page
    return 0.5;
}

- (float)heightAdjustLimit
{
    // allow up to half a page to be bumped to
    // the next page
    return 0.5;
}

- (void)adjustPageHeightNew:(float *)newBottom
                        top:(float)top
                     bottom:(float)proposedBottom
                      limit:(float)bottomLimit
{
    // inherit the superclass behaviuor
   [super adjustPageHeightNew:newBottom
                          top:top
                       bottom:proposedBottom
                        limit:bottomLimit];
    // adjust the page such that any partial images are
```

```
    // bumped to the next page
   *newBottom=top-((int)((top-proposedBottom) / [self imageDistribution])
                  * [self imageDistribution]);
}

@end
```

The output from running the application AdjustedPagination is shown in Figure 25.8. Notice how all the desks are now printed without being broken at a page break.

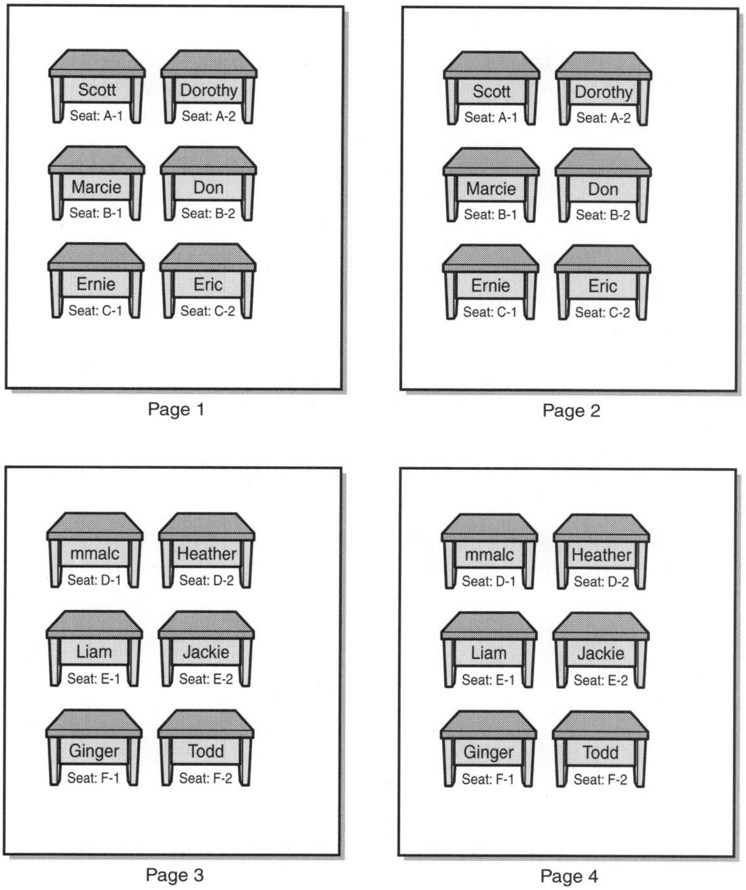

FIGURE 25.8 The printed output respects the location of the desks when cutting pages with adjusted pagination.

The location on the page where the printing takes place can be customized by implementing `-locationOfPrintRect:`. This method is called for each page, passing an `NSRect` representing the printable rectangle of the current page with the origin at 0.0,0.0. A subclass should return an `NSPoint` with the location to use to place the rectangle on the page. Alternately, it can call the super implementation to inherit the standard behavior. Overriding this method and not calling super removes the effectiveness of the `NSPrintInfo` `-setHorizontallyCentered:` and `-setVerticallyCentered:` methods.

CustomPagination

An application may require still more control over the areas that are printed. In that case, custom pagination may be the solution. CustomPagination requires the application to determine the number of pages available, be able to return an `NSRect` for each page upon request and optionally specify the position on the page that the printed area will appear.

If an `NSView` subclass implements CustomPagination, it must override and implement the method `-knowsPageRange:`. The subclass modifies the contents of the `NSRangePointer` argument to return the first page, and the number of pages that can be printed, and returns `YES`. If `-knowsPageRange:` returns `NO`, AutomaticPagination is used instead.

For each page an application using CustomPagination is expected to return an `NSRect` describing the location in the view to be printed for a given page. This is accomplished by implementing `-rectForPage:`. This method has one argument, an integer, which is the page number that the `NSRect` should represent. This method is not called when AutomaticPagination is used.

The PaginationDemos example application CustomPagination implements `-knowsPageRange:` and `-rectForPage:` and causes each desk to be printed on a separate page (suitable for labeling a child's desk perhaps). The implementation is again in a separate Category `ClassDeskView+CustomPagination.m`.

```
//
//  ClassDeskView+CustomPagination.m
//  CustomPagination
//
//  Created by Scott Anguish on Tue Jun 04 2002.
//

#import "ClassDeskView+CustomPagination.h"

@implementation ClassDeskView(CustomPagination)
```

```
- (BOOL)knowsPageRange:(NSRangePointer)aRange
{
    aRange->location=1;
    aRange->length=[self numberOfHorizontalItems]
        * [self numberOfVerticalItems];
    return YES;
}
- (NSRect)rectForPage:(int)page {
    float x=(int)((page-1) % [self numberOfHorizontalItems]);
    float y=(int)((page-1)/[self numberOfHorizontalItems]);
    return NSMakeRect(x*[self imageDistribution],
                      y*[self imageDistribution],
                      [self imageDistribution],
                      [self imageDistribution]);
}

@end
```

Example output from the CustomPagination example is shown in Figure 25.9.

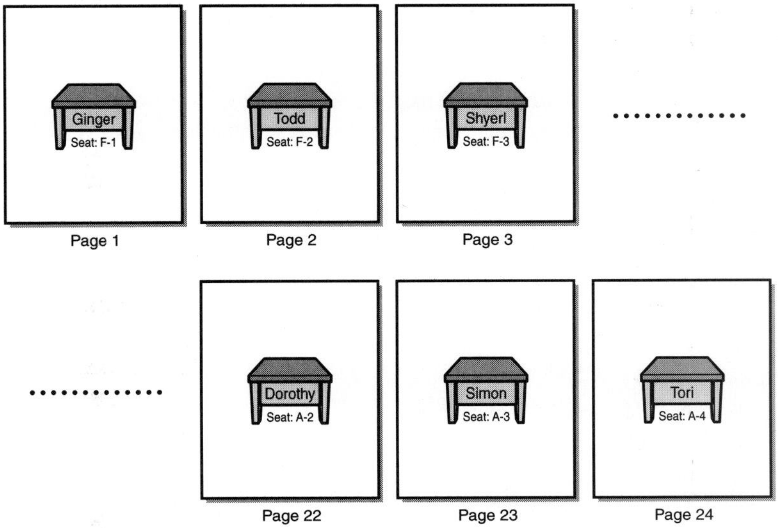

FIGURE 25.9 The printed output has one desk per page when custom pagination is used.

Alternative Pagination Technique

Often Cocoa's CustomPagination capabilities rely on the technique of dividing a single large view into smaller page-sized rectangles. There are occasions, however, where this may not be the optimum solution.

An alterative method to this would be to determine the page that is currently being printed in the `-drawRect:` implementation and draw only the contents of that page. This requires the implementation of both the `-knowsPageRange:` and `-rectForPage:` methods in the `NSView` subclass.

```
//
//  AltPrintView.m
//  AlternativePrintingStrategy
//

#import "AltPrintView.h"


@implementation AltPrintView

- (NSAttributedString *)attributedStringForPageNumber:(int)i
{
    NSAttributedString *pageString;
    NSString *page;
    page=[NSString stringWithFormat:@"PAGE %d",i];
    pageString=[[[NSAttributedString alloc] initWithString:page] autorelease];
    return pageString;
}


- (void)drawRect:(NSRect)rect {
    if (![[NSGraphicsContext currentContext] isDrawingToScreen])
    {
        int page;
        NSAttributedString *attrString;
        NSRect destRect;

        page=[[NSPrintOperation currentOperation] currentPage];
        attrString=[self attributedStringForPageNumber:page];
        destRect=[self rectForPage:page];
        [attrString drawInRect:destRect];
    }
```

```
}

- (BOOL)knowsPageRange:(NSRangePointer)aRange
{
    aRange->location=1;
    aRange->length=6;
    return YES;
}

- (NSRect)rectForPage:(int)page {
    NSAttributedString *attrString;
    NSSize attrStringSize;
    attrString=[self attributedStringForPageNumber:page];
    attrStringSize=[attrString size];
    return NSMakeRect(0.0,0.0,
                      attrStringSize.width,
                      attrStringSize.height);
}


@end
```

In this example the -knowsPageRange: causes six pages to be printed. Each time a page is generated the -rectForPage: determines the size of page required to display the NSAttributedString containing the page number. The -drawRect: method is called for each page as well, and draws the string on the page.

Printing in NSDocument-Based Applications

An NSDocument-based Cocoa application provides cover for more of the printing functionality, isolating the developer even further from direct NSPageLayout and NSPagePanel interaction.

Each NSDocument contains its own NSPrintInfo instance, which is accessible through the method -printInfo. The document's NSPrintInfo instance can be set using the method -setPrintInfo: and passing the NSPrintInfo as the argument.

NOTE

Overriding -setPrintInfo: in an NSDocument subclass provides an opportunity to react to a user having changed the page orientation, scale, or page type. The subclass's implementation of -setPrintInfo: can cause any views to redraw as required.

NSPageLayout Interaction

There are several opportunities to customize behavior when an NSDocument application is going to present the Page Setup panel. When the user selects the Page Setup menu item, the NSDocument subclass will receive the message -runPageLayout: passing the sender object as the argument. The normal behavior of this method is to call -runModalPageLayoutWithPrintInfo:delegate:didRunSelector:contextInfo: with the NSDocument's NSPrintInfo. If the user clicks the OK button in a presented Page Setup panel, the NSDocument method -shouldChangePrintInfo is called with the NSPrintInfo instance passed as the argument. This method returns YES by default, allowing changes.

If an NSDocument subclass overrides -shouldChangePrintInfo: it can modify the NSPrintInfo data and return YES, or simply return NO to disallow the changes.

NOTE

Overriding -shouldChangePrintInfo: provides another opportunity to react to a user having changed the page orientations, scale, or paper type. A subclass implementation of -showChangePrintInfo: could notify NSView instances that need to redraw and then return YES.

The display of an NSPageLayout panel is done using one of the following methods:

```
-runModalPageLayoutWithPrintInfo:
-runModalPageLayoutWithPrintInfo:delegate:
        didRunSelector:contextInfo:
```

The method -runModalPageLayoutWithPrintInfo: returns an int value of NSOKButton or NSCancelButton depending on the user's actions. The more complete method -runModalPageLayoutWithPrintInfo:delegate:didRunSelector:contextInfo: allows setting of a delegate and didRunSelector method to act after the print function is complete. The didRunSelector method should have the following signature:

```
- (void)documentDidRunModalPageLayout:(NSDocument *)document
                             accepted:(BOOL)accepted
                          contextInfo:(void *)contextInfo
```

When the OK or Cancel button is clicked, the delegate receives a message to the didRunSelector method with the current document passed as an argument, along with an optional user-provided contextInfo object. The didRunSelector and the delegate can both be nil, if no action needs to be taken as a result of the panel dismissal.

When these methods are used to run the NSPageLayout panel, the application is given a further opportunity to modify the NSPageLayout object, by overriding -preparePageLayout:. This method provides the opportunity to send the NSPageLayout instance (passed as an argument to -preparePageLayout:) messages such as -setAccessoryView: to add an accessory view to the panel. A subclass implementation of -preparePageLayout: should return YES if the NSPageLayout panel was successfully prepared, and NO if there was a failure.

Printing Documents

In an NSDocument application, the Print menu item is configured to send the action -printDocument: to the First Responder. The NSDocument implementation of -printDocument: simply calls -printShowingPrintPanel: passing YES as the argument.

The method -printShowingPrintPanel: is always overridden in NSDocument applications that want to print. The subclass implementation needs to create an NSPrintOperation, configure it to display the panels using the passed BOOL argument and then run the print operation.

The print operation can be run using this NSDocument method:

```
- (void)runModalPrintOperation:(NSPrintOperation *)printOperation
                      delegate:(id)delegate
                didRunSelector:(SEL)didRunSelector
                   contextInfo:(void *)contextInfo;
```

The method expects an NSPrintOperation as the first argument, the delegate object that receives the didRunSelector message as the second and third arguments, and an optional contextInfo object. The didRunSelector method must have a signature like the following:

```
- (void)documentDidRunModalPrintOperation:(NSDocument *)document
                                  success:(BOOL)success
                              contextInfo:(void *)contextInfo
```

When the OK or Cancel button is clicked, the delegate receives a message to the didRunSelector method with the current document passed as an argument, along with an optional user-provided contextInfo object. The didRunSelector and the delegate can both be nil, if no action needs to be taken as a result of the panel dismissal.

The following code provides the -printShowingPrintPanel implementation from the PaginationDemo project:

```
- (void)printShowingPrintPanel:(BOOL)flag
{
    NSPrintOperation *printOp;

    printOp=[NSPrintOperation printOperationWithView:demoView
                                              printInfo:[self printInfo]];
    [printOp setShowPanels:flag];
    [self runModalPrintOperation:printOp
                        delegate:nil
                  didRunSelector:NULL
                     contextInfo:NULL];
}
```

The example creates the new `NSPrintOperation` for the `demoView` with the document's `NSPrintInfo` instance, sets the print operation's panels flag to the value passed to `-printShowingPrintPanel:`, and then calls the `NSDocument` method `-runModalPrintOperation:delegate:didRunSelector:contextInfo:` with the `NSPrintOperation`, `nil` for the delegate, and `NULL` for `didRunSelector` and `contextInfo`.

NOTE

Be aware that an `NSDocument` can have multiple `NSWindowController` instances and, therefore, multiple windows associated with it. In these examples, the `demoView` is hardwired to the `NSDocument` because each document is known to have only a single window.

Summary

Cocoa's basic `NSView` printing support is sufficient for many applications and complex printing support is available, if needed. The Cocoa classes provide hooks for extending the basic printing behavior to handle each application's needs. Adding printing support to Cocoa applications is seldom a large task. Cocoa programmers are able to focus on the unique features of each application instead of printing.

Chapter 26, "Application Requirements, Design, and Documentation," delves into the subtleties of application design using Cocoa. A simple game called TransparentTetris is developed to illustrate each step in the process of developing a representative complete Cocoa application.

PART III

Cocoa Techniques

IN THIS PART

26

Application Requirements, Design, and Documentation

IN THIS CHAPTER

- Designing an Application with Requirements
- Designing TransparentTetris
- Implementing the Design
- Using AutoDoc

In this chapter, the design of a Cocoa application is described by using the requirements, design, and documentation of a very simple Cocoa game that is similar to the classic Tetris puzzle game. Learning by example is often the most efficient method. Other chapters provide examples that highlight the use of Cocoa classes and the details of the API. Through examples, this chapter explains why an application is designed and implemented in a particular way. In some cases, alternate designs are described to illustrate the trade-offs and reasoning employed. The chapter also outlines a process for application development, which starts with a description of the goal and ends with documentation.

The TransparentTetris example illustrates universal design techniques and also delves into the subtleties of application design using Cocoa. Application requirements, specification, application design, and the use of the Model/View/Controller architecture apply to any application. Cocoa idioms and best practices used in this application include one way to implement graphical animation, use of notifications to decouple code (separate Model from Controller), use of categories to decouple code (separate Model from View), use of user defaults/preferences, a simple subclass of `NSView`, hiding and showing a view, coordinate system transformations, simple display optimization, and one way to automatically generate documentation.

Designing an Application with Requirements

Application design is an essential stage of application development. Small applications are often designed entirely within the imagination of a single programmer, but every application benefits from a design. Software development projects have become very complex and expensive. Few people would consider building a house without a plan, yet all but the smallest software projects are much more complex than the construction of a typical house, and can cost as much money to complete. A design does not necessarily imply a bureaucracy. The purpose of a design is to communicate the plan to individual developers. Sometimes one page or a diagram on a white board is sufficient.

Before a design can be written, a set of objectives or requirements must be defined. It is not possible to explain design decisions without first listing the requirements that influenced the decisions. Requirements answer the question, "What is being built?" The design answers the question, "How is it being built?" After a design has been developed, it can be evaluated to determine how well it meets the requirements. Again, the requirements and the design do not need to be a chore. Their purpose is to aid communication and avoid wasted or misguided effort.

Most successful applications are guided to completion by one or more people who have a vision of the complete application. Expressing any complex idea is very difficult and frustrating. Pictures, diagrams, and even prototypes or demonstrations can help, but written requirements and design are the best and most reliable way to make sure an application achieves the designer's vision. Unfortunately, requirements are hard to write and are never complete. Designs often change during implementation. Written requirements and a design do not guarantee successful application development; they are merely the best technique available.

Describing the Goal

The first step in the development of requirements is to describe the goal. Figure 26.1 shows the TransparentTetris game designed in this chapter.

TransparentTetris is a puzzle game in which a block falls from the top of a game board that is organized in a grid pattern. The falling block might have several different shapes relative to the game grid. The player can shift the falling block left or right, and rotate it in increments of 90°. When the falling block can not fall any farther without leaving the game board or colliding with another object, the falling block's motion stops. When the falling block's motion stops, the falling block occupies the positions within the game grid, which correspond to the block's shape and position when it has stopped falling. If blocks occupy any complete rows within the grid, the filled rows of blocks are removed from the game. Any blocks in rows above the rows that were removed fall to fill the space left by the removed rows. Then, a new block with a randomly selected shape starts falling from the top. When there is no room for a new block that has just started falling from the top to fall without colliding with blocks already displayed, the game is over. The player's score increases every time a row of blocks is removed from the game. The player's goal is to maximize the score by shifting the falling blocks left or right and rotating them to create the maximum number of filled rows that are removed before the game is over. As the game progresses, the falling blocks fall faster and faster, making game play more difficult. The player can change the color of the blocks and can even make the blocks transparent, so that a background can be seen through the blocks.

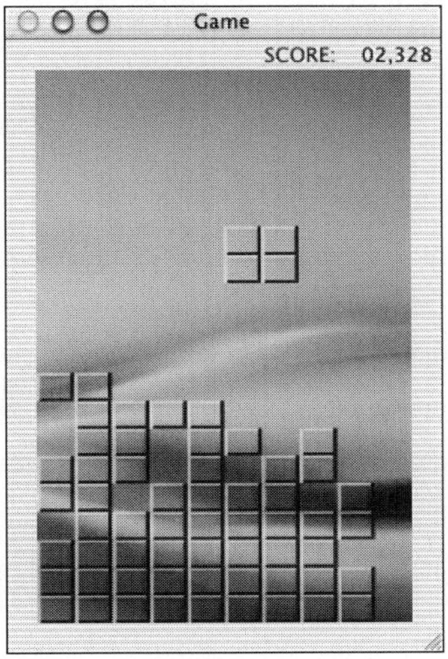

FIGURE 26.1 TransparentTetris is implemented with the two windows shown.

The description does not include the finer points of the game such as the shapes of the falling blocks; the size of the game grid; the speed at which blocks fall, what background is visible; how the player shifts and rotates blocks; how shifting, rotating, and falling are animated; what sounds, if any, are played; and how the player changes the color of the blocks. These finer points are design decisions that can impact the value of the game, but do not fundamentally alter the nature of the game.

Deriving Requirements from a Description

Given the description of the game, requirements can be derived. The requirements should be as general as possible. Requirements should not dictate design decisions, but they should be specific enough that any design that meets all the requirements will result in an application that is satisfactory. Of course, it is always better when a design and implementation exceed the minimum standard of satisfactory.

Programmers and designers (like most people) want to create high art whenever possible, but losing sight of the requirements may cause the result to be beautiful, but unsatisfactory.

In the context of a requirement, certain words have specific meaning. The word shall is used in formal requirement clauses. Any design that does not satisfy all shall requirement clauses will not be satisfactory. The word should is used to describe features that are expected but not required. A design that does not satisfy some of the should clauses might still be satisfactory. The word may is used to describe an optional implementation. The word may should be used sparingly and only to clarify a shall or a should clause.

The TransparentTetris game has the following requirements derived directly from the game description:

> Requirement 1—There shall be a game board.
>
> Requirement 2—The game board shall consist of a rectangular grid (the subblock grid) that subblocks (game pieces) may occupy.
>
> Requirement 3—At the start of a game, no subblocks shall occupy positions in the subblock grid.
>
> Requirement 4—During game play, there shall be exactly one falling block at all times.
>
> Requirement 5—A falling block shall consist of some number of subblocks arranged in a pattern.
>
> Requirement 6—It shall be possible for the subblocks of a falling block to be arranged in several different patterns.
>
> Requirement 7—During game play, the falling block shall be animated to fall from the top of the game board toward the bottom.
>
> Requirement 8—The pattern of subblocks in a falling block shall be randomly selected from the set of available patterns when the falling block first starts falling.
>
> Requirement 9—It shall be possible for the player to shift the falling-block left or right as long as doing so does not cause any part of the falling block to leave the game board.
>
> Requirement 10—It shall be possible for the player to rotate the falling block clockwise or counterclockwise in increments of 90° as long as doing so does not cause any part of the falling-block to leave the game board.
>
> Requirement 11—When the falling block cannot fall any farther without either leaving the game board or overlapping a subblock that occupies a position in the subblock grid, the displayed falling block shall stop falling.
>
> Requirement 12—When a falling block stops falling, subblocks shall be placed in the subblock grid so that they occupy positions corresponding to the subblock positions in the falling block given the falling block's position and orientation when it stopped falling.

Requirement 13—After subblocks have been added to the subblock grid, any rows that are completely filled with subblocks shall be removed from the game.

Requirement 14—When a row of subblocks is removed from the game, the players score shall be increased.

Requirement 15—When a row of subblocks is removed from the game, all subblocks above the removed row shall be moved down one row in the grid to fill the space formerly occupied by the removed row.

Requirement 16—After sub-blocks have been placed in the subblock grid, the falling-block shall be removed from the game.

Requirement 17—After a falling-block has been removed from the game, a new falling-block with a randomly selected pattern shall be placed at the top of the game board and start falling.

Requirement 18—Each new falling-block that is placed at the top of the game board shall fall faster than the preceding falling block.

Requirement 19—If a new falling-block at the top of the game board cannot fall without overlapping one or more subblocks already in the subblock grid, the game shall be over.

The following requirements are implied even though they do not appear in the game description. The game description cannot include all the details and features that puzzle games on Mac OS X can be assumed to have.

Requirement 20—It should be possible for the player to specify the color of the subblocks including any transparency.

Requirement 21—The game board should be displayed in a window.

Requirement 22—It should be possible for a game to be paused. (All game animation will halt and the game state should not change until the game is resumed.)

Requirement 23—It should be possible to resume a paused game.

Requirement 24—It should be possible to start a new game. (When starting a new game, all windows and state of previously started games may be discarded.)

Requirement 25—A sound should be played when a row of subblocks is removed and at other times when events of interest to the player occur.

Requirement 26—It should be possible to disable sound playing.

Requirement 27—Any player selected subblock color and transparency should be saved as a user preference and used in subsequent game play sessions.

Selecting an Architecture

Now that the requirements of the application being designed are known, the next step is to define the architecture. An application's architecture is sometimes called top-level design. The purpose of the architecture is to factor the application into subsystems that can be developed independently. A small application, such as this one, can easily be developed by a single person in a short time. Most applications, however, require multiple programmers and will be in development for months or years. The architecture is a means to divide the work so different teams of programmers can work in parallel, and so that everybody knows how the application will fit together in the end. The architecture can also simplify future software maintenance by preventing changes in one part of the application from requiring changes to other parts.

This example uses the Model-View-Controller (MVC) architecture described in Chapter 6, "Cocoa Design Patterns." The MVC architecture partitions the application into three subsystems: the model, the view, and the controller. Every application has different architectural needs. MVC will not apply in every case, but it is well-suited to most graphical applications, including TransparentTetris.

Designing TransparentTetris

Designing classes to meet requirements is largely magic. There are many schools of thought and modeling techniques. Every application can be decomposed into classes in an infinite number of ways. The collection of classes used can have a dramatic impact on the quality and success of an implementation, yet there is no modeling technique that guarantees an optimal implementation or even a successful implementation. The best approach is to rely on the intuition of experienced application designers and copy related successful designs.

The top-level design (architecture) can reduce the complexity of the application design by breaking it into multiple subsystems that can be designed independently. This divide and conquer approach can be extended to the subsystems to break them into smaller pieces, but the utility of that usually diminishes before the granularity of individual classes is achieved. When the divide and conquer approach is overapplied, opportunities for shared classes and class reuse are missed. A popular approach is to model the application's objects on their real-world equivalents. That can work well if the application models the real world. For some applications, a successful technique is to use the nouns in the application description and requirements as a starting point.

The design of TransparentTetris consists of five classes organized within the MVC architecture as follows:

Model: `MYGameModel`, `MYBlock`, `MYSubBlock`

View: `MYBlockView`

Controller: `MYGameController`

Not all designs should specify the precise classes that will be implemented. In most large applications, only the classes that play a major role, or encapsulate specific critical data, should be identified by name in the design. However, TransparentTetris is a very simple application, and the emphasis of this chapter is an explanation of the rationale behind the design and implementation. The TransparentTetris design is over detailed to provide a context for the rationale.

TransparentTetris Model

All the mandatory requirement clauses for TransparentTetris apply the model subsystem. The model must contain a game grid, subblocks that can occupy space in the grid, a falling block that is composed of subblocks, an API to move the falling block left or right, and an API to rotate the falling block clockwise or counterclockwise. The model must define several different subblock patterns that a falling block can have. The model must be able to select the subblock pattern randomly. The model must be able to detect when moving or rotating the falling block would cause some portion of the falling block to leave the game board and prevent such actions. The model must be able to detect when a falling block can no longer fall and when the game is over. The model must be able to place subblocks into the grid appropriately when the falling block stops falling. The model must be able to detect full rows of subblocks and remove them. The model must move subblocks that are above a removed row. The model must store a score and increase the score when rows are removed.

The model in the TransparentTetris application consists of three classes, `MYSubBlock`, `MYBlock`, and `MYGameModel`. `MYSubBlock` encapsulates the subblocks described in the application requirements. Subblocks are stored in a game grid and in falling blocks. The `MYBlock` class encapsulates the falling block including its position, rotation, and collection of subblocks in a variety of patterns. Finally, `MYGameModel` encapsulates the entire model including the game grid that stores subblocks, the falling block, the score, and the game over state. Given this decomposition, each of the classes has distinct responsibilities.

`MYSubBlock` Class

Each subblock occupies a single position in the game grid or in a falling block. Therefore, the data encapsulated by an instance of `MYSubBlock` is a position. In all cases, the position of a subblock is relative to the coordinate system of its container, the grid, or a falling block. The position is stored as two integer values on the assumption that subblocks always occupy integral (x, y) positions in a coordinate system. The use of only integral positions has the desirable consequence that subblocks with different positions will not overlap. Several requirements imply the capability to detect the collision (overlap) of subblocks during game play. The foresight to specify integer positions in the design yields the benefit that subblock collision can be detected by simply comparing positions for equality. This foresight is a small example of the magical element in design.

Designers must anticipate implementation problems. When designing one part of an application, designers must use intuition and analysis to side step potential problems in other parts of the application. The following code defines the interface to the `MYSubBlock` class, which will be used to represent the parts that compose the pattern of a block within the model.

```
//
//  MYSubBlock.h
//  TransparentTetris
//

#import <Foundation/Foundation.h>

@class NSButtonCell;
@class NSView;
@class NSColor;


@interface MYSubBlock : NSObject
{
  int            _myXPosition;     /*" integral X position "*/
  int            _myYPosition;     /*" integral Y position "*/
}

/*" Designated initializer "*/
- (id)initX:(int)x y:(int)y;

/*" Overridden initializer "*/
- (id)init;

/*" Accessors "*/
- (int)xPosition;
- (int)yPosition;
```

```
- (void)setXPosition:(int)x;
- (void)setYPosition:(int)y;

@end
```

NOTE

Specially formatted comments appear in the class declarations and also in the implementation code. The comments that begin with the sequence `/*"` and end with `"*/`, can be automatically extracted with a tool called AutoDoc to produce formatted documentation. Documentation generation is described in this chapter.

The position of a subblock within a falling block is determined by the pattern of the falling block. The position of a subblock within the game grid is determined by the subblock's position within the falling block when the falling block stops falling. It is implied that a subblock's position can change; first it is set relative to a position in the falling block, and then it is set to a position in the game grid. Therefore, accessor methods are provided to change a subblock's position. An alternative approach would be to make a subblock's position immutable after initialization. Then, when a falling block stops falling, rather than placing the falling block's existing subblock instances in the game grid and changing their positions to match, new subblock instances are created and initialized with positions in the grid. Both approaches are reasonable. The decision to enable the modification of a subblock's position via accessors was arbitrary.

There is no need for the `MYSubBlock` class to override its inherited `-dealloc` method because the `MYSubBlock` class does not allocate any memory or copy or retain any objects.

`MYBlock` Class

The `MYBlock` class implements the falling block. Each instance of `MYBlock` must have a position, a rotation, and some number of subblocks arranged in a pattern. The position of a falling block is always relative to the coordinate system of the game grid. As an instance of `MYBlock` falls, or is moved by the player, its position must change. The rotation must also change. Therefore, accessors to set the position and rotation must be available.

To enable smooth animation as a block falls or moves side to side, the falling block's position is stored as floating-point values. Using floating-point values for the position of a block means that the falling block can occupy positions with fractional offsets from the integral grid positions. As a block moves, it can be between grid positions rather than snapping from grid intersection to grid intersection.

Smooth movement of falling blocks was not a requirement. Designers should anticipate nice features that might not be required, but can enhance the quality of the application. Smooth movement of falling blocks is easy to implement if it is anticipated in the design. This is another example of the "magic" inherent in design.

Even though the falling block can occupy positions between grid intersections, the subblocks within the falling block occupy integral positions in a coordinate system defined by the falling block. As the falling block moves relative to the grid, the subblocks within the falling block remain in the same positions relative to the falling block.

The header file for the `MYBlock` class includes the definition of the number of subblocks stored in a block. The definition is in the header rather than the implementation file, so that storage can be reserved in the class interface, and so that other classes can easily reference a block's subblocks by index. To access the subblocks by index, the calling code must know how many subblocks are available. The pivot point for blocks is also defined in the header. The pivot point is the point within the block around which the block rotates.

```
////////////////////////////////////////////////////////////////////////////////
//  MYBlock.h
//  TransparentTetris
//

#import <Foundation/Foundation.h>

#define MYNUM_SUBBLOCKS_IN_BLOCK (4)     /*" Num sub-blocks in block "*/
#define MYBLOCK_PIVOT_X (2)  /*" X pos about which block rotates "*/
#define MYBLOCK_PIVOT_Y (2)  /*" Y pos about which block rotates "*/
```

The requirements dictate that a sound should be played when events of interest to the player occur. Interesting events might include the movement of a block left or right or the rotation of a block. Furthermore, the display of special visual effects after such events can be anticipated even though it is not required. The `MYBlock` class is an obvious place to detect the events, but the `MYBlock` class is part of the model in the MVC architecture. The model should not have knowledge about, or dependencies on, playing sounds and displaying visual effects that belong in the view or controller subsystems.

The use of notifications is one Cocoa technique that enables satisfaction of the requirements without violating the MVC architecture. Notifications provide a way to transfer information from the model to the other subsystems without creating an inappropriate coupling or dependence. The `MYBlock` class can broadcast notifications of events to anonymous observers. The sender of a notification does not know anything about the observers of the notification, if any.

The `MYBlock` class sends two notifications:

```
/*" Notification Names "*/
#define MYBLOCK_DID_SLIDE_NOTIFICATION (@"MYSubBlockDidSlideNotification")
#define MYBLOCK_DID_ROTATE_NOTIFICATION (@"MYSubBlockDidRotateNotification")
```

In addition to the position and rotation of the block, a target position and a target rotation are stored. These instance variables enable a technique called a low-pass filter to smooth large changes in position into several gradual changes. During each game update, the falling block will move half the distance from its actual position and rotation to its target position and rotation.

```
@class MYSubBlock;
@class MYGameModel;

@interface MYBlock : NSObject
{
  MYSubBlock    *_mySubBlocks[MYNUM_SUBBLOCKS_IN_BLOCK];    /*" sub-blocks
                                                            compose block "*/
  NSPoint       _myPosition;                /*" Pos of block in sub-block grid"*/
  NSPoint       _myTargetPosition;          /*" Target position of block "*/
  float         _myRotationDegrees;         /*" Degrees (-180 to 180) "*/
  float         _myTargetRotationDegrees;   /*" Deg. (-180 to 180) (should be
                                                0, 90, 180, or 270) "*/
}


/*" Designated initializer "*/
- (id)init;
```

The low-pass filter is time based. An `-update` method is needed to implement the filter and should be called at regular time intervals.

```
/*" Update "*/
- (void)update;
```

This is yet another magical aspect of design. The thought process that resulted in the specification of an `-update` method in the `MYBlock` class progressed as follows: First, smooth motion of blocks was anticipated even though it is not required. Then, a low-pass filter was selected to implement smooth motion from an actual position and rotation to a target position and rotation. Finally, the `-update` method was needed to implement the filter. The need to call the `-update` method at regular time intervals effects the design of the other classes that must call it. Each design decision has rippling effects. A designer must consider each design decision, anticipate the consequences, and judge the merits. Different designers will invariably make different subjective judgments.

Accessor methods are needed to set and get the actual and target positions and rotations.

```
/*" Positioning & rotation "*/
- (void)setPosition:(NSPoint)aPosition;
- (NSPoint)position;
- (BOOL)canFallDelta:(float)aDelta inModel:(MYGameModel *)aModel;
- (void)fallDelta:(float)delta inModel:(MYGameModel *)aModel;
- (void)moveTargetPositionLeftInModel:(MYGameModel *)aModel;
- (void)moveTargetPositionRightInModel:(MYGameModel *)aModel;
- (void)moveTargetRotationClockwiseInModel:(MYGameModel *)aModel;
- (void)moveTargetRotationCounterclockwiseInModel:(MYGameModel *)aModel;
```

The requirement to place subblocks into the game grid based on the position and orientation of the falling block, implies the need to be able to convert subblock positions from the coordinate system of the falling block to the coordinate system of the grid.

```
/*" Conversion to grid coordinates "*/
- (void)convertSubBlocksToGrid;
```

The need to place the subblocks contained in the falling block into the grid suggests that an accessor method is needed. The most direct approach is to access subblocks by index. Some equally valid approaches include the use of a custom enumerator, or an accessor that returns an array containing the subblocks.

```
/*" Sub-block access "*/
- (MYSubBlock *)subBlockAtIndex:(int)anIndex;

/*" Clean-up: "*/
- (void)dealloc;
```

Finally, the `MYBlock` class must override its inherited `-dealloc` method to release the contained subblocks.

```
@end
```

MYGameModel Class

MYGameModel is the final class in the model subsystem. This class defines and stores the game grid data structure and indirectly stores all game state. The -update method must be called periodically to update the game state. In this design, the game update rate is determined by the controller subsystem, which calls -update. A reasonable alternative design includes the periodic game update in the model itself. In this game, each time the model is updated, the view should also be updated. The controller subsystem has access to both the model and the view, making it an ideal location to update both. If game update was handled entirely within the model, a notification sent from the model could be used to trigger view updates.

```
//
//  MYGameModel.h
//  TransparentTetris
//

#import <Foundation/Foundation.h>
```

The size of the game grid is available in the class interface rather than hidden in the implementation so that other classes can use the information. The MYBlock class and MYSubBlock class can use the information to detect attempts to position subblocks outside the bounds of the grid. Classes in the view or controller subsystems can use the information.

In this design, the grid dimensions are specified with symbolic constants. An alternative approach would be to provide methods to obtain the grid dimensions. If the grid dimensions were only accessed through methods the grid dimensions could be variable. For variety, they could be different every time the game is played. Using methods exclusively would also improve encapsulation and avoid the necessity of recompiling all classes that use the dimensions whenever the dimensions are changed.

The primary reason for using symbolic constants rather than methods is that storage for the game grid is defined using a two-dimensional C array. Multidimensional C arrays must be declared with constant sizes. If the size of the grid was not a constant expression evaluated at compile time, the storage for the grid would have to be allocated explicitly in the implementation introducing additional complexity. In a more complicated application, the additional complexity in the implementation might be justified by the improved encapsulation and flexibility provided by methods. In this case, simple is better, but it is a close judgement call.

```
#define MYGAME_GRID_HEIGHT (20)   /*" number of rows in sub-block grid "*/
#define MYGAME_GRID_WIDTH (10)    /*" number of columns in sub-block grid "*/
```

Just as notifications were used to inform interested, anonymous observers about events in the MYBlock class, they are used by MYGameModel when the falling block stops falling, when a row of subblocks is removed from the grid, and when individual subblocks are removed from the grid. Classes in the controller or view subsystems can observe these notifications to play sounds or display visual effects as appropriate. The key to the design is that the MYGameModel class has no dependencies on classes outside the model.

```
/*" Notification Names "*/
#define MYROW_WAS_REMOVED_NOTIFICATION (@"MYRowWasRemovedNotification")
#define MYSUBBLOCK_WILL_BE_REMOVED_NOTIFICATION (\
    @"MYSubBlockWillBeRemovedNotification")
#define MYSBLOCK_WAS_PLACED_IN_GRID_NOTIFICATION (\
    @"MYBlockWasPlacedInGridNotification")

@class MYSubBlock;
@class MYBlock;
```

The MYGameModel class stores the game grid, the current falling block, the status of the game, the score, and the distance that the falling block should fall during each game update.

```
@interface MYGameModel : NSObject
{
    /*" Sub-blocks grid "*/
  MYSubBlock     *_mySubBlockGrid[MYGAME_GRID_HEIGHT][MYGAME_GRID_WIDTH];
  MYBlock        *_myFallingBlock;    /*" block that is falling "*/
  BOOL           _myIsRunning;        /*" YES iff game running (not paused) "*/
  BOOL           _myIsGameOver;       /*" YES iff the game is over "*/
  BOOL           _myIsDropping;       /*" YES iff falling block was dropped "*/
  int            _myScore;            /*" Score "*/
  float          _myCurrentFallDelta; /*" Increases-> game more difficult "*/
}

/*" Designated Initializer "*/
- (id)init;
```

The need for periodic game updates is implied by the game description. The fact that a block moves, rotates, and falls implies time-based changes in game state. The need for update is also dictated by the design decisions made in the MYBlock class. The MYGameModel class is responsible for calling the -update method of the current falling block at regular time intervals.

```
/*" Periodic update "*/
- (void)update;
```

Methods must be provided, so that the controller subsystem can query and modify the game state as the result of player actions.

```
/*" Game State "*/
- (void)reset;
- (BOOL)isRunning;
- (BOOL)isGameOver;
- (void)pause;
- (void)resume;
- (int)score;

/*" falling block "*/
- (MYBlock *)fallingBlock;
- (BOOL)fallingBlockCanFall;
- (void)moveFallingBlockLeft;
- (void)moveFallingBlockRight;
- (void)dropFallingBlock;
- (void)rotateFallingBlockClockwise;
- (void)rotateFallingBlockCounterclockwise;
```

The subblocks at specific grid positions are accessible so that other classes can detect collisions, and so that the model can be displayed.

```
/*" sub-block grid access "*/
- (MYSubBlock *)subBlockAtX:(int)column y:(int)row;

/*" Clean-up: "*/
- (void)dealloc;
```

The `MYGameModel` class must override its inherited `-dealloc` method to release the falling block and the subblocks stored in the game grid.

```
@end
```

TransparentTetris View

The view subsystem is implemented with one custom class, some categories on model classes, and the object instances stored in the application's `.nib` file. As usual with Cocoa applications, very little code is required for the view subsystem. The `MYBlockView` class has only five methods.

MYBlockView Class

Ideally, the view subsystem should not have dependencies on the model or controller subsystems. In this case, the MYBlockView class contains an instance variable to directly reference the model. The additional complexity required to limit model access strictly to the controller subsystem would defeat the purpose of the MVC architecture in this application. The goals of MVC should be applied in the following order of decreasing importance for Cocoa applications:

- Limit dependencies between the model and other subsystems
- Limit the complexity of the controller subsystem
- Limit the dependencies between the view and other subsystems

The primary justification for ordering the goals this way is the relative simplicity of view subsystems in Cocoa. Other development environments make the view subsystem so difficult and inflexible that almost any degree of complexity can be tolerated in the controller subsystem to simplify and isolate the view subsystem. Given Interface Builder, most changes to the view subsystem in Cocoa applications do not require any code. The controller subsystem of Cocoa applications, therefore, becomes the most prone to expensive code changes throughout the life of the application. To reduce the cost of the code changes, the controller subsystem should be kept as simple as possible, even at the expense of increased dependencies in the view subsystem.

There is no need to override the initializer inherited from the NSView class. No special initialization is required.

```
//
//  MYBlockView.h
//  TransparentTetris
//

#import <AppKit/AppKit.h>

@class MYGameModel;


@interface MYBlockView : NSView
{
  MYGameModel           *_myGameModel;    /*" Reference: model to display "*/
}
```

```
/*" Model access "*/
- (MYGameModel *)gameModel;
- (void)setGameModel:(MYGameModel *)aModel;

/*" Drawing configuration "*/
- (void)setBaseColor:(NSColor *)aColor;

/*" Drawing "*/
- (void)drawRect:(NSRect)aRect;

/*" Clean-up: "*/
- (void)dealloc;
@end
```

TransparentTetris Controller

The controller subsystem in TransparentTetris is implemented in just one class, `MYGameController`. The purpose of the controller is to accept actions from the user interface in the view subsystem and translate them into messages to the model. The controller must keep the information presented by the view consistent with the information stored in the model. The controller must, therefore, tell the view subsystem to redraw the game board, update the displayed score, and update the status of user interface elements such as menus to reflect the state of the model.

`MYGameController` Class

An instance of the `MYGameController` class is instantiated in Interface Builder, and set as the application object's delegate. Classes in the controller subsystem are commonly implemented as singletons, meaning that only one instance is ever allocated. The application's delegate is usually an object from the controller subsystem. For example, an instance of `NSDocumentController` can be the application's delegate in multidocument applications built using the Project Builder template provided by Apple, and there is only one instance of `NSDocumentController` in such applications.

The `MYGameController` class registers as an observer of several notifications that are sent by the classes in the model subsystem. When notifications are received, the controller plays sounds as required. `MYGameController` also manages user preferences for colors, and sounds.

In this design, the controller is responsible for the periodic update of the game. The controller must call the `-update` method of the `MYGameModel` class at regular intervals as long as the game is not over and not paused. The technique used to enable periodic updates is described in the implementation of this class.

The MYGameController class does not implement an initializer. Game state initialization is performed in the -applicationDidFinishLaunching: delegate method that is called automatically by the application object.

```
//
//  MYGameController.h
//  TransparentTetris
//

#import <Foundation/Foundation.h>
#import <AppKit/AppKit.h>

@class MYGameModel;
@class MYBlockView;
@class NSTextField;


@interface MYGameController : NSObject
{
  MYGameModel              *_myGameModel;          /*" model that stores game
                                                       board data "*/
  // Outlets
  IBOutlet MYBlockView     *_myBlockView;          /*" View: display model "*/
  IBOutlet NSImageView     *_myBackgroundView;     /*" View: display background
                                                       image "*/
  IBOutlet NSTextField     *_myScoreField;         /*" Field: display score "*/
  IBOutlet NSTextField     *_myGameOverField;      /*" Field: display
                                                       GAME OVER "*/
  IBOutlet NSButton        *_myEnableSoundButton;  /*" Button: enable sound "*/
  IBOutlet NSColorWell     *_mySubBlockColorWell;  /*" Color well: display/set
                                                       sub-block color "*/
}

/*" Actions "*/
- (IBAction)rotateCounterclockwise:(id)sender;
- (IBAction)rotateClockwise:(id)sender;
- (IBAction)moveLeft:(id)sender;
- (IBAction)moveRight:(id)sender;
- (IBAction)drop:(id)sender;
- (IBAction)togglePause:(id)sender;
- (IBAction)reset:(id)sender;
- (IBAction)takeSubBlockBaseColorFrom:(id)sender;
- (IBAction)takeSoundEnabledFrom:(id)sender;
```

```
/*" Application delegate methods "*/
- (void)applicationDidFinishLaunching:(NSNotification *)aNotification;
- (void)applicationDidBecomeActive:(NSNotification *)aNotification;
- (void)applicationDidResignActive:(NSNotification *)aNotification;

/*" Automatic menu validation "*/
- (BOOL)validateMenuItem:(NSMenuItem *)anItem;

/*" Clean-up: "*/
- (void)dealloc;

@end
```

The `-togglePause:` action method is used to implement a common idiom in Cocoa applications. A single menu item is connected to the `-togglePause:` action. Each time the action is sent, the pause state of the application is changed. The title of the menu item is changed to indicate the result of the next invocation of the action. When the game is running, the menu's title is Pause. When the game is paused, the same menu item's title is Resume. The title of the menu item is controlled by the automatic menu validation logic in the `-validateMenuItem:` method. Menu validation is described in Chapter 16, "Menus."

Implementing the Design

The design has defined the roles and public interfaces of the various classes in TransparentTetris. The implementation of each class is straightforward. In some cases, private methods and private categories are needed. Several idioms that are unique to Cocoa applications are described along with their uses in the implementations.

The user interface is built in Interface Builder. A `MYBlockView` instance is used to display the game board. An instance of the `MYGameController` class is instantiated in Interface Builder and made the application object's delegate. An instance of `NSImageView` is used to provide a background behind the game board, and made editable so that the user can set the background image via drag and drop at runtime. Text fields are used for the score and the "Game Over" indication. A utility panel with five buttons is used to enable the player to move the falling block left, move it right, rotate it clockwise, rotate it counterclockwise, and drop it.

The best way to understand the interface and the connections between the objects is to examine the application's `.nib` file in Interface Builder. One tool that is missing from the standard Cocoa tool set is an application to document the connections made in .nib files. At least one commercial tool was available for use with previous versions of Interface Builder, but it doesn't work with the latest versions.

MYSubBlock Class

The designated initializer for the MYSubBlock class is the - initX:y: method. The -init method inherited from the NSObject class is overridden to call -initX:y: with default arguments. Whenever the designated initializer for a class is different from the designated initializer of the superclass, the designated initializer of the superclass must be overridden to call the new designated initializer. The new designated initializer must call the superclass's designated initializer.

The most common Cocoa idiom for the introduction of a new designated initializer is used in the MySubBlock class. The new designated initializer contains a line of the form self = [super oldDesignetedInitializer]; MYSubBlock also overrides the inherited designated initializer to call the new designated initializer with a line similar to return [self newDesignatedInitializer];.

Assertions are used to verify that the arguments to the initializer are within acceptable constraints. If the condition in an assertion evaluates to NO, an NSAssertionFailed exception is raised with the exception's argument set to the textual description of the assertion expression.

```
//
//  MYSubBlock.m
//  TransparentTetris
//

#import "MYSubBlock.h"
#import "MYGameModel.h"


@implementation MYSubBlock
/*"
Each instance of this class represents either a sub-block that occupies a
position in the grid or a sub-block that is part of the falling block. Each
sub-block stores its position (either in the grid or in a falling block). A
sub-block's position is always stored in whole numbers so that its position
lines up with the sub-block grid or with the other sub-blocks in a falling
block.
"*/

- (id)initX:(int)x y:(int)y
/*"
```

```
  Designated initializer: Initializes the receiver with the specified
position.
"*/
{
  // Always call the super-class's designated initializer
  self = [super init];

  // Sanity check the position
  NSAssert(x >= 0 && x < MYGAME_GRID_WIDTH,
      @"Attempt to init sub-block outside grid");
  NSAssert(y >= 0 && y < MYGAME_GRID_HEIGHT,
      @"Attempt to init sub-block outside grid");

  // Set the position
  myXPosition = x;
  myYPosition = y;

  return self;
}


- (id)init
/*" Implemented to return [self initX:0 y:0] "*/
{
  return [self initX:0 y:0];
}


// Accessors
- (int)xPosition
/*" Returns the receiver's X position "*/
{
  return _myXPosition;
}

- (int)yPosition
/*" Returns the receiver's Y position "*/
{
  return _myYPosition;
}
```

```
- (void)setXPosition:(int)x
/*" Sets the receiver's X position "*/
{
  _myXPosition = x;
}


- (void)setYPosition:(int)y
/*" Sets the receiver's Y position "*/
{
  _myYPosition = y;
}

@end
```

MYBlock Class

The requirements state that within falling blocks several different patterns of subblocks must be available. The available patterns of subblocks are defined as static data in the implementation. The patterns could have been stored in a data file for more flexibility, but the extra flexibility is not needed for this application. From a design and implementation standpoint, any time more than a few lines of static data are declared, consider using a data file instead.

The required random selection of a pattern from the set of available patterns is incorporated in the designated initializer.

Requirements 5, 6, and 8 are satisfied by this class. This class assists the MYGameModel class satisfaction of requirements 9, 10, 11, and 12.

```
//
//  MYBlock.m
//  TransparentTetris
//

#import "MYBlock.h"
#import "MYSubBlock.h"
#import "MYGameModel.h"

/*" The number of block shapes (patterns) defined for the game "*/
#define _MYNUM_BLOCK_SHAPES (7)
```

```
@implementation MYBlock
/*"
Instances of this class encapsulate the falling block in the game. A block
consists of some number of sub-blocks arranged in a pattern. The block can be
moved side to side as it falls. The block can also be rotated in increments of
90 degrees. Side to side motion and rotation are animated smoothly using a
simple low-pass filter. When a block is moved or rotated, its new target
position and rotation are stored. Each time a block is updated, it's position
and rotation are adjusted half the distance toward the target values. The
visual effect is that the block slides left or right and rotates smoothly
rather than jumping between integral positions in the sub-block grid. Call
-fallDelta:inModel: to move the block down and simulate falling. The speed at
which the block falls is determined by the delta argument to
-fallDelta:inModel:.

Notifications Posted:

MYBLOCK_DID_SLIDE_NOTIFICATION   : Sent when block slides left or right.
                                         ARGUMENT: The block that is sliding.

     MYBLOCK_DID_ROTATE_NOTIFICATION  : Sent whenever a block rotates.
                                         ARGUMENT: The block that rotated.

"*/


/*" Type used to store flags that indicate which sub-blocks are used by a
block shape (pattern) "*/
typedef struct {
  BOOL    subBlockIsPresent[MYNUM_SUBBLOCKS_IN_BLOCK][MYNUM_SUBBLOCKS_IN_BLOCK];
} _MYBlockShapeData;
```

Figure 26.2 shows the block patterns defined by the following data.

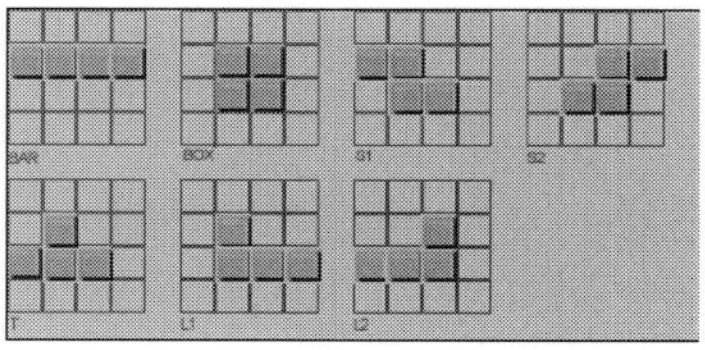

FIGURE 26.2 The blocks in TransparentTetris have these patterns.

```
/*" Defines the available block shapes (patterns) "*/
static _MYBlockShapeData    myBlockShapes[_MYNUM_BLOCK_SHAPES] = {
{{{NO, NO, NO, NO},           // Bar shape
 {YES, YES, YES, YES},
 {NO, NO, NO, NO},
 {NO, NO, NO, NO}}},
{{{NO, NO, NO, NO},           // Square shape
 {NO, YES, YES, NO},
 {NO, YES, YES, NO},
 {NO, NO, NO, NO}}},
{{{NO, NO, NO, NO},           // S Shape 1
 {YES, YES, NO, NO},
 {NO, YES, YES, NO},
 {NO, NO, NO, NO}}},
{{{NO, NO, NO, NO},           // S Shape 2
 {NO, NO, YES, YES},
 {NO, YES, YES, NO},
 {NO, NO, NO, NO}}},
{{{NO, NO, NO, NO},           // T Shape
 {NO, YES, NO, NO},
 {YES, YES, YES, NO},
 {NO, NO, NO, NO}}},
{{{NO, NO, NO, NO}            // L Shape 1
 {NO, YES, NO, NO},
 {NO, YES, YES, YES},
 {NO, NO, NO, NO}}},
{{{NO, NO, NO, NO},           // L Shape 2
 {NO, NO, YES, NO},
 {YES, YES, YES, NO},
 {NO, NO, NO, NO}}}};

- (id)init
/*" Designated initializer: Initializes the receiver with a randomly selected
shape (pattern) "*/
{
  int                            i, j;
  int                            numberOfSubBlocksFound = 0;
  const _MYBlockShapeData        *selectedBlockShape;

  // Always call the designated initializer of the super-class
  self = [super init];
```

```
  // Randomly select one of the pre-defined shapes
  selectedBlockShape = &myBlockShapes[random() % _MYNUM_BLOCK_SHAPES];

  // Set the initial actual and target position and rotation
  myPosition = _myTargetPosition = NSZeroPoint;
  myRotationDegrees = _myTargetRotationDegrees = 0.0;

  // Create the sub-blocks according to the selected shape
  for(j = 0; j < MYNUM_SUBBLOCKS_IN_BLOCK; j++) {
    for(i = 0; i < MYNUM_SUBBLOCKS_IN_BLOCK; i++) {
      if(selectedBlockShape->subBlockIsPresent[i][j]) {
        // We should not find more sub-blocks than we can store!
        NSAssert(numberOfSubBlocksFound < MYNUM_SUBBLOCKS_IN_BLOCK,
            @"Too many sub blocks in block shape definition");

        // Allocate, initialize, and store a new sub-block
        _mySubBlocks[numberOfSubBlocksFound] = [[MYSubBlock alloc] initX:i
                                                                  y:j];
        numberOfSubBlocksFound++;
      }
    }
  }

  return self;
}
```

The falling block must send an `-update` message periodically so that the low pass filter logic can be applied. In this design, an instance of the `MYGameModel` class is responsible for calling the falling block's `-update` method.

```
// Update
- (void)update
/*"
    Call this method periodically. This method adjusts the receiver's
position and rotation half the distance toward the target values. The
effect is that the block slides left or right and rotates smoothly rather
than jumping between integral positions in the sub-block grid.

"*/
{
  if(!NSEqualPoints(_myPosition, _myTargetPosition)) {
    // Move the position half the distance to target position
```

```
    _myPosition.x += (_myTargetPosition.x - _myPosition.x) / 2.0;
    _myPosition.y += (_myTargetPosition.y - _myPosition.y) / 2.0;
  }

  if(_myRotationDegrees != _myTargetRotationDegrees) {
    // Rotate half the angular distance to target angle
    float          deltaAngle = (_myTargetRotationDegrees - _myRotationDegrees);

    // Limit the delta to range (180 to 180) so that direction of rotation is
    // preserved even across zero boundaries
    // There are always two angular distances (clockwise or counterclockwise)
    // to any target angle. This code makes sure that the shorter angular
    // distance is used.
    if(deltaAngle > 180.0) {
      deltaAngle -= 360.0;
    } else if(deltaAngle < -180.0) {
      deltaAngle += 360.0;
    }

    // Adjust the angle half the angular distance to the target angle
    _myRotationDegrees += deltaAngle / 2.0;

    // Limit to (-180 to 180) so comparisons to _myTargetRotationDegrees
    // will work.
    // Adding deltas can cause the angle to be less than -180 or greater
    // than +180 degrees. We convert the angle to its equivalent in the
    // (-180 to 180) range so that comparisons for equality will be
    // simpler.

    if(_myRotationDegrees > 180.0) {
     _ myRotationDegrees -= 360.0;
    } else if(_myRotationDegrees < -180.0) {
      _myRotationDegrees += 360.0;
    }
  }
}
```

Setting the position of a block also sets the target position. Otherwise, each update after the position is set will change the block's position until it equals the target position. By setting both the position and the target position, the block can be moved and it will stay at its new position until moved again or until the target position is set independently.

```
// Positioning
- (void)setPosition:(NSPoint)aPosition
/*"
Set the receiver's position on a unit grid. Fractional values in aPosition
specify fractional offsets from integral grid alignment. Supporting fractional
offsets makes the smooth motion possible.

"*/
{
  _myPosition = aPosition;
  _myTargetPosition = aPosition;
}


- (NSPoint)position
/*" Returns the receiver's position "*/
{
  return _myPosition;
}
```

When a block stops falling, the subblocks contained in the block must be placed in the game grid. The conversion from a position in the falling block to a position in the game grid is implemented here. The falling block's position, pattern, and rotation are the inputs to the algorithm for converting positions. Because all the inputs to the algorithm are available within the `MYBlock` class, the `MYBlock` class is a natural place to put the algorithm. Alternatively, the algorithm could be implemented in the `MYGameModel` class, and use the available accessors of the `MYBlock` class to obtain the inputs to the algorithm.

```
- (void)_myConvertPositionX:(int *)xPtr y:(int *)yPtr forAngle:(float)degrees
/*"
     Returns by reference in xPtr and yPtr the approximate integral positions
for a sub-block that is rotated degrees  within the receiver. Use this method
to calculate the integral position at which a sub-block at (*xPtr, *yPtr)
within the receiver would be placed within the sub-blocks grid.

"*/
{
  float     positiveDegrees = fmod(degrees + 360.0, 360.0); // constrain to
                                                             // positive degrees
                                                             // for simplicity
```

```
  int       resultX;            // value to be returend
  int       resultY;            // value to be returned

  NSAssert(NULL != xPtr && NULL != yPtr, @"Invalid argument");

  if(positiveDegrees > 270.0 + 45.0 || positiveDegrees < 45.0) {
    // heading for 0 degrees so result position is same as position passed in
    resultX = *xPtr;
    resultY = *yPtr;

  } else if(positiveDegrees > 180.0 + 45.0) {
    // heading for 270 degrees so invert x and swap x and y
    resultY = (MYNUM_SUBBLOCKS_IN_BLOCK - 1) - *xPtr;
    resultX = *yPtr;

  } else if(positiveDegrees > 90.0 + 45.0) {
    // heading for 180 degrees so invert x and y
    resultX = (MYNUM_SUBBLOCKS_IN_BLOCK - 1) - *xPtr;
    resultY = (MYNUM_SUBBLOCKS_IN_BLOCK - 1) - *yPtr;
  } else {
    // heading for 90 degrees so invert y and swap x and y
    resultY = *xPtr;
    resultX = (MYNUM_SUBBLOCKS_IN_BLOCK - 1) - *yPtr;
  }

  // Return the results by reference
  *xPtr = resultX;
  *yPtr = resultY;
}


- (void)convertSubBlocksToGrid
/*"
    Converts the positions of all sub-block of the receiver to integral
grid aligned coordinates. After calling this method, the sub-blocks of
the receiver can be placed directly in the sub-block grid. Do not call
-update or -fall:inModel: after calling this method because the sub-block's
positions will have been altered in a way that will make -update or
-fall:inModel: work incorrectly!
```

```
"*/
{
  int              i;

  // For each sub-block
  for(i = 0; i < MYNUM_SUBBLOCKS_IN_BLOCK; i++) {
    MYSubBlock          *tempSubBlock = [self subBlockAtIndex:i];
    int                 subBlockPositionX = [tempSubBlock xPosition];
    int                 subBlockPositionY = [tempSubBlock yPosition];
    int                 gridPositionX;
    int                 gridPositionY;

    // Convert sub-block position by accounting for block's rotation
    [self _myConvertPositionX:&subBlockPositionX y:&subBlockPositionY
        forAngle:_myTargetRotationDegrees];

    // Offset the position based on the block's position
    gridPositionX = subBlockPositionX + _myTargetPosition.x - MYBLOCK_PIVOT_X;
    gridPositionY = subBlockPositionY + _myTargetPosition.y - MYBLOCK_PIVOT_Y;

    // grid pos may be outside game grid if block has not completely
    // fallen into the game board
    [tempSubBlock setXPosition:gridPositionX];
    [tempSubBlock setYPosition:gridPositionY];
  }
}
```

The `MYBlock` class determines whether it can occupy a particular position in the game grid. This private method is used internally to validate requests to set the block's target position and rotation. In Objective-C, no method is truly private. The Objective-C runtime allows messages to any method in any loaded class from any context. To indicate that a method is private and should not be used except by the maintainers of the method, start the method name with an underscore and a unique prefix. Don't declare private methods in the class interface. When using a class, respect other developers' clear intentions for methods. Don't call methods that are not declared in the interface of a class or one of its superclasses. Don't call or override methods that begin with an underscore unless absolutely necessary.

```
- (BOOL)_myCanOccupyPositionInModel:(MYGameModel *)aModel x:(int)x y:(int)y
    withRotation:(float)degrees
/*"
```

```
  Returns YES iff the falling block could occupy the integral grid-aligned
position specified without any sub-blocks hanging outside the sub-block grid
and without overlapping any existing sub-blocks in the sub-block grid.

*/
{
  int               i;
  BOOL              result = YES;

  for(i = 0; i < MYNUM_SUBBLOCKS_IN_BLOCK && result; i++) {
    MYSubBlock       *tempSubBlock = [self subBlockAtIndex:i];
    int              subBlockPositionX = [tempSubBlock xPosition];
    int              subBlockPositionY = [tempSubBlock yPosition];
    int              gridPositionX;
    int              gridPositionY;

    [self _myConvertPositionX:&subBlockPositionX y:&subBlockPositionY
        forAngle:degrees];

    gridPositionX = subBlockPositionX + x - MYBLOCK_PIVOT_X;
    gridPositionY = subBlockPositionY + y - MYBLOCK_PIVOT_Y;

    if(gridPositionX < 0 || gridPositionX >= MYGAME_GRID_WIDTH) {
      // Position is outside grid
      result = NO;

    } else if(gridPositionY < 0) {           // Don't check > MYGAME_GRID_
                  // HEIGHT because we want block to fall in
      // Position is outside grid
      result = NO;
    } else if(nil != [aModel subBlockAtX:gridPositionX y:gridPositionY]) {
      // Position is occupied
      result = NO;
    }
  }

  return result;
}


- (BOOL)canFallDelta:(float)aDelta inModel:(MYGameModel *)aModel
/*"
```

```
     Returns YES iff the receiver can occupy the position in the sub-block grid
that would result from lowering the receiver's position by aDelta.

"*/
{
  return ([self _myCanOccupyPositionInModel:aModel x:(_myTargetPosition.x)
      y:(_myTargetPosition.y - aDelta) withRotation:_myTargetRotationDegrees]);
}
```

The -fallDelta:inModel: method must be called periodically. Both the target position and the actual position are modified by the same delta, so that the low-pass filtering is not applied to falling. If only the target position was set, the block would seem to speed up and slow down as it approached its target height. Falling only applies to the vertical component of the block's position.

```
- (void)fallDelta:(float)delta inModel:(MYGameModel *)aModel
/*"
     If the receiver can occupy the position in the sub-block grid that
would result from lowering the receiver's position by aDelta this method
lowers the receiver's position and target position by delta. Otherwise
this method does nothing.

"*/
{
  if([self canFallDelta:delta inModel:aModel]) {

    _myPosition.y -= delta;
    _myTargetPosition.y -= delta;
  }
}
```

In each of the movement methods, if the commanded movement or rotation can occur without causing the block to leave the game grid or overlap subblocks in the game grid, then the target position or rotation are modified appropriately. Target rotation values are stored in the range –180°–+180°, so that angles can be easily compared and so the direction of the difference between two angles is known. In the default-coordinate system used by Cocoa applications, positive angular differences indicate counterclockwise rotation, whereas negative differences imply clockwise rotation. For example, if angles were stored in the common 0°–360° Range when the block was rotated –90°from 0, the target angle would be 270°. However, when the target angle and the actual angle are compared, the difference is +270, indicating counterclockwise rotation when in fact the block was rotated –90° (clockwise). The angle 270° and the angle –90° are identical except for the sign. Storing angles in the range –180°–180° preserves the sign, and hence the direction of rotation in a way that the range 0°–360° does not.

```
- (void)moveTargetPositionLeftInModel:(MYGameModel *)aModel
/*"
     If the receiver can occupy the position in the sub-block grid that
would result from sliding the receiver's position left by one integral
position then this method moves the receiver's target position one integral
position left and sends the MYBLOCK_DID_SLIDE_NOTIFICATION notification to
the default notification center. Otherwise this method does nothing.

"*/
{
  if([self _myCanOccupyPositionInModel:aModel x:(_myTargetPosition.x - 1.0)
      y:_myTargetPosition.y withRotation:_myTargetRotationDegrees]) {

    _myTargetPosition.x -= 1.0;

    [[NSNotificationCenter defaultCenter]
        postNotificationName:MYBLOCK_DID_SLIDE_NOTIFICATION object:self];
  }
}


- (void)moveTargetPositionRightInModel:(MYGameModel *)aModel
/*"
     If the receiver can occupy the position in the sub-block grid that would
result from sliding the receiver's position right by one integral position then
this method moves the receiver's target position one integral position right
and sends the MYBLOCK_DID_SLIDE_NOTIFICATION notification to the default
notification center. Otherwise this method does nothing.
"*/
{
  if([self _myCanOccupyPositionInModel:aModel x:(_myTargetPosition.x + 1.0)
      y:_myTargetPosition.y withRotation:_myTargetRotationDegrees]) {

    _myTargetPosition.x += 1.0;
```

```
    [[NSNotificationCenter defaultCenter]
        postNotificationName:MYBLOCK_DID_SLIDE_NOTIFICATION object:self];
  }
}


- (void)moveTargetRotationClockwiseInModel:(MYGameModel *)aModel
/*"
     If the receiver can occupy the position in the sub-block grid that would
result from rotating the receiver clockwise by 90 degrees then this method
moves the receiver's target rotation by 90 degrees clockwise and sends the
MYBLOCK_DID_ROTATE_NOTIFICATION notification to the default notification
center. Otherwise this method does nothing.

"*/
{
  float         proposedTargetAngle = _myTargetRotationDegrees -90.0;

  // Limit to range (-180 to 180)
  if(proposedTargetAngle < -180.0) {
    proposedTargetAngle += 360.0;
  }

  if([self _myCanOccupyPositionInModel:aModel x:_myTargetPosition.x
      y:_myTargetPosition.y withRotation:proposedTargetAngle]) {

    _myTargetRotationDegrees = proposedTargetAngle;

    [[NSNotificationCenter defaultCenter]
        postNotificationName:MYBLOCK_DID_ROTATE_NOTIFICATION object:self];
  }
}


- (void)moveTargetRotationCounterclockwiseInModel:(MYGameModel *)aModel
/*"
     If the receiver can occupy the position in the sub-block grid that would
result from rotating the receiver counterclockwise by 90 degrees then this
method moves the receiver's target rotation by 90 degrees counterclockwise and
sends the MYBLOCK_DID_ROTATE_NOTIFICATION notification to the default
notification center. Otherwise this method does nothing.
```

```
"*/
{
  float        proposedTargetAngle = _myTargetRotationDegrees + 90.0;

  // Limit to range (-180 to 180)
  if(proposedTargetAngle > 180.0) {
    proposedTargetAngle -= 360.0;
  }

  if([self _myCanOccupyPositionInModel:aModel x:_myTargetPosition.x
      y:_myTargetPosition.y withRotation:proposedTargetAngle]) {

    _myTargetRotationDegrees = proposedTargetAngle;

    [[NSNotificationCenter defaultCenter]
        postNotificationName:MYBLOCK_DID_ROTATE_NOTIFICATION object:self];
  }
}


// Sub-block access
- (MYSubBlock *)subBlockAtIndex:(int)anIndex
/*"
     Returns indexed sub-block of receiver.
anIndex must be >= 0 and < MYNUM_SUBBLOCKS_IN_BLOCK.

"*/
{
  NSAssert(anIndex >= 0 && anIndex < MYNUM_SUBBLOCKS_IN_BLOCK,
      @"Invalid sub-block index");

  return _mySubBlocks[anIndex];
}
```

The subblocks retained by an instance of `MYBlock` must be released in `-dealloc`. If the subblocks have been retained in the game grid they will not be deallocated here.

```
- (void)dealloc
/*" Clean-up: Releases the receiver's sub-blocks. "*/
{
  int              i;
```

```
  for(i = 0; i < MYNUM_SUBBLOCKS_IN_BLOCK; i++) {
    [_mySubBlocks[i] release];
    _mySubBlocks[i] = nil;
  }

  [super dealloc];
}

@end
```

MYGameModel Class

Most of the logic of the game is implemented in this class. The implementation is fairly long in printed form and contains several private methods, but it is straightforward. The controller accesses the model by calling the methods of this class.

This class directly or indirectly implements the following requirements:

- Stores the game board, which consists of a rectangular grid that stores subblocks. [Requirements 1, 2]
- Initializes the grid so that no subblocks are stored in the grid when the game starts. [Requirement 3]
- Creates and stores the falling block making sure that exactly one falling block exists at all times. [Requirement 4]
- Is implemented to cause the falling block to fall during game updates. [Requirement 7]
- Provides methods that move the falling block's target position left or right. [Requirement 9]
- Provides methods that change the falling block's target rotation in increments of 90°. [Requirement 10]
- Detects when the falling block must stop falling, stops it, and adds subblocks to the grid. [Requirements 11, 12]
- Stores the score, removes complete rows of subblocks in the grid, increases the score, and moves subblocks above removed rows down. [Requirements 13, 14, 15]
- Removes the falling block when it has stopped falling, creates a new falling block with a randomly selected pattern, places the new falling block at the top of the game grid, increases the distance that the falling block falls during each update of the game, and causes the block to fall. [Requirements 16, 17, 18]

- Stores the game over status, detects when a new falling block at the top of the game grid cannot fall without overlapping one or more subblocks already in the grid, and sets the game over status. [Requirement 19]
- Stores sufficient game state so that a game can be paused and resumed. [Requirements 22, 23]

The following code implements the `MYGameModel` class defined in the TransparentTetris design.

```
//
//  MYGameModel.m
//  TransparentTetris
//

#import "MYGameModel.h"
#import "MYSubBlock.h"
#import "MYBlock.h"
```

Arbitrary constants are used to control the game difficulty and scoring logic. Try different constants to see their impact on game play.

```
#define _MYINITIAL_FALL_DELTA (0.1)      /*" Relatively slow (game easy) "*/
#define _MYMAX_FALL_DELTA (1.0)          /*" Very Fast (game hard) "*/
#define _MYFALL_DELTA_INCREASE_PER_BLOCK (0.005)  /*" Reach maximum speed
                                                  after 200 blocks "*/
#define _MYINITIAL_SCORE_MULTIPLIER (10) /*" Initial number of point for each
                                                  sub-block removed "*/
#define _MYSCRORE_MULTIPLIER_DELTA_PER_ROW (10)  /*" Additional points for each
                                                  sub-block in consecutive removed
                                                  rows "*/
```

The format of the comments results in attractive documentation generated by the AutoDoc application. Two or more blank lines in the comments are necessary to persuade AutoDoc to leave a blank line in the documentation. AutoDoc removes individual blank lines.

```
@implementation MYGameModel
/*"
In the model/view/controller (MVC) architecture, this class is the principal
component of the model. The majority of the application's state and data
structures are encapsulated by this class. The model is self contained. It
```

```
does not have any dependencies on code that is not part of the model such as
classes that are part of the view or controller portions of the application.
The firm separation between the model and the view/control portions of an
application can have dramatic positive influences on an application's design,
implementation, and maintainability. Ideally, the same model can be used with
any number of different views.

This class sends several notifications in order to inform the view and/or
controller portions of the application that something important has happened.
The other portions of the application can observe the notifications and act
appropriately when they are received. For instance, the controller might play
a sound when a row is removed from the sub-block grid.

Notifications Posted:

     MYROW_WAS_REMOVED_NOTIFICATION  : Sent after a row is removed.
                             ARGUMENT: NSNumber of removed row number

     MYSUBBLOCK_WILL_BE_REMOVED_NOTIFICATION : Sent before sub-block removed.
                                     ARGUMENT: The block that was removed.

     MYSBLOCK_WAS_PLACED_IN_GRID_NOTIFICATION : Sent after placed in grid.
                                      ARGUMENT: nil

"*/

// Initializer
- (id)init
/*" Designated initializer: Calls [self reset] to initialize game state. "*/
{
  // Always call super-class's designated initializer
  self = [super init];

  // Reset the game state
  [self reset];

  return self;
}


- (void)pause
/*" Pause the game  "*/
```

```
{
  _myIsRunning = NO;
}


- (void)resume
/*" Resume the game "*/
{
  if(!_myIsGameOver) {

    _myIsRunning = YES;
  }
}


- (float)_myMaximumFallDeltaPerUpdate
/*" Returns maximum distance that falling block can fall in one update "*/
{
  return _MYMAX_FALL_DELTA;
}


- (float)_myFallDeltaPerUpdate
/*"
     Returns the distance that the falling block should fall during the
current update. The distance gradually increases as the game is played
to make the game get harder and harder. If the -dropFallingBlock method
has been called since the current falling block was created then the
distance returned is the maximum distance that the falling block can fall
in one update.

"*/
{
  float        result = _myCurrentFallDelta;  // Use current distance by default

  if(_myIsDropping) {
    // return the maximum distance
    result = [self _myMaximumFallDeltaPerUpdate];
  }

  return result;
}
```

```
- (void)_mySetSubBlock:(MYSubBlock *)aBlock atX:(int)x y:(int)y
/*"
     Set the sub-block at the specified position in the sub-block grid.
"*/
{
  // Sanity check the specified position
  NSAssert(x >= 0 && x < MYGAME_GRID_WIDTH, @"Set sub-block outside grid");
  NSAssert(y >= 0 && y < MYGAME_GRID_HEIGHT,
      @"Attempt to set sub-block outside grid");

  // Normal "set" accessor idiom
  [aBlock retain];
  [_mySubBlockGrid[y][x] release];
  _mySubBlockGrid[y][x] = aBlock;

  // Make the sub-block's stored position consistent with its actual position
  [aBlock setXPosition:x];  // make sure the sub block knows its position
  [aBlock setYPosition:y];  // make sure the sub block knows its position
}


- (void)_myPlaceFallingBlock
/*"
     This method is called when the falling block can no longer fall. This
method places the sub-blocks that compose the falling block into the sub-block
grid. Sends the MYSBLOCK_WAS_PLACED_IN_GRID_NOTIFICATION with a nil argument.
Observers of the notification might draw special effects or play a sound to
highlight this event.

"*/
{
  int         i;

  // Force falling block to convert all of its sub-block positions into the
  // sub-block grid's coordinate system. Assures correct placement of
  // sub-blocks in a rotated falling block.
  [_myFallingBlock convertSubBlocksToGrid];

  // Place each sub-block in the falling block into the sub-block grid
  for(i = 0; i < MYNUM_SUBBLOCKS_IN_BLOCK; i++) {
```

```
    MYSubBlock       *tempSubBlock = [_myFallingBlock subBlockAtIndex:i];
    int              gridPositionX;
    int              gridPositionY;

    gridPositionX = [tempSubBlock xPosition]; // provides grid position after
                                              // call -convertSubBlocksToGrid
    gridPositionY = [tempSubBlock yPosition]; // provides grid position after
                                              // call -convertSubBlocksToGrid

    if(gridPositionX < 0 || gridPositionX >= MYGAME_GRID_WIDTH) {
      // Error: Position is outside grid

    } else if(gridPositionY < 0 || gridPositionY >= MYGAME_GRID_HEIGHT) {
      // Error: Position is outside grid

    } else if(nil != [self subBlockAtX:gridPositionX y:gridPositionY]) {
      // Error: Position is occupied

    } else {
      // Place the sub-block in the sub-block grid
      [self _mySetSubBlock:tempSubBlock atX:gridPositionX y:gridPositionY];
    }
  }

  // Send notification
  [[NSNotificationCenter defaultCenter] postNotificationName:
      MYSBLOCK_WAS_PLACED_IN_GRID_NOTIFICATION object:nil];
}


- (void)_myGenerateRandomFallingBlockAtPosition:(NSPoint)aPoint
/*"
     Releases the current falling block and allocates a new falling block
positioned at aPoint in game board coordinates.

"*/
{
  [_myFallingBlock release];                  // Release current falling block
  _myFallingBlock = [[MYBlock alloc] init];  // Allocate/init new falling block
```

```
  [_myFallingBlock setPosition:aPoint];      // Set new falling block's pos
  _myIsDropping = NO;                        // Reset flag so new block
                                             // will fall slowly
}


- (BOOL)_myRemoveAndScoreCompleteRowsWithMultiplyer:(int)scoreMultiplyer
/*"
     This method is called when a falling block can no longer fall. This
method searches the sub-block grid for a complete row of sub-blocks. If a
complete row is found, the sub-blocks in that row are removed from the
sub-block grid. Each time a sub-block is removed, the MYSUBBLOCK_WILL_BE_
REMOVED_NOTIFICATION notification is sent to the default notification center.
The argument to the notification is an NSValue containing an NSPoint that
identifies the x,y position of the sub-block that is about to be removed from
the sub-block grid. Observers of the notification may draw special effects or
play a sound for each block removed. After the row of sub-block is removed,
the rows above the removed row are moves down to fill in the empty row.
Finally, the score is increased by (MYGAME_GRID_WIDTH * scoreMultiplyer).

     If a row is removed by this method, this method returns YES. Otherwise
it returns NO. At most one row will be removed each time this method is
called. Therefore, this method should be called repeatedly in a loop until
it returns NO indicating that there are no more complete rows to remove.
Each time this method is called in the loop, the scoreMultiplyer can be
increase so that removing multiple rows increases the score.

"*/
{
  int                 i, j;                 // Loop index
  BOOL                foundFullRow = NO;    // YES iff a full row is found

  // Search bottom to top for full row of sub-blocks in the sub-block grid
  for(j = 0; j < MYGAME_GRID_HEIGHT && !foundFullRow; j++) {
    int           numSubBlocksInRow = 0;    // Num sub-blocks found so far

    // Search for sub-blocks in the row
    for(i = 0; i < MYGAME_GRID_WIDTH; i++) {
      if(nil != [self subBlockAtX:i y:j]) {
```

```
          numSubBlocksInRow++;
        }
      }
      foundFullRow = (numSubBlocksInRow == MYGAME_GRID_WIDTH);

      if(foundFullRow) {
        // A complete row of sub-blocks was found

        // Remove each sub-block in the row
        for(i = 0; i < MYGAME_GRID_WIDTH; i++) {
          // Notify any observers that a sub-block will be removed
          [[NSNotificationCenter defaultCenter] postNotificationName:
              MYSUBBLOCK_WILL_BE_REMOVED_NOTIFICATION object:
              [NSValue valueWithPoint:NSMakePoint(i, j)]];

          // Remove the sub-block
          [self _mySetSubBlock:nil atX:i y:j];
        }

        // Copy all of the rows above the removed row down
        for(; j < (MYGAME_GRID_HEIGHT - 1); j++) {
          for(i = 0; i < MYGAME_GRID_WIDTH; i++) {
            [self _mySetSubBlock:[self subBlockAtX:i y:j+1] atX:i y:j];
            [self _mySetSubBlock:nil atX:i y:j+1]             }
        }

        // Increase the score
        _myScore += (MYGAME_GRID_WIDTH * scoreMultiplyer);
      }
    }

    return foundFullRow;
  }


  - (BOOL)isRunning
  /*"
      Returns YES iff the game is NOT paused.
  "*/
  {
    return _myIsRunning;
  }
```

```
- (BOOL)isGameOver
/*"
     Returns YES iff the game is not over. The game is over when a newly
created falling block can not fall because the sub-block grid is too full.

"*/
{
  return _myIsGameOver;
}


- (void)reset
/*"
     Removes all sub-blocks in the sub-block grid. Releases the current
falling block if any. Sets the score to zero. Sets the current fall delta
to its initial default value (slow), and sets the game over flag to NO.

"*/
{
  int           i, j;

  // Clear out sub-block grid
  for(j = 0; j < MYGAME_GRID_HEIGHT; j++) {
    for(i = 0; i < MYGAME_GRID_WIDTH; i++) {
      [self _mySetSubBlock:nil atX:i y:j];    // Releases any blocks in grid
    }
  }

  // forget falling block
  [_myFallingBlock release];
  _myFallingBlock = nil;

  // reset score, falling delta, and game over state
  _myScore = 0;
  _myCurrentFallDelta = _MYINITIAL_FALL_DELTA;
  _myIsGameOver = NO;
}


- (int)score
/*"
     Returns the current score.
```

```
"*/
{
  return _myScore;
}
```

In this design, the MYGameController class calls the -update method at regular time intervals. The -update method in turn calls the -update method of the falling block.

```
- (void)update
/*"
     Call this method at regular intervals. This method implements the
TransparentTetris game update logic. If the current falling block can not
fall without leaving the game board or colliding with sub-blocks in the
sub-block grid then the component sub-blocks of the falling block are
removed and placed in the sub-block grid. Then any complete rows are removed
and the score is increased appropriately. Each time a row is removed, the
 MYROW_WAS_REMOVED_NOTIFICATION notification with an NSNumber argument that
identifies the row number removed is posted to the default notification
center. Then a new falling block is created at the top center of the game
board. If the new falling block can not fall then the game is over.

In all cases, the current falling block is told to fall and update so that
smooth motion in the sub-block grid can be simulated.

"*/
{
  if(![self fallingBlockCanFall]) {
    int         scoreMultiplyer;          // Increase score when multiple
                                          // rows are removed at once
    int         numberOfRowsRemoved = 0; // The falling block is done falling!

    [self _myPlaceFallingBlock];          // Add sub-block of falling block to
                                          // the sub-block grid

    // Score and remove rows that are complete after falling block placed
    // in the grid
    for(scoreMultiplyer = _MYINITIAL_SCORE_MULTIPLIER; [self
        _myRemoveAndScoreCompleteRowsWithMultiplyer:scoreMultiplyer];
        scoreMultiplyer += _MYSCRORE_MULTIPLIER_DELTA_PER_ROW) {
```

```
      numberOfRowsRemoved++;

      [[NSNotificationCenter defaultCenter] postNotificationName:
          MYROW_WAS_REMOVED_NOTIFICATION object:
          [NSNumber numberWithInt:numberOfRowsRemoved]];
    }

    // Start a new random block at the center top
    [self _myGenerateRandomFallingBlockAtPosition:
        NSMakePoint(MYGAME_GRID_WIDTH / 2, MYGAME_GRID_HEIGHT)];

    // If the falling block that was just placed at the top of the grid
    // can not fall then the game is over
    _myIsGameOver = ![self fallingBlockCanFall];
  }

  // Make the falling block fall if possible. -_myFallDeltaPerUpdate returns
  // increasing values as the game progresses causing the falling blocks to
  // fall faster and faster making the game harder and harder
  [_myFallingBlock fall:[self _myFallDeltaPerUpdate] inModel:self];  // Fall

  // Give the falling block a chance to rotate and move side to side
  [_myFallingBlock update];
}


- (MYSubBlock *)subBlockAtX:(int)column y:(int)row
/*"
    Returns the sub-block if any at the specified position in the sub-block
grid.

"*/
{
  MYSubBlock          *result = nil;

  if(column >= 0 && column < MYGAME_GRID_WIDTH && row >= 0 &&
      row < MYGAME_GRID_HEIGHT) {

    result = _mySubBlockGrid[row][column];
  }
```

```
  return result;
}


- (MYBlock *)fallingBlock
/*"
    Returns the current falling block if any.

"*/
{
  return _myFallingBlock;
}


- (BOOL)fallingBlockCanFall
/*"
    Returns YES if the current falling block can fall without leaving the
game board or colliding with an existing sub-block in the sub-block grid.

"*/
{
  return (_myFallingBlock != nil && [_myFallingBlock canFallDelta:
      [self _myFallDeltaPerUpdate] inModel:self]);
}


- (void)moveFallingBlockLeft
/*"
    Moves the current falling block's target position to the left. The
falling block will progressively move toward its target position on successive
updates creating smooth animation.

"*/
{
  [_myFallingBlock moveTargetPositionLeftInModel:self];
}


- (void)moveFallingBlockRight
/*"
```

```
     Moves the current falling block's target position to the right. The
falling block will progressively move toward its target position on
successive updates creating smooth animation.

"*/
{
  [_myFallingBlock moveTargetPositionRightInModel:self];
}


- (void)dropFallingBlock
/*"
     This method sets a flag that causes the falling block to fall as fast as
possible until it can not fall without leaving the game board or colliding
with an existing sub-block in the sub-block grid. This method also increases
the score by the height of the falling block when this method is called in
order to reward the player for dropping it. When the next falling block is
generated, the flag that causes blocks to fall as fast as possible is reset
so that the new block will fall as a more sedate rate.

"*/
{
  _myIsDropping = YES;

  // Increase score proportional to height at which drop starts
  _myScore += (int)[_myFallingBlock position].y;
}


- (void)rotateFallingBlockClockwise
/*"
     Moves the current falling block's target rotation angle 90 degrees
clockwise. The falling block will progressively rotate toward its target
rotation angle on successive updates creating smooth animation.

"*/
{
  [_myFallingBlock moveTargetRotationClockwiseInModel:self];
}
```

```
- (void)rotateFallingBlockCounterclockwise
/*"
     Moves the current falling block's target rotation angle 90 degrees
counterclockwise. The falling block will progressively rotate toward its
target rotation angle on successive updates creating smooth animation.

"*/
{
  [_myFallingBlock moveTargetRotationCounterclockwiseInModel:self];
}
```

The `-dealloc` method calls `-reset` to release the falling block and any subblocks in the grid. `-reset` is also called from `-init`. Using a single method that sets an instance to a default state results in a single point of maintenance in the code. The use of such a method in both `-init` and `-dealloc` can save lines of code when new instance variables are added to the class. In this case, only the `-reset` method needs to be changed if new instance variables are added.

```
- (void)dealloc
/*"
   Clean-up: Calls reset to release sub-blocks and falling block if any.

"*/
{
  // Release the falling block and all of the sub-blocks
  [self reset];

  // Always call super-class's dealloc
  [super dealloc];
}

@end
```

The `MYBlockView` class and the application's `.nib` file compose the view subsystem of TransparentTetris. The purpose of the view subsystem is to present the data stored in the model subsystem to users and accept input from users.

One traditional difficulty encountered when implementing the MVC architecture is that some classes seemingly need to be in multiple subsystems. In this application, blocks and subblocks need to be drawn. The natural implementation of drawing that maximizes opportunities for polymorphism is to include drawing methods in the

MYBlock and MYSubBlock classes. However, drawing is clearly a role of the view subsystem, and the MYBlock and MYSubBlock classes are part of the model. Blocks and subblocks could be drawn any number of different ways. It should be possible to have alternate view subsystems that draw the model in different ways. If drawing code is implemented in the model, then each time the appearance of the game is changed the model will need to be changed.

Objective-C provides an elegant solution to the problem. The methods for drawing blocks and subblocks can be added in categories from within the view subsystem. The added methods take full advantage of opportunities for polymorphism, and the code is implemented in the most appropriate subsystem. The implementation of the classes within the model is complete, self contained, and separately usable. The view subsystem adds methods to the model classes to help implement the view. Other views could add different methods without conflict.

In this implementation, the -_myBlockViewDraw method is added to both the MYSubBlock and MYBlock classes. These methods are only called from the MYBlockView class. The drawing code is kept together in one subsystem. The interfaces for the two categories are private, and defined within the implementation of the MYBlockView class. As a result, they are not readily accessible outside the MYBlockView class, and they are maintained along with the MYBlockView class where they are used.

The implementation of this class and the application's .nib file directly or indirectly satisfy the following requirements:

- The color and transparency used to draw subblocks can be set. A preferences panel with a color well and access to the standard color panel are provided in the application's .nib file. [Requirement 20]
- This class is a subclass of NSView, and can be used in any Cocoa window. A window containing an instance of this class is provided in the application's .nib file. [Requirement 21]
- Menu items to start/reset a game as well as pause and resume a game are provided in the application's .nib file. [Requirement 22, 23, 24]
- A preferences panel with a toggle button to enable or disable sound play is provided in the application's .nib file. [Requirement 26]

```
//
//  MYBlockView.m
//  TransparentTetris
//
```

```
#import "MYBlockView.h"
#import "MYGameModel.h"
#import "MYSubBlock.h"
#import "MYBlock.h"


@interface MYSubBlock (_MYBlockViewDrawingSupport)
/*" Private category for drawing sub-blocks in an instance of _MYBlockView "*/

/*" Base color configuration "*/
+ (void)reinitColorsWithBaseColor:(NSColor *)aColor;

/*" Drawing "*/
- (void)_myBlockViewDraw;

@end


@interface MYBlock (_MYBlockViewDrawingSupport)
/*" Private category for drawing blocks in an instance of _MYBlockView "*/

/*" Drawing "*/
- (void)_myBlockViewDraw;

@end
```

The use of private categories can be a very powerful technique. As with most powerful techniques, this one is prone to abuse. To avoid spaghetti code and maintenance hassles, follow theses guidelines:

- The methods added via a private category in another class's implementation should not modify the state of the extended class or have side effects on the extended class.
- The methods added via a private category in another class should only be used within the source file where they are declared.

```
@implementation MYBlockView
/*"
In the MVC architecture, an instance of this class is the principal "view"
component. This class draws the game model so that the game grid fits the
view's bounds exactly. Within this file, specialized drawing methods for
```

```
sub-blocks and blocks are added to the relevant classes via categories. As a
result, all drawing code is implemented in this file. The MVC partitioning
is maintained. The model knows nothing about drawing. Another view could draw
the same model differently by implementing its own drawing methods in separate
categories. In fact, multiple different views of the same model could exist
simultaneously without conflict.

"*/

- (void)setBaseColor:(NSColor *)aColor
/*" Set the base color to use when drawing sub-blocks "*/
{
  [MYSubBlock reinitColorsWithBaseColor:aColor];
}


- (MYGameModel *)gameModel
/*" Returns the model that will be drawn by the receiver "*/
{
  return _myGameModel;
}


- (void)setGameModel:(MYGameModel *)aModel
/*" Sets the model that will be drawn by the receiver "*/
{
  [aModel retain];
  [_myGameModel release];
  _myGameModel = aModel;
}
```

The `MYBlockView` instance defined in the application's `.nib` file is configured to resize along with the window that contains it. Scaling the coordinate system to represent one unit in the game grid as one unit when drawing, simplifies drawing. The use of floating-point positions enables simple fractional offsets from grid positions. The drawing of subblocks can be defined in terms of fractions of a unit square area.

```
- (void)drawRect:(NSRect)aRect
/*"
     This method is called automatically by the application whenever the view
should be drawn. This method is implemented to scale the current coordinate
```

```
system so that the game model's sub-block grid will fit exactly in the
receiver's bounds when drawn. Then the sub-blocks if any in the model's grid
are drawn. Finally the model's falling block if any is drawn.

"*/
{
  NSAffineTransform    *translateTransform = [NSAffineTransform transform];
  int             i, j;
  float           xScaleFactor = [self bounds].size.width / MYGAME_GRID_WIDTH;
  float           yScaleFactor = [self bounds].size.height / MYGAME_GRID_HEIGHT;

  // scale coordinate system so that correct number of sub blocks will fit
  // regardless of the size of the bounds
  [translateTransform scaleXBy:xScaleFactor yBy:yScaleFactor];
  [translateTransform concat];

  // Draw all of the model's sub-blocks
  for(j = 0; j < MYGAME_GRID_HEIGHT; j++) {
    for(i = 0; i < MYGAME_GRID_WIDTH; i++) {
      [[[self gameModel] subBlockAtX:i y:j] _myBlockViewDraw];
    }
  }

  // Draw the model's falling block
  [[[self gameModel] fallingBlock] _myBlockViewDraw];
}

@end
```

The subblocks are drawn as five rectangles representing the center of a subblock and four bezels. The colors of the five rectangles are derived from a color that can be set with the `+reinitColorsWithBaseColor` class method; defined in the `_MYBlockViewDrawingSupport` category of the `MYSubBlock` class. A class method is used because the color is shared by all instances of `MYSubBlock`.

```
@implementation MYSubBlock (_MYBlockViewDrawingSupport)
/*"
     Private category for drawing sub-blocks in an instance of_MYBlockView.
This code is part of the view in the MVC design. My extending the MYSubBlock
class with a category that is part of the view, the implementation of
MYSubBlock within the model can remain generic and not contain any code that
is view specific.
```

```
"*/

/*" The number of rectangles needed to draw a sub-block. "*/
#define _MYNUM_SUB_BLOCK_RECTS (5)

/*"
     The colors of the rectangles needed to draw a sub-block.  Each sub-block
is represented by a central rectangle and four surrounding rectangles that
simulate bezels. These are the colors of the central rectangle and the bezels.

"*/
static NSColor    *mySharedSubBlockColors[_MYNUM_SUB_BLOCK_RECTS] = {
  nil,
  nil,
  nil,
  nil,
  nil
};

/*"
     The rectangles needed to draw a sub-block (defined within an unit
square). Each sub-block is represented by a central rectangle and four
surrounding rectangles that simulate bezels

"*/
static NSRect      mySharedSubBlockRects[_MYNUM_SUB_BLOCK_RECTS] = {
  {{0.0, 0.0}, {0.8, 0.8}}, // center
  {{0.0, 0.0}, {0.1, 1.0}}, // left
  {{0.1, 0.0}, {0.9, 0.1}}, // bottom
  {{0.9, 0.1}, {0.1, 0.9}}, // right
  {{0.1, 0.9}, {0.8, 0.1}}  // top
};
```

Static variables can be used to store data shared by all instances of a class. This is a common idiom in Cocoa applications. Class methods should be used to access the static data.

```
+ (void)reinitColorsWithBaseColor:(NSColor *)aColor
/*"
     Re-initializes the table of colors used to draw the rectangles that
represent a sub-block. aColor is used as the color of the center of the
sub-block. The other rectangles are drawn with either a highlighted variant
of aColor or a shadowed variant of aColor.
```

```
"*/
{
  NSColor       *baseColor = [aColor copy];

  [mySharedSubBlockColors[0] release];
  mySharedSubBlockColors[0] = baseColor;
  [mySharedSubBlockColors[1] release];
  mySharedSubBlockColors[1] = [[baseColor highlightWithLevel:0.6] retain];
  [mySharedSubBlockColors[2] release];
  mySharedSubBlockColors[2] = [[baseColor shadowWithLevel:0.9] retain];
  [mySharedSubBlockColors[3] release];
  mySharedSubBlockColors[3] = [[baseColor shadowWithLevel:0.9] retain];
  [mySharedSubBlockColors[4] release];
  mySharedSubBlockColors[4] = [[baseColor highlightWithLevel:0.6] retain];
}
```

The `MYBlockView` class is implemented to draw by scaling its view coordinates to fit the size of the game grid. Because this category of `MYSubBlock` is implemented in the same file, the implementation detail of `MYBlockView` can safely be used to implement the `-_myBlockViewDraw` method in `MYSubBlock`. The encapsulation (implementation hiding) of the `MYBlockView` class is preserved. No dependence on the implementation of `MYBlockView` leaks into the model or even out of the file in which `MYBlockView` is implemented. However, if the implementation of the `-drawRect:` method in `MYBlockView` is changed, the `-_myBlockViewDraw` method will also have to change. Note such dependencies in the method documentation.

```
- (void)_myBlockViewDraw
/*"
Saves the current coordinate system, translates the current coordinate system
so that the origin is coincident with the receiver's position, draws the
colored rectangles that represent the receiver within a unit square, and then
restores the previous coordinate system. Before calling this method, make sure
that the current coordinate system has been scaled so that a unit square is
the appropriate size on the display.

"*/
{
  NSAffineTransform     *translateTransform = [NSAffineTransform transform];

  [NSGraphicsContext saveGraphicsState];
  [translateTransform translateXBy:_myXPosition yBy:_myYPosition]; // Assumes
```

```
                                          // current coordinate system scaled
                                          // to grid dimensions
  [translateTransform concat];
  NSRectFillListWithColorsUsingOperation(mySharedSubBlockRects,
      mySharedSubBlockColors, _MYNUM_SUB_BLOCK_RECTS, NSCompositeSourceOver);
  [NSGraphicsContext restoreGraphicsState];
}

@end


@implementation MYBlock (_MYBlockViewDrawingSupport)
/*"
     Private category for drawing blocks in an instance of _MYBlockView. This
code is part of the view in the MVC design. My extending the MYBlock class
with a category that is part of the view, the implementation of MYSubBlock
within the model can remain pure and not contain any code that is view
specific.

"*/



// Drawing
- (void)_myBlockViewDraw
/*"
Saves the current coordinate system, translates the current coordinate system
so that the origin is coincident with the receiver's position, draws the
colored sub-blocks that compose the receiver, and then restores the previous
coordinate system. Before calling this method, make sure that the current
coordinate system has been scaled so that a unit square is the appropriate
size on the display.

"*/
{
  int                   i;

  NSAffineTransform    *translateTransform = [NSAffineTransform transform];

  // Save the state
  [NSGraphicsContext saveGraphicsState];
```

```
  // Create a coordinate system for drawing the block
  [translateTransform translateXBy:_myPosition.x yBy:_myPosition.y];
                                  // Translate to center of rotation
  [translateTransform rotateByDegrees:_myRotationDegrees];      // Rotate
  [translateTransform translateXBy:-MYBLOCK_PIVOT_X yBy:-MYBLOCK_PIVOT_Y];
                                  // Make center of block coincident with
                                  // block position
  [translateTransform concat];

  // Draw all of the sub-blocks in the grid
  for(i = 0; i < MYNUM_SUBBLOCKS_IN_BLOCK; i++) {
    [_mySubBlocks[i] _myBlockViewDraw];
  }

  // Restore the state
  [NSGraphicsContext restoreGraphicsState];
}

@end
```

`MYGameController` Class

An instance of this class acts as a bridge between the view of the game and the model of the game. Following the MVC architecture, this class is the controller. Controllers should be kept as simple and small as possible. Most importantly, controllers should store little or no program state information. Program state (other than purely display state) belongs in the model. A common mistake is to make the controller portion of an application too big, too complex, and too full of important state information. When that happens, the whole MVC architecture breaks down because if either the model or view part of the system changes, the controller portion usually changes. If too much code is implemented in the controller the benefits of keeping the portions separate are greatly diminished.

This class principally consists of outlets to view subsystem objects provided in the application's `.nib` file, and action methods that are invoked from objects in the applications `.nib` file. The outlets are used to keep the user interface objects consistent with the state of the model. The action methods are used to change the state of the model.

One crucial element of the TransparentTetris design that has been left for implementation in the class is the periodic game update. As long as the game is not over and not paused, this class sends `-update` messages to the a `MYGameModel` instance at regular time intervals.

This class stores the user's sound and color preferences in the his defaults database. Management of user preferences can be part of the controller or the model in the MVC architecture. The color is saved and restored to satisfied requirement 27.

```
//
//  MYGameController.m
//  TransparentTetris
//

#import "MYGameController.h"
#import "MYGameModel.h"
#import "MYBlockView.h"
#import "MYSubBlock.h"
#import "MYBlock.h"

#define _MYPAUSE_TITLE (@"Pause")   /*" Title when game can be paused "*/
#define _MYRESUME_TITLE (@"Resume") /*" Title when game can be resumed "*/
#define _MYGAME_UPDATE_PERIOD (0.05)/*" Game update period: 50ms (1/20 seconds)
                                    —> 20 Hz "*/


@implementation MYGameController
/*"
     An instance of this class acts as a bridge between the view of the game
and the model of the game. Following the model/view/controller (MVC)
architecture, this class is the controller. There may be any number of
different ways to view the game such as where the score is displayed, if there
is a background, the size of the window in which the game is played, how the
"game over" message is displayed, how user input is collected, etc. None of
the different ways to view the game have any impact on the game data in the
model. Similarly, there may be many different models with different ways to
represent the game data itself. This class, the controller, ties the model and
the view together. The view should know as little as possible about the model
or else the view will have to be changed every time the model changes. The
model should know absolutely nothing about the view or else the model will
have to change every time the view changes. (In most applications, the model
stabilizes, but the views continually evolve)  This class knows about both the
model and the view, and as a result any significant changes to the model or
the view will require changes to this class.
```

```
Observed Notifications:

    MYROW_WAS_REMOVED_NOTIFICATION

    MYSBLOCK_WAS_PLACED_IN_GRID_NOTIFICATION

    MYBLOCK_DID_SLIDE_NOTIFICATION

    MYBLOCK_DID_ROTATE_NOTIFICATION

"*/
```

The Game Over view is a simple noneditable text field configured in the application's `.nib` file. The view is added and removed from the window that contains the `MYBlockView` instance to show or hide the Game Over text. The Game Over view is referenced by the `_myGameOverField` instance variable, and retained so that it is not deallocated when it is removed from the view hierarchy.

```
- (void)_myShowGameOver
/*"
     This method inserts the "game over" field into the view hierarchy (thus
making it visible) if it is not already in the view hierarchy.

"*/
{
  if(nil == [_myGameOverField superview]) {
    // _myGameOverField is NOT already in the view hierarchy
    [_myGameOverField setFrame:[_myBackgroundView bounds]];
                                 // size "game over" to fill the game area
    [_myBackgroundView addSubview:_myGameOverField];
                                 // add it to the view hierarchy
                                 // (make it visible)

    // Display the background view and indirectly the "game over" view also
    [_myBackgroundView displayIfNeeded];
  }
}


- (void)_myHideGameOver
/*"
```

```
     This method removes the "game over" field from the view hierarchy
(thus making it invisible) if it is in the view hierarchy

"*/
{
  if(nil != [_myGameOverField superview]) {
    // _myGameOverField IS in the view hierarchy
    // Remove _myGameOverField from the view hierarchy
    // _myGameOverField will NOT be deallocated NOW because we retained it in
    // -applicationDidFinishLanching:
    [_myGameOverField removeFromSuperview];

    // Display the background view and indirectly erase the "game over"
    // view also
    [_myBackgroundView displayIfNeeded];
  }
}
```

The `-_myRunStep:` method is called by the `-togglePause:` method and the `-reset` method to start the periodic update of the game. This is one technique for implementing periodic update and animation. Each time `-_myRunStep:` is called, any previously scheduled calls to `-_myRunStep:` are canceled. If the game is still running, another call to `-_myRunStep:` is scheduled after a delay, via the `-performSelector:withObject:afterDelay:` method declared in a category of `NSObject` within `NSRunLoop.h`. The facility to call an arbitrary method after an arbitrary delay is very handy. For another way to schedule periodic messages to an object, see the `NSTimer` class.

Each time `-_myRunStep:` is called, the game model is updated via a call to `MYGameModel`'s `-update` method. Then, `-setNeedsDisplayInRect:` is sent to the view that displays the game grid and falling block. The integer value of the field that displays the score is set, causing the field to redraw if necessary. Finally, if the game is over, the `-_myShowGameOver` method is called.

A small optimization of display update is used in `-myRunStep:`. The `-setNeedsDisplayInRect:` method is used rather than `-setNeedsDisplay:` so that only the area that actually needs display will be redrawn. Only the rectangle that encloses the falling block and a little margin above and to the sides changes during a single update. The extra margin is needed to erase the space where the falling block might have been drawn on the last update. If `-setNeedsDisplay:` was used, the entire view would be redrawn after every update of the game model.

Use the -setNeedsDisplay and -setNeedsDisplayInRect: methods rather than -display or -displayInRect:. This will enable the ApplicationKit to better queue drawing and minimize unnecessary drawing. The -setNeedsDisplay and -setNeedsDisplayInRect: methods take advantage of the ApplicationKit's autodisplay features. No matter how many times you call -setNeedsDisplay for a view, it will only be redrawn at most once per user event. Calling -display forces the view to immediately redraw. Using the application kit to optimize drawing can simplify your code. Use the QuartzDebug.app in /Developer/Applications to see how the TransparentTetris game redraws.

```
// Periodic action
- (void)_myRunStep:(id)sender
/*"
    Call this method to execute one update of the game. If the game is not
paused and the game is not over, this method automatically schedules another
call to this method after a short delay. As a result, once this method is
called, the game will continue to "play" until it is paused or over.

"*/
{
  NSPoint fallingBlockOrigin;
  float  xScaleFactor = [_myBlockView bounds].size.width / MYGAME_GRID_WIDTH;
  float  yScaleFactor = [_myBlockView bounds].size.height / MYGAME_GRID_HEIGHT;

  // Cancel any previously scheduled calls to this method so that we do not
  // inadvertently get called too often
  [[self class] cancelPreviousPerformRequestsWithTarget:self
      selector:@selector(_myRunStep:) object:nil];

  if([_myGameModel isRunning] && ![_myGameModel isGameOver]) {
    // Schedule another call to this method
    [self performSelector:@selector(_myRunStep:) withObject:nil
        afterDelay:_MYGAME_UPDATE_PERIOD];
  }

  // Update the game model. The update may result in the game being over
  [_myGameModel update];

  // Tell the game view that it must refresh the rectangle that encloses the
  // falling block plus a little margin above and to the sides to erase the
  // space where the falling block may have been drawn on the last update.
  // This block of code could be replaced by a simple [_myBlockView
```

```
  // setNeedsDisplay:YES], but that would cause the entire view to redraw when
  // only the rectangle around the falling block really needs to be redrawn.
  fallingBlockOrigin = [[_myGameModel fallingBlock] position];
  [_myBlockView setNeedsDisplayInRect:NSMakeRect(((fallingBlockOrigin.x -
      (MYNUM_SUBBLOCKS_IN_BLOCK / 2)) - 1) * xScaleFactor,
      (fallingBlockOrigin.y - (MYNUM_SUBBLOCKS_IN_BLOCK / 2)) * yScaleFactor,
      (MYNUM_SUBBLOCKS_IN_BLOCK + 2) * xScaleFactor,
      (MYNUM_SUBBLOCKS_IN_BLOCK + 1) * yScaleFactor)];

  // Refresh the score
  [_myScoreField setIntValue:[_myGameModel score]];

  if([_myGameModel isGameOver]) {
    // The game is now over so show the "game over" indication
    [self _myShowGameOver];
  }
}
```

Before playing any sounds, this class checks the user's preference for sound playing. In this implementation, the user's preference is stored in the user's defaults database. There is no need to maintain an instance variable for the user's preference. It can be found in the defaults database each time it is needed. The first time the default values are accessed, an `NSDictionary` containing the user's preferences is loaded into memory. Subsequent queries about a default value are fast.

```
- (void)_myModelRowWasRemoved:(NSNotification *)aNotification
/*"
     This method is called when a MYROW_WAS_REMOVED_NOTIFICATION notification
is received. This method plays a sound effect and updates the display.

"*/
{
  if([[NSUserDefaults standardUserDefaults] boolForKey:@"isSoundEnabled"]) {
    NSSound      *submarine = [NSSound soundNamed:@"Submarine"];

    [submarine play];
  }

  // Display immediatly so that user sees each row removed
  [_myBlockView setNeedsDisplay:YES];
}
```

```
- (void)_myModelBlockWasPlacedInGrid:(NSNotification *)aNotification
/*"
     This method is called when a MYSBLOCK_WAS_PLACED_IN_GRID_NOTIFICATION
notification is received. This method plays a sound effect and updates the
display.

"*/
{
  if([[NSUserDefaults standardUserDefaults] boolForKey:@"isSoundEnabled"]) {
    NSSound       *funk = [NSSound soundNamed:@"Funk"];

    [funk play];
  }

  [_myBlockView setNeedsDisplay:YES];
}


- (void)_myModelBlockDidSlideInGrid:(NSNotification *)aNotification
/*"
     This method is called when a MYBLOCK_DID_SLIDE_NOTIFICATION notification
or a MYBLOCK_DID_ROTATE_NOTIFICATION notification is received. This method
plays a sound effect and updates the display.

"*/
{
  if([[NSUserDefaults standardUserDefaults] boolForKey:@"isSoundEnabled"]) {
    NSSound      *tink = [NSSound soundNamed:@"Tink"];

    [tink play];
  }
}


- (IBAction)rotateCounterclockwise:(id)sender
/*" Asks the model to rotate the falling block counterclockwise "*/
{
  [_myGameModel rotateFallingBlockCounterclockwise];
}
```

```
- (IBAction)rotateClockwise:(id)sender
/*" Asks the model to rotate the falling block clockwise "*/
{
  [_myGameModel rotateFallingBlockClockwise];
}


- (IBAction)moveLeft:(id)sender
/*" Asks the model to move the falling block left "*/
{
  [_myGameModel moveFallingBlockLeft];
}


- (IBAction)moveRight:(id)sender
/*" Asks the model to move the falling block right "*/
{
  [_myGameModel moveFallingBlockRight];
}


- (IBAction)drop:(id)sender
/*" Asks the model to drop the falling block. (make it fall faster) "*/
{
  [_myGameModel dropFallingBlock];
}


- (IBAction)togglePause:(id)sender
/*"
    If the model is not paused then this method asks the model to pause.
Otherwise, this method asks the model to resume and then starts the periodic
update of the model and the view.

"*/
{
  if([_myGameModel isRunning]) {
    [_myGameModel pause];          // Pause the model
```

```
  } else {
    [_myGameModel resume];          // Resume the model
    [self _myRunStep:nil];          // start the periodic update
  }
}


- (IBAction)reset:(id)sender
/*"
     Resets the game model, hides the "game over" message if it is visible and
starts the periodic update of the game model and view.

"*/
{
  [self _myHideGameOver];     // Hide the "game over" (harmless if not visible)
  [_myGameModel reset];       // Reset the model
  [_myGameModel resume];      // Make sure the model is not paused
  [self _myRunStep:nil];      // start the periodic update
}
```

In addition to setting the color used to draw subblocks, the -takeSubBlockBaseColorFrom: method saves the color in the user's defaults database. When a Cocoa application is quit, any changes made to the default's database are automatically saved in a file in the user's home directory. In this application, the user's preferences are reloaded from the defaults database in the -_myUpdateUIWithDefaults method, which is called from -applicationDidFinishLaunching:.

```
- (IBAction)takeSubBlockBaseColorFrom:(id)sender
/*"
     sender must respond to the -color message and return a color. This method
sets the base color used by the model to represent sub-blocks and stores the
color as a user default so that the same color will be used the next time the
game is launched by the same user.

"*/
{
  NSData         *encodedColorData;

  NSAssert([sender respondsToSelector:@selector(color)],
      @"Attempt to take a color value from a sender that can not provide one");
```

```
  // The the model what color to use
  [_myBlockView setBaseColor:[sender color]];

  // Tell the view that it needs to refresh
  [_myBlockView setNeedsDisplay:YES];

  // Set user sub-block base color preference
  // This trick of encoding the color simplifies storing colors in the defaults
  // database
  encodedColorData = [NSArchiver archivedDataWithRootObject:[sender color]];
  if(nil != encodedColorData) {
    [[NSUserDefaults standardUserDefaults] setObject:encodedColorData
        forKey:@"subBlockBaseColorData"];
  }
}


- (IBAction)takeSoundEnabledFrom:(id)sender
/*"
     sender must respond to the -intValue message and return an int. This
method stores the boolean representation of the int value as a user default
so that the preference for enabling sound will be used the next time the
game is launched by the same user.

"*/
{
  NSAssert([sender respondsToSelector:@selector(intValue)],
      @"Attempt to take an int value from a sender that can not provide one");

  // Set user sound enabled preference
  [[NSUserDefaults standardUserDefaults] setBool:(BOOL)[sender intValue]
      forKey:@"isSoundEnabled"];
}
```

The `-validateMenuItem:` method is called automatically by the Cocoa-menu handling classes unless automatic menu validation has been disabled by sending `setAutoenablesItems:NO` to the `NSMenu` object.

In this implementation, if the action of the `anItem` argument is `-togglePause:`, then `anItem`'s title is set to reflect the action that will be performed if the user selects `anItem`. If the game is running the title is set to Pause because selecting the menu item will pause the game. If the game is already paused, the title is set to Resume because selecting the menu will resume the game. This method disables `anItem` if the game is over.

```
- (BOOL)validateMenuItem:(NSMenuItem *)anItem
/*"
     If an instance of this class in the responder chain and automatic menu
validation is enabled (it is enabled unless programmatically disabled) then
this method is called automatically when a menu item is exposed. If anItem's
action is -togglePause: then this method sets anItem's title to "Pause" or
"Resume" as appropriate based on the model's state and disables anItem if
the game is over. If the game is not over and/or anItem's action is not
-togglePause: then this method returns YES which enables anItem by default.

"*/
{
  BOOL          result = YES;         // Default return value to enable anItem

  if([anItem action] == @selector(togglePause:)) {
    // anItem toggles the game's running status
    NSAssert([anItem respondsToSelector:@selector(setTitle:)],
        @"Invalid sender: does not respond to -setTitle:");

    if([_myGameModel isGameOver]) {
      // The game is over so disable anItem and set its title to "Pause"
      result = NO;
      [anItem setTitle:_MYPAUSE_TITLE];
    } else {
      // The game is not over
      if([_myGameModel isRunning]) {
        // Game is running therefore pressing anItem will pause the game so set
        // the title to "Pause"
        [anItem setTitle:_MYPAUSE_TITLE];
      } else {
        // Game is paused therefore pressing anItem will resume the game so set
        // the title to "Resume"
        [anItem setTitle:_MYRESUME_TITLE];
      }
    }
  }

  // Returns YES if anItem should be enabled
  return result;
}
```

```
- (void)_myUpdateUIWithDefaults
/*"
     Updates the relevant user interface elements so that they reflect the
user's preference values.

"*/
{
  NSData       *encodedColorData;

  // Get user sound preference
  [_myEnableSoundButton setIntValue:[[NSUserDefaults standardUserDefaults]
      boolForKey:@"isSoundEnabled"]];

  // Get user tile color preference
  encodedColorData = [[NSUserDefaults standardUserDefaults]
      objectForKey:@"subBlockBaseColorData"];

  if(nil != encodedColorData) {
    NSColor   *encodedColor = [NSUnarchiver
        unarchiveObjectWithData:encodedColorData];

    [_mySubBlockColorWell setColor:encodedColor];
    [_myBlockView setBaseColor:encodedColor];

  } else {
    // No previous default has been set
    NSColor    *defaultColor = [NSColor colorWithCalibratedRed:0.7 green:1.0
blue:0.7
        alpha:0.2];

    [_mySubBlockColorWell setColor:defaultColor];
    [_myBlockView setBaseColor:defaultColor];
  }
}


// Application delegate methods
- (void)applicationDidFinishLaunching:(NSNotification *)aNotification
/*"
This method is called automatically once after the application has fully
launched if an instance of this class is the delegate of the application's
application object. This method is implemented to seed the random number
```

```
generator with a time value so that the sequence of blocks will be different
in every game. The shared color panel is configured to allow the user to
select transparent colors. Without transparent colors this would not be
"TransparentTetris". The user's default preferences are loaded if any.
The game model is created and the game view is given access to the game model.
NOTE: It is usually a bad idea for a "view" object to have direct access to
a "model" object. However, this is a simple application and the "view" will
not modify the model. In this case the simplest design enables the view to
directly represent the model since the controller can not contribute any
value by interceding and we know that the view does not modify the model
behind the controllers back.

"*/
{
  // Initialize the random number generator so that the same sequence
  // is not repeated each time the game starts
  srandom([NSDate timeIntervalSinceReferenceDate]);

  // Configure shared color panel to allow transparency
  [[NSColorPanel sharedColorPanel] setShowsAlpha:YES];

  // Read user preferences and update UI
  [self _myUpdateUIWithDefaults];

  // Create the game model
  _myGameModel = [[MYGameModel alloc] init];

  // Configure view of model & background
  [_myBlockView setGameModel:_myGameModel];
  [_myBackgroundView setImage:[NSImage imageNamed:@"DefaultBackground"]];

  // Retain _myGameOverField so this it will not be deallocated if/when removed
from
  // the view hierarchy
  [_myGameOverField retain];

  // Register for notification of interesting events in the model
  [[NSNotificationCenter defaultCenter] addObserver:self
      selector:@selector(_myModelRowWasRemoved:)
      name:MYROW_WAS_REMOVED_NOTIFICATION object:nil];
  [[NSNotificationCenter defaultCenter] addObserver:self
      selector:@selector(_myModelBlockWasPlacedInGrid:)
```

```
        name:MYSBLOCK_WAS_PLACED_IN_GRID_NOTIFICATION object:nil];
    [[NSNotificationCenter defaultCenter] addObserver:self
        selector:@selector(_myModelBlockDidSlideInGrid:)
        name:MYBLOCK_DID_SLIDE_NOTIFICATION object:nil];
    [[NSNotificationCenter defaultCenter] addObserver:self
        selector:@selector(_myModelBlockDidSlideInGrid:)
        name:MYBLOCK_DID_ROTATE_NOTIFICATION object:nil];

    // Start playing
    [self reset:nil];
}


- (void)applicationDidBecomeActive:(NSNotification *)aNotification
/*"
     This method is called automatically once after the application becomes
active if an instance of this class is the delegate of the application's
application object. This method is implemented to resume the game if it is
paused and start the periodic update of the game.

"*/
{
    [_myGameModel resume];
    [self _myRunStep:nil];       // start the periodic update
}


- (void)applicationDidResignActive:(NSNotification *)aNotification
/*"
     This method is called automatically once after the application resigns
being active if an instance of this class is the delegate of the application's
application object. This method is implemented to pause the game so that it
does not continue while the user is not paying attention.

"*/
{
    [_myGameModel pause];
}
```

```
- (void)dealloc
/*" Clean-up: Releases objects allocated or retained by the receiver "*/
{
  // Remove observer from from association with the notification center so that
  // there is no chance that a notification will be sent after the instance is
  // deallocated
  [[NSNotificationCenter defaultCenter] removeObserver:self];

  // Release model that was allocated in -applicationDidFinishLaunching:
  [_myGameModel release];
  _myGameModel = nil;

  // We retained _myGameOverField in -applicationDidFinishLaunching: so we must
  // release it now
  [_myGameOverField release];
  _myGameOverField = nil;

  [super dealloc];
}

@end
```

Using AutoDoc

The code in this application is annotated with specially formatted comments that are extracted by a tool called AutoDoc. AutoDoc can be freely obtained from `www.misckit.com`. Examples of the output from AutoDoc are available along with this example at `www.cocoaprogramming.net`.

AutoDoc is an open-source utility to generate documentation for Objective-C classes, categories, and protocols by extracting comments imbedded in source-code files. AutoDoc will also produce documentation for functions, static inline functions, definitions, macros, typedefs, and global variables. AutoDoc can be used to generate documentation for just one file at a time or for all files in a project. Documentation can be generated in either RTF, HTML, or [PDF]LaTeX format.

Most of the documentation formatting is done using template files that enable a large degree of flexibility in what the generated documentation looks like. AutoDoc comes with three default templates, one each for RTF, HTML, and [PDF]LaTeX. The RTF template file generates NeXTSTEP-style documentation. The HTML template generates documentation similar to Apple's current Cocoa class documentation. The LaTeX template generates a file meant to be further processed by 'pdflatex' to produce PDF documentation. 'pdflatex' can be found at `http://www.tug.org/teTeX/`. If pure LaTeX is needed, then the template needs to be modified slightly to remove the hyperlink commands.

If desired, alternate templates can be specified. Support for other (text-based) document formats should be relatively easy to add, but it cannot be done purely externally. Much of the work is simply writing the template file, but a small amount of programmatic support is necessary as well. The open-source nature of AutoDoc ensures that changes can be made to support other output formats as they arise.

Summary

TransparentTetris is a small application that is just large enough to include most of the design elements of large Cocoa applications. In this chapter, a technique for deriving requirements from a description of the goal was employed without imposing a burdensome process. The rationale for selecting a software architecture was explored. Although TransparentTetris is not a traditional productivity application, it nevertheless benefited from the Model/View/Controller architecture that is commonly, and successfully, used for traditional applications with graphical user interfaces. Within the architecture, classes were designed and implemented to satisfy the requirements. Finally, class documentation was extracted from the code. One iteration of the software development cycle was completed, and resulted in a small but useful application.

As with most applications, the first version of TransparentTetris lacks some features that users might want. The natural next step in the development cycle is to use the application (play the game), gather feedback, revise the requirements based on the feedback, revise the design to meet the new requirements, and implement the new design.

TransparentTetris is a standalone application that is built upon the Cocoa frameworks provided by Apple. In larger projects, and any time you want to simplify the reuse of code by other programmers, consider creating new frameworks to contain the functions, classes, and resources that you create. A framework packages all the related code and data into one convenient unit of reuse. Chapter 27, "Create Your Own Frameworks," describes the process of creating your own frameworks for use by others.

27

Creating Custom Frameworks

IN THIS CHAPTER

As a developer uses Cocoa, it is common to build up a library of objects that are reused by several applications. If there are very few modifications to the code from one application to the next, it might be worth putting that code into a custom framework. A framework is a special kind of bundle that packages a dynamic shared library with localizable image, string, sound, and interface resources required by the library.

By placing reusable objects into frameworks, it is easier to include that code in new projects. It is also easier to maintain the code because the reused source code is in the framework project itself and not copied into every project. Project Builder is able to build applications faster if much of the code has already been compiled and is included in a framework. A framework can be used by multiple applications simultaneously. Sharing code can save virtual memory and hard drive space.

The main downsides are that framework projects are a little bit more difficult to set up than application projects. Frameworks are harder to debug than application projects, and writing objects that are truly reusable takes longer and is harder than writing objects that aren't. The setup complexities of framework projects aren't terrible, and they only have to be dealt with once per framework. This chapter guides you through the process. The debugging and other issues involved in designing generic, reusable objects could easily take up a whole other book, so they'll only be briefly discussed in this chapter.

Creating and Using a Framework

To start a new framework project, choose the New Project item (Cmd-Shift-N) from Project Builder's File menu. This opens the New Project assistant. Choose Cocoa Framework under the "Frameworks" heading. Click the Next button to advance to the next page in the assistant. Enter the new framework's name in the Project Name field and click the Finish button. After clicking the Finish button, a new framework project is created and opened.

Objective-C classes, C++ classes, and C source files can all be added to the new project in the same ways they would be added to an application project. Resources such as nib files, strings files, images, and sounds can all be added in the usual way as well. After the framework's elements are all present, the build settings should be configured.

Install Location

Apple recommends that applications be installable by drag and drop. In order for this to be possible for an application that uses custom frameworks, the frameworks need to be packaged inside the application bundle. A framework can only be used from the install location. A framework built for embedding inside an application will not work when installed in `/Library/Frameworks`. A framework built to be installed at `/Library/Frameworks` cannot be embedded inside an application.

To build a framework that is embeddable, which is the preferred approach, the framework needs to be told that it will be used from within an application bundle. This is done by setting the framework's install location. To do this, select the framework's target in the project's Targets tab, and then select the Build Settings tab. The Path field of the Install Location section should be set to `@executable_path/../Frameworks`. Figure 27.1 shows a project with this setting in place.

If the framework will not be packaged inside an application bundle, set the install location to where it is supposed to be installed. Paths such as `/Library/Frameworks` or `/Local/Library/Frameworks` might make sense. To gain the benefits of sharing a single framework between multiple applications, the framework must be installed external to the applications. Doing this, however, makes an application more difficult for users to install and uninstall because the frameworks aren't packaged with the application anymore. This should generally be avoided unless the frameworks are so large that the extra hassle for the user is far outweighed by the savings in hard drive space.

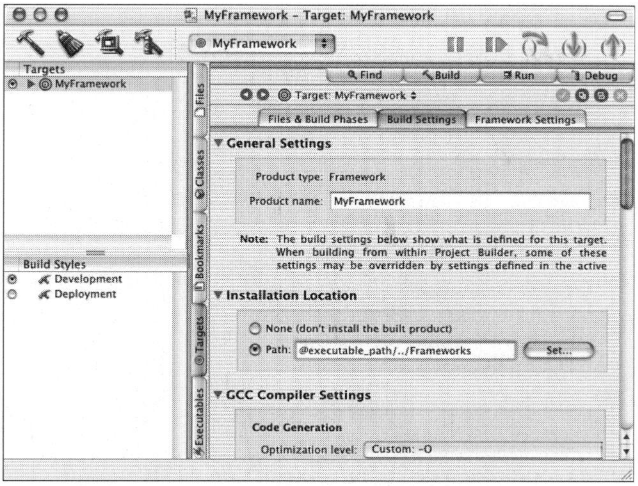

FIGURE 27.1 Setting a framework's install location.

Prebinding

When an application launches, it needs to be linked with any dynamic frameworks it uses. Part of this process includes assigning memory addresses to all the code segments of each framework used by the application—this is called binding. Binding can be time consuming, so Apple uses a technique called prebinding to speed it up. A prebound framework has already been assigned a specific range of memory addresses. When an application using a prebound framework launches, that framework's addresses are already assigned so that the address assignment, or binding, step can be skipped.

The downside to prebinding is that if two frameworks are prebound to the same address area, the application will ignore the prebinding when it launches. It is important, therefore, to attempt to choose addresses that will not conflict with any other frameworks. Because of the difficulties and limitations involved with prebinding, some developers will choose to not bother with it. For smaller frameworks, the speed penalty for using a framework that isn't prebound is minimal. For the large frameworks that Cocoa uses, it is significant and worth the trouble.

NOTE

When an application is built, warnings will be generated if any of the frameworks it uses are not prebound. This can be fixed by prebinding the frameworks and rebuilding the framework. Warnings are also generated if two prebound frameworks have conflicting memory address assignments. To fix this, one of the conflicting frameworks needs to be rebuilt using a different address.

To enable prebinding, a setting needs to be added to the Build Settings table at the bottom of the Build Settings tab. In the `OTHER_LDFLAGS` row of the table, add the flag `-seg1addr <address>`. The address is an eight digit hexadecimal number such as `0x3fff000`. Figure 27.2 shows a project with this setting in place.

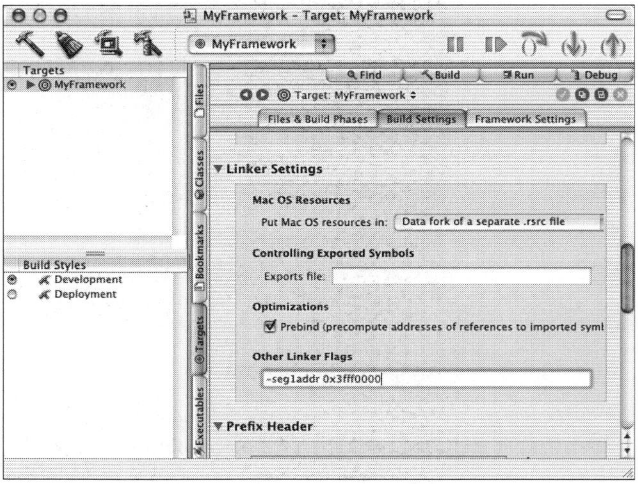

FIGURE 27.2 Setting a framework's install location.

When choosing an address for prebinding, there are two things to know. First, Apple has reserved the addresses `0x40000000` and higher. Never pick an address in that range. Second, the application's code is prebound starting at address `0x00000000`. An address higher than that should be selected. A good process to try is to choose an address as high as possible while being sure that the framework doesn't overlap into the `0x40000000` range. When a framework builds, the build log will provide the framework's built size, so it is possible to calculate a good address range with a little hexadecimal math.

When multiple custom frameworks are used, it is best to use the same address selection process, but start by putting the most often used frameworks at the highest address. The next framework should be at a lower address, and so on, working the way down. If two frameworks will never be used together, they can be assigned the same address. This approach will leave more space for the program's code, which starts at `0x00000000` and works its way up. If third-party frameworks are used, they might already have claimed some addresses, so care should be taken to take that into account.

Because the addresses are statically assigned at build time, selecting the right address for prebinding can be a painful process. Each developer has to decide whether it is worth the trouble. There are several other issues with prebinding that are described in the Mac OS X developer documentation. Start with the file `/Developer/Documentation/ReleaseNotes/Prebinding.html`.

Building a Custom Framework

With install location and prebinding set up, a framework can be built. Frameworks that are used external to an application can be built, and then be installed with a `pbxbuild install DSTROOT=/` from the command line. Frameworks to be embedded inside of an application should not be built with an install build. They should be built with a normal build only. In this case, the built framework is located in the project's `build` directory by default.

Using a Custom Framework

To use a framework from within an application, add the framework as would be done for any built-in Mac OS X framework. In Project Builder's Project menu, select the Add Frameworks item (Option-Cmd-F). Select the framework in the open sheet, and add the framework to the project by clicking the Open button.

The framework search path probably needs to be updated. This is the case if the framework can't be found when building the application. Select the application's target in the projects Targets tab, and then select the Build Settings tab. Near the bottom of the options is an area labeled Search Paths. Add the path to the framework, excluding the framework's name to the Frameworks path. For example, the path `/Local/Library/Frameworks` would be added so that the build process could find `/Local/Library/Frameworks/Myframework.framework`.

For frameworks that are embedded inside of an application's bundle, there is more to do. Project Builder won't automatically copy the framework into the built application. Instead, a copy files build phase needs to be added to the project. Go to the Project menu and New Build Phase submenu. Select New Copy Files Build Phase.

NOTE

The menu item might not be enabled. If not, go to the Files and Build Phases tab of the application target and select one of the build phases. Selecting a build phase should enable the menu item to add a new copy phase.

If necessary, drag the newly added copy files build phase so that it is right before the Frameworks & Libraries build phase. Select Frameworks from the pop-up. Drag the custom frameworks into the Files area. All the frameworks that need to be copied into the application bundle should appear in the Files list. Figure 27.3 shows what this build phase looks like in Project Builder.

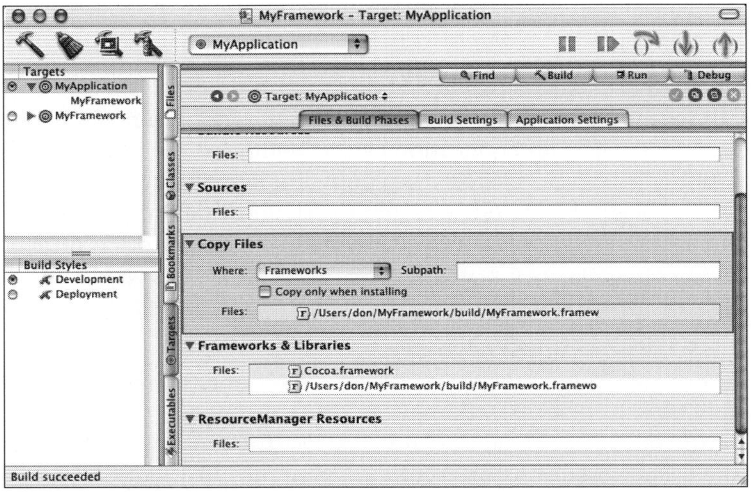

FIGURE 27.3 A new copy files phase added to the Project Builder framework target.

After the project is set up to find and include the frameworks, it should be possible to build and run the application like normal.

Header Files

A framework's files are its public interface. All code that wants to use the framework must include one or more of its headers. Project Builder offers a few options for dealing with header files that are of interest to framework builders. The first, precompiling, makes for faster compiles. The second, private headers, makes it possible to separate internal and external interfaces.

Precompiled Headers

To make compiles run faster when using a framework, it is possible to precompile the framework's headers. Precompiling avoids the time that would be spent by the compiler to parse the headers. To do this in a framework project, create a master header file that imports all the public headers files in the project. (Look at a header such as the `AppKit.h` header inside of `AppKit.framework` for an example.)

Add the master header to the Prefix Header section of the framework target's Build Settings tab. There is a check box to the left of the header name. If the check box is on, ProjectBuilder will precompile the header. Designating a header as a prefix header causes it to be included as part of every source file in the project. Therefore, every source file in the framework project will be compiled as if it started with an `#import` statement that includes the precompiled header.

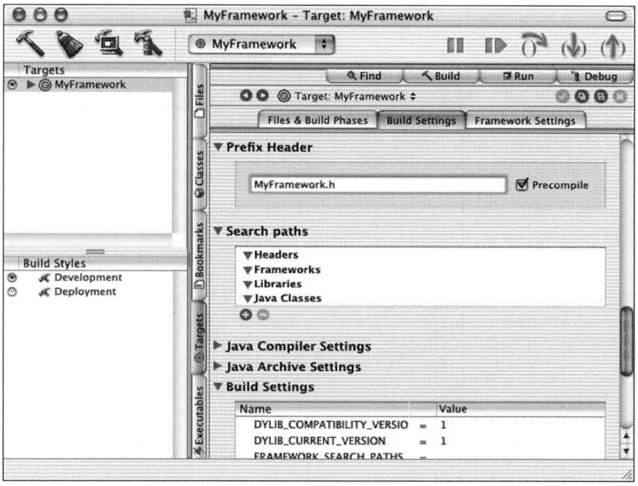

FIGURE 27.4 Precompiling a prefix header.

Public Versus Private API

When a framework is built, the headers are copied into the build product. It is possible to control which headers are copied into the framework bundle. This is desirable because functionality that is a private, internal implementation detail of a framework should not be published. Publishing a private interface tempts users to use it.

When designing objects for a framework, it should be decided which methods are public and should be in the public headers files. The remaining methods are private, and should be placed in a separate header file that won't be copied into the framework when it is built.

All headers, whether public or private, are listed in the Headers build phase on the framework target's Files & Build Phases tab. If a header is public, the Public switch should be checked. By checking the public switch, the build process will know to copy the header into the `Headers` folder inside the framework bundle. Figure 27.5 shows the public and private switches.

NOTE

It is tempting to check the Private switch for private headers—don't. Checking the Private switch will cause the header to be copied into the `PrivateHeaders` folder inside the framework. This is usually not desirable. By checking nothing, the header will not be copied anywhere, which is usually the desired result.

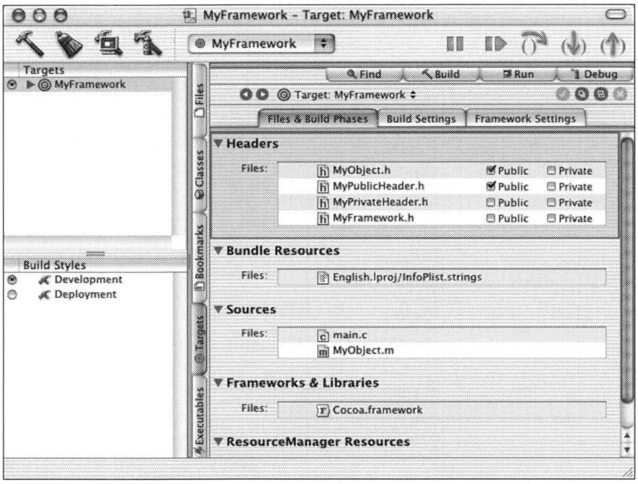

FIGURE 27.5 Public and private header settings.

The headers are strictly necessary for building products that link to the framework. When a framework is distributed for use as a runtime library, it is safe to delete the `Headers` folder inside the framework bundle. This applies especially to frameworks that are embedded inside of applications. Such frameworks don't need to waste disk space for headers when installed at their final locations. When building an application that embeds frameworks, it is often convenient to add a shell script build phase after the copy files phase that copies the framework into the `.app` wrapper. The shell script simply deletes the header files from the installed frameworks. A script used by one of the authors in his projects looks like this:

```
echo "Remove the framework headers...."
cd $BUILD_PATH/../<Application Name>.app/Contents/Frameworks
rm -rf */Headers
rm -rf */Versions/*/Headers
rm -rf */Versions/*/PrivateHeaders
rm -rf */Versions/*/Resources/*/Contents/Headers
exit 0
```

This deletes the header files from any and all installed frameworks. To work correctly, this script's build phase must be placed after the copy files phase, which copies the frameworks into the application.

Providing Backward Compatibility

The dynamic nature of Objective-C partially solves a problem known as the "fragile base class problem," but it doesn't solve it completely. The main issue in the fragile base class problem is that whenever an object's interface changes, all objects that interact with the changed object need to be recompiled. With Objective-C, a recompile is only needed if the number or order of instance variables change, and usually only subclasses of the changed object need to be recompiled.

NOTE

More experienced programmers will recognize that this is an oversimplification of the issues and solutions involving the fragile base class problem. Many good articles are scattered across the Web that discuss this problem. Those interested in learning the precise details should look a few of them up. Good starting points are "The Fragile Base Class Problem and Its Solution" by Mikhajlov and Sekerinski at `http://www.tucs.fi/Publications/techreports/tMiSe97.php` and "What's the Fragile Base Class (FBC) Problem?" by Peter Potrebic at `http://2f.ru/holy-wars/fbc.html`.

The main thing to know about the fragile base class problem is that changes to Objective-C objects cause fewer repercussions to collaborating classes, which is good news for framework designers. On the other hand, changing the number or order of instance variables in an object does cause problems, which is bad news. It means that care must still be taken from one version of a framework to the next to ensure compatibility.

One way to avoid incompatibilities between framework versions is to reserve an extra instance variable in each object. It can be given a name such as `_myPrivateIvars`. This variable should be listed in the public headers as a `void` pointer. In the first version of a class, it would be empty and unused. In later versions, it would contain an `NSMutableDictionary` to store added instance variables by name. Instance variables stored this way are slower to access than those stored as part of the object's structure, but at least new variables can be added as needed without forcing recompiles as the framework is enhanced.

NOTE

The technique of using a dictionary to add instance variables to a class is common in the implementation of Cocoa. Look carefully at a few of the Cocoa objects' headers to see evidence.

Sometimes incompatibility between framework versions is unavoidable. When this happens, it is important to change the framework's version. This isn't the public version number, but a special identifier that is used by the linker to keep different incompatible revisions of a framework from interfering with each other.

The framework version is found in the Build Settings tab of the framework's target. In the Build Settings area near the bottom of the Build Settings tab is a key named `FRAMEWORK_VERSION`. The default value for this key is `A`. When an incompatible change is made in the framework, it is customary to change this to `B`, then `C`, and so on each time a new, incompatible version is built for distribution. Some developers prefer to use the year or some other, longer string as the identifier. Any string that is a valid filename, such as `2002D` is fine. Figure 27.6 shows a framework set to the default version `A`.

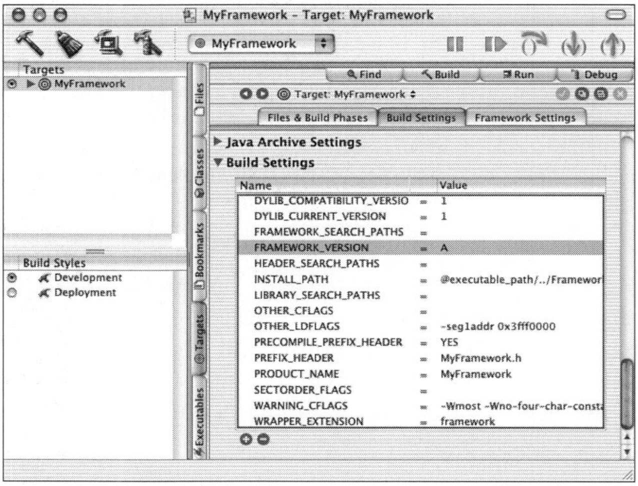

FIGURE 27.6 Setting a framework's version.

Debugging Frameworks

Debugging frameworks is an extremely difficult task. The integration between the gdb debugger and Project Builder's capability to display a breakpoint's source code doesn't work as seamlessly with frameworks. The best advice that can be given regarding debugging frameworks is to come up with a workflow that removes the need for it.

An old programming adage says that the code that doesn't need to be debugged is the easiest code to debug. Because using the debugger with frameworks can be tricky at best, it is better to fully debug code before adding it to a framework. It is common practice to create a test application to use as a debugging harness. The test application makes it easy to exercise all the features of an object. Because debugging an application is generally easier than debugging a framework, it gives a good setting for any debugging sessions. When the object works as it should, it can then be added to the framework.

Following this workflow should reduce the need for debugging the framework itself. Features are simply never put into the framework until they work.

Summary

Building frameworks can be a helpful means of packaging code that is meant to be reused between multiple applications. There are a few wrinkles to the process, but on the whole it is not difficult to create multiple frameworks. Frameworks can be packaged inside an application's bundle. When frameworks are embedded inside an application, they become a programmer convenience that doesn't impact users. The end user never needs to know about what, if any, frameworks are needed to make an application run.

The next chapter discusses packaging applications for distribution and installing applications. The various options available for packaging are covered. Multiple installation approaches are explained in detail, including a technique that enables users to simply drag and drop an application to install it.

28 Distributing Applications

IN THIS CHAPTER

- Package Directories
- Using Disk Images
- Application Installation

After an application is developed using the Cocoa frameworks, the application still needs to be prepared for installation by users. Applications consist of many files. For example, each resource used by the application is in its own file. An application that supports multiple languages and cultures might have many different versions of each resource file. The application executable itself is a file, and the application might depend on dynamically loaded library files. When an application is installed on a user's computer, all the files must be correctly copied. Furthermore, users might move the application, copy it to a different computer, or delete the application. All files associated with the application need to be moved or deleted as a unit in such cases. This chapter explains how to prepare a Cocoa application for distribution to users.

Two general techniques are available for installing Cocoa applications on user's computers. The simplest and usually the best way to install applications is to enable users to copy the application's package directory from a CD-ROM or other media into the preferred location on the user's own hard disk. The other general technique is to use a dedicated installer application. Installer applications can copy files to multiple locations on the user's hard disk and modify the user's system configuration, if necessary.

Package Directories

A Cocoa application's executable and all associated files are stored in a single directory called a package. Apple's Finder application identifies package directories and displays them just like single files. From the user's perspective, applications seem to consist of only one file that can be easily moved or dragged into the desktop's trash can. The complexity and multitude of files that a developer uses to create an application are hidden from end users. Cocoa's `NSFileWrapper` and `NSBundle` classes for interacting with package directories are described in Chapter 7 and Chapter 8.

NOTE

Apple's Finder provides a contextual menu accessible by Ctrl-clicking a package. Select Show Package Contents from the menu and Finder will show the hidden files inside the package directory. In most cases, a folder called Contents within the package directory actually contains all of the application's files.

Apple's Project Builder application automatically creates package directories when Cocoa applications are built. Installing a Cocoa application on a developer's machine is often as easy as copying the package directory created by Project Builder into another folder on the same hard disk. However, special precautions and extra steps are needed to ensure that the installation process is as easy as possible for other users of the application.

NOTE

The terms *package* and *wrapper* are sometimes used interchangeably in Apple's documentation. Package is the preferred term for directories that appear to users as single files in Finder. However, Apple's Cocoa documentation often uses the term wrapper interchangeably with package. In addition, the term package can cause confusion because the same term is used to describe directories of files installed by Apple's Installer application.

Using Disk Images

If a Cocoa application is distributed on a CD-ROM, installation of the application can often be simple. Users just drag a package directory from the CD-ROM to a location on the local hard disk. Even if a special installer application is needed, users can simply double-click the icon for a file on the CD-ROM to start the installation. Apple's Finder application ensures that the application's package directory appears to be a single file on both the CD-ROM and the hard disk. Users do not see the multitude of files that actually compose the application, so there is no chance of confusing users. Users cannot accidentally copy only some of the needed files or change the organization of the files. However, many applications are distributed electronically via the Internet. Special precautions are needed to ensure that installation of Cocoa applications from the Internet is as simple as possible.

For Internet distribution, the Cocoa application must be stored in archive files containing the various files that make up the applications. There are several reasons for this. Operating systems other than Max OS X do not conceal the files within application package directories. Users might be confused by the many files exposed when attempting to download an application's package directory via an FTP client or a web browser. Other operating systems do not necessarily preserve Mac OS X specific file information. A specially constructed archive is needed to preserve that information on many systems. Finally, application files should be compressed to reduce download times. A single compressed archive containing all of the application's files minimizes download times.

Apple recommends the use of the Disk Image format (commonly referred to as DMG) as the archive format for Mac OS X applications. Standard Unix tools, such as `gnutar` and `gzip`, can also be used. Tools for creating and using DMG files are included with Mac OS X. When a user downloads a DMG file, it appears on their desktop like another hard disk. Double-clicking a DMG archive launches Apple's Disk Copy application. The user can then install the application from the DMG or even run the application directly from the DMG with an experience similar to installing from a CD-ROM.

DMG files are simple archives that eliminate the need to use a secondary encoding, such as `MacBinary` or `BINHEX`, to preserve traditional Mac resource forks and file type and creator information. DMG archives include support for compression and reduce the need for additional compression tools.

There are two methods of creating DMG archives: Use Apple's `Disk Copy` application which provides a graphical user interface for managing DMG archives, or use the command-line `hdiutil` tool to manage the archives. Both have their place in the development process. Regardless of the method used, the general steps are as follows:

1. Create an empty, writable DMG archive of the appropriate size, and mount it in the Finder.
2. Copy the files to the DMG archive, and then unmount the DMG.
3. Make a read-only, compressed version of the DMG archive.

Creating a DMG Using Disk Copy

Disk Copy is an application included with Mac OS X and installed at `/Applications/Utilities/Disk Copy`.

For this example, create a 10Mb DMG archive called Our Cocoa Application, and save it as `CocoaApplication-Writable.dmg`. Figure 28.1 shows Disk Copy's `New Blank Image` panel that is used to create an empty DMG archive.

1. Launch Disk Copy.
2. Select Image, New Blank Image... to open the New Blank Image panel, as shown in Figure 28.1.

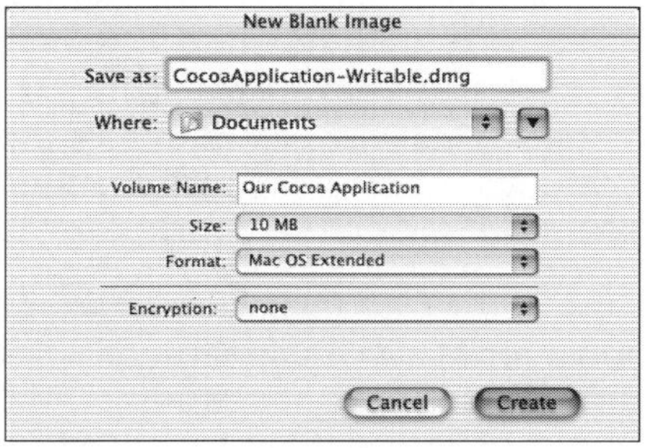

FIGURE 28.1 Disk Copy's New Blank Image panel is displayed with the data that will be entered in steps 3 and 4.

3. In the New Blank Image panel, set Size to 10MB, Format to Mac OS Extended, and Encryption to none.
4. Enter **`Our Cocoa Application`** in the Volume Name field, and **`CocoaApplication-Writable.dmg`** in the Save as field.
5. Click Create.

Disk Copy creates the new empty archive and mounts it as a volume in the Finder, as shown in Figure 28.2. Mac OS X uses the term volume to refer to any file system that can be viewed in Finder. Depending on the user's preferences, the new DMG volume can also be shown on the user's desktop. Use Finder to copy the application, documentation, and any other files to be distributed with the application to the Our Cocoa Application volume.

The copied application files in the DMG are shown in Figure 28.3.

Next, unmount the DMG by dragging it to the trash, or by selecting the DMG in the Finder, Ctrl-click on the volume to bring up the context menu, and select Eject.

The final step is to make a read-only version of the DMG archive.

1. Launch Disk Copy.
2. Select the Image, Convert Image menu item to open Disk Copy's Convert Image panel shown in Figure 28.4.

3. Select the `CocoaApplication-Writable.dmg` file when prompted for the image to convert.
4. When the panel appears, select the Compressed option of the Image Format pop-up button.
5. Enter a filename into the Save as: field to use when saving the converted and compressed DMG. A good practice is to use the application's name and version number as the name of the read-only compressed DMG archive.
6 Click Convert.

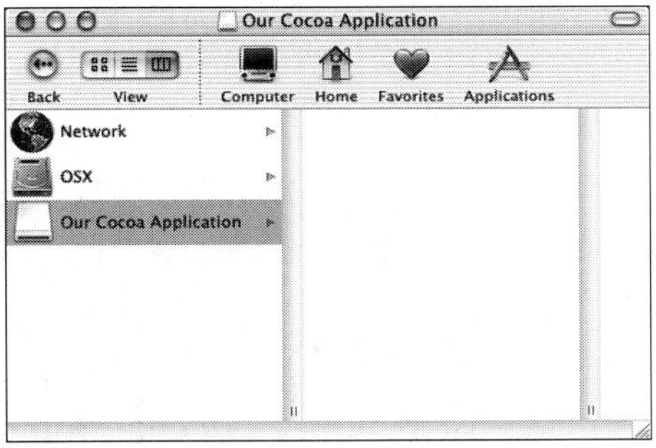

FIGURE 28.2 The new empty DMG archive is displayed as a volume in Finder.

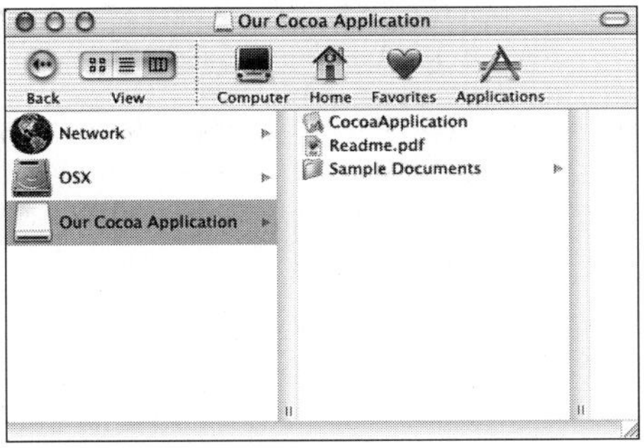

FIGURE 28.3 Finder shows the copied application files in the DMG.

When the read-only compressed DMG archive is saved, it is ready for distribution. Be sure to test the DMG and ensure that it is read-only.

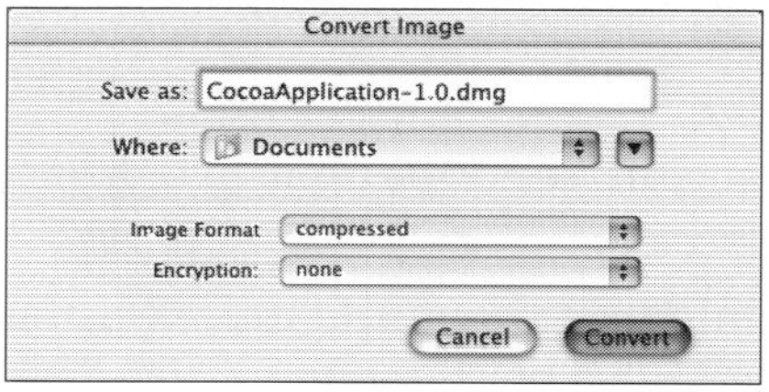

FIGURE 28.4 Disk Copy's Convert Image panel is used to convert a writable DMG archive into a read-only compressed archive.

Creating a DMG File from the Command Line

DMG archives can be created from the command line instead of using the Disk Copy application. As a result, creation of DMG archives can be integrated and automated with the application build process.

Use the following command line to create a writable DMG archive:

```
hdiutil create -megabytes 10 CocoaApplication-Writable.dmg -layout NONE
➥-partitionType Apple_HFS
```

Next, mount the DMG image without the notifying Finder with the following command:

```
hdid -nomount CocoaApplication-Writable.dmg
```

The hdid command will return the disk device that the volume is mounted as in the format /dev/disk<*somenumber*> where <*somenumber*> is chosen by the operating system. This disk volume device returned is used in some of the following steps. In each case, replace the text disk<*somenumber*> in the commands with the actual name assigned by the operating system.

The mounted DMG image needs to be formatted as an HFS+ volume and given a name that will be shown when the DMG is seen in Finder. Formatting requires authenticating as an administrator. Use the following command to format the DMG and set its name to "Our Cocoa Application":

```
sudo newfs_hfs -v "Our Cocoa Application"  /dev/disk<somenumber>
```

The newfs command requires authentication via sudo, and will request the user password.

Unmount the newly formatted archive with the following command:

```
hdiutil eject /dev/disk<somenumber>
```

The writable DMG is now ready for use. Mount it again, but this time, provide notification to the Finder.

```
hdid CocoaApplication-Writable.dmg
```

Finder now shows Our Cocoa Application as an available disk drive. The hdid command creates a file named /dev/disk<*somenumber*>, which is the file shown in Finder. If the DMG will be unmounted from the command line, it is necessary to keep track of the file created by hdid.

Copy the application and other files to the DMG archive. This can be done in the Finder or by using command-line tools. Figure 28.3 shows the copied files in Finder.

Unmount the Our Cocoa Application DMG by dragging it to the trash, or by selecting the DMG in the Finder, Ctrl-clicking it to bring up the context menu, and selecting Eject. This can also be done using the following command:

```
hdiutil eject /dev/disk<somenumber>
```

Note that in this case, <*somenumber*> is the value returned when the volume was mounted hdid.

Finally, to convert the writable DMG file into a read-only compressed version, use the following command:

```
hdiutil convert -format UDZO CocoaApplication-Writable.dmg -o
➥CocoaApplication-1.0.dmg -noext
```

This will create a new file called CocoaApplication-1.0.dmg, which is ready to be distributed.

One advantage of creating DMG archives using the command-line method is that it can be automated with Unix shell scripts and integrated into the application build process. Shell scripts can be included as ProjectBuilder targets and executed by Project Builder. A Stepwise article at http://www.stepwise.com/Articles/Technical/2001-05-28.01.html explains how to integrate DMG archive creation with Project Builder.

Customizing DMG Archives

DMG archives can be configured via Disk Copy to open in Finder with a particular default view. For example, by setting a DMG's default view to as Icon and enlarging the icon size using Finder's View, Show View Options menu, large icons are centered in the window, as shown in Figure 28.3.

Another bit of customization that is possible is to set a background image that will frame the application icons. This is accomplished by copying an image to the DMG volume; then setting the background image using the Finder's View, Show View Options menu, and specifying the copied image file. Unmount the DMG archive, remount it, and delete the copied image file. The background image is retained. This can be used to great effect, as shown in the DMG file for Omni Group's OmniGraffle application in Figure 28.5.

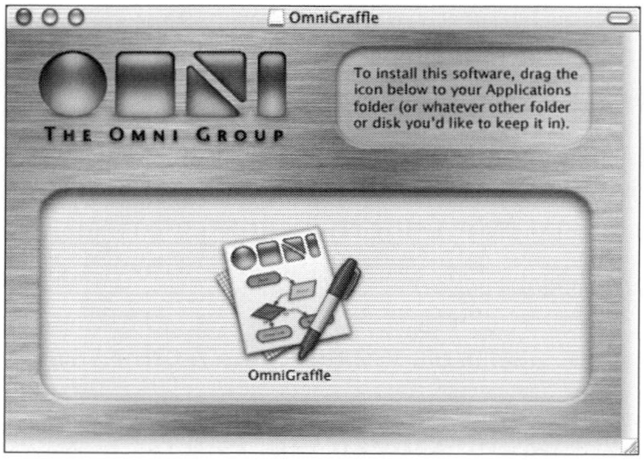

FIGURE 28.5 The Omni Group's OmniGraffle application is distributed in a DMG archive with a background image.

Application Installation

Using DMG archives simplifies the process of downloading applications. When a user has a DMG containing an application displayed in Finder, there are two common ways of installing the application. The easiest way is to just drag the application from the DMG archive into a folder on the local hard disk, but sometimes a more complex installation process using a dedicated installer application is needed.

A dedicated installer application might be required if the application being installed has any of the following characteristics:

- The application shares frameworks or resources with other applications.
- The application is made up of multiple components that must be installed in different locations.
- The application requires that specific software be started upon rebooting the computer.
- The application requires specific system permissions or ownership (commonly only Unix applications).

Drag in the File System

The vast majority of user applications for Mac OS X should be installed by dragging an application wrapper icon from a disk image and dropping it into the Applications folder on a local hard disk.

Applications that require multiple components installed in different locations can still be installed via drag and drop. The application itself can adjust components as needed (create file system links or copy files) when it is run and finds some aspect of its installation missing. This approach's advantage is that the application is self-repairing in the event that a user has deleted a needed file or inappropriately changed the file system. The disadvantage is that special logic must be implemented in the application to support self-repair. As long as the advantages outweigh the disadvantages, the drag and drop style of installation should be used.

In some cases, the temptation to install multiple components of an application in different locations is great, but it should be avoided. A common situation is that an application uses custom frameworks. It might be tempting to use an installation process in which the frameworks are copied into the standard `/Library/Frameworks` directory or some other location outside the application's wrapper. A much better solution is to have the application look for custom frameworks within its own application wrapper. Multiple copies of the frameworks might waste disk space when several installed applications use the same frameworks, but it provides a much more friendly installation for the user. It also enables the user to simply copy the application to another machine without the need to identify and copy separate frameworks.

Installer

There are some applications that require a dedicated installer application and a complex installation process. Apple provides one dedicated installer option called Installer with Mac OS X. Installer uses special package directories with the `.pkg` extension that are created by another application called PackageMaker. Finder shows `.pkg` package directories as single files even though they are actually directories that contain many files. Finder also hides the extension on `.pkg` package directories under certain circumstances. The `.pkg` package directories contain application files as well as scripts that are run at various stages of the installation process.

NOTE

The `.pkg` package directories can be stored in DMG archives to avoid revealing the fact that multiple files are present during a download.

To build a `.pkg` package directory, create the directory hierarchy that the application being installed needs to have after installation. Copy the application files into the directories. Use the PackageMaker application included with Apple's Developer tools in the /Developer/Applications/PackageMaker folder to specify the directory that will be stored in a .pkg package directory. Any preinstall or postinstall scripts that must be run as well as any basic information about the package such as its name, description, and owner are specified with PackageMaker. PackageMaker then creates the .pkg package directory.

Multiple .pkg package directories can be combined into a single metapackage package directory with the .mpkg extension. Users can select which .pkg package directories within a larger .mpkg package directory to install and which to skip. Documentation for the PackageMaker and Installer applications is available from the respective application's Help menu.

PackageMaker makes constructing packages deceptively simple. Unless great care is taken in the creation of packages, an installation can seriously damage the user's installed copy of Mac OS X. The PackageMaker documentation describes some of the pitfalls. Be careful to avoid these problems when using PackageMaker and Installer. This is especially important if the package being installed requires the user to authenticate as an administrator.

Many of the problems with Mac OS X software installation are described in articles on Stepwise. A tutorial for making PackageMaker .pkg package directories is available at http://www.stepwise.com/Articles/Technical/Packages/BuildingAPackage.html. An article titled, "Beware of Installers bearing packages (Part II)" is available at http://www.stepwise.com/Articles/Technical/Packages/InstallerOnX.html. Another article titled "Packaging and Distributing Your Software on Mac OS X" is available at http://www.stepwise.com/Articles/Technical/2001-05-11.01.html.

File Ownership and Permissions

PackageMaker and Installer can corrupt file ownership and permission data. This is only a serious problem when authentication is required for installation. Ensure that all the files and directories in the .pkg package directory have the appropriate permissions. Any permissions that are incorrect and any unusual file ownership will be carried over to the user's installation. It's best to make the ownership of files be "root," if possible. By doing this, users who install a package but are not root will have the file ownership set to an appropriate value.

If an installation inadvertently changes the ownership or permissions on system directories and files, it might not be possible to start Mac OS X when the machine is rebooted.

Symbolic Links

PackageMaker uses the Unix tool, PAX, for archiving. PAX is single-minded about file types. If the .pkg package directory has a normal directory stored, but the operating system installation has a symbolic link in that location (to perhaps allow storage of items on another hard disk) PAX will replace the symbolic link with a normal directory. This can be disastrous in some cases. For example, if during the construction of the directory hierarchy for a `.pkg` package directory, a directory called `/etc` is created, installing the resulting `.pkg` might make the Mac OS X machine unable to boot. On Mac OS X, a directory called `/etc` already exists but is normally hidden from users by Finder. Actually, the `/etc` directory is a file system link to another directory called `/private/etc` that stores essential operating system configuration data. When a `.pkg` package directory containing the `/etc` directory is installed, PAX overwrites the link from `/etc` to `/private/etc`. The next time the user reboots, startup will fail.

Safety Rules for Using Installer

If a `.pkg` must be installed in a directory such as `/usr/local/bin`, it is better to create a package with the contents of only the `bin` directory. Set the installation directory in PackageMaker to `/usr/local/bin`. If the installation directory is the root directory, `/`, and there are any symbolic links in the installation path, files will be destroyed. If a package must install files into multiple locations such as `/Library/StartupItems`, `/Applications`, and `/usr/local/bin`, it is better to create three packages that are grouped in a `.mpkg` package directory than to have them all in a single `.pkg` that installs at `/`.

Pre-install and post-install scripts should be space safe. It is imperative that the install scripts that run before or after an installation handle paths that have space characters in them. This requires some extra care during the authoring of these scripts. Failure to handle spaces in filenames can lead to accidental file deletion or incomplete installs. Apple released a version of their iTunes application that didn't handle spaces in filenames correctly and users suffered badly (including massive data loss).

Third-Party Installers

Third-party installer applications are available with varying degrees of support for Mac OS X. One or more of the following installers could be useful, but some might have shortcomings when used with Mac OS X:

- StuffIt InstallerMaker from Aladdin Systems (`http://www.aladdinsys.com`)
- InstallerVise from MindVision Software, Inc. (`http://www.mindvision.com`)
- InstallAnywhere from Zero G (`http://www.installanywhere.com/`)

Summary

Installing Cocoa applications should be made as simple as possible for users. The best technique is to let users copy the application's package directory to their local file system with Finder. Apple provides the Installer application for use in the rare cases when a dedicated installer application is needed. However, special care is needed to avoid damaging a user's file system when applications are installed with Installer. Apple's DMG archives or other archive file formats can be used to simplify the process of downloading Cocoa applications over the Internet.

PART IV
Appendixes

IN THIS PART

A

Unleashing the Objective-C Runtime

IN THIS APPENDIX

- Objective-C Objects
- Messaging with IMPs and Selectors
- Common Runtime Functions
- Forwarding, Distributed Objects, and Proxies
- Examples

Apple's Objective-C runtime consists of a few key data structures and functions that implement Objective-C's message sending semantics. This appendix describes Apple's runtime, and most of the information here applies to the Gnu runtime. This appendix provides information about the implementation of Objective-C, which is not required to use the language. Most languages do not provide any programmer access to internal implementation details.

Directly manipulating the runtime enables many powerful uses of Objective-C including the integration of Objective-C with scripting languages, performance optimizations, and a high degree of introspection. Using the runtime, it is possible to find information about every class in an application or library. Information about every method implemented by an object can be discovered including the method name, the number and type of arguments, and the return type. Most language compilers discard this information, but Objective-C preserves it for possible use in running applications.

The Objective-C runtime can even be used to implement different languages. Apple sells a version of its WebObjects product that includes support for the WebScript language. WebScript is essentially an interpreted version of Objective-C that is implemented with the Objective-C runtime and can, therefore, interoperate with compiled objects.

Objective-C Objects

From a C programmer's point of view, Objective-C objects are just C structures with the following layout defined in `objc.h`:

```
typedef struct objc_object {
       Class isa;
} *id;
```

The `objc.h` file, and the others that implement Apple's Objective-C runtime, are available as part of Apple's Darwin open-source project at `http://www.opensource.apple.com/projects/darwin/`.

The `objc_object` structure declaration shows that the only requirement for memory to be used as an object is the presence of the `isa` element, and any such memory can be referenced by the type `id`.

The `isa` Element

The essential element in every Objective-C object is the `isa` element with the type `Class`. The type `Class` is described in its own section in this appendix. For now, it is enough to note that the `isa` element is a pointer to memory that represents a class object, and the class object stores all the methods understood by instances of the class. In Chapter 4, "Objective-C," objects are loosely defined as anything that can receive messages. The presence of the `isa` element is the key that enables the runtime to find a method to invoke when a message is received.

Extra Bytes

A rarely used feature of Objective-C is the capability to allocate an arbitrary number of extra bytes when the memory for an object is allocated. The only requirement for memory to be used as an object is the presence of the `isa` element; therefore, bytes after the `isa` element have no impact and are usually ignored by the runtime.

Extra bytes can be used for any purpose. For example, the extra bytes can store an ASCII string or an array of integers. Because Cocoa does not use the extra bytes, programmers are free to use the feature in any way desired.

It is not possible to allocate extra bytes using Cocoa directly, but Apple's Objective-C runtime includes a function that can allocate extra bytes.

```
id class_createInstance(Class aClass, unsigned idxIvars);
```

The `class_createInstance(Class, unsigned idxIvars)` function and the other functions of the Objective-C runtime do not conform to the Cocoa naming conventions and are not technically part of Cocoa. However, they can be used in Cocoa applications. The `class_createInstance(Class, unsigned idxIvars)` function returns a pointer to enough newly allocated memory to store an instance of the class `aClass` as well as extra bytes specified by `idxIvars`. The following function serves the same purpose and enables the specification of a memory zone to use when allocating memory:

```
id class_createInstanceFromZone(Class, unsigned idxIvars, void *z);
```

Memory zones are described in the "Using Memory Zones" section of Chapter 5, "Cocoa Conventions."

Class

Each object's `isa` element points to objects defined by the following structure:

```
typedef struct objc_class {
        struct objc_class *isa;
        struct objc_class *super_class;
        const char *name;
        long version;
        long info;
        long instance_size;
        struct objc_ivar_list *ivars;
        struct objc_method_list **methodLists;
        struct objc_cache *cache;
        struct objc_protocol_list *protocols;
} *Class;
```

The key to the definition of the Class structure is that it contains an `isa` element just like the objc_object structure. The first bytes of an `objc_class` structure have the same meaning as an `objc_object` structure. As a result, Objective-C classes are objects that can receive messages and can be used in any situation that any other object can be used.

After the `isa` element, the elements of the `objc_class` structure provide information used by the runtime to find methods to invoke when messages are received. The information is also available for use with runtime object introspection.

The `super_class` Element

The `super_class` element is returned from the `+superclass` method implemented by the `NSObject` base class. The `NSObject` class also provides the `+class` method, and it returns the class of the receiver.

NOTE

Almost all features of the `NSObject` base class are implemented with runtime-C functions and the `objc_class` structure. The `NSObject` class and the runtime are closely coupled and cannot be easily used separately.

The `super_class` element points to the class that is used by the runtime to find a method to invoke if the receiver of a message does not provide such a method itself or when a message is sent to `super`. Details about the use of the `super_class` element are presented in the "Messaging with `IMP`s and Selectors" section of this appendix.

The `name` Element

This element stores a pointer to the ACSII string name of the class. All class names used in a single application must be unique, and the runtime guarantees that. Any attempt to load a class into a program that already contains a class with the same name fails and an error is generated.

The name is used by runtime functions such as `objc_lookUpClass(const char *name)` that return a pointer to the class with the specified name. The name is also returned by the `-className` method implemented by `NSObject`.

The `version` Element

The version is returned by `NSObject`'s `+version` method. The version is used to detect old versions of a class when initializing objects previously encoded. The initialization code can use the version number to convert between versions as necessary. If the version of a class has never been explicitly set, it defaults to zero.

The `NSCoder` class's `-versionForClassName:` method and the runtime's `class_getVersion(Class class)` function also use the version element.

The `info` Element

The `info` element is reserved for use by Apple's particular implementation of the runtime. No functions or methods are provided to access this element. Currently, the runtime uses it to identify the purpose of each class and determine whether the class is fully initialized.

The `instance_size` Element

The `instance_size` element specifies the number of bytes needed to store an instance of the class. The minimum instance size on Mac OS X is the 4 bytes needed to store the `isa` element. Each element beyond the `isa` element requires additional storage and increases the instance size.

The `class_createInstance(Class, unsigned idxIvars)` and `class_createInstanceFromZone(Class, unsigned idxIvars, void *z)` runtime functions reference a class's `instance_size` element to allocate the correct amount of memory.

The `ivars` Element

The `ivars` element stores a pointer to a dynamically allocated array of structures containing the name and type of each instance variable.

The following runtime functions are provided to directly access instance variables:

```
Ivar object_setInstanceVariable(id, const char *name, void *);
Ivar object_getInstanceVariable(id, const char *name, void **);
Ivar class_getInstanceVariable(Class, const char *);
```

The `Ivar` type is a structure containing the following elements that provide the name, type, and offset of an instance variable within the bytes that represent an object instance:

```
typedef struct objc_ivar {
        char *ivar_name;
        char *ivar_type;
        int ivar_offset;
}  *Ivar;
```

The `ivar_type` element of the `objc_ivar` structure stores a type encoding string produced by the `@encode()` compiler directive introduced in Chapter 4. Details about type encoding are provided in Apple's online document at `http://developer.apple.com/techpubs/macosx/Cocoa/ObjectiveC/4MoreObjC/index.html`.

An `objc_ivar_list` structure provides storage for a variable number of `objc_ivar` structures.

```
struct objc_ivar_list {
       int ivar_count;
       struct objc_ivar ivar_list[1]; /* variable length */
};
```

NOTE

The technique of defining a structure with a count variable followed by an array with only one element is used to create variable length arrays. Memory is dynamically allocated to store the number of values specified by the count variable. The pointer to the allocated memory is cast to the structure to enable array index semantics without C compiler warnings.

The methodLists Element

The methodLists element stores a pointer to a dynamically allocated array of arrays of structures containing the name, return type, argument types, and implementation of each instance method implemented by the class.

The following runtime functions use the instance_methods element:

```
void class_addMethods(Class, struct objc_method_list *);
void class_removeMethods(Class, struct objc_method_list *);
unsigned method_getNumberOfArguments(Method);
unsigned method_getSizeOfArguments(Method);
unsigned method_getArgumentInfo(Method m, int arg, const char **type, int *offset);
struct objc_method_list *class_nextMethodList(Class, void **);
```

Methods can be added and removed from classes, and information about existing methods can be obtained from the runtime. These features provided by the runtime enable a high degree of dynamism.

The methodLists element is declared as objc_method_list **methodLists. The double pointer is used because multiple arrays of methods are stored. At a minimum, instance methods and class methods are stored in separate arrays.

The objc_method structure stores the following information about each method:

```
Typedef struct objc_method {
        SEL method_name;
        char *method_types;
        IMP method_imp;
} *Method;
```

The SEL and IMP types have already been introduced in Chapter 4 and are covered again with more detail in the "Messaging with IMPs and Selectors" section of this appendix. The method_types variable stores a sequence of type encoding characters produced by the @encode() compiler directive.

An objc_method_list structure uses the same technique for implementing a variable length array that was used for instance variable lists.

```
struct objc_method_list {
        int method_count;
        struct objc_method method_list[1];    /* variable length */
};
```

The cache Element

Each class stores a cache of information about recently received messages and the methods that implement them. The cache is an optimization that works on the assumption that any message recently received is likely to be received again soon. Using the cache to lookup the method to invoke when a message is received is much faster than using other techniques.

Details about how the cache is used are provided as part of the explanation of messaging in the "Messaging with IMPs and Selectors" section of this appendix. The cache is implemented with the following hash table data structure:

```
typedef struct objc_cache {
        unsigned int mask;            /* total = mask + 1 */
        unsigned int occupied;
        Method buckets[1];
} *Cache;
```

The performance improvements provided by the cache are the result of the hashing function used to map message selectors to method implementations. Hashing functions and hash tables are common programming tools that are explained in almost every introductory data structures textbook. An excellent introduction is available at http://ciips.ee.uwa.edu.au/~morris/Year2/PLDS210/hash_tables.html. An advanced description of hashing functions is available at http://www.cris.com/~Ttwang/tech/inthash.htm.

The protocols Element

Each class can conform to any number of protocols. The protocols are stored in a linked list of arrays. The unusual combination of data structures used to store protocols is a remnant of the earliest implementation of distributed objects. Protocols are used to aid static typing, enable multiple-interface inheritance, and optimize distributed messaging.

The Objective-C runtime declares a class called Protocol. The following structure defines a variable length list of Protocol instances:

```
@class Protocol;

struct objc_protocol_list {
        struct objc_protocol_list *next;
        int count;
        Protocol *list[1];
};
```

Categories

Categories are not stored in the `objc_class` structure. The methods added to a class by a category are added to the method lists already stored for the class. Nevertheless, the Objective-C runtime defines a structure for categories.

```
typedef struct objc_category {
        char *category_name;
        char *class_name;
        struct objc_method_list *instance_methods;
        struct objc_method_list *class_methods;
        struct objc_protocol_list *protocols;
} *Category;
```

The category name and the name of the class extended are stored as well as the instance methods, class methods, and protocols implemented by the category. Apple's compiler embeds one or more `objc_category` structures in the `.o` files generated for modules that contain category implementations. When an `.o` file is loaded into a running application, the runtime is notified so that it can read the embedded `objc_category` structures and copy the methods and protocols from the categories into the extended classes. When the methods and protocols are copied, the `objc_category` structures are no longer needed.

Messaging with IMPs and Selectors

The Objective-C runtime contains two functions that implement messaging:

```
id objc_msgSend(id self, SEL op, ...);
id objc_msgSendSuper(struct objc_super *super, SEL op, ...);
```

The `objc_msgSend(id self, SEL op, ...)` function is the key to the dynamism and flexibility of Objective-C. All the runtime's data structures exist either to make the implementation of `objc_msgSend(id self, SEL op, ...)` possible or to optimize the implementation. The capability to add methods to an existing class, have one class pose as another, implement distributed messaging, and implement polymorphism results from the existence of `objc_msgSend(id self, SEL op, ...)`.

When the Objective-C compiler encounters a messaging expression such as `[receiver someMessageSelector]`, it replaces that expression with code to call `objc_msgSend(receiver, @selector(someMessageSelector))` in the output binary file.

The `objc_msgSend(id self, SEL op, ...)` function finds a method implemented by the receiver that corresponds to the specified selector and invokes that method. To find a suitable method, `objc_msgSend(id self, SEL op, ...)` first finds the class that describes the receiver by referencing the receiver's isa variable. It then looks in the cache and method lists of the receiver's class for a method that corresponds to the selector. If one isn't found, objc_msgSend(id self, SEL op, ...) looks in the receiver class's super_class variable and so on until a method is found or there are no more superclasses. More details about the search for a method that corresponds to a selector are provided in the "Searching for a Method" section of this appendix.

Apple includes a diagram in the "How Messaging Works" section of http://developer.apple.com/techpubs/macosx/Cocoa/XObjC/XObjC.pdf that shows how objc_msgSend(id self, SEL op, ...) searches for an IMP.

If no suitable method is found by objc_msgSend(id self, SEL op, ...), code is called to forward the message represented by the selector to another object. Forwarding is described in the section on "Forwarding, Distributed Objects, and Proxies" in this appendix.

If a suitable method is found by objc_msgSend(id self, SEL op, ...), the function that implements the method is called. The function called is referenced by the method_imp element of the objc_method structure that describes the method. The method_imp variable stores an IMP, and an IMP is just a pointer to a C function with the following type:

```
typedef id              (*IMP)(id self, SEL _cmd, ...);
```

The first two arguments to the function referenced by an IMP are the receiver and selector passed as arguments to objc_msgSend(id self, SEL op, ...). Within the method implemented by the IMP, the receiver argument to objc_msgSend(id self, SEL op, ...) is the self variable used by the method. Additional arguments to a method are passed from the stack to the function referenced by the IMP. Apple's Objective-C runtime uses assembly language to change the CPU's stack pointer so that the additional arguments are available to the function called. The GNU Objective-C runtime uses portable C code to adjust the stack and as a result suffers a small performance penalty when used with some CPU families.

The objc_msgSendSuper(struct objc_super *super, SEL op, ...) function works exactly the same way as objc_msgSend(id self, SEL op, ...) except that objc_msgSendSuper(struct objc_super *super, SEL op, ...) begins the search for a method with the receiver's superclass and does not consider any methods implemented by the receiver itself. The Objective-C compiler generates a call to objc_msgSendSuper(struct objc_super *super, SEL op, ...) when it encounters a messaging expression containing the super keyword such as [super someMessageSelector].

Searching for a Method

Searching for a method to invoke can be time consuming. Apple's Objective-C runtime avoids the search in most cases by caching the `IMP` for each selector within the class itself. The cache has already been described as part of the `objc_class` data structure. When `objc_msgSend(id self, SEL op, ...)` is called, it checks the cache for an `IMP` that corresponds to the specified selector. If an `IMP` is found in the cache, no search takes place. The `IMP` is called immediately. If the correct `IMP` is not found in the cache, the search for a method `IMP` is performed. When the `IMP` is found, it is placed in the cache to avoid future searches.

NOTE

Apple's Objective-C runtime finds the correct `IMP` in the cache 85% to 90% of the time in tested applications. Calling an `IMP` that was found in the cache requires a pointer dereference followed by a jump instruction. In such cases, the performance of Objective-C message dispatch is roughly equivalent to the performance of calling a C++ virtual member function.

Selectors identify messages and are used to find corresponding method `IMP`s. The important attributes of selectors are that every different message has a different selector and selectors can be efficiently used as an index into a class's method cache. Pointers to global variables make ideal selectors because the existing C linkers can be used to guarantee that every selector is unique. Pointers are also easily converted to indexes into the cache.

The selector type is declared in `obcj.h` as follows:

```
typedef struct objc_selector     *SEL;
```

The most important thing about the `SEL` type is that it is a pointer. It doesn't matter what it points to. When Apple's Objective-C compiler encounters an `@selector()` compiler directive, it generates object code for a pointer to a global variable corresponding to the selector. Each unique selector in a program must have a corresponding global variable. When Objective-C programs are linked, the linker resolves all the references to global variables. A similar process takes place when Objective-C objects are dynamically loaded.

Because C allows the conversion of pointers to integers, many programmers use the `SEL` type interchangeably with integers. Because the selectors are guaranteed by the linker to be unique, two selectors can be compared using simple pointer comparison. For example, the following function returns a nonzero value if the two selector arguments are equal:

```
BOOL MYSelectorCompare(SEL selector1, SEL selector2)
{
  return (selector1 == selector2);
}
```

Apple provides information about messaging with selectors and `IMP`s at `http://developer.apple.com/techpubs/macosx/Cocoa/ObjectiveC/3CoreObjC/iHow_Messaging_Works.html`.

Common Runtime Functions

Several runtime functions are commonly used in Cocoa applications. The `NSStringFromSelector(SEL)` function converts selectors into strings. The following line of code can be placed in any method implementation to output the name of the method:

```
NSLog(@"%@", NSStringForSelector(_cmd));
```

The `NSSelectorFromString(NSString *)` function returns the selector if any that corresponds to a string.

The `NSClassFromString(NSString *)` function returns the class identified by a string name. The following lines of code can be used to send a user specified message to a user specified class object:

```
void MYSendMessageToAClass(NSString *className, NSString *messageName)
{
  [NSClassFromString(className) performSelector:
      NSSelectorFromString(messageName)];
}
```

The capability to implement a function such as `MYSendMessageToAClass(NSString *className, NSString *messageName)` that can translate user input strings into messages to objects is one of the advantages of Objective-C.

NOTE

When the runtime tries to find a named class and fails, it calls a function that raises an exception. Users can replace the default function with an alternative implementation by calling `void objc_setClassHandler(int (*)(const char *))`. A function set this way can be implemented to dynamically load more code in an attempt to find the named class.

Chapter 4 described a technique for optimizing Objective-C by using the following methods implemented by the `NSObject` class:

```
- (IMP)methodForSelector:(SEL)aSelector;
+ (IMP)instanceMethodForSelector:(SEL)aSelector;
```

The basic technique is to look up the `IMP` for a particular receiver and selector pair once, and then call the `IMP` multiple times without incurring the lookup cost each time. These methods use the following runtime functions in their implementation:

```
IMP class_lookupMethod(Class, SEL);
IMP class_lookupMethodInMethodList(struct objc_method_list *mlist, SEL);
IMP class_lookupNamedMethodInMethodList(struct objc_method_list *mlist,
    const char *meth_name);
IMP _class_lookupMethodAndLoadCache(Class, SEL);
```

In almost all cases, the methods provided by `NSObject` should be used, but the C functions are available for special cases. For example, the runtime's C functions can be used to optimize code compiled with an ANSI C compiler rather than an Objective-C compiler.

Forwarding, Distributed Objects, and Proxies

When `objc_msgSend(id self, SEL op, ...)` and `objc_msgSendSuper(struct objc_super *super, SEL op, ...)` fail to find a method that corresponds to the selector of a received message, the `-forwardInvocation:` method implemented by the `NSObject` class is called. The argument to `-forwardInvocation:` is an instance of the `NSInvocation` class initialized with information about the message that could not be handled including the selector and any arguments.

The default implementation of `-forwardInvocation:` calls `[self doesNotRecognizeSelector:aSelector]`. The `-doesNotRecognizeSelector:` method raises an exception. If `-forwardInvocation:` is overloaded, it can be implemented to find another receiver for the message that could not be handled. The online `NSObject` class documentation describes techniques for implementing `-forwardInvocation:` in a variety of ways. The forwarding topic at `http://developer.apple.com/techpubs/macosx/Cocoa/ObjectiveC/5RunTime/Forwarding.html` describes a technique for simulating multiple inheritance in Objective-C with forwarding.

Some Cocoa technologies that use `-forwardInvocation:` include the Application Kit's built-in undo and redo support as well as Apple's implementation of distributed objects. Proxy objects in the application that sends distributed messages represent distributed objects in other processes. A proxy object implemented by the `NSProxy` class is a root class like `NSObject`. Unlike `NSObject`, the `NSProxy` class implements very few methods. When the proxy object receives a message, it forwards the message over a network connection to a receiver in a different process.

A full description of Apple's distributed objects technology is provided at `http://developer.apple.com/techpubs/macosx/Cocoa/TasksAndConcepts/ProgrammingTopics/DistrObjects/index.html`. Apple's implementation is very good, but the same general approach can be used for custom solutions as well. The `-forwardInvocation:` method can be implemented to support cross-platform, standard CORBA distributed objects, and the Gnustep project at `http://www.gnustep.org/` provides its own implementation of distributed objects for Objective-C.

Examples

This section contains examples that use the Objective-C runtime to obtain detailed information about the objects in an application. None of the examples are complete. They each show just enough to illustrate how to perform a certain task using the runtime. The examples need to be incorporated into larger Cocoa applications to be of any practical use.

Get a List of All Classes

The `MYShowAllClasses()` function, in this example, prints the name of every class linked to a Cocoa application. Call this function from within a Cocoa application that is run in Project Builder or from a Terminal to see the output. This function can be trivially modified to return an `NSArray` containing the `NSString` names of all classes linked into an application. The `NSArray` version of this function is available at `www.cocoaprogramming.net`.

```
#import <objc/objc-runtime.h>

void MYShowAllClasses()
/*"
Print to stdout the names of all classes known to the
Objective-C runtime.

"*/
{
  Class   *classes;
  Class   *currentClass;
  int     numberOfClasses;
  int     i;
```

```
  // Get the number of classes known by the runtime
  numberOfClasses = objc_getClassList(NULL, 0);

  // Allocate storage for the correct number of classes
  classes = (Class *)malloc(sizeof(Class) * numberOfClasses);

  // Fill the storage with classes know by the runtime
  objc_getClassList(classes, numberOfClasses);

  // Print the name of each class
  currentClass = classes;
  for(i = 0; i < numberOfClasses; i++) {
    NSLog("%s", (*currentClass)->name);
    currentClass++;
  }

  // Free the allocated storage
  free(classes);
}
```

Get a List of All Instance Variables

The `MYShowAllInstanceVariables(Class)` function prints a list of all instance variables defined for instances of a specified class.

```
void MYListAllInstanceVariables(Class aClass)
{
  struct objc_ivar_list   *ilist = aClass->ivars;
  const int                  numInstanceVariables = ilist->ivar_count;
  int                       i;

  for(i = 0; i < numInstanceVariables; i++)
  {
    Ivar    currentInstanceVariable = &ilist->ivar_list[i];

    NSLog(@"%s %s %d", currentInstanceVariable->ivar_name,
        currentInstanceVariable->ivar_type,
        currentInstanceVariable->ivar_offset);
  }
}
```

Get a List of All Methods

In this example, the `MYShowAllMethods(Class)` function prints a list of all methods implemented by a class and the address of each implementation.

```
void MYShowAllMethods(Class aClass)
{
  void                         *iterator = NULL;
  struct objc_method_list      *mlist;

  while(mlist = class_nextMethodList(aClass, &iterator ))
  {
    const int         numMethods = mlist->method_count;
    int                 i;

    for(i = 0; i < numMethods; i++)
    {
      Method     currentMethod = &mlist->method_list[i];

      NSLog(@"%@ %p", NSStringFromSelector(currentMethod->method_name),
          currentMethod->method_imp);
    }
  }
}
```

Store the `IMP` for a Replaced Method

Categories are one of Objective-C's most powerful features. With categories, individual methods of a class can be replaced with alternate implementations even without source code to the methods being replaced. One limitation of categories is that there is no convenient way to call the original implementation of a method from the version that replaces it. The following example shows one technique for calling the replaced implementation of a method. The `MYTest` class implements the `-testMethod` method. A category of the `MYTest` class replaces the original implementation of the `-testMethod` method, but is still able to call the original implementation.

```
File MYTest.h:
#import <Foundation/Foundation.h>

@interface MYTest : NSObject
{
}
```

```
- (void)testMethod;

@end
```

Each of the `+load`, `+initialize`, and `-testMethod` methods implemented by the `MYTest` class outputs text indicating that it was called.

```
File MYTest.m:
#import "MYTest.h"

@implementation MYTest

+ (void)load
{
  NSLog(@"Original load");
}

+ (void)initialize
{
  NSLog(@"Original initialize");
}

- (void)testMethod
{
  NSLog(@"Original testMethod");
}

@end
```

The following category replaces methods of the `MYTest` class.

```
File MYTest_MYTest.m:
#import "MYTest.h"
#import <objc/objc-class.h>

@implementation MYTest (MYTest)

static IMP _myOriginalTestMethod = NULL;

+ (void)load
{
  Method        originalMethod;
```

```
  NSLog(@"Category load");

  // Save original IMP
  originalMethod = class_getInstanceMethod(self, @selector(testMethod));
  if(NULL != originalMethod)
  {
    _myOriginalTestMethod = originalMethod->method_imp;
  }
}

+ (void)initialize
{
  NSLog(@"Category initialize");
}

- (void)testMethod
{
  if(NULL != _myOriginalTestMethod)
  {
    // Call original IMP
    (*_myOriginalTestMethod)(self, _cmd);
  }

  NSLog(@"Category testMethod");
}

@end
```

Use the following `main(int, const char *)` function to call the `-testMethod` method.

```
File main.m:
#import <Foundation/Foundation.h>
#import "MYTest.h"

int main (int argc, const char * argv[])
{
  NSAutoreleasePool   *pool = [[NSAutoreleasePool alloc] init];
  MYTest             *test = [[MYTest alloc] init];

  [test testMethod];
  [test release];
```

```
  [pool release];
  return 0;
}
```

This is the output from the example:

```
2002-04-02 10:21:55.159 TestCachedIMP[359] Original load
2002-04-02 10:21:55.160 TestCachedIMP[359] Category load
2002-04-02 10:21:55.160 TestCachedIMP[359] Category initialize
2002-04-02 10:21:55.161 TestCachedIMP[359] Original testMethod
2002-04-02 10:21:55.161 TestCachedIMP[359] Category testMethod

TestCachedIMP has exited with status 0.
```

The output shows that the `+load` method is called separately for both the original implementation of `MYTest` and the category. The `+load` method is a special case handled by the runtime. The runtime sends `+load` to each class and category that implements it when the class or category is first loaded. The `+load` method is the only method that is called in a class, even if a category that implements the same method is loaded at the same time.

The `MYTest (MYTest)` category implements `+load` to obtain the original implementation of the `-testMethod` method. That original implementation is stored and used within the category's implementation of `-testMethod`. As a result, the category is able to call the replaced method.

The output from the example shows first that the `MYTest` class's implementation of `+load` is called. Then, the implementation of `+load` in the category is called. Only the category's implementation of `+initialize` is called even though the `MYTest` class also implements `+initialize`. The category has already replaced the original implementation by the time the runtime calls `+initialize`. When `-testMethod` is called from `main()`, the category's implementation is used, but the category is able to call the original implementation that was saved.

This technique can be used with any class, but there are several critical limitations. The runtime `class_getInstanceMethod(Class)` function must be used rather than `NSObject`'s `+instanceMethodForSelector:` method because at the time `+load` is called, the `NSObject` class might not be loaded yet. The `+load` method is seldom used in part because it is not safe to call any methods within it. This example works with the implementation of the Objective-C runtime in Mac OS X version 10.1.3 and earlier. The Objective-C runtime implementation always calls the category's version of `+load` after the original class's implementation of `+load`. Apple does not guarantee that this behavior will be preserved in future versions. Finally, this example produces unpredictable results if multiple categories replace the same method.

An alternate approach is to replace the `IMP` stored for an existing method with the `IMP` for a different method that has the same arguments. In other words, rather than replacing an existing method directly with a category, add a similar method that takes the same arguments. At runtime, switch the `IMP` stored for the original method with the one for the added method. After that's done, selectors for the added method and the original method end up calling the same `IMP`. The original `IMP` can be called from the added method.

```
File NSObject_MYReplaceIMP.m:
#import <Foundation/Foundation.h>
#import <objc/objc-class.h>
extern _objc_flush_caches(Class);

@implementation NSObject (MYReplaceIMP)

static IMP _myOriginalRelease = NULL;

+ (void)installCustomRelease
{
  Method     originalMethod;

  if (originalMethod = class_getInstanceMethod(self, @selector(release)))
  {
    // Store original IMP
    _myOriginalRelease = originalMethod->method_imp;

    // Replace IMP
    originalMethod->method_imp = [self instanceMethodForSelector:
        @selector(_myRelease)];
    // The following is needed to keep NSObject's state consistent
    _objc_flush_caches(self);  // Private: found in runtime source
  }
}

- (void)_myRelease
{
  NSLog(@"Released instance: %@ %p", [[self class] description], self);
  (*_myOriginalRelease)(self, @selector(release));
}

@end
```

The +installCustomRelease method added to NSObject must be called sometime early in the program's execution. When +installCustomRelease is called, every time NSObject's -release method is called, the code that implements -_myRelease is executed. The -_myRelease method calls the original implementation.

Access Any Class From a Scripting Language

Several popular scripting languages have already been extended to use the Objective-C runtime and, therefore, can access Cocoa objects. One recent example is the open source RubyCocoa project at http://sourceforge.net/projects/rubycocoa/. Another example is F-Script at http://www.fscript.org/.

A scripting language must be extensible to be integrated with Cocoa. As long as it is possible to dynamically map language elements of a scripting language to Objective-C selectors, almost any Cocoa object can be used from the scripting language.

A simple example that makes Cocoa accessible from the popular TCL scripting language is available at www.cocoaprogramming.net. In TCL, new commands can be added by calling the Tcl_CreateObjCommand() function after creating a TCL interpreter with the Tcl_CreateInterp() function. The Tcl_CreateObjCommand() function associates a string command name with a function that will be called whenever the interpreter encounters the command string in an appropriate context.

Very little code is needed to provide access to all Cocoa from TCL. One technique only requires the addition of two new commands to the TCL interpreter using Tcl_CreateObjCommand(). Add one command called classWithName which takes a single argument that is the name of a class and returns a reference to the named Objective-C class. Add a second command called sendMessage that sends a named message to a specified object. The classWithName command is implemented with NSClassFromString(NSString *). The sendMessage command is implemented with NSSelectorFromString(NSString *) and the -performSelector: method.

The following TCL code uses the new commands to load image data from the hard disk:

```
bundle = classWithName NSBundle;
path = sendMessage [sendMessage $bundle mainBundle] pathToResource:ofType:
    testImage tiff;
image = sendMessage [sendMessage [ClassWithName NSImage] alloc]
    initWithPath: $path;
```

The next TCL code sample converts a Fahrenheit value obtained from one objective-C object and sets the value of another Objective-C object to the equivalent Celsius value. The arg1 and sender values are previously defined objects.

```
sendMessage $arg1 setFloatValue: [expr 5 * (
    [sendMessage sender floatValue] - 32 )  / 9 ];    # Fahrenheit to Celsius
```

An example at www.cocoaprogramming.net uses the Fahrenheit to Celsius code to implement a Cocoa temperature converter with a slider and a text field.

Summary

The Objective-C runtime is one of the strengths of Cocoa and provides many advantages over other languages for certain applications. The Objective-C runtime can also be misused. The techniques and information presented in this appendix are not needed to implement the vast majority of Cocoa applications. The almost unparalleled flexibility and power enabled by the runtime make detailed introspection, the integration of scripting languages, and sophisticated optimizations possible, but it is necessary to use low-level C code and it is very easy to introduce hard to track bugs unless great care is taken.

Appendix B, "Optimizing and Finding Memory Leaks," describes several techniques for debugging and optimizing Cocoa applications. Cocoa provides many hooks for error detection and debugging. Apple provides developer tools to help optimize Cocoa applications, and Appendix B describes how they are used.

B

Optimizing and Finding Memory Leaks

IN THIS APPENDIX

- Optimizing Applications
- Finding Memory Leaks

This appendix describes techniques for optimizing Cocoa applications and finding memory leaks. A Cocoa application called `LotsOfWords` is developed and revised several times within the appendix to demonstrate various optimizations. `LotsOfWords` displays strings with random positions, font sizes, and colors. The application is small but realistic. It could form the basis of a screen saver, but more importantly, the optimizations that apply to `LotsOfWords` also apply to larger applications. Finally, techniques for finding memory leaks are provided.

Optimizing Applications

Several general principals apply to optimizing applications. The first and most important principal is not to optimize prematurely. Another important principal is that most applications spend 80% of the their time executing only 20% of the code. When optimizing an application, it is important to concentrate on optimizations that will have a noticeable affect on performance. Optimizing the 80% of the program that consumes 10% of the execution time has no noticeable affect on performance.

Premature Optimization

The famous computer scientist Donald Knuth is quoted in nearly every book that describes optimizations. He said, “Premature optimization is the root of all evil.” There are many reasons to avoid optimizing at all.

- Optimizing an application often introduces new bugs.
- Optimizing an application’s code usually makes that code harder to read and maintain.
- A lot of time can be spent optimizing code for little gain in performance.

Before optimizing an application, consider whether the application needs to be optimized at all. In many cases, applications are fast enough without any specific optimizations. The decision to optimize cannot be made until the application is substantially complete. Therefore, any optimization before the application is nearly complete is premature.

NOTE

The temptation to prematurely optimize strikes all programmers sooner or later. The best practice is to resist the temptation. Wait until the time spent optimizing can be spent where it will provide the best performance improvements.

The 80/20 Rule

A rule of thumb, which was alluded to earlier, is that 80% of a program's execution time is spent on 20% of the code. In the rare case that an application spends the same amount of time in every module of code, the task of optimizing is gigantic. In such cases, every module must be optimized to be able to get noticeable improvements. For most applications, after the critical 20% of the code has been identified, focused optimization of only that code can provide maximum benefit for minimum effort. The key is finding the critical code.

In some Cocoa applications, the code that consumes the most execution time is inside the Cocoa frameworks. This is particularly true for graphical Cocoa applications. Most of the drawing code used by Cocoa applications is inside the frameworks. It is not realistic to modify the Cocoa frameworks when optimizing applications. In many cases, the Cocoa frameworks are already highly optimized. If an application spends most of its time executing framework code, the best optimization technique is to execute framework code less often. For example, drawing as little as possible results in fewer calls into the framework's drawing code and can yield dramatic performance improvements.

The `LotsOfWords` Application

The `LotsOfWords` application displays words randomly selected from a text file at `/usr/share/dict/words`, which is part of Mac OS X's BSD subsystem. The application can be trivially modified to use words from another source. No word is displayed more than once before all words have been displayed at least once. The application has been stripped to its minimum features so that this chapter can focus on optimizing without the distraction of extraneous features. The complete source code for the `LotsOfWords` application is available at `www.cocoaprogramming.net`.

The `LotsOfWords` application is implemented with three custom classes: `MYWordView`, `_MYWord`, and `MYWordController`. An instance of the `MYWordView` class is used to draw instances of the _MYWord class. An instance of the MYWordController class acts as the NSApplication's delegate; it keeps track of the application's update rate and provides the _MYWord instances that MYWordView draws. Figure B.1 shows the LotsOfWords application displaying words with random colors, random amounts of transparency, random font sizes, and random positions.

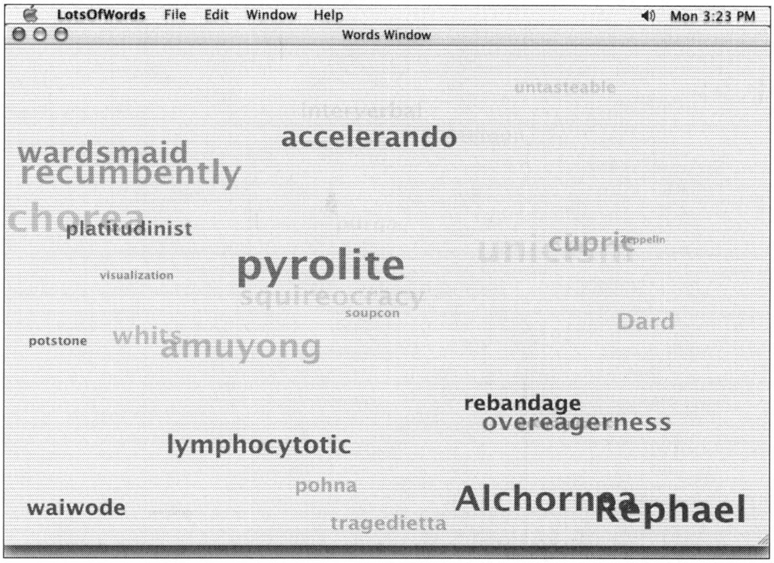

FIGURE B.1 The LotsOfWords application displays words with random attributes.

The LotsOfWords application loosely follows the MVC design described in Chapter 6, "Design Patterns." The _MYWord class comprises most of the model. The MYWordView class and the application's nib file implement the view subsystem. The MYWordController class implements the controller subsystem and manages an array of _MYWord instances to be displayed.

The code in this section implements a working application, but it is only a starting point. The code is optimized throughout the remainder of the appendix. The following code defines the interface of the _MYWord class:

File _MYWord.h

```
#import <Cocoa/Cocoa.h>
```

```
@interface _MYWord : NSObject
{
  NSString        *_myWord;               /*" The word "*/
  NSPoint         _myPosition;            /*" The word's position "*/
  NSDictionary       *_myAttributes;        /*" The word's attributes "*/
}

/*" Class methods "*/
+ (void)initializeWordSetWithPath:(NSString *)aPath;
+ (NSString *)nextWordInSet;

/*" Designated Initializer "*/
- (id)initWithWord:(NSString *)aWord inRect:(NSRect)aFrame;

/*" Alternate Initializers "*/
- (id)initWithNextWordInRect:(NSRect)aFrame;
- (id)init;

/*" Drawing "*/
- (void)drawRect:(NSRect)aRect;

/*" Accessors "*/
- (NSString *)word;

@end
```

The code that implements the `_MYWord` class includes methods that are not exposed in the class's interface. The hidden methods are used to obtain random attributes for words and manage initialization.

```
File _MYWord.m

#import "_MYWord.h"

@implementation _MYWord
/*" Instances of the _MYWord class store a string, a position, and attributes
to use when drawing the string at the position.
"*/

static NSMutableSet    *_MYWordSet = nil;        /*" Set of words to draw "*/
static NSEnumerator    *_MYWordEnumerator = nil; /*" Keeps pos in set "*/
```

```
+ (void)initializeWordSetWithPath:(NSString *)aPath
/*" Call this method to specify a file to use as a source of words. Each word
in the file at aPath is stored in a set that is later used to provide words
for display. This method should be called before +nextWordInSet or
-initWithNextWordInRect:. Each time this method is called it replaces the set
of words specified with the previous call. If the file at aPath can not be
read or does not conatin any words, the set of words will be empty. "*/
{
  NSString        *wordsSource = [NSString stringWithContentsOfFile:aPath];

  [_MYWordSet release];
  _MYWordSet = [[NSMutableSet alloc] init];

  if(nil != wordsSource)
  {
    NSScanner          *scanner = [NSScanner scannerWithString:wordsSource];
    NSCharacterSet     *interestingSet = [NSCharacterSet letterCharacterSet];
    NSString           *results;

    [scanner scanUpToCharactersFromSet:interestingSet intoString:NULL];
    while([scanner scanCharactersFromSet:interestingSet intoString:&results])
    {
      // ignore one letter words
      if(1 < [results length])
      {
        [_MYWordSet addObject:results];
      }
      [scanner scanUpToCharactersFromSet:interestingSet intoString:NULL];
    }
  }
}


+ (NSString *)nextWordInSet
/*" Returns the next word in the set of words produced by calling
+initializeWordSetWithPath:. No word is returned more than once until every
word in the set has been returend at least once. If all words in the set have
been previously returned, this method starts over returning words from the
set. If no set of words is available or the set is empty, this method returns
@"None". "*/
{
  NSString          *result;
```

```
  if (nil == (result = [_MYWordEnumerator nextObject]))
  {
    // there is no next object so try getting a new enumerator
    [_MYWordEnumerator release];
    _MYWordEnumerator = [[_MYWordSet objectEnumerator] retain];
    if (nil == (result = [_MYWordEnumerator nextObject]))
    {
      // there is still no next word so no words are available
      result = @"None";
    }
  }

  return result;
}


/*" Minimum point size of font used to draw words "*/
#define _MYMINIMUM_FONT_SIZE (9)

/*" Maximum point size of font used to draw words "*/
#define _MYMAXIMUM_FONT_SIZE (45)

+ (NSFont *)_myRandomFont
/*" Returns the user's default bold system font with a size randomly selected
between _MYMINIMUM_FONT_SIZE points and _MYMAXIMUM_FONT_SIZE points. "*/
{
  const int  fontSizeDelta = (_MYMAXIMUM_FONT_SIZE - _MYMINIMUM_FONT_SIZE);
  const int  shiftFactor = 512; // least significant bits returned by random()
                                // are not very random. Constant used to shift
                                // to more random bits
  const int  shiftedFontSizeDelta = fontSizeDelta * shiftFactor;

  return [NSFont boldSystemFontOfSize:(float)(
      random() % shiftedFontSizeDelta) / (float)shiftFactor +
      _MYMINIMUM_FONT_SIZE];
}


+ (NSColor *)_myRandomColor
/*" Returns a color with randomly selected red, green, blue, and alpha
components. "*/
{
```

```
  const int     shiftFactor = 512; // least significant bits returned by random()
                                  // are not very random. Constant used to shift
                                  // to more random bits
  const float floatShiftFactor = (float)shiftFactor;
  const float red = (float)(random() % shiftFactor) / floatShiftFactor;
  const float green = (float)(random() % shiftFactor) / floatShiftFactor;
  const float blue = (float)(random() % shiftFactor) / floatShiftFactor;
  const float alpha = (float)(random() % shiftFactor) / floatShiftFactor;

  return [NSColor colorWithCalibratedRed:red green:green blue:blue
      alpha:alpha];
}


+ (NSPoint)_myRandomPointInRect:(NSRect)aRect
/*" Returns a random point within aRect or NSZeroPoint if aRect has no area.
"*/
{
  NSPoint        result;

  if(aRect.size.width > 0.0 || aRect.size.height > 0.0)
  {
    // there is room for the word
    result = NSMakePoint((random() % (int)aRect.size.width) + aRect.origin.x,
                         (random() % (int)aRect.size.height) + aRect.origin.y);
  }
  else
  {
    // there is no room for the word so any point is as good as another
    result = NSZeroPoint;
  }

  return result;
}


- (id)_myReinitWithWord:(NSString *)aWord inRect:(NSRect)aFrame
/*" Called by -initWithWord:inRect:. This method does the actual work of
initializing an instance. "*/
{
  NSSize        stringSize;
  NSRect        validPositionArea;
```

```
  id            attributes[2];
  id            keys[2];

  // copy the word
  aWord = [aWord copy];
  [_myWord release];
  _myWord = aWord;

  // release any existing attributes
  [_myAttributes release];

  // store random attributes in the attributes dictionary
  attributes[0] = [[self class] _myRandomFont];
  attributes[1] = [[self class] _myRandomColor];
  keys[0] = NSFontAttributeName;
  keys[1] = NSForegroundColorAttributeName;
  _myAttributes = [[NSDictionary alloc] initWithObjects:attributes
                                        forKeys:keys count:2];

  // get the size of specified word drawn with specified attributes
  // and subtract from specified frame so that entire word will be
  // visible if drawn inside the frame.
  stringSize = [_myWord sizeWithAttributes:_myAttributes];
  validPositionArea = aFrame;
  validPositionArea.size.width -= stringSize.width;
  validPositionArea.size.height -= stringSize.height;

  // store random position
  _myPosition = [[self class] _myRandomPointInRect:validPositionArea];

  return self;
}


- (id)initWithWord:(NSString *)aWord inRect:(NSRect)aFrame
/*" Initializes receiver with aWord, a random position within aFrame, and
random attributes. "*/
{
  self = [super init];

  if(self)
  {
```

```
    [self _myReinitWithWord:aWord inRect:aFrame];
  }

  return self;
}


- (id)initWithNextWordInRect:(NSRect)aFrame
/*" Initializes the receiver with the next word obtained by calling
+nextWordInSet. "*/
{
  self = [self initWithWord:[[self class] nextWordInSet] inRect:aFrame];

  return self;
}


- (id)init
/*" Initializes receiver with the word "None" at NSZeroPoint with random
attributes. "*/
{
  return [self initWithWord:@"None" inRect:NSZeroRect];
}


- (void)drawRect:(NSRect)aRect
/*" Draws receiver's word at receiver's position with receiver's
attributes. "*/
{
  [_myWord drawAtPoint:_myPosition withAttributes:_myAttributes];
}


- (NSString *)word
/*" Returns the receiver's stored word. "*/
{
  return _myWord;
}


- (void)dealloc
/*" Cleanup "*/
```

```
{
  [_myWord release];
  _myWord = nil;
  [_myAttributes release];
  _myAttributes = nil;

  [super dealloc];
}

@end
```

The `MYWordView` class is almost as simple as an `NSView` subclass can be. An instance of `MYWordView` stores an array of `_MYWord` instances and draws those instances as needed. The array of `_MYWord` instances is set with the only method that `MYWordView` adds to `NSView`, `-setWordsToView:`.

```
File MYWordView.h

#import <Cocoa/Cocoa.h>

@interface MYWordView : NSView
{
  NSArray      *_myWordsArray;     /*" The array of words to display "*/
}

/*" Accessors "*/
- (void)setWordsToView:(NSArray *)anArray;

@end
```

The `MYWordView` class overrides the inherited implementation of `-drawRect:` to draw the words set with `-setWordsToView:`.

```
File MYWordView.m

#import "MYWordView.h"
#import "_MYWord.h"

@implementation MYWordView
/*" Draws an array of _MYWord instances set with -setWordsToView:. "*/

- (void)setWordsToView:(NSArray *)anArray
/*" Set the array of words to draw. "*/
```

```
{
  [anArray retain];
  [_myWordsArray release];
  _myWordsArray = anArray;
}


- (void)drawRect:(NSRect)aRect
/*" Draw the words set with -setWordsToView: "*/
{
  NSEnumerator            *enumerator = [_myWordsArray objectEnumerator];
  _MYWord                *currentWord;

  while(nil != (currentWord = [enumerator nextObject]))
  {
    [currentWord drawRect:aRect];
  }
}


- (void)dealloc
/*" Clean-up "*/
{
  [_myWordsArray release];
  _myWordsArray = nil;

  [super dealloc];
}

@end
```

An instance of the `MYWordController` class is used as the application's delegate. The `-applicationDidFinishLaunching:` and `-applicationWillTerminate:` delegate methods are used to setup and shut down the application, respectively. While the application is running, the `MYWordController` instance uses a timer to redraw the `MYWordView` as fast as possible, adding a new word every time it is drawn. The `MYWordController` instance also keeps track of timing information so that it can log reports about its own performance.

```
File MYWordController.h

#import <Cocoa/Cocoa.h>
#import "MYWordView.h"
```

```
@interface MYWordController : NSObject
{
  IBOutlet MYWordView     *wordView;             /*" Connect in IB: word view"*/
  int                    _myNumberOfWordsToView; /*" Num simultaneous words "*/
  NSMutableArray         *_myWordsArray;         /*" Words being displayed "*/
  NSTimer                *_myTimer;              /*" Used to add words+display"*/
  NSTimeInterval         _myStartTime;           /*" Used to calc update rate"*/
  NSTimeInterval         _myLastReportTime;      /*" Used to calc update rate"*/
  int                    _myUpdateCounter;       /*" Used to calc update rate"*/
}

/*" Application delegate methods "*/
- (void)applicationDidFinishLaunching:(NSNotification *)aNotification;
- (void)applicationWillTerminate:(NSNotification *)aNotification;

@end
```

The MYWordController class is designed to be used as an applications delegate. MYWordController provides an outlet that must be connected to an instance of MYWordView to draw anything.

```
File MYWordController.m

#import "MYWordController.h"
#import "_MYWord.h"

@implementation MYWordController
/*" Use an instance of this class as the application's delegate. Forces an
instance of MYWordView to periodically redraw with a new word and logs
information about the redraw rate. "*/

- (void)_mySetNumberOfWords:(int)aNumber
/*" Set the number of words to draw each time. "*/
{
  _myNumberOfWordsToView = MAX(0, aNumber);

  // remove as many words as necessary to get down to aNumber words stored.
  while([_myWordsArray count] > _myNumberOfWordsToView)
  {
    [_myWordsArray removeObjectAtIndex:0];
  }
}
```

```
- (void)_myAddNextWord
/*" Add a word to draw. Removes a word if necessary to ensure that no more
than the number of words specified with -_mySetNumberOfWords: are drawn. "*/
{
  if(_myNumberOfWordsToView > 0)
  {
    if([_myWordsArray count] >= _myNumberOfWordsToView)
    {
      [_myWordsArray removeObjectAtIndex:0];
    }

    [_myWordsArray addObject:[[_MYWord alloc] initWithNextWordInRect:
        [wordView bounds]]];
    [wordView setNeedsDisplay:YES];
  }
}


/*" The number of seconds between update rate logs "*/
#define _MYNUM_SECONDS_BETWEEN_LOGS (10.0f)

- (void)addWord:(id)sender
/*" Called repeatedly from a timer. Adds a new word to draw replacing an old
one if necessary. Logs the cumulative redraw rate periodically. "*/
{
  NSTimeInterval    _currentTime = [NSDate timeIntervalSinceReferenceDate];

  // Add a word to draw.
  [self _myAddNextWord];

  _myUpdateCounter++;

  if(_MYNUM_SECONDS_BETWEEN_LOGS <= (_currentTime - _myLastReportTime))
  {
    // ten seconds or more has elapsed since last log
    NSLog(@"%f Hz", (double)_myUpdateCounter / (_currentTime -
                                             _myLastReportTime));

    _myLastReportTime = _currentTime;
    _myUpdateCounter = 0;
  }
}
```

```
/*" The number of words to view for each redraw "*/
#define _MYDEFAULT_NUM_WORDS_TO_VIEW (30)

/*" Path to file containing words to display "*/
#define _MYDEFAULT_PATH_TO_WORDS_FILE (@"/usr/share/dict/words")

- (void)applicationDidFinishLaunching:(NSNotification *)aNotification
/*" Called automatically if receiver is application's delegate. Schedules a
timer that calls -addWord: at periodic intervals but no more than once per
cycle of the application's run loop. "*/
{
  _myWordsArray = [[NSMutableArray alloc] init];
  [self _mySetNumberOfWords:_MYDEFAULT_NUM_WORDS_TO_VIEW];

  // Initialize the set of words to display
  [_MYWord initializeWordSetWithPath:_MYDEFAULT_PATH_TO_WORDS_FILE];

  // Tell the wordView what words to draw
  [wordView setWordsToView:_myWordsArray];

  // set up a repeating timer
  _myTimer = [NSTimer scheduledTimerWithTimeInterval:0.0
      target:self selector:@selector(addWord:) userInfo:nil repeats:YES];
  [_myTimer retain];

  // store information for redraw rate log
  _myStartTime = [NSDate timeIntervalSinceReferenceDate];
  _myLastReportTime = _myStartTime;
  _myUpdateCounter = 0;
}


- (void)applicationWillTerminate:(NSNotification *)aNotification
/*" Called automatically if receiver is application's delegate. Shuts down
the timer that caused redraws. "*/
{
  [_myTimer invalidate];
  [_myTimer release];
  _myTimer = nil;
}
```

```
- (void)dealloc
/*" Clean-up"*/
{
  [_myWordsArray release];
  _myWordsArray = nil;

  [super dealloc];
}

@end
```

The only other code in the `LotsOfWords` application is the unmodified `main.m` file that Project Builder generated when the project was created.

To run this application, download the complete project from `www.cocoaprogramming.net`, or create a new Project Builder project using the Cocoa Application template. Add the `MYWordView`, `_MYWord`, and `MYWordController` classes to the project. Edit the project's `MainMenu.nib` file so that it contains one window filled with an instance of the `MYWordsView` class. Use Interface Builder to create an instance of the `MYWordController` class. Connect the `MYWordsView` instance to the `MYWordController` instances's `wordView` outlet. Make the `MYWordController` instance the application's delegate. Build the project and run it with project Builder to see the log output. On a 450 MHz G4 computer, this implementation of `LotsOfWords` redraws at approximately 12 Hz. In the remainder of this appendix, the application will be optimized so that it redraws at 70 Hz or more on the same computer. The almost 600% increase results primarily from graphics optimizations.

First Optimize Graphics

The first, and most important, optimization for graphical applications is to reduce drawing as much as possible. For most applications, changing the color of even one pixel onscreen is time consuming in comparison to the time spent executing application logic. Modern computers are much faster at mathematical operations than they are at memory operations. To draw a button onscreen, Cocoa must set the values of every pixel in the button. If the button includes any transparency, Cocoa must read the values of the pixels that will be replaced by the pixels of the button, combine them with the pixels of the button, and then set the values of the combined pixels of the button. After Cocoa has drawn the button, Mac OS X's window server must copy the memory that stores the pixel values for the button from the computer's main memory to the memory of its graphic card. It is common for drawing graphics to consume 90% of an application's time. Little benefit arises from optimizing an application's logic until its drawing is fully optimized. The bottom line is that almost any amount of processing to avoid drawing is justified.

Finding Excess Drawing

The first step in optimizing drawing is finding excess drawing that can be eliminated. Drawing fewer pixels each time an application updates can yield large performance improvements.

Apple provides a tool called Quartz Debug, which is located in the `/Developer/Applications` folder. When running, Quartz Debug communicates with Mac OS X's window server process and highlights areas of the screen that are being redrawn. Quartz Debug works with all Mac OS X applications. It is instructional to use Quartz Debug to analyze how much drawing takes place in Apple's applications, including Project Builder. Figure B.2 shows Quartz Debug being used with `LotsOfWords` to show the areas of the screen being redrawn.

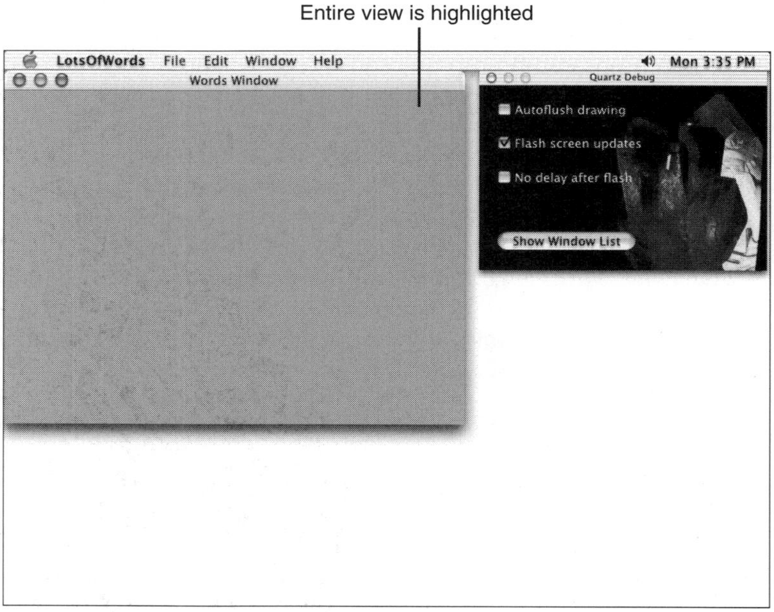

FIGURE B.2 Quartz Debug indicates the areas of the screen being redrawn by drawing a colored highlight rectangle over those areas.

As shown in Figure B.2, the `LotsOfWords` application is very sloppy with its drawing. The whole `MYWordView` instance is redrawn every time a word is added.

Reducing Excess Drawing Part I

The LotsOfWords application adds one word each time the MYWordView is redrawn. At most one word is removed each time the MYWordView is redrawn. The first step to reducing drawing in LotsOfWords is to take advantage of these facts and redraw only the area of a MYWordView that is covered by an added word or a removed word.

To implement the first optimization, it is necessary to know the area of the MYWordView that is covered by each word. Fortunately, that area is already calculated when each word is added so that no part of the word is drawn outside the bounds of the MYWordView. The _MYWord class must be modified to store the area covered by the word rather than just the position of the word.

Replace the definition of the _myPosition instance variable in the _MYWord class with the _myRect instance variable, as shown in the following redefinition of _MYWord's instance variables.

```
@interface _MYWord : NSObject
{
  NSString        *_myWord;          /*" The word "*/
  // _myPosition is replaced by _myRect
  //NSPoint        _myPosition;     /*" The word's position "*/
  NSRect          _myRect;         /*" The word's position & size "*/
  NSDictionary    *_myAttributes;   /*" The word's attributes "*/
}
```

Add the accessor method, -rect, to _MYWord's interface. The -rect method will return the _myRect instance variable.

```
/*" Accessors "*/
- (NSString *)word;
- (NSRect)rect;        // added as part of first optimization
```

Change the implementation of the _MYWord class to use _myRect instead of _myPosition. In the -_myReinitWithWord: inRect: method, replace the line that sets _myPosition with the following code:

```
  // Replaced code that sets _myPosition with code to set _myRect
  //_myPosition = [[self class] _myRandomPointInRect:validPositionArea];
  _myRect.origin = [[self class] _myRandomPointInRect:validPositionArea];
  _myRect.size = stringSize;
```

Rewrite _MYWord's -drawRect: method to use the _myRect instance variable and only draw the word if _myRect intersects that rectangle argument passed to -drawRect:.

```
- (void)drawRect:(NSRect)aRect
/*" "*/
{
  // Replaced next line that always draws the word
  // [_myWord drawAtPoint:_myPosition withAttributes:_myAttributes];

  // Draw only if word's rectangle intersects aRect
  if(NSIntersectsRect(_myRect, aRect))
  {
    [_myWord drawInRect:_myRect withAttributes:_myAttributes];
  }
}
```

Testing for the intersection of `_myRect` and the rectangle passed as an argument to `-drawRect:` has a lot of potential to reduce drawing, but for it to help, the rectangle passed to `-drawRect:` must be minimized. If the rectangle passed to `-drawRect:` is always the full bounds of a view, the optimizations made so far do not reduce drawing at all.

To help the `LotsOfWords` application minimize the rectangles passed to `_MYWord`'s `-drawRect:` method, other classes need to know the rectangle covered by each word before it is added and removed. To provide that information, implement the `-rect` accessor method as follows:

```
- (NSRect)rect
/*" Returns the rectangle covered by receiver's stored word. "*/
{
  return _myRect;
}
```

The next step is to modify the `MYWordView` class so that it draws correctly even if the rectangle passed to its `-drawRect:` method is smaller than the view's bounds. In `MYWordView.m`, add a line to clip the current graphics context to the rectangle passed in to `MYWordView`'s `-drawRect:` method. The following code implements the modified method:

```
- (void)drawRect:(NSRect)aRect
/*" Draw the words set with -setWordsToView: "*/
{
  NSEnumerator        *enumerator = [_myWordsArray objectEnumerator];
  _MYWord             *currentWord;

  // Add this line to clip to aRect
  NSRectClip(aRect);
```

```
  while(nil != (currentWord = [enumerator nextObject]))
  {
    [currentWord drawRect:aRect];
  }
}
```

Some of the words might partially overlap the area being redrawn and, therefore, need to be redrawn. However, such words might also overlap other words that do not overlap the area being redrawn. The clipping is necessary to prevent the words that are being redrawn from inappropriately obscuring overlapping words that are not redrawn. After the modifications for this optimization are complete, experiment by commenting the call to `NSRectClip()` to see its effects.

Finally, modify the `MYWordController` class so that it uses the rectangles obtained from `MYWord`'s `-rect` method and only tells the `MYWordView` class to redraw the areas covered by the added word and any removed word. Change the implementation of `MYWordController`'s `-_myAddNextWord:` method to the following:

```
- (void)_myAddNextWord
/*" Add a word to draw. Removes a word if necessary to ensure that no more
than the number of words specified with -_mySetNumberOfWords: are drawn. "*/
{
  if(_myNumberOfWordsToView > 0)
  {
    _MYWord        *newWord = [[_MYWord alloc] initWithNextWordInRect:
        [wordView bounds]];

    if([_myWordsArray count] >= _myNumberOfWordsToView)
    {
      NSRect      obsoleteRect = [[_myWordsArray objectAtIndex:0] rect];

      [_myWordsArray removeObjectAtIndex:0];

      // Tell wordView it needs to redraw rect covered by removed word
      [wordView setNeedsDisplayInRect:obsoleteRect];
    }

    [_myWordsArray addObject:newWord];
    [wordView setNeedsDisplayInRect:[newWord rect]];
  }
}
```

With these modifications, rebuild the `LotsOfWords` application and run it in Project Builder. There is already a dramatic speedup, but more can be done. Figure B.3 shows the results of the first optimization reflected in Quartz Debug.

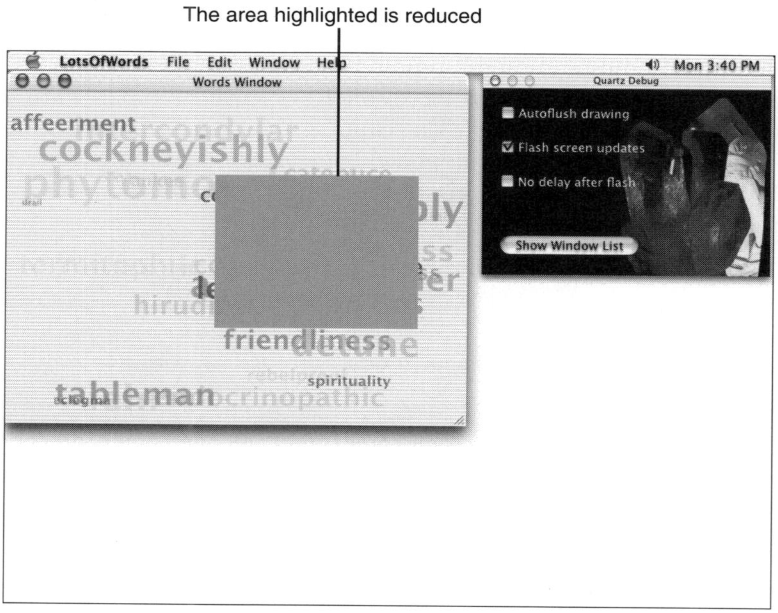

FIGURE B.3 Now only part of the `MYWordView` is redrawn.

Large areas of the `MYWordView` are still redrawn, but the whole `MYWordView` is no longer redrawn every time. The reason for this is Cocoa's abysmal implementation of `NSView`'s `-setNeedsDisplayInRect:` method in Mac OS X version 10.1.3 Each time the `-setNeedsDisplayInRect:` message is sent to a view, the view stores the smallest rectangle that encloses the argument to `-setNeedsDisplayInRect:` as well as the rectangles specified by all previous calls to `-setNeedsDisplayInRect:` since the last redraw. When the view is finally redrawn, it redraws the rectangle that encloses all the rectangles set via `-setNeedsDisplayInRect:`.

In the `LotsOfWords` application, if the word that is removed is in one corner of the `MYWordsView` and the word that is added is in the opposite corner, the entire view ends up being redrawn because the rectangle that encloses both words covers the entire view.

Reducing Excess Drawing Part II

The next optimization modifies the LotsOfWords application so that it does not use -setNeedsDisplayInRect:. The -setNeedsDisplayInRect: method exists to improve drawing performance by accumulating the rectangles that need to be redrawn and redrawing them all at once under optimal conditions. It is ironic that Cocoa's poor implementation of the -setNeedsDisplayInRect: method actually degrades efficiency compared to alternatives.

NOTE

Apple's class documentation recommends the use of -setNeedsDisplayInRect: instead of -displayRect:. In reality, applications should almost always use -displayRect: instead of -setNeedsDisplayInRect: at least until Apple improves the implementation of -setNeedsDisplayInRect:.

The principal alternative to using -setNeedsDisplayInRect: is to use -displayRect:. Unlike -setNeedsDisplayInRect:, which accumulates rectangles for future display, -displayRect: forces its receiver to redraw the specified rectangle immediately.

Replace each occurrence of -setNeedsDisplayInRect: with -displayRect: within MYWordController's implementation so that its -_myAddNextWord: method is implemented as follows:

```
- (void)_myAddNextWord
/*" Add a word to draw. Removes a word if necessary to ensure that no more
than the number of words specified with -_mySetNumberOfWords: are drawn. "*/
{
  if(_myNumberOfWordsToView > 0)
  {
    _MYWord        *newWord = [[_MYWord alloc] initWithNextWordInRect:
        [wordView bounds]];

    if([_myWordsArray count] >= _myNumberOfWordsToView)
    {
      NSRect      obsoleteRect = [[_myWordsArray objectAtIndex:0] rect];

      [_myWordsArray removeObjectAtIndex:0];

      // Tell wordView it needs to redraw rect covered by removed word
      [wordView displayRect:obsoleteRect];
    }
```

```
    [_myWordsArray addObject:newWord];
    [wordView displayRect:[newWord rect]];
  }
}
```

On a 450 MHz G4, this version of LotsOfWords redraws at more than 70 Hz. Figure B.4 shows the results of the latest optimization reflected in Quartz Debug.

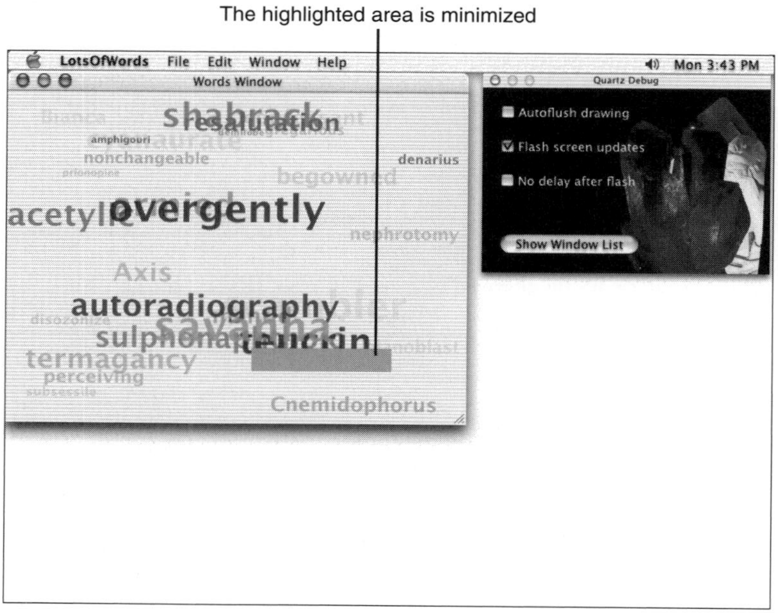

FIGURE B.4 MYWordView now redraws the minimum area.

An interesting effect of this optimization is that the application actually runs faster with its window maximized than it does with a very small window. The time needed to draw the optimized MYWordView is proportional to the number of words drawn. Because the words are randomly placed within the MYWordView, a large bounds size means that it is not likely for words to overlap. With a very small bounds size, almost all words overlap, and the minimum redraw must redraw many overlapping words. With a large bounds, most likely only the word removed and the word added need to be drawn. Running with its window maximized, LotsOfWords updates at more than 70 Hz on the system tested.

Optimizing Nongraphical Code

Optimizing drawing is crucial, but nongraphical Cocoa applications and applications that already have highly optimized drawing can benefit from other optimizations. The developer tools that come with Mac OS X include several applications that help identify nongraphics code that can benefit from optimization.

Finding Performance Bottlenecks

The task of identifying which lines of code are called most often and which lines of code take the longest time to execute is called profiling. Mac OS X comes with two profiling applications: Sampler, and gprof. Each uses a different technique to identify performance bottlenecks.

Sampler works by periodically interrupting an application's execution and checking the call stack to determine which function or method is currently being executed. After Sampler has interrupted an application many times, a statistical profile is generated that estimates the percentage of the application's execution time spent in each function or method.

Sampler can be used with any application. When the Sampler application has been launched, its File, New menu item is used to specify an application to launch and sample. Applications that are already running can be sampled by using Sampler's File, Attach menu item. Figure B.5 shows Sampler's statistical analysis of the `LotsOfWords` application that has optimized graphics.

Even with optimized graphics, `LotsOfWords` is executing code called from `MYWordView`'s `-drawRect:` method in 4,377 samples out of 6,482. That means that approximately 68% of the application's time is spent for custom drawing. Drawing is actually even more expensive than that. Further analysis with Sampler reveals that an additional 15% of the execution time is spent flushing graphics from main memory to the graphics card. In total, 83% of the application's time is needed for drawing. There is little to gain from optimizing the parts of `LotsOfWords` that does not involve drawing.

NOTE

Additional graphical optimizations for `LotsOfWords` require heroic efforts beyond the scope of this appendix. For example, it is possible to use OpenGL rather than Apple's Quartz to draw the words, but doing so will probably degrade the quality of the drawing.

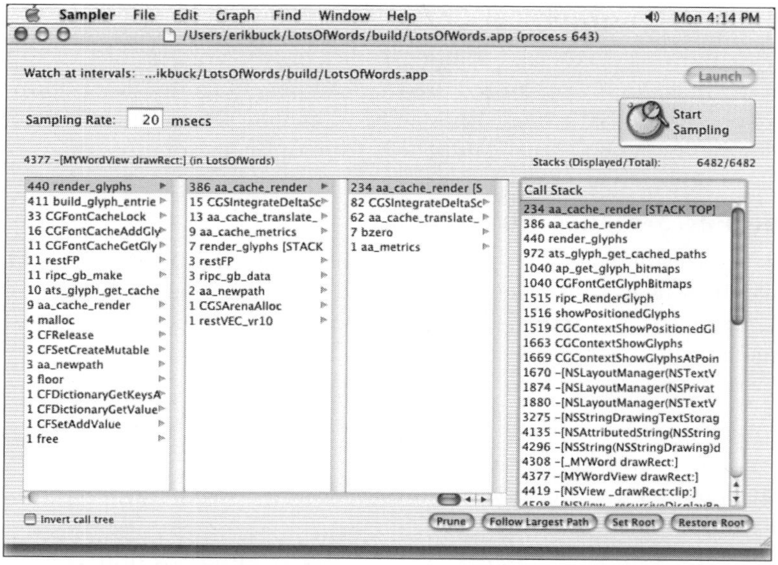

FIGURE B.5 Sampler shows that the vast majority of samples are spent inside `MYWordView`'s `-drawRect:` method.

To describe techniques for optimizing nongraphical code, the remainder of the optimizations in this section are applied to a version of `LotsOfWords` that does not draw anything. The techniques described here are best applied to nongraphical applications. Download the `LotsOfWordsNoDraw` project from `www.cocoaprogramming.net`, or make changes to `LotsOfWords` so that it no longer draws. To disable drawing, comment out the two `-displayRect:` messages in `MYWordController`'s `-_myAddNextWord` method as follows:

```
- (void)_myAddNextWord
/*" Add a word to draw. Removes a word if necessary to ensure that no more
than the number of words specified with -_mySetNumberOfWords: are drawn. "*/
{
  if(_myNumberOfWordsToView > 0)
  {
    _MYWord             *newWord = [[_MYWord alloc] initWithNextWordInRect:
        [wordView bounds]];

    if([_myWordsArray count] >= _myNumberOfWordsToView)
    {
```

```
        // Comment the following line to eliminate warning
        // generated if drawing is disabled
        //NSRect      obsoleteRect = [[_myWordsArray objectAtIndex:0] rect];

        [_myWordsArray removeObjectAtIndex:0];

        // Comment the following line to disable drawing
        //[wordView displayRect:obsoleteRect];
      }

      [_myWordsArray addObject:newWord];

      // Comment the following line to disable drawing
      //[wordView displayRect:[newWord rect]];
    }
  }
```

The declaration of `obsoleteRect` in the `-_myAddNextWord` method is also commented so that the compiler does not generate a warning that the variable is declared, but not used when drawing is disabled.

Even though the periodic redraw of the `LotsOfWords` application is disabled by modifying `MYWordController`'s `-_myAddNextWord` method, the application will still redraw for other reasons. For example, resizing the window containing the `MYWordView` instance causes a redraw. However, unless the window is continuously resized while sampling, the number of samples that the Sampler application finds inside the drawing code should drop to close to zero.

Optimize Only the Bottlenecks

When Sampler is used with the version of `LotsOfWords` that does not draw, it is clear that the most time is spent inside the `NSFont` class's `-boldSystemFontOfSize:` method called from `_MYWord`'s `-_myRandomFont` method. Figure B.6 shows that 3,575 samples out of 5,851 (or 61%) are spent inside `-_myRandomFont`. The `NSFont` class's `-boldSystemFontOfSize:` method is clearly the bottleneck to performance.

The `LotsOfWords` application uses a small number of different sizes of the user's default bold system font. Because it is not practical to change the implementation of `-boldSystemFontOfSize:`, the best optimization is to not call it as often. To avoid calling `-boldSystemFontOfSize:` every time `_MYWord`'s `-_myRandomFont` method is called, the collection of fonts needed can be cached and reused. Add the following `-_myCachedFontWithSize:` method to the `_MYWord` class's implementation right before the implementation of `-_myRandomFont`.

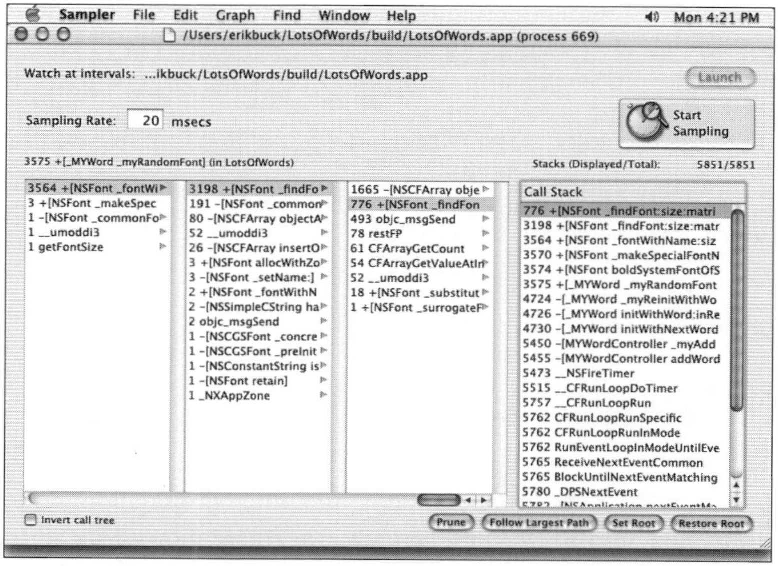

FIGURE B.6 The `-boldSystemFontOfSize:` method consumes most of the time in the version of `LotsOfWords` that does not draw.

```
/*" Cached fonts to avoid lookups "*/
static NSMutableArray    *_MYCachedFonts = nil;

+ (NSFont *)_myCachedFontWithSize:(int)aSize
/*" Returns the cached font with the specified size or nil if aSize is not
available. "*/
{
  NSFont        *result = nil;

  if(aSize >= _MYMINIMUM_FONT_SIZE && aSize <= _MYMAXIMUM_FONT_SIZE)
  {
    if(nil == _MYCachedFonts)
    {
      // create the cache & fill with fonts
      int        i;

      _MYCachedFonts = [[NSMutableArray alloc] init];
      for(i = _MYMINIMUM_FONT_SIZE; i <= _MYMAXIMUM_FONT_SIZE; i++)
      {
```

```
        [_MYCachedFonts addObject:[NSFont boldSystemFontOfSize:(float)i]];
      }
    }

    result = [_MYCachedFonts objectAtIndex:aSize - _MYMINIMUM_FONT_SIZE];
  }

  return result;
}
```

The `_myCachedFontWithSize:` method stores an instance of `NSFont` in the `_MYCachedFonts` array for each font size used.

Next, rewrite the `-_myRandomFont` method to call `-_myCachedFontWithSize:` instead of `-boldSystemFontOfSize:` as follows:

```
+ (NSFont *)_myRandomFont
/*" Returns the user's default bold system font with a size randomly selected
between _MYMINIMUM_FONT_SIZE points and _MYMAXIMUM_FONT_SIZE points. "*/
{
  const int  fontSizeDelta = (_MYMAXIMUM_FONT_SIZE - _MYMINIMUM_FONT_SIZE);
  const int     shiftFactor = 512; // least significant bits returned by random()
                               // are not very random. Constant used to shift
                               // to more random bits
  const int  shiftedFontSizeDelta = fontSizeDelta * shiftFactor;

  // Use the cached fonts rather than NSFont's -boldSystemFontOfSize:
  return [self _myCachedFontWithSize:(random() % shiftedFontSizeDelta) /
      shiftFactor + _MYMINIMUM_FONT_SIZE];
}
```

After the modification to use a font cache, Sampler shows that, with the exception of start-up time spent initializing the set of words, more than 90% of the samples are inside Apple's Core Foundation code that handles the event loop and the timer. No more optimizations that will have a significant impact on performance are practical for `LotsOfWords`.

Using `gprof` to Profile

The Gnu gprof application is provided with Apple's developer tools. The gprof application provides detailed analysis of the number of times each function or method is called, which functions and methods call other functions or methods, and the number of computer cycles spent in each function or method. Applications must be recompiled specifically for use with gprof to be able to use it.

Project Builder is configured to compile source code that includes gprof profiling information by setting the `PROFILING_CODE` build setting to `YES`. Figure B.7 shows the Build Settings tab for the `LotsOfWords` target in Project Builder. The `PROFILING_CODE` build setting is not always in the table of build settings for a target. If it is not already in the table, add it and set its value to `YES`.

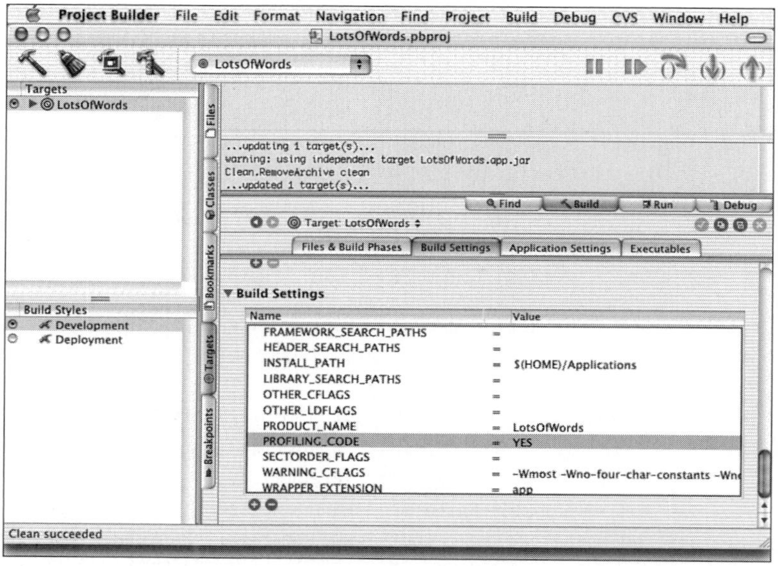

FIGURE B.7 The `PROFILING_CODE` build setting is highlighted in the Build Settings table for the `LotsOfWords` target.

To get profile information for functions and methods inside frameworks, the application being profiled must be configured to run with the profiling versions of the frameworks. Figure B.8 shows the Executables tab for the `LotsOfWords` target. The Dynamic Library Runtime Variant pop-up button is set to Profile.

It is possible to profile an application that uses the standard versions of the system frameworks, but without profiling information for the frameworks, the value of the information provided by gprof is diminished. It becomes impossible to determine which application methods are called as the result of framework code.

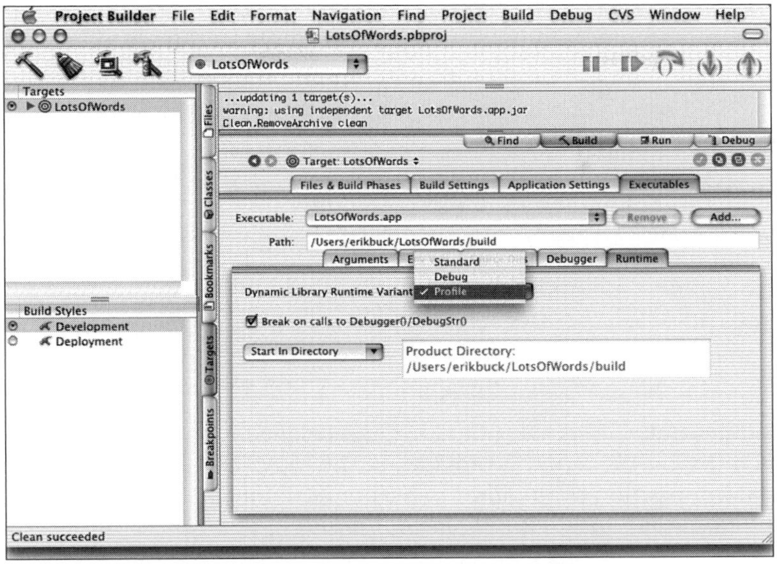

FIGURE B.8 A target is configured to use the Profile variant of each dynamic library via the Executables tab for the target.

NOTE

If the system libraries have been updated through Apple's Software Update application, it might not be possible to use the profiling versions of system frameworks. The profiling versions of the system frameworks must be from the same build as the standard versions, but because the profile versions are only distributed with the developer tools, any update that installs system frameworks newer than the developer tools prevents profiling.

After Project Builder is configured to include profiling information and optionally use the profiling versions of frameworks, the application must be completely rebuilt. Clean the application target and rebuild it.

The next time the application is run, it writes a file named `gmon.out` to the application's current directory. The `gmon.out` file includes all the profiling information gathered during the run. The gprof application generates a report from the data in the `gmon.out` file.

To run gprof and generate the profiling report, start the Terminal application. Change Terminal's current directory to the directory where the `gmon.out` file was generated. The command to execute gprof requires the full path to the executable for the profiled application and the path to the `gmon.out` file.

The following command line was used to generate a profiling report for the `LotsOfWords` application:

```
gprof /Users/erikbuck/LotsOfWords/build/LotsOfWords.app/Contents/MacOS/
➥LotsOfWords ./gmon.out
```

The path to the executable will be different for each user. The executable for a Cocoa application is in the `Contents/MacOS/` folder within the application package. Use Finder's context menu to open the application's package and see the folders inside.

The report generated by gprof is too long and detailed to include here. Information about each field in the report is provided at the top of the report that is generated. Additional information about gprof and its report format is available at `www.gnu.org/manual/gprof-2.9.1/gprof.html`.

Optimizing Rules of Thumb

The following rules of thumb apply to optimizing large Cocoa applications:

- Using a better algorithm yields bigger performance improvements than any number of low-level optimizations.
- Graphics usually consume the vast majority of an application's time. Optimize graphics before anything else.
- After graphics, the next most time consuming code is usually dynamic memory allocation. Avoid dynamic memory allocation when possible.
- Extremely low-level optimizations such as using `NSObject`'s `-methodForSelector:` to obtain a pointer to the function that implements a method rarely improves performance. Use low-level techniques only as a last resort.

Keep the optimizing rules of thumb in mind when optimizing Cocoa applications. The choice of algorithms to use in an application is beyond the scope of this book. This appendix has already described techniques to optimize graphics. Low-level optimizations using `NSObject`'s `-methodForSelector:` are described in Chapter 4, "Objective-C" and Appendix A, "Profiling, Optimizing, and Detecting Memory Leaks." Additional low-level optimizations are explained at `www.mulle-kybernetik.com/artikel/Optimization`. One feature of Cocoa applications that commonly consumes a lot of time, but has not been adequately described is dynamic memory allocation. The next section describes a technique for avoiding dynamic memory allocation.

Avoiding Dynamic Memory Allocation

Dynamic memory allocation is one of the slowest services provided by modern operating systems. One reason dynamic memory allocation is slow is its need to communicate with the operating system's kernel to obtain additional memory. Freeing memory is also slow. The operating system and system libraries need to do a lot of work to avoid memory fragmentation when memory is freed. Consider the following: 1000 bytes is allocated followed by 4 bytes followed by another 1000 bytes. When the 4 byte block is freed, the operating system might have to shuffle memory around to avoid leaving a 4 byte block of memory that cannot be easily reused because of the large blocks on either side of it.

The dynamic memory allocation functions provided by Mac OS X are optimized and automatically avoid memory fragmentation, but they are still a common source of performance problems. The problem is exacerbated by the fact that most objects only require a few bytes of storage. Frequent allocation and deallocation of objects puts the maximum memory allocation burden on the system. The following `MYShortString` class shows one way to reduce dynamic memory allocation for objects.

The `MYShortString` Class

In a particular large Cocoa application, profiling revealed that a large percentage of processing time was being spent allocating and deallocating `NSString` instances. The strings were usually very short, but thousands of them were allocated and deallocated every second. Because one of the primary requirements of the application was string processing, a solution to avoid the dynamic allocation of string objects was needed. The `MYShortString` class presented here, and available at `www.cocoaprogramming.net`, provided the solution.

The `MYShortString` class only handles short strings. Instances of `MYShortString` are allocated as needed, but are seldom deallocated. Instead of being deallocated, the `MYShortString` instances are added to a pool of available instances. When a new `MYShortString` instance is needed, one of the unused instances in the pool is reused rather than allocating a new one.

Creating the `MYShortString` subclass of `NSString` is complicated because `NSString` is the abstract interface to a class cluster. Class clusters are described in Chapter 6, and Apple provides documentation on class clusters at `http://developer.apple.com/techpubs/macosx/Cocoa/TasksAndConcepts/ProgrammingTopics/Foundation/Concepts/ClassClusters.html`. To create a new concrete subclass of a class cluster's abstract class, the following rules should be followed:

- The new class must override the superclass's primitive methods.
- The new class must override all the superclass's initializer methods or risk exceptions.
- Every initializer in the new class must call its superclass's designated initializer, which is always `-init` for abstract interface to a class cluster.

Primitive methods provide the core features common to all classes in a class cluster. Apple's class documentation identifies the primitive methods of the public classes in class clusters. The other methods declared for a class cluster are implemented using the primitive methods. The existence of primitive methods reduces the number of methods that must be overridden in a subclass of a class cluster. By implementing just the primitive methods for a class cluster, a new concrete subclass ensures that the other inherited methods operate properly.

`NSString`'s primitive methods are `-length` and `-characterAtIndex:`. According to the rules for subclassing class clusters, the `MYShortString` class must implement `-length` and `-characterAtIndex:` as well as all `NSString`'s initializers. The following code defines the class interface for the `MYShortString` class.

```
File MYShortString.h

#import <Foundation/Foundation.h>

#define _MYMAX_SHORT_STRING_LENGTH (40)


@interface MYShortString : NSString
{
  unichar       _myBuffer[_MYMAX_SHORT_STRING_LENGTH+1]; /*" the string "*/
  unsigned int    _myLength;           /*" num unichars not counting null "*/
}

/*" Overridden allocator "*/
+ (id)allocWithZone:(NSZone *)aZone;

/*" Shared resource cleanup "*/
+ (void)cleanup;

/*" Reuse statistics "*/
+ (unsigned int)numberOfAvailableInstances;
+ (unsigned int)totalNumberOfInstances;
```

```
/*" Encoding support "*/
+ (BOOL)isSupportedEncoding:(NSStringEncoding)anEncoding;

/*" Overridden designated initializer "*/
- (id)init;

/*" Undocumented method that MUST be overridden in a concrete subclass of
NSString "*/
- (id)initWithBytes:(const void *)bytes length:(unsigned)length
encoding:(NSStringEncoding)encoding;

/*" Overridden initializers "*/
- (id)initWithCharacters:(const unichar *)characters length:(unsigned)length;
- (id)initWithCString:(const char *)bytes length:(unsigned)length;
- (id)initWithString:(NSString *)aString;
- (id)initWithData:(NSData *)data encoding:(NSStringEncoding)encoding;

/*" Overridden NSString primitive methods "*/
- (unsigned int)length;
- (unichar)characterAtIndex:(unsigned)index;

/*" Overridden NSString performance methods "*/
- (void)getCharacters:(unichar *)buffer;
- (void)getCharacters:(unichar *)buffer range:(NSRange)aRange;

@end
```

The rule that every initializer in the class cluster's interface must be overridden to avoid exceptions is particularly difficult to follow in this case because Apple failed to document one of `NSString`'s most important initializers. The `-initWithBytes:length:encoding:` method is called frequently by the Cocoa frameworks, but it does not appear anywhere in Apple's documentation.

Failure to override all the class cluster's initializers in a subclass does not automatically mean that the subclass cannot be used. The initializers that are overridden will work correctly. Attempts to use initializers that are not overridden will raise exceptions that must be handled. Just keep in mind that any of the initializers might be called from code inside the Cocoa frameworks where it is not easy to handle exceptions.

The `MYShortString` class deliberately does not override some of `NSString`'s initializers and raises exceptions from some of the initializers it does override. The primary reason is that `MYShortString` cannot handle strings that are longer than

MYMAX_SHORT_STRING_LENGTH (40). It is better to raise an exception in situations where MYShortString cannot determine the length of the string it is being asked to store or it knows the string is too long, rather than fail silently or truncate the stored string. The following code implements the MYShortString class:

```
#import "MYShortString.h"
#import <objc/objc-class.h>


@implementation MYShortString
/*" This class helps alleviate the overhead of memory allocation for short
strings.  As long as the string values are short, this class can be used more
efficiently than the built in NSString concrete classes. Instances of this
class are seldom deallocated and can be reused repeatedly without penalty. "*/

/*" Collection of shared instances "*/
static NSMutableArray        *_MYShortStringCache = nil;

/*" Number of instances allocated "*/
static unsigned int            _MYTotalNumberOfInstances = 0;

static BOOL                    _MYCacheIsDisabled = NO;


+ (NSMutableArray *)_myShortStringCache
/*" Return the shared array of available instances. "*/
{
  if(nil == _MYShortStringCache && !_MYCacheIsDisabled) {
    _MYShortStringCache = [[NSMutableArray alloc] init];
  }

  return _MYShortStringCache;
}


+ (void)cleanup;
/*" Releases all of the shared short string instances that are available for
reuse "*/
{
  id         temp = _MYShortStringCache;

  _MYShortStringCache = nil;
```

```
  _MYCacheIsDisabled = YES;    // prevent re-caching when instances released
  [temp release];
  _MYCacheIsDisabled = NO;
}


+ (unsigned int)numberOfAvailableInstances
/*" Returns number of MYShortString instances available for reuse. "*/
{
  return [[self _myShortStringCache] count];
}

+ (unsigned int)totalNumberOfInstances
/*" Returns total number of MYShortString instances ever allocated. "*/
{
  return _MYTotalNumberOfInstances;
}

  /*" Encoding support "*/
+ (BOOL)isSupportedEncoding:(NSStringEncoding)anEncoding
/*" Returns YES if instances of receiver support anEncoding. Only
NSASCIIStringEncoding and NSUnicodeStringEncoding are currently supported. "*/
{
  BOOL      result = NO;

  if(anEncoding == NSASCIIStringEncoding ||
      anEncoding == NSUnicodeStringEncoding)
  {
    result = YES;
  }

  return result;
}


+ (id)allocWithZone:(NSZone *)aZone
/*" Reuses any available existing instance before creating a new one. "*/
{
  NSMutableArray    *shortStringCache;
  MYShortString        *result = nil;
```

```
  shortStringCache = [self _myShortStringCache];
  if([shortStringCache count] > 0) {
    // there is an available instance to reuse
    result = [shortStringCache lastObject];
    [result retain];                       // retain (next line will release)
    [shortStringCache removeLastObject]; // release result

  } else {
    // create a new instance (Can't use +alloc without infinite recursion)
    result = NSAllocateObject([self class], 0, aZone);
    _MYTotalNumberOfInstances++;
  }

  return result;
}


- (unichar *)_myBuffer
/*" Returns the fixed size buffer used to store strings "*/
{
  return _myBuffer;
}


- (id)init
/*" Overridden designated initializer "*/
{
  _myBuffer[0] = '\0';
  _myLength = 0;

  return self;
}


- (id)initWithCharacters:(const unichar *)characters length:(unsigned)length
/*" Initializes receiver. Raises NSRangeException if length is too long. "*/
{
  id        result;

  self = [self init];
  result = self;
```

```
  if(length < _MYMAX_SHORT_STRING_LENGTH)
  {
    memcpy(_myBuffer, characters, (length * sizeof(unichar)));
    _myLength = length;
  }
  else
  {
    [self release];
    self = nil;
    [NSException raise:NSRangeException format:@""];
  }

  return result;
}


- (id)initWithCString:(const char *)bytes length:(unsigned)length
/*" Initializes receiver. Raises NSRangeException if length is too long. "*/
{
  id          result;

  self = [self init];
  result = self;

  if(length < _MYMAX_SHORT_STRING_LENGTH)
  {
    int           i;

    for(i = 0; (i < length) && ('\0' != bytes[i]); i++) {
      _myBuffer[i] = bytes[i];
    }
    _myBuffer[i] = '\0';
    _myLength = i;
  }
  else
  {
    [self release];
    self = nil;
    [NSException raise:NSRangeException format:@""];
  }
```

```
  return result;
}


- (id)initWithCString:(const char *)bytes
/*" Initializes the receiver. Calls -initWithCString:length:. "*/
{
  return [self initWithCString:bytes length:strlen(bytes)];
}


- (id)initWithString:(NSString *)aString
/*" Initializes receiver. Raises NSRangeException if aString is too long. "*/
{
  id             result;
  const int      length = [aString length];

  self = [self init];
  result = self;

  if(length < _MYMAX_SHORT_STRING_LENGTH)
  {
    NSRange         copyRange = NSMakeRange(0, length);

    [aString getCharacters:_myBuffer range:copyRange];
    _myBuffer[length] = '\0';
    _myLength = length;
  }
  else
  {
    [self release];
    self = nil;
    [NSException raise:NSRangeException format:@""];
  }

  return result;
}


- (id)initWithBytes:(const void *)bytes length:(unsigned)length
encoding:(NSStringEncoding)encoding
/*" Apple's super secret undocumented method that MUST be overridden in every
```

```
concrete subclass of NSString. Only NSASCIIStringEncoding and
NSUnicodeStringEncoding are supported. Any othe encoding causes
NSInvalidArgumentException. "*/
{
  if(encoding == NSASCIIStringEncoding)
  {
    self = [self initWithCString:(char *)bytes length:length];
  }
  else if(encoding == NSUnicodeStringEncoding)
  {
    self = [self initWithCharacters:(unichar *)bytes
                             length:length / sizeof(unichar)];
  }
  else
  {
    [self release];
    self = nil;
    [NSException raise:NSInvalidArgumentException format:@""];
  }

  return self;
}


- (id)initWithData:(NSData *)data encoding:(NSStringEncoding)encoding
  /*" Initializes the receiver. Calls -initWithBytes:length:encoding: "*/
{
  return [self initWithBytes:[data bytes] length:[data length]
      encoding:encoding];
}


/*" Overridden NSString primitive methods "*/
- (unsigned int)length
/*" Returns receiver's length in Unicode charaters "*/
{
  return _myLength;
}


- (unichar)characterAtIndex:(unsigned)index
/*" Returns receiver's charater at index. Raises NSRangeException if index is
```

```
not available. "*/
{
  if(index >= _myLength)
  {
    [NSException raise:NSRangeException format:@""];
  }
  return _myBuffer[index];
}


/*" Overridden NSString primitive methods "*/
- (void)getCharacters:(unichar *)buffer
/*" Copies the receiver's characters into buffer. This method does not NULL
terminate buffer.  Buffer must be able to store the number of Unicode
characters stored by the receiver. "*/
{
  memcpy(buffer, _myBuffer, ((_myLength) * sizeof(unichar)));
}


- (void)getCharacters:(unichar *)buffer range:(NSRange)aRange
/*" Copies the receiver's characters from aRange into buffer. This method does
not NULL terminate buffer.  Buffer must be able to store aRange.length Unicde
characters. Raises NSRangeException if any character specified by aRange are
not available in the receiver. "*/
{
  if((aRange.length + aRange.location) > _myLength || aRange.location < 0)
  {
    [NSException raise:NSRangeException format:@"-getCharacters: %@",
        [[self class] description]];

  } else {
    memcpy(&buffer[aRange.location], _myBuffer,
        ((aRange.length) * sizeof(unichar)));
  }
}

- (void)release
/*" Overloaded to cache unused instances for reuse. "*/
{
  if([self retainCount] == 1) {
```

```
    [[[self class] _myShortStringCache] addObject:self];
  }

  [super release];
}

- (void)dealloc
/*" Clean-up "*/
{
  _MYTotalNumberOfInstances--;

  [super dealloc];
}

@end
```

The key to the implementation of `MYShortString` is that it overrides the `-release` method to store unused instances for later reuse rather than deallocating them. The `+allocWithZone:` method reuses stored instances rather than creating new ones whenever it can. The number of instances available for reuse is obtained from the `+ numberOfAvailableInstances` method. The total number of instances that have been allocated is returned from the `+ totalNumberOfInstances` method. The `+cleanup` method is used to release and deallocate all the instances that are available for reuse and reduces the total number of instances to the minimum number in use at one time.

The `MYShortString` class is not required to override the `-getCharacters:` and `-getCharacters:range:` methods inherited from `NSString` because they are not primitive methods. However, these two methods are called frequently by other `NSString` methods. The `NSString` class includes implementations of `-getCharacters:` and `-getCharacters:range:` based on the primitive methods, but the implementations provided in `MYShortString` are much faster because they avoid many unnecessary calls to the primitive methods.

The `MYShortString` class can be used directly in application code. Instances can be created by calling `[MYShortString alloc]` and initialized by calling any of the provided initializers. However, Cocoa classes that return strings do not automatically take advantage of the `MYShortString` class. For example, calling `NSString`'s `+stringByAppendingString:` method will return an instance of one of Cocoa's private concrete `NSString` subclasses rather than an instance of `MYShortString`. Even if `+stringByAppendingString:` is sent to a `MYShortString` instance, the string returned will not be a `MYShortString`.

It is possible to force Cocoa to use a custom subclass of a class cluster and return the custom class from framework methods. An example is available at www.cocoaprogramming.net that shows how to force Cocoa to use MYShortString instances whenever possible and automatically fall back to Cocoa's own private NSString subclasses when MYShortString can't handle a string.

Finding Memory Leaks

Unlike optimizations, which are unnecessary for many applications, memory leaks are usually bugs that need to be fixed. Memory leaks and other memory errors are described in Chapter 5, "Cocoa Conventions." Memory leaks can cause long running applications to crash, and they can reduce the performance of the operating system by consuming memory that is needed for other applications.

Apple explains how to efficiently use and debug memory at the following URL: http://developer.apple.com/techpubs/macosx/Essentials/Performance/VirtualMemory/Allocating__eing_Memory.html.

Apple provides developer tools for finding memory leaks. The easiest tool to use is ObjectAlloc, and can be used with any Cocoa application. Another tool is MallocDebug, which provides detailed information about memory leaks in Carbon and Cocoa applications. MallocDebug scans an application's memory for areas that are no longer referenced elsewhere in the application. Such areas are usually leaks. Finally, the Objective-C runtime and Cocoa frameworks contain features for finding memory leaks.

ObjectAlloc

ObjectAlloc is located in /Developer/Applications and documented at http://developer.apple.com/techpubs/macosx/Essentials/Performance/PerformanceTools/Observing_A_ObjectAlloc.html. It provides animated bar charts that show how many instances of each class are allocated over time. It can also show how many bytes are used. Figure B.9 shows ObjectAlloc's analysis of the LotsOfWords application. It shows the roughly 230,000 strings that store the words loaded from /usr/share/dict/words. Watching ObjectAlloc's bar charts over time highlights a memory leak in LotsOfWords. The number of _MYWord instances grows continuously, and each _MYWord instance stores both a dictionary and a color.

Armed with the information that _MYWord instances are leaking, a quick inspection of the LotsOfWords code reveals the problem. The -_myAddNextWord method in the MYWordController class violates Cocoa's reference-counted, memory-management conventions. It allocates instances of _MYWord, but it never releases them. The following implementation of -_myAddNextWord adds the necessary -release message and an appropriate comment:

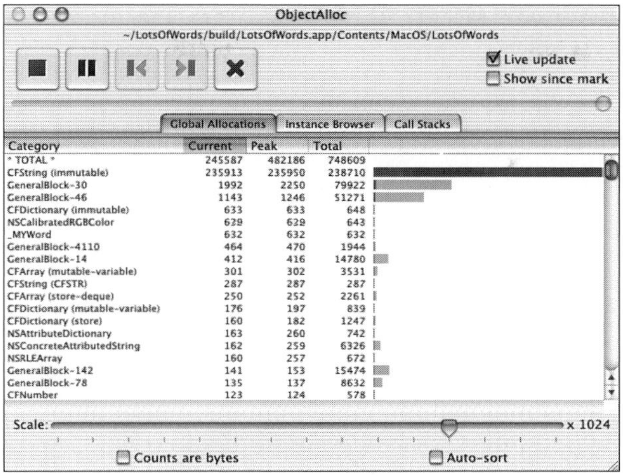

FIGURE B.9 ObjectAlloc highlights a memory leak in `LotsOfWords`.

```
- (void)_myAddNextWord
/*" Add a word to draw. Removes a word if necessary to ensure that no more
than the number of words specified with -_mySetNumberOfWords: are drawn. "*/
{
  if(_myNumberOfWordsToView > 0)
  {
    // The following line allocates new _MYWordInstances
    _MYWord        *newWord = [[_MYWord alloc] initWithNextWordInRect:
        [wordView bounds]];

    if([_myWordsArray count] >= _myNumberOfWordsToView)
    {
      NSRect      obsoleteRect = [[_myWordsArray objectAtIndex:0] rect];

      [_myWordsArray removeObjectAtIndex:0];

      // Tell wordView it needs to redraw rect covered by removed word
      [wordView displayRect:obsoleteRect];
    }

    [_myWordsArray addObject:newWord];
    [newWord release];        // !!! Must release newWord
```

```
    [wordView displayRect:[newWord rect]];
  }
}
```

With this small modification, the LotsOfWords application no longer leaks.

NOTE

ObjectAlloc shows the number of allocated objects and memory blocks changing continuously. As long as the numbers do not continually increase, there is no leak. It is normal for the number of allocations to count up, and then go back down over time.

MallocDebug

MallocDebug is located in /Developer/Applications and documented at http://developer.apple.com/techpubs/macosx/Essentials/Performance/PerformanceTools/Debugging_A_MallocDebug.html. It uses a conservative algorithm for detecting unreferenced blocks of memory. MallocDebug searches an application's memory for pointers to each allocated block. MallocDebug cannot always definitively identify memory leaks. It classifies memory blocks as either leaked, possibly leaked, or not leaked.

MallocDebug provides the call stack that resulted in the allocation of memory classified as a leak. Use the call stack to determine what went wrong and fix the problem. Possible leaks pose a much trickier problem. The best way to determine if possible leaks are actual leaks is to watch the total amount of memory allocated by the functions that allocated the possible leaks. If the total amount of memory allocated by those functions grows and never shrinks, there is most likely a leak.

MallocDebug can detect a wide variety of memory misuse bugs. It detects memory overruns and underruns. It also detects the use of already freed memory. The reports produced my MallocDebug often contain so much information that important details are easily missed in the mass of unimportant statistics. The real trick to using MallocDebug is learning to filter the information and selecting only the important parts. Unfortunately, that is not easy to do, and the important information for one application might be unimportant for another. It is usually best to start looking for leaks with ObjectAlloc and only resort to using MallocDebug to narrow down the cause of a leak that ObjectAlloc already detected.

Using Cocoa Frameworks to Find Leaks

Cocoa's Foundation framework includes a header file named NSDebug.h. Searching for NSDebug in Project Builder reveals a multitude of useful memory debugging information. NSDebug.h lists a group of environment variables that can be set to control how Cocoa's memory-management conventions are enforced. For example, when the NSZombieEnabled environment variable is set to YES, no objects are deallocated. Instead, the class of each object that would have been deallocated is changed to a special debugging class that logs all messages it receives. As a result, messages to objects that would have been deallocated are logged to an error report. Setting NSZombieEnabled to YES makes it easy to isolate attempts to use or release already deallocated objects.

Another useful environment variable is NSAutoreleaseFreedObjectCheckEnabled. Setting this variable to YES degrades the performance of autorelease pools, but makes it easy to identify when an already released object is still in an autorelease pool. This environment variable helps detect one of the most common bugs in Cocoa applications.

The NSDebug.h file also contains a category that extends the NSAutoreleasePool class with methods to aid in leak detection. In particular, the +showPools method displays the state of all autorelease pools in the current thread.

When a reference counting bug has been identified, one technique for tracking down the specific problem is to override the -retain and -release methods inherited from NSObject to log the call stack each time -retain or -release is called. The following versions of the -retain and -release methods show one technique:

```
- (id)retain
{
  NSLog(@"RETAIN <%p> %d %@", self, [self retainCount],
      [[self class] description]);
  return [super retain];
}

- (void)release
{
  NSLog(@"RELEASE <%p> %d %@", self, [self retainCount],
      [[self class] description]);
  [super release];
}
```

The address of self output to the log enables you to differentiate between instances of the same class. The call stacks can be analyzed in gdb to determine which calls were made in error by setting break points on the overridden -retain and -release methods.

Summary

Optimizing and memory-leak detection are large topics that are not completely covered in this appendix, but enough information is provided to meet the needs of most applications. The rules of thumb provided represent best practices that can save a lot of time and effort optimizing and debugging. Apple provides a collection of documents related to performance optimization and memory debugging at the following location: `http://developer.apple.com/techpubs/macosx/Essentials/Performance/`. Many of the documents referenced in this appendix are also available indirectly through that URL.

Appendix C, "Finding Third-Party Resources," lists many additional resources available to help Cocoa programmers. A large and diverse community of Cocoa programmers provides content for Web sites and mailing lists. Apple provides detailed Cocoa reference information on its own site. Finally, many Cocoa example programs are available for use as references. Example programs often contain the exact line of code or algorithm that is needed for a new Cocoa application.

APPENDIX C

Finding Third-Party Resources

IN THIS APPENDIX

Many topics covered within this book could easily be book topics on their own. Apple provides reference documentation with their developer tools and via the Web. Tremendous amounts of example code as well as complete frameworks and applications are available for reference and for use in applications. Several Web sites are dedicated solely to Cocoa topics, and more cover Cocoa as part of their overall Mac coverage. Finally, mailing lists are some of the best resources dedicated to Cocoa development issues.

Apple-Provided Documentation

Apple provides developer documentation with the standard Mac OS X Developer Tools. The best place to start looking for answers to specific questions is in the Apple documentation. Search tools such as Apple's own Sherlock as well as MTLibrarian (`http://www.montagetech.com/MTLibrarian.html` can be used to search the documentation.)

Apple updates the developer documentation from time to time, and the latest version is available on their Web site at `http://developer.apple.com/techpubs/index.html`. Apple also provides an excellent search interface to these documents along with technical notes at `http://developer.apple.com/search/search.html`.

Cocoa Developer Documentation

`http://developer.apple.com/techpubs/macosx/Cocoa/CocoaTopics.html`

This is a general portal to all of Apple's Cocoa developer documentation, including reference materials, tutorials, and various programming topic notes. It leads to the individual documentation for each of the various components related to Cocoa provided by Apple.

Core Foundation

`/Developer/Documentation/CoreFoundation/corefoundation_carbon.html`

The procedural C library, CoreFoundation, is the basis for some of Cocoa's Foundation framework classes. Most features of CoreFoundation are best used through Cocoa's objects, but CoreFoundation offers some additional functionality beyond the Foundation framework. Some features unique to CoreFoundation that might be of interest to Cocoa programmers include Utility Services and XML Services. Utility Services contain functions to perform byte swapping and convert numbers to and from property lists. XML Services provide an XML parser to read and extract data from XML format files.

Carbon Frameworks

`/Developer/Documentation/Carbon/carbon.html`

Until Cocoa has Objective-C wrappers for all the functionality available on Mac OS X, Carbon can be used for some tasks.

Developer Tools

`/Developer/Documentation/DeveloperTools/devtools.html`

Apple is working very hard to make the developer tools the best possible. They are updated several times a year, and new features are constantly being added. There is a general developer tool index that points to the various components, such as Project Builder, Interface Builder, gcc, gdb, and FileMerge. Also, be sure to read the Project Builder release notes (they are displayed every time ProjectBuilder starts).

Release Notes

`/Developer/Documentation/ReleaseNotes`

Always read the release notes. They are updated with most developer releases and often have great details that you might otherwise miss. They're also an excellent place to keep up with the newest features being added to the Cocoa Frameworks. These cover not only Cocoa, but also the other technologies that you encounter during your Mac OS X development projects: Carbon, Foundation, CoreFoundation, the developer tools, and Java technologies.

Example Code

Examining others' work is a great aid to understanding how things can be done. A good amount of source code is available for Cocoa developers to examine.

Cocoa Sample Code

`http://developer.apple.com/samplecode/Sample_Code/Cocoa.htm`

`/Developer/Examples/AppKit`

`/Developer/Examples/Foundation`

`/Developer/Examples/InterfaceBuilder`

Apple provides sample code with the Mac OS X Developer Tools installation, and more is available online in the Sample Code pages of the Developer Connection.

Omni Group Frameworks

`http://www.omnigroup.com/developer/sourcecode/`

Omni Group, the developers of OmniWeb and many other Mac OS X applications, have very generously made a great deal of their source code available in what is commonly referred to as the OmniFrameworks. It is made up of several individual frameworks that benefit from their years of Cocoa (and before that OpenStep) development.

The frameworks include

- OmniBase: a series of debugging aids, alternate assertions, and runtime manipulation aids. All the Omni Frameworks rely on this base class.
- OmniFoundation: Classes that extend and compliment Apple's Foundation/CoreFoundation frameworks. This includes Unicode-friendly regular expression, its own implementation of NSScanner, some Carbon wrappers, custom NSFormatters and more. That includes about 130 classes/categories in all.
- OmniAppKit: Widgets, widgets, and more widgets. Dozens of UI-oriented classes, including its own implementation of Apple's Aqua buttons, calendar views, chasing arrows, preference-panel implementations, and inspectors. OmniAppKit includes more than 90 classes in all.
- OmniNetworking: An Objective-C wrapper around basic BSD-level sockets. They've also released an example for an FTP server that uses this framework.

- OWF: This is the Omni Web Framework and is responsible for a good amount of the underlying architecture of OmniWeb itself. It includes content fetching, HTML parsing, and more.
- OmniExpat: A wrapper around the James Clark's expat XML-parsing framework.

All these are available for use in your own applications, and include full-source code. They're covered by the Omni Source License (a straightforward, open license).

The Omni Group provides information and examples for building Open GL-based games for Mac OS X. Game related information is available at `http://www.omnigroup.com/developer/gamedevelopment/`. Omni provides the OmniTimer framework for high-performance, low-overhead timing. Slides and sample code from a presentation made at the 2001 Game Developer's Conference about developing Mac OS X games are available.

MiscKit Frameworks

`http://www.misckit.com/`

The MiscKit is a collection of frameworks and classes that provide additional functionality to both Apple's Cocoa and Foundation frameworks. Originally, developed under NeXTSTEP, they've been updated for the Cocoa frameworks. The MiscKit is a community-driven, developed effort and submissions are welcome.

The MiscKit is the home for AutoDoc, an Objective-C documentation tool similar to JavaDoc. AutoDoc can read comments in source code and generate HTML or RTF-formatted output in the style of Apple's documentation.

MOKit Frameworks

`http://www.lorax.com/FreeStuff/MOKit.html`

The MOKit is a collection of useful objects written by Mike Ferris. This framework includes a regular-expression class implemented as a wrapper around Henry Spencer's Unicode-capable, regular-expression implementation. Classes to implement field completion, and an NSFormatter palette that utilizes regular expressions for validation are available.

Mike Ferris also provides TextExtras that can be installed to enhance the features of Apple's Cocoa text-handling classes. When installed, all Cocoa applications benefit. Every place text is manipulated in a Cocoa application, a staggering number of new features become available. More information is available at `http://www.lorax.com/FreeStuff/TextExtras.html`.

EDCommon Frameworks

http://www.mulle-kybernetik.com/software/ALX3000/edcommon.html

http://www.mulle-kybernetik.com/software/ALX3000/edinternet.html

The EDCommon Frameworks are a set of frameworks written by long-time developer Erik Dörnenburg as part of the ALX3000 Cocoa newsreader project. They consist of three parts: EDInternet, EDCommon, and EDPalette.

- EDInternet is designed to make interacting with network and mail protocols easier. It includes classes for communicating with SMTP mail servers, creating MIME messages, as well as writing applications that utilize BSD sockets. Categories on various Foundation classes offer access to the underlying utilities for MIME encoding NSData and NSString objects.
- EDCommon consists of utility classes and categories. Functionality includes several new Collection objects (EDObjectPair, EDStack, EDRedBlackTree, EDNumberSets, and EDSparseClusterArray), and extensions to Foundation classes (EDRange, EDLightWeightLock, EDBitmapCharacterSet, EDStringScanner, EDIRCObject, EDLRUCache and EDObjectReference). It also includes convenience enhancements for the Application Kit and several additional user interface widgets.
- EDPalette is an Interface Builder palette that enables the drag and drop creation of EDTableView, EDActivityIndicator, EDCanvas, and EDObjectWell from within Interface Builder.

Web Sites

Many Web sites are dedicated to Mac news and developer information. Some sites cover all information relevant to Mac users, and some specialize in just Mac OS X or just developer issues.

Stepwise

http://www.stepwise.com/

Stepwise has been serving the NeXTStep, OpenStep, Rhapsody, and Mac OS X communities since March 1993. Stepwise includes information for developers just getting started with Cocoa as well as Cocoa technical articles, editorials, and news. Stepwise provides search utilities and links of interest to Cocoa programmers.

The authors of this book are all Stepwise contributors. Scott Anguish owns and operates Stepwise. Don Yacktman is a frequent contributor and is on the Stepwise editorial board. Erik Buck is a contributor and likes to hang out with the Stepwise crowd.

Softrak

`http://www.stepwise.com/Softrak`

Softrak is a service of Stepwise. It's a self-managed archive of Mac OS X software. Each developer creates and maintains their own entries, and full search capabilities are available. Often developers make source code and frameworks available. Softrak has a special category for applications that include source code, and it is possible to search for applications using the criteria that have source code available.

O'Reilly Mac DevCenter

`http://www.oreillynet.com/mac`

Although the O'Reilly Mac DevCenter publishes articles addressing the Unix side of Mac OS X, they often have good Cocoa articles available as well.

CocoaDev

`http://www.cocoadev.com`

CocoaDev is a collaborative site for the Mac OS X developer community. Readers can add or edit any existing articles.

MacTech

`http://www.mactech.com`

MacTech is the grand daddy of the Macintosh-developer magazines. Although mainly a print oriented resource, they do maintain a Web site with current information and links.

Mailing Lists

Several active mailing lists are available for Cocoa developers. They are often read by Apple engineers as well as long time Cocoa developers and are excellent resources.

Each of these mailing lists represents a community of sorts, and it's best to understand the community standards before beginning to rant.

cocoa-dev

`http://www.lists.apple.com/cocoa-dev`

Hosted by Apple, this a great place to get started with your Cocoa questions. It covers all aspects of Cocoa development in both Objective-C and Java.

Project Builder

`http://www.lists.apple.com/projectbuilder-users`

Also hosted by Apple, this list is a must for users of Apple's development environment. Questions about Apple provided developer tools are answered here, often by the developers of the tools.

macosx-dev

`http://www.omnigroup.com/developer/mailinglists/macosx-dev`

The Omni Group hosts this list. It is another of the "must read" lists and is populated by new developers and veterans. It's oriented toward technical/development issues.

Summary

Mac OS X Cocoa development has a thriving community that is constantly growing on the Internet. The previous information is current as of publication. Up-to-date pointers are available on `http://www.cocoaprogramming.net`. The authors of this book have created the `http://www.cocoaprogramming.net` to provide updated information as needed.

D

Cocoa Additions in Mac OS X Version 10.2

IN THIS APPENDIX

- Quartz Extreme
- Handwriting Recognition
- Address Book and vCard
- Universal Access
- Updated Tools
- Framework Enhancements

Mac OS X version 10.2, code named Jaguar, is a significant update that includes many features not available in previous versions. This appendix introduces many of the new features and explains how they impact Cocoa applications. Some of the new features are implemented in the frameworks so that existing Cocoa programs automatically take advantage of them without even being recompiled for Jaguar. Other features are introduced with entirely new programming interfaces. Applications need new code to use those features, and such applications will not work with prior releases of Mac OS X.

Quartz Extreme

One of the most highly anticipated new features in Jaguar is Quartz Extreme. Quartz consists of a window server process and a powerful library of 2D drawing functions based on Adobe's Portable Document Format (PDF) imaging model. The window server is a process that runs in the background and controls display access by applications. The window server manages the layering of windows owned by different applications and implements features such as translucency, live-window dragging, and color correction. The window server can reposition windows, apply translucent drop shadows, and layer translucent windows without interrupting other applications. Quartz Extreme enhances the window server to use hardware accelerated graphics operations when possible. Cocoa applications benefit from Quartz Extreme automatically.

OpenGL Accelerated 2D

Quartz Extreme uses OpenGL to access available graphics hardware on a computer. OpenGL is most often associated with high-performance 3D graphics, but it can also be used for 2D. The Quartz Extreme window server is able to store the images that represent windows using a special format called an OpenGL texture. Textures can be stored in memory on the graphics card instead of the computer's main memory. Modern graphics cards enable very fast manipulation of textures with translucency and many other effects.

By using OpenGL and graphics-card hardware, operations such as dragging windows, hiding windows, and drawing drop shadows are accelerated. In some cases, scrolling can be accelerated also. With much of the graphics work offloaded to the graphics card, the main CPU chip(s) have more cycles available for nongraphics operations.

The 2D line and font drawing features of Quartz are not accelerated by Quartz Extreme. The high-quality, device-independent PDF imaging model used by Quartz is incompatible with the accelerated drawing features supported by OpenGL and common graphics hardware. Graphics cards are optimized to simply draw graphics on a single device, the computer screen, as fast as possible. Features such as What You See Is What You Get (WYSIWYG) drawing that can be output to high-resolution printers as well as the computer screen are not supported by the current generation of graphics cards.

The Quartz PDF imaging model is used to draw the lines and fonts that are displayed in each window. Quartz draws the contents of each window into a memory buffer. With the introduction of Quartz Extreme, that memory buffer can be used as an OpenGL texture, and further operations such as dragging the window onscreen take advantage of the hardware acceleration available when using textures.

Multiple Layers per Window

Another feature made possible by Quartz Extreme is the use of multiple layers within each window. The Window Server already manages a buffer for each window and draws the buffers to the screen to implement overlapping layered windows. By enabling multiple buffers per window, Quartz Extreme can accelerate the drawing of overlapping layers within windows.

Requirements

Quartz Extreme requires modern graphics hardware. At a minimum, the graphics card must support 2x AGP and provide 16 Mb of memory on the card. Recent ATI and nVidia brand cards shipped with new Macs have the required features. If the required hardware is not available, Quartz Extreme falls back to the all-software system used in Mac OS X versions prior to 10.2.

Handwriting Recognition

Cocoa applications automatically benefit from the handwriting input and recognition features named Ink that Apple provides with Jaguar. When used with an input tablet, Ink enables input of text via a stylus. Users accustomed to using a tablet can use Ink to avoid switching to the keyboard. Advanced handwriting recognition software automatically converts handwritten input into text.

In all versions of Mac OS X, Cocoa text input objects use a plug-in architecture called Input Managers to obtain input from a variety of sources. Input Managers are described in the "Input Managers" section of Chapter 10, "Views and Controls." The Ink technology is exposed to Cocoa programmers as another Input Manager. As a result, handwriting can be input to any Cocoa text object. From the programmer's perspective the source of the input is not important.

Address Book and vCard

Mac OS X 10.2 comes with a new Address Book application that is used to organize contact information such as names, addresses, and email addresses. Address Book uses an underlying database that is compatible with an emerging operating system independent standard called vCards. The vCards standard simplifies the storage and exchange of information. In addition to typical business card information, vCards support graphics and multimedia including photographs, company logos, and audio clips. More information about vCards is available at `http://www.imc.org/pdi/vcardoverview.html`.

Apple makes the vCards-compatible database of information accessible from Cocoa programs through a new Address Book framework. The framework provides both Objective-C classes and a C API. With the new classes, Cocoa applications gain the capability to read and modify contact information that can be easily exchanged between applications and across devices. A whole new breed of applications that collect and unify information as diverse as cell phone speed dial numbers and photographs is possible; however, new applications that link with the Address Book framework will only run on Mac OS X 10.2 and subsequent versions.

Universal Access

There are aspects of computer usage that many people find physically difficult. Jaguar includes technology intended to make the computer more accessible to users with disabilities. The entire screen can be magnified to assist users with vision impairments. The magnified screen can be panned, and the zoom factor can be changed to accommodate a wide range of needs. Jaguar also includes a flexible text-to-speech technology that can be used to read any onscreen text to the user. These features are implemented as operating system services. Existing Cocoa applications work seamlessly with the new features.

Jaguar also includes enhancements to many of the standard Cocoa user interface control classes. The enhancements provide more keyboard access than prior versions so that, in theory, it is possible to use applications without the mouse. The enhancements also provide features such as near universal text to speech. For example, users can have the text portion of each user interface item read to them whether the item is a menu or a button. Existing Cocoa applications benefit from the enhancements automatically in most cases, but custom controls need to be revised to support the enhancements.

Custom controls must implement new accessibility methods and call the inherited implementations as appropriate. In addition, several new notifications and exceptions related to accessibility features have been added in Jaguar.

Updated Tools

Many of the software tools and system services provided with Mac OS X have been updated and enhanced in version 10.2. Apple's own developer tools as well as the gcc compiler and standard Unix tools are all improved.

GCC 3.1

The Gnu Compiler Collection (GCC) shipped with Jaguar is version 3.1, and it is a major update from previous versions. Numerous bug fixes and performance enhancements have been made. Integration of the compiler with Apple's Project Builder Integrated Development Environment (IDE) has been improved. The new compiler generates much more efficient code for Apple's PPC architecture.

GCC 3.1 includes support for the ISO C99 standard which provides many benefits for C programmers. The Objective-C language also benefits from the upgrade to C99. In particular, because C99 allows the declaration of variables anywhere in a programming block, Objective-C now allows that as well.

GCC 3.1 offers much closer to conformance with ANSI/ISO standard C++ than previous versions of GCC provide. GCC now supports code that uses newer features of C++ and the Standard Template Library (STL). The improvements to C++ greatly simplify the task of porting C++ code to Mac OS X. The improvements to C++ support also apply to the Objective-C++ language.

More information about GCC 3.1 is available at `http://gcc.gnu.org/gcc-3.1`.

BSD Tools

Jaguar includes updated versions of many BSD Unix command-line programs and tools, and keeps Mac OS X roughly up-to-date with other Unix-based operating systems. The updates include the Apache Web server software, Kerberos Network Authentication Protocol software, the Samba file sharing server, and more.

IPv6

Internet Protocol Version 6 (IPv6) is the next-generation protocol designed to be a new international standard. IPv6 will gradually replace the current version of the Internet Protocol, which is Internet Protocol Version 4 (IPv4). IPv4 is nearly twenty years old and has served well in spite of its age, but it has limitations. Almost all IPv4 addresses have already been allocated, and a new address is needed for each computer added to the Internet. IPv6 solves the address shortage and provides other improvements such as improved routing and improved network autoconfiguration options.

Apple has contributed technology and protocol definitions called Zero Configuration Networking to international standards organizations and the Internet Engineering Task Force (IETF) to improve future opportunities for automatic configuration of computers when they are added to heterogeneous networks. The technology attempts to simplify configuration of industry-standard TCP/IP networking using IPv6.

IPv6 is completely backward compatible with IPv4, which means that the transition to IPv6 can be gradual, but only computers that support IPv6 will be able to take advantage of new network services. The inclusion of IPv6 in Mac OS X 10.2 keeps the Mac up-to-date with other operating systems and ensures continued access and compatibility with the Internet.

Many of the networking APIs in Mac OS X have been improved to support IPv6. Apple's `CFNetworking` component in the Core Foundation framework has been greatly expanded from prior versions. Cocoa programmers can use `CFNetworking` to access network resources. The BSD sockets API in Jaguar has also been expanded.

Updated Cocoa Spell Checking Support

The English spelling dictionary provided by Apple is dramatically improved and expanded in Jaguar. All Cocoa applications are able to take advantage of the built in spell checking support provided by Cocoa's text classes and Mac OS X's system services. Apple provides hooks for using any spelling dictionary with Cocoa, but most users are content to stick with the one installed by default. Because of the enhancements to the default spelling dictionary, spell checking is automatically improved in all Cocoa applications.

Framework Enhancements

Many of Apple's frameworks have been improved and expanded in Jaguar. In almost all cases, new features have been added, and pre-existing features have been preserved. Table D.1 describes the components and classes that have undergone the most changes:

TABLE D.1 New and Significantly Changed Components in Jaguar

Component	Description
`CFNetworking`	Improved communication with the standard services on the Web. Support for detecting and broadcasting to network services, configuring socket streams, encryption, and firewalls.
`NSURLHandle`	Enhanced to use features of `CFNetworking`.
`NSNetServices`	Partial Cocoa interface to `CFNetworking`.
`NSText` classes	Support for bidirectional text and new input managers.
`NSResponder`, `NSTabView`, `NSToolBar`, `NSWindow`	Additional support for keyboard navigation.
`NSThread`	Enhanced threading support and simplified access to an application's main thread.
`NSUserDefaults`	Introduction of new preferences domains and locked preferences.
`NSFileManager`	Enhanced support for traditional Mac OS/HFS+ file attributes.
Keyed archiving system	A new system for encoding and decoding object graphs in a human readable text format.
New CD Burning API	Simplifies addition of CD- and DVD-writing features to Cocoa applications.
New digital Camera support API	Simplifies addition of digital camera support to Cocoa applications.
New text to speech classes	Simplifies addition of text to speech features to Cocoa applications.

Summary

Many Cocoa classes have been expanded and improved in the Jaguar release of Mac OS X. Several entirely new frameworks have been added including support for industry standard vCard databases, accessibility features, CD and DVD writing, digital camera access, and text to speech. The Quartz 2D graphics system has been improved and benefits from graphics hardware acceleration in some cases. Apple has made substantial enhancements to the networking layers of the operating system and the BSD Unix tools.

Cocoa applications written with previous versions of Mac OS X continue to work, and in some cases they automatically gain new features when run on Mac OS X 10.2. Most of the enhancements add value to all Cocoa applications. Cocoa applications that use new frameworks introduced with Jaguar will not work with prior versions.

Symbols

A

B

C

D

E

F

G

H

I

J - K

L

M

N

O

P

Q

S

T

U

V

W - Z